Séfer haḤinnuch סֵפֶר הַחִנּוּךְ

THE BOOK OF [MITZVAH] EDUCATION

סֵפֶר הַחִנּוּךְ

כנראה מאת רבנו פנחס
(אחיו של רבנו אהרן) הלוי
איש ברצלונה

מהדורה מנוקדת, מבוססת על
ההוצאה הראשונה (ונציה רפ"ג)
בהשוואה עם ארבעה כתבי-יד עתיקים,
עם תרגום והערות באנגלית, מאת
אלחנן וֶנגרוֹב

כרך שלישי: ספר ויקרא, חלק שני

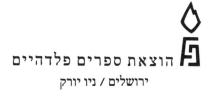

הוצאת ספרים פלדהיים
ירושלים / ניו יורק

Séfer haḤinnuch

THE BOOK OF [MITZVAH] EDUCATION

evidently by Rabbi Pinḥas
(brother of Rabbi Aaron) haLévi
of Barcelona

the Hebrew text (with *n'kudoth*)
based on the first edition (Venice 1523)
compared with four old manuscripts,
with a translation and notes, by
Charles Wengrov

VOLUME III: LEVITICUS, PART 2

FELDHEIM PUBLISHERS
Jerusalem / New York

כל הזכויות שמורות
למוציאים לאור
הוצאת ספרים פלדהיים בע״מ
ירושלים

First published 1984
ISBN 0-87306-297-3
(The set: ISBN 0-87306-145-4)

Philipp Feldheim Inc.
200 Airport Executive Park
Spring Valley, NY 10977

Feldheim Publishers Ltd
POB 6525 / Jerusalem, Israel

Printed in Israel

כי נר מצוה ותורה אור

נר
לנשמה הטהורה
של רעיתי אהובתי
רוזה (שושנה) בת ר' יצחק
נ"ע
נלב"ע כ"ג חשון תשמ"ג

ת נ צ ב ה

"שלי ושלכם שלה הוא"

מכתב ברכה

ממרן הגאון ר' מרדכי גיפטר שליט"א

YESHVAT TELSHE
Kiryat Telshe Stone
Jerusalem

Rabbi Mordechai Gifter
President

ישיבת טלז
קרית טלז-סטון
ירושלים

הרב מרדכי גיפטר
ראש הישיבה

ב"ה

ידידי עוז נכבד ר' ישראל נ"י, שלום וברכה נצח!

לשמחה רבה היא לי הבשורה שכת"ר עומד להוציא לאור את ספר החינוך בתרגום אנגלי.
החינוך הרי הוא מיוסד על סדר הלמוד של תרי"ג מצות ה', לפי סדרת הפרשיות, ויש בו לכן
שימוש נפלא לחנך הנער בעצם קדושת התורה והמצוות בקביעות ההלכה שבכל מצוה,
ובא "מנחת חינוך" ז"ל הפליא להגדיל בזה.

ואף טעמי המצות שביאר החינוך ז"ל בכל מצוה - אשר בזה לא דנו ספרי ההלכה -
דרכו שעמד לרוב בזה שטעמי המצות לפי פשטות הדברים - וכבר שאם
ספרו לבני הנוער - דרכם של רבותינו הראשונים ז"ל להלביש הדברים
מתאימים עטיפה הדור והראשון בטעם המצות, וראה פנימיות התוכן
משמש להבנת גדר ההלכה. והדברים מעוררים לב ונפש למען יהא הלב
המצוה המצוה ושרה עומדת אשר רק היא מצוה כהלכתה, אשר קדושתה
בלבד מתורתה התורה הקדושה - כמבואר בס' "נפש החיים" - כי נר מצוה
ותורה אור, שכל מצוה נושאת בקרבה מאתו אור ה' הצפון בתורה.

ודברי הקדושים של החינוך בהקדמתו מעוררים לב ונפש
~~[illegible]~~ בדרכו של עשה ומצוה, למען יקבל המתחנך מושג
התשוקה לקיום מצותיו.

ואסמוך ידי שבזכות המתרגם שהוא בעצמו נאמן לרוח
החינוך והדברים יהא לפני עיני ר"ח שיבקרו הדברים לנקותם
מכל שגיאה. ויביא תשואת חן ברכה להגדלה הבוחרים לדבר
ה' אשר השפה האנגלית קרובה להם, ומעוררת בהם להתקרב
לדברים גם במקורם.

ויזכהו ה' לברך את המעשה. באהבה,

משפטי

List of abbreviations, etc.

§	numbered section or *mitzvah*
ad loc.	*ad locum*, at the place
b.	*ben*, the son of
cf.	*confer*, compare
col.	column
Deut.	the Book of Deuteronomy (*d'varim*)
ed.	edition of; edited by; editor
e.g.	*exempli gratia*, for example
et al.	*et alii*, and others (i.e. people)
etc.	*et cetera*, and others
et seq.	*et sequentes*, and the following
Ex., Exod.	the Book of Exodus (*sh'moth*)
ff.	and pages following
Gen.	the Book of Genesis (*b'réshith*)
Guide	Rambam (R. Moshe b. Maimon, Maimonides), *Guide of the Perplexed* (*Moreh N'vuchim*)
ibid.	*ibidem*, at the (same) place
idem	the same (person)
i.e.	*id est*, that is
l.	line
Lev.	the Book of Leviticus (*va-yikra*)
loc. cit.	*loco citato*, in the place cited
MdRSbY	*Midrash d'Rabbi Shimon b. Yohai* (ed. Epstein-Melamed)
MH	R. Joseph Babad, *Minhath Hinnuch* (commentary on the *Hinnuch*)
MhG	*Midrash haGadol*, anthology of Midrash, etc. compiled in Yemen, 14th century
MS (plural, MSS)	*manuscriptum*, manuscript (plural, *manuscripta*, manuscripts)
MT	Rambam (R. Moshe b. Maimon, Maimonides), *Mishneh Torah* (also known as *Yad Hazakah*)
MY	R. Yitzhak *ha-kohén* Aronovsky, *Minhath Yitzhak* (commentary on the *Hinnuch*)
n.s.	new series
Num.	the Book of Numbers (*ba-midbar*)
op. cit.	*opera citato*, in the work cited
o.s.	old series
p. / pp.	page / pages
q.v.	*quod vide*, which see
R.	Rabbi, Rabbénu, Rav
ShM	Rambam (Maimonides), *Séfer haMitzvoth*
sic	so, thus (i.e. something that looks peculiar is so in the source cited)
s.v.	*sub verbo*, *sub voce*, under the word (or words)
TB	*Talmud Bavli*, Babylonian Talmud
TJ	*Talmud Yerushalmi*, Jerusalem Talmud
viz.	*videlicet*, namely

Séfer haḤinnuch סֵפֶר הַחִנּוּךְ

THE BOOK OF [MITZVAH] EDUCATION

ספר ויקרא

סדרות קדושים – בחוקותי

LEVITICUS

SIDROTH K'DOSHIM—B'HUKOTHAI

סֵפֶר וַיִּקְרָא

🕎 🕎 🕎 🕎 🕎 🕎

חֵלֶק שֵׁנִי

🕎 קְדוֹשִׁים תִּהְיוּ

יֵשׁ בָּהּ נ"א מִצְווֹת, י"ג מִצְווֹת עֲשֵׂה ול"ח מִצְווֹת לֹא־תַעֲשֶׂה

[מִצְוַת יְרְאַת אָב וָאֵם]

רִיב לִירָא מֵהָאָבוֹת, כְּלוֹמַר שֶׁיִּתְנַהֵג הָאָדָם עִם אִמּוֹ וְאָבִיו הַנְהָגָה שֶׁאָדָם נוֹהֵג עִם מִי שֶׁיָּרֵא מִמֶּנּוּ, שֶׁנֶּאֱמַר: אִישׁ אִמּוֹ וְאָבִיו תִּירָאוּ. וּלְשׁוֹן סִפְרָא: אֵי זֶהוּ מוֹרָא, לֹא יֵשֵׁב בִּמְקוֹמוֹ וְלֹא יְדַבֵּר בִּמְקוֹמוֹ וְלֹא סוֹתֵר אֶת דְּבָרָיו.

מִשָּׁרְשֵׁי הַמִּצְוָה, כָּתַבְתִּי בְמִצְוַת כִּבּוּד הָאָבוֹת בְּפָרָשַׁת וַיִּשְׁמַע יִתְרוֹ [סי' ל"א].

מִדִּינֵי הַמִּצְוָה, מַה שֶּׁאָמְרוּ זִכְרוֹנָם לִבְרָכָה: עַד הֵיכָן מוֹרָאַת אָב וָאֵם, שֶׁאֲפִלּוּ הִכּוּהוּ וְיָרְקוּ בְּפָנָיו לֹא יַכְלִים אוֹתָן; וְאַף־עַל־פִּי־כֵן צִוּוּ חֲכָמִים לְבַל יַכֶּה אָדָם בְּנוֹ הַגָּדוֹל, לְפִי שֶׁיֵּשׁ בַּדָּבָר מִשּׁוּם "וְלִפְנֵי עִוֵּר", וּמְנַדִּין עַל כָּךְ.

וְאָמְרוּ זִכְרוֹנָם לִבְרָכָה בְּחֹמֶר מִצְוָה זוֹ שֶׁאֲפִלּוּ נִטְרְפָה דַעַת הָאָב וְהָאֵם, שֶׁיִּשְׁתַּדֵּל הַבֵּן לִנְהֹג עִמָּהֶם דֶּרֶךְ כָּבוֹד לְפִי דַעְתָּם, אֲבָל אִם נִשְׁתַּטּוּ בְּיוֹתֵר יָכוֹל

---

§212   1. The paragraph is based on ShM positive precept §211.
2. TB Kiddushin 31a.
3. I.e. inducing a person to come to grief: because goaded thus beyond control, the son may turn contumacious (Rashi, Me'iri) or may strike his father back (R. Ḥanan'el; *Nimmuké Yoséf*) so incurring a penalty of death: TB Mo'éd Katan 17a.
4. TB Kiddushin 31b.

LEVITICUS

ψψψψψψψψψψ

part two

sidrah k'doshim

(Leviticus 19–20)

There are fifty-one precepts in it: 13 positive and 38 negative precepts.

212 [THE MITZVAH OF REVERENCE FOR FATHER AND MOTHER] to have a reverent fear of parents; in other words, a man should behave toward his mother and father in the way one behaves toward a person of whom he stands in awe: for it is stated, *You shall fear every man his mother and his father* (Leviticus 19:3). In the language of the Midrash *Sifra*: What constitutes reverent fear?—one should not sit in his [parent's] place, should not speak in his place, and should not contradict his words.[1]

The root reason for the precept, I wrote in the precept of respect for parents (§31), in *sidrah yithro*.

Among the laws of the precept, there is what the Sages of blessed memory taught:[2] How far should reverent fear of a father and mother go?—even if they beat him and spat in his face, he should not put them to shame. Nevertheless, the Sages ordained that a man should not strike his grown son, because there is in the matter an element of "before the blind you shall not put a stumbling-block" (Leviticus 19:14; §232);[3] and a person is to be excommunicated for this.

Then our Sages of blessed memory said,[4] on the severity of this precept, that even if the mind of the father and mother became deranged, the son should endeavor to deal with them in a respectful way, in accord with their understanding. But if they became excessively

⟨3⟩

לְהַנִּיחָם וִיצַוֶּה אֲחֵרִים עֲלֵיהֶם לְהַנְהִיגָם כָּרָאוּי אִם יֵשׁ לוֹ.

וְהַמַּמְזֵר חַיָּב בִּכְבוֹד הָאָבוֹת וּמוֹרָאָם, אַף־עַל־פִּי שֶׁפָּטוּר מִן הַמִּשְׁפָּט עַל מַכָּתָם וְקִלְלָתָם. וְהוֹרוּנוּ זִכְרוֹנָם לִבְרָכָה בְּעִנְיָן זֶה שֶׁאִם צִוּוּ הָאָבוֹת לַעֲבֹר עַל דִּבְרֵי תוֹרָה, וַאֲפִלּוּ עַל מִצְווֹת דְּרַבָּנָן, שֶׁאֵין שׁוֹמְעִין לָהֶם; וְיֶתֶר פְּרָטֶיהָ, בִּמְקוֹמוֹת בַּתַּלְמוּד, וְהָרֹב בְּקִדּוּשִׁין לְפִי דַעְתִּי.

וְנוֹהֶגֶת בְּכָל מָקוֹם וּבְכָל זְמַן, בַּזְּכָרִים וּנְקֵבוֹת. וְעוֹבֵר עָלֶיהָ וְהֵקֵל בְּיִרְאָתָם, בִּטֵּל עֲשֵׂה זֶה, אֶלָּא־אִם־כֵּן מִדַּעַת הָאָב וּבִמְחִילָתוֹ, שֶׁהָאָב שֶׁמָּחַל עַל כְּבוֹדוֹ, כְּבוֹדוֹ מָחוּל.

[שֶׁלֹּא לִפְנוֹת אַחַר עֲבוֹדָה זָרָה לֹא בְּמַחֲשָׁבָה וְלֹא בְּדִבּוּר וְלֹא בְּהַבָּטָה]

ריג שֶׁלֹּא לִפְנוֹת אַחַר עֲבוֹדָה זָרָה בְּמַחֲשָׁבָה אוֹ בְּדִבּוּר אוֹ אֲפִלּוּ בִּרְאִיָּה לְבַד, כְּדֵי שֶׁלֹּא יָבוֹא מִתּוֹךְ כָּךְ לַעֲבֹד אוֹתָהּ, שֶׁנֶּאֱמַר: אַל תִּפְנוּ אֶל הָאֱלִילִים; וְאָמְרוּ זִכְרוֹנָם לִבְרָכָה בְּסִפְרָא: אִם פּוֹנֶה אַתְּ אַחֲרֵיהֶם אַתְּ עוֹשֶׂה אוֹתָם אֱלֹהוֹת, כְּלוֹמַר אִם אַתָּה מִתְעַסֵּק בְּעִנְיָנֶיהָ, כְּלוֹמַר לְהַרְהֵר אַחֲרֵי הַשִּׁגְעוֹנוֹת אֲשֶׁר יֹאמְרוּ הַמַּאֲמִינִים בָּהּ, שֶׁמַּזָּל פְּלוֹנִי אוֹ כוֹכָב פְּלוֹנִי יַעֲשֶׂה פְּעֻלָּה כֵּן וָכֵן בִּקְטֹרֶת פְּלוֹנִית אוֹ בַעֲבוֹדָה פְּלוֹנִית, אוֹ תַבִּיט תָּמִיד בַּצּוּרוֹת שֶׁעוֹשִׂין עוֹבְדֶיהָ כְּדֵי לָדַעַת אֵיכוּת עֲבוֹדָתָהּ, מִכָּל זֶה יִהְיֶה סִבָּה שֶׁתִּהְיֶה נִפְתֶּה אַחֲרֶיהָ וְתַעַבְדֶהָ.

וּבְפֵרוּשׁ נֶאֱמַר שָׁם בְּסִפְרָא שֶׁאֲפִלּוּ הַהַבָּטָה לְבַד אֲסוּרָה, שֶׁאָמְרוּ שָׁם: רַבִּי יְהוּדָה אוֹמֵר: אַל תִּפְנֶה לִרְאוֹתָן; וְהָעִנְיָן מִן הַטַּעַם שֶׁאָמַרְנוּ, שֶׁהוּא סִבָּה לְטָעוּת אַחֲרֶיהָ, וְכֵן כְּדֵי שֶׁלֹּא יְבַטֵּל חֵלֶק מֵהַזְּמַן וְיִתְעַסֵּק בְּאוֹתָן הַהֲבָלִים, וְהָאָדָם אֵינֶנּוּ נִבְרָא רַק לַעֲסֹק בַּעֲבוֹדַת בּוֹרְאוֹ.

וְזֶהוּ שֶׁאָמְרוּ זִכְרוֹנָם לִבְרָכָה בְּשַׁבָּת פֶּרֶק שׁוֹאֵל אָדָם מֵחֲבֵרוֹ: וְדִיּוֹקְנֵי עַצְמָהּ אֲפִלּוּ בְּחֹל אָסוּר לְהִסְתַּכֵּל בָּהּ, מִשּׁוּם שֶׁנֶּאֱמַר: אַל תִּפְנוּ אֶל הָאֱלִילִים; מַאי

---

5. I.e. someone born to forbidden consaguineous relations or adulterers, for whom conjugal intimacy is punishable by *karéth*; TB Yevamoth 22a (MT *bilchoth mamrim* vi 11.)

6. TB Bava M'tzi'a 32a.

7. MT *bilchoth mamrim* vi 6, based on TB B'rachoth 19b (see *Kessef Mishneh*).

§213   1. Sifra, *k'doshim, parashah* 1, 6.

deranged, he can leave them and instruct others about them, to attend to them properly, if he has [others to assign]. A bastard[5] has the obligation of respect toward parents, and reverent fear—even though he is not liable to sentencing for beating or cursing them.

Further, our Sages instructed us about this subject,[6] that if parents should command someone to transgress the words of the Torah, even if only a precept decreed by the Sages,[7] they are not to be heeded. The rest of its details are in various places in the Talmud, mostly in the tractate *Kiddushin*, I believe.

It applies in every place and every time, for both man and woman. If a person transgresses it and is negligent about reverent fear for them, he disobeys this positive precept, unless it is with the father's knowledge and consent: For if a father renounces his right to respect, the respect due him is thereby renounced.

[NOT TO TURN ASTRAY AFTER IDOL-WORSHIP IN THOUGHT OR WORD]

213 not to turn to an idol in thought or speech, or even by looking alone, so as not to be led thus to worship it—as it is stated, *Do not turn to the idols* (Leviticus 19:4); and our Sages of blessed memory said in the Midrash *Sifra*: If you turn after them, you thus make them into gods. In other words, if you occupy yourself with its concepts, i.e. to ponder on the nonsense that those who believe in it say—that this constellation or that star will achieve this-and-this effect through this kind of incense, or upon that kind of worship—or if you constantly study the images that its worshippers make in order to understand the nature of its worship—out of all this a motivation will form for you to be persuaded after it and to worship it.

There, in the Midrash *Sifra*, it was stated explicitly[1] that even watching alone is forbidden. For it is taught there: R. Judah said: "Do not turn"—to see them. This is on account of the reason we have stated: that it becomes a cause of being misled by it; and so is it also in order that one should not waste any part of his time by occupying himself with those vapid matters of nonsense. For a man was created for nothing else but to busy himself with the worship of his Creator.

This is why the Sages of blessed memory said in chapter 23 of the Talmud tractate *Shabbath* (149a): As for an idolatrous image itself, even on a common weekday it is forbidden to gaze at it, because it is stated, *Do not turn to the idols.* How is this derived [from the verse]?

תַּלְמוּדָא, אָמַר רַבִּי יוֹחָנָן: אַל תִּפְנוּ אֶל מַדַּעְתְּכֶם.

וְנִכְפַּל לָאו זֶה, כְּלוֹמַר בְּאִסוּר הַמַּחֲשָׁבָה בַּעֲבוֹדָה זָרָה, בְּמָקוֹם אַחֵר, שֶׁנֶּאֱמַר: הִשָּׁמְרוּ לָכֶם פֶּן יִפְתֶּה לְבַבְכֶם וְסַרְתֶּם וַעֲבַדְתֶּם וְגוֹמֵר, כְּלוֹמַר שֶׁאִם יַרְבֶּה לְבָךְ לַחְשֹׁב בָּהּ, יִהְיֶה סָבָד לִנְטוֹתְךָ מִן הַדֶּרֶךְ הַיְשָׁרָה וּלְהִתְעַסֵּק בַּעֲבוֹדָתָהּ; וְעוֹד נֶאֱמַר בְּזֶה הָעִנְיָן: וּפֶן תִּשָּׂא עֵינֶיךָ הַשָּׁמַיְמָה וְרָאִיתָ וְגוֹמֵר, שֶׁאֵין הָעִנְיָן שֶׁלֹּא יִשָּׂא הָאָדָם רֹאשׁוֹ וְיַבִּיט בַּשָּׁמַיִם, אֲבָל הַכַּוָּנָה בַּדָּבָר שֶׁלֹּא יַבִּיט בָּהֶם בְּעֵין הַלֵּב לָדַעַת כֹּחָן וְעִנְיָנָן כְּדֵי לְעָבְדָן, וּכְמוֹ שֶׁנֶּאֱמַר בְּמָקוֹם אַחֵר: וּפֶן תִּדְרֹשׁ לֵאלֹהֵיהֶם לֵאמֹר אֵיכָה יַעַבְדוּ הַגּוֹיִם אֶת אֱלֹהֵיהֶם וְאֶעֱשֶׂה־כֵּן גַּם אָנִי, שֶׁיִּמְנָעֵנוּ הַכָּתוּב מִלִּשְׁאֹל עַל אֵיכוּת עֲבוֹדָתָהּ, לְפִי שֶׁכָּל זֶה הוּא סָבָּה לִטְעוֹת בָּהּ.

שֹׁרֶשׁ רִחוּק עֲבוֹדָה זָרָה וְכָל אַבִיזָרֶיהָ יָדוּעַ לְכָל אָדָם.

דִּינֵי הַמִּצְוָה וּפְרָטֶיהָ יִתְבָּאֲרוּ בְּהַרְבֵּה מְקוֹמוֹת בַּגְּמָרָא בְּפִזּוּר, שֶׁהִזְהִירוּנוּ זִכְרוֹנָם לִבְרָכָה שֶׁלֹּא לְהַרְהֵר בְּמַחֲשֶׁבֶת עֲבוֹדָה זָרָה; וְאָמְרוּ זִכְרוֹנָם לִבְרָכָה שֶׁלֹּא מַחֲשֶׁבֶת עֲבוֹדָה זָרָה בִּלְבַד אֲסוּרָה, אֶלָּא כָל מַחֲשָׁבָה הַגּוֹרֶמֶת לוֹ לְאָדָם לַעֲקֹר דָּבָר מִן הַתּוֹרָה; וּבְפֵרוּשׁ הִזְהִיר הַכָּתוּב עַל זֶה בְּמָקוֹם אַחֵר, דִּכְתִיב: וְלֹא תָתוּרוּ אַחֲרֵי לְבַבְכֶם. וְאָמְרוּ זִכְרוֹנָם לִבְרָכָה שֶׁאֵין הַקָּדוֹשׁ־בָּרוּךְ־הוּא מְחַשֵּׁב לְיִשְׂרָאֵל מַחֲשֶׁבֶת עֲבֵרָה כְּמַעֲשֶׂה, חוּץ מִמַּחֲשֶׁבֶת עֲבוֹדָה זָרָה, שֶׁהִיא נֶחֱשֶׁבֶת לוֹ לְאָדָם כְּמַעֲשֶׂה.

וְנוֹהֵג אִסּוּר זֶה בְּכָל מָקוֹם וּבְכָל זְמַן, בַּזְּכָרִים וּנְקֵבוֹת. וְעוֹבֵר עָלֶיהָ וּפָנָה אַחַר עֲבוֹדָה זָרָה בְּדֶרֶךְ שֶׁיְּהֵא עוֹשֶׂה בָהּ מַעֲשֶׂה, לוֹקֶה.

<hr />

2. So R. Nathan b. Yeḥiél, 'Aruch, explains the Talmudic words; Rashi: Do not turn to the god you create from your own mind.

3. The last three paragraphs are based on ShM negative precept §30.

4. TB B'rachoth 12b.

5. TB Kiddushin 40a, etc.

6. It is a standard rule that where no physical action is involved in violating a negative precept, whiplashes are not given (TB Sanhedrin 63b).   ⟨6⟩

Said R. Yoḥanan: [We understand it to signify] "Do not turn God
out of your thoughts." [2]

This injunction, i.e. which prohibits thinking about an idol, was
repeated elsewhere: for it is stated, *Take heed to yourselves lest your
heart be deceived, and you turn aside and serve,* etc. (Deuteronomy 11:16):
In other words, if your heart will ponder on it very much, it will be a
motivation for you to turn away from the right path and occupy
yourself with its worship. Then it was stated further about this subject,
*and beware lest you lift up your eyes to heaven, and when you see the sun
and the moon and the stars, all the host of heaven, you be drawn away and
worship them,* etc. (Deuteronomy 4:19). Here the sense is not that a
man should not lift up his head and look at the heavens. It is rather
meant to convey that one should not contemplate them with the eye
of the heart to know their power and significance, which means in effect
in order to worship them. As it is stated elsewhere, *and lest you inquire
about their gods, saying, "How did these nations serve their gods? So will I do
likewise"* (Deuteronomy 12:30). Thus the Writ restrains us from inquiring about the nature of its worship, because all this is a causative
factor to go astray about it. [3]

The root reason for removing idolatry and whatever pertains to it,
is known to everyone.

The laws of the precept and its details are elucidated in many
places in the Talmud, scattered about. Our Sages of blessed memory
adjured us not to contemplate any thought of idolatry. And they
(of blessed memory) said that not only any thought of idolatry is
forbidden, but any conception that causes a man to uproot something
from the Torah. [4] Well, elsewhere the Writ expressly cautioned about
this: for it is written, *and that you shall not search astray after your heart*
(Numbers 15:39); and the Sages of blessed memory taught [5] that the
Holy One, blessed is He, reckons no thought of sin as the equivalent
of the deed for an Israelite, except the thought of idol-worship: this
is reckoned for a man like the deed [itself].

This prohibition is in effect everywhere, at every time, for both
man and woman. If someone transgressed it and turned to an idol in
such a way as to do some act [of worship] toward it, he should receive
whiplashes. [6]

⟨7⟩

[שֶׁלֹּא לַעֲשׂוֹת עֲבוֹדָה זָרָה לֹא לְעַצְמוֹ וְלֹא לְזוּלָתוֹ]

רִיד שֶׁלֹּא לַעֲשׂוֹת עֲבוֹדָה זָרָה לְמִי שֶׁיַּעַבְדֶנָּה, בֵּין לְעַצְמוֹ בֵּין לְזוּלָתוֹ, וַאֲפִלּוּ יִהְיֶה הַמְצֻוֶּה לַעֲשׂוֹתָהּ גּוֹי, שֶׁנֶּאֱמַר: וֵאלֹהֵי מַסֵּכָה לֹא תַעֲשׂוּ לָכֶם, וְאָמְרוּ זִכְרוֹנָם לִבְרָכָה בִּסְפָרָא: אֲפִלּוּ לַאֲחֵרִים. וְשָׁם נֶאֱמַר: הָעוֹשֶׂה עֲבוֹדָה זָרָה לְעַצְמוֹ עוֹבֵר מִשּׁוּם שְׁתֵּי אַזְהָרוֹת, כְּלוֹמַר מִשּׁוּם "לֹא תַעֲשׂוּ" וּמִשּׁוּם "לֹא... לָכֶם".

שֹׁרֶשׁ רִחוּק עֲבוֹדָה זָרָה יָדוּעַ.

מִדִּינֶיהָ, מַה שֶּׁאָמְרוּ זִכְרוֹנָם לִבְרָכָה: מַה בֵּין עֲבוֹדָה זָרָה שֶׁל יִשְׂרָאֵל לַעֲבוֹדָה זָרָה שֶׁל גּוֹי, עֲבוֹדָה זָרָה שֶׁל גּוֹי אֲסוּרָה בַּהֲנָאָה מִיָּד, שֶׁנֶּאֱמַר: פְּסִילֵי אֱלֹהֵיהֶם תִּשְׂרְפוּן בָּאֵשׁ וְגוֹמֵר, מִשֶּׁפְּסָלוֹ נַעֲשָׂה לוֹ אֱלוֹהַּ; וְשֶׁל יִשְׂרָאֵל אֵינָהּ אֲסוּרָה בַּהֲנָאָה עַד שֶׁתֵּעָבֵד, שֶׁנֶּאֱמַר: וְשָׂם בַּסֵּתֶר, עַד שֶׁיַּעֲשֶׂה לָהּ דְּבָרִים שֶׁבַּסֵּתֶר, שֶׁהֵן עֲבוֹדָתָהּ.

וּמְשַׁמְּשֵׁי עֲבוֹדָה זָרָה בֵּין שֶׁל גּוֹי אוֹ שֶׁל יִשְׂרָאֵל אֵינָם אֲסוּרִין עַד שֶׁיִּשְׁתַּמְּשׁוּ בָּהֶן לַעֲבוֹדָה זָרָה; וְהָעוֹשֶׂה עֲבוֹדָה זָרָה אַף־עַל־פִּי שֶׁהוּא לוֹקֶה שְׂכָרוֹ מֻתָּר, וַאֲפִלּוּ עֲשָׂאָהּ לְגוֹי, שֶׁהִיא אֲסוּרָה מִשֶּׁנִּגְמְרָה אֲפִלּוּ קֹדֶם שֶׁתֵּעָבֵד, מִכָּל־מָקוֹם אֵינָהּ אֲסוּרָה עַד שֶׁתִּגָּמֵר, וּמַכּוֹשׁ אַחֲרוֹן שֶׁגּוֹמְרָהּ אֵין בּוֹ שָׁוֶה פְּרוּטָה; וְיֶתֶר רַבֵּי פְּרָטֶיהָ, בְּמַסֶּכֶת עֲבוֹדָה זָרָה.

וְנוֹהֶגֶת אִסּוּרָהּ בְּכָל מָקוֹם וּבְכָל זְמַן, בַּזְּכָרִים וּנְקֵבוֹת. וְעוֹבֵר וְעָשָׂה עֲבוֹדָה זָרָה לְזוּלָתוֹ, בֵּין עֲשָׂאָהּ לְגוֹי אוֹ לְיִשְׂרָאֵל, לוֹקֶה מַלְקוּת אַחַת; וְאִם עֲשָׂאָהּ לְעַצְמוֹ לוֹקֶה שְׁתֵּי מַלְקִיּוֹת כְּמוֹ שֶׁאָמַרְנוּ, וּשְׁנֵיהֶם מִשּׁוּם הָעֲשִׂיָּה לְבַד לְכַוָּנַת עֲבוֹדָה, וְאַף־עַל־פִּי שֶׁלֹּא עֲבָדָהּ.

§214

1. The paragraph is based on ShM negative precept §3.
2. TB ʿAvodah Zarah 51b, etc.
3. Which an Israelite would not do openly, fearing punishment.
4. *Ibid.* 51b–52a.
5. It becomes an idol, from which all benefit is forbidden, only with the final few hammer-blows that put the finishing touches on it; but the heathen would quite certainly pay the Israelite craftsman in full even if he did not add these unimportant last touches. Hence in essence the Israelite receives his fee for his work on the object before it becomes ranked as an idol (*tosafoth* s.v. *makkosh*); *ibid.* 19b. (The last two paragraphs are based on MT *hilchoth ʿavodath kochavim* vii 4–5).

⟨8⟩

[TO MAKE NO IDOL, FOR ONESELF OR FOR ANYONE
ELSE]

214 not to make an idol for one who would worship it, whether thus for himself or for someone else—and even if the one ordering it made is a heathen: for it is stated, *and molten gods shall you not make for yourselves* (Leviticus 19:4); whereupon our Sages of blessed memory said in the Midrash *Sifra*: not even for others. It was further taught there: If a person makes an idol for himself, he sins on account of two injunctions—in other words, on account of "you shall not make" and on account of "for yourselves." [1]

The root reason for removing idolatry is known.

Among its laws there is what the Sages of blessed memory taught: [2] What difference is there [in law] between the idol of an Israelite and the idol of a heathen? It becomes forbidden at once to have any benefit from the idol of a heathen, for it is stated, *The graven images of their gods you shall burn with fire*, etc. (Deuteronomy 7:25): once it is cast into form it becomes a god for him. As for that of an Israelite, it does not become forbidden to benefit from it until it is worshipped: for it is stated, *Cursed be the man who makes a graven or molten image ... and sets it up in secret* (ibid. 27:15)—not until he does secret [unavowable] things with it, which are its way of worship. [3]

Objects for serving an idol, whether it is a heathen's or an Israelite's, do not become forbidden until they are used for the idol. [4] If someone makes an idol, even though he receives whiplashes, the benefit of his wages is permissible. Even if he made it for a heathen, so that it becomes forbidden from the time it is finished, yet before it is worshipped, it nevertheless does not become forbidden until it is actually completed, and the final blow of the hammer that completes it is not worth a *p'rutah*. [5] The rest of its many details are in the Talmud tractate *'Avodah Zarah*.

Its prohibition is in force in every place and every time, for both man and woman. If a person violated it and made an idol for someone else, whether he made it for an Israelite or a heathen, he should be whipped with one set of lashes. If he made it for himself, he should be whipped with two sets of lashes, as we stated—and both merely on account of making it with the intention of worship, even if he did not worship it [afterward].

[שֶׁלֹּא לֶאֱכֹל נוֹתָר]

רטו שֶׁלֹּא לֶאֱכֹל נוֹתָר, וְהוּא מַה שֶׁנִּשְׁאַר מִבְּשַׂר הַקֳּדָשִׁים מִקָּרְבָּן שֶׁקָּרֵב כְּמִצְוָתוֹ, אַחַר זְמַן הָרָאוּי לְאָכְלוֹ—שֶׁנֶּאֱמַר בַּמִּלּוּאִים: לֹא יֵאָכֵל כִּי קֹדֶשׁ (הֵם) [הוּא], וּבָא הַפֵּרוּשׁ עַל זֶה: כָּל שֶׁבַּקֹּדֶשׁ פָּסוּל, לִתֵּן לֹא־תַעֲשֶׂה עַל אֲכִילָתוֹ; וְזֶה יִרְמֹז הַכָּתוּב בְּאָמְרוֹ כִּי קֹדֶשׁ (הֵם) [הוּא], זֶה הַנִּסְתָּר שֶׁהוּא (הֵם) [הוּא], הוּא כּוֹלֵל כָּל מַה שֶׁנִּפְסָד מִן הַקֳּדָשִׁים.

וְאֵין לָנוּ לִלְמֹד בְּכָךְ שֶׁנַּחֲשֹׁב הַפִּגּוּל וְהַנּוֹתָר לְלָאו אֶחָד, כִּי שְׁנֵי שֵׁמוֹת הֵן, וּכְמוֹ שֶׁכָּתַבְתִּי לְמַעְלָה בְּאִסּוּר סֵדֶר צַו, לֹא־תַעֲשֶׂה ו' [סי' קמ"ד]. וּמָצִינוּ שֶׁבָּאוּ בָהֶן שְׁנֵי כְתוּבִים לְגַבֵּי הָעֹנֶשׁ, דִּכְתִיב בְּפִגּוּל בְּסֵדֶר צַו: וְאִם הֵאָכֹל יֵאָכֵל וְגוֹמֵר, וּכְתִיב בַּתְרֵיהּ: וְהַנֶּפֶשׁ הָאֹכֶלֶת מִמֶּנּוּ עֲוֹנָהּ תִּשָּׂא, וּנְשִׂיאַת עָוֹן זֶה הוּא כָרֵת, כְּמוֹ שֶׁנִּלְמַד בִּגְזֵרָה שָׁוָה מִנּוֹתָר, וּכְתִיב הָכָא גַבֵּי נוֹתָר: וְהַנּוֹתָר עַד יוֹם הַשְּׁלִישִׁי... פִּגּוּל הוּא לֹא יֵרָצֶה וְאֹכְלָיו עֲוֹנוֹ יִשָּׂא כִּי אֶת קֹדֶשׁ יי חִלֵּל וְנִכְרְתָה וְגוֹמֵר. וְעַל־כֵּן, אַף־עַל־פִּי שֶׁאַזְהָרַת שְׁנֵיהֶם מִמִּקְרָא אֶחָד, לֹא נִמָּנַע מִפְּנֵי־כֵן לַחְשְׁבָם שְׁנֵי לָאוִין. וְכֵן אָמְרוּ בִמְעִילָה: הַפִּגּוּל וְהַנּוֹתָר אֵין מִצְטָרְפִין זֶה עִם זֶה, מִפְּנֵי שֶׁהֵן שְׁנֵי שֵׁמוֹת וְכוּלֵי, כְּמוֹ שֶׁמְּפֹרָשׁ שָׁם שֶׁיֵּשׁ דְּבָרִים שֶׁאֵין מִצְטָרְפִין בָּהֶן וְיֵשׁ שֶׁמִּצְטָרְפִין בָּהֶן.

מִשָּׁרְשֵׁי הַמִּצְוָה, כָּתַבְתִּי בְּאִסּוּר פִּגּוּל מַה שֶׁיָּדַעְתִּי.

מִדִּינֵי הַנּוֹתָר, מַה שֶׁאָמְרוּ זִכְרוֹנָם לִבְרָכָה: אָכַל מִן הָעוֹר אוֹ מִן הַמָּרָק אוֹ מִן הַתַּבְלִין אוֹ מִן הָאָלָל אוֹ מִן הַמָּרְאָה אוֹ מִן הַגִּידִין וּמִן הַקַּרְנַיִם וּמִן הַטְּלָפַיִם וּמִן הַצִּפָּרְנַיִם וּמִן הַחַרְטוֹם, מִבֵּיצֵי הָעוֹף, מִן הַנּוֹצָה, אֵינוֹ חַיָּב כָּרֵת; וְכֵן בְּדָם אֵין בָּהּ

1. I.e. after it has become thus disqualified, either by improper thought (intention) or deed; TB Me'ilah 17b, etc. Both in this and the next sentence, the original text reads "because they (hém) are holy" (Exodus 29:33); and in the next sentence the original text continues, "this third-person pronoun, hém"; but verse 33 deals with proper, acceptable holy sacrifices, and is thus inappropriate. See *Torah Shelémah* on Exodus 29:34, §105, note, that this is a matter of confusion, generally, among the early commentaries and authorities. In ShM negative precept §131 the verse is correctly given.

2. An offering that becomes disqualified because the man who brings it or the *kohen* who offers it up has an improper intention about it, e.g. to eat some of it after the permitted time; see §144.

3. See §144, fourth paragraph, that although the verse speaks of actually eating the meat of an offering after the permitted time, it is interpreted as referring to an earlier intention to do so.

4. I.e. meat of two offerings that were thus respectively disqualified—in order to constitute the minimal amount that renders the hands ritually unclean; for the sin of eating them, though, the two can be considered as one, as our author writes at the end.

⟨10⟩

[THE PROHIBITION OF EATING LEFT-OVER MEAT OF SACRIFICES]

215 not to eat *nothar*, i.e. what is left over of the meat of holy sacrifice from an offering that was brought according to its precept, after the proper time for eating it: for it is stated about the [ram of] consecration [of the *mishkan*, the Tabernacle], *it shall not be eaten, because it is holy* (Exodus 29:34); and the interpretation was given [that this refers to] everything in a holy offering [through which it can become] disqualified, unacceptable—to make eating it then[1] the violation of a negative precept. This is what Scripture intimates by saying, *because it is holy*: this third-person pronoun, *hu*, "it," is meant to include everything of holy offerings that becomes spoiled [disqualified].

Yet we are not to learn from this that we should reckon *piggul*[2] and *nothar* as one negative precept, since they are two separate terms (categories), as I wrote above, in regard to the prohibition of *piggul*, in the sixth negative precept of *sidrah tzav* (§144). And so we find that two verses occur about them in regard to the punishment: About *piggul* it is written in *sidrah tzav*, *And if any . . . shall be at all eaten, etc.*[3] (Leviticus 7:18); then it is written afterward, *and the soul that eats of it shall bear iniquity* (ibid.), this "bearing of iniquity" denoting *karéth* [Divine severance of existence], as we learn by *g'zérah shavah* [identity of terms in two verses] from *nothar*. For here, in regard to *nothar*, it is written, *and if anything remains until the third day . . . it is a vile thing; it will not be accepted; and every one who eats it shall bear his iniquity, because he has profaned a holy thing of the Lord; and that soul shall be cut off*, etc. (Leviticus 19:6–8).

Therefore, even though the injunction about both is derived from one verse, we need not refrain for this reason from considering them two negative precepts; and so it was stated in the Talmud tractate *Me'ilah* (17b): *piggul* and *nothar* cannot be considered joined together,[4] because they are two [different] categories, etc.—as this is explained there, that for certain matters they cannot be considered joined together, as one, and for certain matters they can.

As to the root reason for the precept, I have written in regard to the ban on *piggul* (§144) what I know.

Among the laws of *nothar*, there is what the Sages of blessed memory taught:[5] if a person ate of the skin, broth, seasoning, bits of flesh clung to skin, crop [of fowl], sinews, horns, hooves, claws or beak, or of the eggs of a fowl or its down, he does not deserve *karéth*.[6]

⟨11⟩

חַיָּיב מִשּׁוּם נוֹתָר, וְכֵן בַּלְּבוֹנָה וְהַקְּטֹרֶת וְהָעֵצִים, וּכְמוֹ שֶׁכְּתַבְנוּ בְּפִגּוּל; אָכַל מִן הַשָּׁלִיל אוֹ מִן הַשִּׁלְיָא, חַיָּיב כָּרֵת, וְכֵן מַה שֶּׁאָמְרוּ כִּי קָדְשֵׁי הַגּוֹיִם, כְּלוֹמַר נְדָרִים וּנְדָבוֹת שֶׁמְּקַבְּלִין מֵהֶן, אֵין בָּהֶן מִשּׁוּם נוֹתָר וּפִגּוּל; וְיֶתֶר פְּרָטֵי אִסּוּר הַנּוֹתָר וְגַם הַפִּגּוּל, יִתְבָּאֲרוּ בְּהַרְבֵּה מְקוֹמוֹת מִסֵּדֶר קָדָשִׁים.

וְנוֹהֵג אִסּוּר זֶה בִּזְמַן הַבַּיִת בִּזְכָרִים וּנְקֵבוֹת. וְעוֹבֵר עָלָיו וְאָכַל כַּזַּיִת נוֹתָר בְּמֵזִיד, חַיָּיב כָּרֵת; בְּשׁוֹגֵג, חַיָּיב לְהָבִיא חַטַּאת קְבוּעָה. וְכֵן הַדִּין אִם אָכַל כַּזַּיִת מִנּוֹתָר וּפִגּוּל בְּיַחַד, דִּלְעִנְיַן אֲכִילָה מִצְטָרְפִין הֵן.

[מִצְוַת פֵּאָה]

רטז לְהַנִּיחַ פֵּאָה מִן הַתְּבוּאָה, שֶׁנֶּאֱמַר "לֶעָנִי וְלַגֵּר תַּעֲזֹב אֹתָם" אַחַר שֶׁנִּזְכַּר "לֹא תְכַלֶּה פְּאַת שָׂדְךָ". וּפֵרוּשׁ גֵּר זֶה גֵּר צֶדֶק, וְכֵן כָּל גֵּר הָאָמוּר בְּמַתְּנוֹת עֲנִיִּים, שֶׁהֲרֵי כָּתוּב בְּמַעְשַׂר עָנִי "לַגֵּר לַיָּתוֹם וְלָאַלְמָנָה", וְזֶה וַדַּאי גֵּר צֶדֶק הוּא מִן הַסְּתָם, שֶׁעֵדָיו בְּצִדּוֹ, וְהוּא הַדִּין לְכָל מַתְּנוֹת עֲנִיִּים. וְאַף־עַל־פִּי־כֵן אָמְרוּ זִכְרוֹנָם לִבְרָכָה שֶׁאֵין מוֹנְעִין אוֹתָן מֵעֲנִיֵּי גוֹיִים, מִפְּנֵי דַרְכֵי שָׁלוֹם.

וְעִנְיַן הַפֵּאָה הוּא שֶׁיַּנִּיחַ הָאָדָם בְּעֵת שֶׁיִּקְצֹר תְּבוּאָתוֹ מְעַט מִן הַתְּבוּאָה בְּקָצֶה הַשָּׂדֶה. וְאֵין לְשִׁיּוּר זֶה שִׁעוּר מִן הַתּוֹרָה, אֲבָל חֲכָמִים נָתְנוּ שִׁעוּר לַדָּבָר, וְהוּא חֵלֶק אֶחָד מִשִּׁשִּׁים.

מִשָּׁרְשֵׁי הַמִּצְוָה, כִּי הַשֵּׁם בָּרוּךְ הוּא רָצָה לִהְיוֹת עַמּוֹ אֲשֶׁר בָּחַר מְעֻטָּרִים בְּכָל מִדָּה טוֹבָה וִיקָרָה, וְשֶׁיִּהְיֶה לָהֶם נֶפֶשׁ בְּרָכָה וְרוּחַ נְדִיבָה. וּכְבָר כָּתַבְתִּי כִּי

---

5. TB Z'vaḥim 35a–b, Ḥullin 121a; Mishnah, Tohoroth i 2 (see MY); MT *bilchoth p'sulé ha-mukdashin* xviii 22.

6. Because these are not properly of the flesh of the offering. I have rendered 'alal as bits of flesh clung to skin, because very likely our author would have so explained it had he added clarification. He generally follows Rambam (unless he has a reason to differ), and thus Rambam specifically explains it in MT *ibid.* xiv 7, and in his commentary to Mishnah, Z'vaḥim iii 4, Ḥullin ix 1, and Tohoroth i 2. Rashi defines it as the hard tendons in an animal's throat, which are soft and edible in fowl, however. For *mur'ab* I thought it best to give the general meaning of the crop or gizzard in fowl, although here again Rambam gives a different meaning: a thin membrane or layer between skin and flesh, which is not fit to eat (MT *ibid.*). But while his explanation of 'alal has a firm basis in the view of Resh Lakish (TB Ḥullin 121a), for his view on *mur'ab* I find only a tentative suggestion of a reason in *Kessef Mishneh* on MT *ibid.*

7. TB Z'vaḥim 45b.

8. Brought for the altar; i.e. if there was delay in burning these; *ibid.*

9. From an offering that became *nothar*; *ibid.* 35a.

10. TB Z'vaḥim 35a; MT *bilchoth p'sulé ha-mukdashin* xviii 24.

11. Explained in § 121.

So too with blood, there is no guilt on account of *nothar*;[7] and likewise
with the frankincense, incense and wood,[8] as we wrote in connection
with *piggul* (§144). But if one ate of an embryo or a placenta,[9] he is
punishable by *karéth*. Then there is, likewise, what the Sages said:[10]
that for holy sacrifices of non-Jews, i.e. vowed and voluntary offerings
that are accepted from them, the laws of *nothar* and *piggul* do not
apply. The remaining details of the prohibition of *nothar* as well as
piggul are clarified in many places in the Talmudic order of *Kodashim*.

This prohibition is in effect when the Temple exists, for both
man and woman. If someone violated it and ate an olive's amount of
nothar, if it was done willfully, he would deserve *karéth*; if it was
inadvertent, he would be obligated to bring a fixed, unvarying *hattath*
(sin-offering).[11] The law is the same if one ate an olive's amount of
nothar and *piggul* together: for in regard to eating they can join together
[to be considered one transgression].

[THE MITZVAH OF LEAVING AN EDGE OF ONE'S FIELD
UNREAPED, FOR THE POOR]

216 to leave over an unreaped part of a field of produce: for it is
stated, *you shall leave them for the poor and for the stranger* (Leviticus
19:10), this after the text, *you shall not reap every last edge of your field*
(*ibid.* 9). Now, the meaning of "stranger" (*gér*) is a full, righteous
convert to Judaism,[1] and so every occurrence of the term *gér* in regard
to gifts for the poor. For about the tithe for the poor it is written,
to the gér *(stranger), to the orphan, and to the widow* (Deuteronomy
26:12); and this quite certainly means a full, righteous proselyte,
since its witnesses are beside it.[2] Then the same holds true for all gifts
to the poor. Nevertheless, the Sages of blessed memory ruled that they
are not to be withheld from poor non-Jews, for the sake of peace.[3]

In substance, the obligation of the unreaped part is that when
reaping his produce, a man should leave a little of the produce over at
the edge of the field. There is no set amount for this remainder by the
law of the Torah; the Sages, however, set a minimal amount for the
matter, which is one sixtieth.[4]

At the root of the precept lies the reason that the Eternal Lord,
blessed is He, wished that His people, whom He chose, should be
adorned with every good and precious quality, and that they should
have a blessed soul and a generous spirit. I have written previously
that as a result of one's activities, the soul is influenced accordingly,

מִתּוֹךְ הַפְּעֻלּוֹת תִּתְפַּעֵל הַנֶּפֶשׁ, וְתִהְיֶה טוֹבָה וְתָחוּל בִּרְכַּת הַשֵּׁם בָּהּ. וְאֵין סָפֵק כִּי בְהוֹתִיר הָאָדָם חֵלֶק אֶחָד מִפֵּרוֹתָיו בְּשָׂדֵהוּ וְיַפְקִירֵם שֶׁיֶּהֱנוּ בוֹ הַצְּרִיכִים, תֵּרָאֶה בְנַפְשׁוֹ שֹׂבַע רָצוֹן וְרוּחַ נָכוֹן וּמְבֹרָךְ, וְכִי הַשֵּׁם הִשְׂבִּיעוֹ בְטוּבוֹ, וְגַם נַפְשׁוֹ בְּטוֹב תָּלִין.

וְהַמְאַסֵּף הַכֹּל אֶל הַבַּיִת וְלֹא יַשְׁאִיר אַחֲרָיו בְּרָכָה שֶׁיֶּהֱנוּ בָם הָאֶבְיוֹנִים אֲשֶׁר רָאוּ הַשָּׂדֶה בְּקָמוֹתֶיהָ וְיִתְאַוּוּ תַאֲוָה אֵלֶיהָ לְמַלֵּא נַפְשָׁם בָּהּ כִּי רָעֵבוּ, יוֹרֶה בְנַפְשׁוֹ בְּלִי סָפֵק רֹעַ לֵב וְנֶפֶשׁ רָעָה, וְגַם רָעָה תְבוֹאֵהוּ, וּכְמוֹ שֶׁאָמְרוּ זִכְרוֹנָם לִבְרָכָה: בְּמִדָּה שֶׁאָדָם מוֹדֵד, בָּהּ מוֹדְדִין לוֹ. וְזֶה הָעִנְיָן יַסְפִּיק לָנוּ עַל צַד הַפְּשָׁט גַּם בְּלֶקֶט וְשִׁכְחָה וּפֶרֶט הַכֶּרֶם וְעוֹלְלוֹת.

מִדִּינֵי הַמִּצְוָה, כְּגוֹן מַה שֶׁאָמְרוּ זִכְרוֹנָם לִבְרָכָה שֶׁאֶחָד הַקּוֹצֵר אוֹ הַתּוֹלֵשׁ חַיָּב בְּפֵאָה, וְאַף־עַל־פִּי שֶׁכָּתוּב קוֹצֵר, לָאו דַּוְקָא; וְאִם עָבַר וְקָצַר הַכֹּל, נוֹתֵן מְעַט מִן הַקָּצוּר לָעֲנִיִּים; וּמַה שֶׁאָמְרוּ זִכְרוֹנָם לִבְרָכָה שֶׁאֵין בְּמַתְּנוֹת עֲנִיִּים אֵלּוּ טוֹבַת הֲנָאָה לַבְּעָלִים אֶלָּא הֵם נוֹטְלִין אוֹתָן בְּעַל כָּרְחָן; וְדִין מֵאֵימָתַי כָּל אָדָם מֻתָּרִין בָּהֶם; וּמַה שֶׁאָמְרוּ זִכְרוֹנָם לִבְרָכָה שֶׁאִם אֵין עֲנִיִּים שֶׁיִּטְּלוּ הַפֵּאָה, שֶׁמֻּתָּר לְבַעַל הַשָּׂדֶה לִטְּלָהּ, שֶׁנֶּאֱמַר: לֶעָנִי וְלַגֵּר, וְדָרְשׁוּ זִכְרוֹנָם לִבְרָכָה: וְלֹא לָעוֹרְבִים וְלָעֲטַלֵּפִים.

וּכְלָל זֶה נָתְנוּ זִכְרוֹנָם לִבְרָכָה בְּחִיּוּב הַפֵּאָה, בֵּין בְּפֵאָה שֶׁל תְּבוּאָה אוֹ שֶׁל אִילָן: כָּל אֹכֶל שֶׁגִּדּוּלוֹ מִן הָאָרֶץ וְנִלְקָט כֻּלּוֹ כְּאֶחָד וּמַכְנִיסִין אוֹתוֹ לְקִיּוּם, כְּגוֹן הַתְּבוּאָה וְהַקִּטְנִית וְהֶחָרוּבִין וְהָאֱגוֹזִים וּשְׁקֵדִים וַעֲנָבִים וְזֵיתִים וּתְמָרִים, וְכָל כַּיּוֹצֵא בָאֵלּוּ שֶׁיֵּשׁ בָּהֶן חָמֵשׁ דְּבָרִים אֵלּוּ שֶׁאָמַרְנוּ, חַיָּב בְּפֵאָה,

---

§216   1. As opposed to *gér toshav*, a heathen who merely renounced idolatry, accepting only the seven precepts which the Torah imposes on all mankind.

    2. I.e. the two listed with "the stranger," the orphan and the widow, attest that the term denotes a full convert to Judaism (as observant of the precepts as they); derived from Sifra, *k'doshim, perek* 3, 4.

    3. Literally, on account of the ways of peace; i.e. for the sake of peaceful relations; TB Gittin 59b.

    4. Mishnah, Pé'ah i 2.

    5. TB Sotah 8b.

    6. TB Ḥullin 137a.

    7. TB Bava Kamma 94a, etc.

    8. I.e. by choosing the particular poor people whom he would give the produce of the unreaped part of the field — e.g. friends, or those who would do him favors; TB Ḥullin 131a.

    9. Mishnah, Pé'ah viii 1 (see Rashi, TB Ta'anith 6b, s.v. *mi-she-yélchu*).

    10. I.e. there is no need to let it go to waste; TB Ḥullin 134b.

    11. Mishnah, Pé'ah i 4-5.

and it thus becomes good, so that the blessing of the Eternal Lord is bestowed upon it. Well, there is no doubt that when a man leaves over one part of the produce in his field and makes it ownerless, so that those in need can benefit from it, you will perceive in his soul a fulfilling satisfaction and a decent and blessed spirit, whereupon the Eternal Lord will satisfy him with His goodness, and *his soul shall abide in good fortune* (Psalms 25:13).

On the other hand, if someone gathers everything into the house, leaving no blessing behind him, so that the poor could benefit from it, having seen the field with the crops grown tall and thus felt a yearning desire for it to fill their souls with it when they grow hungry—he displays in his soul, past any doubt, an evil heart and a mean spirit. Then evil will equally befall him. As the Sages of blessed memory said:[5] By the yardstick with which a man measures, by that is he measured. And this reason will be enough, too, by way of the plain meaning, [to explain] about gleanings (§218), forgotten sheaves (§592), single grapes in the vineyard (§222), and small single bunches of grapes (§220).

Among the laws of the precept, there is, for example, what the Sages of blessed memory taught:[6] that whether one cuts or plucks [picks, in reaping] he has the obligation to leave a bit of area unreaped; even though the term "cutting" is used in the verse, this is not meant specifically. If one went ahead and reaped everything, he is to give a bit of the harvested produce to the poor.[7] Then we have what the Sages of blessed memory taught: that with these gifts to the poor, the owner may derive no pleasure by giving them,[8] but they can rather take them against their will. And there is the law about the time when they become permissible to everyone.[9] Further, there is what the Sages of blessed memory said: that if there are no poor to take [the produce of] the left-over part, the owner of the field is permitted to take it: For it is stated, *for the poor and for the stranger* (Leviticus 19:10), and our Sages of blessed memory interpreted: but not for the ravens and the bats.[10]

Further, our Sages of blessed memory gave this rule for the duty of leaving an unreaped part of the field, whether it is a bit of a field of produce or a part of an orchard: All food that is grown from the earth, watched (tended), gathered all at once, and taken somewhere to keep it—for instance, grains, legumes, carob, nuts, almonds, grapes, olives, dates, and everything similar that has these five characteristics that we said—is subject to the obligation of leaving an unreaped part.[11]

אֲבָל אִיסְטִיס וּפוּאָה וְכַיוֹצֵא בָהֶן פְּטוּרִין, מִפְּנֵי שֶׁאֵינָן אֹכֶל; וְכֵן כְּמֵהִין וּפִטְרִיוֹת
פְּטוּרִין [לְפִי שֶׁאֵין גִּדּוּלֵיהֶן מִן הָאָרֶץ כִּשְׁאָר פֵּרוֹת הָאָרֶץ; וְכֵן הַהֶפְקֵר פָּטוּר]
לְפִי שֶׁאֵינוֹ נִשְׁמָר; וְכֵן תְּאֵנִים אֵינָם חַיָּבִין, לְפִי שֶׁאֵין לְקִיטָתָן כְּאֶחָד; וְכֵן הַיָּרָק
פָּטוּר, לְפִי שֶׁאֵין מַכְנִיסִין אוֹתוֹ לְקִיּוּם.

וְכֵן מַה שֶּׁאָמְרוּ זִכְרוֹנָם לִבְרָכָה שֶׁאֵין הַפֵּאָה חַיָּב אֶלָּא לְאַחַר שֶׁהֵבִיאוּ
הַפֵּרוֹת שְׁלִישׁ, וְשֶׁאֵין מַנִּיחִין הַפֵּאָה אֶלָּא בְּסוֹף הַשָּׂדֶה, כְּדֵי שֶׁיֵּדְעוּ הָעֲנִיִּים
מְקוֹמָהּ.

וְדִין הָאַחִין שֶׁחָלְקוּ שֶׁהַשָּׂדֶה מַה דִּינָהּ בְּפֵאָה, וְכֵן הַשֻּׁתָּפִין שֶׁחָלְקוּ, וְדִין הַמּוֹכֵר
מְקוֹמוֹת מִשָּׂדֵהוּ לַאֲנָשִׁים; וְדִין עָנִי אֶחָד אוֹמֵר לַחֲלֹק הַפֵּאָה בֵּינֵיהֶם וַחֲבֵרָיו
אוֹמְרִים לָבוֹז, שֶׁשּׁוֹמְעִין לָאֶחָד, וַאֲפִלּוּ כְּנֶגֶד כַּמָּה, לְפִי שֶׁהוּא אוֹמֵר כַּהֲלָכָה;
וְדִין בְּאֵי זֶה עוֹנוֹת בַּיּוֹם מְחַלְּקִין הַפֵּאָה; וְדִין עָנִי שֶׁנָּטַל מִקְצָת פֵּאָה וְזָרַק עַל
הַשְּׁאָר אוֹ שֶׁפֵּרֵס טַלִּיתוֹ עָלֶיהָ; וְדִין עֲנִיִּים הָעוֹמְדִים עַל הַפֵּאָה, שֶׁאִם בָּא עָנִי
וּנְטָלָהּ זָכָה בָּהּ, לְפִי שֶׁאֵין עָנִי זוֹכֶה בְּלֶקֶט שִׁכְחָה וּפֵאָה וְלֹא כָל אָדָם בִּסְלַע שֶׁל
מְצִיאָה עַד שֶׁיַּגִּיעוּ לְיָדוֹ; וְכֵן מַה שֶּׁאָמְרוּ זִכְרוֹנָם לִבְרָכָה שֶׁאָדָם חַיָּב לְהוֹסִיף
בְּפֵאָה לְפִי גֹדֶל הַשָּׂדֶה וּלְפִי רֹב הָעֲנִיִּים וּלְפִי בִּרְכַּת הַזֶּרַע; וְיֶתֶר רַבֵּי פְּרָטֶיהָ,
בַּמַּסֶּכְתָּא הַבְּנוּיָה עַל זֶה, וְהִיא מַסֶּכֶת פֵּאָה.

וְנוֹהֶגֶת מִן הַתּוֹרָה בִּזְכָרִים וּנְקֵבוֹת, בֵּין בְּיִשְׂרָאֵל בֵּין בְּכֹהֵן וְלֵוִי, וּבְאֶרֶץ
יִשְׂרָאֵל דַּוְקָא, וּבִזְמַן שֶׁיִּשְׂרָאֵל שָׁם, כִּתְרוּמָה וּמַעַשְׂרוֹת, כְּדַעַת הָרַמְבַּ"ם זִכְרוֹנוֹ
לִבְרָכָה, שֶׁאָמַר כִּי תְרוּמָה וּמַעַשְׂרוֹת אֵינָן נוֹהֲגִין אֶלָּא בָּאָרֶץ וּבִזְמַן שֶׁיִּשְׂרָאֵל
שָׁם דַּוְקָא, וּכְמוֹ שֶׁנִּכְתֹּב בְּעֶזְרַת הַשֵּׁם בְּסֵדֶר שׁוֹפְטִים עָשֶׂה ו' [סִי' תק"ז].

---

12. TB Shabbath 68a. The bracketed addition is to correct an evident scribal error noted in MH. It is based on MT *hilchoth mat'noth aniyyim* ii 2, which our author has clearly followed here. Something like this must have been present in the original, and was omitted by an early copyist, by a jump of the eye between similar words; for without it the text is untenable: mushrooms, etc. (which are held to derive their sustenance for growth from the air) need not necessarily grow untended and unwatched.

13. TJ Pé'ah iv 4.

14. I.e. when and where the reaping is ended; TB Shabbath 23a (see Rashi s.v. *l'sof sadéhu*, and 23b, s.v. *umip'né*).

15. Mishnah, Pé'ah iii 5.

16. *Ibid.* iv 1 (where it is too dangerous, however, for an ordinary person to attempt to reach the left-over produce, it is the accepted law that the owner is to obtain and distribute it: *ibid.* 2).

17. *Ibid.* iv 5.

18. I.e. in order to claim it; *ibid.* 5.

19. *Ibid.*

20. TB Bava M'tzi'a 118a and 2a.

⟨16⟩

But woad (*isatis tinctoria*), dyer's madder (*rubia tinctorum*), and so forth, are not subject to this obligation, because they are not foods; likewise morels and mushrooms, [because their growth-sustenance is not from the earth, like other produce of the soil; and ownerless produce is likewise free of the obligation] because it is not watched (tended). Similarly figs do not impose the obligation, because their gathering is not done all at once. So too are green vegetables not subject to the duty, because they are not taken in for storage.[12]

We have, likewise, what the Sages of blessed memory taught:[13] that the duty of leaving an unreaped part comes only when the produce has attained a third of its growth. The part left over should be nowhere but at the end of the field,[14] so that the poor will know its place.

Moreover, we have the law of two brothers who divided a field, what is their duty in regard to the left-over part;[15] and so too if partners divided a field.[15] And there is the law of one who sells sections of his field to people;[15] and the law if one poor man says to divide the left-over part among them, and his fellows say to plunder it—that the one is heeded, even against any number [of opponents], because he speaks according to the accepted law.[16] And there is the law about which times of the day the produce of the left-over part is shared out;[17] the law if a poor man took some of the left-over produce and threw it over the rest, or if he spread his cloak over it;[18] and the law that if poor people are standing about a left-over part and an indigent man comes and takes it [its produce] he gains it[19]—because a poor man cannot establish a claim to gleanings, forgotten sheaves, or an unreaped corner, nor any man to a coin that he finds, until it gets into his hand.[20] Likewise, there is what the Sages of blessed memory said:[21] that a man is duty-bound to add to the unreaped part according to the size of the field, according to the greater number of poor, and according to the blessing in the yield. The rest of its many details are in the Mishnah tractate composed about this: the tractate *Pē'ah*.

By the law of the Torah it applies to both man and woman, to an ordinary Israelite, a *kohen*, and a Levite—but specifically in the land of Israel, and at the time that the Israelites are there; as [the law is for] *t'rumah* [the part of the produce given a *kohen*] and *ma'as'roth* (tithes). So according to Rambam of blessed memory,[22] who stated that *t'rumah* and *ma'as'roth* are in force to be observed only in the land, and at the time that the Israelites are there, as we will write, with the Eternal Lord's help, in the sixth positive precept of *sidrah shof'tim*

וּמִדְּרַבָּנָן נוֹהֶגֶת אֲפִלּוּ בְּחוּצָה לָאָרֶץ. וְכָתַב הוּא זִכְרוֹנוֹ לִבְרָכָה שֶׁיֵּרָאֶה לוֹ
דְּהוּא הַדִּין לִשְׁאָר מַתְּנוֹת עֲנִיִּים שֶׁהֵן כֻּלָּן נוֹהֲגוֹת בְּחוּצָה לָאָרֶץ מִדִּבְרֵי סוֹפְרִים.

וְעוֹבֵר עָלֶיהָ וְלֹא הִנִּיחַ פֵּאָה בָּאָרֶץ בִּזְמַן שֶׁהִיא בְּיִשּׁוּבָהּ, בִּטֵּל עֲשֵׂה זֶה וְחַיָּב
לָתֵת מִן הַפֵּרוֹת שִׁעוּר הַפֵּאָה לַעֲנִיִּים; וְאִם אָבְדוּ אוֹ נִשְׂרְפוּ כָּל הַפֵּרוֹת קֹדֶם
שֶׁיִּתֵּן מֵהֶם כְּלוּם לַעֲנִיִּים, לוֹקֶה מִשּׁוּם לָאו דְּלֹא תְכַלֶּה פְּאַת שָׂדְךָ, מִכֵּיוָן שֶׁאֵין
בְּיָדוֹ עוֹד לְתַקֵּן הַלָּאו; אֲבָל כָּל זְמַן שֶׁיֵּשׁ בְּיָדוֹ מִן הַפֵּרוֹת נוֹתֵן מֵהֶן וּפָטוּר בְּכָךְ,
לְפִי שֶׁהַלָּאו הַזֶּה הוּא לָאו שֶׁנִּתַּק לַעֲשֵׂה, וְכֵן לָאו דְּלֶקֶט, כְּמוֹ שֶׁהִתְבָּאֵר בְּפֵאָה
וּבְמַכּוֹת.

[שֶׁלֹּא לְכַלּוֹת הַפֵּאָה בַּשָּׂדֶה]

ריז שֶׁלֹּא לִקְצֹר כָּל הַנִּזְרוֹעַ אֲבָל יַעֲזֹב מִמֶּנּוּ שְׁאֵרִית לָעֲנִיִּים בִּקְצֵה הַשָּׂדֶה,
שֶׁנֶּאֱמַר: לֹא תְכַלֶּה פְּאַת שָׂדְךָ לִקְצֹר. וְזֶה הַלָּאו נִתָּק לַעֲשֵׂה, שֶׁנֶּאֱמַר: לֶעָנִי וְלַגֵּר
תַּעֲזֹב אֹתָם וְגוֹמֵר, כְּלוֹמַר שֶׁאִם עָבַר וְקָצַר כָּל הַשָּׂדֶה, שֶׁיִּתֵּן לָעֲנִיִּים מִן הַקָּצוּר
שִׁעוּר פֵּאָה; וְהוּא חֵלֶק אֶחָד מִשִּׁשִּׁים מִדְּרַבָּנָן, שֶׁחִיְּבוּנוּ כֵן, אֲבָל מִן הַתּוֹרָה אֵין
לָהּ שִׁעוּר, כִּדְתְנַן: אֵלּוּ דְבָרִים שֶׁאֵין לָהֶם שִׁעוּר, הַפֵּאָה וְכוּלֵי.

מִשָּׁרְשֵׁי הַמִּצְוָה וְדִינֶיהָ וְכָל עִנְיָנֶיהָ, כָּתַבְתִּי לְמַעְלָה בְּמִצְוַת עֲשֵׂה ב' שֶׁבְּסֵדֶר
זֶה [סִי' רֵ"ז] מַה שֶּׁיָּדַעְתִּי בָהּ.

[מִצְוַת לֶקֶט]

ריח לַעֲזֹב הַלֶּקֶט לַעֲנִיִּים, וְהוּא מַה שֶּׁנּוֹפֵל מִתּוֹךְ הַמַּגָּל בִּשְׁעַת קְצִירָה אוֹ
מִתּוֹךְ הַיָּד בִּשְׁעַת תְּלִישָׁה, שֶׁנֶּאֱמַר בְּלֶקֶט: לֶעָנִי וְלַגֵּר תַּעֲזֹב אֹתָם.

21. Mishnah Pé'ah i 2.
22. MT *bilchoth t'rumoth* i 26.
23. MT *bilchoth mat'noth aniyyim* i 14.

§217   1. I.e. the amount of produce they would have gathered from a left-over, unreaped part of a field.
2. Mishnah, Pé'ah i 2.
3. *Ibid.* 1.

(§ 507). By the ruling of the Sages, however, it is in effect even outside the land. And he (of blessed memory) wrote²³ that it seems to him the same law holds for the other gifts to the poor—that they are all in force, to be observed, outside the land, by the ruling of the Sages.

If someone transgressed it and did not leave an unreaped part [of his field] in the land [of Israel] at a time that it was in its settled, inhabited state, he would disobey this positive precept, and he would be obligated to give of the produce the amount of an unreaped part, to the poor. If all the produce was lost or burned before he gave any of it to the poor, he should be whipped with lashes, on account of the negative precept, *you shall not wholly reap your field, to its very edge* (Leviticus 19:9), since he no longer has the means to make amends for the negative precept. But as long as he has some of the produce in his possession, he gives of it, and is thus free of penalty, because this negative precept is one whose violation is linked to a positive precept [to be made right by it]; and so too the negative precept about gleanings (§ 219), as explained in the tractates *Pē'ah* and *Makkoth* (15b).

217 [NOT TO REAP THE VERY LAST END OF ONE'S FIELD] not to reap the entire crop, but rather to leave a remnant of it over for the poor at the edge of the field: for it is stated, *you shall not wholly reap your field, to its very end* (Leviticus 19:9). This negative precept's transgression is given over to a positive precept for rectification: for it is stated, *you shall leave them for the poor and for the stranger* (*ibid*. 10). In other words, if a person transgressed and reaped the entire field, he is to give the poor out of the produce the amount of an unreaped part,¹ which is one sixtieth by the ruling of the Sages, who so obligated us.² By the law of the Torah it has no fixed amount, as we learned in the Mishnah:³ "These are things for which there is no fixed amount: the unreaped part," etc.

The root reason for the precept, its laws, and all its subject matter, I wrote above, in the second positive precept of this *sidrah* (§ 216)— what I knew of it.

218 [THE PRECEPT OF LEAVING THE GLEANINGS OF THE HARVEST FOR THE POOR] to leave the gleanings for the poor, these being what falls from the sickle during the reaping or from the hand during the picking: for it is stated in regard to gleanings, *you shall leave them to the poor and to the stranger* (Leviticus 19:10).

מִשָּׁרְשֵׁי הַמִּצְוָה, כָּתַבְתִּי בְמִצְוַת הַפֵּאָה מַה שֶּׁיָּדַעְתִּי.

מִדִּינֵי הַמִּצְוָה, כְּגוֹן מַה שֶּׁאָמְרוּ זִכְרוֹנָם לִבְרָכָה: שִׁבֹּלֶת אַחַת אוֹ שְׁתַּיִם לֶקֶט, שָׁלֹשׁ אֵינָם לֶקֶט, כְּלוֹמַר שֶׁאִם נָפְלוּ שָׁלֹשׁ שִׁבֳּלִים אוֹ יוֹתֵר בְּיַחַד מִיַּד הַקּוֹצֵר, שֶׁלְּשָׁתָּן לְבַעַל הַשָּׂדֶה, שֶׁאֵין דִּין לֶקֶט אֶלָּא בְּמוּעָט; וְדַוְקָא שֶׁנָּפַל הַלֶּקֶט מִיַּד הַקּוֹצֵר בְּלֹא אֹנֶס, אֲבָל הִכָּהוּ קוֹץ בְּיָדוֹ וְנָפַל, אֵין זֶה לֶקֶט. וְסָפֵק לֶקֶט — לֶקֶט, שֶׁנֶּאֱמַר: עָנִי וָרָשׁ הַצְדִּיקוּ, צַדֵּק מִשֶּׁלְּךָ וְתֵן לוֹ. וְדִין תְּבוּאָה הַנִּמְצֵאת בְּחוֹרֵי הַנְּמָלִים; וְדִין שִׁבֹּלֶת שֶׁל לֶקֶט שֶׁנִּתְעָרְבָה בְגָדִישׁ; וְיֶתֶר פְּרָטֶיהָ, מְבֹאָרִים בְּמַסֶּכֶת פֵּאָה. וּלְעִנְיַן בְּאֵי זֶה מָקוֹם נוֹהֶגֶת וּמִי חַיָּב בָּהּ וְעֹנֶשׁ הָעוֹבֵר עָלֶיהָ, הַכֹּל כְּמוֹ בְּפֵאָה.

[שֶׁלֹּא לָקַחַת שִׁבֳּלִים הַנּוֹפְלִים בִּשְׁעַת הַקָּצִיר]

רי**ט** שֶׁלֹּא לָקַחַת שִׁבֳּלִים הַנּוֹפְלִים בִּשְׁעַת הַקָּצִיר, אֲבָל נַעֲזֹב אוֹתָם לָעֲנִיִּים, שֶׁנֶּאֱמַר: וְלֶקֶט קְצִירְךָ לֹא תְלַקֵּט. וְזֶה גַם־כֵּן נִתָּק לַעֲשֵׂה, כְּמוֹ שֶׁבֵּאַרְנוּ בְּפֵאָה. וְכָל עִנְיַן מִצְוָה זוֹ גַם־כֵּן כְּתַבְתִּיו לְמַעְלָה בְּסֵדֶר זֶה, בְּמִצְוַת עֲשֵׂה שֶׁל לֶקֶט, ג׳.

[מִצְוַת הַנַּחַת פְּאַת הַכֶּרֶם]

ר**כ** לְהַנִּיחַ פֵּאָה בַּכֶּרֶם; וּפֵאָה זוֹ שֶׁל כֶּרֶם הוֹצִיאָהּ הַכָּתוּב בִּלְשׁוֹן עוֹלְלוֹת, כְּלוֹמַר שֶׁנִּצְטַוֵּינוּ שֶׁנַּשְׁאִיר כָּל הָעוֹלְלוֹת שֶׁבַּכֶּרֶם לְפֵאָה, וְזֶהוּ דִּכְתִיב "לֶעָנִי וְלַגֵּר תַּעֲזֹב אֹתָם" אַחַר שֶׁנֶּאֱמַר "וְכַרְמְךָ לֹא תְעוֹלֵל"; זֶהוּ דַעַת הָרַמְבַּ"ם זִכְרוֹנוֹ לִבְרָכָה.

§218

1. Mishnah, Pé'ah vi 5.
2. *Ibid.* iv 10.
3. *Ibid.* 11.
4. I.e. give him the benefit of the doubt; TB Ḥullin 134a.
5. Mishnah, Pé'ah iv 11; TB *ibid.* (MT *bilchoth mat'noth aniyyim* iv 9).
6. Mishnah, Pé'ah v 2.

§220

1. The Hebrew verb is *th'olél*, from the same root as *ol'loth*; hence it denotes, "do not strip it bare of *ol'loth*, the small single bunches."

2. According to Ramban, *Commentary (hassagoth) to ShM*, Introduction to the details of the precepts, Rambam writes in ShM, root-principle 9, that the Divine injunctions *you shall not strip your vineyard bare* and *When you beat your olive tree, you shall not go over (th'fa'ér) the boughs behind you* (Deuteronomy 24:20) "are one restriction, on one point: that you are not to gather all the fruit. The left-overs of grapes are called *ol'loth* [see note 1] and of olives, *po'roth*" (from the same root as *th'fa'ér*). As MY notes here, this was evidently in the first version of ShM, which R. Abraham b. Ḥisdai translated (R. Moses ibn Tibbon mentions the version and the translation — both no longer extant — in his introduction to *his* translation). It might be noted tangentially that

As to the root purpose of the precept, I wrote in the precept of the unreaped part of the field (§216) what I knew.

Among the laws of the precept there is, for example, what the Sages of blessed memory said:[1] one or two ears [of grain] are gleanings; three are not gleanings. In other words, if three ears or more fell together from the reaper's hand, all three belong to the owner; for the law of gleanings applies only to a smaller amount. Then, this holds specifically when the gleanings fell from the reaper's hand where there was no compulsion; but if a thorn struck his hand and they fell, they are not gleanings [for the poor].[2] Where there is doubt if certain ears, etc. are gleanings, they are [considered] gleanings:[3] for it is stated, *grant the afflicted and the destitute right* (Psalms 82:3)—grant [him] the right to what is yours and give it to him.[4] Then there is the law of grain found in ant-holes;[5] and the law of an ear from gleanings that became mixed up in a stack.[6] The rest of its details are explained in the Mishnah tractate *Pé'ah*. Regarding the location where it is in effect, who bears the obligation to observe it, and the punishment of a person who transgresses it, all is the same as for the left-over, unreaped part of the field (§216).

[NOT TO GATHER STALKS OF GRAIN THAT FELL AWAY DURING THE HARVEST]

219 not to take ears [of grain] that fall during the reaping, but we should rather leave them for the poor: as it is stated, *neither shall you gather the gleanings of your harvest* (Leviticus 19:9). The transgression of this too is given over to [rectification by] a positive precept, as we explained about the left-over part of the field. And everything concerning this precept I have likewise written above, in this *sidrah*, in the third positive precept, about gleanings (§218).

[THE PRECEPT OF LEAVING A PART OF A VINEYARD UNREAPED, FOR THE POOR]

220 to leave over an unharvested part in a vineyard; Scripture used the term *ol'loth* to denote this unharvested part, which is to say that we were commanded to leave all the *ol'loth* in the vineyard, as the unharvested part; and this is why it is written, *you shall leave them for the poor and for the stranger* (Leviticus 19:10) after Scripture mentions, *And you shall not strip your vineyard bare*[1] (ibid.). This is the view of Rambam of blessed memory about the small single bunches

בְּעוֹלְלוֹת הַכֶּרֶם, שֶׁהֵם בִּמְקוֹם פֵּאָה שֶׁבִּשְׁאָר אִילָנוֹת; וְהָרַמְבַּ"ן זִכְרוֹנוֹ לִבְרָכָה
לֹא פֵּרַשׁ כֵּן. וּבְלָאו דְּ"וְכַרְמְךָ לֹא תְעוֹלֵל", שֶׁהוּא בְּסֵדֶר זֶה [סִי' רכ"א], אֶכְתּׂב
עִקַּר מַחְלְקֹתָם בָּאָרֶץ. וְעוֹד אֲבָאֵר שָׁם פֵּאָה בְּכָל הָאִילָנוֹת מִנַּיִן, וְכָל עִנְיְנֵי
הַמִּצְוָה כְּמִנְהָגִי, בְּעֶזְרַת הַשֵּׁם.

[שֶׁלֹּא לְכַלּוֹת פְּאַת הַכֶּרֶם]

רכא שֶׁלֹּא לְכַלּוֹת כָּל פֵּרוֹת הַכֶּרֶם בְּעֵת הַבָּצִיר, אֲבָל יַנִּיחַ מֵהֶם פֵּאָה לָעֲנִיִּים,
שֶׁנֶּאֱמַר: וְכַרְמְךָ לֹא תְעוֹלֵל, וְזֶהוּ פְּאַת הַכֶּרֶם; כֵּן כָּתַב הָרַמְבַּ"ם זִכְרוֹנוֹ לִבְרָכָה.
וְעוֹד אָמַר כִּי מַה שֶּׁכָּתוּב "לֹא תְפָאֵר אַחֲרֶיךָ" בְּזֵיתִים, יוֹרֶה גַם־כֵּן עַל פְּאַת
הַזַּיִת, כִּי פְּאַת הַזֵּיתִים נִקְרָאִים פֵּארוֹת, וּפְאַת הַכֶּרֶם, עוֹלְלוֹת; וּמִשְּׁנֵיהֶם נִלְמַד
לְכָל הָאִילָנוֹת.

וְהָרַמְבַּ"ן זִכְרוֹנוֹ לִבְרָכָה הִשִּׂיג עָלָיו בָּזֶה וְאָמַר כִּי כֻלּוֹ טָעוּת; וְאָמַר כִּי לָאו
דְּ"וְכַרְמְךָ" מְיֻחָד דַּוְקָא בְּכֶרֶם, וְהוּא שֶׁנַּנִּיחַ בָּהּ כָּל הָעֲנָבִים הַקְּטַנִּים שֶׁאֵין לָהֶם
כָּתֵף וְנָטֵף; וּפֵרוּשׁ "כָּתֵף" פְּסִיגִין זֶה עַל גַּבֵּי זֶה, "נָטֵף", תְּלוּיוֹת כֻּלָּן וְיוֹרְדוֹת.
וְנִמְצָא לְפִי זֶה שֶׁעוֹלְלוֹת הֵן הָעֲנָבִים הַקְּטַנִּים הַנִּמְצָאִים בַּכְּרָמִים לִפְעָמִים,
הַנִּקְרָאִין בְּלַעַז גַּטִּימ"שׁ; וְזֶהוּ דָבָר מוּעָט בְּוַדַּאי, לְפִי הַנִּרְאֶה בַּכְּרָמִים שֶׁלָּנוּ. וְכֵן
אָמְרוּ זִכְרוֹנָם לִבְרָכָה: אֵי זֶהוּ עוֹלְלוֹת, כָּל שֶׁאֵין לוֹ לֹא כָתֵף וְלֹא נָטֵף.

וּמִלְּבַד חִיּוּב זֶה שֶׁל עוֹלְלוֹת יֵשׁ עָלֵינוּ חִיּוּב לְהַנִּיחַ פֵּאָה. וּבִפְאַת הַכֶּרֶם לֹא
בָא עָלֶיהָ כָּתוּב מְבֹאָר אֶלָּא דְּגַמְרִינָן אַחֲרֶיךָ מְזֵיתִים, וְכִדְאָמְרִינָן בַּגְּמָרָא
חָלִין בְּפֵרוּשׁ: אַרְבַּע מַתָּנוֹת שֶׁבַּכֶּרֶם, הַפֶּרֶט וְהָעוֹלְלוֹת הַשִּׁכְחָה וְהַפֵּאָה; שְׁנַיִם

according to ed. Heller and ed. Kafaḥ (Arabic-Hebrew, Jerusalem 1971), the last
sentence ("The left-overs" etc.) is not found in the extant Arabic texts of ShM; but it is
present in ibn Tibbon's translation. At any rate, in ShM as *we* have it, the passage in
question regards the two prohibitions as "one injunction, on one point: that one is not to
take what he has forgotten of either grain or fruit, when he is gathering them."

Ramban (*loc. cit.*) continues: "And he [Rambam] wrote in [ShM] positive precept
223 that we were commanded to leave for the poor whatever remains [ed. Kafaḥ: the
leavings that remain] in the vineyard during the grape harvest, this being what is called
ol'loth." Whereas in root principle 9 Rambam evidently revised his text to rank the *ol'loth*
(small single bunches) as "forgotten fruit" rather than *pé'ah* (an unreaped part), here he
has evidently not done so. But this problem must be left for §221, note 2. Suffice it to
conclude here that ShM positive precept 223, taken with the passage in root principle 9,
first version, is the basis for our author's present statement.

§221   1. Generally translated as boughs.

2. In §220 note 2, two passages from ShM as cited by Ramban (*loc. cit.*) were given.
He continues: "And so he [Rambam] wrote further in negative precept 212, that He (be   ⟨22⟩

of grapes in the vineyard [2]—that they are in place of the unharvested part of other trees. However, Ramban of blessed memory did not explain it so. In the negative precept, *you shall not strip your vineyard bare (ibid.—§221)* which is in this *sidrah*, I will write the main point of their difference of opinion, at length. I will also explain there how we learn that an unharvested part of all trees should be left, and so likewise the whole subject-matter of the precept, as it is my custom, with the Eternal Lord's help.

[THE PROHIBITION OF REAPING ABSOLUTELY ALL THE FRUIT OF A VINEYARD]

221 not to remove absolutely all the fruit of a vineyard during the vintage (harvest), but rather to leave over an unharvested part of them for the poor: as it is stated, *And you shall not strip your vineyard bare* (Leviticus 19:10); and this is *pē'ah*, the left-over unharvested part of the vineyard. So Ramban of blessed memory wrote. He said further that the verse, *you shall not go over the boughs behind you* (Deuteronomy 24:20), about olive trees, likewise signifies an unharvested, left-over part of an olive orchard; for the unharvested part of an olive orchard is called *po'roth*,[1] and the unharvested part of a vineyard, *ol'loth*. And from these two we learn [that the law applies] to all trees.[2]

However, Ramban of blessed memory refuted him about this[3] and said it is entirely erroneous. He holds that the negative precept, *you shall not strip your vineyard bare*, applies specifically to a vineyard: it means that we should leave over in it all the small grapes that have neither "shoulder" nor "dripping." The meaning of "shoulder" is sprigs, one over the other; and "dripping" denotes that all hang and go down. Hence, according to this, *ol'loth* are the small grapes found in vineyards at times, which are called *gatimas* in the foreign tongue [Spanish]; and this is certainly something quite little, as it appears in our vineyards. So too did our Sages say:[4] What is defined as *ol'loth*?— whatever has neither "shoulder" nor "dripping."

Now, apart from this duty of *ol'loth*, an obligation lies on us to leave over an unharvested bit, although no explicit verse was given about a left-over part of a vineyard. We rather learn it from [the law on] olive trees, through the identical term "after you" in their verses. As it was stated explicitly in the Talmud tractate Ḥullin (131a): There are four gifts [for the poor] in the vineyard: gleanings, *ol'loth*, forgotten bunches, and an unreaped part;[5] and there are two in an orchard:

שֶׁבָּאִילָן, הַשִּׁכְחָה וְהַפֵּאָה; וְנֶאֱמַר שָׁם פֵּאָה בַּכֶּרֶם מִדִּכְתִיב בָּה "לֹא תְעוֹלֵל
אַחֲרֶיךָ", וְאָמַר רַבִּי לֵוִי: "אַחֲרֶיךָ" זוֹ שִׁכְחָה, כְּלוֹמַר מַה שֶּׁיִּשָּׁאֵר אַחֲרֶיךָ, דְּהַיְנוּ
שִׁכְחָה; וּפֵאָה גַּמְרִינָן אַחֲרֶיךָ אַחֲרֶיךָ מִזֵּיתִים, דְּכְתִיב בְּזַיִת: כִּי תַחְבֹּט זֵיתְךָ לֹא
תְפָאֵר אַחֲרֶיךָ, וְתָנָא דְּבֵי רַבִּי יִשְׁמָעֵאל: שֶׁלֹּא תִּטֹּל תִּפְאַרְתּוֹ מִמֶּנּוּ, דְּהַיְנוּ פֵּאָה.

וְיִלְמַד הָרַמְבַּ"ן זִכְרוֹנוֹ לִבְרָכָה פֵּאָה בְּכָל הָאִילָנוֹת מִזַּיִת, שֶׁחִיֵּב הַכָּתוּב בָּה
פֵּאָה בְּפֵרוּשׁ, וּמִכֶּרֶם, שֶׁלְּמַדְנוּהוּ מִלְּשׁוֹן "אַחֲרֶיךָ". וְאָמַר הוּא זִכְרוֹנוֹ לִבְרָכָה
כִּי הָרַמְבַּ"ם זִכְרוֹנוֹ לִבְרָכָה כָּתַב הָעִנְיָן בְּתִקּוּן בְּחִבּוּרוֹ הַגָּדוֹל.

וּמִכְּלַל מַחֲלָקְתָּם זֶה אֵין לָנוּ תּוֹסֶפֶת וְגֵרוּעַ בְּחֶשְׁבּוֹן הַלָּאוִין, שֶׁאֵין הַמַּחְלֹקֶת
אֶלָּא שֶׁהָרַמְבַּ"ם זִכְרוֹנוֹ לִבְרָכָה יְפָרֵשׁ "לֹא תְעוֹלֵל" לְפֵאָה, וְהָרַמְבַּ"ן זִכְרוֹנוֹ
לִבְרָכָה מְפָרֵשׁ אוֹתוֹ לְעוֹלְלוֹת מַמָּשׁ, וְיִלְמַד מִלְּשׁוֹן "אַחֲרֶיךָ" פֵּאָה בַּכֶּרֶם, כְּמוֹ
שֶׁכָּתַבְנוּ, דְּגַמְרִינָן אַחֲרֶיךָ אַחֲרֶיךָ מִזֵּיתִים.

וְזֶה הַלָּאו גַּם־כֵּן נִתָּק לַעֲשֵׂה, שֶׁאִם עָבַר וְכִלָּה הַכֹּל שֶׁחַיָּב לָתֵת הָעוֹלְלוֹת
לָעֲנִיִּים.

מִשָּׁרְשֵׁי הַמִּצְוָה וְדִינֶיהָ, כָּתַבְתִּי לְמַעֲלָה בְּסֵדֶר זֶה בְּמִצְוַת פֵּאָה [עֲשֵׂה] ב' [סִי'
רט"ז] קְצָת, וְשָׁם כָּתוּב בְּאֵי זֶה מָקוֹם נוֹהֵג הִיא וְכָל שְׁאָר מַתְּנוֹת עֲנִיִּים,
וְשֶׁפְּרָטֵי מִצְוַת פֵּאָה מְבֹאָרִים בְּמַסֶּכֶת פֵּאָה. וְעוֹד יֵשׁ לָנוּ לִכְתֹּב כָּאן מַה שֶּׁאָמְרוּ
זִכְרוֹנָם לִבְרָכָה בְּעוֹלְלוֹת: שֶׁאִם הָיָה הַכֶּרֶם כֻּלּוֹ עוֹלְלוֹת, כֻּלּוֹ הוּא לָעֲנִיִּים,
שֶׁנֶּאֱמַר: וְכַרְמְךָ לֹא תְעוֹלֵל, וְדָרְשׁוּ זִכְרוֹנָם לִבְרָכָה: אֲפִלּוּ כֻּלָּה כֻּלָּהּ עוֹלְלוֹת. וְאֵין

He exalted) stated, *And you shall not strip [your vineyard] bare,* which is an injunction against making a total clean sweep of a vineyard during the grape harvest—but we should rather leave the bunches at the edges for the poor. And such is the law for all the trees, since the restriction was reiterated, about this very matter, for olive trees: for it is stated, *you shall not go over the boughs behind you*; and from the two we learn [that the law applies] to all trees." This is quite exactly what our author has paraphrased here. (Note too that starting two lines above, our author cites, "for the unharvested part of an olive orchard . . . ol'loth," although it is not included in Ramban's version. There is a very similar passage in Ramban's citation from ShM root principle 9, given in §220 note 2. Hence both must derive from Rambam's first version of ShM, and the passage in root principle 9 is not, as claimed in ed. Kafaḥ, an addition by R. Moses ibn Tibbon.)

In the standard edition of R. Moses ibn Tibbon's Hebrew translation, we read instead that one ". . . should leave the *ol'loth* for the poor. And this law applies to other trees which are like the grapevine, for there is the injunction in His statement, 'you shall not beat your olive tree' etc. [*sic!*] which means that one should not take the forgotten fruit from an olive tree; [and thus] you know that other trees are under the law of forgotten fruit. . . ."

While the phrase in Ramban's version (end of first sentence), "at the edges," like our author's words, leaves no doubt that Rambam originally understood *ol'loth* as *pé'ah* in a vineyard, here the point is gone; and at the end the fruit to be left on olive trees is ⟨24⟩

forgotten fruit and an unharvested part. Then [the duty of] an unharvested part in a vineyard is derived there from the verse about it,
you shall not glean it after you (Deuteronomy 24:21): R. Lévi said:
"after you" signifies forgotten bunches—i.e. what will be left behind
you, which means forgotten bunches; and [the duty of] the unharvested
part we learn from [the law on] olive trees, through the identical
term "after you": For it is written about them, *When you beat your
olive-trees, you shall not go over the boughs after you* (ibid. 20), and the
School of R. Ishmael taught that [it means] you shall not take [all]
its pride from it[6]—i.e. [leave] an unharvested part.

So Ramban of blessed memory derives [the obligation of]
an unharvested part for all trees from the olive orchard, for which
Scripture explicitly imposed the duty of a left-over part, and from the
vineyard, for which we learn the obligation through the term "after
you." Then he (of blessed memory) stated further that Rambam (of
blessed memory) wrote the matter correctly in his major work.[7]

Now, from the whole of this difference of opinion between them,
we have neither an addition nor a subtraction in the reckoning of the
negative precepts. For the difference is only that Rambam of blessed
memory would interpret *you shall not glean* (Leviticus 19:9) about
the unharvested part, while Ramban of blessed memory takes it to
mean actual *ol'loth* (single small bunches), and derives the duty of an
unharvested part in a vineyard from the term "after you," as we have
written—that we learn it from olive trees, through the identical term
"after you."

The transgression of this negative precept is likewise given over
for rectification through a positive precept: If someone violated it and
stripped everything bare, he must give the small single bunches[8]
to the poor.

Some of the root reasons for the precept and its laws, I have written
above in this *sidrah*, in the second positive precept, about the unharvested part (§216), to some extent. There it is written in which
location it and all other gifts for the poor are in effect, and that the details
of the precept of the left-over part are explained in the tractate *Pé'ah*.
It remains for us to write here what the Sages of blessed memory
taught about *ol'loth*:[9] that if a vineyard consisted entirely of small
single bunches, it all goes to the poor: for it is written, *And you shall
not glean your vineyard* (Leviticus 19:9), and our Sages of blessed
memory interpreted: even if it is entirely gleanings of *ol'loth*. Then

הֶעָנִיִּים זוֹכִים לְקַח הָעוֹלֵלוֹת עַד שֶׁיַּתְחִיל בַּעַל הַכֶּרֶם לִבְצֹר כַּרְמוֹ, שֶׁנֶּאֱמַר: כִּי תִבְצֹר כַּרְמְךָ לֹא תְעוֹלֵל.

[מִצְוַת הַנַּחַת פֶּרֶט הַכֶּרֶם]

רכב לַעֲזֹב פֶּרֶט הַכֶּרֶם לַעֲנִיִּים, וְהוּא מַה שֶּׁיִּתְפָּרֵד וְיִפֹּל מִן הָעֲנָבִים בִּשְׁעַת בְּצִירָה, שֶׁנֶּאֱמַר "לֶעָנִי וְלַגֵּר תַּעֲזֹב אֹתָם" אַחַר שֶׁזָּכַר "וּפֶרֶט כַּרְמְךָ לֹא תְלַקֵּט". וּבְלָאו דְּ"לֹא תְלַקֵּט" [סי׳ רכ"ט] אֶכְתֹּב כָּל עִנְיְנֵי הַמִּצְוָה בְּעֶזְרַת הַשֵּׁם.

[שֶׁלֹּא לְלַקֵּט פֶּרֶט הַכֶּרֶם]

רכג שֶׁלֹּא נִלְקֹט פֶּרֶט הַכֶּרֶם אֲבָל נַעֲזֹב אוֹתוֹ לָעֲנִיִּים, שֶׁנֶּאֱמַר: וּפֶרֶט כַּרְמְךָ לֹא תְלַקֵּט; וְהוּא הַגַּרְעִינִים הַנּוֹשְׁרִין בִּשְׁעַת קְטִיפַת הָעֲנָבִים. וְהוּא הַדִּין לִשְׁאָר הָאִילָנוֹת הַדּוֹמִין לַכֶּרֶם, שֶׁנִּתְחַיַּבְנוּ שֶׁלֹּא לְלַקֵּט הַגַּרְעִינִין הַנּוֹשְׁרִין. רֶמֶז מִשָּׁרְשֵׁי הַמִּצְוָה בָּעִנְיָן שֶׁכָּתַבְנוּ לְמַעְלָה בְּפֵאָה.

מִדִּינֵי הַמִּצְוָה, מַה שֶּׁאָמְרוּ זִכְרוֹנָם לִבְרָכָה: אֵי זֶהוּ פֶרֶט, זֶה גַּרְגִּיר אֶחָד אוֹ שְׁנֵי גַּרְגִּרִים הַנִּפְרָטִין מִן הָאֶשְׁכּוֹל בִּשְׁעַת הַבְּצִירָה, אֲבָל שְׁלֹשָׁה גַּרְגִּרִים שֶׁנָּפְלוּ בְּבַת אַחַת אֵינוֹ פֶרֶט; הָיָה בּוֹצֵר וּמַשְׁלִיךְ לָאָרֶץ, כְּשֶׁמְּפַנֶּה הָאֶשְׁכּוֹלוֹת אֲפִלּוּ חֲצִי אֶשְׁכּוֹל הַנִּמְצָא שָׁם פֶּרֶט, וְכֵן אֶשְׁכּוֹל שָׁלֵם שֶׁנִּפְרַט שָׁם הֲרֵי הוּא פֶרֶט; וְהַמַּנִּיחַ אֶת הַכַּלְכָּלָה תַּחַת הַגֶּפֶן בְּשָׁעָה שֶׁבּוֹצֵר הֲרֵי זֶה גּוֹזֵל אֶת הָעֲנִיִּים, וְיֶתֶר פְּרָטֶיהָ, בְּמַסֶּכֶת פֵּאָה.

וְעִנְיַן הַמִּצְוָה בְּאֵי זֶה מָקוֹם נוֹהֶגֶת וּבְמִי, כָּתוּב לְמַעְלָה בְּמִצְוַת פֵּאָה [עֲשֵׂה] ב׳ [סי׳ רט"ז].

[שֶׁלֹּא לִגְנֹב שׁוּם מָמוֹן]

רכד שֶׁלֹּא לִגְנֹב שׁוּם מָמוֹן, שֶׁנֶּאֱמַר: לֹא תִּגְנֹבוּ, וְאָמְרוּ זִכְרוֹנָם לִבְרָכָה שֶׁזֶּה

regarded as shich-ḥah, "forgotten fruit"—paralleling the change from Ramban's to ibn Tibbon's version in root principle 9, pointed out in §220 note 2. The fact that in both instances the change is found only in ibn Tibbon's version may justify some doubt as to its exact origin.

Again, in ibn Tibbon's version this law for the vineyard applies not to all trees but to those "which are like the grapevine"; and ed. Heller reads that "this does not apply to other trees, even those similar to the grapevine." Further, while the text in ed. Kafaḥ is very close to Ramban's version, on this point it agrees with ed. Heller. Taken in conjunction with what follows, that the similar law for the olive tree does apply to all trees, one is at a loss to understand either version here, applying the law of ol'loth only to "similar trees" or to no other trees. (Nor, in all humility, do I find the note in English ed. Chavel helpful.)

R. Yosef Kafaḥ, a veteran scholar on Rambam's writings, is forced to conclude that

[we have the law that] the poor do not gain the right to take the small single bunches until the owner begins to harvest his vintage: for it is stated, *And you shall not glean your vineyard.*[10]

[THE PRECEPT OF LEAVING FALLEN GRAPES IN A VINE-
YARD, FOR THE POOR]

222 to leave over the *peret* of the vineyard for the poor, this being what separates and falls from the grapes during the vintage (harvest): for it is written, *you shall leave them for the poor and for the stranger* (Leviticus 19:10), after Scripture has stated, *neither shall you gather the* peret *of your vineyard* (*ibid.*). In the negative precept, "neither shall you gather" (§223) I will write everything concerning this *mitzvah*, with the Eternal Lord's help.

[THE PROHIBITION OF GATHERING THE FALLEN GRAPES
IN A VINEYARD]

223 not to gather fallen grapes in a vineyard, but we should rather leave them for the poor: for it is written, *neither shall you gather* peret, *the fallen fruit* [of your vineyard] (Leviticus 19:10), which means the single grapes that fall off during the picking of the bunches. The same law applies to other trees that are similar to grapevines: we are duty-bound not to gather the single fruits that fall loose.[1]

A suggestion of the root reason for this precept lies in the theme that we wrote above about *pé'ah*. the unharvested part (§216).

Among the laws of the precept, there is what the Sages of blessed memory taught:[2] What is *peret?*—it is one or two grapes that separate from the bunch during the vintage (harvest). But if three grapes fell at once, they are not *peret*. If a person goes picking the grapes and drop-ping them to the ground, then when he removes the bunches, if even half a bunch is found there, it is *peret*; so too a whole bunch that re-mained alone there is *peret*.[3] If someone puts a basket under a vine when he picks the grapes, he thus robs the poor.[4] The rest of its details are in the tractate *Pé'ah*. As to the subject of the location in which this precept is in effect, and for whom, it is written above, in the second positive precept, about the left-over part of the field (§216).

[THE PROHIBITION ON·THE THEFT OF ANYTHING OF
VALUE]

224 not to steal anything of value: for it is stated, *You shall not steal* (Leviticus 19:11), and the Sages of blessed memory taught that

אַזְהָרָה לְגוֹנֵב מָמוֹן. וְעִנְיַן הַגְּנֵבָה הוּא כְּמוֹ שֶׁפֵּרַשְׁנוּ בְּסֵדֶר מִשְׁפָּטִים [סִי׳ נ״ד].

שֹׁרֶשׁ מִצְוָה זוֹ יָדוּעַ, כִּי הִיא מִן הַמִּצְוֹת שֶׁהַשֵּׂכֶל מְחַיְּבָם.

מִדִּינֵי הַמִּצְוָה, מַה שֶּׁאָמְרוּ זִכְרוֹנָם לִבְרָכָה שֶׁאָסוּר מִן הַתּוֹרָה לִגְנֹב אֲפִלּוּ עַל־מְנָת לְמֵקֵט, כְּלוֹמַר כְּדֵי לְהַכְעִיס בַּעַל הַגְּנֵבָה וּלְהַבְהִילוֹ לְשָׁעָה וּלְהַחֲזִיר לוֹ הַדָּבָר אַחַר־כָּךְ; וְכֵן אָמְרוּ בְּסִפְרָא: לְפִי שֶׁנֶּאֱמַר בִּגְנֵבָה "שְׁנַיִם יְשַׁלֵּם", לָמַדְנוּ עֹנֶשׁ; אַזְהָרָה מִנַּיִן, תַּלְמוּד לוֹמַר "לֹא תִּגְנֹבוּ": לֹא תִגְנֹב אֲפִלּוּ עַל־מְנָת לְמֵקֵט, לֹא תִגְנֹב עַל־מְנָת לְשַׁלֵּם אַרְבָּעָה וַחֲמִשָּׁה.

וְדִין הַגּוֹנֵב סֶלַע מִכִּיס חֲבֵרוֹ אוֹ מִבֵּיתוֹ וְהֶחֱזִיר הַדָּבָר הַגָּנוּב לִמְקוֹמוֹ, לְדַעַת בְּעָלָיו אוֹ שֶׁלֹּא לְדַעְתּוֹ, מַה דִּינוֹ; וּבְאֵי זֶה צַד מִנְיָן פּוֹטְרוֹ; וְהַחִלּוּק שֶׁיֵּשׁ בְּעִנְיָן זֶה בֵּין דָּבָר שֶׁיֵּשׁ בּוֹ רוּחַ חַיִּים, כְּגוֹן בְּהֵמוֹת, לְמַה שֶׁאֵין בּוֹ רוּחַ חַיִּים, וּכְמוֹ שֶׁבָּא בְּקַמָּא פֶּרֶק (ז) [י]; וּמַה שֶּׁאָמְרוּ שֶׁאָסוּר לִקְנוֹת מִיָּד גַּנָּב, מִפְּנֵי שֶׁמַּחֲזִיק יְדֵי עוֹבְרֵי עֲבֵרָה; וְכֵן כָּל דָּבָר שֶׁחֶזְקָתוֹ שֶׁהוּא גָנוּב אָסוּר לָקַח אוֹתוֹ, וּלְפִיכָךְ אָמְרוּ זִכְרוֹנָם לִבְרָכָה שֶׁאֵין לוֹקְחִין מִן הָרוֹעִים צֶמֶר, חָלָב וּגְדָיִים, וְכֵן אֵין לוֹקְחִין מִשּׁוֹמְרֵי עֵצִים אוֹ פֵרוֹת אֶלָּא בִּמְקוֹמוֹת יְדוּעִים, וְכֵן אֵין לוֹקְחִין מִן הַנָּשִׁים וּמִן הָעֲבָדִים וּמִן הַקְּטַנִּים אֶלָּא דְבָרִים יְדוּעִים; וְדֶרֶךְ כְּלָל אָמְרוּ: וְכֻלָּם שֶׁאָמְרוּ "הַטְמֵן" אָסוּר לָקַח מֵהֶן.

וּמַה שֶּׁאָמְרוּ כִּי לַגַּנָּב מְפֻרְסָם לֹא עָשׂוּ בוֹ תַּקָּנַת הַשּׁוּק, וּמַחֲזִיר הַלּוֹקֵחַ מִמֶּנּוּ הַכְּלִי בְּלֹא דָמִים, וְהוּא יַעֲשֶׂה דִין עִם הַגַּנָּב; אֲבָל אִם אֵינוֹ מְפֻרְסָם יֵשׁ בּוֹ תַּקָּנַת הַשּׁוּק וּמַחֲזִיר בַּעַל הַגְּנֵבָה מְעוֹתָיו לַלּוֹקֵחַ וְנוֹטֵל כֵּלָיו, וְאַחַר־כָּךְ יַעֲשֶׂה הוּא דִין עִם הַגַּנָּב.

here and in the passages cited in §220 note 2, the great master labored under a temporary misapprehension about the fruit in a vineyard and an olive orchard to be left for the poor. And results of this misapprehension were obviously altered, but not properly corrected, in later versions of ShM. For on this subject ShM is clearly at variance with the Talmud, which our author cites in the next two paragraphs. As R. Kafaḥ states in his Introduction to his Arabic-Hebrew edition of ShM (p. 11), Rambam wrote this work after his Mishnah commentary and before MT. For the rest of his life (R. Kafaḥ notes) Rambam kept revising and correcting his works, but he gave first priority to MT and second priority to his Mishnah commentary. Evidently after ShM, Rambam took full cognizance of the Talmud in writing MT; for there (as Ramban indicates) such misapprehension about the laws of the vineyard is nowhere in evidence. R. Kafaḥ goes on to list other discrepancies between ShM and MT, which Rambam apparently found no opportunity to correct, under the press of a very heavy daily schedule (of which he has left a written record).

3. *Loc. cit.* in §220, note 2.
4. Mishnah, Péʾah vii 4.
5. Hence *olʿloth* and the unreaped part are not identical.

this is an injunction about stealing anything of value.[1] The meaning of stealing is as we explained in *sidrah mishpatim* (§54).

The root reason for this precept is known (evident), since it is one of the commandments that reason necessitates.

Among the laws of the precept, there is what the Sages of blessed memory said: that by the law of the Torah, it is forbidden to steal something even with the intention of [merely] upsetting someone[2]— i.e. in order to enrage the owner and overwhelm him for a while, and return the object to him afterward. And so is it taught in the Midrash *Sifra*:[3] Since it is stated about stealing, *he shall pay double* (Exodus 22:3), we have learned the punishment; from where do we learn the admonition?—Scripture states, *You shall not steal*: you shall not steal even with the mere intent to upset someone;[4] you shall not steal even with the purposeful intent to pay four or five times the theft.[5]

Then there is the law of a person who steals a *sela*[6] from his fellow's purse or house, and he returns the stolen object to its place, with or without its owner's knowledge—what the law is for him;[7] and under what circumstances counting [by the owner] frees him from penalty.[8] And there is the difference that applies in this matter whether [the stolen object was] something living, such as animals, or something inanimate—as it is taught in chapter 10 of the Talmud tractate *Bava Kamma* (118b). Further, there is what the Sages said:[9] that it is forbidden to buy from a thief, because that would strengthen the hands of wrong-doers. So too, if anything is firmly assumed to be stolen property, it is forbidden to buy it.[9] Therefore the Sages of blessed memory ruled[9] that wool, milk and kids should not be bought from shepherds. Similarly, one should not buy from watchmen over wood or fruit, except under certain known conditions.[9] So too, nothing but certain known objects are to be bought from women, servants, and children.[9] As a general rule, the Sages taught:[9] If any of these said, "Hide this," it is forbidden to buy it from them.

Then there is what the Sages said,[10] that for a notorious thief, they did not establish the "amendment of the market" [that if someone buys a stolen object from a thief, the owner is to refund him the money and sue the thief]; anyone who buys a [stolen] object from him is to return it without [receiving his] money, and he can then sue the thief. But if he is not notorious, the "amendment of the market" applies to him: the stolen object's owner returns the buyer his money and takes his object, and afterward he [the owner] can sue the thief.

⟨29⟩

וְכָתַב הָרַמְבַּ״ם זִכְרוֹנוֹ לִבְרָכָה, וְזֶה לְשׁוֹנוֹ: כָּל הַגּוֹנֵב מָשְׁוֶה פְּרוּטָה וּלְמַעְלָה
עוֹבֵר עַל לֹא־תַעֲשֶׂה, שֶׁנֶּאֱמַר "לֹא תִּגְנֹבוּ"; וְאֵין לוֹקִין עַל לָאו זֶה, לְפִי שֶׁנִּתַּן
לְהִשָּׁבוֹן; וְאֶחָד הַגּוֹנֵב מָמוֹן יִשְׂרָאֵל אוֹ הַגּוֹנֵב מָמוֹן עוֹבֵד עֲבוֹדָה זָרָה, וְאֶחָד
הַגּוֹנֵב אֶת הַגָּדוֹל אוֹ אֶת הַקָּטָן; עַד כָּאן; וְיֶתֶר פְּרָטֶיהָ, בְּקַמָּא פֶּרֶק שְׁבִיעִי
וּבִמְקוֹמוֹת אֲחֵרִים.

וְנוֹהֵג אִסּוּר זֶה בְּכָל מָקוֹם וּבְכָל זְמָן, בִּזְכָרִים וּנְקֵבוֹת. וְעוֹבֵר עַל לָאו זֶה וְגָנַב,
חַיָּב לְשַׁלֵּם, כְּמוֹ שֶׁמְּפֹרָשׁ בַּכָּתוּב. אִם גָּנַב דִּינָר אוֹ כְּסוּת אוֹ חֲמוֹר אוֹ גָמָל,
מְשַׁלֵּם שְׁנַיִם בִּדְמֵיהֶם, וְנִמְצָא מַפְסִיד כַּשִּׁעוּר שֶׁבִּקֵּשׁ לְחַסֵּר חֲבֵרוֹ. וְתַשְׁלוּמֵי
כֶּפֶל נוֹהֲגִין בְּכָל דָּבָר חוּץ מִשּׁוֹר וָשֶׂה, שֶׁיֵּשׁ בָּהֶן צְדָדִין שֶׁמְּשַׁלְּמִין עֲלֵיהֶן אַרְבָּעָה
וַחֲמִשָּׁה, כְּגוֹן שֶׁטָּבַח וּמָכַר, כְּמוֹ שֶׁבָּא בַכָּתוּב מְבֹאָר.

וּכְשֶׁמְּשַׁלֵּם כֶּפֶל, אוֹ אַרְבָּעָה וַחֲמִשָּׁה בְּשׁוֹר וָשֶׂה, דַּוְקָא שֶׁהֵעִידוּ עָלָיו עֵדִים,
וְשִׁלֵּם עַל פִּיהֶם בְּבֵית־דִּין; אֲבָל מוֹדֶה מֵעַצְמוֹ פָּטוּר עִם תַּשְׁלוּם הַקֶּרֶן לְבַד,
שֶׁנֶּאֱמַר: אֲשֶׁר יַרְשִׁיעֻן אֱלֹהִים יְשַׁלֵּם שְׁנַיִם, וְדָרְשׁוּ זִכְרוֹנָם לִבְרָכָה: פְּרָט
לְמַרְשִׁיעַ אֶת עַצְמוֹ; וְהוּא הַדִּין לְכָל קְנָסוֹת, שֶׁהַמּוֹדֶה בָּהֶן פָּטוּר. וּכְבָר כָּתַבְתִּי
לְמַעְלָה שֶׁאֵין דָּנִין דִּינֵי קְנָסוֹת אֶלָּא בָּאָרֶץ.

[שֶׁלֹּא נְכַחֵשׁ עַל מָמוֹן שֶׁיֵּשׁ לְאַחֵר בְּיָדֵינוּ]

רכה שֶׁלֹּא נְכַחֵשׁ בַּמֶּה שֶׁהֻפְקַד בְּיָדֵינוּ וּבְכָל מַה שֶּׁיֵּשׁ לְזוּלָתֵנוּ עָלֵינוּ,
שֶׁנֶּאֱמַר: וְלֹא תְכַחֲשׁוּ, וּבָא הַפֵּרוּשׁ שֶׁבְּמָמוֹן הַכָּתוּב מְדַבֵּר. וּלְשׁוֹן סִפְרָא: לְפִי
שֶׁנֶּאֱמַר "וְכִחֶשׁ בָּהּ וְנִשְׁבַּע עַל שָׁקֶר", לָמַדְנוּ עֹנֶשׁ; אַזְהָרָה מִנַּיִן, תַּלְמוּד לוֹמַר:

6. The Hebrew verb *tb'fa'ér*, generally understood to refer to *po'roth*, boughs, is now connected with *tif'ereth*, pride or splendor, which is equally understood to denote the boughs, the pride of an olive tree.

7. MT *bilchoth mat'noth aniyyim* iv 17.

8. Which he picked in violation of the law.

9. Mishnah, Pé'ah viii 8.

10. I.e. while harvesting; hence only then can there be left-over bunches which become a gift to the poor; *ibid*.

§223 1. This last sentence is found in the two oldest manuscripts and in the first edition. In the next two manuscripts, by a scribal error, a jump of the eye between the two words *ba-nosh'rim* ("that fall off" or "loose"), everything between them is missing. In later editions the sentence has been dropped, apparently because it was found difficult. From Tosefta, Pé'ah ii 13 (cited in TB Ḥullin 131a) it seems clear that the law of *peret* applies only to a vineyard and not to trees—of whatever kind. Our author derived this sentence, however, from ShM negative precept 213, in its original version: for while it is not in R. Moses ibn Tibbon's text (nor in ed. Kafaḥ), it is found in three manuscripts of the Arabic

Now, Rambam of blessed memory wrote this—these being his words:[11] Whoever steals from a *p'rutah*'s worth and up transgresses a negative precept, for it is written, *You shall not steal* (Leviticus 19:11); but whiplashes are not given over this injunction, because it is given over to correction [by repayment]. It is all one whether a person steals the goods of an Israelite or an idol-worshipper; and so is it all one whether a person steals from an adult or from a child. Thus far his words. The rest of its details are in chapter 7 of the Talmud tractate *Bava Kamma*, and in other places.

This prohibition applies everywhere, at every time, for both man and woman. If someone transgresses this injunction and steals, he is duty-bound to make compensation, as it is stated directly in the Writ (Exodus 21:37). If someone stole a *dinar*, a garment, a donkey or a camel, he is to pay back the value of two of them.[12] Consequently, he loses the amount that he wanted to make his fellow lose. The law of double payment applies to everything, except an ox and a sheep: with them there are certain instances when four and five times their value [respectively] have to be paid—if, for example, a person slew or sold one, as it is explicitly stated in the Writ (Exodus 21:37).

Now, this matter of paying double the value, or four or five times for an ox or a sheep, is specifically when witnesses testify about it, whereupon payment is made in the court on the basis of their word. But if a person confesses by his own will, he acquits himself by payment of the principal alone.[13] For it is stated, *he whom the judges will condemn shall pay double*[14] (Exodus 22:8). And the law is the same for all fines: whoever confesses in regard to them, is free of the obligation. I have already written above (§49) that cases of fines are judged nowhere but in the land [of Israel].[15]

[NOT TO DENY IT WHEN SOMETHING OF VALUE THAT BELONGS TO ANOTHER IS IN OUR POSSESSION]

225 that we should not lie about something that was given us for safekeeping, or about anything of someone else's that we have: for it is stated, *neither shall you deny falsely* (Leviticus 19:11), for which the explanation was given [in the Oral Tradition][1] that the verse applies to goods. In the language of the Midrash *Sifra*:[2] Since it is written, *and has lied about it and sworn falsely* (Leviticus 5:22), we have learned the punishment;[3] where do we find the injunction?—Scripture

וְלֹא תְכַחֲשׁוּ. גַּם זֹאת מִן הַמִּצְוֹת שֶׁהַשֵּׂכֶל מֵעִיד בָּהֶן.

מִדִּינֵי הַמִּצְוָה, מַה שֶּׁאָמְרוּ זְכָרוֹנָם לִבְרָכָה שֶׁהַכּוֹפֵר בְּפִקָּדוֹן פָּסוּל לְעֵדוּת, וְאַף־עַל־פִּי שֶׁלֹּא נִשְׁבַּע; וְאָמְרוּ בַּגְּמָרָא: וְדַוְקָא דְּאָמְרֵי סָהֲדֵי דְּהַהִיא שַׁעְתָּא הֲוָה פִּקָּדוֹן בְּבֵיתֵיהּ; וְיֶתֶר פְּרָטֶיהָ, מְבֹאָרִין בִּמְקוֹמוֹת מִמַּסֶּכֶת שְׁבוּעוֹת.

וְנוֹהֵג אִסּוּר זֶה בְּכָל מָקוֹם וּבְכָל זְמַן, בַּזְּכָרִים וּנְקֵבוֹת. וְעוֹבֵר עָלֶיהָ וְכִחֵשׁ בַּעֲמִיתוֹ בְּדָבָר שֶׁבְּמָמוֹן, עָבַר עַל לָאו זֶה, וְהוּא כְעוֹבֵר עַל מִצְוַת מֶלֶךְ, אֲבָל אֵין בּוֹ מַלְקוֹת.

[שֶׁלֹּא לְשָׁבַע עַל כְּפִירַת מָמוֹן]

רכו שֶׁלֹּא נִשָּׁבַע עַל הַהַכְחָשָׁה, שֶׁנֶּאֱמַר: וְלֹא תְשַׁקְּרוּ, כְּלוֹמַר שֶׁאִם כָּפַר אִישׁ בְּפִקָּדוֹן עָבַר עַל "לֹא תְכַחֲשׁוּ", וְאִם נִשְׁבַּע לוֹ עַל הַכְּפִירָה אַחַר־כָּךְ, עָבַר עַל "וְלֹא תְשַׁקְּרוּ", שֶׁכֵּן בָּא לָנוּ פֵּרוּשׁ זֶה הַכָּתוּב, שֶׁהוּא לְהַזְהִיר עַל הַנִּשְׁבָּע בִּכְפִירַת מָמוֹן, וּכְמוֹ שֶׁבָּא בְּסִפְרָא: "וְלֹא תְשַׁקְּרוּ", מַה תַּלְמוּד לוֹמַר; לְפִי שֶׁנֶּאֱמַר "וְנִשְׁבַּע עַל שָׁקֶר", לָמַדְנוּ עֹנֶשׁ; אַזְהָרָה מִנַּיִן, תַּלְמוּד לוֹמַר: וְלֹא תְשַׁקְּרוּ. וְנִתְבָּאֵר בְּמַסֶּכֶת שְׁבוּעוֹת שֶׁכָּל מִי שֶׁיִּשָּׁבַע שְׁבוּעַת שֶׁקֶר עַל כְּפִירַת מָמוֹן עוֹבֵר בִּשְׁנֵי לָאוִין: מִשּׁוּם וְלֹא תִשָּׁבְעוּ בִּשְׁמִי לַשָּׁקֶר, וּמִשּׁוּם וְלֹא תְשַׁקְּרוּ אִישׁ בַּעֲמִיתוֹ.

מִשָּׁרְשֵׁי אִסּוּר הַשְּׁבוּעָה לַשֶּׁקֶר, כָּתַבְתִּי בְּפָרָשַׁת יִתְרוֹ בְּסִימָן (ל"ב) [ל'].

וְדִינֵי מִצְוָה זוֹ בְּפֶרֶק חֲמִישִׁי מִשְּׁבוּעוֹת. וְנוֹהֶגֶת בְּכָל מָקוֹם וּבְכָל זְמַן. וְעוֹבֵר

(as well as a printed edition—see note in Arabic-Hebrew ed. Kafaḥ) and in the Hebrew translation of R. Sh'lomoh ibn Iyyov (ed. Heller, negative precept 212, note 6). See on this §221, note 2; and let it be noted that of this ruling also, no trace is to be found in MT *hilchoth mat'noth aniyyim*. (Might it be wondered if perhaps this was somehow the source of the emendation from the original in negative precept 212 found in ibn Tibbon's version, given above in §221 note 2, second paragraph?)

2. Mishnah, Pé'ah vi 5.

3. MT *hilchoth mat'noth aniyyim* iv 16, based on TJ Pé'ah vi 4 (*Kessef Mishneh*).

4. Because when they fall, the single grapes already belong to the poor; Mishnah, Pé'ah vii 3 (see R. 'Obadiah Bertinoro, commentary).

§224   1. In contrast to Exodus 20:13, whose injunction against stealing is understood to mean kidnapping (§36); TB Sanhedrin 86a.

2. TB Bava M'tzi'a 61b. MS Vatican 163/1 and the first edition read: even with the intention of returning it or [merely] upsetting someone (see MT *hilchoth g'névah* i 2).

3. On Leviticus 19:11—*k'doshim*, *parashah* 2, 1–2.

4. Midrash Sifra adds here, "you shall not steal with the purposeful intent of

states, *neither shall you deny falsely*. This too is one of the precepts to whose need and value reason attests.

Among the laws of the precept, there is what the Sages of blessed memory taught:[4] that a person who falsely denies that something was left with him for safekeeping, is disqualified to serve as a witness, even if he did not swear to it. And it was stated in the Talmud:[4] but this is only when witnesses declare that at the time, the entrusted object was in his house. The rest of its details are in various places in the Talmud tractate *Sh'vu'oth*.

This prohibition is in effect everywhere, at every time, for both man and woman. If a person transgresses it and gives his neighbor a false denial in a matter involving something of value, he violates this negative precept. He is then as one who disobeys a king's command, but no whiplashes are given for it.

[NOT TO SWEAR OVER A FALSE DENIAL ABOUT SOMETHING OF VALUE]

226 that we should not swear to a false denial: for it is stated, *nor shall you lie* (Leviticus 19:11); in other words, if a person falsely denied that an object was given him for safekeeping, he would thus transgress [the injunction] *neither shall you deny falsely* (ibid.), and if he swore to him about the denial afterward, he would thus transgress [the admonition] *nor shall you lie*. For so the explanation was given us about this verse [in the Oral Tradition]: that it is stated to caution us about swearing to a false denial about goods—as we find in the Midrash *Sifra*:[1] "nor shall you lie"—why was this stated? Since Scripture says, *and has sworn falsely*, [etc.] (Leviticus 5:22), we have learned the punishment; where do we find the admonition?—Scripture states, *nor shall you lie*. Now, it is explained in the Talmud tractate *Sh'vu'oth* (49b) that anyone who swears a false oath over an untrue denial concerning goods, transgresses two negative precepts: on account of *you shall not swear by My name falsely* (Leviticus 19:12), and on account of *nor shall you lie to one another*.[2]

The root reason for the prohibition on an oath to a falsehood, I wrote in *sidrah yithro*, §30.

The laws of this precept are in chapter 5 of the tractate *Sh'vu'oth*. It is in effect everywhere, in every time. If a person transgressed it and lied, then swore to the denial deliberately, he should receive whip-

עָלֶיהָ וְשִׁקֵּר וְנִשְׁבַּע עַל הַכְּפִירָה בְּמֵזִיד, לוֹקֶה; וְאַף־עַל־פִּי שֶׁאֵין בּוֹ מַעֲשֶׂה, מֵחֹמֶר הַשְּׁבוּעָה חִיְּבַתּוּ הַתּוֹרָה מַלְקוֹת.

[שֶׁלֹּא נִשָּׁבַע לַשֶּׁקֶר]

רכז שֶׁלֹּא נִשָּׁבַע לַשֶּׁקֶר, שֶׁנֶּאֱמַר: וְלֹא תִשָּׁבְעוּ בִשְׁמִי לַשָּׁקֶר, וּפֵרְשׁוּ זִכְרוֹנָם לִבְרָכָה שֶׁזֶּה הַכָּתוּב יַזְהִיר עַל שְׁבוּעַת בִּטּוּי; וּשְׁבוּעַת בִּטּוּי הִיא מַה שֶׁנֶּאֱמַר בַּתּוֹרָה, "אוֹ נֶפֶשׁ כִּי תִשָּׁבַע לְבַטֵּא בִשְׂפָתַיִם לְהָרַע אוֹ לְהֵיטִיב", וְהִיא נֶחֱלֶקֶת לְאַרְבָּעָה חֲלָקִים, שְׁתַּיִם לֶהָבָא וּשְׁתַּיִם לְשֶׁעָבַר: כְּגוֹן שֶׁנִּשְׁבַּע עַל דָּבָר שֶׁעָבַר שֶׁנַּעֲשָׂה אוֹ לֹא נַעֲשָׂה, וְעַל דָּבָר שֶׁעָתִיד לִהְיוֹת שֶׁיַּעֲשֶׂה אוֹתוֹ אוֹ לֹא יַעֲשֶׂה.

וְאֵין שְׁבוּעַת בִּטּוּי נוֹהֶגֶת אֶלָּא בִּדְבָרִים שֶׁאֶפְשָׁר לוֹ לָאָדָם לַעֲשׂוֹתָן, בֵּין לֶהָבָא אוֹ לְשֶׁעָבַר. כֵּיצַד לְשֶׁעָבַר: אָכַלְתִּי אוֹ לֹא אָכַלְתִּי, וְכֵן זָרַקְתִּי אוֹ לֹא זָרַקְתִּי אֶבֶן לַיָּם; וְכֵיצַד לֶהָבָא: אֹכַל אוֹ לֹא אֹכַל, אוֹ: אֶזְרֹק אוֹ לֹא אֶזְרֹק. אֲבָל בִּדְבָרִים שֶׁיֵּשׁ בָּהֶן מוֹנֵעַ מִן הַתּוֹרָה אֵין שְׁבוּעַת בִּטּוּי נוֹהֶגֶת בָּהֶן, שֶׁאֵין הַשְּׁבוּעָה חָלָה אֶלָּא עַל דְּבַר הָרְשׁוּת, שֶׁאִם רָצָה עוֹשֵׂהוּ וְאִם רָצָה לֹא יַעֲשֵׂהוּ, שֶׁנֶּאֱמַר: לְהָרַע אוֹ לְהֵיטִיב; אֲבָל בְּכָל דְּבַר מִצְוָה חִיּוּב עָלָיו לַעֲשׂוֹתוֹ, לְפִיכָךְ אֵין שְׁבוּעַת בִּטּוּי חָלָה עָלָיו בֵּין בֵּין לֶהָבָא בֵּין לְשֶׁעָבַר: כְּגוֹן שֶׁנִּשְׁבַּע לְקַיֵּם מִצְוָה וְלֹא קִיְּמָהּ, וְכֵן אִם נִשְׁבַּע שֶׁקִּיֵּם מִצְוָה וְהוּא לֹא קִיְּמָהּ, דִּכְמוֹ שֶׁאֵין חִיּוּב חָל בִּדְבַר מִצְוָה לֶהָבָא, כֵּן אֵינוֹ חָל עָלָיו לְשֶׁעָבַר. וְכֵן מִתְבָּאֵר הָעִנְיָן בִּמְקוֹמוֹ בִּשְׁבוּעוֹת.

וּמִן הַטַּעַם הַזֶּה שֶׁאָמַרְנוּ, שֶׁאֵין חִיּוּב הַשְּׁבוּעָה חָל אֶלָּא בְּמַה שֶׁהוּא בִּרְשׁוּתוֹ לַעֲשׂוֹת, פָּטְרוּ זִכְרוֹנָם לִבְרָכָה גַּם־כֵּן מִשְּׁבוּעַת בִּטּוּי כָּל הַנִּשְׁבָּע לְהָרַע לַאֲחֵרִים, מִפְּנֵי שֶׁהוּא מְצֻוֶּה שֶׁלֹּא לְהָרַע לַחֲבֵרוֹ. וְכָתַב הָרַמְבַּ"ם זִכְרוֹנוֹ לִבְרָכָה כִּי יֵרָאֶה לוֹ שֶׁהוּא לוֹקֶה מִכָּל־מָקוֹם מִשּׁוּם שְׁבוּעַת שָׁוְא.

וְהַנִּשְׁבָּע לְהָרַע לְעַצְמוֹ, אַף־עַל־פִּי שֶׁאֵינוֹ רַשַּׁאי, חַיָּב מִשּׁוּם שְׁבוּעַת בִּטּוּי

paying double compensation"; but this is likewise omitted in ShM negative precept 244—evidently because what follows conveys the same point. It is clear from MT *hilchoth g'nevah* i 1 that Rambam knew of this passage in the Midrash; hence the omission was evidently for the sake of brevity.

5. "If someone is a poor man of good parentage and will not accept charity, let a man not say: I will steal from him, so that I will become obligated by law to pay him double, or four or five times the value—because his spirit will become attached [accustomed, addicted] to theft": R. Hillel of Greece, *Commentary on Sifra*. The penalty for theft is generally double payment (the stolen object, or its value if it cannot be returned in its original condition, and another like it, or twice the value—Exodus 22:3); for stealing an ox the thief must make fourfold compensation, and for stealing a sheep, fivefold (Exodus 21:37).

6. A coin; i.e. a sum of money.

lashes. Even though the violation involves no physical action,[3] because of the seriousness of an oath the Torah sentenced him to lashes.

[THE PROHIBITION AGAINST SWEARING FALSELY]

227 that we should not swear falsely: for it is stated, *And you shall not swear by My name falsely* (Leviticus 19:12), and the Sages of blessed memory explained[1] that this verse enjoins us against an oath of expression. Now, an oath of expression is what we find in the Torah: *or if anyone swears clearly with his lips to do harm or to do good* (Leviticus 5:4); and it divides into four types—two in the past and two in the future: for instance, if one swears about something that is past, that it was done or was not done; or about something that is going to be—that he will do it or will not do it.[2]

An oath of expression is one that can apply only to things which a man is able to do, either in the past or in the future. How in the past?— "I ate" or "I did not eat"; so too, "I threw—or, I did not throw—a stone into the sea." And how in the future?—"I will eat" or "I will not eat"; or again, "I will throw" or "I will not throw."[3] However, to things on which there is a restriction of the Torah, no oath of expression can apply: because an oath can take effect on nothing but a voluntary matter, which if he wishes he may do, and if he wishes he may not do—as it is stated, *to do harm or to do good* (Leviticus 5:4). But about every subject of a precept there lies an obligation on him to do it; therefore no oath of expression can take effect about it, whether it concerns the past or the future: for example, if a person swore to observe a *mitzvah* and did not observe it; and likewise if he swore that he had observed a precept, and he had not observed it. For just as [an added] obligation cannot take effect about a *mitzvah* in the future, so can it have no effect on him about a *mitzvah* in the past;[4] and so the matter was explained in its proper place in the tractate *Sh'vu'oth* (27a).

Now, for this reason that we stated, that the obligation of an oath becomes binding only on something that it is a person's free right to do, the Sages of blessed memory likewise freed of penalty for an oath of expression anyone who swore to harm others, since he is commanded not to do ill to others.[5] But Rambam of blessed memory wrote[6] that it seems to him that the person should receive whiplashes nonetheless, on account of a vain oath (§30).

If someone swore to harm himself, even though he is not permitted ⟨35⟩ to do so, he is punishable for an oath of expression if he did not so harm

אִם לֹא הֵרַע. נִשְׁבַּע לְהֵיטִיב לַאֲחֵרִים בְּדָבָר שֶׁהוּא בְּיָדוֹ לַעֲשׂוֹת וְלֹא עָשָׂה, חַיָּב מִשּׁוּם שְׁבוּעַת בִּטּוּי.

וְיֶתֶר רְבֵי פְּרָטֵי הַשְּׁבוּעוֹת וְעִנְיַן הֶתֵּרָן, יִתְבָּאֵר הַכֹּל יָפֶה בַּמַּסֶּכְתָּא הַבְּנוּיָה עַל זֶה, וְהִיא מַסֶּכֶת שְׁבוּעוֹת. וּכְבָר כָּתַבְתִּי יוֹתֵר מִזֶּה בְּעִנְיַן מִצְוָה זוֹ, וְהֶאֱרַכְתִּי בְּשָׁרְשָׁהּ, בְּמִצְוַת לֹא תִשָּׂא שֵׁמַע שָׁוְא וַיִּשְׁמַע יִתְרוֹ [סִי' ל'].

וְנוֹהֵג זֶה אִסּוּר בְּכָל מָקוֹם וּבְכָל זְמַן, בַּזְּכָרִים וּבַנְּקֵבוֹת. וְעוֹבֵר עָלֶיהָ, אִם הָיָה מֵזִיד לוֹקֶה, וְדַוְקָא בְּעֵדִים וְהַתְרָאָה, כְּמוֹ שֶׁיָּדוּעַ בְּכָל הַמִּצְוֹת; וְאִם שׁוֹגֵג, חַיָּב לְהָבִיא קָרְבָּן עוֹלֶה וְיוֹרֵד; וְכֵן אָמְרוּ שָׁם בִּשְׁבוּעוֹת: זוֹ הִיא שְׁבוּעַת בִּטּוּי, שֶׁחַיָּבִין עַל זְדוֹנָהּ מַלְקוֹת וְעַל שִׁגְגָתָהּ קָרְבָּן עוֹלֶה וְיוֹרֵד. וְזֶה שֶׁאָמְרוּ "זוֹ הִיא", אֵין שָׁם חִדּוּשׁ אַחֵר אֶלָּא מִצַּד שֶׁהַקָּרְבָּן הוּא עוֹלֶה וְיוֹרֵד.

[שֶׁלֹּא לַעֲשׁק]

רכח שֶׁלֹּא נַחֲזִיק בְּמַה שֶּׁיִּהְיֶה בְּיָדֵינוּ מִגְּזוּלָתֵנוּ דֶּרֶךְ אֹנֶס אוֹ דֶּרֶךְ דְּחִיָּה וְרַמָּאוּת, כְּמוֹ אַנְשֵׁי אֹנֶן אָוֶן שֶׁדּוֹחִים בְּנֵי־אָדָם לֵאמֹר לָהֶם "לֵךְ וָשׁוּב" כְּדֵי לְסַבֵּב שֶׁיִּשָּׁאֵר לָהֶם מַה שֶּׁבְּיָדָם מִגְּזוּלָתָם. וְזֹאת הִיא מִדָּה רָעָה בְּיוֹתֵר, וְהִרְחִיקַתְנוּ תוֹרָתֵנוּ הַשְּׁלֵמָה מִמֶּנָּה וְהִזְהִירָה בְּכָךְ בְּזֶה הַמִּקְרָא, דִּכְתִיב: לֹא תַעֲשֹׁק אֶת רֵעֲךָ; כִּי מַחֲזִיק בְּמָמוֹן מִגְּזוּלָתוֹ בְּזֶה הָעִנְיָן שֶׁאָמַרְנוּ נִקְרָא עוֹשֵׁק.

וּבִכְלָל עוֹשֵׁק הוּא גַּם־כֵּן כָּל שֶׁחַיָּב לַחֲבֵרוֹ מָמוֹן מֵעִנְיָן וְעוֹשֵׁק אוֹתוֹ, כְּגוֹן כּוֹבֵשׁ שְׂכַר שָׂכִיר וְכַיּוֹצֵא בּוֹ; דְּלָא בָעֵינַן שֶׁיָּבוֹא מַמָּשׁ מָמוֹן מִיַּד הֶעָשׁוּק לְיַד הָעוֹשֵׁק, אֲבָל כָּל שֶׁיֵּשׁ לוֹ אֶצְלוֹ תְּבִיעַת מָמוֹן מֵעִנְיָן, וְהוּא דּוֹחֶה אוֹתוֹ מֵחֲמַת

---

7. Whether he is quit of all responsibility; TB Bava Kamma 118a.

8. I.e. where the owner knows from the counting that whatever was stolen has been returned; *ibid.*

9. TB Bava Kamma 118b.

10. *Ibid.* 115a.

11. MT *hilchoth g'névah* i 1.

12. Exodus 22:3.

13. I.e. of the stolen object alone; TB Bava Kamma 75a.

14. But not a person who condemns himself.

15. In keeping with what our author writes below, in §491, this means more specifically that when there is an ordained, authorized court in the land of Israel, such cases can be tried in other countries as well, by justices acting as the deputies of this *beth din*, as is evident from TB Bava Kamma 83b.

§225   1. TB Sh'vu'oth 37b. (The standard translations render the verse, "neither shall you deal falsely.")

2. On the above verse—*k'doshim, parashah* 2, 3.

himself.[5] If someone swore to do good to others in a matter where it is in his power to act, and then he did not do so, he is punishable on account of an oath of expression.[5]

The rest of the very many details about oaths, and the matter of release from them, are all well explained in the Talmud tractate built about this theme, which is the tractate *Sh'vu'oth*. I have written previously more than this in regard to this precept, and explained at length about its root reason, in the precept of not taking the Lord's name in vain (§30), in *sidrah yithro*.

This prohibition is in effect in every place, at every time, for both man and woman. If someone transgressed it, if he did so willfully, he should be given whiplashes, but this specifically if there were witnesses and a warning, as is known in regard to all the precepts. If he did so unwittingly, he would be obligated to bring an offering of greater or lesser value.[7] And so was it expressed there in the tractate *Sh'vu'oth* (27b): This is an oath of expression, which if taken deliberately is punishable by whiplashes, and if inadvertently, requires an offering of greater or lesser value. As to why it is said there, "This is," there is nothing especial or novel there except the fact that the offering is to be one of greater or lesser value.

[NOT TO WITHHOLD ANOTHER PERSON'S PROPERTY WRONGLY]

228 that we should not retain the property of another person that is in our possession, either through force or by procrastination and trickery, like wrongdoers who put people off, saying, "Go and come back," so as to arrange matters that the other's property which they hold should remain with them. This is an extremely bad way of behavior, and our complete, perfect Torah withdrew us from it and adjured us about it in this verse: as it is written, *You shall not maltreat* (tha'ashok) *your neighbor* (Leviticus 19:13)—because anyone who holds on to another's goods in this way that we have stated is called *'oshék* (a "maltreater").

Included in the category of *'oshék* is anyone who owes his fellow a specific amount of money and he cheats him out of it: for instance, if one holds back the wages of a hired worker, and so on; because it is not necessary that actual money or goods should have passed from the hand of the maltreated one to the hand of the *'oshék*. Rather, if anyone has a claim against a person for a specific amount and the

אַלְמוּת שֶׁיֵּשׁ בּוֹ, אוֹ כָּל צַד רַמָּאוּת, נִקְרָא עוֹשֵׁק.

וְאַף־עַל־פִּי שֶׁהָעֹשֶׁק וְהַגְּזֵלָה וְהַגְּנֵבָה עִנְיָן אֶחָד הוּא עִם הֱיוֹת שֶׁהַמַּעֲשֶׂה חָלוּק זֶה מִזֶּה, כִּי כַּוָּנַת שְׁלָשְׁתָּן שֶׁלֹּא יִקַּח הָאָדָם מָמוֹן מִזּוּלָתוֹ מִשּׁוּם צַד, לְפִי שֶׁבִּשְׁלֹשָׁה דְרָכִים אֵלּוּ יַחְמְסוּ בְּנֵי־אָדָם זֶה אֶת זֶה פֵּרְטָם הַכָּתוּב כֻּלָּן וְהִזְהִיר בְּכָל אֶחָד בִּפְנֵי עַצְמוֹ; וּכְעִנְיָן מַה שֶּׁאָמְרוּ זִכְרוֹנָם לִבְרָכָה בִּמְצִיעָא פֶּרֶק הַמַּקְבֵּל: רָבָא אָמַר: זֶהוּ עֹשֶׁק זֶהוּ גֵּזֶל, וְלָמָּה חִלְּקָן הַכָּתוּב, לַעֲבֹר עָלָיו בִּשְׁנֵי לָאוִין.

וּפֵרוּשׁ עִנְיָן זֶה וְעִקַּר הַטַּעַם לְפִי דַעְתִּי הוּא מִשְּׁנֵי צְדָדִין: הָאֶחָד, שֶׁכָּל שֶׁרָצָה הָאֵל בָּרוּךְ הוּא לְהַרְחִיק מִמֶּנּוּ לְטוֹבָתֵנוּ רָחוֹק גָּדוֹל, הִרְבָּה לָנוּ בּוֹ אַזְהָרוֹת רַבּוֹת. וְעוֹד תּוֹעֶלֶת לָנוּ נִמְצָא בְּרִבּוּיֵ הָאַזְהָרוֹת, וְהוּא כְּמוֹ שֶׁאָמְרוּ זִכְרוֹנָם לִבְרָכָה שֶׁרָצָה הַמָּקוֹם לְזַכּוֹת אֶת יִשְׂרָאֵל וּלְפִיכָךְ הִרְבָּה לָהֶם מִצְווֹת, וְהַכַּוָּנָה' לָהֶם בְּאָמְרָם מִצְווֹת גַּם עַל הָאַזְהָרוֹת, שֶׁהִרְבָּה לָהֶם אַזְהָרוֹת הַרְבֵּה בְּמַה שֶׁיִּהְיֶה אֶפְשָׁר לְהוֹדִיעַ בְּאַזְהָרָה אַחַת, כְּמוֹ בְכָאן, שֶׁהָיָה אֶפְשָׁר לְהַזְהִירֵנוּ דֶּרֶךְ כְּלָל "לֹא תִקְחוּ מָמוֹן מִזּוּלַתְכֶם שֶׁלֹּא כַדִּין", וְנִתְרַבּוּ הָאַזְהָרוֹת לָנוּ בַּדָּבָר, כְּדֵי שֶׁנְּקַבֵּל שָׂכָר הַרְבֵּה עַל הַפְּרִישָׁה מִן הָעֲבֵרָה.

וּכְמוֹ־כֵן בְּכָל מָקוֹם שֶׁאָמְרוּ זִכְרוֹנָם לִבְרָכָה "לַעֲבֹר עָלָיו בְּהַרְבֵּה לָאוִין" כֵּן נִפְרָשׁ הַדָּבָר, שֶׁאֵין לְפָרֵשׁ חָלִילָה שֶׁיִּרְצֶה הָאֵל לָבוֹא בַּעֲלִילָה עַל בְּרִיּוֹתָיו, וְלָכֵן שֶׁיִּרְבֶּה הַנָּקָם עֲלֵיהֶם, כִּי חָפֵץ הַשֵּׁם, בָּרוּךְ הוּא וּבָרוּךְ שְׁמוֹ, לְזַכּוֹת בְּרִיּוֹתָיו, לֹא לְחַיֵּב, אֲבָל יָזָרֵז אוֹתָם זֵרוּז אַחַר זֵרוּז לְמַעַן יִלְמְדוּ יִקְחוּ מוּסָר וְיִזְכּוּ בְּהִתְרַחֲקָם מִן הָעֲבֵרָה זְכוּת רָב. וְזֶה הַטַּעַם לְיוֹדְעֵי דַעַת, דְּבַשׁ וְחָלָב.

3. Given in the continuation of the verse.

4. TB Bava M'tzi'a 5b, etc.

§226   1. On the above verse—*k'doshim, parashah* 2, 3.

2. The paragraph is based on ShM negative precept §249.

3. And we have a standing rule that over such a negative precept, no whiplashes are given (TB Sanhedrin 63b).

§227   1. TB Sh'vu'oth 21a.

2. So MT *hilchoth sh'vu'oth* i 1.

3. So *ibid.* 2.

4. For some reason our author does not follow MT *hilchoth sh'vu'oth* v 19, which gives the ruling that such an oath about a past matter does incur guilt (MH).

5. TB Sh'vu'oth 27a.

6. MT *hilchoth sh'vu'oth* v 16.

7. Explained in §123.

§228   1. I.e. essentially, any form of cheating someone out of what belongs to him is merely another way of robbing him.

other puts him off because of some trait of lawlessness that he has, or some trait of trickery, he is called *'oshék.*

Now, illegal retention [of another's property], robbery and theft are [essentially] one matter, despite the fact that the three respective actions are different from one another. For the purpose of all three [injunctions] is that no man should take the possessions of another in any way whatever, since in these three ways people despoil one another. Nevertheless, Scripture gave them all in detail and adjured us about each one by itself, in keeping with what the Sages of blessed memory taught in chapter 9 of the tractate *Bava M'tzi'a* (111a): Rava said: *'oshek* (illegal retention) and robbery are one and the same;[1] then why did Scripture divide them [into two precepts]?—to make such an act the violation of two negative precepts.

The meaning of this theme and its main import, to my mind, lies in two directions: one, that the more God, blessed is He, wished to remove us, for our good, a great distance [from something], the more He increased for us the number of injunctions about it. Then we find yet another benefit in the increase of the injunctions, which is as the Sages of blessed memory said:[2] that the omnipresent God wished to make the Israelites (Jewry) meritorious, and He therefore gave them a great many *mitzvoth*; and in saying *mitzvoth*, they meant the injunctions as well—that He added on for them a great many prohibitions where it would be possible to give them the same instruction in one expression of warning—such as here: It was possible to adjure us in a general way, "Do not take anything of value from other people unjustly." Yet the injunctions about the matter were increased for us, so that we can receive increased reward for abstaining from the transgression.

Similarly, wherever our Sages of blessed memory said, "It is to make this deed the violation of many negative precepts," we will explain the matter so. For it is not to be explained—perish the thought— that God desires to trump up charges against His creatures, and this in order to increase the vengeance wreaked upon them. The Eternal Lord, blessed is He and blessed His name, desires to make His creatures meritorious, not to make them guilty. Then He rather alerts them time after time in order that they will learn to accept the moral chastisement and will merit great reward by moving far away from the transgression. And this reason, for those who know reason, [will be as sweet as]

⟨39⟩ *honey and milk* (Song of Songs 4:11).

שֹׁרֶשׁ הַמִּצְוָה יָדוּעַ, כִּי הִיא מִן הַמִּצְווֹת שֶׁהַשֵּׂכֶל מְחַיֵּב אוֹתָן. דִּינֵי הַמִּצְוָה
בְּבָבָא קַמָּא, וְעִקָּר בְּפֶרֶק תְּשִׁיעִי וּבְפֶרֶק עֲשִׂירִי.

וְנוֹהֵג אִסּוּר זֶה בְּכָל מָקוֹם וּבְכָל זְמָן. וְעוֹבֵר עָלָיו וְעָשַׁק אֶת חֲבֵרוֹ, עָבַר עַל
לָאו זֶה; וְהוּא לָאו הַנִּתָּק לַעֲשֵׂה, כְּלוֹמַר שֶׁיָּשִׁיב הֶחָמָס אֲשֶׁר בְּכַפָּיו וִירַצֶּה אֶת
חֲבֵרוֹ עַל שֶׁהִקְנִיטוֹ וְהִכְעִיסוֹ. וּכְבָר הוֹדִיעוּנוּ זִכְרוֹנָם לִבְרָכָה שֶׁגָּדוֹל כֹּחַ בַּעֲלֵי
תְּשׁוּבָה.

וְהָרַב הַצָּרְפָתִי כָּתַב בְּחֶשְׁבּוֹן הַמִּצְווֹת: מִכֵּיוָן דְּאַשְׁכְּחָן דַּאֲמַר רָבָא דְּעֹשֶׁק
וְגָזֵל הוּא חַד, לֹא נִמְנֶה לָאו דְּעֹשֶׁק בְּמִנְיַן הַלָּאוִין; וְהוּא יִמְנֶה בְּמָקוֹם זֶה ״וְלֹא
יִהְיֶה כְקֹרַח וְכַעֲדָתוֹ״, כְּלוֹמַר שֶׁלֹּא נַחֲזִיק בְּמַחֲלֹקֶת. וּלְדַעְתֵּנוּ אָנוּ אֵין כַּוָּנַת רָבָא
שֶׁלֹּא יִמָּנוּ בִּשְׁנֵי לָאוִין, אֶלָּא לַעֲבֹר בְּגֶזֶל בִּשְׁנֵי לָאוִין, וּבְעֹשֶׁק גַּם־כֵּן; וּמִכֵּיוָן
שֶׁעִנְיָנָן חָלוּק נִמְנֶה אוֹתָן לִשְׁנַיִם כְּמוֹ הַגְּזֵלָה וְהַגְּנֵבָה, שֶׁאַף־עַל־פִּי שֶׁעִנְיַן שְׁנֵיהֶם
הוּא שֶׁלֹּא נִקַּח מָמוֹן מְזוּלָּתֵנוּ, אֵין סָפֵק כִּי לִשְׁנֵי לָאוִין הֵם נֶחְשָׁבִין בְּתרי״ג
מִצְווֹת.

[שֶׁלֹּא לִגְזֹל]

רכט שֶׁלֹּא לִגְזֹל, כְּלוֹמַר שֶׁלֹּא נִטֹּל מַה שֶׁאֵין לָנוּ זְכוּת בּוֹ בְּכֹחַ וּבִזְרוֹעַ
בְּפַרְסוּם, שֶׁנֶּאֱמַר: וְלֹא תִגְזֹל; וּבָא הַפֵּרוּשׁ עָלָיו שֶׁלְּשׁוֹן גְּזֵלָה נוֹפֵל עַל הַחוֹטֵף
דָּבָר מִיַּד חֲבֵרוֹ אוֹ הוֹצִיאוֹ מֵרְשׁוּתוֹ בְּעַל־כָּרְחוֹ דֶּרֶךְ אֹנֶס וּבְפַרְסוּם, כָּעִנְיָן
שֶׁנֶּאֱמַר: וַיִּגְזֹל אֶת הַחֲנִית מִיַּד הַמִּצְרִי.

שֹׁרֶשׁ הַמִּצְוָה יָדוּעַ, שֶׁהוּא דָּבָר שֶׁהַשֵּׂכֶל מְחַיֵּב, וְרָאוּי לְהַרְחִיקוֹ, כִּי
יוֹדֵעַ הַגּוֹזֵל הֶחָלוּשׁ מִמֶּנּוּ כִּי בְּבוֹא עָלָיו תַּקִּיף מִמֶּנּוּ הָיָה גַּם הוּא נִגְזָל, וְהִיא סִבָּה
לְחָרְבַּן הַיִּשּׁוּב.

2. TB Makkoth 23b.

3. So *ibid.* 16a, etc.

4. R. Moses of Coucy, *Séfer Mitzvoth Gadol*, negative precept §156.

5. So the oldest manuscript and most editions: *shelo' yimnu*; in the next three
manuscripts, *shelo'* was omitted; and in the first three editions the reading is *she-yimnu*,
"that they should be counted."

6. So too ShM negative precepts §§245, 247.

§229   1. TB Bava Kamma 79b.

2. The paragraph is based on ShM negative precept §245.

The root purpose of the precept is known (evident), as it is one of the commandments that reason necessitates. The laws of the precept are in the Talmud tractate *Bava Kamma*, mainly in chapters 9 and 10.

This prohibition is in force everywhere, at every time. If someone transgresses it and illegally withholds his fellow's property, he violates this negative precept; but it is an injunction whose violation is given over to a positive precept for correction:[3] in other words, he is to return the ill-gotten gains which he holds, and pacify his fellow for having vexed and angered him. Long ago our Sages of blessed memory taught us that great is the force of those who repent.

Now, the French rabbi [R. Moses of Couçy] wrote in [his] reckoning of the precepts:[4] "Since we find that Rava said that illegal retention and robbery are one thing, we will not count the injunction against illegal retention in the reckoning of the precepts." In its place he counts *and he shall not be as Korah and as his company* (Numbers 17:5), which is to say that we should not support a controversy. To our mind, though, it was not Rava's intention that they should not be counted as two negative precepts,[5] but only that robbery should be punished as the violation of two injunctions, and illegal retention likewise. Yet since their subject matter is different, we list them [thus] as two [negative precepts],[6] like robbery and stealing: even though the point of both is that we should not take another's possessions, there is no doubt that they are reckoned as two negative precepts among the 613 *mitzvoth*.

229 [THE PROHIBITION AGAINST COMMITTING ROBBERY] not to commit robbery: in other words, that we should not take something to which we have no right, by might and main force, openly—for it is stated, *neither shall you rob him* (Leviticus 19:13), and the explanation was given about it[1] that the expression of *g'zélah*, robbery, applies to one who snatches something from his fellow or takes it out of his possession against his will, by means of force, openly, in the vein of the verse, *and he snatched the spear out of the Egyptian's hand* (II Samuel 23:21).[2]

The root reason for the precept is known (evident), since it is something that reason strongly repudiates. And it is right to repudiate it: for one who robs someone weaker than himself knows that should someone stronger than he attack him, he will be equally robbed—and this is a cause of ruin for a settled community.

מִדִּינֵי הַמִּצְוָה, מַה שֶּׁאָמְרוּ זִכְרוֹנָם לִבְרָכָה שֶׁאָסוּר דְּאוֹרַיְתָא לִגְזֹל אֲפִלּוּ כָּל־
שֶׁהוּא, אֲבָל לָאו דְּלֹא תִגְזֹל אֵינוֹ חָל אֶלָּא בְּשָׁוֶה פְּרוּטָה, כִּי הַתּוֹרָה לֹא תְחַיֵּב
אֶלָּא בְּדָבָר שֶׁהוּא מָמוֹן, וּפָחוֹת מִשָּׁוֶה פְּרוּטָה אֵינוֹ נִקְרָא מָמוֹן, אֲבָל מִכָּל־מָקוֹם
אָסוּר הוּא דְּבַר תּוֹרָה, כְּמוֹ חֲצִי שִׁעוּר, שֶׁאֵין לוֹקִין עָלָיו וְהוּא אָסוּר דְּאוֹרַיְתָא.

וְכָתַב הָרַמְבַּ״ם זִכְרוֹנוֹ לִבְרָכָה: אֲפִלּוּ גּוֹי וְעוֹבֵד עֲבוֹדָה זָרָה אָסוּר לְגָזְלוֹ אוֹ
לַעֲשָׁקוֹ, וְאִם גְּזָלוֹ אוֹ עֲשָׁקוֹ יַחֲזִיר; וּבַגְּמָרָא אָמְרוּ זִכְרוֹנָם לִבְרָכָה שֶׁאֲפִלּוּ
אֲנָשִׁים שֶׁמֻּתָּר לְאַבֵּד גּוּפָן, כְּגוֹן הַמִּינִין, אָסוּר לְאַבֵּד מָמוֹנָם וְלִגְזֹל אוֹ לִגְנֹב לָהֶם;
וְאָמְרוּ בְּטַעַם זֶה דְּשֶׁמָּא יֵצֵא מֵהֶן זֶרַע רָאוּי, וְיִהְיֶה מָמוֹנָם לָהֶם. וְעוֹד אֶפְשָׁר
לוֹמַר שֶׁנְּתָנָתָם זִכְרוֹנָם לִבְרָכָה בְּהַרְחִיקָם זֶה כְּדֵי שֶׁלֹּא יַרְגִּיל הָאָדָם טִבְעוֹ בְּכָךְ,
כִּי גְרִיעוּת יִהְיֶה בַּנֶּפֶשׁ בְּהַרְגִּילָהּ בַּמִּדּוֹת הַפְּחוּתוֹת וְהָרָעוֹת, וְהוּא חֶבֶל חָזָק
לִמְשֹׁךְ הֶעָוֹן.

וְכֵן מִדִּינֵי הַמִּצְוָה, מַה שֶּׁאָמְרוּ זִכְרוֹנָם לִבְרָכָה שֶׁהַגּוֹזֵל חַיָּב לְהַחֲזִיר הַגְּזֵלָה
עַצְמָהּ, שֶׁנֶּאֱמַר: הַגְּזֵלָה אֲשֶׁר גָּזָל, וּפֵרְשׁוּ זִכְרוֹנָם לִבְרָכָה: יַחֲזִיר כְּעֵין שֶׁגָּזָל;
וּמִפְּנֵי־כֵן אָמְרוּ כִּי בְּדִין הוּא שֶׁאֲפִלּוּ גָזַל מָרִישׁ, פֵּרוּשׁ קוֹרָה, וּבְנָאָהּ בְּבִירָה,
מְקַעְקֵעַ כָּל הַבִּירָה וּמַחֲזִיר מָרִישׁ לִבְעָלָיו; אֶלָּא מִפְּנֵי תַקָּנַת הַשָּׁבִים תִּקְּנוּ, נוֹתֵן
אֶת דָּמֶיהָ וְיִפָּטֵר. וּכְבָר כָּתַבְנוּ לְמַעְלָה אֵיךְ יֵשׁ כֹּחַ בְּיַד חֲכָמִים בָּזֶה.

וְדִין הַגּוֹזֵל חֲבֵרוֹ בַּיִּשּׁוּב וְרָצָה לְהַחֲזִיר לוֹ בַּמִּדְבָּר מַה דִּינוֹ, וְדִין הַגּוֹזֵל חֲבֵרוֹ
וְהִבְלִיעַ לוֹ בְּחֶשְׁבּוֹן, שֶׁיָּצָא יְדֵי חוֹבָתוֹ בְּכָךְ, וְאִם הֶחֱזִיר לְכִיסוֹ יָצָא, וְהוּא שֶׁיֵּשׁ

---

3. TB Sanhedrin 57a.

4. Even though the victim will later forgive the robber if he took less than a
p'rutah's worth (see further), at the moment he suffers; *ibid.*

5. MT *hilchoth g'zelah* i 2.

6. TB Bava Kamma 119a.

7. Literally, in moving it far away.

8. Our author echoes here Isaiah 5:18, *Woe to them that draw iniquity with ropes of
vanity.*

9. TB Bava Kamma 98b.

10. For if the robber actually had to tear down his house and return the beam, he
would be dismayed and would never attempt repentance (Rashi, TB Gittin 55a, s.v.
mip'ne).

11. TB Bava Kamma 118a; MT *hilchoth g'zelah* i 7.

12. In such a way that the owner is unaware of it, so as to avoid embarrassment;
ibid. 118b; MT *ibid.* 8.

Among the laws of the precept, there is what the Sages of blessed memory taught:[3] that by the Torah's law it is forbidden to seize anything at all in robbery,[4] but the negative precept, *neither shall you rob him*, applies to nothing less than a *p'rutah*'s worth: for the Torah imposes punishment only for something that is a possession of value, and anything worth less than a *p'rutah* is not called a possession of value. Nevertheless, it is forbidden by Torah law as half a minimal amount, for which whiplashes are not given, but it is yet prohibited by the law of the Torah.

Now, Rambam of blessed memory wrote:[5] Even a non-Jewish idol-worshipper—it is forbidden to rob or maltreat him (by illegally retaining his property); and if someone robbed or thus maltreated him, he is to return [what he took]. In the Talmud, the Sages of blessed memory taught[6] that even those people whom it is permitted to destroy physically, such as sectarian heretics—it is forbidden to destroy their possessions, rob them, or steal from them. And they said as a reason for this that perhaps worthy offspring will emerge from them, and their possessions will become theirs. It can be said, further, that the intention of the Sages of blessed memory in establishing this restriction[7] is that a man should not accustom his nature to this. For the spirit will acquire a defect by becoming accustomed to inferior and evil traits of character; and this becomes a strong rope to draw iniquity.[8]

Likewise, among the laws of the precept, there is what the Sages of blessed memory taught:[9] that a robber is obligated to return the seized object itself; since it is stated, *he shall restore what he took by robbery* (Leviticus 5:23), which the Sages explained to mean: he is to return it just as he seized it.[9] For this reason they taught that by law, even if someone seized a wooden beam in robbery and built it into a structure, he ought to demolish the entire structure and return the beam to its owner. It is only on account of the "amendment for the repentant" that the Sages made a ruling that he should give its value in money, and thus be quit of his obligation.[10] We have already written above (§130) how the Sages have the power to do this.

Then there is the law of one who robs his fellow in the settled community and wishes to return the seized object to him in the wilderness—what his law is;[11] the law that if one robs his fellow and then absorbs [the value of what he took] into an account [that he settles with him],[12] he acquits himself of his obligation with this; and if he

⟨43⟩

בָּהּ מָעוֹת, דְּקַיְמָא לָן כְּרַבִּי יִצְחָק דְּאָמַר: אָדָם עָשׂוּי לְמַשְׁמֵשׁ בְּכִיסוֹ וְיִמְנֶה מָעוֹתָיו, וּמִנְיָן שֶׁלֹּא מִדַּעַת פּוֹטֵר בְּמַה שֶּׁאֵינוֹ בַעַל־חַיִּים.

וְדִין הַגּוֹזֵל וָמֵת, בֵּין שֶׁהֶאֱכִיל הַגְּזֵלָה לַבָּנִים קֹדֶם יֵאוּשׁ אוֹ אַחַר יֵאוּשׁ, אִם הִנִּיחַ קַרְקַע חַיָּבִים הַבָּנִים לְשַׁלֵּם דְּמֵי הַגְּזֵלָה, אֲבָל מִן הַמִּטַּלְטְלִים לֹא יִהְיוּ חַיָּבִין הַיְּתוֹמִים לְשַׁלֵּם, אֶלָּא מִפְּנֵי תַקָּנַת הַגְּאוֹנִים שֶׁתִּקְּנוּ כֵן שֶׁאֲפִלּוּ בְמִלְוֶה־עַל־פֶּה יִשְׁתַּעְבְּדוּ מְטַלְטְלֵי דְיַתְמֵי מִפְּנֵי תִקּוּן הָעוֹלָם.

וְדִין הַלּוֹקֵחַ מִן הַגַּזְלָן כְּדִין הַלּוֹקֵחַ מִן הַגַּנָּב, שֶׁיֵּשׁ חִלּוּק בֵּין מְפֻרְסָם לְשֶׁאֵינוֹ מְפֻרְסָם. וּמַה שֶּׁאָמַרְנוּ שֶׁאָסוּר לֵהָנוֹת מֵאָדָם שֶׁחֶזְקָתוֹ שֶׁכָּל שֶׁיֵּשׁ לוֹ מִן הַגֵּזֶל, אֲבָל אִם הָיָה קְצָת מַה שֶּׁבְּיָדוֹ שֶׁלֹּא מִן הַגֵּזֶל, אַף־עַל־פִּי שֶׁהוּא מוּעָט, מֻתָּר לֵהָנוֹת מִמֶּנּוּ עַד שֶׁיֵּדַע בְּבֵרוּר שֶׁאוֹתוֹ דָבָר מַמָּשׁ שֶׁהוּא נֶהֱנֶה בּוֹ גָזוּל. וְיֶתֶר דִּינֵי גְזֵלָה וְדִינֵי יֵאוּשׁ וְשִׁנּוּי רְשׁוּת וּשְׁאָר פְּרָטֵיהֶן, מְבֹאָרִין בְּפֶרֶק תְּשִׁיעִי וַעֲשִׂירִי מִקַּמָּא, וּקְצָת מֵהֶן כָּתַבְתִּי בְסֵדֶר וַיִּקְרָא בְמִצְוַת עֲשֵׂה י"א [סִי' ק"ל].

וְנֹהַג אִסּוּר זֶה בְּכָל מָקוֹם וּבְכָל זְמַן, בַּזְּכָרִים וּנְקֵבוֹת. וְעוֹבֵר עָלָיו וְגָזַל מִשְׁוֶה פְרוּטָה וּלְמַעְלָה עָבַר עַל לָאו, אֲבָל אֵין לוֹקִין עַל לָאו זֶה לְפִי שֶׁהוּא נִתָּק לַעֲשֵׂה דַהֲשָׁבָה, שֶׁנֶּאֱמַר: וְהֵשִׁיב אֶת הַגְּזֵלָה וְגוֹמֵר, וַאֲפִלּוּ בִטֵּל עֲשֵׂה שֶׁבָּהּ, כְּלוֹמַר שֶׁשָּׂרַף אֶת הַגְּזֵלָה אוֹ הִשְׁלִיכָהּ לַיָּם הַגָּדוֹל, מָקוֹם שֶׁאֵינָה נִמְצֵאת לְעוֹלָם, אֵינוֹ לוֹקֶה, לְפִי שֶׁהוּא לָאו שֶׁנִּתָּן לְתַשְׁלוּמִין, שֶׁיְּשַׁלֵּם מַה שֶּׁהֱזִיקָה שָׁנָה. וְאִם כָּפַר בָּהּ

---

13. Given to fingering and counting the contents of his purse, shortly after he receives his money from the other he will count it, find more than was due him, and will realize that what he lost in robbery has been returned him (Rashi, *ibid.* s.v. *'adam*).

13a. Because of their value or significance, the owner is wont to count such objects every so often, and hence he will be aware of no loss. Therefore the robber need do no more — in keeping with the previous ruling; TB Bava Kamma 118a; MT *ibid.* and *hilchoth g'nevah* iv 11–12. (MY, however, considers this a scribal error, and would remove the word *shelo'*, making it read, "*with* the knowledge"; see there.)

14. Since the obligation to pay was essentially their father's; MT *hilchoth g'zelah* v 5.

15. Literally, for the sake of the rectification of the world — i.e. for the sake of good business relations, that people should not hesitate to lend money, etc.

16. MT *ibid.* 7 (see *Maggid Mishneh*).

17. MT *ibid.* 9, based on TB Bava Kamma 119a.

18. So TB Makkoth 16a.

returns it to the other's purse, he is equally quit of obligation—provided there is money in it. For we hold to the view of R. Yitzḥak, who said: A man is used to fingering about in his purse; and thus he will count his money.[13] Where [objects that one is given to] counting [were taken and returned] without the knowledge [of the owner], one is free of penalty if the objects were nothing living (inanimate).[13a]

We have, further, the law of one who took something in robbery and died, whether he gave the seized object [first] to his sons before loss of hope [by the owner] or afterward: If he left [them] land, the sons are obligated to pay the value of what was seized, but out of movable goods the orphans should not be obligated to pay[14]— except for the amendment of the *ge'onim*, who so ruled: that even for a loan given orally [without a promissory note] the movable goods of the orphans become collateral, for the sake of good relations in the community.[15]

The law for one who buys from a robber is as the law of one who buys from a thief, i.e. that it makes a difference whether [the robber] is thus known or not.[16] And there is what the Sages said: that it is forbidden to derive any benefit from a man about whom it is firmly held that all he had [he acquired] by robbery; but if some part of what he has was not gained by robbery, even if it is only a small part, it is permitted to derive benefit from him, until one knows for certain that the actual object from which he benefits was taken in robbery.[17] The remaining laws of robbery, the laws about [the owner's] loss of hope and a change of possession [of the seized object], and the rest of their details, are explained in chapters 9 and 10 of the tractate *Bava Kamma*. Some of them I wrote in the eleventh positive precept of *sidrah va-yikra* (§130).

This prohibition is in force in every place, at every time, for both man and woman. If a person transgressed it and took from a *p'rutah*'s worth and up, he thus violated this negative precept; but whiplashes would not be given over this injunction, because its violation is given over for correction to the positive precept (§130) of returning [the seized property], as it is stated, *and he shall restore what was taken in robbery*, etc. (Leviticus 5:23). Even if one disobeyed the positive precept concerning it—in other words, he burned the seized object or threw it into the Great Sea, where it can nevermore be found—he is not given whiplashes: because it is a negative precept whose violation can be made right by compensation, when he pays what it was worth.[18]

וְנִשְׁבַּע לַשֶּׁקֶר, יוֹסִיף הַחֹמֶשׁ וְיַקְרִיב אָשָׁם, כְּמוֹ שֶׁהִתְבָּאֵר בְּקַמָּא וּבְסוֹף מַכּוֹת.

[שֶׁלֹּא נְאַחֵר שְׂכַר שָׂכִיר]

רל שֶׁלֹּא נְאַחֵר שְׂכַר שָׂכִיר, שֶׁנֶּאֱמַר: לֹא תָלִין פְּעֻלַּת שָׂכִיר אִתְּךָ עַד בֹּקֶר. וְזֶה הַכָּתוּב אָמְרוּ זִכְרוֹנָם לִבְרָכָה שֶׁמְּדַבֵּר בִּשְׂכִיר יוֹם, וְהֶאֱרִיכָה הַתּוֹרָה זְמַן פֵּרָעוֹנוֹ כָּל הַלַּיְלָה, שֶׁנֶּאֱמַר: עַד בֹּקֶר; וּבִשְׂכִיר לַיְלָה לָמַדְנוּ בְמָקוֹם אַחֵר שֶׁזְּמַן פֵּרָעוֹנוֹ כָּל הַיּוֹם, שֶׁנֶּאֱמַר: בְּיוֹמוֹ תִתֵּן שְׂכָרוֹ וְלֹא תָבוֹא עָלָיו הַשֶּׁמֶשׁ, וּפֵרְשׁוּ זִכְרוֹנָם לִבְרָכָה שֶׁזֶּה הַכָּתוּב מְדַבֵּר בִּשְׂכִיר לַיְלָה. וּלְשׁוֹן הַמִּשְׁנָה: שְׂכִיר יוֹם גּוֹבֶה כָּל הַלַּיְלָה וּשְׂכִיר לַיְלָה גּוֹבֶה כָּל הַיּוֹם.

וְאַף־עַל־פִּי שֶׁבָּאוּ בְּמִצְוָה זוֹ שְׁנֵי כְתוּבִים אֵינָם אֶלָּא מִצְוָה אַחַת, וְהָאֶחָד נֶאֱמַר לְהַשְׁלִים דִּין הַמִּצְוָה, וְאֵין לָנוּ לִמְנוֹת מַה שֶּׁיָּבוֹא בַתּוֹרָה לְתַשְׁלוּם דִּין הַמִּצְוָה, מִצְוָה בִּפְנֵי עַצְמָהּ.

וְעִנְיַן מִצְוָה זוֹ הוּא, שֶׁלֹּא נְאַחֵר לַשָּׂכִיר פֵּרָעוֹנוֹ אֲבָל נִפְרָעֵהוּ תּוֹךְ זְמַן קָצוּב, זֶהוּ יְסוֹד הַמִּצְוָה; וְעִם שְׁנֵי הַלָּאוִין אֵלּוּ הַנִּזְכָּרִים בָּהּ, יָדַעְנוּ זְמַן הַפֵּרָעוֹן בִּשְׂכִירִים, בֵּין שְׂכִיר יוֹם בֵּין שְׂכִיר לַיְלָה, מָתַי הוּא. וּזְכֹר זֶה הָעִקָּר בְּכָל הַמִּצְוֹת, כִּי עִקָּר גָּדוֹל הוּא בְּחֶשְׁבּוֹן הַמִּצְוֹת, וְהוּא הָעִקָּר שֶׁהִסְכִּימוּ עָלָיו שְׁנֵי עַמּוּדֵי הָעוֹלָם, הָרַמְבַּ"ם זִכְרוֹנוֹ לִבְרָכָה וְהָרַמְבַּ"ן זִכְרוֹנוֹ לִבְרָכָה.

מִשָּׁרְשֵׁי הַמִּצְוָה, לְפִי שֶׁהַשֵּׁם בָּרוּךְ הוּא חָפֵץ בְּקִיּוּם הָאָדָם אֲשֶׁר בָּרָא, וְיָדוּעַ כִּי בְאִחוּר הַמְּזוֹנוֹת יֹאבַד הַגּוּף, וְעַל־כֵּן צִוָּנוּ לָתֵת שְׂכַר שָׂכִיר, כִּי אֵלָיו הוּא נוֹשֵׂא אֶת נַפְשׁוֹ לְהִתְפַּרְנֵס בּוֹ, וּלְפִי הַנִּרְאֶה עַל־כֵּן שָׂם שָׁם גְּבוּל זְמַנּוֹ יוֹם אֶחָד וְלֹא יוֹתֵר, כִּי דֶרֶךְ בְּנֵי־אָדָם לְהִתְעַנּוֹת יוֹם אֶחָד לִפְעָמִים. וּבְפֵרוּשׁ הוֹדִיעַ הַכָּתוּב טַעַם

§230
1. TB Bava M'tzi'a 110b.
2. Mishnah, Bava M'tzi'a ix 11 (TB *ibid.*).
3. "This principle" is the concept indicated in the second paragraph, that when the Torah commands something twice, but the instructions in the two instances do not repeat but complement one another, we have one precept, not two; ShM negative precept 238, root principle 9, etc. Ramban evidently concurs, since in his commentary (*hassagoth*) he raises no objections.
4. Hence the night following a day of work, or the day following a night, is a period that the worker can tolerate, waiting for his pay.

If he denied it and swore falsely, he must add on a fifth of the seized object's value, and bring an 'asham (guilt-offering), as explained in the tractate *Bava Kamma* and toward the end of *Makkoth*.

230 [THAT PAYMENT OF A HIRED MAN IS NOT TO BE DELAYED] that we should not delay the wages of a hired worker: for it is stated, *you shall not keep the wages of a hired servant with you all night until the morning* (Leviticus 19:13); and the Sages of blessed memory said[1] that this verse speaks of a day-laborer, in which case the Torah extended the time for paying him throughout the night, as it is written, *until the morning.* About a night-worker we learned elsewhere that the time for paying is the entire [following] day: for it is stated, *On the same day you shall give him his hire, that the sun shall not go down over it* (Deuteronomy 24:15); and the Sages of blessed memory explained[1] that this verse deals with a laborer hired for the night. In the language of the Mishnah:[2] A person hired for the day is to collect [his wages at any time] during the entire night, and one hired for the night is to collect [at any time] during the entire day.

Now, although two verses are given about this commandment, it is no more than one precept, the other verse being stated to complete the law of the precept; and we cannot count what is given in the Torah to complete the law of a precept as a precept in its own right.

The substance of this precept is that we should not delay the wages of a hired worker, but should pay him within a fixed period. This is the basic demand of the precept; and with these two injunctions about it, given above, we know the time-period for the payment of all hired workers, whether day-laborers or night-workers—when it is. Now, remember this principle for all the precepts, because it is an important rule in the reckoning of the *mitzvoth*, and it is a rule on which the two pillars of the world are agreed: Rambam and Ramban of blessed memory.[3]

At the root of the precept lies the reason that the Eternal Lord, blessed is He, delights in the sustenance of the human beings He created; and it is known that by the delay of food, the body begins to perish. He therefore commanded us to give the pay of a hired worker, because he sets his heart on it to be sustained by it. And apparently, for this reason He set the time limit for it at one day and no more, because it is

⟨47⟩ the way of people to fast one day at times.[4] The Torah explicitly

הַדָּבָר בְּאָמְרוֹ "וְאֵלָיו הוּא נוֹשֵׂא אֶת נַפְשׁוֹ". וְאַף־עַל־פִּי שֶׁדָּרְשׁוּ בּוֹ זִכְרוֹנָם
לִבְרָכָה עִנְיָן אַחֵר, פְּשָׁטֵיהּ דִּקְרָא כְּמוֹ שֶׁכָּתַבְנוּ מַשְׁמָע.

מִדִּינֵי הַמִּצְוָה, מַה שֶּׁאָמְרוּ זִכְרוֹנָם לִבְרָכָה שֶׁאֶחָד שְׂכַר הָאָדָם וְהַבְּהֵמָה
וְהַכֵּלִים, יֵשׁ בָּהֶם מִשּׁוּם "בְּיוֹמוֹ תִתֵּן שְׂכָרוֹ" וּמִשּׁוּם "בַּל תָּלִין", וְכֵן מַה
שֶּׁפֵּרְשׁוּ זִכְרוֹנָם לִבְרָכָה שֶׁשְּׂכִיר שָׁעוֹת שֶׁל יוֹם גּוֹבֶה כָּל יוֹם, וּשְׂכִיר שָׁעוֹת שֶׁל
לַיְלָה גּוֹבֶה כָּל הַלַּיְלָה; שְׂכִיר חֹדֶשׁ, שְׂכִיר שַׁבָּת, שְׂכִיר שָׁנָה, שְׂכִיר שָׁבוּעַ, יָצָא
בַּיּוֹם גּוֹבֶה שְׂכָרוֹ כָּל הַיּוֹם, יָצָא בַּלַּיְלָה גּוֹבֶה שְׂכָרוֹ כָּל הַלַּיְלָה.

וְדִין נָתַן טַלִּיתוֹ לְאֻמָּן, גְּמָרָהּ וְהוֹדִיעוֹ, שֶׁכָּל זְמַן שֶׁהַטַּלִּית בְּיַד אֻמָּן אֵינוֹ
עוֹבֵר, נְתָנָהּ לוֹ וְלֹא פְּרָעוֹ בַּיּוֹם שֶׁנְּתָנָהּ לוֹ, עוֹבֵר, שֶׁהַקַּבְּלָנוּת כִּשְׂכִירוּת, כֵּן
פֵּרְשׁוּ זִכְרוֹנָם לִבְרָכָה.

וְדִין שָׁלִיחַ שֶׁשָּׂכַר פּוֹעֲלִים, מִי עוֹבֵר מִשּׁוּם בַּל תָּלִין, הוּא אוֹ בַּעַל הַבַּיִת,
שֶׁהַכֹּל הוֹלֵךְ לְפִי הַלָּשׁוֹן שֶׁאָמַר לַפּוֹעֲלִים; וּמַה שֶּׁאָמְרוּ שֶׁאֵין הַשּׂוֹכֵר עוֹבֵר אֶלָּא
בִּזְמַן שֶׁתְּבָעוֹ הַשָּׂכִיר וְלֹא נָתַן לוֹ, אֲבָל אִם לֹא תְבָעוֹ אֵינוֹ עוֹבֵר; תּוֹסֶפֶת: אוֹ
שֶׁתְּבָעוֹ וְלֹא הָיָה לוֹ מַה שֶּׁיִּתֵּן לוֹ, אֵינוֹ עוֹבֵר, עַד כָּאן. וְכֵן אִם הִמְחָהוּ לַפּוֹעֵל
אֵצֶל אַחֵר שֶׁיִּפְרַע לוֹ הַשָּׂכָר וְקִבֵּל הַפּוֹעֵל, פָּטוּר הַשּׂוֹכֵר אַף־עַל־פִּי שֶׁלֹּא פְּרָעוֹ
הָאַחֵר אַחַר כֵּן.

וּמַה שֶּׁאָמְרוּ זִכְרוֹנָם לִבְרָכָה שֶׁהַמַּשְׁהֶה שְׂכַר שָׂכִיר עַד אַחַר זְמַנּוֹ, אַף־עַל־פִּי
שֶׁכְּבָר עָבַר בַּעֲשֵׂה וְלֹא־תַעֲשֶׂה, חַיָּב לִתֵּן לוֹ מִיָּד שֶׁיִּתְבָּעֵהוּ, וְכָל זְמַן שֶׁיַּשְׁהֶה לוֹ

---

5. In TB Bava M'tzi'a 112b the verse is taken to mean that for the sake of the wages
the worker was willing to toil and risk his life, and further, that withholding his pay is
like taking his life.

6. TB Bava M'tzi'a 110b–111a.

7. *Ibid.* 111a.

8. Because the Torah only enjoins withholding the wages, and an employer is
guilty of withholding them only if he has the money and will not give it; *ibid.* 112a. This
sentence, preceded by the word *tosefeth* (literally, "addition"), would seem to be a
marginal gloss that was incorporated into the text; it was possibly added by the author
himself to rectify an omission (it is present in the oldest manuscripts), as it derives
directly from MT *hilchoth s'chiruth* xi 4, our author's immediate source. The first edition
reads, ". . . to pay him, nor could he find anyone to lend him the amount, he [likewise],"
etc. But as this extra phrase is not in the oldest manuscripts, it would seem to be a still
later addition.

conveys the reason for the matter by saying, *and he sets his heart on it* (Deuteronomy 24:15). Even though the Sages of blessed memory interpreted it in a different manner,[5] the plain meaning of the verse seems to be as we have written.

Among the laws of the precept, there is what the Sages of blessed memory taught:[6] that whether it is the hire of a man, an animal, or equipment, the commandments to "give him his hire on that day" and not to let it remain through the night, apply to it. Then there is what the Sages of blessed memory explained:[6] that someone hired for certain hours of the day is to collect [his wages at some time] during the entire day, while a person hired for certain hours of the night is to collect at some time during the whole night. As for a person hired for a month, a week, a year, or seven years, if he left [ended] by day, he is to collect [at some time] that entire day; if he left [ended] at night, he is to collect his wages [some time] during the whole night.[6]

Then there is the law of one who gave his cloak to an artisan [for repairs, etc.] who finished it and let him know—that as long as the cloak remains in the artisan's hands, he commits no sin [by delaying payment]. If he gave it back to him and then he did not pay him on the day he returned it to him he would thus commit a transgression: because payment for contracted work is like wages for hired labor. So our Sages of blessed memory explained.[7]

Then we have the law of an agent who hired workers: who transgresses the precept not to let payment wait all night—he or the employer? It all depends on the language he used in speaking to the workers.[1] And there is what the Sages said:[7] that an employer commits no transgression except at the time that the hired man demands his wages from him and he does not give it to him; but if he does not demand it of him, he commits no transgression. To add a corollary: If he demanded it of him and he did not have the means to pay him, he [likewise] commits no transgression.[8] Thus far the addition. So too, if he handed over the worker to someone else to pay him the wages and the worker acquiesced, the employer is free of guilt [over this injunction] even if the other man does not pay him afterward.[1]

[Going further, we have] what the Sages of blessed memory taught:[1] that if a person holds back the wages of a hired hand beyond its proper time, even though he has already violated the positive and the negative precepts, he is yet obligated to pay him at once when [the worker] demands it of him. And so long as he delays his payment

⟨49⟩

פְּרָעֲונוֹ אֲפִלּוּ אַחַר הַזְּמַן, עוֹבֵר עוֹד עַל לָאו שֶׁל דִּבְרֵיהֶם זִכְרוֹנָם לִבְרָכָה, וְסָמְכוּ לָזֶה מִקְרָא שֶׁכָּתוּב: אַל תֹּאמַר לְרֵעֲךָ לֵךְ וָשׁוּב.

וְדִין הַשָּׂכִיר שֶׁנִּשְׁבָּע וְנוֹטֵל כָּל זְמַן שֶׁתָּבַע שְׂכָרוֹ תוֹךְ זְמַנּוֹ, וַאֲפִלּוּ הָיָה הַשָּׂכִיר קָטָן, גַּם הוּא נִשְׁבָּע וְנוֹטֵל; וְנָתְנוּ זִכְרוֹנָם לִבְרָכָה טַעַם בָּזֶה, לְפִי שֶׁבַּעַל הַבַּיִת טָרוּד בְּפוֹעֲלָיו. וְיֶתֶר פְּרָטֶיהָ, מְבֹאָרִים בְּפֶרֶק תְּשִׁיעִי מִמְּצִיעָא.

וְנוֹהֶגֶת בְּכָל מָקוֹם וּבְכָל זְמַן. וְעוֹבֵר עָלֶיהָ וְעִכֵּב שְׂכַר שָׂכִיר עַד אַחַר זְמַן הַמְגֻבָּל, בִּטֵּל עֲשֵׂה וְעוֹבֵר עַל לָאו; וְאֵין לוֹקִין עַל לָאו זֶה, לְפִי שֶׁנִּתָּן לְהִשָּׁבוֹן, שֶׁהֲרֵי חַיָּב הוּא לְשַׁלֵּם שְׂכָרוֹ בְּכָל עֵת. וְעוֹד אָמְרוּ זִכְרוֹנָם לִבְרָכָה בְּכוֹבֵשׁ שְׂכַר שָׂכִיר, עַל דֶּרֶךְ הָאַזְהָרָה, שֶׁעוֹבֵר מִשּׁוּם בַּל תַּעֲשֹׁק וּבַל תִּגְזֹל וּבַל תָּלִין וּמִשּׁוּם לֹא תָבוֹא עָלָיו הַשָּׁמֶשׁ. וְאָמְרוּ בְּגֵר תּוֹשָׁב שֶׁיֵּשׁ בּוֹ מִשּׁוּם בְּיוֹמוֹ תִתֵּן שְׂכָרוֹ, אֲבָל אֵין עוֹבְרִין בּוֹ מִשּׁוּם בַּל תָּלִין; וְזֶה הַדִּין דְּגֵר תּוֹשָׁב מְפֹרָשׁ בַּמִּשְׁנָה פֶּרֶק הַמְקַבֵּל. וְכָתַב הָרַמְבַּ"ם זִכְרוֹנוֹ לִבְרָכָה דְּהוּא הַדִּין לְבֶן נֹחַ.

[שֶׁלֹּא לְקַלֵּל אֶחָד מִיִּשְׂרָאֵל בֵּין אִישׁ בֵּין אִשָּׁה]

רלא שֶׁלֹּא לְקַלֵּל אֶחָד מִיִּשְׂרָאֵל, בֵּין אִישׁ בֵּין אִשָּׁה, וְאַף־עַל־פִּי שֶׁאֵינוֹ שׁוֹמֵעַ הַקְּלָלָה, שֶׁנֶּאֱמַר: לֹא תְקַלֵּל חֵרֵשׁ; וּבָא הַפֵּרוּשׁ עָלָיו: מִי שֶׁאֵינוֹ שׁוֹמֵעַ קִלְלָתְךָ, וְכֵן תִּרְגֵּם אֻנְקְלוֹס. וּלְשׁוֹן סִפְרָא: אֵין לִי אֶלָּא חֵרֵשׁ; מִנַּיִן לְרַבּוֹת כָּל אָדָם, תַּלְמוּד לוֹמַר: בְּעַמְּךָ לֹא תָאֹר; אִם־כֵּן לָמָּה נֶאֱמַר חֵרֵשׁ, מַה חֵרֵשׁ מְיֻחָד

8a. Although, as MH points out, the Torah's prohibition is violated only at the initial failure to pay the worker on time.

9. So MT *hilchoth s'chiruth* xi 6, as cited by Rabad (who differs); there is, however, another version in MT: see *Kessef Mishneh*.

10. Hence he could be mistaken about the matter more readily than the employee; but as a precaution against his lying, we require an oath of the worker; *ibid.* 112b.

11. Hebrew, *la'ashok*; see §228, first paragraph.

12. Literally, for a descendant of Noah (but since all except Noah and his family were annihilated in the flood, this means all mankind); ShM positive precept §200.

§231   1. On the above verse—*k'doshim, parashah* 2, 13.

even after the proper time, he violates yet another prohibition, by the ruling of the Sages of blessed memory,[8a] which they substantiated by the Scriptural verse, *Do not say to your neighbor, "Go and come again, and tomorrow I will give it," when you have it with you* (Proverbs 3:28).

Moreover, there is the law that a hired hand can take an oath and collect as long as he claims his wages in the proper time;[7] even if the worker is a minor, he too may swear an oath and collect.[9] Our Sages of blessed memory gave a reason for this: it is because the master [employer] is busy, distracted with his workers.[10] The rest of its details are explained in chapter 9 of the Talmud tractate *Bava M'tzi'a*.

It remains in effect in every place and every time. If someone transgresses it and withholds the wages of a hired worker past the set time, he disobeys a positive precept and violates a negative precept. No whiplashes are given over this injunction, though, since its violation is "given over" to compensation: for here he remains obligated to pay his wages at any time. Moreover, our Sages of blessed memory said about a person who suppresses a hired worker's wages, by way of admonition, that he violates the injunctions, *Do not maltreat*[11] ... *nor rob ... nor let the wages ... remain all night* (Leviticus 19:13), as well as the injunction, *neither shall the sun go down on it* (Deuteronomy 24:15).[7] They taught, too,[7] that the precept, *On the same day you shall give him his hire* (ibid.) applies [equally] to a *gér toshav*, a heathen who renounced idolatry; but one does not transgress the commandment not to let the wages "remain all night" in regard to him. This law about a *gér toshav* is in chapter 9 of the Mishnah tractate *Bava M'tzi'a* (ix 12). And Rambam of blessed memory wrote that the law is the same for anyone in the world.[12]

[THE PROHIBITION ON CURSING ANY JEW, MAN OR WOMAN]

231 not to curse any Jew, whether man or woman, even if he does not hear the curse: for it is stated, *You shall not curse the deaf* (Leviticus 19:14), and this is explained [in the 'Oral Tradition] to mean one who does not hear your curse; and so Onkelos rendered it. In the language of the Midrash *Sifra*:[1] Thus I know it only about a deaf man; how do I know to extend its application to every man?— Scripture states, *among your people you shall not curse* (Exodus 22:27). In that case, why was "the deaf" stipulated?—Since it is a characteristic

שֶׁהוּא בַּחַיִּים, יָצָא הַמֵּת, שֶׁאֵינוֹ בַּחַיִּים.

אַף־עַל־פִּי שֶׁאֵין בָּנוּ כֹּחַ לָדַעַת בְּאֵי זֶה עִנְיָן תָּנוּחַ הַקְּלָלָה בַּמְּקֻלָּל וְאֵי זֶה כֹּחַ בַּדִּבּוּר לַהֲבִיאָהּ עָלָיו, יָדַעְנוּ דֶּרֶךְ כְּלָל מִכָּל בְּנֵי הָעוֹלָם שֶׁחוֹשְׁשִׁין לַקְּלָלוֹת, בֵּין יִשְׂרָאֵל בֵּין שְׁאָר הָאֻמּוֹת, וְיֹאמְרוּ שֶׁקִּלְלַת בְּנֵי־אָדָם, גַּם קִלְלַת הֶדְיוֹט, תַּעֲשֶׂה רֹשֶׁם בַּמְּקֻלָּל וְתַדְבִּיק בּוֹ הַמְּאֵרָה וְהַצַּעַר.

וְאַחַר דַּעְתֵּנוּ דָבָר זֶה מִפִּי הַבְּרִיּוֹת, נֹאמַר כִּי מְשָׁרְשֵׁי הַמִּצְוָה, שֶׁמְּנָעָנוּ הַשֵּׁם מֵהַזִּיק בְּפִינוּ לְזוּלָתֵנוּ כְּמוֹ שֶׁמְּנָעָנוּ מֵהַזִּיק לָהֶם בְּמַעֲשֶׂה; וּכְעֵין עִנְיָן זֶה אָמְרוּ זִכְרוֹנָם לִבְרָכָה: בְּרִית כְּרוּתָה לַשְּׂפָתַיִם, כְּלוֹמַר שֶׁיֵּשׁ כֹּחַ בְּדִבְרֵי פִי אָדָם.

וְאֶפְשָׁר לָנוּ לוֹמַר לְפִי עֲנִיּוּת דַּעְתֵּנוּ, כִּי בִּהְיוֹת הַנֶּפֶשׁ הַמְדַבֶּרֶת שֶׁבָּאָדָם חֵלֶק עֶלְיוֹנִי, וּכְמוֹ שֶׁכָּתוּב: וַיִּפַּח בְּאַפָּיו נִשְׁמַת חַיִּים, וְתִרְגֵּם אָנְקְלוֹס: לְרוּחַ מְמַלְּלָא, נָתַן בָּהּ כֹּחַ רַב לִפְעֹל אֲפִלּוּ בְּמַה שֶׁהוּא חוּץ מִמֶּנָּה, וְעַל כֵּן יָדַעְנוּ וְנִרְאֶה תָמִיד כִּי לְפִי חֲשִׁיבוּת נֶפֶשׁ הָאָדָם וּדְבֵקוּתָהּ בָּעֶלְיוֹנִים בְּנֶפֶשׁ הַצַּדִּיקִים וְהַחֲסִידִים, יְמַהֲרוּ דִבְרֵיהֶם לִפְעֹל בְּכָל מַה שֶׁיְּדַבְּרוּ עָלָיו, וְזֶה דָּבָר יָדוּעַ וּמְפֻרְסָם בֵּין יוֹדְעֵי דַעַת וּמְבִינֵי מַדָּע.

וְאֶפְשָׁר לוֹמַר עוֹד, כִּי הָעִנְיָן לְהַשְׁבִּית רִיב בֵּין בְּנֵי־אָדָם וְלִהְיוֹת בֵּינֵיהֶם שָׁלוֹם, כִּי עוֹף הַשָּׁמַיִם יוֹלִיךְ אֶת הַקּוֹל, וְאוּלַי יָבוֹאוּ דִבְרֵי הַמְּקַלֵּל בְּאָזְנֵי מִי שֶׁקֻּלָּל.

וְהָרַמְבָּ"ם זִכְרוֹנוֹ לִבְרָכָה אָמַר בְּטַעַם מִצְוָה זוֹ, כְּדֵי שֶׁלֹּא יָנִיעַ נֶפֶשׁ הַמְקֻלָּל אֶל הַנְּקָמָה וְלֹא יַרְגִּילָהּ לַכַּעַס; וְעוֹד הֶאֱרִיךְ בָּעִנְיָן בְּסִפְרוֹ. וְנִרְאֶה לִי מִדְּבָרָיו, שֶׁלֹּא יֵרָאֶה הוּא בְּדַעְתּוֹ נֶזֶק אֶל הַמְקֻלָּל בַּקְּלָלָה, אֶלָּא שֶׁתַּרְחִיק הַתּוֹרָה הָעִנְיָן

---

2. That whatever they utter should have an effect; TB Mo'éd Katan 18a.
3. ShM negative precept §317.

of a deaf person that he is alive, a dead person is excluded, as he is not alive.

Now, even though it is not in our power to know in what way a malediction takes effect on a cursed person, and what force speech has to bring this [effect] upon him, we know generally from all the people in the world that they are fearful about curses—both Jewry and other peoples. They say that anyone's malediction, even the curse of a commoner, leaves a mark on the cursed person, and the imprecation and the pain cling to him.

Well, knowing this concept from people's words, we would say that at the root of the precept lies the reason that the Eternal Lord has restrained us from causing harm with our mouths to anyone else, as He has restrained us from harming others by action. In a vein akin to this theme, our Sages of blessed memory said: A covenant (pact) was made with the lips.[2] In other words, there is a force in the words of a man's mouth.

Now, we could possibly say, by the paucity of our understanding, that inasmuch as the spirit that speaks in man is a supernal element—as it is written, *and He breathed into his nostrils the soul of life [and man became a living spirit]* (Genesis 2:7), which Onkelos renders as "a talking spirit"—He endowed it with a great power to act, even on what is outside of itself. Therefore we know and see constantly that according to the significance and worth of a human spirit, and its adherence to supernal entities—to the spirits of the righteous and the pious—his words are swift to take effect in regard to whatever he speaks about. This is something accepted and widely recognized among those who know wisdom and understand knowledge.

It could be said, further, that it is a matter of stopping contention among people and having peace rule among them: *For a bird of heaven will carry the voice* (Ecclesiastes 10:20), and the words of the one who uttered the malediction will perhaps come to the ears of the one he cursed.

Rambam of blessed memory wrote about the reason for this precept[3] that it is in order that the spirit of the one uttering the curse should not be moved to vengeance, nor should he accustom it to rage; and he continued at length about the theme in his work. Well, it appears to me, from his words, that to his mind, he sees no harm in store for the cursed person from the malediction; it is only that the Torah prohibits the matter for the sake of the one uttering the curse—

מִצַּד הַמְקַלֵּל שֶׁלֹּא יַרְגִּיל נַפְשׁוֹ אֶל הַנְּקָמָה וְהַכַּעַס וְאֶל פְּחִיתוּת הַמִּדּוֹת. וְכָל דִּבְרֵי רַבֵּנוּ נְקַבֵּל, עִם הֱיוֹת לְבֵּנוּ נֶאֱחָז בְּמַה שֶׁכָּתַבְנוּ יוֹתֵר.

מִדִּינֵי הַמִּצְוָה, מַה שֶׁאָמְרוּ זִכְרוֹנָם לִבְרָכָה שֶׁאָסוּר לְקַלֵּל בְּשׁוּם עִנְיָן, וּמִכָּל-מָקוֹם אֵינוֹ לוֹקֶה אֶלָּא הַמְקַלֵּל בְּשֵׁם מִן הַשֵּׁמוֹת, כְּגוֹן יָהּ, שַׁדַּי וֶאֱלוֹהַּ וְכַיּוֹצֵא בָהֶן, אוֹ בְכִנּוּי מִן הַכִּנּוּיִין, כְּגוֹן חַנּוּן, קַנּוֹא וְכַיּוֹצֵא בָהֶן;, וּבְכָל לָשׁוֹן שֶׁקִּלֵּל בְּשֵׁם אוֹ בְכִנּוּי חַיָּב, שֶׁהַשֵּׁמוֹת שֶׁקּוֹרְאִין בָּהֶן הַגּוֹיִים לְהַקָּדוֹשׁ בָּרוּךְ הוּא הֲרֵי הֵן בִּכְלַל הַכִּנּוּיִן.

וּמַה שֶׁאָמְרוּ שֶׁאָפִלּוּ הַמְקַלֵּל אֶת עַצְמוֹ לוֹקֶה, שֶׁנֶּאֱמַר: הִשָּׁמֶר לְךָ וּשְׁמֹר נַפְשְׁךָ מְאֹד; וּמַה שֶׁאָמְרוּ בִמְכִילְתָּא: "לֹא תְקַלֵּל חֵרֵשׁ", בַּאֲמֵלָלִין שֶׁבָּאָדָם; וְעוֹד אָמְרוּ שָׁם: כְּשֶׁהַכָּתוּב אוֹמֵר "וְנָשִׂיא בְעַמְּךָ לֹא תָאֹר", אֶחָד דַּיָּן וְאֶחָד נָשִׂיא בְמַשְׁמָע, וּמַה תַּלְמוּד לוֹמַר "אֱלֹהִים לֹא תְקַלֵּל" — לְחַיֵּב עַל זֶה בִּפְנֵי עַצְמוֹ וְעַל זֶה בִּפְנֵי עַצְמוֹ; מִכָּאן אָמְרוּ: יֵשׁ מְדַבֵּר דָּבָר אֶחָד וְחַיָּב עָלָיו מִשּׁוּם אַרְבָּעָה דְבָרִים: בֶּן נָשִׂיא שֶׁקִּלֵּל אָבִיו חַיָּב עָלָיו מִשּׁוּם הָאָב וּמִשּׁוּם דַּיָּן וּמִשּׁוּם נָשִׂיא וּמִשּׁוּם בְּעַמְּךָ לֹא תָאֹר.

וְנוֹהֶגֶת בְּכָל מָקוֹם וּבְכָל זְמַן, בִּזְכָרִים וּנְקֵבוֹת. וְעוֹבֵר עָלֶיהָ וְקִלֵּל בַּשֵּׁם אוֹ בַכִּנּוּי אֶחָד מִיִּשְׂרָאֵל בְּמֵזִיד וְיֵשׁ עֵדִים וְהַתְרָאָה, לוֹקֶה, שֶׁזֶּהוּ אֶחָד מִשְּׁלֹשָׁה לָאוִין שֶׁאַף-עַל-פִּי שֶׁאֵין בָּהֶן מַעֲשֶׂה לוֹקִין עֲלֵיהֶן; וְהַשְּׁנַיִם הָאֲחֵרִים הֵם נִשְׁבַּע וּמֵמֵר, כְּמוֹ שֶׁכָּתַבְנוּ כְּבָר.

[שֶׁלֹּא לְהַכְשִׁיל תָּם בְּדַרְכּוֹ]

רלב שֶׁלֹּא לְהַכְשִׁיל בְּנֵי יִשְׂרָאֵל לָתֵת לָהֶם עֵצָה רָעָה, אֲבָל נַיְשִׁיר אוֹתָם כְּשֶׁיִּשְׁאָלוּ עֵצָה, בְּמַה שֶׁנַּאֲמִין שֶׁהוּא יָשָׁר וְעֵצָה טוֹבָה, שֶׁנֶּאֱמַר: וְלִפְנֵי עִוֵּר לֹא

---

4. TB Sh'vu'oth 35a.

5. Several examples of Divine names are now given in the Hebrew text.

6. MT hilchoth sanhedrin xxvi 3, derived from TB Sanhedrin 60a.

7. TB Sh'vu'oth 36a; MT ibid.

8. Mechilta on Exodus 22:27.

9. While e-lo-him generally means God (hence JPS 1917, "You shall not revile God"), it often has this meaning, and it is so understood here by the Sages.

10. Literally, a prince, or a patriarch; the nassi was the religious head of Israel, who served as head of the Sanhedrin (the supreme court); hence he was also a justice.

§232   1. MH queries this, since, as our author himself makes it clear later, it is equally forbidden to seek to mislead a non-Jew, as ruled explicitly in the Talmud (e.g. TB P'saḥim 22b). To this MY replies that perhaps our author holds to the view that while the Torah does forbid mistreating or misleading a non-Jew (even if he is an idol-worshipper), the

so that he should not accustom his spirit to vengeance and anger, and a degeneration of character traits. Let us accept all the words of our master [Rambam] even though our heart holds more strongly to what we have written.

Among the laws of the precept, there is what the Sages of blessed memory taught:[4] that while it is forbidden to curse in any way whatever, nevertheless, only he receives whiplashes who curses by one of the Divine names,[5] or by one of the attributive names, such as Compassionate One, Vengefully Jealous One, and so on. If a person curses in any language by a Divine name or a substitute, he incurs punishment; for the names by which the nations call the Holy One, blessed is He, are included in the category of substitute names.[6]

Then we have what the Sages of blessed memory taught:[7] that even one who curses himself is given whiplashes; for it is stated, *Only take care for yourself, and guard yourself greatly* (Deuteronomy 4:9). And there is what they said in the Midrash *Mechilta*:[8] "You shall not curse the deaf"—this denotes the unfortunate among men. They taught there further: when Scripture states, *nor shall you curse a ruler of your people* (Exodus 22:27), both a judge and a ruler are implied; then why does Scripture say, *You shall not curse a judge*[9] (*ibid.*)?—to impose punishment for this one separately and for that one separately. Hence they said:[8] A person can say one thing and incur punishment over it for four things: If the son of a *nassi*[10] cursed his father, he is punishable for it because he is his father (§260), because he is a judge (§69), because he is a *nassi* (§71), and because of the injunction, *among your people you shall not curse* (*ibid.*).

It applies everywhere, at every time, for both man and woman. If someone transgressed it and cursed an Israelite, by a Divine or substitute name, deliberately, and there were witnesses and a warning, he should receive whiplashes; for this is one of three negative precepts over which lashes are given even though their violation involves no physical action—the two others being swearing [in vain] (§30) and exchanging [holy offerings] (§351), as we have written previously (§62).

[NOT TO MAKE A TRUSTING PERSON STUMBLE THROUGH
MISLEADING ADVICE]

232 not to bring Israelites[1] to grief by giving them bad counsel, but we should rather guide them aright when they ask advice, by

⟨55⟩ what we believe to be an honest way and a good plan—as it is stated,

תִּתֵּן מִכְשׁׁל. וּלְשׁוֹן סִפְרָא: לִפְנֵי סוּמָא בַּדָּבָר וְהָיָה נוֹטֵל מִמְּךָ עֵצָה, אַל תִּתֵּן לוֹ עֵצָה שֶׁאֵינָהּ הוֹגֶנֶת לוֹ. וְאָמְרוּ זִכְרוֹנָם לִבְרָכָה: אַל יֹאמַר אָדָם לַחֲבֵרוֹ "מְכֹר שָׂדְךָ וְקַח חֲמוֹר", וְהוּא עוֹקֵף עָלָיו וְנוֹטְלָהּ הֵימֶנּוּ.

וְזֶה הַלָּאו כּוֹלֵל כְּמוֹ־כֵן מִי שֶׁיַּעֲזֹר עוֹבֵר עֲבֵרָה, שֶׁהוּא מֵבִיא אוֹתוֹ שֶׁיִּתְפַּתֶּה בְּזוּלַת זֶה לַעֲבֹר פְּעָמִים אֲחֵרִים עוֹד; וּמִזֶּה הַצַּד אָמְרוּ זִכְרוֹנָם לִבְרָכָה בְּמַלְוֶה וְלוֹוֶה בְּרִבִּית שֶׁשְּׁנֵיהֶם עוֹבְרִים בְּלִפְנֵי עִוֵּר וְגוֹמֵר.

שֹׁרֶשׁ הַמִּצְוָה יָדוּעַ, כִּי תִקּוּן הָעוֹלָם וְיִשּׁוּבוֹ הוּא לְהַדְרִיךְ בְּנֵי־אָדָם וְלָתֵת לָהֶם בְּכָל מַעֲשֵׂיהֶם עֵצָה טוֹבָה.

מִדִּינֵי הַמִּצְוָה, מַה שֶּׁאָמְרוּ זִכְרוֹנָם לִבְרָכָה בְּרֵישׁ מַסֶּכֶת עֲבוֹדָה זָרָה דְּאַלְּפְנֵי מִפְקְדִינָן, אֲבָל לִפְנֵי דְלִפְנֵי לָא מִפְקְדִינָן; וּמִפְּנֵי־כֵן פֵּרְשׁוּ שָׁם דְּכִי אִיבַּעְיָא לָן בַּגְּמָרָא טַעְמָא דְּמַתְנִיתִין, אִי מְשׁוּם דְּאָזִיל וּמוֹדֶה אִי מְשׁוּם לִפְנֵי עִוֵּר, דְּלָא הֲוָה מִסְתַּפֵּק בְּטַעְמָא דְּמַתְנִיתִין אֶלָּא בְּלֶשֵׁאת וְלָתֵת עִמָּהֶם, דְּיָהֵיב לֵיהּ לְגוֹי מִידֵי דַחֲזֵי לְתִקְרוֹבֶת, וּבְכִי הַאי גַּוְנָא אֶפְשָׁר דְּאִכָּא בֵּיהּ מְשׁוּם וְלִפְנֵי עִוֵּר; אֲבָל שְׁאָר מַתְנִיתִין כֻּלָּהּ, כְּגוֹן לְהַלְוֹותָן וּלְפָרְעָן וּלְהַשְׁאִילָן, מְשׁוּם דְּאָזִיל וּמוֹדֶה הוּא אִסּוּרָא, דִּמְשׁוּם לִפְנֵי עִוֵּר לֵכָּא לְמֵימַר, דִּשְׁאָלָה בְּעֵינָהּ הָדְרָא; וּלְהַלְוֹותָן וּלְפָרְעָן נַמִּי, זוּזֵי יַהֲבִינָן לְהוּ, וְזוּזֵי לָא חֲזוּ לְתִקְרוֹבֶת; מַאי אָמַרְתְּ, דִּילְמָא זָבֵין בְּהוּ תִקְרוֹבֶת, הֲוָה לֵיהּ לִפְנֵי דְלִפְנֵי, וּבְכִי הַאי לָא מַפְקְדִינָן, כְּמוֹ שֶׁאָמַרְנוּ; וְכֵן כָּל כַּיּוֹצֵא בָזֶה.

specific negative precept about "a stumbling-block before the blind" is violated only if the victim is a member of Jewry; and here our author is giving the basic meaning of the negative precept, without regard to auxiliary laws. For such a view, that something may be forbidden by the Torah yet no specific negative precept is violated if that something is done, MY (q.v.) finds some basis in MT *hilchoth s'chiruth* xi 1, in conjunction with *hilchoth g'zélah* i 2.

2. In Sifra on the verse.

3. By giving him the feeling that such behavior is acceptable.

4. Because each thus helps the other violate the prohibition on interest; TB Bava M'tzi'a 75b. (The first two paragraphs are based on ShM negative precept §299).

5. Literally, for it is the improvement of the world and its settlement.

6. E.g. it is forbidden to sell an animal suitable for an offering to an idol-worshipper on his religious holiday, because he is then likely to sacrifice it to his idol; hence this is "putting a stumbling-block before the blind," since we are taught that idolatry was forbidden to all mankind. However, it is not forbidden to sell such an animal to a heathen dealer who will then sell it to the idol-worshipper—because that is called "before the before," since the heathen dealer himself is not prohibited from putting a stumbling-block before his customer (leading him into grief).

7. In the commentary of R. Nissim, TB 'Avodah Zarah, beginning (also early authorities cited in Ritba *ibid.* 2a).

nor shall you put a stumbling-block before the blind (Leviticus 19:14).
In the language of the Midrash *Sifra*: [This means] before one who is
blind about some matter, and he would take advice from you; do
not give him counsel that is not suitable for him. And our Sages of
blessed memory said:[2] Let a man not tell his fellow, "Sell your field
and buy a donkey," so that he can then scheme around him and take
it [the field] from him.

This injunction includes, likewise, a person who would help
someone committing a transgression—for he would thus induce
him to be persuaded, apart from this, to commit the sin other times
as well.[3] In this vein, the Sages of blessed memory taught that when
one lends and another borrows at interest, both violate the injunction
not to put a stumbling-block before the blind.[4]

The root reason for the precept is known (evident): for it serves
to improve society and order its communal life[5] to guide people
and give them good advice in all their activities.

Among the laws of the precept, there is what the Sages of blessed
memory taught at the beginning of the tractate *'Avodah Zarah* (14a):
that about matters [directly] "before [the blind]" we are commanded
[to be careful], but about matters "before the before" we were not
commanded.[6] Therefore it was explained there[7] that when it is asked
in the Talmud[8] whether the reason of the Mishnah [that forbids
doing business with idol-worshippers for three days before their
sacred holiday] is that they will go and give thanks[9] or so as not to
"put a stumbling-block before the blind,"[10] the doubt about the
Mishnah's reason is only about doing business with them whereby
the Israelite gives the heathen something suitable for an offering.
In such a case it is possible that the injunction about a stumbling-block
before the blind is involved. But as to the entire rest of the passage
in the Mishnah—for instance, about lending or repaying them money,
or lending them things—it is because he will go and give thanks that
they are forbidden. For "a stumbling-block before the blind" cannot
be said to be involved here: because a borrowed object is returned
intact; and as for lending or repaying them money, there too it is
coins that are given them, and coins are not suitable for an offering.
Then what would you say?—perhaps they will buy an offering with
them [the coins]? This is "before the before," and in such a case we
are not commanded [to beware], as we have stated. And so everyting

similar.

וְכֵן מַה שֶּׁאָמְרוּ זִכְרוֹנָם לִבְרָכָה שֶׁאָסוּר לִמְכֹּר כָּל כְּלֵי מִלְחָמָה וְכָל דָּבָר שֶׁיֵּשׁ
בּוֹ נֶזֶק לָרַבִּים, לַגּוֹיִם, אֶלָּא־אִם־כֵּן מוֹכְרָן כִּי הֵיכִי דִמְגַנּוּ עֲלָן; וְכֵן אָסוּר לְמָכְרוֹ
לְיִשְׂרָאֵל הַמּוֹכְרוֹ לְגוֹי, וְכֵן לְיִשְׂרָאֵל לִיסְטִים; וְאָסְרוּ הַכֹּל מִשּׁוּם וְלִפְנֵי עִוֵּר
וְגוֹמֵר. וְיֵתֶר פְּרָטֶיהָ, בִּמְקוֹמוֹת מֵהַתַּלְמוּד בְּפִזּוּר.

וְנוֹהֶגֶת בְּכָל מָקוֹם וּבְכָל זְמַן, בִּזְכָרִים וּנְקֵבוֹת. וְעוֹבֵר עָלֶיהָ וְהִשִּׂיא אֶת חֲבֵרוֹ
לָדַעַת עֵצָה שֶׁאֵינָהּ הוֹגֶנֶת לוֹ, אוֹ סִיַּע אוֹתוֹ בִּדְבַר עֲבֵרָה, כְּגוֹן הַמּוֹשִׁיט כּוֹס יַיִן
לְנָזִיר וְכָל כַּיּוֹצֵא בָזֶה, עָבַר עַל לָאו זֶה, וְהוּא כְּעוֹבֵר עַל מִצְוַת מֶלֶךְ, וְאֵין לוֹקִין
עָלָיו, לְפִי שֶׁאֵין בּוֹ מַעֲשֶׂה.

[שֶׁלֹּא לְעַוֵּל הַמִּשְׁפָּט]

רלג שֶׁלֹּא יַעֲשֶׂה הַדַּיָּן עָוֶל בַּדִּין; וְהָעָוֶל יִהְיֶה בְּכָל עֵת שֶׁיַּעֲבֹר עַל מַה שֶּׁצִּוְּתָה
לָנוּ הַתּוֹרָה בְּעִנְיַן הַדִּין, אֶלָּא־אִם־כֵּן עָשָׂה בְרָצוֹן בַּעֲלֵי הַדִּין; וְעַל זֶה נֶאֱמַר: לֹא
תַעֲשׂוּ עָוֶל בַּמִּשְׁפָּט.

שֹׁרֶשׁ הַמִּצְוָה יָדוּעַ, כִּי בְמִשְׁפַּט צֶדֶק יִתְקַיֵּם יִשּׁוּב בְּנֵי־אָדָם.

מִדִּינֵי הַמִּצְוָה, מַה שֶּׁאָמְרוּ זִכְרוֹנָם לִבְרָכָה שֶׁהַמְעַנֶּה אֶת הַדִּין בִּכְלַל מְעַוֵּל
הַמִּשְׁפָּט הוּא; וּמַה שֶּׁאָמְרוּ: הֱווּ מְתוּנִים בַּדִּין, כְּדֵי שֶׁלֹּא יָבוֹאוּ לְעַוֵּל הַמִּשְׁפָּט;
וְאָמְרוּ זִכְרוֹנָם לִבְרָכָה שֶׁרָאוּי לְמִי שֶׁדָּן, לְהַמְלֵךְ עִם גָּדוֹל מִמֶּנּוּ אִם הוּא אֶצְלוֹ.

וְאָמְרוּ בְּאַזְהָרַת עִנְיָן זֶה: כָּל הַמּוֹנֵעַ עַצְמוֹ מִן הַדִּין מוֹנֵעַ מִמֶּנּוּ אֵיבָה וְגָזֵל
וּשְׁבוּעַת שָׁוְא. וְכָל זֶה לְלַמְּדֵנוּ שֶׁהַדָּבָר צָרִיךְ מָתוּן וְיִשּׁוּב הַדַּעַת הַרְבֵּה כְּדֵי שֶׁלֹּא
יִטְעוּ בַדִּין, כִּי הַרְבֵּה דְרָכִים יֵשׁ בַּדִּינִים, וְחָכָם גָּדוֹל צָרִיךְ לִהְיוֹת בַּדִּין, וּכְמוֹ שֶׁאָמְרוּ

---

8. TB 'Avodah Zarah 6a.

9. To their idol for making profit from the transaction, etc. (§86).

10. By selling them something which they can offer up to the idol.

11. TB 'Avodah Zarah 15b.

12. Whose vow to be a *nazir* forbids him to drink it (Numbers 6:3).

13. See §13, note 5.

§233   1. Or the execution of justice; TB K'thuboth 105a (MT *hilchoth sanhedrin* xx 6); see also Mishnah, 'Avoth v 8.

2. *Ibid.* i 1.

3. TB Yevamoth 109b.

4. Mishnah, 'Avoth iv 7.

5. Enmity by giving a wrong judgment against someone; robbery by unjustly giving one person's property to another; and vain oaths by making parties to a lawsuit swear needlessly.

6. TB Bava Bathra 175b.

Likewise, there is what the Sages of blessed memory taught:[11] that it is forbidden to sell any weapon of war, or anything which can bring harm to many, to the heathen, unless they are sold to them so that they can defend us. So too is it forbidden to sell it [such equipment] to an Israelite who will then sell it to a heathen; and likewise [not] to an Israelite bandit. They banned all this on the strength of the injunction about a stumbling-block before the blind. The rest of its details are in various places in the Talmud, scattered about.

It is in force everywhere, at every time, for both man and woman. If a person violated it and knowingly gave his fellow-man advice that was not suitable for him, or if he helped him in a sinful matter— for instance, if one held out a cup of wine to a *nazir*,[12] or anything like that—he thus transgressed this negative precept. He is as a person who disobeys a royal command, but no whiplashes are given for it, because the violation entails no physical action.[13]

233 [NOT TO PERVERT JUSTICE IN A CIVIL JUDGMENT] that a judge should not do any injustice at a trial, it being an injustice whenever he will transgress what the Torah has commanded us regarding a trial, unless he does it with the consent of the contending parties. About this it was stated, *You shall do no injustice in judgment* (Leviticus 19:15).

The root purpose of the precept is known (evident); for by righteous judgment, the settled community of human beings endures.

Among the laws of the precept, there is what the Sages of blessed memory said: that one who delays a verdict[1] is included in the category of those who do wrong in judgment. And there is what they said [further]:[2] "Be deliberate in judgment," so that [the judges] should not be led to distort a judgment. Our Sages of blessed memory said, too,[3] that it is fitting for a person judging a case to take counsel with someone greater than himself, if he is there.

Now, as an admonition about this matter they declared:[4] Whoever keeps himself away from [sitting in] judgment keeps away from himself enmity, robbery, and vain oaths[5]—all this to teach us that the matter needs patience and a great amount of calm reflection, so that one should not make an error in trying a case. For there are many ways [to proceed] in trials, and a case requires a very wise scholar. As our

〈59〉 Sages of blessed memory said:[6] whoever would become wise, let

זִכְרוֹנָם לִבְרָכָה: הָרוֹצֶה לְהִתְחַכֵּם יַעֲסֹק בְּדִינֵי מָמוֹנוֹת, שֶׁאֵין מִקְצוֹעַ בַּתּוֹרָה גָּדוֹל
מֵהֶן, שֶׁהֵן כְּמַעְיָן הַנּוֹבֵעַ. וְהִזְהִירוּנוּ גַם־כֵּן שֶׁיְּהֵא חָבִיב עָלֵינוּ דִּין שֶׁל פְּרוּטָה
כְּדִין שֶׁל מֵאָה מָנֶה, לָדוּן אוֹתוֹ לַאֲמִתּוֹ. וּמִפְּנֵי חֹמֶר הַדִּין שִׁבְּחוּ הַרְבֵּה מִי
שֶׁיָּכוֹל לְהַטִּיל פְּשָׁרָה בֵּין בַּעֲלֵי הָרִיב, וְעָלָיו נֶאֱמַר: אֱמֶת וּמִשְׁפַּט שָׁלוֹם שְׁפָטוּ,
שֶׁזֶּהוּ מִשְׁפַּט שֶׁל שָׁלוֹם, וְכֵן בְּדָוִד הוּא אוֹמֵר: וַיְהִי דָוִד עֹשֶׂה מִשְׁפָּט וּצְדָקָה לְכָל
עַמּוֹ: אֵי זֶהוּ מִשְׁפָּט שֶׁיֵּשׁ עִמּוֹ צְדָקָה, הֱוֵי אוֹמֵר זֶהוּ מְצוּעַ. וְיֶתֶר רַבֵּי הָאַזְהָרוֹת
שֶׁהִזְהִירוּנוּ זִכְרוֹנָם לִבְרָכָה בְּהַשְׁוָיַת הַדִּין, וּשְׁאָר פְּרָטֵי הַמִּצְוָה, הֵם בִּפְזוּר בְּסֵדֶר
נְזִיקִין, וְהָעִקָּר בְּמַסֶּכֶת סַנְהֶדְרִין.

וְנוֹהֶגֶת בְּכָל מָקוֹם וּבְכָל זְמַן בִּזְכָרִים, כִּי לָהֶם הַמִּשְׁפָּט. וְעוֹבֵר עָלֶיהָ וְעָשָׂה
עָוֶל בְּמִשְׁפָּט, כְּלוֹמַר שֶׁדָּן שֶׁלֹּא כְדִין תּוֹרָה, לְדַעַת, עָבַר עַל לָאו זֶה, אֲבָל אֵין
לוֹקִין עָלָיו, דְּלָאו שֶׁאֵין בּוֹ מַעֲשֶׂה אֶלָּא דִּבּוּר לְבָד, אֵין לוֹקִין עָלָיו, חוּץ מֵאוֹתָן
שֶׁמָּנִינוּ לְמַעְלָה. וְעוֹד, שֶׁהֲרֵי כָּל הַדָּן שֶׁלֹּא כְדִין תּוֹרָה, דִּינוֹ חוֹזֵר, וּלְפִיכָךְ אֵין
לוֹקִין עָלָיו; וּכְדְאַמְרִינָן בְּסַנְהֶדְרִין פֶּרֶק אֶחָד דִּינֵי מָמוֹנוֹת, שֶׁכָּל טוֹעֶה בְּדָבָר
מִשְׁנָה, לְעוֹלָם חוֹזֵר. וְהָעִנְיָן לוֹמַר שֶׁכָּל הַטּוֹעֶה לָדוּן בְּמַה שֶׁהוּא הֵפֶךְ כַּוָּנַת
הַתּוֹרָה, בְּלִי סָפֵק דִּינוֹ בָּטֵל לְגַמְרֵי, וַהֲרֵי הוּא כְּאִלּוּ לֹא נֶאֱמַר.

וְשָׁם יִתְבָּאֵר שֶׁיֵּשׁ צְדָדִין שֶׁאִם דָּן הַדַּיָּן בְּהֵפֶךְ הָאֱמֶת, שֶׁדִּינוֹ דִין וְחַיָּב לְשַׁלֵּם
מִבֵּיתוֹ לְמִי שֶׁעִוֵּת לוֹ דִינוֹ; וּמִכָּל זֶה לֹא יִתְחַיֵּב מַלְקוֹת, וַאֲפִלּוּ עָשָׂה בּוֹ מַעֲשֶׂה,
וּכְגוֹן שֶׁנָּשָׂא וְנָתַן בְּיָד; מִן הַכְּלָל שֶׁבְּיָדֵינוּ, שֶׁכָּל לָאו שֶׁנִּתָּן לְתַשְׁלוּמִין אֵין לוֹקִין
עָלָיו.

7. TB Sanhedrin 8a.

8. *Ibid.* 6b.

9. Because it is an amicable settlement, with no winner and loser, and thus with no rancor.

10. Literally, from his house.

him occupy himself with the civil laws, on goods and possessions—
because there is no greater branch of the Torah; they are like a flowing
wellspring.

Our Sages likewise warned us that a case about a *p'rutah* should be
as precious to us as a case of a hundred *maneh*, to judge it truly.[7] Then,
because of the serious nature of a trial, they greatly praised a person
who can achieve a compromise between the parties to the controversy
[who wish the trial];[8] to him the verse applies, *render truth and a judgment
of peace* (Zechariah 8:16), because this is a judgment of peace.[9] So
is it stated of David: *and David rendered judgment and righteousness
to all his people* (II Samuel 8:15); what is judgment with which there
is righteousness?—you must say: a compromise settlement.[8] The
rest of the very many admonitions which the Sages of blessed memory
gave us about making a trial equitable, and the other details of the
precept, are scattered through the Talmudic order of *N'zikin*, mainly
in the tractate *Sanhedrin*.

It applies everywhere, at every time, for men, since judgment
is their province. If someone transgressed it and did something unjust
in a judgment, i.e. he judged not according to the law of the Torah—
if he did it deliberately, he would violate this negative precept; but
no whiplashes are given for it, since over a negative precept whose
violation requires no physical action, but merely speech, lashes are
not given—except for those we listed above (§231). Moreover,
whoever judges a trial not in accord with the laws of the Torah, his
verdict is overturned. Hence no whiplashes are given over it. As
stated in chapter 4 of the tractate *Sanhedrin* (33a), if anyone makes
an error in a law of the Mishnah, it is always retracted. In substance, it
is to say that if anyone errs and gives a verdict which is the opposite
of the Torah's intention without any doubt, his verdict is completely
null and void, and it is as if it had never been pronounced.

There it is further explained that under certain circumstances,
if the judge rendered a verdict which is the opposite of the truth,
his verdict stands, and he is duty-bound to pay out of his own funds[10]
to the one for whom he perverted justice. Yet for all this he does
not become punishable by whiplashes, even if he did some physical
action in connection with it—for example, if he took [from one]
and gave [the other] with [his own] hand—by the principle we have
that over any negative precept whose transgression is correctable
by compensation, no lashes are given.

וְאִם לֹא שֶׁיֶּאֱרַךְ הָעִנְיָן וְנֵצֵא מִגֶּדֶר מְלַאכְתֵּנוּ, בָּאנוּ לְפָרֵשׁ בְּכָאן כָּל הַצְּדָדִין שֶׁהַדִּין חוֹזֵר, וְהַצְּדָדִין שֶׁאֵינוֹ חוֹזֵר וְחַיָּב הַבֵּית־דִּין לְשַׁלֵּם מִבֵּיתוֹ, וְהַצְּדָדִין שֶׁאֵינוֹ חוֹזֵר וּפָטוּר הַבֵּית־דִּין לְשַׁלֵּם. וּכְלָלָא דְמִילְתָא, לְפִי הַנִּרְאֶה, דְּכָל הֵיכָא שֶׁדָּנוּ בְּלֹא קַבָּלָה וְאִיכָּא בָּעִיר גָּדוֹל מֵהֶם, וְטָעוּ אֲפִלּוּ בְּשִׁקּוּל הַדַּעַת, וְהוּא שֶׁלֹּא נָשְׂאוּ וְנָתְנוּ בְּיָד, שֶׁאֵלּוּ נָשְׂאוּ וְנָתְנוּ בְּיָד, אֵין דִּינָם חוֹזֵר אֲבָל חַיָּבִין לְשַׁלֵּם; בְּעִנְיָן אַחֵר אֵין דִּינָם חוֹזֵר.

וְהֵיכָא שֶׁדָּנוּ בִּרְשׁוּת, דְּלֵיכָּא לְמֵימָר דַּהֲווּ פּוֹשְׁעִים כְּשֶׁבָּאוּ לָדוּן, פְּטוּרִים מִלְּשַׁלֵּם; וְהֵיכָא דְּלָאו בִּרְשׁוּת, אִי נַמֵי בְּכָל צַד דְּאִיכָּא לְמֵימָר דַּהֲווּ פּוֹשְׁעִים כְּלָל כְּשֶׁבָּאוּ לָדוּן, חַיָּבִים לְשַׁלֵּם.

וְכָל הֵיכָא דְּאָמְרִינָן דִּינָם חוֹזֵר, אֲפִלּוּ נֶאֱבַד אוֹ נֶאֱכַל הַדָּבָר שֶׁדָּנוּ עָלָיו, פְּטוּרִין מִלְּשַׁלֵּם, אֶלָּא־אִם־כֵּן נָשְׂאוּ וְנָתְנוּ בְּיָדָם מַמָּשׁ, דְּכֵיוָן שֶׁכֵּן, מִדִּין מַזִּיקִין, מֵיחַת חַיָּבִים לְשַׁלֵּם; הָא לָאו הָכִי, פְּטוּרִין.

וְהָא דְּאָמְרִינָן לְעֵיל דְּכָל שָׁטוּעֶה בְּדָבָר מִשְׁנָה לְעוֹלָם חוֹזֵר, פֵּרְשׁוּ לָנוּ מוֹרֵי יִשְׁמְרֵם אֵל, דְּלָאו דַּוְקָא מִשְׁנָה מַמָּשׁ, אֶלָּא אַף כָּל שֶׁהוּא מְפֹרָשׁ בַּתַּלְמוּד בְּדִבְרֵי הָאָמוֹרָאִים שֶׁהוּא הֲלָכָה, וְטָעָה בָּהּ הַדַּיָּן, גַּם זֶה טוֹעֶה בְּדָבָר מִשְׁנָה יִקָּרֵא.

וְעוֹד הִפְרִיזוּ עַל מִדוֹתָם לוֹמַר עוֹד, שֶׁאֲפִלּוּ הַטּוֹעֶה בְּדָבָר אֶחָד שֶׁפָּסַק אֶחָד מִן הַגְּאוֹנִים אוֹ מִן הַחֲכָמִים הַמְפֻרְסָמִים בֵּינֵינוּ בְּחָכְמָה, כְּטוֹעֶה בְּדָבָר מִשְׁנָה מַשְׁוִינָן לֵיהּ, אֶלָּא אִם־כֵּן יֹאמַר אוֹתוֹ הַבֵּית־דִּין שֶׁאַף־עַל־פִּי שֶׁהָיָה יוֹדֵעַ וְנִזְכָּר דַּעַת אוֹתוֹ הַגָּאוֹן אוֹ הֶחָכָם, לֹא הָיָה דָן כָּמוֹהוּ וְלֹא יָשׁוּב בִּשְׁבִילוֹ מִלָּדוּן דִּינָיו כְּדַעְתּוֹ — וְהוּא שֶׁיְּהֵא רָאוּי לְכָךְ.

11. Literally, from its house.

12. E.g. if the Talmud contains a difference of opinion between two Sages, without deciding on either view, and the *beth din* now ruled according to one of them, not knowing that authorities had generally accepted the other view as binding (MT *hilchoth sanhedrin* vi 2).

13. I.e. from the highest Torah authorities in the area.

14. Having caused someone an unjust loss.

15. TB Sanhedrin 33a (hence the mention of "my master teachers" above refers not to this particularly, since this is a Talmudic ruling, but to the next paragraph).

16. Authorities cited by R. 'Ashér, Sanhedrin iv, §6.

17. I.e. the head of the *beth din* must himself be a great Torah scholar, who can reason from the Talmudic sources to defend his ruling. MY notes that in this last point, our author's master teacher (see note 15) agrees with none of the authorities cited by R. 'Ashér (see note 16), but gives a compromise of his own.

If the subject would not be so long, taking us beyond the framework of our task, we would proceed to explain at length all the instances when a verdict is overturned and the instances when it is not overturned, the *beth din* (court) then being obligated to pay out of its own funds[11] [to the wronged party], and those circumstances where the verdict is not overturned, yet the *beth din* is free of any duty to make compensation. The sum of the matter, as it would seem, is that wherever they hold a trial without acceptance [of their authority by the parties to the trial], and there is someone in the city greater than they are, then if they erred even in their reasoning,[12] their verdict is overturned—provided they did not take [from one] and give [the other] with their own hands. For if they gave and took with their own hands, their verdict is not overturned, but they are rather obligated to make compensation. In any other circumstances, their verdict is not upset.

Now, where they held trial with permission,[13] so that they cannot be said to be willful wrongdoers when they came to give a verdict, they are free of any duty to make payment. But where it was without permission, or else, if it was done in any way whereby they could be said at all to be willful wrongdoers when they came to give the verdict, they are obligated to make compensation.[14]

Wherever the rule is that their verdict is overturned, even if the object about which they held the trial was lost or consumed, they have no obligation to pay for it unless they took and gave it with their very own hands: for in that case, by the law of damagers they are at any rate required to pay. But otherwise, they are free of penalty.

As to what was said above, that if anyone erred in a law of the Mishnah, the verdict is always overturned, my master teacher (may God protect him) explained that this does not specifically mean the Mishnah literally, but rather anything explicitly taught in the Talmud, in the words of the *amora'im* (the later Sages), which is accepted law: If a judge erred in that, it is also considered as "an error in a law of the Mishnah."[15]

Moreover, the Sages[16] went yet much further, to say that even if a person erred about something that one of the *ge'onim* or scholars renowned for his wisdom among us had decided, we rank it as making an error in a Mishnah law—unless that *beth din* says that although it knew and remembered the ruling of that *ga'on* or scholar, it would not so decide the matter, and it will not retract on his account from deciding its cases by its view—but this [only] if it is worthy for this.[17]

⟨63⟩

[שֶׁלֹּא לְכַבֵּד גָּדוֹל בַּדִּין]

רלד שֶׁלֹּא יְכַבֵּד הַדַּיָּן אֶחָד מִבַּעֲלֵי הַדִּין בִּשְׁעַת הָרִיב, וַאֲפִלּוּ הָיָה גָּדוֹל וְנִכְבָּד וּנְשׂוּא פָנִים, שֶׁנֶּאֱמַר: וְלֹא תֶהְדַּר פְּנֵי גָדוֹל: וְאָמְרוּ בְסִפְרָא: שֶׁלֹּא תֹאמַר עָשִׁיר הוּא זֶה, בֶּן גְּדוֹלִים הוּא, הֵיאַךְ אֲבַיְּשֶׁנּוּ, כְּלוֹמַר שֶׁלֹּא יְכַבֵּד אוֹתוֹ יוֹתֵר מִבַּעַל דִּינוֹ שֶׁאֵינוֹ גָדוֹל כָּמוֹהוּ, לְכָךְ נֶאֱמַר: וְלֹא תֶהְדַּר פְּנֵי גָדוֹל.

שֹׁרֶשׁ הַמִּצְוָה יָדוּעַ, וּכְתַבְתִּיו בְּרֹאשׁ הַסֵּדֶר מִצְוַת עֲשֵׂה ו' [סִי' רל"ה].

מִדִּינֵי הַמִּצְוָה, מַה שֶּׁאָמְרוּ זִכְרוֹנָם לִבְרָכָה שֶׁלֹּא יְהֵא אֶחָד יוֹשֵׁב וְאֶחָד עוֹמֵד, אֶלָּא שְׁנֵיהֶן עוֹמְדִין: כִּי בִּהְיוֹתָם לִפְנֵי הַבֵּית-דִּין רָאוּי לָהֶם לַעֲמֹד כְּאִלּוּ הֵם לִפְנֵי שְׁכִינָה, כִּי רוּחַ אֱלֹהִים שׁוֹכֵן בְּתוֹךְ עֲדַת דַּיָּנֵי יִשְׂרָאֵל, כְּמוֹ שֶׁנֶּאֱמַר: אֱלֹהִים נִצָּב בַּעֲדַת אֵל. וּמִכָּל-מָקוֹם אָמְרוּ זִכְרוֹנָם לִבְרָכָה שֶׁאִם רָצוּ לְהוֹשִׁיב בַּעֲלֵי הַדִּין, הָרְשׁוּת בְּיָדָם; וּבַמֶּה דְּבָרִים אֲמוּרִים, בִּשְׁעַת מַשָּׂא וּמַתָּן, אֲבָל בִּגְמַר דִּין, מִן הַחִיּוּב הוּא בַּעֲמִידָה, כְּמוֹ שֶׁנֶּאֱמַר: וַיַּעֲמֹד הָעָם עַל מֹשֶׁה; אֶלָּא שֶׁנָּהֲגוּ בְכָל בָּתֵּי-דִּינֵי יִשְׂרָאֵל מְאַחַר הַתַּלְמוּד לְהוֹשִׁיבָם מִפְּנֵי הַמַּחֲלֹקֶת; וַאֲפִלּוּ הָעֵדִים, שֶׁכָּתוּב בָּהֶם "וְעָמְדוּ שְׁנֵי הָאֲנָשִׁים", נָהֲגוּ גַם-כֵּן הַיּוֹם לְהוֹשִׁיב. וְיֶתֶר פְּרָטֶיהָ, בִּמְקוֹמוֹת מִסַּנְהֶדְרִין וּשְׁבוּעוֹת.

וְנוֹהֶגֶת בְּכָל מָקוֹם וּבְכָל זְמַן בִּזְכָרִים, כִּי לָהֶם הַמִּשְׁפָּט. וְעוֹבֵר עָלֶיהָ וְכִבֵּד בַּעַל-דִּין אֶחָד יוֹתֵר מֵחֲבֵרוֹ, בְּמֵזִיד, עָבַר עַל לָאו זֶה וּבִטֵּל עֲשֵׂה, שֶׁכָּתוּב "בְּצֶדֶק תִּשְׁפֹּט". וּמַה שֶּׁהִתִּירוּ זִכְרוֹנָם לִבְרָכָה בְּזֶה בְּיִתְרוֹן הֶחָכָם עַל עַם-הָאָרֶץ, עִם קְצָת שְׁאָר דִּינֵי הַמִּצְוָה, כָּתוּב לְמַעְלָה בְּרֹאשׁ הַסֵּדֶר מִצְוַת עֲשֵׂה ו' [סִי' רל"ה].

---

§234   1. The paragraph is based on ShM negative precept §275.

2. As noted previously, in the original arrangement by our author all positive precepts in each *sidrah* were dealt with first; hence §235 appeared earlier.

3. TB Sh'vu'oth 30a.

4. *Ibid.* 30b.

5. MT *hilchoth sanhedrin* xxi 5.

6. I.e. this is the positive precept; see §235.

[NOT TO HONOR AN EMINENT PERSON AT A TRIAL]
234 that a judge should not honor one of the parties to a lawsuit
during the [court] controversy, even if he is notable, respectable and
distinguished: for it is stated, *nor shall you favor the person of the great*
(Leviticus 19:15); and it was taught in the Midrash *Sifra*: that you
should not say, "This man is rich; he is the son of great men; how
can I disgrace him?" This means, then, that he should not honor
him more than his opponent at the trial, who is not as great as he.
It is therefore stated, *nor shall you favor the person of the great*.[1]

The root purpose of the precept is known (evident), and I have
written it in this *sidrah*, in the sixth positive precept (§235).[2]

Among the laws of the precept, there is what the Sages of blessed
memory taught:[3] that one [of the parties to the lawsuit] should not
sit and the other stand, but rather both should stand. When they are
before the court, it is fitting for them to stand, as though they were
before the *shechinah* (Divine Presence)—because the spirit of God
abides with the community of Israelite judges, as it is stated, *God
stands in the congregation of God; in the midst of the judges, He judges*
(Psalms 82:1). Nevertheless, the Sages of blessed memory said that if
[the judges] wished to seat the parties to the lawsuit, the right is in
their hands. Now, when does this apply?—during the negotiations;
but at the end of the trial [when the verdict is given] it is compulsory
to stand[4]—as it is stated, *and the people stood about Moses* (Exodus
18:13). However, it became the custom in every *beth din* of Jewry
after the time of the Talmud to have them seated, for the sake of
avoiding controversy. Even the witnesses, of whom it is written,
then both the men shall stand (Deuteronomy 19:17), it has become the
custom today equally to seat.[5] The rest of its details are in various
places in the tractates *Sanhedrin* and *Sh'vu'oth*.

It is in effect in every place and time, for men, as judgment is
for them [to effect]. If someone transgressed it and deliberately honored
one party more than the other in a lawsuit, he would violate this
negative precept and disobey a positive precept: for it is written,
in righteousness shall you judge (Leviticus 19:15).[6] What the Sages of
blessed memory permitted in this regard in [recognition of] the
superiority of a wise scholar over an ignoramus, as well as a few other
laws of the precept, I have written above, at the beginning of this
sidrah, in the sixth positive precept (§235).[2]

[מִצְוַת שׁוֹפֵט שֶׁיִּשְׁפֹּט בְּצֶדֶק]

רלה לִשְׁפֹּט בְּצֶדֶק, שֶׁנֶּאֱמַר: בְּצֶדֶק תִּשְׁפֹּט עֲמִיתֶךָ; וּבָא הַפֵּרוּשׁ שֶׁנִּצְטַוּוּ הַדַּיָּנִין לְהַשְׁווֹת בַּעֲלֵי הָרִיב, כְּלוֹמַר שֶׁלֹּא יְכַבֵּד הַדַּיָּן אֶחָד מִבַּעֲלֵי הַדִּין יוֹתֵר מִן הָאַחֵר; וְכֵן אָמְרוּ בִּסְפָרָא: שֶׁלֹּא יְהֵא אֶחָד מְדַבֵּר כָּל צָרְכּוֹ וְאֶחָד אוֹמֵר לוֹ קַצֵּר דְּבָרֶיךָ. וְכֵן בְּפֶרֶק שְׁבוּעַת הָעֵדוּת, תָּנוּ רַבָּנָן: "בְּצֶדֶק תִּשְׁפֹּט עֲמִיתֶךָ", שֶׁלֹּא יְהֵא אֶחָד עוֹמֵד וְאֶחָד יוֹשֵׁב, וְאֶחָד מְדַבֵּר כָּל צָרְכּוֹ וְאֶחָד אוֹמֵר לוֹ קַצֵּר דְּבָרֶיךָ.

וְכֵן בִּכְלַל מִצְוָה זוֹ שֶׁכָּל אִישׁ שֶׁהוּא חָכָם בְּדִינֵי הַתּוֹרָה וְיָשָׁר בִּדְרָכָיו, שֶׁהוּא מְצֻוֶּה שֶׁיָּדִין דִּין תּוֹרָה בֵּין בַּעֲלֵי הָרִיב אִם יֵשׁ כֹּחַ בְּיָדוֹ; וַאֲפִלּוּ יָחִיד יָכוֹל לָדוּן מִדִּין תּוֹרָה, וּכְמוֹ שֶׁאָמְרוּ זִכְרוֹנָם לִבְרָכָה: אֶחָד דָּן אֶת חֲבֵרוֹ דִּין תּוֹרָה, שֶׁנֶּאֱמַר: בְּצֶדֶק תִּשְׁפֹּט עֲמִיתֶךָ; וַחֲכָמִים הִזְהִירוּ שֶׁלֹּא יְהֵא אָדָם דָּן יְחִידִי. וְעוֹד יֵשׁ בִּכְלַל מִצְוָה זוֹ שֶׁרָאוּי לְכָל אָדָם לָדוּן אֶת חֲבֵרוֹ לְכַף זְכוּת, וְלֹא יְפָרֵשׁ מַעֲשָׂיו וּדְבָרָיו אֶלָּא לְטוֹב.

שֹׁרֶשׁ הַמִּצְוָה נִגְלֶה הוּא, כִּי בְהַשְׁוָיַת הַדִּין יִתְיַשֵּׁב הָעוֹלָם, וְאִם יְכַבֵּד הַדַּיָּן אֶחָד מִבַּעֲלֵי הַדִּין עַל הָאַחֵר יִפָּחֵד בַּעַל הָרִיב מִלְּהַגִּיד כָּל טַעֲנוֹתָיו לְפָנָיו, וּמִתּוֹךְ כָּךְ יֵצֵא הַמִּשְׁפָּט מְעֻקָּל. וּבַמֶּה שֶׁאָמַרְנוּ שֶׁמִּצְוָה עַל הֶחָכָם בְּדִינֵי הַתּוֹרָה וְהוּא אִישׁ יָשָׁר לָדוּן בֵּין הַחוֹלְקִים, שֶׁזֶּהוּ בִּכְלַל הַמִּצְוָה כְּמוֹ־כֵן, גַּם בָּזֶה תּוֹעֶלֶת, כִּי הֶחָכָם וְהַיָּשָׁר יָדִין דִּין אֱמֶת; וְאִם הוּא הַיּוֹדֵעַ לֹא יִרְצֶה לִשְׁפֹּט, יִשְׁפְּטוּם שְׁאָר בְּנֵי־אָדָם שֶׁאֵינָם חֲכָמִים וְיַטּוּ הַדִּין עַל הָאֶחָד מִבְּלִי יְדִיעָה.

גַּם בַּמֶּה שֶׁאָמַרְנוּ שֶׁכָּל אָדָם חַיָּב לָדוּן חֲבֵרוֹ לְכַף זְכוּת, שֶׁהוּא בִּכְלַל הַמִּצְוָה,

1. TB Sanhedrin 3a.
2. Mishnah, 'Avoth iv 8.
3. The first two paragraphs are based on ShM positive precept §177.

[THE PRECEPT THAT A JUDGE SHOULD RENDER JUDGMENT
WiTH RIGHTEOUSNESS]

235 to judge in righteousness, as it is stated, *in righteousness shall you judge your neighbor* (Leviticus 19:15); and the explanation was given that the judges were [thus] commanded to treat the contending parties equally: in other words, that a judge should not honor one of the parties to the lawsuit more than the other. So was it stated in the Midrash *Sifra*: that one should not speak as long as he needs, whereas he [the judge] tells the other, "Shorten your words." And so in chapter 4 of the Talmud tractate *Sh'vu'oth* (30a): Our Sages taught: "in righteousness shall you judge your neighbor"—that one should not stand and the other sit, one speak his full need whereas he [the judge] tells the other, "Shorten your words."

Likewise included in this precept is [the indication] that every man who is learned in the laws of the Torah and honest in his ways is commanded to judge by the Torah's law between parties to a controversy, if he has the power to do so. Even one individual person is able to judge by the law of the Torah; as the Sages of blessed memory said:[1] one person [learned in the law] may judge his fellow by the Torah's law, for it is stated, *in righteousness shall you judge your neighbor*. However, the Sages cautioned that a man should not judge alone.[2] Included as well in the meaning of this precept is the point that it is fitting for every man to judge his fellow favorably, toward the side of virtue, explaining his actions and words in nothing but a good, favorable way.[3]

The root purpose of the precept is obvious, since by equal treatment [of the parties] at a trial, life in the world is settled. Should the judge honor one of the contending parties more than the other, this opponent will be afraid to present all his arguments before him, and as a result the judgment will come out distorted. As to what we said, that it is a *mitzvah* for a scholar learned in the Torah's laws who is an honest man, to judge between those who quarrel and contend, which is equally included in the meaning of the precept—there is a useful advantage in this too: For a learned and honest scholar will render true judgment; while if he who has the knowledge will not wish to act as judge, other people, who are not learned scholars, will judge them, unwittingly perverting justice for one [of the contending parties].

<67>   In what we said, too, that every man is obligated to judge his

יִהְיֶה סִבָּה לִהְיוֹת בֵּין אֲנָשִׁים שָׁלוֹם וְרֵעוּת. וְנִמְצָא שֶׁעִקַּר כָּל כַּוָּנוֹת הַמִּצְוָה לְהוֹעִיל בְּיִשּׁוּב בְּנֵי־אָדָם עִם יֹשֶׁר הַדִּין, וְלָתֵת בֵּינֵיהֶם שָׁלוֹם עִם סִלּוּק הַחֲשָׁד אִישׁ בְּאִישׁ.

מִדִּינֵי הַמִּצְוָה, מַה שֶּׁאָמְרוּ זִכְרוֹנָם לִבְרָכָה שֶׁשְּׁנֵי בַעֲלֵי דִין שֶׁהָיָה הָאֶחָד לָבוּשׁ בְּגָדִים יְקָרִים וְהַשֵּׁנִי בְּגָדִים בְּלוּיִים, אוֹמְרִים לַמְּכֻבָּד "הַלְבִּישֵׁהוּ כְּמוֹתְךָ אוֹ לְבַשׁ כְּמוֹתוֹ וְאַחַר־כָּךְ נָדִין בֵּינֵיכֶם, כְּדֵי שֶׁתִּהְיוּ שָׁוִין"; וְעַכְשָׁיו בִּזְמַנֵּנוּ לֹא רָאִינוּ בֵּית־דִּין שֶׁעָשָׂה כֵן.

וְעוֹד אָמְרוּ זִכְרוֹנָם לִבְרָכָה שֶׁמִּצְוָה לְהוֹשִׁיבָם בְּשָׁוֶה וְלֹא הָאֶחָד לְמַעְלָה מֵחֲבֵרוֹ אוֹ הָאֶחָד בִּישִׁיבָה וְהָאַחֵר בַּעֲמִידָה, רַק בְּתַלְמִיד חָכָם וְעַם הָאָרֶץ, שֶׁאָמְרוּ בָהֶם: מוֹשִׁיבִין הֶחָכָם וְאוֹמְרִים לְעַם הָאָרֶץ, שֵׁב; וְאִם לֹא יֵשֵׁב אֵין מַקְפִּידִין עַל כָּךְ; וְאָמְרוּ זִכְרוֹנָם לִבְרָכָה שֶׁאִם בָּאוּ לְפָנֶיךָ הַרְבֵּה דִינִין וְיֵשׁ בֵּינֵיהֶם דִּין יָתוֹם וְאַלְמָנָה, שֶׁמִּצְוָה לְהַקְדִּימָן, שֶׁנֶּאֱמַר: שִׁפְטוּ יָתוֹם רִיבוּ אַלְמָנָה, כְּלוֹמַר שֶׁבְּדִינָם נִצְטַוֵּינוּ לְזָרֵז יוֹתֵר מִבְּדִין אֲחֵרִים. וְכֵן אָמְרוּ זִכְרוֹנָם לִבְרָכָה שֶׁדִּין תַּלְמִיד חָכָם קוֹדֵם לָדִין עַם הָאָרֶץ, וְדִין אִשָּׁה קוֹדֵם לָדִין אִישׁ, לְפִי שֶׁבֹּשֶׁת הָאִשָּׁה מְרֻבָּה; וְכָל זֶה שֶׁאָמַרְנוּ, בִּכְלַל "בְּצֶדֶק תִּשְׁפֹּט" הוּא.

וְעִנְיָנִים אֵלּוּ עִם יֶתֶר פִּרְטֵי הַמִּצְוָה, בִּמְקוֹמוֹת מְפֻזָּרִים בַּתַּלְמוּד, וּמֵהֶן הַרְבֵּה בְּסַנְהֶדְרִין וּשְׁבוּעוֹת.

וְנוֹהֶגֶת מִצְוָה זוֹ בְּכָל מָקוֹם וּבְכָל זְמָן, בִּזְכָרִים, שֶׁהֵן חַיָּבִין לָדוּן וְלֹא הַנְּקֵבוֹת. וְאוּלָם גַּם הַנְּקֵבוֹת חַיָּבוֹת בְּמַה שֶּׁאָמַרְנוּ שֶׁהוּא בִּכְלַל מִצְוָה זוֹ, וְהוּא לָדוּן הֶחָבֵר לְכַף זְכוּת.

[שֶׁלֹּא לְרַגֵּל]

רלו שֶׁנִּמְנַעְנוּ מִן הָרְכִילוּת, שֶׁנֶּאֱמַר: לֹא תֵלֵךְ רָכִיל. וְהָעִנְיָן הוּא שֶׁאִם נִשְׁמַע אָדָם מְדַבֵּר רַע בַּחֲבֵרוֹ, שֶׁלֹּא נֵלֵךְ אֵלָיו וּנְסַפֵּר לוֹ "פְּלוֹנִי מְדַבֵּר בְּךָ כָּךְ וְכָךְ",

---

4. TB Sh'vu'oth 31a.

5. So MT *hilchoth sanhedrin* xxi 5, and Raaban (R. 'Eli'ezer b. Nathan), cited by *Sifthé Kohen* to *Shulḥan 'Aruch Ḥoshen Mishpat* §17, 2.

6. Tanhuma, *shof'tim* 7 (ed. Buber, 4); MT *ibid.* 3.

7. TB Sh'vu'oth 30b.

8. MT *ibid.* 6, derived from TB K'thuboth 105b.

9. Which she can suffer while waiting for a trial; TB K'thuboth 100a.

fellow favorably, toward the side of merit, which is included in the sense of the precept—in this lies a reason for peace and friendship among people. Thus we find that the main point of the purposes of this precept is to provide benefit for the settled communal life of human beings by the upright honesty of the law, and to spread peace among them by the removal of one man's suspicion of another.

Among the laws of the precept, there is what the Sages of blessed memory taught:[4] that if two people having a lawsuit were dressed one in expensive clothing and the second in ragged, worn-out clothes, the more distinguished man is told, "Clothe him like yourself or dress like him, and then we will judge between you, so that you should be equal." Yet now, in our time, we have seen no *beth din* observe this.[5]

Our Sages of blessed memory said further[6] that it is a duty to place them equally, and not one higher than the other, or one sitting and the other standing—except for a Torah scholar and an ignoramus: About them the Sages said:[7] The scholar is seated, and the ignoramus is told, "Sit"; but if he does not sit, no attention is paid to the matter. Then our Sages of blessed memory taught[8] that if many cases come before you [to be tried] and among them there is a lawsuit of an orphan or a widow, it is a *mitzvah* (religious duty) to try that first; for it is stated, *judge the orphan, champion the widow* (Isaiah 1:17), which means that we were commanded to be more alert [for them] than with the lawsuits of others. So too did our Sages of blessed memory teach that the suit of a Torah scholar takes precedence over that of an ignoramus;[8] and the suit of a woman takes precedence over a man's—because the shame of a woman[9] is the greater. All this that we have stated is included in the charge, *in righteousness shall you judge.*

These matters, along with the remaining details of the precept, are [to be found] scattered in various places in the Talmud, many of them in the tractates *Sanhedrin* and *Sh'vu'oth*. This precept is in effect everywhere, at every time, for men, since they are obligated to hold trials, but not for women. However, women are equally duty-bound to observe what, as we said, is included under this precept: i.e. to judge a fellow human being favorably, toward the side of virtue.

[THE PROHIBITION ON GOSSIPING SLANDEROUSLY]

236 that were were restrained from talebearing, as it is stated, *You shall not go about as a talebearer* (Leviticus 19:16): This means that if we hear a man telling something bad about his fellow, we should not

אֶלָּא־אִם־כֵּן תִּהְיֶה כַוָּנָתֵנוּ לְסִלּוּק הַנְּזָקִין וּלְהַשְׁבִּית רִיב. וְאָמְרוּ זִכְרוֹנָם לִבְרָכָה בְּפֵרוּשׁ רָכִיל: רַךְ לָזֶה וְקָשֶׁה לָזֶה; דָּבָר אַחֵר: לֹא תְהֵא כְּרוֹכֵל, מַטְעִין דְּבָרִים וְהוֹלֵךְ.

מִשָּׁרְשֵׁי הַמִּצְוָה, כִּי הַשֵּׁם חָפֵץ בְּטוֹבַת הַבְּרִיּוֹת אֲשֶׁר בָּרָא, וְצִוָּנוּ בָזֶה כְּדֵי לִהְיוֹת שָׁלוֹם בֵּינֵינוּ, כִּי הָרְכִילוּת סִבָּה לְרִיב וּמַצָּה.

פְּרָטֵי הַמִּצְוָה וְרֹב הָאַזְהָרוֹת שֶׁהִזְהִירוּנוּ זִכְרוֹנָם לִבְרָכָה עַל הָרְכִילוּת וְעַל לָשׁוֹן הָרַע שֶׁתָּפוּ, יִתְבָּאֲרוּ בִּמְקוֹמוֹת מֵהַתַּלְמוּד וּבַמִּדְרָשׁוֹת בְּפִזּוּר. וּבְפֵרוּשׁ אָמְרוּ בַּלָּשׁוֹן הָרַע, שֶׁמֵּמִית הָאוֹמְרוֹ וְהַמְּקַבְּלוֹ וְהַנֶּאֱמַר עָלָיו; וְהַמְּקַבְּלוֹ יוֹתֵר מִכֻּלָּן. וְהִזְהִירוּ הַרְבֵּה עָלָיו, עַד שֶׁאָמְרוּ דֶּרֶךְ מָשָׁל: מַאן דְּאִית זְקִיפָא בִּדְיָקְתֵּיהּ, לָא לֵימָא לֵיהּ "זְקוֹף בִּינִיתָא". וְאָמְרוּ כִּי בִּכְלָל לָשׁוֹן הָרַע אָבָק הוּא הַמְשַׁבֵּחַ חֲבֵרוֹ בִּפְנֵי שׂוֹנְאוֹ, שֶׁנֶּאֱמַר: מְבָרֵךְ רֵעֵהוּ וְגוֹמֵר.

וְנוֹהֶגֶת בְּכָל מָקוֹם וּבְכָל זְמַן, בִּזְכָרִים וּנְקֵבוֹת. וְעוֹבֵר עָלֶיהָ וְרָגַל עַל לְשׁוֹנוֹ, עוֹבֵר עַל לָאו, וְהוּא כְעוֹבֵר עַל מִצְוַת מֶלֶךְ, וְאֵין בּוֹ מַלְקוֹת, לְפִי שֶׁהוּא לָאו שֶׁאֵין בּוֹ מַעֲשֶׂה. וְכַמָּה שְׁלוּחִים לַמָּקוֹם לְהַלְקוֹת מִלְּבַד רְצוּעָה שֶׁל עֵגֶל וְשֶׁל פָּרוֹת.

וְאַף־עַל־פִּי שֶׁאֵין בַּלָּאו הַזֶּה מַלְקוֹת, לְפִי שֶׁאֵין בּוֹ מַעֲשֶׂה, פְּעָמִים שֶׁיֵּשׁ בּוֹ אֲפִלּוּ חִיּוּב מִיתָה, כַּיָּדוּעַ בְּדִין מוֹסֵר; וְזֶה הַדִּין הִתִּירוּ חֲכָמִים לַעֲשׂוֹת אֲפִלּוּ בְחוּצָה לָאָרֶץ, לְתִקּוּן הָעוֹלָם: מוּטָב יָמוּת אִישׁ אֶחָד וְלֹא יַזִּיק וִיאַבֵּד לָרַבִּים גּוּפָם אוֹ אֲפִלּוּ מָמוֹנָם.

וְאֶכְתֹּב לְךָ בְּנֵי מְעַט מִמַּה שֶּׁיֵּשׁ בַּגְּמָרָא בְּעִנְיָן זֶה, וְאִם תִּזְכֶּה לָדַעַת, תִּרְאֶה

§236   1. Sifra on the verse — *k'doshim, parashah* 4, 5; TB K'thuboth 46a.

2. TB *ibid.*

3. Hebrew, *lashon ha-ra*: literally, a tongue of evil.

4. TB 'Arachin 15b.

5. MT *bilchoth dé'oth* vii 3 (see Mechilta on Exodus 23:1).

5a. The text in the manuscripts and editions has ברוקתיה; the Talmud editions, however, have בדיוקתיה; but one MS reads בדרוקתיה; and similarly, דוקתא occurs three times in *She'iltoth d'R. Aḥai*, §41; cf. Jastrow s.v. דיוקתא. (It is known that in the early manuscripts scribal errors are found fairly frequently in unfamiliar words.)

6. Even though this is not talebearing or slander, it is "a tongue of evil" (see note 3), which can cause pain by touching a raw nerve; TB Bava M'tzi'a 59b.

7. Literally, dust of slander: i.e. it has a touch or an intimation of the character of slander about it; TB 'Arachin 15a.

8. Since it will only make the listener malign the person, in reaction (MT *bilchoth dé'oth* vii 4).

9. Expression based on Psalms 15:3.

10. Although capital punishment generally may be carried out only when there is a properly ordained and authorized *beth din* in the land of Israel, which can pass death

go to him and tell him, "So-and-so is saying this-and-this about you"—unless it is our intention [thus] to remove or avoid injury, or to stop a quarrel. Our Sages of blessed memory said in explanation of the word *rachil* (talebearer): *rach*, soft (kind), to one, and harsh to another.[1] Another meaning: do not be as a *rochél* (peddler), loading up with words and going [to "peddle" them].[2]

At the root of the precept lies the reason that the Eternal Lord desires good for the human beings He created. Hence He commanded us about this, so that there should be peace among us; for evil gossip is a cause of contention and quarrel.

The details of the precept and the many admonitions that our Sages of blessed memory gave us about evil gossip and its partner, slander,[3] are clarified in various places in the Talmud and Midrashim, scattered about. They taught distinctly[4] that slander brings death to the one who says it, the one who receives it, and the one about whom it is told—but most of all to the one who receives it.[5] They warned us greatly about it, to the extent that they said by way of illustration: If a person has in his family record[5a] one who was hanged [from the gallows], he should not be told, "Hang the fish."[6] And they said, further, that included in the category of the echo of slander[7] is the act of a man who praises his fellow before a person who hates him;[8] as it is stated, *He who blesses his neighbor...it will be counted as a curse to him* (Proverbs 27:14).

It is in force everywhere, at every time, for both man and woman. If a person transgresses it and slanders with his tongue,[9] he violates a negative precept. He is as one who violates a royal command, but no whiplashes are given for it, because it is a negative precept involving no physical action. Yet how many agents the omnipresent God has to inflict whiplashes apart from the strip of leather [from the hide] of a calf or of cows.

Now, even though this injunction brings no punishment of lashes, because it involves no physical action, sometimes there is even a penalty of death over it, as is known in the law of an informer—and the Sages permitted carrying out this law even outside the land [of Israel],[10] for the sake of proper communal life:[11] It is better that one man should die and not harm or destroy many physically, or even [so injure] their property.

Let me write you, my son, a bit of what there is in the Talmud

about this matter, and if you will merit to gain knowledge, you will

הַכֹּל בִּמְקוֹמוֹ. גַּרְסִינָן בְּפֶרֶק הַגּוֹזֵל בַּתְרָא: הַהוּא גַּבְרָא דְּאַחְוֵי כַּרְיָא דְחִטֵּי דְּבֵי
רֵישׁ גָּלוּתָא, חַיְבֵיהּ רַב נַחְמָן לְשַׁלּוּמֵי; וְטַעְמָא מִשּׁוּם דִּינָא דְגַרְמֵי. וְדַוְקָא
שֶׁהֶרְאָה מֵעַצְמוֹ, אֲבָל מִתּוֹךְ הָאֹנֶס פָּטוּר, וְכִדְתַנְיָא: יִשְׂרָאֵל שֶׁאֲנָסוּהוּ גוֹיִם
וְהֶרְאָה מָמוֹן חֲבֵרוֹ, פָּטוּר. וּפֵרְשׁוּ מוֹרֵינוּ (זִכְרוֹנָם לִבְרָכָה) דְּלֹא סוֹף דָּבָר
אֲנָסוּהוּ בְגוּפוֹ, אֶלָּא אֲפִלּוּ אֲנָסוּהוּ בְמָמוֹן, שֶׁיִּקְחוּ לוֹ מָמוֹן אִם לֹא יַרְאֶה מָמוֹן
חֲבֵרוֹ, וְהֶרְאָהוּ, פָּטוּר; דְּכָל מַרְאֶה עַל־יְדֵי אֹנֶס פָּטוּר, וְאֵינוֹ חַיָּב אֶלָּא בְמַרְאֶה
מֵעַצְמוֹ; וְכֵן כָּתַב הָרַב רַבִּי אַבְרָהָם בַּר רַבִּי דָוִד זִכְרוֹנוֹ לִבְרָכָה.

וְאִם נָשָׂא וְנָתַן בַּיָּד חַיָּב, וַאֲפִלּוּ עַל־יְדֵי אֹנֶס נַפְשׁוֹת. וְאִם תֹּאמַר: אֵין לְךָ
דָּבָר שֶׁעוֹמֵד בִּפְנֵי פִּקּוּחַ נֶפֶשׁ — יֵשׁ לוֹמַר: מִי אַמְרִינַן לֵיהּ יָמוּת וְלֹא יִתֵּן, יִתֵּן
וִישַׁלֵּם קָאַמְרִינַן לֵיהּ, וְלֹא יַצִּיל עַצְמוֹ בְמָמוֹן חֲבֵרוֹ; וַאֲפִלּוּ בְנִרְדָּף שֶׁהָיָה בּוֹרֵחַ
מִפְּנֵי רוֹדֵף וְשָׁבַר כֵּלִים, חַיָּב, וְאַף־עַל־פִּי שֶׁלֹּא שָׁבְרָן בְּכַוָּנָה אֶלָּא בְלֹא כַוָּנָה
וּבְשָׁעָה שֶׁהָיָה בּוֹרֵחַ לְהִנָּצֵל; וְכָל־שֶׁכֵּן נָשָׂא וְנָתַן בַּיָּד, שֶׁחַיָּב בְּתַשְׁלוּמִין.

וְאִם לְאַחַר שֶׁהֶרְאָה מִתּוֹךְ הָאֹנֶס נָשָׂא וְנָתַן בַּיָּד, מִשָּׁעָה שֶׁהֶרְאָה רוֹאִין אֶת
הַדָּבָר כְּאִלּוּ נִשְׂרָף, וְשׁוּב אֵינוֹ מִתְחַיֵּב עָלָיו מִשּׁוּם נָשָׂא וְנָתַן; וּמִשּׁוּם שֶׁהֶרְאָה
נַמִּי אֵינוֹ חַיָּב, כֵּיוָן שֶׁהֶרְאָה מִתּוֹךְ הָאֹנֶס, כִּדְכָתִיבְנָא. וְהָכִי אַמְרִינַן הָתָם: הַהוּא
גַּבְרָא דְּאַחְוֵי חַמְרָא דְרַב מָרִי וְרַב פִּנְחָס בְּנֵי דְרַב פַּפָּא, פֵּרוּשׁ מִתּוֹךְ הָאֹנֶס, אָמְרֵי
לֵיהּ "דְּרֵי וְאַמְטִי", דָּרָא וְאַמְטִי; וְאַסִּיקְנָא דְּכֵיוָן דְּאוֹקְמִינְהוּ עֲלַוֵּיהּ, מִיקְלָא
קַלְיֵא, וְשׁוּב אֵינוֹ מִתְחַיֵּב עָלָיו.

sentences and can deputize Jewish courts abroad to so act with its authority.

11. Literally, for the improvement of the world. (Whoever knows Jewish history will realize how warranted and necessary this ruling was, in view of the enormous harm done to entire communities by informers and slanderers).

12. I.e. the house of the religious head of Jewry in exile (Babylonia).

13. I.e. he was the cause of the loss of the entire stock of wheat; TB Bava Kamma 117b.

14. A teaching by the Sages of the Mishnah which was not included in the Mishnah; *ibid.* 117a.

15. Rashba (R. Sh'lomoh ibn 'Adreth), Responsa, I §980, follows Rabad generally, citing other laws of this topic; and this particular ruling by Rabad is found in *Shittah M'kubetzeth* to Bava Kamma 117b (ed. Tziyoni, Tel Aviv 1963, 801b, sixth paragraph).

16. Rabad, cited in *Shittah M'kubetzeth ibid.*

16a. This is in accord with Rif to Bava Kamma *loc. cit.* and Rashba, in *Shittah M'kubetzeth* there.

17. I.e. at the other's expense; R. Isaac 'Alfasi, Bava Kamma x: MT *hilchoth hovél* viii 4.

18. TB Bava Kamma 117b, Sanhedrin 74a.

19. Hopelessly beyond saving.

20. TB Bava Kamma 117a.

see everything in its place. We read in the last chapter of the Talmud
tractate *Bava Kamma* (116b): There was a man who showed the
stock of wheat of the exilarch's house[12] [to robbers], and R. Naḥman
sentenced him to pay for it—the reason being on account of the law of
cause.[13] Yet this is valid only if he showed it of his own free will;
if it was under compulsion, he is free of penalty—as we learned in a
baraitha:[14] If a Jew was forced by non-Jews and he showed [them]
the wares of his fellow, he is free of penalty. And our master teacher
of blessed memory explained:[15] Nor is this the law only if they applied
physical force to him; even if they compelled him through property—
[threatening] that they would take his goods if he would not show
[them] the wares of his fellow—and he showed them, he incurs no
penalty. For whoever reveals [another's property to robbers] under
compulsion goes free, incurring no penalty—unless he revealed it of
his own free will; and so R. Abraham b. David of blessed memory
wrote.[16]

Now, if he took [another's property] and gave [it to the robbers]
with [his own] hand, he is obligated [to pay] even if it was under a
threat to his life.[16a] Yet you might ask: Surely nothing must stand fast
before a threat to human life? It can be answered: Are we then telling
him he should die and not give it? We tell him that he should give it,
but he is to pay for it, and not save himself by his fellow's property.[17]
Even a pursued man who was fleeing from his pursuer—if he broke
utensils [while fleeing] he is obligated [to pay]—and this even if he
did not break them intentionally, but only by accident, at the time he
was running away to save himself.[18] Then all the more certainly,
if one took and gave [another's property to robbers] with [his own]
hand, he has a duty to make compensation.

On the other hand, if after revealing [another's goods to robbers]
under force, a person then took and gave it over by hand, from the
time he showed it we regard the object as though burnt,[19] and he
can no longer be obligated over it for taking and giving it; and because
he revealed it he can equally not be held liable, since he showed it
[to the robbers] under compulsion, as we wrote. And so is it taught
there:[20] There was a certain man who showed the wine of R. Mari and
R. Pinḥas, the sons of R. Papa, [to robbers]—i.e. under compulsion.
They told him, "Take and bring it"; and he took and brought it.
And it was concluded that once he brought them to it, [in effect]
⟨73⟩ he burned it, and he could no longer incur guilt over it.

וְהֵיכָא דְהֶרְאָה מֵעַצְמוֹ בְּלֹא טַעֲנַת אֹנֶס, חַיָּב מִיתָה וְתַשְׁלוּמִין, דְּגַרְסִינָן הָתָם: הַהוּא גַּבְרָא דַּהֲוָה בָּעֵי דְּנַחְוֵי בֵּי תִבְנָא דְּחַבְרֵיהּ; אָתָא לְקַמֵּיהּ דְּרַב, אָמַר לֵיהּ רַב "לָא תַעֲבֵד הָכִי", כְּלוֹמַר הַתְרָה בּוֹ; לָא הֲוָה צָאֵית; הֲוָה יָתִיב רַב קַמֵּיהּ דְּרַב, קָם רַב כַּהֲנָא שַׁמְטֵיהּ לְקוֹעֵיהּ, כְּלוֹמַר הֲרָגוֹ; וְהָכִי מוּכַח הָא דַאֲמַר לֵיהּ רַב לְרַב כַּהֲנָא: הָאִידָּנָא מַלְכוּתָא דְּפַרְסָאֵי הִיא, וְקַפְּדֵי אַשְׁפִיכוּת דָּמִים. וְאַמְרִינָן נַמֵּי בִגְמָרָא גַּבֵּי מַאי דְּבָעֵיָא לָן: מָמוֹן מוֹסֵר אִם מֻתָּר לְאַבְּדוֹ, וּמְהַדְּרִינָן: לֹא יְהָא מָמוֹנוֹ חָמוּר מִגוּפוֹ; אַלְמָא דְגוּפוֹ מֻתָּר לְאַבְּדוֹ.

מִיהוּ דַּוְקָא בִּשְׁעַת מַעֲשֶׂה וְעַל יְדֵי הַתְרָאָה, וּכְמַעֲשֶׂה דְּרַב כַּהֲנָא; וְאֵינוֹ צָרִיךְ שֶׁיְּקַבֵּל עָלָיו הַתְרָאָה כִּשְׁאָר חַיָּבֵי מִיתוֹת. וּמִי שֶׁמֻּחְזָק לִמְסוֹר, נִרְאֶה שֶׁהוּא כְּמַתְרֶה וְעוֹמֵד, וּמֻתָּר לְהָרְגוֹ בְּכָל שָׁעָה.

וְדַעַת הָרַמְבַּ"ם זִכְרוֹנוֹ לִבְרָכָה שֶׁכָּתַב בְּדִין מוֹסֵר כָּךְ הוּא: כֵּיוָן שֶׁאָמַר הֲרֵינִי מוֹסֵר פְּלוֹנִי בְּגוּפוֹ אוֹ בְּמָמוֹנוֹ, וַאֲפִלּוּ מָמוֹן קַל, הֲרֵי זֶה הִתִּיר עַצְמוֹ לְמִיתָה, וּמַתְרִין בּוֹ וְאוֹמְרִין לוֹ "אַל תִּמְסֹר"; אִם הֵעִיז פָּנָיו וְאָמַר "לֹא כִי אֶלָּא אֶמְסֹר", מִצְוָה לְהָרְגוֹ וְכָל הַקּוֹדֵם לְהָרְגוֹ זָכָה. עָשָׂה הַמּוֹסֵר אֲשֶׁר זָמַם וּמָסַר, יֵרָאֶה לִי שֶׁאָסוּר לְהָרְגוֹ, אֶלָּא-אִם-כֵּן הֻחְזַק לִמְסוֹר הֲרֵי זֶה יֵהָרֵג, שֶׁמָּא זֶה יִמְסֹר אֲחֵרִים. עַד כָּאן לְשׁוֹן הָרַב.

הִצְרִיךְ הַתְרָאָה לְמִי שֶׁאֵינוֹ מֻחְזָק לִמְסוֹר, וְשֶׁיְּקַבֵּל הַתְרָאָה; וּלְמִי שֶׁהוּא מֻחְזָק לִמְסוֹר, נִרְאֶה מִתּוֹךְ דְּבָרָיו שֶׁאֵינוֹ צָרִיךְ הַתְרָאָה. וְאֵין הַמּוֹסֵר יָכוֹל לוֹמַר "בִּשְׁבִיל שֶׁפְּלוֹנִי מֵצֵר לִי, אֲנִי מוֹסְרוֹ בְּיַד גּוֹיִם", שֶׁאֵין זֶה פּוֹטְרוֹ מֵעָנְשׁוֹ; אֲבָל הַמֵּצֵר לַצִּבּוּר, מֻתָּר לַצִּבּוּר לְמָסְרוֹ בְּיַד גּוֹיִם, וְכֵן כָּתַב הָרַמְבַּ"ם זִכְרוֹנוֹ לִבְרָכָה.

21. Being Rav's disciple.

22. Literally, harder, stricter; TB Bava Kamma 119a.

23. For them to be liable to a death sentence, it is necessary that they should hear the warning and answer that they are going ahead nevertheless.

24. MT hilchoth hovél viii 10–11.

25. I.e. for others to have the right to kill him.

However, where a person reveals [such property] of his own accord, with no argument of compulsion, he is punishable by death and the obligation to pay. For we read there:[20] There was a certain man who wanted to show the store of straw of his fellow [to robbers], and he came before Rav [to ask him]. Rav told him, "Do not do so." In other words, he warned him. But the other did not listen. R. Kahana was then sitting before Rav;[21] so R. Kahana arose and wrung his neck. In other words, he killed him; this is shown by what Rav then said to R. Kahana: "Now we have a Persian government, and they are strict about shedding blood." We likewise read in the Talmud, in regard to the question asked there, whether it is permissible to destroy the property of an informer, this answer that was given: Let his property not be more sacred[22] than his person. Hence it is permitted to destroy his person.

However, this is the law specifically at the time the act is about to be done and upon a warning being given him, as in the case of R. Kahana; but it is not necessary that he should accept the warning, like others who incur the penalty of death.[23] Yet if someone has a firm reputation as an informer, apparently it is as though he has received a standing warning, and it is permitted to kill him at any time.

The view of Rambam of blessed memory, which he wrote on the law of an informer, is this:[24] Once he says, "I am going to inform about so-and-so's person," or "about his property," even about some insignificant possession, he has made himself vulnerable to death. He is then warned and told, "Do not inform"; and if he is arrogant and says, "No! I shall certainly inform," it is a religious duty to kill him, and whoever is the first to slay him gains the merit [for it]. If the informer did what he planned and conveyed the information, it seems to me that it is forbidden to kill him, unless he becomes firmly held to be a [chronic] informer: then he is to be killed because he may inform on others. Thus far the language of the master.

[So] he requires that a warning be given one who is not firmly reputed to be an informer, and that he accept the warning; but as for a person held to be an informer, it appears from his words that he does not require a warning.[25] Nor can an informer say, "Because so-and-so persecutes me, I will give him over into the power of the heathens"— because this does not free him of his punishment. However, if someone oppresses a community, the community is allowed to give him over into the power of heathens; and so Rambam of blessed memory

⟨75⟩

וְאָסוּר לְאַבֵּד מָמוֹן מוֹסֵר, מִשּׁוּם "יָכִין וְצַדִּיק יִלְבָּשׁ", כִּדְאַסִּיקְנָא בְּפֶרֶק הַגּוֹזֵל.

[שֶׁלֹּא לַעֲמֹד עַל דַּם רֵעִים]

רלז שֶׁלֹּא נִמָּנַע מִלְּהַצִּיל נֶפֶשׁ מִיִּשְׂרָאֵל כְּשֶׁנִּרְאֵהוּ בְּסַכָּנַת הַמִּיתָה וְהָאֲבֵדָה וְיִהְיֶה לָנוּ יְכֹלֶת לְהַצִּילוֹ בְּשׁוּם צַד, שֶׁנֶּאֱמַר: לֹא תַעֲמֹד עַל דַּם רֵעֶךָ. וְאָמְרִינָן בְּסַנְהֶדְרִין: תַּנְיָא, מִנַּיִן לְרוֹאֶה אֶת חֲבֵרוֹ שֶׁטּוֹבֵעַ בַּנָּהָר אוֹ חַיָּה גוֹרַרְתּוֹ אוֹ לִיסְטִים בָּאִים עָלָיו, שֶׁהוּא חַיָּב לְהַצִּילוֹ בְּנַפְשׁוֹ, שֶׁנֶּאֱמַר: לֹא תַעֲמֹד עַל דַּם רֵעֶךָ. וְלָא מִבַּעְיָא אַצוֹלֵיהּ בְּנַפְשֵׁיהּ דִּמְחַיָּב, אֶלָּא מִטְרַח וְאָגִיר נַמֵּי אֲגִירֵי חַיָּב.

וְעוֹד כָּלְלוּ זִכְרוֹנָם לִבְרָכָה זוֹ שֶׁלֹּא לִכְבֹּשׁ עֵדוּת, כְּדֵי שֶׁלֹּא יְאַבֵּד חֲבֵרוֹ מָמוֹנוֹ; וְכֵן הוּא בְּסִפְרָא: מִנַּיִן שֶׁאִם נוֹדַע לוֹ עֵדוּת, שֶׁאֵינוֹ רַשַּׁאי לִשְׁתֹּק עָלֶיהָ, שֶׁנֶּאֱמַר: לֹא תַעֲמֹד עַל דַּם רֵעֶךָ. וּמִנַּיִן שֶׁאִם רְאִיתוֹ טוֹבֵעַ בַּנָּהָר וְכוּלֵי. וּמִנַּיִן לְרוֹדֵף אַחַר חֲבֵרוֹ לְהָרְגוֹ, שֶׁאַתָּה חַיָּב לְהַצִּילוֹ בְּנַפְשׁוֹ — שֶׁנֶּאֱמַר: לֹא תַעֲמֹד עַל דַּם רֵעֶךָ וְגוֹמֵר.

שֹׁרֶשׁ מִצְוָה זוֹ יָדוּעַ, כִּי כְּמוֹ שֶׁיַּצִּיל אֶת הָאֶחָד הָאָדָם כֵּן חֲבֵרוֹ יַצִּיל אוֹתוֹ, וְיִתְיַשֵּׁב הָעוֹלָם בְּכָךְ, וְהָאֵל חָפֵץ בְּיִשּׁוּבוֹ, כִּי לָשֶׁבֶת יְצָרָהּ. וּכְבָר נִתְבָּאֲרוּ דִּינֵי מִצְוָה זוֹ בְּמַסֶּכֶת סַנְהֶדְרִין.

וְנוֹהֶגֶת בְּכָל מָקוֹם וּבְכָל זְמַן, בַּזְּכָרִים וּנְקֵבוֹת. וְעוֹבֵר עָלֶיהָ וְנִמְנַע מִלְּהַצִּיל וְיֵשׁ יְכֹלֶת בְּיָדוֹ, עָבַר עַל לָאו, וְאֵין לוֹקִין עָלָיו, לְפִי שֶׁהוּא לָאו שֶׁאֵין בּוֹ מַעֲשֶׂה, דְּקַיְמָא לָן אֵין לוֹקִין עָלָיו.

---

26. MT *ibid.* 11.

27. I.e. he may leave a worthy son or grandson, who will put his possessions to good use. Three words follow in the text, which were inadvertently omitted in the English version; they are to be translated: as we conclude in the tenth chapter of the Talmud tractate *Bava Kamma* (119a). While in the Talmud, opinion on the matter is divided, this is the *halachah* as given in *Rif* (the compendium of R. Isaac Alfasi) and MT *loc. cit.*

§237   1. See §236, note 14.

2. This last part, "by his own efforts" (*b'nafshéh*), is not in our editions of the Talmud, but see *Dikduké Sof'rim*.

3. This last sentence is not in Sifra, but rather in TB Sanhedrin 73a.

4. Since the transgression is the failure to save another's life.

5. TB Sanhedrin 63b, etc.

wrote.[26] [In any case, though] it is forbidden to destroy an informer's possessions, on account of the principle that *a wicked man . . . may prepare it, and the righteous will wear it* (Job 27:13, 17).[27]

[NOT TO STAND IDLY BY WHEN SOMEONE'S BLOOD IS SHED]

237 that we should not refrain from saving the life of an Israelite when we see him in danger of death and perdition, and we have the ability to rescue him in some way: For it is stated, *you shall not stand idly by the blood of your neighbor* (Leviticus 19:16); and we read in the Talmud tractate *Sanhedrin* (73a): It was taught in a *baraitha*:[1] How do we know that if someone sees his fellow drowning in the river, or a wild beast dragging him off, or bandits coming upon him, that he is duty-bound to save him by his own efforts?[2]—because it is stated, *you shall not stand idly by the blood of your neighbor*. And not only is one obligated to save him by his own efforts, but he is even duty-bound to trouble himself to hire others.

Moreover, our Sages of blessed memory included under this injunction the duty not to suppress testimony in order that one's fellow should lose his property. And so was it taught in the Midrash *Sifra*: How do we know that if someone knows testimony on behalf of another, he is not allowed to keep silent about it?—because it is stated, *you shall not stand idly by the blood of your neighbor*. And how do we know that if he saw him drowning in the river, etc. [as above]. And how do we know that if someone is pursuing his fellow-man to kill him, you are obligated to save him by [taking] the other's life?—because it is stated, *you shall not stand idly by your neighbor's blood*, etc.[3]

The root purpose of this precept is known (evident): for just as one person will save his fellow, so will the other save him [when necessary], and the world will thus remain settled; and God delights in its communal life, since *He formed it to be inhabited* (Isaiah 45:18).

The laws of this precept have been explained in the past in the Talmud tractate *Sanhedrin*. It applies everywhere, at every time, for both man and woman. If a person disobeys it and refrains from rescuing someone when he has the ability to do so, he violates this negative precept; but whiplashes are not given for it, because it is an injunction that entails no physical action in its transgression,[4] in which case we have a standing rule[5] that there is no penalty of a whipping.

[שֶׁלֹּא לִשְׂנֹא אַחִים]

רלח שֶׁלֹּא לִשְׂנֹא שִׂנְאַת הַלֵּב אֶחָד מִיִּשְׂרָאֵל, שֶׁנֶּאֱמַר: לֹא תִשְׂנָא אֶת אָחִיךָ
בִּלְבָבֶךָ. וּלְשׁוֹן סִפְרָא: לֹא אָמַרְתִּי אֶלָּא שִׂנְאָה שֶׁהִיא בַּלֵּב. וּכְמוֹ כֵן בַּעֲרָכִין:
בְּשִׂנְאָה שֶׁבַּלֵּב הַכָּתוּב מְדַבֵּר. אֲבָל כְּשֶׁיַּרְאֶה לוֹ שִׂנְאָה וְיָדוּעַ שֶׁהוּא שׂוֹנְאוֹ, אֵינוֹ
עוֹבֵר עַל זֶה הַלָּאו. אָמְנָם הוּא עוֹבֵר עַל "לֹא תִקֹּם וְלֹא תִטֹּר", וְעוֹבֵר כְּמוֹ־כֵן
עַל עֲשֵׂה, שֶׁנֶּאֱמַר: וְאָהַבְתָּ לְרֵעֲךָ כָּמוֹךָ. וּמִכָּל־מָקוֹם שִׂנְאַת הַלֵּב הִיא קָשָׁה מִכָּל
הַשִּׂנְאָה הַגְּלוּיָה, וְעָלֶיהָ תַּזְהִיר הַתּוֹרָה בְּיוֹתֵר.

שֹׁרֶשׁ הַמִּצְוָה יָדוּעַ, כִּי שִׂנְאַת הַלֵּב גּוֹרֶמֶת רָעוֹת גְּדוֹלוֹת בֵּין בְּנֵי־אָדָם, לִהְיוֹת
תָּמִיד חֶרֶב אִישׁ בְּאָחִיו וְאִישׁ בְּרֵעֵהוּ, וְהוּא סִבָּה לְכָל הַמְּסִירוֹת הַנַּעֲשׂוֹת בֵּין
אֲנָשִׁים, וְהִיא הַמִּדָּה הַפְּחוּתָה וְהַנִּמְאָסָה תַּכְלִית הַמָּאוּס בְּעֵינֵי כָּל בַּעַל שֵׂכֶל.

פְּרָטֵי הַמִּצְוָה וְרֻבֵּי הָאַזְהָרוֹת שֶׁהִזְהִירוּנוּ זִכְרוֹנָם לִבְרָכָה עָלֶיהָ, שֶׁלֹּא לְהַרְגִּיל
נַפְשֵׁנוּ בְּמִדָּה רָעָה זוֹ, מְבֹאָרִים בַּתַּלְמוּד בְּפִזּוּר וּבַמִּדְרָשׁוֹת.

וְנוֹהֶגֶת בְּכָל מָקוֹם וּבְכָל זְמַן, בִּזְכָרִים וּנְקֵבוֹת. וְעוֹבֵר עָלֶיהָ וְקָבַע שִׂנְאָה בְּלִבּוֹ
לְאֶחָד מִכָּל יִשְׂרָאֵל הַכְּשֵׁרִים, עָבַר עַל לָאו זֶה; וְאֵין לוֹקִין עָלָיו, לְפִי שֶׁאֵין בּוֹ
מַעֲשֶׂה. אֲבָל בְּשִׂנְאַת הָרְשָׁעִים אֵין בּוֹ אִסּוּר, אֶלָּא מִצְוָה לְשָׂנְאָן שֶׁנּוֹכִיחַ
אוֹתָם עַל חֶטְאָם פְּעָמִים הַרְבֵּה וְלֹא רָצוּ לַחֲזֹר בָּהֶן, שֶׁנֶּאֱמַר: הֲלֹא מְשַׂנְאֶיךָ יְיָ
אֶשְׂנָא וּבִתְקוֹמְמֶיךָ אֶתְקוֹטָט.

[מִצְוַת תּוֹכָחָה לְיִשְׂרָאֵל שֶׁאֵינוֹ נוֹהֵג כַּשּׁוּרָה]

רלט לְהוֹכִיחַ אֶחָד מִיִּשְׂרָאֵל שֶׁאֵינוֹ מִתְנַהֵג כַּשּׁוּרָה, בֵּין בִּדְבָרִים שֶׁבֵּין אָדָם
לַחֲבֵרוֹ אוֹ בֵּין אָדָם לַמָּקוֹם, שֶׁנֶּאֱמַר: הוֹכֵחַ תּוֹכִיחַ אֶת עֲמִיתֶךָ וְלֹא תִשָּׂא עָלָיו
חֵטְא. וְאָמְרוּ בְּסִפְרָא: מִנַּיִן אִם הוֹכַחְתּוֹ (ארבעה וחמשה) [אַרְבַּע וְחָמֵשׁ] פְּעָמִים

[THE PROHIBITION AGAINST HATING ONE'S BRETHREN]

238 not to bear hatred in the heart for any Israelite—as it is stated, *You shall not hate your brother in your heart* (Leviticus 19:17). In the language of the Midrash *Sifra*: I can apply this only to hatred that is in the heart. And so too in the Talmud tractate *'Arachin* (16b): The verse speaks of hatred that is in the heart. But when one shows the other his hatred and it is known that he detests him, he does not transgress this negative precept. However, he does transgress the injunction, *You shall not take vengeance nor bear any grudge* (*ibid.* 18); and he likewise disobeys a positive precept: for it is stated, *you shall love your neighbor as yourself* (*ibid.*). Yet in any case, the hatred of the heart is more serious than any open hatred, and the Torah warned against it the more strongly. [1]

The root reason for the precept is known (evident): for the hatred of the heart causes great evils among people, so that *every man's sword is against his brother* (Ezekiel 38:21) and against his neighbor. It is the cause of all instances of informing that occur among people; and it is the worst and most utterly despicable quality in the eyes of every intelligent human being. As for the laws of the precept and the many admonitions that our Sages of blessed memory gave us about it, not to accustom our spirit in this evil quality, they are explained in scattered places in the Talmud, and in the Midrashim.

It is in force everywhere, at every time, for both man and woman. If a person violates it and sets hatred firmly in his heart for anyone among worthy Israelites, he transgresses this negative precept; but whiplashes are not given for it, since no physical action is involved. On the hatred of wicked people, though, there is no prohibition; it is rather a religious duty to hate them after we reprove them many times about their sins and they yet do not wish to retract them; for it is stated, *Do I not hate those, O Lord, who hate Thee, and strive with those that rise against Thee?* (Psalms 139:21). [2]

[THE RELIGIOUS DUTY TO REBUKE A FELLOW-JEW FOR IMPROPER BEHAVIOR]

239 to rebuke an Israelite who does not behave properly either in matters between man and his fellow-man, or between man and the omnipresent God—as it is stated, *you shall surely reprove your neighbor, and not bear sin because of him* (Leviticus 19:17). In the Midrash *Sifra* it was taught: How do we know that if you rebuked him four or five

וְלֹא חָזַר, שֶׁאַתָּה חַיָּב לַחֲזֹר וּלְהוֹכִיחַ, תַּלְמוּד לוֹמַר: הוֹכֵחַ תּוֹכִיחַ. וְעוֹד אָמְרוּ
רַבּוֹתֵינוּ זִכְרוֹנָם לִבְרָכָה בַּגְּמָרָא: "הוֹכֵחַ תּוֹכִיחַ", אֲפִלּוּ מֵאָה פְּעָמִים.

וְאָמְרוּ שָׁם בְּסִפְרָא: יָכוֹל מוֹכִיחוֹ וּפָנָיו מִשְׁתַּנּוֹת, תַּלְמוּד לוֹמַר: וְלֹא תִשָּׂא
עָלָיו חֵטְא. וְזֶה מְלַמֵּד שֶׁבִּתְחִלַּת הַתּוֹכָחָה שֶׁרָאוּי לְאָדָם לְהוֹכִיחַ בַּסֵּתֶר וּבְלָשׁוֹן
רַכָּה וְדִבְרֵי נַחַת, כְּדֵי שֶׁלֹּא יִתְבַּיֵּשׁ. וְאֵין סָפֵק שֶׁאִם לֹא חָזַר בּוֹ בְּכָךְ, שֶׁמְּכַלְּמִין
אוֹתוֹ הַחוֹטֵא בָּרַבִּים וּמְפַרְסְמִין חֶטְאוֹ וּמְחָרְפִין אוֹתוֹ עַד שֶׁיַּחֲזֹר לְמוּטָב.

מִשָּׁרְשֵׁי הַמִּצְוָה, לְפִי שֶׁיֵּשׁ בָּזֶה שָׁלוֹם וְטוֹבָה בֵּין אֲנָשִׁים, כִּי כְּשֶׁיֶּחֱטָא אִישׁ
לְאִישׁ וְיוֹכִיחֶנּוּ בְּמִסְתָּרִים, יִתְנַצֵּל לְפָנָיו וִיקַבֵּל הִתְנַצְּלוּתוֹ וְיַשְׁלָם עִמּוֹ; וְאִם לֹא
יוֹכִיחֶנּוּ יִשְׂטְמֶנּוּ בְּלִבּוֹ וְיַזִּיק אֵלָיו לְפִי שָׁעָה אוֹ לִזְמַן מִן הַזְּמַנִּים, כְּמוֹ שֶׁנֶּאֱמַר
בָּרְשָׁעִים: וְלֹא דִבֶּר אַבְשָׁלוֹם עִם אַמְנוֹן וְגוֹמֵר. וְכָל דַּרְכֵי הַתּוֹרָה דַּרְכֵי נֹעַם
וּנְתִיבוֹתֶיהָ שָׁלוֹם.

מִדִּינֵי הַמִּצְוָה, מַה שֶּׁאָמְרוּ זִכְרוֹנָם לִבְרָכָה שֶׁחִיּוּב מִצְוָה זוֹ עַד הַכָּאָה, כְּלוֹמַר
שֶׁחַיָּב הַמּוֹכִיחַ לְהַרְבּוֹת תּוֹכְחוֹתָיו אֶל הַחוֹטֵא עַד כְּדֵי שֶׁיִּהְיֶה קָרוֹב הַחוֹטֵא
לְהַכּוֹת אֶת הַמּוֹכִיחַ; וּמִכָּל־מָקוֹם אָמְרוּ זִכְרוֹנָם לִבְרָכָה גַּם־כֵּן שֶׁאִם יִרְאֶה
הַמּוֹכִיחַ שֶׁאֵין בְּדִבְרֵי תּוֹכְחוֹתָיו שׁוּם תּוֹעֶלֶת נִמְצָא, מִתּוֹךְ גֹּדֶל רֶשַׁע הַחוֹטֵא, אוֹ
שֶׁהוּא אִישׁ אִלֵּם וְרָשָׁע בְּיוֹתֵר וּמִתְיָרֵא מִמֶּנּוּ שֶׁלֹּא יַעֲמֹד עָלָיו וְיַהַרְגֶנּוּ, שֶׁאֵינוֹ
חַיָּב בְּמִצְוָה זוֹ בְּאִישׁ כָּזֶה; וְזֶהוּ אָמְרָם זִכְרוֹנָם לִבְרָכָה: כְּשֵׁם שֶׁמִּצְוָה לוֹמַר דָּבָר
הַנִּשְׁמָע, כָּךְ מִצְוָה לִשְׁתֹּק בְּמָקוֹם שֶׁאֵין הַדָּבָר נִשְׁמָע—לְפִי שֶׁיִּהְיֶה בָּעִנְיָן קָלוֹן
לַמּוֹכִיחַ וְלֹא תוֹעֶלֶת לַאֲשֶׁר הוּכַח.

וּמִכָּל־מָקוֹם יֵשׁ לְהִתְיַשֵּׁב לְכָל בַּעַל נֶפֶשׁ וּלְהַשְׂגִּיחַ הַרְבֵּה בָּעִנְיָנִים אֵלֶּה,
וְלַחֲשֹׁב וְלִרְאוֹת אִם יִהְיֶה תּוֹעֶלֶת בִּדְבָרָיו אֶל הַחוֹטֵא שֶׁיּוֹכִיחֶנּוּ, וְיִבְטַח בַּשֵּׁם כִּי

---

§239   1. Literal translation of the phrase generally rendered (as above) "you shall surely
rebuke him"; i.e. the Hebrew verb is doubled, thus implying, "rebuke him time and
again."

2. TB Bava M'tzi'a 31a.

3. E.g. the blood drains from his face (he turns pale) because he is shaken by too
strong a rebuke.

4. I.e. the sin of needlessly shaming or hurting him.

5. MT *hilchoth dé'oth* vi 8.

6. Our author echoes here MT *ibid.* 6.

7. TB 'Arachin 16b (MT *ibid.* 7).

8. TB Yevamoth 65b.

times and the other did not retract, you are obligated to rebuke him yet again?—Scripture states, *rebuke shall you rebuke him*.[1] Our Sages of blessed memory said further, in the Talmud:[2] *rebuke shall you rebuke him*—even a hundred times.

Then it was taught there in the Midrash *Sifra*: I might think that he should reprove him even if the other's countenance is altered?[3]— Scripture states, *and you shall not bear sin because of him*.[4] This teaches that at the beginning of the reproof, it is proper for a man to chide [the other] in secret, with soft language and gentle words, so that the other will not be ashamed. But there is no doubt that if the other does not retract [from his evil practice] through this, the sinner is to be disgraced in public, his misdeed made widely known, and he vilified, until he returns to the good, right path.[5]

At the root of the precept lies the reason that this makes for peace and goodness among people. For when one man sins toward another and he reproves him in secret, he will apologize to him, and the other will accept his apology and make peace with him. But if the other will not rebuke him, he will hate him in his heart, and will cause him harm either then or at some other time—as it is stated of the wicked, *And Absalom spoke with Amnon neither good nor bad* (II Samuel 13:22).[6] All the ways of the Torah, though, *are ways of pleasantness, and her paths are peace* (Proverbs 3:17).

Among the laws of the precept, there is what the Sages of blessed memory said,[7] that the obligation of this precept is "until a beating": in other words, the one giving the reproof has a duty to increase his rebuke until the sinner comes close to striking the admonisher. Nevertheless, our Sages of blessed memory also said that if the admonisher sees that no useful effect results from the words of his reproof, because of the great wickedness of the sinner, or if he is an extremely violent and wicked man, and the other fears him, that he may rise up against him and kill him—he is not duty-bound to fulfill this precept for that man. This is why the Sages of blessed memory said:[8] Just as it is a religious obligation to say something that will be heeded, so is it a religious duty to be still in an instance where the word will not be heeded—because there will be disgrace for the admonisher, and no useful benefit for the man rebuked.

Yet in any case, everyone with a scrupulous, aware spirit should consider and take great care in these matters, to ponder and see if there will be any benefit in his words to the sinner should he rebuke him.

הוּא יַעְזְרֵנוּ בְּהִלָּחֲמוֹ עִם שׂוֹנְאָיו; וְאַל יֵרַךְ לְבָבוֹ וְלֹא יִירָא, כִּי יי שׁוֹמֵר אֶת כָּל אוֹהֲבָיו וְכָל הָרְשָׁעִים יַשְׁמִיד; וְאִם יָשׁוּב הַחוֹטֵא מֵחֶטְאוֹ, יִהְיֶה לוֹ בָזֶה שָׂכָר גָּדוֹל. וּמִי שֶׁבְּיָדוֹ לַהֲשִׁיבוֹ וְלִמְחוֹת בּוֹ וְלֹא מִחָה, הוּא נִתְפָּשׂ עַל חֶטְאוֹ; וְזֶה דָבָר בָּרוּר מִדִּבְרֵי רַבּוֹתֵינוּ, גַּם מִן הַכְּתוּבִים.

וְעוֹד אָמְרוּ זִכְרוֹנָם לִבְרָכָה שֶׁאֲפִלּוּ הַקָּטָן חַיָּב לְהוֹכִיחַ הַגָּדוֹל אִם יִרְאֶה הַגָּדוֹל הוֹלֵךְ בְּדֶרֶךְ לֹא טוֹב; וְיֶתֶר פְּרָטֵי מִצְוָה זוֹ, נִתְבָּאֲרוּ בִּמְקוֹמוֹת מְפֻזָּרִים בַּתַּלְמוּד.

וְנוֹהֶגֶת מִצְוָה זוֹ בְּכָל מָקוֹם וּבְכָל זְמַן, בִּזְכָרִים וּנְקֵבוֹת. וְעוֹבֵר עָלֶיהָ וְלֹא הוֹכִיחַ בָּעִנְיָן שֶׁאָמַרְנוּ, בִּטֵּל עֲשֵׂה; וְעוֹד שֶׁהוּא מִכַּת הָרְשָׁעִים שֶׁעוֹשִׂים כֵּן.

[שֶׁלֹּא לְהַלְבִּין פְּנֵי אָדָם מִיִּשְׂרָאֵל]

רמ שֶׁלֹּא לְבַיֵּשׁ אֶחָד מִיִּשְׂרָאֵל, וְזֶה הֶעָוֹן יִקְרָאוּ רַבּוֹתֵינוּ זִכְרוֹנָם לִבְרָכָה "מַלְבִּין פְּנֵי חֲבֵרוֹ בָּרַבִּים"; וְהַלָּאוּ הַבָּא עַל זֶה הוּא מַה שֶּׁכָּתוּב: הוֹכֵחַ תּוֹכִיחַ אֶת עֲמִיתֶךָ וְלֹא תִשָּׂא עָלָיו חֵטְא. וְאָמְרוּ בְּסִפְרָא: מִנַּיִן שֶׁאִם הוֹכַחְתּוֹ אֲפִלּוּ אַרְבָּעָה אוֹ חֲמִשָּׁה פְעָמִים, חֲזוֹר וְהוֹכֵחַ—שֶׁנֶּאֱמַר: הוֹכֵחַ תּוֹכִיחַ. יָכוֹל אֲפִלּוּ פָּנָיו מִשְׁתַּנּוֹת, תַּלְמוּד לוֹמַר: וְלֹא תִשָּׂא עָלָיו חֵטְא.

שֹׁרֶשׁ הַמִּצְוָה יָדוּעַ, לְפִי שֶׁהֲבֹשֶׁת צַעַר גָּדוֹל לַבְּרִיּוֹת, אֵין גָּדוֹל מִמֶּנּוּ, וְעַל-כֵּן מְנָעָנוּ הָאֵל מִלְּצַעֵר בְּרִיּוֹתָיו כָּל-כָּךְ, כִּי אֶפְשָׁר לְהוֹכָחָה בְּיָחוּד וְלֹא יִתְבַּיֵּשׁ הַחוֹטֵא כָּל כָּךְ.

מִדִּינֵי הַמִּצְוָה, מַה שֶׁאָמְרוּ זִכְרוֹנָם לִבְרָכָה שֶׁלֹּא בְּכָל הַדְּבָרִים הֻזְהַרְנוּ בְכָךְ, אֶלָּא בִּדְבָרִים שֶׁבֵּין אָדָם לַחֲבֵרוֹ; אֲבָל בְּדִבְרֵי שָׁמַיִם, אִם לֹא חָזַר מִן הַתּוֹכֵחָה שֶׁבַּסֵּתֶר, מִצְוָה לְהַכְלִימוֹ בָּרַבִּים וּלְפַרְסֵם חֶטְאוֹ וּלְבַזּוֹתוֹ וּלְקַלְּלוֹ עַד שֶׁיַּחֲזוֹר

9. TB Shabbath 54b: Whoever has the power to prevent the members of his household [from sinning] and does not prevent them, he is gripped by guilt over them; if the people of his city, he is gripped by guilt over them; etc.

10. Ibid. 55a: It is written, *The Lord will enter into judgment with the elders of His people and its princes* (Isaiah 3:14). If the princes sinned, how did the elders sin?... because they did not prevent the princes.

11. TB Bava M'tzi'a 31a.

§240   1. Because the shock and pain of the disgrace make the other pale as the blood drains from his face. Our author now uses this idiom throughout the section on this precept to denote shaming a fellow-man.

2. Sifra, *k'doshim, parashah* 4, 8.

3. See §239, note 1.

4. See *ibid.* note 3.

And let him trust in the Eternal Lord, that He will help him when he battles His enemies. Let his heart not weaken and let him not be afraid: for *the Lord preserves all who love Him, but all the wicked He will destroy* (Psalms 145:20). And if the sinner repents, he will have great reward for it. On the other hand, if he has the power to make him turn back and to prevent him [from sinning] and he does not prevent him, he is seized [by guilt] for the other's sin. This is something clear from the words of our Sages,[9] and even from Scripture.[10]

Our Sages of blessed memory taught further[11] that even a minor is obligated to reprove an adult, if he sees the adult going in a way that is not good. The remaining details of this precept are explained in scattered places in the Talmud.

This precept applies in every place, at every time, for both man and woman. If a person violates it and does not give reproof in the way that we have stated, he disobeys a positive precept. Moreover, he is [thus] of the sect of the wicked who act like that.

240 [THE PROHIBITION AGAINST SHAMING A JEW] not to shame any Israelite. Our Sages of blessed memory would call this sin "whitening one's fellow's face in public";[1] the injunction which applies to this is the verse, *you shall surely rebuke your neighbor, and not bear sin because of him* (Leviticus 19:17); and it was taught in the Midrash *Sifra*:[2] How do we know that if you rebuked him even four or five times, you are to go back and rebuke [him again]?— because it is stated, *rebuke shall you rebuke.*[3] I might think this applies even if his countenance changes?[4]—Scripture states, *and you shall not bear sin because of him.*[5]

The root reason for the precept is known (evident)—because shame is a great anguish for human beings; there is none greater. Therefore God restricted us from inflicting too much anguish on His creatures: because it is possible to give reproof when they are alone, so that the sinner will not feel so much shame.

Among the laws of the precept, there is what the Sages of blessed memory said:[6] that not in regard to everything were we adjured about this, but only in regard to matters between man and his fellow-man. Concerning matters of Heaven, however,[7] if [the sinner] did not repent through the reproof in private, it is a religious duty to

⟨83⟩ shame him publicly, announce his sin, and contemn and curse him,

לְמוּטָב, כְּדֶרֶךְ שֶׁעָשׂוּ הַנְּבִיאִים לְיִשְׂרָאֵל.

וּמַה שֶּׁאָמְרוּ זִכְרוֹנָם לִבְרָכָה עַל דֶּרֶךְ אַזְהָרָה בְּעִנְיָן זֶה: נוֹחַ לוֹ לְאָדָם שֶׁיַּפִּיל עַצְמוֹ לְכִבְשַׁן הָאֵשׁ וְאַל יַלְבִּין פְּנֵי חֲבֵרוֹ בָּרַבִּים; מְנָא לָן, מִתָּמָר, שֶׁלֹּא רָצְתָה לְהַלְבִּין פְּנֵי חָמִיהָ לֵאמֹר בְּפַרְסוּם שֶׁמִּמֶּנּוּ הִיא הָרָה, וְלוּלֵי שֶׁמְּצָאָה הָעֵרָבוֹן וְהוֹדִיעוּ הַדָּבָר בְּרֶמֶז, הָיְתָה נִדּוֹנֶת בִּשְׂרֵפָה וְלֹא תַלְבִּין פָּנָיו. וּשְׁאָר פְּרָטֵי הַמִּצְוָה, בִּמְקוֹמוֹת מֵהַתַּלְמוּד בְּפִזּוּר וּבַמִּדְרָשׁוֹת.

וְנוֹהֶגֶת בְּכָל מָקוֹם וּבְכָל זְמָן. וְעוֹבֵר עָלֶיהָ וְהִלְבִּין פְּנֵי חֲבֵרוֹ בָּרַבִּים בְּמֵזִיד, שֶׁלֹּא מֵחֲמַת עֲבֵרָה, עַל הָעִנְיָן שֶׁאָמַרְנוּ, עָבַר עַל מִצְוַת מֶלֶךְ, אֲבָל אֵינוֹ לוֹקֶה, לְפִי שֶׁאֵין בּוֹ מַעֲשֶׂה; וְכַמָּה שְׁלוּחִים לַמָּקוֹם לְהִפָּרַע מֵעוֹבְרֵי רְצוֹנוֹ.

[שֶׁלֹּא לִנְקֹם]

רמא שֶׁלֹּא לִנְקֹם, כְּלוֹמַר שֶׁנִּמְנַעְנוּ מִלָּקַחַת נְקָמָה מִיִּשְׂרָאֵל. וְהָעִנְיָן הוּא כְּגוֹן יִשְׂרָאֵל שֶׁהֵרַע אוֹ צִעֵר לַחֲבֵרוֹ בְּאֶחָד מִכָּל הַדְּבָרִים, וְנוֹהֵג רֹב בְּנֵי אָדָם שֶׁבָּעוֹלָם הוּא שֶׁלֹּא יָסוּרוּ מִלַּחֲשֹׂב אַחַר מִי שֶׁהֵרַע לָהֶן עַד שֶׁיִּגְמְלוּהוּ כְּמַעֲשֵׂהוּ הָרַע אוֹ יַכְאִיבוּהוּ כְּמוֹ שֶׁהִכְאִיבָם. וּמִזֶּה הָעִנְיָן מְנָעָנוּ הַשֵּׁם בָּרוּךְ הוּא בְּאָמְרוֹ "לֹא תִקֹּם". וּלְשׁוֹן סִפְרָא: עַד הֵיכָן כֹּחָהּ שֶׁל נְקָמָה, אָמַר לוֹ "הַשְׁאִילֵנִי מַגָּלְךָ" וְלֹא הִשְׁאִילוֹ; לְמָחָר אָמַר לוֹ "הַשְׁאִילֵנִי קַרְדֻּמְּךָ", אָמַר לוֹ "אֵינִי מַשְׁאִילְךָ כְּדֶרֶךְ שֶׁלֹּא הִשְׁאַלְתָּ לִי מַגָּלְךָ"; לְכָךְ נֶאֱמַר לֹא תִקֹּם. וְעַל כְּגוֹן זֶה הֻקַּשׁ כָּל הָעִנְיָנִים.

מִשָּׁרְשֵׁי הַמִּצְוָה, שֶׁיֵּדַע הָאָדָם וְיִתֵּן אֶל לִבּוֹ כִּי כָל אֲשֶׁר יִקְרֵהוּ, מִטּוֹב עַד רַע,

---

5. See *ibid.* note 5. (The paragraph is based on ShM negative precept §303).

6. MT *hilchoth dé'oth* vi 8, apparently based on TB Yoma 86b and Sh'vu'oth 30b, etc. (MY).

7. I.e. sins toward the Almighty which affect no one else.

8. TB K'thuboth 67b, etc.

9. See Genesis 38. Our author echoes here a Midrashic tradition recorded in TB Sotah 10b (and see Rashi s.v. *v'al yalbin*), Targum Yerushalmi and Jonathan; see also *Torah Shelémah ad loc.* note to §106, and §§103–104.

§241   1. Sifra, *k'doshim, parashah* 4, 10.
         2. The paragraph is based on ShM negative precept §304.

until he returns to good conduct—in the way that the prophets did to the Israelites.

Then there is what the Sages of blessed memory said by way of admonition about this matter:[8] It were better for a man to throw himself into a fiery furnace rather than shame his fellow-man in public. How do we know this?—from Tamar, who did not want to shame her father-in-law by announcing publicly that she was with child from him; and had she not found the pledge and informed him of the fact by a hint, she would have been punished by burning and would not have put him to shame.[9] The remaining details of the precept are in various places in the Talmud, scattered, and in the Midrashim.

It applies in every place and every time. If a person transgresses it and disgraces his fellow-man in public, deliberately, and not on account of a sin in an instance that we have described, he disobeys a command of the Divine King; but he receives no whipping of lashes, since no physical action is involved in the transgression. Yet how many agents the omnipresent God has to exact punishment from those who transgress His will.

241 [THE PROHIBITION AGAINST TAKING REVENGE]

not to avenge oneself; in other words, that we were prohibited from taking revenge of an Israelite. It applies, for example, if an Israelite harmed or inflicted pain on another in any kind of matter where it would be the way of most people in the world not to turn aside from seeking after the one who harmed them until they paid him back in kind for his evil action, or until they gave him pain as he had given them. From this sort of thing the Eternal Lord, blessed is He, restricted us by saying, *You shall not take vengeance* (Leviticus 19:18). In the language of the Midrash *Sifra*:[1] How far does the force of vengeance reach?—If one asked another, "Lend me your sickle," and the other did not lend it to him, then the next day the other asked him, "Lend me your pickaxe," whereupon he told him, "I will not lend it to you, in the same way that you did not lend me your sickle"— about this it was said, *You shall not take vengeance.* Thus it applies to all situations similar to this illustration.[2]

At the root of the precept lies the purpose that a man should

know and reflect that whatever happens to him, good or bad, is

הוּא סִבָּה שֶׁתָּבוֹא עָלָיו מֵאֵת הַשֵּׁם בָּרוּךְ הוּא, וּמִיַּד הָאָדָם מִיַּד אִישׁ אָחִיו לֹא
יִהְיֶה דָבָר בִּלְתִּי רְצוֹן הַשֵּׁם בָּרוּךְ הוּא; עַל־כֵּן כְּשֶׁיְצַעֲרֵהוּ אוֹ יַכְאִיבֵהוּ אָדָם, יֵדַע
בְּנַפְשׁוֹ כִּי עֲווֹנוֹתָיו גָּרְמוּ, וְהַשֵּׁם (יִתְבָּרֵךְ) גָּזַר עָלָיו בְּכָךְ, וְלֹא יָשִׁית מַחְשְׁבוֹתָיו
לִנְקֹם מִמֶּנּוּ, כִּי הוּא אֵינוֹ סִבַּת רָעָתוֹ, כִּי הֶעָוֹן הוּא הַמְסַבֵּב, וּכְמוֹ שֶׁאָמַר דָּוִד
עָלָיו הַשָּׁלוֹם: הַנִּחוּ לוֹ וִיקַלֵּל כִּי אָמַר לוֹ הַשֵּׁם (יִתְבָּרֵךְ); תָּלָה הָעִנְיָן בְּחֶטְאוֹ וְלֹא
בְשִׁמְעִי בֶּן גֵּרָא. וְעוֹד נִמְצָא בַּמִּצְוָה תּוֹעֶלֶת רַב לְהַשְׁבִּית רִיב וּלְהַעֲבִיר
הַמַּשְׂטֵמוֹת מִלֵּב בְּנֵי־אָדָם, וּבִהְיוֹת שָׁלוֹם בֵּין אֲנָשִׁים יַעֲשֶׂה הַשֵּׁם שָׁלוֹם לָהֶם.

דִּינֵי הַמִּצְוָה קְצָרִים, כְּבָר זָכַרְנוּ מֵהֶן לְפִי הַנִּרְאֶה.

וְנוֹהֶגֶת בְּכָל מָקוֹם וּבְכָל זְמַן, בִּזְכָרִים וּנְקֵבוֹת. וְעוֹבֵר עָלֶיהָ וְקָבַע בְּלִבּוֹ לִשְׂנֹא
חֲבֵרוֹ עַל שֶׁהֵרַע לוֹ, עַד שֶׁיִּגְמְלֵהוּ כְּרָעָתוֹ, עָבַר עַל לָאו זֶה, וְרָעָתוֹ רַבָּה, כִּי הוּא
סִבָּה לְתַקָּלָה מְרֻבָּה; אֲבָל אֵין לוֹקִין עַל לָאו זֶה, לְפִי שֶׁאֵין בּוֹ מַעֲשֶׂה. וּכְכָל זֶה
יִהְיֶה בְיָדְךָ בְּכָל מָקוֹם שֶׁנֶּאֱמַר לָאו שֶׁאֵין בּוֹ מַעֲשֶׂה אֵין לוֹקִין עָלָיו: שֶׁאַף־עַל־פִּי
שֶׁעָשָׂה בּוֹ שׁוּם מַעֲשֶׂה, אֵינוֹ לוֹקֶה עָלָיו מִפְּנֵי־כֵן, מִכֵּיוָן שֶׁאֶפְשָׁר לַעֲבֹר עַל
הַלָּאו מִבְּלִי מַעֲשֶׂה. וְתִזְכֹּר דָּבָר זֶה בְּכָלָל, כִּי דָּבָר בָּרוּר הוּא, אֵין צֹרֶךְ לִשְׁנוֹתוֹ
בְּמָקוֹם אַחֵר.

[שֶׁלֹּא לִנְטֹר]

רמב שֶׁלֹּא לִנְטֹר, כְּלוֹמַר שֶׁנִּמָּנַעְנוּ מִלִּנְטֹר בִּלְבָבֵנוּ מַה שֶׁהֵרַע לָנוּ אֶחָד
מִיִּשְׂרָאֵל, וְאַף־עַל־פִּי שֶׁנַּסְכִּים בְּנַפְשׁוֹתֵינוּ שֶׁלֹּא לְשַׁלֵּם לוֹ גְּמוּל עַל מַעֲשָׂיו,
אֲפִלּוּ בִּזְכִירַת חֶטְאוֹ בַּלֵּב לְבַד נִמְנַעְנוּ, וְעַל זֶה נֶאֱמַר: וְלֹא תִטֹּר. וּלְשׁוֹן סִפְרֵי: עַד
הֵיכָן כֹּחָהּ שֶׁל נְטִירָה, אָמַר לוֹ "הַשְׁאִילֵנִי מַגָּלְךָ" וְלֹא הִשְׁאִילוֹ, לְמָחָר אָמַר לוֹ

---

3. The expression is taken from Genesis 9:5.

4. Cf. Tanḥuma, *va-yikra* 7 (ed. Buber, 18): not on account of a man's goodness
does he hear calumnies and invective, but on account of the sins he accumulated
[literally, that there are in his hand]—as it is stated, *If a soul shall sin, then it shall bear a
voice of cursing* (Leviticus 5:1, in a literal translation).

5. Since it is possible to hurt another vengefully with words alone, as in the
illustration in the first paragraph.

6. I.e. for all negative precepts to which it can apply.

caused by the Eternal Lord, blessed is He, to occur to him; from a human hand, from a man's brother's hand,[3] nothing can be without the will of the Eternal Lord, blessed is He. Therefore, should a man inflict suffering or pain on him, let him know in his soul that his bad deeds were the cause,[4] and the Eternal Lord (be He blessed) decreed this upon him; and let him not set his thoughts to take revenge from him. For the other is not the [primary] cause of his trouble, since it is sin that brought it about. As David (peace be with him) said, "*So let him curse, because the Lord has told him*" (II Samuel 16:10): he attributed the matter to his sin, not to Shim'i b. Gérah. Moreover, there is another great benefit resulting from the precept: [it serves] to stop contention and remove hates from people's hearts. And when there is peace among people, the Eternal Lord grants them peace.

The laws of the precept are brief. As it would seem, we have already made mention of them.

It is in force everywhere, at every time, for both man and woman. If a person transgresses it and determines firmly in his heart to hate his fellow-man because he harmed him, until he can repay him in kind for his bad deed, he violates this negative precept. His wickedness is great, as he is [thus] the cause of great misfortune. However, no whipping of lashes is given over this negative precept, because no physical action is [necessarily] involved in its violation.[5] This rule should be in your hand: Wherever a negative precept is stated that does not apply to physical action, whiplashes are not given over it. Even if a person did some physical action in [violating] it, he receives no lashes on account of that, since it is possible to transgress the negative precept without action. Then remember this rule for them all,[6] because it is a clear matter; there is no need to repeat it anywhere else.

242 [THE PROHIBITION AGAINST BEARING A GRUDGE]
not to bear a grudge; in other words, we were forbidden to keep in our heart any ill-feeling over the harm that any Jew did to us. Even if we should resolve not to repay him in kind for his deeds, the mere remembrance of his sin in the heart was forbidden us; hence it was stated, *nor shall you bear a grudge* (Leviticus 19:18). In the language of the Midrash *Sifra*:[1] How far does the force of a grudge go?—If one asks another, "Lend me your sickle," and he does not lend it to

"הַשְׁאִילֵנִי קַרְדֻּמְּךָ", אָמַר לוֹ "הֵילָךְ, וְאֵינִי כְּמוֹתְךָ שֶׁלֹּא הִשְׁאַלְתָּנִי מַגָּלְךָ"; לְכָךְ נֶאֱמַר וְלֹא תִטֹּר.

כָּל עִנְיָן מִצְוָה זוֹ כְּמִצְוַת הַנְּקִימָה הַקּוֹדֶמֶת.

[מִצְוַת אַהֲבַת יִשְׂרָאֵל]

רמג לֶאֱהֹב כָּל אֶחָד מִיִּשְׂרָאֵל אַהֲבַת נֶפֶשׁ, כְּלוֹמַר שֶׁנַּחְמֹל עַל יִשְׂרָאֵל וְעַל מָמוֹנוֹ כְּמוֹ שֶׁאָדָם חוֹמֵל עַל עַצְמוֹ וּמָמוֹנוֹ, שֶׁנֶּאֱמַר: וְאָהַבְתָּ לְרֵעֲךָ כָּמוֹךָ. וְאָמְרוּ זִכְרוֹנָם לִבְרָכָה: דַּעֲלָךְ סְנֵי, לְחַבְרָךְ לָא תַעֲבִיד. וְאָמְרוּ בְסִפְרֵי: אָמַר רַבִּי עֲקִיבָא: זֶה כְּלָל גָּדוֹל בַּתּוֹרָה; כְּלוֹמַר שֶׁהַרְבֵּה מִצְווֹת שֶׁבַּתּוֹרָה תְּלוּיִין בְּכָךְ; שֶׁהָאוֹהֵב חֲבֵרוֹ כְנַפְשׁוֹ לֹא יִגְנֹב מָמוֹנוֹ וְלֹא יִנְאַף אֶת אִשְׁתּוֹ וְלֹא יוֹנֵהוּ בְּמָמוֹן וְלֹא בִדְבָרִים וְלֹא יַסִּיג גְּבוּלוֹ וְלֹא יַזִּיק לוֹ בְּשׁוּם צַד. וְכֵן כַּמָּה מִצְווֹת אֲחֵרוֹת תְּלוּיוֹת בָּזֶה, יָדוּעַ הַדָּבָר לְכָל בֶּן דַּעַת.

שֹׁרֶשׁ הַמִּצְוָה יָדוּעַ, כִּי כְּמוֹ שֶׁיַּעֲשֶׂה הוּא בַחֲבֵרוֹ כֵּן יַעֲשֶׂה חֲבֵרוֹ בּוֹ, וּבָזֶה יִהְיֶה שָׁלוֹם בֵּין הַבְּרִיּוֹת.

וְדִינֵי מִצְוָה זוֹ כְּלוּלִים הֵם בְּתוֹךְ הַמִּצְוָה, שֶׁכְּלַל הַכֹּל הוּא שֶׁיִּתְנַהֵג הָאָדָם עִם חֲבֵרוֹ כְּמוֹ שֶׁיִּתְנַהֵג עִם עַצְמוֹ, לִשְׁמֹר מָמוֹנוֹ וּלְהַרְחִיק מִמֶּנּוּ כָּל נֶזֶק; וְאִם יְסַפֵּר עָלָיו דְּבָרִים יְסַפְּרֵם לָשֶׁבַח וְיָחוּס עַל כְּבוֹדוֹ וְלֹא יִתְכַּבֵּד בִּקְלוֹנוֹ, וּכְמוֹ שֶׁאָמְרוּ זִכְרוֹנָם לִבְרָכָה: הַמִּתְכַּבֵּד בִּקְלוֹן חֲבֵרוֹ אֵין לוֹ חֵלֶק לָעוֹלָם הַבָּא; וְהַמִּתְנַהֵג עִם חֲבֵרוֹ דֶּרֶךְ אַהֲבָה וְשָׁלוֹם וְרֵעוּת וּמְבַקֵּשׁ תּוֹעַלְתָּם וְשָׂמֵחַ בְּטוּבָם, עָלָיו הַכָּתוּב אוֹמֵר: יִשְׂרָאֵל אֲשֶׁר בְּךָ אֶתְפָּאָר.

וְנוֹהֶגֶת מִצְוָה זוֹ בְּכָל מָקוֹם וּבְכָל זְמָן. וְעוֹבֵר עָלֶיהָ וְלֹא נִזְהָר בְּמָמוֹן חֲבֵרוֹ לְשָׁמְרוֹ, וְכָל-שֶׁכֵּן אִם הִזִּיק אוֹתוֹ בְּמָמוֹן אוֹ צִעֲרוֹ בְּשׁוּם דָּבָר לָדַעַת, בִּטֵּל עֲשֵׂה

---

2. The paragraph is based on ShM negative precept §305.

§243   1. Literally, to have compassion on.
        2. TB Shabbath 31a.
        3. Sifra, k'doshim, parashah 4, 12.
        4. To usurp part of his land (§522).
        5. TJ Hagigah ii 1.

him, then the next day the other says to him, "Lend me your pickaxe," whereupon he replies, "Here it is; I am not like you; you would not lend me your sickle"—about this it was stated, *nor shall you bear a grudge*. The entire subject-matter of this precept is like that of the preceding *mitzvah*, about vengeance.[2]

243 [THE PRECEPT OF AFFECTION FOR A FELLOW-JEW] to love every Israelite with a profound affection, which is to say that we are to be concerned about[1] an Israelite and his property as a man is concerned about himself and his property—for it is stated, *you shall love your neighbor as yourself* (Leviticus 19:18); and the Sages of blessed memory explained:[2] What is hateful to you, do not do to your fellow-man. Then, in the Midrash *Sifra* it was taught:[3] Said R. Akiva: This is a great principle in the Torah. In other words, many commandments in the Torah depend on it: Thus, a person who loves another as himself will not steal from him, will not commit adultery with his wife, will not cheat him of goods or oppress him with words, will not move his boundary,[4] and will not harm him in any way. So are many other religious duties bound up with it; the matter is evident to every understanding person.

The root reason for the *mitzvah* is known (apparent): for as a person treats another, so will the other treat him; and with this there will be peace among human beings.

The laws of the precept are summed up in the precept: for it includes everything to say that a man should behave toward his fellow-man as he behaves toward himself—to guard his property and remove all harm from him. And if he relates things about the other one, let him relate them in his praise and have a care for the other's esteem, and not find honor in the other's disgrace. As the Sages of blessed memory said:[5] Whoever derives honor through the disgrace of his fellow-man, has no share in the world-to-come. On the other hand, when a man behaves toward his fellow in a way of love and peace and friendship, seeking his advantage and rejoicing in his good fortune, Scripture refers to him in the verse, *Israel, in whom I will be glorified* (Isaiah 49:3).

This precept is in force everywhere, at every time. If a person transgresses it and is not careful about his fellow-man's property to guard it, and all the more certainly if he causes him some damage

זֶה, מִלְּבַד הַחִיּוּב שֶׁבּוֹ לְפִי הָעִנְיָן שֶׁהִזִּיקוֹ, כְּמוֹ שֶׁמְּפֹרָשׁ בִּמְקוֹמוֹ.

[שֶׁלֹּא לְהַרְבִּיעַ בְּהֵמָה עִם מִין שֶׁאֵינוֹ מִינוֹ]

רמד שֶׁלֹּא לְהַרְבִּיעַ בְּהֵמָה כִּלְאַיִם, כְּלוֹמַר שֶׁלֹּא נַרְבִּיעַ הַזָּכָר עַל שׁוּם מִין בְּהֵמָה אוֹ חַיָּה שֶׁאֵינוֹ מִינוֹ, שֶׁנֶּאֱמַר: בְּהֶמְתְּךָ לֹא תַרְבִּיעַ כִּלְאַיִם; וּבְבֵאוּר אָמְרוּ זִכְרוֹנָם לִבְרָכָה שֶׁאֵין הַחִיּוּב עַד שֶׁיַּכְנִיס כְּמִכְחוֹל בִּשְׁפוֹפֶרֶת, וְאָז יִלְקֶה.

מִשָּׁרְשֵׁי הַמִּצְוָה, כִּי הַשֵּׁם בָּרוּךְ הוּא בָּרָא עוֹלָמוֹ בְחָכְמָה בִּתְבוּנָה וּבְדַעַת, וְעָשָׂה וְצִיֵּר כָּל הַצּוּרוֹת לְפִי מַה שֶׁהָיָה צֹרֶךְ עִנְיָנוֹ רָאוּי לִהְיוֹת מְכֻנָּנוֹת כִּוּוּן הָעוֹלָם, וּבָרוּךְ הוּא הַיּוֹדֵעַ; וְזֶהוּ שֶׁנֶּאֱמַר בְּמַעֲשֵׂה בְרֵאשִׁית: וַיַּרְא אֱלֹהִים אֶת כָּל אֲשֶׁר עָשָׂה וְהִנֵּה טוֹב מְאֹד; וּרְאִיָּתוֹ בָּרוּךְ הוּא, הִיא יְדִיעָתוֹ וְהִתְבּוֹנְנוּתוֹ בַּדְּבָרִים, כִּי הוּא בָּרוּךְ הוּא, לְגֹדֶל מַעֲלָתוֹ, אֵינוֹ צָרִיךְ לִרְאִיַּת הָעַיִן אֶל הַדְּבָרִים אַחַר מַעֲשֶׂה, כִּי הַכֹּל נִגְלֶה וְיָדוּעַ וְנִרְאֶה לְפָנָיו קֹדֶם מַעֲשֶׂה כְּמוֹ אַחַר מַעֲשֶׂה.

אֲבָל הַתּוֹרָה תְדַבֵּר לִבְנֵי-אָדָם בְּמִלּוֹת מוּבָנוֹת אֲלֵיהֶם, וּתְכַנֶּה בְשֵׁם דְּבָרִים כַּדְּבָרִים הַמְּכֻנִּים בָּהֶם, שֶׁאִי אֶפְשָׁר לְדַבֵּר עִם בְּרִיָּה אֶלָּא בְּמַה שֶׁיָּדוּעַ אֵלָיו, כִּי מִי יָבִין מַה שֶׁאֵין בְּכֹחוֹ לְהָבִין. וְעַל כַּיּוֹצֵא בָזֶה יֹאמְרוּ זִכְרוֹנָם לִבְרָכָה: כְּדֵי לְשַׁבֵּר אֶת הָאֹזֶן מַה שֶׁהִיא יְכוֹלָה לִשְׁמֹעַ.

וּבִהְיוֹת יוֹדֵעַ אֱלֹהִים כִּי כָל אֲשֶׁר עָשָׂה הוּא מְכֻנָּן בִּשְׁלֵמוּת לְעִנְיָנוֹ שֶׁהוּא צָרִיךְ בְּעוֹלָמוֹ, צִוָּה לְכָל מִין נָמִין לִהְיוֹת עוֹשֶׂה פֵרוֹתָיו לְמִינֵהוּ, כְּמוֹ שֶׁכָּתוּב בְּסֵדֶר בְּרֵאשִׁית, וְלֹא יִתְעָרְבוּ הַמִּינִין, פֶּן יֶחְסַר שְׁלֵמוּתָן וְלֹא יְצֻוֶּה עֲלֵיהֶן בִּרְכָתוֹ. וּמִזֶּה הַשֹּׁרֶשׁ, לְפִי הַנִּרְאֶה בְּמַחֲשַׁבְתֵּנוּ, נִמְנַעְנוּ מֵהַרְבִּיעַ הַבְּהֵמוֹת כִּלְאַיִם; וּכְמוֹ-

1. TB Bava M'tzi'a 91a.

2. Literally, "to hear"; Mechilta, Exodus 19:18. On this reason in general, cf. Ramban, commentary, Leviticus 19:20.

SIDRAH
K'DOSHIM

through his property, or causes him anguish in some way—if it is deliberate, he thus disobeys this positive precept, apart from any obligation incurred according to the way he harmed him, as it is explained in its place.

[THE PROHIBITION ON MATING TWO ANIMALS OF DIFFERENT SPECIES]

244 not to mate two species of animal: in other words, that we should not couple a male beast with any kind of domestic or wild animal that is not of its species—as it is stated, *you shall not let your cattle breed with a different kind* (Leviticus 19:19). In explanation, our Sages of blessed memory said[1] that guilt is not incurred until one effects intromission [copulation], "as a brush in a paint-tube"; then he is to be given whiplashes.

At the root of the precept lies the reason that the Eternal Lord, blessed is He, created His world with wisdom, understanding and knowledge, and He made and shaped all the forms, each according to what its object required, prepared to fit into the purpose of the world; and blessed is He who has [this] knowledge. This is why it is written in the account of the creation, *And God saw everything that He had made, and behold, it was very good* (Genesis 1:31). His vision is His knowledge and understanding of things: for He, blessed is He, in the greatness of His excellence, does not need the eye's sight of matters after they have come into being, since all is revealed, known and visible before Him before an act just as after the act.

The Torah, however, speaks to people in words understandable to them, and ascribes to the Eternal Lord things like those which are ascribed to them [people]. For it is impossible to speak with a human being in any other terms but those known to him, because who will understand what it does not lie in his power to understand? About something like this our Sages used the expression, "in order to make the ear accept what it is able to comprehend."[2]

Now, since God knows that everything He wrought is perfectly suited to its purpose, as it is needed in His world, He commanded each and every species to produce its offspring of its own kind, as it is written in *sidrah b'réshith* (Genesis 1:11,21,24)—and the species should not be mingled, lest they become lacking in their perfection, and He will then not command His blessing for them. For this root reason, as it seems to our mind, we were forbidden to mate different species

⟨91⟩

כֵּן הִזְהַרְנוּ בְּכָךְ מִזֶּה הַטַּעַם בְּצֵרוּף טַעַם אַחֵר, שֶׁכָּתַבְנוּ כְּבָר עַל מִינֵי הַזְּרָעִים וְהָאִילָנוֹת.

מִדִּינֵי הַמִּצְוָה, מַה שֶּׁאָמְרוּ זִכְרוֹנָם לִבְרָכָה דְּלָאו דַּוְקָא בְּהֵמָה לְבַד הוּא בְּאִסּוּר זֶה, אֶלָּא אֲפִלּוּ חַיָּה וָעוֹף, כָּל שֶׁהִרְבִּיעָן בְּשֶׁאֵינָן מִינָן לוֹקֶה; וַאֲפִלּוּ הִרְבִּיעַ בְּהֵמָה אוֹ חַיָּה בְּמִינֵי חַיָּה שֶׁבַּיָּם, לוֹקֶה עֲלֵיהֶן; וְאֶחָד בְּהֵמָה חַיָּה וָעוֹף שֶׁלּוֹ אוֹ שֶׁל חֲבֵרוֹ, לוֹקֶה עֲלֵיהֶן.

וּמַה שֶּׁאָמְרוּ שֶׁמֻּתָּר לְהַכְנִיס שְׁנֵי מִינִין לְסַהַר אֶחָד, וְאִם רָבְעוּ זֶה אֶת זֶה, אֵין זָקוּק לְהַפְרִישָׁן; וּמַה שֶּׁאָמְרוּ שֶׁאָסוּר לְיִשְׂרָאֵל לְהַרְבִּיעַ בְּהֶמְתּוֹ כִּלְאַיִם עַל יְדֵי גוֹי; וְכֵן מַה שֶּׁאָמְרוּ שְׁמֵי שֶׁעָבַר וְהִרְכִּיב בְּשֶׁאֵינוֹ מִינוֹ, הַנּוֹלָד מֵהֶן מֻתָּר הוּא בַּהֲנָאָה וּבַאֲכִילָה, וּבִלְבַד שֶׁשְּׁתֵּיהֶן בְּהֵמוֹת טְהוֹרוֹת.

וְכָל שֶׁהֵן שְׁנֵי מִינִין, אַף־עַל־פִּי שֶׁדּוֹמִין זֶה לָזֶה; וְכָל שֶׁהֵן מִין אֶחָד, אַף־עַל־פִּי שֶׁהָאֶחָד מִדִּבְרֵי וְהָאֶחָד יְשׁוּבִי, מֻתָּרִין; אֲבָל אַוָּז הַבָּר וְאַוָּז יְשׁוּבִי אֵינָן בְּהֶתֵּר זֶה, לְפִי שֶׁהֵן שְׁנֵי מִינִין, שֶׁהַיְּשׁוּבִי בֵּיצָיו מִבְּפְנִים וְהַמִּדְבָּרִי מִבַּחוּץ. וְהַכּוֹי כִּלְאַיִם עִם בְּהֵמָה וְחַיָּה, וְאֵין לוֹקִין עָלָיו, מִפְּנֵי שֶׁהוּא סָפֵק.

וּבְעִנְיַן אִסּוּר זֶה, הַכֹּל הוֹלֵךְ אַחַר הָאֵם, שֶׁאֵין חוֹשְׁשִׁין לְזֶרַע הָאָב, לְפִי הַנִּרְאֶה מִפְּסַק הָרַב אַלְפָסִי זִכְרוֹנוֹ לִבְרָכָה. וְיֵשׁ מְפָרְשִׁים אֲחֵרִים שֶׁפָּסְקוּ כִּי מִפְּנֵי שֶׁנִּסְתַּפְּקוּ בְּעִנְיָן זֶה בַּגְּמָרָא, אִם חוֹשְׁשִׁין לְזֶרַע הָאָב אוֹ אֵין חוֹשְׁשִׁין, אַזְלִינָן בֵּיהּ לְחֻמְרָא לְעוֹלָם.

וּלְעִנְיַן "אוֹתוֹ וְאֶת בְּנוֹ" חוֹשְׁשִׁין לְזֶרַע הָאָב וְאֵין שׁוֹחֲטִין הָאָב עִם הַבֵּן אִם

---

3. TB Bava Kamma 54b. In this and the next two paragraphs our author basically follows MT *hilchoth kil'ayim* ix 1–5.

4. TB Bava Kamma 55a states, "One who mates two species that are in the sea is to receive whiplashes"; and *tosafoth* s.v. *ha-marbi'a* demonstrates that it must refer to sea animals, not fish. MT *ibid.* 1 likewise writes of "one who mounts a male on a female that is not of its species . . . even among the species of animal that are in the sea." Our author's direct source seems to be R. Moses of Couçy, *Séfer Mitzvoth Gadol (S'mag)* negative precept 281: "and it is stated in chapter 5 of TB Bava Kamma that even if one mates [another kind of creature] with any species of animal in the sea, he is to receive whiplashes by the law of the Torah." (Either he had a different reading in the Talmud, or, more likely, he inferred it from the Talmudic ruling.)

4a. Sifra, *k'doshim, perek* 4, 14.

5. TB Bava M'tzi'a 91b.

6. Ibid. 90a; MT *hilchoth kil'ayim* ix 2.

7. Mishnah, Kil'ayim viii 1.

8. TB Ḥullin 115a.

9. Mishnah, Kélim i 6.

10. TJ Kil'ayim viii 4.

10a. TB Bava Kamma 55a.

of animals; and we were likewise adjured for the same reason, in
conjunction with another reason that we wrote previously (§62),
about plants and trees.

Among the laws of the precept, there is what the Sages of blessed
memory taught:[3] that not particularly a domestic beast alone is
covered by this ban, but even a wild animal and fowl: Whatever
one mates with a creature not of its species, he is to be given whiplashes
for it. Even if one couples a domestic or wild animal with one of the
species of sea animals, he is punishable by whiplashes on account
of them.[4] And whether it is a domestic or wild animal or a fowl of
his or his fellow-man's, he is **equally given lashes because of them.**[4a]

Then there is what the Sages taught:[5] that it is permissible to put
animals of two different species into one pen, and if they couple,
he is not required to separate them. And there is what they said further,[6]
that it is forbidden for an Israelite to mate his beast with another species
even by means [of the services] of a non-Jew. There is, too, what
they taught: that if someone transgressed and coupled a creature with
one of a different species, it is permitted to have benefit from the offspring born to them,[7] and to eat it, provided that both are pure (permissible) animals.[8]

Whatever creatures are of two species, they are included under
this prohibition, even if they resemble one another;[9] and whatever
creatures are of one species, even if one is wild and the other domestic,
it is permitted to mate them.[10] However, this permission does not
apply to the wild-goose and the domestic goose, because they are of
two species:[10a] the domestic kind has its testes within, and the wild
kind without. The *koy*[11] is considered another species in regard to
both domestic and wild animals, but no whiplashes are given for it,
because it is in doubt.[12]

In regard to this prohibition, everything is determined according
to the dam (mother),[13] for no attention is paid to the contribution
of the sire (father), as it would appear from the ruling of R. Isaac
'Alfasi of blessed memory.[14] There are other authorities,[15] however,
who ruled that since there was doubt about this in the Talmud, whether
we should take the contribution of the sire into account or not, we
always take a strict course about it.[16]

Now, in regard to "it and its young" (Leviticus 22:28), we take
the sire's role into account, and the sire is not to be ritually slain together
with its young, if we recognize it. But concerning mating, plowing,

אָנוּ מַכִּירִין אוֹתוֹ; וּלְעִנְיַן הַרְבָּעָה וַחֲרִישָׁה וְהַנְהָגָה זֶה עִם זֶה, אֵין חוֹשְׁשִׁין לְזֶרַע
הָאָב לִהְיוֹת נֶחְשָׁב מִין אֶחָד עִם הַבֵּן, כָּל זְמַן שֶׁהָאֵם מִין אַחֵר. זֶהוּ הָעוֹלֶה מִן
הַשְּׁמוּעָה עִם הַפֵּרוּשׁ הַטּוֹב, בְּחֶלְקִין פֶּרֶק אוֹתוֹ וְאֶת בְּנוֹ. וְשָׁם הִזְכִּירוּ לָנוּ בַּגְּמָרָא
סִימָנִים לְהַכִּיר מִין הַפְּרָדִים שֶׁיִּהְיוּ מֵאֵם אַחַת: בְּאָזְנַיִם וְזָנָב וְקוֹל; וְאֵין סָפֵק כִּי
בִהְיוֹת מִין אִמָּן שֶׁל פְּרָדִים שָׁוֶה, מִין אֲבִיהֶן שָׁוֶה גַּם־כֵּן; זֶה יָדוּעַ לְכָל אָדָם.
וְיֶתֶר פְּרָטֵי הַמִּצְוָה, בְּמַסֶּכֶת כִּלְאַיִם.

וְנוֹהֶגֶת בְּכָל מָקוֹם וּבְכָל זְמַן, בִּזְכָרִים וּנְקֵבוֹת. וְעוֹבֵר עָלֶיהָ וְהִרְבִּיעַ כִּלְאַיִם,
וְהוּא שֶׁהִכְנִיס כְּמִכְחוֹל בִּשְׁפוֹפֶרֶת, לוֹקֶה מִן הַתּוֹרָה; וְאִם הֶעֱלָם זֶה אוֹ זֶה אוֹ
שֶׁעֲזָרָן בְּקוֹל, מַכִּין אוֹתוֹ מַכַּת מַרְדּוּת.

[שֶׁלֹּא לִזְרֹעַ כִּלְאֵי זְרָעִים וְלֹא נַרְכִּיב אִילָן בְּשׁוּם מָקוֹם בָּאָרֶץ]

רמה שֶׁלֹּא לִזְרֹעַ שְׁנֵי מִינֵי זְרָעִים, כְּגוֹן חִטָּה וּשְׂעוֹרָה אוֹ פוֹל וַעֲדָשָׁה, בְּיַחַד,
בְּאֶרֶץ יִשְׂרָאֵל דַּוְקָא, שֶׁנֶּאֱמַר: שָׂדְךָ לֹא תִזְרַע כִּלְאָיִם, וּבָא הַפֵּרוּשׁ עָלָיו שֶׁבַּשָּׂדֶה
שֶׁיִּהְיֶה לָנוּ בָאָרֶץ הַכָּתוּב מְדַבֵּר.

מִשָּׁרְשֵׁי הַמִּצְוָה, כָּתַבְתִּי מַה שֶּׁיָּדַעְתִּי בַּמִּצְוָה הַקּוֹדֶמֶת, וְכֵן בְּמִצְוַת מְכַשֵּׁפָה
בְּסֵדֶר מִשְׁפָּטִים מִצְוַת לֹא־תַעֲשֶׂה ה' [סִי' ס"ב].

מִדִּינֵי הַמִּצְוָה, מַה שֶּׁאָמְרוּ זִכְרוֹנָם לִבְרָכָה שֶׁאֶחָד הַזּוֹרֵעַ וְאֶחָד הַמְּנַכֵּשׁ אוֹ
הַמְּחַפֶּה בֶעָפָר, כֻּלָּן בִּכְלַל זְרִיעָה הֵן לִלְקוֹת עֲלֵיהֶן; וּבֵין שֶׁחִפָּה אוֹתָן בְּיָדוֹ אוֹ
בְּרַגְלוֹ אוֹ אֲפִלּוּ בִּכְלִי, עַל כֻּלָּן לוֹקֶה; וְהַזּוֹרֵעַ בְּעָצִיץ נָקוּב כְּזוֹרֵעַ בָּאָרֶץ מַמָּשׁ
הוּא.

וּמַה שֶּׁאָמְרוּ שֶׁאֵין אָסוּר מִשּׁוּם כִּלְאֵי זְרָעִים אֶלָּא זְרָעִים הָרְאוּיִין לְמַאֲכַל
אָדָם, אֲבָל זְרָעִים הַמָּרִים, אֲפִלּוּ עוֹמְדִים לִרְפוּאוֹת בְּנֵי־אָדָם, אֵין בָּהֶן מִשּׁוּם
כִּלְאֵי זְרָעִים; וְכִלְאֵי אִילָנוֹת הֲרֵי הֵן בִּכְלַל לָאו זֶה שֶׁל "שָׂדְךָ לֹא תִזְרַע כִּלְאָיִם",

11. An animal with characteristics of both domestic animals and hunted (wild) beasts (Mishnah, Bikkurim ii 8-11); hence its particular species remains a matter of doubt. See §187, note 5.

12. MT hilchoth kil'ayim ix 5.

13. In deciding on the species of an animal from mixed parentage.

14. Rif, Ḥullin v, beginning.

15. Literally, commentators; i.e. authors of commentary on the Talmud.

16. In every question arising about an animal of mixed parentage, we decide stringently; tosafoth to TB Ḥullin 79a, s.v. 'ayil. Thus two animals of mixed breed may not be mated unless the two sires were of one species, and so also the two dams.

17. Literally, this is what rises.

18. TB Ḥullin 79a; MT ibid. 6.

19. Hence all mules which share these characteristics are certainly of one species, born from the same kind of dam.

and leading with the two together, we do not consider the sire's role, that it should be reckoned as of the same species as its young, as long as the dam is of another species. This is what we gather[17] from the Oral Tradition, with its good explanation, in chapter 5 of the Talmud tractate *Ḥullin*. There in the Talmud,[18] the Sages gave us signs to recognize animals of the species called mule, which are of one [kind of] dam—by the ears, tail and voice.[19] And there is no doubt that as the species of the dam of mules is [always] the same, the species of their sire is likewise [always] the same. This is known to every man.

The remaining details of the precept are in the Mishnah tractate *Kil'ayim*. It applies in every place and every time, for both man and woman. If a person violated it and mated two different species, provided that he effected intromission [copulation] "as a brush in a paint-tube," he should be given whiplashes by the law of the Torah. If he mounted one on another or urged them on with his voice, he should be given lashes for disobedience.[20]

[NOT TO SOW DIFFERENT KINDS OF SEED TOGETHER, ETC. IN THE LAND OF ISRAEL]

245 not to plant two species of crops, such as wheat and barley, or beans and lentils, together—specifically in the land of Israel: for it is stated, *you shall not sow your field with two kinds of seed* (Leviticus 19:19); and the explanation was given for it [in the Oral Tradition][1] that the verse means in a field that we would have in the land.

About the root reason for the precept, I wrote what I knew in the preceding precept, and so too in the commandment about a sorceress (§62)—the fifth negative precept in *sidrah mishpatim*.

Among the laws of the precept, there is what the Sages of blessed memory taught:[2] that whether a person sows [two species], weeds them, or covers the roots with earth, these activities are all included under planting for whiplashes to be incurred [given] for them. And whether a person covered the roots with his hand, his foot, or even a tool, whiplashes are given for all. If a person plants them in a perforated pot,[3] it is like planting them in the actual ground.[4]

Then there is what the Sages said:[5] that the ban on sowing two species of plants applies only to plants fit for human food; but on bitter plants, even if they are suitable for medicinal purposes for humans, there is no ban on planting two species. Two species of trees are included [forbidden] under this negative precept, *you shall not sow your field*

וְאָמְנָם אֵין הָאִסּוּר בְּכִלְאֵי הָאִילָנוֹת אֶלָּא דֶּרֶךְ הַרְכָּבָה, כְּגוֹן שֶׁהִרְכִּיב יְחוּר שֶׁל תַּפּוּחַ בְּאֶתְרוֹג וְכֵן כָּל כַּיּוֹצֵא בָזֶה שֶׁהֵן שְׁנֵי מִינִין, אֲבָל דֶּרֶךְ זְרִיעָה, כְּגוֹן לִזְרֹעַ זֶרַע אִילָן עִם זְרָעִים, דָּבָר זֶה מֻתָּר אֲפִלּוּ לְכַתְּחִלָּה, חוּץ מִן הַכֶּרֶם, כְּמוֹ שֶׁנִּפְרָשׁ בְּסֵדֶר כִּי תֵצֵא לַאו י' [סִי' תקמ"ט] בְּעֶזְרַת הַשֵּׁם.

וְאָמְרוּ זִכְרוֹנָם לִבְרָכָה שֶׁהַזּוֹרֵעַ זְרָעִים כִּלְאַיִם, וְכֵן הַמַּרְכִּיב אִילָנוֹת כִּלְאַיִם, אַף־עַל־פִּי שֶׁיֵּשׁ מַלְקוֹת בְּכָל אֶחָד מֵאֵלּוּ הֲרֵי אֵלּוּ מֻתָּרִין בַּאֲכִילָה, שֶׁלֹּא נֶאֱסַר אֶלָּא זְרִיעָתָן לְבָד. וְכֵן הִתִּירוּ לִטַּע יְחוּר שֶׁל אִילָן שֶׁהִרְכַּב כִּלְאַיִם אוֹ לִזְרֹעַ מִזֶּרַע שֶׁנִּזְרַע כִּלְאַיִם.

וְהַזְּרָעִים נֶחְלָקִים לִשְׁלשָׁה חֲלָקִים וּשְׁלשָׁה שֵׁמוֹת, וְאֵלּוּ הֵן: תְּבוּאָה, קִטְנִית, זֵרְעוֹנֵי גִנָּה; וְיֵשׁ מִזֵּרְעוֹנֵי הַגִּנָּה קְצָתָם שֶׁנִּקְרָאִין מִינֵי יָרָק. וְאַף־עַל־פִּי שֶׁנֶּאֶסְרוּ לָנוּ לְעָרֵב כָּל שְׁנֵי מִינֵי זְרָעִים, וְאַף־עַל־פִּי שֶׁהֵם מִשֵּׁם אֶחָד, כְּגוֹן חִטָּה וּשְׂעוֹרָה, שֶׁשְּׁנֵיהֶן נִקְרָאִין תְּבוּאָה, וְכֵן פּוֹל וַעֲדָשָׁה, אַף־עַל־פִּי שֶׁשְּׁנֵיהֶן נִקְרָאִין קִטְנִית, מִכָּל־מָקוֹם חִלּוּק יֵשׁ בָּהֶן קְצָת בְּשִׁנּוּי הַשֵּׁם.

כֵּיצַד, שֶׁאִם נִתְעָרֵב שֶׁלֹּא בְכַוָּנָה חִטָּה עִם שְׂעוֹרָה חֵלֶק אֶחָד בְּיֶתֶר מִג' וְעֶשְׂרִים, אֵין צָרִיךְ לָבוֹר אוֹתָן; בְּפָחוֹת מִכֵּן יָבוֹר אוֹתָן. וְאִם נִתְעָרְבָה בְּאֶחָד מִזֵּרְעוֹנֵי גִנָּה, שֶׁעִיּוּרָן אֶחָד מֵעֶשְׂרִים וְאַרְבָּעָה מִמַּה שֶׁזּוֹרְעִין בְּבֵית סְאָה מֵאוֹתוֹ הַמִּין שֶׁל זֵרְעוֹנֵי גִנָּה. וּתְבוּאָה וְקִטְנִית לְעִנְיָן זֶה כְּמִין אֶחָד הוּא, וְשִׁעוּרָן בְּעֶשְׂרִים וְאַרְבָּעָה בִּתְבוּאָה.

וְאָמְרוּ זִכְרוֹנָם לִבְרָכָה שֶׁבְּאֶחָד בַּאֲדָר מַשְׁמִיעִין עַל הַשְּׁקָלִים וְעַל הַכִּלְאַיִם, וְכָל אֶחָד יוֹצֵא לְגִנָּתוֹ וּלְשָׂדֵהוּ וּמְנַקֶּה אוֹתוֹ מֵהֶן. וְכָל שֶׁהֵן שְׁנֵי מִינִין, אַף־עַל־פִּי שֶׁדּוֹמִין בְּצוּרָתָן, אֲסוּרִין מִשּׁוּם כִּלְאַיִם; וְכָל שֶׁהוּא מִין אֶחָד, אַף־עַל־פִּי

---

20. See § 24, note 14.

§245

1. TB Kiddushin 39a.

2. TB Mo'éd Katan 2b, etc.

3. I.e. with a hole at the bottom large enough to let a small root descend (Mishnah, 'Uktzin ii 10).

4. Mishnah, Kil'ayim vii 8.

5. MT hilchoth kil'ayim i 4, derived from TJ Kil'ayim i 1.

6. I.e. not merely tolerated after the fact; Tosefta, Kil'ayim i; MT hilchoth kil'ayim i 6.

7. Mishnah, Kil'ayim viii 1.

8. Tosefta, Kil'ayim ii, 15.

9. MT ibid. 8–9.

10. I.e. to remove it; the proportion is too small to matter.

11. Mishnah, Kil'ayim ii 1; MT hilchoth kil'ayim ii 1.

12. I.e. if this amount of garden-plant seed became mixed with twenty-three

with two kinds of seed. However, the prohibition on two kinds of trees applies only to the method of grafting: [1] for example, if someone grafted a shoot of an apple tree onto an *'ethrog* (citron) tree; and so anything similar, where they are of two species. By the way of planting, however—for instance, to sow the seed of a tree with other seeds— this is permissible even from the start, [6] except in a vineyard, as we will explain in the tenth negative precept of *sidrah ki thétzé* (§ 549), with the Eternal Lord's help.

Our Sages of blessed memory said further[7] that if a person sows two species of plants together, and so likewise if he grafts different species onto trees, even though whiplashes are given in each of these instances, it is permitted to eat their yield, because nothing more than the planting alone was forbidden. So, too, they permitted planting a shoot of a tree that was grown by grafting two species, or to sow some of the seed [obtained] by sowing two species together. [8]

Now, plants are divided into three groups, bearing three names, which are: grains, legumes, and garden plants; and there are some garden plants that are called varieties of vegetables. [9] Although we were forbidden to commingle any two species of plants, and although some bear one name—for instance, wheat and barley, which are both called grains; and so beans and lentils: even though both are called legumes—nevertheless, there is a slight differentiation between them on account of the difference in name.

How [is the law then applied to them]? If wheat became un- intentionally mixed with barley, one part in more than twenty-three parts, there is no need to pick it out; [10] but in a smaller quantity, they should be picked [separated] out. [11] If it became mixed with one of the garden plants, the minimal amount [to make it forbidden as two species] is one twenty-fourth the quantity needed to sow a *beth se'ah* (land fifty by fifty cubits) with this species of garden plant. [12] In this respect, grains and legumes are considered as one species, the minimal amount for them [to impose the restriction being one part] in twenty- four of grain. [13]

Moreover, our Sages of blessed memory said[14] that on the first of Adar, a proclamation would be made about the [half] shekels (§ 105) and mixed species of plants; then everyone would go out to his garden and field, and rid them of them. Whatever plants are of two species, even if they are similar in their forms, they are forbidden under the ban on mixed species; [15] but whatever are of one kind,

⟨97⟩

שֶׁמְּשַׁנִּין בְּצוּרָתָן מֵחֲמַת שִׁנּוּי הַמְּקוֹמוֹת אוֹ שִׁנּוּי עֲבוֹדַת הָאָרֶץ, הֲרֵי הוּא כְּמִין אֶחָד.

וְדִינֵי שְׁעוּרֵי הַהַרְחָקָה הַצְּרִיכָה בֵּין שְׁנֵי הַמִּינִין, רַבִּים; וְשִׁעוּר הַרְחָקַת שְׁנֵי מִינֵי יָרָק, שֶׁלֹּא יִינְקוּ זֶה מִזֶּה, אָמְרוּ זִכְרוֹנָם לִבְרָכָה שֶׁהוּא טֶפַח וּמֶחֱצָה לְכָל אֶחָד, שֶׁנִּמְצָא רֶוַח בֵּין שְׁנֵיהֶם שְׁלֹשָׁה טְפָחִים. וּמַה שֶּׁאָמְרוּ בַּמִּשְׁנָה בְּכִלְאַיִם פֶּרֶק ג', וְהֵבִיאוּ אוֹתָהּ גַּם-כֵּן בְּשַׁבָּת פֶּרֶק אָמַר רַבִּי עֲקִיבָא, שֶׁעֲרוּגָה שֶׁהִיא שִׁשָּׁה עַל שִׁשָּׁה טְפָחִים, זוֹרְעִין לְתוֹכָהּ חֲמִשָּׁה זֵרְעוֹנִין; וּלְפִי דְבָרֵנוּ הָיָה לָהֶם לוֹמַר תִּשְׁעָה: שְׁמֹנָה בְּאַרְבַּע רוּחוֹתֶיהָ וְאֶחָד בָּאֶמְצַע—אֵין זֶה קָשֶׁה, שֶׁכְּבָר תֵּרְצוּ אוֹתָהּ בִּירוּשַׁלְמִי כִּי בַעֲרוּגָה שֶׁבַּעֲרוּגוֹת הִיא מַתְנִיָא.

וְהַכְּלָל הָעוֹלֶה בְּיָדֵינוּ מִדִּבְרֵיהֶם זִכְרוֹנָם לִבְרָכָה בְּעִנְיַן כִּלְאֵי הַזְּרָעִים הוּא שֶׁכָּל זְמַן שֶׁיֵּשׁ בֵּין שְׁנֵי הַמִּינִין הַרְחָקָה הָרְאוּיָה, וְהוּא טֶפַח וּמֶחֱצָה, כְּמוֹ שֶׁאָמַרְנוּ, אֲפִלּוּ נִתְעָרְבוּ הֶעָלִים אֵין חוֹשְׁשִׁין לָהֶם; וְכֵן כָּל זְמַן שֶׁיֵּרָאוּ מֻבְדָּלִין זֶה מִזֶּה, כְּגוֹן שֶׁהֹטָּה עָלִין שֶׁבָּעֲרוּגָה הָאַחַת לְצַד אֶחָד וְעָלִין שֶׁבָּעֲרוּגָה שֶׁבְּצִדָּהּ לְצַד אַחֵר, אַף-עַל-פִּי שֶׁהֵן יוֹנְקִין זֶה מִזֶּה אֵין חוֹשְׁשִׁין לִינִיקָתָן, דְּבִשְׁנֵיהֶם יַחַד הַקְפִּידָה תּוֹרָה, שֶׁיִּינְקוּ זֶה מִזֶּה וְתֵרָאֶה יְנִיקָתָן לְעֵינֵי הָרוֹאִים לְהָדְיָא.

וּבַמֶּה דְּבָרִים אֲמוּרִים שֶׁצָּרִיךְ הַרְחָקָה אוֹ דָבָר הַמַּבְדִּיל, בְּשֶׁזָּרַע בְּתוֹךְ שָׂדֵהוּ; אֲבָל אִם הָיְתָה שָׂדֵהוּ זְרוּעָה חִטִּים, מֻתָּר לַחֲבֵרוֹ לִזְרוֹעַ בְּצִדָּהּ שְׂעוֹרִים, שֶׁנֶּאֱמַר: שָׂדְךָ לֹא תִזְרַע כִּלְאַיִם, כְּלוֹמַר שָׂדְךָ דַּוְקָא, שֶׁלֹּא נֶאֱמַר: הָאָרֶץ לֹא תִזְרַע כִּלְאָיִם. וְעוֹד לָמְדוּ זִכְרוֹנָם לִבְרָכָה, מִדִּכְתִיב "שָׂדְךָ", לוֹמַר דְּדַוְקָא בְּאֶרֶץ הוּא שֶׁנּוֹהֵג אִסּוּר כִּלְאֵי זְרָעִים, אֲבָל לֹא בְחוּצָה לָאָרֶץ. וְאַף-עַל-גַּב דְּלְעִנְיַן הַרְכָּבַת אִילָן, דְּנָפְקָא לָן גַּם-כֵּן מִ"שָׂדְךָ", לֹא אָמְרוּ כֵן, אֶלָּא שֶׁנּוֹהֵג בְּכָל מָקוֹם, וּכְדְאָמַר

---

twenty-fourths of a *se'ah* of grain or legumes (MT *ibid.* 3). The amount of garden-plant seed needed to sow a *beth se'ah* (fifty by fifty cubits of land) varies with each kind.

13. I.e. in a total of twenty-four parts, hence one part of the first species in twenty-three of the second, as above; and as our author indicates, it makes no difference if the two species are both grains, both legumes, or one of each; Mishnah *ibid.* and MT *ibid.* 2–3.

14. Mishnah, Sh'kalim i 1.

15. Mishnah, Kil'ayim i 4–5.

16. *Ibid.* 1–2.

17. So Rashi, TB Shabbath 84b, s.v. *v'ehad b'emtza.*

18. As the Mishnah itself continues: four along the four sides, and one in the middle.

19. I.e. one in each corner, and one at the midpoint of each side; as the bed measures six by six handbreadths, there would yet remain three handbreadths of space between any two.

20. TJ Shabbath ix 2.

even if they are different in form on account of a change in location
or a change in the [way of] working the earth, they are as one kind. [16]

Then we have the many laws of the measure of distance required
between two species. As to the amount of distance between two kinds
of vegetables, that they should not derive sustenance from one another,
our Sages said it is one and a half handbreadths for each one, so that
as a result, the space between the two is three handbreadths. [17] And
there is what they said in the Mishnah tractate *Kil'ayim*, chapter 3
(iii 1), which they also cited in chapter 9 of the Talmud tractate *Shabbath*
(84b): that in a garden bed measuring six handbreadths by six, five
kinds of seeds may be planted. [18] According to our words, though,
they should have said nine: eight along its four sides, [19] and one in the
middle. This is no difficulty, however, as it was answered long ago
in the Jerusalem Talmud [20]—that this refers to one garden bed among
others. [21]

The rule that we gather from the words of the Sages of blessed
memory in regard to mixed species of plants is that as long as there is
the proper distance between two kinds, which is one and a half handbreadths, as we stated, then even if the leaves became intermingled,
we need not be concerned about them. And as long as they appear
separated from one another—for instance, if the leaves in one garden
bed were turned to one side, and the leaves in the next garden bed to
another side—then even if they derive sustenance from one another,
we need not be concerned about this sustenance, since the Torah objects
only when the two are together, so that they draw sustenance from
each other and this [mutual] sustenance of theirs is plainly visible to
onlookers. [22]

Now, when was it said that distance or something that divides
is needed?—when a person plants within his field. But if his field is
planted with wheat, his neighbor is permitted to plant barley alongside
it. For it is stated, *you shall not sow your field with two kinds of seed*—i.e.
specifically "your field," since it does not say, "you shall not sow the
land with two kinds of seed." [23] Moreover, our Sages of blessed
memory learned from Scripture's phrase, "your field," to rule that
specifically in the land [of Israel] the prohibition of mixed kinds of
plants prevails, but not outside the land. [1] Nevertheless, regarding
tree grafting, whose prohibition we derive also from the phrase,
"your field," they did not say so; it is rather in force everywhere,
as Sh'mu'él taught in the first chapter of the Talmud tractate *Kiddushin*

שְׁמוּאֵל בְּפֶרֶק קַמָּא דְּקִדּוּשִׁין, דְּמַקִּישׁ הַרְכָּבַת אִילָן לְהַרְבָּעַת בְּהֵמָה, שֶׁנּוֹהֵג בְּכָל מָקוֹם, כְּבָר תֵּרְצוּ הַדָּבָר זִכְרוֹנָם לִבְרָכָה שָׁם בְּקִדּוּשִׁין, וְאִם חָפֵץ בְּנֵי לָדַעַת, תִּרְאֶנּוּ מִשָּׁם. וְיֶתֶר רַבֵּי פְּרָטֶיהָ, מְבֹאָרִין בְּמַסֶּכֶת כִּלְאָיִם.

וְנוֹהֵג אִסּוּר כִּלְאֵי זְרָעִים בִּזְכָרִים וּנְקֵבוֹת, בְּאֶרֶץ יִשְׂרָאֵל בִּלְבַד, כְּמוֹ שֶׁאָמַרְנוּ; אֲבָל בְּחוּצָה לָאָרֶץ מֻתָּר לְעָרֵב הַזְּרָעִים לְכַתְּחִלָּה וּלְזָרְעָן; וַאֲפִלּוּ בָּאָרֶץ אֵין הָאִסּוּר אֶלָּא לְיִשְׂרָאֵל, אֲבָל מֻתָּר לוֹמַר לְגוֹי לִזְרֹעַ לוֹ כִּלְאָיִם; וּמִכָּל־מָקוֹם אָסוּר לְקַיְּמָן לִכְשֶׁיִּגְדְּלוּ בְּשָׂדֵהוּ.

וְכָל זֶה שֶׁאָמַרְנוּ, דַּוְקָא בְּכִלְאֵי זְרָעִים, אֲבָל כִּלְאֵי הָאִילָנוֹת, כְּלוֹמַר הַרְכָּבָה, שֶׁהִיא אֲסוּרָה בָּהֶן, נוֹהֶגֶת אֲפִלּוּ בְּחוּצָה לָאָרֶץ, כְּמוֹ שֶׁאָמַרְנוּ. וְאָסוּר לְיִשְׂרָאֵל לְהַנִּיחַ לְגוֹי לְהַרְכִּיב אִילָנוֹ, אֲפִלּוּ בְּחוּצָה לָאָרֶץ.

וְעוֹבֵר עַל זֶה, בֵּין אִישׁ אוֹ אִשָּׁה, וְזָרַע כִּלְאֵי זְרָעִים בְּאֶרֶץ יִשְׂרָאֵל, חַיָּב מַלְקוֹת. וְהַמַּרְכִּיב אִילָן בְּאִילָן שֶׁאֵינוֹ מִינוֹ אוֹ יָרָק בְּאִילָן, אוֹ אִילָן בְּיָרָק, אֲפִלּוּ בְּחוּצָה לָאָרֶץ, וְכָל־שֶׁכֵּן בָּאָרֶץ, חַיָּב גַּם־כֵּן מַלְקוֹת.

[שֶׁלֹּא לֶאֱכֹל עָרְלָה]

רמו שֶׁלֹּא נֹאכַל מִפֵּרוֹת הָאִילָן תּוֹךְ זְמַן עָרְלָתוֹ, וְהֵן שָׁלֹשׁ שָׁנִים רִאשׁוֹנוֹת לִנְטִיעָתוֹ, וְאֶחָד הַנּוֹטֵעַ נְטִיעָה אוֹ יְחוּר מִן הָאִילָן—שֶׁנֶּאֱמַר: שָׁלֹשׁ שָׁנִים יִהְיֶה לָכֶם עֲרֵלִים לֹא יֵאָכֵל.

מִשָּׁרְשֵׁי מִצְוָה זוֹ, כָּתַבְתִּי בְּמִצְוַת נֶטַע רְבָעִי, ט׳ בְּזֶה הַסֵּדֶר [סִי׳ רמ״ז], בְּשֵׁם הָרַמְבַּ״ם זִכְרוֹנוֹ לִבְרָכָה.

מִדִּינֵי הַמִּצְוָה, מַה שֶּׁאָמְרוּ זִכְרוֹנָם לִבְרָכָה שֶׁהַנּוֹטֵעַ לִסְיָג וּלְקוֹרוֹת, פָּטוּר מִן הָעָרְלָה, דְּ״עֵץ מַאֲכָל״ כָּתוּב; כְּלוֹמַר, שֶׁלֹּא יַטַּע אוֹתוֹ לָדַעַת שֶׁיֹּאכַל פֵּרוֹתָיו

---

21. I.e. directly next to others; then if there will be plants both at the corners and at the midpoints of the edges, those at the sides of adjacent beds will be too close to one another; but if only five are planted per bed, in one bed the corners can be used, and in the next bed the midpoints of the edges.

22. MT *hilchoth kil'ayim* iv 16.

23. Mishnah, Kil'ayim ii 7; MT *ibid.* iii 16.

24. MT *ibid.* i 3.

§246   1. So Sifra, *k'doshim, parashah* vi 3, that the period begins at the planting.

2. So *ibid.* 2.

3. In this as in most Hebrew editions, this appears later, not above, as our author indicates. However, as noted previously, in our author's original version, the positive precepts in each *sidrah* were given first, then the negative. Hence §247, being a positive precept, appeared there earlier.

4. Mishnah, 'Orlah i 1.

(39a), equating tree grafting with the mating of animals [of different species], whose prohibition is in force everywhere. However, the Sages of blessed memory resolved this difficulty long ago, there in the tractate *Kiddushin*. If it is your desire to know this, my son, you can see it there. The rest of its many details are in the Mishnah tractate *Kil'ayim*.

The prohibition on sowing two kinds of plants together applies to both man and woman, in the land of Israel alone, as we stated. Outside the land, though, it is permitted to mix seeds initially and plant them.[1] And even in the land, the prohibition prevails only for an Israelite; he is permitted, however, to tell a non-Jew to plant mixed species for him. Nevertheless, he is forbidden to keep them when they grow in his field.[24]

All this that we have said applies specifically to mixed species of plants. As for mingling kinds of trees, i.e. grafting, which is forbidden, this ban is in force even outside the land, as we stated. And an Israelite is forbidden to allow a non-Jew to graft his tree, even outside the land.[1]

If someone transgressed this, whether a man or a woman, and sowed mixed kinds of plants together in the land of Israel, he would be punishable by whiplashes. If someone grafts a tree onto another tree that is not of its species, or a vegetable onto a tree, or a tree [shoot] onto a vegetable plant—this even in other countries, and all the more certainly in the land—he is equally punishable by lashes.

[NOT TO EAT THE FIRST THREE YEARS' PRODUCE OF A TREE]

246 that we should not eat of the fruit of a tree within the period when it is 'orlah [forbidden], which is the first three years after its planting;[1] and it is all one whether a sapling or a shoot of a tree is planted[2]—as it is stated, *three years it shall be forbidden to you; it shall not be eaten* (Leviticus 19:23).

The root reason for this commandment I wrote in the ninth positive precept of this *sidrah* (§247),[3] about the fourth year's fruit, in the name of Rambam of blessed memory.

Among the laws of the precept, there is what the Sages of blessed memory taught:[4] that if a person plants [trees] for a fence or to [provide] wooden beams, he is free of the obligation of 'orlah,[5] since it is written, *trees for food* (ibid.); in other words, if he does not plant it with the knowledge (intention) that he will eat its fruit, but rather that the

אֶלָּא שֶׁיִּהְיֶה הָאִילָן סְיָג סָבִיב גַּנָּתוֹ, אוֹ לָדַעַת שֶׁיַּעֲשֶׂה מִמֶּנּוּ קוֹרָה לְבֵיתוֹ. נָטַע לִסְיָג אוֹ לְקוֹרָה וְחָזַר וְחָשַׁב עָלָיו לְמַאֲכָל, חַיָּב בְּעָרְלָה; כֵּיוָן שֶׁעֵרַב בּוֹ מַחֲשֶׁבֶת חִיּוּב, חַיָּב.

וְשׁוֹמֵר הַפְּרִי חַיָּב בְּעָרְלָה, וּכְמוֹ שֶׁדָּרְשׁוּ: "אֶת פִּרְיוֹ", אֶת הַטָּפֵל לְפִרְיוֹ, כְּלוֹמַר שׁוֹמֵר הַפְּרִי; וּבַתְּנָאִים הַיְדוּעִים לְרַבּוֹתֵינוּ זִכְרוֹנָם לִבְרָכָה, הוּא שֶׁיֵּאָסֵר הַשּׁוֹמֵר, וְהֵם שֶׁיְּהֵא הַשּׁוֹמֵר עוֹמֵד בַּפְּרִי עַד שָׁעָה שֶׁיַּגִּיעַ הַפְּרִי לִכְלַל אִסּוּר עָרְלָה, וְעוֹד שֶׁיְּהֵא הַפְּרִי צָרִיךְ אֵלָיו כָּל־כָּךְ דְּאִי שָׁקְלִית לֵיהּ לַשּׁוֹמֵר, מָאִית פֵּירָא; וּלְפִיכָךְ אָמְרוּ זִכְרוֹנָם לִבְרָכָה שֶׁהַצַּלָּף חַיָּב בְּעָרְלָה מִן הָאֲבִיּוֹנוֹת בִּלְבָד; אֲבָל הַקַּפְרִיסִין מֻתָּר, מִזֶּה הַטַּעַם שֶׁאָמַרְנוּ, כִּי יָדוּעַ הוּא דְּאִי שָׁקְלִית לֵיהּ לַקַּפְרִיס מִקַּמֵּי דְּמָטֵי פֵּירָא לְאִסּוּר עָרְלָה, לָא מָאִית פֵּירָא.

וְדִין הַנּוֹטֵעַ לָרַבִּים; וְהַנּוֹטֵעַ לְמִצְוָה; וְהַנּוֹטֵעַ בְּעָצִיץ שֶׁאֵינוֹ נָקוּב, שֶׁחַיָּב בְּעָרְלָה; וְדִין יַלְדָּה שֶׁסִּבְּכָה בִזְקֵנָה; וְיֶתֶר פְּרָטֶיהָ, מְבֹאָרִין בְּמַסֶּכֶת עָרְלָה.

וְנוֹהֶגֶת בְּכָל מָקוֹם וּבְכָל זְמַן, בַּזְּכָרִים וּנְקֵבוֹת. וְכָתַב הָרַמְבַּ"ם זִכְרוֹנוֹ לִבְרָכָה, וְזֶה לְשׁוֹנוֹ: וְאִסּוּר עָרְלָה בְּחוּצָה לָאָרֶץ הֲלָכָה לְמֹשֶׁה מִסִּינַי, אָמְנָם לְשׁוֹן הַתּוֹרָה הוּא בָּאָרֶץ בִּלְבָד; עַד כָּאן — לְפִי שֶׁבַּתּוֹרָה נֶאֱמַר בְּפֵרוּשׁ "וְכִי תָבֹאוּ אֶל הָאָרֶץ וּנְטַעְתֶּם", דְּמַשְׁמַע דַּוְקָא בָאָרֶץ. וּבְפֵרוּשׁ אָמְרוּ זִכְרוֹנָם לִבְרָכָה בְּעִנְיַן הָעָרְלָה כִּי כָךְ נֶאֶמְרָה עָלֶיהָ הַהֲלָכָה לְמֹשֶׁה מִסִּינַי: וַדַּאָה אָסוּר, סְפֵקָה מֻתָּר; כְּלוֹמַר שֶׁאֵין עִנְיַן עָרְלָה אִסּוּרָהּ כְּמוֹ שְׁאָר אִסּוּרִין שֶׁבַּתּוֹרָה, שֶׁכָּל זְמַן שֶׁיִּתְחַדֵּשׁ עָלֵינוּ סָפֵק בְּדָבָר שֶׁהוּא אָסוּר מִן הַתּוֹרָה, יֵשׁ לָנוּ לֶאֱסֹר אוֹתוֹ מִסָּפֵק, דְּקַיְמָא לָן סְפֵק אָסוּר

---

5. I.e. he need not abstain from eating the fruit in the first three years after the planting.

6. Tosefta, 'Orlah i; TJ i 1.

7. TB B'rachoth 36b; the derivation which follows is inferred from the extra particle 'eth.

8. *Ibid.*

9. For public use or a public need; Mishnah, 'Orlah i 2.

10. E.g. to grow an *'ethrog* (citron) for use on *Sukkoth* (§ 324); TJ 'Orlah i 1.

11. TJ 'Orlah i 2.

12. TB N'darim 57b.

13. ShM negative precept § 192; MT *hilchoth ma'achaloth 'asuroth* x 10.

14. I.e. fruit which definitely grew in the first three years after a tree was planted.

15. TB Kiddushin 39a.

tree will be a protective barrier about his garden, or with the intention
that he will make of it a beam for his house. If he [thus] planted for a
fence or for a beam, then thought better of it and intended it for
[providing] food, he has the obligation of 'orlah: [6] Once he has involved
a duty-imposing thought with it, he has the obligation.

That which protects the fruit [its shell or rind, etc.] is subject to
the obligation of 'orlah; as the Sages taught: [7] *its fruit* (ibid.)—that
which is subsidiary to its fruit; i.e. the protector of the fruit. But only
under conditions known to our Sages of blessed memory does the
protection [shell, rind, etc.] become forbidden: i.e. if the protection
remains with the fruit until the time when the fruit reaches the stage
of the prohibition of 'orlah. Moreover, the fruit must need it to such
an extent that if you removed the protection, the fruit would die.
Therefore the Sages of blessed memory ruled [8] that for a caper tree
there is the obligation of 'orlah in regard to the berries alone; however,
the blossoms are permissible [the first three years] for this reason
that we have stated: for it is known that if the blossom is taken away
before the fruit comes to be forbidden as 'orlah, the fruit will not
perish.

Then there is the law of one who plants [trees] for the sake of
the public; [9] one who plants [trees] for the sake of a *mitzvah* (religious
duty); [10] and one who plants [a tree] in an unperforated plant-holder
(tub) [11]—who does have the obligation of 'orlah. Further, there is
the law about a young tree [less than three years old] that was grafted
onto an old tree. [12] The rest of its details are explained in the tractate
'Orlah.

It is in effect everywhere, at every time, for both man and woman.
Rambam of blessed memory wrote, in these words: [13] that the prohibition of 'orlah is in effect in other countries, outside the land [of Israel],
is a law [given orally] to Moses at Sinai. By the Torah's expression,
though, it prevails only in the land alone. Thus far his words. For we
read distinctly in the Torah, *And when you shall come into the land
and plant* (Leviticus 19:23), which would mean in the land only.
But our Sages of blessed memory said explicitly regarding 'orlah, that
so was the law given about it [orally] to Moses at Sinai: That which is
certain [14] is forbidden; what is in doubt is permissible. [15] This is to
say that the nature of its prohibition is not like that of other forbid-
dances in the Torah: [Generally] whenever any doubt arises in a

⟨103⟩ matter that is forbidden by Torah law, it is for us to forbid it on account

דְּאוֹרַיְתָא אָסוּר, וּכְמוֹ־כֵן בֵּאַרְנוּ עִם הַפֵּרוּשִׁים הַטּוֹבִים, שֶׁסָּפֵק הֲלָכָה לְמֹשֶׁה מִסִּינַי, לְחָמְרָא; וּבְעִנְיַן אִסוּר עָרְלָה קִבַּלְנוּ כִּי בְּפֵרוּשׁ נֶאֱמַר לְמֹשֶׁה שֶׁיְּהֵא סְפֵקָא מְתָּר.

וְכֵיוָן שֶׁכֵּן הוּא, שֶׁאֵין אִסּוּר עָרְלָה חָל כְּלָל בִּסְפֵיקָא, יִשְׂרָאֵל שֶׁיֵּשׁ לוֹ אִילָן שֶׁל עָרְלָה בְּגִנָּתוֹ וּבָא חֲבֵרוֹ וְאָכַל מִמֶּנּוּ, אֵינוֹ נִזְקָק לְהוֹדִיעוֹ כְּלָל שֶׁהוּא עָרְלָה. וּבְעִנְיַן זֶה מָצָאנוּ בַּגְּמָרָא שֶׁאָמְרוּ זִכְרוֹנָם לִבְרָכָה: סָפֵק לִי וַאֲנָא אֲכוּל, כְּלוֹמַר שֶׁכָּל זְמַן שֶׁלֹּא יָדַע הָאָדָם בְּוַדַּאי שֶׁהִיא עָרְלָה, שָׁרֵי לֵיהּ לְמֵיכַל מִינָהּ.

וְעוֹבֵר עַל מִצְוָה זוֹ וְאָכַל כְּזַיִת מִפֵּרוֹת הָאִילָן תּוֹךְ שְׁנֵי עָרְלָה, אוֹ אֲפִלּוּ מִשּׁוֹמֵר הַפְּרִי, אוֹתוֹ הַיָּדוּעַ שֶׁנֶּאֱסַר עִמּוֹ, חַיָּב מַלְקוֹת.

[מִצְוַת נֶטַע רְבָעִי]

רמז לִהְיוֹת נֶטַע רְבָעִי כֻּלּוֹ קֹדֶשׁ, פֵּרוּשׁ כָּל פֵּרוֹת הַיּוֹצְאִין בָּאִילָן בַּשָּׁנָה הָרְבִיעִית לִנְטִיעָתוֹ הֵם קֹדֶשׁ, כְּלוֹמַר שֶׁהֵם נֶאֱכָלִים לַבְּעָלִים כְּמוֹ מַעֲשֵׂר שֵׁנִי בִּירוּשָׁלַיִם, וְזוֹ הִיא קְדֻשָּׁתָן—שֶׁנֶּאֱמַר: וּנְטַעְתֶּם כָּל עֵץ מַאֲכָל... וּבַשָּׁנָה הָרְבִיעִית יִהְיֶה כָּל פִּרְיוֹ קֹדֶשׁ הִלּוּלִים לַיָי; וּבָא הַפֵּרוּשׁ שֶׁהֵם לַבְּעָלִים; וּפֵרוּשׁ "הִלּוּלִים" הוּא שֶׁיֹּאכְלוּהוּ הַבְּעָלִים בִּירוּשָׁלַיִם, וְזֶהוּ הַהִלּוּל; וְזֶה יִקְרְאוּ חֲכָמִים בְּכָל מָקוֹם נֶטַע רְבָעִי.

וּבְסִפְרֵי דּוֹרֵשׁ שֶׁנֶּטַע רְבָעִי הוּא לַבְּעָלִים מִדִּכְתִיב: וְאִישׁ אֶת קֳדָשָׁיו לוֹ יִהְיוּ, שֶׁאָמְרוּ שָׁם: "אִישׁ אֶת קֳדָשָׁיו" וְגוֹמֵר, מָשַׁךְ [הַכָּתוּב] כָּל הַקֳּדָשִׁים וּנְתָנָם לַכֹּהֲנִים, וְלֹא שִׁיֵּר מֵהֶם אֶלָּא תּוֹדָה וּשְׁלָמִים וּפֶסַח וּמַעֲשֵׂר בְּהֵמָה וּמַעֲשֵׂר שֵׁנִי

16. Not to risk transgressing a law of the Torah.

17. Since the law has the same authority as though written in the Torah; Ramban, commentary to ShM, root principle 2, s.v. *v'hinnéh*.

18. I.e. in the first three years since it was planted.

§247　　1. Because in TB Kiddushin 54b it is equated in its laws with the Second Tithe, which Deuteronomy 14:23 declares to belong to its owner.

2. So Rashi on the verse.

3. Sifré, Numbers § 6.

of the doubt;[16] for we have a standing rule: where there is doubt
whether something is forbidden by Torah law, it is forbidden. We
have similarly explained, in accord with the good commentaries,
that where there is doubt in a matter of a law given orally to Moses
at Sinai, we decide stringently.[17] Yet regarding the prohibition of
'orlah, we have received an Oral Tradition that Moses was expressly
told that anything doubtful should be permissible.

Well, since this is the case, that the prohibition of *'orlah* does not
prevail at all in a matter of doubt, if an Israelite has a tree of *'orlah*[18]
in his garden and his neighbor comes and eats of its fruit, he is not
duty-bound to inform him at all that it is *'orlah*. In this matter we
find in the Talmud[15] that the Sages of blessed memory used the
expression, "It is a doubt to me, and I will eat"; in other words, as
long as a man does not know for certain that it is *'orlah*, he is allowed
to eat of it.

If someone transgressed this precept and ate an olive's amount
of fruit from a tree within its years of *'orlah*, or even of such protection
of the fruit [shell, rind, etc.] which was known to be forbidden along
with it, he would be punishable by whiplashes.

[THE PRECEPT OF THE FRUIT OF A TREE'S FOURTH
YEAR]

247 that fourth-year fruit should be entirely sacred, which means
that all fruit that appears on a tree in the fourth year since its planting,
is hallowed; in other words, it is to be eaten by its owner like the
Second Tithe, in Jerusalem; this is its sacredness. For it is stated, *you
shall plant every kind of tree for food . . . and in the fourth year all its fruit
shall be holy, for praise-giving to the Lord* (Leviticus 19:23–24); and the
explanation was given [in the Oral Tradition] that it belongs to the
owner,[1] while the meaning of "praises" is that the owner should eat
it in Jerusalem, this being the "praise-giving."[2] This the Sages call
throughout. "fourth-year fruit."

In the Midrash *Sifre*[3] it is derived that fourth-year fruit belongs
to the owner, since it is written, *every man's hallowed things shall be his*
(Numbers 5:10). Thus it was stated there: "every man's hallowed
things," etc.—the Writ withdrew all the holy foods and gave them to
the *kohanim*, and left of them nothing but the *todah* (thanks-offering),
sh'lamim (peace-offering), the Passover offering, the tithe of animals,

וְנֶטַע רְבָעִי, שֶׁיִּהְיוּ לַבְּעָלִים.

מִשָּׁרְשֵׁי הַמִּצְוָה, שֶׁרָצָה הָאֵל לִהְיוֹת הָאָדָם מִתְעוֹרֵר לְהַלֵּל הַשֵּׁם בָּרוּךְ הוּא
בִּתְחִלַּת מִבְחַר פֵּרוֹת אִילָנוֹתָיו, כְּדֵי שֶׁיָּנוּחַ עָלָיו נֹעַם הַשֵּׁם וּבִרְכָתוֹ וְיִתְבָּרְכוּ
פֵּרוֹתָיו, כִּי הָאֵל הַטּוֹב חָפֵץ בְּטוֹב בְּרִיּוֹתָיו, וְלָכֵן צִוָּנוּ לְהַעֲלוֹתָן וְלֶאֱכֹל אוֹתָן
בַּמָּקוֹם שֶׁבָּחַר מִימֵי קֶדֶם לַעֲבוֹדָתוֹ בָּרוּךְ הוּא, כִּי שָׁם צִוָּה יי אֶת הַבְּרָכָה, וּמִבְחַר
פֵּרוֹת הָאִילָן הֵם הַיּוֹצְאִים בַּשָּׁנָה הָרְבִיעִית.

וְעוֹד יֵשׁ תּוֹעֶלֶת לָאָדָם בִּהְיוֹתוֹ מְצֻוֶּה לֶאֱכֹל הַהוּא בַּמָּקוֹם קְצָת פֵּרוֹתָיו, כְּגוֹן
זֶה וּמַעֲשֵׂר שֵׁנִי וְגַם מַעֲשַׂר בְּהֵמָה, כִּי מִתּוֹךְ כָּךְ יִקְבַּע מוֹשָׁבוֹ אוֹ מוֹשַׁב קְצָת
מִבָּנָיו בְּאוֹתוֹ הַמָּקוֹם לִלְמֹד תּוֹרָה שָׁם, כִּי שָׁם מוֹרֵי הַתּוֹרָה וְעִקַּר הַחָכְמָה, וּכְמוֹ
שֶׁנִּכְתֹּב בְּמִצְוַת מַעֲשֵׂר שֵׁנִי [סִי׳ תע״ג] בְּעֶזְרַת הַשֵּׁם.

וְהָרַמְבַּ״ן זִכְרוֹנוֹ לִבְרָכָה כָּתַב בְּטַעַם מִצְוָה זוֹ בְּפֵרוּשָׁיו: כְּדֵי לְכַבֵּד הַשֵּׁם
מֵרֵאשִׁית כָּל תְּבוּאָתֵנוּ וְלֹא נֹאכַל מֵהֶם עַד שֶׁנָּבִיא כָּל פְּרִי שָׁנָה אַחַת הַלּוּלִים
לַיי; וְהִנֵּה אֵין הַפְּרִי בְּתוֹךְ שָׁלֹשׁ רָאוּי לְהַקְרִיבוֹ לְפִי שֶׁהוּא מוּעָט, גַּם שֶׁאֵין נוֹתֵן
בְּפֵרְיוֹ טַעַם אוֹ רֵיחַ טוֹב, גַּם כִּי רֹב הָאִילָנוֹת לֹא יוֹצִיאוּ פֵּרוֹת כְּלָל עַד שָׁנָה
רְבִיעִית לִנְטִיעָתָן, וּלְכָךְ נַמְתִּין לְכֻלָּן; וְהַמִּצְוָה הַזֹּאת דּוֹמָה לַבִּכּוּרִים. וְעוֹד כָּתַב
כִּי אֱמֶת הַדָּבָר עוֹד שֶׁהַפְּרִי בִּתְחִלַּת נְטִיעָתוֹ, עַד הַשָּׁנָה הָרְבִיעִית, רַב הַלַּחוּת דָּבֵק
מְאֹד, מַזִּיק לַגּוּף וְאֵינֶנּוּ טוֹב לַאֲכִילָה, כְּדָג שֶׁאֵין לוֹ קַשְׂקֶשֶׂת וְהַמַּאֲכָלִים
הַנֶּאֱסָרִים בַּתּוֹרָה, שֶׁהֵם רָעִים גַּם לַגּוּף.

מִדִּינֵי הַמִּצְוָה, מַה שֶּׁאָמְרוּ זִכְרוֹנָם לִבְרָכָה שֶׁהָרוֹצֶה לִפְדּוֹת נֶטַע רְבָעִי פּוֹדֵהוּ
כְּמוֹ מַעֲשֵׂר שֵׁנִי שֶׁהוּא נִפְדֶּה, כְּלוֹמַר שֶׁפּוֹדֶה הַפֵּרוֹת בְּכֶסֶף וּמַעֲלֶה הַכֶּסֶף
לִירוּשָׁלַיִם. וְאִם פּוֹדֵהוּ לְעַצְמוֹ מוֹסִיף חֹמֶשׁ, שֶׁבֵּן הוּא הַדִּין בְּמַעֲשֵׂר שֵׁנִי
מִדִּכְתִיב בֵּיהּ: וְאִם גָּאֹל יִגְאַל אִישׁ מִמַּעַשְׂרוֹ [חֲמִשִׁיתוֹ יֹסֵף עָלָיו]; אֲבָל הַפּוֹדֶה

---

4. I.e. the verse denotes that originally all hallowed foods which a man separated
and consecrated were to belong to him, but elsewhere the Torah allotted all but these to
others; hence fourth-year fruit remains his. The first two paragraphs are based on ShM
positive precept §119.

5. Our author echoes here the Talmudic teaching that the site of the Sanctuary was
one of seven entities created before the world (TB P'saḥim 54a).

6. To Leviticus 19:23.

7. Which would explain why 'orlah, the fruit of the first three years, is forbidden.

8. TB B'rachoth 35a.

9. I.e. exchange it for money (see below) so that it is no longer sacred and may be
eaten anywhere.

10. Mishnah, Pé'ah vii 6.

the Second Tithe, and fourth-year fruit—that they should belong to their owners. [4]

At the root of the precept lies the reason that God wished that man should be stirred to praise the Eternal Lord, blessed is He, with the beginning of the choice fruit of his trees, so that the grace of the Eternal Lord and His blessing will rest upon him, and his fruit will be blessed; for the good God delights in good for His human beings. Therefore he bade us take it up and eat it in the location He chose since days of yore [5] for His worship, blessed is He; *for there* [in Jerusalem] *the Lord commanded the blessing* (Psalms 133:3); and the choice fruits of a tree are those which appear in the fourth year.

There is another useful advantage for a man in being ordered to eat some of his fruit in that location—such as this, the Second Tithe (§473), and also the animal tithe (§360): As a result of this, he will make his home, or the home of some of his sons, in that location, to study Torah there; for there *the* instructors of Torah and the main core of wisdom are found, as we will write in the precept of the Second Tithe (§473), with the Eternal Lord's help.

Ramban of blessed memory wrote as a reason for this precept, in his commentary, [6] that it is in order to honor the Eternal Lord with the first of all our produce, not eating of it until we bring the entire fruit of one year for praise-giving to the Lord. Now, in the first three years, the yield is not fit to bring, because it is little, and moreover, it does not impart to its fruit any taste or good scent; in addition, most trees will not produce fruit at all until the fourth year after their planting; and therefore we wait with them all. This precept is [thus] similar to *bikkurim* (first-fruits, §91). Then he wrote as well that it is true, furthermore, that from the start of its planting till the fourth year, there is a great amount of moisture (humor) in a tree's fruit that clings strongly; it is harmful to the body and not good to eat, like a fish without scales and [other] foods forbidden by the Torah, which are equally harmful for the body. [7]

Among the laws of the precept, there is what the Sages of blessed memory taught: [8] that if someone wishes to redeem fourth-year fruit, [9] he can redeem it like the Second Tithe, which is redeemable (Deuteronomy 14:24–26). In other words, he exchanges the fruit for money, and takes the money up to Jerusalem. If he redeems it for himself, he is to add on a fifth, [10] since this is the law for the Second
Tithe, as it is written of it, *And if a man will redeem any of his tithe,*

מַעֲשֵׂר שֵׁנִי לַאֲחֵרִים אֵין מוֹסִיף חֹמֶשׁ.

וְאֵין פּוֹדִין אוֹתוֹ עַד שֶׁיַּגִּיעַ לְעוֹנַת הַמַּעֲשֵׂר, שֶׁנֶּאֱמַר בּוֹ: לְהוֹסִיף לָכֶם תְּבוּאָתוֹ, וְדָרְשׁוּ זִכְרוֹנָם לִבְרָכָה: עַד שֶׁיַּעֲשֶׂה תְבוּאָה, כְּלוֹמַר שֶׁהַגִּיעַ לְעוֹנַת מַעֲשֵׂר, וְהוּא שְׁלִישׁ בִּשׁוּלוֹ. וְאֵין פּוֹדִין אוֹתוֹ בִּמְחֻבָּר, כְּמוֹ מַעֲשֵׂר, לְדַעַת הָרַמְבַּ"ם זִכְרוֹנוֹ לִבְרָכָה; וַאֲחֵרִים פֵּרְשׁוּ דַאֲפִלּוּ בִּמְחֻבָּר פּוֹדִין אוֹתוֹ.

וְהוּא נִקְרָא מָמוֹן גָּבוֹהַּ כְּמוֹ מַעֲשֵׂר, וּלְפִיכָךְ אֵינוֹ נִקְנֶה בְּמַתָּנָה אֶלָּא־אִם־כֵּן נְתָנוֹ בְּעוֹדוֹ בֹּסֶר, שֶׁעֲדַיִן לֹא חָל עָלָיו הַחִיּוּב, כְּמוֹ שֶׁאָמַרְנוּ.

וְדִינוֹ בִּשְׁאָר הַדְּבָרִים, כְּגוֹן אֲכִילָה שְׁתִיָּה וְסִיכָה, כְּמַעֲשֵׂר. וּבְמִצְוַת מַעֲשֵׂר שֵׁנִי בְּפָרָשַׁת רְאֵה אָנֹכִי [סי' תע"ג] נַאֲרִיךְ עוֹד בָּזֶה בְּעֶזְרַת הַשֵּׁם.

וְהַפּוֹדֶה כֶרֶם רְבָעִי, רָצָה פּוֹדֵהוּ עֲנָבִים, רָצָה פּוֹדֵהוּ יַיִן; וְכֵן הַזֵּיתִים, אֲבָל שְׁאָר הַפֵּרוֹת פּוֹדֶה אוֹתָן קֹדֶם שֶׁיִּשְׁתַּנּוּ מִבְּרִיָּתָן. וְהַפִּדְיוֹן הוּא שֶׁאוֹמְרִים "פֵּרוֹת אֵלּוּ יִהְיוּ מְחֻלָּלִין עַל כֶּסֶף זֶה", וַהֲרֵי הֵן מְחֻלָּלִין בְּכָךְ; וּמַעֲלֶה הַכֶּסֶף וְאוֹכְלוֹ בִּירוּשָׁלַיִם. וְאָמַר שְׁמוּאֵל בַּגְּמָרָא, שֶׁהֶקְדֵּשׁ שָׁוֶה מָנֶה שֶׁחִלְּלוֹ עַל שָׁוֶה פְרוּטָה, מְחֻלָּל, אֲבָל לֹא בְּפָחוֹת מִשָּׁוֶה פְרוּטָה, שֶׁאֵין לוֹ דִין כֶּסֶף לְשׁוּם דָּבָר; וְהוּא הַדִּין לְפֵרוֹת רְבָעִי.

וְכֶרֶם רְבָעִי אֵין לוֹ שִׁכְחָה וּפֵאָה וְלֹא פֶרֶט וְעוֹלְלוֹת, וְאֵין מַפְרִישִׁין מִמֶּנּוּ תְּרוּמָה וּמַעֲשְׂרוֹת, אֶלָּא כֻּלּוֹ עוֹלֶה לִירוּשָׁלַיִם, אוֹ נִפְדֶּה וְיַעֲלוּ הַדָּמִים, וְיֵאָכְלוּ בִּירוּשָׁלַיִם.

וְדִין מַה שֶּׁאָמְרוּ זִכְרוֹנָם לִבְרָכָה: מֵאֵימָתַי מוֹנִין רֹאשׁ הַשָּׁנָה לִרְבָעִי, וְכֵן מַה שֶּׁאָמְרוּ שֶׁכָּל שֶׁהוּא חַיָּב בְּעָרְלָה חַיָּב בִּרְבָעִי; וּבְמִצְוַת עָרְלָה נַאֲרִיךְ בָּזֶה בְּעֶזְרַת

---

11. In Sifra on the verse—*k'doshim, parashah* 6, 10.

12. And thus each fruit has its own time when it becomes subject to the obligation of the tithe, and then the tithe may be redeemed. So *tosafoth*, TB Rosh haShanah 12b, s.v. *ha-t'vu'ah.*

13. MT *bilchoth ma'asér shéni* ix 2.

14. See *tosafoth*, TB Bava Kamma 69a, s.v. *'éma.* So also Rashba, *Responsa ascribed to Ramban*, §156; see also *idem, Responsa* I §744.

15. TB Kiddushin 52b.

16. I.e. before it has attained a third of its growth: see the preceding paragraph; *ibid.* 54b; MT *ibid.*

17. One may redeem either them or the oil made from them; Tosefta, Ma'asér Shéni, toward the end.

18. Derived from Mishnah, T'rumoth xi 11.

19. TB Kiddushin 11b, etc.

20. A *maneh*, worth 19,200 times as much as a *p'rutah*, contained and was worth 480 grams of silver.

21. Mishnah, Ma'asér Shéni v 3; MT *bilchoth ma'asér shéni* ix 4.

he shall add a fifth part of it to it (Leviticus 27:31). But if a person redeems
Second Tithe for others, he does not add the fifth.

It is not to be redeemed until the season of the tithe arrives:
because it is stated about it, *that it may increase its yield for you* (Leviticus
19:25), and the Sages of blessed memory interpreted:[11] [wait] until
it forms produce; in other words, until it reaches the time for the
tithe, which is at one third of its full growth.[12] Nor is it to be redeemed
while attached [to the tree], like the tithe—this by the view of Rambam
of blessed memory.[13] But others explained[14] that even while attached [to the tree] it may be redeemed.

Now, this is called "Heaven's property," like the tithe.[15] Therefore
it cannot be acquired as a gift, unless it is given while it is yet unripe,
when the obligation has not yet taken effect on it, as we said.[16]

Then there is its law in regard to other matters, such as eating,
drinking, and spreading oil on the skin—as with the tithe. In the precept
of the Second Tithe, in *sidrah r'éh* (§473), we will deal further with
this, at length, with the Eternal Lord's help.

When a person redeems the fourth-year fruit of a vineyard, if he
wishes he may redeem it as grapes, and if he wishes he may redeem
it as wine; and so too olives.[17] Other fruits, however, are to be redeemed before they change from their original state.[18] The redemption
consists of saying, "These fruits shall become non-holy in exchange
for this money"; and they are thus made non-holy. Then one takes
the money and eats [food bought with] it in Jerusalem. In the Talmud,[19]
Sh'mu'él taught that if hallowed food worth a *maneh* is thus exchanged
for a *p'rutah*,[20] the exchange takes effect; but not if for less than a
p'rutah, since that is not considered money in regard to anything.
Well, the law is the same for fourth-year fruit.

The fourth-year fruit of a vineyard carries no obligation of forgotten grapes (§592) or of an unharvested part (§220), nor of fallen grapes
(§222) or of small single bunches (§221). Neither are *t'rumah* [the
kohen's portion] and the tithes separated from it; but the whole is
rather taken up to Jerusalem, or redeemed, and the money is then
taken up and used for food in Jerusalem.[21]

There is, further, the law that the Sages of blessed memory
taught:[22] From when is the beginning of the year reckoned for the
fourth-year fruit? So too, there is what they said,[23] that whatever
has the obligation of *'orlah* has the obligation of fourth-year fruit.
⟨109⟩ In the precept of *'orlah* (§246) we will deal at length with this,[24]

הַשֵּׁם, וְנִכְתָּב אִי זֶה אִילָן חַיָּב בָּהּ וְאִי זֶה דָבָר שֶׁבָּאִילָן, וּמִמֶּנָּה נִלְמַד לְרִבְעִי;
וְיֶתֶר כָּל פְּרָטֶיהָ, מְבֹאָרִים בְּפֶרֶק אַחֲרוֹן מִמַּעֲשֵׂר שֵׁנִי.

וְנוֹהֶגֶת מִצְוָה זוֹ בִּזְמַן הַבַּיִת בָּאָרֶץ, בִּזְכָרִים וּנְקֵבוֹת, אֲבָל לֹא בְחוּצָה לָאָרֶץ;
וְכֵן כָּתַב הָרַמְבַּ״ם זִכְרוֹנוֹ לִבְרָכָה: כְּשֵׁם שֶׁאֵין מַעֲשֵׂר שֵׁנִי בְּסוּרְיָא כָּךְ אֵין נֶטַע
רְבָעִי בְּסוּרְיָא, עַד כָּאן—וְכָל שֶׁכֵּן בְּחוּצָה לָאָרֶץ. וְיֵשׁ מֵרַבּוֹתֵינוּ שֶׁהוֹרוּנוּ, הַשֵּׁם
יִשְׁמְרֵם וִיחַיֵּם, שֶׁחִיּוּב מִצְוָה זוֹ הוּא אֲפִלּוּ עַכְשָׁיו בָּאָרֶץ, וַאֲפִלּוּ בְחוּצָה לָאָרֶץ
נוֹהֵג כֶּרֶם רְבָעִי מִדְּרַבָּנָן; וּלְפִי זֶה צָרִיךְ כָּל אָדָם עַכְשָׁיו לִפְדּוֹת פֵּרוֹת כֶּרֶם רְבָעִי
שֶׁלּוֹ עַל שָׁוֶה פְרוּטָה אוֹ יוֹתֵר. גַּם אָמְרוּ שֶׁמְּבָרְכִין עַל הַפְּדִיָּה, וְאַחַר־כָּךְ מַשְׁלִיךְ
הַפִּדְיוֹן לְיָם הַמֶּלַח, כְּלוֹמַר לְמָקוֹם הָאָבֵד, כְּדֵי שֶׁלֹּא יֵהָנֶה בּוֹ בְּרִיָּה, לְפִי שֶׁהוּא
קָדוֹשׁ הַיּוֹם מִדְּרַבָּנָן; וְאַחַר־כָּךְ אוֹכֵל פֵּרוֹת כַּרְמוֹ. אֲבָל נֶטַע רְבָעִי אֵינוֹ נוֹהֵג כְּלָל
בְּחוּצָה לָאָרֶץ אֲפִלּוּ מִדְּרַבָּנָן.

וְעוֹבֵר עַל מִצְוָה זוֹ וְלֹא הֶעֱלָה הַפֵּרוֹת לִירוּשָׁלַיִם אוֹ פְּדִיוֹנָן בִּזְמַן הַבַּיִת, אוֹ
שֶׁלֹּא פְדָאָן בָּאָרֶץ כְּדַעַת קְצָת הַמְפָרְשִׁים אֲפִלּוּ עַכְשָׁיו, בִּטֵּל עֲשֵׂה זֶה, וְלֹא חָפֵץ
בִּבְרָכָה; וּמְקַיְּמָהּ יִהְיֶה בָרוּךְ.

[שֶׁלֹּא לֶאֱכֹל וְלִשְׁתּוֹת כְּדֶרֶךְ זוֹלֵל וְסוֹבֵא]

רמח שֶׁלֹּא לְהַרְבּוֹת בַּאֲכִילָה וּשְׁתִיָּה בִּימֵי הַנַּעֲרוּת בַּתְּנָאִים הַנִּזְכָּרִים בְּבֵן
סוֹרֵר וּמוֹרֶה כַּכָּתוּב, עִם מַה שֶּׁפֵּרְשׁוּ בּוֹ חֲכָמֵינוּ זִכְרוֹנָם לִבְרָכָה בְּמַסֶּכֶת
סַנְהֶדְרִין; וְהָאַזְהָרָה לָנוּ עַל זֶה מִדִּכְתִיב: לֹא תֹאכְלוּ עַל הַדָּם, שֶׁכֵּן אָמְרוּ בְּפֵרוּשׁ
בְּסַנְהֶדְרִין: אַזְהָרָה לְבֵן סוֹרֵר וּמוֹרֶה מְנַּיִן, תַּלְמוּד לוֹמַר: לֹא תֹאכְלוּ עַל הַדָּם—

22. TB Rosh haShanah 9b.

23. TJ 'Orlah i 1.

24. See §246, note 3.

25. MT *hilchoth ma'asér shéni* ix 1; however, in *hilchoth ma'achaloth 'asuroth* x 15 he writes that the law of "fourth-year fruit" applies in the land of Israel both when the Temple is extant and when it is not; yet the obligation to observe it when the Temple is not in existence would seem to be only by the ruling of the Sages, while our author follows the law of the Torah here (MY).

26. Since the Sages imposed the obligation of observing the tithes and the seventh (sabbatical) year (§84) on Jews in Syria, so that Jews in Israel should not be tempted to move there (MT *hilchoth ma'achaloth 'asuroth* x 15).

27. Rashba (R. Sh'lomoh ibn 'Adreth), R. 'Ashér, and *Ba'al haMa'or* to R. Isaac 'Alfasi, on TB B'rachoth 35a, following R. Yitzḥak in *tosafoth* to TB Yevamoth 82b s.v. *y'rushah* (as cited in *Tur Yoreh Dé'ah* §331). Instead of this phrase of blessing, the oldest manuscripts and all editions but the first read "today" (*ha-yom*). Evidently the original was either היו׳ an abbreviation of the phrase in the first edition, or היו short for *ha-yom*. In the context the first seems more likely. (For sources see also Rashba, *Responsa* I §744; and R. Aḥa'i, *She'iltoth, k'doshim* §100.)

with the Eternal Lord's help, and will write which tree brings the obligation, and which product on the tree; and from that we will learn [the law] for fourth-year fruit. All the rest of its details are explained in the last chapter of the Mishnah tractate *Ma'asér Shéni*.

This precept is in effect when the Temple is in existence, in the land [of Israel], for both man and woman—but not outside the land. So Rambam of blessed memory wrote:[25] just as the Second Tithe is not observed in Syria, so is "fourth-year fruit" not observed in Syria. Thus far his words. Then all the more certainly is it so in other countries.[26] Yet there are some of our sages, may the Eternal Lord guard them and give them life,[27] who have instructed us that the obligation of this precept exists even now in the land [of Israel];[28] and even in other countries, the law of "fourth-year fruit" of a vineyard is to be observed by the ruling of the Sages.[29] Hence, every man must now redeem the fourth-year produce of his vineyard for the worth of a *p'rutah* or more; and they[30] ruled further that a benediction is to be recited over the redemption [the exchange]; then the coin of the redemption is to be thrown into the Dead Sea—i.e. into a place of total loss,[31] so that no one can benefit from it, since it is sacred today by the ruling of the Sages. After this one may eat the fruit of his vineyard. However, the law of [other] fourth-year fruit is not in force at all outside the land [of Israel], even by the ruling of the Sages.

If a person violated this precept and did not take the fruits or the money of their redemption to Jerusalem at the time the Temple stood, or, in the view of some authorities, if he does not redeem them in the land [of Israel] even now, he would thus disobey this positive precept, having no wish for blessing. But he who observes it will be blessed.

[NOT TO EAT OR DRINK IN THE MANNER OF A GLUTTON
OR DRUNKARD]

248 not to overindulge in eating and drinking in the days of youth, under the conditions mentioned about the stubborn and rebellious son in Scripture (Deuteronomy 21:18), according to what the Sages of blessed memory explained about him in the Talmud tractate *Sanhedrin*. The admonition given us about it lies in the verse, *You shall not eat with the blood* (Leviticus 19:26); for it was so stated explicitly in *Sanhedrin* (63a): Where do we find an admonition about a stubborn and rebellious son?—Scripture states, *You shall not eat with*

כְּלוֹמַר לֹא תֹאכְלוּ אֲכִילָה שֶׁהִיא מְבִיאָה לִשְׁפֹּךְ דָּם, וְהִיא אֲכִילַת זוֹלֵל וְסוֹבֵא, שֶׁחַיָּב עַל אוֹתָהּ אֲכִילָה הָרָעָה מִיתָה.

וְכָתַב הָרַמְבַּ"ם זִכְרוֹנוֹ לִבְרָכָה: וְאַף־עַל־פִּי שֶׁזֶּה הַלָּאו הוּא לָאו שֶׁבִּכְלָלוּת, כְּמוֹ שֶׁבֵּאַרְנוּ בָּעִקָּר הַתְּשִׁיעִי, אֵינוֹ רָחוֹק כִּי כְשֶׁיִּהְיֶה הָעֹנֶשׁ מְפֹרָשׁ, כְּלוֹמַר עֹנֶשׁ בֵּן סוֹרֵר וּמוֹרֶה, דְּהַיְנוּ מִשְׁפָּטוֹ שֶׁהוּא בִּסְקִילָה מְפֹרָשׁ בַּכָּתוּב, אֵינִי חוֹשֵׁשׁ עַל הָאַזְהָרָה אִם הִיא מִן לָאו שֶׁבִּכְלָלוּת.

וְנָתַן טַעַם לִדְבָרָיו, כְּמוֹ שֶׁכָּתַב בְּסִפְרוֹ מִצְוַת לֹא־תַעֲשֶׂה קצ"ה וּבָעִקָּר הַתְּשִׁיעִי. וְהָרַמְבַּ"ן זִכְרוֹנוֹ לִבְרָכָה תָּפַשׂ עָלָיו הַרְבֵּה בְּכָאן; וְאוּלָם שְׁנֵיהֶם מוֹדִים כִּי זֶה הַלָּאו דְּ"לֹא תֹאכְלוּ עַל הַדָּם" וְכָל כַּיּוֹצֵא בוֹ, שֶׁכּוֹלֵל דְּבָרִים רַבִּים, כְּמוֹ שֶׁנִּכְתּוֹב כָּאן, וְאֵין עִנְיָנָם וְטַעַם אִסּוּרָן שָׁוֶה, אֶלָּא שֶׁהַכָּתוּב אֲסָרָם כֻּלָּם בְּלָאו אֶחָד וְשֵׁם אֶחָד, כִּי לָאו שֶׁבִּכְלָלוּת הוּא נִקְרָא, וַהֲלָכָה הִיא: לָאו שֶׁבִּכְלָלוּת אֵין לוֹקִין עָלָיו.

אֲבָל הָרַמְבַּ"ם זִכְרוֹנוֹ לִבְרָכָה יֹאמַר כִּי מִפְּנֵי־כֵן יֵעָנֵשׁ הַבֵּן מִיתָה בַּאֲכִילָה זוֹ אַף־עַל־פִּי שֶׁהָאַזְהָרָה מִזֶּה הַלָּאו, לְפִי שֶׁהַכָּתוּב גִּלָּה בְּפֵרוּשׁ שֶׁעָנְשׁוֹ בִּסְקִילָה בְּמָקוֹם אַחֵר; וְהוּא בֵאֵר בְּהַקְדָּמַת סִפְרוֹ שֶׁכָּל מַה שֶׁיִּתְחַיֵּב הַכָּתוּב בּוֹ כָּרֵת אוֹ מִיתַת בֵּית־דִּין הוּא מִצְוַת לֹא־תַעֲשֶׂה, חוּץ מִפֶּסַח וּמִילָה, שֶׁיֵּשׁ בָּהֶן כָּרֵת וְהֵן מִצְוַת עֲשֵׂה. וּמִן הַכְּלָל הַזֶּה יָצָא לוֹ לָרַב שֶׁאַזְהָרַת בֵּן סוֹרֵר וּמוֹרֶה, אַף־עַל־פִּי שֶׁהִיא לְמוֹדָה מִלָּאו שֶׁבִּכְלָלוּת, דִּינָהּ כִּשְׁאָר אַזְהָרוֹת, מִכֵּיוָן שֶׁהַכָּתוּב פֵּרַשׁ בּוֹ עֹנֶשׁ מִיתָה.

וְהָרַמְבַּ"ן זִכְרוֹנוֹ לִבְרָכָה לֹא יַחֲזִיק בְּזֶה הַדֶּרֶךְ וְלֹא יִטֶּה אֵלָיו, וּלְעוֹלָם יְחַזֵּר לִהְיוֹת הָאַזְהָרָה מְפֹרֶשֶׁת עַל הַלּוֹקֶה אוֹ עַל הַמּוּמָת וְלֹא מִלָּאו שֶׁבִּכְלָלוּת; וַאֲפִלּוּ

28. I.e. by the law of the Torah, not merely by the Sages' ruling, as Rambam holds (see note 25—MY).

29. So *tosafoth* to TB B'rachoth 35a, s.v. *u-l'man*.

30. I.e. the authorities listed in note 27.

31. From which it cannot be recovered.

§248   1. That he eats as a glutton and guzzler, with money stolen from his parents, in the company of low, scurrilous types; hence it is predictable that when he is older he will rob and kill to obtain the money to continue such behavior (Rashi to Deuteronomy 21:18, based on Sifre to *ibid.* 21 and TB Sanhedrin 72a).

2. ShM negative precept §195.

3. I.e. prohibiting several different, unrelated things; see seven paragraphs below.

4. That this verse should provide the warning or admonition against the bad deed of the stubborn and rebellious son, in fulfillment of the rule of the Sages that the Torah does not impose punishment for any offense unless it also admonishes us not to do it. 〈112〉

the blood. In other words, you should not eat something that leads to bloodshed—which means the meal of a stubborn and rebellious boy,[1] for which evil act of eating he is punishable by death.

Now, Rambam of blessed memory wrote:[2] Even though this injunction is a general, omnibus negative precept,[3] as we explained in the ninth principle, it is not far-fetched:[4] for when the punishment is plainly stated—i.e. the punishment of the stubborn and rebellious son, meaning his sentence, which is death by stoning, is distinctly stated in the Writ[5]—I am not concerned about the admonition if it comes from a general, omnibus negative precept.

He gave a reason for his words, too, as it is written in his *Book of Precepts*, negative precept §195, and in the ninth principle [there]. However, Ramban of blessed memory refuted him greatly about this.[6] Yet both are in agreement that this injunction, *You shall not eat with the blood*, and any other like it which includes many matters (as we will write here) whose subject matter is not the same, nor the reasons for their prohibition, but Scripture merely forbade them all with one injunction and one name—is called a general, omnibus negative precept; and the definitive law is: over a general, omnibus negative precept, no whiplashes are given.

Nevertheless, Rambam of blessed memory would say that for this reason the [stubborn and rebellious] son should be punished by death for this kind of eating even though the admonition is from this negative precept: because Scripture distinctly revealed elsewhere (Deuteronomy 21:21) that his penalty is death by stoning. And he explained in the foreword to his work[7] that anything which Scripture makes punishable by *karéth* [Divine severance of existence] or death by sentence of the *beth din* (court), is [the subject of] a negative precept, except for the Passover sacrifice (§5) and circumcision (§2), which entail the penalty of *karéth*, yet are positive precepts. Thus, from this rule, the master [Rambam] drew the conclusion that the injunction about a stubborn and rebellious son, although learned from a general, omnibus negative precept, has the same law as other injunctions, since the Writ specified a death penalty for him.

However, Ramban of blessed memory would not follow such a way or incline to it, but would always seek about for an explicit admonition for a person who should receive whiplashes or be put to death, and not [one learned] from a general, omnibus negative precept.

⟨113⟩ Even if Scripture should specify [some sinner's] death a hundred

יְפָרֵשׁ הַכָּתוּב מִיתָתוֹ מֵאָה פְעָמִים, עֲדַיִן יֹאמַר הָרַב לֹא עָנַשׁ אֶלָּא כֵן אִם כֵּן הִזְהִיר, וְלָאו שֶׁבִּכְלָלוּת לֹא יַחְשְׁבֵהוּ לְאַזְהָרָה בִּמְקוֹם מַלְקוּת, מִמַּה שֶׁבְּדִינוּ הֲלָכָה רוֹוַחַת: אֵין לוֹקִין עַל לָאו שֶׁבִּכְלָלוּת.

וְעַל כֵּן אָמַר הוּא זִכְרוֹנוֹ לִבְרָכָה כִּי כְבָר הֵעִידוּ בַגְּמָרָא מֵאֵי זֶה מִקְרָא לָמַדְנוּ לְהַלְקוֹת בֶּן סוֹרֵר וּמוֹרֶה, וְאָמְרוּ בְסַנְהֶדְרִין: מַלְקוּת בְּבֶן סוֹרֵר וּמוֹרֶה הֵיכָא כְּתִיבָא, כִּדְרַבִּי אַבָּהוּ, דְּאָמַר רַבִּי אַבָּהוּ: לָמַדְנוּ מַלְקוּת בְּמוֹצִיא שֵׁם רַע, דִּכְתִיב בֵּיהּ "וְיִסְּרוּ אֹתוֹ", מ"וְיִסְּרוּ" דִּכְתִיב בְּבֶן סוֹרֵר, וּבֶן מִבֶּן: "וְהָיָה אִם בֵּן הַכּוֹת הָרָשָׁע".

וְעוֹד בָּזֶה קוּשְׁיָא לָרַמְבַּ"ם זִכְרוֹנוֹ לִבְרָכָה, בַּמֶּה שֶׁאָמַר בָּעִקָּר הַשֵּׁנִי שֶׁאֵין מַלְקִין מִכֹּחַ גְּזֵרָה שָׁוָה. וְעוֹד הִקְשָׁה עַל הָרַב מַאֲמָרוֹ כִּי הַבֵּן הַסּוֹרֵר יִתְחַיֵּב מִיתָה עַל רִבּוּי הָאֲכִילָה, וְלֹא חָלַק כְּלָל לַהֲמִיתוֹ בֵּין אֲכִילָה רִאשׁוֹנָה לַשְּׁנִיָּה; וּבְפֵרוּשׁ אָמְרוּ בַגְּמָרָא בְּסַנְהֶדְרִין שֶׁאֲכִילָה רִאשׁוֹנָה שֶׁל בֶּן סוֹרֵר וּמוֹרֶה אֵין עוֹשָׂהּ מִיתָה אֶלָּא מַלְקוּת, כְּמוֹ שֶׁאָמְרוּ: מַתְרִין בּוֹ בִּפְנֵי שְׁנַיִם וּמַלְקִין אוֹתוֹ בִּפְנֵי שְׁלֹשָׁה; חָזַר וְנִתְקַלְקֵל, נִדּוֹן בְּעֶשְׂרִים וּשְׁלֹשָׁה. וְעוֹד כָּתַב הוּא זִכְרוֹנוֹ לִבְרָכָה, וְזֶה לְשׁוֹנוֹ: וְהָרְאוּי לְהַעֲלוֹת מִזֶּה שֶׁאֲכִילָה רִאשׁוֹנָה נִמְנַעַת וְעָנְשָׁהּ מַלְקוּת, וְהַשְּׁנִיָּה עָנְשָׁהּ מִיתָה, וְהֵן שְׁתֵּי מְנִיעוֹת בְּחֶשְׁבּוֹן הַמִּצְווֹת, וְנִכְלְלוּ בְּ"לֹא תֹאכְלוּ עַל הַדָּם". עַד כָּאן.

וְהִנֵּה אַזְכִּיר לְךָ מִן הַדְּבָרִים שֶׁפֵּרְשׁוּ לָנוּ זִכְרוֹנָם לִבְרָכָה, שֶׁנִּכְלָלִין בַּלָּאו הַזֶּה:

5. Deuteronomy 21:21.

6. In his commentary to ShM, there.

7. ShM root principle 14, toward the end.

8. Identical in the Hebrew, *v'yisru 'otho*, although translated slightly differently in the English, on account of the contexts.

9. Identical in the Hebrew spelling, though vocalized differently; and vocalization marks (*n'kudoth*) are not written in the text of a Torah scroll.

10. In "a stubborn and rebellious son" the Hebrew for "son" is *ben* (the standard word for it).

11. Then Scripture goes on to order that such a person (wicked enough to deserve a beating) should be given lashes. Hence we learn (as our author writes in the next paragraph) that a stubborn and rebellious son is given a whipping for his first act of gluttony and guzzling through theft from his parents (death by stoning being the punishment for the second such act).

12. Of his *Séfer haMitzvoth* (ShM).

13. Yet the Talmudic passage cited above clearly derives this as the punishment of a stubborn and rebellious son, through a *g'zérah shavah*.

14. See note 11.

15. I.e. witnesses, who rebuke and warn him before he commits the wrong.

times, this master would still say, "It does not give the punishment unless it gives an admonition," and he would not consider a general, omnibus negative precept as an admonition in an instance entailing whiplashes, in view of the well-established rule we have: No lashes are given over a general, omnibus negative precept.

Therefore he (of blessed memory) said that long ago it was asserted in the Talmud from which verse we learn to give whiplashes to a stubborn and rebellious son. Thus it was taught in the tractate *Sanhedrin* (71b): Where are lashes prescribed for a stubborn and rebellious son?—it is as R. 'Abbahu taught; for R. 'Abbahu said: We learn that lashes are to be given one who brings an evil name [on his bride] because it is written of him, *and they shall chastise him* (Deuteronomy 22:18) [thus deriving it] from [the identical phrase][8] *and they chastise him* (ibid. 21:18) written about the stubborn and rebellious son; and [we learn that this means lashes for him from the identical Hebrew words] *ben* and *bin*,[9] [respectively, in his appellation][10] and in the verse, *if the wicked man* bin, *deserve, to be beaten* (ibid. 25:2).[11]

A further difficulty lies in this for Rambam of blessed memory, inasmuch as he said in the second principle[12] that whiplashes are not to be given on the strength of a *g'zérah shavah* [equation of two cases through identical terms in their Scriptural verses].[13] In addition, he [Ramban] objected to the master's [Rambam's] saying that the stubborn son incurs the death penalty over the excessive eating, and he made no distinction at all, in regard to executing him, between the first eating and the second.[14] Yet it was stated distinctly in the Talmud tractate *Sanhedrin* (71a) that the first [gluttonous act of] eating does not incur death but only lashes of the whip—as it was taught: He is warned before two,[15] and whipped before three;[16] if he repeated his bad behavior, he is to be tried by [a court of] twenty-three [judges].[17]

Then he (of blessed memory) wrote further, these being his words: What it is proper to gather from this is that the first [gluttonous act of] eating is forbidden, and its punishment is whiplashes, while the second act carries a penalty of death; and these are two prohibitions in the reckoning of the precepts, included in the injunction, *You shall not eat with the blood.* Thus far his words.

Now let me mention to you some of the matters that our Sages of
⟨115⟩ blessed memory explained to us, which are included in this injunction.

אָמְרוּ זִכְרוֹנָם לִבְרָכָה שֶׁיֵּשׁ בּוֹ אַזְהָרָה לְאוֹכֵל מִבְּהֵמָה קֹדֶם שֶׁתֵּצֵא נַפְשָׁהּ; וְכֵן
לְאוֹכֵל בְּשַׂר קָדָשִׁים קֹדֶם זְרִיקַת הַדָּם, וּכְמוֹ שֶׁאָמְרוּ: לֹא תֹאכְלוּ הַבָּשָׂר וַעֲדַיִן
דָּם בַּמִּזְרָק; וְכֵן לָמְדוּ מִמֶּנּוּ שֶׁאֵין מַבְרִין עַל הֲרוּגֵי בֵית-דִּין; וְכֵן סַנְהֶדְרִין שֶׁהָרְגוּ
אֶת הַנֶּפֶשׁ, שֶׁאֵין טוֹעֲמִין כְּלוּם כָּל אוֹתוֹ הַיּוֹם; וְשֶׁלֹּא יִטְעַם אָדָם כְּלוּם עַד
שֶׁיִּתְפַּלֵּל; וְכֵן אַזְהָרָה לְבֵן סוֹרֵר וּמוֹרֶה, כְּמוֹ שֶׁאָמַרְנוּ.

מִשָּׁרְשֵׁי הַמִּצְוָה, לְפִי שֶׁרֹב חַטֹּאת בְּנֵי-אָדָם יֵעָשׂוּ בְּסִבַּת רִבּוּי הָאֲכִילָה
וְהַשְּׁתִיָּה, כְּמוֹ שֶׁכָּתוּב ״וַיִּשְׁמַן יְשֻׁרוּן וַיִּבְעָט״, וְכֵן ״שָׁמַנְתָּ עָבִיתָ כָּשִׂיתָ וַיִּטֹּשׁ
אֱלוֹהַּ עָשָׂהוּ״; וְכֵן אָמְרוּ זִכְרוֹנָם לִבְרָכָה: מִי גָרַם לָךְ שֶׁתִּבְעָטִי בִי, כַּרְשִׁינִין
שֶׁהֶאֱכַלְתִּיךְ, וְדֶרֶךְ כְּלָל אָמְרוּ: מְלֹא כְרֵסָא זָנֵי בִישָׁא, כְּלוֹמַר אַחַר מִלּוּי הַכֶּרֶס
יָבוֹא בֶן-אָדָם לַעֲשׂוֹת חֲטָאִים רָעִים.

וְהָעִנְיָן הוּא לְפִי שֶׁהַמְּזוֹנוֹת הֵם עִסַּת הַחֹמֶר, וְהַהִתְבּוֹנְנוּת בַּמֻּשְׂכָּל וּבְיִרְאַת
אֱלֹהִים וּבְמִצְווֹתָיו הַיְקָרוֹת הִיא עִסַּת הַנֶּפֶשׁ, וְהַנֶּפֶשׁ וְהַחֹמֶר הֲפָכִים גְּמוּרִים, כְּמוֹ
שֶׁכָּתַבְתִּי בְּרֹאשׁ הַסֵּפֶר; וְעַל-כֵּן בְּהִתְגַּבֵּר עִסַּת הַחֹמֶר תֶּחֱלַשׁ קְצָת עִסַּת הַנֶּפֶשׁ.
וּמִזֶּה הַשֹּׁרֶשׁ הָיוּ מִן הַחֲכָמִים זִכְרוֹנָם לִבְרָכָה שֶׁלֹּא הָיוּ נֶהֱנִין בִּמְזוֹנוֹת רַק לְמַה
שֶׁצָּרִיךְ לְהַחֲיוֹת נַפְשָׁם לְבַד, וּכְמוֹ שֶׁכָּתוּב: צַדִּיק אֹכֵל לְשֹׂבַע נַפְשׁוֹ.

וְעַל כֵּן תִּמְנָעֵנוּ תּוֹרָתֵנוּ הַשְּׁלֵמָה לְטוֹבָתֵנוּ מֵהַרְבּוֹת בַּאֲכִילָה וּשְׁתִיָּה יוֹתֵר
מִדַּי, פֶּן יִתְגַּבֵּר הַחֹמֶר עַל הַנֶּפֶשׁ הַרְבֵּה עַד שֶׁיַּחֲלִיאָהּ וִיאַבֵּד אוֹתָהּ לְגַמְרֵי, וְלָכֵן,
לְהַרְחִיק הָעִנְיָן עַד תַּכְלִית, הִזְהַרְנוּ עַל זֶה בְּעֹנֶשׁ חָזָק, וְהוּא עֹנֶשׁ הַמִּיתָה. זֶהוּ
הַנִּרְאֶה לִי בָּעִנְיָן.

וְהֻזְהַר הָאָדָם עַל זֶה בִּתְחִלַּת תֹּקֶף חֹם בַּחֲרוּתוֹ וּבְרֵאשִׁית בּוֹאוֹ בְחִיּוּב שְׁמִירַת

---

16. Three judges, who constitute the *beth din* (court) that sentences him to whiplashes.

17. Since he is then on trial for his life.

18. TB Sanhedrin 63a.

19. Derived from the plain sense of the verse, in view of Scripture's statement that the blood is the life of an animal (Deuteronomy 12:23).

20. Ordinarily, when someone dies, the first meal for the mourners after the burial should be prepared by others, as "the mourner's meal of consolation" (*se'udath havra'ah*); in such a case, though, since the dead person's blood was shed by sentence of the *beth din*, we learn from the verse that such a meal is not to be eaten "over his blood" (the Hebrew for the phrase "with the blood" in the verse means literally "over the blood").

21. They too are not to eat "over his blood" (see note 20).

22. The verse is understood to imply: Do not eat before you have prayed for your life (in keeping with Scripture's statement that the blood is a being's life — Leviticus 17:11, Deuteronomy 12:23); TB B'rachoth 10b.

23. I.e. the food that nourished and strengthened the base animal element; *ibid.* 32a.

They (of blessed memory) taught[18] that it contains an admonition about eating part of an animal before its life expires;[19] and so too about eating the flesh of holy offerings before the sprinkling of the blood; as they put it, "you shall not eat the flesh while the blood is yet in the bowl." They learned from it, as well, that the mourner's meal of consolation is not to be eaten over those put to death by sentence of the *beth din* (court);[20] and a *sanhedrin* (court of twenty-three) that sent someone to his death is not to taste any food that day.[21] Nor is any man to taste any food until he prays.[22] So is it also an admonition to a stubborn and rebellious son, as we stated.

At the root of the precept lies the reason that most sins of human beings are done because of overindulgence in food and drink—as it is written, *But Jeshurun grew fat and kicked out* (Deuteronomy 32:15); so too, *you grew fat, you grew thick, you became gross; and he forsook the God who made him* (ibid.); and so our Sages of blessed memory said: "Who caused you to kick out against Me?—the horse-beans I gave you to eat."[23] In general, they taught:[24] Full stomach, the commission of sin. In other words, after the belly is full, a person comes to do evil sins.

The reason is that food is the "dough" (nourishment) of the physical matter [of the body], while reflection on wise thought and on the fear of God and His precious precepts is the "dough" of the spirit; and the spirit and the material body are complete opposites, as I wrote at the beginning of the work. Therefore, as the "dough" (sustenance) of the physical body grows stronger, the nourishment of the spirit grows somewhat weaker. And for this root reason there were some Sages of blessed memory who would have no benefit of food beyond what was necessary just to keep their spirit alive— as it is written, *The righteous eats to the satisfaction of his spirit* (Proverbs 13:25).

Therefore the complete, perfect Torah would restrain us, for our good, from increasing our food and drink inordinately, for fear that the physical matter may prevail greatly over the spirit [in the body] until it sickens and destroys it entirely. Hence, to remove the matter [from us] to the ultimate degree, we were adjured about it [and threatened] with a strong punishment, i.e. the death penalty. This is how I perceive the matter.

Now, a man is adjured about this when the warmth of his youth begins in strength, at the start of his entry into the obligation of caring

נַפְשׁוֹ, וְהֵם שְׁלֹשָׁה חֲדָשִׁים הָרִאשׁוֹנִים מִשֶּׁהִתְחִיל לְהָבִיא שְׁתֵּי שְׂעָרוֹת עַד שֶׁיַּקִּיף כָּל הַגִּיד. וּמֵאוֹתוֹ הַזְּמַן יִקַּח מוּסָר לְכָל יָמָיו; כִּי מִהְיוֹת דְּבַר הַמָּזוֹן עִנְיָן תְּמִידִי בָּאָדָם, אִי־אֶפְשָׁר לוֹ זוּלָתוֹ, לֹא חִיְּבַתּוּ הַתּוֹרָה עָלָיו בְּכָל עֵת, רַק שְׁחֲרוֹ מוּסָר בִּזְמַן אֶחָד, לְהוֹעִיל לוֹ לְכָל הַזְּמַנִּים.

מִדִּינֵי הַמִּצְוָה, מַה שֶּׁאָמְרוּ זִכְרוֹנָם לִבְרָכָה שֶׁאֵין בֵּן סוֹרֵר וּמוֹרֶה חַיָּב עַד שֶׁיִּגְנֹב מִשֶּׁל אָבִיו וְיִקְנֶה בָּשָׂר וְיַיִן בְּזוֹל, וְיֹאכַל אוֹתָן חוּץ מֵרְשׁוּת אָבִיו בַּחֲבוּרָה שֶׁכֻּלָּם רֵיקָנִין וּפְחוּתִין, וְיֹאכַל הַבָּשָׂר חַי וְאֵינוּ חַי כְּדֶרֶךְ שֶׁהַגַּנָּבִים אוֹכְלִים, וְיִשְׁתֶּה הַיַּיִן מָזוּג וְאֵינוּ מָזוּג כְּדֶרֶךְ שֶׁהַגַּרְגְּרָנִים שׁוֹתִין; וְהוּא שֶׁיֹּאכַל מִשְׁקַל חֲמִשִּׁים דִּינָר מִבָּשָׂר זֶה בְּלֻגְמָא אַחַת וְיִשְׁתֶּה חֲצִי לֹג מִיַּיִן זֶה בְּבַת אֶחָת.

וּמַה שֶּׁאָמְרוּ שֶׁאִם אָכַל אֲכִילָה זוֹ הַמֻּכְלֶּרֶת מִבָּשָׂר אָסוּר, אוֹ בְּיוֹם שֶׁאָסוּר בַּאֲכִילָה, וַאֲפִלּוּ בְּתַעֲנִית דְּרַבָּנָן, שֶׁאֵינוֹ חַיָּב, שֶׁנֶּאֱמַר: אֵינֶנּוּ שֹׁמֵעַ בְּקֹלֵנוּ — מִי שֶׁאֵינוֹ עוֹבֵר בְּאוֹתָהּ אֲכִילָה אֶלָּא עַל קוֹלָם, יָצָא זֶה שֶׁעוֹבֵר בָּהּ אַף עַל דִּבְרֵי תוֹרָה.

וּמַה שֶּׁאָמְרוּ שֶׁאִם אָכַל כָּל מַאֲכָל וְלֹא אָכַל בָּשָׂר בְּהֵמָה, שָׁתָה כָּל מַשְׁקֶה וְלֹא שָׁתָה יַיִן, פָּטוּר; וְהַטַּעַם מִן הַשֹּׁרֶשׁ שֶׁכָּתַבְנוּ לְמַעְלָה, לְפִי שֶׁאֵין הַטֶּבַע נִמְשָׁךְ אַחַר שׁוּם דָּבָר כָּל־כָּךְ כְּמוֹ בְּאֵלּוּ.

וְעִנְיָן כֵּיצַד דָּנִין אוֹתוֹ, וְכֵיצַד מַתְרִין בּוֹ, וְכֵיצַד מַכְרִיזִין עָלָיו; וּמַה שֶּׁאָמְרוּ שֶׁאֵין נַעֲשֶׂה דִין סוֹרֵר וּמוֹרֶה אֶלָּא בְּשֶׁהָאָב וְהָאֵם שְׁנֵיהֶם רוֹצִים בְּכָךְ, שֶׁנֶּאֱמַר: וְתָפְשׂוּ בוֹ אָבִיו וְאִמּוֹ; וְאִם הָיָה אֶחָד מֵהֶם גִּדֵּם [אוֹ חִגֵּר] אוֹ אִלֵּם אוֹ סוּמָא אוֹ חֵרֵשׁ, אֵינוֹ נַעֲשֶׂה בֵּן סוֹרֵר וּמוֹרֶה: שֶׁנֶּאֱמַר "וְתָפְשׂוּ בוֹ" וְלֹא גִדְמִין, "וְהוֹצִיאוּ אוֹתוֹ" וְלֹא חִגְּרִין, "וְאָמְרוּ" וְלֹא אִלְּמִין, "בְּנֵנוּ זֶה" וְלֹא סוּמִין, "אֵינֶנּוּ שֹׁמֵעַ

---

24. *Ibid.*

25. TB Sanhedrin 70a.

26. Literally, raw yet not raw.

27. Literally, mixed yet not mixed. In Talmudic times wine was made strong and had to be mixed with a certain proportion of water to be fit to drink. A guzzler, in his eager haste, would not bother adding sufficient water.

28. And it is a transgression of Torah law to disobey even a ruling of the Sages. This and the previous paragraph are based on MT *hilchoth mamrim* vii 2.

29. TB Sanhedrin 71a; MT *ibid.* 7.

30. TB *ibid.*

31. TB *ibid.* 89a; MT *ibid.* 13.

32. TB Sanhedrin 71a.

33. I.e. they should be able to take hold of him normally, with both hands.

34. I.e. going normally, on two feet.

for his spirit, this being the first three months from the time he begins to produce two [pubic] hairs, until the entire membrum is encircled [by hair]. And from that period he will learn his moral lesson for all his days. For as the matter of food is something constant with a person, as he cannot do without it, the Torah would not punish him for this at every time, but would only "chasten him early" (Proverbs 13:24) at one period [of his life] so that it should benefit him at all times.

Among the laws of the precept there is what the Sages of blessed memory taught:[25] that a stubborn and rebellious son incurs no punishment until he steals from his father and buys meat and wine cheaply, and consumes them outside his father's premises in the company of those who are all empty louts and inferior lowly types, eating the meat partly cooked,[26] in the way that thieves eat it, and drinking the wine partly mixed,[27] as guzzlers drink it—and this [only] if he eats fifty *dinars'* weight of this meat in one mouthful, and drinks half a *log* of this wine at once.

Then there is what the Sages said:[25] that if he ate in this repugnant way of forbidden meat, or on a day when eating is forbidden, even on a day of fasting by the ruling of the Sages, he does not incur guilt: because it is stated [that the parents are to report] *he does not hearken to our voice* (Deuteronomy 21:20), [meaning] one who disobeys by that eating nothing more than their voice—which excludes one who thereby transgresses the words of the Torah.[28]

There is, further, what the Sages said,[25] that if he ate any food at all but not animal flesh, or if he drank any beverage at all but not wine, he is free of guilt. This is for the root reason we wrote above: because the [body's] nature is not drawn after anything else as much as after these.

Then there is the matter of how he is judged,[29] how he is warned,[30] and how proclamation is made about him.[31] And there is, too, what the Sages said:[32] that the law of the stubborn and rebellious son is not carried out unless both the father and the mother wish it: for it is stated, *then his father and his mother shall take hold of him* (Deuteronomy 21:19). If one of them was one-handed, [lame] mute, blind, or deaf, he does not become [judged as] a stubborn and rebellious son: for it is stated that they "shall take hold of him," [meaning] not one-handed people;[33] *and they shall take him out* (ibid.)[34] —not the lame; *and they shall say* (ibid. 20)—not the mute; *This*

⟨119⟩

בְּקֹלֵנוּ" וְלֹא חֵרְשִׁין.

וּמִפְּנֵי כָל עִנְיָנִים אֵלֶּה הַצְּרִיכִים בּוֹ, הָיוּ מִן הַחֲכָמִים שֶׁאָמְרוּ (בַּגְּמָרָא) כִּי מֵעוֹלָם לֹא נַעֲשָׂה דִין סוֹרֵר וּמוֹרֶה; וְיֵשׁ מֵהֶם מִי שֶׁהֵעִיד שֶׁרָאָה אוֹתוֹ וְגַם יָשַׁב עַל קִבְרוֹ.

וּמַה שֶּׁאָמְרוּ כִּי בִתְחִלָּה מַלְקִין אוֹתוֹ, שֶׁנֶּאֱמַר "וְיִסְּרוּ אֹתוֹ", וּפֵרְשׁוּ זִכְרוֹנָם לִבְרָכָה: וְיִסְּרוּ אוֹתוֹ, זֶה מַלְקוּת; וְיֵתֶר פְּרָטֶיהָ, בְּפֶרֶק ח' מִסַּנְהֶדְרִין.

וְנוֹהֶגֶת בְּאֶרֶץ יִשְׂרָאֵל בִּלְבַד, שֶׁאֵין דָּנִין דִּינֵי נְפָשׁוֹת אֶלָּא שָׁם, וּבְבֵית־דִּין שֶׁל עֶשְׂרִים וּשְׁלֹשָׁה לְכָל הַפָּחוֹת. וְאֵין דִּין זֶה נוֹהֵג אֶלָּא בַזְּכָרִים, אֲבָל לֹא בַנְּקֵבוֹת, שֶׁאֵין דַּרְכָּן לְהַמְשֵׁךְ בַּאֲכִילָה וּשְׁתִיָּה כְּמוֹ הָאֲנָשִׁים, וְזֶהוּ שֶׁנֶּאֱמַר "בֵּן סוֹרֵר (וּמוֹרֶה)" וְלֹא בַת; וְלֹא טוּמְטוּם וְאַנְדְּרוֹגִינוֹס, וַאֲפִלּוּ טוּמְטוּם שֶׁנִּקְרַע וְנִמְצָא זָכָר אֵינוֹ נַעֲשֶׂה בֵן סוֹרֵר, שֶׁנֶּאֱמַר "כִּי יִהְיֶה לְאִישׁ בֵּן סוֹרֵר", עַד שֶׁיִּהְיֶה בֶן מִשְׁעַת הֲוָיָה.

וְעוֹבֵר עַל זֶה וְנַעֲשָׂה בֵן סוֹרֵר וּמוֹרֶה עַל־פִּי כָל הַדְּבָרִים שֶׁכָּתַבְנוּ, נִסְקָל, וַהֲרֵי הוּא כְּכָל הֲרוּגֵי בֵית־דִּין, שֶׁמָּמוֹנָם לְיוֹרְשֵׁיהֶם, שֶׁאַף־עַל־פִּי שֶׁאָבִיו גָּרַם לוֹ סְקִילָה, הֲרֵי הוּא יוֹרֵשׁ כָּל נְכָסָיו.

[שֶׁלֹּא לְנַחֵשׁ]

רמט שֶׁלֹּא נֵלֵךְ אַחֲרֵי נָחָשִׁים, שֶׁנֶּאֱמַר: לֹא תְנַחֲשׁוּ; וְנִכְפַּל בְּמָקוֹם אַחֵר, שֶׁנֶּאֱמַר: לֹא יִמָּצֵא בְךָ וְגוֹמֵר וּמְנַחֵשׁ. וְאָמְרוּ בְסִפְרֵי: מְנַחֵשׁ, כְּגוֹן הָאוֹמֵר "נָפְלָה פִתִּי מִפִּי, נָפְלָה מַקֵּל מִיָּדִי, עָבַר נָחָשׁ מִימִינִי וְשׁוּעָל מִשְּׂמֹאלִי", וְיִמָּנַע מִפְּנֵי־כֵן מֵעֲשׂוֹת שׁוּם מַעֲשֶׂה.

וּבְסִפְרָא אָמְרוּ: "לֹא תְנַחֲשׁוּ", כְּגוֹן אֵלּוּ הַמְנַחֲשִׁים בְּחֻלְדָּה וּבְעוֹפוֹת

---

35. Because the phrase implies that they can see him and point to him.

36. Because the deaf could not hear if they spoke to him properly, thus to know if he did not heed them.

37. I.e. a "stubborn and rebellious son" who was tried and put to death.

38. I.e. the first time he does the repugnant deed.

39. This is a general statement, whose more specific meaning is given in §491; see also §47, note 7.

40. TB Sanhedrin 68b.

41. MT hilchoth mamrim vii 11.

42. MT ibid.

43. Literally, torn — i.e. the membrane covering the organs of generation (which is what makes the tumtum's gender uncertain).

44. TB Bava Bathra 126b; MT ibid. 12.

45. TB Sanhedrin 48b; MT ibid. 14.

our son (ibid.)—not the blind;[35] *he does not hearken to our voice (ibid.)*— not the deaf.[36]

Now, because of all these conditions that are required for it, there were some Sages who said in the Talmud[32] that the sentence of a stubborn and rebellious son was never carried out. Yet there was one of them who attested that he had seen one[37] and had sat on his grave.

Then there is what the Sages said,[32] that at first[38] he is given whiplashes; for it is written, *and they shall chastise him (ibid.* 18), and they (of blessed memory) explained: "and they shall chastise him"— this denotes whiplashes. [These] and its further details are in chapter 8 of the Talmud tractate *Sanhedrin.*

It is in force in the land of Israel alone, as capital cases are judged nowhere but there[39]—and this in a *beth din* of at least twenty-three [judges]. Moreover, this law applies only to males, but not to females,[40] as it is not their way to be drawn to food and drink like men;[41] this is why it is "a stubborn and rebellious *son*," not a daughter, a *tumtum* [one of uncertain gender] or a hermaphrodite.[42] Even if a *tumtum* was examined surgically[43] and found to be male, he cannot become a "stubborn and rebellious son," because it is stated, *If a man has a stubborn and rebellious son* (Deuteronomy 21:18)—he must be a son [for certain] from the time he existed.[44]

If someone transgressed it and became a "stubborn and rebellious son" in accordance with all the things [conditions] we wrote, he should be stoned to death. Then he is like all those put to death by order of the *beth din,* whose property goes to their heirs. Thus, although his father caused him to be stoned to death, he would inherit all his property.[45]

249 [THE PROHIBITION AGAINST PRACTICING AUGURY] that we should not heed omens: for it is stated, *you shall not practice augury* (Leviticus 19:26); and this was repeated elsewhere, as it is stated, *There shall not be found among you . . . one that uses augury* (Deuteronomy 18:10). It was taught in the Midrash *Sifre:* "one that uses augury"—for instance, if a person says, "My bread fell from my mouth"; "a stick fell from my hand"; "a snake passed at my right, and a fox at my left"—and he will hold back on account of this from carrying out some action.

In the Midrash *Sifra*[1] it was taught: "you shall not practice augury"—like, for example, those who practice foretokening with a

וּבְכוֹכָבִים וְכַיּוֹצֵא בָהֶן, עַד כָּאן. וְכֵן כְּגוֹן מַה שֶׁאָמְרוּ הַמּוֹנֵי הָעַמִּים הַסְּכָלִים, "כֵּיוָן שֶׁשָּׁבַתִּי מִדַּרְכִּי שֶׁהָיִיתִי הוֹלֵךְ", אוֹ צָבִי הִפְסִיקוֹ, אוֹ עוֹרֵב צוֹעֵק עוֹבֵר עַל רֹאשׁוֹ, אוֹ "כֵּיוָן שֶׁרָאִיתִי דָּבָר פְּלוֹנִי בִּתְחִלַּת הַיּוֹם לֹא אַרְוִיחַ הַיּוֹם", אוֹ שׁוּם מִקְרֶה רַע יְבוֹאֵהוּ; וְכָל הַמַּעֲשִׂים הָאֵלּוּ וְכַיּוֹצֵא בָהֶן הֵם בִּכְלַל לָאו זֶה.

מִשָּׁרְשֵׁי הַמִּצְוָה, לְפִי שֶׁעִנְיָנִים אֵלֶּה הֵם דִּבְרֵי שִׁגָּעוֹן וְסִכְלוּת גְּמוּרָה, וּלְעַם קָדוֹשׁ אֲמִתִּי אֲשֶׁר בָּחַר הָאֵל לֹא יֵאוֹת לָהֶם שֶׁיִּשְׁעוּ בְּדִבְרֵי שֶׁקֶר; וְעוֹד שֶׁהֵם סִבָּה לְהַדִּיחַ הָאָדָם מֵאֱמוּנַת הַשֵּׁם וּמִתּוֹרָתוֹ הַקְּדוֹשָׁה, וְלָבוֹא מִתּוֹכָם לִכְפִירָה גְּמוּרָה, שֶׁיַּחְשֹׁב כָּל טוֹבָתוֹ וְרָעָתוֹ מִכָּל אֲשֶׁר יִקְרֵהוּ שֶׁהוּא דָּבָר מִקְרִי, לֹא בְּהַשְׁגָּחָה מֵאֵת בּוֹרְאוֹ, וְנִמְצָא יוֹצֵא בְּכָךְ מִכָּל עִקְּרֵי הַדָּת. עַל־כֵּן, כִּי חָפֵץ הַשֵּׁם בְּטוֹבָתֵנוּ, צִוָּנוּ לְהָסִיר מִלִּבֵּנוּ מַחֲשָׁבָה זוֹ וְלִקְבֹּעַ בְּלִבֵּנוּ כִּי כָל הָרָעוֹת וְהַטּוֹב מִפִּי עֶלְיוֹן תֵּצֶאנָה לְפִי מַעֲשֵׂה הָאָדָם, אִם טוֹב וְאִם רָע, וְהַנְּחָשִׁים לֹא מַעֲלִין וְלֹא מוֹרִידִין, וּכְמוֹ שֶׁכָּתוּב: כִּי לֹא נַחַשׁ בְּיַעֲקֹב וְלֹא קֶסֶם בְּיִשְׂרָאֵל.

פְּרָטֵי הַמִּצְוָה בְּפֶרֶק שְׁבִיעִי מִשַּׁבָּת וּבְתוֹסֶפְתָּא דְּשַׁבָּת.

וְנוֹהֶגֶת בְּכָל מָקוֹם וּבְכָל זְמַן, בִּזְכָרִים וּנְקֵבוֹת. וְעוֹבֵר עָלֶיהָ וְעָשָׂה שׁוּם מַעֲשֶׂה עַל־פִּי הַנַּחַשׁ בְּעֵדִים וְהַתְרָאָה, לוֹקֶה, וְדַוְקָא בְּבֵית־דִּין (שֶׁל עֶשְׂרִים וּ)שְׁלֹשָׁה, וְכֵן בְּכָל מָקוֹם שֶׁבְּכָתַבְנוּ בְּמַה שֶׁקָּדַם. וּבְמַה שֶׁנִּכְתַּב "לוֹקֶה", הַכַּוָּנָה הִיא בָּאָרֶץ הַקְּדוֹשָׁה, שֶׁהִיא מְקוֹם הַמִּשְׁפָּט שֶׁל עֶשְׂרִים וּשְׁלֹשָׁה, שֶׁאֵין דָּנִין דִּינֵי נְפָשׁוֹת בְּחוּצָה לָאָרֶץ אֶלָּא בְּמָסוֹר לְבַד, לְפִי שֶׁמִּיתָתוֹ הַצָּלָה וּתְחִיָּה לַאֲחֵרִים טוֹבִים מִמֶּנּוּ.

[שֶׁלֹּא לְעוֹנֵן]

רן שֶׁלֹּא לְעוֹנֵן, שֶׁנֶּאֱמַר: וְלֹא תְעוֹנֵנוּ. וּפֵרוּשׁ הָעִנְיָן כְּמוֹ שֶׁאָמְרוּ בְּסִפְרָא,

§249   1. Sifra, k'doshim, perek 6, 2.

2. Expression based on Exodus 5:9.

3. Literally, do not raise and do not lower.

4. The Hebrew has twenty-three; but our author's words in §594 make it clear that this can only be a scribal error. In the oldest manuscripts it is written not as עשרים ושלשה but as כ"ג (using Hebrew letters as numbers); hence the postulated error need have been only the addition of one letter, not a word; and it was quite possibly added under the influence of the next sentence (where twenty-three is quite correct).

5. I.e that a punishment of whiplashes should be given.

6. I.e. to decide whether a person deserves death. Our author evidently bases himself here on the teaching of Rava in TB Sanhedrin 10a that whiplashes are a substitute penalty for death; hence he states that they can be given only under the conditions where a death sentence can be carried out. See MY here, and also §47, note 7, and below, §491.

mole or fowl, or by the stars, and similar things. Thus far the Midrash. So too, there is, for example, what the foolish masses of people say: "Since I have turned back from my way that I was taking," or "a deer crossed it," or "a shrieking crow is passing over my head," or "since I saw that certain thing at the beginning of the day—I will make no profit today," or some evil occurrence will befall him. All these activities and their like are included under this injunction.

At the root of the precept lies the reason that these things are matters of utter lunacy and folly, and for the truly holy people that God chose, it is not fitting that they should pay regard to lying words.[2] Moreover, they are a factor that thrusts a man away from faith in the Eternal Lord and from His sacred Torah, to set him going from their midst to complete heresy: For he will reckon that all his good and bad fortune, all that happens to him, is a matter of chance occurrence, not by watchful care on the part of his Creator. In consequence, he will thus abandon all the principles of the religion. Therefore, since the Eternal Lord desires our good, He commanded us to remove this thought from our heart, and to set firmly in our heart that all evil and good issue by the word of the One on high, according to a man's deeds, be they good or bad. And omens neither help nor hinder[3]—as it is written, *For there is no augury with Jacob, nor divination with Israel* (Numbers 23:23).

The details of the precept are in chapter 7 of the Talmud tractate *Shabbath*, and in the Tosefta of the tractate. It applies everywhere, at every time, for both man and woman. If a person violates it and does any action according to omens, with witnesses [present, who give him due] warning, he is given whiplashes—but this specifically through a *beth din* of three [judges];[4] and so in every instance that we have written previously.[5] And when we write that whiplashes are given, the meaning is in the holy land, as that is the place for a trial by twenty-three [justices].[6] For capital cases are not tried in other countries, except for an informer alone (§236), because his death [means] rescue and survival for others who are better than he is.

[THE PROHIBITION AGAINST THE PRACTICE OF CONJUR-
ING]

250 not to conjure: as it is stated, *nor shall you conjure* (Leviticus 19:26). The explanation of this subject is as it was given in the Midrash *Sifra*,[1] that [the Hebrew verb, th'onénu, connotes] the sense of 'onah,

שֶׁהוּא לְשׁוֹן עוֹנָה, כְּלוֹמַר שֶׁלֹּא נִקְבַּע עוֹנוֹת לוֹמַר: שָׁעָה פְּלוֹנִית טוֹבָה לַעֲשׂוֹת
בָּהּ מַעֲשֶׂה פְּלוֹנִי, וְיַצְלִיחַ כָּל הָעוֹשֶׂה אוֹתוֹ בְּאוֹתָהּ שָׁעָה, וְהָעוֹשֶׂה אוֹתוֹ בְּשָׁעָה
פְּלוֹנִית לֹא יַצְלִיחַ — כְּמוֹ שֶׁיֹּאמְרוּ הַמַּהְבִּילִים בַּעֲלֵי הַכִּשּׁוּף. וְנִכְפַּל הַלָּאו בְּזֶה
הָעִנְיָן בְּסֵדֶר שׁוֹפְטִים, דִּכְתִיב שָׁם: לֹא יִמָּצֵא בְךָ וְגוֹמֵר מְעוֹנֵן.

וּבִכְלַל לָאו זֶה דִּמְעוֹנֵן אָמְרוּ זִכְרוֹנָם לִבְרָכָה שֶׁהוּא מַעֲשֶׂה אֲחִיזַת עֵינַיִם
שֶׁיַּעֲשׂוּ בְּנֵי־אָדָם, וּכְמוֹ שֶׁאָמְרוּ זִכְרוֹנָם לִבְרָכָה: מְעוֹנֵן, זֶה הָאוֹחֵז אֶת הָעֵינַיִם.
וְעִנְיָן זֶה הוּא מִין גָּדוֹל מֵהַתַּחְבּוּלָה יֶחָבַּר אֵלֶיהָ קַלּוּת הַיָּד וּגְבוּרַת מְהִירוּתָהּ עַד
שֶׁיִּדְמֶה לִבְנֵי־אָדָם הַמִּתְחַבֵּל עִנְיָנִים שֶׁל פֶּלֶא, כְּלוֹמַר דְּבָרִים שֶׁהֵם חוּץ
מִן הַטֶּבַע, כְּמוֹ שֶׁיַּעֲשׂוּ תָמִיד הַמִּשְׁתַּדְּלִים בָּזֶה, שֶׁיִּקְחוּ חֶבֶל וְיָשִׂימוּ אוֹתוֹ בִּכְנַף
בִּגְדָם לְעֵינֵי אֲנָשִׁים, וְאַחַר־כֵּן יוֹצִיאוּהוּ נָחָשׁ; וְכֵן יַשְׁלִיכוּ טַבַּעַת בָּאֲוִיר וְאַחַר־
כֵּן יוֹצִיאוּהוּ מִפִּי אֶחָד מֵהָעוֹמְדִים לִפְנֵיהֶם; וְכַיּוֹצֵא בְעִנְיָנִים אֵלּוּ רַבִּים.

וְכָל אֶחָד מֵהַמַּעֲשִׂים הָרָעִים אֵלּוּ הוּא אָסוּר, וְהָעוֹשׂוֹ נִקְרָא אוֹחֵז הָעֵינַיִם,
וְהוּא בִּכְלַל לָאו דִּמְעוֹנֵן, וְלוֹקִין עָלָיו. וְאַף־עַל־פִּי שֶׁנֶּאֱמַר מְעוֹנֵן אֵצֶל מְכַשֵּׁף
בְּכָתוּב אֶחָד, אֵינוֹ מִין כִּשּׁוּף מַמָּשׁ, שֶׁאִלּוּ הָיָה בּוֹ מִשּׁוּם לָאו דִּמְכַשֵּׁף,
לֹא הָיִינוּ מַלְקִין עָלָיו, מִשּׁוּם דְּלָאו דִּמְכַשֵּׁף נִתַּן לְאַזְהָרַת מִיתַת בֵּית־דִּין,
שֶׁנֶּאֱמַר: מְכַשֵּׁפָה לֹא תְחַיֶּה, וְקַיְמָא לָן כָּל דְּלָאו שֶׁנִּתַּן לְאַזְהָרַת מִיתַת בֵּית־דִּין
אֵין לוֹקִין עָלָיו.

מִשָּׁרְשֵׁי הַמִּצְוָה, מַה שֶּׁכָּתַבְנוּ בְּלָאו דִּמְנַחֵשׁ, סָמוּךְ. וְעוֹד הֶפְסֵד גָּדוֹל מְאֹד
נִמְצָא בָזֶה, לְפִי שֶׁיָּשׁוּבוּ אֵצֶל הֶהָמוֹן וְהַנָּשִׁים וְהַנְּעָרִים הָעִנְיָנִים הַנִּמְנָעִים
בְּתַכְלִית הַמְּנִיעָה אֶפְשָׁרִיִּים, וְיֶעֱרַב לְדַעְתָּם לְקַבֵּל הַנִּמְנָע הֱיוֹתוֹ אֶפְשָׁר מִבִּלְתִּי
הֱיוֹת הָעִנְיָן נֵס מֵאֵת הַבּוֹרֵא, וְאוּלַי יֵצֵא לָהֶם מִזֶּה סִבָּה רָעָה לִכְפֹּר בָּעִקָּר וְהִכָּרֵת
נַפְשָׁם; וְהָבֵן זֶה.

פְּרָטֵי הַמִּצְוָה שָׁם בְּסִפְרָא וּבִמְקוֹמוֹת בַּגְּמָרָא וּבַמִּדְרָשׁוֹת.

§250   1. R. 'Akiva's teaching in Sifra, *k'doshim, perek* 6, 2. (The verb "conjure" is used for *'onén* for lack of anything better. While for the basic meaning that follows, "practice soothsaying" of JPS 1917 might be somewhat better, and S. R. Hirsch's "observe times" is exact, the term must also cover the meaning in the next paragraph: the creation of optical illusions.

2. Literally, one who seizes the eyes; TB Sanhedrin 65b and Sifra *ibid.*

3. From the beginning to here is based on ShM negative precept §32.

4. TB 'Eruvin 17b.

5. This paragraph is likewise based on ShM *ibid.*

a proper time—i.e. that we should not determine set times, to say that this hour is good for doing that activity in it, and whoever does it at that time will succeed, whereas whoever does it at this other time will not succeed—as the deluding masters of sorcery say. The injunction was repeated about this subject in *sidrah shof'tim*, for it is written there, *There shall not be found among you . . . a conjurer* (Deuteronomy 18:10).

Now, within the scope of this injunction against a conjurer, our Sages of blessed memory said that it refers to any act of optical illusion that people may do; as they (of blessed memory) said: "a conjurer" is one who creates an optical illusion.[2] This matter is a widespread kind of trickery which combines a lightness (deftness) of the hand and an intensification of its speed, until it appears to people that the trickster is doing matters of wonder, i.e. things that are beyond nature— as those who strive at this always do: They take a cord and put it inside their clothing before people's eyes, and afterward they take it out as a snake. So too, they throw a ring into the air, and afterward take it out of the mouth of one of those standing before them; and so are there many matters like these.

Well, every one of these wicked deeds is forbidden. A person who does any is called a prestidigitator, and he is included under the scope of this injunction, for whose transgression a whipping of lashes is given.[3] And although a conjurer is named near a sorcerer in one verse (Deuteronomy 18:10), this is not actually a kind of sorcery. For if its prohibition were on account of the injunction against a sorcerer, we would not give whiplashes for it: because the injunction against a sorcerer is capable of involving a warning of death by sentence of the *beth din*, since it is written, *You shall not permit a sorceress to live* (Exodus 22:17); and we have a standing rule[4] that over any injunction that can entail a warning of a death sentence, no lashes are given.

At the root of the precept lies the reason that we wrote about the adjacent injunction against one who practices augury (§249). And another very great damage lies in this: because among the masses and the women and young lads, matters which are impossible to the utmost degree will be taken to be possible, and it will delight their minds to accept the impossible, that it can be, without the matter being a miracle from the Creator; and perhaps the result of this for them will be an evil reason to deny the main truth [of His existence] and thus have their souls cut off [from eternal life]. Understand this.[5]

The details of the precept are there in the Midrash *Sifra*, and in

וְנוֹהֶגֶת אִסּוּרָהּ בְּכָל מָקוֹם וּבְכָל זְמַן, בַּזְּכָרִים וּבַנְּקֵבוֹת. וְעוֹבֵר עָלֶיהָ וּמַגִּיד
לִבְנֵי־אָדָם עֲוֹנוֹת שֶׁיַּעֲשׂוּ מַעֲשֵׂיהֶם בָּהֶן כְּדֵי שֶׁיַּצְלִיחוּ, וְגַם הוּא עוֹשֶׂה מַעֲשָׂיו
לְפִי הָעֲוֹנוֹת, חַיָּב מַלְקוֹת; וְהָאִישׁ הַשּׁוֹאֵל אֶל הַיּוֹדֵעַ אֵין עָלָיו חִיּוּב מַלְקוֹת
בִּשְׁאֵלָה לְבַד, עַד שֶׁיְּכַוֵּן פְּעֻלָּתוֹ אֶל הָעֵת הַיְּדוּעָה וְיַעֲשֶׂה מְלַאכְתּוֹ בָהּ, וְאָז יִלְקֶה
בַּעֲבוּרוֹ, מִכֵּיוָן שֶׁעָשָׂה מַעֲשֶׂה.

[שֶׁלֹּא לְהַקִּיף פַּאֲתֵי הָרֹאשׁ]

רנא שֶׁלֹּא לְהַקִּיף פַּאֲתֵי הָרֹאשׁ, שֶׁנֶּאֱמַר: לֹא תַקִּפוּ פְּאַת רֹאשְׁכֶם; וּפֵרְשׁוּ
זִכְרוֹנָם לִבְרָכָה שֶׁהָעִנְיָן הוּא שֶׁאָסוּר לְיִשְׂרָאֵל לְגַלֵּחַ וּלְהַשְׁווֹת שַׂעֲרוֹת רֹאשׁוֹ
לְאָחוֹר אָזְנָיו וּלְפַדַּחְתּוֹ, כְּמוֹ שֶׁעוֹשִׂים גַּם הַיּוֹם עוֹבְדֵי עֲבוֹדָה זָרָה וְכוֹמָרֵיהֶם;
וְזֶהוּ שֶׁאָמְרוּ זִכְרוֹנָם לִבְרָכָה בְּמַסֶּכֶת מַכּוֹת: אֵיזֶהוּ פְּאַת הָרֹאשׁ, זֶה הַמַּשְׁוֶה
צְדָעָיו לַאֲחוֹרֵי אָזְנָיו וּלְפַדַּחְתּוֹ.

מִשָּׁרְשֵׁי הַמִּצְוָה, כְּדֵי לְהַרְחִיק מִמֶּנּוּ וּלְהַשְׁכִּיחַ מִבֵּין עֵינֵינוּ וּמִכָּל מַעֲשֵׂינוּ כָּל
עִנְיַן עֲבוֹדָה זָרָה וְכָל הַנַּעֲשֶׂה בִּשְׁבִילָהּ; וּבָאָה הָאַזְהָרָה מְפֹרֶשֶׁת בְּדָבָר שֶׁיַּעֲשׂוּ לָהּ
בְּנֵי־אָדָם בְּגוּפוֹתָם, מִפְּנֵי שֶׁהִיא לְמַזְכֶּרֶת עָוֹן תָּמִיד, אַחַר שֶׁהִיא דָבָר קָבוּעַ
בַּגּוּף. וּמִפְּנֵי שֶׁזֶּה מֵעִקְּרֵי טַעַם הַמִּצְוָה, הָיוּ צְרִיכִין זִכְרוֹנָם לִבְרָכָה שֶׁיְּבָאֲרוּ כִּי
הַקָּפַת כָּל הָרֹאשׁ גַּם־כֵּן בִּכְלַל הַלָּאו, שֶׁלֹּא תֹאמַר מַה שֶׁנֶּאֱסַר כְּדֵי
שֶׁלֹּא נִדְמֶה לָהֶם, וְהֵם לֹא יְגַלְּחוּ כָּל הָרֹאשׁ כֻּלּוֹ, לִמְּדוּנוּ שֶׁגַּם זֶה בִּכְלַל הָאָסוּר
הוּא, כְּמוֹ שֶׁבָּא בִּיבָמוֹת, שֶׁאָמְרוּ שָׁם: הַקָּפַת כָּל הָרֹאשׁ שְׁמָהּ הַקָּפָה; וְאֶפְשָׁר כִּי
הַתּוֹרָה אָסְרָה הַכֹּל מִשּׁוּם דּוֹמֶה לְדוֹמֶה.

מִדִּינֵי הַמִּצְוָה, מַה שֶׁאָמְרוּ זִכְרוֹנָם לִבְרָכָה בְּמַכּוֹת, שֶׁאֶחָד הַמְגַלֵּחַ וְאֶחָד

1. Our author perhaps alludes here to the tonsure of certain medieval monks and friars. In at least one old manuscript the passage was inked out by a censor.
2. I.e. it is a way of showing and being reminded of loyalty to idolatry. Cf. *Guide* III 37.
3. I.e. shaving the head above the level of the forehead, or even entirely.
4. I.e. because shaving the entire head is not unlike shaving the temples to leave a tonsure. (The last three sentences are based on ShM negative precept §43).

various places in the Talmud and Midrashim. Its prohibition is in force in every place and every time, for both man and woman. If someone transgresses it and tells people special times when they should carry out their activities so that they should succeed, and he does his actions too according to those times, he is punishable by a whipping of lashes. However, a man who enquires of one who is "knowledgeable" [in such matters] does not incur a penalty of lashes merely for asking—not until he arranges his activity for that certain time and does his work in it; then he should be whipped on account of it, since he did a deed [acted on it].

[THE PROHIBITION AGAINST ROUNDING OFF THE TEMPLES OF THE HEAD]

251 not to round off the corners of the head, as it is stated, *You shall not round off the corners of your heads* (Leviticus 19:27); and our Sages of blessed memory explained that the meaning is that it is forbidden an Israelite (Jew) to shave and even off the hair of his head level with the area behind his ears and with his forehead, as idol-worshippers and their priests do even this day.[1] In this sense our Sages of blessed memory said in the Talmud tractate *Makkoth* (20b): What does "the corner of the head" mean? It signifies a person who evens off his temples level with the area behind his ears and with his forehead.

At the root of the precept lies the purpose to remove far from us, take away from [the mind] between our eyes and from all our deeds and cast into oblivion, every matter of idol-worship and everything that is done for its sake. The admonition was given explicitly about this matter that people do to their physical selves as it constantly *brings iniquity to remembrance*[2] (Ezekiel 21:28), since it is something set in the human body. And because this is a main core of the reason for the precept, it was necessary for the Sages of blessed memory to explain that rounding off the entire head[3] is also included under the prohibition. In order that you should not say that the end-purpose of the prohibition is that we should not resemble them, and they do not shave the entire head, they taught us that this too is included under the prohibition— as we find that they said this, in the Talmud tractate *Yevamoth* (5a): The rounding (shaving) of the entire head is called (considered) "rounding off." It is possible that the Torah thus forbade [shaving] it all because this "resembles the resemblance."[4]

Among the laws of the precept, there is what the Sages of blessed

הַמִּתְגַּלֵּחַ כָּל זְמַן שֶׁסִּיֵּעַ, שְׁנֵיהֶם חַיָּבִים; אֲבָל לֹא סִיֵּעַ, אֵין חַיָּב אֶלָּא הַמְּגַלֵּחַ;
וְהַמְּגַלֵּחַ אֶת הַקָּטָן, חַיָּב. וּבְשִׁעוּר פְּאַת הָרֹאשׁ לֹא נָתְנוּ חֲכָמִים שִׁעוּר. וְכָתַב
הָרַמְבַּ"ם זִכְרוֹנוֹ לִבְרָכָה: שָׁמַעְנוּ מִזְּקֵנֵינוּ שֶׁאֵין מַנִּיחִין פָּחוֹת מֵאַרְבָּעִים שְׂעָרוֹת,
זֶהוּ לְשׁוֹנוֹ. וּמֻתָּר לְגַלֵּחַ הַפֵּאָה בְּמִסְפָּרַיִם, שֶׁלֹּא אָסְרָה הַתּוֹרָה אֶלָּא הַשְׁחָתָה שֶׁל
תַּעַר (אוֹ מַשְׁוֶה צְדָעָיו לַאֲחוֹרֵי אָזְנָיו; וְשָׁמַעְתִּי דְּבִפְאַת הָרֹאשׁ אַף בְּמִסְפָּרַיִם
כְּעֵין תַּעַר, אָסוּר). וְיֶתֶר פְּרָטֶיהָ, בְּסוֹף מַכּוֹת.

וְנוֹהֶגֶת בְּכָל מָקוֹם וּבְכָל זְמַן, בִּזְכָרִים, אֲבָל לֹא בִנְקֵבוֹת — בֵּין גִּלְּחוּ בֵּין
נִתְגַּלְּחוּ פְּטוּרוֹת; וּכְמוֹ שֶׁדָּרְשׁוּ זִכְרוֹנָם לִבְרָכָה: "לֹא תַקִּפוּ פְּאַת רֹאשְׁכֶם וְלֹא
תַשְׁחִית אֵת פְּאַת זְקָנֶךָ", כָּל שֶׁיֶּשְׁנוֹ בְּבַל תַּשְׁחִית וְגוֹמֵר. וּמִכָּל־מָקוֹם אָסוּר לָהֶן
לְגַלֵּחַ הַזָּכָר, וַאֲפִלּוּ קָטָן. וְהָעֲבָדִים, אַף־עַל־פִּי שֶׁהֵם בִּגְדֶר הַנָּשִׁים בְּהַרְבֵּה
מִצְווֹת, בְּזוֹ חַיָּבִים הֵם בָּהּ, הוֹאִיל וְיֵשׁ לָהֶם זָקָן. וְטוּמְטוּם וְאַנְדְּרוֹגִינוֹס הֲרֵי הֵם
סָפֵק, וְנוֹתְנִין עֲלֵיהֶם חֻמְרֵי זָכָר וּנְקֵבָה בְּזוֹ וּבְכָל מָקוֹם, וְחַיָּבִין בַּכֹּל; אֲבָל אִם
עָבְרוּ, אֵינָם לוֹקִין מִסָּפֵק.

וּבְגִדְרַת עִנְיָן זֶה אֶכְתֹּב הַכְּלָל שֶׁלִּמְּדוּנוּ זִכְרוֹנָם לִבְרָכָה בְּמִצְווֹת הַנָּשִׁים, אַף־
עַל־פִּי שֶׁדַּרְכִּי לְכָתְבוֹ בִּפְרָט בְּכָל מִצְוָה וּמִצְוָה, כִּי מִתּוֹךְ הַכְּלָל וְהַפְּרָט יִזְכְּרֵהוּ
הַקּוֹרֵא; וְזֶהוּ: כָּל מִצְוַת לֹא־תַעֲשֶׂה שֶׁבַּתּוֹרָה, אֶחָד אֲנָשִׁים וְאֶחָד נָשִׁים חַיָּבִין,
חוּץ מִבַּל תַּקִּיף וּבַל תַּשְׁחִית וּבַל תִּטַּמָּא לְמֵתִים; וְכָל מִצְוַת עֲשֵׂה שֶׁהַזְּמַן גְּרָמָא,
נָשִׁים פְּטוּרוֹת, חוּץ מִקִּדּוּשׁ וּמַצָּה וַאֲכִילַת פֶּסַח וְהַקְהֵל וְשִׂמְחָה. וְהֵם אָמְרוּ גַם־

---

5. TB Nazir 57b.

6. MT *hilchoth 'avodath kochavim* xii 6.

7. Literally, to shave; i.e. to cut very close.

8. Literally, the destruction.

9. This part in parentheses is not in the oldest manuscripts, nor in any edition but the first. It would therefore seem to be a later interpolation, by a learned reader.

10. TB Nazir 57b, Kiddushin 35b.

11. I.e. whoever has a beard — a male.

12. See MY for the source. They would not be whipped with lashes for it, though, since the basic injunction does not apply to them directly; MT *hilchoth 'avodath kochavim* xiii 5, based on TB *ibid.*

13. MT *ibid.* 2.

14. If they are male or female.

15. Tosefta, Bikkurim ii; *tosafoth* to TB Yevamoth 83a, s.v. *b'ri-yah*; MT *ibid.* xii 4.

16. I.e. which precepts they have the duty to observe.

17. Whether the particular precept applies to women.

18. Literally, every positive precept which time causes; i.e. which has to be observed at a particular time.

memory taught in the tractate *Makkoth* (20b): that both the one who does the shaving and the one who is shaved—as long as [the latter] assists—the two are equally guilty; but if he did not assist, only the one who did the shaving is guilty. If a person thus shaves a child, he is guilty.[5] As for the minimal amount of the "corner of the head" [that must be left], the Sages gave no measure. Rambam of blessed memory wrote:[6] We have heard from our elders that no fewer than forty hairs are to be left over. These are his words [in continuation]: "But it is permissible to clip[7] the corner [temple] with scissors, as the Torah forbade no more than the total removal[8] by a razor" (or making the temples level with the area behind the ears; yet I heard that for the "corner" of the head, even [to crop it close] with scissors as with a razor is forbidden).[9] The rest of its details are toward the end of the Talmud tractate *Makkoth*.

It is in effect everywhere, at every time, for males, but not for women: whether they did the shaving or were thus shaven, they are free of guilt. As the Sages of blessed memory interpreted:[10] *You shall not round off the corners of your heads, nor shall you mar the edges of your beard* (Leviticus 19:27)—whoever is subject to the injunction, *nor shall you mar*,[11] is subject to the admonition, *You shall not round off*, etc. Nevertheless, they are forbidden thus to shave a male, even a child.[12] As to servants, although they are in the same category as women for many precepts, they are obligated by this, since they have a beard.[13] A *tumtum* [one of uncertain gender] and a hermaphrodite are cases of doubt;[14] hence the stringencies applicable to either male or female are imposed on them, both in this and in every instance, and they are obligated to observe everything. Yet if they transgressed this, they would not receive whiplashes, because it is a doubt.[15]

Now, to define the matter, I will write the rule that our Sages taught us about the precepts of women,[16] even though it is my way to write it in detail for each and every precept;[17] for between the rule and the detail, the reader will remember it. This is it: By every negative precept in the Torah, both man and woman are obligated—except [the present ones] *You shall not round off . . . nor shall you mar*, and the injunction not to become defiled by the dead (§263). As for every positive precept whose obligation is brought on by time,[18] women are free of its duty, except for sanctification [of the Sabbath, etc.] (§31), eating *matzah* (§10) and the Passover sacrifice (§6), assembly (§612), and rejoicing [on the festivals] (§488). Yet the Sages said, too,

כֵּן שֶׁאֵין לְמֵדִין מִן הַכְּלָלוֹת, וַאֲפִלּוּ בְּמָקוֹם שֶׁנֶּאֱמַר שֶׁנֶּאֱמַר בָּהֶן "חוּץ": כִּי הַכּוֹלֵל, כְּדֵי
לְקַצֵּר כְּלָלָיו, לֹא יָחוּשׁ לִדְבָרִים מְעַטִּים הַיּוֹצְאִים מִן הַכְּלָל, לְהַעֲלוֹתָן עַל סֵפֶר.

וְעוֹבֵר עַל זֶה וְגִלַּח פֵּאָה אַחַת מִן הָרֹאשׁ, חַיָּב מַלְקוֹת אַחַת; וְאִם גִּלַּח שְׁנֵי
צְדָעָיו, וַאֲפִלּוּ בְּבַת אַחַת וְהַתְרָאָה אַחַת, חַיָּב שְׁתֵּי מַלְקִיּוֹת. וְכָתַב הַמַּעְתִּיק בְּשֵׁם
הָרַמְבַּ"ם זִכְרוֹנוֹ לִבְרָכָה: וְהָרָאוּי שֶׁלֹּא נִמְנֶה אֵלֶּה לִשְׁתֵּי מִצְווֹת אַף-עַל-פִּי
שֶׁלּוֹקֶה שְׁתַּיִם, לְפִי שֶׁשְּׁנֵיהֶם כְּתוּבִים תַּחַת לָאו אֶחָד; שֶׁאִלּוּ אָמַר "לֹא תַקִּיפוּ
פְּאַת רֹאשְׁכֶם מִיָּמִין וּפְאַת רֹאשׁ מִשְּׂמֹאל" וּמָצָאנוּ אוֹתָן מְחַיְּבִין עֲלֵיהֶם שְׁתַּיִם,
אָז הָיָה רְשׁוּת לוֹמַר שֶׁנִּמְנֶה אוֹתָן שְׁתֵּי מִצְווֹת. אָמְנָם בִּהְיוֹתוֹ מִלָּה אַחַת וְעִנְיָן
אֶחָד, בֶּאֱמֶת שֶׁהוּא מִצְוָה אַחַת; וְאַף עַל פִּי שֶׁבָּא בְּפֵרוּשׁ שֶׁמְּנִיעָה זוֹ הִיא כּוֹלֶלֶת
חֲלָקִים מִשְׁתַּנִּים מֵהַגּוּף וְשֶׁהוּא חַיָּב עַל כָּל חֵלֶק מֵהֶם לְבַד, עִם כָּל זֶה לֹא זֶה יִתְחַיֵּב
שֶׁיִּהְיוּ מִצְווֹת הַרְבֵּה. עַד כָּאן לְשׁוֹנוֹ.

[שֶׁלֹּא לְהַשְׁחִית פְּאַת זָקָן]

רנב שֶׁלֹּא לְגַלֵּחַ פְּאַת הַזָּקָן, שֶׁנֶּאֱמַר: וְלֹא תַשְׁחִית אֶת פְּאַת זְקָנֶךָ. וְחָמֵשׁ
פֵּאוֹת יֵשׁ בּוֹ בַּזָּקָן, וּבְכָל אַחַת יֵשׁ בָּהּ חִיּוּב מַלְקוֹת, אֲפִלּוּ נְטָלָן כֻּלָּן כְּאַחַת
וּבְהַתְרָאָה אֶחָת; וְאֵלּוּ הֵן: לְחִי הָעֶלְיוֹן וְהַתַּחְתּוֹן מִיָּמִין, וְהָעֶלְיוֹן וְהַתַּחְתּוֹן
מִשְּׂמֹאל, הֲרֵי אַרְבָּעָה, וְשִׁבֹּלֶת הַזָּקָן וְהוּא מְקוֹם חִבּוּר הַלְּחָיַיִם לְמַטָּה הַנִּקְרָא
בְּלַעַז מוֹנְטוֹן; הֲרֵי חֲמִשָּׁה. וּלְשׁוֹן הַמִּשְׁנָה: וְעַל הַזָּקָן חָמֵשׁ, שְׁתַּיִם מִכָּאן וּשְׁתַּיִם
מִכָּאן וְאַחַת מִלְּמַטָּן.

וְכָתַב הַמַּעְתִּיק בְּשֵׁם הָרַמְבַּ"ם זִכְרוֹנוֹ לִבְרָכָה: וּבָאָה הַמְּנִיעָה בָּזֶה בְּאֵלֶּה
הַמִּלּוֹת, "וְלֹא תַשְׁחִית אֶת פְּאַת זְקָנֶךָ", וְלֹא אָמַר "לֹא תַשְׁחִית זְקָנֶךָ", וְאַף-עַל-
פִּי שֶׁהַכֹּל יִקָּרֵא זָקָן, יִרְצֶה לוֹמַר בָּזֶה שֶׁלֹּא תְגַלֵּחַ אֲפִלּוּ פֵּאָה אַחַת מִכְּלַל הַזָּקָן,

---

19. I.e. whether or not they include a particular instance.

20. The paragraph is based on TB Kiddushin 29a and 34a.

21. TB Makkoth 20a.

22. ShM negative precept §43; the work was translated from the original Arabic into Hebrew; our author's version differs somewhat from our editions, as he apparently had the translation of R. Abraham b. Ḥisdai, from an earlier version of ShM (MY). In a good number of small points, however, this text agrees with ed. Kafaḥ (a new Hebrew rendering of the Arabic), suggesting perhaps a greater fidelity to the Arabic original than by R. Moses ibn Tibbon.

§252   1. Mishnah, Makkoth iii 5 (TB 20a).

2. The paragraph is based on ShM negative precept §44.

3. ShM *ibid*. See §251, note 22, which applies equally here. On our author's root reason cf. *Guide* III 37.

that nothing is to be inferred [specifically] from general rules,[19] even where the word "except" is used about them. For one who sums matters up succinctly to make his rules short will not pay heed to a few things that do not fit the rule, to put them in writing.[20]

If a person violates this and shaves off one corner (temple) of the head, he deserves one whipping of lashes; if he shaved off both his temples, even if at once and upon one warning, he is punishable by two whippings of lashes.[21] But the translator wrote in the name of Rambam of blessed memory:[22] It is seemly, though, that we should not count these as two precepts, even though one is given two sets of whiplashes—because the both are written under one injunction. Had Scripture stated, "You shall not round off the corner of your head at the right and the corner of the head at the left," and we found it imposing two punishments for it, we would then have the right to say that we should count them as two precepts. But since it is one word and one matter, in truth it is but one precept. Even though it was taught in the [traditional] explanation that this prohibition applies to different parts of the body, and punishment is incurred over each part separately, it is nevertheless not inevitable that it should comprise many commandments. Thus far his words.

[THE PROHIBITION AGAINST MARRING THE EDGES OF THE BEARD]

252 not to shave off the edges of the beard, as it is stated, *nor shall you mar the edges of your beard* (Leviticus 19:27). There are five "edges" in a beard, and for each there is a penalty of whiplashes, even if he removed them all at once and upon one warning. These are: the upper and lower cheek at the right, and the upper and lower one at the left, making four; and the pointed end of the beard, the place where the cheeks are joined below, which is called *menton* in the foreign tongue (Spanish); thus five. In the language of the Mishnah:[1] For [shaving] the beard, five [sets of whiplashes are given]: two for one side, two for the other side, and one for the area below.[2]

In the name of Rambam of blessed memory, the translator wrote:[3] The prohibition of this was given in these words: *nor shall you mar the edges of your beard*; and it does not say, "nor shall you mar your beard," even though all of it is called "the beard." Scripture means to say by this that you should not shave off even one edge from the whole beard, and a whipping of one set of lashes is given

⟨131⟩

וְלוֹקִין עַל כָּל אַחַת מַלְקוּת אַחַת; וַאֲפִלּוּ גִּלְּחָן בְּבַת אַחַת כֻּלָּם, חַיָּבִין עֲלֵיהֶם חָמֵשׁ מַלְקֻיּוֹת.

מִשָּׁרְשֵׁי הַמִּצְוָה, מַה שֶּׁכָּתַבְנוּ בַּמִּצְוָה הַקּוֹדֶמֶת, לְהַרְחִיק כָּל עִנְיַן עֲבוֹדָה זָרָה, וְזֶה גַם־כֵּן הָיָה מִנְהַג כּוֹמְרֵי עֲבוֹדָה זָרָה, לְהַשְׁחִית פְּאַת זְקָנָם. וְעוֹד כָּתַב, וְזֶה לְשׁוֹן הַמַּעְתִּיק: וַאֲשֶׁר יְחַיֵּב שֶׁלֹּא יִמְנוּ חָמֵשׁ פֵּאוֹת שֶׁבַּזָּקָן חָמֵשׁ מִצְווֹת, הוּא בַעֲבוּר שֶׁבָּאָה הַמְּנִיעָה בְּמִלָּה נִפְרֶדֶת, וְהוּא עִנְיָן נִפְרָד, כְּמוֹ שֶׁבֵּאַרְנוּ בַּמִּצְוָה שֶׁלְּפָנֶיהָ. עַד כָּאן.

דִּינֵי הַמִּצְוָה, כְּגוֹן מַה שֶּׁאָמְרוּ זִכְרוֹנָם לִבְרָכָה שֶׁאֵין הַחִיּוּב אֶלָּא בְּגִלּוּחַ שֶׁל תַּעַר, שֶׁנֶּאֱמַר ״וְלֹא תַשְׁחִית״, גִּלּוּחַ שֶׁיֵּשׁ בּוֹ הַשְׁחָתָה דַּוְקָא, וְזֶהוּ תַּעַר; כֵּן פֵּרְשׁוּ זִכְרוֹנָם לִבְרָכָה. וְכָתַב הָרַמְבַּ״ם זִכְרוֹנוֹ לִבְרָכָה: וְאִם גָּלַח בְּמִסְפָּרַיִם, פָּטוּר. נִרְאֶה מִדְּבָרָיו דְּדַוְקָא פָּטוּר הוּא, אֲבָל אָסוּר לַעֲשׂוֹת כֵּן; וְאֶפְשָׁר שֶׁיִּהְיֶה הָעִנְיָן בְּמִסְפָּרַיִם כְּעֵין תַּעַר, וּכְמוֹ שֶׁנִּרְאָה הָעִנְיָן כֵּן בְּמַסֶּכֶת נָזִיר, שֶׁאָמְרוּ שָׁם: וְהַשָּׂפָם מֻתָּר לְגַלְּחוֹ בְּתַעַר, שֶׁאֵין שָׁם חֲשַׁשׁ פֵּאָה כְּלָל. וְיֵשׁ מִן הַגְּדוֹלִים שֶׁהֶחְמִירוּ שֶׁלֹּא לְהַעֲבִיר תַּעַר עַל כָּל הַבָּשָׂר. וְיֶתֶר פְּרָטֶיהָ, מְבֹאָרִים בְּסוֹף מַכּוֹת.

וְנוֹהֶגֶת בְּכָל מָקוֹם וּבְכָל זְמַן, בִּזְכָרִים; אֲבָל הַנְּקֵבוֹת מֻתָּרוֹת הֵן בְּהַשְׁחָתַת זָקָן אִם יֵשׁ לָהֶן שֵׂעָר בָּהֶן; גַּם אִם הִשְׁחִיתָה הָאִשָּׁה זְקַן הָאִישׁ, פְּטוּרָה. וְהָעֲבָדִים חַיָּבִים בְּהַשְׁחָתַת זָקָן, כְּמוֹ שֶׁכָּתַבְנוּ לְמַעְלָה; וְכֵן טוּמְטוּם וְאַנְדְּרוֹגִינוֹס, מִסָּפֵק.

[שֶׁלֹּא נִכְתֹּב בִּבְשָׂרֵנוּ כְּתֹבֶת קַעֲקַע]

רנג שֶׁלֹּא נִכְתֹּב בִּבְשָׂרֵנוּ כְּתֹבֶת קַעֲקַע, שֶׁנֶּאֱמַר: וּכְתֹבֶת קַעֲקַע לֹא תִתְּנוּ (בבשרכם) [בָּכֶם]. וְהָעִנְיָן הוּא כְּמוֹ שֶׁעוֹשִׂין הַיּוֹם יִשְׁמְעֵאלִים, שֶׁכּוֹתְבִים

---

4. TB Makkoth 21a.

5. MT hilchoth 'avodath kochavim xii 7.

6. If he already did this.

7. The first edition reads: . . . he is free of guilt—as the matter would appear from the Talmud tractate *Nazir* (58b); for it was taught there: Rav said: A man may trim the hair of his entire body with a razor; and it was established that this means with a pair of scissors in the manner of [used as] a razor—but this except the armpits and the pubes, which it is forbidden [to shave] even thus.

8. Literally, to pass a razor over any [part] of the flesh.

9. Literally, "destroyed"; similarly in the next sentence.

10. That perhaps they are male.

for each one. Even if he shaved them all off at once, a person is punishable for them by five whippings.

At the root of the precept lies the purpose we wrote for the
preceding *mitzvah*: to remove every matter of idol-worship. This
too was a custom of priests of idolatry—to mar [remove utterly] the
edges of their beards. Now, he [Rambam] of blessed memory wrote
further, about this, in this wording of the translator:[3] What determines
our conclusion that the five edges of the beard are not to be counted
as five precepts is the fact that the prohibition is given in one distinct
expression, so that it is one matter, as we explained in the previous
precept. Thus far his words.

The laws of the precept are, for example, what the Sages of
blessed memory taught:[4] that punishment is incurred by nothing
other than shaving with a razor; for it is stated, *nor shall you mar* (literally,
destroy)—[i.e. by] a shave that specifically has destruction [of the
hair completely] in it, which denotes a razor. Thus our Sages of blessed
memory explained it. Hence Rambam of blessed memory wrote:[5]
and if a person shaved with scissors, he is free of guilt. It would seem
from his words that one is only free of guilt,[6] but it is forbidden
[originally] to do so. Perhaps this is the case when one [actually]
shaves with the scissors as with a razor, as the matter would appear
from the Talmud tractate *Nazir* (58b)—for it was taught there:
As for the mustache, it is permissible to shave it with a razor, since
there is no suspicion at all that it might be an "edge" [of the beard].[7]
Yet there are some great authorities who ruled stringently that it is
forbidden to use a razor on any part of the body.[8]

The rest of its details are explained toward the end of the tractate
Makkoth. It is in force everywhere, at every time, for men. Women,
however, are allowed to utterly remove a beard, if they have hair
[growing] there. Even if a woman razor-shaved[9] a man's beard,
she is free of guilt. Slaves, however, would bear guilt for razor-shaving
their beard, as we wrote above (§251). So too a *tumtum* [one of uncertain,
concealed gender] and a hermaphrodite, on account of the doubt.[10]

[THE PROHIBITION AGAINST INSCRIBING ANY TATTOO
IN ONE'S FLESH]

253 that we should not inscribe in our flesh any tattoo marks:
as it is stated, *nor shall you put any tattoo marks on yourselves*[1] (Leviticus
19:28). This matter is as Ishmaelites do today, inscribing in their

בְּבְשָׂרָם כְּתָב מְחֻקֶּה וְתָקוּעַ שֶׁאֵינוֹ נִמְחָק לְעוֹלָם. וְאֵין הַחִיּוּב אֶלָּא בִּכְתָב חָקוּק
וְרָשׁוּם בִּדְיוֹ אוֹ בְּכָחָל אוֹ בִּשְׁאָר צִבְעוֹנִין הָרוֹשְׁמִין; וְכֵן אָמְרוּ בְּמַכּוֹת: קָעַקַע
וְלֹא כָתַב, כְּלוֹמַר שֶׁלֹּא רָשַׁם בְּצֶבַע, כָּתַב וְלֹא קָעַקַע, כְּלוֹמַר שֶׁרָשַׁם בִּבְשָׂרוֹ
בְּצֶבַע אֲבָל לֹא עָשָׂה שְׂרִיטָה בִּבְשָׂרוֹ, אֵינוֹ חַיָּב — עַד שֶׁיִּכְתֹּב וִיקַעֲקַע בִּדְיוֹ
וּבְכָחָל וּבְכָל דָּבָר שֶׁהוּא רוֹשֵׁם.

מִשָּׁרְשֵׁי הַמִּצְוָה, מַה שֶׁכָּתַבְנוּ בְּהַקָּפַת הָרֹאשׁ וּבְהַשְׁחָתַת זָקָן, סָמוּךְ: לְהַרְחָקַת
כָּל עִנְיְנֵי עֲבוֹדָה זָרָה מִגּוּפֵנוּ וּמִבֵּין עֵינֵינוּ. וְגַם זֶה מִן הַשֹּׁרֶשׁ הַזֶּה בְּעַצְמוֹ, שֶׁהָיָה
מִנְהַג הַגּוֹיִים שֶׁרוֹשְׁמִים עַצְמָם לַעֲבוֹדָה זָרָה שֶׁלָּהֶם, כְּלוֹמַר שֶׁהוּא עֶבֶד נִמְכָּר לָהּ
וּמְרֻשָּׁם לַעֲבוֹדָתָהּ.

מִדִּינֵי הַמִּצְוָה, מַה שֶׁאָמְרוּ זִכְרוֹנָם לִבְרָכָה שֶׁכָּל מָקוֹם שֶׁבַּגּוּף, בֵּין מְגֻלֶּה בֵּין
מְכֻסֶּה בִּבְגָדִים, בִּכְלַל אִסּוּר זֶה; וְיֶתֶר פְּרָטֶיהָ, בְּסוֹף מַסֶּכֶת מַכּוֹת.

וְנוֹהֶגֶת בְּכָל מָקוֹם וּבְכָל זְמַן, בַּזְּכָרִים וּנְקֵבוֹת. וְעוֹבֵר עַל זֶה וְכָתַב אֲפִלּוּ אוֹת
אַחַת בְּכָל מָקוֹם שֶׁבַּגּוּפוֹ בָּעִנְיָן זֶה שֶׁאָמַרְנוּ, שֶׁיִּהְיֶה חָקוּק וְרָשׁוּם בְּאֶחָד מִמִּינֵי
הַצְּבָעִין הָרוֹשְׁמִין, לוֹקֶה; וְאִם רָשְׁמוּ בּוֹ אֲחֵרִים, אֵינוֹ לוֹקֶה אֶלָּא אִם כֵּן סִיַּע, מִן
הַכְּלָל הַיָּדוּעַ: לָאו שֶׁאֵין בּוֹ מַעֲשֶׂה אֵין לוֹקִין עָלָיו.

[מִצְוַת הַיִּרְאָה מִן הַמִּקְדָּשׁ]

רנד לִירֹא מִן הַמִּקְדָּשׁ, כְּלוֹמַר שֶׁנַּעֲמִידֵהוּ בְּנַפְשׁוֹתֵינוּ מָקוֹם הַפַּחַד וְהַיִּרְאָה,
כְּדֵי שֶׁיִּתְרַכְּכוּ לְבָבֵנוּ בְּבוֹאֵנוּ שָׁם לְהִתְפַּלֵּל אוֹ לְהַקְרִיב קָרְבָּנוֹת, שֶׁנֶּאֱמַר:
וּמִקְדָּשִׁי תִּרָאוּ. וּפֵרְשׁוּ זִכְרוֹנָם לִבְרָכָה בְּסִפְרָא וּבִבְרָכוֹת כְּמוֹ־כֵן: אֵי זֶהוּ מוֹרָא,
לֹא יִכָּנֵס לְהַר הַבַּיִת בְּמַקְלוֹ וּבְמִנְעָלוֹ וּבְאַפֻנְדָּתוֹ וּבָאָבָק שֶׁעַל רַגְלָיו וּבַמָּעוֹת

§253   1. So MT *hilchoth 'avodath kochavim* xii 11.
   2. *Ibid.* (see *Kessef Mishneh*).
   3. TB Sanhedrin 63b, etc.

§254   1. Literally, *softened*.
   2. Sifra, *k'doshim, perek* 7, 9.

flesh a permanent, adhered "script" which can never be erased. The
guilt is incurred for nothing but an incised inscription, marked in
ink or paint or any other marking color. And so was it taught in the
tractate *Makkoth* (21a): If a person incised [something beneath the
skin] but did not write—i.e. he did not mark it with color; or if he
wrote [something] but did not incise [it]—i.e. he marked his flesh
(skin) with color, but did not make any incision in his flesh—he is
not guilty, until he writes (marks) and incises [something] in ink or
paint or anything that makes a mark.

At the root of the precept lies the purpose we wrote in the nearby
sections about rounding off the head and shaving the beard with a
razor (§§251, 252): to remove all matters of idolatry from our bodies
and from [the mind] between our eyes. This too is for that reason, as it
was a custom of the heathens that they would [thus] mark themselves
for their idol-worship—i.e. [to show] that he [such a person] was a
servant dedicated to it, marked for its service.[1]

Among the laws of the precept, there is what the Sages of blessed
memory said: that every area of the body, whether [generally] exposed
or covered by clothing, is included under this prohibition.[1] The
rest of its details are toward the end of the Talmud tractate *Makkoth*.

It is in effect everywhere, at every time, for both man and woman.
If a person violates it and inscribes even one letter anywhere on his
body in the manner we have stated—incised and drawn with one of
the kinds of coloring matter that leaves a mark, he should be given
whiplashes. If others so marked [tattooed] him, he is not to be whipped,
unless he assisted[2]—this by the known rule:[3] over a negative precept
involving no physical action [in its violation] one is not given lashes.

254 [THE PRECEPT OF REVERENT AWE FOR THE SANCTUARY]
to have a reverent fear of the Sanctuary: in other words,
that we should regard and establish it in our souls as the place of awe
and veneration, so that our hearts will be moved[1] when we come
there to pray or to bring offerings; for it is stated, *and you shall reverence
My sanctuary* (Leviticus 19:30). Our Sages of blessed memory explained in the Midrash *Sifra*,[2] and likewise in the Talmud tractate
B'rachoth (54a), what such reverence means: One should not enter
the Temple Mount with his walking-stick, with his shoes on, with
his money-bag or purse, with the dust [of travel] on his feet, or with

הַצְּרוּרִים לוֹ בְּסְדִינוֹ, וְלֹא יַעֲשֵׂנּוּ קַפַּנְדַּרְיָא, כְּלוֹמַר שֶׁיִּכָּנֵס מִפֶּתַח זֶה וְיֵצֵא מִפֶּתַח שֶׁכְּנֶגְדּוֹ כְּדֵי לְקַצֵּר הַדֶּרֶךְ לְבַד, וּרְקִיקָה מִקַּל וָחֹמֶר, פֵּרוּשׁ וְאֵין צָרִיךְ לוֹמַר שֶׁאָסוּר הַמָּקוֹם בִּרְקִיקָה.

וּבֵאֲרוּ גַּם־כֵּן בַּסַּנְהֶדְרִין שֶׁאֵין כָּלָל רָאוּי לָשֶׁבֶת בָּעֲזָרָה, כִּי־אִם לְמַלְכֵי בֵית דָּוִד, מִשּׁוּם כְּבוֹד מַלְכוּת, שֶׁנֶּאֱמַר: וַיָּבֹא הַמֶּלֶךְ דָּוִד וַיֵּשֶׁב לִפְנֵי יי. וְאָמְרוּ בְסִפְרָא: לֹא מִן הַמִּקְדָּשׁ אַתָּה יָרֵא אֶלָּא מִמִּי שֶׁפָּקַד עַל הַמִּקְדָּשׁ.

מִשָּׁרְשֵׁי מִצְוָה זוֹ כָּתַבְתִּי לְמַעְלָה בְּמִצְוַת "וְעָשׂוּ לִי מִקְדָּשׁ", סֵדֶר וַיִּקְחוּ לִי תְרוּמָה [סִי׳ צ״ה], וּבִמְקוֹמוֹת אֲחֵרִים.

מִדִּינֵי הַמִּצְוָה, מַה שֶּׁאָמְרוּ זִכְרוֹנָם לִבְרָכָה שֶׁאֵין אָדָם נִכְנָס בְּכָל הַר הַבַּיִת אֶלָּא לִדְבַר מִצְוָה; וְכָל מִי שֶׁהִשְׁלִים עֲבוֹדָה בַּבַּיִת וְנִסְתַּלֵּק, מְהַלֵּךְ אֲחוֹרַנִּית מְעַט מְעַט, וְכֵן אַנְשֵׁי מִשְׁמָר וְאַנְשֵׁי מַעֲמָד וּלְוִיִּם מְדוּכָנָם, כָּךְ הֵם יוֹצְאִים מִן הַמִּקְדָּשׁ.

וּמַה שֶּׁאָמְרוּ זִכְרוֹנָם לִבְרָכָה: אָסוּר שֶׁיִּפָּנֶה אוֹ יִישַׁן לְעוֹלָם בֵּין מִזְרָח לְמַעֲרָב, מִפְּנֵי שֶׁהַהֵיכָל הוּא בְמַעֲרָב; וְכֵן אָסוּר לְאָדָם לִבְנוֹת בַּיִת תַּבְנִית הֵיכָל, וְאַכְסַדְרָה תַבְנִית אוּלָם, חָצֵר תַּבְנִית הָעֲזָרָה—וְכָל זֶה לְמוֹרָאַת הַמָּקוֹם; וְיֶתֶר פְּרָטֵי כְּבוֹד הַבַּיִת וּמוֹרָאוֹ, בְּמִדּוֹת וְתָמִיד.

וְנוֹהֶגֶת מִצְוָה זוֹ בִּזְכָרִים וּנְקֵבוֹת בְּכָל מָקוֹם, שֶׁאַף־עַל־פִּי שֶׁהַמִּקְדָּשׁ חָרֵב הַיּוֹם בַּעֲוֹנוֹתֵינוּ, חַיָּב כָּל אָדָם בְּמוֹרָאוֹ, וְלֹא יִכָּנֵס אֶלָּא בְּמָקוֹם שֶׁהוּא מֻתָּר לְהִכָּנֵס בּוֹ בִּבְנִינֵנוּ, וְלֹא יֵשֶׁב אֲפִלּוּ בָעֲזָרָה, וְלֹא יָקֵל רֹאשׁוֹ כְּנֶגֶד שַׁעַר הַמִּזְרָח, שֶׁנֶּאֱמַר: אֶת שַׁבְּתוֹתַי תִּשְׁמֹרוּ וּמִקְדָּשִׁי תִּירָאוּ, וְאָמְרוּ בְסִפְרָא: מַה שְּׁמִירַת שַׁבָּת

---

3. *Ibid.* 7; so too TB Yevamoth 6b.

4. The first two paragraphs are based on ShM positive precept §21.

5. MT *hilchoth béth ha-b'hirah* vii 2, based on TB M'gillah 28b.

6. MT *ibid.* 4, based on TB Yoma 52b.

7. At the time of the Second Temple, the *kohanim* were divided into "watches" (family groups), each serving a week at the Temple.

8. Just as there were twenty-four "watches" of *kohanim* (see note 7), there were twenty-four groups of Israelites, each spending a week at the Temple as representatives of the entire people, to stand by, with the *kohanim* and Levites, as offerings were brought on behalf of the people; they were called *anshé ma'amad*, "the members of the post."

9. TB Yoma 53a.

10. TB B'rachoth 61b and 5b.

11. The Temple "palace," which included the *'ulam* (entrance hall), the holy chamber, and the holy of holies (§95).

12. TB Rosh haShanah 24a.

13. Sifra, *k'doshim*, perek 7, 8; so too TB Yevamoth 6b.

14. From the paragraph's second sentence to here is based on MT *hilchoth béth ha-b'hirah* vii 7.

his money gathered in his tunic; and he should not use it for a crosscut path—i.e. that he should enter from this doorway and leave through the opposite doorway merely in order to shorten the route; and expectoration by *kal va-ḥomer* [reasoning from the less to the more]— i.e. there is no need to say that expectoration is forbidden at the site.

It was likewise explained in the tractate *Sanhedrin* (101b) that it is not right at all to sit in the Temple forecourt, except for kings of the House of David, on account of the honor due royalty: for it is stated, *Then David the king went in and sat before the Lord* (II Samuel 7:18). In the Midrash *Sifra*[3] the Sages declared: Not of the Sanctuary should you be in awe, but of the One who ordered [us] about the Sanctuary.[4]

About the root reason for this precept I wrote above, in the commandment, *And let them make Me a sanctuary* (Exodus 25:8), in *sidrah t'rumah* (§95), and in other places.

Among the laws of the precept, there is what the Sages of blessed memory taught:[5] that a man is not to enter anywhere on the Temple mount except for a matter of *mitzvah* (religious duty). Whoever completed some service at the Temple and withdrew, should walk backwards little by little.[6] So too, the members of the watch,[7] the members of the post,[8] and the Levites [returning] from their stand of service, would thus go out from the Sanctuary.[9]

Then there is what the Sages of blessed memory said further:[10] It is forever forbidden for a man to relieve himself, or to sleep, in a position between east and west, because the *héchal*[11] was at the west. So too is it forbidden for a man to build a house on the model of the *héchal*,[11] a porch or terrace on the model of the *'ulam*, or a courtyard on the model of the Temple court[12]—all this out of reverent fear of the place. The remaining details of honor and awe toward the Temple are in the tractates *Middoth* and *Tamid*.

This precept is in effect for both man and woman, everywhere. For even if the Sanctuary is today destroyed, for our sins, every man is duty-bound to venerate it. He may enter no area but where it was permitted to enter when it was standing; he may not sit even in the Temple forecourt; and he may not act irreverently directly opposite the east gate—for it is stated, *You shall keep My sabbaths and reverence My sanctuaries* (Leviticus 19:30); and it was taught in the Midrash *Sifra*:[13] Just as the observance of the Sabbath is forever, even so should the veneration of the Sanctuary be forever.[14] If a person violated it and

לְעוֹלָם אַף מוֹרָא מִקְדָּשׁ לְעוֹלָם. וְעוֹבֵר עָלֶיהָ וְנָהַג קַלּוּת רֹאשׁ בְּעִנְיָנִים אֵלּוּ שֶׁאָמַרְנוּ, בִּטֵּל עֲשֵׂה זֶה.

[שֶׁלֹּא לַעֲשׂוֹת מַעֲשֵׂה אוֹב]

רנה שֶׁלֹּא לַעֲשׂוֹת מַעֲשֵׂה אוֹב וְלֹא נִפְנֶה אַחֲרָיו, כְּלוֹמַר שֶׁלֹּא נִשְׁאַל בּוֹ, שֶׁנֶּאֱמַר: אַל תִּפְנוּ אֶל הָאֹבֹת. וְהָעִנְיָן הוּא שֶׁמַּקְטִירִין קְטֹרֶת יְדוּעָה וְעוֹשִׂין מַעֲשִׂים יְדוּעִים, וּבְאוֹתָם הָעִנְיָנִים יְדַמֶּה לְאָדָם שֶׁיִּשְׁמַע דִּבּוּר מִתַּחַת הַשֶּׁחִי שֶׁיַּעֲנֶה לוֹ בְּמַה שֶּׁיִּשְׁאַל; זֶהוּ מִין אֶחָד מִמִּינָיו. וּלְשׁוֹן סִפְרָא: אוֹב זֶה פִּיתוֹם הַמְדַבֵּר מִשֶּׁחְיוֹ.

מִשָּׁרְשֵׁי מִצְוָה זוֹ, מַה שֶּׁכָּתַבְנוּ בְּאִסּוּר מְנַחֵשׁ, וּמִכֵּיוָן שֶׁכָּל אֵלּוּ הַהֲבָלִים גּוֹרְמִין לוֹ לְאָדָם לְהַנִּיחַ דַּת הָאֱמֶת הָעִקָּרִית וֶאֱמוּנַת הַשֵּׁם וְיִפְנֶה אַחַר הַהֶבֶל וְיַחְשֹׁב כִּי כָל אֲשֶׁר יִקְרֵהוּ יִהְיֶה עָלָיו דֶּרֶךְ מִקְרֶה, וְשֶׁיִּהְיֶה בְּיָדוֹ לְהֵיטִיב לְעַצְמוֹ וּלְסַלֵּק מֵעָלָיו כָּל נֶזֶק בְּאוֹתָן שְׁאֵלוֹת וְאוֹתָן תַּחְבּוּלוֹת שֶׁיַּעֲשֶׂה; וְכָל זֶה אֵינֶנּוּ שָׁוֶה לוֹ, כִּי הַכֹּל נִגְזַר מֵאֵת אֲדוֹן הָעוֹלָם, וּלְפִי מַעֲשֵׂה הַכָּשֵׁר אוֹ הַחֵטְא אֲשֶׁר יַעֲשֶׂה הָאָדָם יִתְחַדְּשׁוּ עָלָיו מַעֲשִׂים, אִם טוֹב וְאִם רָע, כְּמוֹ שֶׁכָּתוּב: כִּי פֹעַל אָדָם יְשַׁלֶּם לוֹ; וְעַל זֶה רָאוּי לוֹ לְאָדָם לְהַשְׁכִּין מַחְשְׁבוֹתָיו וּלְכַוֵּן כָּל דְּרָכָיו, וְזוֹ הִיא מַחְשֶׁבֶת כָּל אָדָם מִבְּנֵי-יִשְׂרָאֵל הַטּוֹבִים. וְעוֹד שֶׁיֵּשׁ בְּעִנְיָן זֶה שֶׁל אוֹב וְיִדְּעוֹנִי צַד עֲבוֹדָה זָרָה.

פְּרָטֵי הַמִּצְוָה, בְּפֶרֶק שְׁבִיעִי מִסַּנְהֶדְרִין.

וְנוֹהֶגֶת בְּכָל מָקוֹם וּבְכָל זְמַן, בִּזְכָרִים וּנְקֵבוֹת. וְעוֹבֵר עָלֶיהָ וְעָשָׂה מַעֲשֵׂה הָאוֹב בְּמֵזִיד וְעֵדִים, נִסְקָל; וְאִם אֵין עֵדִים וְהַתְרָאָה, בְּכָרֵת; בְּשׁוֹגֵג, מֵבִיא חַטָּאת קְבוּעָה; וְהַנִּשְׁאָל בָּהֶן, בְּלָאו, וְאִם כִּוֵּן מַעֲשָׂיו וְעָשָׂה כְּמַאֲמָרָן, לוֹקֶה.

---

1. I.e. one form of mediumistic activity.
2. Sifra, k'doshim, perek 7, 10; so too TB Sanhedrin 65a.
3. The paragraph is based on ShM negative precept §8.
4. Expression based on Esther 5:13.
5. Explained in §121.
6. For which he is not given lashes, however, since he did no physical action in merely inquiring. Actually, the injunction involved is not the present one, but §513, which see.

acted irreverently in any of these ways that we have described, he
would [thus] disobey this positive precept.

[THE PROHIBITION AGAINST ACTING AS AN 'OV—A
MEDIUM]

255 not to perform the act of an 'ov (a medium), nor should we
turn to follow him—i.e. we should not ask anything of him: for it is
stated, *Do not turn to the* 'ovoth (Leviticus 19:31). In essence, they
burn a certain incense and do certain actions, and through these
methods a man imagines that he hears [human] speech from under
the [medium's] armpit which answers him on what he asks. This
is one of its forms.[1] In the language of the Midrash *Sifra*:[2] An 'ov
is a conjurer who speaks from his armpit.[3]

At the root of this precept lies the reason we wrote about the
prohibition on practicing augury (§249). For all these forms of vapid
nonsense cause a man to leave the essential, true religion and belief
in the Eternal Lord, and he will thus turn to follow the nonsense;
and he will believe that all that happens to him comes upon him
by way of chance, and it lies in his power to better his fortune and
remove every harm from himself by those questions [to the medium]
and those tricks that he will do. Yet all this will avail him nothing,[4]
since everything is decreed by the Lord and Master of the world, and
according to the worthy or sinful activity that a man will do, new
events, good or bad, will occur for him—as it is written, *For according
to the work of a man will He requite him* (Job 34:11). It is fitting for a
man to center all his thoughts and attune all his affairs about this.
This is the way of thinking of every man among good, worthy Israelites.
Moreover, in this business of the medium and the wizard there is an
element of idolatry.

The details of the precept are in chapter 7 of the Talmud tractate
Sanhedrin. It applies in every place and every time, for both man and
woman. If a person violated it and did the act of an 'ov (a medium)
deliberately, before witnesses, he should be stoned to death. If there
were no witnesses or no warning, he would incur *karéth* [Divine
severance of existence]. And if it was done unwittingly, he should bring
a standard unvarying *hattath* (sin-offering).[5] If someone consults them,
it is the violation of an injunction;[6] hence if he attuned his deeds
and acted according to their words, he should receive whiplashes.

[שֶׁלֹּא לַעֲשׂוֹת מַעֲשֵׂה יִדְעוֹנִי]

רנו שֶׁלֹּא נַעֲשֶׂה מַעֲשֵׂה הַיִּדְעוֹנִי, שֶׁנֶּאֱמַר: אַל תִּפְנוּ וְגו' וְאֶל הַיִּדְעֹנִים; וּפֵרֵשׁ הָרַמְבַּ"ם זִכְרוֹנוֹ לִבְרָכָה, וְזֶה לְשׁוֹנוֹ: שֶׁהַיִּדְעָנִי הוּא שֶׁיִּקַּח עֶצֶם עוֹף שֶׁשְּׁמוֹ יִדּוֹעַ וְיִשִׂימֵהוּ בְּפִיו וְיַקְטִיר לוֹ בְּמִינֵי הַקְּטֹרֶת וְיַשְׁבִּיעַ הַשְּׁבָעוֹת וְיַעֲשֶׂה פְּעֻלּוֹת עַד שֶׁיִּתְחַבֵּר לוֹ עִנְיָן (הנופל מחולי) [מֵחֲלֵי הַנּוֹפֵל] כְּמוֹ הַחֳלִי הַנִּקְרָא סַבָּאת, וִידַבֵּר בַּעֲתִידוֹת. וְכֵן אָמְרוּ זִכְרוֹנָם לִבְרָכָה: יִדְעוֹנִי מַנִּיחַ עֶצֶם יִדּוֹעַ בְּפִיו וְהוּא מְדַבֵּר מֵאֵלָיו. וְאַל תַּחֲשֹׁב שֶׁזֶּהוּ לָאו שֶׁבִּכְלָלוֹת, שֶׁהוּא כְּבָר הִפְרִישָׁם כְּשֶׁזָּכַר הָעֹנֶשׁ, אָמַר "אוֹב אוֹ יִדְעוֹנִי", וְחִיֵּב עַל כָּל אַחַת מִשְּׁנֵיהֶם סְקִילָה וְכָרֵת לְמֵזִיד; וְהוּא אָמְרוּ "וְאִישׁ אוֹ אִשָּׁה כִּי יִהְיֶה בָהֶם אוֹב אוֹ יִדְעֹנִי מוֹת יוּמָתוּ" (וְגוֹמֵר). וּלְשׁוֹן סִפְרָא: לְפִי שֶׁהוּא אוֹמֵר "וְאִישׁ אוֹ אִשָּׁה כִּי יִהְיֶה בָהֶם אוֹב אוֹ יִדְעֹנִי מוֹת יוּמָתוּ" וְגוֹמֵר, עֹנֶשׁ שָׁמַעְנוּ; אַזְהָרָה מִנַּיִן—תַּלְמוּד לוֹמַר: אַל תִּפְנוּ אֶל הָאֹבֹת וְאֶל הַיִּדְעֹנִים.

כָּל עִנְיַן יִדְעוֹנִי יַגִּיד עָלָיו רֵעוֹ אוֹב שֶׁכָּתַבְנוּ. וְשָׁם בְּסַנְהֶדְרִין פֶּרֶק (ו) [ז] יִתְבָּאֲרוּ דִּינָיו גַּם־כֵּן.

[מִצְוַת כְּבוֹד חֲכָמִים]

רנז לְכַבֵּד הַחֲכָמִים וְלָקוּם מִפְּנֵיהֶם, שֶׁנֶּאֱמַר "מִפְּנֵי שֵׂיבָה תָּקוּם", וְתִרְגֵּם אָנְקְלוֹס: מִן קֳדָם דְּסָבַר בְּאוֹרַיְתָא תְּקוּם; "וְהָדַרְתָּ פְּנֵי זָקֵן", פֵּרְשׁוּ זִכְרוֹנָם לִבְרָכָה: אֵין זָקֵן אֶלָּא מִי שֶׁקָּנָה חָכְמָה. וְזֶה שֶׁהוֹצִיא הַכָּתוּב הֶחָכָם בִּלְשׁוֹן זָקֵן, הַטַּעַם מִפְּנֵי שֶׁהַבָּחוּר הֶחָכָם רָאָה מַה שֶׁרָאָה הַזָּקֵן בְּרֹב שָׁנָיו.

מִשָּׁרְשֵׁי הַמִּצְוָה, לְפִי שֶׁעִקַּר הֱיוֹת הָאָדָם נִבְרָא בָּעוֹלָם הוּא מִפְּנֵי הַחָכְמָה,

---

1. ShM negative precept §9 (and MT *hilchoth 'avodath kochavim* vi 2); but see §251, note 21, which applies here. (Here our author is content to cite Rambam that "one takes a bone of a fowl" etc. In §514, however, where he does not cite Rambam, he follows the view of other early scholars that *yiddo'a* is a certain kind of beast.)

2. TB Sanhedrin 65a.

3. I.e. the entire verse, which refers to both an *'ov* (medium) and a *yid'oni* (kind of wizard).

4. Sifra, *k'doshim, perek* 9, 1.

5. Expression taken from Job 36:33 (where, however, its meaning in the context is rather different); i.e. it is entirely similar to the previous precept.

§257   1. TB Kiddushin 32b.

256 [NOT TO FUNCTION AS A YID'ONI, A KIND OF WIZARD]

that we should not do any act of a *yid'oni* (a kind of wizard):
for it is stated, *Do not turn to* . . . yid'onim (Leviticus 19:31). Rambam
of blessed memory explained, in these words:[1] In substance it means
that one takes a bone of a fowl whose name is *yiddo'a*, and puts it in
his mouth; then he burns certain kinds of incense to it, imposes oaths,
and performs certain acts, until he is taken by a form of falling sickness
[epilepsy], like the illness called *saba'th*, and he utters predictions. So our
Sages of blessed memory said too:[2] A *yid'oni* places a bone of a *yiddo'a*
in his mouth, and it speaks of itself. Now, do not think this is
one general, omnibus negative precept:[3] for Scripture definitely
separates them in mentioning the punishment for them, stating,
an 'ov or a yid'oni (Leviticus 20:27), and imposing on each of the two
death by stoning and *karéth* [Divine severance of existence] for willfully
acting thus. So Scripture says, *And a man or a woman, if there shall be*
an 'ov or a yid'oni *among them, they shall surely be put to death,* etc.
(*ibid.*). And the Midrash *Sifra* expounds:[4] Since it says, "And a man
or a woman, if there shall be an *'ov* or a *yid'oni* among them, they shall
surely be put to death," etc. we have heard the punishment; from
where do we derive the admonition? Hence Scripture states, *Do not*
turn to mediums or yid'onim.

As for the entire subject of the *yid'oni*, "his companion" the
'ov (medium) "will relate about him"[5]—as we have written (§255).
There in the Talmud tractate *Sanhedrin*, chapter 7 (65a-b), its laws
are equally elucidated.

257 [THE MITZVAH OF HONORING WISE SCHOLARS]

to honor Torah scholars and rise before them: for it is stated,
You shall rise up before the hoary head (Leviticus 19:32), which Onkelos
translated, "You shall rise up before one who studies Torah"; *and*
honor the face of an old man (*ibid.*)—on which our Sages of blessed
memory explained:[1] "an old man" means none else but one who has
acquired wisdom. As to why the Writ expresses the concept of a
Torah scholar by the term "an old man," the reason is that a·young
Torah scholar sees through his wisdom what an old man sees through
the multitude of his years.

At the root of the precept lies the reason that the main point of
man's having been created in the world is for the sake of wisdom,

כְּדֵי שֶׁיַּכִּיר בּוֹרְאוֹ; עַל־כֵּן רָאוּי לִבְנֵי־אָדָם לְכַבֵּד מִי שֶׁהִשִּׂיג אוֹתָהּ, וּמִתּוֹךְ כָּךְ יִתְעוֹרְרוּ הָאֲחֵרִים עָלֶיהָ. וּמִזֶּה הַשֹּׁרֶשׁ פֵּרֵשׁ אִיסִי בֶּן יְהוּדָה בַּגְּמָרָא בְּקִדּוּשִׁין שֶׁאֲפִלּוּ זָקֵן אַשְׁמַאי, כְּלוֹמַר שֶׁאֵינוֹ חָכָם, הוּא בִּכְלַל הַמִּצְוָה, שֶׁרָאוּי לְכַבְּדוֹ מִפְּנֵי שֶׁרֹב שָׁנָיו רָאָה וְהִכִּיר קְצָת בְּמַעֲשֵׂי הַשֵּׁם וְנִפְלְאוֹתָיו, וּמִתּוֹךְ כָּךְ רָאוּי לְכָבוֹד; וְהַיְנוּ דְּאָמַר רַבִּי יוֹחָנָן שָׁם בְּקִדּוּשִׁין: הֲלָכָה כְּאִיסִי בֶּן יְהוּדָה; וְזֶה שֶׁאָמְרוּ, בִּתְנַאי שֶׁלֹּא יִהְיֶה בַּעַל עֲבֵרוֹת, שֶׁאִם כֵּן מָנַע עַצְמוֹ מִכָּבוֹד.

מִדִּינֵי הַמִּצְוָה, מַה שֶּׁאָמְרוּ זִכְרוֹנָם לִבְרָכָה שֶׁאֵין צָרִיךְ לוֹמַר שֶׁמִּי שֶׁאֵינוֹ חָכָם חַיָּב בִּכְבוֹד הֶחָכָם, אֶלָּא אֲפִלּוּ הֶחָכָם חַיָּב בִּכְבוֹד הֶחָכָם, כְּמוֹ שֶׁאָמְרוּ זִכְרוֹנָם לִבְרָכָה: תַּלְמִידֵי חֲכָמִים שֶׁבְּבָבֶל עוֹמְדִים זֶה מִפְּנֵי זֶה. וּמַה שֶּׁבֵּאֲרוּ גַם־ כֵּן, כִּי בִּכְבוֹד הָרַב עַל הַתַּלְמִיד יֵשׁ תּוֹסֶפֶת גָּדוֹל עַל הַכָּבוֹד שֶׁחַיָּב לְכָל חָכָם אַחֵר; וְהִפְלִיגוּ בָּזֶה עַד שֶׁאָמְרוּ: מוֹרָא רַבָּךְ כְּמוֹרָא שָׁמַיִם.

וּכְבֵאוּר אָמְרוּ: אָבִיו וְרַבּוֹ, רַבּוֹ קוֹדֵם בְּכָבוֹד וּבַאֲבֵדָה וּבְמַשָּׂא וּבִשְׁבִיָה; אֲבָל אִם הָיָה אָבִיו חָכָם, אַף־עַל־פִּי שֶׁאֵינוֹ שָׁקוּל כְּרַבּוֹ, אָבִיו קוֹדֵם. וּבְפֶרֶק חֵלֶק אָמְרוּ: כָּל הַחוֹלֵק עַל רַבּוֹ כְּחוֹלֵק עַל הַשְּׁכִינָה, שֶׁנֶּאֱמַר: בְּהַצֹּתָם עַל יְיָ; וְשָׁם הֶאֱרִיכוּ בָּעִנְיָן הַרְבֵּה.

וּמַה שֶּׁאָמְרוּ זִכְרוֹנָם לִבְרָכָה בְּמוֹרָאת רַבּוֹ, שֶׁלֹּא יֵשֵׁב בִּמְקוֹמוֹ וְלֹא יַכְרִיעַ דְּבָרָיו וְלֹא יִסְתֹּר דְּבָרָיו וְלֹא יוֹרֶה בְּפָנָיו לְעוֹלָם, וַאֲפִלּוּ תּוֹךְ שְׁנֵים־עָשָׂר מִיל עִמּוֹ אָסוּר לְהוֹרוֹת; וְאִם רָאָהוּ עוֹבֵר עַל דִּבְרֵי תוֹרָה כֵּיצַד יִמְנָעֶנּוּ; וְהַחִלּוּק שֶׁבֵּין רַבּוֹ

2. I.e. they will be moved to wish to attain it.

3. So TB Sanhedrin 85a, that such a person deserves no honor even from his son.

4. TB Bava M'tzi'a 33a.

5. Mishnah, 'Avoth iv 12.

6. TB K'rithoth 28a, Bava M'tzi'a 33a.

7. Thus Scripture equates conflict with Moses and Aaron to conflict with the Almighty.

8. Derived from a similar teaching about one's father in TB Kiddushin 31b, since it was noted in the previous paragraph that a teacher of Torah ranks yet higher.

9. I.e. if his teacher has an argument or difference of opinion with someone, he should not say whose view appears right or better to him.

10. TB Sanhedrin 5b.

so that he will become aware of his Creator. It is therefore fitting for a man to honor one who has attained it. As a result, others will be bestirred about it.[2] And for this root reason, 'Issi b. Judah explained in the Talmud tractate *Kiddushin* (32b) that even an uneducated old man, i.e. who is not wise, is included in this precept: it is right to honor him—because in his great number of years he has seen and recognized a bit of the workings of the Eternal Lord and His wonders; hence he is deserving of esteem. This is why R. Yoḥanan said there in the tractate *Kiddushin*: The definitive law is as 'Issi b. Judah [taught]. Yet this [rule] that they stated holds only on condition that he is not a confirmed sinner; for if he is, he has deprived himself of honor.[3]

Among the laws of the precept, there is what the Sages of blessed memory taught: that needless to say, one who is not a wise scholar has the obligation of honoring a wise scholar; but even he who is one himself is also required to honor a wise person. As our Sages of blessed memory recounted:[4] The Torah scholars in Babylonia rise up before one another. Then there is what they equally explained: that in the honor due a Torah teacher from a student, there is a great deal more [required] than in the esteem he owes every other scholar. They indeed went so far as to say:[5] The reverent fear of your Torah teacher should be as the reverent fear of Heaven.

In explanation, they taught:[6] Between one's father and Torah teacher, his teacher takes precedence in regard to honor, [returning] a lost object, [helping with] a load, and [ransoming from] captivity. But if one's father is a Torah scholar, even if he is not the equal of his teacher, his father takes precedence. Then, in chapter 11 of *Sanhedrin* (110a), the Sages taught: Whoever disputes his Torah teacher, it is as though he disputed the *shechinah* (Divine Presence)—as it is stated, *who strove against Moses and against Aaron . . . when they strove against the Lord* (Numbers 26:9).[7] And there they dwelt at great length on the matter.

In addition, there is what the Sages of blessed memory said about reverent fear for one's Torah teacher:[8] that he should not sit in his place, should not decide about his words,[9] should not contradict his words, nor ever give a ruling in his presence. If he is even within twelve mils of his teacher, it is forbidden for him to give a ruling.[10] Then, if he saw him transgressing the words of the Torah, [there is the law] how he should dissuade him;[8] and there is the difference [in his obligation] between one's outstanding (master) teacher—i.e. from

מִבְהָק, כְּלוֹמַר שֶׁרַב חָכְמָתוֹ מִמֶּנּוּ, לְרַבּוֹ שֶׁאֵין רַב חָכְמָתוֹ מִמֶּנּוּ; וּמֵאֵימָתַי חַיָּב לַעֲמֹד מִפְּנֵי רַבּוֹ וּמִפְּנֵי חָכָם אַחֵר, וּבְאֵי זֶה מָקוֹם וּבְאֵי זֶה עִנְיָן פָּטוּר מִן הַקִּימָה.

וְיֶתֶר רֻבֵּי פְּרָטֵי עִנְיָנִים אֵלֶּה, בְּקִדּוּשִׁין פֶּרֶק רִאשׁוֹן וּבִמְקוֹמוֹת אֲחֵרִים. וְכֵן מִדִּינֵי הַמִּצְוָה הָעִנְיָנִים שֶׁפּוֹטְרִין מֵהֶן הַחֲכָמִים מִצַּד כְּבוֹדָם וּמוֹרָאָם, כְּגוֹן בְּעִנְיָן וַחֲפִירוֹת הַמְּדִינָה וְכַיּוֹצֵא בָהֶן, וְכֵן הַמִּסִּין שֶׁמַּטִּילִין הַמְּלָכִים עַל אַנְשֵׁי הָאָרֶץ, בֵּין מַס שֶׁהוּא קָצוּב עַל כָּל בְּנֵי הָעִיר יַחַד אוֹ שֶׁהוּא קָצוּב עַל כָּל אִישׁ וָאִישׁ אוֹ שֶׁאֵינוֹ קָצוּב כְּלָל — מִכָּל זֶה הֵם פְּטוּרִים, שֶׁנֶּאֱמַר: גַּם כִּי יִתְנוּ בַגּוֹיִם עַתָּה אֲקַבְּצֵם וַיָּחֵלּוּ מְעָט מִמַּשָּׂא מֶלֶךְ וְשָׂרִים.

וְנוֹהֶגֶת בְּכָל מָקוֹם וּבְכָל זְמַן, בִּזְכָרִים וּנְקֵבוֹת. וְעוֹבֵר עָלֶיהָ, בִּטֵּל עֲשֵׂה וְעָנְשׁוֹ גָּדוֹל, לְמַעַן כִּי זֶה יְסוֹד חָזָק בַּדָּת.

[שֶׁלֹּא לְהוֹנוֹת בַּמִּדּוֹת וְכָל הַמִּדּוֹת בִּכְלָל]

רנח שֶׁלֹּא לְהוֹנוֹת בְּמִדּוֹת הַלַּח וְהַיָּבֵשׁ וְלֹא בְּמֹאזְנַיִם; וּבִכְלָל מִדּוֹת הוּא גַם־ כֵּן מְדִידַת הַקַּרְקָעוֹת, וְכָל דָּבָר הַנִּמְדָּד בֵּין בְּנֵי אָדָם, כְּגוֹן בְּגָדִים — שֶׁנֶּאֱמַר: לֹא תַעֲשׂוּ עָוֶל בַּמִּשְׁפָּט בַּמִּדָּה בַּמִּשְׁקָל וּבַמְּשׂוּרָה. וּפֵרְשׁוּ זִכְרוֹנָם לִבְרָכָה כִּי מְשׂוּרָה הִיא מִדַּת הַלַּח וְהַיָּבֵשׁ, וְהִיא מִדָּה קְטַנָּה בְּיוֹתֵר, שֶׁהִיא אֶחָד מל"ג בְּלֹג; וְלָמְדָנוּ מִכַּאן כִּי הַתּוֹרָה הִקְפִּידָה עַל הַמִּדּוֹת בְּכָל־שֶׁהוּא, כְּלוֹמַר שֶׁאַף־עַל־פִּי שֶׁבִּשְׁאָר גְּזֵלוֹת לֹא תַקְפִּיד הַתּוֹרָה אֶלָּא בִּפְרוּטָה, בְּעִנְיַן הַמִּדּוֹת תַּקְפִּיד בְּכָל שֶׁהוּא.

וּפֵרוּשׁ הַכָּתוּב כֵּן: לֹא תַעֲשׂוּ עָוֶל בַּמִּשְׁפָּט, וּמַהוּ הַמִּשְׁפָּט הַשָּׁנוּי כָּאן, הוּא הַמִּדָּה וְהַמִּשְׁקָל וְהַמְּשׂוּרָה. וְלָמְדוּ זִכְרוֹנָם לִבְרָכָה מִזֶּה שֶׁהִזְכִּיר הַכָּתוּב בְּכָאן

---

11. TB Bava M'tzi'a 33a–b; MT *hilchoth talmud torah* v 9.

12. TB Kiddushin 33a–b.

13. *Ibid.* 32b.

14. I.e. where the inhabitants are drafted into a labor force by the government; TB Bava Bathra 8a.

15. This is how the Talmud interprets Hosea 8:10, the text quoted there; *ibid.*

§258   1. TB Bava M'tzi'a 61b.

   2. Sifra on Leviticus 19:35—*k'doshim, perek* 8, 5.

whom he acquired the greater part of his wisdom—and his Torah
teacher from whom he did not acquire most of his wisdom. [11] [There
is also the law] from what time one is obligated to rise before his
teacher, and before any other Torah scholar; [12] and in which place
and in which situation he is free of the duty to rise. [13]

[These] and the many other details about these topics are in the
first chapter of the Talmud tractate *Kiddushin* and elsewhere. Likewise,
among the laws of the precept, there are those situations where Torah
scholars are freed of obligation on account of the honor and veneration
due them—such as the construction and digging work of the country, [14]
and so forth; and so too the taxes which kings impose on the inhabitants
of the land, whether it is a single amount of tax set for all the people
in a city together, or it is an amount set for each and every man to
pay, or it is not fixed at all—from all this they are free; for it is stated,
"If all study [Torah], now will I gather them; and if but a few of them,
let them be exempt from the burden of king and princes." [15]

It is in effect everywhere, at every time, for both man and woman.
A person who transgresses it disobeys a positive precept; and his
punishment will be great, because this is a firm foundation in our
religion.

[THE PROHIBITION AGAINST CHEATING WITH ANY
KIND OF MEASURE]

258 not to cheat in liquid and dry measures, nor with scales;
and included in "measures" is likewise the measurement of lands,
and so anything measured among people, such as [cloth for] garments,
and so forth—for it is stated, *You shall do no wrong in judgment, in
measure of length, in weight, or in* m'surah, *measure of quantity* (Leviticus
19:35). Our Sages of blessed memory explained [1] that *m'surah* (measure
of quantity) is both a liquid and dry standard, which is the smallest
measure, being one thirty-third of a *log*. Thus we learn from this
that the Torah is particular in regard to measures about any amount at
all. In other words, even though in other ways of robbery the Torah
is concerned with nothing less than a *p'rutah* [in value], in regard to
measures it is strict about any amount at all.

Now, this is the sense of the verse: *You shall do no wrong in judgment*;
and what is the judgment meant here?—it is [any] measure of length,
weight, or measure of quantity. Well, from the fact that Scripture
mentions "judgment" here, the Sages of blessed memory learned [2]

‏"מִשְׁפָּט", שֶׁהַמּוֹדֵד נִקְרָא דַיָּן, וְאִם שִׁקֵּר בַּמִּדָּה, הֲרֵי הוּא כִּמְקַלְקֵל אֶת הַדִּין‏
‏וְקָרוּי עַוָּל וּמְשֻׁקָּץ חֵרֶם וְתוֹעֵבָה, וְגוֹרֵם לַחֲמִשָּׁה דְבָרִים הָאֲמוּרִים בַּדָּיָן: מְטַמֵּא‏
‏אֶת הָאָרֶץ, וּמְחַלֵּל אֶת יי וּמְסַלֵּק אֶת הַשְּׁכִינָה וּמַפִּיל אֶת יִשְׂרָאֵל בַּחֶרֶב וּמַגְלֶה‏
‏אוֹתָן מֵאַרְצָם. וְעוֹד הִפְלִיגוּ בְחֹמֶר מִצְוָה זוֹ וְאָמְרוּ כִּי גָדוֹל עָנְשָׁן מֵעֹנֶשׁ עֲרָיוֹת,‏
‏שֶׁזֶּה בֵּין אָדָם לַמָּקוֹם וְזֶה בֵּינוֹ וַחֲבֵרוֹ.‏

‏שֹׁרֶשׁ הַמִּצְוָה יָדוּעַ, כְּמוֹ שֶׁכָּתַבְתִּי לְמַעְלָה בְּמִצְוַת עֲשֵׂה יב בְּסֵדֶר זֶה [סי'‏
‏רנ"ט].‏

‏מִדִּינֵי הַמִּצְוָה, מַה שֶּׁאָמְרוּ שֶׁהַמּוֹדֵד אוֹ הַשּׁוֹקֵל בְּעָוֶל, אַף־עַל־פִּי שֶׁהוּא גוֹנֵב‏
‏בְּלִי סָפֵק, אֵינוֹ מְשַׁלֵּם תַּשְׁלוּמֵי כֶפֶל אֶלָּא מְשַׁלֵּם לוֹ מַה שֶּׁחִסֵּר מִן הַמִּדָּה אוֹ‏
‏הַמִּשְׁקָל. וְכֵן מַה שֶּׁאָמְרוּ זִכְרוֹנָם לִבְרָכָה לְמִשְׁמֶרֶת מִצְוָה זוֹ, שֶׁסֶּלַע שֶׁנִּפְגְּמָה מִן‏
‏הַצַּד לֹא יַעֲשֶׂנָּה מִשְׁקָל, שֶׁמָּא יָפְגֹם מִמֶּנּוּ יוֹתֵר וְיִהְיֶה הַמִּשְׁקָל חָסֵר; וְלֹא יַנִּיחֶנָּה‏
‏בְּמָקוֹם שֶׁיּוּכְלוּ אֲחֵרִים לַעֲשׂוֹתָהּ מִשְׁקָל; וּמַה שֶׁהֶאֱרִיכוּ בָזֶה לוֹמַר שֶׁאִם סָאָה חֲסֵרָה‏
‏וְעָמְדָה עַל מֶחֱצָה בְּכִוּוּן, יְקַיֵּם; וּמַה שֶּׁאָמְרוּ: עוֹשֶׂה אָדָם מִדּוֹתָיו סְאָה וַחֲצִי סְאָה‏
‏וְכוּלֵי, אֲבָל לֹא יַעֲשֶׂנָּה קַבַּיִם, שֶׁלֹּא תִתְחַלֵּף בְּרֹבַע הַסְּאָה, שֶׁהוּא קַב וּמֶחֱצָה; וְכֵן‏
‏בְּמִדּוֹת הַלַּח, עוֹשֶׂה הִין וַחֲצִי הִין וְכוּלֵי, כִּדְאִיתָא בַּבְּרַיְתָא בְּבָבָא בַּתְרָא.‏

‏וּמַה שֶּׁאָמְרוּ שֶׁהַמּוֹדֵד אֶת הַקַּרְקַע בְּחֶבֶל לֹא יָמֹד לְאֶחָד בִּימוֹת הַחַמָּה‏
‏וּלְאֶחָד בִּימוֹת הַגְּשָׁמִים, מִפְּנֵי שֶׁהַחֶבֶל מִתְקַצֵּר בִּימוֹת הַחַמָּה; וּמַה שֶּׁאָמְרוּ‏
‏שֶׁצָּרִיךְ כָּל אָדָם לְדַקְדֵּק הַרְבֵּה בִּמְשִׁיחַת הַקַּרְקַע, לְפִי שֶׁיֵּשׁ חִלּוּקִין הַרְבֵּה‏
‏בִּמְשִׁיחַת הַקַּרְקַע בֵּין הָהָר וְהַגַּיְא; וְיֵשׁ לָעַיֵּן בּוֹ גַם־כֵּן בֵּין הָעֲגוּלִין וְהָרְבּוּעִין‏
‏וְהָאֲלַכְסוֹנִין.‏

‏וְעוֹד הַרְבֵּה עִנְיָנִים הַמִּתְבָּאֲרִים בְּסִפְרֵי חָכְמַת הַחֶשְׁבּוֹן וְהַגֵּמַטְרִיָאוֹת,‏

---

3. Literally, fells the Israelites by the sword, and exiles them.

4. TB Bava Bathra 88b.

5. This is a point well worth noting: that in the teaching of the Talmud, sin toward other human beings is more serious than sin toward the Almighty.

6. In our author's original version, all positive precepts in each *sidrah* are treated before the negative precepts; hence §259 occurs earlier. We follow the standard printed editions, where the precepts are arranged strictly by the order of their Scriptural verses; hence §259 appears below.

7. MT *bilchoth g'névah* vii 2, based on TB Bava M'tzi'a 61b.

8. As a thief is ordinarily obligated to do (Exodus 22:3).

9. I.e. any coin; as coins were then made with an exact amount of metal in each, they were used as weights.

10. TB Bava M'tzi'a 52a–b.

11. TB Bava Bathra 89b–90a.

12. On the measure of a *se'ah*, see §111, note 13.

13. A *hin* is twelve *log*. A *log* is 345.6 cubic centimeters according to one view; 597 according to a more stringent view (*Chazon Ish*).

that one who does measuring is called "a judge"; and so, if there is
falsehood in the measure, he is as one who impairs justice at a trial.
It is called injustice, something loathsome, disgrace, and abomination;
and it causes five things that were said about a judge: He defiles the
land, desecrates the Divine name of the Lord, repels the *shechinah*
(Divine Presence), makes the Israelites fall by the sword, and causes
their exile[3] from their land. The Sages emphasized the seriousness
of this precept yet further, saying[4] that the punishment over it is
greater than the penalty for forbidden conjugal relations: because
the latter is between a man and the omnipresent God, while the former
is between one person and another.[5]

The root reason for the precept is known (evident), as I have
written above, in the twelfth positive precept of this *sidrah* (§259).[6]

Among the laws of the precept, there is what the Sages said:[7]
that when a person measures or weighs unjustly, even though he
steals past any doubt, he does not pay double the amount,[8] but only
pays the other person what was lacking in the measure or the weight.
Likewise, there is what they (of blessed memory) ruled as a "protective
barrier" about this precept: that if a *sela*[9] became damaged (defective)
at the edge, it should not be used as a weight, as it might become
further defective, and be lacking in the weight.[10] Nor should it be
left in a place where others would be able to use it for a weight.[10]
There is, too, what they went on to teach about this, saying that if it
became further lacking and remained at precisely the half, it may be
kept.[10] And there is what they said further:[11] A man should make
his measures a *se'ah*, half a *se'ah*, etc.[12] but should not make one of
two *kav*, so that it should not be substituted for a quarter of a *se'ah*,
which is one and a half *kav*. Similarly, for liquid measure, one should
make a *hin*, half a *hin*, etc.[13]—as stated in a *baraitha* in the tractate
Bava Bathra (89b–90a).

Then we have what the Sages taught:[14] that if someone measures
land with a cord, he should not measure for one person in the sunny
season and for another in the rainy season, because the cord becomes
shorter (contracts) in the sunny season. And there is, too, what they
said:[15] that a man needs to be very precise in surveying land, because
there are great differences in land surveying between a hill and a valley.
One should also carefully study it [to differentiate] between circles,
rectangles and diagonals.

⟨147⟩ There are many more matters that are elucidated in works of

שֶׁיִּחַלְקוּ בֵּין זָוִית נִצָּבָה לְזָוִית נִרְוַחַת וְזָוִית חַדָּה, וְאֵלּוּ שָׁלֹשׁ צוּרוֹתֵיהֶן כְּסֵדֶר:
וּבֵין מְשֻׁלָּשׁ שָׁוֶה הַצְּלָעוֹת וְהַמְשֻׁלָּשׁ אֲשֶׁר שְׁתֵּי הַצְּלָעוֹת בִּלְבַד ◁ △ △
שָׁווֹת, וְהוּא נִקְרָא מְשֻׁלָּשׁ שָׁוֶה הַשּׁוֹקַיִם, וּבֵין מְשֻׁלָּשׁ שֶׁאֵין צֶלַע מִכָּל צַלְעוֹתָיו
שָׁוֶה, וְהוּא הַנִּקְרָא מִתְחַלֵּף הַצְּלָעוֹת; וּבֵין מְרֻבָּע רְבוּעַ שָׁוֶה לְמַרְבֵּעַ אָרֹךְ,
וּמְרֻבָּע מְעֻיָּן כָּזֶה: ◇ וּמְרֻבָּע דּוֹמֶה לִמְעֻיָּן כָּזֶה: ◇ וְכַמָּה צְדָדִין בְּאֵלּוּ, לֹא
יָכִיל קֻלְף גָּדוֹל לְרֹב הַצּוּרוֹת שֶׁעָשׂוּ בָזֶה בַּעֲלֵי חָכְמַת הַתִּשְׁבֹּרֶת וְהַשִּׁעוּרִין
הַנִּקְרָאִין אַלְהַנְדָּסָא בָּעִנְיָנִים אֵלֶּה. וּמִכָּל צַד צְרִיכִין אָנוּ לְהִזָּהֵר הַרְבֵּה בִּמְדִידַת
הַקַּרְקָעוֹת.

וְתִזְכֹּר עִם זֶה כִּי הַכְּלָלִים שֶׁכָּלְלוּ חֲכָמִים זִכְרוֹנָם לִבְרָכָה בְּעִנְיְנֵי הַחֶשְׁבּוֹן,
כְּגוֹן מַה שֶׁאָמְרוּ: כָּל אַמְּתָא בְרִבּוּעָא, אַמְּתָא וּתְרֵי חוּמְשֵׁי בַּאֲלַכְסוֹנָא; וְכֵן כָּל
שֶׁיֵּשׁ בְּהֶקֵּפוֹ שְׁלֹשָׁה טְפָחִים יֵשׁ בּוֹ רֹחַב טֶפַח; וְכֵן כַּמָּה מְרֻבָּע יָתֵר עַל הָעֲגוּל,
רָבִיעַ; וְכַיּוֹצֵא בִכְלָלִים אֵלּוּ—שֶׁלֹּא אָמְרוּ זִכְרוֹנָם לִבְרָכָה עַל הַכִּוּוּן הַגָּמוּר כִּי
אִם בְּקֵרוּב, וְלָכֵן אַל תִּסְמֹךְ בָּזֶה בַּחֲלֻקַּת הַדְּבָרִים בֵּין בְּנֵי־אָדָם.

וְאַל תִּתְמַהּ: אֵיךְ יִכָּתְבוּ דָבָר בִּלְתִּי מְכֻוָּן וְהֵם אַנְשֵׁי אֱמֶת אֲשֶׁר אֱלֹהִים נִצָּב
בַּעֲדָתָם—כִּי הֵם לֹא נִצְרְכוּ אֶל הַחֶשְׁבּוֹנוֹת כִּי־אִם בְּחֶשְׁבּוֹן תְּחוּמֵי שַׁבָּת אוֹ
בִּזְרִיעַת הַכִּלְאַיִם וּנְטִיעָתָם וְכַיּוֹצֵא בְּאֵלּוּ הַדְּבָרִים, וּבָזֶה מַה שֶׁלֹּא כְוָנוּ בוֹ מֵבִיא
אוֹתָנוּ לִידֵי חֻמְרָא וְאֵינוֹ מַזִּיק לְשׁוּם אָדָם בְּמָמוֹנוֹ; וְאַף־עַל־פִּי־כֵן הֵעִידוּ בְּרֹב
מְקוֹמוֹת אֵלּוּ שֶׁאֵין הַחֶשְׁבּוֹן מְדֻקְדָּק שָׁם, שֶׁאָמְרוּ בְּכָל מָקוֹם וּמָקוֹם כְּפִי הָרָאוּי
בּוֹ, הַיְנוּ דְּלָא דָק וּלְחֻמְרָא לָא דָק, וְכַיּוֹצֵא בָזֶה—שֶׁהוֹדִיעוּנוּ מִכָּל־מָקוֹם שֶׁלֹּא
נִתְלֶה בָּהֶם מְעוּט הַהַשְׁגָּחָה וִידִיעָה בְּדָבָר מִכָּל הַדְּבָרִים. וְיֶתֶר פְּרָטֵי הַמִּצְוָה,
בְּבַתְרָא וּבִמְקוֹמוֹת אֲחֵרִים.

וְנוֹהֶגֶת בְּכָל מָקוֹם וּבְכָל זְמַן, בַּזְּכָרִים וּנְקֵבוֹת. וְעוֹבֵר עָלֶיהָ וְשִׁקֵּר בְּמִדָּה
בְּמִשְׁקָל וּבִמְשׂוּרָה, עָבַר עַל לַאו, אֲבָל אֵין לוֹקִין עָלָיו, לְפִי שֶׁהוּא נִתַּן
לְתַשְׁלוּמִין. וְכָתַב הָרַמְבַּ"ם זִכְרוֹנוֹ לִבְרָכָה שֶׁאִם מָדַד בְּמִדּוֹת שֶׁקֶר אֲפִלּוּ לְגוֹי עוֹבֵד

14. TB Bava M'tzi'a 61b, Bava Bathra 89b.

15. TB Bava M'tzi'a 107b; MT hilchoth g'névah viii 1.

16. The Hebrew adds: and these are their three shapes, respectively. MS Vatican 163/1 shows the three angles in order (and they are so shown in our Hebrew text), while MS Parma 741 shows them as parts of triangles and labels them. But they do not appear in the printed editions.

17. The Hebrew adds, "like this," and the figures are shown; likewise MSS Parma 928 and 741 and MS Vatican 163/1 have appropriate diagrams.

18. I.e. the ratio of the length of a square's diagonal to the length of its side (more precisely it is 1.4142, the square root of 2); TB 'Eruvin 57a.

19. The ratio of a circle's circumference to its diameter (pi, more precisely, 3.1416); ibid. 13b.

mathematics and geometry that differentiate between a right angle, an obtuse angle, and an acute angle,[16] between an equilateral triangle, a triangle with only two equal sides, which is called an isosceles triangle, and a triangle with no equal sides at all, which is called "variously-sided." Then [they differentiate] between a square, a rectangle, a rhomb (equilateral parallelogram),[17] and a rhomboid (non-equilateral parallelogram).[17] There are many aspects to these topics; a large sheet would not contain the very many shapes that the masters of the science of geometry and measurement drew in regard to these matters. Under any circumstances, we need to take great care in the measurement of land areas.

Along with this, remember that the rules which the Sages of blessed memory gave in matters of mathematics—for example, what they said, "Every cubit in a square shape is one and two-fifths cubits [times its length] in the diagonal";[18] and so too, "Whatever is three handbreadths in its circumference has a width of one handbreadth";[19] and again, "By how much does a square exceed a circle?—one·fourth";[20] and so on with these rules—our Sages did not state them with absolute precision but only as approximations.[21] Therefore do not rely on this in regard to divisions of matters [of land] among people.

Nor should you wonder how they could write something inexact, when they are people of truth, in whose congregation God stands.[22] For they had no need of calculations except for the reckoning of the permitted Sabbath limits,[23] or for sowing different kinds of plants or planting trees,[24] and matters like these. And there, where they were not exact, it leads us to be more stringent, and. causes no one damage in his possessions. Nevertheless, in most of these instances where the calculation is imprecise, they attested that they ruled in every single place as it was appropriate—meaning that they were inexact, but on the side of stringency, etc. Thus they made it clear to us that we should not assume about them any inadequacy of care or knowledge in any of these matters.

The rest of its details are in the tractate *Bava Bathra* and in other places. It applies everywhere, at every time, for both man and woman. If a person transgresses it and cheats with a measure of length, a weight, or a measure of quantity, he violates a negative precept; but whiplashes are not given for it, because it can be rectified by payment. Now, Rambam of blessed memory wrote[25] that if someone cheats even a

עֲבוֹדָה זָרָה, עוֹבֵר בְּלֹא־תַעֲשֶׂה וְחַיָּב לְהַחֲזִיר; וְכֵן אָסוּר לְהַטְעוֹת הַגּוֹיִים
בְּחֶשְׁבּוֹן, שֶׁנֶּאֱמַר: וְחִשַּׁב עִם קוֹנֵהוּ — אַף־עַל־פִּי שֶׁהוּא כָּבוּשׁ תַּחַת יָדֶיךָ, קַל
וָחֹמֶר לְגוֹי שֶׁאֵינוֹ כָּבוּשׁ תַּחַת יָדֶיךָ; וַהֲרֵי הוּא אוֹמֵר: כִּי תוֹעֲבַת יי . . . כָּל עוֹשֵׂה
עָוֶל, מִכָּל־מָקוֹם.

[מִצְוַת צִדּוּק הַמֹּאזְנַיִם וְהַמִּשְׁקָלִים וְהַמִּדּוֹת]

רנט לְצַדֵּק הַמֹּאזְנַיִם וְהַמִּשְׁקָלִים וְהַמִּדּוֹת וּלְיַשֵּׁר אוֹתָם, וּלְהִשָּׁמֵר מְאֹד בָּם,
שֶׁנֶּאֱמַר: מֹאזְנֵי צֶדֶק אַבְנֵי צֶדֶק אֵיפַת צֶדֶק וְהִין צֶדֶק יִהְיֶה לָכֶם; וּלְשׁוֹן סִפְרֵי:
"מֹאזְנֵי צֶדֶק", צַדֵּק הַמֹּאזְנַיִם יָפֶה יָפֶה, כְּלוֹמַר שֶׁתִּהְיֶינָה הַמֹּאזְנַיִם מְיֻשָּׁרוֹת.
וְיֵשׁ בְּעִנְיַן הַמֹּאזְנַיִם כִּוּוּנִין גְּדוֹלִים לְפִי שֶׁאֶפְשָׁר לַעֲשׂוֹת בָּהֶם כַּמָּה מִינֵי שְׁקָרִים,
יָדוּעַ הַדָּבָר. "אַבְנֵי צֶדֶק", צַדֵּק אֶת הַמִּשְׁקָלוֹת יָפֶה יָפֶה. גַּם בְּמִשְׁקָלוֹת גַּם־כֵּן
אֶפְשָׁר לַעֲשׂוֹת בָּהֶן הַרְבֵּה מִינֵי שֶׁקֶר, וּכְעֵין מַה שֶּׁאָמְרוּ זִכְרוֹנָם לִבְרָכָה: אֲנִי
עָתִיד לִפָּרַע מִמִּי שֶׁטּוֹמֵן מִשְׁקְלוֹתָיו בְּמֶלַח. "אֵיפַת צֶדֶק", צַדֵּק אֶת הָאֵיפוֹת
יָפֶה; "וְהִין צֶדֶק", צַדֵּק אֶת הַהִינִין יָפֶה.

וְהָאֵיפָה הִיא מִדַּת הַיָּבֵשׁ, וְהִין מִדַּת הַלַּח; וְהִזְהִירַתְנוּ הַתּוֹרָה בְּכָל אֶחָד וְאֶחָד
מִדְּבָרִים אֵלּוּ בִּפְרָט לְחֹמֶר הָעִנְיָן, וְאַף־עַל־פִּי שֶׁהַכֹּל נִכְלָל בִּכְלָל "לֹא תוֹנוּ אִישׁ
אֶת עֲמִיתוֹ". וּלְשׁוֹן סִפְרָא: עַל תְּנַאי כָּךְ הוֹצֵאתִי אֶתְכֶם מֵאֶרֶץ מִצְרַיִם, שֶׁתְּקַבְּלוּ
עֲלֵיכֶם מִצְוַת מִדּוֹת. וְאָמְרוּ גַם־כֵּן זִכְרוֹנָם לִבְרָכָה: אֲנִי שֶׁהִבְחַנְתִּי בְּמִצְרַיִם בֵּין
טִפָּה שֶׁל בְּכוֹר לְטִפָּה שֶׁאֵינָהּ שֶׁל בְּכוֹר, אֲנִי עָתִיד לִפָּרַע מִמִּי שֶׁטּוֹמֵן מִשְׁקְלוֹתָיו
בְּמֶלַח כְּדֵי לְהוֹנוֹת הַבְּרִיּוֹת שֶׁאֵין מַכִּירִין בָּהֶן.

שֹׁרֶשׁ מִצְוַת הַיֹּשֶׁר וְהַרְחָקַת הַגֵּזֶל וְהַתַּרְמִית מִבֵּין בְּנֵי־אָדָם יָדוּעַ לְכָל בֶּן
דָּעַת.

20. Where the side of the square equals the diameter of the circle (here too, *pi* is
assumed to be 3); *ibid.* 14b.

21. So *tosafoth* to TB 'Eruvin 57a, s.v. *kol*, and to *ibid.* 14a, s.v. *v'ha'ikka*; and
Rambam, commentary to Mishnah, 'Eruvin i 5.

22. Expression based on Psalms 82a.

23. I.e. the distance one may walk beyond a settled community on the Sabbath
(§ 24).

24. I.e. the minimal distance that must be left between them.

25. MT *bilchoth g'névah* vii 8.

26. I.e. if a Hebrew sold himself into servitude to a *gér toshav*, a non-Jew in the land
of Israel who renounced idolatry, his period of servitude would be until the jubilee year.
If a relative came to redeem him, he and his master were to calculate how many years
were past and how many remained till the jubilee; and for these remaining years, when
the *gér toshav* would not have the servant's labor, he was to be refunded a proportional
share of the purchase price he had paid.

27. I.e. the *gér toshav*, being an isolated foreigner among the Hebrews.

non-Jewish idol-worshipper with false measures, he violates a negative
precept, and is obligated to return [the withheld amount]. So too is it
forbidden to mislead a non-Jew in calculation: for it is stated, *And
he shall reckon with him that bought him*[26] (Leviticus 25:50), even though
he is subservient under your dominion;[27] then all the more certainly
[must we treat with justice] a non-Jew who is not subservient under
your dominion. And then Scripture states, *For an abomination to the
Lord are . . . all who do injustice* (Deuteronomy 25:16)—in any way.

[THE PRECEPT THAT SCALES, WEIGHTS AND MEASURES
SHOULD BE MADE CORRECT]

259 to make scales, weights and measures just, correct them,
and be very careful with them—as it is stated, *Just balances, just weights,
a just éphah, and a just hin shall you have* (Leviticus 19:36). In the language
of the Midrash *Sifra*:[1] "Just balances"—adjust your scales very finely;
in other words, that the scales should be made true. There are many
adjustments [to be made] in a scale, because it is possible to make many
kinds of falsifications with it; this is a known matter. "Just weights"—
adjust the weights very finely. With weights too, it is equally possible
to make many kinds of falsification—in keeping with what the Sages
of blessed memory said,[2] "I am destined to exact payment from one
who immerses his weights in salt."[3] "A just *éphah*"—adjust the
éphah measures finely; "and a just *hin*"—adjust the *hin* measures
finely.

The term *éphah* denotes dry measure; the term *hin*, liquid measure.
And the Torah adjured us about each and every one of these items
in detail, in view of the seriousness of the matter, even though everything was generally included under the injunction, *And you shall not
wrong one another* (Leviticus 25:17).[4] In the language of the Midrash
Sifra:[5] "On this condition did I take you out of the land of Egypt:
that you shall accept the precept about measures."[6] Our Sages of
blessed memory said equally,[7] "I who discriminated in Egypt between
the seminal drop of a firstborn [that engendered him] and a seminal
drop that was not of a firstborn [that did not engender one][8]—I
am destined to exact payment from one who immerses his weights
in salt in order to cheat people who do not detect them."

The root reason· for a precept of fairness and honesty and the
avoidance[9] of robbery and cheating among people, is known (evident)
to every person of sense.

מִדִּינֵי הַמִּצְוָה, מַה שֶּׁאָמְרוּ זִכְרוֹנָם לִבְרָכָה שֶׁאֵין עוֹשִׂין מִשְׁקָלוֹת שֶׁל בְּדִיל
וְעוֹפֶרֶת וְכָל שְׁאָר מִינֵי מַתָּכוֹת, מִפְּנֵי שֶׁמַּעֲלִין חֲלוּדָה וּמִתְחַסְּרִין, אֲבָל עוֹשִׂין
אוֹתָן שֶׁל אֶבֶן וּזְכוּכִית וְכַיּוֹצֵא בָּהֶן; וְהַדְּבָרִים שֶׁאָמְרוּ בִּמְדִידַת הַקַּרְקַע, וּמַה
שֶּׁלִּמְּדוּנוּ בְּצוּרַת הַמַּחַק שֶׁקּוֹרִין בְּלַעַז רְשׁוּרַא; וְאָמְרוּ גַם-כֵּן שֶׁלֹּא יַרְתִּים בְּמִדַּת
הַלַּח בְּעֵת שֶׁמּוֹדֵד, וַאֲפִלּוּ הָיְתָה מִדָּה קְטַנָּה בְּיוֹתֵר, שֶׁהֲרֵי מָצִינוּ שֶׁהַתּוֹרָה
הִקְפִּידָה עַל הַמִּדּוֹת בְּכָל-שֶׁהוּא, שֶׁנֶּאֱמַר בַּתּוֹרָה: לֹא תַעֲשׂוּ עָוֶל... בַּמִּדָּה
בַּמִּשְׁקָל וּבַמְּשׂוּרָה, וְהַמְּשׂוּרָה הִיא מִדָּה קְטַנָּה בְּיוֹתֵר, שֶׁהִיא חֵלֶק אֶחָד מִשְּׁלֹשָׁה
וּשְׁלֹשִׁים בְּלֹג.

וְהַשִּׁעוּרִים שֶׁנָּתְנוּ זִכְרוֹנָם לִבְרָכָה בְּאֹרֶךְ קְנֵה הַמֹּאזְנַיִם וּבְאֹרֶךְ הַחוּטִים,
וְהַחִלּוּקִים שֶׁאָמְרוּ בֵּין מֹאזְנַיִם הֶעָשׂוּיִין לִשְׁקֹל מִין אֶחָד לְמֹאזְנַיִם שֶׁל מִין אַחֵר;
וּמַה שֶּׁאָמְרוּ שֶׁחַיָּבִין בֵּית-דִּין לְהַעֲמִיד שׁוֹטְרִים בְּכָל מָקוֹם וּמָקוֹם לִהְיוֹת
מְחַזְּרִים לְצַדֵּק הַמֹּאזְנַיִם וְהַמִּשְׁקָלוֹת, וְיֵשׁ לָהֶם רְשׁוּת לִקְנֹס בְּמָמוֹנוֹ גַם בְּגוּפוֹ כָּל
שֶׁנִּמְצָא עִמּוֹ מִשְׁקָל חָסֵר; וְיֶתֶר פְּרָטֶיהָ, בְּפֶרֶק חֲמִישִׁי מִבָּתְרָא.

וְנוֹהֶגֶת בְּכָל מָקוֹם וּבְכָל זְמַן, בִּזְכָרִים וּנְקֵבוֹת. וְעוֹבֵר עָלֶיהָ בִּטֵּל עֲשֵׂה, מִלְּבַד
שֶׁעָבַר עַל לָאו דְּאוֹנָאָה וּגְזֵלָה וּגְנֵבָה אִם יֵשׁ בָּהּ שָׁוֶה פְּרוּטָה. וּמַה שֶּׁיְּקַשֶּׁה בָּעִנְיָן
יוֹתֵר, כִּי הַמַּשְׁקֵר בַּמִּדּוֹת לֹא יִתֵּן לֵב לְכָל הַלּוֹקְחִים וְאֵינוֹ יוֹדֵעַ לְמִי גָּזַל שֶׁיַּחֲזִיר
אֵלָיו גְּזֵלוֹ; וְזֶהוּ שֶׁאָמְרוּ זִכְרוֹנָם לִבְרָכָה כִּי קָשֶׁה מְאֹד עָנְשָׁן שֶׁל מִדּוֹת.

[שֶׁלֹּא לְקַלֵּל אָב וָאֵם]

רס שֶׁלֹּא לְקַלֵּל אָב וָאֵם, שֶׁנֶּאֱמַר: אִישׁ אִישׁ אֲשֶׁר יְקַלֵּל אֶת אָבִיו וְאֶת אִמּוֹ,

§259

1. Sifra, *k'doshim, perek* 8, 7.

2. Explaining the significance of the Almighty's words in the rest of the verse cited
above: *I am the Lord your God;* TB Bava M'tzi'a 61b.

3. To reduce their actual weight (MT *hilchoth g'névah* viii 7), so that they will
balance on the scales against less of his goods that he sells.

4. This should evidently rather be Leviticus 25:14, *you shall not wrong one another.*
According to the Talmud (TB Bava M'tzi'a 58b) it refers to exploitation, cheating or
extortion of goods, while verse 17 refers to oppressing with words.

5. Sifra *ibid.* 10. This too (see note 2) interprets the second part of the opening
verse: *I am the Lord your God who brought you out of the land of Egypt.*

6. From the beginning to here is based on ShM positive precept §208.

7. TB Bava M'tzi'a 61b.

8. If a woman committed adultery, the first son she bore after marriage might not
be a firstborn to his real father, while sons whom she bore later might be firstborn to
their real fathers. Thus, when the tenth plague killed out all of Egypt's firstborn, only the
Almighty could know who they actually were.

9. More literally, the removal to a distance.

10. TB Bava Bathra 89a–b.

11. See §258, fifth paragraph.

Among the laws of the precept, there is what the Sages of blessed
memory taught:[10] that weights are not to be made of tin alloy,
lead, or any other kind of metal—because they grow rusty and continually become diminished; but they may rather be made of stone,
glass, and similar materials. Then there are those matters which they
said about the measurement of land;[11] and what they taught us about
the form of the "leveler,"[12] called *rasero* in the foreign tongue
[Spanish]. They taught further[10] that one should not cause bubbling
and foaming [when pouring] into a liquid measure,[13] at the time a
measure is taken—this even if it is the very smallest measuring container: for here we find that the Torah is strict about any measure
whatever, since it is stated in the Torah, *You shall do no wrong . . . in
measure of length, in weight, or in* m'surah (*measure of quantity*; Leviticus
19:35), and *m'surah* denotes the very smallest measure, which is one
thirty-third of a *log.*[14]

Moreover, we have the measurements that the Sages of blessed
memory gave[10] for the horizontal lever of the balance (scales)[15] and
for the length of the cords.[16] And there are the differences they stipulated[10] between scales made to measure one sort and scales for another
kind. There is, too, what they said:[10] that the court is obligated to
appoint officers in every single location, to go about and adjust the
scales and weights, and they should have the right to impose a fine
on property, and even physical penalty, on anyone who is found
to have a short weight. The rest of its details are in chapter 5 of the
Talmud tractate *Bava Bathra.*

It is in force in every place, at every time, for both man and woman.
If a person violates it, he disobeys a positive precept—apart from
transgressing the injunctions against illegal retention of property,
robbery and theft, if [at least] a *p'rutah's* worth is involved. What
is worst of all in the matter is that the one who cheats with his measures
will pay no attention to all the customers, and will not know whom
he robbed, to be able to return to each the amount of which he robbed
him. This is why the Sages of blessed memory said[17] that the punishment in regard to measures is very severe.

[THE PROHIBITION AGAINST CURSING ONE'S FATHER
OR MOTHER]

260 not to curse a father or a mother, as it is stated, *whatever man
there may be who curses his father or his mother, he shall surely be put to*

וְגוֹמֵר. וְהָאֱמֶת שֶׁעִקַּר הָאַזְהָרָה בְּקִלְלַת אָב נָאֶה מִן הַמִּקְרָא הַזֶּה, כִּי בְּכָאן לֹא יַזְכִּיר רַק הָעֹנֶשׁ בִּמְקַלֵּל, וְכֵן מַה שֶׁכָּתוּב בְּסֵדֶר מִשְׁפָּטִים "וּמְקַלֵּל אָבִיו וְאִמּוֹ מוֹת יוּמָת", שָׁם גַּם־כֵּן לֹא דִּבֵּר אֶלָּא בָּעֹנֶשׁ.

וְזֶהוּ שֶׁאָמְרוּ בִּמְכִלְתָּא: "וּמְקַלֵּל אָבִיו וְאִמּוֹ" וְכוּלֵי, עֹנֶשׁ שָׁמַעְנוּ, אַזְהָרָה מִנַּיִן; תַּלְמוּד לוֹמַר "אֱלֹהִים לֹא תְקַלֵּל": אִם דַּיָּן הוּא אָבִיךָ הֲרֵי הוּא בִכְלָל "אֱלֹהִים לֹא תְקַלֵּל", וְאִם נָשִׂיא הוּא הֲרֵי הוּא בִכְלָל "וְנָשִׂיא בְעַמְּךָ לֹא תָאֹר", וְאִם בּוּר הוּא הֲרֵי הוּא בִכְלָל "לֹא תְקַלֵּל חֵרֵשׁ"; הֲרֵי אַתָּה דָן בִּנְיַן אָב מִשְּׁלָשְׁתָּן וְכוּלֵי, עַד: הַצַּד הַשָּׁוֶה שֶׁבָּהֶן שֶׁהֵם בְּעַמְּךָ וְאַתָּה מֻזְהָר עַל קִלְלָתָן; אַף אָבִיךָ שֶׁבְּעַמְּךָ אַתָּה מֻזְהָר עַל קִלְלָתוֹ.

וְכֵן אָמְרוּ גַם־כֵּן בְּסִפְרָא: "אִישׁ אִישׁ אֲשֶׁר יְקַלֵּל", עֹנֶשׁ שָׁמַעְנוּ וְכוּלֵי, כְּמוֹ הַלָּשׁוֹן אֲשֶׁר בִּמְכִלְתָּא בְּשָׁוֶה. וּמִפְּנֵי שֶׁאֵין לָאַזְהָרָה זוֹ לָאו מְיֻחָד אֶלָּא שֶׁהוּא יוֹצֵא מִכְּלַל שְׁלֹשָׁה לָאוִין שֶׁכָּתַבְנוּ, כְּתַבְתִּיו עַל מִקְרָא זֶה שֶׁמְּדַבֵּר בָּעֹנֶשׁ, וּכְמוֹ־ כֵן כָּתְבוּ הָרַמְבַּ"ם זִכְרוֹנוֹ לִבְרָכָה בְּ"מְקַלֵּל אָבִיו וְאִמּוֹ מוֹת יוּמָת", שֶׁהוּא מְדַבֵּר בָּעֹנֶשׁ.

מִשָּׁרְשֵׁי הַמִּצְוָה, כָּתַבְתִּי בְּמִשְׁפָּטִים מִצְוַת לֹא־תַעֲשֶׂה ג' [סִי' מ"ח].

מִדִּינֵי הַמִּצְוָה, כְּגוֹן מַה שֶׁאָמְרוּ שֶׁחַיָּב קִלְלַת הָאָב וְהָאֵם הוּא בֵּין בְּחַיֵּיהֶם אוֹ אֲפִלּוּ אַחַר מוֹתָן, מַה שֶׁאֵין כֵּן בְּהַכָּאָה, שֶׁאֵין הַחִיּוּב בָּהּ כִּי אִם בְּחַיֵּיהֶם, אֲבָל לְאַחַר מִיתָה פָּטוּר עַל הַכָּאָתָם.

---

12. Which levels off the excess of what has to be measured flat; TB *ibid.*

13. By pouring fast and from a height; the bubbles and foam will make the container look full when it actually is not.

14. See §258, first paragraph.

15. Which is balanced at its midpoint on a fulcrum.

16. Which hang from its ends to hold the two pans.

17. TB Bava Bathra 89a.

§260   1. This passage from Mechilta is abridged, as it is in ShM negative precept §318 (although it may equally be a variant, shorter version); here our author breaks off with "etc."

    2. I.e. who observes the Torah and is not sinful.

    3. Sifra, *k'doshim, perek* 9, 7.

    4. ShM negative precept §318.

    5. TB Sanhedrin 85b.

death (Leviticus 20:9). Now, in truth, the main admonition about cursing a father or mother is not [learned] from this verse, since here only the punishment for the one who utters the curse is mentioned. So too the verse in *sidrah mishpatim: And he that curses his father or his mother shall surely be put to death* (Exodus 21:17)—there also only the punishment is mentioned.

This is why it was stated in the Midrash *Mechilta*: "And he that curses his father or his mother shall surely be put to death"—thus we have heard the punishment; where do we find the admonition? Scripture states, *You shall not curse a judge* (Exodus 22:27): Now, if your father is a judge, he is included under the ban, "you shall not curse a judge" (§69); if he is a ruler, he is clearly included under the ban, *nor shall you curse a ruler of your people* (ibid.—§71); and if he is an illiterate commoner, he is clearly included under the ban, *You shall not curse the deaf* (Leviticus 19:14—§231). Thus you deduce a standing rule from the three:[1] the characteristics of a judge are not like those of a ruler [in law], nor are the characteristics of a ruler like those of a judge [in law]; nor are the characteristics of either [in law] like those of a deaf man, and neither are those of a deaf man like theirs. Their common denominator is that they are "of your people" (Exodus 22:27) and you are adjured against cursing them. Thus you are adjured too against cursing your father who is "of your people."[2]

So was it stated likewise in the Midrash *Sifra*:[3] "whatever man there may be who curses . . . "—thus we have heard the punishment, etc.—exactly like the exposition in *Mechilta*. Well, since this injunction has no specific negative precept [in Scripture] but is derived from the sum total of the three negative precepts that we noted, I have written it for this verse, which speaks of the punishment. So too did Rambam of blessed memory write it[4] in conjunction with the verse, *he that curses his father or his mother shall surely be put to death* (Exodus 21:17), which speaks of the penalty.

As to the root reason for the commandment, I wrote it in the third negative precept of *sidrah mishpatim* (§48).

Among the laws of the precept, there is, for example, what the Sages taught:[5] that punishment for cursing a mother or father is incurred whether [it is done] in their lifetime or even after their death—which is not the case about striking them: there punishment is incurred only [if it is done] while they are alive, but after their death one goes free of penalty for striking them.

⟨155⟩

וּמַה שֶּׁאָמְרוּ שֶׁאֵין חַיּוּב מִיתָה לַבֵּן עַד שֶׁיְּקַלְּלֵם בְּשֵׁם מִן הַשֵּׁמוֹת הַמְיֻחָדִים;
אֲבָל הַמְקַלְּלָן בְּכִנּוּי, פָּטוּר מִסְּקִילָה, וְלוֹקֶה כְּדֶרֶךְ שֶׁלּוֹקֶה עַל קִלְלַת אָדָם כָּשֵׁר.
וּמַה שֶּׁאָמְרוּ שֶׁהַמְקַלֵּל אֲבִי אָבִיו אוֹ אֲבִי אִמּוֹ, דִּינוֹ כִּמְקַלֵּל אֶחָד מִשְּׁאָר
הַקָּהָל; וְהָאָב שֶׁנִּתְחַיֵּב שְׁבוּעָה, אֵין הַבֵּן מַשְׁבִּיעוֹ בִּשְׁבוּעַת הָאָלָה, אֶלָּא מַשְׁבִּיעוֹ
שְׁבוּעָה שֶׁאֵין בָּהּ אָלָה; וְאָמְרוּ גַם־כֵּן שֶׁאָסוּר לְבַזּוֹתוֹ כְּלָל, שֶׁלֹּא עַל הַקְּלָלָה
הִקְפִּידָה תוֹרָה אֶלָּא אַף עַל הַבִּזָּיוֹן; וְהַמְבַזֵּהוּ הֲרֵי הוּא בְּ"אָרוּר", שֶׁנֶּאֱמַר: אָרוּר
מַקְלֶה אָבִיו וְאִמּוֹ, וְיֵשׁ לְבֵית־דִּין לְהַכּוֹת הָעוֹשֶׂה זֶה וְלַעֲנשׁ כְּפִי הָרָאוּי; וְיֶתֶר
פְּרָטֶיהָ, בְּפֶרֶק שְׁבִיעִי מִסַּנְהֶדְרִין.

וְנוֹהֶגֶת בְּכָל מָקוֹם וּבְכָל זְמַן, בִּזְכָרִים וּנְקֵבוֹת, וְכֵן בְּטוּמְטוּם וְאַנְדְּרוֹגִינוֹס.
וּשְׁתוּקִי חַיָּב עַל אִמּוֹ וְאֵינוֹ חַיָּב עַל אָבִיו, אַף־עַל־פִּי שֶׁנִּבְדְּקָה אִמּוֹ וְאָמְרָה: בֶּן
פְּלוֹנִי הוּא. וּלְפִי הַדּוֹמֶה שֶׁמַּמְזֵר חַיָּב עַל קִלְלַת אָבִיו וְאִמּוֹ, שֶׁהֲרֵי הוּא רָאוּי
לִירַשׁ אוֹתָם מִדִּין תּוֹרָה, וְדִין בֵּן כָּשֵׁר יֵשׁ לוֹ גַם־כֵּן לְעִנְיַן אֲבֵלוּת וּלְכָל דָּבָר;
אֲבָל הַבֵּן מִן הַשִּׁפְחָה וּמִן הַנָּכְרִית אֵינוֹ חַיָּב עַל קִלְלָתָן. וְכֵן גֵּר שֶׁהוֹרָתוֹ שֶׁלֹּא
בִקְדֻשָּׁה אַף־עַל־פִּי שֶׁנּוֹלַד בִּקְדֻשָּׁה, כְּגוֹן שֶׁנִּתְגַּיְּרָה אִמּוֹ כְּשֶׁהָיְתָה מְעֻבֶּרֶת, אֵינוֹ
חַיָּב עַל קִלְלַת אָבִיו; וּכְשֵׁם שֶׁאֵינוֹ חַיָּב עַל קִלְלַת אָבִיו, כָּךְ אֵינוֹ חַיָּב עַל (קִלְלַת)
אִמּוֹ, אַף־עַל־פִּי שֶׁהִיא יְהוּדִית כְּשֶׁיְּלָדַתּוּ, וּכְמוֹ שֶׁדָּרְשׁוּ זִכְרוֹנָם לִבְרָכָה:
"וּמְקַלֵּל אָבִיו וְאִמּוֹ", אֶת שֶׁהוּא חַיָּב עַל אָבִיו חַיָּב עַל אִמּוֹ וְכוּלֵי. וְאֵין לְהַקְשׁוֹת
עַל דְּרָשָׁה זוֹ מִשְּׁתוּקִי, שֶׁחַיָּב עַל אִמּוֹ לְבַדָּהּ, לְפִי שֶׁאֵין הָאָב יָדוּעַ וְנִכָּר.

וְהַגֵּר אָסוּר לְקַלֵּל אֲבִי אָבִיו הַגּוֹי, מִדְּרַבָּנָן, כְּדֵי שֶׁלֹּא יֹאמְרוּ: בָּא מִקְּדֻשָּׁה חֲמוּרָה

6. TB Sh'vu'oth 35a.

7. Which designate the Almighty alone.

8. Such as the Almighty, the Merciful One, etc.

9. MT *hilchoth mamrim* v 2 (see *Kessef Mishneh, Leḥem Mishneh*).

10. Sifra, *k'doshim, perek* 9, 8; Mechilta d'R. Simeon b. Yoḥai, Exodus 21:17 (MT *ibid.* 3).

11. I.e. calling down Heaven's anathema, etc. upon him if the subject of his oath is not true; MT *ibid.* 15; according to R. Moses of Couçy, *Séfer Mitzvoth Gadol* (*S'mag*), negative precept §219, this is a ruling of the *ge'onim*.

12. MT *hilchoth mamrim* v 15.

13. I.e. whiplashes of disobedience (see §24, note 14).

14. Whether one's gender is in doubt or he is both genders, it makes no difference here, since it applies to both male and female; Mechilta, Exodus 21:17; MT *ibid.* 1.

15. MT *ibid.* 9. Sifra, *k'doshim, perek* 9, 9.

16. I.e. a son born to consanguineous relations or adulterers, for whom conjugal intimacy is punishable by *karéth* (Divine severance of existence); TB Yevamoth 22b.

17. Because he is not ranked as a Jew; MT *ibid.*

18. Because converts to Judaism are as newborn infants, hence no longer related to previous kin; MdRSbY, Exodus 21:17; MT *ibid.*

Then there is what the Sages said:[6] that no death penalty is due the son until he curses them by one of the particular Divine names;[7] but if one curses them by a substitute (attributive) name,[8] he is free of the penalty of stoning; he is given lashes (a whipping) however, as he would be whipped for cursing any worthy person (§231).[9]

We have, further, what the Sages said:[10] that if someone curses his father's father or his mother's father, his sentence is as for cursing anyone else in the community. If a father became obligated to swear an oath, his son is not to administer to him an oath of imprecation,[11] but rather administers to him an oath containing no imprecation. They said, likewise,[12] that it is forbidden to disgrace him [one's father] at all; for not merely about cursing did the Torah object, but about disgrace also; and one who disgraces him [his father] lies under an imprecation, for it is stated, *Cursed be he who dishonors his father or his mother* (Deuteronomy 27:16). It is for the court to whip the one who does this and to administer suitable punishment.[13] The rest of its details are in chapter 7 of the Talmud tractate *Sanhedrin.*

It is in force everywhere, at every time, for both man and woman, as well as a *tumtum* [one of uncertain gender] and a hermaphrodite.[14] A *sh'tuki* [of uncertain fatherhood] is punishable over his mother but not over his father, even if his mother was examined (questioned) and she said, "He is so-and-so's son."[15] A bastard[16] is evidently punishable for cursing his father or his mother: for he is fit to inherit them by the law of the Torah, and he also is a proper, acceptable son under the law in regard to mourning and everything [similar]. However, a son by a female slave or a heathen woman is not punishable for cursing them;[17] so too a convert to Judaism who was not conceived in holiness, even if he was born in holiness—for instance, if his mother converted while she was pregnant—he is not liable to punishment for cursing his father.[18] And just as he is not punishable for malediction of his father, so is he not liable for cursing his mother, even though she was Jewish when she bore him. As our Sages of blessed memory expounded:[19] "And he that curses his father or his mother" (Exodus 21:17)—one who would incur punishment over his father is punishable over his mother, etc. Now, this exposition cannot be refuted by the case of a *sh'tuki* [one of uncertain fatherhood]: he is punishable over his mother alone because the father is not identified and known.[20]

A convert to Judaism is forbidden to curse his non-Jewish father by the ruling of the Sages: so that it should not be said, "He went from

לִקְלָלָה; אֲבָל הָעֶבֶד אֵין לוֹ יָחוּס, וַהֲרֵי אָבִיו כְּמִי שֶׁאֵינוֹ אָבִיו לְכָל דָּבָר, וְאַף לְאַחַר שֶׁנִּשְׁתַּחְרֵר.

וְעוֹבֵר עַל זֶה וְקִלְלָם בְּשֵׁם מִן הַשֵּׁמוֹת, נִסְקָל, וְהוּא שֶׁיֵּשׁ שָׁם עֵדִים וְהַתְרָאָה, כְּמוֹ שֶׁיָּדוּעַ בְּכָל הַמִּצְווֹת; וְאִם קִלְּלָן בְּאֶחָד מִן הַכִּנּוּיִין, לוֹקֶה.

[מִצְוַת שֶׁיִּשָּׂרְפוּ מִי שֶׁיִּתְחַיֵּב שְׂרֵפָה]

רס א לִהְיוֹת בֵּית־דִּין שׂוֹרְפִין בָּאֵשׁ, כְּלוֹמַר שֶׁנִּצְטַוּוּ הַבֵּית־דִּין לַעֲשׂוֹת מִשְׁפָּט בִּשְׂרֵפָה בְּמִקְצָת עֲבֵרוֹת, וְאַחַת מֵהֶן הִיא הַבָּא עַל אִשָּׁה וְעַל אִמָּהּ, שֶׁנֶּאֱמַר: וְאִישׁ אֲשֶׁר יִקַּח אֶת אִשָּׁה וְאֶת אִמָּהּ זִמָּה הִיא בָּאֵשׁ יִשְׂרְפוּ אוֹתוֹ וְאֶתְהֶן וְגוֹמֵר. וּכְבָר כָּתַבְתִּי לְמַעְלָה, בְּסֵדֶר אַחֲרֵי מוֹת בְּמִצְוַת לֹא־תַעֲשֶׂה י״ח [סי׳ ר״י״ג], בְּאֵי זֶה עִנְיָן יִתְחַיֵּב אֲשֶׁר יִקַּח אִשָּׁה וּבִתָּהּ, וְשֶׁאֵין בִּכְלָל הַחִיּוּב אֶלָּא הָאַחַת, וְהִיא הָאַחֲרוֹנָה. וּמַה שֶּׁכָּתוּב "וְאֶתְהֶן", פֵּרוּשׁ אַחַת מֵהֶן, שֶׁכֵּן בָּא הַפֵּרוּשׁ בְּמַסֶּכֶת סַנְהֶדְרִין, וְאָמְרוּ שָׁם שֶׁכֵּן בְּמָקוֹם פְּלוֹנִי קוֹרִין לְאַחַת הֵן, וְכוּלֵי, כְּמוֹ שֶׁכָּתַבְתִּי שָׁם.

מִשָּׁרְשֵׁי אִסּוּר הָעֲרָיוֹת כָּתַבְתִּי לְמַעְלָה בְּאַחֲרֵי מוֹת [סי׳ ק״צ] מַה שֶּׁיָּדַעְתִּי וְשָׁמַעְתִּי בְּעִנְיָנָן.

מִדִּינֵי הַמִּצְוָה, מַה שֶּׁאָמְרוּ זִכְרוֹנָם לִבְרָכָה: מִצְוַת הַנִּשְׂרָפִין, שֶׁהָיוּ מְשַׁקְּעִין אוֹתוֹ בְּזֶבֶל עַד אַרְכּוּבּוֹתָיו, וְנוֹתְנִין סוּדָר קָשֶׁה בְּתוֹךְ סוּדָר רַךְ וְכוֹרֵךְ עַל צַנָּארוֹ, וּשְׁנֵי עֵדָיו זֶה מוֹשֵׁךְ אֶצְלוֹ וְזֶה מוֹשֵׁךְ אֶצְלוֹ עַד שֶׁהוּא פוֹתֵחַ אֶת פִּיו, וּמַתְּיכִין אֶת הַבְּדִיל וְהָעוֹפֶרֶת וְכַיּוֹצֵא בָהֶן וְזוֹרֵק לְתוֹךְ פִּיו, וְהִיא יוֹרֶדֶת וְשׂוֹרֶפֶת אֶת בְּנֵי מֵעָיו; וְיֶתֶר פְּרָטֶיהָ, בְּפֶרֶק שְׁבִיעִי מִסַּנְהֶדְרִין.

וְנוֹהֶגֶת מִצְוָה זוֹ בִּזְכָרִים כִּי לָהֶם הַמִּשְׁפָּט, וּבְאֶרֶץ יִשְׂרָאֵל בִּלְבַד כִּי הִיא

---

19. MdRSbY, Exodus 21:17; Sifra, k'doshim, perek 9, 9.

20. Hence he is liable over both parents, but in regard to his father the punishment cannot be given because that parent cannot be identified with certainty; Sifra *ibid*.

21. I.e. as a Gentile he was forbidden to curse his father, and now that he is a Jew he is permitted!—MT *bilchoth mamrim* v 11, based on TB Yevamoth 22a (*Kessef Mishneh*).

22. MT *ibid*.

23. As our author wrote four paragraphs above.

§261   1. I.e. the second of the two whom he married, since he committed no sin in marrying the first.

2. This is the reading in TB Shabbath 31b, Mo'éd Katan 28a, and Nazir 8b; our editions of TB read here *béna*. Jacob Levy, *Wörterbuch über die Talmudim und Midrashim*, s.v. הין III, links the word with the Greek *en*; Jastrow, s.v. הֵינָא, with the Greek *ena*—both meaning "one."

a stricter state of holiness to a lighter one." [21] A slave, however, has no relations by law, and his father is regarded as not being his father in any respect—this also after he is set free. [22]

If a person violates this and curses them [either of the parents] by one of the Divine names, he should be stoned to death—this if there were witnesses and a warning, as is known about all the precepts. If he cursed [either of] them by one of the substitute (attributive) names, he should be given whiplashes. [23]

[THE PRECEPT THAT WHOEVER INCURS DEATH BY
BURNING IS TO BE BURNED]

261 that a *beth din* (court) should execute by burning with fire; in other words, that the *beth din* was charged to render a verdict of burning for some transgressions, one of them being [the sin of] a person who is conjugally intimate with a woman and with her mother—for it is stated, *And if a man takes a wife and her mother, it is wickedness; they shall be burned with fire, both he and they,* etc. (Leviticus 20:14). I have already written, above, in the eighteenth negative precept of *sidrah aharé moth* (§203) under what circumstances one who takes a woman and her daughter becomes guilty, and that only one [woman] is subject to the penalty, this being the later one; [1] as for Scripture's term *v'eth-hen*, "and they," it means one of them. For so is the explanation given in the tractate *Sanhedrin* (76b); and it was stated there: for in that certain region, they call one (female) *hen*, [2] etc.—as I wrote there.

As to the root reason for the ban on forbidden conjugal relations, I wrote above, in *sidrah aharé moth* (§190), what I have known and heard about the subject.

Among the laws of the precept, there is what the Sages of blessed memory taught: [3] The precept for any person to be burned to death is that he would be immersed in dung up to his knees. A hard cloth would be wrapped in a soft cloth; it would be wound about his neck, and his two witnesses then pulled each [one end] to himself, until he opened his mouth. Tin alloy, lead, and so forth would be melted, and hurled into his mouth; [4] it would descend and burn his innards. The rest of its details are in chapter 7 of the tractate *Sanhedrin*.

This precept applies to men, as judgment is for them [to carry out], and this in the land of Israel alone, for that is the place of judgment. [5] If [the judges of] a court transgressed it and did not sentence a

מְקוֹם הַמִּשְׁפָּט. וּבֵית־דִּין שֶׁעָבְרוּ עָלֶיהָ וְלֹא דָנוּ הַחַיָּב כְּדִינוֹ, בִּטְּלוּ עֲשֵׂה, וְעָנְשׁוֹ גָּדוֹל, כִּי בְמִשְׁפָּט יִתְיַשֵּׁב הָעוֹלָם.

וּכְבָר כָּתַבְתִּי לְמַעְלָה בְּסֵדֶר מִשְׁפָּטִים מִצְוַת עֲשֵׂה ד' [סִי' מ"ז], כִּי הָרַמְבַּ"ן זִכְרוֹנוֹ לִבְרָכָה לֹא יִמְנֶה בְחֶשְׁבּוֹן הַמִּצְווֹת הַמִּצְווֹת בַּסֵּפֶר שֶׁלּוֹ אַרְבַּע מִיתוֹת בֵּית־דִּין, וְשָׁם הֵבֵאתִי קְצָת הַטַּעַם שֶׁכָּתַב הוּא בָּעִנְיָן.

[שֶׁלֹּא לָלֶכֶת בְּחֻקּוֹת הַגּוֹיִם]

רסב שֶׁלֹּא לָלֶכֶת בְּחֻקּוֹת הָאֱמוֹרִי, וְכֵן בְּחֻקּוֹת הַגּוֹיִם, שֶׁנֶּאֱמַר "וְלֹא תֵלְכוּ בְּחֻקֹּת הַגּוֹי אֲשֶׁר אֲנִי מְשַׁלֵּחַ מִפְּנֵיכֶם", וְהוּא הַדִּין לְכָל שְׁאָר הַגּוֹיִם, כִּי הָעִנְיָן מִפְּנֵי שֶׁהֵם סָרִים מֵאַחֲרֵי הַשֵּׁם וְעוֹבְדִין עֲבוֹדָה זָרָה.

וְעִנְיַן הַמִּצְוָה הוּא שֶׁלֹּא נִתְנַהֵג כָּהֶם בְּמַלְבּוּשֵׁינוּ וְעִנְיָנֵינוּ; וּכְמוֹ שֶׁאָמְרוּ בְּסִפְרֵי: "וּבְחֻקֹּתֵיהֶם לֹא תֵלֵכוּ", שֶׁלֹּא תֵלְכוּ בְנִמוֹסוֹת שֶׁלָּהֶם, בַּדְּבָרִים הַחֲקוּקִים לָהֶם, כְּגוֹן טֵיַטְרָאוֹת וְקִרְקְסָאוֹת וְהָאִסְטַרְיָאוֹת. וְכָל אֵלּוּ הֵם מִינֵי שְׂחוֹק שֶׁעוֹשִׂין בְּקִבּוּצֵיהֶן כְּשֶׁמִּתְקַבְּצִין לַעֲשׂוֹת שִׁגְעוֹנוֹת וּזְנוּת וַעֲבוֹדַת הָאֱלִילִים.

וְאָמְרוּ שָׁם: "בְּחֻקּוֹת הַגּוֹי", רַבִּי מֵאִיר אוֹמֵר: אֵלּוּ דַרְכֵי הָאֱמוֹרִי שֶׁמָּנוּ חֲכָמִים; רַבִּי יְהוּדָה בֶן בְּתֵירָה אוֹמֵר: שֶׁלֹּא תְגַדֵּל צִיצַת הָרֹאשׁ כָּהֶם וְלֹא תְסַפֵּר קוֹמֵי, כְּלוֹמַר שֶׁלֹּא יְגַלַּח מִן הַצְּדָדִין וְיַנִּיחַ שֵׂעָר בָּאֶמְצַע, וְזֶהוּ הַנִּקְרָא בְּלוֹרִית.

וְנִכְפַּל זֶה הַלָּאו בְּמָקוֹם אַחֵר בְּמִלּוֹת אֲחֵרוֹת, שֶׁנֶּאֱמַר: הִשָּׁמֶר לְךָ פֶּן תִּנָּקֵשׁ אַחֲרֵיהֶם. וּלְשׁוֹן סִפְרֵי: "הִשָּׁמֶר", בְּלֹא־תַעֲשֶׂה; "פֶּן", בְּלֹא־תַעֲשֶׂה; "תִּנָּקֵשׁ אַחֲרֵיהֶם", שֶׁמָּא תִדְמֶה לָהֶם וְתַעֲשֶׂה כְּמַעֲשֵׂיהֶם וְיִהְיוּ לְךָ לְמוֹקֵשׁ: שֶׁלֹּא תֹאמַר: הוֹאִיל וְהֵן יוֹצְאִין בְּאַרְגָּמָן אֲנִי אֵצֵא בְאַרְגָּמָן, הוֹאִיל וְהֵן יוֹצְאִין בִּכְלוֹסִין אֲנִי

---

3. TB Sanhedrin 52a.

4. This is the reason for immersing him up to his knees—that he should not thrash about and receive the hot molten metal on his body instead.

5. See §47, note 7, and below, §491, for the more precise meaning of this brief general statement.

§262   1. I.e. our conduct.

2. Sifra, aḥaré moth, perek 13, 9.

3. Or, legislated; Rambam (note 5): established for them from [the time of] their fathers.

4. E.g. in TB Shabbath 67a.

5. Hebrew, בכלוסין, and so the Vilna Gaon reads in Sifra (בכלוסין); in our ed. Sifra, בתולסין (ShM negative precept §30, בתלוסין); Yalkut Shim'oni, Deuteronomy § 885, בקלוסין. Cf. Jastrow s.v. קולס.

guilty person according to his law, they would thus disobey a positive precept; and their punishment would be great, for by judgment the world is settled.

Now, I have already written above, in the fourth positive precept of *sidrah mishpatim* (§47), that Ramban of blessed memory does not list the four forms of death imposed by the *beth din* in the reckoning of the *mitzvoth* in his work. And there I cited a bit of the reason that he wrote about the matter.

[THE PROHIBITION AGAINST FOLLOWING CUSTOMS AND
WAYS OF THE AMORITES]

262 not to follow the customs of the Amorites, and equally the customs of the heathen—for it is stated, *And you shall not walk in the customs of the nation which I am casting out before you* (Leviticus 20:23); and the same law holds for all other nations, because the reason is that they turn away from following the Eternal Lord and worship idols.

The substance of the precept is that we should not behave like them in our way of dress and our affairs.[1] As it was taught in the Midrash *Sifra*:[2] "neither shall you walk in their customs" (Leviticus 18:3)—that you should not follow their practices in matters that are established[3] for them, such as theaters, circuses, and amphitheater spectacles. These are all forms of sport and entertainment that they enact in their mass gatherings, when they assemble to commit lunatic acts, immorality, and idol-worship.

It was taught there: "in the customs of the nation"—R. Me'ir said: These are the ways of the Amorites that the Sages listed.[4] R. Judah b. Bathyra said: It denotes that you should not grow the locks of the head and should not trim the pate. In other words, one should not trim closely at the sides and leave the hair in the middle, which is called a crest.

This injunction was repeated elsewhere, in different words, as it is stated, *take heed to yourself that you be not ensnared to follow them* (Deuteronomy 12:30). In the language of the Midrash *Sifre*: "take heed"—it is the subject of a negative precept; "that you be not"— [another] negative precept; "ensnared to follow them"—perhaps you will emulate them and do things like them; and so they will be a snare for you. Thus you should not say, "Since they go out in velvet, I will go out in velvet"; "because they go out in helmets, I will go out in a helmet"[5]—this being one of the pieces of armor of the horse-

אֵצֵא בִּכְלוּסִין, וְהוּא מִין מִמִּינֵי זִיּוּן הַפָּרָשִׁים. וּלְשׁוֹן סִפְרֵי הַנְּבוּאָה: וְעַל כָּל הַלְבָשִׁים מַלְבּוּשׁ נָכְרִי.

מִשָּׁרְשֵׁי הַמִּצְוָה, כְּדֵי לְהִתְרַחֵק מֵהֶם וּלְגַנּוֹת כָּל הַנְהָגוֹתֵיהֶם, וַאֲפִלּוּ בְמַלְבּוּשׁ.

מִדִּינֵי הַמִּצְוָה, כָּתַבְנוּ קְצָתָם, וְהֵבִיאוּ זִכְרוֹנָם לִבְרָכָה מֵאֵלוּ קְצָת, עִם יֶתֶר פְּרָטֶיהָ, פֶּרֶק שְׁבִיעִי מִשַּׁבָּת וּבְתוֹסֶפְתָּא דְשַׁבָּת.

וְנוֹהֶגֶת בְּכָל מָקוֹם וּבְכָל זְמַן, בַּזְּכָרִים וּנְקֵבוֹת. וְעוֹבֵר עַל זֶה וְעָשָׂה דָבָר מֵאֵלוּ הַדְּבָרִים שֶׁזָּכַרְנוּ לְהִדַּמוֹת אֲלֵיהֶם, חַיָּב מַלְקוֹת. וְהַמִּתְרַחֵק מִכָּל הַנְהָגוֹתֵיהֶם וּמִכָּל נִמּוּסֵיהֶם וְיָשִׂים כָּל לִבּוֹ וּמַחְשְׁבוֹתָיו אֶל הַשֵּׁם וּבְמִצְוֹתָיו הַיְקָרוֹת, נַפְשׁוֹ בְטוֹב תָּלִין לְעוֹלָם וְזַרְעוֹ יִירַשׁ אָרֶץ.

☙ אֱמֹר אֶל הַכֹּהֲנִים

יֵשׁ בָּהּ כ״ד מִצְוֹת עֲשֵׂה וְל״ט מִצְוֹת לֹא־תַעֲשֶׂה

[שֶׁלֹּא יִטַּמֵּא כֹהֵן הֶדְיוֹט בְּמֵת זוּלָתִי בַּקְּרוֹבִים הַמְבֹאָרִים בַּכָּתוּב]

רסג שֶׁלֹּא יִטַּמֵּא כֹהֵן הֶדְיוֹט בְּמֵת, זוּלָתִי בַּקְּרוֹבִים הַמְבֹאָרִים בַּכָּתוּב, שֶׁנֶּאֱמַר: [לְנֶפֶשׁ] לֹא יִטַּמָּא בְּעַמָּיו, כְּלוֹמַר כָּל אֶחָד מִן הַכֹּהֲנִים לֹא יִטַּמֵּא לְנֶפֶשׁ מֵת. וְאַף־עַל־פִּי שֶׁנֶּפֶשׁ טוֹבָה לֹא תָמוּת, יְכַנֶּה הַכָּתוּב הַגּוּף בְּשֵׁם הַנֶּפֶשׁ, כִּי הִיא הָעִקָּר.

מִשָּׁרְשֵׁי הַמִּצְוָה, לְפִי שֶׁהַכֹּהֲנִים נִבְחֲרוּ לַעֲבוֹדַת הַשֵּׁם בָּרוּךְ הוּא, כְּמוֹ שֶׁאָמַר הַכָּתוּב "קְדֹשִׁים יִהְיוּ לֵאלֹהֵיהֶם", עַל־כֵּן הִרְחִיקָם מִן הַמֵּת; וּכְבָר כָּתַבְתִּי לְמַעְלָה שֶׁעִנְיַן הַטֻּמְאָה דָבָר נִמְאָס וְנֶאֱלָח, וְגוּף הָאָדָם הַמֵּת פֵּרְשׁוּ חֲכָמִים שֶׁהוּא אֲבִי אֲבוֹת הַטֻּמְאָה, כְּלוֹמַר שֶׁיֵּשׁ לוֹ טֻמְאָה חֲזָקָה עַד מְאֹד, לְמַעְלָה מִכָּל טָמֵא.

---

6. The past three paragraphs are based on ShM negative precept §30.
7. I.e. in the preceding paragraphs.

1. I.e. not a *kohen gadol*, chief among the *kohanim*, who had more sacred duties and more restrictions than the others.
2. Listed in Leviticus 21:2–3: *except...for his mother, his father, his son, his daughter, his brother, or his virgin sister...who has had no husband...*
3. I.e. it endures after death, to live in the world-to-come.
4. Literally, the father of fathers.

men. In the phrasing of the Books of the Prophets, [*I will punish . . .*]
all who clothe themselves in foreign attire (Zephaniah 1:8).[6]

At the root of the precept lies the purpose to have us move far
away from them and despise all their customs, even the way of dress.

As to the laws of the precept, we have written some of them;[7]
and the Sages of blessed memory set forth a few of these, with the
rest of its details, in chapter 7 of the Talmud tractate *Shabbath*, and in
the Tosefta of *Shabbath*.

It applies in every place and every time, for both man and woman.
If a person transgressed this and did any one of the things we have
mentioned, in order to emulate them, he would be punishable by
lashes of the whip. But if a person moves well away from all their
customs and ways, and sets all his heart and thoughts on the Eternal
Lord and His precious *mitzvoth*, then *his spirit shall abide in good fortune,
and his progeny shall inherit the land* (Psalms 25:13).

sidrah 'emor

(Leviticus 21–24)

It contains twenty-four positive and thirty-nine negative precepts.

[AN ORDINARY KOHEN SHOULD MAKE HIMSELF RITUALLY
UNCLEAN ONLY AT THE DEATH OF CERTAIN RELATIVES]

263 that an ordinary *kohen*[1] should not defile himself with the
dead, except for relatives clearly specified in the Writ:[2] for it is stated,
none shall defile himself by a soul among his people (Leviticus 21:1);
in other words, no one among the *kohanim* should become defiled
by a dead soul. Even though the good soul does not die,[3] Scripture
designates the body by the term "soul" because that is the main,
important element.

At the root of the precept lies the reason that the *kohanim* were
chosen for the service of the Eternal Lord, blessed is He—as Scripture
states, *They shall be holy to their God* (Leviticus 21:6); therefore He
removed them from the dead. I have written previously, above (§159),
that in substance, ritual uncleanness is something repugnant and
foul; and as for the body of a dead man, the Sages explained that it is the
uttermost source[4] of ritual defilement; in other words, it possesses
⟨163⟩ an utmost intensity of uncleanness, beyond any other uncleanness.

וְהָעִנְיָן הוּא כִּי בְּהִפָּרֵד מֵעָלָיו צוּרַת הַשֵּׂכֶל הַחַיָּה הַטּוֹבָה וְיִשָּׁאֵר הוּא לְבַדּוֹ, בְּשַׁגַּם הוּא בָשָׂר פָּחוּת וְנָגוּעַ וּמְשֻׁתָּק אֶל הָרָעוֹת, וְגַם בְּרַעְתּוֹ רַבָּה הֶחֱטִיא הַנֶּפֶשׁ הַיְקָרָה בְּעוֹדָהּ שׁוֹכֶנֶת אֶצְלוֹ, עַל־כֵּן רָאוּי שֶׁיִּטַּמֵּא כָל סְבִיבָיו בְּהִתְפַּשֵּׁט מֵעָלָיו כָּל הוֹדוֹ, שֶׁזֶּהוּ נַפְשׁוֹ, וְלֹא נִשְׁאָר בּוֹ כִּי־אִם הַחֹמֶר הָרָע.

וְרָאוּי בֶּאֱמֶת לִמְשָׁרְתֵי הַשֵּׁם לְהִתְרַחֵק מִמֶּנּוּ, זוּלָתִי בַקְּרוֹבִים שֶׁהֻתַּר לָהֶם, כִּי אֲחֵיהֶם בְּשָׂרָם הוּא, וְכָל דַּרְכֵי הַתּוֹרָה נֹעַם וּנְתִיבוֹתֶיהָ שָׁלוֹם, וְלֹא רָצְתָה לְצַעֲרָם כָּל־כָּךְ כִּי יֵחַם כִּי לְבָבָם עַל הַקָּרוֹב הַמֵּת, שֶׁלֹּא יוּכְלוּ לְהִתְקָרֵב תּוֹךְ הָאֹהֶל אֲשֶׁר הוּא בְתוֹכוֹ וְלִשְׁפֹּךְ אֶת רוּחָם וּלְהַשְׁבִּיעַ נַפְשָׁם בִּבְכִי עָלָיו.

וְרָאִיתִי רֶמֶז אֶל הַטַּעַם הַזֶּה שֶׁכָּתַבְתִּי בְּטֻמְאַת הַמֵּת, שֶׁאָמְרוּ זִכְרוֹנָם לִבְרָכָה כִּי הַצַּדִּיקִים גְּמוּרִים אֵינָם מְטַמְּאִין, וּלְפִי הַדּוֹמֶה כִּי הַכַּוָּנָה לְפִי שֶׁגּוּפָם טָהוֹר וְנָקִי וְלֹא הֶחֱטִיא נַפְשָׁם, אֲבָל סִיַּע לְזַכּוֹתָהּ, וְעַל־כֵּן תַּעֲלֶה נַפְשָׁם בִּנְשִׁיקָה, וְעַל גּוּנָם יִשְׁכֹּן אוֹר זָרוּעַ לְעוֹלָם.

מִדִּינֵי הַמִּצְוָה, מַה שֶּׁאָמְרוּ זִכְרוֹנָם לִבְרָכָה שֶׁהַמֵּת מְטַמֵּא בְּמַגָּע וּבְמַשָּׂא וּבְאֹהֶל; וְטֻמְאַת מַשָּׂא לְמֵדוּהָ זִכְרוֹנָם לִבְרָכָה מִקַּל וָחֹמֶר מִטֻּמְאַת נְבֵלָה, וְטֻמְאַת מַגָּע הָאֲמוּרָה בְּכָל מָקוֹם, בֵּין בְּמֵת בֵּין בִּשְׁאָר הַמְּטַמְּאִין, עִנְיָנָהּ הוּא שֶׁיִּגַּע הָאָדָם בַּטֻּמְאָה עַצְמָהּ, בֵּין בְּיָדוֹ בֵּין בְּרַגְלוֹ אוֹ בִשְׁאָר גּוּפוֹ, אֲפִלּוּ בִלְשׁוֹנוֹ נְגִיעָה הִיא. וְהָרַמְבַּ"ם זִכְרוֹנוֹ לִבְרָכָה כָּתַב שֶׁאֲפִלּוּ נְגִיעָה בְּצִפֹּרֶן אוֹ בְשִׁנַּיִם נְגִיעָה הוּא, כְּגוּף הֵם נֶחְשָׁבִים.

וְטֻמְאַת מַשָּׂא הָאֲמוּרָה בְּכָל מָקוֹם, הוּא שֶׁיִּשָּׂא אָדָם הַטֻּמְאָה אַף־עַל־פִּי שֶׁלֹּא נָגַע בָּהּ; אֲפִלּוּ הָיָה בֵינוֹ לְבֵינָהּ כַּמָּה כֵלִים, הוֹאִיל וּנְשָׂאָהּ נִטְמָא. וְאֶחָד הַנּוֹשֵׂא אוֹתָהּ בְּיָדוֹ אוֹ בְכָל דָּבָר שֶׁבְּגוּפוֹ, הֲרֵי זֶה בִכְלָל נוֹשֵׂא, וְטָמֵא.

---

5. TJ B'rachoth iii 1; see *tosafoth* to TB K'thuboth 103b, s.v. 'otho ha-yom.

6. According to TB B'rachoth 8a, this is the easiest of 903 forms of death. D'varim Rabbah 11, 10 (end) states that this is how Moses died; and TB Bava Bathra 17a indicates that this holds true also for Aaron and Miriam, which signifies that the angel of death had no power over them.

7. MT *hilchoth tum'ath méth* i 1.

8. I.e. whoever, whatever is with a dead person within a tent, or any covering structure, becomes defiled (Numbers 19:14).

9. Of which it is written, *and he who carries the carcass shall wash his clothes and be unclean* (Leviticus 11:40); hence this should apply all the more certainly to a corpse; Sifre, Numbers § 127; MT *ibid.* 2.

10. Since it can protrude, it is not considered to belong to a "hidden, enclosed part" (see two paragraphs below).

11. MT *hilchoth tum'ath méth* i 3.

12. *Ibid.* 6.

The reason is that when the good, living mode of intelligence departs from him [from a human being] he remains devoid, being mere flesh, inferior and debased, a lure for evils; moreover, in its great wickedness, [the flesh, the body] made the precious spirit sinful while it abided with it. Therefore it is right that it should defile everything around it when it is divested of all its splendor, which is the spirit, and nothing remains but the bad physical matter.

Then it is truly fitting for those who minister to the Eternal Lord to move and keep well away from it—except for the relatives that were permitted them,[2] since they are their flesh-and-blood kin-brothers. All the ways of the Torah are *pleasantness, and its paths are peace* (Proverbs 3:17). So it did not wish to distress them too much, since their heart would be agitated about a dead close kin if they could not go near within the tent where he lies, to pour out their emotion. and solace their spirit in weeping for him.

Now, I have seen an intimation of this reason that I have written, about the ritual uncleanness of the dead, in what the Sages of blessed memory said:[5] that the utterly righteous do not cause defilement [when dead]. Apparently the reason is that their body was ever pure and clean, and did not lead their soul to sin, but rather helped it gain merit. Therefore their soul expires with a [Divine ethereal] kiss,[6] while an implanted [Divine] light dwells about their body forever.

Among the laws of the precept, there is what the Sages of blessed memory taught:[7] that a dead person causes defilement on being touched or carried, and in a tent.[8] As for the defilement on carrying him, they (of blessed memory) inferred it by *kal va-ḥomer* (reasoning from the less to the more) from the defilement of a carcass.[9] Wherever defilement by touch is mentioned, whether in regard to a dead man or any other source of uncleanness, it means if a man touches the object of uncleanness itself, whether with his hand or foot or any other part of his body. Even with his tongue, it constitutes touching.[10] And Rambam of blessed memory wrote[11] that even touching with a fingernail or the teeth is considered as touching with the body.

As for defilement by carrying which is mentioned everywhere, it means if a man carries the defiling matter, even if he does not touch it. Even if there are many objects or garments between him and it, because he carries it he becomes defiled. Whether one carries it in his hand or by any other part of his body, it is included in the category of carrying, and he becomes ritually unclean.[12]

⟨165⟩

וּמֵסִיט בִּכְלָל נוֹשֵׂא הוּא גַם־כֵּן; וְכֵיצַד הוּא הַהֶסֵּט, כְּגוֹן שֶׁיֵּשׁ בְּרֹאשׁ קוֹרָה טְמֵאָה, מִכֵּיוָן שֶׁהֵנִיד הָאָדָם הַקּוֹרָה בְּשׁוּם צַד, הוֹאִיל וּמִכֹּחוֹ הֱנִידָהּ, וְאַף־עַל־פִּי שֶׁהַטֻּמְאָה בָּרֹאשׁ הָאַחֵר שֶׁל קוֹרָה, וְהָאָדָם הֱנִידָהּ בָּרֹאשׁ הָאַחֵר, הֲרֵי זוֹ מֵסִיט וְטָמֵא. וְזוֹ וְכָל כַּיּוֹצֵא־בּוֹ הוּא טֻמְאַת הֶסֵּט הָאֲמוּרָה בְּכָל מָקוֹם.

וְטֻמְאַת בֵּית הַסְּתָרִים, אַף־עַל־פִּי שֶׁאֵינָהּ מְטַמְּאָה מִשּׁוּם נְגִיעָה, שֶׁאֵין בֵּית הַסְּתָרִים בִּכְלָל נוֹגֵעַ, מְטַמְּאָה הִיא מִדִּין נוֹשֵׂא, שֶׁהַנּוֹשֵׂא בְּבֵית הַסְּתָרִים נוֹשֵׂא נִקְרָא, וְטָמֵא.

וְאֵין מִתְטַמֵּא בְמַשָּׂא בְּלֹא נְגִיעָה אֶלָּא הָאָדָם בִּלְבַד, וְלֹא הַכֵּלִים; וְטֻמְאַת אֹהֶל אֵינָהּ זוּלָתִי בְּטֻמְאַת מֵת בִּלְבַד וְלֹא בִשְׁאָר הַטֻּמְאוֹת; וְהַצָּרַעַת, אַף־עַל־פִּי שֶׁמְּטַמְּאָה בְבִיאָה, אֵינָהּ מְטַמְּאָה בְּאֹהֶל; וְהַמֵּת מְטַמֵּא בְּאֹהֶל בֵּין אָדָם בֵּין כֵּלִים אוֹ אֳכָלִין וּמַשְׁקִין; וְאֶחָד הָאָדָם שֶׁנִּכְנַס כֻּלּוֹ לְאֹהֶל הַמֵּת, אוֹ אֲפִלּוּ מִקְצָתוֹ, כְּגוֹן שֶׁהִכְנִיס שָׁם יָדוֹ אוֹ רָאשֵׁי אֶצְבְּעוֹתָיו אוֹ חָטְמוֹ, הֲרֵי זֶה נִטְמָא כֻלּוֹ.

וְהַנְּפָלִים אַף־עַל־פִּי שֶׁלֹּא נִתְקַשְּׁרוּ אֵיבְרֵיהֶם מְטַמְּאִין; וּכְזַיִת בָּשָׂר מִן הַמֵּת, וְאֵבֶר אֶחָד שָׁלֵם שֶׁנֶּחְתַּךְ מִן הָאָדָם אַף־עַל־פִּי שֶׁאֵין בּוֹ כְזַיִת בָּשָׂר, כָּל אֵלּוּ מְטַמְּאִין בְּמַגָּע וּבְמַשָּׂא וּבְאֹהֶל; וְאֵבֶר נִקְרָא כָל אֶחָד מֵרמ"ח אֵיבָרִים שֶׁבָּאָדָם, שֶׁבְּכָל אֶחָד מֵהֶם יֵשׁ בָּשָׂר וְגִידִים וַעֲצָמוֹת; וְאֵין הַשְּׁנַיִם מִן הַמִּנְיָן.

עַצְמוֹת הַמֵּת, אַף־עַל־פִּי שֶׁאֵין עֲלֵיהֶם בָּשָׂר, אִם הָיְתָה נִכֶּרֶת בָּהֶם צוּרַת הָאָדָם מְטַמְּאִין אֲפִלּוּ בְּאֹהֶל. וְאֵלּוּ הֵן הָעֲצָמוֹת שֶׁאָמְרוּ זִכְרוֹנָם לִבְרָכָה שֶׁמְּטַמְּאִין אֲפִלּוּ בְּאֹהֶל: הַשִּׁדְרָה וְהַגֻּלְגֹּלֶת וְרֹב בִּנְיָנוֹ שֶׁל גּוּף וְרֹב מִנְיָנוּ, כְּלוֹמַר רֹב מִנְיַן הָעֲצָמוֹת. וְשִׁדְרָה וְגֻלְגֹּלֶת שֶׁאָמְרוּ, דַּוְקָא כְּשֶׁהֵן שְׁלֵמוֹת, אֲבָל חָסְרָה

---

13. *Ibid.* 7.

14. E.g. the throat or rectum.

15. The term is understood to refer only to outer parts of the body; with them one touches.

16. MT *hilchoth tum'ath méth* i 8.

17. *Ibid.* 9.

18. *Ibid.* 10: As indicated in note 8, "tent" is not used here in any literal sense but only in the sense of covering: If a dead body is above or below anything or anyone, or the two are beneath one covering object or material of any sort, the dead body transmits defilement, even if there is no physical contact between the two.

19. I.e. he thus defiles everything in the house, by his entry; Mishnah, N'ga'im xiii 11. While the rule of the "tent" does not apply to him, this special law does, even if the man with the *tzara'ath* touches nothing in the house: "because Scripture states of such a man [a m'tzora], *outside the camp shall his habitation be* (Leviticus 13:46), whence the Oral Tradition (Sifra, *thazri'a, perek* 12, 14) teaches that 'his habitation' [any dwelling in which he is found] is ritually unclean" (Rambam, Commentary to Mishnah, Kélim i 4).

20. Derived from Numbers 19:14.

A "shaker" is included in the category of the carrier. How does shaking occur? If, for example, there is an object of uncleanness at the end of a beam, once a man bestirs the beam in any way, since he has moved it by his power, even if the object of uncleanness is at one end of the beam and the man who moved it is at the other end, this constitutes "shaking," and he becomes ritually defiled. This and anything similar is the uncleanness of shaking (budging) which is mentioned everywhere.[13]

Regarding defilement through a hidden, enclosed part of the body,[14] although it does not bring ritual uncleanness on account of touch, because a hidden, enclosed part is not included in the meaning of "touch,"[15] it does bring defilement under the law of carrying;[16] for if someone carries something in a hidden, enclosed part of the body, this is called carrying; hence he becomes ritually unclean.

None but a human being alone becomes defiled by carrying [a source of uncleanness] without touching [it], but not objects.[17] Defilement in a tent occurs with nothing but the uncleanness of the dead, but not with other sources of defilement.[18] As for a man with a *tzara'ath* ailment, though he defiles upon entry [into a house],[19] he does not cause defilement by the law of the tent. In a tent a corpse defiles both a person, objects, and food and drink.[20] And whether a man enters the tent of a dead person entirely or even partly—for instance, if he puts his hand, his fingertips, or his nose inside, he becomes entirely defiled.[21]

Infants that do not survive birth, even if their limbs did not become well knit, cause defilement.[22] [So too] an olive's amount of flesh from a corpse, or one whole limb that was cut from a human body, even if it does not contain an olive's amount of flesh—all these bring defilement through touch or carrying, and in a tent.[23] "A limb" means any one of the 248 limbs and organs in a man; for in every one of them there are flesh, sinews and bones;[24] but teeth are not included.[25]

As to bones of a corpse, even if there is no flesh on them, if the human form is recognizable in them, they cause defilement even in a tent. Now, these are the bones of which the Sages of blessed memory said that they cause defilement even in a tent: the spine, the cranium, the majority of the structure of the body, and the majority of its number—i.e. the majority of the number of bones. As for the spine and the cranium which they listed, this means only when they are

שִׁדְרָה אֲפִלּוּ חוּלְיָא אַחַת, וְגֻלְגֹּלֶת כְּסֶלַע, אֵין מְטַמְּאִין בְּאֹהֶל; וּשְׁתֵּי שׁוֹקָיו שֶׁל אָדָם וְיָרֵךְ אַחַת, זֶהוּ רֹב בִּנְיָנוֹ; חָסֵר כָּל־שֶׁהוּא, אֵינוֹ מְטַמֵּא בְּאֹהֶל; וְרֹב מִנְיָנוֹ הוּא קכ"ה עֲצָמוֹת מִן רמ"ח אֵיבָרִים שֶׁיֵּשׁ בָּאָדָם. שְׁאָר עֲצָמוֹת שֶׁאֵין בָּהֶן רֹב בִּנְיָן וְרֹב מִנְיָן, אִם יֵשׁ בָּהֶם רֹבַע קַב עֲצָמוֹת מְטַמְּאִין אֲפִלּוּ בְּאֹהֶל, וְאִם לָאו אֵין מְטַמְּאִין בְּאֹהֶל.

וְטֻמְאַת הַמֵּת הִיא שִׁבְעַת יָמִים; וְיֶתֶר פְּרָטֶיהָ, מְבֹאָרִים בְּסֵדֶר טָהֳרוֹת וּבְרֹב בְּמַסֶּכֶת אָהֳלוֹת.

וְנוֹהֶגֶת מִצְוָה זוּ בַּכֹּהֲנִים הַזְּכָרִים, בְּכָל מָקוֹם וּבְכָל זְמַן, אֲבָל לֹא בַנְּקֵבוֹת, שֶׁכֵּן בָּא הַפֵּרוּשׁ: "אֱמֹר אֶל הַכֹּהֲנִים בְּנֵי אַהֲרֹן" . . . "לְנֶפֶשׁ לֹא יִטַּמָּא", בְּנֵי אַהֲרֹן דַּוְקָא וְלֹא בְּנוֹת אַהֲרֹן. וְכֹהֵן הָעוֹבֵר עַל זֶה וְנִטְמָא לְשׁוּם מֵת חוּץ מֵחֲמִשָּׁה מֵתֵי מִצְוָה, בְּמֵזִיד, לוֹקֶה.

[מִצְוַת עִנְיַן טֻמְאַת הַכֹּהֲנִים לִקְרוֹבֵיהֶם, וּבִכְלָלָהּ שֶׁיִּתְאַבְּלוּ כָּל אֶחָד מִיִּשְׂרָאֵל עַל שִׁשָּׁה מִקְרוֹבָיו הַיְדוּעִים]

רסד שֶׁיִּטַּמְּאוּ הַכֹּהֲנִים לִקְרוֹבִים הַנִּזְכָּרִים בַּתּוֹרָה, שֶׁנֶּאֱמַר: לָהּ יִטַּמָּא, וְזֶה מִצְוַת עֲשֵׂה, שֶׁכֵּן בָּא הַפֵּרוּשׁ עָלָיו, וְכֵן הוּא מְפֹרָשׁ בַּסִּפְרָא: "לָהּ יִטַּמָּא", מִצְוָה; לֹא רָצָה לְטַמֵּא, מְטַמְּאִין אוֹתוֹ בְּעַל כָּרְחוֹ.

וְלוּלֵי שֶׁקִּבַּלְנוּ מֵחֲכָמֵינוּ הַפֵּרוּשׁ כֵּן, הָיִיתִי סָבוּר לוֹמַר שֶׁיִּהְיֶה רְשׁוּת, אִם רָצָה מְטַמֵּא וְאִם רָצָה אֵינוֹ מִטַּמֵּא, לְפִי שֶׁהַכָּתוּב מְנָעוֹ מֵהִטַּמֵּא לִשְׁאָר קְרוֹבִים, וְהָיִיתִי אוֹמֵר שֶׁבְּאֵלּוּ הַנִּזְכָּרִים בַּפָּרָשָׁה הִרְשׁוּהוּ לְהִטַּמֵּא אִם יִרְצֶה. עַל כֵּן בָּא לָנוּ הַפֵּרוּשׁ עָלָיו שֶׁאֵין זֶה רְשׁוּת אֶלָּא מִצְוָה. וְהִזְכִּירוּ חֲכָמִים זִכְרוֹנָם לִבְרָכָה מַעֲשֶׂה שֶׁבָּא בְּיוֹסֵף הַכֹּהֵן, שֶׁמֵּתָה אִשְׁתּוֹ בְּעֶרֶב פֶּסַח וְלֹא רָצָה לְטַמֵּא וּדְחָפוּהוּ

---

21. TB Nazir 43a; this is not the case when a man with a *tzara'ath* infection is in a tent or house; see Mishnah, Kélim i 4, and R. 'Obadiah Bertinoro, commentary, there.

22. TB Nazir 50a.

23. Mishnah, 'Oholoth ii 1, i 7–8.

24. Tosefta, 'Oholoth i.

25. Since they contain no flesh or sinews; MT *hilchoth tum'ath méth* ii 1–3, 7.

26. Based on Mishnah 'Oholoth ii 3 and TB B'choroth 37b.

27. TB B'choroth 45a.

28. Mishnah, 'Oholoth ii 1; MT *hilchoth tum'ath méth* ii 8.

29. Mishnah *ibid.* 9. A *kav* is one sixth of a *se'ah.*

30. Numbers 19:11, 14.

31. Sifra, *'emor, parashah* 1, 1; TB Kiddushin 35b.

32. I.e. for whom he has an obligation (§264) to defile himself in conjunction with their burial; see note 2. (While Leviticus 21:2–3 lists six relatives, ShM negative precept § 166 also has "five" — see ed. Heller there and positive precept §37 note 1; evidently the sister is omitted, since he may defile himself in her case only if she never married.)

whole; but if the spine is missing even one vertebra, or the cranium an amount the size of a *sela*, they do not cause defilement in a tent.[26] The two shanks of a man and one thigh constitute "the majority of his structure";[27] if any of this is at all lacking, it does not cause defilement in a tent. The "majority of its number" means 125 bones from the 248 limbs that a man has.[28] As for other bones, which do not constitute most of the structure or most of the number, if they make up a quarter of a *kav* of bones, they cause defilement even in a tent; if not, they do not cause ritual impurity in a tent.[29]

Defilement by a corpse lasts seven days.[30] The rest of its details are elucidated in the Talmud order of *Tohoroth*, mostly in the tractate *'Oholoth*.

This precept applies to male *kohanim* everywhere, at every time, but not to the women; for so was the interpretation given:[31] *Speak to the* kohanim *the sons of Aaron . . . none shall defile himself* (Leviticus 21:1)—specifically "the sons of Aaron" and not "the daughters of Aaron." If a *kohen* violates this and defiles himself deliberately by any dead person other than the five dead people of religious obligation,[32] he should be given whiplashes.

264 [THAT A KOHEN SHOULD DEFILE HIMSELF, AND A JEW SHOULD MOURN, FOR A DECEASED CLOSE RELATIVE] that the *kohanim* should become defiled by the [deceased] relatives mentioned in the Torah; as it is stated, *for her he shall defile himself* (Leviticus 21:3), and this is a positive precept—for so was the explanation given for it. And so is it taught in the Midrash *Sifra*:[1] "for her he shall defile himself"—it is a religious duty; if one does not wish to become ritually unclean, he is defiled against his will.

Now, had we not received the interpretation thus from our Sages, I would be inclined to say that it is a matter of free choice: if he wishes, he may defile himself, and if he wishes [in turn], he need not defile himself, inasmuch as Scripture restricted him from becoming defiled for other relatives; and so I would say that for those mentioned in the section he was allowed to defile himself if he should so wish. Therefore the interpretation was given us about it that it is not a matter of choice, but a *mitzvah*, a religious duty. The Sages of blessed memory recounted an incident that occurred with Joseph the *kohen*:[2] His wife died the day before Passover, and he did not wish to become ritually unclean,[3]

חֲכָמִים וְטִמְּאוּהוּ עַל כָּרְחוֹ.

וְכָתַב הָרַמְבַּ"ם זִכְרוֹנוֹ לִבְרָכָה: וְזֹאת בְּעַצְמָהּ הִיא מִצְוַת אָבוּל, כְּלוֹמַר שֶׁכָּל
אִישׁ מִיִּשְׂרָאֵל חַיָּב לְהִתְאַבֵּל עַל קְרוֹבָיו, כְּלוֹמַר שִׁשָּׁה מֵתֵי מִצְוָה הַנִּזְכָּרִים
בַּכָּתוּב. וְהַמִּקְרָא שֶׁהֵבִיא הָרַב עַל מִצְוַת אָבוּל מַה הוּא מַה שֶּׁנֶּאֱמַר בְּאַהֲרֹן: וְאָכַלְתִּי
חַטָּאת הַיּוֹם הַיִּיטַב בְּעֵינֵי יְיָ; וְאָמַר: וּמֵחֵזֶק הַחוֹבָה הַזֹּאת, בֵּאֲרוֹ בְכֹהֵן, שֶׁהוּא
מֻזְהָר עַל הַטֻּמְאָה, שֶׁיְּטַמֵּא עַל־כָּל־פָּנִים כִּשְׁאָר יִשְׂרָאֵל, בִּשְׁבִיל שֶׁלֹּא יֶחֶלְשׁוּ
מִשְׁפְּטֵי הָאֲבֵלוּת. וּכְבָר נִתְבָּאֵר שֶׁאֲבֵלוּת יוֹם רִאשׁוֹן דְּאוֹרַיְתָא, וְהוּא יוֹם מִיתָה
וּקְבוּרָה; וּבְבֵאוּר אָמְרוּ בְּמוֹעֵד קָטָן: אָבֵל אֵינוֹ נוֹהֵג אֲבֵלוּתוֹ בָּרֶגֶל, אֲתֵי עֲשֵׂה
דְּרַבִּים וְדָחֵי עֲשֵׂה דְּיָחִיד. הִנֵּה הִתְבָּאֵר שֶׁחִיּוּב הָאֲבֵלוּת דְּאוֹרַיְתָא וְשֶׁהוּא מִצְוַת
עֲשֵׂה, אֲבָל בְּיוֹם רִאשׁוֹן בִּלְבַד, וְנִשְׁאֲרוּ הַשִּׁשָּׁה דְּרַבָּנָן; וַאֲפִלּוּ הַכֹּהֵן יִנְהַג
אֲבֵלוּתוֹ בְּיוֹם רִאשׁוֹן וְיִטַּמֵּא לִקְרוֹבָיו; וְהָבֵן זֶה. עַד כָּאן.

מִשָּׁרְשֵׁי הַמִּצְוָה, מַה שֶּׁכָּתַבְתִּי פְּעָמִים הַרְבֵּה בַּמִּצְווֹת הַקּוֹדְמוֹת: כִּי הָאָדָם
נִפְעָל כְּפִי פְּעֻלּוֹתָיו שֶׁיַּעֲשֶׂה; כִּי מִהְיוֹתוֹ בַּעַל חֹמֶר לֹא יִתְפַּעֵל לְדָבָר בְּכֹחַ עַד
שֶׁיּוֹצִיא הָעִנְיָנִים מִן הַכֹּחַ אֶל הַפֹּעַל; עַל־כֵּן בְּבוֹא אֵלָיו עֹנֶשׁ מִקְרֶה מָוֶת בְּאֶחָד
מִקְרוֹבָיו אֲשֶׁר הַטֶּבַע מְחַיֵּב הָאַהֲבָה לָהֶם, תְּחַיְּבֶנּוּ הַתּוֹרָה לַעֲשׂוֹת מַעֲשִׂים
בְּעַצְמוֹ אֲשֶׁר יְעוֹרְרוּהוּ לִקְבֹּעַ מַחֲשַׁבְתּוֹ עַל הַצַּעַר שֶׁהִגִּיעַ אֵלָיו, וְאָז יֵדַע וְיִתְבּוֹנֵן
בְּנַפְשׁוֹ כִּי עֲווֹנוֹתָיו גָּרְמוּ לוֹ לְהַגִּיעַ אֵלָיו הַצַּעַר הַהוּא, כִּי הַשֵּׁם לֹא יְעַנֶּה מִלִּבּוֹ
וַיַּגֶּה בְּנֵי־אִישׁ כִּי־אִם מִצַּד חֲטָאִים; וְזֹאת הִיא אֱמוּנָתֵנוּ הַשְּׁלֵמָה, אֲנַחְנוּ בַּעֲלֵי
דָת יְהוּדִית הַיְקָרָה; וּבְתֵת הָאָדָם אֶל לִבּוֹ עִנְיָן זֶה בְּמַעֲשֵׂה הָאֲבֵלוּת, יָשִׁית דַּעְתּוֹ
לַעֲשׂוֹת תְּשׁוּבָה וְיַכְשִׁיר מַעֲשָׂיו כְּפִי כֹחוֹ.

וְהִנֵּה מָצָאנוּ עִם זֶה בְּמִצְוַת הָאָבוּל תּוֹעֶלֶת רַב לִבְנֵי־אָדָם. וְהַמִּתְחַכְּמִים

§264   1. Sifra, 'emor, parashah 1, 12 (the translation of the verse is literal; it is usually rendered, "he may defile himself").

2. TB Z'vaḥim 100a.

3. So as not to become disqualified from eating the Passover offering in the evening.

4. ShM positive precept §37 (on which, moreover, the first two paragraphs are based).

5. I.e. for whom this precept imposes a duty on a *kohen* to become defiled, in conjunction with their burial; see §263, note 2. The present precept is thus understood to signify, more widely, that every Jew is duty-bound to observe mourning for these near kin.

6. MT *hilchoth 'evel* i 1. I.e. Aaron refrained from eating the flesh of the offering, although he was obligated to do so, because he was in mourning for his two sons. He thus demonstrated the religious duty of mourning.

7. To rejoice on a festival (§488).

8. Literally, when there comes upon him the punishment.

9. In attending to the burial, etc.

whereupon the Sages thrust him forward and made him defiled against his will.

Rambam of blessed memory wrote:[4] This is itself [in essence] the *mitzvah* (religious obligation) of mourning. In other words, every man in Jewry is obligated to observe mourning for his kin, which means the six dead of religious duty[5] who are mentioned in the Torah. The verse which the master [Rambam] cited for the *mitzvah* of mourning is what Aaron said, *If I had eaten the ḥattath (sin-offering) today, would it have been pleasing in the sight of the Lord?* (Leviticus 10:19).[6] And he continued:[4] On the strength of this obligation, it was explained about a *kohen*, who is adjured against ritual uncleanness, that he must nevertheless defile himself [for these kin] like any Israelite (Jew), so that the norms of mourning should not be relaxed. Long ago it was clarified that mourning on the first day is an obligation by the law of the Torah—this being the day of death and burial. In elucidation it was taught in the tractate *Mo'éd Katan* (14b): but one's mourning is not to be observed on a festival; the positive public precept[7] comes and thrusts aside the positive individual precept. Thus it was made clear that the obligation of mourning is by the law of the Torah, and it is a positive precept. Yet this is on the first day only, the other six remaining [a duty] by the ruling of the Sages. Then even a *kohen* is to observe his mourning on the first day, becoming defiled for his kin. Now understand this. Thus far his words.

At the root of the precept lies the principle that I have written many times in the earlier precepts: that a man is influenced in accord with his actions that he does. For since he is a physical being, he will not be affected by anything potential, until he carries matters out from the potential to the actual. Therefore, when he suffers the blow[8] of the occurrence of death for one of his near kin, for whom nature makes affection inevitable, the Torah obligates him to do certain things himself[9] which will move him to focus his thought on the grief that has come to him. Then he will know and understand in his soul that his sins have caused him to be visited with this grief. For the Eternal Lord *does not willingly afflict or grieve the children of men* (Lamentations 3:33) except by reason of sins. This is our complete belief—we of the treasured Jewish faith. Then as a man ponders this theme in his heart during the activity of mourning, he will set his mind to achieve repentance and will make his deeds worthy according to his ability.

⟨171⟩ So we have hereby found in the religious duty of mourning a

הַכּוֹפְרִים הַמַּהְבִּילִים כָּל דִּבְרֵי הָעוֹלָם וּמַעֲשֵׂי הַשֵּׁם הַנּוֹרָאִים, יָשִׂיתוּ אָוֶן בְּלִבָּם הָרַע, יִתְלוּ מוֹת בְּנֵי-אִישׁ לְמִקְרֶה הַזְּמַן, וְיַחְשְׁבוּ בְּמַחְשְׁבוֹתָם הָרָעִים כִּי מִקְרֶה הָאָדָם וְהַבְּהֵמָה מִקְרֶה אֶחָד לָהֶם, כְּמוֹת זֶה כֵּן מוֹת זֶה; וְעַל-כֵּן כָּתְבוּ בְּסִפְרֵיהֶם, שֶׁיִּשְׂרְפוּ: הָאֻמְלָל מִי שֶׁיִּדְאַג כְּלָל. וְלַעֲקֹר וּלְשָׁרֵשׁ מִלְּבָבֵנוּ אֱמוּנָתָם זֹאת הָרָעָה, חִיְּבַתְנוּ הַתּוֹרָה בְּמִצְוָה זוֹ, מִלְּבַד הַתּוֹעֶלֶת בְּמַה שֶּׁנַּזְכִּירֶנּוּ.

מִדִּינֵי הַמִּצְוָה, מַה שֶּׁאָמְרוּ זִכְרוֹנָם לִבְרָכָה שֶׁיּוֹם רִאשׁוֹן הוּא דְאוֹרַיְתָא וְהַשְּׁשָׁה דְרַבָּנָן; וְאַף-עַל-פִּי שֶׁנֶּאֱמַר בַּתּוֹרָה: וַיַּעַשׂ לְאָבִיו אֵבֶל שִׁבְעַת יָמִים, נִתְּנָה תוֹרָה וְנִתְחַדְּשָׁה הֲלָכָה. וּמִכָּל-מָקוֹם אָמְרוּ זִכְרוֹנָם לִבְרָכָה כִּי מֹשֶׁה רַבֵּנוּ תִּקֵּן לָהֶם לְיִשְׂרָאֵל ז' יְמֵי אֲבֵלוֹת וְז' יְמֵי הַמִּשְׁתֶּה.

וְאָמְרוּ זִכְרוֹנָם לִבְרָכָה שֶׁאֵין חִיּוּב הָאֲבֵלוּת חָל עַד שֶׁיִּסָּתֵם הַגּוֹלֵל, כְּלוֹמַר אַחַר שֶׁכִּסּוּ גוּפוֹ שֶׁל מֵת בַּקֶּבֶר; אֲבָל כָּל זְמַן שֶׁלֹּא נִקְבַּר, אֵין הָאָבֵל אָסוּר בְּדָבָר מִכָּל דִּבְרֵי אֲבֵלוּת; וּמִפְּנֵי טַעַם זֶה רָחַץ דָּוִד הַמֶּלֶךְ וְסָךְ כְּשֶׁמֵּת הַיֶּלֶד, קֹדֶם שֶׁיִּקָּבֵר.

וּמַה שֶּׁאָמְרוּ שֶׁכָּל שֶׁלֹּא שָׁהָה שְׁלֹשִׁים יוֹם בָּאָדָם, אֵין מִתְאַבְּלִין עָלָיו, לְפִי שֶׁהוּא סָפֵק; וּבַגְּמָרָא אָמְרוּ זִכְרוֹנָם לִבְרָכָה, שֶׁאִם יָדַעְנוּ בְּבֵרוּר שֶׁשָּׁלְמוּ לוֹ חֳדָשָׁיו, שֶׁדִּינוֹ כִשְׁאָר מֵתִים לְעִנְיַן אֲבֵלוּת; וְכֵן לְכָל שְׁאָר הַדְּבָרִים דִּינוֹ כְּאָדָם שָׁלֵם.

וְכֵן אָמְרוּ זִכְרוֹנָם לִבְרָכָה שֶׁהַפּוֹרְשִׁים עַצְמָם מִכָּל דַּרְכֵי צִבּוּר, וְכֵן הַמִּינִין וְהַמְשֻׁמָּדִים וְהַמַּסוֹרוֹת, כָּל אֵלּוּ אֵין מִתְאַבְּלִין עֲלֵיהֶן כְּלָל, שְׁמִיתָתָן שִׂמְחָה הִיא לָעוֹלָם, וְאֵין זֶה עֹנֶשׁ לַקְּרוֹבִים, אֲבָל זְכוּת הוּא לָהֶם; וְכָל זֶה מִן הַשֹּׁרֶשׁ שֶׁכָּתַבְתִּי, וַעֲלֵיהֶם נֶאֱמַר: הֲלוֹא מְשַׂנְאֶיךָ יְיָ אֶשְׂנָא. וְכֵן הַמֵּמִית עַצְמוֹ לָדַעַת, אֵין

---

10. In keeping with the philosophy expressed in Isaiah 22:13, *Let us eat and drink, for tomorrow we die.* As noted by R. Yeruḥam Leiner in ed. Chavel, this is cited as a saying of Socrates in Ramban, *Torath ha'Adam*, preface (*Kithvé Rabbénu Mosheh b. Naḥman*, ed. Chavel, II p. 14).

11. *Halachoth G'doloth, bilchoth 'ével*; R. Isaac 'Alfasi, Mo'éd Katan iii (289b), in the name of the ge'onim; MT *bilchoth 'ével* i 1.

12. TJ K'thuboth i 1; i.e. by tradition it is an enactment made by Moses orally, like any Rabbinic law established by the Sages; MT *ibid.*

13. TB Mo'éd Katan 27a.

14. MT *bilchoth 'ével* i 2.

15. TB Shabbath 136a; MT *ibid.* 6.

16. I.e. nine whole months; TB *ibid.* MT *ibid.* 7.

17. Talmud, minor tractate S'maḥoth ii 10; MT *ibid.* 10.

great benefit for human beings. But those overly wise heretics who make vapid nonsense of all the matters of the world and the awesome works of the Eternal Lord, wreak wickedness in their evil heart by ascribing the death of the children of men to chance events of time, thinking in their evil minds that what befalls man and beast is *one common fate for both: as one dies, so dies the other* (Ecclesiastes 3:19). Therefore they wrote in their books, that should be burned: He is unfortunate who has any care at all.[10] To uproot and extirpate from our hearts this evil belief of theirs, the Torah gave us the obligation of this precept—apart from the useful benefit that we mentioned.

Among the laws of the precept, there is what the Sages of blessed memory said:[11] that the first day [of mourning] is [obligatory] by Torah law, and the six [remaining days] by the ruling of the Sages. Even though it is stated in the Torah, *and he made a mourning for his father seven days* (Genesis 50:10), the Torah was given [thereafter] and a new law established. Nevertheless, they (of blessed memory) said that Moses instituted for the Israelites [the norms of] seven days of mourning and seven days of wedding festivity.[12]

Our Sages of blessed memory taught too[13] that the obligation of mourning does not go into effect until the grave is closed—in other words, until the dead person's body has been covered in the grave; but as long as he has not been [thus] buried, nothing is forbidden the mourner out of all that is banned during mourning. For this reason King David washed and spread oil on his body when the child died (II Samuel 12:20) before he was buried.[14]

Then we have what the Sages said,[15] that over any human being who did not endure thirty days, there should be no mourning, because it is doubtful [if he was born fit to survive]. In the Talmud they (of blessed memory) taught that if we know for certain that his months [of gestation] were completed for him,[16] the law is the same for him as for other dead in regard to mourning; and so for all other matters, the law is the same for him as for a fully normal person.

Our Sages of blessed memory likewise taught[17] that for those who separate themselves from all the ways [mores] of the community, and so too for sectarian heretics, apostates and informers—for all these no mourning at all is held: because their death is a joy for the world, and it is no punishment for the near kin, but rather a source of merit—all this for the root reason that I wrote. Of them is it said

[in Scripture], *Those that hate Thee, O Lord, I surely hate* (Psalms 139:21).

מִתְאַבְּלִין עָלָיו; וּבְמְקוֹמוֹ מִתְחָבֵּר כֵּיצַד גֵדַע שֶׁלְּדַעַת אִבֵּד עַצְמוֹ.

וְכֵן מִדִּינֵי הַמִּצְוָה הַדְּבָרִים שֶׁאָמְרוּ זִכְרוֹנָם לִבְרָכָה שֶׁהָאָבֵל אָסוּר בָּהֶם בְּיוֹם רִאשׁוֹן מִן הַתּוֹרָה, וּבִשְׁאָר הַיָּמִים מִדְּרַבָּנָן; וְדִין שִׁבְעָה וּשְׁלֹשִׁים, וְדִין י״ב חֹדֶשׁ, בַּאֲבֵלוּת אָב וָאֵם; וְדִין קְרִיעָה, מִי הֵם הַקְּרוֹבִים שֶׁקּוֹרְעִין וְאֵי זֶה זְמַן וְכֵיצַד עַל הַקְּרוֹבִים, וְכֵיצַד עַל אָב וָאֵם, וְעַל מִי מִקְּרוֹבָיו וּמִמְּלַמְּדָיו וּמִגְּדוֹלָיו, וְעַל אֵי זֶה מְקוֹמוֹת בְּחָרַבָּנָן; וְדִינֵי הַקְּרָעִים שֶׁשּׁוֹלְלִין אוֹתוֹ מִיָּד אוֹ לְאַחַר זְמַן, וְדִין הָאִשָּׁה שֶׁשּׁוֹלֶלֶת מִיָּד, כְּדֵי שֶׁלֹּא תִתְבַּזֶּה.

וְדִין הָרְגָלִים, שֶׁמַּפְסִיקִין וְאֵינָן עוֹלִין; וּמַה שֶּׁאָמְרוּ שֶׁכָּל הַקּוֹבֵר מֵתוֹ אֲפִלּוּ שָׁעָה אַחַת קֹדֶם הָרֶגֶל, בָּטְלָה מִמֶּנּוּ גְּזֵרַת שִׁבְעָה; וְאִם עָבְרוּ שִׁבְעָה קֹדֶם הָרֶגֶל וְנִכְנַס אֲפִלּוּ שָׁעָה אַחַת תּוֹךְ שְׁלֹשִׁים, בָּטְלוּ מִמֶּנּוּ גְּזֵרַת שְׁלֹשִׁים; וְרֹאשׁ הַשָּׁנָה וְיוֹם הַכִּפּוּרִים דִּינָן כִּרְגָלִים שֶׁל פֶּסַח שָׁבוּעוֹת וְסֻכּוֹת.

וּמַה שֶּׁאָמְרוּ שֶׁאַף־עַל־פִּי שֶׁאֵין אֲבֵלוּת נוֹהֵג בְּחָלּוֹ שֶׁל מוֹעֵד, קוֹרֵעַ אָדָם עַל מֵתוֹ שֶׁחַיָּב לְהִתְאַבֵּל עָלָיו; וְדִין שְׁמוּעָה רְחוֹקָה לְאַחַר שְׁלֹשִׁים יוֹם, שֶׁאֵין נוֹהֲגִין אֲבֵלוּת אֶלָּא יוֹם אֶחָד, וְאֵינוֹ קוֹרֵעַ, דְּאָמַר הָכִי בִּגְמָרָא מַשְׁקִין; אֲבָל עַל אָבִיו וְעַל אִמּוֹ קוֹרֵעַ אֲפִלּוּ בִּשְׁמוּעָה רְחוֹקָה לְדַעַת הָרַמְבָּ״ן זִכְרוֹנוֹ לִבְרָכָה, וְלֹא לְדַעַת הָרַב רַבִּי אַבְרָהָם בְּרַבִּי דָוִד זִכְרוֹנוֹ לִבְרָכָה.

18. Talmud *ibid.* 1; MT *ibid.* 11.

19. Talmud *ibid.* 2; MT *ibid.*

20. TB Mo'éd Katan 21a; MT *bilchoth 'ével* v 1.

21. I.e. laws of observance for the first seven days since the burial (MT *ibid.* v) and for the first thirty days (*ibid.* vi).

22. TB Mo'éd Katan 22b; MT *ibid.* vi 7.

23. I.e. all who are required to observe mourning; Ramban, *Torath ha'Adam* 12b; see also TB Mo'éd Katan 26b and MT *bilchoth 'ével* viii 5.

24. TB Mo'éd Katan 24a; MT *ibid.* xi 1.

25. TB Mo'éd Katan 22b.

26. Those for whom mourning is required; see note 23.

27. TB Mo'éd Katan 26a.

28. *Ibid.* 22b, 26a.

29. If a festival day falls amid the seven days of mourning, the mourning ceases then.

30. If a close relative dies during a festival, the seven days of mourning must begin after the festival, as its days cannot be counted among the seven; TB Mo'éd Katan 19a.

31. *Ibid.* 20a.

32. *Ibid.* 19b.

33. *Ibid.* 19a.

34. MT *bilchoth 'ével* xi 1, based on TB Mo'éd Katan 24b.

35. Literally, a distant report.

36. Ramban, *Torath ha'Adam*, *bilchoth kri'ah*, 61b (citing R. Isaac 'Alfasi); ed. Venice 1595, fol. 21a.

Similarly, if someone takes his own life deliberately, he is not to be mourned.[18] In its proper place[19] it is clarified how we can know if he destroyed himself deliberately.

So also, among the laws of the precept, there are those matters which, the Sages of blessed memory taught, are forbidden for a mourner on the first day [of his mourning] by the law of the Torah, and on the other days by the ruling of the Sages.[20] There is the law of the seven [days of mourning] and thirty [days];[21] and the law of twelve months of mourning for a father or a mother.[22] And there is the law of rending [clothing]: who are the relatives who rend [their garments],[23] at which time,[24] how for [other] relatives and how for a father or mother,[25] and for which of a person's relatives[26] and teachers, and great luminaries;[27] and likewise, over which places [of the holy land] in their state of ruin [is a garment to be rent].[27] Then there is the law of the rents in the garments: if they may be resewn raggedly, unevenly, at once or after a period of time;[28] and the law about a woman, that she may resew it raggedly at once so that she should not suffer disgrace.

Further, there is the law of the festivals: that they interrupt [mourning],[29] and are not counted [for it].[30] There is, too, what the Sages taught,[31] that whoever buries his dead even one hour before a festival, the requirement of the seven [days of mourning] is nullified for him. And if the seven [days] passed by before the festival, and he began even for one brief moment the thirty [days of mourning before the festival], the requirement of the thirty days becomes nullified for him.[32] For *Rosh haShanah* and *Yom Kippur* the law is the same as for the festivals of Passover, *Shavu'oth* and *Sukkoth*.[33]

[Going further] there is what the Sages said,[34] that even though mourning is not observed on the intermediate days of a festival, a man does rend [his clothing then] over his dead for whom he would be required to mourn. We have, too, the law of a late report[35] [of the death of kin—received] after thirty days [past the time of death], when mourning is observed for no more than one day, and clothing is not rent; for the definitive law follows R. Mani, who so rules in the Talmud tractate *Mo'éd Katan* (20b); over one's father or mother, though, clothing is rent even upon a late report, in the view of Ramban of blessed memory,[36] but not according to R. Abraham b. David [Rabad] of blessed memory.[37]

⟨175⟩　　　　Then we have the subject of the eulogy (funeral oration): for

וְעִנְיַן הַהֶסְפֵּד: עַל מִי מַסְפִּידִין, וְכֵיצַד, וְשַׁבָּת וְיוֹם טוֹב וְחֻלּוֹ שֶׁל מוֹעֵד וַחֲנֻכָּה
וּפוּרִים מַה הֵן בְּהֶסְפֵּד; וְעַל מִי מְבַטְּלִין תַּלְמוּד תּוֹרָה בְּמוֹתוֹ, וְעִנְיַן צְדּוּק הַדִּין
וְהַבְּרָכוֹת וְהַנֶּחָמוֹת שֶׁעוֹשִׂין בְּבֵית הָאָבֵל; וְעִנְיַן לִקּוּט עֲצָמוֹת שֶׁל קְרוֹבִים, וְכֵן
לִקּוּט עַצְמוֹת אָבִיו וְאִמּוֹ.

וּמַה שֶּׁאָמְרוּ שֶׁהַקְּרוֹבִים שֶׁמִּתְאַבְּלִים עֲלֵיהֶם, מִתְאַבְּלִים עִמָּהֶם בִּפְנֵיהֶם
מִדִּבְרֵי סוֹפְרִים, לִכְבוֹדָם; וּמַה שֶּׁאָמְרוּ שֶׁמִּתְאַבֵּל אָדָם עַל אִשְׁתּוֹ, וְהִיא עַל
בַּעְלָהּ, וְעַל אַחִים מִן הָאֵם, מִדִּבְרֵי סוֹפְרִים; וּבְנוֹ אוֹ אָחִיו מִן הַשִּׁפְחָה וּמִן
הַנָּכְרִית, אֵין מִתְאַבְּלִין עֲלֵיהֶם אֲפִלּוּ נִתְגַּיְּרוּ, לֹא מִדִּבְרֵי תוֹרָה וְלֹא מִדִּבְרֵי
סוֹפְרִים; וְהַכֹּהֵן מִטַּמֵּא לְאִשְׁתּוֹ: אַף־עַל־פִּי שֶׁאֲבֵלוּת אָדָם עַל אִשְׁתּוֹ מִדִּבְרֵי
סוֹפְרִים, עָשׂוּ אוֹתָהּ לוֹ כְּמֵת מִצְוָה; וּמֵאַחַר שֶׁנִּסְתַּם הַגּוֹלָל, אֵין מִטַּמֵּא כֹהֵן עוֹד;
וּמַה שֶּׁאָמְרוּ שֶׁחִיּוּב אֲבֵלוּת בִּשְׁלֹשָׁה קְרוֹבִים, דְּרַבָּנָן, וְאֵלּוּ הֵם: אָח אוֹ אָחוֹת
מֵאֵם, וְאָחוֹת נְשׂוּאָה אוֹ אֲרוּסָה, בֵּין מֵאָב בֵּין מֵאֵם, וּבֵין אֲנוּסָה וּמְפֻתָּה;
וּלְפִיכָךְ אֵין כֹּהֵן מִטַּמֵּא בְאֵלּוּ. וְאֵלּוּ הָעִנְיָנִים עִם יֶתֶר פְּרָטֶיהָ מְבֹאָרִים בְּמַסֶּכֶת
מַשְׁקִין וּבִמְקוֹמוֹת מִבְּרָכוֹת וּכְתֻבּוֹת וִיבָמוֹת, וּבִסְפָרָא בְּפָרָשַׁת אֱמֹר אֶל הַכֹּהֲנִים.

וְנוֹהֶגֶת מִצְוָה זוֹ שֶׁל חִיּוּב הַטֻּמְאָה בְּמֵת הַקָּרוֹב בְּכֹהֵן, בְּכָל מָקוֹם וּבְכָל זְמַן
בִּזְכָרֵי כְהֻנָּה; אֲבָל הַנָּשִׁים אֵינָן בְּחִיּוּב זֶה, שֶׁכֵּן בָּא הַפֵּרוּשׁ שֶׁמִּי שֶׁנִּמְנַע
מִלְּהִטַּמֵּא לְזוּלַת הַקְּרוֹבִים הוּא שֶׁנִּצְטַוָּה לְהִטַּמֵּא לַקְּרוֹבִים, אֲבָל הַנָּשִׁים
הַכֹּהֲנוֹת, אַחַר שֶׁלֹּא נִמְנְעוּ מִלְּהִטַּמֵּא בְמֵת, כְּמוֹ שֶׁמְּבֹאָר בִּמְקוֹמוֹ, כְּמוֹ־כֵן לֹא
נִצְטַוּוּ לְהִטַּמֵּא לַקְּרוֹבִים עַל כָּל פָּנִים. אֲבָל מִתְאַבְּלוֹת הֵן מִכָּל־מָקוֹם, וְלָהֶן

---

37. As cited by Ramban *ibid.* (so too MT *ibid.* viii 6).

38. TB Mo'éd Katan 24b; MT *ibid.* xii 5.

39. See *Tur* and *Shulḥan 'Aruch Yoreh Dé'ah,* §344, 1.

40. TB Mo'éd Katan 27a, Shabbath 21b, M'gillah 5b; MT *ibid.* xi 3.

41. TB K'thuboth 17a.

42. TB B'rachoth 19a, 46b; K'thuboth 8b; Ramban, *Torath ha'Adam* 25a.

43. Literally, the bones.

44. TB Mo'éd Katan 8a; R. 'Ashér *ad loc.* §10.

45. MT *hilchoth 'ével* ii 4, based on TB Mo'éd Katan 20b.

46. E.g. if a man's son lost his child, the son (the child's father) must rend his clothing by Torah law; in this son's presence at the time, the man (his father) must also rend his clothing, by the ruling of the Sages.

47. For a brother (or virgin sister) from one father, mourning is required by Torah law; see §263, note 2.

48. MT *hilchoth 'ével* ii 1 (see *Kessef Mishneh, Leḥem Mishneh*).

49. Derived from TB Yevamoth 22a–b; see §260, notes 17, 18.

50. Literally, a corpse of religious obligation. If a person finds an abandoned, unidentifiable corpse, the duty to bury it falls upon him, and this duty overrides all other considerations of religious obligation, ritual purity, etc.

whom is a eulogy given,[38] and how;[39] and the Sabbath, a festival day, the intermediate days of a festival, Ḥanukkah and Purim—what the law is then regarding a eulogy;[40] and for whom Torah study is interrupted when he dies.[41] Then there is the subject of acknowledging the justice of Heaven's sentence of death, and the benedictions and consolations uttered in the house of a mourner.[42] There is, too, the subject of the gathering of the remains[43] of near kin [for reburial], and likewise the gathering of the remains of one's father or mother.[44]

There is, further, what the Sages said:[45] that regarding those relatives whom one is required to mourn [upon their death, the law is that] one mourns with them in their presence, by the ruling of the Scribes—in homage to them;[46] and there is what they said, that a man is to mourn for his wife, and she for her husband, and so [one should observe mourning] for brothers from one mother,[47] by the ruling of the Scribes.[48] As for a son or a brother from a female slave or a non-Jewish woman, one does not mourn for them even if they were converted to Judaism—neither by Torah law nor by the ruling of the Sages.[49] A *kohen* is to defile himself for his wife. Even though the mourning of a man for his wife is required only by the ruling of the Sages, they gave her the status of a *méth mitzvah*[50] for him.[51] From the time the grave has been closed [though] a *kohen* is not to defile himself any more.[52] There is, moreover, what the Sages said,[53] that there exists an obligation of mourning for three relatives by the ruling of the Sages, these being a brother or sister from one mother,[47] and a married or betrothed sister, whether from one father or one mother, and [equally] whether she had been raped or seduced.[54] For this reason[55] a *kohen* does not defile himself for these. These subjects, with the rest of its details, are clarified in the Talmud tractate *Moʻéd Katan*, in certain places in the tractates *B'rachoth*, *K'thuboth* and *Yevamoth*, and in the Midrash *Sifra* on *sidrah 'emor*.

This precept, of the duty of defilement for near kin by a *kohen*, is in effect everywhere, at every time—for male *kohanim*. Women, however, are not under this obligation: for the interpretation was given that whoever was restricted from defiling himself for any but near relatives, was commanded to defile himself to close kin; as for women *kohanim*, though, since they were not restricted from defiling themselves by the dead, as this is explained in its proper place (§263, end), they were likewise not commanded to defile themselves to near kin under any particular circumstances. Nevertheless, they should

הַבְּחִירָה לְהִטַּמֵּא אִם יִרְצוּ. וְדַע זֶה וְזָכְרֵהוּ.

וּמִצְוַת חִיּוּב הָאֲבֵלוּת הַנִּגְרֶרֶת עִם מִצְוָה זוֹ, כְּמוֹ שֶׁאָמַרְנוּ, נוֹהֶגֶת בְּכָל מָקוֹם וּבְכָל זְמַן וּבְכָל אָדָם, בֵּין כֹּהֵן בֵּין יִשְׂרָאֵל, וּבִזְכָרִים וּנְקֵבוֹת.

וְכֹהֵן הָעוֹבֵר עַל זֶה וְלֹא רָצָה לְהִטַּמֵּא לְשִׁשָּׁה הַקְּרוֹבִים הַנִּזְכָּרִים בַּכָּתוּב, וְכֵן כֹּהֵן אוֹ יִשְׂרָאֵל שֶׁלֹּא רָצוּ לְהִתְאַבֵּל עַל קְרוֹבֵיהֶם בַּדְּבָרִים שֶׁמָּנוּ חֲכָמִים בְּחִיּוּב עִקַּר הָאֲבֵלוּת בְּיוֹם רִאשׁוֹן, בִּטְּלוּ עֲשֵׂה זֶה. וּכְבָר כָּתַבְתִּי לְמַעְלָה שֶׁבֵּית־דִּין כּוֹפִין עַל בִּטּוּל עֲשֵׂה.

וְיֵשׁ מִן הַמְפָרְשִׁים שֶׁכָּתְבוּ שֶׁאֵין מִצְוַת אָבוּל נֶחְשֶׁבֶת לְמִצְוָה דְאוֹרַיְתָא. אוּלַי דַּעְתָּם לוֹמַר שֶׁאַף־עַל־פִּי שֶׁאוֹנֵן אָסוּר בְּקָדָשִׁים דְּאוֹרַיְתָא, כָּל עִנְיַן אֲבֵלוּת מִיהָא דְרַבָּנָן הוּא.

[שֶׁלֹּא יְשַׁמֵּשׁ כֹּהֵן טְבוּל יוֹם עַד שֶׁיַּעֲרִיב שִׁמְשׁוֹ]

רסה שֶׁלֹּא יְשַׁמֵּשׁ כֹּהֵן טְבוּל יוֹם עַד שֶׁיַּעֲרִיב שִׁמְשׁוֹ; וְאַף־עַל־פִּי שֶׁטָּבַל וְטָהַר, צָרִיךְ הַעֲרֵב שֶׁמֶשׁ, לְפִי שֶׁהוּא כְּשֵׁנִי לְטֻמְאָה עַד שֶׁיַּעֲרִיב שִׁמְשׁוֹ, שֶׁכֵּן פֵּרְשׁוּ זִכְרוֹנָם לִבְרָכָה: "בַּמַּיִם יוּבָא וְטָמֵא עַד הָעֶרֶב וְטָהֵר", הַכָּתוּב קָרָא לִטְבוּל יוֹם טָמֵא אַף־עַל־פִּי שֶׁטָּבַל, עַד שֶׁיַּעֲרִיב שִׁמְשׁוֹ; אֲבָל מִכָּל־מָקוֹם אֵינוֹ טָמֵא כְּמוֹ שֶׁהָיָה קֹדֶם טְבִילָה, כִּי מִתְּחִלָּה הָיָה רִאשׁוֹן לְטֻמְאָה, וְאַחַר הַטְּבִילָה נִקְרָא שֵׁנִי לְטֻמְאָה; וְעַל זֶה נֶאֱמַר: וְלֹא יְחַלְּלוּ שֵׁם אֱלֹהֵיהֶם, שֶׁכֵּן בָּא עָלָיו הַפֵּרוּשׁ הַמְקֻבָּל, וְכֵן הוּא בְּפֶרֶק תְּשִׁיעִי מִסַּנְהֶדְרִין, שֶׁאָמְרוּ שָׁם: "קָדָשִׁים יִהְיוּ לֵאלֹהֵיהֶם וְלֹא יְחַלְּלוּ שֵׁם אֱלֹהֵיהֶם", אִם אֵינוֹ עִנְיָן לְטָמֵא, שֶׁכְּבָר נִתְבָּאֵר, תְּנֵהוּ עִנְיָן לִטְבוּל יוֹם

51. TB Yevamoth 89b; MT *ibid.* 7.
52. Minor tractate S'maḥoth iv 10–11.
53. TB Mo'éd Katan 20b; Ramban, *Torath ha'Adam, sha'ar ha'ével*, beginning.
54. In all these instances she is no longer "his virgin sister who is near to him, who has not been with any man" (Leviticus 21:3), for whom mourning is obligatory by the Torah's law.
55. I.e. that the obligation of mourning was imposed only by the Sages.
56. So ShM positive precept §37.
57. I.e. it is all by the decree of the Sages: R. Yitzḥak (of *tosafoth*) cited in R. 'Ashér, Mo'éd Katan iii 2.

§265   1. Literally, "immersed by day"; if a *kohen* became defiled for one day, he was to undergo ritual immersion by day, then wait for the sun to set and night to come, to be ritually pure; between the immersion and nightfall he is called a *t'vul yom*. As our author notes two paragraphs below, the term applies equally to ritually unclean objects, and to one who was defiled for seven days, on the final day.
2. So MT *hilchoth she'ar 'avoth ha-tum'ah* x 1, based on Mishnah, Zavim v 12; TB P'saḥim 14a, Shabbath 14b.

⟨178⟩

observe mourning; and the choice is theirs to become defiled if they wish. So know this and remember it. [56]

The *mitzvah* of the [general] obligation of mourning, which follows as a corollary of this precept, as we said, applies in every place and every time, and for everyone, whether *kohen* or Israelite, man or woman.

If a *kohen* violates this and does not wish to defile himself for the six close relatives mentioned in the Writ (Leviticus 21:2–3)—and likewise a *kohen* or Israelite who does not wish to mourn his near kin in those ways that the Sages listed in the obligation of the main observance of mourning on the first day—they disobey this positive precept. And I have already written above (§6) that the *beth din* should apply coercive force against the disobedience of a positive precept.

There are some authorities who wrote that the *mitzvah* of mourning is not reckoned as a precept of the Torah. [57] Perhaps their view is to hold that even though an *'onén* [in grief over the dead before burial] is forbidden meat of holy offerings by the Torah's law, the entire matter of mourning is nevertheless by the ruling of the Sages.

[THAT A KOHEN DEFILED FOR A DAY WHO UNDERGOES RITUAL IMMERSION SHOULD NOT SERVE AT THE SANCTUARY TILL SUNSET]

265 that a *kohen* who is a *t'vul yom* [1] should not serve [at the Temple] until his sun goes down, because he is in the second degree of ritual uncleanness until his sun sets. For so our Sages of blessed memory explained: "it must be put into water, and it shall be unclean until the evening; then it shall be clean" (Leviticus 11:32)—Scripture calls a *t'vul yom* ritually unclean, even though he or it underwent ritual immersion, until the sun sets. [2] But in any event, he is not as impure as he was before the immersion: for originally he was in the first degree of ritual uncleanness, and after the immersion he is ranked in the second degree of impurity. In regard to this it is stated, *and they shall not profane the name of their God* (Leviticus 21:6); for so was the traditional explanation given for it; and so we read in chapter 9 of the Talmud tractate *Sanhedrin* (83b), as it was taught there: "They shall be holy to their God, and they shall not profane the name of their God"—if this is not needed for one who is defiled, as that was already elucidated, [3] apply it to the subject of a *t'vul yom* who serves

שֶׁיְּשַׁמֵּשׁ; וְיָלִיף לָהּ הָתָם מֵחִלּוּל חִלּוּל.

מִשָּׁרְשֵׁי הַמִּצְוָה, לְפִי שֶׁהַכֹּהֵן הוּא הַשָּׁלִיחַ בֵּין יִשְׂרָאֵל לַאֲבִיהֶם שֶׁבַּשָּׁמַיִם, וּמִתּוֹךְ מַעֲשָׂיו וְקָרְבְּנוֹתָיו יִתְרַצֶּה הָאָדָם לִפְנֵי בּוֹרְאוֹ וִיכַפֵּר עֲוֹנוֹ; עַל־כֵּן חוֹבָה עָלָיו לִהְיוֹת נְקִי הַגּוּף בְּתַכְלִית בְּעֵת הָעֲבוֹדָה, וְאוּלַי רוּחַ הַטֻּמְאָה לֹא יַעֲבֹר לְגַמְרֵי מֵעָלָיו עַד הֶעָרֵב הַשֶּׁמֶשׁ; וּבָרוּךְ אֲדוֹן הַחָכְמָה, כִּי הוּא הַיּוֹדֵעַ וְלֹא אֲנַחְנוּ עַד אֵי זֶה עֵת יִכְשַׁר לְמִי שֶׁנִּטְמָא לַעֲסֹק בַּעֲבוֹדָתוֹ בָּרוּךְ הוּא, וְהוֹדִיעָנוּ כִּי הוּא עֵת בּוֹא הַשֶּׁמֶשׁ לִקְצָת הַטֻּמְאוֹת.

מִדִּינֵי הַמִּצְוָה, מַה שֶּׁאָמְרוּ זִכְרוֹנָם לִבְרָכָה שֶׁאֶחָד טְבוּל יוֹם מִטֻּמְאָה חֲמוּרָה, כְּגוֹן שֶׁטָּבַל מִטֻּמְאַת מֵת וְזִיבוֹת וְצָרָעוֹת, אוֹ מִטֻּמְאָה קַלָּה, כְּגוֹן טֻמְאַת שֶׁרֶץ וְכַיּוֹצֵא בָהּ, טָעוּן הֶעָרֵב שֶׁמֶשׁ; וְזֶה הָעִנְיָן הוּא בֵּין בְּאָדָם בֵּין בְּכֵלִים, בֵּין בְּטֻמְאָה דְאוֹרַיְתָא אוֹ אֲפִלּוּ בְּטֻמְאָה דְרַבָּנָן, צָרִיךְ הֶעָרֵב שֶׁמֶשׁ.

וּפֵרוּשׁ טְבוּל יוֹם, כְּלוֹמַר מִי שֶׁטָּבַל וְלֹא הֶעֱרִיב שִׁמְשׁוֹ, זֶהוּ פֵּרוּשׁוֹ בְּכָל מָקוֹם. וְאִם נָגַע בְּאָכְלֵי תְרוּמָה וּמַשְׁקִין שֶׁל תְּרוּמָה, פּוֹסֵל אוֹתָן וְעוֹשֶׂה אוֹתָן שְׁלִישִׁי לְטֻמְאָה, לְפִי שֶׁהוּא כְּשֵׁנִי לְטֻמְאָה, כְּמוֹ שֶׁאָמַרְנוּ; נָגְעוּ הֵן אַחַר־כֵּן בַּאֲכָלִין אֲחֵרִים, אֵינָן פּוֹסְלִין אוֹתָן, שֶׁאֵין שְׁלִישִׁי עוֹשֶׂה רְבִיעִי בַּתְּרוּמָה; וְאִם נָגַע טְבוּל יוֹם בְּאָכְלֵי קֹדֶשׁ אוֹ בְמַשְׁקִין, עֲשָׂאָן רְבִיעִי, כְּלוֹמַר שֶׁפְּסָלָן, אֲבָל אֵין חוֹזְרִין הֵן לְטַמֵּא אֲחֵרִים: שֶׁאַף־עַל־פִּי שֶׁשְּׁלִישִׁי עוֹשֶׂה רְבִיעִי בַּקֹּדֶשׁ, טֻמְאַת טְבוּל יוֹם אֵינָהּ חֲמוּרָה כָּל־כָּךְ שֶׁתְּטַמֵּא לִרְבִיעִי; אֲבָל אִם נָגַע טְבוּל יוֹם בְּאָכְלֵי חֻלִּין אוֹ בְמַשְׁקִין, הֲרֵי הֵן טְהוֹרִין, שֶׁאֵין שֵׁנִי עוֹשֶׂה שְׁלִישִׁי בְּחֻלִּין; כֵּן קִבַּלְנוּ הַדְּבָרִים מֵחֲכָמֵינוּ זִכְרוֹנָם לִבְרָכָה.

---

3. I.e. that a *kohen* who is defiled, ritually unclean, is not to serve at the Sanctuary, is derived from another verse (§278).

4. In Leviticus 22:9, interpreted as referring to eating *t'rumah* (the *kohen*'s portion from all crops and produce) while defiled, we read, *and they shall die thereby if they profane it*. Hence if a *t'vul yom* serves in the Sanctuary, the penalty is similarly death, since Leviticus 21:6, applied to this sin, reads, *and they shall not profane*, etc.—the two verses have the identical verb, "profane." (The paragraph is based on ShM negative precept § 76).

5. Based on TB Yoma 18b.

6. MT *hilchoth she'ar 'avoth ha-tum'ah* x 2, based on Tosefta, etc. (*Kessef Mishneh*).

7. TB Me'ilah 8b.

8. I.e. if the *t'rumah* that he defiled touches other *t'rumah*.

9. Mishnah, Tohoroth ii 4.

10. TB Sotah 29a, etc.

[at the Temple]. And [the penalty] is derived there [from *t'rumah*] through the identical terms of *ḥillul* (profanation).[4]

At the root of the precept lies the reason that the *kohen* is a messenger between the Israelites and their Father in heaven.[5] Through his deeds and offerings, a man becomes acceptable before his Creator, and his sin is atoned. Therefore an obligation lies upon him to be utmostly clean in body at the time of the service: and perhaps the spirit of uncleanness does not leave him completely until the setting of the sun. Blessed is the Lord of wisdom: for He knows, not we, at which time it becomes suitable for one who was defiled to engage in His service (blessed is He); and He informed us that this is the time when the sun goes down, for some instances of defilement.

Among the laws of the precept, there is what the Sages of blessed memory taught:[6] that whether one is a *t'vul yom* from a severe defilement—for instance, if he underwent ritual immersion after defilement by a corpse, or after discharges or leprous ailments—or from a light uncleanness, such as defilement by a swarming creature, and so forth—he requires the setting of the sun. This rule holds whether [the *t'vul yom*] is a man or utensils, and whether it was a defilement by Torah law or even by the ruling of the Sages—the setting of the sun is [always] necessary.[6]

Now, the meaning of *t'vul yom* is to signify that someone underwent ritual immersion and his sun did not go down yet; this is its sense everywhere. If he touches food and drink of *t'rumah* [the *kohen*'s portion of produce] he disqualifies it[7] and makes it defiled in the third degree of uncleanness, because he is in the second degree of uncleanness, as we said. If they should touch other food afterward,[8] they do not disqualify it, since the third degree of uncleanness does not engender a fourth degree in *t'rumah*.[9] If a *t'vul yom* touches hallowed food or drink [of offerings] he makes it defiled in the fourth degree of uncleanness.[7] In other words, he disqualifies it, but it in turn cannot make anything else unclean; for even though the third degree of uncleanness does engender a fourth in holy things, the impurity of a *t'vul yom* is not so severe that it can give rise to a fourth degree. However, if a *t'vul yom* touched ordinary, non-holy food or drink, that would remain ritually pure, since a second degree of uncleanness does not create a third degree in non-holy food.[10] So we received these matters from our Sages of blessed memory.

⟨181⟩ It thus becomes clear from this that neither the third degree of

וְהִנֵּה יִתְבָּאֵר מִזֶּה שֶׁאֵין שְׁלִישִׁי שֶׁבִּתְרוּמָה, וְלֹא רְבִיעִי שֶׁבַּקֹּדֶשׁ, מְטַמְּאִין מַשְׁקֶה אַחֵר וְאֹכֶל אַחֵר; וְאֵין צָרִיךְ לוֹמַר שֶׁאֵין מְטַמְּאִין כֵּלִים, שֶׁאָדָם וְכֵלִים אֵין מְקַבְּלִין טֻמְאָה אֶלָּא מֵאַב הַטֻּמְאָה; וְכָל הַמְּטַמְּאִין, בֵּין חֲמוּרִים בֵּין קַלִּים, מַשְׁקִין הַיּוֹצְאִין מֵהֶן, כְּגוֹן רֻקָּן וּמֵימֵי רַגְלֵיהֶם, דִּינָן כְּמַשְׁקִין שֶׁנָּגְעוּ בָּהֶן; וְיֶתֶר פְּרָטֶיהָ, בְּמַסֶּכֶת טְבוּל יוֹם.

וְנוֹהֶגֶת מִצְוָה זוֹ בַּכֹּהֲנִים הַזְּכָרִים בִּזְמַן הַבַּיִת, שֶׁהֵם הֻזְהֲרוּ עַל הָעֲבוֹדָה וּלְהִזָּהֵר מֵהַטֻּמְאָה, וְלֹא הַכֹּהֲנוֹת. וּמִי שֶׁעָבַר עַל זֶה וְשִׁמֵּשׁ טְבוּל יוֹם, חַיָּב מִיתָה בִּידֵי שָׁמַיִם. וְלֹא בָא עַל חִיּוּב זֶה כָּתוּב מְבֹאָר בַּתּוֹרָה, אֶלָּא שֶׁלָּמְדוּ חֲכָמִים זִכְרוֹנָם לִבְרָכָה הָעִנְיָן שָׁם בְּסַנְהֶדְרִין, בִּגְזֵרָה שָׁוָה דְּחִלּוּל חִלּוּל.

[שֶׁלֹּא יִשָּׂא כֹהֵן אִשָּׁה זוֹנָה]

רסו שֶׁלֹּא יִשָּׂא כֹהֵן, בֵּין כֹּהֵן גָּדוֹל בֵּין כֹּהֵן הֶדְיוֹט, אִשָּׁה זוֹנָה לְאִשָּׁה, שֶׁנֶּאֱמַר: אִשָּׁה זוֹנָה וַחֲלָלָה לֹא יִקָּחוּ, וּלְשׁוֹן קִיחָה מַשְׁמַע דֶּרֶךְ אִישׁוּת, עַל־כֵּן אֵינוֹ לוֹקֶה עָלֶיהָ אֶלָּא כְּשֶׁנִּשָּׂאָהּ וּבְעָלָהּ, שֶׁכֵּן בָּא הַפֵּרוּשׁ שֶׁאֵין הַחִיּוּב עַד שֶׁיִּבְעָלֶנָּה, כְּמוֹ שֶׁנִּכְתֹּב בְּעֶזְרַת הַשֵּׁם.

מִשָּׁרְשֵׁי הַמִּצְוָה, לְפִי שֶׁהַכֹּהֲנִים נִבְחֲרוּ לַעֲבֹד עֲבוֹדַת הַשֵּׁם תָּמִיד, רָאוּי וּמְחֻיָּב לִהְיוֹתָם קְדוֹשִׁים וּנְקִיִּים יוֹתֵר מִכָּל שְׁאָר הָעָם בְּכָל עִנְיְנֵיהֶם, אַף־כִּי בְּעִנְיַן הַזִּוּוּג, שֶׁהוּא דָבָר עִקְרִי בָאָדָם, וּקְצָת מַחְשְׁבוֹת הָאָדָם עַל בַּת זוּגוֹ תָּמִיד. לָכֵן נִתְחַיֵּב שֶׁלֹּא לָשֵׂא הַזּוֹנָה, שֶׁמְּזוּגָהּ רַע נָמֵר, פֶּן תְּסִירֵנוּ וְתַטֵּנוּ בְּרֹב לְקַחְתָּהּ מִדַּרְכוֹ הַטּוֹבָה וְכַוָּנָתוֹ הָרְצוּיָה; גַּם הִיא בֹשֶׁת וּפְגָם אֶל כָּל הַקָּרֵב אֵלֶיהָ, שֶׁכָּל הָעָם מְרַנְּנִים אַחֲרֶיהָ בְּטֻמְאָתָהּ אֲשֶׁר בְּשׁוּלֶיהָ.

---

11. MT *hilchoth she'ar 'avoth ha-tum'ah* x 5.

12. Tosefta, Kélim vi, beginning; TB Bava Kamma 2b.

13. Mishnah, T'vul Yom ii 1; MT *ibid.* 4.

§266 1. The Hebrew, *zonah*, is generally understood as harlot; but as our author proceeds to explain, in our Oral Tradition the term applies only in certain instances of immorality; a less pejorative English term has therefore been chosen.

2. MT *hilchoth 'issuré bi'ah* xvii 2, based on his understanding of TB Kiddushin 78a (*Maggid Mishneh*).

3. Expression based on Lamentations 1:9.

ritual uncleanness in *t'rumah* nor the fourth degree in hallowed food can impart defilement to other drink or other food; and there is no need to add that they do not impart defilement to utensils, [11] since a man and utensils (objects) can receive defilement only from a "father" (primary source) of uncleanness. [12] As to all sources of defilement, whether severe or light, if liquid issues from them, such as their spittle or urine, its law is like that of liquid which touched them. [13] The rest of its details are in the Mishnah tractate *T'vul Yom*.

This precept applies to male *kohanim* at the time the Temple exists, as they were adjured about the Temple service, and to beware of ritual uncleanness; but not to women *kohanim*. If someone violated this and served while he was a *t'vul yom*, he would incur death at Heaven's hands. No clear verse is given in the Torah about this penalty, but the Sages of blessed memory learned the matter there in the tractate *Sanhedrin* (83b) by a *g'zérah shavah* [identity in two verses] of the term *ḥillul* (profanation). [4]

[THAT A KOHEN IS PROHIBITED FROM MARRYING A
WANTON]

266 that a *kohen*, whether a *kohen gadol* or an ordinary one, should not take a wanton [1] for a wife, as it is stated, *They shall not take a woman that is wanton or profaned* (Leviticus 21:7); and the term "take" signifies by marriage. Therefore one does not receive whiplashes on account of her until he weds her and is conjugally intimate with her; for so the explanation was given [in the Oral Tradition] [2]—"until he is conjugally intimate with her"—as we will write, with God's help.

At the root of the precept lies the reason that since the *kohanim* were chosen to carry out the service of the Eternal Lord, it is right and necessary constantly that they should be holy and clean, more than all the rest of the people, in all their affairs, indeed including the matter of matrimony, which is a matter of main importance for a man; and some of a man's thoughts are always on his helpmeet. Therefore was he duty-bound not to marry a wanton, whose temperament is bad and bitter, for fear that she might turn him and lead him astray, *with her abundant sweet talk* (Proverbs 7:21), away from his good path and acceptable intentions. Moreover, she is a disgrace and a blemish for anyone who becomes close to her, since all the people murmur about her, regarding "her uncleanness that is in her skirts." [3]

⟨183⟩   Among the laws of the precept, there is what the Sages of blessed

מִדִּינֵי הַמִּצְוָה, מַה שֶּׁאָמְרוּ זִכְרוֹנָם לִבְרָכָה שֶׁהַזּוֹנָה הָאֲמוּרָה כָּאן הִיא כָּל
שֶׁאֵינָהּ בַּת יִשְׂרָאֵל, דְּכֻלָּן בִּכְלַל זוֹנוֹת הֵן; וְעוֹד, שֶׁכֵּיוָן שֶׁאֵין קִדּוּשִׁין תּוֹפְשִׂין
בָּהֶן, זוֹנָה הִיא; וְכֵן תִּקָּרֵא זוֹנָה כָּל בַּת יִשְׂרָאֵל שֶׁנִּבְעֲלָה לְאָדָם שֶׁהִיא אֲסוּרָה
לִנָּשֵׂא לוֹ אִסּוּר הַשָּׁוֶה בַכֹּל — לְאַפּוּקֵי אַלְמָנָה שֶׁנִּבְעֲלָה לְכֹהֵן גָּדוֹל, אוֹ גְרוּשָׁה
לְכֹהֵן הֶדְיוֹט, שֶׁאֵין זֶה אִסּוּר בְּכָל אָדָם, וְאֵינָהּ נַעֲשֵׂית זוֹנָה בְּכָךְ.

וְכֵן נַמֵּי תִּקָּרֵא זוֹנָה כָּל שֶׁנִּבְעֲלָה לְכֹהֵן חָלָל, וְאַף־עַל־פִּי שֶׁהִיא מֻתֶּרֶת
לְהִנָּשֵׂא לוֹ, שֶׁאֵין הֱיוֹתָהּ זוֹנָה תָּלוּי בִּבְעִילָה שֶׁל אִסּוּר אֶלָּא בִּפְגִימָה, וּמִפִּי
הַשְּׁמוּעָה לָמַדְנוּ שֶׁאֵינָהּ פְּגוּמָה אֶלָּא מֵאָדָם הָאָסוּר לָהּ שֶׁתִּנָּשֵׂא לוֹ אוֹ מִכֹּהֵן
חָלָל.

וְלָמַדְנוּ מֵעַתָּה שֶׁהַנִּרְבַּעַת לִבְהֵמָה, אַף־עַל־פִּי שֶׁהִיא בִּסְקִילָה, לֹא נַעֲשֵׂית
זוֹנָה, דְּדַוְקָא בִּבְעִילַת אָדָם הוּא שֶׁעוֹשָׂהּ אוֹתָהּ זוֹנָה. וְכֵן אִם נִבְעֲלָה בְּעוֹדָהּ נִדָּה
לְמִי שֶׁרְאוּיָה שֶׁתִּנָּשֵׂא לוֹ, אֵינָהּ נַעֲשֵׂית זוֹנָה בְּכָךְ, וְאַף־עַל־פִּי שֶׁהִיא בְּכָרֵת. וְכֵן
הַבָּא עַל הַפְּנוּיָה, אֲפִלּוּ הָיְתָה קְדֵשָׁה, כְּלוֹמַר שֶׁהִפְקִירָה עַצְמָהּ לַכֹּל, אֵינָהּ
נַעֲשֵׂית זוֹנָה, כָּל זְמַן שֶׁלֹּא נִבְעֲלָה לְמִי שֶׁאֲסוּרָה לְהִנָּשֵׂא לוֹ, כְּלוֹמַר שֶׁהִיא עֶרְוָה
עָלָיו; וַאֲפִלּוּ מְחַיָּבֵי לָאוִין אוֹ אֲפִלּוּ מְחַיָּבֵי עֲשֵׂה בִּכְלַל אִסּוּר זֶה. וּלְפִיכָךְ אָמְרוּ
שֶׁגּוֹי אוֹ עֶבֶד, אוֹ נָתִין אוֹ מַמְזֵר, אוֹ גֵּר עַמּוֹנִי וּמוֹאָבִי אוֹ מִצְרִי אוֹ אֲדוֹמִי רִאשׁוֹן
וְשֵׁנִי, אוֹ פְצוּעַ דַּכָּא וּכְרוּת שָׁפְכָה, שֶׁבָּא אֶחָד מֵהֶן עַל יְהוּדִית, עֲשָׂאָהּ זוֹנָה
וּנְפָסְלָה לִכְהֻנָּה; וְאִם הִיא כֹהֶנֶת נִפְסְלָה מִן הַכְּהֻנָּה.

וְכָל הַנִּבְעֶלֶת לְמִי שֶׁעוֹשֶׂה אוֹתָהּ זוֹנָה, בֵּין בְּאֹנֶס בֵּין בְּרָצוֹן בֵּין בְּשִׁגְגָה, בֵּין

---

4. I.e. who was converted or manumitted (freed) from servitude; for an ordinary non-Jewish woman is forbidden to all Jews, not merely a *kohen*; TB Yevamoth 61a.

5. Since it is assumed that before conversion she was conjugally intimate with a heathen or a slave—which, by the rule in the next sentence, would put a Jewish woman in this category; Rashi to *ibid.*

6. I.e. their prior marital bond with a heathen or slave; it is thus as if they had been conjugally intimate with a man whom they are forbidden to marry (see the rule which follows).

7. MT *hilchoth 'issuré bi'ah* xviii 1 (sources in *Maggid Mishneh*).

8. *Ibid.* 5.

9. TB Yevamoth 59b.

10. Derived from *ibid.* 60a; MT *ibid.* 5.

11. TB Yevamoth 61b; MT *ibid.* 2.

12. I.e. by being conjugally intimate with her.

13. Born to a man and woman for whom conjugal intimacy is punishable by *karéth* (Divine severance of existence), i.e. consanguineous relations or adulterers; Deuteronomy 23:3.

14. All these, from "an Ammonite" to here, are forbidden to marry into the Jewish community: Deuteronomy 23:4, 8–9, 2.

15. TB Yevamoth 68a, 70a; MT *hilchoth 'issuré bi'ah* xviii 3.

memory taught: that the "wanton" spoken of here denotes anyone who is not an Israelite (Jewish),[4] for they all are included in the category of wantons;[5] moreover, since the marital bond does not take effect with them, it is wantonness, immorality.[6] So too would the term "wanton" apply to any daughter of Israel (Jewess) who was conjugally intimate with a man whom she is forbidden to marry by a ban that applies equally to all[7]—which excludes a widow that was conjugally intimate with a *kohen gadol*, or a divorced woman with an ordinary *kohen*: the ban [in their cases] does not apply equally to every man, and she does not thus become a wanton.

So would any woman be called wanton if she was conjugally intimate with a profaned *kohen* (disqualified by lineage), even though she is permitted to marry him;[7] for becoming a wanton depends not on forbidden conjugal intimacy, but on damage to status; and by the Oral Tradition we learned that her status is damaged only by a man whom she is forbidden to marry, or by a profaned *kohen*.[8]

Hence we learn that if a woman was conjugally intimate with a beast, even though she is liable to death by stoning, she does not thus become a wanton[9]—for it is specifically conjugal intimacy with a man that makes her a wanton. So likewise, if she was thus intimate while unclean from the menses with someone whom she is fit to marry, she does not become a wanton for that,[10] even though she incurs *karéth* [Divine severance of existence]. Similarly, if someone is thus intimate with a single woman, even if she is a harlot, i.e. who has made herself available to all, she does not become a wanton[11]— not as long as she had no conjugal intimacy with someone whom she is forbidden to marry, i.e. if she is a consanguineous relation to him. Yet even those who bring guilt over a negative precept, or even over a positive precept,[12] are included in this prohibition. It was therefore taught that if a heathen, a slave, a *nathin* [descendant of the Gibeonites; Joshua 9:27], a bastard,[13] an Ammonite or Moabite convert, a first or second generation Egyptian or Edomite convert, or a man with crushed or maimed testes[14] was conjugally intimate with a Jewess, he thus made her a wanton, and she is disqualified to marry a *kohen*; and if she is a woman *kohen*, she is disqualified from the privileges of *kohanim*.[15]

Moreover, if anyone is conjugally intimate with a man who can thus make her a wanton, whether it was by compulsion (rape) or free will, or unintentional, and whether they had natural or unnatural

כְּדַרְכָּהּ בֵּין שֶׁלֹּא כְדַרְכָּהּ, מִשֶּׁהֶעֱרָה בָהּ נִפְסְלָה מִשּׁוּם זוֹנָה, וּבִלְבַד שֶׁתִּהְיֶה בַּת שָׁלֹש שָׁנִים וְיוֹם אֶחָד וָמַעְלָה וְיִהְיֶה הַבּוֹעֵל בֶּן תֵּשַׁע שָׁנִים וְיוֹם אֶחָד וָמַעְלָה.

וְכֵן מֵעִנְיַן הַמִּצְוָה מַה שֶּׁאָמְרוּ בְּאֵשֶׁת כֹּהֵן שֶׁאָמְרָה לְבַעְלָהּ "נֶאֱנַסְתִּי", וַאֲפִלּוּ עֵד אֶחָד מֵעִיד לוֹ עָלֶיהָ שֶׁכֵּן הוּא כִּדְבָרֶיהָ, שֶׁזִּנְּתָה, שֶׁאֵינָהּ אֲסוּרָה עָלָיו בְּכָךְ, דְּאַמְרִינָן שֶׁמָּא עֵינֶיהָ נְתוּנָה בְאַחֵר; וּמִכָּל-מָקוֹם אֲסוּרָה לְכָל כֹּהֵן אַחַר מוֹת אִישָׁהּ, דְּשַׁוִּיתָה נַפְשָׁהּ חֲתִיכָה דְּאִסּוּרָא. וְאִם הָיְתָה נֶאֱמֶנֶת לוֹ, אוֹ הָעֵד נֶאֱמָן לוֹ, הֲרֵי זֶה יוֹצִיאֶנָּה עַל-כָּל-פָּנִים, לָצֵאת יְדֵי סָפֵק.

וְהוֹרוּנוּ מוֹרֵינוּ יִשְׁמְרֵם אֵל דְּדַוְקָא שֶׁבָּאַתָה לוֹמַר כֵּן, הִיא אוֹ הָעֵד, מִתּוֹךְ שָׁלוֹם שֶׁבֵּינוֹ לְבֵינָהּ; אֲבָל אָמְרָה כֵן, בֵּין הִיא בֵּין הָעֵד, מִתּוֹךְ קְטָטָה שֶׁיֵּשׁ בֵּינוֹ לְבֵינָהּ, יֵשׁ לָדוּן בַּדָּבָר שֶׁאֵינוֹ זָקוּק לְהוֹצִיאָהּ עַל-כָּל-פָּנִים, שֶׁחֲזָקָה הִיא דְּשַׁקּוּרֵי מְשַׁקְּרָא, וְאֵין רָאוּי לְהַאֲמִינָהּ בִּדְבוּרָהּ בְּעֵד אֶחָד אֶלָּא בִּשְׁנֵי עֵדִים כְּשֵׁרִים; אֲבָל מִכָּל-מָקוֹם אִם דַּעְתּוֹ סוֹמֶכֶת בִּדְבָרֶיהָ אוֹ בְּדִבְרֵי הָעֵד הַרְבֵּה, רָאוּי לוֹ לַחֲשֹׁ מִלָּבוֹא עָלֶיהָ. וְיֵתֶר רַבֵּי פְרָטֵי הַמִּצְוָה, בִּיבָמוֹת וּבְקִדּוּשִׁין.

וְנוֹהֶגֶת בְּכֹהֲנִים בְּכָל מָקוֹם וּבְכָל זְמָן. וְכֹהֵן הָעוֹבֵר עָלֶיהָ וְנָשָׂא אִשָּׁה זוֹנָה מֵאֵלּוּ שֶׁבֵּאַרְנוּ, דֶּרֶךְ אִישׁוּת, וּבְעָלָהּ, לוֹקֶה.

[שֶׁלֹּא יִשָּׂא כֹהֵן אִשָּׁה חֲלָלָה]

רסז שֶׁלֹּא יִשָּׂא כֹהֵן, בֵּין גָּדוֹל בֵּין הֶדְיוֹט, חֲלָלָה, שֶׁנֶּאֱמַר: אִשָּׁה זוֹנָה וַחֲלָלָה לֹא יִקָּחוּ; וַחֲלָלָה תִּקָּרֵא שֶׁנּוֹלְדָה מִפְּסוּלֵי כְהֻנָּה, כְּגוֹן בַּת אַלְמָנָה מִכֹּהֵן גָּדוֹל, אוֹ בַּת גְּרוּשָׁה מִכֹּהֵן הֶדְיוֹט, אוֹ שֶׁנִּתְחַלְּלָה עַל-יְדֵי בִיאַת אֶחָד מִן הַפְּסוּלִין לִכְהֻנָּה.

16. MT *ibid.* 6, based on TB Yevamoth 35a, 56b, 53b; Niddah 44b, 45a.
17. I.e. by her words she is forbidden to a *kohen*; TB N'darim 90b, K'thuboth 9a.
18. Derived from TB Kiddushin 66a; MT *ibid.* 8–9.
19. Rashba (R. Sh'lomoh ibn 'Adreth), *Responsa*, I §1237.

§267   1. I.e. a woman is ranked as profaned if she was conjugally intimate with a *kohen* with whom marriage would be forbidden, or if she was born from such a relationship; TB Kiddushin 77a.

relations, from the time he intromits the corona she is disqualified as a wanton—provided she is three years and a day old or more, and the male is nine years and a day old or more.[16]

It is likewise part of the subject-matter of this precept what the Sages taught about the wife of a *kohen* who told her husband, "I was raped": Even if one witness testifies about her that her words are true, that she [thus] became wanton, she does not become forbidden to him thereby—for we say: perhaps her eyes are cast on another man. However, she is forbidden to any *kohen* after her husband's death, since she made herself a forbidden entity.[17] But if he believed her, or believed the witness, he should divorce her in any event, to be quit of doubt.[18]

Yet our master teacher, may God protect him, taught us[19] that this holds only if she or the witness came to say this amid a situation of peace between him and her. But if she or the witness said this amid quarrel and strife that existed between him and her, it can be ruled in such a case that he need not be impelled to divorce her in any event, for it is a firm assumption that she was lying. It is therefore not right to believe her word with one witness [to support her], but only with two worthy, acceptable witnesses. Under any circumstances, though, if his mind places great reliance on her words or on the words of the witness, it is right for him to beware of being conjugally intimate with her.

The many remaining details of the precept are in the Talmud tractates *Yevamoth* and *Kiddushin*. It applies to *kohanim* everywhere, at every time. If a *kohen* violates it and takes a wanton as a wife—one of those types that we have elucidated—in marriage, and is conjugally intimate with her, he should be given whiplashes.

[THAT A KOHEN IS PROHIBITED FROM MARRYING A PROFANED WOMAN]

267 that a *kohen*, whether a *kohen gadol* or an ordinary one, should not marry a profaned woman: for it is stated, *They shall not take a woman that is wanton or profaned* (Leviticus 21:7). A woman is called profaned if she was born from [any of the marriages] disqualified among *kohanim*—for instance, the daughter of a widow by a *kohen gadol*, or the daughter of a divorced woman by an ordinary *kohen*; or if she was profaned by conjugal intimacy with one of those [with whom marital relations are] disqualified among *kohanim*.[1]

מִשָּׁרְשֵׁי הַמִּצְוָה, מַה שֶּׁכָּתַבְתִּי בְּאִסוּר זוֹנָה הַקּוֹדֶם לָזֶה.

מִדִּינֵי הַמִּצְוָה, מַה שֶּׁאָמְרוּ זִכְרוֹנָם לִבְרָכָה שֶׁאֵין חַיָּב הַמַּלְקוֹת לְכֹהֵן הַנּוֹשֵׂא חֲלָלָה עַד שֶׁיִּבְעַל, אֲבָל נְשָׂאָהּ וְלֹא בָעַל אֵינוֹ לוֹקֶה, שֶׁאֵין חַיָּב הַמַּלְקוֹת אֶלָּא בִּבְעִילָה, וְהוּא וְהִיא לוֹקִין. וְזֶה שֶׁאָמְרוּ לִבְרָכָה, לֹא הֻזְהֲרוּ כְשֵׁרוֹת לִנָּשֵׂא לִפְסוּלִין, אֵינוֹ מֵעִנְיַן זֶה כְּלָל, וּלְמַטָּה בְּדַף זֶה נְפָרֵשׁ הַדָּבָר; דְּוַדַּאי זוֹ אַחַר שֶׁהִיא נִבְעֶלֶת לְמִי שֶׁהִיא אֲסוּרָה עָלָיו בְּלָאו, בִּכְלָל הַחִיּוּב הִיא גַם-כֵּן, וּכְעִנְיָן שֶׁאָמְרוּ זִכְרוֹנָם לִבְרָכָה, שֶׁאֵין הֶפְרֵשׁ בֵּין אִשָּׁה לְאִישׁ לְכָל עֲנָשִׁין שֶׁבַּתּוֹרָה חוּץ מִשִּׁפְחָה חֲרוּפָה, כְּמוֹ שֶׁכָּתַבְתִּי לְמַעְלָה בְּסֵדֶר וַיִּקְרָא מִצְוַת עֲשֵׂה י' [סי' קכ"ט].

וְכֵן מִדִּינֵי הַמִּצְוָה מַה שֶּׁאָמְרוּ זִכְרוֹנָם לִבְרָכָה שֶׁהַכֹּהֵן שֶׁעוֹבֵר שֶׁעוֹבֵר הָעֲבֵרָה שֶׁהוּא בָא עַל הַחֲלָלָה, אֵין גּוּפוֹ מְחֻלָּל בְּכָךְ, אַף-עַל-פִּי שֶׁזַּרְעוֹ מְחֻלָּל; וּבֵין שֶׁנִּבְעֲלָה בְּאֹנֶס אוֹ בִשְׁגָגָה, בֵּין כְּדַרְכָּהּ בֵּין שֶׁלֹּא כְדַרְכָּהּ, מִשֶּׁהֶעֱרָה בָהּ, וְהוּא שֶׁיִּהְיֶה הַכֹּהֵן בֶּן ט' שָׁנִים וְיוֹם אֶחָד וָמַעְלָה וְהִיא מִבַּת ג' שָׁנִים וְיוֹם אֶחָד וָמַעְלָה, נִתְחַלְּלָה.

וּמַה שֶּׁאָמְרוּ שֶׁאֵינָהּ נַעֲשֵׂית חֲלָלָה אֶלָּא בִבְעִילָה, אֲבָל בְּקִדּוּשִׁין לְבַד לֹא נִתְחַלְּלָה; אֲבָל בְּנִשּׂוּאִין, אַף-עַל-פִּי שֶׁלֹּא נִבְעֲלָה נַעֲשֵׂית חֲלָלָה, מִפְּנֵי שֶׁכָּל נְשׂוּאָה בְּחֶזְקַת בְּעוּלָה, וְאַף-עַל-פִּי שֶׁנִּמְצֵאת בְּתוּלָה.

וּמַה שֶּׁאָמְרוּ שֶׁכֹּהֵן שֶׁבָּא עַל הַנִּדָּה, אַף-עַל-פִּי שֶׁהִיא בְּכָרֵת לֹא חִלְלָהּ, שֶׁאֵין עִנְיַן הַחִלּוּל אֶלָּא בְּאִסּוּר הַמְיֻחָד בַּכֹּהֲנִים, כְּמוֹ אַלְמָנָה וּגְרוּשָׁה וַחֲלָלָה זוֹנָה, אוֹ הַנִּבְעֶלֶת לְאֶחָד מִן הַפְּסוּלִין לִכְהֻנָּה, כְּמוֹ הַחֲלָלִין.

2. Source in § 266, note 2.

3. TB Yevamoth 84b.

4. For living with him in marriage, since in such a case (e.g. a divorced woman and a *kohen*) each is equally forbidden to marry the other.

5. TB Sotah 23a.

6. He does not become disqualified to serve at the Sanctuary, etc.

7. MT *hilchoth 'issuré bi'ah* xix 2 (sources in §266, note 16).

8. TB Yevamoth 56b; MT *ibid.* 3.

9. See §35, note 8.

10. We assume that the marriage was nevertheless consummated, without the rupture of the hymen.

11. TB Yevamoth 60a; Kiddushin 77a; MT *hilchoth 'issuré bi'ah* xix 6.

12. I.e. in relation to a *kohen gadol* (Leviticus 21:14).

13. I.e. one born from a woman who was not a proper, legitimate wife for his father (a *kohen*) to have married.

At the root of the precept lies the reason I wrote about the ban on a wanton, which precedes this.

Among the laws of the precept, there is what the Sages of blessed memory taught:[2] that a *kohen* who marries a profaned woman incurs no punishment of whiplashes until they are conjugally intimate; but if he married her and effected no consummation, he is not whipped, as the penalty of lashes is only for conjugal intimacy, for which both he and she are whipped. As for what the Sages of blessed memory said,[3] that women of qualified status are not adjured against marrying disqualified [*kohanim*], that is not part of this subject at all; yet we will elucidate the matter below, on this leaf. For certainly, after such a woman is conjugally intimate with a man to whom she is forbidden by an injunction, she is equally included in the liability to the punishment[4]—in keeping with what the Sages of blessed memory said,[3] that there is no difference between a man and a woman in regard to punishments, except for a betrothed female slave, as I wrote above, in the tenth positive precept of *sidrah va-yikra* (§129).

Likewise, among the laws of the precept, there is what they of blessed memory taught:[5] that the *kohen* himself who commits the transgression by being conjugally intimate with a profaned woman, is not personally profaned thereby,[6] even though his offspring will be profaned (of disqualified status). Whether the intimacy occurs by rape or unwittingly, and whether by natural or unnatural relations, once he intromits the corona she becomes profaned—provided the *kohen* is nine years and a day or older, and she three years and a day or older.[7]

Then there is what the Sages taught,[8] that she becomes profaned by nothing other than conjugal intimacy; upon betrothal alone, though,[9] she is not profaned. With marriage, however, even if there was no consummation, she becomes profaned: because every married woman is firmly assumed to have had conjugal intimacy—this, even if she should be found to be a virgin.[10]

We have, further, what the Sages taught,[11] that if a *kohen* is thus intimate with a woman ritually impure from the menses, although it is punishable by *karéth* [Divine severance of existence] he does not thus profane her. For the matter of profanation is produced through nothing but a prohibition that applies uniquely to *kohanim*, such as with a widow,[12] a divorced woman, or a wanton (§266), or when there is conjugal intimacy by males who are disqualified as *kohanim*, such as profaned ones.[13]

⟨189⟩

וּמַה שֶּׁאָמְרוּ זִכְרוֹנָם לִבְרָכָה שֶׁיֵּשׁ חֲלָלִים מִדִּבְרֵי סוֹפְרִים; כֵּיצַד: כְּגוֹן כֹּהֵן
שֶׁבָּעַל חֲלוּצָה, (ו)שֶׁהִיא אֲסוּרָה לְכֹהֵן מִדְּרַבָּנָן, וְשֶׁהִיא חֲלָלָה מִדְּרַבָּנָן וְזַרְעָהּ
חֲלָלִים מִדְּרַבָּנָן; אֲבָל כֹּהֵן שֶׁבָּא עַל אַחַת מִן הַשְּׁנִיּוֹת אֵין זַרְעוֹ מִמֶּנָּה חֲלָלִים
אֲפִלּוּ דְרַבָּנָן, לְפִי שֶׁהוּא אִסּוּר הַשָּׁוֶה בַּכֹּל וְאֵינוֹ מְיֻחָד בְּכֹהֲנִים, וּכְמוֹ שֶׁכָּתַבְתִּי
לְמַעְלָה.

כֹּהֵן שֶׁבָּא עַל סָפֵק זוֹנָה, כְּגוֹן סָפֵק גִּיוֹרֶת וּמְשֻׁחְרֶרֶת, אוֹ עַל סָפֵק גְּרוּשָׁה, וְכֵן
כֹּהֵן גָּדוֹל שֶׁבָּא עַל סָפֵק אַלְמָנָה, הֲרֵי זוֹ סָפֵק חֲלָלָה וְהַנּוֹלָד סָפֵק חָלָל.

נִמְצְאוּ הַחֲלָלִים שְׁלֹשָׁה: חָלָל מִן הַתּוֹרָה, חָלָל מִדִּבְרֵיהֶם, וְסָפֵק חָלָל; וְכָל
סָפֵק חָלָל אוֹ חָלָל מִדִּבְרֵיהֶם, נוֹתְנִין עָלָיו חֻמְרֵי כֹהֲנִים וְחֻמְרֵי יִשְׂרָאֵל: אֵינוֹ
אוֹכֵל בִּתְרוּמָה וְאֵינוֹ מְטַמֵּא לְמֵתִים, וְצָרִיךְ לִשָּׂא אִשָּׁה הָרְאוּיָה לְכֹהֵן; וְאִם אָכַל
תְּרוּמָה אוֹ נִטְמָא אוֹ נָשָׂא גְרוּשָׁה וַחֲלָלָה זוֹנָה, מַכִּין אוֹתוֹ מַכַּת מַרְדּוּת; אֲבָל
חָלָל שֶׁל תּוֹרָה הַוַּדַּאי, הֲרֵי הוּא כְזָר, וְנוֹשֵׂא גְרוּשָׁה וּמִטַּמֵּא לְמֵתִים, שֶׁנֶּאֱמַר:
אֱמֹר אֶל הַכֹּהֲנִים בְּנֵי אַהֲרֹן — אַף־עַל־פִּי שֶׁהֵם בְּנֵי אַהֲרֹן, עַד שֶׁיִּהְיוּ בִכְהֻנָּתָן.

וְעוֹד קִבְּלוּ זִכְרוֹנָם לִבְרָכָה בְּפֵרוּשׁ זֶה הַכָּתוּב: "בְּנֵי אַהֲרֹן" וְלֹא בְּנוֹת אַהֲרֹן,
מִכָּאן שֶׁלֹּא הֻזְהֲרוּ כְשֵׁרוֹת לְהִנָּשֵׂא לִפְסוּלִין; וְעַל־כֵּן הַכֹּהֶנֶת מֻתֶּרֶת לְהִנָּשֵׂא
לְחָלָל וּלְגֵר וְלִמְשֻׁחְרָר. וּלְפִיכָךְ אָמְרוּ זִכְרוֹנָם לִבְרָכָה שֶׁהַגֵּר מֻתָּר לִשָּׂא כֹהֶנֶת

---

14. TB Yevamoth 24a, 85a.

15. Those relations whom the Sages forbade to marry as consanguineous, in addition to the ones thus forbidden by the Torah.

16. I.e. it occurred in her very early years, for if it took place in her older years, she is considered definitely wanton: see § 266, third paragraph, and notes 4–6. (The doubt here is whether the process in question took place, or if it was legally valid.)

17. MT hilchoth 'issuré bi'ah xix 9.

18. Because the Sages' decree is only to add restriction, not to grant privilege; ibid. 10, based on TB Yevamoth 99b.

19. Being equated with an Israelite.

20. Being equated with a kohen.

21. The penalty for violating a ruling of the Sages; see §24, note 12.

22. MT hilchoth 'issuré bi'ah xix 10, based on Sifra, 'emor, parashah 1, 2, etc.

23. Sifra ibid. 1.

[Going further] there is what the Sages of blessed memory said:[14] that there are profaned *kohanim* by the decree of the Scribes. How so?—if a *kohen* was conjugally intimate with a woman who underwent *halitzah*, release from the obligation of levirate marriage: She is forbidden to a *kohen* [in marriage] by the ruling of the Sages; then she becomes a profaned woman by the Sages' decree, and her progeny are profaned *kohanim* by the Sages' decree. If, however, a *kohen* is conjugally intimate with one of the "secondary ones,"[15] his children by her are not profaned *kohanim* even by the Sages' decree,[14] because the ban involved here is one that applies equally to everyone, and is not unique to *kohanim*—as I have written above.

If a *kohen* was conjugally intimate with a woman who is doubtfully wanton—for example, if she was doubtfully converted to Judaism or freed from servitude,[16] or if with a woman who was doubtfully divorced, and so too if a *kohen gadol* was thus intimate with one who is doubtfully a widow—she becomes doubtfully profaned, and so is her child.[17]

Thus we find that there are three kinds of profaned *kohanim*: one profaned by Torah law, one by the Sages' decree, and one who is doubtfully profaned. On everyone who is profaned doubtfully or by the Sages' decree, the severities that apply to both *kohanim* and ordinary Israelites are applied:[18] He may not eat *t'rumah* [the *kohen*'s share of crops and produce],[19] and may not defile himself for the dead; and he must marry a woman who is suitable for a *kohen*.[20] If he ate *t'rumah*, defiled himself, or married a divorced, profaned or wanton woman, he should be whipped with lashes of disobedience.[21] However, if a *kohen* is definitely profaned by Torah law, he is clearly like an outsider [a non-*kohen*], and he may marry a divorced woman and may defile himself with the dead: for it is stated, *Speak to the* kohanim *the sons of Aaron* (Leviticus 21:1): even if they are the sons [descendants] of Aaron, [this does not apply] until they have the status of a *kohen*.[22]

Moreover, our Sages of blessed memory received [in the Oral Tradition] as the interpretation of this verse:[23] *the sons of Aaron*, and not the daughters of Aaron. Hence we learn that young women of qualified status [among them] were not adjured against marrying disqualified, unacceptable men; and therefore a female *kohen* is permitted to marry a profaned *kohen*, a convert to Judaism, or a freed slave.

⟨191⟩ And for the same reason the Sages of blessed memory ruled that a

וּמַמְזֶרֶת: כֹּהֶנֶת מִפְּנֵי טַעַם זֶה שֶׁאָמַרְנוּ, שֶׁלֹּא הֻזְהֲרוּ לְהִנָּשֵׂא לִפְסוּלִין; מַמְזֶרֶת מִשּׁוּם דִּקְהַל גֵּרִים לָא אִקְרֵי קָהָל, וּבְאִסּוּר מַמְזֵר כְּתִיב: לֹא יָבֹא מַמְזֵר בִּקְהַל יי.

וּמַה שֶּׁאָמְרוּ שֶׁחָלָל שֶׁנָּשָׂא כְשֵׁרָה, כָּל זַרְעוֹ חֲלָלִים וּפְסוּלִין לִכְהֻנָּה; אֲבָל יִשְׂרָאֵל שֶׁנָּשָׂא חֲלָלָה, כָּל זַרְעוֹ מִמֶּנָּה כְּשֵׁרִים לִכְהֻנָּה — שֶׁהַנּוֹלָד בְּעִנְיָן זֶה הוֹלֵךְ אַחַר הַזָּכָר, שֶׁנֶּאֱמַר: וַיִּתְיַלְדוּ עַל מִשְׁפְּחוֹתָם; וּמִשְׁפָּחָה שֶׁנִּתְעָרֵב בָּהּ סְפֵק חָלָל, כָּל אַלְמָנָה מֵאוֹתָהּ מִשְׁפָּחָה אֲסוּרָה לְכֹהֵן לְכַתְּחִלָּה; וְאִם נִשֵּׂאת לֹא תֵצֵא, לְפִי שֶׁיֵּשׁ כָּאן שְׁתֵּי סְפֵקוֹת, וּבִסְפֵק-סְפֵקָא אֲפִלּוּ בְּדְאוֹרַיְתָא לָא חַיְשִׁינָן; אֲבָל נִתְעָרֵב בְּמִשְׁפָּחָה וַדַּאי חָלָל, כָּל אִשָּׁה מֵהֶן אֲסוּרָה לְכֹהֵן עַד שֶׁיִּבְדֹּק, וְיֵתֵּר פְּרָטֶיהָ, בְּקִדּוּשִׁין וּבִיבָמוֹת.

וְנוֹהֶגֶת בְּכָל מָקוֹם וּבְכָל זְמָן. וְעוֹבֵר עָלֶיהָ וְנָשָׂא חֲלָלָה וַדָּאִית וּבְעָלָהּ, חַיָּב מַלְקוּת. נָשָׂא סְפֵק חֲלָלָה אוֹ חֲלָלָה מִדִּבְרֵיהֶן, מַכִּין אוֹתוֹ מַכַּת מַרְדּוּת. וְזֶה יִהְיֶה בִּזְמַן שֶׁיִּשְׂרָאֵל דָּנִין דִּינֵי נְפָשׁוֹת, אֲבָל בַּזְּמַן הַזֶּה אֵין מַלְקִין, וּכְמוֹ שֶׁנִּכְתֹּב לְמַטָּה בְּעֶזְרַת הַשֵּׁם בְּסֵדֶר כִּי-תֵצֵא בְּמִצְוַת עֲשֵׂה דְמַלְקוּת [סִי' תקצ"ד].

[שֶׁלֹּא יִשָּׂא כֹהֵן אִשָּׁה גְרוּשָׁה]

רסח שֶׁלֹּא יִשָּׂא כֹהֵן, בֵּין גָּדוֹל בֵּין הֶדְיוֹט, גְּרוּשָׁה, שֶׁנֶּאֱמַר: וְאִשָּׁה גְרוּשָׁה מֵאִישָׁהּ לֹא יִקָּחוּ.

מִשָּׁרְשֵׁי הַמִּצְוָה, מַה שֶּׁכָּתַבְתִּי בְּאִסּוּר זוֹנָה הַקּוֹדֵם.

24. A girl born to a man and woman for whom conjugal intimacy is punishable by *karéth*, i.e. forbidden consanguineous relations and adulterers; TB Kiddushin 73a.

25. TB Kiddushin 77a.

26. And it is not known or remembered exactly who he was.

27. Whether she is the widow of that particular *kohen*, and if so, whether he was actually profaned.

28. TB K'thuboth 14a; MT *hilchoth 'issuré bi'ah* xix 23.

29. TB Kiddushin 76a; MT *ibid*.

30. I.e. in an authorized *beth din* of twenty-three ordained justices; but the proper degree of ordination ended in Israel in ancient times, and was never formally renewed.

male convert is allowed to marry a female *kohen* or bastard:[24] a female *kohen*, for this reason that we have stated—that they were not adjured against marrying any disqualified men; and a female bastard, because the community of proselytes is not called an "assembly," and about the ban on a bastard it is written, *A bastard shall not enter into the assembly of the Lord* (Deuteronomy 23:3).

In addition, we have what the Sages said:[25] that if a profaned *kohen* married a woman of qualified rank, all his children are profaned and disqualified as *kohanim*; but if an ordinary Israelite married a profaned woman, all his children by her are of qualified status [for marriage] to *kohanim*—since the child in this regard acquires the status of the male [parent], as it is stated, *and they gave their pedigrees after their families, by their fathers' houses* (Numbers 1:18). If a doubtfully profaned *kohen* became mixed into a family,[26] every widow from that family is forbidden to a *kohen* originally, at the start; but if she married him, she need not leave [him with a divorce], because there are two doubts here,[27] and where there is a doubt upon a doubt, we need have no misgivings, even in a matter of Torah law.[28] However, if a definitely profaned *kohen* became mixed into a family, every woman in it is forbidden to a *kohen* until he investigates.[29] The rest of its details are in the Talmud tractates *Kiddushin* and *Yevamoth*.

It applies in every place, at every time. If someone transgressed it and married a definitely profaned woman and was conjugally intimate with her, he should be punished with whiplashes. If he married someone who was doubtfully profaned, or who was profaned by the ruling of the Sages, he should be whipped with lashes of disobedience.[21] But this would be only at the time that the Israelites try capital cases;[30] at the present time, though, whiplashes are not given, as we will write below, with the Eternal Lord's help, in *sidrah ki thétzé*, in the precept of lashes (§594).

[THAT A KOHEN IS PROHIBITED FROM MARRYING A DIVORCED WOMAN]

268 that a *kohen*, whether a *kohen gadol* or an ordinary one, should not marry a divorced woman, as it is stated, *neither shall they take a woman divorced from her husband* (Leviticus 21:7).

At the root of the precept lies the reason I wrote about the earlier precept of the wanton (§266).

Among the laws of the precept, there is what the Sages of blessed

מִדִּינֵי הַמִּצְוָה, מַה שֶּׁאָמְרוּ זִכְרוֹנָם לִבְרָכָה שֶׁגְּרוּשָׁה הִיא נִקְרֵאת אֲפִלּוּ מִן
הָאֵרוּסִין, וְאֵין צָרִיךְ לוֹמַר מִן הַנִּשּׂוּאִין; אֲבָל הַמְמָאֶנֶת, אֲפִלּוּ גֵּרְשָׁהּ בְּגֵט
וְהֶחֱזִירָהּ וּמֵאֲנָה בּוֹ, הֲרֵי זוֹ מֻתֶּרֶת לְכֹהֵן. וְהַחֲלוּצָה, כְּלוֹמַר אִשָּׁה שֶׁיָּצְאָה מִתַּחַת
יַד יָבָם בַּחֲלִיצָה, אֲסוּרָה לְכֹהֵן מִדְּרַבָּנָן, מִפְּנֵי שֶׁנָּתְנוּ לָהּ דִּין גְּרוּשָׁה. וְכֹהֵן שֶׁכָּנַס
סְפֵק גְּרוּשָׁה אוֹ זוֹנָה וַחֲלָלָה, מוֹצִיאָהּ בְּגֵט; אֲבָל כָּנַס סְפֵק חֲלוּצָה, אֵין מוֹצִיאָהּ,
שֶׁלֹּא גָזְרוּ חֲכָמִים אֶלָּא עַל חֲלוּצָה וַדָּאִית.

וְכֹל שֶׁאֵינָהּ רְאוּיָה לַחֲלֹץ, אִם נֶחְלְצָה לֹא נִפְסְלָה לְכֹהֻנָּה; יָצָא עָלֶיהָ קוֹל
שֶׁהִיא חֲלוּצָה, אֵין חוֹשְׁשִׁין לְאוֹתוֹ קוֹל, שֶׁחֲכָמִים הוּא שֶׁגָּזְרוּ עַל הַחֲלוּצָה
לִהְיוֹתָהּ כִּגְרוּשָׁה, וְהֵם הֵקֵלּוּ בָהּ בָּעִנְיָנִים אֵלּוּ שֶׁאָמַרְנוּ; וְיֶתֶר פְּרָטֶיהָ, בְּקִדּוּשִׁין,
וּבִיבָמוֹת.

וְנוֹהֶגֶת בַּכֹּהֲנִים בְּכָל מָקוֹם וּבְכָל זְמָן. וְעוֹבֵר עָלֶיהָ וְנָשָׂא גְּרוּשָׁה וּבָעַל, חַיָּב
מַלְקוֹת; אֲבָל כָּל זְמָן שֶׁלֹּא בָעַל אֵינוֹ מִתְחַיֵּב מַלְקוֹת; וַאֲפִלּוּ כֹהֵן גָּדוֹל, שֶׁחַיָּב
שְׁנֵי לָאוִין, מִשּׁוּם "לֹא יִקָּח" וּמִשּׁוּם "לֹא יְחַלֵּל", וּכְמוֹ שֶׁנִּכְתֹּב לְמַטָּה בְּעֶזְרַת
הַשֵּׁם, וְלוֹקֶה עַל שְׁנֵיהֶם, אֵינוֹ לוֹקֶה לְעוֹלָם עַל אֶחָד מֵהֶם אֶלָּא אַחַר שֶׁבָּעַל; אֲבָל
לֹא בָעַל, אֵינוֹ לוֹקֶה מִשּׁוּם "לֹא יִקָּח", דְּ"לֹא יִקָּח", דְּ"לֹא יְחַלֵּל" אָגִיד הוּא בְּלָאו דְּ"לֹא
יְחַלֵּל".

וּפְעָמִים שֶׁיִּתְחַיֵּב גָּדוֹל כֹּהֵן אַרְבַּע מַלְקִיּוֹת בְּבִיאָה אַחַת, וּכְגוֹן שֶׁהִיא אַלְמָנָה
וְנַעֲשֵׂית גְּרוּשָׁה וְנַעֲשֵׂית חֲלָלָה וְנַעֲשֵׂית זוֹנָה; וְעַל כַּיּוֹצֵא בָזֶה יֹאמְרוּ חֲכָמִים
זִכְרוֹנָם לִבְרָכָה "אָסוּר מוֹסִיף", שֶׁהֲרֵי בַּתְּחִלָּה הָאַלְמָנָה הָיְתָה מֻתֶּרֶת לְכֹהֵן
הַהֶדְיוֹט, וּכְשֶׁנִּתְגָּרְשָׁה נִתְוַסֵּף בָּהּ אִסּוּר שֶׁנֶּאֶסְרָה לְהֶדְיוֹט; וַעֲדַיִן הִיא מֻתֶּרֶת לֶאֱכֹל

1. TB Yevamoth 59a.
2. See § 202, note 2.
3. TB Yevamoth 108a. If an orphan girl with no father was married off by her mother or brother as a child with her consent, she may refuse her consent afterward, and by her refusal the marriage is annulled without any need of a divorce, as though it had never been.
4. TB Yevamoth 24a.
5. Since she may be forbidden to him by Torah law. (The doubt can be if the process in question occurred at all, or if it was legally valid.)
6. TB Gittin 89a, version of R. Isaac 'Alfasi, et al.
7. MT hilchoth 'issuré bi'ah xvii 7, based on his understanding of TB Kiddushin 78a (Maggid Mishneh).
8. TB Kiddushin 77a; MT ibid. 9–10. (See §266 paragraph 3 et seq. on the term "wanton" as it is used here. Neither this nor the Hebrew original, zonah, has its usual sense here.)

memory taught:[1] that a woman is called divorced even [if the marital bond is sundered] after *'érusin* [betrothal, the first stage of marriage]; and there is no need to add, after *kiddushin* [the second stage].[2] But if a girl refused her consent, then even if the man gave her a bill of divorce and took her back, and she refused him again, she is permissible to a *kohen*.[3] If a woman undergoes *halitzah*, i.e. she is released by her brother-in-law from the duty of levirate marriage, she is forbidden to a *kohen* by the ruling of the Sages, because they gave her the legal rank of a divorced woman.[4] If a *kohen* wed a woman who was doubtfully divorced, wanton (§266), or profaned (§267), he has to send her away with a divorce.[5] But if he wed a woman who doubtfully underwent *halitzah*, he need not divorce her; for the Sages imposed their decree on none but a woman who certainly underwent *halitzah*.[4]

Whoever was not fit to properly undergo *halitzah*, if she did undergo it, she would not be disqualified [thereby] for a *kohen*. If a rumor spread about someone that she underwent *halitzah*, no attention need be paid to the rumor:[6] For it is the Sages who decreed that a woman after *halitzah* should be [ranked] as a divorced woman, and they were lenient about it in those instances that we have described. The rest of its details are in the Talmud tractates *Kiddushin* and *Yevamoth*.

It applies to *kohanim* everywhere, in every time. If someone transgresses it and marries a divorced woman and is conjugally intimate with her, he deserves lashes of the whip; but as long as he did not consummate the marriage, he would not incur lashes. Even a *kohen gadol*—who is punishable for two negative precepts, *he shall not take* (Leviticus 21:14) and *he shall not profane* (ibid. 15), as we will write below with the Eternal Lord's help, and he should be whipped for the two—is never given lashes for either of them until after he has effected consummation.[7] If he did not do so, however, he is not given lashes for violating *he shall not take*, because this injunction is bound together with the injunction, *he shall not profane*.

Sometimes, though, a *kohen gadol* can incur four whippings for one act of conjugal intimacy: for instance, if she was a widow who was then divorced, became profaned (§267) and became wanton (§266). About a case like this the Sages of blessed memory would say:[8] the forbiddance is cumulative. For here, at the start the widow was permissible to an ordinary *kohen*; when she was divorced, a prohibition was added about her, as she became forbidden to an

בִּתְרוּמָה, וּכְשֶׁנִּתְחַלְּלָה נִתְוַסֵּף בָּהּ אִסּוּר שֶׁנֶּאֶסְרָה מִלֶּאֱכֹל בִּתְרוּמָה; וַעֲדַיִן הִיא
מֻתֶּרֶת לְיִשְׂרָאֵל, וּכְשֶׁנַּעֲשֵׂית זוֹנָה נִתְוַסֵּף בָּהּ אִסּוּר לְגַבֵּי יִשְׂרָאֵל, שֶׁהֲרֵי מָצִינוּ
אִסּוּר בְּיִשְׂרָאֵל בְּזוֹנָה, שֶׁהַמְזַנָּה בִּרְצוֹן תַּחַת בַּעֲלָהּ, אֲסוּרָה לַבַּעַל וְלַבּוֹעֵל.

אֲבָל אִם נִשְׁתַּנָּה סֵדֶר זֶה וּכְגוֹן שֶׁנַּעֲשֵׂית תְּחִלָּה זוֹנָה וְכוּלֵי, אֵין חַיָּבִין עַל
בִּיאָתָהּ אֶלָּא מַלְקוּת אַחַת, לְפִי שֶׁאֵין שָׁם אִסּוּר מוֹסִיף. וּכְלָל גָּדוֹל בְּכָל אִסּוּרִין
שֶׁבַּתּוֹרָה: אֵין אִסּוּר חָל עַל אִסּוּר, אֶלָּא־אִם־כֵּן הָיוּ הָאִסּוּרִין בָּאִין כְּאֶחָד אוֹ
שֶׁהָיָה הָאֶחָד אִסּוּר מוֹסִיף דְּבָרִים אֲחֵרִים, כְּמוֹ שֶׁאָמַרְנוּ, אוֹ אִסּוּר כּוֹלֵל.

[מִצְוַת קִדּוּשׁ זֶרַע אַהֲרֹן]

רסט לְקַדֵּשׁ זֶרַע אַהֲרֹן, כְּלוֹמַר לְקַדְּשָׁם וּלְהַכְנִיסָם לְקָרְבָּן, וְזֶהוּ עִקַּר הָעֲשֵׂה,
וְכֵן לְהַקְדִּימָם לְכָל דָּבָר שֶׁבִּקְדֻשָּׁה; וְלוּ מֵאֲנוּ בָּזֶה, לֹא נִשְׁמַע אֲלֵיהֶם; וְזֶה כֻּלּוֹ
לִכְבוֹד הַשֵּׁם יִתְעַלֶּה, אַחַר שֶׁהוּא לְקָחָם וּבְחָרָם לַעֲבוֹדָתוֹ; שֶׁנֶּאֱמַר: וְקִדַּשְׁתּוֹ כִּי
אֶת לֶחֶם אֱלֹהֶיךָ וְגוֹמֵר, וּבָא הַפֵּרוּשׁ, "וְקִדַּשְׁתּוֹ" לְכָל דָּבָר שֶׁבִּקְדֻשָּׁה: לִפְתֹּחַ
רִאשׁוֹן יְבָרֵךְ רִאשׁוֹן וְלִטֹּל מָנָה יָפָה רִאשׁוֹן.

וּלְשׁוֹן סִפְרָא: "וְקִדַּשְׁתּוֹ", עַל כָּרְחוֹ, כְּלוֹמַר שֶׁזֹּאת הַמִּצְוָה אֲנַחְנוּ נִצְטַוִּינוּ
בָּהּ, וְאֵין זֶה בִּבְחִירַת הַכֹּהֵן. וְעוֹד אָמְרוּ: "קְדֹשִׁים יִהְיוּ לֵאלֹהֵיהֶם", עַל כָּרְחָם;
"וְהָיוּ קֹדֶשׁ", לְרַבּוֹת בַּעֲלֵי מוּמִין, שֶׁלֹּא נֹאמַר: אַחַר שֶׁזֶּה אֵינוֹ רָאוּי לְהַקְרִיב
לֶחֶם אֱלֹהֵיהֶם, לָמָּה זֶה נַקְדִּימֵהוּ וּנְכַבְּדֵהוּ; עַל־כֵּן אָמְרוּ: "וְהָיוּ קֹדֶשׁ", כְּלוֹמַר

9. If she was a female *kohen* (*koheneth*) by birth.

10. E.g. if *Yom Kippur* falls on a Sabbath, the restrictions of both take effect together when the day is ushered in by its consecration.

11. E.g. if one eats non-kosher food on *Yom Kippur*: it is already forbidden as non-kosher; but because *Yom Kippur* brings a wider range of prohibition for the day, it adds its ban as well to the eating of non-kosher food; TB *ibid*.

§269   1. TB Gittin 59b.

2. In the congregational reading of the Torah or in a gathering (Rashi to TB Gittin 59b, s.v. *lifto-aḥ*).

3. To lead in the grace after meals (*ibid*.).

4. If he is one of a group among whom portions of food are shared, he is to be told, "Choose and take whichever you want" (*ibid*.).

5. Sifra on the verse.

ordinary *kohen*; but she could still be allowed to eat *t'rumah* [the *kohen*'s portion of all produce];[9] when she became profaned, a prohibition was added about her, as she became forbidden to eat *t'rumah*; yet she was still permissible to an ordinary Israelite. When she became wanton, however, a prohibition was added about her in regard to an ordinary Israelite (Jew)—since indeed we find a ban for an Israelite in regard to a wanton: If a woman willingly acts licentiously while bound to her husband, she becomes forbidden to both the husband and the adulterer.[8]

However, if this order was altered and, for example, she became wanton at the start, etc. one incurs no punishment for conjugal intimacy with her other than one whipping of lashes, because there is no additive prohibition in that case. It is a paramount rule about all prohibitions in the Torah: One prohibition cannot take effect over another, unless the two prohibitions came as one [together],[10] or one was a prohibition adding some other elements, as we stated, or it is a general, wide-ranging prohibition.[11]

[THE PRECEPT OF THE SANCTIFICATION OF AARON'S DESCENDANTS]

269 to consecrate the progeny of Aaron; in other words, to hallow them and enter them in [the service of] offerings, this being the core element of the positive precept; and so also to give them precedence in every matter of holiness—and if they refuse anything of this, we are not to listen to them. This is entirely for the glory of the Eternal Lord, since He took them and chose them for His service—as it is stated, *Therefore you shall consecrate him, for he offers the bread of your God* (Leviticus 21:8); and the interpretation was given:[1] "you shall consecrate him"—in every matter of holiness, he should open, as the first,[2] and be the first to utter blessing,[3] and take a fine portion as the first.[4]

In the language of the Midrash *Sifra*: "you shall consecrate him"— [even] against his will. In other words, we were commanded this precept, and it is not left to the free choice of the *kohen*. The Sages said further:[5] "They shall be holy to their God" (Leviticus 21:6)— [even] against their will; "and they shall be holy" (*ibid.*)—to add those with disfiguring blemishes or impairments: so that we should not say, "Since this one is not fit to offer up *the bread of their God* (*ibid.*) why should we then give him precedence and honor him?" Therefore

הַזֶּרַע הוּא מְיֻחָס כֻּלּוֹ, תָּמִים וּבַעַל מוּם.

מִשָּׁרְשֵׁי הַמִּצְוָה, לְפִי שֶׁיָּדוּעַ כִּי מִכְּבוֹד הָאָדוֹן כִּי לְכַבֵּד אֶת מְשָׁרְתָיו, וּבְכָל עֵת כַּבְּדֵנוּ הַכֹּהֲנִים, נִזְכֹּר וְנִקְבַּע בְּמַחֲשַׁבְתֵּנוּ כְּבוֹדוֹ בָּרוּךְ הוּא וְגָדְלוֹ; וּבִזְכוּת הַמַּחֲשָׁבָה הַזַּכָּה וְהַמַּעֲלָה וְהָרָצוֹן הַטּוֹב, תָּחוּל בִּרְכָתוֹ בָּרוּךְ הוּא וְטוּבוֹ הַגָּדוֹל עָלֵינוּ; וְהוּא חָפֵץ בְּבִרְכָה, כַּאֲשֶׁר הוֹדִעָנוּ כַּמָּה פְעָמִים.

מִדִּינֵי הַמִּצְוָה, מַה שֶּׁאָמְרוּ זִכְרוֹנָם לִבְרָכָה שֶׁסֵּדֶר קְרִיאַת הַתּוֹרָה בְּצִבּוּר זֶהוּ: שֶׁהַכֹּהֵן קוֹרֵא רִאשׁוֹן לְעוֹלָם, וְאַחֲרָיו לֵוִי, וְאַחֲרָיו יִשְׂרָאֵל; וְאִם אֵין שָׁם כֹּהֵן, נִתְפָּרְדָה חֲבִילָה; וְאִם אֵין שָׁם לֵוִי, כֹּהֵן קוֹרֵא שְׁנֵי פְעָמִים; וְכֹהֵן אַחַר כֹּהֵן לֹא יִקְרָא, מִשּׁוּם פְּגָמוֹ שֶׁל רִאשׁוֹן; וְלֵוִי אַחַר לֵוִי לֹא יִקְרָא, מִשּׁוּם פְּגַם פְּגַם שְׁנֵיהֶם.

וְכָבוֹד זֶה נַעֲשָׂה לָהֶם כְּשֶׁרְאוּיִין לְכָךְ, אֲבָל הָיוּ בַּעֲלֵי עֲבֵרוֹת, נִמְנָעִים מִכָּבוֹד; וּכְבָר אָמְרוּ זִכְרוֹנָם לִבְרָכָה שֶׁמַּמְזֵר תַּלְמִיד חָכָם קוֹדֵם לְכֹהֵן עַם־הָאָרֶץ; וְעַכְשָׁיו בַּזְּמַן הַזֶּה לֹא רָאִינוּ מִי שֶׁהִקְדִּים עַצְמוֹ לִשׁוּם כֹּהֵן מִפְּנֵי חָכְמָתוֹ, וְעֵקֶב עֲנָוָה יִרְאַת יְיָ; וְיֶתֶר פְּרָטֶיהָ, נִתְבָּאֲרוּ בִּמְקוֹמוֹת חֲלוּקִים מִן גְּמָרָ[א] מַכּוֹת וְחֻלִּין וּבְכוֹרוֹת וְשַׁבָּת וְזוּלָתָם.

וְנוֹהֶגֶת בְּכָל מָקוֹם וּבְכָל זְמַן, בִּזְכָרִים וּנְקֵבוֹת, שֶׁמִּצְוָה עַל כֻּלָּן לְכַבֵּד זֶרַע אַהֲרֹן. וְעוֹבֵר עַל זֶה וְלֹא כִבְּדָם בְּמָקוֹם שֶׁרָאוּי וְכֹהֵן הָרָאוּי לְכָבוֹד, בִּטֵּל עֲשֵׂה זֶה.

[שֶׁלֹּא יִכָּנֵס כֹּהֵן גָּדוֹל בְּאֹהֶל הַמֵּת]

רע שֶׁלֹּא יִכָּנֵס כֹּהֵן גָּדוֹל בְּאֹהֶל הַמֵּת, וַאֲפִלּוּ לְשִׁשָּׁה מֵתֵי מִצְוָה, שֶׁנֶּאֱמַר: וְעַל

6. The first two paragraphs are based on ShM positive precept §32.

7. TB Gittin 59a–b.

8. In Talmudic times it was the practice for each person called to the Torah to read his own portion aloud. In the tradition current today, one reader chants all the portions, on behalf of those called to the Torah, as their deputy. (Yemenite Jewry, however, retains the Talmudic practice.)

9. Then it is equally unnecessary to call a Levite before an Israelite.

10. Since he is also a Levite, of the tribe of Lévi (as Aaron was a descendant of Lévi), he reads (or is called to) the Levite's portion as well.

11. I.e. as though the second had to be called because something disqualifying was discovered about the first; therefore, in the absence of a Levite, the same *kohen* is called for the first two portions.

12. It could be conjectured that the second was called because something disqualifying was discovered about the first, or that the second was called because his claim to be a Levite is spurious, and he is really an ordinary Israelite (Rashi to TB Gittin 59b, s.v. *lifto-ah*).

13. Just as a sinful parent loses his right to honor by his son: TB Yevamoth 22b, Sanhedrin 85a.

Scripture stated, *and they shall be holy*: as much as to say, the progeny is entirely of noble rank, both the whole in body and the disfigured and impaired.[6]

At the root of the precept lies the reason that it is an honor to the Lord and Master to honor His ministers; and at every instance when we honor the *kohanim,* we will remember and set firmly in our mind His honor and grandeur (blessed is He). Then, by the merit of the pure, exalted thought and the good wish, His blessing and great goodness will be bestowed upon us. And He has delight in blessing, as we have conveyed many times.

Among the laws of the precept, there is what the Sages of blessed memory taught:[7] that the order of reading the Torah in public is this: that a *kohen* always reads the first,[8] and after him a Levite, and after him an ordinary Israelite. If there is no *kohen* there, "the bond is severed" [they need not be linked in this order].[9] And if no Levite is present, a *kohen* reads twice.[10] One *kohen* should not read directly after another, because [it implies] a defect in the first.[11] Nor should one Levite read directly after another, because [it implies] a defect in both.[12]

Now, this honor is to be paid them when they are worthy of it. But if they are sinful, they are to be deprived of the honor.[13] Long ago our Sages of blessed memory said[14] that a bastard who is a Torah scholar takes precedence over a *kohen* who is an ignoramus. Now, however, in the present time, we have not seen anyone who would put himself ahead of any *kohen* on account of his wisdom; *in the wake of humility there is fear of the Lord* (Proverbs 22:4).[15] The rest of its details are elucidated in various places in the Talmud tractates *Makkoth,* *Ḥullin, B'choroth, Shabbath,* and others.

It is in effect everywhere, at every time, for both man and woman: for a religious duty lies on all to honor the descendants of Aaron. If a person transgresses this and does not honor them in an instance where it is proper, and where the *kohen* is worthy of honor, he disobeys this positive precept.

[THAT A KOHEN GADOL IS PROHIBITED FROM ENTERING
THE TENT OF A DEAD MAN]

270 that a *kohen gadol* should not enter the tent of a dead person, even for the six dead [relatives] of religious duty;[1] for it is stated, *neither shall he go in to any dead body* (Leviticus 21:11); in other words,

כָּל נַפְשֹׁת מֵת לֹא יָבֹא, כְּלוֹמַר לֹא יָבוֹא בְתוֹךְ הַבַּיִת עִמָּהֶם, דְּלִישׁוֹן בִּיאָה בִּיאַת בַּיִת מַשְׁמָע.

מִשָּׁרְשֵׁי הַמִּצְוָה, מַה שֶּׁכָּתַבְתִּי לְמַעְלָה בְּמִצְוַת לֹא־תַעֲשֶׂה אַ' בְּסֵדֶר זֶה [סִי' רס"ג], שֶׁעִנְיַן הַטֻּמְאָה רָאוּי לְהִתְרַחֵק מִן הַכֹּהֲנִים, שֶׁהֵם קְדוֹשִׁים עוֹשֵׂי מְלֶאכֶת הַשֵּׁם תָּמִיד; וְהַכֹּהֵן הַגָּדוֹל, הַנִּבְדָּל לִהְיוֹת קֹדֶשׁ קָדָשִׁים, עִם הֱיוֹתוֹ בַּעַל גּוּף, נַפְשׁוֹ תִשְׁכֹּן תָּמִיד בְּתוֹךְ הַמְשָׁרְתִים הָעֶלְיוֹנִים, עַל־כֵּן לֹא תָחוּשׁ הַתּוֹרָה עָלָיו לְהַתִּיר לוֹ טֻמְאָה לְעוֹלָם, וַאֲפִלּוּ בַּקְּרוֹבִים כְּמוֹ לְכֹהֲנִים הַדְיוֹטִים, שֶׁכָּתַבְתִּי לְמַעְלָה דְּחָס רַחֲמָנָא עֲלֵיהֶם שֶׁיִּשְׁפְּכוּ נַפְשָׁם בְּבֵית הַמֵּת כִּי יֵחַם לְבָבָם עַל קְרוֹבֵיהֶם, מַה שֶּׁאֵינוּ כֵן בְּכֹהֵן גָּדוֹל, כִּי מֵרֹב דְּבֵקוּת נַפְשׁוֹ לְמַעְלָה יִתְפַּשֵּׁט לְגַמְרֵי מִטֶּבַע בְּנֵי־אִישׁ, וְיַשְׁכִּיחַ מִלִּבּוֹ כָּל עֵסֶק הָעוֹלָם הַזֶּה הַנִּפְסָד, וְעַל חֶבְרַת הַקָּרוֹב לֹא תִבְכֶּה נַפְשׁוֹ, כִּי כְבָר הוּא נִפְרָד מִמֶּנּוּ בְּעוֹדֶנּוּ בַּחַיִּים.

וּבְדִינֵי טֻמְאַת הַמֵּת וְאֹהֶל הַמֵּת דִּבַּרְתִּי מְעַט כְּמִנְהָגִי בְּסֵדֶר זֶה, אֵין רָאוּי לְהַחֲזִירוֹ, פֶּן יִכְבַּד עַל הַקּוֹרֵא.

וְנוֹהֵג אִסּוּר זֶה בִּזְמַן הַבַּיִת, שֶׁיֵּשׁ שָׁם כֹּהֵן גָּדוֹל; וּבְכָל מָקוֹם שֶׁיִּהְיֶה, וַאֲפִלּוּ אִם הָיָה מִקְרֶה שֶׁיֵּצֵא לְחוּצָה לָאָרֶץ, מֻזְהָר מֵהִכָּנֵס בְּאֹהֶל הַמֵּת. וְאִם עָבַר וְנִכְנַס שָׁם בְּמֵזִיד, וַאֲפִלּוּ אָבִיו אוֹ אִמּוֹ מֵתִים בַּבַּיִת, לוֹקֶה.

[שֶׁלֹּא יִטַּמֵּא כֹהֵן גָּדוֹל בְּשׁוּם טֻמְאָה בְּמֵת]

רעא שֶׁלֹּא יִטַּמֵּא כֹהֵן גָּדוֹל אֲפִלּוּ בְּמֵת מִקְרוֹבָיו, וְכָל־שֶׁכֵּן בְּכָל שְׁאָר הַמֵּתִים שֶׁבָּעוֹלָם, בְּמִין מִמִּינֵי הַטֻּמְאָה, בֵּין בִּנְגִיעָה בֵּין בְּמַשָּׂא, שֶׁנֶּאֱמַר: לְאָבִיו וּלְאִמּוֹ לֹא יִטַּמָּא — כְּלוֹמַר אֲפִלּוּ לְאֵלּוּ שֶׁהֵם קְרוֹבָיו; וְאַף־עַל־פִּי שֶׁבָּרֹאשׁ

14. TB Horayoth 13a.

15. I.e. it is a mark of praiseworthy, rewarding humility that no one ever seeks to put this rule into effect; so MT *hilchoth t'fillah* xii 18.

§270   1. For whom it is generally a religious duty to become defiled, in connection with the burial, etc. See § 263, note 2.

2. Literally, their spirit, or soul.

3. Cf. P'sikta d'R. Kahana §27, end (ed. Buber, 178a): Said R. 'Abbahu: Was the *kohen gadol* then not a man? It is rather as R. Pinḥas taught: When the holy spirit dwelt on him, his countenance would blaze like torches ... (So too Va-yikra Rabbah 21, 12). And cf. MT *hilchoth k'lé ha-mikdash* v 7: It was to his splendor and honor that he would stay in the Sanctuary all day and not go out to his home except at night, or for an hour or two by day.

4. By the rule in TB Kiddushin 37a, that any personal, physical obligation applies both in the land of Israel and outside it.

he should not enter any house [where he will be] with them—for "go in" denotes entering a house.

At the root of the precept lies the reason I wrote above, in the first negative precept of this *sídrah* (§263): that it is right and proper for the essence of ritual uncleanness to be removed far from the *kohanim*, since they are the hallowed ones who do the labor of the Eternal Lord constantly. Now, the *kohen gadol* is set apart to be the "holy of the holy"; then even though he is possessed of a physical body, his spirit should abide constantly among the supernal Divine ministers. Therefore the Torah shows no concern for him, to permit him any defilement ever, even for close kin, as it does ordinary *kohanim*, of whom I wrote above (§263) that the merciful God had compassion on them, [to permit] that they should pour out their heart[2] in the house of the deceased when their heart is emotionally aroused over their kin. This is not the case, however, with the *kohen gadol*. For in the immense clinging of his spirit [to the realm] above, he must divest himself completely from [ordinary] human nature and cast out of his heart into oblivion every concern of this temporal, perishing world.[3] Then for the companionship of the [departed] near kin, his spirit is not to weep, since he separated from him previously, while he was yet alive.

About the laws of the ritual uncleanness of the dead and the tent of the dead, I have spoken a bit, as is my custom, in this *sidrah* (§263); it would not be suitable to repeat it, for fear that it would overburden the reader.

This prohibition is in effect at the time that the Temple exists, when there is a *kohen gadol* there, and wherever he may be. Even if it should happen that he goes abroad, outside the land [of Israel], he is adjured against entering the tent of a deceased person.[4] If he transgressed and entered there deliberately, even if his father or mother lay dead in that house, he should be given whiplashes.

[THAT A KOHEN GADOL SHOULD NOT MAKE HIMSELF RITUALLY UNCLEAN OVER ANY DEAD MAN]

271 that a *kohen gadol* should not defile himself even for a dead person among his close kin, and all the more certainly not for any other dead person in the world, in any of the ways of defilement, whether by touching or by carrying—for it is stated, *nor shall he defile himself for his father or for his mother* (Leviticus 21:11), meaning even for those who are [merely] his close kin. Now, even though at the

הַפָּסוּק אָסַר עָלָיו מֵהִטַּמֵּא עַל כָּל נַפְשׁוֹת, זֶהוּ טֻמְאַת בִּיאָה לְאֹהֶל הַמֵּת, כְּמוֹ שֶׁפֵּרַשְׁנוּ (שָׁם), שֶׁהֲרֵי כָּתוּב שָׁם "לֹא יָבֹא", דְּמַשְׁמַע בִּיאָה לְאֹהֶל, וְכָאן יֶאֱסֹר עָלָיו כָּל שְׁאָר מִינֵי הַטֻּמְאָה בִּכְלָל.

וְאַל תַּחְשֹׁב שֶׁזֶּה שֶׁנֶּאֱמַר "לְאָבִיו וּלְאִמּוֹ" וְגוֹמֵר, הוּא פֵּרוּשׁ לְרֹאשׁ הַמִּקְרָא שֶׁאָמַר: וְעַל כָּל נַפְשׁוֹת וְגוֹמֵר — שֶׁאֵין הַדָּבָר כֵּן, אֲבָל הֵם שְׁנֵי לָאוִין, "לֹא יָבֹא" וְ"לֹא יְטַמָּא". וּלְשׁוֹן סִפְרָא: חַיָּב בְּ"לֹא יָבֹא" וְחַיָּב בְּ"לֹא יְטַמָּא"; וּכְמוֹ־כֵן אָמְרוּ זִכְרוֹנָם לִבְרָכָה שֶׁחַיָּב כֹּהֵן הֶדְיוֹט בְּ"לֹא יָבֹא" וְ"לֹא יְטַמָּא", אַף־עַל־פִּי שֶׁלֹּא נִכְתַּב בּוֹ, מִדִּין גְּזֵרָה שָׁוָה, דִּשְׁנֵיהֶם נֶאֶסְרוּ מֵהִטַּמֵּא בְּנֶפֶשׁ, וּכְמוֹ שֶׁבָּא (בגמרא) [בְסִפְרָא].

וְאָמְנָם אֵין לִמְנוֹת בְּמִנְיַן הַלָּאוִין "לֹא יָבֹא" וְ"לֹא יְטַמָּא" בַּכֹּהֵן הֶדְיוֹט לִשְׁנַיִם לָאוִין כְּמוֹ שֶׁמָּנִינוּ אוֹתָן בְּכֹהֵן גָּדוֹל, לְפִי שֶׁבְּכֹהֵן גָּדוֹל נִכְתְּבוּ בְּפֵרוּשׁ וּבְכֹהֵן הֶדְיוֹט נִלְמַד הָאֶחָד בִּגְזֵרָה שָׁוָה, וּכְבָר הוֹרָה זָקֵן, הוּא הָרַמְבַּ"ם זִכְרוֹנוֹ לִבְרָכָה, שֶׁאֵין לָנוּ לִמְנוֹת בְּמִנְיַן תרי"ג מִצְוֹת אֶלָּא הַמְּפֹרָשׁוֹת בַּכָּתוּב, אֲבָל לֹא הַנִּלְמָדוֹת בְּמִדּוֹת שֶׁהַתּוֹרָה נִדְרָשֶׁת.

מִשָּׁרְשֵׁי הַמִּצְוָה, מַה שֶּׁכָּתַבְנוּ בַּמִּצְוָה הַקּוֹדֶמֶת לְזוֹ. וְהוּא הַדִּין וְהוּא הַטַּעַם, כִּי כַּוָּנַת שְׁתֵּיהֶן, בַּל יָבוֹא וּבַל יִטַּמָּא, עִנְיָן אֶחָד הוּא.

וּבְדִינֵי טֻמְאַת הַמֵּת, כְּבָר כָּתַבְתִּי לְמַעְלָה בְּסֵדֶר זֶה מִצְוַת לֹא־תַעֲשֶׂה א' [סִי' רס"ג] קְצָת מֵהֶן.

וְנוֹהֵג אִסּוּר זֶה בִּזְמַן הַבַּיִת, כִּי אָז יִהְיֶה שָׁם כֹּהֵן גָּדוֹל, וּבְכָל מָקוֹם שֶׁהַכֹּהֵן שָׁם, גַּם־כֵּן נוֹהֵג אִסּוּר זֶה. וְאִם עָבַר וְנִטְמָא, וַאֲפִלּוּ לִקְרוֹבָיו, בְּמִין מִמִּינֵי הַטֻּמְאָה, חַיָּב מַלְקוֹת.

---

§271   1. See §263, note 8.

2. Sifra, 'emor, parashah 2, 4.

3. For the ordinary *kohen* it is written, *None shall defile himself,* etc. (Leviticus 21:1); and for the *kohen gadol* there is our opening verse, *nor shall he be defile himself,* etc. (*ibid.* 11)—the verbs are identical.

4. A Talmudic expression: TB Shabbath 51a, Yevamoth 108b.

5. ShM root principle 2.

6. The first three paragraphs are based on ShM negative precept §168.

7. See §270, note 4.

beginning of the verse Scripture forbade him from becoming defiled for anyone, that refers to defilement upon entering the tent of the dead,[1] as we explained there (§270); for you see, it is written there, *neither shall he go in* (*ibid.*), which denotes entering a tent. Here, though, Scripture bans all other kinds (ways) of defilement in general for him.

Now, do not think that this Scriptural statement, *for his father or for his mother*, etc. is an explanation of the first part of the verse, which states, *neither shall he go in to any dead body*. This is not so, as they are rather two negative precepts: "neither shall he go in" and "nor shall he defile himself." In the language of the Midrash *Sifra*:[2] he is punishable for "neither shall he go in" and he is punishable for "nor shall he defile himself." And our Sages of blessed memory likewise taught[2] that an ordinary *kohen* is [equally] punishable for "neither shall he go in" and for "nor shall he defile himself," even though they were not written about him—by the rule of *g'zérah shavah* [identical terms in two verses], since both were forbidden to defile themselves for a dead person,[3] as we read in the (Talmud) [Midrash *Sifra*].[2]

Nevertheless, the two admonitions for an ordinary *kohen*, "neither shall he go in" and "nor shall he defile himself," are not to be reckoned as two injunctions in the list of negative precepts, as we count them in regard to the *kohen gadol*: For about the *kohen gadol* they were written explicitly, while regarding an ordinary *kohen* we infer one of them by a *g'zérah shavah*; and "the elder has already instructed"[4] [us]—i.e. Rambam of blessed memory[5]—that we are to list in the reckoning of the 613 *mitzvoth* none but those given explicitly in the Writ, but not those derived by the rules with which the Torah is interpreted.[6]

At the root of the *mitzvah* lies the reason we wrote in the precept before this (§270); it is essentially the same law, for the same reason; for the purpose of both, "neither shall he go in" and "nor shall he defile himself," is one concept.

As to the laws of the defilement of a dead person, I have previously written some of them, above, in the first negative precept of this *sidrah* (§263).

This prohibition is in effect when the Temple is extant, for then there is a *kohen gadol* there; and wherever the *kohen gadol* is, there this prohibition is equally in force.[7] If he transgressed and became defiled, even for one of his near kin, by any one of the kinds (ways) of defilement, he would deserve whiplashes.

[מִצְוַת כֹּהֵן גָּדוֹל לִשָּׂא נַעֲרָה בְתוּלָה]

רעב שֶׁיִּשָּׂא כֹהֵן גָּדוֹל נַעֲרָה בְתוּלָה, שֶׁנֶּאֱמַר: וְהוּא אִשָּׁה בִבְתוּלֶיהָ יִקָּח;
וְהָרְאָיָה שֶׁזֶּה נֶחְשָׁב מִכְּלַל מִצְוַת עֲשֵׂה, מַה שֶּׁאָמְרוּ זִכְרוֹנָם לִבְרָכָה: עוֹשֶׂה הָיָה
רַבִּי עֲקִיבָה מַמְזֵר אֲפִלּוּ מְחַיָּבֵי עֲשֵׂה, וּבֵאֲרוּ זֶה בְּשֶׁיִּהְיֶה כֹהֵן גָּדוֹל בָּא עַל אִשָּׁה
שֶׁאֵינָהּ בְּתוּלָה, שֶׁהִיא אֲסוּרָה עָלָיו בַּעֲשֵׂה, שֶׁהָעִקָּר הוּא אֶצְלֵנוּ: לָאו הַבָּא מִכְּלַל
עֲשֵׂה—עֲשֵׂה. וְעוֹד אָמְרוּ זִכְרוֹנָם לִבְרָכָה: מֻזְהָר עַל הָאַלְמָנָה וּמְצֻוֶּה עַל
הַבְּתוּלָה.

מִשָּׁרְשֵׁי הַמִּצְוָה, לְפִי שֶׁהָעִקָּר הַטּוֹב הוּא שֶׁיִּהְיֶה לוֹ מַחֲשֶׁבֶת טְהָרָה
וּנְקִיּוּת, כִּי אַחֲרֵי הַמַּחֲשָׁבוֹת יִמָּשֵׁךְ מַעֲשֵׂה הַגּוּפוֹת; עַל־כֵּן רָאוּי לוֹ לַמְשָׁרֵת
הַגָּדוֹל לְהִדָּבֵק בְּאִשָּׁה שֶׁלֹּא קָבְעָה מַחְשַׁבְתָּהּ בְּאִישׁ אַחֵר זוּלָתִי בוֹ, שֶׁהוּא קֹדֶשׁ
קָדָשִׁים, וּמִתּוֹךְ כָּךְ יִהְיֶה הַזֶּרַע אֲשֶׁר יִתֵּן לוֹ הַשֵּׁם מִמֶּנָּה טָהוֹר וְנָקִי, רָאוּי לַעֲבֹד
בִּקְדֻשָּׁה.

וְשֶׁמָּא תֹאמַר: וּמִי יוֹדֵעַ אִם גַּם הַבְּתוּלָה קָבְעָה מַחֲשַׁבְתָּהּ (בְּאִישׁ זוּלָתִי בוֹ)
וְנָתְנָה עֵינֶיהָ בְּאַחֵר? הַתְּשׁוּבָה בָּזֶה שֶׁכָּל זְמַן שֶׁלֹּא יָצְאָה מַחֲשַׁבְתָּהּ מִן הַכֹּחַ אֶל
הַפֹּעַל, אֵינָהּ נִפְסֶלֶת, אֲבָל כָּל זְמַן שֶׁנִּבְעָלָה, נִפְסְלָה. וְאַף־עַל־פִּי שֶׁאָמְרוּ זִכְרוֹנָם
לִבְרָכָה דְּמִשֶּׁתִּתְבַּגֵּר אֲסוּרָה עָלָיו, הָעִנְיָן הוּא דְּמִכֵּיוָן שֶׁהִיא גְדוֹלָה כָּל־כָּךְ, יֵצֶר
מַחֲשֶׁבֶת לִבָּהּ רַק רָע, וְאוּלַי קָבְעָה מַחֲשַׁבְתָּהּ בְּאָדָם אַחֵר, וּמַחֲשַׁבְתָּהּ רָעָה, מִכֵּיוָן
שֶׁהִיא גְדוֹלָה, נֶחְשֶׁבֶת לָהּ כְּמַעֲשֶׂה.

וְכֵן מִזֶּה הַטַּעַם אָמְרוּ גַם־כֵּן שֶׁאִם נִתְאַלְמְנָה מִן הָאֵרוּסִין, אֲפִלּוּ בְעוֹדָהּ
קְטַנָּה, אֲסוּרָה הִיא לַכֹּהֵן, דְּמִכֵּיוָן שֶׁנַּעֲשָׂה בָּהּ מַעֲשֵׂה הַקִּדּוּשִׁין, כְּבָר קָבְעָה
מַחֲשַׁבְתָּהּ מְאֹד בְּאִישׁ אַחֵר מִתּוֹךְ מַעֲשֵׂה הָאֵרוּסִין, וְנִפְסְלָה, דְּמַעֲשֶׂה פּוֹסֵל אֲפִלּוּ

---

§272   1. TB K'thuboth 30a.

    2. I.e. by their conjugal intimacy, which led to the birth of the child.

    3. Thus, in this case, from the positive precept that a *kohen gadol* should marry a virgin we infer the injunction that he should not marry one who is not. Hence, if he does marry a non-virgin, he does not violate a negative precept, but rather this positive one.

The paragraph is taken from ShM negative precept 9. It should be noted, however, that the statement about R. Akiva is by no means a Talmudic quotation, and needs to be clarified. In TB K'thuboth 29b we read that R. Yeshévav said (in contrast to R. Akiva's original statement in the Talmud, and R. Sima'i's citation in his name), "Come, let us cry out against Akiva ben Yosef, who used to say: Whoever has no [permission for] conjugal intimacy [with a particular woman] in Jewry—the child [from their union] is a bastard." The Talmud (30a) then considers that R. Yeshévav may have meant only those forbidden conjugal intimacy by a prohibition (negative precept) or perhaps also those forbidden by a positive precept (as explained above). If the latter (concludes the Talmud) it would *not* apply to conjugal relations between a *kohen gadol* and a non-virgin, because R. Akiva's rule as cited by R. Yeshévav refers only to a ban that applies equally to all, and this ban applies solely to a *kohen gadol*.

[THE PRECEPT THAT THE KOHEN GADOL SHOULD TAKE
A VIRGIN FOR A WIFE]

272 that a *kohen gadol* should marry a virgin maiden, as it is stated, *And he shall take a wife in her virginity* (Leviticus 21:13). The proof that this is reckoned in the category of the positive precepts, lies in what the Sages of blessed memory said:[1] R. Akiva would declare a bastard even [the child] of those punishable for [disobeying] a positive precept;[2] and they explained this [to refer to] when a *kohen gadol* is conjugally intimate with a woman (wife) who was not a virgin, since she is forbidden to him by a positive precept. For it is a main principle for us: an injunction derived from a positive precept is a positive precept.[3] Our Sages of blessed memory said further:[4] He is adjured against a widow, and commanded about a virgin.

At the root of the precept lies the reason that the main good element in man is that he should harbor thoughts of purity and immaculateness; for after the thoughts, the activity of the physical self is drawn. It is therefore fitting for the great ministering servant [at the Sanctuary] to unite himself with a wife who has not fixed her thoughts on any other man but him, who is the "holy of holies."[5] As a result, the offspring which the Eternal Lord will give him by her will be pure and faultless, fit to serve in holiness.

Yet you might ask: But who knows if even a virgin has [not perhaps] set her mind (on some other man than him) and cast her eye on another? The answer is that as long as her thought has not been converted from the potential into the actual [into action] she is not disqualified;[6] but at any time that she participates in conjugal intimacy, she is disqualified.[7] In any event, though, our Sages of blessed memory taught[8] that once she reaches maturity,[9] she is forbidden to him [to marry]. The reason is that since she has become this grown, "every imagination of the thought of her heart is only evil,"[10] and perhaps she has set her heart[11] on another man; and then, since she is a grown maiden, her evil thought is reckoned for her as a deed.

For this reason the Sages likewise taught[8] that if a girl became a widow after 'érusin (betrothal),[12] even if while she was yet a child, she is forbidden to the *kohen* [*gadol*]. For since she experienced the act of consecration for matrimony, she already set her heart[11] very much on another man, by virtue of the act of 'érusin (betrothal), and she thus became disqualified. For an act makes her unacceptable even in childhood,[13] and thought in her grown state. Thus they

⟨205⟩

בְּקַטְנוּת, וּמַחֲשָׁבָה בְּגַדְלוּת. וְכֵן אָמְרוּ שֶׁאִם נִבְעֲלָה שֶׁלֹּא כְדַרְכָּהּ, גַּם־כֵּן פְּסוּלָה, שֶׁכְּבָר נַעֲשָׂה בָהּ מַעֲשֵׂה רַב, אַף־עַל־פִּי שֶׁבְּתוּלֶיהָ קַיָּמִין.

וְכֵן אָמְרוּ שֶׁאַף מַכַּת עֵץ פְּסוּלָה; וְהַטַּעַם בָּהּ לְפִי הַדּוֹמֶה לְפִי שֶׁאֵינָהּ קוֹבַעַת עוֹד מַחֲשַׁבְתָּהּ הַרְבֵּה בְּכֹהֵן גָּדוֹל, דְּמִכֵּיוָן שֶׁנֶּאֶבְדוּ בְתוּלֶיהָ אֵינָהּ כּוֹרֶתֶת בְּרִית חָזָק לְעוֹלָם לְאִישׁ; וּכְעֵין מַה שֶׁאָמְרוּ זִכְרוֹנָם לִבְרָכָה: אֵינָהּ אִשָּׁה כּוֹרֶתֶת בְּרִית אֶלָּא לְמִי שֶׁעֲשָׂאָהּ כֶּלִי, וַהֲרֵי זוֹ לֹא עֲשָׂאָהּ שׁוּם אָדָם כֶּלִי; וּמִכָּל־מָקוֹם לֹא הֶחְמִירוּ זִכְרוֹנָם לִבְרָכָה בְּאֵלּוּ הַרְבֵּה, וְאָמְרוּ שֶׁאִם נָשָׂא בוֹגֶרֶת אוֹ מֻכַּת עֵץ, דִּיעֲבַד יְקַיֵּם.

מִדִּינֵי הַמִּצְוָה, מַה שֶׁאָמְרוּ זִכְרוֹנָם לִבְרָכָה שֶׁאֶחָד כֹּהֵן גָּדוֹל הַמָּשׁוּחַ בְּשֶׁמֶן הַמִּשְׁחָה אוֹ הַמְרֻבֶּה בִּבְגָדִים, וְאֶחָד כֹּהֵן גָּדוֹל הָעוֹבֵד, אוֹ כֹהֵן גָּדוֹל שֶׁמִּנּוּהוּ וְעָבַר, וְכֵן כֹּהֵן מְשׁוּחַ מִלְחָמָה, כֻּלָּם מְצֻוִּין עַל הַבְּתוּלָה וַאֲסוּרִין בְּאַלְמָנָה; וּמַה שֶׁאָמְרוּ שֶׁאֵפְלוּ אֵרַס הַקְּטַנָּה וּבָגְרָה תַחְתָּיו קֹדֶם נִשּׂוּאִין, הֲרֵי זֶה לֹא יִכְנֹס, וְאִם כָּנַס אֵינוֹ מוֹצִיא; וּמַה שֶׁאָמְרוּ שֶׁאֵינוֹ נוֹשֵׂא שְׁתַּיִם נָשִׁים לְעוֹלָם, שֶׁנֶּאֱמַר: וְהוּא אִשָּׁה בִבְתוּלֶיהָ יִקָּח, דַּוְקָא אִשָּׁה אַחַת אֲבָל לֹא שְׁתַּיִם; וּמַה שֶׁאָמְרוּ שֶׁאִם כָּנַס הָאַלְמָנָה בְּעוֹדוֹ הֶדְיוֹט וְנִתְמַנָּה גָּדוֹל, שֶׁאֵינוֹ מוֹצִיאָהּ; וַאֲפִלּוּ אֵרְסָהּ קֹדֶם שֶׁנִּתְמַנָּה גָדוֹל, כּוֹנְסָהּ לְאַחַר שֶׁנִּתְמַנָּה; וְיֶתֶר פְּרָטֶיהָ, בְּפֶרֶק שִׁשִּׁי מִיְּבָמוֹת וּבִמְקוֹמוֹת מִכְּתֻבּוֹת וְקִדּוּשִׁין.

וְנוֹהֵג בָּאָרֶץ בִּזְמַן הַבַּיִת וְהָעֲבוֹדָה, כִּי אָז יִתְמַנֶּה הַכֹּהֵן גָּדוֹל, לֹא בְמָקוֹם אַחֵר. וְכֹהֵן גָּדוֹל הָעוֹבֵר עַל זֶה וְנָשָׂא בְעוּלַת אִישׁ שֶׁאֵינָהּ לֹא אַלְמָנָה וְלֹא גְרוּשָׁה, בִּטֵּל עֲשֵׂה, וּמוֹצִיאָהּ בְּגֵט.

Yet the point remains, that the Talmud did consider that a rule regarding a positive precept should apply to the case of a *kohen gadol* and a non-virgin, and it excludes the case only for a specific reason about the rule. Hence we do have proof that their conjugal intimacy *is* banned by a positive precept. (So R. Yosef Kafaḥ in ShM, Arabic-Hebrew ed.)

4. TB Horayoth 11b.

5. Derived from I Chronicles 23:13, *and Aaron was separated that he should be sanctified as the holy of holies.*

6. For thoughts of a young person (see the next sentence in the text) that are not converted into action will pass away, leaving no permanent effect. (The phrase in parentheses in the paragraph's first sentence is not in the manuscripts. It is thus apparently a later interpolation, and it is in fact superfluous.)

7. Since the thought led to action, her heart will remain focused on the participant.

8. TB Yevamoth 59a.

9. By definitive religious law, this is after the age of twelve and a half, at six months after the appearance of two pubic hairs.

likewise taught[8] that if she participated in unnatural carnal relations she is equally disqualified, since a major act was done with her, even though her virginity is intact.

So they taught, too,[8] that even one whose virginity was terminated by an accident[14] is disqualified. The reason, it would seem, is that she would no longer set her mind greatly on a *kohen gadol*; since she lost her virginity, she cannot ever form a strong bond with any man— in keeping with what the Sages of blessed memory said:[15] A woman plights her troth to none but him who makes of her an instrument [for marital love and life];[16] and as for this one, no man whatever made an instrument of her. Nevertheless, the Sages of blessed memory were not overly stringent with these, and they ruled[17] that if he married a grown girl or one with accidentally destroyed virginity, then having done so, after the fact, he may keep her.

Among the laws of the precept, there is what the Sages of blessed memory said:[18] that it is all one whether he is a *kohen gadol* who was anointed with anointing oil (§107) or by virtue of the additional [special] garments;[19] whether he is a *kohen gadol* who serves [at the Sanctuary] or one who was appointed and passed by; and so likewise a *kohen* anointed for war (§526)—all are commanded about [marrying] a virgin, and forbidden a widow. Then there is what they taught:[20] that even if he betrothed a child and she grew up under him [during the betrothal period] before the marriage,[12] he should then not marry her; but if he did, he is not to divorce her.[21] There is, further, what the Sages taught:[8] that he was never to be married to two wives: for it is stated, *And he shall take* a wife *in her virginity*—specifically one wife, but not two.[22] We have, too, what they said:[23] that if he married a widow while yet an ordinary *kohen* and he was then appointed *kohen gadol*, he is not to divorce her, and this even if he betrothed her before he was appointed *kohen gadol* and he married her after his appointment. [These] and the rest of its details are in chapter 6 of the Talmud tractate *Yevamoth* and in various places in *K'thuboth* and *Kiddushin*.

It is in force in the land [of Israel], at the time the Temple and its service are extant: for then a *kohen gadol* is appointed, and nowhere else. If a *kohen gadol* transgresses this and marries a woman who experienced conjugal intimacy, who is neither widowed nor divorced, he disobeys a positive precept, and he is to send her away with a divorce.

〈207〉

[שֶׁלֹּא יִשָּׂא כֹהֵן גָּדוֹל אַלְמָנָה]

רעג שֶׁלֹּא יִשָּׂא כֹהֵן גָּדוֹל לְבַד אַלְמָנָה, שֶׁנֶּאֱמַר: אַלְמָנָה וּגְרוּשָׁה וַחֲלָלָה זוֹנָה
אֶת אֵלֶּה לֹא יִקָּח. וְלֹא הָיָה צָרִיךְ הַכָּתוּב לַחֲזֹר אִסּוּר גְּרוּשָׁה וַחֲלָלָה זוֹנָה בְּכֹהֵן
גָּדוֹל, שֶׁכְּדֶרֶךְ כְּלָל נֶאֶסְרוּ עַל כָּל כֹּהֵן, וְהוּא רֹאשׁ הַכֹּהֲנִים; וְעַל־כֵּן פֵּרְשׁוּ זִכְרוֹנָם
לִבְרָכָה כִּי לְלַמֵּד לָנוּ עִנְיָן בָּא כֵּפֶל הָאַזְהָרָה בִּגְרוּשָׁה וַחֲלָלָה זוֹנָה בְּכֹהֵן גָּדוֹל;
וְאָמְרוּ בִּגְמָרָא קִדּוּשִׁין שֶׁבָּא לְלַמֵּד שֶׁבִּזְמַן שֶׁיְּקָרֶה שֶׁיִּהְיוּ כָּל אִסּוּרִין אֵלּוּ בְּאִשָּׁה
אַחַת כַּסֵּדֶר הַזֶּה, שֶׁבַּתְּחִלָּה תִּתְאַלְמֵן וְאַחַר־כָּךְ תִּתְגָּרֵשׁ וְאַחַר־כָּךְ תִּתְחַלֵּל וְאַחַר־
כָּךְ תֵּעָשֶׂה זוֹנָה, וּבָא עָלֶיהָ כֹּהֵן גָּדוֹל, שֶׁחַיָּב עַל בִּיאָה אַחַת אַרְבַּע מַלְקִיּוֹת, וְהוּא
שֶׁהֻזְהַר בְּאַרְבַּעַת הַלָּאוִין; וְאִם בָּא עָלֶיהָ כֹּהֵן הֶדְיוֹט, לוֹקֶה שָׁלֹשׁ.

וְהַטַּעַם שֶׁיִּתְחַיְּבוּ עָלֶיהָ הַרְבֵּה מַלְקִיּוֹת כְּשֶׁהִיא כַּסֵּדֶר הַזֶּה, לְפִי שֶׁיֵּשׁ בָּהּ
בְּעִנְיָן זֶה אִסּוּר מוֹסִיף, וּכְמוֹ שֶׁכָּתַבְנוּ לְמַעְלָה סָמוּךְ בְּמִצְוַת לֹא־תַעֲשֶׂה ה׳ [סִי׳
רס״ח] שֶׁאֵין אִסּוּר חָל עַל אִסּוּר אֶלָּא כְּשֶׁיִּהְיֶה אִסּוּר מוֹסִיף אוֹ אִסּוּר כּוֹלֵל אוֹ
אִסּוּרִין בָּאִין כְּאַחַת, כְּמוֹ שֶׁמִּתְבָּאֵר בְּמַסֶּכֶת כְּרֵתוֹת. וְאֵין צָרִיךְ לוֹמַר שֶׁאִם בָּעַל
אַרְבַּע נָשִׁים וְאַחַת מֵהֶן אַלְמָנָה וְאַחַת גְּרוּשָׁה וְאַחַת חֲלָלָה וְאַחַת זוֹנָה, וְהִתְרָה
עַל כֻּלָּן, שֶׁחַיָּב אַרְבָּעָה מַלְקִיּוֹת, בֵּין שֶׁיָּבֹא עֲלֵיהֶן כַּסֵּדֶר אוֹ שֶׁלֹּא כַּסֵּדֶר, הוֹאִיל
וְהֵן גּוּפִין מְחֻלָּקִין.

וְאִם תִּשְׁאַל וְתֹאמַר: וְאֵיךְ יִלְקֶה הַרְבֵּה מַלְקִיּוֹת, בֵּין בְּאִשָּׁה אַחַת בֵּין בְּהַרְבֵּה,
וְהָא קַיְמָא לָן אֵין לוֹקִין עַל לָאו שֶׁבִּכְלָלוּת, וַהֲרֵי זֶה לָאו שֶׁבִּכְלָלוּת הוּא, שֶׁהֲרֵי
בְּכֻלָּן בָּאָה הַמְּנִיעָה בְּלָאו אֶחָד, וּכְמוֹ שֶׁכָּתַבְנוּ לְמַעְלָה לְדַעַת הָרַמְבַּ״ם זִכְרוֹנוֹ
לִבְרָכָה.

הַתְּשׁוּבָה: דַּע שֶׁכְּבָר בֵּאֲרוּ זִכְרוֹנָם לִבְרָכָה עִנְיָן זֶה, וְזֶהוּ אָמְרָם בִּגְמָרָא

10. Expression based on Genesis 6:5.
11. Literally, her thought.
12. See § 35, note 8.
13. So TB Ḥullin 12b.
14. Literally, one wounded by a piece of wood.
15. TB Sanhedrin 22b.
16. By terminating her virginity in marital intimacy.
17. TB Yevamoth 60a.
18. TB Horayoth 12b.
19. That were only for a *kohen gadol* to wear. In the time of the Second Temple there was no anointing oil, and the *kohen gadol* became invested with the authority of his office on putting on these garments (MT *hilchoth k'lé ha-mikdash* i 9).
20. TB Yevamoth 58b.
21. Since he need not divorce his wife even if he betrothed and wed her after she was grown, as stated at the end of the previous paragraph; MT *hilchoth 'issuré bi'ah* xvii 17.
22. MT *ibid.* 13.
23. TB Yevamoth 61a.

273 that a *kohen gadol* particularly[1] is not to marry a widow, as it is stated, *A widow or a divorced, profaned, or wanton woman, these he shall not take* (Leviticus 21:14). Now, Scripture did not need to repeat the prohibition on a divorced, profaned or wanton woman for a *kohen gadol*, for they were generally forbidden to every *kohen*, and he is the head of the *kohanim*. Therefore our Sages of blessed memory explained that in order to teach us something, the admonition about a divorced, profaned or wanton woman was repeated for the *kohen gadol*. It was stated in the Talmud tractate *Kiddushin* (77a) that it comes to teach us that should it happen at some time that all these prohibitions apply to one woman in this order—first she becomes widowed, then divorced, then profaned (§267), then wanton (§266)— and a *kohen gadol* is conjugally intimate with her, he is punishable for the one act of intimacy by four sets of whiplashes—but this, if he was warned about the four injunctions. If an ordinary kohen is thus intimate with her, he receives three sets of whiplashes.[2]

Now, the reason why they are punishable by several whippings when she [becomes the object of the prohibitions] in this order, is that there is a cumulative forbiddance in the matter. As we wrote recently above, in the fifth negative precept (§268),[3] one prohibition cannot take effect upon another, unless it is an additive prohibition [that adds something new], a general, wide-ranging prohibition, or a ban that comes simultaneously [together with the first], as explained in the Talmud tractate *K'rithoth* (14b). Needless to say, if he was conjugally intimate with four women, one widowed, one divorced, one profaned, and one wanton, and he was warned about them all, he is punishable by four sets of whiplashes, whether he was thus intimate with them in order or not in order—because they are separate entities.[4]

You might ask and say, however: But how can he be whipped several times, whether for one woman or more? We have a standing rule: no lashes are given over a general, omnibus negative precept! For surely this is a general, omnibus injunction, since the restriction about all is given in one negative commandment, as we wrote above (§7),[5] by the view of Rambam of blessed memory?

The answer is this: Know that long ago the Sages of blessed memory clarified this matter. In this respect they said in the Talmud

קִדּוּשִׁין בְּמַה שֶּׁכָּתוּב בְּכֹהֵן הֶדְיוֹט: "וְאִשָּׁה גְרוּשָׁה מֵאִישָׁהּ לֹא יִקָּחוּ", שֶׁמִּפְּנֵי־
כֵן נִפְרְדָה הַגְּרוּשָׁה בְּלָאו, לְלַמֵּד שֶׁמַּלְקִין עַל הַגְּרוּשָׁה בִּפְנֵי עַצְמָהּ; וּכְמוֹ
שֶׁמַּלְקִין עַל הַגְּרוּשָׁה בִּפְנֵי עַצְמָהּ, כָּךְ מַלְקִין עַל הַחֲלָלָה וְעַל הַזּוֹנָה בִּפְנֵי עַצְמָן;
וְאָמְרוּ שָׁם: כְּשֵׁם שֶׁחֲלוּקָה גְּרוּשָׁה מֵחֲלָלָה וְזוֹנָה בְּכֹהֵן הֶדְיוֹט, כָּךְ חֲלוּקָה בְּכֹהֵן
גָּדוֹל; וּלְלַמֵּד דְּבָרִים אֵלּוּ נִכְפְּלָה הַמַּנִּיעָה בְּכֹהֵן גָּדוֹל, כְּמוֹ שֶׁאָמַרְנוּ.

מִשָּׁרְשֵׁי הַמִּצְוָה, לְפִי שֶׁיֵּשׁ בְּנִשּׂוּאֵי הָאַלְמָנָה (מחשבת) [מַחֲשָׁבוֹת] זָרוֹת,
כָּעִנְיָן מַה שֶּׁאָמְרוּ זִכְרוֹנָם לִבְרָכָה שֶׁבָּחוּר שֶׁנָּשָׂא אַלְמָנָה, שָׁלֹשׁ דֵּעוֹת בַּמִּטָּה,
וְכוּלֵּי.

מִדִּינֵי הַמִּצְוָה, מַה שֶּׁאָמְרוּ זִכְרוֹנָם לִבְרָכָה שֶׁאַלְמָנָה הִיא נִקְרֵאת אֲפִלּוּ מִן
הָאֵרוּסִין; וְכֹהֵן גָּדוֹל שֶׁמֵּת אָחִיו אֲפִלּוּ מִן הָאֵרוּסִין, הֲרֵי זֶה לֹא יְיַבֵּם אֶלָּא אֶלָּא חוֹלֵץ;
הָיְתָה מְקֻדֶּשֶׁת סָפֵק קִדּוּשִׁין וּמֵת אֲרוּסָהּ, הֲרֵי זוֹ סָפֵק אַלְמָנָה, וַאֲסוּרָה, שֶׁכָּל
סָפֵק דְּאוֹרַיְתָא אָסוּר הוּא מִן הַתּוֹרָה, וְעַל כֵּן אָמְרוּ זִכְרוֹנָם לִבְרָכָה בְּכָל מָקוֹם
שֶׁסְּפֵקָא דְאוֹרַיְתָא לְחֻמְרָא; וְיֶתֶר פְּרָטֶיהָ, בִּיבָמוֹת, בִּקִדּוּשִׁין.

וְכֹהֵן גָּדוֹל הָעוֹבֵר עַל זֶה וְקִדֵּשׁ אַלְמָנָה וּבְעָלָהּ, לוֹקֶה שְׁתֵּי מַלְקִיּוֹת, אַחַת
מִשּׁוּם "אַלְמָנָה לֹא יִקָּח", וְאַחַת מִשּׁוּם "וְלֹא יְחַלֵּל זַרְעוֹ בְּעַמָּיו", שֶׁהוּא לָאו
בִּפְנֵי עַצְמוֹ, וּכְמוֹ שֶׁנִּכְתַּב אוֹתוֹ בְּסָמוּךְ; אֲבָל קִדֵּשׁ וְלֹא בְעָלָה אַחַר כָּךְ,
אֵינוֹ לוֹקֶה כְּלָל, וַאֲפִלּוּ מִשּׁוּם "לֹא יִקָּח", וּכְמוֹ שֶׁאָמְרוּ שָׁם בְּקִדּוּשִׁין: בָּעַל
לוֹקֶה, לֹא בָעַל אֵינוֹ לוֹקֶה, דְּמַה טַּעַם קָאָמַר: מַה טַּעַם "לֹא יִקָּח", מִשּׁוּם "לֹא
יְחַלֵּל".

אֲבָל בָּעַל בְּעַל הָאַלְמָנָה אַף־עַל־פִּי שֶׁלֹּא קִדְּשָׁהּ, לוֹקֶה אַחַת, מִשּׁוּם לָאו דְּ"לֹא

---

§273

1. Literally, alone; i.e. this injunction applies solely to him.

2. Because as a widow she is forbidden only to a *kohen gadol*, but not to him.

3. Next to the last paragraph, where this theme is similarly discussed.

4. Hence there the rule that one prohibition cannot take effect over another is not relevant.

5. So also toward the end of §117.

6. The first four paragraphs are based on ShM negative precept §161.

7. Derived directly from TB P'saḥim 112a: if a divorced man married a divorced woman, there are four minds in the bed; and if you like, this may equally be said of a widow ...

8. TB Yevamoth 59a.

9. See §202, note 2.

10. TB Yevamoth 20a.

11. I.e. there is doubt if it was legally valid.

12. MT *hilchoth 'issuré bi'ah* xvii 12.

13. A biblical term denoting his progeny, the children and descendants that may issue from him.

14. TB Kiddushin 78a.

tractate *Kiddushin* (77b) on the verse written about an ordinary *kohen*, *neither shall they take a woman divorced by her husband* (Leviticus 21:7), that for this reason a divorced woman was forbidden in a separate injunction, to teach that whiplashes are inflicted for a divorced woman separately; and just as a whipping is given over a divorced woman separately, so is it given over a profaned woman or a wanton alone. And they taught there: Just as the divorced woman is separated from the profaned woman and the wanton in regard to an ordinary *kohen*, so is she separated in regard to a *kohen gadol*; and in order to teach this concept, the restriction was repeated for a *kohen gadol*—as we stated.[6]

At the root of the precept lies the reason that in marriage to a widow, alien thoughts are involved—in accord with what the Sages of blessed memory said: that if a young bachelor marries a widow, there are three minds in the bed, etc.[7]

Among the laws of the precept, there is what the Sages of blessed memory taught:[8] that a woman is called a widow even [if her husband died] after the *'érusin* (betrothal);[9] and if the brother of a *kohen gadol* died even after his betrothal, he should not take his sister-in-law in levirate marriage, but should release her with *halitzah*.[10] If a woman was betrothed by a doubtful consecration,[11] and her betrothed man died, she has a doubtful status of widow,[12] and is forbidden [to a *kohen gadol*]—for every matter of doubt involving a law of the Torah is forbidden by the ruling of the Torah. For this reason the Sages of blessed memory said everywhere that in a matter of doubt on a Torah law, we decide stringently. The rest of its details are in the tractates *Yevamoth* and *Kiddushin*.

If a *kohen gadol* transgressed this and married a widow and was conjugally intimate with her, he should be given two sets of whiplashes, once on account of "A widow ... he shall not take," and once on account of "And he shall not profane his seed[13] among his people" (Leviticus 21:15),[14] which is a negative precept by itself, as we will write shortly (§274). If, however, he wed her and did not consummate the marriage afterward, he receives no whiplashes at all, not even on account of "he shall not take." As the Sages said here, in the tractate *Kiddushin* (78a): If he was conjugally intimate, he is whipped; if he was not thus intimate, he is not whipped; for [Scripture] states what the reason is: for what reason *shall he not take?*—so that "he shall not profane."

However, if he was conjugally intimate with a widow, then even if he did not wed her, he should receive a whipping on account of

יְחַלֵּל", שֶׁהֲרֵי חִלְּלָהּ לָאַלְמָנָה וַעֲשָׂאָהּ זוֹנָה, וְהוּא מֻזְהָר שֶׁלֹּא יְחַלֵּל כְּשֵׁרִים,
דְּבִכְלַל לָאו דְּ"לֹא יְחַלֵּל" מַשְׁמַע, שֶׁכֵּן פֵּרְשׁוּ זִכְרוֹנָם לִבְרָכָה: "וְלֹא יְחַלֵּל", לֹא
לָהּ וְלֹא זַרְעוֹ; וְכֵן אָמְרוּ שָׁם בְּקִדּוּשִׁין: וּמוֹדֶה רָבָא בְּכֹהֵן גָּדוֹל בְּאַלְמָנָה שֶׁאִם
בָּעַל וְלֹא קִדֵּשׁ, לוֹקֶה; מַאי טַעְמָא, "וְלֹא יְחַלֵּל זַרְעוֹ" אָמַר רַחֲמָנָא, וַהֲרֵי חִלֵּל,
כְּלוֹמַר דְּבִכְלַל "וְלֹא יְחַלֵּל" מַשְׁמַע דְּלֹא יְחַלֵּל כְּשֵׁרִים וְלֹא זַרְעוֹ.

[שֶׁלֹּא יִבְעַל כֹּהֵן גָּדוֹל אַלְמָנָה]

רעד שֶׁלֹּא יִבְעַל כֹּהֵן גָּדוֹל אַלְמָנָה וַאֲפִלּוּ בְּלֹא קִדּוּשִׁין, שֶׁנֶּאֱמַר: וְלֹא יְחַלֵּל
זַרְעוֹ בְּעַמָּיו; וְאָמְרוּ בְּקִדּוּשִׁין: כֹּהֵן גָּדוֹל בְּאַלְמָנָה לוֹקֶה שְׁתַּיִם, מִשּׁוּם "לֹא
יִקָּח" וּמִשּׁוּם "וְלֹא יְחַלֵּל", כְּלוֹמַר שֶׁאִם נְשָׂאָהּ וּבְעָלָהּ, לוֹקֶה שְׁתֵּי מַלְקִיּוֹת;
וְאִם בְּעָלָהּ מִבְּלִי שֶׁקִּדְּשָׁהּ, לוֹקֶה אַחַת, מִשּׁוּם "לֹא יְחַלֵּל", וּכְמוֹ שֶׁאָמַר רָבָא
שָׁם: וּמוֹדֶה רָבָא בְּאַלְמָנָה לְכֹהֵן גָּדוֹל שֶׁאִם בָּעַל וְלֹא קִדֵּשׁ, לוֹקֶה; מַאי טַעְמָא,
"וְלֹא יְחַלֵּל" אָמַר רַחֲמָנָא, וַהֲרֵי חִלֵּל; קִדְּשָׁהּ וְלֹא בְּעָלָהּ, אֵינוֹ לוֹקֶה מִשּׁוּם "לֹא
יִקָּח", דְּהָא אָמְרִינָן הָתָם דְּמַה טַעַם קָאָמַר: מַה טַּעַם "לֹא יִקָּח", מִשּׁוּם "לֹא
יְחַלֵּל"; מַשְׁמַע דְּכָל־זְמַן שֶׁלֹּא חִלֵּל אֵינוֹ לוֹקֶה.

וְזֶה הַטַּעַם לְמָדְנוּהוּ אַף בְּכֹהֵן הֶדְיוֹט בַּנָּשִׁים הָאֲסוּרוֹת לוֹ; וְאַף־עַל־פִּי
שֶׁכָּתוּב זֶה דְּ"לֹא יְחַלֵּל" בְּכֹהֵן גָּדוֹל הוּא וּבְאַלְמָנָה, לָמַדְנוּ מִמֶּנּוּ שֶׁאֵין הַהֶדְיוֹט

2. I.e. the widow, by being conjugally intimate with her out of wedlock; and his
seed, if the act of coition was completed (TB Kiddushin 78a).

"he shall not profane," since here he profaned the widow and made her a wanton, and he is adjured not to profane people of qualified rank, since this is included in the sense of "and he shall not profane." For so the Sages of blessed memory interpreted: *and he shall not profane*— neither her nor his seed. And so was it stated there in the tractate *Kiddushin* (78a): Rava concedes about a *kohen gadol* and a widow that if he was conjugally intimate with her and did not marry her, he should receive whiplashes; for what reason?—the merciful God said, "and he shall not profane his seed," and he did cause profanation. In other words, included in the meaning of "he shall not profane" lies the directive that he should profane neither people of worthy status nor his seed [*qua* progeny].

[THAT CONJUGAL INTIMACY WITH A WIDOW IS FORBIDDEN A KOHEN GADOL]

274 that a *kohen gadol* should not be conjugally intimate with a widow even if without marriage: for it is stated, *And he shall not profane his seed*[1] *among his people* (Leviticus 21:15); and it was taught in the Talmud tractate *Kiddushin* (78a): If a *kohen gadol* transgressed with a widow, he·is to be given two whippings: on account of "he shall not take" (*ibid*. 14) and on account of "he shall not profane." In other words, if he married her and they were conjugally intimate, he should be flogged with two sets of lashes. Hence, if he was thus intimate with her without having married her, he should receive one whipping, for violating "he shall not profane"—as Rava said there; for we read: And Rava agrees about a widow with a *kohen gadol*, that if they were conjugally intimate and did not marry, he should receive whiplashes; for what reason?—the merciful God said, *he shall not profane*, and here he did profane.[2] If he married her and they were not conjugally intimate, he is not whipped on account of "he shall not take"; for we learn there that Scripture gave the reason for it: for what reason shall he not take [a widow]?—so that "he shall not profane";[2] hence this implies that as long as he did not profane [her] he receives no whiplashes.

Now, we have learned that this reason applies also to an ordinary *kohen* in regard to the women forbidden to him. Although this verse, *he shall not profane*, refers to a *kohen gadol* with a widow, we derive from it that neither does an ordinary *kohen* incur a whipping of lashes for the women forbidden to him until he goes through marriage and

גַּם־כֵּן חַיָּב מַלְקוּת בַּנָּשִׁים הָאֲסוּרוֹת לוֹ עַד שֶׁיִּקַּח וְיִבְעַל, דְּוַדַּאי לֹא הֶחְמִיר הֶדְיוֹט מִגָּדוֹל.

וּכְמוֹ שֶׁבֵּאֲרוּ שָׁם בְּקִדּוּשִׁין: בָּעַל לוֹקֶה, לֹא בָעַל אֵינוֹ לוֹקֶה; וְאָמְרוּ שֶׁדִּין זֶה גַּם־כֵּן בְּכֹהֵן הֶדְיוֹט, שֶׁאֵינוֹ חַיָּב עַל הַנָּשִׁים הָאֲסוּרוֹת לוֹ עַד שֶׁיְּקַדֵּשׁ תְּחִלָּה וְאַחַר־כָּךְ יִבְעַל; אֲבָל בָּעַל זוֹנָה אוֹ גְרוּשָׁה וַחֲלָלָה בְּלֹא קִדּוּשִׁין, אַף־עַל־פִּי שֶׁזֶּה אָסוּר לוֹ וּפוֹסְלוֹ לִכְהֻנָּה, אֵינוֹ לוֹקֶה, מִכֵּיוָן שֶׁלֹּא נִתְבָּאֲרָה הַמְּנִיעָה בּוֹ מִזֶּה בְּפֵרוּשׁ, דְּ"לֹא יְחַלֵּל" בְּפָרָשַׁת כֹּהֵן גָּדוֹל הוּא כָתוּב וּבְאַלְמָנָה דַּוְקָא, אֲבָל בְּזוֹנָה וּגְרוּשָׁה וַחֲלָלָה אַף הַכֹּהֵן גָּדוֹל גַּם־כֵּן אֵינוֹ לוֹקֶה עֲלֵיהֶן אֶלָּא מַלְקוּת אַחַת בְּשֶׁנָּשָׂא אוֹתָן וְאַחַר־כָּךְ בְּעָלָן; אֲבָל בְּעָלָן בְּלֹא קִדּוּשִׁין, אַף־עַל־פִּי שֶׁזֶּה אָסוּר לוֹ וּפוֹסְלוֹ מִן הַכְּהֻנָּה, אֵין לוֹ בָזֶה חִיּוּב מַלְקוּת, אֶלָּא דִינוֹ בָזֶה כְּמוֹ כֹהֵן הֶדְיוֹט בְּשָׁוֶה; שֶׁלְּעִנְיַן הָאַלְמָנָה דַּוְקָא הוּא שֶׁנִּתְיַחֵד הַלָּאו בְּכֹהֵן גָּדוֹל לְחַיְּבוֹ בְּ"לֹא יְחַלֵּל", כְּלוֹמַר בִּבְעִילָה בְּלֹא קִדּוּשִׁין, כְּמוֹ שֶׁאָמַרְנוּ, אֲבָל לֹא בַּשָּׁלֹשׁ הָאֲחֵרוֹת, שֶׁלֹּא נִכְפְּלוּ הַשָּׁלֹשׁ הָאֲחֵרוֹת בְּכֹהֵן גָּדוֹל אֶלָּא לְאוֹתוֹ עִנְיָן שֶׁאָמַרְנוּ לְמַעְלָה — לְחַלֵּק, כְּלוֹמַר לְחַיֵּב עַל כָּל אַחַת וְאַחַת.

וְעוֹד יֵשׁ טַעַם אַחֵר בַּדָּבָר: שֶׁבָּאַלְמָנָה יֵשׁ בָּהּ חִלּוּל בִּבְעִילָה, שֶׁהָיְתָה כְשֵׁרָה לְהֶדְיוֹט וְנִפְסְלָה בִּבְעִילָה, וְעַל־כֵּן יֵשׁ לְחַיְּבוֹ מַלְקוּת עָלֶיהָ מִשּׁוּם "לֹא יְחַלֵּל", אֲבָל בַּשָּׁלֹשׁ הָאֲחֵרוֹת אֵין לְחַיְּבוֹ מַלְקוּת בִּבְעִילָה מִבְּלִי קִדּוּשִׁין, שֶׁהֲרֵי אֵין לָנוּ לוֹמַר בָּהֶן חִלּוּל, שֶׁהֲרֵי מְחֻלָּלוֹת וְעוֹמְדוֹת אַף לְכֹהֵן הֶדְיוֹט קֹדֶם בְּעִילָה.

מִשָּׁרְשֵׁי הַמִּצְוָה, בַּקּוֹדֶמֶת לָהּ, וּקְצָת דִּינֶיהָ גַּם־כֵּן.

וְנוֹהֶגֶת מִצְוָה זוֹ בִּזְמַן הַבַּיִת, שֶׁהָיָה לָנוּ כֹהֵן גָּדוֹל. עָבַר וּבָעַל אַלְמָנָה אֲפִלּוּ

---

3. Perhaps in the sense that any children born from this relationship are not qualified to function as *kohanim*; or perhaps this means that it could disqualify his Temple service if he intended the intimacy to form a marital bond: see Mishnah, Kiddushin i 1, B'choroth vii 7. Or·*ufos'lo* (literally, "and it disqualifies him") may be a scribal error for *ufos'lah*, "and he disqualifies her" (see §267, third and fifth paragraphs). He himself, however, is not disqualified by this act *per se*, as our author wrote in §267.

4. See note 3.

5. And as it would seem, if he completes the act of coition he violates more specifically (or in addition) the injunction, *he shall not profane his seed*.

6. I.e. they were disqualified from the start for marriage to a *kohen*.

conjugal intimacy: for certainly [the Torah] would not be more stringent with an ordinary *kohen* than with a *kohen gadol.*

As it was clarified there in the tractate *Kiddushin* (78a): If he had conjugal intimacy, he receives whiplashes; if he did not, he does not receive whiplashes. And it was then stated that this law applies also to an ordinary *kohen*: neither is he punishable for the women forbidden to him until he weds first and then has conjugal intimacy; but if he was thus intimate with a wanton or with a divorced or profaned woman without marriage, even though this is forbidden him and it causes him disqualification as a *kohen*,[3] he is not whipped, since this restriction was not clearly stated [in the Writ] explicitly about him. For the injunction, *he shall not profane*, was written about a *kohen gadol*, and specifically with a widow; but with a wanton or a divorced or profaned woman, the *kohen gadol* too is likewise given whiplashes over them no more than once, upon marrying them and then being conjugally intimate with them. If, however, he was thus intimate with them without marriage, even though this is forbidden him and it causes him disqualification as a *kohen*,[4] the law for him in this respect is the same as the law for an ordinary *kohen*. For it is specifically in regard to a widow that the particular injunction was written for the *kohen gadol.* to make him punishable for the precept, *he shall not profane*[2]—i.e. for conjugal intimacy without marriage, as we have said. But this does not apply to the three other [forbidden] women, since the three others were repeated in regard to the *kohen gadol* for nothing but the reason we stated above (§273)—to separate—i.e. to impose punishment for each of them separately.

Moreover, there is another reason for the matter: With a widow, there is profanation in the conjugal intimacy, since she was [previously] permissible to an ordinary *kohen*, and she became disqualified by this intimacy. Hence he is to be punished with whiplashes on her account because of the injunction, *he shall not profane* [her].[5] With the other three, however, he cannot be punished with a whipping for conjugal intimacy without marriage, for here we cannot speak of profanation in regard to them, since they were in the status of profaned women,[6] even for an ordinary *kohen*, yet before this intimacy.

The root purpose of the precept [will be found] in the previous one (§273), and so too a few of its laws.

This precept is in effect when the Temple stands, when we have a 〈215〉 *kohen gadol*. If one transgressed and was conjugally intimate with a

בְּלֹא קִדּוּשִׁין, לוֹקֶה מִשּׁוּם "לֹא יְחַלֵּל", שֶׁהֲרֵי חִלֵּל לָאַלְמָנָה, שֶׁהָיְתָה רְאוּיָה
לַכֹּהֵן הֶדְיוֹט וְעַכְשָׁיו אֲסוּרָה לוֹ; וּכְבָר אָמַרְנוּ שֶׁהוּא חַיָּב שֶׁלֹּא יְחַלֵּל לֹא לָהּ וְלֹא
זַרְעוֹ. וְחִלּוּל זַרְעוֹ שַׁיָּךְ לוֹמַר בְּשֶׁבָּא עַל גְּרוּשָׁה חֲלָלָה זוֹנָה, שֶׁהֵן מְחֻלָּלוֹת,
וּכְשֶׁהוּא בָא עֲלֵיהֶן אֵינוֹ מְחַלְּלָן, שֶׁהֲרֵי מְחֻלָּלוֹת וְעוֹמְדוֹת הֵן, אֲבָל זַרְעוֹ הוּא
שֶׁמְּחַלֵּל, שֶׁזַּרְעוֹ בִּמְקוֹם חִלּוּל.

וְחִלּוּל הָאִשָּׁה שַׁיָּךְ לוֹמַר בְּבָא עַל הָאַלְמָנָה, שֶׁהִיא כְּשֵׁרָה עֲדַיִן לְכֹהֵן הֶדְיוֹט,
וּבְבִיאָה זוֹ שֶׁל כֹּהֵן גָּדוֹל נַעֲשֵׂית זוֹנָה, וַהֲרֵי חִלְּלָהּ מִכַּשְׁרוּתָהּ; וְאֵין סָפֵק כִּי גַם
הַזֶּרַע מְחֻלָּל הוּא בָהּ מִמֵּילָא; אֲבָל הַחִלּוּק שֶׁיֵּשׁ בֵּין הַחִלּוּל שֶׁבָּהּ לְחִלּוּל הַזֶּרַע,
שֶׁהִיא מְחֻלֶּלֶת בְּהַעֲרָאָה, וְהַזֶּרַע בְּגוֹמֵר בִּיאָתוֹ, כִּדְאִיתָא בַּגְּמָרָא.

[שֶׁלֹּא יַעֲבֹד כֹּהֵן בַּעַל מוּם]

רעה שֶׁלֹּא יַעֲבֹד כֹּהֵן בַּעַל מוּם בַּעֲבוֹדַת בֵּית הַמִּקְדָּשׁ, שֶׁנֶּאֱמַר: אִישׁ מִזַּרְעֲךָ
לְדֹרֹתָם אֲשֶׁר יִהְיֶה בוֹ מוּם לֹא יִקְרַב לְהַקְרִיב לֶחֶם אֱלֹהָיו, כְּלוֹמַר לֹא יִקְרַב
לַעֲבוֹדָה, כִּי כָל עִנְיְנֵי מַאֲכָל קָרוּי לֶחֶם בְּהַרְבֵּה מְקוֹמוֹת.

וּמוּם זֶה עִנְיָנוֹ מוּם קָבוּעַ, שֶׁכֵּן פֵּרְשׁוּ בְּסִפְרָא: "אֲשֶׁר יִהְיֶה בוֹ מוּם לֹא
יִקְרַב", אֵין לִי אֶלָּא מוּם קָבוּעַ; מוּם עוֹבֵר מִנַּיִן, תַּלְמוּד לוֹמַר בְּאוֹתָהּ פָּרָשָׁה: כָּל
אִישׁ אֲשֶׁר בּוֹ מוּם לֹא יִקְרַב.

וּמוּם קָבוּעַ הוּא כְּגוֹן שֶׁבֶר יָד אוֹ שֶׁבֶר רֶגֶל; וּמוּם עוֹבֵר, כְּגוֹן גָּרָב אוֹ יַלֶּפֶת,
וְהִיא הַחֲזָזִית.

7. TB Kiddushin 78a.

§275   1. By an obvious error the oldest manuscripts read here, *Whatever man of the
progeny of Aaron* (Leviticus 22:4); so too one MS of ShM negative precept §70 (ed.
Heller).

2. So Rashi on the verse, citing Daniel 5:1 as an example; and so too Rashi on
Genesis 31:54.

3. Sifra, *'emor, parashah* 3, 5.

4. I.e. it is derived from another verse, and thus is another precept (§276); but the
verse in the first paragraph applies only to a permanent defect.

widow even without marriage, he should be given a whipping of lashes on account of the injunction, *he shall not profane*, since here he profaned the widow: She had been fit [acceptable as a wife] for an ordinary *kohen*, and now she is forbidden to him. And we stated previously that he is punishable because he ought not profane either her or his seed. Now, it is possible to speak of the profanation of his seed [alone] when he is conjugally intimate with a divorced, profaned or wanton woman, since they are profaned [disqualified to marry a *kohen*] and when he is thus intimate with them he does not profane them, as they already have the status of profaned women. He does, however, profane his seed, as his seed is thus in a place of profanation.

Again, it is possible to speak of profanation of the woman when he is conjugally intimate with a widow: for she was yet acceptable [as a wife] for an ordinary *kohen*, but by this intimacy with a *kohen gadol* she becomes a wanton, and thus he profanes (disqualifies) her from her worthy, acceptable state. And beyond any doubt, the seed is also profaned: that occurs automatically. There is, however, a difference between her profanation and that of the seed: she becomes profaned upon intromission, and the seed at the completion of his act of intimacy, as this is conveyed in the Talmud.[7]

[THAT A KOHEN WITH A BLEMISHING DEFECT SHOULD NOT SERVE AT THE SANCTUARY]

275 that a *kohen* with a disfiguring blemish should not take part in the service at the Sanctuary: as it is stated, *Any man of your descendants throughout their generations*[1] *who has a blemish, let him not approach to offer the bread of his God* (Leviticus 21:17); in other words, he should not approach to [join in] the service; for all matters of food are called "bread" in many instances.[2]

Now, this blemish means in essence a permanent disfigurement; for it was so interpreted in the Midrash *Sifra*:[3] "who has a blemish, let him not approach"—thus I know only about a permanent disfigurement; where do I learn about a passing blemish?—Scripture states (in the same section), *For any man who has a blemish shall not draw near* (ibid. 18).[4]

A permanent disfigurement is, for example, a broken hand or a broken foot. A passing blemish is, for example, a scurvy or a scab,

⟨217⟩ which means a lichen.

מִשָּׁרְשֵׁי הַמִּצְוָה, לְפִי שֶׁרַב פְּעֻלוֹת בְּנֵי־אָדָם רְצוּיוֹת אֶל לֵב רוֹאֵיהֶם לְפִי חֲשִׁיבוּת עוֹשֵׂיהֶן, כִּי בִּהְיוֹת הָאָדָם חָשׁוּב בְּמַרְאֵהוּ וְטוֹב בְּמַעֲשָׂיו, יִמְצָא חֵן וְשֵׂכֶל טוֹב בְּכֹל אֲשֶׁר יַעֲשֶׂה בְּעֵינֵי כָל רוֹאָיו; וְאִם יִהְיֶה בְּהֶפֶךְ מִזֶּה, פָּחוּת בְּצוּרָתוֹ וּמְשֻׁנֶּה בְּאֵיבָרָיו, וְאִם יָשָׁר בִּדְרָכָיו, לֹא יֵאוֹתוּ פְּעֻלוֹתָיו כָּל־כָּךְ אֶל לֵב רוֹאָיו. עַל־כֵּן, בֶּאֱמֶת, רָאוּי לִהְיוֹת הַשָּׁלִיחַ שֶׁהַכַּפָּרָה תְּלוּיָה עָלָיו אִישׁ חֵן, יְפֵה תֹאַר וִיפֵה מַרְאֶה, וְנָאֶה בְּכָל דְּרָכָיו, לְמַעַן יִתְפְּשׂוּ מַחְשְׁבוֹת בְּנֵי־אִישׁ אַחֲרָיו. וּמִלְּבַד זֶה אֶפְשָׁר שֶׁיֵּשׁ בִּשְׁלֵמוּת צוּרָתוֹ רֶמֶז לְעִנְיָנִים שֶׁמִּתּוֹךְ מַחְשְׁבוֹת הָאָדָם בָּהֶן תִּטְהַר נַפְשׁוֹ וְתִתְעַלֶּה. וְלָכֵן אֵין רָאוּי בְּשׁוּם צַד שֶׁיִּהְיֶה בּוֹ שִׁנּוּי צוּרָה מִכָּל צוּרוֹתָיו, פֶּן תִּתְפַּזֵּר נֶפֶשׁ הַמְחַשֵּׁב מִצַּד הַשִּׁנּוּי וְתָנוּד מִן הַחֵפֶץ.

מִדִּינֵי הַמִּצְוָה, מַה שֶּׁאָמְרוּ זִכְרוֹנָם לִבְרָכָה שֶׁשְּׁלֹשָׁה מִינֵי מוּמִין הֵן: יֵשׁ מוּמִין שֶׁפּוֹסְלִין הַכֹּהֵן מֵלַעֲבֹד, וְאִם הֵן בַּבְּהֵמָה פּוֹסְלִין אוֹתָהּ מִלִּקָּרֵב; וְיֵשׁ מוּמִין אֲחֵרִים שֶׁפּוֹסְלִין הָאָדָם בִּלְבַד מֵלַעֲבֹד וְלֹא הַבְּהֵמָה מִלִּקָּרֵב; וְיֵשׁ מוּמִין שֶׁאֵין פּוֹסְלִין לֹא אָדָם וְלֹא בְהֵמָה אֶלָּא מִשּׁוּם מַרְאִית הָעַיִן; וְכָל כֹּהֵן שֶׁיֵּשׁ בּוֹ אֶחָד מִשְּׁלֹשֶׁת מִינֵי מוּמִין אֵלּוּ, אֵינוֹ עוֹבֵד.

אֵין פּוֹסְלִין בָּאָדָם אֶלָּא מוּמִין שֶׁבְּגָלוּי, אֲבָל מוּמִין שֶׁבַּחֲלַל הַגּוּף, כְּגוֹן שֶׁנִּטַּל כָּלְיָתוֹ אוֹ טְחוֹל שֶׁלּוֹ אוֹ נִקְּבוּ מֵעָיו, אַף־עַל־פִּי שֶׁיֵּעָשֶׂה בָּהֶן טְרֵפָה, עֲבוֹדָתוֹ כְּשֵׁרָה, שֶׁנֶּאֱמַר "שֶׁבֶר רָגֶל אוֹ שֶׁבֶר יָד": מָה אֵלּוּ בְּגָלוּי, אַף כָּל שֶׁהוּא בְּגָלוּי.

וּמָנוּ חֲכָמִים שֶׁהַמּוּמִין שֶׁהֵם פּוֹסְלִין בֵּין בָּאָדָם וּבַבְּהֵמָה הֵם חֲמִשִּׁים, מִלְּבַד שֶׁיֵּשׁ מוּמִין מְיֻחָדִים בַּבְּהֵמָה וְהֵם כ״ג, וְנִמְצְאוּ בַּבְּהֵמָה ע״ג; וְיֵשׁ גַּם־כֵּן מוּמִין

---

5. I.e. the *kohen*, whom our author thus describes in the second paragraph of § 265, as the mediator between the Israelite and his Creator.

6. Expression taken from Genesis 39:6.

7. TB B'choroth 43a–b; MT *hilchoth bi'ath ha-mikdash* vi 5.

8. TB *ibid.* 45b.

9. MT *ibid.* 7.

10. What follows in this and the next four paragraphs is given in detail in MT *ibid.* vii and viii.

〈218〉

At the root of the precept lies the reason that most actions of people are acceptable, appealing to the heart of those who see them, in accordance with the eminence of those who do them. For when a man is distinguished in his appearance and good in his actions, he *will find grace and good understanding* (Proverbs 3:4) with all that he does, in the eyes of all who observe him. Should he be, however, the opposite of this—inferior in his form, or peculiar in his limbs, then even if he is straight in his ways, his activities will not be so attractive to the heart of those who see him. It is therefore truly fitting that the messenger,[5] on whom atonement depends, should be a man of grace, handsome in appearance and fair in features,[6] and pleasing in all his ways—that the minds of men may be drawn to him. And apart from this, it is possible that in the perfection of his form lies an intimation of matters through which, as a man's thoughts dwell on them, his spirit will be cleansed and exalted. It is therefore not right in any way that there should be in him [the *kohen*] any deviation in form from all His forms, for fear that the spirit of the contemplator will be distracted on account of the peculiarity and will wander from the desired goal.

Among the laws of the precept there is what the Sages of blessed memory said,[7] that there are three kinds of blemishes: There are disfigurements that disqualify a *kohen* from serving [at the Sanctuary], and if they are in an animal, they disqualify it from being brought as an offering. There are other blemishes, which disqualify only a man from serving, but not a beast from being offered up. And there are blemishes which disqualify neither a man nor an animal, but [impose restriction] only for appearance sake. And any *kohen* who has any one of these three kinds of disfigurements, does not serve [at the Sanctuary].

None but blemishes that are open, visible, disqualify a man; but with defects in a body cavity—for instance, if one's kidney or spleen was removed, or his viscera were perforated—even if he thus becomes fatally wounded, his service [at the Temple] is acceptable.[8] For it is stated, *broken in foot or broken in hand* (Leviticus 21:19): just as these are in the open, exposed, so anything [else] that is in the open.[9]

Now, the Sages calculated[10] that the blemishes which disqualify both man and animal are fifty in number. Apart from these, there are blemishes peculiar to beasts, which are twenty-three in number; thus, consequently, there are seventy-three [altogether that can be found] in animals. Then there are also blemishes unique to man, which

מְיֻחָדִים בָּאָדָם וְהֵם תִּשְׁעִים; נִמְצְאוּ הַפּוֹסְלִים בָּאָדָם מֵאָה וְאַרְבָּעִים.

וְזֶהוּ כְּלַל הַתִּשְׁעִים הַמְיֻחָדִים בָּאָדָם: שְׁמוֹנָה יֵשׁ בָּרֹאשׁ וּשְׁנַיִם בַּצַּוָּאר, אַרְבָּעָה בָאָזְנַיִם וַחֲמִשָּׁה בַּגְּבִינִים, אַרְבָּעָה בְּרִיסֵי הָעֵינַיִם, אֶחָד־עָשָׂר בָּעֵינַיִם, שִׁשָּׁה בַחֹטֶם, שְׁלֹשָׁה בַשְּׂפָתַיִם וּשְׁלֹשָׁה בַּבֶּטֶן וּשְׁלֹשָׁה בְּגַבּוֹ שֶׁל אָדָם וְשִׁשָּׁה בַיָּדַיִם, אַרְבָּעָה בְּאִיבְרֵי הַזֶּרַע, חֲמִשָּׁה־עָשָׂר בַּשּׁוֹקַיִם וּבָרַגְלַיִם, אַרְבָּעָה בְּכָל הַגּוּף, שְׁמוֹנָה בְּעוֹר הַבָּשָׂר; וְעוֹד אַרְבָּעָה מוּמִין גְּדוֹלִים מְיֻחָדִים בָּאָדָם וְאֵינָם בְּגָלוּי, וְאֵלּוּ הֵן: חֵרֵשׁ, שׁוֹטֶה, נִכְפֶּה וַאֲפִלּוּ לְיָמִים, וּמִי שֶׁרוּחַ רָעָה מְבַעֲתַתּוֹ, אֲפִלּוּ בְעִתִּים יְדוּעִים.

וּמִלְּבַד אֵלֶּה, יֵשׁ עוֹד שְׁנַיִם שֶׁפּוֹסְלִין מִפְּנֵי מַרְאִית הָעַיִן, וְאֵלּוּ הֵן: מִי שֶׁנָּשְׁרוּ רִיסֵי עֵינָיו אַף־עַל־פִּי שֶׁנִּשְׁאַר הַשֵּׂעָר בְּעִקָּרָן, וּמִי שֶׁנִּטְּלוּ שִׁנָּיו.

וְזֶהוּ כְּלַל הַחֲמִשִּׁים הַפּוֹסְלִין בָּאָדָם וּבַבְּהֵמָה: חֲמִשָּׁה בָאֹזֶן, שְׁלֹשָׁה בְּרִיס שֶׁל עַיִן, וּשְׁלֹשָׁה אֵלּוּ בִּכְלַל חָרוּץ הָאָמוּר בַּתּוֹרָה; שְׁמוֹנָה בָעַיִן, שְׁלֹשָׁה בַחֹטֶם, שִׁשָּׁה בַפֶּה, שְׁנֵים־עָשָׂר בְּאִיבְרֵי הַזֶּרַע, שִׁשָּׁה בַיָּדַיִם וּבָרַגְלַיִם, אַרְבָּעָה רְאוּיִין לִהְיוֹת בְּכָל הַגּוּף, וְאֵלּוּ הֵן: גָּרָב, וְהוּא הָאָמוּר בַּתּוֹרָה; ב' יַבֶּלֶת שֶׁיֵּשׁ בּוֹ עֶצֶם, וְזֶהוּ יַבֶּלֶת הָאָמוּר בַּתּוֹרָה; ג' מִי שֶׁיֵּשׁ בּוֹ חֲזָזִית הַמִּצְרִית כָּל־שֶׁהוּא, וְזוֹ הִיא יַלֶּפֶת הָאֲמוּרָה בַּתּוֹרָה; ד' כָּל עֶצֶם שֶׁבְּגָלוּי שֶׁנֶּחֱרַץ בּוֹ חֶרֶץ, וְהוּא בִּכְלַל חָרוּץ הָאָמוּר בַּתּוֹרָה; וְאֵין הַצְּלָעוֹת בִּכְלַל עֲצָמוֹת שֶׁבְּגָלוּי.

וְעוֹד שְׁלֹשָׁה אֲחֵרִים: הַזָּקֵן שֶׁהִגִּיעַ לִהְיוֹת רוֹתֵת וְרוֹעֵד כְּשֶׁהוּא עוֹמֵד; ב' הַחוֹלֶה שֶׁהוּא רוֹעֵד מִפְּנֵי חָלְיוֹ וְכִשְׁלוֹן כֹּחוֹ; אֲבָל הַטְּרֵפָה, כָּשֵׁר בָּאָדָם וּפָסוּל בַּבְּהֵמָה, וְכֵן יוֹצֵא דֹפֶן כָּשֵׁר בָּאָדָם וּפָסוּל בַּבְּהֵמָה; ג' הַמְזֹהָם — הֲרֵי חֲמִשִּׁים; וְיֶתֶר פְּרָטֶיהָ, בְּמַסֶּכֶת בְּכוֹרוֹת פֶּרֶק שְׁבִיעִי.

10a. The source is Mishnah, B'choroth vii 6 (TB 45b), and by the Mishnah's own rule (T'rumoth i 2) ḥérésh means a deaf-mute. Yet as commentaries note (R. Samson of Sens, R. 'Ovadyah Bertinoro), in the Talmud there are exceptions to the rule, where the term denotes only deafness (Ḥagigah 2b; Yevamoth 104b). Paḥad Yitzḥak, s.v. ḥérésh, cites a sound view that where sense (knowledge, intelligence) is required, only a deaf-mute is excluded, because in Talmudic law he is ranked with a witless person and a small child. As Rambam explains (commentary to Mishnah, ibid.), a child born deaf would not have the stimulus of hearing to develop the power of speech, and thus would be a deaf-mute; and lacking this basic means of social communication, he would not develop any normal intelligence and sense. Thus he should indeed be classed with the witless and small children. Where sense and intelligence are not relevant factors, however, ḥérésh should denote only a deaf person. MH indeed queries if here ḥérésh could mean a deaf-mute; and R. Ezekiel Landau notes that since the Mishnah lists it as a defect disqualifying a kohen but not an animal intended for an offering, it would seem to denote deafness only, as muteness can certainly not be a factor in the disqualification of animals (Noda' biYhudah, 1st series, Even ha'Ezer, §53).

11. Generally translated as maimed or mutilated.

are ninety in number; hence there are 140 [altogether] that can disqualify a man.

This, in sum, is an outline of the ninety that are unique to man: There are eight in the head, two in the neck, four in the ears, five in the eyebrows, four in the eyelids and eyelashes, eleven in the eyes, six in the nose, three in the lips, three on the belly, three on a man's back, six in the hands, four in the organs of procreation, fifteen in the thighs and feet, four over the entire body, eight on the skin of the flesh, and another four major blemishes unique to man which are not visible: these are a deaf person,[10a] a witless person, an epileptic, even if only on certain days, and one whom an evil spirit throws into terror (deranges), even if only at certain times.

Apart from these, there are another two that disqualify on account of their appearance; these are: one whose eyelashes fell out, even if the hairs remained in their follicles, and one whose teeth were removed.

Now, this is an outline of the fifty that disqualify in both man and beast: five in the ear, three in the eyelid and lash—these three being included under the term *harutz*[11] that is given in the Torah (Leviticus 22:22), eight in the eye, three in the nose, six in the mouth, twelve in the organs of procreation, six in the hands and feet, and four that can occur anywhere on the body. These are: (1) a scabrous itch, which is mentioned in the Torah (Leviticus 21:20); (2) a hardened cyst containing a bone, which is *yabeleth* (a wen) mentioned in the Torah (ibid. 22:22); (3) whoever has any kind of Egyptian lichen (scabs) whatever, this being *yalefeth* that is mentioned in the Torah (ibid.); (4) any bone that is exposed, in which a groove was formed, this being included under the term *harutz* (grooved) mentioned in the Torah (ibid.). The ribs, though, are not included among the exposed bones [that constitute a blemish].

There are yet three more: (1) an old man who has reached the stage of quivering and shaking when he stands; (2) a sick man who quivers on account of his illness and the breakdown of his strength; a fatal wound or illness, however, is acceptable in a man and disqualifying in a beast; likewise, birth by Caesarian operation is acceptable for a man and disqualifying for an animal; (3) one with an offensive odor. Thus we have fifty.

The rest of its details are in chapter 7 of the Talmud tractate *B'choroth*. It applies at the time the Temple stands, to the *kohanim*.

וְנוֹהֶגֶת בִּזְמַן הַבַּיִת, בְּלֹהֲנִים. וְכֹהֵן הָעוֹבֵר עַל זֶה וְעָבַד וְהוּא בַּעַל מוּם, אִם
הוּא מִן הַמּוּמִין הַפּוֹסְלִים בָּאָדָם וּבַבְּהֵמָה, בֵּין שׁוֹגֵג בֵּין מֵזִיד עֲבוֹדָתוֹ פְּסוּלָה;
וְאִם הָיָה מֵזִיד, חַיָּב מַלְקוֹת. וְכֵן אָמְרוּ בְּסִפְרָא: אֵין בַּעַל מוּם בְּמִיתָה אֶלָּא
בְּאַזְהָרָה. וְאִם הוּא מִן הַתִּשְׁעִים מוּמִין הַמְּיֻחָדִין בָּאָדָם, אַף־עַל־פִּי שֶׁהוּא לוֹקֶה
לֹא חִלֵּל עֲבוֹדָתוֹ. וְאִם הוּא מִן הַמּוּמִין שֶׁפְּסְלוּתָן אֵינוֹ אֶלָּא מִפְּנֵי מַרְאִית הָעַיִן,
אֵינוֹ לוֹקֶה, וַעֲבוֹדָתוֹ כְּשֵׁרָה.

[שֶׁלֹּא יַעֲבֹד כֹּהֵן בַּעַל מוּם עוֹבֵר]

רעו שֶׁלֹּא יַעֲבֹד כֹּהֵן בַּעַל מוּם עוֹבֵר, שֶׁנֶּאֱמַר: כָּל אִישׁ אֲשֶׁר בּוֹ מוּם מִזֶּרַע
אַהֲרֹן הַכֹּהֵן לֹא יִגַּשׁ. "כָּל" רִבּוּיָא הוּא וּמַרְבֶּה אֲפִלּוּ מוּם עוֹבֵר; כִּי בַתְּחִלָּה
יַזְהִיר עַל מוּם קָבוּעַ, וְהָיִיתִי סָבוּר שֶׁהוּא מֻתָּר לַעֲבֹד בְּמוּם עוֹבֵר, שֶׁהוּא קַל
מִמֶּנּוּ; לְפִיכָךְ הִזְהִיר גַּם עַל הָעוֹבֵר, וְהוּא הַגָּרָב וְהַיַּלֶּפֶת.

מִשָּׁרְשֵׁי הַמִּצְוָה, כְּעִנְיָן שֶׁכָּתַבְנוּ בַּמִּצְוָה הַקּוֹדֶמֶת לָהּ.

מִדִּינֵי הַמִּצְוָה, מַה שֶּׁאָמְרוּ זִכְרוֹנָם לִבְרָכָה שֶׁאֶחָד מוּם קָבוּעַ אוֹ מוּם עוֹבֵר
פּוֹסֵל הָעֲבוֹדָה, וְלוֹקֶה הַכֹּהֵן עָלָיו אִם עָבַד בְּמֵזִיד; וּמַה שֶּׁאָמְרוּ זִכְרוֹנָם לִבְרָכָה
שֶׁבֵּית־דִּין הַגָּדוֹל הָיוּ יוֹשְׁבִין בְּלִשְׁכַּת הַגָּזִית, וְעִקַּר מַעֲשֵׂיהֶם בְּהַתְמָדָה שֶׁהָיוּ
בוֹדְקִין הַכֹּהֲנִים בְּיוּחֲסִין וּבְמוּמִין; וְכָל כֹּהֵן שֶׁנִּמְצָא פָּסוּל בְּיוּחֲסִין, לוֹבֵשׁ
שְׁחוֹרִים וּמִתְעַטֵּף שְׁחוֹרִים וְיוֹצֵא מִן הָעֲזָרָה; וְכָל מִי שֶׁנִּמְצָא שָׁלֵם וְכָשֵׁר, לוֹבֵשׁ
לְבָנִים וְנִכְנָס וּמְשַׁמֵּשׁ עִם אֶחָיו הַכֹּהֲנִים; וּמִי שֶׁנִּמְצָא כָּשֵׁר בְּיִחוּסוֹ וְנִמְצָא בוֹ

---

12. Sifra, 'emor, perek 3, 10.

13. According to our standard version of the Talmud, B'choroth 43b, he thus violates only a positive precept, and would not be whipped (see Rashi, s.v. 'aseh); but Rambam had a different version (see *Tosafoth Yom Tov* to Mishnah, B'choroth vii 3, s.v. *mip'né*), which our author follows.

14. Thus the only admonition to a *kohen* with one of these is that initially he should not serve.

§276   1. I.e. when it is apparently superfluous, it is interpreted as adding something to the precept, extending its force to cover something not evident in the plain meaning of the verse.

2. MT *hilchoth bi'ath ha-mikdash* vi 4 gives these as examples.

3. TB B'choroth 43a.

4. Sifra, 'emor, perek 3, 10.

5. Mishnah, Middoth v 4; MT *ibid.* 11.

If a *kohen* transgressed this and served [at the Sanctuary] while he had a disfiguring defect, if it was one of the blemishes that disqualify both man and beast, then whether he acted deliberately or inadvertently, his service is disqualified (unacceptable); and if it was deliberate, he should be given lashes of the whip. And so it was stated in the Midrash *Sifra*:[12] A man with a blemish is not liable to a death penalty, as he merely violates a negative precept. If it was one of the ninety disfigurements that are unique to man, then even though he would be whipped,[13] his [Temple] service would not be profaned (unacceptable). And if it was one of those blemishes that disqualify only because of the appearance, then he would receive no whiplashes, and his service would be acceptable.[14]

[THAT A KOHEN WITH A TEMPORARY BLEMISH IS

FORBIDDEN TO SERVE AT THE SANCTUARY]

276 that a *kohen* with a passing (temporary) blemish should not serve [at the Sanctuary]: for it is stated, *kol 'ish, any man, of the descendants of Aaron the* kohen *who has a blemish shall not come near* (Leviticus 21:21); and the word *kol* [any; literally, all] is an additive term:[1] it adds even a passing blemish. For at first Scripture admonishes about a permanent blemish (§275), and thus I might have thought that one is permitted to serve [at the Sanctuary] with a passing disfigurement, since that is less serious. Therefore Scripture adjures also about the passing kind, which means a scabrous itch and scurvy.[2]

At the root of the precept lies a reason similar to the one we wrote about the precept before this (§275).

Among the laws of he precept, there is what the Sages of blessed memory said,[3] that whether it is a permanent or a passing blemish, it disqualifies his [Temple] service, and the *kohen* is given a whipping of lashes on its account if he performed his service deliberately.[4] Then there is what the Sages of blessed memory said:[5] that the great *beth din* (supreme court) would sit in the chamber of hewn stone [at the Sanctuary], and their principal activity, continually, was that they would investigate and examine the *kohanim* in regard to lineage and blemishes. Any *kohen* found to be disqualified through lineage would wear black and wrap himself in black, and go out of the Temple court. Whoever was found to be sound and worthy [in lineage] would dress in white and enter and serve with his brother-*kohanim*.

If one was found worthy in his lineage but a blemish was discovered

מוּם, יוֹשֵׁב בְּלִשְׁכַּת הָעֵצִים וּמְתַלֵּעַ עֵצִים לַמַּעֲרָכָה, וְחוֹלֵק בַּקֳּדָשִׁים עִם אַנְשֵׁי
בֵית־אָב שֶׁלּוֹ וְאוֹכֵל, שֶׁנֶּאֱמַר: לֶחֶם אֱלֹהָיו מִקָּדְשֵׁי הַקֳּדָשִׁים וּמִן הַקֳּדָשִׁים יֹאכֵל;
וְיֶתֶר דִּינֵי כָל הַמּוּמִין, בִּבְכוֹרוֹת פֶּרֶק שְׁבִיעִי.

וְנוֹהֶגֶת בִּזְמַן הַבַּיִת בְּכֹהֲנִים. עָבַר וְעָבַד בְּמוּם עוֹבֵר בְּמֵזִיד, לוֹקֶה.

וְהָרַמְבַּ"ן זִכְרוֹנוֹ לִבְרָכָה לֹא יִמְנֶה זֶה שֶׁל מוּם עוֹבֵר לְלָאו בִּפְנֵי עַצְמוֹ,
וְכָתַב דְּבִכְלַל לָאו דְּמוּם קָבוּעַ הוּא, וְהוּא כְמוֹ חֵלֶק מֵחֶלְקֵי הַמִּצְוָה; וּכְבָר
הִסְכִּימוּ הוּא וְהָרַמְבַּ"ם זִכְרוֹנוֹ לִבְרָכָה, וְדָבָר בָּרוּר הוּא, שֶׁאֵין לַחֲשֹׁב חֵלֶק
הַמִּצְוָה מִצְוָה בִּפְנֵי עַצְמָהּ.

[שֶׁלֹּא יִכָּנֵס בַּעַל מוּם בַּהֵיכָל]

רעז שֶׁלֹּא יִכָּנֵס בַּעַל מוּם בַּהֵיכָל בִּכְלָלוֹ, כְּלוֹמַר אֶל הַמִּזְבֵּחַ וּבֵין הָאוּלָם
וְלַמִּזְבֵּחַ וּבְכָל שְׁאָר הַמְּקוֹמוֹת שֶׁבַּהֵיכָל, שֶׁנֶּאֱמַר: אַךְ אֶל הַפָּרֹכֶת לֹא יָבֹא וְאֶל
הַמִּזְבֵּחַ לֹא יִגַּשׁ; וְנִתְבָּאֵר בְּסִפְרָא שֶׁשְּׁנֵי לָאוִין אֵלֶּה, שֶׁל הַפָּרֹכֶת וְהַמִּזְבֵּחַ, לֹא
יַסְפִּיק אֶחָד מֵהֶם בִּלְתִּי חֲבֵרוֹ, וּשְׁנֵיהֶם בָּאוּ לְהַשְׁלִים הַדִּין בְּעִנְיָן אֶחָד, וְהוּא
לְהַרְחִיק הַמָּקוֹם הָאָסוּר עֲלֵיהֶם לְהִכָּנֵס בּוֹ.

מִשָּׁרְשֵׁי הַמִּצְוָה, לְהַגְדִּיל כְּבוֹד הַבַּיִת וַהֲדָרָהּ, עַל־כֵּן אֵין רָאוּי לָבֹא שָׁם בַּעַל
מוּם, כִּי הוּא מְקוֹם הַשְּׁלֵמוּת, אֵינוֹ בְדִין לַעֲמֹד שָׁם מִי שֶׁיֵּשׁ בּוֹ שׁוּם חִסָּרוֹן.
וּכְבָר כָּתַבְתִּי לְמַעֲלָה הַרְבֵּה פְעָמִים הַתּוֹעֶלֶת הַנִּמְצָא לָנוּ בְּהַגְדִּילֵנוּ מַעֲלַת הַבַּיִת
הַקָּדוֹשׁ וְתִפְאַרְתּוֹ.

דִּינֵי הַמִּצְוָה, כְּלוֹמַר מַה הֵן הַמּוּמִין שֶׁבִּשְׁבִילָן יִמָּנַע הַכֹּהֵן מִלִּכָּנֵס, וְזָכַרְתִּים
לְמַעֲלָה סָמוּךְ בְּרֶמֶז בְּאַזְהָרַת בַּעַל מוּם קָבוּעַ; וְשָׁם הוֹדַעְתִּי מְקוֹמָן בַּגְּמָרָא וְכָל
הָעִנְיָן, כְּמִנְהָגִי.

6. Mishnah *ibid.* ii 5; MT *ibid.* 12.
7. See §152, note 18.
8. So TB Z'vahim 98b, etc.
9. MT *hilchoth bi'ath ha-mikdash* vi 12.
10. Ramban, commentary to ShM negative precept §71.
11. So ShM root principle 11, and Ramban, commentary, there.

§277　　1. See §95, fourth paragraph before end.
2. Sifra, *'emor, perek* 3, 10.
3. The veil was a curtain in the holy chamber separating it from the holy of holies;
the altar was in the Temple forecourt. Hence (says the Sifra) Scripture specifies the altar:
although not within the holy chamber, it too was forbidden to a blemished *kohen*. The
altar was used regularly in the Temple service; the veil was not. Hence (says the Sifra)
Scripture specifies the veil: although it was not used in the Temple service (and he was
forbidden *to serve* at the Sanctuary—Leviticus 21:21), a blemished *kohen* might not go
there either.

upon him, he would sit in the chamber of the wood and weed out wormy pieces in preparing piles of wood for the altar.[6] And he would share in the holy offerings with the members of his "father's house"[7] and eat,[8] as it is stated, *He may eat of the bread of his God, both of the most holy and of the holy* (Leviticus 21:22).[9] The remaining laws about all the blemishes are in chapter 7 of the Talmud tractate *B'choroth*.

It applies when the Temple exists, for the *kohanim*. If one transgressed and served [at the Sanctuary] with a passing blemish deliberately, he should be given whiplashes.

Now, Ramban of blessed memory does not count this injunction concerning a temporary blemish as a negative precept in its own right; he wrote[10] that it is to be included under the negative precept about a permanent blemish, thus being as one of the parts of the precept. And previously he and Rambam of blessed memory were in accord, this being a clear matter, that part of a precept is not to be reckoned as a *mitzvah* by itself.[11]

[THAT A KOHEN WITH A BLEMISHING DEFECT IS NOT TO ENTER THE HOLY TEMPLE]

277 that a *kohen* with a blemish should not enter the *héchal* (Temple "palace") anywhere within its area, i.e. to the altar, and between the *'ulam* (entrance hall) and the altar, and in all other places in the *héchal*[1]— as it is stated, *But he shall not go in to the veil, nor come near the altar* (Leviticus 21:23). It was explained in the Midrash *Sifra* concerning these two injunctions, about the veil and the altar,[2] that one of them would not be enough without the other,[3] and so both were given, to complete the law about one matter, i.e. to make the place where it is forbidden for them to enter, well removed [from them].[4]

At the root of the precept lies the purpose to magnify the glory of the Temple and its splendor. It is therefore not fitting for a blemished, disfigured man to go in there. For it is the place of wholeness, perfection; it is not right that a person who has any defect should stand there. I have written previously, above, many times, the useful benefit we will find in magnifying the excellence of the holy Temple and its majesty.

As to the laws of the precept, i.e. what the blemishes are, because of which the *kohen* must refrain from entering, I have mentioned them shortly above, in connection with the injunction about one with a permanent defect (§275). There I gave their location in the Talmud, and the entire subject-matter, as my custom is.

וְכָתַב הָרַמְבַּ"ן זִכְרוֹנוֹ לִבְרָכָה שֶׁאֵין לָנוּ לַחְשֹׁב זֶה הַלָּאו בְּמִנְיַן הַלָּאוִין,
שֶׁאִסּוּר הִכָּנֵס בַּעַל מוּם בַּהֵיכָל, וְגַם פְּרוּעֵי רֹאשׁ וּקְרוּעֵי בְגָדִים וְשָׁתוּי, אֵינוֹ
אֶלָּא מַעֲלָה מִדִּבְרֵיהֶם זִכְרוֹנָם לִבְרָכָה, וְלֹא בָא הַכָּתוּב הַזֶּה אֶלָּא לֶאֱסֹר מֵהֶם
קְרִיבָה לָעֲבוֹדָה, וְזֶה בִּכְלַל לָאו דְּבַעַל מוּם שֶׁלֹּא יַעֲבֹד הוּא. וְכָתַב עוֹד שֶׁאַף הֵם
לֹא אָסְרוּ אֶלָּא הַמָּקוֹם הַנִּקְרָא בֵּין הָאוּלָם וְלַמִּזְבֵּחַ, שֶׁהוּא כ"ב אַמָּה, אֲבָל כְּנֶגֶד
הַמִּזְבֵּחַ עַצְמוֹ, שֶׁהוּא ל"ב אַמָּה, לֹא אָסְרוּ, וּכְמוֹ שֶׁכָּתַבְתִּי לְמַעְלָה בְּסֵדֶר "וַיְהִי
בַיּוֹם הַשְּׁמִינִי" בְּאַזְהָרַת פְּרוּעַ רֹאשׁ [סִי' קמ"ט], בְּשֵׁם הָרַב זִכְרוֹנוֹ לִבְרָכָה.

[שֶׁלֹּא יַעֲבֹד כֹּהֵן טָמֵא]

רעח שֶׁלֹּא יַעֲבֹד כֹּהֵן בְּעוֹדוֹ טָמֵא, שֶׁנֶּאֱמַר: וְיִנָּזְרוּ מִקָּדְשֵׁי בְנֵי יִשְׂרָאֵל וְלֹא
יְחַלְּלוּ אֶת שֵׁם קָדְשִׁי; וְאָמְרוּ זִכְרוֹנָם לִבְרָכָה בְּפֶרֶק תְּשִׁיעִי מִסַּנְהֶדְרִין: מִנַּיִן
לְטָמֵא שֶׁשִּׁמֵּשׁ שֶׁהוּא בְמִיתָה, כְּלוֹמַר מִיתָה בִּידֵי שָׁמַיִם, דִּכְתִיב: דַּבֵּר אֶל אַהֲרֹן
וְאֶל בָּנָיו וְיִנָּזְרוּ מִקָּדְשֵׁי בְנֵי יִשְׂרָאֵל וְלֹא יְחַלְּלוּ, וּכְתִיב בְּמָקוֹם אַחֵר: וּמֵתוּ בוֹ כִּי
יְחַלְּלֻהוּ.

מִשָּׁרְשֵׁי הַמִּצְוָה, מַה שֶּׁכָּתַבְנוּ בִּמְקוֹמוֹת רַבִּים, כִּי לִכְבוֹד הַבַּיִת וּמַעֲלַת
הָעֲבוֹדָה נִתְרַחֵק מִמֶּנָּה כָּל דָּבָר שֶׁאֵינוֹ בְּמַעֲלָתוֹ וַחֲשִׁיבוּתוֹ; וּמַעֲלַת הָאָדָם
בְּטָהֳרָה יָדוּעַ לְכָל מֵבִין.

דִּינֵי הַמִּצְוָה, כְּגוֹן מַה הֵן הַטֻּמְאוֹת הַמְּטַמְּאוֹת מִדְּאוֹרַיְתָא וְהַמְטַמְּאוֹת
מִדְּרַבָּנָן, וּבְאֵי זֶה עִנְיָן יִטְהַר הַטָּמֵא מִטֻּמְאָתוֹ, וְאֵי זוֹ טֻמְאָה צְרִיכָה הַזָּאָה וְקָרְבָּן
לְטָהֳרָתָהּ, וְאֵי זוֹ אֵינָהּ צְרִיכָה אֶלָּא טְבִילָה וְהֶעֱרֵב שֶׁמֶשׁ; וּמִכְּלַל הָעִנְיָן שֶׁאִי־

---

4. The paragraph is based on ShM negative precept §69.
5. Ramban, commentary to ShM *ibid.*

Now, Ramban of blessed memory wrote[5] that we ought not reckon this injunction in the list of negative precepts: For the ban on a blemished man's entering the *héchal*, and so too on those with overgrown hair or torn clothing, and those intoxicated, is no more than a higher standard set by the ruling of the Sages of blessed memory; and this verse comes only to forbid them coming close in order to serve, which is included under the negative precept about a blemished man, that he should not serve [at the Temple]. He wrote further that even the Sages forbade no more than the area called "between the *'ulam* and the altar," which is twenty-two cubits; but directly opposite the [entire] altar, which measured thirty-two cubits, they did not forbid—as I wrote above, in *sidrah sh'mini*, at the injunction about overgrown hair (§ 149), in the name of the master [Ramban] of blessed memory.

[THAT A RITUALLY UNCLEAN KOHEN IS FORBIDDEN TO SERVE AT THE HOLY TEMPLE]

278 that a *kohen* should not serve [at the Sanctuary] while he is ritually unclean, for it is stated, *that they should keep apart from the holy things of the Israelites . . . and not profane My holy name* (Leviticus 22:2); and the Sages of blessed memory taught in chapter 9 of the Talmud tractate *Sanhedrin* (83b): How do we derive that if a defiled [*kohen*] served [in the Sanctuary], he incurs a death penalty—i.e. death at Heaven's hands?—because it is written, *Speak to Aaron and his sons, that they should keep apart from the holy things of the Israelites . . . and not profane*, and it is written elsewhere, *and they shall die thereby when they profane it* (ibid. 9).

At the root of the precept lies what we have written in many instances, that for the glory of the Temple and the exaltation of the service, everything that was not in its [proper state of] excellence and eminence was removed from it. And the exalted level of a man in a state of purity is something known (evident) to every person of understanding.

The laws of the precept are, for example, which are the ritual impurities that defile by Torah law, and which by the ruling of the Sages; in what way a defiled person is purified from his ritual uncleanness; which uncleanness requires sprinkling [with lustral water; § 399] and an offering for its purification, and which needs no more than ritual immersion and the setting of the sun. As a general rule

אֶפְשָׁר לְעוֹלָם לַעֲלוֹת מִשּׁוּם טֻמְאָה כִּי־אִם בִּטְבִילָה; וְאֵי זוֹ טֻמְאָה צְרִיכָה שִׁבְעָה
יָמִים לְטָהֳרָתָהּ, וְאֵיזוֹ יַסְפִּיק לָהּ יוֹם אֶחָד; וְיֶתֶר רֻבֵּי פִרְטֵי עִנְיָנִים אֵלֶּה, אֲשֶׁר
רַבּוּ לְמַעְלָה, יִתְבָּאֲרוּ כֻלָּם בְּסֵדֶר טָהֳרוֹת.

וְנוֹהֶגֶת בְּכֹהֲנִים בִּזְמַן הַבַּיִת. וְכֹל הָעוֹבֵר עָלֶיהָ וְעָבַד בְּטֻמְאָה, חַיָּב מִיתָה
בִּידֵי שָׁמַיִם.

[שֶׁלֹּא יֹאכַל כֹּהֵן טָמֵא תְּרוּמָה]

רעט שֶׁלֹּא יֹאכַל כֹּהֵן טָמֵא תְּרוּמָה, שֶׁנֶּאֱמַר: אִישׁ אִישׁ מִזֶּרַע אַהֲרֹן וְכוּלֵי
בַקֳּדָשִׁים לֹא יֹאכַל עַד אֲשֶׁר יִטְהָר; וְאָמְרִינָן בְּמַסֶּכֶת מַכּוֹת: אַזְהָרָה לִתְרוּמָה
מִנַּיִן, כְּלוֹמַר שֶׁלֹּא יֹאכְלֶנָּה טָמֵא — שֶׁנֶּאֱמַר: אִישׁ אִישׁ וְגוֹמֵר, אֵי זֶהוּ דָבָר
שֶׁהוּא שָׁוֶה בְזַרְעוֹ שֶׁל אַהֲרֹן, כְּלוֹמַר שֶׁיֹּאכְלֵהוּ הַזֶּרַע כֻּלּוֹ, זְכָרִים וּנְקֵבוֹת, הֱוֵי
אוֹמֵר זוֹ תְרוּמָה.

וְנִכְפְּלָה הָאַזְהָרָה בָּזֶה הָעִנְיָן, כְּמוֹ שֶׁכָּתוּב: וְשָׁמְרוּ אֶת מִשְׁמַרְתִּי, וּכְמוֹ
שֶׁאָמְרוּ בְסַנְהֶדְרִין פֶּרֶק תְּשִׁיעִי גַּבֵּי מְחֻיָּבֵי מִיתָה בִּידֵי שָׁמַיִם, שֶׁיִּלְמְדוּ שָׁם טָמֵא
הָאוֹכֵל תְּרוּמָה מִ"וְשָׁמְרוּ אֶת מִשְׁמַרְתִּי וְלֹא יִשְׂאוּ עָלָיו חֵטְא".

מִשָּׁרְשֵׁי הַמִּצְוָה, לְהַגְדִּיל וּלְיַקֵּר בְּלֵב כָּל אָדָם כָּל אֲשֶׁר בַּקֹּדֶשׁ, וּכְבָר זָכַרְתִּי
כַּמָּה פְעָמִים רַבּוֹת הַתּוֹעֶלֶת הַנִּמְצָא לָנוּ בַּדָּבָר; וּמַעֲלוֹת הַקֹּדֶשׁ לְאָכְלוֹ בְּטָהֳרָה,
יָדוּעַ.

מִדִּינֵי הַמִּצְוָה, מַה שֶּׁאָמְרוּ זִכְרוֹנָם לִבְרָכָה שֶׁכֹּהֵן טָמֵא שֶׁאָכַל תְּרוּמָה
טְהוֹרָה, הוּא בְמִיתָה וְלוֹקֶה עָלֶיהָ; אֲבָל אָכַל תְּרוּמָה טְמֵאָה, אַף־עַל־פִּי שֶׁהוּא
בְלָאו, אֵינוֹ לוֹקֶה, לְפִי שֶׁאֵינָהּ קֹדֶשׁ.

וּמַה שֶּׁאָמְרוּ שֶׁהַטְּמֵאִים אוֹכְלִים בִּתְרוּמָה בְּהֶעֱרֵב הַשֶּׁמֶשׁ וְיֵרָאוּ בָרָקִיעַ

§278   1. As our author goes on to state, the details of the laws are "very many" indeed, and it is not feasible to give references for those given in this paragraph, beyond the Mishnah order of Tohoroth, which he mentions below (MY).

§279   1. For meat from offerings of major holiness might be eaten by the male *kohanim* alone.
    2. Not to eat *t'rumah* while ritually impure (Rashi on the verse).
    3. And the verse concludes: *and die thereby if they profane it.*
    4. TB Sanhedrin 83a; MT *hilchoth t'rumoth* vii 1. (The death mentioned below means at Heaven's hands, as our author noted two paragraphs above.)
    5. TB B'rachoth 2a, Shabbath 35b; MT *ibid.* 2.

for the subject, it is never possible to emerge from any defilement without ritual immersion. [Then we have the law on] which ritual uncleanness requires seven days for its purification, and for which one day is enough.[1] [These] and the rest of the very many details of these matters, which are more than numerous, are all clarified in the Mishnah order of *Tohoroth*.

It applies to the *kohanim* when the Temple is extant. If a *kohen* violated ît and served in ritual uncleanness, he would be punishable by death at Heaven's hands.

[THAT A RITUALLY UNCLEAN KOHEN IS FORBIDDEN TO EAT T'RUMAH]

279 that a ritually impure *kohen* should not eat *t'rumah* [the *kohen's* portion of produce]: for it is stated, *Everyone of the progeny of Aaron . . . shall not eat of the holy things until he is clean* (Leviticus 22:4); and it was taught in the Talmud tractate *Makkoth* (14b): Where do we learn an admonition about *t'rumah*—i.e. that one should not eat it while ritually impure?—Scripture states, *Everyone of the progeny of Aaron,* etc. What entity is there that applies equally among the progeny (descendants) of Aaron?—i.e. which all the progeny eat, both the males and the females?—we have to say, *t'rumah.*[1]

The admonition about this matter was repeated: for it is written, *They shall therefore keep My charge* (Leviticus 22:9), and as it was taught in chapter 9 of the tractate *Sanhedrin* (83a), about those who incur death at Heaven's hands, the Sages there infer this [penalty] for a defiled [*kohen*] who eats *t'rumah* from the verse, *They shall therefore keep My charge,*[2] *and not bear sin for it*[3] (ibid.).

At the root of the precept lies the aim to make great and dear in the heart of every man all that there is in holiness. I have previously mentioned many times the useful benefit that results for us in the matter. And it is known that it is among the high levels of holiness to eat it [*t'rumah*] in ritual purity.

Among the laws of the precept, there is what the Sages of blessed memory taught:[4] that if a defiled *kohen* eats ritually pure *t'rumah*, he incurs death and receives whiplashes for it; but if he [thus] ate defiled *t'rumah*, even though it is forbidden by an injunction, he receives no whiplashes, because it was not hallowed.

Then there is what they said,[5] that defiled [*kohanim*] are to eat

t'rumah when the sun goes down and they see three medium-sized

שְׁלֹשָׁה כּוֹכָבִים בֵּינוֹנִיּוֹת, וְזֶה הָעֵת הוּא כְּמוֹ שְׁלִישׁ שָׁעָה אַחַר שְׁקִיעַת הַחַמָּה; וּמַה שֶּׁאָמְרוּ זִכְרוֹנָם לִבְרָכָה בְּמִי שֶׁהָיָה אוֹכֵל תְּרוּמָה וְהִרְגִּישׁ שֶׁנִּזְדַּעְזְעוּ אֵיבָרָיו לְהוֹצִיא שִׁכְבַת זֶרַע, וּמַה שֶּׁאָמְרוּ בְּרוֹכְבֵי גְמַלִּים; וּמַה שֶּׁאָמְרוּ בִּתְרוּמַת חוּצָה לָאָרֶץ שֶׁהִיא מֻתֶּרֶת לְכֹהֵן שֶׁאֵין שֶׁמָּא טֻמְאָה יוֹצֵאָה עָלָיו מִגּוּפוֹ, כְּגוֹן קָטָן שֶׁלֹּא רָאָה קֶרִי וּקְטַנָּה שֶׁלֹּא פֵּרְסָה נִדָּה; וּמַה שֶּׁאָמְרוּ שֶׁכָּל עַמֵּי הָאָרֶץ בְּחֶזְקַת טֻמְאָה הֵן, וְעַל־כֵּן אֵין נוֹתְנִין הַתְּרוּמָה אֶלָּא לְכֹהֲנִים הַיּוֹדְעִים לְשָׁמְרָהּ בְּטָהֳרָה. וְדִינֵי הַטֻּמְאוֹת זָכַרְתִּי לְמַעְלָה גַּם־כֵּן קִצְתָן בִּכְלָל וּבִפְרָט.

וְנוֹהֶגֶת בְּכֹהֲנִים בִּזְכָרִים וּנְקֵבוֹת, בָּאָרֶץ וּבִזְמַן שֶׁהִיא בְּיִשּׁוּבָהּ, כִּי אָז שָׁם חַיּוּב הַתְּרוּמָה דְּאוֹרַיְתָא כְּדַעַת הָרַמְבַּ״ם זִכְרוֹנוֹ לִבְרָכָה. וְעוֹבֵר עַל זֶה וְאָכַל תְּרוּמָה בְּמֵזִיד וְהוּא טָמֵא, חַיָּב מִיתָה בִּידֵי שָׁמַיִם, וּכְמוֹ שֶׁנִּזְכַּר בְּסַנְהֶדְרִין פֶּרֶק תְּשִׁיעִי, שֶׁמָּנוּ שָׁם מְחַיְּבֵי מִיתָה וּמִכְּלָלָם מָנוּ כֹהֵן טָמֵא שֶׁאָכַל תְּרוּמָה. וּבִזְמַן הַזֶּה אָסוּר דְּרַבָּנָן בְּפֵרוֹת אֶרֶץ יִשְׂרָאֵל.

[שֶׁלֹּא יֹאכַל שׁוּם זָר תְּרוּמָה]

רפ שֶׁלֹּא יֹאכַל שׁוּם זָר תְּרוּמָה, שֶׁנֶּאֱמַר: וְכָל זָר לֹא יֹאכַל קֹדֶשׁ, וּבָא הַפֵּרוּשׁ הַמְקֻבָּל שֶׁזֶּה הַקֹּדֶשׁ הוּא הַתְּרוּמָה לְבַד וְכָל מַה שֶּׁנִּקְרָא תְּרוּמָה, אֲבָל לֹא בָא לְהַזְהִיר בְּכָאן עַל קָדָשִׁים אֲחֵרִים. וּמַהוּ שֶׁנִּקְרָא תְּרוּמָה גַּם־כֵּן, אֵלּוּ הַבִּכּוּרִים; וּכְמוֹ שֶׁדָּרְשׁוּ זִכְרוֹנָם לִבְרָכָה מִן הַקַּבָּלָה: "וּתְרוּמַת יָדְךָ", אֵלּוּ הַבִּכּוּרִים.

מִשָּׁרְשֵׁי הַמִּצְוָה, בַּמִּצְוָה הַקּוֹדֶמֶת. וּמִמַּעֲלוֹת הַקֹּדֶשׁ שֶׁיֹּאכְלוּהָ מְשָׁרְתֵי הַשֵּׁם וּנְשֵׁיהֶם וּבְנֵיהֶם וַעֲבָדֵיהֶם אֲשֶׁר קָנוּ לָהֶם, וְיִתְּנוּהָ לִבְהֶמְתָּם וּלְכָל חַיָּתָם, וְלֹא לַאֲחֵרִים.

---

6. So R. Moses of Coucy, *Séfer Mitzvoth Gadol, bilchoth t'rumoth,* negative precept § 257. (The *kohen* is also required to have undergone ritual immersion during the day: Leviticus 22:6–7; Sifra, *'emor, perek* 4, 7; TB Yevamoth 74b).

7. TB Niddah 40a; MT *ibid.* 4.

8. Ibid. 14a (see Rashi); MT *ibid.* 6.

9. TB B'choroth 27a; MT *ibid.* 8.

10. MT *ibid.* 9.

11. TB Ḥullin 130b; MT *ibid.* vi 2.

12. MT *ibid.* i 26.

§280   1. TB P'saḥim 23a, etc.

2. The name is also applied to "*t'rumah* of the tithe," given by Levites from their share (tithe) of the produce of Israelites; *ḥallah* (the *kohen*'s portion of dough or bread); and *bikkurim* (first-fruits; see the next sentence); MT *bilchoth t'rumoth* xv 2.

3. TB P'saḥim 36b, etc.

stars in the sky—this time being about a third of an hour after sunset.[6] We have, further, what the Sages of blessed memory said about one who was eating t'rumah and his limbs quivered to emit semen;[7] and what they said about camel-riders;[8] then, what they taught about t'rumah abroad, outside the land [of Israel][9]—that it is permitted a kohen whose source of defilement does not originate for him from his own body—for instance, a young boy who experienced no pollution, and a young girl who did not begin her menses.[10] [Going further, we have] what they taught:[11] that all ignoramuses are firmly assumed to be in a state of ritual uncleanness, and therefore t'rumah is to be given only kohanim who know how to keep it in ritual purity. I also mentioned some laws of ritual uncleanness above (§159), both generally and in detail.

It applies to kohanim, both male and female, in the land [of Israel], at the time it is in its inhabited, settled state; for then there is the obligation of t'rumah by the law of the Torah, in the view of Rambam of blessed memory.[12] If someone violated this and deliberately ate t'rumah while defiled, he would be punishable by death at Heaven's hands—as it is mentioned in chapter 9 of Sanhedrin (83a), where those who deserve [such] death are listed, and among them is included a ritually unclean kohen who ate t'rumah. At the present time there is a prohibition by the ruling of the Sages on the produce of the land of Israel.

[THAT ANY AND EVERY NON-KOHEN IS FORBIDDEN TO EAT T'RUMAH]

280 that no outsider [non-kohen] whatever should eat t'rumah: for it is stated, *And no outsider shall eat of a holy thing* (Leviticus 22:10); and the interpretation received [in the Oral Tradition] was given[1] that this "holy thing" means solely t'rumah and whatever [else] is called t'rumah;[2] but Scripture did not come here to adjure about other holy things. Now, "whatever is called t'rumah" means also bikkurim, first-fruits; as the Sages of blessed memory interpreted by the Oral Tradition:[3] *nor the t'rumah (heave-offering) of your hand* (Deuteronomy 12:17)—this denotes the first-fruits.

The precept's root purpose is given in the previous precept (§279). It is one of the high favors of holiness that the ministering servants of the Lord should eat it, along with their wives and children, and their [non-Jewish] slaves whom they bought for themselves, and they should

מִדִּינֵי הַמִּצְוָה, מַה שֶּׁאָמְרוּ זִכְרוֹנָם לִבְרָכָה שֶׁעֶבֶד כֹּהֵן שֶׁבָּרַח אוֹכֵל בִּתְרוּמָה,
דְּקִנְיַן כַּסְפּוֹ הוּא מִכָּל-מָקוֹם; וְכֵן אֵשֶׁת כֹּהֵן שֶׁמָּרְדָה הֲרֵי הִיא אוֹכֶלֶת, וְכָל אֵשֶׁת
כֹּהֵן אוֹכֶלֶת, אֲפִלּוּ הִיא בַת ג׳ שָׁנִים וְיוֹם אֶחָד; וְגַם הָאֲרוּסָה לוֹ הָיְתָה רְאוּיָה
לֶאֱכֹל, אֶלָּא שֶׁחֲכָמִים גָּזְרוּ שֶׁלֹּא תֹאכַל עַד שֶׁתִּנָּשֵׂא, כְּמוֹ שֶׁבָּא בְּרֵישׁ פֶּרֶק
(קמא) [ה׳] דִּכְתֻבּוֹת.

עֶבֶד עִבְרִי שֶׁל כֹּהֵן אֵינוֹ אוֹכֵל, שֶׁהֲרֵי אָסְרָה הַתּוֹרָה שְׂכִיר עוֹלָם וּשְׂכִיר
שָׁנִים, כְּמוֹ שֶׁכָּתוּב: תּוֹשָׁב כֹּהֵן וְשָׂכִיר לֹא יֹאכַל קֹדֶשׁ; אֲבָל עֶבֶד כְּנַעֲנִי אוֹכֵל,
דְּקִנְיַן כַּסְפּוֹ הוּא; וְגַם אִם קָנָה הָעֶבֶד עֲבָדִים, גַּם הֵם אוֹכְלִים עַל-יָדוֹ, מִשּׁוּם
דִּכְתִיב "כִּי יִקְנֶה נֶפֶשׁ קִנְיָן", שֶׁיֵּשׁ בְּמַשְׁמָע שֶׁהַנֶּפֶשׁ יַעֲשֶׂה קִנְיָן; אֲבָל אִם הָעֶבֶד
הַשֵּׁנִי קָנָה שְׁלִישִׁי אֵינוֹ אוֹכֵל, דְּכִי יִקְנֶה הַנֶּפֶשׁ "קִנְיָן" אָמַר רַחֲמָנָא, וְלֹא "קִנְיַן
הַקִּנְיָן."

וְכָל כֹּהֶנֶת שֶׁנִּבְעֲלָה לִפְסוּלֵי כְהֻנָּה אֲסוּרָה לֶאֱכֹל בִּתְרוּמָה לְעוֹלָם; וְגַם
אַנְדְּרוֹגִינוֹס גַּם-כֵּן בֵּין שֶׁנִּבְעַל דֶּרֶךְ זִכְרוּתוֹ אוֹ דֶּרֶךְ נַקְבוּתוֹ; וְאַף מָשׁוּךְ, וְהוּא מִי
שֶׁנִּמְשְׁכָה עָרְלָתוֹ עַד שֶׁנִּרְאָה כְּאִלּוּ לֹא מָל, אָסוּר לֶאֱכֹל מִדְּרַבָּנָן עַד שֶׁיִּמּוֹל פַּעַם
שְׁנִיָּה; וְיֶתֶר פְּרָטֶיהָ רַבִּים, יִתְבָּאֲרוּ בְּמַסֶּכֶת תְּרוּמוֹת.

וְנוֹהֵג אִסּוּר אֲכִילַת הַתְּרוּמָה לְזָרִים בְּכָל יִשְׂרָאֵל, זְכָרִים וּנְקֵבוֹת, בְּכָל מָקוֹם
שֶׁיֵּשׁ שָׁם תְּרוּמָה דְּאוֹרַיְתָא, דְּהַיְנוּ בִּזְמַן שֶׁאֶרֶץ יִשְׂרָאֵל בְּיִשּׁוּבָהּ, כִּי אָז חִיּוּב
הַתְּרוּמָה דְּאוֹרַיְתָא, כְּמוֹ שֶׁנִּכְתָּב בְּסֵדֶר שׁוֹפְטִים עֲשֵׂה ו׳ [סִי׳ תק״ז], בְּעֶזְרַת
הַשֵּׁם. וּבַזְּמַן הַזֶּה נוֹהֵג אֲסוּרָהּ מִדְּרַבָּנָן בְּפֵרוֹת אֶרֶץ-יִשְׂרָאֵל, כְּמוֹ שֶׁנִּכְתָּב שָׁם.

וְעוֹבֵר עַל זֶה וְאָכַל תְּרוּמָה וְהוּא זָר, כְּגוֹן יִשְׂרָאֵל שֶׁהוּא זָר, אוֹ אֲפִלּוּ כֹּהֵן אוֹ

---

4. TB Gittin 12b.

5. TB Niddah 44b.

6. For fear that she may receive a cup of wine that is *t'rumah* in her father's house, from her betrothed man's family, and she will give her brothers and sisters some. (On betrothal, see § 202, note 2.)

7. I.e. a Hebrew slave who chooses to remain with his master after the usual six years of servitude. Scripture states, *he shall serve him for ever* (or, *for life*; Exodus 21:6), but he goes free at the jubilee (Mechilta, based on Leviticus 25:10).

8. I.e. an ordinary Hebrew slave, since his servitude lasts only six years (Exodus 21:2); TB Yevamoth 70a.

9. Literal translation; understood to mean the Hebrew slave described in note 7 (*ibid.*).

10. Because the Hebrew for "if he buys a soul, the purchase," taken by itself, out of context, could also mean, "if the soul buys a purchase" (see next sentence); TB Yevamoth 66a.

11. TB Yevamoth 68a, etc.

12. MT *hilchoth t'rumoth* vii 16 (see *Kessef Mishneh*).

13. TB Yevamoth 72a.

give it to their domestic beasts and all their livestock, but not to others.

Among the laws of the precept, there is what the Sages of blessed memory said:[4] that if a *kohen*'s slave fled, he may eat *t'rumah*, because in any event he is "the purchase of his money" (Leviticus 22:11); so too, if a *kohen*'s wife ran away, she may eat it. Every wife of a *kohen* may eat it, even if she is but three years and a day in age.[5] Anyone betrothed to him should be equally entitled to eat of it, but the Sages decreed that she should not eat until she is married to him[6]—as this is conveyed at the beginning of the (first) [fifth] chapter of the Talmud tractate *K'thuboth* (57b).

The Hebrew servant of a *kohen* does not eat it: for you see, the Torah forbade a person hired for life[7] and one hired for [a few] years,[8] as it is written: *a settler*[9] *of a* kohen *or a hired servant*[8] *shall not eat of a holy thing* (Leviticus 22:10). A heathen slave, however, does eat it, as he is "the purchase of his money" (*ibid.* 11). Even if the slave purchased slaves, they too eat [*t'rumah*] with him; for it is written, [*But a* kohen,] *if he buys a soul, the purchase* [*of his money*] (*ibid.*)—which carries the implication that the "soul" can make a purchase [in turn].[10] However, if the second servant bought a third, he does not eat it: for the merciful God said, "if the soul buys a purchase," and not "if the purchase buys a purchase."

Any woman *kohen* (*koheneth*) who was conjugally intimate with someone disqualified as a *kohen*, is forbidden to eat *t'rumah* forever after;[11] so too a hermaphrodite, whether he was thus intimate by way of his maleness or his femaleness.[12] So also one with drawn skin, i.e. whose prepuce was stretched until he appears as if uncircumcised—he is forbidden to eat it by the decree of the Sages, until he undergoes circumcision a second time.[13] Its many remaining details are elucidated in the Mishnah tractate *T'rumoth*.

The prohibition on outsiders' eating *t'rumah* applies to all Jews, both men and women, wherever there is *t'rumah* by the law of the Torah—which means at the time that the land of Israel is in its settled, inhabited state, for then the obligation of *t'rumah* prevails by Torah law, as we will write in *sidrah shof'tim*, in the sixth positive precept (§507), with the Eternal Lord's help. At the present time, its ban is in effect, by the decree of the Sages, on the produce of the land of Israel, as we will write there.

If someone transgressed this and ate *t'rumah* though he was an outsider—for instance, an Israelite [non-*kohen*], who is an outsider,

כֹּהֶנֶת שֶׁנִּתְחַלְּלוּ מִן הַכְּהֻנָּה בְּאֶחָד מִמִּינֵי הַחִלּוּל הַיְדוּעִים שֶׁהוֹרוּנוּ חֲכָמִים זִכְרוֹנָם לִבְרָכָה, חַיָּב מִיתָה בִּידֵי שָׁמַיִם, כְּמוֹ שֶׁבָּא בְּסַנְהֶדְרִין פֶּרֶק תְּשִׁיעִי, מִדִּכְתִיב "וּמֵתוּ בוֹ כִּי יְחַלְּלֻהוּ", וְאַחֲרָיו "וְכָל זָר לֹא יֹאכַל קֹדֶשׁ".

[שֶׁלֹּא יֹאכַל תּוֹשַׁב כֹּהֵן וְשָׂכִיר תְּרוּמָה]

רפא שֶׁלֹּא יֹאכַל תּוֹשַׁב כֹּהֵן וּשְׂכִירוֹ תְּרוּמָה, שֶׁנֶּאֱמַר: תּוֹשַׁב כֹּהֵן וְשָׂכִיר לֹא יֹאכַל קֹדֶשׁ.

שֹׁרֶשׁ הַמִּצְוָה וְכָל עִנְיָנָהּ נִכְלָל בַּמִּצְוָה הַקּוֹדֶמֶת, כִּי טַעַם אִסּוּרָן מִפְּנֵי שֶׁנֶּחְשְׁבוּ כְּמוֹ זָר, אַחַר שֶׁאֵינָן קִנְיַן כַּסְפּוֹ, כִּי הַתּוֹשַׁב הוּא שְׂכִיר עוֹלָם, וְהַשָּׂכִיר הוּא שְׂכִיר שָׁנִים.

[שֶׁלֹּא יֹאכַל עָרֵל תְּרוּמָה]

רפב שֶׁלֹּא יֹאכַל עָרֵל תְּרוּמָה, כְּלוֹמַר כֹּהֵן שֶׁלֹּא נִמּוֹל, בֵּין שֶׁהוּא מֵזִיד אוֹ שׁוֹגֵג אוֹ אָנוּס, וּכְגוֹן שֶׁמֵּתוּ אֶחָיו מֵחֲמַת מִילָה, שֶׁיִּרְאַת הַמָּוֶת מְנָעַתּוּ מִלָּמוֹל — בְּכָל עִנְיָן שֶׁיִּהְיֶה, מִכֵּיוָן שֶׁהוּא עָרֵל אָסוּר לֶאֱכֹל בַּתְּרוּמָה; וְהוּא הַדִּין שֶׁאָסוּר בִּשְׁאָר קָדָשִׁים.

וּמְנִיעָה זוֹ לֹא נִתְבָּאֲרָה בַּכָּתוּב, אֲבָל נִלְמְדָה בִּגְזֵרָה שָׁוָה. וְכָתַב הַמַּעְתִּיק בְּשֵׁם הָרַמְבַּ"ם זִכְרוֹנוֹ לִבְרָכָה: וּבֵאֲרוּ הַמְקַבְּלִים עִם זֶה שֶׁזֶּה הָאִסּוּר הוּא מִדְּאוֹרַיְתָא, לֹא מִדְּרַבָּנָן; וּלְשׁוֹן יְבָמוֹת: מִנַּיִן לְעָרֵל שֶׁאֵינוֹ אוֹכֵל תְּרוּמָה, נֶאֱמַר "תּוֹשָׁב וְשָׂכִיר" בַּפֶּסַח וְנֶאֱמַר "תּוֹשָׁב וְשָׂכִיר" בַּתְּרוּמָה, מַה "תּוֹשָׁב וְשָׂכִיר"

---

§281   1. See §280, note 7.

     2. See §280, note 8.

     3. See §280, notes 8–9.

     4. Hence these two are not his property, part of his domicile and domain, like a heathen slave or livestock (see §280, second paragraph). So TB Yevamoth 70a (see §280, note 8).

§282   1. So Rashi to TB Yevamoth 70a, s.v. *he'orél*.

     2. ShM negative precept §135. Our author refers to "the translator" because Rambam wrote the work in Arabic, and it was later rendered into Hebrew. The standard edition was translated by R. Moses ibn Tibbon; our author's version, both here and in other quotations, differs slightly, and would seem to be from the translation of R. Abraham b. Ḥisdai, mentioned by R. Moses ibn Tibbon in his introduction as having been made from a first version by Rambam.

     3. See §281, last sentence.

     4. Respectively, Exodus 12:45 and Leviticus 22:10.

or even a man or woman *kohen* who became profaned (disqualified) from functioning as a *kohen* in one of the known ways of profanation of which the Sages of blessed memory informed us—he incurs death at Heaven's hands, as we read in chapter 9 of the tractate *Sanhedrin* (83b): since it is written, *and they shall die thereby if they profane it* (Leviticus 22:9), and [immediately] afterward, *an outsider shall not eat of a holy thing* (ibid. 10).

[THAT NEITHER A PERMANENT NOR A TEMPORARY HEBREW SLAVE OF A KOHEN IS TO EAT T'RUMAH]

281 that a *kohen*'s "settler" [Hebrew slave till the jubilee][1] or his "hired worker" [ordinary Hebrew slave][2] is not to eat *t'rumah*: for it is stated, *a settler of a* kohen *or a hired servant shall not eat of a holy thing*[3] (Leviticus 22:10).

The root purpose of the precept and its subject-matter are included in the preceding *mitzvah* (§280): because the reason why they are forbidden is that they are reckoned as outsiders, since they are not "the purchase of his money" (ibid. 11); for the "settler" is [in effect] a worker hired forever [until the jubilee],[1] while the "hired servant" is one hired for a number of years.[4]

[THAT AN UNCIRCUMCISED PERSON IS FORBIDDEN TO EAT T'RUMAH]

282 that an uncircumcised person should not eat *t'rumah*, i.e. a *kohen* who was not circumcised, whether he [lives thus] deliberately, inadvertently, or under compulsion—for example, if his brothers died on account of circumcision, so that the fear of death has restrained him from being circumcised.[1] However it may be, since he is uncircumcised, he is forbidden to eat *t'rumah*; and it is equally the law that he is forbidden to eat any other holy food.

Now, this restriction is not made clear in the Writ, but we learn it by a *g'zérah shavah* [identical terms in two verses]. The translator wrote in the name of Rambam of blessed memory:[2] Those who received [the Oral Tradition] clarified about this that this prohibition is by Torah law, and not by the ruling of the Sages. In the language of the tractate *Yevamoth* (70a): How do we learn that an uncircumcised person is not to eat *t'rumah*?—"a settler" and "a hired servant"[3] are mentioned in regard to the Passover offering and in regard to *t'rumah*.[4] Just as when "a settler" and "a hired servant" are mentioned

הָאָמוּר בַּפֶּסַח עָרֵל אָסוּר בּוֹ, אַף "תּוֹשָׁב וְשָׂכִיר" הָאָמוּר בִּתְרוּמָה עָרֵל אָסוּר
בָּהּ; וְהוּא הַדִּין לִשְׁאָר קָדָשִׁים. וְזֶה כְמוֹ־כֵן לְשׁוֹן סִפְרָא, וְשָׁם נֶאֱמַר: רַבִּי עֲקִיבָה
אוֹמֵר: "אִישׁ אִישׁ", לְרַבּוֹת אֶת הֶעָרֵל; וְשָׁם נִתְבָּאֵר, כְּלוֹמַר בַּגְּמָרָא יְבָמוֹת,
שֶׁדִּבֶּר תּוֹרָה מָשׁוּךְ אוֹכֵל בִּתְרוּמָה, וּמִדִּבְרֵיהֶם גָּזְרוּ עָלָיו מִפְּנֵי שֶׁנִּרְאָה כְּעָרֵל;
וּמָשׁוּךְ הוּא שֶׁנִּמְשְׁכָה הָעָרְלָה בְּעִנְיָן שֶׁנִּרְאָה כְּמִי שֶׁאֵינוֹ מָהוּל אַחַר שֶׁנִּמּוֹל. הִנֵּה
כְבָר הִתְבָּאֵר לְךָ שֶׁעָרֵל אָסוּר בִּתְרוּמָה מִן הַתּוֹרָה, וְהַמָּשׁוּךְ אָסוּר מִדְּרַבָּנָן, וְהָבֵן
זֶה. וְשָׁם נֶאֱמַר: מָשׁוּךְ צָרִיךְ שֶׁיִּמּוֹל מִדְּרַבָּנָן. עַד כָּאן.

וּלְפִי הַדּוֹמֶה, כָּל אֲרִיכוּת דְּבָרָיו כָּאן הוּא מִפְּנֵי שֶׁכָּתַב בָּעִקָּר הַשֵּׁנִי מִסְּפֶר
הַמִּצְוֹת שֶׁאֵין כָּל מַה שֶׁיִּלָּמֵד בְּאַחַת מִי"ג מִדּוֹת שֶׁהַתּוֹרָה נִדְרֶשֶׁת בָּהֶן אוֹ בְּרִבּוּי
רָאוּי לִמְנוֹתוֹ בְּמִנְיָן הַמִּצְוֹת, וְהִנֵּה הַגְּזֵרָה שָׁנָה אַחַת מִי"ג מִדּוֹת הִיא, וְהִנֵּה הוּא
בְּעַצְמוֹ יִמְנֶה אִסּוּר הֶעָרֵל בִּתְרוּמָה בְּאַחַת, וְאַף־עַל־פִּי שֶׁהוּא נִלְמַד כֵּן. וְלָכֵן
יִתְנַצֵּל בְּאָמְרוֹ כִּי הַמְקַבְּלִים בֵּאֲרוּ שֶׁזֶּה הָאָסוּר מִדְּאוֹרַיְתָא, לֹא מִדְּרַבָּנָן. וְנִרְאֶה
כִּי כַוָּנָתוֹ לוֹמַר שֶׁכָּל זְמַן שֶׁיְּבָאֲרוּ חֲכָמִים זִכְרוֹנָם לִבְרָכָה בְּפֵרוּשׁ שֶׁהָעִנְיָן
מִדְּאוֹרַיְתָא, נִמְנֶה אוֹתוֹ לְמִצְוָה, וְאַף־עַל־פִּי שֶׁהוּא נִלְמַד בְּאַחַת מִן הַמִּדּוֹת, אַחַר
שֶׁחֲכָמִים יָעִידוּ עַל הַדָּבָר שֶׁהוּא דְּאוֹרַיְתָא.

וְאִם לֹא שֶׁרָאוּי לְהִזָּהֵר מְאֹד בְּגַחֶלֶת הָרַב וְאֵירָא, הָיִיתִי אוֹמֵר כִּי מְדֻחָק גָּדוֹל
נִכְנַס לְזֹאת הַפִּשְׁרָה; וּכְבָר תָּפַשׁ עָלָיו בָּזֶה הָרַמְבַּ"ן זִכְרוֹנוֹ לִבְרָכָה בְּסֵפֶר
הַמִּצְוֹת שֶׁלּוֹ בָּעִקָּר הַשֵּׁנִי וְהִרְבָּה עָלָיו רְאָיוֹת מִדִּבְרֵי הַגְּמָרָא וּמִן הַמִּדְרָשׁוֹת,
כַּמָּה רַבּוּ הַדְּבָרִים, עַד שֶׁלֹּא יְכִילוּם שִׁבְעָה דַּפִּין גְּדוֹלִים. וְסוֹף דָּבָר אָמַר הָרַב,

5. As stated in Exodus 12:48.
6. The Hebrew for "every one" means literally "a man, a man"; hence the repetition can be considered superfluous, so that we may derive from it something further to be included in the application of the law.
7. Our author echoes here Mishnah, 'Aboth ii 10, about relating to masters of the Torah: "and beware of their glowing embers."

about the Passover offering, an uncircumcised person is forbidden it,[5] so too when "a settler" and "a hired servant" are mentioned concerning *t'rumah*, an uncircumcised person is forbidden it; and the law is the same in regard to other hallowed food. This is likewise the expression of the Midrash *Sifra*; and there it is stated: R. Akiva said: "Every one" (Leviticus 22:4)—to include an uncircumcised person. [6] It was also elucidated there (i.e. in the tractate *Yevamoth*) that by the law of the Torah, one with drawn skin may eat *t'rumah*, but by their ruling the Sages decreed it forbidden to him, because he appears uncircumcised. "One with drawn skin" denotes that the prepuce was stretched so that after he underwent circumcision he yet appears as an uncircumcised person. Thus it has now been made clear to you that an uncircumcised person is forbidden *t'rumah* by Torah law, and one with drawn skin by the ruling of the Sages; so understand it. And it was said there: One with drawn skin has to be circumcised by the law of the Sages. Thus far his words.

As it would seem, the entire lengthy flow of his words here is because he wrote in the second root principle of the *Book of Precepts* that whatever is derived by one of the thirteen rules by which the Torah is interpreted, or through an amplifying term, it is not proper to list it in the count of the *mitzvoth*; yet the *g'zérah shavah* [identical terms in two verses] is one of the thirteen rules, and still he himself counts the ban on *t'rumah* for an uncircumcised person as one [precept], even though it is so derived. Therefore he excuses himself by saying that those who received the Oral Tradition explained that this forbiddance is by Torah law and not by the ruling of the Sages. Apparently it was his intention to convey that as long as the Sages of blessed memory distinctly explain that a certain matter is by the law of the Torah, we count it as a precept, even though it is derived by one of the rules of interpretation, since the Sages attest about the matter that it is by Torah law.

Now, if not for the fact that it is well to beware greatly of the glowing embers of the master teacher [Rambam][7] and I am fearful, I would say that it is with a very forced approach that he entered into this way of resolution. In the past, Ramban of blessed memory disputed him about this in his *Book of Precepts*, in the second root principle, and he amassed proofs about it from the words of the Talmud and from the Midrashim. The discussion multiplied so greatly, until seven large folio sheets would not contain it. In summary, the master

כִּי סֵפֶר מִצְווֹת הָרַמְבַּ״ם זִכְרוֹנוֹ לִבְרָכָה לְבָרְכָה עִנְיָנָיו מַמְתַּקִּים וְכֻלּוֹ מַחֲמַדִּים מִלְּבַד הָעִקָּר הַזֶּה, שֶׁהוּא עוֹקֵר הָרִים.

מִשָּׁרְשֵׁי הַמִּצְוָה, לְפִי שֶׁהֶעָרֵל כְּמוֹ זָר נֶחְשָׁב, אַחַר שֶׁלֹּא נִכְנַס עִם יִשְׂרָאֵל בִּבְרִית הַמִּילָה, שֶׁהוּא עִנְיָן גָּדוֹל; וְהַרְחָקַת זָר מִן הַתְּרוּמָה וְהַטְּמֵאִים מִן הַקֹּדֶשׁ שֹׁרֶשׁ אֶחָד לָהֶם, וְכָתוּב לְמַעְלָה סָמוּךְ.

וְנוֹהֶגֶת בַּכֹּהֲנִים בְּכָל מָקוֹם שֶׁיֵּשׁ שָׁם תְּרוּמָה דְּאוֹרַיְתָא, כְּמוֹ שֶׁאָמַרְנוּ בַּמִּצְוָה הַקּוֹדֶמֶת. וּמִי שֶׁעָבַר עַל זֶה וְאָכַל תְּרוּמָה, בֵּין טְהוֹרָה בֵּין טְמֵאָה, וְהוּא עָרֵל, חַיָּב מַלְקוֹת.

[שֶׁלֹּא תֹאכַל חֲלָלָה מִן הַקֹּדֶשׁ]

רפג שֶׁלֹּא תֹאכַל הַחֲלָלָה מִן הַקֹּדֶשׁ, כְּלוֹמַר מִן הַתְּרוּמָה וְחָזֶה וְשׁוֹק, שֶׁרְאוּיוֹת בְּנוֹת אַהֲרֹן הַכְּשֵׁרוֹת לְאָכְלָן, שֶׁנֶּאֱמַר: וּבַת כֹּהֵן כִּי תִהְיֶה לְאִישׁ זָר הִיא בִּתְרוּמַת הַקֳּדָשִׁים לֹא תֹאכֵל; וְאָמְרִינָן בִּגְמָרָא יְבָמוֹת: ״כִּי תִהְיֶה לְאִישׁ זָר״, כְּגוֹן שֶׁנִּבְעֲלָה לְפָסוּל לָהּ, שֶׁפְּסָלָהּ מִן הַכְּהֻנָּה. וּמֵאֲשֶׁר כָּתוּב ״בִּתְרוּמַת הַקֳּדָשִׁים״, אָמְרוּ זִכְרוֹנָם לִבְרָכָה: בְּמוּרָם מִן הַקֳּדָשִׁים לֹא תֹאכֵל, כְּלוֹמַר חָזֶה וְשׁוֹק. וְשָׁם נֶאֱמַר: לִכְתוֹב קְרָא ״בַּקֳּדָשִׁים לֹא תֹאכֵל״, מַאי בִּתְרוּמַת הַקֳּדָשִׁים, שְׁמַעַתְּ מִנַּהּ תַּרְתֵּי: חֲדָא שֶׁהִיא כְּשֶׁנִּבְעֲלָה לְפָסוּל נִפְסְלָה מִלֶּאֱכֹל בִּתְרוּמָה וְחָזֶה וְשׁוֹק; וְעוֹד אַחֶרֶת, שֶׁהִיא כְּשֶׁתִּהְיֶה נְשׂוּאָה לְזָר וּמֵת בַּעְלָהּ, שֶׁחוֹזֶרֶת לֶאֱכֹל בִּתְרוּמָה וְאֵינָהּ חוֹזֶרֶת לְחָזֶה וְשׁוֹק.

וְנִמְצָא שֶׁיִּהְיֶה בִּכְלַל זֶה הַלָּאו אַזְהָרַת הַחֲלָלָה מִלֶּאֱכֹל הַקֹּדֶשׁ, וְאַזְהָרַת כֹּהֶנֶת שֶׁנִּשֵּׂאת לְזָר שֶׁלֹּא תֹאכַל חָזֶה וְשׁוֹק אַף־עַל־פִּי שֶׁמֵּת בַּעְלָהּ אוֹ גֵרְשָׁהּ, מַה שֶּׁלֹּא

---

8. I.e. it runs seriously counter to discussions and conclusions in the Talmud (Ramban, commentary to ShM root principle 2, end).

§283   1. The standard portion for the *kohen* from every *sh'lamim* (peace-offering): Leviticus 7:31–32.

2. TB Yevamoth 68b.

3. The term *t'rumah* literally means "lifting up" or that which is lifted up.

4. The paragraph is based on ShM negative precept §137.

[Ramban] stated that the *Book of Precepts* · by Rambam of blessed memory is sweet in its subject-matter and is all delights, except for this *root* principle, which up*roots* mountains. [8]

At the root of the precept lies the reason that an uncircumcised person is reckoned as an outsider (§280), since he did not enter (join) the Israelite (Jewish) people by the covenant of circumcision, which is a matter of great significance. And for the removal of the outsider from *t'rumah* and of the ritually unclean from holy food, there is one root reason, which was recently written above (§314).

It applies to *kohanim* wherever there is *t'rumah* by the law of the Torah, as we said in the previous precept (§281). If someone transgressed this and ate *t'rumah*, whether it was ritually clean or defiled, while he was uncircumcised, he would be punishable by whiplashes.

[THAT A PROFANED WOMAN IS FORBIDDEN TO EAT HALLOWED FOOD]

283 that a profaned woman should not eat of holy food, i.e. of *t'rumah* and the breast and thigh [of animal offerings],[1] which the daughters of Aaron of acceptable rank are fit to eat: for it is stated, *And if a* kohen's *daughter shall be to an outsider, she shall not eat of the* t'rumah *(separated part) of holy things* (Leviticus 22:12); and it was taught in the Talmud tractate *Yevamoth* (68b): "if she shall be to an outsider"—for instance, if she was conjugally intimate with someone who is disqualified (unacceptable) for her, he disqualifies her from her status of *kohen*. As for Scripture's expression, "of the *t'rumah* (separated part) of holy things," our Sages of blessed memory said[2] it means, "what is lifted off[3] from holy offerings, she shall not eat"—i.e. the breast and thigh. Then it was said there: But let Scripture [merely] write, then, "of holy things she shall not eat"; why "of the *t'rumah* of holy things"?—You can learn two things from it: one, that when she is conjugally intimate with a disqualified man, she is disqualified to eat *t'rumah* and the breast and thigh; and another thing, that if she should be married to an outsider and her husband dies, she returns to eating *t'rumah*, but does not revert to eating the breast and thigh.[4]

Thus we find that included in this negative precept is an injunction to a profaned woman against eating any holy food, and an injunction to a woman *kohen* (*koheneth*) who married an outsider that she should not eat the breast and thigh [from offerings][1] even if her husband died or divorced her—which is not the ruling for *t'rumah*: for if a

נָדִין כֵּן בִּתְרוּמָה, שֶׁכֹּהֶנֶת שֶׁנִּשֵּׂאת לְזָר וּמֵת בַּעֲלָהּ, חוֹזֶרֶת הִיא לֶאֱכֹל בִּתְרוּמָה.

וּמַשְׁמָעוּת הַכָּתוּב כֵּן: כִּי תִהְיֶה לְאִישׁ זָר בִּתְרוּמַת הַקֳּדָשִׁים לֹא תֹאכֵל, כְּלוֹמַר כְּשֶׁתִּבָּעֵל לְאִישׁ זָר, כְּלוֹמַר שֶׁהוּא פָּסוּל לָהּ, וְזֶהוּ זָרוּתוֹ, לֹא תֹאכֵל בִּתְרוּמַת הַקֳּדָשִׁים, דְּהַיְנוּ תְּרוּמָה וְחָזֶה וְשׁוֹק, כְּדִפָרִישִׁית; וְעוֹד יֵשׁ גַּם־כֵּן בְּמַשְׁמָעוּת הַכָּתוּב "כִּי תִהְיֶה לְאִישׁ זָר" לְמִי שֶׁאֵינוֹ כֹהֵן; וְכֵן כָּתַב רַשִׁ"י זִכְרוֹנוֹ לִבְרָכָה: לְאִישׁ זָר, לֵוִי אוֹ יִשְׂרָאֵל, כְּלוֹמַר שֶׁהוּא זָר מִן הַכְּהֻנָּה, בִּתְרוּמַת הַקֳּדָשִׁים אֵינָהּ אוֹכֶלֶת בְּעֵת הֱיוֹתָהּ לוֹ; אֲבָל אַחַר מוֹתוֹ אוֹ שֶׁגֵּרְשָׁהּ, שֶׁהִיא אוֹכֶלֶת בִּתְרוּמַת הַקֳּדָשִׁים, שֶׁהֲרֵי יָצְאָת מִתַּחַת יְדֵי הַזָּר; לֹא תֹאכַל בְּחָזֶה וְשׁוֹק, דְּמִכֵּיוָן שֶׁנִּשֵּׂאת לְזָר נִפְסְלָה בְחָזֶה וְשׁוֹק לְעוֹלָם.

וְאוּלָם תֵּדַע כִּי אִסּוּר אֲכִילַת כֹּהֶנֶת בִּתְרוּמָה בְּעוֹדָהּ תַּחַת בַּעֲלָהּ יִשְׂרָאֵל, לֹא לְמַדְנוּהוּ מִזֶּה הַכָּתוּב כְּלָל, שֶׁלֹּא בָא עָלָיו הַפֵּרוּשׁ לִדְרֹשׁ בּוֹ כָּךְ אֶלָּא מַה שֶׁכָּתַבְנוּ, אֲבָל זֶה הָאִסּוּר לְמָדוּהוּ חֲכָמִים זִכְרוֹנָם לִבְרָכָה בַּעֲלֵי הַקַּבָּלָה מִמָּקוֹם אַחֵר, מִדִּכְתִיב "וְכָל זָר לֹא יֹאכַל קֹדֶשׁ", שֶׁבָּא עָלָיו הַפֵּרוּשׁ שֶׁכָּל זְמַן שֶׁהָאִשָּׁה תַּחַת בַּעֲלָהּ, דְּהַיְנוּ בַּעֲלָהּ הַיִּשְׂרָאֵל, שֶׁהוּא זָר מִן הַכְּהֻנָּה, לֹא תֹאכַל קֹדֶשׁ, כִּי אֵשֶׁת הַזָּר נֶחְשֶׁבֶת כְּזָר: הֲרֵי הִיא כְּמוֹ אַחַת מִצַּלְעוֹתָיו. וְדַע זֶה וְקַבְּלֵהוּ, כִּי־כֵן הָאֱמֶת הַמְקֻבָּל.

וְנוֹהֶגֶת מִצְוָה זוֹ בְּכָל מָקוֹם וּבְכָל זְמַן שֶׁיֵּשׁ שָׁם תְּרוּמָה דְאוֹרַיְתָא, כְּמוֹ שֶׁאָמַרְנוּ בַּמִּצְווֹת הַקּוֹדְמוֹת. עָבְרָה הַכֹּהֶנֶת וְאָכְלָה תְּרוּמָה אוֹ חָזֶה וְשׁוֹק וְהִיא חֲלָלָה, כְּלוֹמַר שֶׁנִּבְעֲלָה לְמִי שֶׁפּוֹסְלָהּ מִן הַכְּהֻנָּה, וְכֵן אִם עָבְרָה וְאָכְלָה חָזֶה וְשׁוֹק אַחַר שֶׁמֵּת בַּעֲלָהּ הַיִּשְׂרָאֵל אוֹ נִתְגָּרְשָׁה מִמֶּנּוּ, וְכֵן אִם עָבְרָה וְאָכְלָה תְּרוּמָה אוֹ חָזֶה וְשׁוֹק בְּעוֹדָהּ תַּחַת בַּעֲלָהּ הַיִּשְׂרָאֵל, בְּכָל צְדָדִין אֵלּוּ חַיֶּבֶת מַלְקוֹת.

---

5. This is an alternative meaning of 'ish zar ("an outsider").

6. In his commentary, on the verse (Leviticus 22:12).

7. TB Yevamoth 68b.

8. Based on Genesis 2:21–23, that Eve was formed and developed from one of Adam's ribs; cf. also TB Kiddushin 2b, explaining why a man courts a woman and not vice versa: It can be compared to a man who lost something.... The one who suffered the loss goes about looking for the lost object. (The paragraph is based on ShM negative precept §137.)

koheneth married an outsider and her husband died, she reverts to eating *t'rumah.*

Then the meaning of the verse will be this: "if she shall be to an outsider, she shall not eat of the *t'rumah* (separated part) of holy things"; in other words, if she will be conjugally intimate with a strange, alien man,[5] i.e. who is disqualified, unacceptable for her, this being his strangeness, she is not to eat of the "*t'rumah* of holy things"—meaning *t'rumah* and the breast and thigh, as it was explained. Then there also lies in the meaning of the verse, "if she shall be to an outsider," i.e. to one who is not a *kohen*; so Rashi of blessed memory wrote:[6] "an outsider"—a Levite or an Israelite; in other words, he is outside the realm of the *kohen*; then "she shall not eat of the *t'rumah* of holy things" while she is with him; but after his death, or if he divorces her, whereupon she may eat "the *t'rumah* of holy things," she is not to eat the breast and thigh; for once she was married to an outsider, she became disqualified for the breast and thigh forever.

You should know, however, that as to the prohibition on a *koheneth* not to eat *t'rumah* while she is with her Israelite [non-*kohen*] husband, we do not derive it from this verse at all: for the explanation was not given about it [in the Oral Tradition] to interpret it so, but only what we have written. This forbiddance, however, the Sages of blessed memory, masters of the Oral Tradition, learned from another place[7]—because it is written, *And no outsider shall eat of a holy thing* (Leviticus 22:10), for which the interpretation was given that as long as the woman is with her husband—i.e., her Israelite husband, who is an outsider to the realm of the *kohen*, she is not to eat holy food: for the wife of an outsider is ranked as an outsider; she is as one of his ribs.[8] Know this and accept it, for this is the traditionally accepted truth.

This precept is in effect in every place and every time where there is *t'rumah* by the law of the Torah, as we said about the preceding *mitzvoth.* If a *koheneth* transgressed and ate *t'rumah* or breast and thigh although she was profaned, which means that she had been conjugally intimate with someone who disqualified her from the status of *kohen*; and so likewise if she transgressed and ate of breast and thigh after her Israelite husband died or she was divorced from him; and so too if she transgressed and ate *t'rumah* or breast and thigh while living with her Israelite husband—in all these instances, she would deserve whip-

〈241〉 lashes.

[שֶׁלֹּא לֶאֱכֹל טֶבֶל]

רפד שֶׁלֹּא לֶאֱכֹל טֶבֶל, בֵּין יִשְׂרָאֵל בֵּין כֹּהֵן, וְהוּא הַדָּבָר שֶׁלֹּא נִטְלָה מִמֶּנּוּ
תְּרוּמָה וּמַעַשְׂרוֹת, שֶׁנֶּאֱמַר: וְלֹא יְחַלְּלוּ אֶת קָדְשֵׁי בְּנֵי יִשְׂרָאֵל אֵת אֲשֶׁר יָרִימוּ
לַיי, וּבָא הַפֵּרוּשׁ הַמְקֻבָּל עַל זֶה שֶׁבָּאוֹכֵל טֶבֶל הַכָּתוּב מְדַבֵּר.

וְעִנְיַן הַכָּתוּב לוֹמַר שֶׁלֹּא יְחַלְּלוּ הַקֳּדָשִׁים בְּעוֹדָן מְעֹרָבִין עִם הַחֻלִּין, וְזֶהוּ
לְשׁוֹן "אֵת אֲשֶׁר יָרִימוּ" שֶׁהוּא לְשׁוֹן עָתִיד, כְּלוֹמַר שֶׁעֲדַיִן לֹא הֵרִימוּ. וְכֵן הוּא
בִּגְמָרָא סַנְהֶדְרִין: מִנַּיִן לְאוֹכֵל טֶבֶל שֶׁהוּא בְּמִיתָה, שֶׁנֶּאֱמַר: וְלֹא יְחַלְּלוּ אֶת קָדְשֵׁי
בְּנֵי יִשְׂרָאֵל אֵת אֲשֶׁר יָרִימוּ לַיי — בַּעֲתִידִים לְהָרִים הַכָּתוּב מְדַבֵּר, וְיָלִיף חִלּוּל
חִלּוּל מִתְּרוּמָה, שֶׁכָּתוּב עָלֶיהָ: וְאֶת קָדְשֵׁי בְּנֵי יִשְׂרָאֵל לֹא תְחַלְּלוּ וְלֹא תָמוּתוּ,
וְהִיא בְּמִיתָה, כְּמוֹ שֶׁכָּתַבְנוּ לְמַעְלָה, מִדִּכְתִיב: וּמֵתוּ בוֹ כִּי יְחַלְּלוּהוּ, וּסְמִיךְ לֵיהּ:
וְכָל זָר לֹא יֹאכַל קֹדֶשׁ.

וְעוֹד אָמְרוּ זִכְרוֹנָם לִבְרָכָה בַּגְּמָרָא מַכּוֹת בְּעִנְיָן זֶה: יָכוֹל לֹא יְהוּ חַיָּבִין אֶלָּא
עַל הַטֶּבֶל שֶׁלֹּא הוּרַם מִמֶּנּוּ כָּל-עִקָּר, אֲבָל נִטְלָה מִמֶּנּוּ תְּרוּמָה גְדוֹלָה וְלֹא נִטְלָה
מִמֶּנּוּ תְּרוּמַת מַעֲשֵׂר אוֹ מַעֲשֵׂר רִאשׁוֹן אוֹ מַעֲשֵׂר שֵׁנִי, וַאֲפִלּוּ מַעְשַׂר עָנִי, מִנַּיִן,
כְּלוֹמַר מִנַּיִן שֶׁיִּהְיֶה בַּדָּבָר חִיּוּב — תַּלְמוּד לוֹמַר: לֹא תוּכַל לֶאֱכֹל בִּשְׁעָרֶיךָ,
וּלְהַלָּן הוּא אוֹמֵר: וְאָכְלוּ בִשְׁעָרֶיךָ וְשָׂבֵעוּ; מַה לְּהַלָּן מַעְשַׂר עָנִי אַף כָּאן מַעְשַׂר
עָנִי, וְאָמַר רַחֲמָנָא "לֹא תוּכַל".

אָמְנָם זֶה הַחִיּוּב הוּא לְמַלְקוֹת, אֲבָל עֲווֹן מִיתָה אֵינוֹ אֶלָּא עַל הַטֶּבֶל שֶׁלֹּא
נִטְלָה מִמֶּנּוּ תְּרוּמָה גְדוֹלָה, וְכֵן נַמִּי בְּאוֹכֵל מַעֲשֵׂר קֹדֶם שֶׁנִּטְלָה מִמֶּנּוּ תְּרוּמַת

§284   1. TB Sanhedrin 83a.

2. The standard Talmudic term for regular *t'rumah*, the portion taken from produce to be given a *kohen*, which he is obligated to eat in ritual purity.

3. Another portion for the *kohen*, given by a Levite out of the "first tithe" that he received; it had to be one tenth, "a tithe of a tithe" (Numbers 18:26).

4. So TB Makkoth 16b, and MT *hilchoth ma'achaloth 'asuroth* x 20.

[NOT TO EAT TEVEL—PRODUCE FROM WHICH T'RUMAH
AND THE TITHES WERE NOT SEPARATED]

284 not to eat *tevel*, either an Israelite [non-*kohen*] or a *kohen*, this being anything from which *t'rumah* and the tithes have not been separated: for it is stated, *And they shall not profane the holy things of the people of Israel, which they will lift off to the Lord* (Leviticus 22:15); and the traditional interpretation was given about it[1] that the verse refers to one who eats *tevel*.

Now, the purpose of the verse is to convey that holy food should not be profaned while it is yet mixed with non-holy food. This is the sense of the phrase, "which they will lift off": it is in the future tense; i.e. it did not have its holy portions lifted off and separated as yet. And so we read in the Talmud tractate *Sanhedrin* (83a): How do we learn that if someone eats *tevel* [produce from which *t'rumah* and the tithes were not separated] he incurs death?—because it is stated, *And they shall not profane the holy things of the people of Israel, which they will lift off to the Lord*: The verse speaks of that which has yet to have its holy portions taken off; and we learn [the penalty of death] from *t'rumah*, through the identical verbs of profanation: for about it [*t'rumah*] it is written, *and you shall not profane the holy things of the people of Israel, so that you shall not die* (Numbers 18:32). It is punishable by death [at Heaven's hand], as we have written above (§280), since it is written, *and they shall die thereby if they profane it* (Leviticus 22:9), and directly after it, *no outsider shall eat of a holy thing* (ibid. 10).

Our Sages of blessed memory taught further in the tractate *Makkoth* (16b) on this subject: I might think that this penalty would be incurred only over *tevel* from which nothing whatever was lifted off; but if the major *t'rumah*[2] was taken from it while the *t'rumah* of tithe,[3] First Tithe, the Second Tithe, or even the tithe for the poor was not separated, how do we know? In other words, how do we learn that this matter too imposes the guilt?—Scripture states, *You may not eat within your gates* (Deuteronomy 12:17), and further on it says, *that they may eat within your gates and be satisfied* (ibid.26:12); just as the second verse refers to the tithe for the poor, so here too it connotes the tithe for the poor—and the merciful God said, "You may not."

This guilt, however, incurs a whipping of lashes;[4] but guilt deserving death is incurred only with *tevel* from which the major *t'rumah* was not separated; and likewise if someone eats of the tithe before *t'rumah* of the tithe was separated from it. Such is the sense of what was stated

מַעֲשֵׂר, וְזֶהוּ שֶׁנֶּאֱמַר בְּצַוָּאַת הַלְוִיִּים כְּשֶׁנָּם לְהוֹצִיא מַעֲשֵׂר מִן הַמַּעֲשֵׂר "וְאֶת קׇדְשֵׁי בְנֵי יִשְׂרָאֵל לֹא תְחַלְּלוּ וְלֹא תָמוּתוּ", שֶׁזּוֹ הִיא מְנִיעָה שֶׁלֹּא לֶאֱכֹל מַעֲשֵׂר רִאשׁוֹן בְּטׇבְלוֹ; כֵּן פֵּרְשׁוּהוּ זִכְרוֹנָם לִבְרָכָה; וּלְפִיכָךְ חַיָּבִין עָלָיו מִיתָה, כְּמוֹ שֶׁנִּתְבָּאֵר בְּמַסֶּכֶת דְּמַאי.

נִמְצָא מִכְּלַל דְּבָרֵינוּ שֶׁהָאוֹכֵל הַטֶּבֶל קֹדֶם שֶׁנִּטְּלָה מִמֶּנּוּ תְּרוּמָה גְּדוֹלָה, וּכְמוֹ כֵן קֹדֶם שֶׁנִּטְּלָה מִמֶּנּוּ תְּרוּמַת מַעֲשֵׂר, הוּא בְמִיתָה; וְאִם אָכַל מִמֶּנּוּ אַחַר שֶׁנִּטַּל מִמֶּנּוּ הַתְּרוּמָה גְּדוֹלָה וְנִטַּל מִמֶּנּוּ תְּרוּמַת מַעֲשֵׂר, וּכְגוֹן שֶׁהִקְדִּים לִטֹּל תְּרוּמַת מַעֲשֵׂר קֹדֶם מַעֲשֵׂר, אַף־עַל־פִּי שֶׁעֲדַיִן הוּא טָבוּל לִשְׁנֵי הַמַּעַשְׂרוֹת, דְּהַיְנוּ מַעֲשֵׂר רִאשׁוֹן וְשֵׁנִי, אוֹ מַעֲשֵׂר עָנִי, אֵינוֹ בְחִיּוּב מִיתָה, אֲבָל הוּא בְחִיּוּב מַלְקוּת, וְכֵן כָּל זְמַן שֶׁהוּא טָבוּל אֲפִלּוּ לְאֶחָד מִן הַמַּעַשְׂרוֹת, בְּמַלְקוּת. וְאַזְהָרוֹתֶיהָ מִ"לֹּא תוּכַל לֶאֱכֹל בִּשְׁעָרֶיךָ" וְגוֹמֵר, וּכְמוֹ שֶׁנִּכְתָּב לְמַטָּה בְּסֵדֶר רְאֵה. וּשְׁמֹר עִנְיָן זֶה, כִּי כֵן תִּמְצָא הָאֱמֶת אִם תִּזְכֶּה לִלְמֹד דִּבְרֵי חֲכָמֵינוּ בַּעֲלֵי הַקַּבָּלָה זִכְרוֹנָם לִבְרָכָה.

מִשָּׁרְשֵׁי הַמִּצְוָה, מַה שֶּׁכָּתַבְתִּי לְמַעְלָה. סָמוּךְ בְּלָאו דְּכֹהֵן טָמֵא, בְּאַזְהָרַת י"ד [סִי' רע"ט].

מִדִּינֵי הַמִּצְוָה, מַה שֶּׁאָמְרוּ זִכְרוֹנָם לִבְרָכָה בְּאִסּוּר הַטֶּבֶל שֶׁאוֹסֵר שֶׁאֶפְשָׁר תַּעֲרׇבְתּוֹ בְּכָל שֶׁהוּא, מַה שֶּׁאֵינוֹ כֵן בִּשְׁאָר אִסּוּרִין שֶׁבַּתּוֹרָה, חוּץ מִיַּיִן נֶסֶךְ וְחָמֵץ בְּפֶסַח, כְּמוֹ שֶׁכָּתַבְתִּי בִּמְקוֹמוֹ. וְנָתְנוּ טַעַם בְּטֶבֶל, מִפְּנֵי שֶׁאִסּוּרוֹ כְּמוֹ הֶתֵּרוֹ: מַה הֶתֵּרוֹ בְּכׇל־שֶׁהוּא, כְּמוֹ שֶׁאָמְרוּ זִכְרוֹנָם לִבְרָכָה, שֶׁאֵין לַתְּרוּמָה שִׁעוּר מִן הַתּוֹרָה אֶלָּא אֲפִלּוּ חִטָּה אַחַת פּוֹטֶרֶת כְּרִי גָּדוֹל שֶׁל חִטִּים, אַף אִסּוּרוֹ כְּמוֹ־כֵן, בְּכָל־שֶׁהוּא; וְנִמְצָא שֶׁאִם נִתְעָרְבוּ מְעַט חִטִּים שֶׁל טֶבֶל בְּכַמָּה שֶׁל חֻלִּין, שֶׁכֻּלָּן אֲסוּרִין.

וּבְסֵדֶר זְרָעִים וּבְמַסֶּכֶת תְּרוּמוֹת וּמַעֲשֵׂר וּמַעַשְׂרוֹת שֵׁנִי וּמַעַשְׂרוֹת יִתְבָּאֵר אֵי זֶה דָבָר

---

5. I.e. with the *t'rumah* of the tithe not yet taken out.

6. TB Yevamoth 86a.

7. I.e. it is evident from teachings in the Mishnah tractate, although not stated there directly; Rambam, however, writes this explicitly at the beginning of his commentary to *D'mai*; and like our author, he gives this reference in ShM negative precept §153, on which this and the previous paragraph are based.

8. Instead of *be'az-harath yod da-leth* ("in the fourteenth negative precept") three of the oldest manuscripts have *bit'rumah yod da-leth* ("with *t'rumah*, the fourteenth"). Very possibly the original reading was *bit'rumah be'az-harath yod da-leth*, i.e. "about a defiled *kohen* with *t'rumah*, in the fourteenth negative precept."

9. I.e. if any amount of *tevel* becomes mixed into other food, the entire lot becomes forbidden. TB 'Avodah Zarah 73b.

10. TB Ḥullin 137b.

in the command to the Levites, when He bade them separate a tithe of the tithe, *and you shall not profane the holy things of the people of Israel, so that you shall not die* (Numbers 18:32); for this is an admonition not to eat the First Tithe when it is in its state of *tevel*.[5] So the Sages of blessed memory interpreted it;[6] and therefore it is punishable by death, as it is elucidated in the Mishnah tractate *D'mai*.[7]

What emerges from the sum of our words is that if a person eats *tevel* before the major *t'rumah* was taken from it, and likewise before the *t'rumah* of the tithe was taken from it, it is punishable by death [at Heaven's hand]. If he ate of it after he took from it the major *t'rumah* and likewise separated from it the *t'rumah* of the tithe—for instance, if he hastened to take off the *t'rumah* of the tithe before the tithe itself—then although it is yet *tevel* in respect of the two tithes, i.e. the First Tithe along with the Second, or with the tithe for the poor, it does not involve a death penalty; but it does entail a whipping of lashes. And so too, as long as it is *tevel* in respect of even one of the tithes, lashes are given. The admonition about these matters derives from the verse, *You may not eat within your gates*, etc. (Deuteronomy 12:17), as we will write below, in *sidrah r'éh*. Keep this theme in mind, for so will you find the truth to be, if you merit to learn the words of our Sages, the masters of the Oral Tradition, of blessed memory.

At the root of the precept lies the reason that I wrote shortly above, at the injunction about a defiled *kohen*, in the fourteenth negative precept[8] (§279).

Among the laws of the precept, there is what the Sages of blessed memory taught about the ban on *tevel*, that the forbiddance [caused by] its mixture is by any amount[9]—which is not the case with other foods prohibited by Torah law, except for wine of libation and *hametz* (leavened food) on Passover, as I wrote in its proper place (§111). Well, the Sages gave a reason [for this] in regard to *tevel*:[9] it is because its prohibition is like [equated to] its permissibility: Just as it becomes permissible through any amount [given as *t'rumah*]—as our Sages of blessed memory said,[10] there is no minimal amount for *t'rumah* by the law of the Torah, but rather, one ear of wheat can free a huge pile of wheat from the obligation—so is its prohibition by any amount. Consequently, if a small amount of *tevel* wheat was mixed into any amount of ordinary, non-holy wheat, the whole is forbidden.

In the Mishnah order *Z'ra'im*, tractates *T'rumoth, Ma'asér Sheni* and *Ma'as'roth*, it is explained what food has the obligation of *t'rumah*

חַיָּב בִּתְרוּמָה וּמַעַשְׂרוֹת וְהֵן טוֹבְלִין הַפֵּרוֹת, וְאֵי זֶה דָבָר פָּטוּר, וְאֵי זֶה דָבָר חַיָּב מִן הַתּוֹרָה וְאֵי זֶה מִדִּבְרֵי סוֹפְרִים. וְיֶתֶר מִשְׁפְּטֵי הַטֶּבֶל שָׁם, וּבִמְקוֹמוֹת מִן מַסֶּכֶת דְּמַאי.

וְנוֹהֵג אִסּוּר זֶה שֶׁל טֶבֶל בְּכָל יִשְׂרָאֵל, בְּזְכָרִים וּנְקֵבוֹת, וַאֲפִלּוּ בְּכֹהֲנִים וּלְוִיִּם, אַף-עַל-פִּי שֶׁהֵם הָאוֹכְלִין הַתְּרוּמוֹת, וַאֲפִלּוּ בְּדָגָן שֶׁלָּהֶם; וְכֵן נוֹהֵג הָאִסּוּר בְּכָל מָקוֹם, כְּלוֹמַר שֶׁאָסוּר לֶאֱכֹל שֶׁל הַטֶּבֶל שֶׁל פֵּרוֹת אֶרֶץ יִשְׂרָאֵל בְּכָל מָקוֹם; אֲבָל חִיּוּב תְּרוּמוֹת וּמַעַשְׂרוֹת מִן הַפֵּרוֹת יָדוּעַ הוּא שֶׁלֹּא חִיְּבַתְנוּ הַתּוֹרָה בָּהֶן אֶלָּא בְּאֶרֶץ יִשְׂרָאֵל וּבִזְמַן שֶׁיִּשְׂרָאֵל שָׁם, שֶׁנֶּאֱמַר בִּתְרוּמָה "כִּי תָבֹאוּ" וְדָרְשׁוּ זִכְרוֹנָם לִבְרָכָה: בִּיאַת כֻּלְּכֶם וְלֹא בִיאַת מִקְצַתְכֶם; כֵּן פָּסַק הָרַמְבַּ"ם זִכְרוֹנוֹ לִבְרָכָה. וּלְפִיכָךְ אֵין אִסּוּר הַטֶּבֶל מִדְּאוֹרָיְתָא אֶלָּא בְּפֵרוֹת אֶרֶץ יִשְׂרָאֵל, וּבְדָגָן תִּירוֹשׁ וְיִצְהָר דַּוְקָא, כְּמוֹ שֶׁנִּכְתַּב בְּמִצְוַת מַעֲשֵׂר בְּסֵדֶר "וַיִּקַּח קֹרַח" עֲשֵׂה ד' [סִי' שצ"ה].

וּכְבָר כָּתַבְתִּי קְצָת חִלּוּקִין בִּמְקוֹמוֹת שֶׁסָּבִיב אֶרֶץ יִשְׂרָאֵל לְעִנְיַן שְׁבִיעִית, בְּסֵדֶר "אִם כֶּסֶף תַּלְוֶה", מִצְוַת עֲשֵׂה ד' [מִשְׁפָּטִים סִי' פ"ד], וּתְחוּמֵי אֶרֶץ יִשְׂרָאֵל יְדוּעִים הֵם. וְעוֹד אֶכְתֹּב בְּאַרְכָּה כָּל עִנְיַן תְּרוּמוֹת וּמַעַשְׂרוֹת וְחִלּוּק הַמְּקוֹמוֹת וּמַה שֶּׁהוּא מִדְּאוֹרַיְתָא אוֹ מִדְּרַבָּנָן, בְּסֵדֶר שׁוֹפְטִים בְּמִצְוַת תְּרוּמָה עֲשֵׂה ו' [סִי' תק"ז], וְקָחֶנּוּ מִשָּׁם.

וְעוֹד אוֹדִיעֲךָ שָׁם מַחֲלֹקֶת הַמְּפָרְשִׁים בְּעִנְיַן תְּרוּמָה אִם הִיא מִדְּאוֹרַיְתָא אוֹ דְרַבָּנָן הַיּוֹם, אֲפִלּוּ בָּאָרֶץ. וּמִי שֶׁהוּא בְּמָקוֹם שֶׁיִּהְיֶה מִסְפָּק עָלָיו אִם הוּא מֵאֶרֶץ יִשְׂרָאֵל אִם לֹא, בִּזְמַן שֶׁהָאָרֶץ בְּיִשּׁוּבָהּ רָאוּי לְהַחֲמִיר בַּדָּבָר עַל-כָּל-פָּנִים, לְפִי שֶׁזֶּהוּ סְפֵקָא דְּאוֹרַיְתָא, וְקַיְמָא לָן סְפֵקָא דְּאוֹרַיְתָא לְחֻמְרָא; וּמִן הַדּוֹמֶה שֶׁחֲכָמִים זִכְרוֹנָם לִבְרָכָה הָיוּ מַחְמִירִין אֲפִלּוּ בְּפֵרוֹת שֶׁחִיּוּב הַמַּעֲשֵׂר שֶׁלָּהֶם

---

11. So MT *hilchoth ma'asér* i 3.

12. The Hebrew has Numbers 15:2, *When you shall come into the land* (while the verses are almost similar in the English, they differ appreciably in the original), and so also Rambam (note 14); but it is evidently an early scribal error, as it is verse 18 to which the interpretation which follows refers. (See MY for a detailed discussion.)

13. TB K'thuboth 25a.

14. MT *hilchoth ma'asér* i 26.

15. TB Bétzah 3b, etc.

〈246〉

and the tithes, so that it is the *tevel* of produce, and what food is free of obligation; what has the obligation by Torah law, and what by the decree of the Sages. The rest of the rules about *tevel* are there, and in certain places in the Mishnah tractate *D'mai*.

This prohibition of *tevel* applies to all Israelites, both man and woman, and even to *kohanim* and Levites, although they are the ones who eat the *t'rumah*, and this even in regard to their own grain.[11] So too, the prohibition applies everywhere: i.e. it is forbidden to eat anywhere the *tevel* of the produce of the land of Israel. However, as far as the obligation of *t'rumah* and tithes from produce is concerned, it is known that the Torah did not impose their duty on us anywhere else but in the land of Israel, and at the time that the Israelites (all Jewry) are there. For it is written concerning *t'rumah*, *When you come into the land* (Numbers 15:18),[12] and the Sages of blessed memory interpreted:[13] [it requires] the coming of all of you, and not the coming of some of you. And so Rambam of blessed memory ruled as law.[14] Therefore the prohibition of *tevel* by Torah law applies to nothing but produce of the land of Israel, and specifically to grain, wine and oil, as we will write in the *mitzvah* of the tithe, the fourth positive precept in *sidrah korah* (§395).

I wrote previously some differences [in law that apply] in the regions around the land of Israel, in regard to seventh-year produce — in *sidrah mishpatim*, §84—and the boundaries of the land of Israel are known. I will yet write at length of the entire matter of *t'rumah* and the tithes, the difference among the various regions, and what is by Torah law and what by the ruling of the Sages—in the *mitzvah* of *t'rumah*, the sixth positive precept in *sidrah shof'tim* (§507); so gather it from there.

There I will also inform you of the difference of opinion among the authorities regarding *t'rumah*, whether it is by Torah law or the Sages' decree today, even in the land [of Israel]. If a person lives in a region about which he is in doubt whether it is of the land of Israel or not, at a time when the land is in its settled, inhabited state, it would be proper for him to be stringent in the matter in any event: because it is a doubt in a matter of Torah law, and we have a standing rule:[15] any doubt about a matter of Torah law is decided stringently. It would seem, too, that the Sages of blessed memory were strict even about produce for which the obligation of tithes was by the decree of the Sages, in those locations where they were uncertain if they are of the

⟨247⟩

דְּרַבָּנָן, בַּמְּקוֹמוֹת הַמְסֻפָּקִים לָהֶם אִם הֵם מֵאֶרֶץ יִשְׂרָאֵל, וַאֲפִלּוּ אַחַר חֻרְבַּן הַבַּיִת, אַף־עַל־פִּי שֶׁאִסּוּר זֶה אֵינוֹ נוֹהֵג אֶלָּא בִּפְנֵי הַבַּיִת מִדְּאוֹרַיְתָא.

וְעוֹבֵר עַל זֶה וְאָכַל כְּזַיִת מִן הַטֶּבֶל שֶׁהַפְרִישׁוּ מִמֶּנּוּ תְּרוּמָה גְדוֹלָה, וְכֵן קֹדֶם שֶׁהַפְרִישׁוּ מִמֶּנּוּ תְּרוּמַת מַעֲשֵׂר, חַיָּב מִיתָה בִּידֵי שָׁמַיִם, וּכְמוֹ שֶׁאָמַרְנוּ לְמַעְלָה; וְאִם אָכַל כְּזַיִת טֶבֶל שֶׁנִּטְּלָה מִמֶּנּוּ תְּרוּמָה גְדוֹלָה וּתְרוּמַת מַעֲשֵׂר אֲבָל עֲדַיִן לֹא הִפְרִישׁוּ מִמֶּנּוּ מַעַשְׂרוֹת, וַאֲפִלּוּ לֹא נִשְׁאַר בּוֹ אֶלָּא מַעֲשֵׂר עָנִי, חַיָּב מַלְקוֹת.

וְאִם הוּא טֶבֶל שֶׁל דִּבְרֵיהֶם, כְּלוֹמַר דָּבָר שֶׁאֵין חִיּוּב הַתְּרוּמָה וְהַמַּעַשְׂרוֹת בּוֹ אֶלָּא מִדְּרַבָּנָן, כְּגוֹן כָּל שְׁאָר פֵּרוֹת חוּץ מִדָּגָן תִּירוֹשׁ וְיִצְהָר, וַאֲפִלּוּ בִּזְמַן שֶׁיִּשְׂרָאֵל בָּאָרֶץ, אוֹ אֲפִלּוּ דָגָן תִּירוֹשׁ וְיִצְהָר שֶׁל אֶרֶץ יִשְׂרָאֵל וּבַזְּמַן הַזֶּה, מַכִּין אוֹתוֹ מַכַּת מַרְדּוּת.

וּמַשְׁקִין הַיּוֹצְאִין מִפֵּרוֹת שֶׁהֵן טֶבֶל, אֲסוּרִין כְּמוֹתָן; וּמִכָּל־מָקוֹם, אַף־עַל־פִּי שֶׁהֵן אֲסוּרִין מִן הַתּוֹרָה, אֵין חִיּוּב הַמַּלְקוֹת עַל הַמַּשְׁקִין אֶלָּא עַל גּוּף הַפֵּרוֹת, חוּץ מִיַּיִן וְשֶׁמֶן, שֶׁלּוֹקִין עֲלֵיהֶן כְּדֶרֶךְ שֶׁלּוֹקִין עַל הַזֵּיתִים וְהָעֲנָבִים; וְהַטַּעַם לְפִי הַדּוֹמֶה מִפְּנֵי שֶׁעִקָּרָן שֶׁל אוֹתָן פֵּרוֹת לְמַשְׁקִין הוּא לַבְּרִיּוֹת.

[שֶׁלֹּא נַקְדִּישׁ בַּעֲלֵי מוּמִין לְהַקְרִיבָם לַמִּזְבֵּחַ]

רפה שֶׁלֹּא נַקְדִּישׁ בַּעֲלֵי מוּמִין לְהַקְרִיבָם לַמִּזְבֵּחַ; וְאַף־עַל־פִּי שֶׁלֹּא הִקְרִיבָם, בְּהֶקְדֵּשׁ לְבַד יֵשׁ אִסּוּר לָאו; וְעַל הַהֶקְדֵּשׁ לְבַד נֶאֱמַר "כֹּל אֲשֶׁר בּוֹ מוּם לֹא תַקְרִיבוּ", מִשּׁוּם בַּל תַּקְדִּישׁ.

מִשָּׁרְשֵׁי הַמִּצְוָה, מַה שֶּׁכָּתַבְנוּ לְמַעְלָה בְּלָאו י"ב [סִי' רע"ז] וּבַעֲשֵׂה ד' [סִי' רפ"ו].

וְדִינֵי הַמִּצְוָה, כְּלוֹמַר מַה הֵן הַמּוּמִין הַפּוֹסְלִין וְכַמָּה, כָּתַבְתִּי גַם־כֵּן קְצָת מִזֶּה לְמַעְלָה בְּלָאו י' [סִי' רע"ה], וְהַכֹּל בָּאֲרֻכָּה בְּמַסֶּכֶת בְּכוֹרוֹת.

וְנוֹהֶגֶת בְּכָל מָקוֹם וּבְכָל זְמַן, בִּזְכָרִים וּנְקֵבוֹת. וְכָל הָעוֹבֵר עָלֶיהָ וְהִקְדִּישׁ בַּעַל

---

16. Our author apparently derives this from TB Ḥullin 6b (MY).

17. The paragraph follows MT *hilchoth ma'achaloth 'asuroth* x 19–20.

18. *Ibid.* 21; see §24, note 14.

19. TB Ḥullin 120b.

20. MT *ibid.* 22, derived from Mishnah, T'rumoth xi 3 (*Kessef Mishneh*).

§285   1. So TB T'murah 6a.

2. As already noted, our author originally treated all positive precepts in each *sidrah* first; hence §286, the fourth positive precept in *sidrah 'emor*, occurred earlier. Our arrangement, that of the standard printed editions, follows the order of the verses.

land of Israel—and this even after the destruction of the Temple,[16] although this prohibition prevails only during the existence of the Temple by the law of the Torah.

If a person violates this and eats an olive's amount of *tevel* before the major *t'rumah* was separated from it, and so too before the *t'rumah* of the tithe was taken from it, he incurs death at Heaven's hands, as we said above. If he ate an olive's amount of *tevel* from which the major *t'rumah* and the *t'rumah* of the tithe were taken, but the tithes were not yet separated from it—even if nothing more than the tithe for the poor was left in it, he is punishable by whiplashes.[17]

If it is *tevel* by the Sages' decree, i.e. it is something for which the obligation of *t'rumah* and the tithes is only by the ruling of the Sages—for example, all other produce except grain, wine and oil, even at the time when the Israelites are in the land; or even grain, wine and oil of the land of Israel at the present time—he is whipped with lashes of disobedience.[18]

Liquids that issue from produce that is *tevel* are as forbidden as it.[19] Nevertheless, even though they are forbidden by Torah law, there is no penalty of whiplashes over the liquids (juice), but only over the actual produce—except for wine and oil, over which lashes are given just as for the olives and grapes.[20] The reason is apparently that the main purpose of those fruits, for people, is for the liquids.

[THE PROHIBITION OF CONSECRATING BLEMISHED ANIMALS FOR OFFERINGS]

285 that we should not consecrate blemished, defective creatures to offer them up on the altar. Even if they are not [actually] offered up, on the consecration alone there lies the prohibition of a negative precept; regarding consecration alone it is stated, *Whatever has a blemish, you shall not bring* (Leviticus 22:20), signifying that you shall not consecrate it.[1]

At the root of the precept lies the reason we wrote above, in the twelfth negative and fourth positive precepts (§§277, 286).[2] As for the laws of the precept, i.e. what the blemishes are that bring disqualification, and how many [there are], I have also written some of this above, in the tenth negative precept (§275). It is all presented at length in the Talmud tractate *B'choroth*.

It applies everywhere, at every time, for both man and woman.

Whoever transgresses it and consecrates a blemished animal, even

מוּם, וַאֲפִלּוּ בַזְּמַן הַזֶּה, עָבַר עַל לָאו זֶה. וּמִן הַנִּרְאֶה שֶׁלֹּא יִהְיֶה בָזֶה מַלְקוּת, לְפִי שֶׁאֵין בּוֹ מַעֲשֶׂה; אֲבָל רָאִיתִי הָרַמְבַּ״ם זִכְרוֹנוֹ לִבְרָכָה שֶׁכָּתַב שֶׁהַמַּקְדִּישׁ בַּעַל מוּם לוֹקֶה; וְאוּלַי יַעֲשֵׂהוּ כְמֵמִיר, שֶׁיֵּשׁ בּוֹ מַלְקוּת וְאַף־עַל־פִּי שֶׁאֵין בּוֹ מַעֲשֶׂה, שֶׁזֶּה הֶקְדֵּשׁ הוּא. וְאֵלָיו נִשְׁמַע וְתוֹרָה נְבַקֵּשׁ מִפִּיהוּ, כִּי מַלְאַךְ יְיָ צְבָאוֹת הוּא.

[מִצְוַת הַקָּרְבָּן לִהְיוֹת תָּמִים]

רפו שֶׁיִּהְיֶה כָל קָרְבָּן שֶׁנַּקְרִיבֵהוּ שָׁלֵם בְּמִינוֹ מִן הַמּוּמִין שֶׁבָּאוּ בַכָּתוּב וּמֵאוֹתָן שֶׁבָּאָה הַקַּבָּלָה עֲלֵיהֶם שֶׁהֵם מוּמִין, וְהוּא מַה שֶּׁנֶּאֱמַר עַל זֶה: תָּמִים יִהְיֶה לְרָצוֹן; וְאָמְרוּ בְסִפְרָא: ״תָּמִים יִהְיֶה״, מִצְוַת עֲשֵׂה; וְהֵבִיאוּ רְאָיָה עַל הֱיוֹת הַנְּסָכִים וְסָלְתָּם וְשַׁמְנָם בְּתַכְלִית הַשְּׁלֵמוּת מֵהַהֶפְסֵד, מִדִּכְתִיב: תְּמִימִם יִהְיוּ לָכֶם וְנִסְכֵּיהֶם.

שֹׁרֶשׁ הַמִּצְוָה נִגְלֶה, עִם מַה שֶּׁהִקְדַּמְנוּ לְמַעְלָה בְּעִנְיַן הַקָּרְבָּנוֹת עַל צַד הַפְּשָׁט, שֶׁהֵם לְעוֹרֵר וּלְכַוֵּן מַחְשֶׁבֶת בְּנֵי־אִישׁ אֶל הַשֵּׁם בָּרוּךְ הוּא, כִּי הָאָדָם מִתְפַּעֵל בְּכֹחַ מַעֲשָׂיו; עַל־כֵּן רָאוּי עַל־כָּל־פָּנִים לִהְיוֹת הַקָּרְבָּן בְּלִי מוּם, כִּי מִזְמוֹת בֶּן־אָדָם לֹא יָנוּחוּ וְלֹא יִתְפַּשְּׁטוּ בַּמִּין הַפָּחוּת כְּמוֹ בֶחָשׁוּב, כִּי הַלְּבָבוֹת יִתְעוֹרְרוּ בֶחָשׁוּב וּבַשָּׁלֵם בְּמִינוֹ יוֹתֵר; וְזֶה דָבָר יָדוּעַ לְכָל מֵבִין.

מִדִּינֵי הַמִּצְוָה, הַמּוּמִין שֶׁמָּנוּ חֲכָמִים זִכְרוֹנָם לִבְרָכָה לִפְסוֹל בַּקָּרְבָּן, שֶׁהֵם ע״ג: חֲמִשִּׁים מֵהֶם הֵם בֵּין בְּאָדָם בֵּין בִּבְהֵמָה, וְהַכ״ג מְיֻחָדִין בִּבְהֵמָה וְאֵינָם רְאוּיִין לִהְיוֹת בְּאָדָם; וּכְמוֹ־כֵן יֵשׁ מוּמִין שֶׁהֵן מְיֻחָדִין בְּאָדָם שֶׁאֵינָם רְאוּיִים לִהְיוֹת בִּבְהֵמָה, וְהֵן תִּשְׁעִים, כְּמוֹ שֶׁנִּכְתַּב בְּסֵדֶר זֶה גַּבֵּי מוּמִין הַפּוֹסְלִין בַּכֹּהֵן.

---

3. Because an animal is consecrated merely by an utterance of words.

4. MT *hilchoth 'issuré ha-mizbe-ah* i 1.

5. I.e. both the original consecrated animal and the one he exchanges for it. Hence his words that the two should be exchanged have a major effect; they are not "mere words"; and for this reason he receives whiplashes. And thus Rambam could apply the same principle here.

§286 1. Sifra, *'emor, parashah* 7, 9.

2. So TB M'nahoth 87a and Sifré, Numbers §149, on the verse. (The paragraph is based on ShM positive precept §61).

3. See there, paragraphs 7–11. (Because the present precept is a positive one, in our author's original work it occurs before §275, which is negative—see §285, note 2; hence "as we will write").

at the present time, violates this negative precept. It would seem, though, that no whiplashes are given for it, since it involves no physical action.[3] Yet I have seen that Rambam of blessed memory wrote:[4] If a person consecrates a blemished animal, he is given whiplashes. Perhaps he equates this with exchanging consecrated animals (§351), which incurs a whipping even though no physical activity is involved, since both the one and the other become consecrated.[5] Let us heed him, *and seek the Torah from his mouth, for he is a messenger of the Lord of hosts* (Malachi 2:7).

[THAT AN ANIMAL OFFERING IS TO BE WHOLE, WITHOUT BLEMISH OR DISFIGUREMENT]

286 that every offering we bring should be whole, perfect in its species, free of the blemishes mentioned in Scripture, and of those designated in the Oral Tradition as blemishes. In this sense it is stated about it, *it shall be perfect to be accepted* (Leviticus 22:21); and it was taught in the Midrash *Sifra*:[1] "it shall be perfect"—this is a positive precept. And proof was [likewise] brought for the fact that the libations, flour and oil [brought with offerings] had to be utterly perfect, free of defect, since it is written, *they shall be for you without blemish, and their drink-offering* (Numbers 28:31).[2]

The root purpose of the precept is obvious, taken with what we have previously written, above, about offerings, by way of the plain meaning—that they are [intended] to arouse and focus the thought of human beings toward the Eternal Lord, blessed is He. For a man is influenced by the force of his actions. It is therefore fitting, under all circumstances, that an offering should be without blemish: because human reflection and meditation will not dwell and not develop about an inferior kind as they will about one with distinction. Hearts are bestirred the more by what is distinguished and perfect of its kind; this is something known (evident) to every person of understanding.

Among the laws of the precept, there are the defects which the Sages of blessed memory listed, that disqualify an offering, these being seventy-three in number: fifty of them apply to both man and animal, and twenty-three are unique to beasts, but do not occur in man. There are likewise defects unique to man, which do not occur in animals, these being ninety, as we will write in this *sidrah*, regarding blemishes that disqualify a *kohen* (§275).[3]

There is, further, the distinction that the Sages of blessed memory

וְכֵן מַה שֶּׁחִלְּקוּ זִכְרוֹנָם לִבְרָכָה בֵּין מוּם קָבוּעַ לְמוּם עוֹבֵר; וּמַה שֶּׁאָמְרוּ
שֶׁאֵין הַמּוּמִין פּוֹסְלִין בְּקָרְבַּן עוֹף, שֶׁלֹּא נֶאֱמַר בָּהֶן תָּמִים זָכָר; וּבַמֶּה דְבָרִים
אֲמוּרִים, בְּמוּמִין קְטַנִּים, אֲבָל עוֹף שֶׁיָּבֵשׁ גַּפּוֹ אוֹ נִסְמֵית עֵינוֹ אוֹ נִקְטְעָה רַגְלוֹ,
אָסוּר לְגַבֵּי הַמִּזְבֵּחַ; וְיֶתֶר פְּרָטֶיהָ, מְבֹאָרִים בְּפֶרֶק שְׁמִינִי מִמְּנָחוֹת.

וְנוֹהֶגֶת מִצְוָה זוֹ בִּזְמַן הַבַּיִת. וְעוֹבֵר עָלֶיהָ וְשָׁחַט אוֹ זָרַק הַדָּם אוֹ הִקְטִיר
הָאֵמוּרִין מִבְּהֵמָה בַּעֲלַת מוּם עַל הַמִּזְבֵּחַ, בִּטֵּל עֲשֵׂה זֶה, מִלְּבַד שֶׁעָבַר עַל לָאו,
וּכְמוֹ שֶׁנִּכְתֹּב בְּעֶזְרַת הַשֵּׁם. וְכָתַב הָרַמְבַּ"ם זִכְרוֹנוֹ לִבְרָכָה: נִמְצֵאתָ לָמֵד שֶׁאִם
הִקְדִּישׁ בַּעַל מוּם וּשְׁחָטוֹ וְזָרַק דָּמוֹ וְהִקְטִיר אֵמוּרָיו עַל הַמִּזְבֵּחַ, לוֹקֶה אַרְבַּע
מַלְקִיּוֹת. וְעַל מַה שֶּׁאָמַר שֶׁאִם הִקְדִּישׁ לוֹקֶה, צָרִיךְ תַּלְמוּד.

[שֶׁלֹּא נָתַן מוּם בַּקֳּדָשִׁים]

רפז שֶׁלֹּא נָתַן מוּם בַּקֳּדָשִׁים, כְּלוֹמַר שֶׁלֹּא נַעֲשֶׂה בִבְהֵמָה שֶׁהִיא קְדוֹשָׁה
לַמִּזְבֵּחַ שׁוּם חַבּוּרָה אוֹ שׁוּם שֶׁבֶר שֶׁיִּפְסְלָה לְהַקְרָבָה, שֶׁנֶּאֱמַר: כָּל מוּם לֹא יִהְיֶה
בּוֹ, וְאָמְרוּ זִכְרוֹנָם לִבְרָכָה: קְרִי בֵיהּ "לֹא יְהַיֶּה בּוֹ"; וּלְשׁוֹן סִפְרָא: "כָּל מוּם לֹא
יִהְיֶה בּוֹ" — אַל תִּתֵּן בּוֹ מוּם.

מִשָּׁרְשֵׁי הַמִּצְוָה, לְפִי שֶׁיִּהְיֶה בִּזְיוֹן הַקֳּדָשִׁים; וּכְבָר כָּתַבְתִּי כַּמָּה פְעָמִים
הַתּוֹעֶלֶת הַנִּמְצָא בְּהִתְיַקֵּר כְּבוֹד בֵּית הַמִּקְדָּשׁ וּמְשָׁרְתָיו וְקָרְבְּנוֹתָיו אֶל לֵב בְּנֵי־
אָדָם.

מִדִּינֵי הַמִּצְוָה, מַה שֶּׁאָמְרוּ שֶׁאֶחָד הַמֵּטִיל מוּם בַּקֳּדָשִׁים עַצְמָן אוֹ בִתְמוּרָתָן,
עוֹבֵר בְּלָאו וְלוֹקֶה, חוּץ מִן הַבְּכוֹר וּמִן הַמַּעֲשֵׂר, שֶׁהַמֵּטִיל מוּם בִּתְמוּרָתָן אֵינוֹ
לוֹקֶה, לְפִי שֶׁאֵין רְאוּיִין לְקָרְבָּנוֹת, כְּמוֹ שֶׁמִּתְבָּאֵר בִּתְמוּרָה; וְיֶתֶר פְּרָטֶיהָ,

---

4. TB Ḥullin 130a, B'choroth 14a.

5. TB Z'vaḥim 116a.

6. Below, §§288–290.

7. MT *hilchoth 'issuré ha-mizbé-aḥ* i 4.

8. Because consecration involves no physical action. The problem is raised, and an answer is offered, at the end of §285. In our author's original arrangement (see §285, note 2), this precept occurs well before §285; hence he left it as a question here, expecting to clarify the matter later.

§287   1. I.e. by anyone's direct action; TB M'naḥoth 56b (see Rashi, s.v. *lo' yihyeh*); so too B'choroth 33b, bottom.

2. Sifra, *'emor, parashah* 7, 9.

3. TB T'murah 21a.

made between a permanent defect and a passing one;[4] and their teaching[5] that blemishes do not disqualify an offering of a fowl, since Scripture does not state "a male without blemish" (Leviticus 1:3) about it. Where does this rule hold, however?—in regard to minor blemishes; but if a bird's wing withered, if one of its eyes was blinded, or one of its feet cut off, it is forbidden at the altar.[5] The rest of its details are explained in chapter 8 of the Talmud tractate *M'naḥoth*.

This precept is in force when the Temple exists. If someone transgressed it and ritually slew, sprinkled the blood of, or burned the *'émurim* of an animal with a blemish, on the altar, he would thus disobey this positive precept, apart from transgressing a negative precept, as we will write with the help of the Eternal Lord.[6] And Rambam of blessed memory wrote:[7] Consequently you learn that if a person consecrated a blemished animal, ritually slew it, sprinkled its blood, and burned its *'émurim* on the altar, he should be whipped with four sets of lashes. But his statement that if one consecrated it he should receive whiplashes, requires study.[8]

[THAT WE SHOULD NOT MAKE A BLEMISHING DEFECT
IN CONSECRATED ANIMALS]

287 that we should not make a blemish in holy offerings; in other words, we should not make any wound or fracture in an animal consecrated for the altar, that will disqualify it as an offering: for it is stated, *there shall be no blemish in it* (Leviticus 22:21); and the Sages of blessed memory said: Read it as "no blemish shall come about in it."[1] In the language of the Midrash *Sifra*:[2] "there shall be no blemish in it"—do not make any blemish in it.

At the root of the precept lies the reason that there would be a despisal of holy offerings in this; and I have already written many times the useful benefit to be found in making the honor of the Sanctuary, its ministering servants, and its offerings, dear to the heart of people.

Among the laws of the precept, there is what the Sages said:[3] that whether one makes a defect in holy offerings themselves or in animals exchanged for them, he equally transgresses a negative precept and is to be given a whipping of lashes—except for a firstborn animal (§18) and one from the tithe (§360): if one makes a defect in their substitutes, he receives no lashes, because they are not fit (acceptable) as offerings, as explained in the Talmud tractate *T'murah* (21a). The

מְבֹאָרִים בִּמְקוֹמוֹת מְפֻזָּרִים מְזְבָּחִים וּתְמוּרָה.

וְנוֹהֵג זֶה אִסּוּר זֶה בְּכָל מָקוֹם וּבְכָל זְמַן, בִּזְכָרִים וּנְקֵבוֹת; אֲבָל אֵין חִיּוּב הַמַּלְקִיּוֹת כִּי־אִם בִּזְמַן שֶׁבֵּית הַמִּקְדָּשׁ קַיָּם, שֶׁרְאוּיָה הַבְּהֵמָה לַקָּרְבָּן, כְּמוֹ שֶׁמִּתְבָּאֵר בִּגְמָרָא עֲבוֹדָה־זָרָה.

[שֶׁלֹּא נִזְרֹק דַּם בַּעַל מוּם עַל הַמִּזְבֵּחַ]

רפח שֶׁלֹּא נִזְרֹק דַּם בַּעֲלֵי מוּמִין עַל גַּבֵּי הַמִּזְבֵּחַ, שֶׁנֶּאֱמַר: עַוֶּרֶת אוֹ שָׁבוּר אוֹ חָרוּץ אוֹ יַבֶּלֶת אוֹ גָרָב אוֹ יַלֶּפֶת לֹא תַקְרִיבוּ אֵלֶּה לַיְיָ, וּבָאָה הַקַּבָּלָה שֶׁזֶּה הַלָּאו הוּא מוֹנֵעַ מִזְּרִיקַת דַּם בַּעֲלֵי מוּמִין, וְזֶהוּ דַעַת תַּנָּא קַמָּא בִּגְמָרָא תְמוּרָה, וְכֵן הֲלָכָה, שֶׁאָמְרוּ שָׁם: וְתַנָּא קַמָּא, הַאי "לֹא תַקְרִיבוּ לַיְיָ" לָמָּה לִי — מִבָּעֵי לֵיהּ לִזְרִיקַת דָּמִים.

כָּל עִנְיַן אַזְהָרָה זוֹ כְּאַזְהָרַת נְתִינַת מוּם בְּקָדָשִׁים וּשְׁחִיטַת בַּעַל מוּם וְהַקְטָרַת אֵמוּרִין. אֲבָל אֵין לְחָשְׁבוֹ עִם הָאֲסוּרִים הַנּוֹהֲגִים הַיּוֹם, לְפִי שֶׁאֵין לָנוּ מִזְבֵּחַ, בַּעֲווֹנוֹתֵינוּ.

[שֶׁלֹּא נִשְׁחַט בַּעֲלֵי מוּם לְשֵׁם קָרְבָּן]

רפט שֶׁלֹּא נִשְׁחַט בַּעֲלֵי מוּמִין לְשֵׁם קָרְבָּן, שֶׁנֶּאֱמַר: לֹא תַקְרִיבוּ אֵלֶּה לַיְיָ, וּלְשׁוֹן סִפְרָא: "לֹא תַקְרִיבוּ" מִשּׁוּם בַּל תִּשְׁחַט.

כָּל עִנְיַן מִצְוָה זוֹ מְפֹרָשׁ בַּמִּצְוָה הַקּוֹדֶמֶת לָהּ. אֲבָל אֵין לַחְשֹׁב זֶה עִם הַנּוֹהֲגִים הַיּוֹם, לְפִי שֶׁאֵין לָנוּ מִקְדָּשׁ, בַּעֲווֹנוֹתֵינוּ, לִשְׁחֹט שָׁם קָרְבְּנוֹתֵינוּ.

[שֶׁלֹּא נַקְטִיר אֵמוּרֵי בַּעֲלֵי מוּמִין]

רצ שֶׁלֹּא לְהַקְטִיר אֵמוּרֵי בַּעֲלֵי מוּמִין; פֵּרוּשׁ אֵמוּרִין כָּתַבְתִּי בְּסֵדֶר צַו עֲשֵׂה

§288   1. The pronoun "we" is used here generically, since only *kohanim* might sprinkle the blood of offerings.

2. I.e. Sage of the Mishnah, in the presentation of two opposing views.

3. This is the Scriptural text given in the oldest manuscripts, as in our standard editions of the Talmud. In the editions of this work, part of verse 22 is cited ("you shall not offer *these* to the Lord"), and so too in MT *hilchoth 'issuré ha-mizbé-aḥ* i 4; but in its standard edition, *'éleh* ("these"—the word absent in verse 24) is set in parentheses to indicate that it should be omitted, as *Leḥem Mishneh* writes (for earlier in the same paragraph Rambam cites verse 22 as the text for the prohibition against the ritual slaying of the animal). Likewise in ShM negative precept §93, verse 24 is cited for this precept. Very possibly this passage, *you shall not offer to the Lord,* was the entire proof-text cited here originally in the first sentence. As it follows a ban on emasculated animals (first part of verse 24), which are forbidden as blemished, defective, in essence it equally applies to all defective beasts. The complete verse 22, that we have as proof-text, could be the

⟨254⟩

rest of its details are explained in scattered places in the tractates *Z'vaḥim* and *T'murah*.

This prohibition is in effect everywhere, at every time, for both man and woman. But there is no punishment of whiplashes except at the time that the Sanctuary exists, when the animal could properly be an offering, as it is explained in the Talmud tractate *'Avodah Zarah* (13b).

[NOT TO SPRINKLE THE BLOOD OF DEFECTIVE ANIMALS ON THE ALTAR]

288 that we should not sprinkle of the blood of blemished animals on the altar:[1] for it is stated, *Animals blind or broken-limbed or gashed or with a wen or a scurf or a scab, you shall not offer these to the Lord* (Leviticus 22:22); and the Oral Tradition taught that this injunction forbids sprinkling the blood of a blemished animal. This is the view of the first *tanna*[2] in the Talmud tractate *T'murah* (6b), and it is the definitive law. For it is stated there: Now, for the first *tanna*, why do I need the verse, *you shall not offer to the Lord* (ibid. 24)?[3]—for him it is needed in regard to sprinkling the blood.

The entire subject-matter of this injunction is like that of the admonition against making a disfiguring blemish in a holy offering (§287), ritually slaying a blemished animal (§289), or burning its *'émurim* (§290). However, it is not to be reckoned with those prohibitions that are in force today, since for our sins, we have no altar.

[THE PROHIBITION ON RITUALLY SLAYING DEFECTIVE ANIMALS FOR HOLY OFFERINGS]

289 that we should not ritually slay blemished animals for offerings: for it is stated, *you shall not offer these to the Lord* (Leviticus 22:22),[1] and in the language of the Midrash *Sifra*:[2] "you shall not offer"—this signifies that you shall not ritually slay it.

The entire subject of this precept was explained in a previous one (§287). This prohibition, though, is not to be reckoned among those that apply today,[3] since for our sins we have no Sanctuary where our offerings could be ritually slain.

[THAT WE SHOULD NOT BURN THE PORTIONS FOR THE ALTAR FROM DEFECTIVE ANIMALS]

290 not to burn the *'émurim* of blemished animals on the altar. The meaning of *'émurim* I wrote in the fifth positive precept of *sidrah*

ה׳ [סי׳ קל״ח]; וְעַל זֶה נֶאֱמַר: וְאִשֶּׁה לֹא תִתְּנוּ מֵהֶם עַל הַמִּזְבֵּחַ. עִנְיַן מִצְוָה זוֹ גַּם־כֵּן, וּבֵאוּר מְקוֹם דִּינֶיהָ, כָּתַבְתִּי בַּמִּצְוָה הַקּוֹדֶמֶת לַחֲבֶרְתָּהּ. אֲבָל אֵין לַחֲשֹׁב אִסּוּר זֶה עִם הַנּוֹהֲגִים הַיּוֹם, לְפִי שֶׁאֵין לָנוּ מִקְדָּשׁ, בַּעֲווֹנוֹתֵינוּ, לְהַקְטִיר בּוֹ.

[שֶׁלֹּא לְסָרֵס אֶחָד מִכָּל הַמִּינִין]

רצא שֶׁלֹּא נְסָרֵס אֶחָד מִכָּל הַמִּינִין, לֹא אָדָם וְלֹא בְהֵמָה וְלֹא עוֹף, שֶׁנֶּאֱמַר: וּבְאַרְצְכֶם לֹא תַעֲשׂוּ. אַחַר שֶׁזָּכַר הַכָּתוּב ״וּמָעוּךְ וְכָתוּת וְנָתוּק וְכָרוּת״, שֶׁהוּא נֶאֱמַר כֻּלּוֹ עַל כְּלֵי הַתַּשְׁמִישׁ, אָמַר ״וּבְאַרְצְכֶם לֹא תַעֲשׂוּ״, וּבָא הַפֵּרוּשׁ עָלָיו: כָּל שֶׁבְּאַרְצְכֶם לֹא תַעֲשׂוּ, כְּלוֹמַר לֹא יַעֲשֶׂה זֹאת בְּיִשְׂרָאֵל, אוֹ פֵּרוּשׁוֹ מִכָּל מִין שֶׁבְּאַרְצְכֶם לֹא תַעֲשׂוּ, וְכָל שֶׁבְּאַרְצֵנוּ יִכְלֹל הָאָדָם וְהַבְּהֵמָה וְכָל בַּעֲלֵי הַחַיִּים. וְאֵין עִנְיַן הַכָּתוּב לוֹמַר שֶׁלֹּא יְהֵא הַסֵּרוּס אָסוּר אֶלָּא בָאָרֶץ, וּבְפֵרוּשׁ אָמְרוּ זִכְרוֹנָם לִבְרָכָה בְּשַׁבָּת פֶּרֶק שְׁמֹנָה שְׁרָצִים: תַּנְיָא, מִנַּיִן לְסָרוּס בָּאָדָם שֶׁהוּא אָסוּר, תַּלְמוּד לוֹמַר: וּבְאַרְצְכֶם לֹא תַעֲשׂוּ — בָּכֶם לֹא תַעֲשׂוּ.

מִשָּׁרְשֵׁי הַמִּצְוָה, לְפִי שֶׁהַשֵּׁם בָּרוּךְ הוּא בָּרָא עוֹלָמוֹ בְּתַכְלִית הַשְּׁלֵמוּת, לֹא חִסֵּר וְלֹא יִתֵּר בּוֹ דָבָר מִכָּל הָרָאוּי לִהְיוֹת בּוֹ לִשְׁלֵמוּתוֹ, וְהָיָה מֵרְצוֹנוֹ, וּבֵרַךְ בַּעֲלֵי חַיִּים לִהְיוֹתָם פָּרִים וְרָבִים; וְגַם צִנָּה הַדְּבָרִים מִמִּין הָאָדָם עַל זֶה, לְמַעַן יַעֲמֹדוּ; שֶׁאִם לֹא כֵן, יִהְיֶה הַמִּין כָּלֶה אַחַר שֶׁהַמָּוֶת מְכַלֶּה בָהֶם; וְעַל־כֵּן הַמַּפְסִיד כְּלֵי הַזֶּרַע מַרְאֶה בְנַפְשׁוֹ כְּמִי שֶׁהוּא קָץ בְּמַעֲשֵׂה הַבּוֹרֵא, וְרוֹצֶה בְהַשְׁחָתַת עוֹלָמוֹ הַטּוֹב.

מִדִּינֵי הַמִּצְוָה, מַה שֶּׁאָמְרוּ זִכְרוֹנָם לִבְרָכָה שֶׁאֲפִלּוּ לוֹמַר לְגוֹי לְסָרֵס בְּהֵמָה שֶׁל יִשְׂרָאֵל אָסוּר, אֲבָל אִם לְקָחָהּ הַגּוֹי מֵעַצְמוֹ וְסֵרֵס אוֹתָהּ, מֻתָּר לְלָקְחָהּ מִיָּדוֹ וְלֶאֱכֹל אוֹתָהּ; וְאִם הֶעֱרִים הַיִּשְׂרָאֵל, כְּגוֹן שֶׁאָמַר דְּבָרִים בִּפְנֵי הַגּוֹי מַרְאִין חֶפְצוֹ

"emendation" of a copyist, who added, as he thought, the missing first part of verse 22. (MS Casanatense 134 has this full verse, *Animals blind*, etc., but without 'éleh, "these"! This indeed could have been the original proof-text—a composite from verses 22 and 24.) This postulate is supported by the fact that in the original arrangement (found in the old manuscripts and the first edition) our author has this precept after §290. Since §§ 288–290 are all negative precepts, only the order of the verses could have determined this arrangement; and §§ 289 and 290 cite verse 22, §290 unmistakably so. (See also §289, note 1).

§289   1. MY would emend this to Leviticus 22:24, omitting "these" from the verse, since § 288 was already derived from verse 22; but see §288, note 3.

2. Sifra, 'emor, perek 7, 1. (This paragraph is from ShM negative precept 92.)

3. In contrast to §287, which is (see its last paragraph). MH queries this, however: What basis does our author have for this statement? Perhaps the precept is violated even if one sacrifices a blemished (defective) animal as a holy offering today, on his own premises?

tzav (§138). Concerning this Scripture states, *nor shall you make an offering by fire of them on the altar* (Leviticus 22:22). The subject-matter of this precept too, and the location of its laws, were written in a precept shortly before this (§287). This prohibition, however, is not to be reckoned among those that are in effect today,[1] because we have no Sanctuary, for our sins, in which to do burning on the altar.

[NOT TO EMASCULATE ANY CREATURE OUT OF ALL THE ANIMAL SPECIES]

291 that we should not make any one of all the living species impotent, neither a man, nor a beast nor a fowl: for it is stated, *and in your land you shall not do so* (Leviticus 22:24). After Scripture declares, *And one that is bruised or crushed or torn or cut* (ibid.), all referring to the organs of generation, it states, *in your land you shall not do so*; and the interpretation was given for it:[1] any, or all, that are in your land. In other words, this is not to be done among Israelites;[2] or it means: with any species that is in your land you shall not do this; and "any in our land" would include man, beast, and all living creatures. But it is not the purpose of Scripture to say that the ban on emasculation should apply nowhere but in the land [of Israel].[3] Our Sages of blessed memory said distinctly in the fourteenth chapter of the tractate *Shabbath* (110b): It was taught in a *baraitha*: How do we learn that emasculation of a man is forbidden?—Scripture states, *and in your land you shall not do so*, [which connotes] "among yourselves you shall not do so."[2]

At the root of the precept lies the reason that the Eternal Lord, blessed is He, created His world in utmost perfection; He left nothing lacking and added nothing superfluous, out of all that should properly be in it for its perfection. Now, it was His will, as He blessed the living creatures, that they should reproduce and have offspring. Moreover, He commanded the male of the human species about this (§1), that it might endure. For otherwise, a species would die out after death ended all of its kind. Therefore, if someone incapacitates organs of generation, he shows himself to be as one who cannot tolerate the work of the Creator and desires the destruction of His good world.

Among the laws of the precept, there is what the Sages of blessed memory taught:[4] that it is forbidden even to tell a heathen to emasculate the beast of an Israelite; but if the heathen took it of his own accord and gelded it, it is permissible to take it from his hand and eat it. If, however, the Israelite used guile—for instance, if he said things in

בְּכָךְ, וְכַיּוֹצֵא בָעִנְיָנִים אֵלֶּה, כְּמוֹ שֶׁעוֹשִׂין הַמַּעֲרִימִין הַפְּחוּתִין, קוֹנְסִים אוֹתוֹ שֶׁיּוֹצִיאֶנָּה מִתַּחַת יָדוֹ וְיִמְכְּרֶנָּה לְיִשְׂרָאֵל אַחֵר; וַאֲפִלּוּ לִבְנוֹ גָדוֹל הִתִּירוּ זִכְרוֹנָם לִבְרָכָה לְמוֹכְרָהּ, דְּלֹא גָזְרוּ אֶלָּא שֶׁתֵּצֵא אֶלָּא מִתַּחַת יָדוֹ; אֲבָל לִבְנוֹ קָטָן אֵינוֹ מוֹכְרָהּ וְלֹא נוֹתְנָהּ.

וּמַה שֶּׁאָמְרוּ גַם־כֵּן שֶׁהַמְסָרֵס אַחַר הַמְסָרֵס חַיָּב, וּכְדְאָמַר רַבִּי חִיָּא בַר אַבִּין אָמַר רַבִּי יוֹחָנָן: הַכֹּל מוֹדִין בִּמְחַמֵּץ אַחַר מְחַמֵּץ שֶׁהוּא חַיָּב, שֶׁנֶּאֱמַר "לֹא תֵאָפֶה חָמֵץ" וְ"לֹא תֵעָשֶׂה חָמֵץ"; בִּמְסָרֵס אַחַר מְסָרֵס שֶׁהוּא חַיָּב, שֶׁנֶּאֱמַר "וּמָעוּךְ וְכָתוּת וְנָתוּק וְכָרוּת": אִם עַל כָּרוּת חַיָּב, עַל נָתוּק לֹא־כָּל־שֶׁכֵּן — אֶלָּא לְהָבִיא נוֹתֵק אַחַר כּוֹרֵת, שֶׁהוּא חַיָּב. כֵּיצַד, הֲרֵי שֶׁבָּא אֶחָד וְכָרַת הַגִּיד וּבָא אַחֵר וְכָרַת הַבֵּיצִים אוֹ נִתְּקָן, חַיָּב גַּם הָאַחֲרוֹן; וְכֵן אִם בָּא בָא אֶחָד וּמָעַךְ אֶת הַגִּיד וּבָא אַחֵר וּנְתָקוֹ, כֻּלָּן לוֹקִין, אַף־עַל־פִּי שֶׁהָאַחֲרוֹן אֵינוֹ מְסָרֵס, שֶׁכְּבָר מְסֹרָס הוּא.

וּמַה שֶּׁאָמְרוּ זִכְרוֹנָם לִבְרָכָה שֶׁהַמְסָרֵס אֶת הַנְּקֵבָה, בֵּין בְּאָדָם בֵּין בִּשְׁאָר מִינִין, פָּטוּר; וּמַה שֶּׁאָמְרוּ שֶׁהַמַּשְׁקֶה עִקָּרִין לְאָדָם אוֹ לִשְׁאָר הַבְּרִיּוֹת כְּדֵי לְסָרְסָן, אָסוּר, אֲבָל אֵין לוֹקִין עַל זֶה; וְכֵן הַמּוֹשִׁיב חֲבֵרוֹ בְּמַיִם אוֹ בְּשֶׁלֶג עַד שֶׁיִּבָּטֵל מִמֶּנּוּ כֹּחַ אֵיבְרֵי הַזֶּרַע, אֵינוֹ לוֹקֶה, אֲבָל רָאוּי לְהַכּוֹתוֹ מַכַּת מַרְדּוּת. וְאִשָּׁה מֻתֶּרֶת לִשְׁתּוֹת כּוֹס עִקָּרִין שֶׁמְּסָרְסִין אוֹתָהּ שֶׁלֹּא תֵלֵד, שֶׁהַנָּשִׁים אֵינָן מְצֻוּוֹת עַל פְּרִיָּה וּרְבִיָּה, כְּמוֹ שֶׁכָּתַבְתִּי בְּמִצְוָה רִאשׁוֹנָה שֶׁבַּסֵּפֶר; וְיֶתֶר פְּרָטֶיהָ, מְבֹאָרִין בִּמְקוֹמוֹת מִמַּסֶּכֶת שַׁבָּת וּבִיבָמוֹת.

וְנוֹהֶגֶת בְּכָל מָקוֹם וּבְכָל זְמַן, בִּזְכָרִים וּנְקֵבוֹת, שֶׁאָסוּר גַּם לָהֶן לְסָרֵס הַזְּכָרִים,

In reply, MY cites TB B'choroth 14b, which derives from a Scriptural text that before the Sanctuary was ever constructed, when it was permissible to offer up sacrifices on a private or local *bamah* ("high place"), it was forbidden to sacrifice a blemished animal there (arguably, because the *bamah* was then equal in sanctity to the altar that would later stand at the Sanctuary). Hence (MY contends) we may infer that today, when no site on earth has the sanctity to be used for holy offerings, no prohibition is violated if a person sacrifices a blemished animal somewhere today (his act is without meaning or significance).

§290   1. See §289, note 3.

§291   1. TB Hagigah 14b.
2. I.e. among "all who are in your land."
3. Since it is a ban imposed in regard to the physical self [and is not integrally related to the land]; and any obligation applying to the physical self is in force both in and outside the land (Rashi to Leviticus 22:24).
4. TB Bava M'tzi'a 90b.
5. Literally, he is fined.
6. MT *hilchoth 'issuré bi'ah* xvi 13.
7. TB Shabbath 111a, top.

the heathen's presence which showed that this was his desire, and so in any similar way out of the various methods that lowly, worthless cheats use—he is given the punitive order[5] that he must remove it from his possession and sell it to another Israelite. Even to a grown son, the Sages of blessed memory permitted him to sell it;[4] for they decreed only that it must leave his possession. To his small son, however, he may neither sell it nor give it.[6]

There is further, what the Sages said, that if one after another performs emasculation [on one animal] he incurs punishment. As R. Ḥiyya b. 'Avin said in in the name of R. Yoḥanan:[7] All agree that if one after another causes leavening [in a *minḥah*, a meal-offering] he is guilty, for it is stated, *It shall not be baked with leaven* (Leviticus 6:10), *shall not be made with leaven* (ibid. 2:11);[8] and if one after another causes emasculation, he is guilty: For it is stated, *And one that is bruised or crushed or torn or cut* (Leviticus 22:24)—if one is guilty over [organs of generation that are] cut, surely he is all the more certainly so for those that are torn?[9] It is then only to convey that if one tears them after they were cut, he is punishable. How could this be? If one came along and cut the membrum and then another came and cut the testes or tore them away, the latter is also punishable; so too if one came and crushed the membrum and another came and tore it away, both are to be given whiplashes, even though the latter person did no emasculation, as it [the animal] had already been made impotent.

Then there is what the Sages of blessed memory taught:[10] that if someone sterilizes a female, whether a human being or any other species, he is free of penalty. There is, too, what they said:[11] If someone gives a sterilizing drug to a man or any other creature to drink, to cause impotence, it is forbidden, but whiplashes are not suffered for it. So too if someone immerses another in water or snow until his potency is destroyed, he is not given whiplashes[12]—not until he causes impotence by hand [by direct action on the organs of generation]. He deserves, however, to be whipped in punishment for disobedience.[13] It is permissible, though, for a woman to drink a sterilizing drug that will render her barren, unable to bear children;[11] for women are not commanded to "be fruitful and multiply" (Genesis 1:28), as I wrote in the first *mitzvah* in this work. The rest of its details are clarified in various places in the Talmud tractates *Shabbath* and *Yevamoth*.

It applies everywhere, at every time, for both man and woman—

as they too are forbidden to emasculate a male; but not to make them-

אֲבָל לֹא עַצְמָן בְּכוֹס עִקָּרִין, כְּמוֹ שֶׁאָמַרְנוּ. וְעוֹבֵר עָלֶיהָ וְסֵרַס אֶחָד מִכָּל מִינֵי בַעֲלֵי־חַיִּים, בֵּין אָדָם בֵּין בְּהֵמָה וָעוֹף, בֵּין טְהוֹרִים בֵּין טְמֵאִים, לוֹקֶה.

[שֶׁלֹּא לְהַקְרִיב קָרְבָּן בַּעַל מוּם מִיַּד הַגּוֹיִם]

רצב שֶׁלֹּא לְהַקְרִיב בַּעֲלֵי מוּמִין מִיַּד הַגּוֹיִם, שֶׁנֶּאֱמַר: וּמִיַּד בֶּן נֵכָר לֹא תַקְרִיבוּ אֶת לֶחֶם אֱלֹהֵיכֶם מִכָּל אֵלֶּה—שֶׁלֹּא נֶאֱמַר: אַחַר שֶׁהוּא גוֹי, נַקְרִיב בַּעֲדוֹ בַּעַל מוּם. וְהַצְרָכָה הָאַזְהָרָה בָּזֶה לְפִי שֶׁכְּבָר הִתִּירַתְנוּ הַתּוֹרָה לְקַבֵּל מֵהֶם קָרְבָּנוֹת תְּמִימִים, כְּמוֹ שֶׁנֶּאֱמַר: אִישׁ אִישׁ מִבֵּית יִשְׂרָאֵל וּמִן הַגֵּר בְּיִשְׂרָאֵל אֲשֶׁר יַקְרִיב קָרְבָּנוֹ לְכָל נִדְרֵיהֶם וּלְכָל נִדְבוֹתָם, וּבָא הַפֵּרוּשׁ עָלָיו: "אִישׁ אִישׁ", לְרַבּוֹת הַגּוֹיִם שֶׁנּוֹדְרִים נְדָרִים וּנְדָבוֹת, וּמְקַבְּלִים אוֹתָם מֵהֶם.

מִשָּׁרְשֵׁי הַמִּצְוָה, כְּבוֹד הַבַּיִת, וּכְמוֹ שֶׁכָּתַבְתִּי בְּלָאו כ"א בְּסֵדֶר זֶה [סִי׳ רפ"ז].

מִדִּינֵי הַמִּצְוָה, מַה שֶּׁאָמְרוּ (זִכְרוֹנָם לִבְרָכָה) שֶׁכָּל מוּם מִן הַמּוּמִין הַפּוֹסְלִין בְּקָרְבְּנוֹתֵינוּ, כְּגוֹן הַשִּׁבְעִים וּשְׁלֹשָׁה מוּמִין הַיְּדוּעִין, פּוֹסְלִין גַּם־כֵּן בְּמַה שֶּׁנְּקַבֵּל מֵהֶם, וְלֹא נֶאֱמַר שֶׁלֹּא יִהְיֶה מוּם בְּקָרְבְּנוֹתָם אֶלָּא מַה שֶּׁהֵם מְחַשְּׁבִין אוֹתוֹ מוּם, כְּגוֹן מְחֻסַּר אֵבֶר; וּקְצָת יֶתֶר פְּרָטֶיהָ, מְפֻזָּרִים בִּמְקוֹמוֹת מֵהַתַּלְמוּד.

וְנוֹהֶגֶת בַּכֹּהֲנִים וּבִזְמַן שֶׁיִּשְׂרָאֵל שְׁרוּיִין עַל אַדְמָתָן, כִּי אָז הוּא זְמַן הַהַקְרָבָה. וְכֹהֵן שֶׁעָבַר עַל זֶה וְהִקְרִיב בַּעַל מוּם, אַף־עַל־פִּי שֶׁהוּא מִבֶּן־נֵכָר, לוֹקֶה.

[מִצְוַת הַקָּרְבָּן שֶׁיִּהְיֶה מִשְּׁמֹנָה יָמִים וּלְמַעְלָה]

רצג שֶׁיִּהְיֶה כָּל קָרְבָּן שֶׁנַּקְרִיב מִן הַבְּהֵמָה מִבֶּן שְׁמֹנַת יָמִים וָמַעְלָה, לֹא פָחוֹת מִזֶּה; וְזֹאת הִיא מִצְוַת מְחֻסַּר זְמַן בְּגוּפוֹ; וְהַמִּקְרָא הַמַּזְהִירֵנוּ בָּזֶה הוּא שֶׁכָּתוּב:

8. Hence anyone who adds leaven to it is guilty, whatever its previous state.

9. The word "cut" (charuth) denotes severing the testicles but leaving them in the scrotum (Rashi ibid. s.v. koréth), while "torn" (nathuk) denotes the removal of the scrotum with its contents. If the first is forbidden, the second must certainly be. Thus "or torn" is apparently superfluous, and it is therefore interpreted as adding to the scope of the precept.

10. Sifra, 'emor, perek 7, 12; TB Shabbath 111 a.

11. Tosefta, Yevamoth viii; TB Shabbath 111a; MT hilchoth 'issuré bi'ah xvi 12.

12. MT ibid. based on TB Sanhedrin 76b.

13. MT ibid. (see §24, note 14).

§292

1. So TB T'murah 7a (the sentence is based on ShM negative precept §96).

2. TB M'naḥoth 73b, Ḥullin 13b.

3. The Hebrew for "anyone" means literally "a man, a man"; the apparently superfluous repetition is interpreted as adding something to the scope or meaning of the precept.

4. TB T'murah 7a.

5. See §275, paragraphs 6 and 9.

selves barren with a sterilizing drug, as we have stated. If someone transgressed this and emasculated any one of all the species of living creatures, whether man, animal or fowl, whether clean [kosher] or unclean [non-kosher], he is punishable by whiplashes.

[NOT TO OFFER UP A DEFECTIVE OFFERING RECEIVED FROM A HEATHEN]

292 not to bring blemished offerings from the hand of heathens: for it is stated, *Neither from the hand of a foreigner shall you offer the bread of your God out of any of these* (Leviticus 22:25)—that we should not say, "Since he is a non-Jew, let us offer up a blemished animal for him."[1] The injunction about this was necessary concerning them, because the Torah previously permitted us to accept whole, unblemished offerings from their hand. For it is stated, *Anyone of the house of Israel or of the strangers in Israel who brings his offering, whether out of all their vows or all their freewill offerings* (Leviticus 22:18); and the traditional interpretation was given for it:[2] "Anyone"[3]—to add heathens who pledge vowed or freewill offerings: they are accepted from them.

At the root of the precept lies the theme of the esteem of the Temple, as I wrote in the twenty-first negative precept of this *sidrah* (§287).

Among the laws of the precept, there is what the Sages of blessed memory said,[4] that every one of the blemishes that would disqualify our offerings, such as the seventy-three known defects,[5] equally disqualifies whatever we accept from them; and we should not say that a blemish in their offerings should be no more than what they consider a defect, such as the lack of a limb. Its few remaining details are scattered in various places in the Talmud.

It applies to *kohanim* when the Israelites (all Jewry) abide on their land, for it is then a time of bringing offerings. If a *kohen* transgressed this and offered up a blemished animal, even though it was from a heathen, he should receive whiplashes.

[THE PRECEPT THAT AN ANIMAL OFFERING SHOULD BE AT LEAST EIGHT DAYS OLD]

293 that every animal offering we bring should be from eight days old and up, not less than this. This is a precept about [an animal] of itself lacking time (age);[1] and the verse which adjures us about it is:

שׁוֹר אוֹ כֶשֶׂב אוֹ עֵז כִּי יִוָּלֵד וְהָיָה שִׁבְעַת יָמִים תַּחַת אִמּוֹ וּמִיּוֹם הַשְּׁמִינִי וָהָלְאָה
יֵרָצֶה; וְדִבְרֵי הַתּוֹרָה נוֹטְרִיקוֹן הֵם, וּמוֹרֶה הַכָּתוּב שֶׁקֹּדֶם לָכֵן לֹא יֵרָצֶה הַקָּרְבָּן;
וְזֶה וְכַיּוֹצֵא בּוֹ יִקָּרְאוּ זִכְרוֹנָם לִבְרָכָה; לָאו הַבָּא מִכְּלַל עֲשֵׂה — עֲשֵׂה; וּלְפִיכָךְ
אֵין לוֹקִין עָלָיו, וּכְמוֹ שֶׁבֵּאֲרוּ זִכְרוֹנָם לִבְרָכָה בְּחֻלִּין פֶּרֶק אוֹתוֹ וְאֶת בְּנוֹ, שֶׁאָמְרוּ
שָׁם לְעִנְיַן מַלְקוֹת: הַנַּח לְמְחֻסַּר זְמַן, שֶׁהַכָּתוּב נְתָקוֹ לַעֲשֵׂה.

מִשָּׁרְשֵׁי הַמִּצְוָה, מַה שֶׁהִקְדַּמְנוּ בְּעִנְיַן הַקָּרְבָּן עַל צַד הַפְּשָׁט, כִּי בְּכֹחַ הַפְּעֻלָּה
יִתְעוֹרֵר הָאָדָם לְהַכְשִׁיר מַעֲשֵׂהוּ, וְלָכֵן נִצְטַוָּה לִהְיוֹת פְּעֻלַּת הַדְּבָרִים שֶׁבָּהֶן הֶכְשֵׁר
הַמַּעֲשֶׂה שְׁלֵמָה בְּכָל כֹּחוֹ. וּמִשְּׁלֵמוּת הַקָּרְבָּן שֶׁיִּהְיֶה מִבֶּן שְׁמֹנַת יָמִים וָהָלְאָה, כִּי
קֹדֶם לָכֵן אֵינֶנּוּ רָאוּי לְכָל דָּבָר וְלֹא יַחְמֹד אִישׁ אוֹתוֹ לְאָכְלָה וְלִסְחוֹרָה וְלִתְשׁוּרָה.

מִדִּינֵי הַמִּצְוָה, מַה שֶׁאָמְרוּ זִכְרוֹנָם לִבְרָכָה שֶׁתּוֹרִים שֶׁלֹּא הִגִּיעַ זְמַנָּן, שֶׁהֵן
אֲסוּרִין לְקָרְבָּן כְּמוֹ בְּהֵמָה שֶׁלֹּא הִגִּיעַ זְמַנָּהּ; וְכֵן בְּנֵי יוֹנָה גְּדוֹלִים הַרְבֵּה אֲסוּרִים,
וְהַטַּעַם בָּהֶם שֶׁהַגַּדְלוּת לָהֶן נֶחְשָׁב כְּמוּם; וְדֶרֶךְ כְּלָל אָמְרוּ זִכְרוֹנָם לִבְרָכָה
בַּמִּשְׁנָה בְּתוֹרִים וּבְנֵי יוֹנָה, שֶׁתְּחִלַּת הַצָּהוֹב שֶׁבָּזֶה וְשֶׁבָּזֶה פָּסוּל, לְפִי שֶׁהוּא
גַּדְלוּת בְּיוֹנִים וְקַטְנוּת בְּתוֹרִים.

וְדָרְשׁוּ זִכְרוֹנָם לִבְרָכָה בְּזֶה הַמִּקְרָא: "כִּי יִוָּלֵד", פְּרָט לְיוֹצֵא דֹפֶן, שֶׁפָּסוּל
לַקָּרְבָּן; "תַּחַת אִמּוֹ", פְּרָט לְיָתוֹם, כְּלוֹמַר שֶׁנּוֹלַד אַחַר שֶׁנִּשְׁחֲטָה אִמּוֹ. וּמִן
הַדּוֹמֶה שֶׁבְּכָל זֶה אֶפְשָׁר לוֹמַר שֶׁאֵין הַשְּׁלֵמוּת בָּהֶן כְּמוֹ בַנּוֹלָדִים כְּדַרְכּוֹ שֶׁל
עוֹלָם, וּכְבָר כָּתַבְנוּ כִּי הַחִיּוּב כִּי לִהְיוֹת הַקָּרְבָּן בְּתַכְלִית הַשְּׁלֵמוּת מִכָּל צַד. וְיֶתֶר
פְּרָטֶיהָ, מִתְבָּאֲרִים בְּסִפְרָא וְסוֹף מַסֶּכֶת זְבָחִים.

§293   1. I.e. lacking in the offering, as opposed to a lack or shortage of time in the person
bringing the offering, e.g. a person defiled for seven days who brings his offering of
purification within the seven days.
    2. The paragraph is based on ShM positive precept §60.
    3. Based on TB Ḥullin 22a.
    4. MT bilchoth 'issuré ba-mizbé-aḥ iii 9.
    5. Mishnah, Ḥullin i 5 (TB 22a).
    6. Literally, of yellowing, or gilding; i.e. when the feathers about the neck begin to
turn yellow; Rashi to ibid.
    7. TB Ḥullin 38b; Sifra, 'emor, parashah 8, 3; MT ibid. 4.

When a bullock or sheep or goat is born, it shall remain seven days under its dam; and from the eighth day and thenceforth it shall be acceptable (Leviticus 22:27). The words of the Torah are abbreviated: the verse thus conveys that before this, the offering will not be acceptable. This and anything similar, our Sages of blessed memory call "an injunction that derives from a positive precept, [which has the force of] a positive precept"; and therefore no whiplashes are given for it, as our Sages of blessed memory explained in the fifth chapter of the Talmud tractate *Hullin* (80b), where they said in regard to whiplashes: Let the animal lacking in age be, since the Writ linked it with a positive precept.[2]

At the root of the precept lies what we wrote earlier on the subject of the offering, by way of the plain meaning: that by the force (impact) of an action, a man will be stirred to make his acts worthy; and therefore he was commanded that the implementation of matters by which a deed is made worthy, should be whole and perfect, by all his power. And it is part of the perfection of an offering that it should be from eight days old and up, as before that it is not fit for anything, and no man would desire it for food, trade, or a gift.

Among the laws of the precept, there is what the Sages of blessed memory said:[3] that turtledoves which have not reached their minimal age are forbidden as offerings, like a beast that has not reached its minimal age. Similarly, very mature pigeons are forbidden, the reason about them being that for them age is considered a defect.[4] As a general rule, the Sages of blessed memory said in the Mishnah[5] about turtledoves and young pigeons that the beginning of a sheen[6] in [the feathers of] both the one and the other, brings disqualification, because it marks overmaturity in pigeons and undue youth in turtledoves.

Further, our Sages of blessed memory interpreted this verse:[7] "is born"—this excludes one delivered by Caesarian section, which is thus disqualified as an offering; "under its dam"—this excludes a motherless animal: i.e. that was born after its dam was ritually slain. Now, evidently, about all these it could be said that they do not have the wholeness, the perfection of those born in the normal way; and I have written previously that there is an obligation for an offering to be utmostly whole and perfect from every aspect. The rest of its details are explained in the Midrash *Sifra* and toward the end of the Talmud tractate *Z'vahim*.

It is in force at the time the Temple stands, for male *kohanim*,

וְנוֹהֶגֶת בִּזְמַן הַבַּיִת בִּזְכְרֵי כְהֻנָּה, כִּי לָהֶם מִצְוַת הַקָּרְבָּן וְעַל יָדָם יִתְקָרְבוּ, וְהֵם הֻזְהֲרוּ מִן הַדּוֹמֶה בָּעִנְיָן. אֲבָל מִכָּל מָקוֹם רָאִיתִי לָרַמְבַּ"ם זִכְרוֹנוֹ לִבְרָכָה שֶׁכָּתַב, וְזֶה לְשׁוֹנוֹ: וְכֵן הַמַּקְדִּישׁ מְחֻסַּר זְמַן הֲרֵי הוּא כְמַקְדִּישׁ בַּעַל מוּם עוֹבֵר, וְאֵינוֹ לוֹקֶה, כְּמוֹ שֶׁבֵּאַרְנוּ. עַד כָּאן.

נִרְאֶה מִדְּבָרָיו שֶׁהוּא סוֹבֵר שֶׁחִיּוּב מִצְוָה זוֹ אַף עַל הַיִּשְׂרָאֵל הַמַּקְדִּישׁ אוֹתוֹ. וְכֵיוָן שֶׁכֵּן, יֵשׁ לָנוּ לוֹמַר לְדַעְתּוֹ שֶׁחִיּוּב מִצְוָה זוֹ בֵּין בַּכֹּהֲנִים בֵּין בְּיִשְׂרָאֵלִים, וּבִזְכָרִים וּנְקֵבוֹת. וְעוֹבֵר עַל זֶה וְהִקְרִיב מְחֻסַּר זְמַן, אוֹ הִקְדִּישׁוֹ, לְדַעַת הָרַמְבַּ"ם זִכְרוֹנוֹ לִבְרָכָה, בִּטֵּל עֲשֵׂה, אֲבָל אֵינוֹ לוֹקֶה, לְפִי שֶׁהוּא לָאו הַבָּא מִכְּלָל עֲשֵׂה, כְּמוֹ שֶׁכָּתַבְנוּ.

[שֶׁלֹּא לִשְׁחֹט בְּהֵמָה וּבְנָהּ בְּיוֹם אֶחָד]

רצד שֶׁלֹּא נִשְׁחַט בְּהֵמָה וּבְנָהּ בְּיוֹם אֶחָד, בֵּין בְּקָדָשִׁים בֵּין בְּחֻלִּין, שֶׁנֶּאֱמַר: אֹתוֹ וְאֶת בְּנוֹ לֹא תִשְׁחֲטוּ בְּיוֹם אֶחָד.

מִשָּׁרְשֵׁי הַמִּצְוָה, שֶׁיִּתֵּן הָאָדָם אֶל לִבּוֹ כִּי הַשְׁגָּחַת הַשֵּׁם בָּרוּךְ הוּא עַל כָּל מִינֵי בַעֲלֵי חַיִּים בִּכְלָל, וְעִם הַשְׁגָּחָתוֹ עֲלֵיהֶם יִתְקַיְּמוּ לְעוֹלָם, כִּי הַשְׁגָּחָתוֹ בִּדְבָרִים זֶהוּ קִיּוּמָם, וְעַל־כֵּן לֹא יִבָּטֵל מִן הַמִּינִין לְגַמְרֵי כָּל יְמֵי עוֹלָם.

וְאַף־עַל־פִּי שֶׁהַשְׁגָּחָתוֹ עַל מִין הָאָדָם בִּפְרָט, וּכְמוֹ שֶׁכָּתַבְתִּי לְמַעְלָה בְּסֵדֶר "אִשָּׁה כִּי תַזְרִיעַ" עֲשֵׂה ג' [סִי' קס"ט], לֹא־כֵן מִינֵי שְׁאָר בַּעֲלֵי חַיִּים, אֶלָּא דֶרֶךְ כְּלָל בַּמִּין יָשִׂים הַשֵּׁם הַשְׁגָּחָתוֹ בָּרוּךְ הוּא; וְעַל־כֵּן נִמְנַעְנוּ מִלְּכַלּוֹת הָאִילָן וַעֲנָפָיו בְּיַחַד, לְרַמֵּז זֶה.

וְעוֹד נוּכַל לוֹמַר בָּעִנְיָן עַל צַד הַפְּשָׁט כְּמוֹ־כֵן, שֶׁהוּא לְקַבֵּעַ בְּנַפְשֵׁנוּ מִדַּת הַחֶמְלָה וּלְהַרְחִיק מִדַּת הָאַכְזָרִיּוּת, שֶׁהִיא מִדָּה רָעָה; וְלָכֵן, אַף־עַל־פִּי שֶׁהִתִּיר

---

8. MT *ibid.* 10.

9. The ruling by Rambam cited toward the end of §285, that for consecrating a blemished animal, one *is* given lashes, applies where the blemish is permanent.

§294   1. This principle is found also in R. Aaron haLévi, *P'kudath haLévi*, folio 93, in the name of R. 'Aḥa. See my Translator's Preface.

   1a. Cf. Ramban, commentary, Deuteronomy 22:6.

as the religious duty of offerings lies upon them, and by them they are offered up; and they were seemingly adjured about the matter. Nevertheless, I have seen that Rambam of blessed memory wrote, these being his words:[8] And so too, if a person consecrates an animal lacking in age, he is thus as one who consecrates an animal with a passing blemish, who is not given whiplashes,[9] as we have explained. Thus far his words.

So it would appear from his words that he holds that guilt over this precept would lie also upon an Israelite who consecrates it. In that case, it is for us to say, by his view, that the obligation [to observe] this precept lies on both *kohanim* and ordinary Israelites, both man and woman. If someone transgressed this and offered up an animal lacking in age, or if he consecrated it, in the view of Rambam of blessed memory, he would disobey a positive precept; but he would receive no whiplashes, since this is an injunction that derives from a positive precept, as we have written.

[THE PROHIBITION AGAINST RITUALLY SLAYING BOTH AN ANIMAL AND ITS YOUNG IN ONE DAY]

294 that we should not ritually slay an animal and its young in one day, whether they are consecrated or non-holy: for it is stated, *you shall not slay it and its young in one day* (Leviticus 22:28).

At the root of the precept lies the purpose that a man should reflect in his heart that the watchful care of the Eternal Lord, blessed is He, extends to all the species of living creatures generally, and with His providential concern for them they will endure permanently. For His watchful care over entities is their maintenance. And therefore none of the species will ever become completely null and void in all the days of the world.

Now, although His watchful care over the human species is individual, as I wrote above, in the third positive precept of *sidrah thazri'a* (§169), this is not so with other species of living creatures: Rather, the Eternal Lord bestows His providential concern on a species in a general way;[1] and we were therefore restricted from destroying a tree together with its branches [a mother-animal together with its young] to imply this.[1a]

We can say further about this subject, likewise by way of the plain meaning, that it is in order to instill in our spirit the quality of pity, and to remove the quality of cruelty, which is an evil trait of

לָנוּ הָאֵל מִינֵי בַעֲלֵי חַיִּים לְמִחְיָתֵנוּ, צִוָּנוּ לְבַל נַהֲרֹג אוֹתוֹ וְאֶת בְּנוֹ בְּיַחַד, וְלִקְבֹּעַ
בְּנַפְשֵׁנוּ מִדַּת הַחֶמְלָה.

דִּינֵי הַמִּצְוָה, כְּגוֹן מַה שֶּׁאָמְרוּ זִכְרוֹנָם לִבְרָכָה שֶׁאֵין חִלּוּק בֵּין ״אוֹתוֹ וְאֶת
בְּנוֹ״ אוֹ בְּנוֹ תְחִלָּה וְאַחַר־כָּךְ הָאֵם; וּמַה שֶּׁאָמְרוּ דְּבְאַרְבָּעָה פְרָקִים בַּשָּׁנָה הַמּוֹכֵר
בְּהֵמָה לַחֲבֵרוֹ צָרִיךְ לְהוֹדִיעוֹ ״אִמָּהּ מָכַרְתִּי לִשְׁחֹט״: לְפִי שֶׁבְּאַרְבָּעָה זְמַנִּים אֵלּוּ,
כָּל הַקּוֹנִים, מִן הַסְּתָם לִשְׁחָטָן לְשָׁעָה קוֹנִין; וְאֵלּוּ הֵן: עֶרֶב יוֹם־טוֹב הָאַחֲרוֹן שֶׁל
חַג וְעֶרֶב יוֹם־טוֹב הָרִאשׁוֹן שֶׁל פֶּסַח וְעֶרֶב עֲצֶרֶת וְעֶרֶב רֹאשׁ הַשָּׁנָה; וּכְדִבְרֵי רַבִּי
יוֹסֵי, אַף עֶרֶב יוֹם הַכִּפּוּרִים בַּגָּלִיל. וְהָא דִתְנָן ״צָרִיךְ לְהוֹדִיעוֹ״, דַּוְקָא הַמּוֹכֵר
צָרִיךְ לְהוֹדִיעַ הַדָּבָר, אֲבָל הַלּוֹקֵחַ אֵינוֹ צָרִיךְ לִשְׁאֹל אוֹתוֹ, מִשּׁוּם דְּסָפֵק סְפֵקָא
הוּא עָלָיו: שֶׁמָּא אֵין לָהּ אֵם, וְאִם יֵשׁ לָהּ, שֶׁמָּא לֹא מְכָרָהּ לִשְׁחֹט.

וּמַה שֶּׁאָמְרוּ דִּשְׁנַיִם שֶׁלָּקְחוּ פָּרָה וּבְנָהּ, זֶה שֶׁלָּקַח רִאשׁוֹן יִשְׁחַט רִאשׁוֹן, וְאִם
קָדַם הַשֵּׁנִי וְשָׁחַט שֶׁלֹּא כַדִּין, אָסוּר הָרִאשׁוֹן לִשְׁחֹט; וְדִין הַשּׁוֹחֵט פָּרָה וּשְׁנֵי בָנֶיהָ
אוֹ שְׁנֵי בָנֶיהָ וְאַחַר־כָּךְ הִיא, וְכֵן הִיא וּבִתָּהּ וּבַת בִּתָּהּ. וּמֻתָּר לִשְׁחֹט הָאֵם עִם בַּת
בִּתָּהּ, שֶׁלֹּא אָסַר הַכָּתוּב אֶלָּא ״אֹתוֹ וְאֶת בְּנוֹ״.

וּמַה שֶּׁאָמְרוּ שֶׁאִם שָׁחַט הָאֵם וּבַת בִּתָּהּ וְאַחַר־כָּךְ הַבַּת, שֶׁאֵין סוֹפֵג אֶלָּא
אַרְבָּעִים; וְאַף־עַל־פִּי שֶׁבִּשְׁחִיטַת בַּת זוֹ, עוֹבֵר שְׁנֵי לָאוִין: מִשּׁוּם אֹתוֹ וְאֶת בְּנוֹ,
וּבְנוֹ וְאוֹתוֹ, מִכָּל־מָקוֹם חַד מַעֲשֶׂה הוּא.

וּמַה שֶּׁאָמְרוּ זִכְרוֹנָם לִבְרָכָה שֶׁאָסוּר ״אֹתוֹ וְאֶת בְּנוֹ״ אֵינוֹ נוֹהֵג אֶלָּא
בִּנְקֵבוֹת, שֶׁאָמְרוּ בְּפֵרוּשׁ: ״בְּנוֹ״, מִי שֶׁבְּנוֹ כָרוּךְ אַחֲרָיו, דְּהַיְנוּ הַנְּקֵבָה. וּמִכָּל־
מָקוֹם הָכִי אַסִּיקְנָא בְּחֻלִּין עִם הַפֵּרוּשִׁים הַטּוֹבִים: שֶׁאִם נִתְבָּרֵר לָנוּ הַדָּבָר שֶׁהוּא

---

2. TB Ḥullin 82a.

3. *Ibid.* 83a (Mishnah, v 3). R. Yosé, in the paragraph's second sentence, is R. Yosé of Galilee, so named explicitly in the Talmud.

4. It is the way of Jews to make festive meals then (Rashi to *ibid.* s.v. be'arba'ah).

5. That could have been alive and sold that day.

6. TB Ḥullin 78b.

character. Therefore, although God permitted us living creatures for food for our sustenance, He commanded us not to kill "it and its young" close together in time, and thus to set permanently in our spirit the quality of mercy.

The laws of the precept are, for example, what the Sages of blessed memory taught:[2] that there is no difference whether "it and its young" [are thus ritually slain] or its young first and then the dam. Then there is what they taught:[3] that at four times in the year, whoever sells a domestic animal to his fellow-man is required to tell him, "I sold its dam to be ritually slain": because at these four times, whoever buys [an animal] probably does so to have it ritually slain directly;[4] and these are they: the day before the last festival day of *Sukkoth*, the day before the first festival day of Passover, the day before *Shavu'oth*, and the day before *Rosh haShanah*; and in the view of R. Yosé, also the day before *Yom Kippur* in the Galilee. Now, when we learn in the Mishnah,[3] "he is required to inform him," the seller (vendor) specifically must make the matter known, but the buyer is not required to ask him[3]—because for him it is a doubt upon a doubt: Perhaps it has no mother,[5] and if it has, perhaps he did not sell it to be ritually slain.

We have, further, what the Sages said,[2] that if two bought a cow and its young calf [respectively] the one who made his purchase first may do his ritual slaying first; but if the second went ahead and slew his, unjustly, the first one is then forbidden to do his ritual slaying. Then there is the law of one who ritually slays a cow and its two calves, or its two calves and then it; and likewise [if one ritually slays] a cow, its young (a cow), and the latter's young.[2] It is permissible, though, to ritually slay a dam and the young of its female young; because Scripture forbade no more than "it and its young."

Moreover, there is what the Sages taught:[2] that if one ritually slew a mother beast and the young of its female young, and afterward [he slew] the the female young [the middle one], he is whipped with no more than forty lashes; even though, in slaying it, he transgressed two injunctions—against [slaying] "it and its young" and also "its young and it"—it is but one act nevertheless.

In addition, there is what they of blessed memory said, that the prohibition on "it and its young" applies only to female [parent] animals; for they taught distinctly:[6] "its young"—that follows it in attachment—which means the female [parent animal]. Nevertheless, ⟨267⟩ we conclude thus in the Talmud tractate *Ḥullin* (78b), with the good

אָבִיו וַדַּאי, שֶׁאֵין שׁוֹחֲטִין אוֹתוֹ עִם בְּנוֹ בְּיוֹם אֶחָד, מִשּׁוּם דְּפַסְקִינָן הָתָם הֲלָכָה

כְּרַבִּי יְהוּדָה, וְרַבִּי יְהוּדָה, לְפִי הַנִּשְׁמָע מִדְּבָרָיו, סְפוּקֵי מְסַפְּקָא לֵיהּ אִי חוֹשְׁשִׁין

לְזֶרַע הָאָב אִם לָא, מִדְּקָאָמַר לְעִנְיַן כִּלְאַיִם בִּפְרָדוֹת: אֵין מַרְבִּיעִין עָלֶיהָ לֹא סוּס

וְלֹא חֲמוֹר אֶלָּא מִינָהּ; וְאִי הֲוָה סְבִירָא לֵיהּ דְּאֵין חוֹשְׁשִׁין וַדַּאי לְזֶרַע הָאָב, לֹא

הָיָה אוֹמֵר כֵּן, אֶלָּא הָכִי הֲוָה לֵיהּ לְמֵימַר: אֵין מַרְבִּיעִין עָלֶיהָ אֶלָּא מִינָהּ מִצַּד

אֵם; אֶלָּא וַדַּאי לְרַבִּי יְהוּדָה מְסַפְּקָא לֵיהּ, וְכִי קָאָמַר אֵין חוֹשְׁשִׁין לְזֶרַע

הָאָב, כַּוָּנָתוֹ לוֹמַר שֶׁלֹּא נָחוּשׁ לְזֶרַע הָאָב לְהָקֵל בַּדָּבָר, אֲבָל לְהַחְמִיר, וַדַּאי נָחוּשׁ

לְזֶרַע הָאָב; וּבְכָל מָקוֹם שֶׁיִּהְיֶה חֲמָרָא כְּשֶׁנֹּאמַר שֶׁלֹּא נָחוּשׁ, אָז נֹאמַר שֶׁאֵין

חוֹשְׁשִׁין לוֹ, דְּכֵיוָן דְּסַפּוּקֵי מְסַפְּקָא לֵיהּ אַזְלִינָן לְחֻמְרָא בְּכָל מָקוֹם; וּלְפִי זֶה,

הֵיכָא שֶׁאָנוּ יוֹדְעִין וַדַּאי הַזָּכָר, נָחוּשׁ לוֹ בְּעִנְיַן אוֹתוֹ וְאֶת בְּנוֹ; וְיֶתֶר פְּרָטֶיהָ,

בַּחֲלִין פֶּרֶק שְׁמִינִי.

וְנוֹהֶגֶת בְּכָל מָקוֹם וּבְכָל זְמַן, בִּזְכָרִים וּנְקֵבוֹת. וְעוֹבֵר עַל זֶה וְשָׁחַט אוֹתוֹ וְאֶת

בְּנוֹ בְּיוֹם אֶחָד, אוֹ בְּנוֹ וְאוֹתוֹ, חַיָּב מַלְקוֹת.

[שֶׁלֹּא לַעֲשׂוֹת דָּבָר שֶׁיִּתְחַלֵּל בּוֹ שֵׁם שָׁמַיִם בֵּין בְּנֵי אָדָם]

רצה שֶׁנִּמְנַעְנוּ מֵחִלּוּל הַשֵּׁם, וְהוּא הֵפֶךְ קִדּוּשׁ הַשֵּׁם, שֶׁנִּצְטַוִּינוּ בּוֹ, כְּמוֹ

שֶׁכָּתַבְנוּ לְמַעְלָה בְּסֵדֶר זֶה — שֶׁנֶּאֱמַר: וְלֹא תְחַלְּלוּ אֶת שֵׁם קָדְשִׁי.

וְכָתַב הַמַּעְתִּיק בְּשֵׁם הָרַמְבָּ"ם זִכְרוֹנוֹ לִבְרָכָה: וְהֶעָוֹן הַזֶּה יֵחָלֵק לִשְׁלֹשָׁה

חֲלָקִים, הַשְּׁנַיִם עַל הַכְּלָל וְהָאֶחָד עַל הַפְּרָט. וְהַחֵלֶק הָאֶחָד הַכְּלָלִי, שֶׁכָּל מִי

שֶׁיְּבֻקַּשׁ מִמֶּנּוּ לַעֲבֹר עַל מִצְוָה מִן הַמִּצְווֹת בִּשְׁעַת הַשְּׁמָד וְהָיָה הָאוֹנֶס מְתַכַּוֵּן

לְהַעֲבִיר, בֵּין מִצְווֹת קַלּוֹת בֵּין חֲמוּרוֹת, אוֹ מִי שֶׁיְּבֻקַּשׁ מִמֶּנּוּ לַעֲבֹר עַל עֲבוֹדָה

7. So *tosafoth* to *ibid.* 79a, s.v. '*ayil li.*

8. Literally, about the seed; and so throughout the paragraph.

9. Although a mule results from the union of a donkey with a horse, it may be mated only with another mule from the same kind of dam, but not with the species of the dam.

§295   1. In the original this reads: as we have written above. in this *sidrah*. See §285, n. 2.

2. ShM negative precept §63; see §282, note 2.

commentaries: that if it becomes quite clear to us which male animal is its sire, certainly it and its young are not to be ritually slain in one day. For it is decided there that the definitive law follows the view of R. Judah;[7] and R. Judah, as we gather from his words, is in doubt whether we need be concerned about the relationship[8] of the sire or not, since he states in regard to mixing other species with a mule: It is to be mated with neither a male horse nor a male donkey, but only with its own kind.[9] Now, if he held that we definitely need have no concern about the role[8] of the sire, he would not have expressed it so, but would rather have stated: No male is to be mated with it other than its own kind on the dam's (mother's) side. Then quite certainly R. Judah was in doubt; and when he said, "There need be no concern about the relationship of the sire," he meant to convey that we need not take the role of the sire into account to be lenient in [deciding] any matter; but to decide stringently, we must certainly take the sire's role into account. On the other hand, wherever it would mean a stringent decision if we said we are not concerned [about its share], then we say we are not concerned. For since he was in doubt, we decide strictly in every instance. Accordingly, wherever we know the male [parent animal] for certain, we take it into account in regard to "it and its young." The rest of its details are in chapter 8 of the Talmud tractate Ḥullin.

It applies everywhere, at every time, for both man and woman. If someone transgresses it and ritually slays "it and its young" in one day, or "its young and it," he is punishable by whiplashes.

[TO DO NOTHING BY WHICH THE DIVINE NAME WILL BE PROFANED OR DESECRATED AMONG MEN]

295 that we were forbidden to desecrate the Divine name, this being the opposite of sanctifying the Divine name, which we were commanded to do, as we will write in this *sidrah* (§296)[1]—for it is stated, *And you shall not profane My holy name* (Leviticus 22:32).

Now, the translator wrote in the name of Rambam of blessed memory:[2] This kind of wrongdoing can be divided into three parts, two applying to all in general, and one applying to individuals. One general part is that if it should be asked of any person to transgress any one of the *mitzvoth* at a time of alien religious coercion, whether the one compelling him means to make him transgress minor *mitzvoth* or major, serious ones; or if someone is asked to sin by idol-worship,

זָרָה, גִּלּוּי עֲרָיוֹת אוֹ שְׁפִיכוּת דָּמִים, וַאֲפִלּוּ שֶׁלֹּא בִּשְׁעַת הַשְּׁמָד, הוּא חַיָּב שֶׁיִּמְסֹר
נַפְשׁוֹ וְיֵהָרֵג וְאַל יַעֲבֹר; וְאִם עָבַר וְלֹא נֶהֱרַג, כְּבָר חִלֵּל אֶת הַשֵּׁם בָּרַבִּים, וְעָבַר
עַל אָמְרוֹ "וְלֹא תְחַלְּלוּ אֶת שֵׁם קָדְשִׁי", וְחָטְאוּ עָצוּם מְאֹד.

אָמְנָם אֵינוֹ לוֹקֶה, בַּעֲבוּר שֶׁהוּא אָנוּס: לְפִי שֶׁאֵין לְבֵית-דִּין שֶׁיְּקַיְּמוּ גְּבוּל
מַלְקוּת אוֹ הֶרֶג אֶלָּא בְּמֵזִיד, בְּרָצוֹן, בְּעֵדִים וְהַתְרָאָה. וּלְשׁוֹן סִפְרָא בְּנוֹתֵן מִדַּרְעוֹ
לַמֶּלֶךְ: "וְשַׂמְתִּי אֲנִי אֶת פָּנַי בָּאִישׁ הַהוּא", אָמְרוּ זִכְרוֹנָם לִבְרָכָה: "הַהוּא" וְלֹא
אָנוּס וְלֹא שׁוֹגֵג וְלֹא מֻטְעֶה. וּכְבָר הִתְבָּאֵר לְךָ שֶׁעוֹבֵד עֲבוֹדָה זָרָה בְּאֹנֶס אֵינוֹ
חַיָּב כָּרֵת, וְכָל-שֶׁכֵּן מִיתַת בֵּית-דִּין — וְאָמְנָם עָבַר עַל חִלּוּל הַשֵּׁם.

וְהַחֵלֶק הַשֵּׁנִי הַכְּלָלִי, שֶׁיַּעֲשֶׂה הָאָדָם עֲבֵרָה, אֵין תַּאֲוָה בָּהּ וְלֹא עֲרֵבוּת, אֲבָל
יְכַוֵּן בִּפְעֻלָּתוֹ לְהַכְעִיס, וְזֶה כְּמוֹ-כֵן מְחַלֵּל שֵׁם שָׁמַיִם וְיִלְקֶה, וּלְפִיכָךְ אָמַר: וְלֹא
תִשָּׁבְעוּ בִשְׁמִי לַשָּׁקֶר וְחִלַּלְתָּ אֶת שֵׁם אֱלֹהֶיךָ, שֶׁזֶּה יֵרָאֶה הַכְעָסָה בְּזֶה הַדָּבָר וְאֵין
עֲרֵבוּת גַּשְׁמִי בְּזֶה.

וְהַחֵלֶק אֲשֶׁר עַל הַפְּרָט, שֶׁיַּעֲשֶׂה אִישׁ מְפֻרְסָם בִּגְמִילוּת חֲסָדִים וּמַעֲשִׂים
טוֹבִים מַעֲשֶׂה אֶחָד שֶׁיֵּרָאֶה לָרַבִּים שֶׁהוּא עֲבֵרָה, וְכָגוֹן הַמַּעֲשֶׂה הַהוּא אֵינוֹ רָאוּי
לִכְמוֹ הָאִישׁ הֶחָסִיד הַהוּא שֶׁיַּעֲשֵׂהוּ; אַף-עַל-פִּי שֶׁהוּא מַעֲשֶׂה הֶתֵּר, חִלֵּל אֶת
הַשֵּׁם; וְהוּא אָמְרָם זִכְרוֹנָם לִבְרָכָה: הֵיכִי דָמֵי חִלּוּל הַשֵּׁם, כְּגוֹן אֲנָא דְּשָׁקֵילְנָא
בִּשְׂרָא מִבֵּי טַבָּחָא וְלָא יַהֲבִינָא דָּמֵי לְאַלְתַּר. רַבִּי פְּלוֹנִי אָמַר: כְּגוֹן אֲנָא דְּמַסְגֵּינָא
אַרְבַּע אַמּוֹת בְּלֹא תוֹרָה וּבְלֹא תְפִלִּין. וּכְבָר נִכְפַּל לָאו זֶה וְאָמַר: וְלֹא תְחַלֵּל אֶת
שֵׁם אֱלֹהֶיךָ אֲנִי יי. עַד כָּאן.

3. Cf. TB Yoma 86a: But if one has the desecration of the Divine name on his
record [literally, in his hand] neither does repentance have the power to let it remain
suspended [for the Day of Atonement to clear it away], nor does the Day of Atonement
have the power to atone for it, nor afflictions to wash it away; rather, all leave it
suspended, and death washes it away....

4. Sifra, k'doshim, parashah 10, 5.

5. MH notes that Rambam does not declare such a miscreant liable to whiplashes,
and he wonders at our author for writing this, since an act that desecrates the Divine
name does not necessarily incur such a punishment. In MT bilchoth yesodé ha-torah v 10,
Rambam indeed makes no mention of lashes, but merely writes, "Whoever transgresses
of his own will [literally, mind] without any compulsion, any of the commandments
stated in the Torah, coldly and deliberately, to infuriate [the Creator], thus desecrates the
Divine name." Here, however, our author is citing ShM negative precept 63, and the
term is Rambam's. Some two centuries before MH, though, R. David ibn Abi Zimra
(Radbaz) similarly found such a view in Rambam incomprehensible (M'tzudath David
§ 7; see ShM ed. Heller, ibid. note 8). MY replies, however, that had Rambam meant the
whiplashes as the penalty for the desecration of the Divine name, the objection would be
justified, since this is obviously an omnibus injunction, applying to a wide variety of
deeds, and for violating such an injunction, lashes are never given. Moreover, the Divine
name can equally be desecrated by a failure to do something, e.g. (see note 8) if someone

by consanguineous or adulterous conjugal intimacy, or by the shedding of blood—even if not at a time of alien religious coercion—he is duty-bound to give up his life and be killed rather than commit the transgression. If he does the sin and is [therefore] not to put to death, he has already publicly desecrated the Divine name, and has disobeyed His utterance, *you shall not profane My holy name*; and his sin is enormous.[3]

Nevertheless, he receives no whiplashes, because he was compelled. For it is not for a *beth din* (court) to apply the rule of whiplashes or a death sentence to anything but a deliberate act by free will, where there were witnesses and a warning. In the language of the Midrash *Sifra*, regarding one who gives one of his children to Molech[4] (§208): *then I will set My face against that man* (Leviticus 20:5)—Our Sages of blessed memory said: "against that man," but not against one who was compelled, who acted unwittingly, or acted in error. And it has been made clear to you previously that if a person engages in idol-worship under compulsion, he is not punishable by *karéth* [Divine severance of existence] and certainly not by a death sentence of the *beth din*. He has committed, however, the sin of desecration of the Divine name.

The second general part [of the precept] is that if a man does a sin which involves no craving desire or sweet pleasure, but he [merely] intends to enrage [Heaven], he likewise desecrates the name of Heaven, and should be given a whipping of lashes.[5] For this reason He said, *And you shall not swear by My name falsely, and so profane the name of your God* (Leviticus 19:12)—for here infuriation[6] is plainly visible in the matter, as there is no sweet physical pleasure in it.

The part about individuals is that if a man who is widely known for his acts of kindness and good deeds should do one thing that appears to people at large to be sinful—e.g. if this deed is not seemly for a pious, kindly man like him to do, even if it is a permissible deed—it is a desecration of the Divine name. Hence the Sages said:[7] "How could desecration of the Divine name happen?—for example, if I[8] were to take meat from the butcher and not give him money immediately."[9] Rabbi So-and-so[10] said, "For instance, if I went four cubits without Torah study and *t'fillin* [on me]." This injunction was repeated previously, when Scripture stated, *neither shall you profane the name of your God: I am the Lord* (Leviticus 18:21). Thus far [the words of Rambam].

⟨271⟩ The root reason for this precept, some of its laws, and all its topics,

שֹׁרֶשׁ מִצְוָה זוֹ וּקְצָת דִּינֶיהָ וְכָל עִנְיָנֶיהָ, כְּמִנְהָגִי, כָּתַבְתִּי בְּמִצְוַת קִדּוּשׁ הַשֵּׁם עֲשֵׂה ו' בְּסֵדֶר זֶה [סִי' רצ"ו].

[מִצְוַת קִדּוּשׁ הַשֵּׁם]

רצו שֶׁנִּצְטַוִּינוּ לְקַדֵּשׁ אֶת הַשֵּׁם, שֶׁנֶּאֱמַר: וְנִקְדַּשְׁתִּי בְּתוֹךְ בְּנֵי יִשְׂרָאֵל, כְּלוֹמַר שֶׁנִּמְסֹר נַפְשֵׁנוּ לָמוּת עַל קִיּוּם מִצְוַת הַדָּת. וּכְבָר בֵּאֲרוּ בֵּאֲרוּ זִכְרוֹנָם לִבְרָכָה מִפִּי הַקַּבָּלָה וּמִן הַכְּתוּבִים בְּאֵי זֶה עִנְיָן וּבְאֵי זוֹ מִצְוָה נִצְטַוִּינוּ בָּזֶה. וְאַף־עַל־פִּי שֶׁכָּתוּב בַּתּוֹרָה "וָחַי בָּהֶם", דְּמַשְׁמָע וְלֹא שֶׁיָּמוּת בָּהֶם, כְּבָר קִבְּלוּ הֵם שֶׁלֹּא נֶאֱמַר מִקְרָא זֶה בְּכָל עִנְיָן וּבְכָל עֲבֵרָה, וּמִפִּי הַקַּבָּלָה אָנוּ חַיִּין בְּכָל דִּבְרֵי הַתּוֹרָה.

וּבְפֵרוּשׁ אָמְרוּ זִכְרוֹנָם לִבְרָכָה כִּי ג' מִצְווֹת הֵן שֶׁחַיָּב הָאָדָם שֶׁיֵּהָרֵג עֲלֵיהֶן וְאַל יַעֲבֹר בָּהֶן לְעוֹלָם, וְהֵן: עֲבוֹדָה זָרָה וְכָל אֲבִיזְרָהָא, כְּלוֹמַר כָּל עִנְיָן שֶׁלָּה הָאָסוּר לָנוּ מִכֹּחַ הַלָּאוִין הַמְיֻסָּדִין בָּהּ, וּכְמוֹ שֶׁנִּפְרֵשׁ לְמַטָּה בְּעֶזְרַת הַשֵּׁם; וְכֵן גִּלּוּי עֲרָיוֹת וְכָל אֲבִיזְרָהָא, וּשְׁפִיכוּת דָּמִים: שֶׁאִם יֹאמְרוּ לוֹ לְאָדָם "עֲבֹד עֲבוֹדָה זָרָה אוֹ נַהַרְגֶךָ", יֵהָרֵג וְאַל יַעֲבֹד; וְאַף־עַל־פִּי שֶׁלִּבּוֹ תָּמִים בֶּאֱמוּנַת הַשֵּׁם, אַף־עַל־פִּי־כֵן נִצְטַוָּה שֶׁיֵּהָרֵג וְלֹא יַעֲשֶׂה הַמַּעֲשֶׂה הָרַע הַהוּא, וְלֹא יִתֵּן מָקוֹם אֶל הַמַּעֲבִיר לַחֲשֹׁב שֶׁהוּא כָּפַר בַּשֵּׁם. וּלְשׁוֹן סִפְרֵי: עַל־מְנָת־כֵּן הוֹצֵאתִי אֶתְכֶם מֵאֶרֶץ מִצְרַיִם, שֶׁתַּקְדִּישׁוּ אֶת שְׁמִי בָּרַבִּים. וּכְמוֹ־כֵן בַּשְּׁתַּיִם שֶׁזָּכַרְנוּ, יֵהָרֵג וְאַל יַעֲבֹר, כְּמוֹ שֶׁאָמַרְנוּ.

שֹׁרֶשׁ מִצְוָה זוֹ יָדוּעַ, כִּי הָאָדָם לֹא נִבְרָא רַק לַעֲבֹד בּוֹרְאוֹ, וּמִי שֶׁאֵינוֹ מוֹסֵר גּוּפוֹ עַל עֲבוֹדַת אֲדוֹנָיו אֵינֶנּוּ עֶבֶד טוֹב. וַהֲרֵי בְּנֵי־אָדָם יִמְסְרוּ נַפְשׁוֹתָם עַל אֲדוֹנֵיהֶם; קַל וָחֹמֶר עַל מִצְוַת מֶלֶךְ מַלְכֵי הַמְּלָכִים הַקָּדוֹשׁ בָּרוּךְ הוּא.

like Rav failed to pay his butcher promptly. Rambam's meaning, however (writes MY), is that a whipping is due for the transgression itself, and in addition there is guilt for the desecration of the Name that it causes. This is borne out by the verse that follows: the example that Rambam has in mind is swearing a false oath; and in MT *bilchoth sh'vu'oth* xii 1 he writes: "Although one who swears a vain or false oath is given whiplashes . . . the sin of the oath is not entirely expiated for them . . . until payment is exacted from him over the great Name that he desecrated. . . ."

6. I.e. the intention to infuriate the Almighty.

7. TB Yoma 86a.

8. The noted *'amora* Rav, who says this in the Talmud.

9. If I were late in paying, he would say I was a robber, and would learn from me to treat robbery as a trivial matter (Rashi to *ibid.* s.v. *v'lo'*).

10. I.e. R. Yoḥanan.

11. The original reads, "I wrote"; see §285, note 2.

§296   1. So that generally we regard it as a commandment of the Torah to ignore or violate any precepts when it is necessary in order to save a life.

2. TB Sanhedrin 74a.

in my usual way, I will write[11] in the *mitzvah* of sanctification of the Divine name, the sixth positive precept in this *sidrah* (§296).

[THE MITZVAH OF SANCTIFYING THE ALMIGHTY'S NAME]

296 that we were commanded to sanctify the Divine name: for it is written, *but I will be hallowed among the Israelites* (Leviticus 22:32), which means that we should [be ready to] offer up our lives, to die for observing a precept of our religion. Long ago the Sages of blessed memory clarified, by the Oral Tradition and from verses of Scripture, in which situation and over which *mitzvah* we were commanded this. Now, although it is written in the Torah, *that he shall live by them* (Leviticus 18:5), which implies, but not that he should die by them[1]— they had an early tradition that this verse was not stated [to apply] in every situation and about every transgression; and it is by the utterance of the Oral Tradition that we live with all the words of the Torah.

Now, the Sages of blessed memory said distinctly[2] that there are three precepts over which a man is duty-bound to die [if necessary] and never transgress them. These are: (1) idol-worship and all its appurtenances; in other words, everything pertaining to it that is forbidden us[3] by the force of the injunctions that were established about it,[4] as we will explain below, with the Eternal Lord's help. (2) There are, likewise, consanguineous or adulterous conjugal relations and all that pertains to them, and (3) the shedding of blood. Thus, if a man is told, "Worship the idol, or we will kill you," he is to undergo death and not worship it. Even if he is wholehearted in his faith in the Eternal Lord,[5] he is nevertheless commanded that he should rather be killed and not do that evil act, so as to leave no room for his malefactor[6] to think that he has heretically denied the Eternal Lord. In the language of the Midrash *Sifra:*[7] "On this condition I took you out of the land of Egypt, that you should sanctify My name among the many." And the same holds true for the other two we mentioned: he is to undergo death sooner than transgress, as we stated.

The root reason for this precept is known (obvious): because a man was created for nothing else but to serve his Creator. Anyone who would not offer up his body for the service and worship of his master is not a good servant. Well, here people are ready to give their
lives for their masters. How much more so [should we] over the com-

מִדִּינֵי הַמִּצְוָה, מַה שֶּׁאָמְרוּ זִכְרוֹנָם לִבְרָכָה שֶׁבְּאֵלּוּ הַג' עֲבֵרוֹת שֶׁזָּכַרְנוּ חַיָּב
הָאָדָם לִמְסֹר נַפְשׁוֹ בְּכָל עִנְיָן, בֵּין בִּשְׁעַת שְׁמָד אוֹ שֶׁלֹּא בִּשְׁעַת שְׁמָד, וּבֵין
בְּפַרְהֶסְיָא אוֹ אֲפִלּוּ בְּצִנְעָה, וּבֵין שֶׁיִּתְכַּוֵּן הַגּוֹי אוֹ לְהַעֲבִיר אוֹ אֲפִלּוּ לַהֲנָאַת עַצְמוֹ;
אֲבָל בִּשְׁאָר עֲבֵרוֹת אָמְרוּ דְּשֶׁלֹּא בִּשְׁעַת הַשְּׁמָד וּבְצִנְעָה יַעֲבֹר וְאַל יֵהָרֵג, וַאֲפִלּוּ
יִתְכַּוֵּן הַגּוֹי לְהַעֲבִירוֹ; אֲבָל בְּפַרְהֶסְיָא, כְּלוֹמַר בִּפְנֵי עֲשָׂרָה יִשְׂרָאֵל, אִם לַהֲנָאָתוֹ
מִתְכַּוֵּן הַמַּעֲבִיר, יַעֲבֹר וְאַל יֵהָרֵג, וְאִם לְהַעֲבִירוֹ, יֵהָרֵג וְאַל יַעֲבֹר.

וּבִשְׁעַת הַשְּׁמָד, אֲפִלּוּ בְּצִנְעָה וַאֲפִלּוּ לַהֲנָאָתוֹ וַאֲפִלּוּ עַל מִצְוָה קַלָּה, יֵהָרֵג
וְאַל יַעֲבֹר; וּמִצְוָה קַלָּה הִיא כְּעִין מַה שֶּׁאָמְרוּ זִכְרוֹנָם לִבְרָכָה: אֲפִלּוּ אַעֲרַקְתָּא
דִּמְסָאנָא, כְּלוֹמַר שֶׁלֹּא יַעֲשֶׂה הַיִּשְׂרָאֵל צוּרַת מִנְעָלוֹ כְּמוֹ הַגּוֹיִם הָעוֹבְדִים עֲבוֹדָה
זָרָה, שֶׁלֹּא יִדְמֶה לִהְיוֹת עוֹבֵד עֲבוֹדָה זָרָה כָּהֶם.

וְזֶה שֶׁאָמְרוּ אֲבִיזְרָהָא דַּעֲבוֹדָה זָרָה, הָעִנְיָן הוּא לוֹמַר כָּל מַה שֶּׁנֶּאֱסַר לָנוּ
מִכָּל לָאו הַמְיֻחָד בַּעֲבוֹדָה זָרָה; וּכְעִין מַה שֶּׁאָמְרוּ בְּפֶסַח רִאשׁוֹן: בַּכֹּל מִתְרַפְּאִין
בִּמְקוֹם סַכָּנָה חוּץ מֵעֲצֵי אֲשֵׁרָה, וְאָמְרוּ עָלָה בִּירוּשַׁלְמִי: לֹא סוֹף דָּבָר בְּשֶׁאָמַר
לוֹ רוֹפֵא "הָבֵא לִי עָלִין שֶׁל אֲשֵׁרָה פְּלוֹנִית", דְּמִיחְזֵי כְּמַאן דְּמוֹדֶה בָּהּ, אֶלָּא
אֲפִלּוּ אָמַר לוֹ "הָבֵא לִי עָלִין שֶׁל אִילָן שֶׁל פְּלוֹנִי" סְתָם, וְהָלַךְ וְלֹא מָצָא אֶלָּא שֶׁל
אֲשֵׁרָה, יֵהָרֵג וְאַל יַעֲבֹר.

וְאַף עַל גַּב דְּהָשְׁתָּא כִּי מִיתְּסֵי בַּעֲצֵי אֲשֵׁרָה לָאו עֲבוֹדָה זָרָה מַמָּשׁ הִיא, דְּהָא
לָא פָּלַח לָהּ, אֶלָּא מִכָּל מָקוֹם-מָקוֹם דְּמִתְהַנֵּי מִנַּהּ וְאִיכָּא בְּמִלְּתָא לָאו דְּ"לֹא יִדְבַּק
בְּיָדְךָ מְאוּמָה מִן הַחֵרֶם", דְּהוּא לָאו הַמְיֻחָד בַּעֲבוֹדָה זָרָה. אֲבָל אִסּוּרִין טוּבָא

---

3. Cf. R. Z'raḥyah haLévi, *baMa'or baGadol*, on R. Isaac 'Alfasi, *ibid.*

4. So Ramban, *Milḥamoth haShem*, on *ibid.* and R. Nissim, TB 'Avodah Zarah, 33 8b, s.v. *bakol*, and P'saḥim 1 36b.

5. So that if he carried out the idol-worship demanded of him, it would only be a meaningless act for him. The sentence is based on ShM positive precept §9.

6. Literally, for the one who would cause transgression.

7. Sifra, 'emor, perek 9, 6, interpreting our opening verse and what follows: *but I will be hallowed among the Israelites: I am the Lord who hallow you, who brought you out of the land of Egypt* (Leviticus 22:32–33).

8. The standard editions read . . . ובעת צרה אפילו על מצוה קלה "And, in a time of dire trouble, even over a minor *mitzvah*," etc. The change from ובשעת השמד (. . . a time of alien religious coercion) was quite certainly made in the face of the censorship on published material that prevailed in Christian Europe. The phrase about "his benefit or enjoyment" may well have been omitted because, as noted below, it is at variance with the views of Early Authorities (*rishonim*); and the phrase "even in private" may simply

⟨274⟩

mandment of the supreme King over all kings, the Holy One, blessed is He.

Among the laws of the precept, there is what the Sages of blessed memory taught:[2] that over these three transgressions that we mentioned, a man is duty-bound to be ready to give up his life in every circumstance, whether or not it is a time of alien religious coercion, whether it is in public or even in private, and whether the non-Jew [compelling him] means to make [him] transgress or even intends [only] his own benefit or enjoyment. About other transgressions, however, they said that if it is not a time of alien religious coercion and it is in private, he should commit the sin and not be killed, even if the heathen thus in ends [specifically] to make him sin. In public, though, which means before ten [or more] Jews, if the one compelling him intends his own benefit or enjoyment, he should transgress and not be killed; but if it is to make him sin, let him undergo death and not sin.

Now, if it is a time of alien religious coercion, then even in private, even if it is for his [the heathen's] benefit or enjoyment, and even if it is over a minor *mitzvah*, he should be killed rather than transgress.[8] A minor *mitzvah* means something like what our Sages of blessed memory said:[8a] even about a shoe-strap; in other words, a Jew should not make the form of his shoe as the heathen who worship idols do,[9] so that he should not appear to be an idol-worshipper like them.

Now, the phrase that we mentioned, "the appurtenances of idolatry," is meant to convey, in substance, all that was forbidden us by every injunction that is specifically about idol-worship[4]—such as what the Sages taught in the first part of the tractate *P'saḥim* (25a): Healing may be done by everything in a case of danger to life, except for *'ashérah* trees.[10] And about this it was said in the Jerusalem Talmud:[11] If a physician tells someone, "Bring me leaves from that *'ashérah* tree," so that he seems like a person who acknowledges it [as an idol to be worshipped],[12] this is not all. Even if he tells him unspecifically, "Bring me leaves of that kind of tree," and he goes and finds nothing but an *'ashérah*,[13] let him die[14] sooner than transgress.

Even though now, if someone were to be healed by [something from] *'ashérah* trees, it is not actually idolatry, since he does not worship it, nevertheless he is benefiting from it, and there is an injunction about the matter: *nothing of the forbidden thing shall cling to your hand* (Deuteronomy 13:18); for this is a negative precept (§466) specifically about idolatry. On the other hand, the good number of prohibitions

have gone with the rest. This reading, however, from the first edition, is confirmed by the early manuscripts.

Now, R. Nissim (b. Re'uven Gerondi) writes, "However, where the heathen make the edict [of forced conversion, etc.] for their own personal benefit or enjoyment, then whether in private or in public, as long as one of the other transgressions is involved, excluding idolatry, forbidden carnal relations, and bloodshed, we do not apply the rule that one is to be killed sooner than transgress" (*Ḥiddushé haRan: Sanhedré G'dolah* VII p. 273). This is, in fact, Rambam's view in his *Iggereth haSh'mad*: "As regards all the other commandments, apart from these three, if one is subjected to coercion, let him see: If the other is intent on his own enjoyment, let him transgress and not be killed, be it during a time of alien religious coercion or not, be it in private or in public" (*Igg'roth l'Rabbénu Mosheh b. Maimon*, ed. Kafaḥ, p. 114). Me'iri goes further and states that if the heathen's sole purpose is his own benefit-enjoyment, "even if it is a matter of idolatry or severely forbidden carnal relations, and even if at a time of alien religious coercion, and it is public knowledge — one is to transgress and not be killed." An editor's note adds that in regard to forbidden carnal intimacy, this is also the view of R. Z'raḥyah haLévi and *Séfer Eshkol* (*Béth haB'ḥirah: Sanhedré G'dolah* IV 215b).

As R. Yosef Kafaḥ notes (*op. cit.* p. 105), Rambam evidently wrote *Iggereth haSh'mad* early in his life. In MT, written many years later, he is not explicit on this. He writes: "When does this apply [that under compulsion on pain of death, one should commit a sin and not be killed]? — with other commandments, except idolatry, severely forbidden carnal relations, and bloodshed. With these three, however, if one is told, *Violate one of them or be killed,* let him submit to death and not transgress. Yet when does this [distinction between these three commandments and all others] hold true? — when the heathen is intent on his own enjoyment... but if he is solely intent on making him violate the commandments, if it is in private and ten Jews are not there, let him transgress and not be killed; while if he [the other] applies force to make him commit the act among ten Jews [or more, i.e. in public], let him submit to death and not transgress — even if the other's purpose is to make him transgress only one of the other commandments. But all these rules hold when it is not a time of alien religious coercion. During a time of such coercion, however — that is, when a wicked sovereign like Nebuchadnezzar and his associates arises and issues a decree against Jewry to nullify their religion or one of the commandments — one should be killed sooner than transgress even one of the other commandments, whether he is compelled among ten or in privacy with the heathen" (MT *hilchoth yesodé ha-torah* v 2–3).

Assuming agreement with *Iggereth haSh'mad,* the editor of MT variorum ed. vol. 1 states categorically that the last sentence of the above citation applies solely when the

sovereign's intent is "to nullify their religion," etc. but if the intent is the heathen's enjoyment the law remains: transgress and survive—"and not (the editor adds) as *Ḥiddushé haRan* has understood it." For R. Nissim writes, "But it seems to me that this is not the view of Rambam of blessed memory in chapter 5 of *hilchoth yesodé ha-torah*, since he states, 'But all these rules hold when it is not at a time of alien religious coercion' etc.—after he has permitted [transgressing to save one's life when the heathen's intent is] their own enjoyment—which implies that at a time of an edict [of coercion] there is no permissibility whatever to transgress" (*op. cit.* p. 273). Again, Me'iri states, "There are likewise those who differ, stating that at a time of alien religious coercion, even with all [the commandments] and it is for their [the heathen's] own enjoyment, it is forbidden to transgress" (*op. cit.* p. 217b).

See also in TB Sanhedrin 74b the question on Queen Esther: How could she accept marriage to the heathen Ahasuerus? As it was a matter of common knowledge ("in public"), surely she should have undergone death sooner than submit? And Rava's reply is that Ahasuerus was intent solely on his own pleasure. This is the basis for the ruling that where the heathen's purpose is his own enjoyment, one may transgress so as not to be killed. However, *Nimmuké Yosef* to Rif comments that Esther's marriage was not at a time of alien religious coercion: The only decree in force then which went counter to the Torah was the royal order to gather all maidens in the empire of Ahasuerus for conjugal intimacy with him, so that he might choose one of them as queen. Since this decree was not directed solely at the Jewish people but at the entire population equally (*Nimmuké Yosef* states), it cannot be regarded as "a time of alien religious coercion." Hence our author's view would follow: that where such coercion exists, the fact that the heathen's purpose is personal enjoyment does not remove the obligation to be killed sooner than transgress.

8a. TB Sanhedrin 74b.

9. Since our author gives this as an example of "a minor *mitzvah*," it indicates that he follows R. Isaac 'Alfasi on TB Sanhedrin 74b, that this refers to a situation where the heathen made their shoe-straps in a particular way, e.g. in a certain color, and the Jews made theirs differently, so as not to dress like them—in keeping with the injunction, *you shall not follow the established practices of the nations* (Leviticus 20:23). Rashi (TB *ibid.* s.v. '*ark'tha*) applies this ruling even to a practice adopted by Jewry, e.g. for the sake of modesty (MH, MY). See also *Kessef Mishneh* to MT *hilchoth yesodé ha-torah* v 2.

10. I.e. not a species of trees, but those worshipped in idolatry.

11. TJ Shabbath xiv 4, and 'Avodah Zarah iii 2.

12. Since he calls it by this name; see note 10.

13. I.e. the only tree or trees of the required kind that he finds are objects of idolatrous worship.

14. By failing to bring the leaves needed to heal him.

דְּאִיכָּא בַּעֲבוֹדָה זָרָה דְּיָלְפִינָן לְהוּ מִלָּאו דְּ"לִפְנֵי עִוֵּר לֹא תִתֵּן מִכְשֹׁל", לֵיתְנִהוּ
בִּכְלַל אַבִיזְרַיְהָא דַּעֲבוֹדָה זָרָה לְהֵרָגֵ עֲלֵיהֶם, כֵּיוָן דְּלָאו דְּ"לִפְנֵי עִוֵּר" אֵינוֹ מִיְחָד
בַּעֲבוֹדָה זָרָה מַמָּשׁ, דִּבְכֻלְּהוּ מִצְווֹת נַמֵּי אִיתֵיהּ.

אַחַר שֶׁכָּתַבְתִּי זֶה, מָצָאתִי בְּמִקְצָת חִדּוּשֵׁי מוֹרַי, יִשְׁמְרֵם אֵל, שֶׁכָּתְבוּ כִּי
בִּירוּשַׁלְמִי דַּעֲבוֹדָה זָרָה מַשְׁמַע דְּכָל שֶׁאָמַר לוֹ הָרוֹפֵא עָלָיו סְתָם, יַעֲבֹר וְאַל
יֵהָרֵג.

וְעִנְיַן שְׁפִיכוּת דָּמִים, לָמְדוּ הָעִנְיָן, זִכְרוֹנָם לִבְרָכָה, מִדֶּרֶךְ הַסְּבָרָא, וְאָמְרוּ עַל
דֶּרֶךְ מָשָׁל: מַאי חָזִית דְּדָמָא דִּידָךְ סוּמָק טְפֵי, דִּלְמָא דָּמָא דְּהַהוּא גַּבְרָא סוּמָק
טְפֵי; כְּלוֹמַר הַנִּרְצָח יִהְיֶה רָאוּי לַעֲשׂוֹת יוֹתֵר מִצְווֹת מֵאוֹתוֹ שֶׁהָרָגוֹ, וְעַל־כֵּן אֵינוֹ
בְּדִין שֶׁיַּהֲרֹג שׁוּם אָדָם לַחֲבֵרוֹ, וַאֲפִילּוּ יֵהָרֵג הוּא עַל זֶה.

וְעוֹד אָמְרוּ זִכְרוֹנָם לִבְרָכָה שֶׁאֲפִלּוּ כַּמָּה אֲלָפִים הָיוּ יִשְׂרְאֵלִים וְאָמְרוּ לָהֶם
אַנָּסִים "תְּנוּ לָנוּ אֶחָד מִכֶּם, וְאִם לָאו נַהֲרֹג כֻּלְּכֶם", יֵהָרְגוּ כֻּלָּם וְאַל יִמְסְרוּ נֶפֶשׁ
אַחַת מִיִּשְׂרָאֵל; וְדַוְקָא כְּשֶׁאָמְרוּ לָהֶם "אֶחָד" סְתָם, אֲבָל יִחֲדוּהוּ לָהֶם בְּפֵרוּשׁ,
שֶׁאָמְרוּ "תְּנוּ לָנוּ פְּלוֹנִי, וְאִם לָאו נַהֲרֹג כֻּלְּכֶם", רַשָּׁאִין לִתְּנוֹ, כָּעִנְיָן הַיָּדוּעַ
בְּשֶׁבַע בֶּן בִּכְרִי. וְכֵן הַדִּין בְּנָשִׁים שֶׁאָמְרוּ לָהֶן גּוֹיִם "תְּנוּ לָנוּ אַחַת מִכֶּם" וְכוּלֵי,
כְּדְאִיתָא בְּמַסֶּכֶת תְּרוּמוֹת פֶּרֶק שְׁמִינִי.

וְעִנְיַן עֲרָיוֹת שֶׁנֶּהֱרָגִין עֲלֵיהֶן לָמְדוּ, זִכְרוֹנָם לִבְרָכָה, אוֹתוֹ לְפִי שֶׁהֻקְשָׁה נַעֲרָה
מְאֹרָסָה לְרוֹצֵחַ: מָה רוֹצֵחַ יֵהָרֵג וְאַל יַעֲבֹר, כְּמוֹ שֶׁאָמַרְנוּ, כֵּן נַעֲרָה מְאֹרָסָה יֵהָרֵג
אָדָם וְלֹא יִבְעַל אוֹתָהּ, כִּי הַתּוֹרָה לֹא תִמְשֹׁל מְשָׁלִים חִנָּם, רַק לְלַמֵּד עִנְיָן. וְעוֹד
יֵשׁ לָהֶם בָּזֶה סֶמֶךְ מִן הַקַּבָּלָה, שֶׁהִיא חוֹמַת בַּרְזֶל לְכָל דִּבְרֵיהֶם.

15. See e.g. §232, fourth paragraph.

16. So Ramban, commentary to R. Isaac 'Alfasi, TB Sanhedrin viii, and R. Nissim,
TB P'saḥim 137a.

17. (See two paragraphs above.) So also *tosafoth* to TB 'Avodah Zarah 27b, s.v.
sha'ni, on the basis of TJ Shabbath viii.

18. TJ T'rumoth viii 4.

19. I.e. in Deuteronomy 22:26, *for just as when a man rises against his neighbor and
slays him, even so is this matter.* This is taken as a basis to apply the same laws to both
subjects; so TB P'saḥim 25b and Sanhedrin 74a.

20. Literally: does not give parables for nothing.

21. See Sh'moth Rabbah 16, 2; or it may mean that in general the Sages taught
nothing of their own, but only what they received from their teachers, and their teachers
from their teachers in turn, in a chain of tradition. See Mishnah, 'Avoth i 1.

that there are about idolatry which we derive from the injunction, *before a blind man you shall not put a stumbling-block* (Leviticus 19:14),[15] are not included among "the appurtenances of idolatry" to require undergoing death on their account—since the injunction about the blind man is not specifically about actual idolatry, as it applies also to all the precepts.[16]

After I wrote this, I found in some of the writings of commentary on religious law by my master instructor, God protect him, that he wrote that in the Jerusalem Talmud, tractate *'Avodah Zarah* (ii 2) it is implied that as long as the physician tells him simply, unspecifically, "[Bring me] leaves," one may transgress and not undergo death.[17]

Now, concerning the shedding of blood, the Sages of blessed memory derived the matter through reasoning,[2] and they said by way of illustration, "What have you seen [to make you think] your blood is more red? Perhaps that man's blood is redder." In other words, the one who is to be killed may be fit to fulfill more *mitzvoth* than the one who is to kill him. It is therefore not just that any man should kill his fellow-man, even if he should be killed for it.

Moreover, our Sages of blessed memory taught[18] that even if there were several thousand Jews, and villains told them, "Give us one of you [to kill] or else we will kill you all," they are all to suffer death rather than give up one Jewish soul [to be killed]. This applies, however, only if they told them "one" generally, unspecifically; but if they singled one out distinctly, saying, "Give us so-and-so, or else we will kill you all," they are allowed to give him over, as in the known instance of Sheba the son of Bichri (II Samuel 20:21–22). And the same law applies to women to whom non-Jews say, "Give us one of you," etc. as we read in chapter 8 of the Mishnah tractate *T'rumoth* (viii 12).

As to the subject of consanguineous or adulterous conjugal relations, that one should undergo death on their account, the Sages of blessed memory inferred this because the case of a [raped] betrothed maiden was equated with that of a murderer.[19] Then just as in a matter of murder one should undergo death sooner than commit it, as we stated, so with a betrothed maiden should a man be killed sooner than be conjugally intimate with her. For the Torah does not use figures of speech purposelessly,[20] but only to teach a point. Moreover, the Sages have a basis for this in the Oral Tradition,[21] which is a wall of

⟨279⟩ iron for all their words.

וְכָתְבוּ הָרִאשׁוֹנִים דְּלָא אַמְרִינַן "יֵהָרֵג וְאַל יַעֲבֹר" לְעוֹלָם אֶלָּא לַעֲבֹר עֲבֵרָה,
אֲבָל לְהִבָּטֵל מִמִּצְוָה יַעֲבֹר וְאַל יַעֲשֶׂה הַמִּצְוָה וְאַל יֵהָרֵג; וּכְעֵין מַה שֶׁאָמְרוּ
זִכְרוֹנָם לִבְרָכָה בְּאֶסְתֵּר: קַרְקַע עוֹלָם הָיְתָה, כְּלוֹמַר וְהוּא כְעֵין "שֵׁב וְאַל
תַּעֲשֵׂה", שֶׁהֲרֵי הָאִשָּׁה עַל כָּרְחָהּ נִבְעֶלֶת, וַאֲפִלּוּ סִיְּעָה הָאִשָּׁה בְּתַשְׁמִישׁ לְאַחַר
שֶׁהַלְבִּישָׁהּ הַיֵּצֶר, לֹא תִתְחַיֵּב בְּכָךְ, שֶׁאֵין אֹנֶס גָּדוֹל מִמֶּנּוּ.

וּמַה שֶּׁשָּׁמַעְנוּ מַעֲשִׂים לַחֲסִידִים הָרִאשׁוֹנִים שֶׁנֶּהֱרָגִים עַל בִּטּוּל מִצְוָה, וּכְעֵין
מַה שֶׁאָמְרוּ זִכְרוֹנָם לִבְרָכָה: מַה לָּךְ יוֹצֵא לַסָּקֵל, עַל שֶׁמַּלְתִּי אֶת בְּנִי; מַה לָּךְ
יוֹצֵא לִצָּלֵב, עַל שֶׁנָּטַלְתִּי אֶת הַלּוּלָב—מִדַּת חֲסִידוּת עָשׂוּ הֵם, וְרָאוּ שֶׁהַדּוֹר הָיָה
צָרִיךְ לְכָךְ, וְהָיוּ חֲכָמִים גְּדוֹלִים רְאוּיִין לְכָךְ לְהוֹרוֹת עַל זֶה; שֶׁאִלְמָלֵא־כֵן שֶׁהָיוּ
גְדוֹלִים וַחֲכָמִים, לֹא הָיוּ רַשָּׁאִין לִמְסֹר נַפְשָׁם לָמוּת, שֶׁלֹּא לְכָל אָדָם יֵשׁ רְשׁוּת
לִהָרֵג בַּמֶּה שֶׁלֹּא חִיְּבוּנוּ זִכְרוֹנָם לִבְרָכָה לִהָרֵג עָלָיו; וְלֹא עוֹד אֶלָּא שֶׁמִּתְחַיֵּב
בְּנַפְשׁוֹ הוּא.

וְעוֹד רָאִיתִי בְּעִנְיַן מִצְוָה זוֹ בְּסִפְרֵי מוֹרַי יִשְׁמְרֵם אֵל, שֶׁבְּכָל אִשָּׁה שֶׁקִּדּוּשִׁין
תּוֹפְסִין בָּהּ, כְּגוֹן אַלְמָנָה לְכֹהֵן גָּדוֹל, גְּרוּשָׁה וַחֲלוּצָה לְכֹהֵן הֶדְיוֹט, מַמְזֶרֶת
וּנְתִינָה לְיִשְׂרָאֵל, בַּת יִשְׂרָאֵל לְנָתִין וּמַמְזֵר, שֶׁאֵינָן עֲרָיוֹת לֵהָרֵג עֲלֵיהֶן; (אֲבָל
מִכָּל מָקוֹם לְהוֹרוֹת לָשׁוּם אָדָם לָבוֹא עַל אִשָּׁה וַאֲפִלּוּ פְּנוּיָה אֵין מוֹרִין, אֶלָּא
יָמוּת מֵחֲלָיוֹ אִם הֶעֱלָה לִבּוֹ טִינָא, וְאַל תִּבָּעֵל לוֹ, וְלֹא יְסַפֵּר עִמָּהּ, וְכוּלֵּי—
בְּסַנְהֶדְרִין פֶּרֶק בֶּן סוֹרֵר וּבְסֵפֶר מַדָּע;) וְיֶתֶר פְּרָטֶיהָ, מְבֹאָרִין בְּפֶרֶק ז' מִסַּנְהֶדְרִין
וּבִפְסָחִים וְיוֹמָא וּבִמְקוֹמוֹת אֲחֵרִים.

וְנוֹהֶגֶת מִצְוָה זוֹ בְּכָל מָקוֹם וּבְכָל זְמַן, בִּזְכָרִים וּנְקֵבוֹת. וְעוֹבֵר עָלֶיהָ וְלֹא

---

22. So *Nimmuké Yoséf* to R. Isaac 'Alfasi, TB Sanhedrin viii, end, and R. Nissim, *ibid.*

23. TB Sanhedrin 74b, in answer to the question of how she was permitted to allow the heathen Ahasuerus to marry her.

24. Derived from TB K'thuboth 51b.

25. Mechilta, *baḥodesh* 6, to Exodus 20:6; Va-yikra Rabbah 32, 1; Midrash T'hillim 12, 5; but our author's version, found also in Rashba, commentary to TB Shabbath 130b, differs.

26. The phrase *middath ḥassiduth* (a way of piety) generally connotes a degree of devotion to the Jewish faith which moves a person to go beyond the letter of the law. Taking a different tack, Rashba, *ibid.*, writes that while this is not obligatory, it is permissible, and there is reward for it, etc.

27. So too *Nimmuké Yoséf* to R. Isaac 'Alfasi, TB Sanhedrin viii.

28. So MT *hilchoth yesodé ha-torah* v 4.

29. I.e. although they are forbidden to marry, and if they do they must separate, the marriage takes effect so that the woman needs a divorce to be permitted to remarry.

30. Who then has the status of a divorced woman by the decree of the Sages (see § 268, third paragraph).

Now, the early authorities wrote[22] that we never say, "Let him be killed sooner than transgress" except about committing a sin; but if it is a matter of being idled and stopped from observing a *mitzvah*, let a person disobey and not do the *mitzvah*, and so not be killed—in keeping with what the Sages said about Esther:[23] she was "earth of the world." In other words, it is akin to "sit and do not act," for a woman is taken in conjugal intimacy against her will; and even if a woman participates actively in the intimacy after passion possesses her, she is not guilty for this, as there is no greater compulsion than this.[24]

As to instances that we find about early men of piety, that they were killed over interference with fulfilling a *mitzvah*, such as what the Sages of blessed memory recounted:[25] "Why are you going out to be stoned to death?"—"because I circumcised my son"; "why are you going out to be crucified?"—"because I took the *lulav*"—they observed a way of piety, as they saw that the generation needed it; and they were great Torah scholars, fit to arrive at this decision about the matter.[26] For had they not been great, wise Torah scholars, they would not have been allowed to give up their lives;[27] because not everyone has the right to undergo death where the Sages of blessed memory did not obligate us to be killed for it; and moreover, one would become guilty and punishable in his very soul.[28]

Now, I saw further in regard to this precept, in the volumes of my tutors, God protect them, that any woman with whom the consecration of marriage would take effect,[29] such as a widow with a *kohen gadol*, a divorced woman with an ordinary *kohen*, and likewise one released from levirate marriage by *ḥalitzah*;[30] a female bastard[31] or *nathin*[32] with an ordinary Israelite, or an Israelite woman with a male bastard or *nathin*—these are not included among consanguineous relations, etc. to require being killed over them [sooner than being conjugally intimate with them].[33] (Yet to give anyone a decision to be conjugally intimate with a woman, even an unmarried one—this is not given. Rather, he is to die from his ailment if his heart has developed an improper passion, and he should not be conjugally intimate with her, nor should he even converse with her,[34] etc.—as we read in chapter 8 of the Talmud tractate *Sanhedrin* (75a) and Rambam's *Book of Knowledge*.)[35] The rest of its details are elucidated in the tractates *Sanhedrin*, chapter 7, *P'saḥim*, *Yoma*, and elsewhere.

This precept is in effect everywhere, at every time, for both man and woman. If a person transgressed it and did not sanctify the Divine

קֹדֶשׁ הַשֵּׁם בְּמָקוֹם שֶׁחַיָּב לְקַדְּשׁוֹ, בִּטֵּל עֲשֵׂה זֶה, מִלְּבַד שֶׁעָבַר עַל לָאו דְּ"לֹא
תְחַלְּלוּ אֶת שֵׁם קָדְשִׁי", וּכְמוֹ שֶׁנִּכְתּב בְּסֵדֶר זֶה בְּעֶזְרַת הַשֵּׁם. וַעֲוֹן חִלּוּל הַשֵּׁם
גָּדוֹל וְחָמוּר עַד מְאֹד, עַד שֶׁאָמְרוּ זִכְרוֹנָם לִבְרָכָה שֶׁאֵין כֹּחַ בִּתְשׁוּבָה וְיוֹם
הַכִּפּוּרִים וְיִסּוּרִין לְכַפֵּר, אֶלָּא בְמִיתָה, כְּדְאִיתָא בְּפֶרֶק אַחֲרוֹן מִיּוֹמָא.

[מִצְוַת שְׁבִיתָה בְּיוֹם רִאשׁוֹן שֶׁל פֶּסַח]

רצז לִשְׁבֹּת בְּיוֹם רִאשׁוֹן שֶׁל פֶּסַח, שֶׁנֶּאֱמַר בּוֹ: בַּיּוֹם הָרִאשׁוֹן מִקְרָא קֹדֶשׁ,
וּבְכָל מַה שֶׁנֶּאֱמַר בַּתּוֹרָה "מִקְרָא קֹדֶשׁ" פֵּרְשׁוּ זִכְרוֹנָם לִבְרָכָה: קַדְּשֵׁהוּ, וְעִנְיַן
קְדֻשָּׁתוֹ הוּא שֶׁלֹּא נַעֲשֶׂה בּוֹ מְלָאכָה אֶלָּא מַה שֶׁהוּא מְיֻחָד בַּאֲכִילָה, כְּמוֹ שֶׁבֵּאֵר
הַכָּתוּב: אַךְ אֲשֶׁר יֵאָכֵל לְכָל נֶפֶשׁ הוּא לְבַדּוֹ יֵעָשֶׂה לָכֶם.

וְהָרְאָיָה שֶׁשְּׁבִיתַת יוֹם-טוֹב נֶחְשֶׁבֶת עֲשֵׂה, אָמְרָם זִכְרוֹנָם לִבְרָכָה: הַאי
"שַׁבָּתוֹן" עֲשֵׂה הוּא; וְלָמַדְנוּ מֵעַתָּה שֶׁבְּכָל מָקוֹם שֶׁנֶּאֱמַר בַּתּוֹרָה "שַׁבָּתוֹן" גַּבֵּי
יוֹם-טוֹב הוּא עֲשֵׂה. וּכְבָר בָּא הַרְבֵּה בַּתַּלְמוּד גַּם-כֵּן: יוֹם-טוֹב, עֲשֵׂה וְלֹא-
תַעֲשֶׂה.

מִשָּׁרְשֵׁי הַמִּצְוָה, כְּדֵי שֶׁנַּחְשֹׁב בְּעִנְיַן הַמּוֹעֵד בַּנֵּס שֶׁנַּעֲשָׂה לָנוּ בוֹ, וּנְהַלֵּל
וּנְפָאֵר בְּמַחֲשַׁבְתֵּנוּ מִי שֶׁצִּוָּנוּ, בָּרוּךְ הוּא, עָלָיו וְעָשָׂה לָנוּ נִסִּים בַּזְּמַן הַהוּא; וְאִם
יִהְיֶה הָאָדָם טָרוּד בִּמְלַאכְתּוֹ, לֹא יִהְיֶה לוֹ פְּנַאי לַחְשֹׁב בְּשׁוּם דָּבָר. וְעוֹד נַאֲרִיךְ
בְּשָׁרְשָׁהּ וּבְדִינֶיהָ בְּלָאו דְּאִסּוּר מְלָאכָה בְּיוֹם-טוֹב שֶׁבְּסֵדֶר זֶה, בְּעֶזְרַת הַשֵּׁם.
וְנוֹהֶגֶת בְּכָל מָקוֹם וּבְכָל זְמַן, בַּזְּכָרִים וּנְקֵבוֹת. וְעוֹבֵר עַל זֶה וְעָשָׂה מְלָאכָה

31. Born to consanguineous relations, adulterers, *et al.* for whom conjugal intimacy is forbidden on pain of *karéth.*

32. A descendant of the Gibeonites (Joshua 9:27).

33. So R. Nissim, commentary to TB Sanhedrin 74a.

34. I.e. even if separated by a partition.

35. MT *hilchoth yesodé ha-torah* v 9. If someone threatens to take a person's life unless he violates a Torah law, he may sin to save himself. But if one's life is imperiled because he has become possessed by an unbridled passion, the Torah gives him no such right: the boundaries of morality are not to be moved, no matter what. (These two sentences in parentheses are found, however, only in the first edition, and are not in the oldest manuscripts. They thus seem a later interpolation—especially since our author rarely mentions a specific volume or section of MT.)

36. The original reads, "as we will write in this *sidrah,* with the Eternal Lord's help"; §295, a negative precept, appears in the original, along with all the negative precepts, after the positive ones (see §285, note 2).

37. The passage is cited in §295, note 3.

§297 1. TB Shabbath 25a.

2. The first two paragraphs are based on ShM positive precept §159.

3. Actually, this is "a positive precept that time causes," i.e. a specific time of year ⟨282⟩

name in a situation where he was duty-bound to sanctify it, he would thus disobey this positive precept, apart from violating the negative precept, *you shall not profane My holy name* (Leviticus 22:32), as we have written in this *sidrah*[36] (§295). But the sin of desecrating the Divine name is extremely great and serious—to the extent that the Sages of blessed memory taught that neither repentance nor the Day of Atonement nor suffering has the power to bring atonement, but [it is gained] only through death, as we read in the last chapter of the Talmud tractate *Yoma* (86a).[37]

[THE PRECEPT OF RESTING FROM WORK ON THE FIRST DAY OF PASSOVER]

297 to rest from work on the first day of Passover: for it is stated about it, *On the first day you shall have a holy convocation* (Leviticus 23:7); and whatever [day] has the phrase "a holy convocation" stated about it in the Torah, our Sages of blessed memory interpreted: Sanctify it. In substance, sanctifying it means that we should do no work then, except what is specifically for [the preparation of] food— as Scripture makes clear: *except that which every man must eat, that only may be done by you* (Exodus 12:16).

Now, the proof that to rest from work on a festival day is reckoned as a positive precept is the statement by the Sages of blessed memory:[1] This term *shabbathon* ("a solemn rest"; Leviticus 23:23,39), denotes a positive precept. Hence we have learned that wherever the term *shabbathon* occurs in the Torah about a festival day, it signifies a positive precept; and it was already stated often in the Talmud as well: A festival day means both a positive and a negative precept.[2]

At the root of the precept lies the purpose that we should ponder the theme of the holy season, the miracle that was wrought for us on it; and so we should praise and extol in our thoughts the One who commanded us about it (blessed is He) and wrought miracles for us at that time [of the year]. But if a man will be busied and burdened by his work, he will have no leisure to think and reflect about anything. We shall yet write at length of its root reason and its laws in the negative precept of the prohibition of work on a festival day, in this *sidrah* (§298), with the Eternal Lord's help.

It applies in every location, at every time, for both man and woman.[3] If someone transgresses this and does work that is not needed for [preparing] food for human beings, he disobeys this positive precept,

שֶׁלֹּא לְצֹרֶךְ אֹכֶל נֶפֶשׁ, בִּטֵּל עֲשֵׂה זֶה, מִלְּבַד שֶׁעָבַר עַל לֹא-תַעֲשֶׂה, כְּמוֹ שֶׁנִּכְתֹּב בִּמְקוֹמוֹ.

דִּינֵי הַמִּצְוָה מִתְבָּאֲרִים בְּיוֹם-טוֹב.

[שֶׁלֹּא לַעֲשׂוֹת מְלָאכָה בְּיוֹם רִאשׁוֹן שֶׁל פֶּסַח]

רחצ שֶׁלֹּא נַעֲשֶׂה מְלָאכָה בְּיוֹם רִאשׁוֹן שֶׁל חַג הַפֶּסַח, שֶׁהוּא יוֹם ט"ו בְּנִיסָן, שֶׁנֶּאֱמַר: בַּיוֹם הָרִאשׁוֹן מִקְרָא קֹדֶשׁ יִהְיֶה לָכֶם כָּל מְלֶאכֶת עֲבֹדָה לֹא תַעֲשׂוּ. וּכְבָר הִזְהִיר עַל זֶה הַכָּתוּב בְּסֵדֶר "בֹּא אֶל פַּרְעֹה" בְּצִוּוּי חַג הַפֶּסַח, שֶׁנֶּאֱמַר שָׁם: כָּל מְלָאכָה לֹא יֵעָשֶׂה בָהֶם; וְזֶה הַמִּקְרָא הֵבִיא הָרַמְבַּ"ם זִכְרוֹנוֹ לִבְרָכָה בְּמִנְיָנוֹ, אֲבָל אֲנִי כָּתַבְתִּי זֶה הָאַחֵר כְּדֵי שֶׁיִּהְיוּ הַמּוֹעֲדוֹת סְדוּרִים בְּסֵדֶר אֶחָד; וְהַכֹּל עוֹלֶה עִנְיָן אֶחָד.

וְאָמַר הַכָּתוּב כָּאן "מְלֶאכֶת עֲבֹדָה" וְלֹא אָמַר "כָּל מְלָאכָה", לְפִי שֶׁצָּרְכֵי אֹכֶל נֶפֶשׁ הֻתְּרוּ לַעֲשׂוֹת בְּיוֹם-טוֹב, כְּמוֹ שֶׁבָּא בַכָּתוּב בְּמָקוֹם אַחֵר: אַךְ אֲשֶׁר יֵאָכֵל לְכָל נֶפֶשׁ הוּא לְבַדּוֹ יֵעָשֶׂה לָכֶם; וְזֶהוּ פֵּרוּשׁ "מְלֶאכֶת עֲבֹדָה", כְּלוֹמַר מְלָאכָה שֶׁאֵינָהּ לְצֹרֶךְ אֹכֶל נֶפֶשׁ, כְּעִנְיָן שֶׁנֶּאֱמַר "וּבְכָל עֲבֹדָה בַּשָּׂדֶה", וְכֵן "וַקַּיִן הָיָה עֹבֵד אֲדָמָה", "מֶלֶךְ לְשָׂדֶה נֶעֱבָד", "עֹבֵד אַדְמָתוֹ". אֲבָל הַמְּלָאכָה שֶׁהִיא לְאֹכֶל נֶפֶשׁ, כְּמוֹ הַבִּשּׁוּל וְכַיּוֹצֵא בוֹ, מְלֶאכֶת הֲנָאָה הִיא, לֹא מְלֶאכֶת עֲבוֹדָה; כֵּן פֵּרֵשׁ הָרַמְבַּ"ן זִכְרוֹנוֹ לִבְרָכָה.

וְכָתַב עוֹד שֶׁזֶּה הַפֵּרוּשׁ מִתְבָּאֵר בַּתּוֹרָה, כִּי בְחַג הַמַּצּוֹת, שֶׁאָמַר תְּחִלָּה "כָּל מְלָאכָה לֹא יֵעָשֶׂה בָהֶם" בְּסֵדֶר "בֹּא אֶל פַּרְעֹה", הִצְרַךְ לְפָרֵשׁ "אַךְ אֲשֶׁר יֵאָכֵל לְכָל נֶפֶשׁ הוּא לְבַדּוֹ יֵעָשֶׂה לָכֶם", וּבִשְׁאָר כָּל יָמִים-טוֹבִים יְקַצֵּר וְאָמַר "כָּל מְלֶאכֶת עֲבֹדָה לֹא תַעֲשׂוּ", לֶאֱסֹר כָּל מְלָאכָה שֶׁאֵינֶנָּה אֹכֶל נֶפֶשׁ וּלְהוֹדִיעַ שֶׁאֹכֶל נֶפֶשׁ מֻתָּר בָּהֶן; וְלֹא יֹאמַר הַכָּתוּב לְעוֹלָם בְּאֶחָד מִכָּל שְׁאָר יָמִים-טוֹבִים "כָּל מְלָאכָה" וְלֹא יְפָרֵשׁ בָּהֶם הֶתֵּר אֹכֶל נֶפֶשׁ, כִּי מְלֶאכֶת עֲבֹדָה" יְלַמֵּד עַל זֶה.

brings its obligation; and as a rule, such a precept does not apply to women. However, there is also a negative precept about it (§298), and negative precepts apply equally to women. Hence, as Rambam writes (ShM, at the end of the positive precepts), that precept imposes this as well upon them, in its wake. However, *tosafoth* to TB Kiddushin 34a, s.v. *ma'akeh*, differs.

§298   1. ShM negative precept §323.
             2. Ramban, commentary, Leviticus 23:7.

apart from the fact that he violates a negative precept, as we will write in its proper place (§298). The laws of the precept are explained in *Yom Tov* [the Talmud tractate *Bétzah*].

[THE PROHIBITION OF DOING WORK ON THE FIRST DAY OF PASSOVER]

298 that we should not do work on the first day of the Passover festival, which is the fifteenth of Nissan: for it is stated, *On the first day you shall have a holy convocation; you shall do no laborious work* (Leviticus 23:7). Scripture previously gave an injunction about this in *sidrah bo*, in the commandment of the Passover festival; for it is stated there, *no work shall be done on them* (Exodus 12:16); and Rambam of blessed memory cited that verse in his listing.[1] I, however, have cited this other verse, so that the holy days should be arranged in one order, but it all comes to the same thing.

Now, Scripture states here "laborious work" rather than "no work at all," because necessary preparations for food for living beings are permitted to be done on a festival day—as it is conveyed elsewhere in Scripture: *except that which every man must eat, that only may be done by you* (Exodus 12:16). So this is the meaning of "laborious work"; in other words, work which is not for the need to prepare human food, in keeping with the verse, *and in every laborious work in the field* (Exodus 1:14); so too: *but Cain was a toiling tiller of the soil* (Genesis 4:2); *a king who makes himself servant to the field* (Ecclesiastes 5:8); *He that laboriously tills his soil* (Proverbs 12:11). On the other hand, work that is for [preparing] human food, such as cooking, and so forth, is a labor of enjoyment, and not laborious work. So Ramban of blessed memory explained.[2]

Now, he wrote further that this explanation becomes clear in the Torah: For regarding the Passover festival, where it stated at first, *no work shall be done on them* (Exodus 12:16), in *sidrah bo*, it needed to explain, *except that which every man must eat, that only may be done by you (ibid.)*; but regarding all other festival days, it is brief, stating, *you shall do no laborious work*, to forbid every labor that is not [for preparing] human food, and to convey that [work for making] ordinary food is permitted on them. Thus, the Writ never states about any of the other festival days, "no work," and does not set forth for them the permission [for work to prepare] human food—because the phrase "laborious work" signifies this.

אֲבָל בְּפָרָשַׁת "כָּל הַבְּכוֹר" בְּחַג הַמַּצּוֹת אָמַר: וּבַיּוֹם הַשְּׁבִיעִי עֲצֶרֶת לַיי
אֱלֹהֶיךָ לֹא תַעֲשֶׂה מְלָאכָה, וְהַטַּעַם מִפְּנֵי שֶׁכְּבָר הִתִּיר בּוֹ בְּחַג זֶה בְּפֵרוּשׁ אֹכֶל
נֶפֶשׁ, בְּסֵדֶר "בֹּא אֶל פַּרְעֹה", וְאַחֲרֵי־כֵן בְּסֵדֶר זֶה הִזְכִּיר "מְלֶאכֶת עֲבֹדָה",
דְּמַשְׁמַע בּוֹ גַם־כֵּן הֶתֵּר אֹכֶל נֶפֶשׁ; וּלְפִיכָךְ כְּשֶׁחָזַר וְהִזְכִּירוֹ פַּעַם אַחֶרֶת בְּפָרָשַׁת
"כָּל הַבְּכוֹר" לֹא הֻצְרַךְ לוֹמַר בּוֹ עוֹד בֵּאוּר, וְהִזְכִּיר מְלָאכָה סְתָם, וְסָמַךְ עַל
הַיָּדוּעַ; וּמִכָּל־מָקוֹם לֹא אָמַר "כָּל מְלָאכָה", כְּמוֹ בְּשַׁבָּת וְיוֹם הַכִּפּוּרִים, אֲבָל
אָמַר מְלָאכָה, כְּלוֹמַר הַמְּלָאכָה אֲשֶׁר הִזְהַרְתִּיךָ עָלֶיהָ.

מִשָּׁרְשֵׁי הַמִּצְוָה, כְּדֵי שֶׁיִּזְכְּרוּ יִשְׂרָאֵל הַנִּסִּים הַגְּדוֹלִים שֶׁעָשָׂה הַשֵּׁם לָהֶם
וְלַאֲבוֹתֵיהֶם, וִידַבְּרוּ בָם וְיוֹדִיעוּם לִבְנֵיהֶם וְלִבְנֵי בְנֵיהֶם, כִּי מִתּוֹךְ הַשְּׁבִיתָה
מֵעִסְקֵי הָעוֹלָם יִהְיוּ פְנוּיִים לַעֲסֹק בָּזֶה; שֶׁאִלּוּ הָיוּ מֻתָּרִין בִּמְלָאכָה וַאֲפִלּוּ
בִּמְלָאכָה קַלָּה, הָיָה כָּל אֶחָד וְאֶחָד פּוֹנֶה לְעָסְקוֹ, וּכְבוֹד הָרֶגֶל יִשָּׁכַח מִפִּי עוֹלְלִים
גַּם מִן הַגְּדוֹלִים.

וְעוֹד יֵשׁ תּוֹעָלוֹת רַבּוֹת בַּשְּׁבִיתָה, שֶׁמִּתְקַבְּצִין כָּל הָעָם בְּבָתֵּי כְנֵסִיּוֹת וּבְבָתֵּי
מִדְרָשׁוֹת לִשְׁמֹעַ דִּבְרֵי סֵפֶר וְרָאשֵׁי הָעָם יַדְרִיכוּם וִילַמְּדוּם דַּעַת, וּכְעֵין מַה
שֶּׁאָמְרוּ זִכְרוֹנָם לִבְרָכָה: מֹשֶׁה תִּקֵּן לָהֶם לְיִשְׂרָאֵל שֶׁיִּהְיוּ דוֹרְשִׁין בְּהִלְכוֹת הַפֶּסַח
בְּפֶסַח וְהִלְכוֹת עֲצֶרֶת בַּעֲצֶרֶת.[3]

מִדִּינֵי הַמִּצְוָה, מַה שֶּׁאָמְרוּ זִכְרוֹנָם לִבְרָכָה שֶׁאַף־עַל־פִּי שֶׁהִתִּיר הַכָּתוּב
הַמְּלָאכוֹת לְצֹרֶךְ אֹכֶל נֶפֶשׁ, דַּוְקָא הַדְּבָרִים שֶׁאִי אֶפְשָׁר לַעֲשׂוֹתָן מֵעֶרֶב יוֹם־טוֹב
הוּא שֶׁהִתִּיר הַכָּתוּב — כְּגוֹן לִישָׁה, שְׁחִיטָה, אֲפִיָּה, בִּשּׁוּל, שֶׁכָּל אֵלּוּ הַמְּלָאכוֹת
נִפְסָדוֹת קְצָת בִּשְׁהִיָּתָן; וּכְמוֹ־כֵן מִזֶּה הַטַּעַם הִתִּירוּ לָדוּךְ סַמְמָנִים בְּיוֹם־טוֹב,
מִשּׁוּם דְּמִפִּיגֵי טַעֲמַיְהוּ בִּשְׁהִיָּה אַחַר שֶׁהֵן נִדּוֹכִין; אֲבָל הַמְּלָאכוֹת שֶׁאֶפְשָׁר
לַעֲשׂוֹתָן מֵעֶרֶב יוֹם־טוֹב וְאֵינָן מְקֻבָּלוֹת בָּזֶה שׁוּם הֶפְסֵד, כְּגוֹן קְצִירָה, דִּישָׁה,

3. TB M'gillah 32a.
4. TB Bétzah 28b.

However, toward the end of *sidrah r'éh*, Scripture states, *and on the seventh day there shall be a solemn assembly to the Lord your God; you shall do no work on it* (Deuteronomy 16:8). The reason is that it previously permitted for this festival, explicitly, [work to prepare] human food—in *sidrah bo* (Exodus 12:16). Afterward, in this *sidrah*, it mentions "laborious work" (Leviticus 23:7-8), which likewise denotes the permission for [work to prepare] human food. Therefore, when it returns to mention it once again in the end section of *sidrah r'éh*, it has no need to state there any further explanation. So it mentions "work" generally, alone, relying on what is already known. Nevertheless, it does not state "any work," as in the case of the Sabbath or the Day of Atonement, but it says merely "work"—which is to say, "the work about which I adjured you."

At the root of the precept lies the purpose that the Jewish people should remember the great miracles that the Eternal Lord wrought for them and for their ancestors, and should talk about them and tell their children and grandchildren about them. For as a result of resting from worldly affairs and concerns, they will be free to occupy themselves with this. For if they were permitted to do work, even light work, each and every one would then turn to his business, and the glory of the festival would be forgotten from the mouths of children as well as adults.

There are many further benefits in resting: All the people gather in synagogues and houses of study to hear the words of the [sacred] Book, and the heads of the people can guide them and teach them knowledge—in keeping with what the Sages of blessed memory said:[3] Moses instituted the custom for the Israelites that they should discuss and ask about the laws of Passover on Passover, and the laws of Shavu'oth on Shavu'oth.

Among the laws of the precept, there is what the Sages of blessed memory said:[4] that although Scripture permitted labors needed [to prepare] human food, it is specifically those things that it was not possible to do the day before the festival, which Scripture permitted— such as kneading, ritual slaying, baking and cooking; for [the results of] all these labors become somewhat spoiled if left long. Similarly, for the same reason, the Sages permitted pounding and crushing spices, since their flavor evaporates if they are left to stand after the pounding. But things which can be done the day before the festival and will thus not suffer any spoilage, such as reaping, threshing, winnowing,

בְּרֵרָה, טְחִינָה, רְקִידָה, וְכַיּוֹצֵא בָהֶן, אָסוּר לַעֲשׂוֹתָן בְּיוֹם־טוֹב וְאֵינָן בִּכְלַל צָרְכֵי
אֹכֶל נֶפֶשׁ כְּלָל, וְלוֹקִין עֲלֵיהֶם כְּמוֹ בַחֲרִישָׁה בַשָּׂדֶה, שֶׁהִיא מְלֶאכֶת עֲבוֹדָה
בֶאֱמֶת.

וְעוֹד בֵּאֲרוּ הַמְּפָרְשִׁים הָאַחֲרוֹנִים עִנְיָן זֶה וְאָמְרוּ כֵן: דְּלָא שָׁרֵי קְרָא צֹרֶךְ
אֹכֶל נֶפֶשׁ אֶלָּא מַה שֶּׁנַּעֲשָׂה לְיוֹמוֹ, כְּלוֹמַר לִזְמַן מוּעָט, כְּמוֹ בִשּׁוּל וַאֲפִיָּה
וְכַיּוֹצֵא בָזֶה, כְּמוֹ שֶׁאָמַרְנוּ; וְכֵן מַה שֶּׁדַּעְתּוֹ שֶׁל אָדָם סוֹמֶכֶת בּוֹ לַהֲכִינוֹ לְשַׁעְתּוֹ,
לְאַפּוֹקֵי צֵידָה, שֶׁאֵין דַּעְתּוֹ שֶׁל אָדָם עָלֶיהָ, דְּשֶׁמָּא לֹא תִזְדַּמֵּן לוֹ צֵידָה הַיּוֹם.

וְעוֹד אָמְרוּ דְּכִי שָׁרֵינָן אֹכֶל נֶפֶשׁ בְּמַה שֶּׁנַּעֲשָׂה לְשַׁעְתּוֹ, דַּוְקָא
כְּשֶׁאָדָם מִשְׁתַּמֵּשׁ בְּגוּפָהּ שֶׁל מְלָאכָה, אֲבָל אִם מִשְׁתַּמֵּשׁ בְּסִלּוּקָהּ שֶׁל מְלָאכָה,
אָסוּר; וְזֶהוּ שֶׁאָסְרוּ זִכְרוֹנָם לִבְרָכָה לְכַבּוֹת הַבְּקַעַת אַף־עַל־פִּי שֶׁדַּעְתּוֹ לְכַבּוֹתָהּ
כְּדֵי שֶׁלֹּא תִתְעַשֵּׁן הַקְּדֵרָה. וּלְעִנְיַן צְלִיַּת בָּשָׂר עַל הַגֶּחָלִים, דְּהָיְנוּ בִּשָׂרָא אַגַּמְרֵי
הַנִּזְכָּר בַּגְּמָרָא, אַף־עַל־פִּי שֶׁהָאֵשׁ מִתְכַּבָּה בְּלַחוּת הַבָּשָׂר אֵין זֶה נִקְרָא מִשְׁתַּמֵּשׁ
בְּסִלּוּקָהּ שֶׁל מְלָאכָה, כִּי צֹרֶךְ הַצְּלִיָּה לַעֲשׂוֹתָהּ כֵּן, וּמִשְׁתַּמֵּשׁ בְּגוּפָהּ שֶׁל מְלָאכָה
הוּא, וְשָׁרֵי.

וְכֵן מַה שֶּׁאָמְרוּ זִכְרוֹנָם לִבְרָכָה שֶׁאֵין בִּכְלַל הֶתֵּר צָרְכֵי אֹכֶל נֶפֶשׁ מַה שֶּׁהוּא
אֲכִילָה וּשְׁתִיָּה לְבַד אֶלָּא אַף כָּל דָּבָר הַצָּרִיךְ לוֹ לְאָדָם לְבוֹ־בַּיּוֹם, בֵּין שֶׁהוּא דְבַר
מִצְוָה, כְּגוֹן קָטָן לְמוּלוֹ וְלוּלָב לָצֵאת בּוֹ וְכֵן סֵפֶר תּוֹרָה לִקְרוֹת בּוֹ, דְּכָל יוֹמָא
וְיוֹמָא זְמַן תּוֹרָה הוּא, וּבֵין שֶׁאֵינוֹ דְבַר מִצְוָה אֶלָּא צָרְכֵי גוּף לְבוֹ־בַּיּוֹם, כְּגוֹן
רְחִיצַת רַגְלַיִם בְּמַיִם שֶׁהֵחַמּוּ שֶׁהֻחַמּוּ בְּיוֹם־טוֹב אוֹ לַעֲשׂוֹת מְדוּרָה לְהִתְחַמֵּם בָּהּ,
כָּל דְּבָרִים אֵלּוּ מֻתָּרִין, וּבִכְלַל הֶתֵּר דְּאֹכֶל נֶפֶשׁ נִינְהוּ; כֵּן פֵּרְשׁוּ הַדָּבָר חֲכָמִים
זִכְרוֹנָם לִבְרָכָה.

וּמִיהוּ דַּוְקָא דְּבָרִים הַשָּׁוִים בְּכָל גּוּף אָדָם הוּא שֶׁנַּתִּיר וְנֹאמַר שֶׁהוּא בִכְלַל
הֶתֵּר זֶה שֶׁל אֹכֶל נֶפֶשׁ, כְּגוֹן רְחִיצַת רַגְלַיִם, דְּכֻלֵּי עָלְמָא רָחֲצֵי הָכִי לִפְעָמִים;

---

5. So TJ *Bétzah* i 10, cited in *tosafoth* to TB, 3a, s.v. *g'zérah*.

6. See MT *hilchoth yom tov* i 2 and 7.

7. E.g. Ramban, *Milḥamoth haShem*, TB *Bétzah* iii, beginning.

8. I.e. Scripture's permission to do work on a festival for the preparation of meals extends only to small quantities of food for immediate use, but not to wholesale preparation for storage.

9. TB *Bétzah* 22a. Extinguishing the fire is not something needed for its own sake, but as a means to an end: to save the food from being spoiled. If the food could be saved otherwise without difficulty, it would be equally satisfactory.

Thus, in this and the preceding two paragraphs we have four rules where labor for preparing common food, ordinarily permitted, may not be done on a festival day: (1) where the work could have been done the day before; (2) work to prepare more than enough for immediate (short-range) use; (3) labor that cannot be relied upon to produce food for certain, e.g. hunting; (4) work whose aftermath alone is needed in the preparation.

grinding, sifting, and so on, are forbidden to be done on a festival day, and are not included at all in the category of necessary labors for preparing human food;[5] and whiplashes are given for them[6] just as for plowing in a field, which is laborious work indeed.

The later authorities clarified this subject further,[7] saying that Scripture permitted work needed for preparing human food—no more than what has to be done for its own day—in other words, for a short amount of time, such as cooking, baking, and so forth, as we said; and so too [labor] that a man's mind relies on, to prepare in its proper time[8]—which excludes food from hunting, since a man's mind would not rely on it, for perhaps nothing will happen to come to him that day from hunting or trapping.

They taught further that when work is permitted for preparing human food that is made for that time, as we said, this means specifically when a man uses the product of the labor itself; but if he makes use of the labor's termination, it is forbidden. This is why the Sages of blessed memory forbade extinguishing a burning log,[9] even if one means to put it out so that the contents of the pot should not become smoky. As for roasting meat over coals, which is mentioned in the Talmud,[10] even if the fire is [partly] put out by the juice of the meat, this is not called making use of the removal of the work, because it is necessary for the roasting to do it this way;[11] thus it constitutes a use of the work itself, and is allowed.

There is, likewise, what the Sages of blessed memory taught:[12] that the permission for work required in making human food includes not only what is intended for eating and drinking, but anything a man needs that very day, whether it is a matter of a *mitzvah*, as for instance to circumcise a child or to go out with a *lulav* (§324), and so too with a Torah scroll to read in it, since every single [festival] day is a time for Torah-reading, or, on the other hand, it is not a matter of a *mitzvah*, but for personal physical needs for that very day, such as washing the feet with warm water heated on the festival, or to make a fire to warm oneself by—all these things are permitted, and are included in the permission to make human food. So the Sages of blessed memory explained the matter.

It is, however, things that apply equally to every physical human being that we allow, saying it is included under this permission for essential food—such as washing the feet, since everyone does such washing at times. But what does not apply to every man equally, such

אֲבָל מַה שֶּׁאֵינוֹ שָׁוֶה לְכָל אָדָם, כְּגוֹן מְגַמֵּר, דְּלָאו כֻּלֵּי עָלְמָא מְגַמְּרֵי, כְּדְאָמְרִינָן בִּכְתֻבּוֹת, וַדַּאי אָסוּר הוּא, וְכָל כַּיּוֹצֵא־בָזֶה. וְדַוְקָא בְּעִנְיָנִים אֵלּוּ בָּעֵינַן שֶׁיִּהְיֶה הָעִנְיָן שָׁוֶה בְּכָל אָדָם, אֲבָל לְעִנְיַן אוֹכְלִין, אֲפִלּוּ מַאֲכָל שֶׁאֵין דֶּרֶךְ לַעֲשׂוֹתוֹ אֶלָּא הַמְּלָכִים וְהַשָּׂרִים הַגְּדוֹלִים מֻתָּר לַעֲשׂוֹת אוֹתוֹ כָל אָדָם, דְּמִכָּל־מָקוֹם עִקַּר אֲכִילָה דָּבָר הַשָּׁוֶה בְּכָל נֶפֶשׁ הִיא.

וְכֵן מַה שֶּׁאָמְרוּ בְּאָסוּר הֲכָנָה דְּאֵין יוֹם־טוֹב מֵכִין לְשַׁבָּת וְלֹא שַׁבָּת לְיוֹם־טוֹב; וְלֹא מִשְׁתַּכְּחָה אָסוּר הֲכָנָה מִדְּאוֹרַיְתָא לְדַעְתִּי, כִּי מְעַיַּנְתְּ שַׁפִּיר בְּדִבְרֵי הַגְּמָרָא, כִּי־אִם בְּבֵיצָה בִּלְבַד; וְעִקַּר אָסוּרָהּ הוּא בְּשֶׁנּוֹלְדָה בְּיוֹם־טוֹב שֶׁלְּאַחַר שַׁבָּת אוֹ בְּשַׁבָּת שֶׁלְּאַחַר יוֹם־טוֹב; בְּהָכִי מִתּוֹקְמָא הֲכָנָה דְּרַבָּה בְּבֵיצָה, וּבְהָכִי אָסִירָא אָסוּרָא דְּאוֹרַיְתָא וְלֹא בְּעִנְיָן אַחֵר: דְּהָא דְּאָסְרִינָן לָהּ בְּשֶׁנּוֹלְדָה בְּשַׁבָּת לְיוֹם־טוֹב שֶׁלְּאַחֲרָיו אוֹ בְּשֶׁנּוֹלְדָה בְּיוֹם־טוֹב לְשַׁבָּת שֶׁאַחֲרָיו, וְכֵן כְּשֶׁנּוֹלְדָה בְּיוֹם־טוֹב עַצְמוֹ, מִדְּרַבָּנָן הוּא אָסוּרָא, וְהַכֹּל מִשּׁוּם גְּזֵרָה דְּנוֹלְדָה בְּיוֹם־טוֹב שֶׁלְּאַחַר שַׁבָּת, כִּדְאָמְרָן. וְיַאֲרִיךְ הָעִנְיָן אִם בָּאתִי לְכָתְבוֹ בְּבֵאוּר רָחָב; וּבִמְקוֹמוֹ בְּרֵישׁ בֵּיצָה הֶאֱרַכְתִּי בוֹ, כַּאֲשֶׁר לְמָדוּנִי רַבּוֹתַי יִשְׁמְרֵם אֵל.

וְדִין מַכְשִׁירֵי אֹכֶל נֶפֶשׁ, שֶׁאָסוּר לַעֲשׂוֹתָן, מִשּׁוּם דְּכְתִיב "הוּא לְבַדּוֹ" וְלֹא מַכְשִׁירָיו; וְדִין זִמּוּן הַגּוֹי בְּיוֹם־טוֹב שֶׁאָסוּר, דְּכְתִיב "לָכֶם" וְלֹא לַגּוֹיִם; וְכֵן אֵין אוֹפִין שׁוּם דָּבָר לַכְּלָבִים, דְּכְתִיב "לָכֶם" וְלֹא לַכְּלָבִים.

וּמַה שֶּׁאָמְרוּ זִכְרוֹנָם לִבְרָכָה בִּשְׁנֵי יָמִים־טוֹבִים שֶׁל גָּלֻיּוֹת, דְּנוֹלְדָה בֵּיצָה בָּזֶה מֻתֶּרֶת בָּזֶה, וּמַה שֶּׁנִּתְלַשׁ מִן הַקַּרְקַע בָּזֶה מֻתָּר בָּזֶה, דִּשְׁתֵּי קְדֻשּׁוֹת הֵן, מַה שֶּׁאֵינוֹ

---

10. *Ibid.* 23a.

11. I.e. for the juice to run and put out some of the fire is inevitable, although it serves no purpose and is of no concern to the person roasting the meat.

12. TB Bétzah 12a.

13. This is all explained in TB K'thuboth 7a.

14. TB Bétzah 2b.

15. I.e. if one follows the other directly.

16. Cf. *tosafoth* to TB Bétzah 2b, s.v. *v'hayah*, that writes that the term "preparation" can properly apply only to an egg, since it is a new thing that did not exist before the hen laid it; hence it was "prepared" (produced); but anything baked or cooked existed before, and only required this way of "fixing" it.

17. Whether an egg is laid on a Sabbath following a festival day or on a festival day following a Sabbath, the "preparation" was not at a time that would make it permissible — an ordinary weekday (see note 18).

18. Because any egg laid today is considered to have been completed in the chicken (hence "prepared"—see note 16) the day before.

19. Because by the rule in note 18, the "preparation" was completed on an ordinary weekday; hence no prohibition can apply by the Torah's law.

20. I.e. if the Sages did not impose their prohibition in the first three instances, people might mistakenly think an egg in this instance equally permissible, and here it means a violation of Torah law.

as incense on coals [after the meal], since not everyone thus puts incense on coals, as stated in the tractate *K'thuboth* (7a)—this is certainly forbidden, and so anything similar. Yet it is specifically in these matters that we require that it should be something equally done by every man; but in regard to food, even a dish that is generally made for none but kings and great nobles may be prepared by any man. For in any event, the principal activity of eating is something that applies equally for everyone. [13]

[Going further] we have, too, what the Sages said about a ban on preparation: [14] that a festival day may not [be a time to] prepare [food] for the Sabbath, nor a Sabbath day [to] prepare for a festival. [15] To my mind, though, if you study well the words of the Talmud, this ban on preparation, by the law of the Torah, is encountered nowhere but in the case of an egg alone. [16] Its main prohibition is where it was laid on a festival day after a Sabbath, or on a Sabbath after a festival; to this applies the "preparation" of which Rabbah speaks in the tractate *Bétzah* (2b); [17] and here the ban of the Torah's prohibition applies, [18] but not in any other situation. For the fact that if it is laid on the Sabbath, it is prohibited on the festival day that follows; or, if laid on a festival day, [it is forbidden] on the Sabbath [if] that follows [directly]; and so too when it is laid on a festival day [it is banned on that day] itself—these prohibitions are by the ruling of the Sages [19]— all to provide a protective decree about one laid on a festival day that follows a Sabbath, [20] of which we spoke. The subject would stretch quite long if I came to write it with full clarification. In its proper place, at the beginning of the Talmud tractate *Bétzah*, I have dwelt at length about it, as my master teachers, may God protect them, instructed me.

Then there is the law about preliminary acts for preparing human food [21]—that it is forbidden to do them, [4] since "that only" is written (Exodus 12:16), but not its preliminaries. And we have the law about inviting a heathen to a meal on a festival day, that it is forbidden, since it is written "for you" [22] (*ibid.*), and not for heathens. [23] By the same token, nothing may be baked for dogs, since it is written "for you," and not for dogs. [24]

There is, moreover, what the Sages said about the two festival days [observed] in the exile, that an egg laid on one [day] may be used on the other; and whatever was plucked from the ground on the one is
permitted on the other [25]—because they are two entities of holiness [26]—

כֵּן בִּשְׁנֵי־יָמִים טוֹבִים שֶׁל רֹאשׁ הַשָּׁנָה; וְיֶתֶר פְּרָטֶיהָ רַבִּים, יִתְבָּאֲרוּ כֻּלָּן בָּאֲרֻכָּה בַּמַּסֶּכְתָּא הַבְּנוּיָה עַל זֶה, וְהִיא מַסֶּכֶת יוֹם־טוֹב.

וְנוֹהֶגֶת בְּכָל מָקוֹם וּבְכָל זְמַן, בִּזְכָרִים וּנְקֵבוֹת. וְעוֹבֵר עַל זֶה וְעָשָׂה מְלָאכָה מִמְּלָאכוֹת הָאֲסוּרוֹת בְּיוֹם־טוֹב, בְּמֵזִיד, חַיָּב מַלְקוּת.

[מִצְוַת הַקְרָבַת מוּסָף כָּל שִׁבְעַת יְמֵי הַפֶּסַח]

רצט לְהַקְרִיב קָרְבַּן מוּסָף בְּכָל שִׁבְעַת יְמֵי הַפֶּסַח, שֶׁנֶּאֱמַר: וְהִקְרַבְתֶּם אִשֶּׁה לַיי שִׁבְעַת יָמִים; וְהוּא כְקָרְבַּן רֹאשׁ חֹדֶשׁ: שְׁנֵי פָרִים וְאַיִל אֶחָד וְשִׁבְעָה כְבָשִׂים, הַכֹּל עוֹלוֹת, וּכְמוֹ שֶׁכָּתוּב בְּפֵרוּשׁ עַל כֻּלָּן בְּסֵדֶר פִּנְחָס: אִשֵּׁה עוֹלָה; וּמִשְׁפַּט הָעוֹלָה כְּבָר פֵּרַשְׁתִּיו לְמַעְלָה; וְשָׂעִיר אֶחָד לְחַטָּאת, וְהִיא נֶאֱכֶלֶת.

מִשָּׁרְשֵׁי הַמִּצְוָה, כְּעִנְיָן מַה שֶּׁכָּתַבְנוּ לְמַעְלָה בְּעִנְיַן הַקָּרְבָּן, כִּי הָאָדָם נִפְעָל לְפִי מַעֲשֵׂהוּ, כִּי מִהְיוֹתוֹ בַּעַל חֹמֶר אֵין מַחֲשַׁבְתּוֹ נִדְבֶּקֶת כִּי־אִם עַל־יְדֵי הַמַּעֲשֶׂה; וּמִזֶּה הַשֹּׁרֶשׁ צִוָּנוּ הָאֵל בָּרוּךְ הוּא לַעֲשׂוֹת פְּעֻלָּה מְיֻחֶדֶת לְשֵׁם הַיּוֹם, לְמַעַן נִתְפָּעֵל מִתּוֹךְ כָּךְ לָתֵת אֶל לִבֵּנוּ גֹּדֶל הַיּוֹם וּקְדֻשָּׁתוֹ וְהַנִּסִּים וְהַטּוֹבוֹת שֶׁגְּמָלָנוּ הָאֵל בָּרוּךְ הוּא בְּאוֹתוֹ הַזְּמָן.

מִדִּינֵי הַמִּצְוָה, מַה שֶּׁאָמְרוּ זִכְרוֹנָם לִבְרָכָה בְּפֶרֶק רְבִיעִי מִמְּנָחוֹת: הַתְּמִידִין אֵינָן מְעַכְּבִין אֶת הַמּוּסָפִין, וְלֹא הַמּוּסָפִין מְעַכְּבִין זֶה אֶת זֶה. וְכֵן מַה שֶּׁאָמְרוּ שָׁם: הַפָּרִים וְהָאֵילִים וְהַכְּבָשִׂים אֵינָם מְעַכְּבִים זֶה אֶת זֶה; הַפָּר וְהָאַיִל וְהַכְּבָשִׂים אֵינָן מְעַכְּבִין אֶת הַלֶּחֶם—כְּלוֹמַר מִנְחַת הַסֹּלֶת, שֶׁזֶּהוּ הַלֶּחֶם—וְלֹא הַלֶּחֶם [מְעַכְּבָן]; הַלֶּחֶם מְעַכֵּב אֶת הַכְּבָשִׂים, דִּבְרֵי רַבִּי עֲקִיבָא. אָמַר רַבִּי שִׁמְעוֹן בֶּן נַנָּס: לֹא כִי אֶלָּא הַכְּבָשִׂים מְעַכְּבִין אֶת הַלֶּחֶם, וְהַלֶּחֶם אֵינוֹ מְעַכֵּב אֶת הַכְּבָשִׂים, שֶׁכֵּן מָצִינוּ שֶׁכְּשֶׁהָיוּ יִשְׂרָאֵל בַּמִּדְבָּר אַרְבָּעִים שָׁנָה, קָרְבוּ כְבָשִׂים בְּלֹא לֶחֶם; אַף כָּאן יִקְרְבוּ כְבָשִׂים בְּלֹא לֶחֶם. אָמַר רַבִּי שִׁמְעוֹן: הֲלָכָה כְדִבְרֵי בֶן נַנָּס, אֲבָל אֵין

---

21. E.g. sharpening a knife for ritually slaying an animal.

22. The literal meaning of the phrase generally translated, in the context, "by you."

23. TB Bétzah 21b.

24. *Ibid.* MT *hilchoth yom tov* i 13.

25. MT *ibid.* 24.

26. See § 301, especially the seventh paragraph.

27. See § 301, last paragraph.

§299   1. A lamb offered up as an *'olah* (burnt-offering) every morning and again every evening (Numbers 28:2–4).

    2. E.g. if a *musaf* sacrifice was offered up before the morning *'olah* (see note 1), which had to be the first offering of the day; or if on a Sabbath which was also *rosh hodesh* (new moon day), the respective *musaf* offerings were brought in the wrong order, or the *musaf* offerings for one of these two occasions could not be brought—the sacrifices offered up are acceptable.

SIDRAH 'EMOR which is not the case with the two festival days of *Rosh haShanah*.[27]

The rest of its numerous details are all clarified at length in the Talmud tractate composed about this, which is the tractate *Bétzah*. It is in effect everywhere, at every time, for both man and woman. If a person transgressed this and did any one of the labors forbidden on a festival day, deliberately, he should be punished with whiplashes.

[THE PRECEPT OF THE MUSAF OFFERING ALL THE SEVEN
DAYS OF PASSOVER]

299 to bring a *musaf* (additional) offering on each of the seven days of Passover: as it is stated, *And you shall bring an offering by fire to the Lord seven days* (Leviticus 23:8). This is like the offering on a new-month-day: two bullocks, one ram and seven lambs, all 'olah (burnt) offerings—as it is written explicitly about them all in *sidrah pinhas*: *an offering by fire, a burnt-offering* (Numbers 28:19). As to the proper procedure with an 'olah, I already explained it above (§115). And there was one goat for a *hattath* (sin-offering), which was eaten.

At the root of the precept lies a theme akin to what we have written above regarding offerings (§95), that a man is influenced according to his action; for since he is a material, physical being, his thought does not cling to anything except through some action. For this root reason, God (blessed is He) commanded us to carry out a special act in honor of the day, in order that we should be impressed by it to reflect on the greatness of the day and its holiness, along with the miracles and favors that God (blessed is He) rendered us at that time [of the year].

Among the laws of the precept, there is what the Sages of blessed memory said in chapter 4 of the Talmud tractate *M'nahoth* (49a): The daily offerings[1] do not hold back the *musaf* offerings, nor do the *musaf* offerings hold back one another.[2] There is likewise what they said there:[3] The bullocks, rams and lambs do not hold one another back;[4] the bullock, ram and lambs do not hold back the bread—i.e. the *minhah* (meal-offering) of fine flour, which is the "bread";[5] nor does the bread [hold them back; but the bread does][6] hold back the lambs;[7] thus the words of R. 'Akiva. Said R. Shim'on b. Nannas: Not so, but rather the lambs hold back the bread,[8] while the bread does not hold back the lambs. For so we find, that when the Israelites were in the wilderness forty years, they offered up lambs without bread;[9] then here too one may bring lambs without the bread. Said R.

הַטַּעַם כִּדְבָרָיו, שֶׁכָּל הָאָמוּר בְּחֹמֶשׁ הַפְּקוּדִים, כְּלוֹמַר בְּסֵפֶר בְּמִדְבַּר סִינַי, קָרְבוּ
בַמִּדְבָּר, וְהָאָמוּר בְּתוֹרַת כֹּהֲנִים, כְּלוֹמַר בְּסֵפֶר וַיִּקְרָא, לֹא קָרְבוּ בַמִּדְבָּר; מִשֶּׁבָּאוּ
לָאָרֶץ קָרְבוּ אֵלּוּ וָאֵלּוּ. וּמִפְּנֵי־מָה אֲנִי אוֹמֵר יִקְרְבוּ כְבָשִׂים בְּלֹא לֶחֶם,
שֶׁהַכְּבָשִׂים מַתִּירִין אֶת עַצְמָן, וְלֶחֶם בְּלֹא כְבָשִׂים אֵין לוֹ מִי שֶׁיַּתִּירֶנּוּ.

וְכֵן מַה שֶּׁאָמְרוּ שָׁם פֶּרֶק תְּשִׁיעִי: מְעָרְבִין נִסְכֵּי פָרִים בְּנִסְכֵּי אֵילִים, אֲבָל אֵין
מְעָרְבִין נִסְכֵּי כְבָשִׂים בְּנִסְכֵּי פָרִים וְאֵילִים; וְעוֹד אָמְרוּ שָׁם גַּם־כֵּן: שֶׁבַע מִדּוֹת
שֶׁל לַח הָיוּ בַמִּקְדָּשׁ, הִין וַחֲצִי הִין וְכוּלֵּי; רַבִּי אֶלְעָזָר בְּרַבִּי צָדוֹק אוֹמֵר: שְׁנָתוֹת
הָיוּ בָהִין, עַד כָּאן לַפָּר, עַד כָּאן לָאַיִל, וְעַד כָּאן לַכֶּבֶשׂ; וְיֶתֶר פְּרָטֶיהָ, מְבֹאָרִים
שָׁם וּבִמְקוֹמוֹת מְקֻדָּשִׁים.

וְנוֹהֶגֶת בִּזְמַן הַבַּיִת, בִּזְכָרֵי כְהֻנָּה. וְאִם עָבְרוּ הַכֹּהֲנִים עַל זֶה וְלֹא הִקְרִיבוּ אֶת
קָרְבַּן מוּסָף בְּמוֹעֲדוֹ, בִּטְּלוּ עֲשֵׂה זֶה וְחָטְאָם יִשָּׂאוּ, וּבְנֵי־יִשְׂרָאֵל נְקִיִּים, כִּי
עֲלֵיהֶם מֻטָּל חִיּוּב הַקָּרְבָּנוֹת בְּיוֹתֵר. וְאִם אוּלַי הִרְגִּישׁוּ יִשְׂרָאֵל בַּדָּבָר, גַּם עֲלֵיהֶם
יִהְיֶה הַפֶּשַׁע, כִּי כָל עִנְיַן הַבַּיִת הַקָּדוֹשׁ, וְכָל־שֶׁכֵּן תְּמִידִין וּמוּסָפִין, עַל הַצִּבּוּר
כֻּלָּן הוּא מֻטָּל.

[מִצְוַת שְׁבִיתָה בִּשְׁבִיעִי שֶׁל פֶּסַח]

ש לִשְׁבֹּת בַּיּוֹם הַשְּׁבִיעִי מֵחַג הַפֶּסַח, שֶׁנֶּאֱמַר: בַּיּוֹם הַשְּׁבִיעִי מִקְרָא קֹדֶשׁ; וּכְבָר
כָּתַבְתִּי לְמַעְלָה סָמוּךְ מִצְוָה זוֹ [סִי׳ רצ"ז] שֶׁבְּכָל מָקוֹם שֶׁנֶּאֱמַר בַּתּוֹרָה "מִקְרָא
קֹדֶשׁ" עִנְיָנוֹ לוֹמַר קַדְּשֵׁהוּ שֶׁלֹּא לַעֲשׂוֹת בּוֹ מְלָאכָה, וְהִיא מִצְוַת עֲשֵׂה. וְגַם שָׁם
כָּתוּב רֶמֶז מִשָּׁרְשֵׁי הַמִּצְוָה עַל צַד הַפְּשָׁט. וּקְצָת דִּינֶיהָ כְּמִנְהָגֵנוּ נִכְתֹּב בְּעֶזְרַת
הַשֵּׁם בְּלָאו דְּאִסּוּר מְלָאכָה שֶׁבְּסֵדֶר זֶה [סִי׳ רצ"ח]. וְכָל עִנְיַן שְׁבִיתַת הַשְּׁבִיעִי

---

3. TB M'naḥoth 44b, 45b.

4. On *Shavu'oth* there were two groups of offerings: seven lambs, a bullock and two rams, brought with the two loaves (Leviticus 23:18), and the *musaf* offerings: two bullocks, a ram and seven lambs (Numbers 28:27). The two groups would not hold one another back (see note 2). If one group could not be offered up, the other might be sacrificed separately.

5. This means the two loaves brought on *Shavu'oth*, which were made of fine flour (Leviticus 23:17). The animals mentioned here are the first group in note 4 (hence "ram" denotes rams).

6. The bracketed addition is per MY based on the Talmud, to correct an evident copyist's omission between the two words *ha-leḥem*.

7. Brought with the bread for *sh'lamim*, which the *kohen* waved (Leviticus 23:19–20).

8. The two loaves may not be brought without the lambs.

9. Since the loaves had to be prepared from wheat grown in the land of Israel (Mishnah, Kélim i 6).

10. The lambs could be brought as offerings in their own right; but without them

Shim'on: The definitive law is as ben Nannas said, but the reason is not as he said, for all that is stated in the *Book of Numbers* (28), they offered up in the wilderness, while what is stated in the codex of the *kohanim*, i.e. the *Book of Leviticus* (23), they did not offer in the wilderness. From the time they entered the land, they offered up both these and those. Then why would I say that the lambs might be offered without the bread?—because the lambs permit themselves [to be offered up], while the bread without the lambs would have nothing to make it permitted.[10]

There is likewise what the Sages said there [TB *M'naḥoth*] in the tenth chapter (89a): The libations (offerings of wine) for bullocks might be mixed with the libations for rams; but those for lambs might not be mixed with those for bullocks or rams. They also taught there, further (87b): There were seven liquid measures in the Sanctuary: the *hin*, the half-*hin*, etc. R. 'El'azar b. R. Tzadok said: There were notch marks in the *hin* measure—till here for a bullock, till here for a ram, and till here for a lamb. The rest of its details are explained there and in various places in the Talmud order *Kodashim*.

It is in force at the time the Temple exists, for the male *kohanim*. If the *kohanim* transgressed this and did not sacrifice the *musaf* offering in its proper time, they would disobey this positive precept, and they would bear their sin, while the Israelites would be innocent; for the duty of the offerings is imposed largely upon them. But if Israelites were aware of the matter, then guilt for the crime lies on them too. For the entire matter of the Sanctuary, and especially the daily offerings and the *musaf* offerings, are an obligation that rests on the entire public.

[THE PRECEPT OF RESTING FROM WORK ON THE SEVENTH DAY OF PASSOVER]

300 to rest from work on the seventh day of the Passover festival: for it is stated, *on the seventh day is a holy convocation* (Leviticus 23:8), and I already wrote above, shortly before this precept (§297), that wherever the term "a holy convocation" is stated in the Torah, its purport is to say, "Sanctify it," by doing no work then, this being a positive precept. There I also wrote an intimation of the root reason for the precept, from the aspect of the plain meaning. Some of its laws, in accord with our usual practice, we wrote[1] in the negative precept of the prohibition against work, in this *sidrah* (§298). The entire subject-matter of rest from work on the seventh day is like that of resting on

כִּשְׁבִיתַת יוֹם רִאשׁוֹן, וּשְׁנֵיהֶם כְּרֶגֶל אֶחָד הֵם חֲשׁוּבִין, לָעִנְיָן שֶׁאֵין אוֹמְרִים זְמַן
בַּשְּׁבִיעִי, וְכֵן לְכָל דָּבָר, מַה שֶּׁאֵין כֵּן בִּשְׁמִינִי עֲצֶרֶת, שֶׁהוּא חַג בִּפְנֵי עַצְמוֹ, וּכְמוֹ
שֶׁנִּכְתַּב בִּמְקוֹמוֹ [סִי׳ שכ״ג] בְּעֶזְרַת הַשֵּׁם.

[שֶׁלֹּא לַעֲשׂוֹת מְלָאכָה בְּיוֹם שְׁבִיעִי שֶׁל פֶּסַח]

שׁא שֶׁלֹּא נַעֲשֶׂה מְלָאכָה בְּיוֹם שְׁבִיעִי שֶׁל פֶּסַח, שֶׁהוּא יוֹם אֶחָד וְעֶשְׂרִים
בְּנִיסָן, שֶׁנֶּאֱמַר: בַּיּוֹם הַשְּׁבִיעִי מִקְרָא קֹדֶשׁ כָּל מְלֶאכֶת עֲבֹדָה לֹא תַעֲשׂוּ.

שֹׁרֶשׁ מִצְוָה זוֹ וְכָל עִנְיָנָהּ, כָּתוּב בַּמִּצְוָה הַקּוֹדֶמֶת [סִי׳ רצ״ח] דְּהַיְנוּ יוֹם
רִאשׁוֹן שֶׁל פֶּסַח. וְאוּלָם רָאוּי שֶׁאֲבָאֵר לְךָ בְּנֵי כָּאן עִנְיַן שְׁנֵי יָמִים־טוֹבִים שֶׁל
גָּלֻיּוֹת, לָמָּה נָהֲגְנוּ לַעֲשׂוֹת שְׁנֵי יָמִים־טוֹבִים בְּכָל מוֹעֵד וּמוֹעֵד, וְתוֹרָתֵנוּ לֹא
חִיְּבַתְנוּ כִּי־אִם בְּיוֹם־טוֹב אֶחָד, כְּמוֹ שֶׁבָּא בַּכָּתוּב מְפֹרָשׁ בְּפֶסַח: בַּיּוֹם הָרִאשׁוֹן
מִקְרָא קֹדֶשׁ, וּבַיּוֹם הַשְּׁבִיעִי, וְכֵן בַּעֲצֶרֶת וְרֹאשׁ הַשָּׁנָה וְסֻכּוֹת.

וְהָאֱמֶת כִּי הָעִנְיָן הוּא עַכְשָׁיו מִנְהָג לְבַד, לֹא חִיּוּב אַחֵר: רְצוֹנִי לוֹמַר שֶׁאֵין
אֲנַחְנוּ עוֹשִׂין אוֹתוֹ הַיּוֹם מִפְּנֵי הַסָּפֵק, כִּי כָל יִשְׂרָאֵל בְּקִיאִין בְּקִבּוּעַ
הֶחֳדָשִׁים וְיוֹדְעִים יוֹם הַמּוֹעֵד מְכֻוָּן עַל־פִּי הַחֶשְׁבּוֹן הַמְּקֻבָּל בְּיָדָם, כְּמוֹ שֶׁכָּתַבְתִּי
לְמַעְלָה בְּסֵדֶר ״בֹּא אֶל פַּרְעֹה״ [עֲשֵׂה א׳ סִי׳ ד׳]. וְנִקְבַּע הַמִּנְהָג מִפְּנֵי שֶׁמִּתְּחִלָּה,
כְּשֶׁהָיוּ אֲנָשִׁים סְמוּכִים בָּאָרֶץ, הָיוּ קוֹבְעִין הַחֹדֶשׁ עַל פִּי הָרְאִיָּה, כְּמִצְוַת הַתּוֹרָה,
כְּמוֹ שֶׁכָּתַבְתִּי שָׁם; וְעַל־כֵּן כָּל מְקוֹמוֹת יִשְׂרָאֵל הָרְחוֹקִים מִן הַמָּקוֹם הַנִּבְחָר,
שֶׁהֶקְבּוּעַ שָׁם, שֶׁלֹּא הָיוּ יְכוֹלִין שְׁלוּחִים לְהַגִּיעַ שָׁם לְהוֹדִיעָם יוֹם הַקָּבוּעַ, הָיָה
לָהֶם סָפֵק בְּאֵי זֶה זֶה יוֹם קָבְעוּ הַחֹדֶשׁ, אִם בְּיוֹם שְׁלֹשִׁים אוֹ בִּשְׁלֹשִׁים וְאֶחָד, וְהָיוּ
עוֹשִׂין הַמּוֹעֵד שְׁנֵי יָמִים מִפְּנֵי סָפֵק זֶה.

וְאוּלָם לֹא הָיָה סָפֵק לָהֶם לְעוֹלָם בְּיוֹתֵר מִיּוֹם אֶחָד, לְפִי שֶׁלְּעוֹלָם הָיוּ קוֹבְעִין

the *kohanim* might not eat the two loaves, and there was no point in bringing them.

§300   1. The original has, "we will write, with the Eternal Lord's help"; being a negative precept, §298 occurs later in our author's original work, after all the positive precepts (see §285, note 2).

    2. "Blessed art Thou, Lord, our God, king of the world, who hast given us life, sustained us, and brought us to this season." It is recited only once to sanctify a festival. Having been said at the beginning of Passover, it need not be repeated on the seventh day.

    3. So TB Yoma 2b top, etc.

§301   1. Since every festival has to begin on a specific day of a specific month, e.g. Passover on the fifteenth of Nissan.

the first; and both [days] are considered as one festival, in regard to the fact that the benediction of the season[2] is not said on the seventh day, and.so for every matter—which is not the case with *Sh'mini 'Atzereth* (the Eighth Day of Assembly), which is a festival by itself,[3] as we will write in its proper place (§323), with the Eternal Lord's help.

[THE PROHIBITION AGAINST DOING WORK ON THE SEVENTH DAY OF PASSOVER]

301 that we should not do work on the seventh day of Passover, which is the twenty-first of Nissan: as it is stated, *on the seventh day is a holy convocation; you shall do no laborious work* (Leviticus 23:8).

The root reason for this precept, and all its subject-matter, are written in a previous *mitzvah* (§298), i.e. about the first day of Passover. It is fitting, though, that I should explain you, my son, the subject of the two days of festival in the exile: why we have it as a custom to hold two festival days at every holy season, whereas the Torah obligated us to hold no more than one day of festival, as expressed distinctly in the Writ about Passover, *On the first day you shall have a holy convocation* (Leviticus 23:7), and again on the seventh day (*ibid.* 8); and so likewise about *Shavu'oth*, *Rosh haShanah* and *Sukkoth* (*ibid.* 21, 24, 35, 36).

The truth is that the matter is now only a custom, without any other obligation. By this I mean that we do not observe that [second] day on account of doubt: for all Jewry is knowledgeable today in the determination of the months, and they know the day of a holy season exactly, according to the traditional calculation that they have—as I wrote above, in the first positive precept in *sidrah bo* (§4). The custom became established because originally, when there were ordained, authorized people in the land [of Israel], they would determine each [lunar] month on the basis of the sighting [of the new moon], as the precept of the Torah [required], as I wrote there. Therefore, in all locations of Israel that were distant from the chosen site [Jerusalem] where this determination was made, which messengers could not reach in time to let them know the decided day, they were in doubt as to which day it was on which [the start of] the month was fixed: on the thirtieth or thirty-first [since the beginning of the previous month]. They would therefore observe the holy occasion for two days, on account of this doubt.[1]

However, they were never in doubt over more than one day, because a new month was always set on the thirtieth or thirty-first

רֹאשׁ חֹדֶשׁ בְּיוֹם שְׁלֹשִׁים אוֹ בִּשְׁלֹשִׁים וְאֶחָד, בֵּין בְּעֵדִים אוֹ שֶׁלֹּא בְעֵדִים, כִּי יָדוּעַ הַדָּבָר וּבָרוּר שֶׁאֵין חִדּוּשׁ הַלְּבָנָה מִתְאַחֵר יוֹתֵר; וְעַל־כֵּן, בֵּין יָבוֹאוּ עֵדִים אוֹ לֹא יָבוֹאוּ, הָיוּ קוֹבְעִין רֹאשׁ חֹדֶשׁ בְּיוֹם שְׁלֹשִׁים וְאֶחָד.

וּמִפְּנֵי הַסָּפֵק הַזֶּה שֶׁיֵּשׁ לָרְחוֹקִים מִירוּשָׁלַיִם, קָבְעוּ לָהֶם בַּתְּחִלָּה לַעֲשׂוֹת שְׁנֵי יָמִים יוֹם־טוֹב, וַחֲכָמִים זִכְרוֹנָם לִבְרָכָה תִּקְּנוּ גַּם עַכְשָׁיו לָרְחוֹקִים מִן הָאָרֶץ לַעֲשׂוֹת שְׁנֵי יָמִים, כְּדַת שֶׁהָיוּ עוֹשִׂין בַּזְּמַן הַהוּא, וְאַף־עַל־פִּי שֶׁכָּל יִשְׂרָאֵל הַיּוֹם בְּקִיאִין בִּקְבּוּעַ הַחֹדֶשׁ, כְּמוֹ שֶׁאָמַרְנוּ; אֲבָל הַקְּרוֹבִים וְכָל־שֶׁכֵּן הַדָּרִים בָּאָרֶץ מַמָּשׁ, אֵין רָאוּי שֶׁיַּעֲשׂוּ כִּי־אִם יוֹם אֶחָד, כְּמִנְהָג אַנְשֵׁי הַמָּקוֹם מֵעוֹלָם; וְכֵן נָהֲגוּ, לְפִי מַה שֶּׁשָּׁמַעְנוּ.

וּמִן הַטַּעַם הַזֶּה שֶׁאָמַרְנוּ, שֶׁהַדָּבָר הוּא תַּקָּנַת חֲכָמִים, לֹא סָפֵק, אָמְרוּ מִן הַמְפָרְשִׁים שֶׁלֹּא נֹאמַר עַכְשָׁיו בִּשְׁנֵי יָמִים־טוֹבִים שֶׁל גָּלֻיוֹת "נוֹלְדָה בָזֶה מֵחֶרֶת בָּזֶה", כְּמוֹ שֶׁבָּא בַּגְּמָרָא, דְּבִזְמַן שֶׁהָיָה סָפֵק הַדָּבָר הָיוּ אוֹמְרִין כֵּן, אֲבָל עַכְשָׁיו, מִכֵּיוָן שֶׁמִּתַּקָּנַת חֲכָמִים הוּא וְלֹא מִתּוֹרַת סָפֵק כְּלָל, לֹא נֹאמַר כֵּן, אֶלָּא דִּינָם כִּקְדֻשָּׁה אֶחָת.

וּמֵהֶם שֶׁאָמְרוּ דְּמֵחֲמַת הַסָּפֵק הָרִאשׁוֹן תִּקְנוּם חֲכָמִים זִכְרוֹנָם לִבְרָכָה, וְלֹא נַחְמִיר בָּהֶם יוֹתֵר מִבָּרִאשׁוֹנָה. וְעוֹד, דְּכִי אִתְּמַר בַּגְּמָרָא "נוֹלְדָה בָזֶה מֵחֶרֶת בָּזֶה", כְּבָר הָיָה בָטֵל הַקָּבוּעַ עַל־פִּי הָרְאִיָּה לְפִי הַדּוֹמֶה; וְכֵן נָהֲגְנוּ הַיּוֹם.

וְכָל מַה שֶּׁאָמַרְנוּ, דַּוְקָא בִּשְׁנֵי יָמִים־טוֹבִים שֶׁל מוֹעֲדֵי הַשָּׁנָה חוּץ מֵרֹאשׁ הַשָּׁנָה, דְּאִלּוּ בְרֹאשׁ הַשָּׁנָה, בְּכָל מָקוֹם כִּקְדֻשָּׁה אַחַת הִיא, וְנוֹלְדָה בָזֶה אֲסוּרָה בָזֶה, מִפְּנֵי שֶׁגַּם בְּבֵית הַוַּעַד הָיוּ עוֹשִׂין אוֹתוֹ לִפְעָמִים שְׁנֵי יָמִים יוֹם־טוֹב שֶׁלֹּא מִתּוֹרַת סָפֵק, וּכְגוֹן שֶׁבָּאוּ הָעֵדִים מִן הַמִּנְחָה וּלְמַעְלָה, שֶׁנּוֹהֲגִין אוֹתוֹ הַיּוֹם קֹדֶשׁ

---

2. Cf. TB Bétzah 4b: Now that we know the determination of the month, why do we observe two days?—because they sent word from there [from the land of Israel, to Babylonia]: Be careful of the custom of your fathers [now] in your hands; there are times when a government may issue a decree, and the matter may deteriorate. I.e. the system of determining the lunar months may become hazy or forgotten.

3. MT *hilchoth yom tov* vi 14–15.

4. Because one of the two days was certainly not a true festival day; hence, if a hen laid an egg on the first day and it was eaten on the second, there was no possibility of violating the law of eating food on a holy day prepared on an immediately preceding holy day; see §298.

5. As the two days of *Rosh haShanah* are regarded; see below.

6. Rabad to MT *ibid.*

7. I.e. the later part of the Talmud—discussion and analysis of the Mishnah, that took place in Babylonia, giving rise to the Babylonian Talmud; TB Bétzah 4b.

8. On the first day of *Rosh haShanah*.

[day since the previous month began], whether there were witnesses or not [to report seeing the new moon], since it was a known and clear matter that the renewal of the moon could not occur any later. Therefore, whether witnesses came or not, they [the great *beth din* in Jerusalem] would determine the beginning of the month on the thirty-first day [at the latest].

Thus, because of this doubt that those far from Jerusalem had, they made themselves a set practice originally to observe two festival days. And the Sages of blessed memory instituted the decree that now too, those far from the land [of Israel] should observe two days of festival, like the custom that was observed at that time, even though all Jewry today has clear knowledge of the determination of the months, as we stated. [2] As for those close [to the land of Israel] however, and certainly those who dwell actually in the land, it is not proper that they should observe more than one day, as the custom of the people in that region always was. And this has been their practice, according to what we have heard.

Well, for this reason that we have stated—that the matter is an enactment by the Sages, not a doubt—some authorities have ruled[3] that we should not hold now, regarding the two festival days of the exile, that an egg laid on one is permissible on the other, as we read in the Talmud: For at the time that it was a matter of doubt, they would so rule;[4] but nowadays, since it [our practice] is by an enactment of the Sages and not because of any condition of doubt at all, we should not rule so, but their law should rather be as for one period of holiness.[5]

Yet there are those[6] who said that the Sages of blessed memory made the enactment on account of the original doubt, and we should not be stringent regarding it beyond the law for the original situation. Moreover, when it was said in the *g'mara*,[7] "an egg laid on this day is permissible on that day," apparently the determination on the basis of sighting [by witnesses] had already ceased to be done. And so this is our practice today [that the egg is permitted].

Now, all that we said holds specifically for the two festival days of the holy seasons of the year—except *Rosh haShanah*. For *Rosh haShanah* is everywhere as one entity [period] of holiness, and an egg laid on one day is forbidden on the other—because even in the assembly [of the Sanhedrin] they would establish it at times as two festival days without any cause of doubt: For instance, if the witnesses came[8] from the time for the afternoon offering and on, that day was

וּלְמָחָר קֹדֶשׁ; וּמִכָּל־מָקוֹם גַּם בְּרֹאשׁ הַשָּׁנָה מְתַקְּנַת חֲכָמִים הִיא הַיּוֹם לַעֲשׂוֹת
שְׁנֵי יָמִים בְּכָל מָקוֹם, אַחַר שֶׁאָנוּ בְּקִיאִין בְּקִבּוּעָא דְּיַרְחָא.

[מִצְוַת קָרְבַּן הָעֹמֶר שֶׁל שְׂעוֹרִים בְּיוֹם שֵׁנִי שֶׁל פֶּסַח]

שב שֶׁנַּקְרִיב בְּיוֹם שֵׁנִי שֶׁל פֶּסַח, יָתֵר עַל הַמּוּסָף שֶׁל שְׁאָר יְמֵי הַפֶּסַח, כֶּבֶשׁ
בֶּן שְׁנָתוֹ לְעוֹלָה, וְעֹמֶר אֶחָד שֶׁל שְׂעוֹרִים, הַנִּקְרָא עֹמֶר הַתְּנוּפָה, שֶׁנֶּאֱמַר: כִּי
תָבֹאוּ אֶל הָאָרֶץ...וַהֲבֵאתֶם אֶת עֹמֶר רֵאשִׁית קְצִירְכֶם אֶל הַכֹּהֵן וְהֵנִיף אֶת
הָעֹמֶר...מִמָּחֳרַת הַשַּׁבָּת; וְתַרְגּוּמוֹ: מִבָּתַר יוֹמָא טָבָא, כְּלוֹמַר בְּיוֹם שֵׁנִי שֶׁל
פֶּסַח, שֶׁהֲרֵי בְּפֶסַח אַיְרֵי בַּפָּרָשָׁה שֶׁלְּמַעְלָה מִזֶּה, וְנֶאֱמַר שָׁם: וַעֲשִׂיתֶם בְּיוֹם
הֲנִיפְכֶם אֶת הָעֹמֶר כֶּבֶשׂ תָּמִים בֶּן שְׁנָתוֹ וְגוֹמֵר.

וְקָרְבָּן זֶה שֶׁל עֹמֶר נִקְרָא מִנְחַת בִּכּוּרִים, וְאֵלֶיהָ הוּא הָרֶמֶז בְּאָמְרוֹ יִתְבָּרַךְ:
וְאִם תַּקְרִיב מִנְחַת בִּכּוּרִים לַיי אָבִיב קָלוּי בָּאֵשׁ וְגוֹמֵר. וּלְשׁוֹן מְכִלְתָּא: כָּל
"אִם" וְ"אִם" שֶׁבַּתּוֹרָה רְשׁוּת, חוּץ מִשְּׁלֹשָׁה שֶׁהֵם חוֹבָה; וְזֶה אֶחָד מֵהֶם. וְאָמְרוּ
שָׁם: אַתָּה אוֹמֵר חוֹבָה, אוֹ אֵינוֹ אֶלָּא רְשׁוּת, תַּלְמוּד לוֹמַר "תַּקְרִיב אֶת מִנְחַת
בִּכּוּרֶיךָ", חוֹבָה וְלֹא רְשׁוּת.

וְעִנְיַן הַמִּנְחָה כֵּן: שֶׁהָיוּ מְבִיאִין שְׁלֹשָׁה סְאִין שְׂעוֹרִין וּמוֹצִיאִין מִן הַכֹּל
עִשָּׂרוֹן אֶחָד שֶׁהוּא מְנֻפֶּה בִּשְׁלֹשׁ־עֶשְׂרֵה נָפָה, וְהַשְּׁאָר נִפְדֶּה וְנֶאֱכָל לְכָל אָדָם,
וְחַיָּב בְּחַלָּה וּפָטוּר מִן הַמַּעַשְׂרוֹת; וְלוֹקְחִין זֶה הָעִשָּׂרוֹן שֶׁל סֹלֶת הַשְּׂעוֹרִים
וּבוֹלְלִין אוֹתוֹ בְּלֹג שֶׁמֶן, וְנוֹתְנִין עָלָיו קֹמֶץ לְבוֹנָה כִּשְׁאָר הַמְּנָחוֹת, וּמְנִיפוֹ הַכֹּהֵן
בַּמִּזְרָח, מוֹלִיךְ וּמֵבִיא מַעֲלֶה וּמוֹרִיד, וּמַגִּישׁוֹ כְּנֶגֶד חַדָּהּ שֶׁל קֶרֶן מַעֲרָבִית

---

9. So TB Rosh haShanah 30b.

§302   1. To Exodus 22:24.
       2. TB M'naḥoth 63b.
       3. Exchanged for money, etc. so that it should lose its sanctity.
       4. TB M'naḥoth 66a.

then observed as holy, and also the following day, as holy.[9] Yet in any event, on *Rosh haShanah* too it is an enactment of the Sages to observe it today for two days everywhere, since we are knowledgeable in the determination of the [new] moon.

[ON THE OFFERING OF THE 'OMER OF BARLEY ON THE SECOND DAY OF PASSOVER]

302 that we should offer on the second day of Passover, beyond the *musaf* (additional offerings) of the other days of Passover, a lamb in its first year as an *'olah* (burnt-offering), and one sheaf (*'omer*) of barley, called the sheaf of the wave-offering: For it is stated, *When you come into the land . . . you shall bring the sheaf of the first-fruits of your harvest to the* kohen; *and he shall wave the sheaf . . . on the morrow after the sabbath* (Leviticus 23:10–11), which Onkelos translates, "after the festival day": in other words, on the second day of Passover, since here the section directly above this deals with Passover. And it is stated there, *on the day when you wave the sheaf, you shall offer a male lamb without blemish in its first year*, etc. (ibid. 12).

This offering of the sheaf is called the *minḥah* (meal-offering) of first-fruits; the allusion was to this when He (be He blessed) said, *And if you bring a meal-offering of the first-fruits to the Lord, ears of new grain parched with fire*, etc. (Leviticus 2:14). In the language of the Midrash *Mechilta*:[1] Every word *'im* ("if") in the Torah denotes a matter of free choice, except for three which are obligatory—and this is one of them. Then it was taught there: You say it is obligatory; yet perhaps it is nothing but a matter of choice?—Scripture states, *you shall offer up the meal-offering of your first-fruits* (ibid.): it is obligatory, and not a free choice.

Now, this, in substance, was the *minḥah*: Three *se'ah* of barley would be brought,[2] and out of the whole, one *'issaron* would be taken, which had been sifted through thirteen sieves. The rest would be redeemed,[3] and might be eaten by any man, carrying the obligation of *ḥallah* [first-cake of the dough, for a *kohen*], but free of the obligation of tithes.[4] This *'issaron* of fine barley flour would be taken and mixed with a *log* of oil. Then a handful of frankincense would be added, as with other *minḥah* offerings, and a *kohen* would wave it in the east [of the altar]: he would move it forward and back, then raise it and lower it; and he would then bring it near [the altar], over against the point of the southwestern horn, like other *minḥah* offerings. He would

דְּרוֹמִית כִּשְׁאָר הַמְּנָחוֹת, וְקוֹמֵץ וּמַקְטִיר, וְהַשְּׁאָר נֶאֱכָל לַכֹּהֲנִים כִּשְׁיָרֵי כָּל הַמְּנָחוֹת.

מִשָּׁרְשֵׁי הַמִּצְוָה, כְּדֵי שֶׁנִּתְבּוֹנֵן מִתּוֹךְ הַמַּעֲשֶׂה הַחֶסֶד הַגָּדוֹל שֶׁעוֹשֶׂה הַשֵּׁם בָּרוּךְ הוּא עִם בְּרִיּוֹתָיו, לְחַדֵּשׁ לָהֶם שָׁנָה שָׁנָה תְּבוּאָה לְמִחְיָה; לָכֵן רָאוּי לָנוּ שֶׁנַּקְרִיב לוֹ בָּרוּךְ הוּא מִמֶּנָּה, לְמַעַן נִזְכֹּר חַסְדּוֹ וְטוּבוֹ הַגָּדוֹל טֶרֶם נֵהָנֶה מִמֶּנָּה, וּמִתּוֹךְ שֶׁנִּהְיֶה רְאוּיִין לִבְרָכָה בְּהֶכְשֵׁר מַעֲשֵׂינוּ לְפָנָיו, תִּתְבָּרֵךְ תְּבוּאָתֵנוּ וְיַשְׁלַם חֵפֶץ הַשֵּׁם בָּנוּ, שֶׁחָפֵץ מֵרֹב טוּבוֹ בְּבִרְכַּת בְּרִיּוֹתָיו. וְנִצְטַוֵּינוּ בָּזֶה בַּשֵּׁנִי שֶׁל פֶּסַח וְלֹא בָּרִאשׁוֹן, כְּדֵי שֶׁלֹּא נְעָרֵב שִׂמְחָה בְּשִׂמְחָה, כִּי הָרִאשׁוֹן נָכוֹן לְזֵכֶר הַנֵּס הַגָּדוֹל שֶׁהוֹצִיאָנוּ בָּרוּךְ הוּא מֵעַבְדוּת לְחֵרוּת, מִיָּגוֹן לְשִׂמְחָה.

מִדִּינֵי הַמִּצְוָה, מַה שֶּׁאָמְרוּ זִכְרוֹנָם לִבְרָכָה שֶׁמִּצְוָתוֹ שֶׁל עֹמֶר לַהֲבִיאוֹ מִן הַקָּרוֹב לִירוּשָׁלַיִם שֶׁבְּכָר תְּחִלָּה; לֹא בִכֵּר הַקָּרוֹב, מְבִיאִין אוֹתוֹ מִכָּל מָקוֹם מֵאֶרֶץ־יִשְׂרָאֵל; וּמִצְוָתוֹ לְהַקְצֵר בַּלַּיְלָה, בְּלֵיל י"ו בְּנִיסָן, בֵּין בְּחֹל בֵּין בְּשַׁבָּת; וּמִצְוָתוֹ לַהֲבִיאוֹ מִן הַלַּח, פֵּרוּשׁ כְּדֵי שֶׁיִּהְיֶה נִרְאֶה וְנִכָּר לָעַיִן יוֹתֵר בְּכוּרוֹ; וְכָל הָעֲיָרוֹת הַסְּמוּכוֹת לְשָׁם מִתְכַּנְּסוֹת, כְּדֵי שֶׁיְּהֵא נִקְצָר בְּעֵסֶק גָּדוֹל; וְכָל זֶה מִן הַשֹּׁרֶשׁ שֶׁכָּתַבְנוּ, כְּדֵי שֶׁיִּתְּנוּ הַכֹּל לִבָּם לַדָּבָר הַשֵּׁם מִתּוֹךְ הַמַּעֲשֶׂה וְהַשִּׂמְחָה.

וְשָׁלֹשׁ סְאִין אֵלּוּ הָיוּ קוֹצְרִין אוֹתָן בִּשְׁלֹשָׁה אֲנָשִׁים וְשָׁלֹשׁ קֻפּוֹת וּשְׁלֹשָׁה מַגָּלוֹת; וְכֵיוָן שֶׁחֲשֵׁכָה אוֹמֵר הַקּוֹצֵר לָעוֹמְדִים שָׁם "בָּא הַשֶּׁמֶשׁ", אוֹמְרִין לוֹ הֵן; "בָּא הַשֶּׁמֶשׁ", אוֹמְרִין לוֹ הֵן; "בָּא הַשֶּׁמֶשׁ", אוֹמְרִין לוֹ הֵן, וְכֵן שָׁלֹשָׁה פְעָמִים; "מַגָּל זוֹ", אוֹמְרִין הֵן, וְכֵן שָׁלֹשָׁה פְעָמִים; "קֻפָּה זוֹ", אוֹמְרִין הֵן, וְכֵן שָׁלֹשָׁה פְעָמִים; "אֶקְצֹר", אוֹמְרִין לוֹ "קְצֹר" — שָׁלֹשָׁה פְעָמִים; וְכָל־כָּךְ לָמָּה, מִפְּנֵי הַטּוֹעִין שֶׁיָּצְאוּ שֶׁכְּלָל

---

5. TB M'naḥoth 67b. The paragraph is based on MT *hilchoth t'midin* vii 12.

6. It is a Talmudic principle that "one rejoicing should not be mingled with another" (TB Mo'éd Katan 8b).

7. TB M'naḥoth 64b. What follows, till "from anywhere," is the reading of the manuscripts, verbatim from the Mishnah, there. The first edition and the standard editions each differ, evidently through changes and interpolations by later hands (but in ed. Chavel the variant is not noted).

8. *Ibid.* 83b.

9. *Ibid.* 71a.

10. *Ibid.* 65a.

11. *Ibid.* 63b; on the three *se'ah*, see three paragraphs above.

12. MSS Parma–de Rossi 928 and Casanatense 134, and all editions but the first, omit "him" (*lo*) all three times, in keeping with Mishnah, M'naḥoth x 3 and TB 65a. The word "him" (*lo*), found in MS Vatican 163 and the first edition, is likewise in MT *hilchoth t'midin* vii 11; but there it is also added in the responses about the scythe and the basket, which follow.

take the handful and burn it; and the rest would be eaten by the *kohanim*, like the remainders of all *minḥah* offerings.[5]

At the root of the precept lies the aim that we should reflect, through this act, on the great kindness that the Eternal Lord, blessed is He, does with His human beings, to renew the produce of grain each year for sustenance. It is therefore fitting for us that we should offer up some of it to Him (blessed is He), that we might remember His kindness and great goodness before we enjoy any benefit from it. Having thus become worthy of blessing through the merit of our deeds before Him, our grain produce will be blessed, and the desire of the Eternal Lord regarding us will be fulfilled. For in His abundant goodness, He delights in blessing for His human beings. Now, we were commanded about this for the second day of Passover, not the first, so that we should not mingle one rejoicing with another.[6] For the first day is designated for remembering the great miracle, that He (blessed is He) took us out from servitude to liberty, from sorrow to joy.

Among the laws of the precept, there is what the Sages of blessed memory said:[7] that the *mitzvah* of the 'omer (the sheaf-offering) was to bring it from [barley] which grew close to Jerusalem and ripened first. If what was near did not ripen, it was brought from anywhere in the land of Israel.[8] The religious duty was that it should be cut at night— the night of the sixteenth of Nissan, whether it was a weekday or a Sabbath; and the religious duty was to bring it of moist ears, so that its [new] ripening should be the more visible and recognizable to the eye.[9] All [the people of] the nearby small towns would gather, so that it should be cut amid great activity[10]—and all this for the root reason that we wrote: so that all should give a great amount of attention and thought to the word of the Eternal Lord, through all the activity and the rejoicing.

These three *se'ah* would be cut by three people, with three baskets and three scythes.[11] Once it grew dark, a reaper (cutter) would ask those standing there, "Has the sun set?" and they would answer him, *Yes.* "Has the sun set?"—they would answer him, *Yes.* "Has the sun set?"—they would answer him, *Yes.*[12] "Is this a scythe?"—they would answer, *Yes*—thus three times. "Is this a basket?"—they would answer, *Yes*—thus three times. "Shall I cut?"—they would tell him, *Cut*, three times. Now, why all this?—on account of those who erred, who left the Israelite community at the time of the Second Temple,

⟨303⟩

יִשְׂרָאֵל בְּבַיִת שֵׁנִי וְהָיוּ אוֹמְרִים שֶׁזֶּה שֶׁנֶּאֱמַר בַּתּוֹרָה "מִמָּחֳרַת הַשַּׁבָּת", שֶׁהוּא
שַׁבַּת בְּרֵאשִׁית. וְיֶתֶר פְּרָטֶיהָ, מְתְבָּאֲרִין מָשְׁלָם בְּפֶרֶק עֲשִׂירִי מִמְּנָחוֹת.

וְנוֹהֶגֶת בִּזְמַן הַבַּיִת, בִּזְכָרִים; וַאֲפִלּוּ יִשְׂרָאֵלִים חַיָּבִין לְהִשְׁתַּדֵּל בְּמִצְוָה זוֹ,
שֶׁהֲרֵי שְׁלוּחֵי בֵית-דִּין יוֹצְאִין וְעוֹשִׂין כְּרִיכוֹת בַּשָּׂדוֹת מֵעֶרֶב יוֹם-טוֹב, וּכְמוֹ
שֶׁמְפֹרָשׁ שָׁם בִּמְנָחוֹת; אֲבָל מִכָּל-מָקוֹם עִקַּר הַחִיּוּב הִיא הַהַקְרָבָה וְהַתְּנוּפָה
וְהַהַגָּשָׁה וְהַקְּמִיצָה וְהַהַקְטָרָה, וְכָל זֶה בַּכֹּהֲנִים. וּמִכָּל-מָקוֹם, כֵּיָון שֶׁיֵּשׁ בָּהּ חֵלֶק
לְכָל יִשְׂרָאֵל, וִיסוֹד הַמִּצְוָה הוּא מִפְּנֵי חִדּוּשׁ הַתְּבוּאָה, שֶׁהוּא הַדָּבָר הַצָּרִיךְ לַכֹּל,
יֵשׁ לָנוּ לְכָתְבָהּ בְּחֶשְׁבּוֹן הַמִּצְוֹת הַמֻּטָּלוֹת עַל כָּל בְּנֵי-יִשְׂרָאֵל.

[שֶׁלֹּא לֶאֱכֹל מִתְּבוּאָה חֲדָשָׁה קֹדֶם כְּלוֹת יוֹם י"ו בְּנִיסָן]

שׁג שֶׁלֹּא לֶאֱכֹל לֶחֶם מִתְּבוּאָה חֲדָשָׁה קֹדֶם כְּלוֹת יוֹם שִׁשָּׁה עָשָׂר בְּנִיסָן,
שֶׁנֶּאֱמַר: וְלֶחֶם וְקָלִי וְכַרְמֶל לֹא תֹאכְלוּ עַד עֶצֶם הַיּוֹם הַזֶּה.

מִשָּׁרְשֵׁי הַמִּצְוָה, לְפִי שֶׁעִקַּר מְחִיָתָן שֶׁל בְּרִיּוֹת הִיא בַתְּבוּאוֹת, וְעַל-כֵּן רָאוּי
לְהַקְרִיב מֵהֶן קָרְבָּן לַיי אֲשֶׁר נְתָנָם, טֶרֶם יֵהָנוּ מֵהֶן בְּרִיּוֹתָיו; וּכְעִין מַה שֶּׁאָמְרוּ
זִכְרוֹנָם לִבְרָכָה בְּדוֹמֶה לָזֶה: כָּל הַנֶּהֱנֶה מִן הָעוֹלָם הַזֶּה בְּלֹא בְּרָכָה, מָעַל, וְכָל זֶה
לְהַכְשִׁיר עַצְמֵנוּ שֶׁנִּהְיֶה רְאוּיִין לְקַבֵּל מִטּוּבוֹ, וּכְמוֹ שֶׁכָּתַבְתִּי בַּסֵּפֶר פְּעָמִים
רַבּוֹת. וּבְיוֹם שִׁשָּׁה עָשָׂר בְּנִיסָן הָיִינוּ מַקְרִיבִין בִּזְמַן הַבַּיִת קָרְבָּן הָעֹמֶר מִתְּבוּאָה
חֲדָשָׁה מִן הַשְּׂעוֹרִים, כִּי הִיא הַתְּבוּאָה הַמַּבְכֶּרֶת יוֹתֵר מִן הַחִטִּים, וְהִיא מַתֶּרֶת כָּל
הַתְּבוּאוֹת.

מִדִּינֵי הַמִּצְוָה, מַה שֶּׁאָמְרוּ זִכְרוֹנָם לִבְרָכָה שֶׁחָמֵשׁ תְּבוּאוֹת לְבַד הֵן שֶׁהֵן
בִּכְלָל אִסּוּר הֶחָדָשׁ, וְהֵן: חִטָּה וּשְׂעוֹרָה וְכֻסֶּמֶת וְשִׁבֹּלֶת שׁוּעָל וְשִׁיפּוֹן; וּבִזְמַן
הַבַּיִת, מִשֶּׁקָּרֵב הָעֹמֶר בְּיוֹם י"ו בְּנִיסָן הָיָה מֻתָּר הֶחָדָשׁ בִּירוּשָׁלַיִם, וְהַמְּקוֹמוֹת
הָרְחוֹקִים מֻתָּרִין אַחַר חֲצוֹת, לְפִי שֶׁאֵין בֵּית-דִּין מִתְעַצְּלִין בּוֹ עַד אַחַר חֲצוֹת,

---

13. I.e. a seventh day of the week, set as the Sabbath, a day of rest, by Scripture's
statement about it in the seven days of creation, that then the Almighty rested (Genesis
2:2–3); TB M'naḥoth 65a. (The paragraph is based on MT ḥilḥoth t'midin vii 11).

14. Since it is a positive precept whose obligation is imposed by a specific time—
from which women are exempt as a rule.

15. See above, the fourth paragraph.

§303   1. TB B'raḥoth 35a.

2. Without a benediction, one takes something of the Almighty's without permission; hence it is like taking something holy.

3. TB M'naḥoth 70a.

4. *Ibid.* 68a.

saying that this phrase in the Torah, *on the morrow after the sabbath* (Leviticus 23:11), means a Sabbath as of the Creation. [13]

The rest of its details are completely explained in chapter 10 of the tractate *M'nahoth*. It is in force at the time of the Temple, for the men, [14] even Israelites [non-*kohanim*] being obligated to exert themselves for this precept. For messengers of the *beth din* (Sanhedrin, high court) would go out and tie bunches [of the standing barley] in the fields on the day before the festival, as it is explained in the tractate *M'nahoth* (65a). But in any event, the main part of the obligation is offering it, waving it, bringing it near [the altar], taking the handful and burning it—and all this is [done] by *kohanim*. Nevertheless, since there is a share in it for all Israelites [to do] and the basic significance of the *mitzvah* is on account of the renewal of the crops of grain, [15] which is something needed by all, it is for us to write it in the reckoning of the precepts imposed on all Israelites.

[TO EAT NOTHING OF THE NEW CROP OF CEREAL GRAINS
BEFORE THE END OF THE 16TH OF NISSAN]

303 to eat no bread of new grains before the end of the sixteenth day of Nissan: for it is stated, *And you shall eat neither bread nor parched or fresh grain until this selfsame day, until you have brought the offering of your God* (Leviticus 23:14).

At the root of the precept lies the reason that the main sustenance of human beings is by grains. It is therefore proper to bring an offering of them to the Lord who has given them, before His human beings enjoy their benefit—in keeping with what the Sages of blessed memory taught, similar to this: [1] Whoever derives benefit from this world without a benediction, commits a breach of holiness. [2] All this is to make ourselves worthy, that we should deserve to receive of His goodness, as I have written in this work many times. On the sixteenth of Nissan we used to bring, at the time the Temple stood, the 'omer (sheaf) offering of the new crop of barley, because it is [then] riper than wheat; and it would make all the crops of grain permissible.

Among the laws of the precept, there is what the Sages of blessed memory taught: [3] that there are only five grains included under the prohibition on new crops, these being wheat, barley, spelt, oats and rye. At the time the Temple stood, once the 'omer was offered on the sixteenth of Nissan, new grain was permissible in Jerusalem. [4] Distant ⟨305⟩ locations were permitted [to use new grain] after midday, because the

וְעַל־כֵּן הָיָה מֻתָּר לָהֶם בְּכָל מָקוֹם לִסְמֹךְ עַל חֲזָקָה זוֹ; וְהַיּוֹם בַּעֲוֹנוֹתֵינוּ שֶׁאֵין
מִקְדָּשׁ, אָסוּר מִן הַתּוֹרָה כָּל הַיּוֹם; וּבִמְקוֹמוֹת שֶׁעוֹשִׂין שְׁנֵי יָמִים־טוֹבִים, אָסוּר
כָּל יוֹם שִׁבְעָה עָשָׂר עַד לָעֶרֶב, מִדְּרַבָּנָן; וְיֵתֶר פְּרָטֶיהָ, בִּמְנָחוֹת פֶּרֶק (י') [ו']
וּבִמְקוֹמוֹת מִשְׁבוּעוֹת וּמַעַשְׂרוֹת וְחַלָּה.

וְנוֹהֵג אִסּוּר זֶה בְּכָל מָקוֹם וּבְכָל זְמַן, בֵּין בִּפְנֵי הַבַּיִת בֵּין שֶׁלֹּא בִּפְנֵי הַבַּיִת,
בִּזְכָרִים וּנְקֵבוֹת. וּמִי שֶׁעָבַר עַל זֶה וְאָכַל כְּזַיִת מִפַּת חָדָשׁ קֹדֶם יוֹם הַקְרָבַת
הָעֹמֶר, חַיָּב מַלְקוֹת.

[שֶׁלֹּא לֶאֱכֹל קָלִי מִתְּבוּאָה חֲדָשָׁה עַד הַיּוֹם הַהוּא]

שד שֶׁלֹּא לֶאֱכֹל קָלִי מִתְּבוּאָה חֲדָשָׁה קֹדֶם הַזְּמַן הַנִּזְכָּר, כְּלוֹמַר שֶׁאַף־עַל־פִּי
שֶׁלֹּא עָשָׂה פַת מִן הַתְּבוּאָה וְלֹא טְחָנָהּ וְלֹא רִקְּדָהּ אֶלָּא שֶׁקְּלָאָהּ מִן הַחִטִּים אוֹ מִן
הַשְּׂעוֹרִים בָּאוּר וְאָכַל מֵהֶן, חַיָּב גַּם עֲלֵיהֶם; וְעַל זֶה נֶאֱמַר "וְקָלִי" וְגוֹמֵר. כָּל
עִנְיָנָהּ בַּמִּצְוָה הַקּוֹדֶמֶת; וְחַיָּב הָאוֹכֵל גַּם־כֵּן מַלְקוֹת עַל כְּזַיִת מִן הַקָּלִי.

[שֶׁלֹּא לֶאֱכֹל כַּרְמֶל מִתְּבוּאָה חֲדָשָׁה עַד הַזְּמַן הַנִּזְכָּר]

שה שֶׁלֹּא נֹאכַל כַּרְמֶל חָדָשׁ קֹדֶם הַזְּמַן הַנִּזְכָּר, שֶׁנֶּאֱמַר: וְכַרְמֶל לֹא תֹאכְלוּ.
וְהַכַּרְמֶל נִקְרָא תְּבוּאָה קְלוּיָה בְשַׁבֳּלִים, גְּרָאנְיֵשׁ בְּלַעַז, וְחַיָּבִין עַל הַכַּרְמֶל גַּם־כֵּן
בִּכְזַיִת; וְאָמְרוּ זִכְרוֹנָם לִבְרָכָה: אָכַל מִן הֶחָדָשׁ לֶחֶם וְקָלִי וְכַרְמֶל, חַיָּב עַל כָּל
אַחַת וְאַחַת; וְאָמְרוּ גַם־כֵּן: "קָלִי" לֹא הָיָה צָרִיךְ לְאָמְרוֹ, אֲבָל הִזְכִּירוֹ הַכָּתוּב
לַחֲלֹק, שֶׁמִּתְחַיֵּב עַל קָלִי בִּפְנֵי עַצְמוֹ, וְכֵן עַל כַּרְמֶל וְלֶחֶם. וְאָמְרוּ בַּגְּמָרָא עַל צַד
הַדְּחִיָּה: אוּלַי יִתְחַיֵּב עַל קָלִי בִּפְנֵי עַצְמוֹ אַחַר שֶׁהוּא מְיֻתָּר, וְיִהְיֶה חַיָּב עַל לֶחֶם

5. Ibid. 68a–b.
6. Since the custom of observing two days of festival instead of one derives from the time when there was doubt if a Jewish month began on the thirtieth or thirty-first day since the start of the previous month (§301), we regard the seventeenth of Nissan in the exile as if there were a doubt whether it is not perhaps the sixteenth; *ibid.* 68b. (From the paragraph's second sentence to here is based on MT *hilchoth ma'achaloth 'asuroth* x 2.)

§305   1. TB K'rithoth 5a.
2. Since it could have been inferred from bread and *karmel*.

[great] *beth din* would not be tardy with it [the '*omer* offering] till after midday.[4] It was therefore permissible for people everywhere to rely on this firm assumption. Today, however, when for our sins there is no Sanctuary, it is forbidden by Torah law the entire day.[5] And in those locations where two days of festival are observed, it is forbidden the entire seventeenth day [of Nissan] until the evening, by the ruling of the Sages.[6] The rest of its details are in the sixth chapter of the Talmud tractate *M'naḥoth*, and in certain places in the tractates (*Sh'vu'oth*) [*Sh'vi'ith*], *Ma'as'roth* and *Ḥallah*.

This prohibition applies everywhere and at every time, whether the Temple exists or not, for both man and woman. If someone transgresses this and eats an olive's amount of new bread before the day of the offering of the '*omer*, he deserves whiplashes.

[TO EAT NO PARCHED GRAIN FROM THE NEW CROP TILL THE END OF THE 16TH OF NISSAN]

304 not to eat parched grain of the new crop before the time mentioned [above]; in other words, even if one did not make bread of the grain, and did not grind it and winnow it, but merely roasted wheat or barley on the fire and ate of it, he would be punishable for that too— as it was stated of this, *nor parched grain*, etc. (Leviticus 23:14). All its subject-matter is in the previous *mitzvah* (§303). Anyone who eats it is likewise punishable by whiplashes over an olive's amount of parched grain.

[TO EAT NO FRESH GRAIN FROM THE NEW CROP UNTIL THE END OF THE 16TH OF NISSAN]

305 that we should not eat new *karmel* (fresh grain) before the time mentioned (§303), as it is stated, *nor* karmel (*fresh grain) shall you eat* (Leviticus 23:14). Now, *karmel* is what grain roasted as ears is called— *granès* in the foreign tongue [Spanish]. Guilt is incurred for *karmel* likewise over an olive's amount. And our Sages of blessed memory said:[1] If someone ate bread, parched grain, and *karmel* from the new crop, he is punishable for each and every one [separately]. They likewise taught: There was no need to state "parched grain";[2] but Scripture mentioned it in order to make [each] separate—that punishment is incurred for parched grain by itself, and so for *karmel* and bread. It was then asked in the Talmud,[1] by way of rebuttal: But perhaps punishment is incurred for parched grain by itself, since it is super-

וְכַרְמֶל מַלְקוּת אַחַת. וְהָיְתָה הַתְּשׁוּבָה: לְמַאי הִלְכְתָא כַּתְבֵיהּ רַחֲמָנָא לְקָלִי בְּאֶמְצַע — לוֹמַר לֶחֶם כִּי קָלִי וְכַרְמֶל כִּדְקָלִי, וְיִהְיֶה חַיָּב עַל כָּל אֶחָד וְאֶחָד.

כָּל עִנְיָנָהּ כִּשְׁתֵּי הַמִּצְוֹת הַקּוֹדְמוֹת, חַבְרוֹתֶיהָ.

[מִצְוַת סְפִירַת הָעֹמֶר]

שׁו לִסְפֹּר תִּשְׁעָה וְאַרְבָּעִים יוֹם מִיּוֹם הֲבָאַת הָעֹמֶר, שֶׁהוּא יוֹם שִׁשָּׁה־עָשָׂר בְּנִיסָן, שֶׁנֶּאֱמַר: וּסְפַרְתֶּם לָכֶם מִמָּחֳרַת הַשַּׁבָּת מִיּוֹם הֲבִיאֲכֶם אֶת עֹמֶר הַתְּנוּפָה.

וְהַמִּנְיָן הַזֶּה חוֹבָה, וְעָלֵינוּ לִמְנוֹת בּוֹ הַיָּמִים יוֹם יוֹם, וְכֵן הַשָּׁבוּעוֹת, שֶׁהַכָּתוּב אָמַר: תִּסְפְּרוּ חֲמִשִּׁים יוֹם, וְאָמַר גַּם־כֵּן: שִׁבְעָה שָׁבוּעוֹת תִּסְפָּר לָךְ, וּבְפֵרוּשׁ אָמַר אַבַּיֵּי בַּגְּמָרָא בִּמְנָחוֹת: מִצְוָה לְמִמְנֵי יוֹמֵי וּמִצְוָה לְמִמְנֵי שָׁבוּעֵי.

וְיֵשׁ מִן הַמְּפָרְשִׁים שֶׁהָיָה דַעְתָּם כִּי כַּוָּנַת הַכָּתוּב לִמְנוֹת הַשָּׁבוּעוֹת דַּוְקָא כְּשֶׁהֵן שְׁלֵמוֹת, אֲבָל לְהַזְכִּיר בְּכָל יוֹם וְלוֹמַר שֶׁהֵן כָּךְ וְכָךְ יָמִים וְכָךְ וְכָךְ שָׁבוּעוֹת, אֵין צֹרֶךְ; וְיֵשׁ מֵהֶם שֶׁאָמְרוּ כִּי הַדֶּרֶךְ הַנִּבְחָר לְהַזְכִּיר מִנְיַן הַשָּׁבוּעוֹת עִם הַיָּמִים תָּמִיד בְּכָל יוֹם; וִירֵא שָׁמַיִם יִבְחַר דַּרְכָּם לְהוֹצִיא מִכָּל סָפֵק, וְלֹא יָחוּשׁ לְתִפְאֶרֶת הַמִּלּוֹת. וְכֵן נָהֲגוּ הַיּוֹם בְּכָל הַמְּקוֹמוֹת שֶׁשָּׁמַעְנוּ.

וְכָתַב הָרַמְבַּ״ם זִכְרוֹנוֹ לִבְרָכָה: וְאַל יַטְעֶה אוֹתְךָ אָמְרָם זִכְרוֹנָם לִבְרָכָה "מִצְוָה לְמִמְנֵי יוֹמֵי וּמִצְוָה לְמִמְנֵי שָׁבוּעֵי" וְתַחְשֹׁב שֶׁהֵן שְׁתֵּי מִצְוֹת, שֶׁאֵין הַכַּוָּנָה בָּזֶה לוֹמַר שֶׁתִּהְיֶה מִצְוָה בִּפְנֵי עַצְמָהּ, אֲבָל הוּא חֵלֶק מֵחֶלְקֵי הַמִּצְוָה. וְאָמְנָם הָיוּ שְׁתֵּי מִצְוֹת אִלּוּ אָמְרוּ מִנְיַן הַיָּמִים מִצְוָה וּמִנְיַן הַשָּׁבוּעוֹת מִצְוָה; וְזֶה מַה שֶׁלֹּא נֶעְלַם מִמִּי שֶׁיְּדַקְדֵּק הַדָּבָר וִיבָאֲרֵהוּ: שֶׁאַתָּה כְּשֶׁתֹּאמַר יִתְחַיֵּב שֶׁיַּעֲשֶׂה

---

3. Since each of the two is adjacent to it.

§306   1. E.g. "Today it is eight days, which are one week and one day, of the 'omer."

2. R. Nissim, commentary on R. Isaac 'Alfasi, P'saḥim, toward the end; Rabiah (R. 'Eli'ezer b. R. Yo'él haLévi) citing a ga'on, mentioned in Mord'chai to TB M'gillah ii, toward the end.

3. I.e. when the days make up a number of whole weeks: seven days, fourteen days, etc.

4. R. 'Ashér (Rosh) writes similarly in a responsum (Responsa, xxiv, §13) that this is the generally accepted practice.

5. ShM positive precept §161; see §282, note 2, which applies here.

fluous; yet one should be punishable for both bread and *karmel* by one set of lashes? The answer was: Then for what practical reason in the law did the merciful God write "parched grain" in the middle?—to denote that bread is like parched grain and *karmel* is like parched grain.³ Therefore punishment is incurred for each one separately.

All its subject-matter is like that of its two fellow-precepts, that precede it.

306 [THE PRECEPT OF COUNTING THE 'OMER] to count forty-nine days from the day of the presentation of the *'omer* (sheaf-offering), which is the sixteenth of Nissan: for it is stated, *And you shall count for yourselves from the morrow after the sabbath, from the day that you brought the sheaf of the wave-offering* (Leviticus 23:15).

This counting is obligatory: it is for us to count the days in question, day by day, and so also the weeks—since Scripture says, *you shall count fifty days* (ibid. 16), and it says likewise, *Seven weeks shall you count for yourself* (Deuteronomy 16:9); and Abbaye said distinctly in the Talmud tractate *M'nahoth* (66a): It is a religious duty to count the days, and so a duty to count the weeks.¹

Now, there are some authorities² who held that the meaning of the Writ is that the weeks should be counted specifically when they are complete;³ but to mention them every day, saying, "It is so many days and so many weeks"—this is not necessary. And there are some who said that the preferable way is to mention the number of weeks with the days continually, every day. Well, one who reverently fears Heaven should choose their way, to avoid any doubt, and he should not be concerned about the elegance of the words; and this is the practice followed in all the locations of which we have heard.⁴

Rambam of blessed memory wrote:⁵ Now, do not be misled by what the Sages of blessed memory said, "It is a religious duty to count the days, and so a duty to count the weeks," so that you will think they are two precepts. For the meaning here was not to say that it should be a precept by itself, but rather one of the parts of the precept. Indeed, they would be two precepts had the Sages said, "The counting of the days is a *mitzvah*, and the counting of the weeks is a *mitzvah*." This is something not to be overlooked by one who will examine the matter carefully and clarify it. For when you say, "It is obligatory that

כָּךְ וְכָךְ, לֹא יִתְחַיֵּב מֵהַמַּאֲמָר הַזֶּה שֶׁהָעִנְיָן הַהוּא מִצְוָה בִּפְנֵי עַצְמָהּ. וְהָרְאָיָה הַמְבֹאֶרֶת עַל זֶה, הֱיוֹתֵנוּ מוֹנִין הַשָּׁבוּעוֹת כְּמוֹ־כֵן כָּל לַיְלָה, בְּאָמְרֵנוּ שֶׁהֵן כָּךְ וְכָךְ שָׁבוּעוֹת וְכָךְ וְכָךְ יָמִים, וְאִלּוּ הָיוּ הַשָּׁבוּעוֹת מִצְוָה בִּפְנֵי עַצְמָהּ, לֹא סִדְּרוּ מִנְיָנָהּ אֶלָּא בְּלֵילֵי הַשָּׁבוּעוֹת בִּלְבַד, וְהָיוּ לָהֶן שְׁתֵּי בְּרָכוֹת: אֲשֶׁר קִדְּשָׁנוּ בְּמִצְוֹתָיו וְצִוָּנוּ עַל סְפִירַת יְמֵי הָעֹמֶר, וְעַל סְפִירַת שְׁבוּעֵי הָעֹמֶר; וְאֵין הַדָּבָר כֵּן, אֲבָל הַמִּצְוָה הִיא סְפִירַת הָעֹמֶר יָמָיו וְשָׁבוּעוֹתָיו, כְּמוֹ שֶׁכָּתַבְנוּ. עַד כָּאן.

מִשָּׁרְשֵׁי הַמִּצְוָה עַל צַד הַפְּשָׁט, לְפִי שֶׁכָּל עִקָּרָן שֶׁל יִשְׂרָאֵל אֵינוֹ אֶלָּא הַתּוֹרָה, וּמִפְּנֵי הַתּוֹרָה נִבְרְאוּ שָׁמַיִם וָאָרֶץ וְיִשְׂרָאֵל, וּכְמוֹ שֶׁכָּתוּב: אִם לֹא בְרִיתִי יוֹמָם וָלַיְלָה וְגוֹמֵר, וְהִיא הָעִקָּר וְהַסִּבָּה שֶׁנִּגְאֲלוּ וְיָצְאוּ מִמִּצְרַיִם, כְּדֵי שֶׁיְּקַבְּלוּ הַתּוֹרָה בְּסִינַי וִיקַיְּמוּהָ, וּכְמוֹ שֶׁאָמַר הַשֵּׁם לְמֹשֶׁה: "וְזֶה לְּךָ הָאוֹת כִּי אָנֹכִי שְׁלַחְתִּיךָ בְּהוֹצִיאֲךָ אֶת הָעָם מִמִּצְרַיִם תַּעַבְדוּן אֶת הָאֱלֹהִים עַל הָהָר הַזֶּה", וּפֵרוּשׁ הַפָּסוּק כְּלוֹמַר: הוֹצִיאֲךָ אוֹתָם מִמִּצְרַיִם יִהְיֶה לְךָ אוֹת שֶׁתַּעַבְדוּן אֶת הָאֱלֹהִים עַל הָהָר הַזֶּה, כְּלוֹמַר שֶׁתְּקַבְּלוּ הַתּוֹרָה, שֶׁהִיא הָעִקָּר הַגָּדוֹל שֶׁבִּשְׁבִיל זֶה הֵם נִגְאָלִים וְהִיא תַּכְלִית הַטּוֹבָה שֶׁלָּהֶם; וְעִנְיָן גָּדוֹל הוּא לָהֶם, יוֹתֵר מִן הַחֵרוּת מֵעַבְדוּת, וְלָכֵן יַעֲשֶׂה הַשֵּׁם לְמֹשֶׁה אוֹת צֵאתָם מֵעַבְדוּת לְקַבָּלַת הַתּוֹרָה, כִּי הַטָּפֵל עוֹשִׂין אוֹת לְעוֹלָם אֶל הָעִקָּר.

וּמִפְּנֵי־כֵן, כִּי הִיא כָּל עִקָּרָן שֶׁל יִשְׂרָאֵל וּבַעֲבוּרָהּ נִגְאֲלוּ וְעָלוּ לְכָל הַגְּדֻלָּה שֶׁעָלוּ אֵלֶיהָ, נִצְטַוִּינוּ לִמְנוֹת מִמָּחֳרַת יוֹם־טוֹב שֶׁל פֶּסַח עַד יוֹם נְתִינַת הַתּוֹרָה, לְהַרְאוֹת בְּנַפְשֵׁנוּ הַחֵפֶץ הַגָּדוֹל אֶל הַיּוֹם הַנִּכְבָּד הַנִּכְסָף לְלִבֵּנוּ, כְּעֶבֶד יִשְׁאַף צֵל, וְיִמְנֶה תָּמִיד מָתַי יָבוֹא הָעֵת הַנִּכְסָף אֵלָיו שֶׁיֵּצֵא לְחֵרוּת, כִּי הַמִּנְיָן מַרְאֶה לָאָדָם

6. The verse is so interpreted in TB N'darim 32a, that heaven and earth were created and exist through the merit of Torah study day and night, which honors and maintains this covenant. Hence that is Jewry's basic reason for existence.

7. So the alternative explanation of Rashi on the verse.

8. To escape the gaze of his master and find freedom.

this-and-this should be done," it does not necessarily follow from this statement that the matter is a precept by itself. And the clear proof of this is that we count the weeks as well every night, by saying that it is so many weeks and so many days. Were [the counting of] the weeks a precept by itself, that counting would have been arranged for none but the nights of the [complete] weeks alone, and there would be two benedictions for them: "who has hallowed us with His precepts and commanded us about counting the *days* of the 'omer," and again, "about counting the *weeks* of the 'omer." Yet the matter is not so; rather, the precept is the counting of the 'omer, its days and its weeks, as we have written. Thus far his words.

At the root of the precept, by way of the plain meaning, lies the reason that the entire main element of the life of Jewry is nothing other than the Torah. On account of the Torah, heaven and earth— and Jewry—were created; as it is written, *If not for My covenant* [of the Torah] *day and night, I would not have set the ordinances of heaven and earth* (Jeremiah 33:25).[6] This is the principal element and the reason why they were rescued and went forth out of Egypt—so that they would accept the Torah at Sinai and fulfill it. As the Eternal Lord said to Moses, *this shall be the sign for you that I have sent you: when you have brought forth the people out of Egypt, you shall serve God on this mountain* (Exodus 3:12). The meaning of the verse is as though it said: "Your taking them out of Egypt will be a sign for you that you will serve God on this mountain";[7] in other words, that you will receive the Torah, as this is the great principal purpose for whose sake they were to be redeemed, and this is the ultimate good for them; and this is a greater matter for them than the liberation from servitude. Therefore the Eternal Lord made their emergence from slavery a sign for Moses of their [eventual] acceptance of the Torah: For a less important, subsidiary matter is always made a sign or token for a matter of main importance.

Now, for this reason—because it is the main core of the Israelites' life, and for its sake they were redeemed and rose to all the distinction that they attained—we were commanded to count [the days] from the morrow after the festival day of Passover till the day the Torah was given—to show with our very souls our great yearning for that distinguished day, for which our heart longs *as a servant eagerly longs for the shadow*[8] (Job 7:2), and constantly counts [and reckons] when his longed-for time will come when he will go out to freedom. For

כִּי כָל יִשְׁעוֹ וְכָל חֶפְצוֹ לְהַגִּיעַ אֶל הַזְּמַן הַהוּא.

וְזֶהוּ שֶׁאָנוּ מוֹנִין לָעֹמֶר, כְּלוֹמַר כָּךְ וְכָךְ יָמִים עָבְרוּ מִן הַמִּנְיָן, וְאֵין אָנוּ מוֹנִין כָּךְ וְכָךְ יָמִים יֵשׁ לָנוּ לַזְּמַן, כִּי כָל זֶה מַרְאֶה בָּנוּ הָרָצוֹן הֶחָזָק לְהַגִּיעַ אֶל הַזְּמַן, וְעַל-כֵּן לֹא נִרְצֶה לְהַזְכִּיר בִּתְחִלַּת חֶשְׁבּוֹנֵנוּ רִבּוּי הַיָּמִים שֶׁיֵּשׁ לָנוּ לְהַגִּיעַ לְקָרְבַּן שְׁתֵּי הַלֶּחֶם שֶׁל עֲצֶרֶת.

וְאַל יִקְשֶׁה עָלֶיךָ לוֹמַר: אִם-כֵּן, אַחַר שֶׁעָבְרוּ רֹב הַיָּמִים שֶׁל שִׁבְעָה שָׁבוּעוֹת אֵלוּ, לָמָּה לֹא נַזְכִּיר מְעוּט הַיָּמִים הַנִּשְׁאָרִים — לְפִי שֶׁאֵין לְשַׁנּוֹת מַטְבֵּעַ הַחֶשְׁבּוֹן בְּאֶמְצָעוֹ. וְאִם תִּשְׁאַל: אִם-כֵּן, לָמָּה אָנוּ מַתְחִילִין אוֹתוֹ מִמָּחֳרַת הַשַּׁבָּת וְלֹא מִיּוֹם רִאשׁוֹן — הַתְּשׁוּבָה כִּי הַיּוֹם הָרִאשׁוֹן נִתְיַחֵד כֻּלּוֹ לְהַזְכָּרַת הַנֵּס הַגָּדוֹל, וְהוּא יְצִיאַת מִצְרַיִם, שֶׁהוּא אוֹת וּמוֹפֵת בְּחִדּוּשׁ הָעוֹלָם וּבְהַשְׁגָּחַת הַשֵּׁם עַל בְּנֵי-הָאָדָם, וְאֵין לָנוּ לְעָרֵב בְּשִׂמְחָתוֹ וּלְהַזְכִּיר עִמּוֹ שׁוּם עִנְיָן אַחֵר; וְעַל-כֵּן נִתְקַן הַחֶשְׁבּוֹן מִיּוֹם שֵׁנִי מִיָּד.

וְאֵין לוֹמַר "הַיּוֹם כָּךְ-וְכָךְ יָמִים לְיוֹם שֵׁנִי שֶׁל פֶּסַח", שֶׁלֹּא יִהְיֶה חֶשְׁבּוֹן רָאוּי לוֹמַר לְיוֹם שֵׁנִי, וְעַל-כֵּן הֻתְקַן לִמְנוֹת לַמִּנְיָן מִמַּה שֶּׁנַּעֲשָׂה בּוֹ, וְהוּא קָרְבַּן הָעֹמֶר, שֶׁהוּא קָרְבָּן נִכְבָּד שֶׁבּוֹ זֵכֶר שֶׁאָנוּ מַאֲמִינִים כִּי הַשֵּׁם בָּרוּךְ הוּא בְּהַשְׁגָּחָתוֹ עַל בְּנֵי-אָדָם רוֹצֶה לְהַחֲיוֹתָם וּמְחַדֵּשׁ לָהֶם בְּכָל שָׁנָה וְשָׁנָה זֶרַע תְּבוּאוֹת לִחְיוֹת בּוֹ.

מִדִּינֵי הַמִּצְוָה, מַה שֶּׁאָמְרוּ זִכְרוֹנָם לִבְרָכָה שֶׁמִּצְוָה לִמְנוֹתָן מִבָּעֶרֶב, כְּדֵי שֶׁיִּהְיוּ תְמִימוֹת, כְּמוֹ שֶׁאָמַר הַכָּתוּב: תְּמִימוֹת תִּהְיֶינָה, וְאָמְרוּ זִכְרוֹנָם לִבְרָכָה: אֵימָתַי הֵן תְּמִימוֹת, בִּזְמַן שֶׁמַּתְחִיל מִבָּעֶרֶב. וּמִכָּל-מָקוֹם פֵּרְשׁוּ הַמְפָרְשִׁים שֶׁאִם שָׁכַח וְלֹא מָנָה מִבָּעֶרֶב, מוֹנֶה לְמָחָר כָּל הַיּוֹם.

---

9. The paragraph echoes Rambam, *Guide* iii 43.

10. That, on the contrary, would be a cause of dismay (or it might even denote an unseemly interest in the great number of days that remain as an "insulating barrier" between us and the granting of the Torah).

11. As the remaining number grows small and dwindles, counting that number would be more in keeping with eagerness to reach the desired day.

12. Since the exodus came about through miracles that defied the laws of nature, produced at the Almighty's wish, it demonstrates that He is the supreme Master of the world and its creation.

13. Since He brought the exodus about, in response to the unjust suffering of the Hebrews, and in fulfillment of His promise to the Patriarchs.

14. See §302, note 6.

15. Cf. §302, fourth paragraph.

16. TB M'naḥoth 66a.

17. Which precedes the day, since in Jewish reckoning, the evening is the beginning of a twenty-four-hour day.

18. Literally, commentators; i.e. authors of commentaries on the Talmud, etc.

counting shows about a person that all his hope of deliverance and all his desire is to reach that time.[9]

This is why we count from the 'omer, i.e. so many days have passed out of the total; and we do not count, "so many days remain for us to that time"—because all this shows the mighty desire in us to reach that time. For this reason we do not wish to mention at the beginning of our reckoning the great number of days that remain for us, to reach the offering of the two loaves on Shavu'oth.[10]

Now, let this not be a difficulty for you, to ask: In that case, after most of the days of these seven weeks have passed, why do we not mention the smaller number of days that remain?[11] The reason is that we cannot change the form of counting in the middle. But you might ask: If so, why do we begin it from "the morrow after the sabbath" and not from the first day [of Passover]? The answer is that the entire first day is designated particularly for recalling the great miracle, the emergence from Egypt, which is a sign and wonder demonstrating the creation of the world out of nothing[12] and the watchful care of the Eternal Lord over human beings.[13] Hence it is not for us to mingle into its joy and mention together with it any other theme.[14] Therefore the reckoning was set to begin directly from the second day.

It should not be said, however, "Today is so many days since the second day of Passover"; because it would not be a seemly reckoning to say "since the second day." It was therefore established to do the counting from that which took place on it, i.e. the 'omer (sheaf) offering: For this is a distinctive offering which bears the connotation that we believe that the Eternal Lord (blessed is He), in His providential care for human beings, desires to sustain them, and He thus renews for them every year the crops of grain, to live on it.[15]

Among the laws of the precept, there is what the Sages of blessed memory taught:[16] that it is a religious duty to count them [the days] from the evening,[17] so that they should be [counted] whole—as Scripture states, complete shall they be (Leviticus 23:15); and they of blessed memory said:[16] When are they complete?—when one begins [counting] from the evening. Nevertheless, the authorities[18] explained that if someone forgot and did not count the day in the [previous] evening, he may do the counting on the morrow, during the entire day.[19]

Now, there are those who ruled that if a person forgot and did not

וְיֵשׁ שֶׁאָמְרוּ שֶׁמִּי שֶׁשָּׁכַח וְלֹא מָנָה יוֹם אֶחָד, שֶׁאֵין יָכוֹל לִמְנוֹת עוֹד בְּאוֹתָהּ
שָׁנָה, לְפִי שֶׁכֻּלָּן מִצְוָה אַחַת הִיא, וּמִכֵּיוָן שֶׁשָּׁכַח מֵהֶן יוֹם אֶחָד הֲרֵי כָּל הַחֶשְׁבּוֹן
בָּטֵל מִמֶּנּוּ; וְלֹא הוֹדוּ מוֹרֵינוּ שֶׁבְּדוֹרֵנוּ לִסְבָרָא זוֹ, אֶלָּא מִי שֶׁשָּׁכַח יוֹם אֶחָד מוֹנֶה
הָאֲחֵרִים עִם כָּל יִשְׂרָאֵל.

וּמִצְוָה מִן הַמֻּבְחָר לִמְנוֹת מְעֻמָּד, וּמְבָרֵךְ "אֲשֶׁר קִדְּשָׁנוּ" וְכוּלֵי; וּמִי שֶׁמָּנָה
בְּלֹא בְרָכָה, יָצָא, וְאֵינוֹ רַשַּׁאי לַחֲזוֹר וְלִמְנוֹת בִּבְרָכָה. וְיֶתֶר פְּרָטֶיהָ, בְּמַסֶּכֶת
מְנָחוֹת.

וְנוֹהֶגֶת מִצְוַת סְפִירַת הָעֹמֶר מִדְּאוֹרַיְתָא בְּכָל מָקוֹם, בִּזְכָרִים, בִּזְמַן הַבַּיִת,
שֶׁיֵּשׁ שָׁם עֹמֶר; וּמִדְּרַבָּנָן בְּכָל מָקוֹם וַאֲפִלּוּ הַיּוֹם, שֶׁאֵין עֹמֶר קָרֵב בַּעֲווֹנוֹתֵינוּ.
וְעוֹבֵר עַל זֶה וְלֹא סָפַר יָמִים אֵלּוּ בִּזְמַן הַבַּיִת, בִּטֵּל עֲשֵׂה.

[מִצְוַת קָרְבַּן מִנְחָה חֲדָשָׁה מִן הַחִטִּים בְּיוֹם עֲצֶרֶת]

שֹׁז לְהַקְרִיב בְּיוֹם חַג הַשָּׁבוּעוֹת לֶחֶם חָמֵץ מִן חִטָּה חֲדָשָׁה, וְזֶה נִקְרָא בַּכָּתוּב
מִנְחָה חֲדָשָׁה, וְהֵם שְׁתֵּי כִכָּרוֹת, כְּמוֹ שֶׁכָּתוּב: מִמּוֹשְׁבֹתֵיכֶם תָּבִיאוּ לֶחֶם תְּנוּפָה
שְׁתַּיִם שְׁנֵי עֶשְׂרֹנִים.

וְהָעִנְיָן הָיָה כֵן: שֶׁהָיוּ מְבִיאִין שָׁלֹשׁ סְאִים חִטִּים חֲדָשׁוֹת וְשָׁפִין אוֹתָן וּבוֹצְעִין
בָּהֶן כְּדֶרֶךְ כָּל הַמְּנָחוֹת, וְטוֹחֲנִין אוֹתָן, וּמְנַפִּין מֵהֶן שְׁנֵי עֶשְׂרוֹנִים בִּשְׁתֵּים עֶשְׂרֵה
נָפָה, וְלוֹקְחִין אוֹתָן וְעוֹשִׂין מֵהֶן שְׁתֵּי חַלּוֹת, וּמֵבִיא שְׂאוֹר וְנוֹתְנוֹ לְתוֹךְ הָעִשָּׂרוֹן;
וְאֹרֶךְ כָּל חַלָּה שִׁבְעָה טְפָחִים וְרָחְבָּהּ אַרְבָּעָה וְגָבְהָהּ אַרְבַּע אֶצְבָּעוֹת, וּמְרֻבָּעוֹת
הָיוּ, וְאוֹפִין אוֹתָן מֵעֶרֶב יוֹם-טוֹב, וּלְמָחָר, אַחַר הֲנָפָתָן, הָיוּ נֶאֱכָלוֹת לַכֹּהֲנִים כָּל
אוֹתוֹ יוֹם וַחֲצִי הַלָּיְלָה.

וְאוֹתָהּ מִנְחָה הִיא רִאשׁוֹנָה לְכָל הַמְּנָחוֹת הַבָּאוֹת מִן הַחִטִּים; וּמַקְרִיבִים עִם

19. So *tosafoth* to TB M'naḥoth 66a, s.v. *zécher*, and MT *hilchoth t'midin* vii 23.
20. So *Halachoth G'doloth*, cited in *tosafoth ibid.* and in *Tur 'Oraḥ Ḥayyim*, §489.
20a. Cf. R. Yeruḥam, *Tol'doth 'Adam v'Ḥavvah*, 5, 4.
21. So R. Hai Ga'on and R. Yitzḥak (of *tosafoth*), cited in R. 'Ashér, P'saḥim, end, §41, and in Tur *ibid.* The first edition reads: . . . that if someone forgot one day, he should say, "Last night it was so [many days, etc. of the *'omer*]," without a benediction, and he may count, etc. As this is not in the oldest manuscripts, it is evidently a later interpolation—and quite inappropriate, since it obviously refers to one who forgot to do the counting at night and remembered about it the following day (mentioned above). Our text, however, refers to one who forgot both at night and the following day.
22. "Blessed art Thou, Lord our God, King of the world, who has hallowed us with His precepts and commanded us about the counting of the *'omer*."
23. MT *hilchoth t'midin* vii 23 and 25.
24. See §302, note 13.

§307   1. TB M'naḥoth 76b.

count one day, he may no longer do the counting that year, because it [the counting of all the days] is all one *mitzvah*, and inasmuch as he forgot one day out of them, the entire reckoning thus becomes stopped, null and void, for him.[20] But our instructors of our generation did not accede to this opinion,[20a] holding rather that if someone forgot one day, he may count the other [days] together with all Jews.[21]

The preferred way of observing the precept is to do the counting standing; and the benediction is said, "who has hallowed us," etc.[22] If someone counts without a benediction, he acquits himself of his obligation, and he is not allowed to count again with a benediction.[23] The rest of its details are in the Talmud tractate *M'nahoth*.

The *mitzvah* of the counting of the 'omer, by the law of the Torah, applies everywhere, to the men,[24] at the time the Temple exists, where there is an 'omer offering; and by the Sages' enactment [it is in effect] everywhere even today, when for our sins the 'omer is not offered up. If someone transgressed it and did not count these [forty-nine] days at the time of the Temple, he would disobey a positive precept.

[THE PRECEPT OF THE MEAL–OFFERING OF NEW WHEAT ON SHAVU'OTH]

307 to offer up on the festival day of *Shavu'oth*, leavened bread of new wheat, which is called in the Writ "a new *minhah* (meal-offering)" (Leviticus 23:16). This is the two loaves of bread, as it is written, *You shall bring from your dwellings two loaves for waving, of two tenths of an 'éphah* (ibid. 17).

This, in substance, was done: Three *se'ah* of new wheat was brought,[1] which was rubbed [by hand] and pounded [by fist],[2] in the way of all *minhah* (meal) offerings.[3] Then it was ground, and two tenths of an 'éphah were sifted out from it through twelve sieves.[1] This was taken, and two loaves were made of it; yeast was brought and added to each tenth of an 'éphah;[4] the length of each loaf was seven handbreadths, its width four, and its height four fingers;[5] and they were of box-like shape.[6] They were baked the day before the festival,[7] and on the morrow, after their waving,[8] they might be eaten by the *kohanim* that entire day and half the night.[9]

That *minhah* was the first of all the *minhah* (meal) offerings that were to be brought of wheat.[10] With the loaves they would offer

הַלֶּחֶם שִׁבְעָה כְבָשִׂים תְּמִימִם וּפַר בֶּן בָּקָר אֶחָד וְאֵילִם שְׁנַיִם, לְעוֹלָה, וְשָׂעִיר
לְחַטָּאת, וּשְׁנֵי כְבָשִׂים לִשְׁלָמִים; וְאֵלּוּ הֵן הַקָּרְבָּנוֹת הָאֲמוּרוֹת בְּחֹמֶשׁ הַפְּקוּדִים.
כָּל זֶה הָיָה קָרֵב עִם הַלֶּחֶם, מִלְּבַד קָרְבַּן מוּסַף הַיּוֹם, שֶׁהוּא שְׁנֵי פָרִים וְאַיִל אֶחָד
וְשִׁבְעָה כְבָשִׂים לְעוֹלָה, וּשְׂעִיר עִזִּים לְחַטָּאת — וְאֵלּוּ הֵן הַקָּרְבָּנוֹת הָאֲמוּרוֹת
בְּסֵפֶר וַיִּקְרָא. וּבְפֵרוּשׁ נִתְבָּאֵר כֵּן בְּפֶרֶק רְבִיעִי מִמְּנָחוֹת, שֶׁזֶּה הַקָּרְבָּן יָבוֹא עִם
הַלֶּחֶם חָלוּק מִמּוּסַף הַיּוֹם; וְאַחַר הֲנָפַת הַלֶּחֶם הָיָה נֶאֱכַל לַכֹּהֲנִים עִם כִּבְשֵׂי
הַשְּׁלָמִים.

מִשָּׁרְשֵׁי הַמִּצְוָה, כָּתַבְתִּי בְּמִצְוַת הָעֹמֶר, י' שֶׁבְּסֵדֶר זֶה [סִי' ש"ב], מַה
שֶּׁמַּסְפִּיק גַּם לִשְׁתֵּי הַלֶּחֶם עַל צַד הַפְּשָׁט. וְעוֹד אוֹמַר לִי לִבִּי בָּעִנְיָן, כִּי מִפְּנֵי זֶה
הָיְתָה הַמִּצְוָה בְּחִטִּים לִהְיוֹת הַמִּנְחָה בְּכִכָּרוֹת שֶׁל לֶחֶם, וּבְמִנְחַת שְׂעוֹרִים בְּקֶמַח,
לְפִי שֶׁהַחִטִּים לְמַאֲכַל אָדָם וְעַל־כֵּן רָאוּי לַהֲכִינָם בְּעִנְיָן שֶׁהָאָדָם נֶהֱנֶה וְנִזּוֹן
מֵהֶם; וְכָל זֶה מִן הַשֹּׁרֶשׁ אֲשֶׁר נָטַעְנוּ בַּתְּחִלָּה בְּעִנְיַן הַקָּרְבָּן עַל צַד הַפְּשָׁט, כִּי
מִתּוֹךְ הַמַּעֲשֶׂה תִּתְעוֹרֵר מַחֲשֶׁבֶת הָאָדָם אֶל הַדְּבָרִים; וְעַל־כֵּן, כְּפִי חֲשִׁיבוּת
הַקָּרְבָּן וַהֲכָנָתוֹ הַטּוֹבָה, לֵב אָדָם מִתְעוֹרֵר עָלָיו יוֹתֵר.

מִדִּינֵי הַמִּצְוָה, מַה שֶּׁאָמְרוּ שֶׁאִם לֹא מָצְאוּ חָדָשׁ יָבִיאוּ מִן הָעֲלִיָּה; וְחִטִּין
שֶׁיָּרְדוּ בֶעָבִים לֹא יָבִיא לְכַתְּחִלָּה, מִפְּנֵי שֶׁיֵּשׁ בָּהֶן סָפֵק אִם אֲנִי קוֹרֵא בָהֶן
"מִמּוֹשְׁבֹתֵיכֶם"; וְאִם הֵבִיא, כָּשֵׁר. לִישָׁתָן שֶׁל שְׁתֵּי הַלֶּחֶם וַעֲרִיכָתָן בַּחוּץ,
וַאֲפִיָּתָן בִּפְנִים כְּכָל הַמְּנָחוֹת, וְאֵין אֲפִיָּתָן דּוֹחָה יוֹם־טוֹב, שֶׁנֶּאֱמַר "יֵעָשֶׂה לָכֶם",
וְלֹא לַגָּבוֹהַּ. הֲנָפַת הַלֶּחֶם עִם שְׁנֵי כִבְשֵׂי הַשְּׁלָמִים הָיְתָה נַעֲשֵׂית בְּעוֹדָן חַיִּים;
וְכֹהֵן גָּדוֹל נוֹטֵל אַחַת מִן הַכִּכָּרוֹת, וְהַשְּׁנִיָּה מִתְחַלֶּקֶת לְכָל הַמִּשְׁמָרוֹת; וְיֶתֶר

2. To make the husks easily removable (Rashi); *ibid.* 76a.

3. *Ibid.*

4. TB M'naḥoth 52b.

5. *Ibid.* 96a, as understood by Rambam, commentary on Mishnah.

6. MT *hilchoth t'midin* viii 9.

7. TB M'naḥoth 100b.

8. See §302, third paragraph.

9. TB *ibid.* and B'rachoth 2a, etc.

10. TB M'naḥoth 68b.

11. I.e. it is eminently a food for man, being the primary staple ingredient for bread.

12. TB M'naḥoth 83b; MT *hilchoth t'midin* viii 2.

13. If in absorbing water vapor from the ocean, the thick clouds absorbed a boatload of wheat too (Rashi, s.v. *she-yor'du*); TB *ibid.* 69b.

14. MT *ibid.* 3.

15. TB M'naḥoth 95b.

16. I.e. it could not thrust aside the prohibition against doing work on the festival, to be allowed to be done then; *ibid.* 100b.

up seven lambs without blemish, one young bullock, and two rams, [all] as *'olah* (burnt) offerings; a male goat as a *hattath* (sin-offering), and two lambs as *sh'lamim* (peace-offerings)—these being the offerings listed in the *Book of Leviticus* (23:18–19). All these were brought with the bread, apart from the *musaf* (additional) offerings, which were two bullocks, one ram and seven lambs, as *'olah* offerings, and a male goat as a *hattath*—these being the offerings listed in the *Book of Numbers* (28:27,30). It is distinctly explained so in chapter 4 of the Talmud tractate *M'nahoth* (45b), that these offerings to be brought with the bread were separate from the *musaf* offerings of the day. After the waving of the bread,[8] it would be eaten by the *kohanim* with the lambs of the *sh'lamim* (peace-offerings).

As to the root reason for this precept, I wrote about the *mitzvah* of the *'omer* (sheaf-offering), the tenth positive precept in this *sidrah* (§302), what will suffice also for the two loaves, by way of the plain meaning. Moreover, my heart tells me about the matter that this is the reason why this *mitzvah* with wheat requires that the *minhah* (meal-offering) should be loaves of bread, while the *minhah* of barley [the *'omer*] was of flour: because wheat is a food for people,[11] and it is therefore fitting to prepare it in a way that a man can benefit and be nourished by it—all this for the root reason we "planted" [set down] at the beginning in regard to offerings (§95), by way of the plain meaning: that in consequence of an act, a man's thought will be stirred about things; and therefore, as the offering is the more ·distinguished, and the better is its preparation, the more moved will a man's heart be about it.

Among the laws of the precept, there is what the Sages said:[12] that if they found no new produce, they might bring it even from the attic; and if wheat came down through thick clouds,[13] it should not be brought initially, because there is a doubt about it, whether the phrase *from your dwellings* (Leviticus 23:17) applies to it; but if it was brought, it is acceptable.[14] The kneading of the two loaves and their shaping took place outside [the Sanctuary forecourt], and their baking within, as with all *minhah* offerings;[15] and their baking did not thrust aside [the law of] the festival,[16] for it is stated, [*that only may be done*] *for you*[17] (Exodus 12:16), but not for Heaven. The waving of the bread with the lambs for *sh'lamim* (peace-offerings) would be done while they were yet alive.[18] The *kohen gadol* would take one of the loaves, while the second was divided up among all the watches.[19] The rest

פְּרָטֶיהָ, מְתֹבָּאֲרִים בְּמְנָחוֹת פֶּרֶק ד' ה' ח' י"א.
וְנוֹהֶגֶת מִצְוָה זוֹ בִּזְכָרִים וְכוּלֵי, כְּמוֹ שֶׁכָּתַבְנוּ בְּמִצְוַת הָעוֹמֶר, י' [סִי' ש"ב].

[מִצְוַת שְׁבִיתָה מִמְּלָאכָה בְּיוֹם עֲצֶרֶת]

שח לִשְׁבֹּת מִכָּל מְלָאכָה, זוּלָתִי מַה שֶּׁמְּיֻחָד לְצֹרֶךְ אֹכֶל נֶפֶשׁ, בְּיוֹם שִׁשָּׁה בְּסִיוָן, שֶׁזֶּהוּ הַנִּקְרָא חַג הַשָּׁבוּעוֹת — שֶׁנֶּאֱמַר: וּקְרָאתֶם בְּעֶצֶם הַיּוֹם הַזֶּה מִקְרָא קֹדֶשׁ; וּכְבָר כָּתַבְתִּי בְּמִצְוַת עֲשֵׂה ז' שֶׁבַּסֵּדֶר הַזֶּה [סִי' רצ"ז] שֶׁבְּכָל מָקוֹם שֶׁנֶּאֱמַר בַּתּוֹרָה "מִקְרָא קֹדֶשׁ" עִנְיָנוֹ לוֹמַר: קַדְּשֵׁהוּ שֶׁלֹּא לַעֲשׂוֹת בּוֹ מְלָאכָה. וְגַם שָׁם כָּתוּב רֶמֶז מִשָּׁרְשֵׁי הַמִּצְוָה שֶׁמַּסְפִּיק עַל צַד הַפְּשָׁט בְּכָל הַיָּמִים־טוֹבִים, וּבְמִי נוֹהֶגֶת. וּקְצָת דִּינֶיהָ, נִכְתָּב בְּלָאו דְּאִסוּר מְלָאכָה דְּיוֹם־טוֹב שֶׁבַּסֵּדֶר הַזֶּה [סִי' רח"צ], בְּעֶזְרַת הַשֵּׁם.

[שֶׁלֹּא לַעֲשׂוֹת מְלָאכָה בְּיוֹם חַג הַשָּׁבוּעוֹת]

שט שֶׁלֹּא לַעֲשׂוֹת מְלָאכָה בְּיוֹם עֲצֶרֶת, שֶׁזֶּהוּ יוֹם שִׁשִּׁי בְּסִיוָן, שֶׁנֶּאֱמַר: וּסְפַרְתֶּם לָכֶם מִמָּחֳרַת הַשַּׁבָּת וְגוֹמֵר תִּסְפְּרוּ חֲמִשִּׁים יוֹם; וּפֵרוּשׁ "מִמָּחֳרַת הַשַּׁבָּת" כְּלוֹמַר מִמָּחֳרַת יוֹם־טוֹב רִאשׁוֹן שֶׁל פֶּסַח, שֶׁבּוֹ דְּבַר תְּחִלָּה; דְּאִי בְּשַׁבָּת בְּרֵאשִׁית, אִם־כֵּן לֹא יוֹדִיעֵנוּ אֵי זֶהוּ. וְנִמְצָא שֶׁחֲמִשִּׁים יוֹם כָּלִים בְּשִׁשָּׁה בְּסִיוָן; כֵּיצַד: ט"ו יָמִים מִנִּיסָן, שֶׁהוּא מָלֵא לְעוֹלָם, וְכ"ט מֵאִיָּר, שֶׁהוּא חָסֵר לְעוֹלָם, וְשִׁשָּׁה מִסִּיוָן, הֲרֵי חֲמִשִּׁים. וּבְיוֹם הַחֲמִשִּׁים זֶה, שֶׁהָיָה יוֹם שֶׁנִּתְּנָה בּוֹ תּוֹרָה, הוּא חַג הָעֲצֶרֶת, וְנִקְרָא גַם־כֵּן חַג הַשָּׁבוּעוֹת. וְכָתוּב בְּסוֹף הַפָּרָשָׁה עַל זֶה הַיּוֹם הַנִּכְבָּד: כָּל מְלֶאכֶת עֲבֹדָה לֹא תַעֲשׂוּ. כְּבָר כָּתַבְנוּ כִּי מְלֶאכֶת עֲבֹדָה נִקְרֵאת כָּל מְלָאכָה שֶׁאֵינָהּ צֹרֶךְ אֹכֶל נֶפֶשׁ.

שֹׁרֶשׁ מִצְוַת הַמּוֹעֵד הַזֶּה רָמוּז בְּמִצְוַת סְפִירַת הָעוֹמֶר שֶׁבְּסֵדֶר זֶה, [מִצְוַת

---

17. I.e. the preparation of food.
18. TB M'naḥoth 61a.
19. I.e. among the twenty-four family groups into which the *kohanim* were divided, each of which served a week at the Sanctuary; TB Yoma 17b.

§308   1. While here §298 appears earlier, in the original work all negative precepts come after the positive precepts in each *sidrah*.

§309   1. See §302, note 12.
2. And so we could not know when to celebrate *Shavu'oth*.
3. A lunar month can have either twenty-nine or thirty-days. One with twenty-nine days is called "lacking" or "defective"; one with thirty is called "full." Nissan invariably has thirty days; as the counting begins after the first day of Passover, which is the fifteenth of Nissan, fifteen days remain to be counted in Nissan. Iyar, which follows,

〈318〉

of its details are explained in the Talmud tractate *M'naḥoth*, chapters 4, 5, 8 and 11.

This precept applies to the men, etc. as I wrote of the *mitzvah* of *'omer*, in the tenth positive precept (§ 302).

308 [THE PRECEPT OF RESTING FROM WORK ON SHAVU'OTH] to rest from all work except what is specifically for [making] sustaining food, on the sixth day of Sivan, which is called the festival of *Shavu'oth*: for it is stated, *And you shall proclaim on this selfsame day a holy convocation* (Leviticus 23:21); and I have written previously, in the seventh positive precept in this *sidrah* (§ 297), that wherever "a holy convocation" is stated in the Torah, its purport is to convey, "Sanctify it," by doing no work in it. There I also wrote a hint of the root reason for the precept that suffices, by way of the plain meaning, for all the festivals, and to whom it applies. And some of its laws I will write in the negative precept about the ban on work on a festival, in this *sidrah*, with the Eternal Lord's help (§ 298).[1]

309 [THE PROHIBITION AGAINST DOING WORK ON THE SHAVU'OTH FESTIVAL] not to do work on the day of *Shavu'oth*, which is the sixth day in Sivan: for it is stated, *And you shall count for yourselves from the morrow after the sabbath . . . you shall count fifty days* (Leviticus 23:15–16); and the meaning of "the morrow after the sabbath" is as though it said, "the morrow after the first festival day of Passover," of which Scripture spoke originally [earlier]; for if it meant a Sabbath as of Creation,[1] it thus does not inform us which one.[2] Now, we find that fifty days thus end on the sixth of Sivan. How so?—fifteen days in Nissan, which is always a full month; twenty-nine in Iyar, which is always defective;[3] and six of Sivan—thus fifty. On this fiftieth day, which is the day on which the Torah was given, we have the festival of the Assembly,[4] that is also called the festival of *Shavu'oth*.[5] And it is written at the end of the section on this eminent day, *no laborious work shall you do* (Leviticus 23:21). We have written previously (§ 298) that the term "servile work" applies to any work that is not necessary for [preparing] human food.

The root reason for the precept of this holy time is intimated in the *mitzvah* of the counting of the *'omer*, the eleventh positive precept

עֲשֵׂה] י״א [סִי׳ שׁ״ו], וְקָחֵנּוּ מִשָּׁם. וְדִינֶיהָ, כָּתַבְתִּי קְצָתָם כְּמִנְהָגִי, בִּשְׁבִיתַת מְלָאכָה בְּיוֹם רִאשׁוֹן שֶׁל פֶּסַח, (עֲשֵׂה כ״ב) [לֹא-תַעֲשֶׂה כ״ט] בְּסֵדֶר זֶה [סִי׳ רח״ץ] וְאֵין צֹרֶךְ לְהַאֲרִיךְ בִּשְׁאָר יְמֵי מוֹעֲדֵי הַשָּׁנָה, כִּי שֵׁשֶׁת יְמֵי הַמּוֹעֲדִים הַיְּדוּעִים, וְהֵן: רִאשׁוֹן וּשְׁבִיעִי שֶׁל פֶּסַח וְרִאשׁוֹן וּשְׁמִינִי שֶׁל חַג וַעֲצֶרֶת וְרֹאשׁ הַשָּׁנָה, דִּין אֶחָד לְכֻלָּן לְכָל הֶתֵּרָן וּלְכָל אִסּוּרָן. וּבֵאוּר כָּל דִּינֵיהֶם בָּאֲרָכָה בַּמַּסֶּכְתָּא הַבְּנוּיָה עַל זֶה, וְהִיא מַסֶּכֶת בֵּיצָה.

[מִצְוַת שְׁבִיתָה בְּיוֹם רֹאשׁ הַשָּׁנָה]

ש״י לִשְׁבּוֹת מִכָּל מְלָאכָה, חוּץ מִמַּה שֶּׁמְּיֻחָד לְצֹרֶךְ אֹכֶל נֶפֶשׁ, בְּיוֹם רִאשׁוֹן שֶׁל חֹדֶשׁ תִּשְׁרֵי, שֶׁנֶּאֱמַר: בַּחֹדֶשׁ הַשְּׁבִיעִי בְּאֶחָד לַחֹדֶשׁ יִהְיֶה לָכֶם שַׁבָּתוֹן; וְחֹדֶשׁ הַשְּׁבִיעִי הוּא חֹדֶשׁ תִּשְׁרֵי, לְפִי שֶׁנִּיסָן רֹאשׁ הַשָּׁנָה לֶחֳדָשִׁים וְרִאשׁוֹן יִקָּרֵא בַכָּתוּב. וּכְתַבְתִּי בְּמִצְוַת עֲשֵׂה שְׁבִיעִי [סִי׳ רצ״ז] מַה שֶּׁאָמְרוּ זִכְרוֹנָם לִבְרָכָה, הַאי ״שַׁבָּתוֹן״ עֲשֵׂה הוּא; וְכָל שְׁאָר עִנְיַן הַמִּצְוָה, כְּמוֹ שֶׁכָּתוּב שָׁם.

[שֶׁלֹּא לַעֲשׂוֹת מְלָאכָה בְּיוֹם רִאשׁוֹן שֶׁל תִּשְׁרֵי]

שׁי״א שֶׁלֹּא לַעֲשׂוֹת מְלָאכָה בְּיוֹם רִאשׁוֹן שֶׁל חֹדֶשׁ תִּשְׁרֵי, שֶׁנֶּאֱמַר: בַּחֹדֶשׁ הַשְּׁבִיעִי בְּאֶחָד לַחֹדֶשׁ... כָּל מְלֶאכֶת עֲבֹדָה לֹא תַעֲשׂוּ, וְחֹדֶשׁ הַשְּׁבִיעִי יִקָּרֵא תִשְׁרֵי, כִּי הוּא שְׁבִיעִי לְנִיסָן, שֶׁהוּא רֹאשׁ הַשָּׁנָה לֶחֳדָשִׁים: וְזֶה הַיּוֹם שֶׁל אֶחָד בְּתִשְׁרֵי, אָמְרוּ זִכְרוֹנָם לִבְרָכָה שֶׁנִּקְרָא רֹאשׁ הַשָּׁנָה לִמְנוֹת מִמֶּנּוּ שָׁנִים וּשְׁמִטִּין וְיוֹבְלוֹת, וְכֵן מוֹנִין מִמֶּנּוּ לִנְטִיעָה וְלִירָקוֹת. וּבַגְּמָרָא דְמַסֶּכֶת רֹאשׁ הַשָּׁנָה בֵּאֲרוּ זִכְרוֹנָם לִבְרָכָה שֶׁהוּא רֹאשׁ הַשָּׁנָה לְעִנְיָנִים אֵלֶּה, לְמַאי הִלְכְתָא.

---

is invariably a "defective" month, with twenty-nine days. Then comes Sivan.

4. It is thus called in the Talmud, etc.

5. I.e. "weeks," since it comes at the end of the counted seven weeks.

6. In counting all these as six days, our author reckons each as one, according to Torah law, not reckoning the second days ordained by the Sages. He thus also counts *Rosh haShanah* as one, as it is mentioned in the Torah (Leviticus 23:24), although in TJ 'Eruvin iii end, it is stated that the early prophets instituted the practice of observing it for two days.

§310   1. So TB Rosh haShanah 2a.

2. Exodus 12:2.

§311   1. See §310.

2. TB Rosh haShanah 2a.

3. The calendar year, reckoned since Creation, the seventh (sabbatical) year, and the jubilee (every fiftieth year) begin on the first of Tishri.

4. A tree planted forty-five days before the first of Tishri is considered after that in

in this *sidrah* (§ 306); so gather it from there. As to its laws, I wrote some of them, as my custom is, about resting from work on the first day of Passover, the twenty-ninth negative precept in this *sidrah* (§ 298); and there is no need to write at length about the other holy times of the year. For the six known days of the holy seasons, which are the first and seventh of Passover, the first and eighth of *Sukkoth*, *Shavu'oth*, and *Rosh haShanah*[6]—have all one law, for all that is permitted and all that is forbidden on them. The elucidation of all their laws at length is in the Talmud tractate built about this, which is the tractate *Bétzah*.

[THE PRECEPT OF RESTING FROM WORK ON ROSH HA-SHANAH]

310 to rest from all work, except what is specifically for the necessity of [preparing] human food, on the first day of the month of Tishri: as it is stated, *In the seventh month, on the first day of the month, it shall be for you* shabbathon, *a solemn rest* (Leviticus 23:24); and the seventh month is the month of Tishri, because Nissan is the start of the year for [the numbering of] the months,[1] being called the first in Scripture.[2] Now, I wrote in the seventh positive precept (§ 297) what the Sages of blessed memory said: This term *shabbathon* ("solemn rest") denotes a positive precept. All the rest of the subject-matter of the precept is as I have written there.

[THE PROHIBITION OF DOING WORK ON ROSH HA-SHANAH]

311 not to do work on the first day of the month of Tishri: for it is stated, *In the seventh month, on the first day of the month . . . You shall do no laborious work* (Leviticus 23:24–25); and the seventh month is called Tishri, that being the seventh starting with Nissan, which is the beginning of the year for [the count of] the months.[1] Now, regarding this first day of Tishri, our Sages of blessed memory said[2] it is called *Rosh haShanah*, the beginning of the year, to reckon from it the years, the seventh-years of *sh'mittah* (§ 84), and the jubilee years;[3] and we likewise reckon from it in regard to tree-planting[4] and [the tithe of] vegetables.[5] In the Talmud tractate *Rosh haShanah* they (of blessed memory) explained what practical difference it makes [in law] that they said it is the start of the year in regard to these matters.[6]

וְעוֹד אָמְרוּ שָׁם שֶׁבְּיוֹם זֶה נִדּוֹנִין כָּל בְּנֵי־הָעוֹלָם, וְאָמְרוּ עַל
דֶּרֶךְ הַמְּלִיצָה, לְבָאֵר שֶׁהַשְׁגָּחָתוֹ בָּרוּךְ הוּא עַל מַעֲשֵׂה כָל אֶחָד וְאֶחָד וְלֹא עַל כָּל
הַמִּין דֶּרֶךְ כְּלָל, שֶׁעוֹבְרִין כָּל בְּנֵי־אָדָם לְפָנָיו כִּבְנֵי מָרוֹן, כְּלוֹמַר אֶחָד וְאֶחָד וְלֹא
בְעִרְבּוּב.

וּמִשָּׁרְשֵׁי מִצְוַת הַמּוֹעֵד הַזֶּה, שֶׁהָיָה מֵחַסְדֵי הָאֵל עַל בְּרוּאָיו לִפְקֹד אוֹתָם
וְלִרְאוֹת מַעֲשֵׂיהֶם יוֹם אֶחָד בְּכָל שָׁנָה וְשָׁנָה, כְּדֵי שֶׁלֹּא יִתְרַבּוּ הָעֲווֹנוֹת וְיִהְיֶה
מָקוֹם לְכַפָּרָה, וְהוּא רַב חֶסֶד מַטֶּה כְּלַפֵּי חֶסֶד, וְכֵיוָן שֶׁהֵם מוּעָטִין מַעֲבִיר עֲלֵיהֶן;
וְאִם אוּלַי יֵשׁ בָּהֶם עֲווֹנוֹת שֶׁצְּרִיכִין מֵרוּק, נִפְרָע מֵהֶם מְעַט מְעַט, וּכְעִין מַה
שֶּׁאָמְרוּ זִכְרוֹנָם לִבְרָכָה: אוֹהֲבוֹ, נִפְרָע מִמֶּנּוּ מְעַט מְעַט; וְאִם לֹא יִפְקְדֵם עַד זְמַן
רַב, יִתְרַבּוּ כָּל־כָּךְ עַד שֶׁיִּתְחַיֵּב הָעוֹלָם כִּמְעַט כְּלָיָה חָלִילָה.

נִמְצָא שֶׁהַיּוֹם הַנִּכְבָּד הַזֶּה הוּא קִיּוּמוֹ שֶׁל עוֹלָם, וְלָכֵן רָאוּי לַעֲשׂוֹת אוֹתוֹ יוֹם־
טוֹב וְלִהְיוֹתוֹ בְּמִנְיַן מוֹעֲדֵי הַשָּׁנָה הַיְּקָרִים. וְאוּלָם, מִהְיוֹתוֹ יוֹם מוֹעֵד לָדוּן כָּל חַי,
רָאוּי לַעֲמֹד בּוֹ בְּיִרְאָה וָפַחַד יוֹתֵר מִכָּל שְׁאָר מוֹעֲדֵי הַשָּׁנָה; וְזֶהוּ עִנְיַן זִכְרוֹן
תְּרוּעָה הַנִּזְכָּרִים בּוֹ, כִּי הַתְּרוּעָה קוֹל שָׁבוּר, לִרְמֹז שֶׁיִּשְׁבֹּר כָּל אֶחָד תֹּקֶף יִצְרוֹ
וְיִתְנַחֵם עַל מַעֲשָׂיו הָרָעִים, וּכְמוֹ שֶׁנִּכְתֹּב בְּמִצְוַת שׁוֹפָר בָּאֲרָכָה בְּסֵדֶר פִּינְחָס
[סִי׳ ת״ה] בְּעֶזְרַת הַשֵּׁם.

וְזֶהוּ הַטַּעַם שֶׁלֹּא קָבְעוּ זִכְרוֹנָם לִבְרָכָה לוֹמַר הַלֵּל בַּמּוֹעֵד הַזֶּה, וּכְמוֹ שֶׁאָמְרוּ,
שֶׁאֵין רָאוּי לוֹ לְאָדָם לוֹמַר שִׁירָה וְהוּא עוֹמֵד בַּדִּין; וְכִדְאָמַר רַבִּי אַבָּהוּ בְּפֶרֶק
אַחֲרוֹן דְּרֹאשׁ הַשָּׁנָה: אָמְרוּ מַלְאֲכֵי הַשָּׁרֵת לִפְנֵי הַקָּדוֹשׁ בָּרוּךְ הוּא: מִפְּנֵי־מָה
אֵין יִשְׂרָאֵל אוֹמְרִים הַלֵּל בְּרֹאשׁ הַשָּׁנָה וְיוֹם הַכִּפּוּרִים, וְכוּלֵי, כִּדְאִיתָא הָתָם.

its second year, in regard to precepts §§ 246 and 247.

5. Produce harvested in one year may not be given as tithe for produce harvested in
another; and the year for vegetables is reckoned from *Rosh haShanah*.

6. TB Rosh haShanah 8b, 9b, 12a, etc.

7. *Ibid.* 16a.

8. I.e. if a person's merits do not outweigh his sins; so *ibid.* 17a.

9. TB 'Avodah Zarah 4a.

Now, they taught there, furthermore,[7] that on this day all human beings in the world are judged for their deeds; and they said further by way of imagery—to make it clear that His providential regard (blessed is He) extends over the activity of every single individual, and not over the species in a general way—that all human beings pass before Him like sheep in single file: in other words, one by one, and not mingled together.

Well, at the root of the precept of this holy season lies the theme that it is of God's kindnesses toward His human beings to recall them and regard their deeds one day in every single year, so that the iniquities should not become a great many, and there should be room for atonement. *Abundant in kindness* (Exodus 32:6), He tips [the scales of justice] toward loving-kindness,[8] and since they [the sins] are few, He pardons and clears them away. And if there are wrong deeds among them, perhaps, that require cleansing, He exacts payment for them bit by bit, in keeping with what the Sages of blessed memory said:[9] From his friend, a man collects [his debt] bit by bit. But if He would not call them to account until a long time, then they [the sins] would become so very many, until the world would almost incur destruction, Heaven forbid.

Consequently, this distinguished day is [ensures] the endurance of the world. It is therefore fitting to make it a festival day, that it should be in the list of the precious holy times of the year. However, since it is the ordained time for everyone alive to be judged, it is proper to behave then with reverent fear and awe, more than on all other holy times of the year. This is the reason for the theme of the "memorial of the *shofar*-sound" (Leviticus 23:24) mentioned with it: for the *t'ru'ah* (*shofar*-sound) is a broken call, to intimate that everyone should break the force of his [evil] inclination and have remorse for his bad deeds, as we will write at length in the precept of the *shofar* (§405), in *sidrah pinḥas*, with the help of the Eternal Lord.

This is the reason, too, why the Sages of blessed memory did not institute that *hallél* (the psalms of praise; Psalms 113–118) should be recited at this holy time; for as they put it, it is not right for a man to utter praise-song while he is standing in judgment. As R. Abbahu taught in the last chapter of the tractate *Rosh haShanah* (32b): Said the ministering angels before the Holy One, blessed is He, "For what reason do the Jewish people not recite *hallél* on *Rosh haShanah* and the

Day of Atonement?" He replied, "Can a King possibly sit on the throne

מִדִּינֵי שְׁבִיתָה בְּיוֹם־טוֹב, כָּתַבְתִּי קְצָתָם כְּמִנְהֲגֵי בְּמִצְוַת מוֹעֵד הַפֶּסַח, (כ״ב)
[לֹא־תַעֲשֶׂה כ״ט — סִי׳ רח״ץ]; וְעוֹד רָאוּי לִכְתּוֹב כָּאן מְעַט מִן הָעִנְיָנִים
הַנִּזְכָּרִים בְּמַסֶּכֶת רֹאשׁ הַשָּׁנָה, שֶׁאָמְרוּ שָׁם שֶׁאַרְבָּעָה רָאשֵׁי שָׁנִים הֵן: בְּאֶחָד
בְּנִיסָן רֹאשׁ הַשָּׁנָה לַמְּלָכִים וְלָרְגָלִים; פֵּרוּשׁ רְגָלִים, כְּלוֹמַר רֶגֶל שֶׁבּוֹ תְחִלָּה
לָרְגָלִים, כֵּן פִּתְרוֹנוֹ בַּגְּמָרָא; בְּאֶחָד בֶּאֱלוּל רֹאשׁ הַשָּׁנָה לְמַעְשַׂר בְּהֵמָה; בְּאֶחָד
בְּתִשְׁרֵי רֹאשׁ הַשָּׁנָה לְמָה שֶׁכָּתַבְנוּ לְמַעְלָה; בְּאֶחָד בִּשְׁבָט רֹאשׁ הַשָּׁנָה לָאִילָן,
כְּדִבְרֵי בֵּית שַׁמַּאי, וּבֵית הִלֵּל אוֹמְרִין בַּחֲמִשָּׁה עָשָׂר בּוֹ. וְשָׁם מִתְבָּאֵר בַּגְּמָרָא
רָאשֵׁי שָׁנִים אֵלּוּ לְאֵי זֶה עִנְיָן.

וְשָׁם אָמְרוּ שֶׁאַרְבָּעָה דְבָרִים מְקָרְעִין גְּזַר דִּינוֹ שֶׁל אָדָם: צְדָקָה, צְעָקָה, שִׁנּוּי
הַשֵּׁם וְשִׁנּוּי מַעֲשֶׂה. וְעִנְיַן שִׁנּוּי הַשֵּׁם הוּא לְפִי הַדּוֹמֶה כְּדֵי שֶׁיַּחְשׁב הָאָדָם כְּאִלּוּ
הוּא אָדָם אַחֵר וְיַכְשִׁיר כָּל דְּרָכָיו, וּבְכָל עֵת שֶׁיִּקָּרֵא זֶה יִזְכּר זֶה וְיִתֵּן לִבּוֹ אֶל הָעִנְיָן.

וּמַה שֶּׁאָמְרוּ שָׁם: שְׁלשָׁה סְפָרִים נִפְתָּחִין בְּרֹאשׁ הַשָּׁנָה, אֶחָד שֶׁל צַדִּיקִים
גְּמוּרִים וְאֶחָד שֶׁל רְשָׁעִים גְּמוּרִים וְאֶחָד שֶׁל בֵּינוֹנִיִּים. וְעִנְיַן פְּתִיחַת הַסְּפָרִים
נֶאֱמַר לְפִי הַדּוֹמֶה עַל דֶּרֶךְ הַמָּשָׁל בְּעִנְיָן הַשְּׁגָּחָתוֹ בָּרוּךְ הוּא עֲלֵיהֶם, כְּדֵי שֶׁיִּכָּנְסוּ
הַדְּבָרִים בְּאָזְנֵי הַשּׁוֹמְעִים, יִדַּבְּרוּ רַבּוֹתֵינוּ לְעוֹלָם בִּמְרֻגָּל בִּבְנֵי אָדָם. צַדִּיקִים
גְּמוּרִים נִכְתָּבִין וְנֶחְתָּמִין לְאַלְתַּר לְחַיִּים; פֵּרַשׁ מוֹרִי: צַדִּיק גָּמוּר בְּכָאן שֶׁכֻּלּוֹ
זַכַּאי; וְכֵן רָשָׁע גָּמוּר בְּכָאן שֶׁכֻּלּוֹ חַיָּב, וּלְפִיכָךְ נֶחְתָּם מִיָּד לְמִיתָה, אַחַר שֶׁאֵין לוֹ
זְכוּת בָּעוֹלָם שֶׁיָּגֵן עָלָיו; בֵּינוֹנִיִּים תְּלוּיִין עַד יוֹם הַכִּפּוּרִים, וְאָז גָּמַר דִּין שֶׁלָּהֶם
נֶחְתָּם.

10. See note 5; the same rule holds here.
11. Similarly MT hilchoth t'shuvah ii 4.

of judgment, with the [account] books of the living and of the dead open before Him, and the Jewish people utter praise-song?"

As for the laws of rest from work on a festival day, I wrote some of them, as it is my custom, in the *mitzvah* of the holy season of Passover, the twenty-ninth negative precept (§ 298). In addition, it is fitting to write here a bit of the themes mentioned in the tractate *Rosh haShanah*. For our Sages said there (2a) that there are four beginnings of the year: on the first of Nissan it is the start of the year for kings and the pilgrimage festivals; the meaning of the latter is that the festival in it [in the month of Nissan] is the start of the pilgrimage festivals; so is it interpreted in the *g'mara* (4a). On the first of Elul it is the start of the year for the tithe of animals;[10] on the first of Tishri it is the start of the year in regard to what we wrote above; and on the first of Sh'vat it is the start of the year for trees, in the ruling of the School of Shammai; but the School of Hillel says it is the fifteenth of that month. And it is elucidated there in the *g'mara* (16b) for what [practical] matters these are [reckoned] the beginnings of the year.

There, too (16b), the Sages taught that four things tear up the decree of judgment against a man: charity, outcry, a change of name, and a change in one's actions. Now, the reason for the change of name, apparently, is in order that a man should consider it as though he is [now] a different person,[11] and he should make all his ways worthy; every time he is called [by name] he will remember this and set his heart to [reflect on] the matter.

Then there is what the Sages taught there (16b): Three [account] books are opened on *Rosh haShanah*: one of the totally righteous, one of the utterly wicked, and one of the middle-range people [between the two extremes]. Now, this theme of the opening of the books was said, as it would seem, by way of metaphor, in reference to His providential watch over them [people]. In order that the words should enter the ears of the listeners, our Sages would always speak in terms familiar to human beings. [The Sages continued:] The totally righteous are written and sealed at once for life. My instructor explained: A totally righteous person here means one who is entirely virtuous, innocent; and similarly, an utterly wicked person here means one who is entirely guilt-laden, and he is therefore [signed and] sealed at once to death, since he has not a virtue in the world that should shield him. The people in the middle range remain suspended until the Day of Atonement, and then the verdict of their judgment is sealed.

וּמַה שֶּׁאָמְרוּ שָׁם בְּסָמוּךְ לָזֶה: בֵּית שַׁמַּאי אוֹמְרִים: שָׁלֹשׁ כִּתּוֹת לְיוֹם הַדִּין,
כְּלוֹמַר אַחַר הַמָּוֶת שֶׁל כָּל אֶחָד וְאֶחָד מִבְּנֵי־אָדָם, שֶׁזֶּה קָרוּי יוֹם הַדִּין; כַּת אֶחָד
שֶׁל צַדִּיקִים גְּמוּרִים וְכַת שֶׁל רְשָׁעִים וְכַת שֶׁל בֵּינוֹנִיִּים. בְּכָאן פֵּרְשׁוּ: צַדִּיק גָּמוּר
וְרָשָׁע גָּמוּר בְּדִינָם; וּבְזֶה הַפֵּרוּשׁ תִּסְתַּלֵּק קוּשְׁיָא גְדוֹלָה מִן הָעִנְיָן; אִם תֹּזְכֶּה,
בְּנִי, תַּרְגִּישׁ בָּהּ וְיָנִיחַ לְךָ עֲמָלִי זֶה.

וּמַה שֶּׁאָמְרוּ שָׁם שֶׁהַצַּדִּיק גָּמוּר בְּדִינוֹ נֶחְתָּם לְאַלְתַּר לְחַיֵּי הָעוֹלָם הַבָּא, אַל
תַּחְשֹׁב שֶׁחַיֵּי הָעוֹלָם הַבָּא דָּבָר הַשָּׁוֶה לְכָל צַדִּיק, כִּי יֵשׁ בְּאוֹתָן הַחַיִּים מַעֲלוֹת עַד
אֵין מִסְפָּר, וְכָל צַדִּיק וְצַדִּיק עוֹלֶה בָּהֶם עַד מָקוֹם הָרָאוּי לוֹ לְפִי שְׂכָרוֹ. וְיֶתֶר
פְּרָטֵי עִנְיָנִים אֵלֶּה, שָׁם בְּרֹאשׁ הַשָּׁנָה פֶּרֶק רִאשׁוֹן.

וְנוֹהֵג אִסּוּר מְלָאכָה בְּיוֹם זֶה בְּכָל מָקוֹם וּבְכָל זְמַן, בַּזְּכָרִים וּנְקֵבוֹת. וְעוֹבֵר
עָלֶיהָ וְעָשָׂה מְלָאכָה שֶׁלֹּא לְצֹרֶךְ אֹכֶל נֶפֶשׁ, חַיָּב מַלְקוּת, כְּמוֹ שֶׁכָּתַבְנוּ בִּשְׁאָר
יְמֵי הַמּוֹעֲדִים.

[מִצְוַת קָרְבַּן מוּסָף בְּיוֹם רֹאשׁ הַשָּׁנָה]

שׁי״ב לְהַקְרִיב קָרְבַּן מוּסָף בְּיוֹם רֹאשׁ הַשָּׁנָה, שֶׁנֶּאֱמַר: וּבַחֹדֶשׁ הַשְּׁבִיעִי
בְּאֶחָד לַחֹדֶשׁ וְגוֹמֵר וַעֲשִׂיתֶם עֹלָה לְרֵיחַ נִיחֹחַ וְגוֹמֵר; וּבְסֵדֶר פִּינְחָס מַזְכִּיר
הַקָּרְבָּן בְּאָרְכָּהּ. וְכָל עִנְיָנֶיהָ כְּמוֹ שֶׁכָּתַבְתִּי בְּמוּסַף הַפֶּסַח בְּמִצְוַת עֲשֵׂה ח׳ בְּסֵדֶר
זֶה [סִי׳ רצ״ט].

[מִצְוַת תַּעֲנִית בְּיוֹם עֲשִׂירִי בְּתִשְׁרֵי]

שׁי״ג לָצוּם בְּיוֹם הָעֲשִׂירִי בְּתִשְׁרֵי, וְהוּא הַנִּקְרָא יוֹם הַכִּפּוּרִים, שֶׁנֶּאֱמַר:
וּבֶעָשׂוֹר לַחֹדֶשׁ...וְעִנִּיתֶם אֶת נַפְשֹׁתֵיכֶם, וּבָא הַפֵּרוּשׁ בְּסִפְרָא: עִנּוּי שֶׁהוּא

12. So Rashba (R. Sh'lomoh ibn 'Adreth), Responsa, I §480.

13. Very likely our author has in mind a question asked by a student of Rashba,
Responsa, I § 480: On this teaching by the School of Shammai, the School of Hillel re-
joins that for the middle-range people, the Almighty tips the scales of justice in favor of
their virtue (TB Rosh haShanah 17a). Why, asked the student, did the School of Hillel
not say this about the middle-range people in the earlier teaching, concerning the three
books opened on *Rosh haShanah*? With this distinction that our author makes, it
becomes understandable: On *Rosh haShanah* a man is judged regarding life on this earth;
then he can repent till the Day of Atonement and win a favorable verdict by his own
efforts. On the final judgment day after death, repentance is no longer possible, and this
kindness of the Almighty is vital. (There is good reason to assume that Rashba was our
author's master teacher. Hence he would very likely have known of this responsum.
There is even a remote possibility that he was the very student who originally asked the
question.)

14. So TB Shabbath 152a.

We have, further, what the Sages taught directly afterward: The School of Shammai says: There are three groups for the day of judgment—in other words, after the death of every single human being, [12] for this is called the day of judgment: the group of the totally righteous, the group of the wicked, and the group of the "middle" people. But here it was explained [that the reference is to people who emerge] entirely righteous or entirely wicked in their [final] judgment. By this explanation a great difficulty is removed from the matter. [13] If you will merit, my son, you will perceive this, and this my labor [here] will set your mind at rest.

Moreover, there is what the Sages taught there (16b), that one who is [found] utterly righteous in his judgment is [signed and] sealed at once for life in the world-to-come. Now, do not think that life in the world-to-come is something equal and the same for every righteous person. For in that life there are levels beyond number, and every single righteous man rises among them to the place that is suited for him according to his reward. [14] The remaining details of these themes are there, in the first chapter of the tractate *Rosh haShanah*.

The prohibition against work on this day is in force everywhere, at every time, for both man and woman. If someone violates it and does work that is not for the necessity of [preparing] human food, he deserves whiplashes, as we wrote about the other days of the holy seasons.

[THE PRECEPT OF THE MUSAF OFFERING ON ROSH HA-SHANAH]

312 to sacrifice the *musaf* (additional) offering on the day of *Rosh haShanah*, as it is stated, *In the seventh month, on the first day of the month . . . and you shall bring an offering of fire to the Lord* (Leviticus 23:24–25); and in *sidrah pinḥas* the offering is described at length (Numbers 29:2–5). All its subject-matter is as I have written about the *musaf* of Passover, in the eighth positive precept in this *sidrah* (§299).

[THE PRECEPT OF FASTING ON THE TENTH OF TISHRI]

313 to fast on the tenth day in Tishri, which is called the Day of Atonement: for it is stated, *And on the tenth day of this seventh month . . . you shall afflict your souls* (Leviticus 23:27); and the explanation was

אֲבוּד נֶפֶשׁ, וְאֵי זֶהוּ, זֶה אֲכִילָה וּשְׁתִיָּה; וּכְמוֹ־כֵן פֵּרְשׁוּהוּ זִכְרוֹנָם לִבְרָכָה
בַּגְּמָרָא. וְעוֹד בָּאָה הַקַּבָּלָה עָלָיו שֶׁהוּא אָסוּר בִּרְחִיצָה וּבְסִיכָה, בִּנְעִילַת הַסַּנְדָּל
וּבְתַשְׁמִישׁ הַמִּטָּה. וּלְשׁוֹן סִפְרָא: מִנַּיִן שֶׁיּוֹם הַכִּפּוּרִים אָסוּר בִּרְחִיצָה וּבְסִיכָה
וּבְתַשְׁמִישׁ הַמִּטָּה [וּבִנְעִילַת הַסַּנְדָּל], תַּלְמוּד לוֹמַר "שַׁבַּת שַׁבָּתוֹן", כְּלוֹמַר כִּי
כְּפֵל הַשְּׁבִיתָה יוֹרֶה עַל שְׁבִיתָה מֵהָעֲסָקִים אֵלֶּה וּשְׁבִיתָה מִמְּזוֹן הַגּוּף.

מִשָּׁרְשֵׁי הַמִּצְוָה, שֶׁהָיָה מֵחַסְדֵּי הַשֵּׁם עַל כָּל בְּרִיּוֹתָיו לִקְבֹּעַ לָהֶם יוֹם אֶחָד
בַּשָּׁנָה לְכַפֵּר עַל הַחֲטָאִים עִם הַתְּשׁוּבָה, וּכְמוֹ שֶׁכָּתַבְתִּי בַּאֲרֻכָּה בְּסֵדֶר אַחֲרֵי־מוֹת
מִצְוַת עֲשֵׂה א' [סִי' קפ"ה], וְלָכֵן נִצְטַוִּינוּ לְהִתְעַנּוֹת בּוֹ, לְפִי שֶׁהַמַּאֲכָל וְהַמִּשְׁתֶּה
וְיֶתֶר הֲנָאוֹת חוּשׁ הַמִּשּׁוּשׁ יְעוֹרְרוּ הַחֹמֶר לְהִמָּשֵׁךְ אַחַר הַתַּאֲוָה וְהַחֵטְא, וְיִבָּטְלוּ
צוּרַת הַנֶּפֶשׁ הַחֲכָמָה מֵחַפֵּשׂ אַחַר שֶׁהוּא אֱמֶת שֶׁהוּא עֲבוֹדַת הָאֵל וּמוּסָרוֹ הַטּוֹב
וְהַמָּתוֹק לְכָל בְּנֵי הַדַּעַת; וְאֵין רָאוּי לְעֶבֶד בְּיוֹם בּוֹאוֹ לְדִין לִפְנֵי אֲדֹנָיו לָבוֹא
בְּנֶפֶשׁ חֲשׁוּכָה וּמְעֻרְבֶּבֶת, מִתּוֹךְ הַמַּאֲכָל וְהַמִּשְׁתֶּה, בְּמַחְשְׁבוֹת הַחֹמֶר אֲשֶׁר הִיא
בְּתוֹכוֹ, שֶׁאֵין דָּנִין אֶת הָאָדָם אֶלָּא לְפִי מַעֲשָׂיו שֶׁבָּאוֹתָהּ שָׁעָה, עַל־כֵּן טוֹב לוֹ
לְהַגְבִּיר נַפְשׁוֹ הַחֲכָמָה וּלְהַכְנִיעַ הַחֹמֶר לְפָנֶיהָ בְּאוֹתוֹ הַיּוֹם הַנִּכְבָּד, לְמַעַן תִּהְיֶה
רְאוּיָה וּנְכוֹנָה לְקַבֵּל כַּפָּרָתָהּ, וְלֹא יִמְנָעֶנָּה מָסַךְ הַתַּאֲווֹת.

מִדִּינֵי הַמִּצְוָה, מַה שֶׁאָמְרוּ זִכְרוֹנָם לִבְרָכָה שֶׁהַשִּׁעוּר הָאֲכִילָה בְּיוֹם הַכִּפּוּרִים
לְחַיֵּב עָלֶיהָ דְּאוֹרַיְתָא מֵאוֹכְלִין הָרְאוּיִין, הוּא כַּכּוֹתֶבֶת הַגַּסָּה; וְהַטַּעַם שֶׁנִּשְׁתַּנָּה
שִׁעוּר הָאֲכִילָה דְיוֹם הַכִּפּוּרִים מִשִּׁעוּר שְׁאָר אֲכִילַת אִסּוּרִין שֶׁבַּתּוֹרָה, שֶׁהֵן
בִּכְזַיִת, מִפְּנֵי שֶׁהַתּוֹרָה אָסְרָה הָאֲכִילָה בְּאוֹתוֹ הַיּוֹם בִּלְשׁוֹן עִנּוּי, וְלֹא נֶאֱמַר עָלֶיהָ
"לֹא תֹאכְלוּ" כְּמוֹ בִּשְׁאָר אִסּוּרִין; וּפֵרְשׁוּ חֲכָמִים שֶׁקִּבְּלוּ הַדְּבָרִים מֵאֲשֶׁר קָדְמוּ

§313   1. Sifra, aḥaré moth, perek 7, 3, on the phrase in Leviticus 16:29, תענו את נפשתיכם.
ShM positive precept §164 cites this phrase as the Scriptural source of the precept,
whereas the four oldest manuscripts cite here (above) ובעשור לחודש וכו' תענו את נפשתיכם—a
composite of Numbers 29:7 and Leviticus 16:29. In the first edition תענו was changed to
ועניתם, giving us the source-text as cited here; but this is actually Numbers 29:7. From the
fourth edition onward, ובעשור was altered to אך בעשור, as we have it in Leviticus 23:27.
This is quite certainly what our author meant to cite, since he follows here the order of
the verses in Leviticus 23; and the reading in the manuscripts must be considered an
oversight. Consequently, our text should be emended accordingly, and the translation
should read, *But on the tenth day*, etc.
  2. TB Yoma 74b.
  3. *Ibid.* 74a.
  4. Sifra, aḥaré moth, perek 8, 3; 'emor, perek 14, 4.
  5. So TB Rosh haShanah 16b.
  6. TB Yoma 80a–b.

given in the Midrash *Sifra*:[1] [it means] an affliction which brings a diminution of the life-force; what is that?—[abstention from] eating and drinking. Our Sages likewise explained it so in the Talmud.[2] Then the Oral Tradition taught further about it[3] that washing, covering the skin with oil, wearing sandals (shoes), and conjugal intimacy are [equally] forbidden. In the language of the Midrash *Sifra*:[4] How do we know that on the Day of Atonement, washing, applying oil to oneself, conjugal intimacy [and wearing sandals] are forbidden? —Scripture states, *It shall be to you* shabbath shabbathon, *a day of rest in solemn rest* (*ibid*. 32). In other words, the doubling of the term for rest denotes both resting (abstaining) from these actions and abstaining from the nourishment of the body.

At the root of the precept lies the point that it was of the kindness of the Eternal Lord toward all His human beings to set one day in the year for them to atone for sins with repentance, as I wrote at length in the first positive precept of *sidrah aḥaré moth* (§185)., Therefore we were commanded to fast on it—because food and drink, and the other pleasures of the sense of touch, arouse the physical self to be drawn after desire and sin; and they can interrupt the form of the spirit of wisdom from seeking after the truth, which is the service of God and His good and sweet moral lessons, for all sensible people. It is not fitting for a servant, on the day he comes for judgment before his master, that he should come with a spirit darkened and confused, on account of food and drink, by thoughts of the material self in which it is lodged. For a man is judged only according to his actions at that time.[5] It is therefore good for him to have his spirit of wisdom prevail and to subdue the material self before it on that estimable day, that it might be suited and prepared to receive its atonement, and the veil of desires should not prevent it.

Among the laws of the precept, there is what the Sages of blessed memory taught:[6] that the minimal amount of food on the Day of Atonement to impose punishment for it by the law of the Torah, out of proper, edible food, is as a bulky date. The reason why the minimal [punishable] quantity of food on the Day of Atonement was made different from that of other forbidden foods in the Torah, for which it is the amount of an olive, is that the Torah forbade eating that day with the expression of affliction, and it was not stated about it, "you shall not eat," as about other forbidden food. Well, our Sages, who received these matters from those who were before them, ex-

לָהֶם, שֶׁאֲכִילָה נִקְרֵאת בִּכְזַיִת, אֲבָל עִנּוּי הוּא בְּאָדָם כָּל זְמַן שֶׁלֹּא אָכַל עַד
כַּכּוֹתֶבֶת, שֶׁאֵין דַּעַת בֶּן־אָדָם מִתְיַשֵּׁב בְּפָחוֹת.

וְשִׁעוּר כּוֹתֶבֶת הוּא יוֹתֵר מִגְּרוֹגֶרֶת וּפָחוֹת מִכְּבֵיצָה, וּפָחוֹת מִשְּׁנֵי זֵיתִים גַּם־
כֵּן, שֶׁשְּׁנֵי זֵיתִים הֵן כְּבֵיצָה. כְּלָל הָעִנְיָן כָּבָר דִּקְדֵּק מִי שֶׁהוּא בָּקִי וְשָׁקַל בַּפֶּלֶס,
שֶׁאֵין בְּמִשְׁקָל י"ב אַרְגִּינֵץ וְעוֹד שִׁעוּר כַּכּוֹתֶבֶת, וְדִינוֹ כַּחֲצִי שִׁעוּר.

וְכֵן מַה שֶּׁאָמְרוּ שֶׁשִּׁעוּר הַשְּׁתִיָּה הִיא מְלֹא לְגֻמָּיו שֶׁל אָדָם, שֶׁהוּא כְּבֵיצָה,
שֶׁכְּבָר שִׁעֲרוּ כִּי בֵיצָה מַחֲזִיק מְלֹא לְגֻמָּיו שֶׁל אָדָם, וּבְפָחוֹת מִכָּאן אֵין בּוֹ אִסּוּר
כָּרֵת אֶלָּא דִינוֹ כַּחֲצִי שִׁעוּר.

וּלְפִיכָךְ מִי שֶׁהוּא חוֹלֶה, אַף־עַל־פִּי שֶׁאֵין בּוֹ סַכָּנָה גְמוּרָה, אִם יִהְיֶה חָלוּשׁ
הַרְבֵּה רָאוּי לְהַאֲכִילוֹ וּלְהַשְׁקוֹתוֹ מְעַט מְעַט כַּשִּׁעוּר שֶׁאָמַרְנוּ, וְנוֹתְנִין רֶוַח בֵּין
אֲכִילָה וּשְׁתִיָּה שֶׁל פַּעַם אַחַת לְפַעַם אַחֶרֶת כְּדֵי שִׁעוּר אֲכִילַת פְּרָס, שֶׁהֵן שָׁלֹשׁ
בֵּצִים כְּדַעַת רֹב הַמְּפָרְשִׁים, כְּדֵי שֶׁלֹּא יִצְטָרְפוּ הָאֲכִילוֹת וְתִהְיֶה נֶחְשֶׁבֶת כַּאֲכִילָה
אַחַת וְשִׁעוּר אֶחָד; אֲבָל בֵּין הָאֲכִילָה וְהַשְּׁתִיָּה אֵין צָרִיךְ לְהַפְסִיק, שֶׁאֵין
מִצְטָרְפִין אֲכִילָה וּשְׁתִיָּה לְעִנְיָן זֶה; וְשִׁעוּר שֶׁבֵּין שְׁתִיָּה לִשְׁתִיָּה, כְּדֵי שְׁתִיַּת
רְבִיעִית; וּמֻתָּר לִשְׁקֹל וּלְשַׁעֵר דְּבָרִים אֵלֶּה בְּיוֹם הַכִּפּוּרִים לְעֵת הַצֹּרֶךְ: מוּטָב
נָחוּשׁ וְנַרְחִיק שֶׁלֹּא לֶאֱכֹל שִׁעוּר וְלֹא נָחוּשׁ לְאִסּוֹר הַמִּשְׁקָל, שֶׁהוּא מִדְּרַבָּנָן.

וְכֵן מֵעִנְיַן הַמִּצְוָה מַה שֶּׁאָמְרוּ זִכְרוֹנָם לִבְרָכָה כִּי אֵלּוּ הָעִנּוּיִין שֶׁהֵן דְּרַבָּנָן,
כְּגוֹן רְחִיצָה וְסִיכָה, לֹא גָזְרוּ בָהֶן רַק שֶׁלֹּא לַעֲשׂוֹתָן שֶׁלֹּא לְצֹרֶךְ, אֲבָל כָּל שֶׁעוֹשֶׂה
אוֹתָן לְצֹרֶךְ לֹא גָזְרוּ: כְּגוֹן מִי שֶׁיֵּשׁ לוֹ חֲטָטִין בְּרֹאשׁוֹ, שֶׁסָּךְ כְּדַרְכּוֹ וְאֵינוֹ חוֹשֵׁשׁ;
וַאֲפִלּוּ לְנָטוֹרֵי פֵּירֵי אָמְרוּ זִכְרוֹנָם לִבְרָכָה שֶׁמֻּתָּר לַעֲבֹר בְּמַיִם עַד הַצַּוָּאר, וְכָל־

---

7. This is so according to MT *hilchoth 'eruvin* i 9 (see *Maggid Mishneh*).

8. TB Yoma 79b.

9. Derived from TB Yoma 80a and K'rithoth 14a (MY). The three oldest manuscripts and the first edition have "the amount of three olives, since three olives," etc. But MS Parma 741 has "two," with a marginal note that this is how it should read. And so all the later editions read.

10. Phrase derived from Isaiah 40:12.

11. Units of weight evidently current in our author's time; since *argentum* is the Latin for silver, these units may have been weights of silver or an alloy. David Rosin gives the word as *arienços* and refers to Zunz, *Zur Geschichte und Literatur*, pp. 554 ff.

12. *Maggid Mishneh* to MT *hilchoth sh'vithath 'asor* ii 1 writes that according to Rambam, an egg weighs 35 argents; and in *ibid*. Rambam writes that a bulky date is only slightly smaller than an egg; hence "twelve *argents*" may well be a scribal error for thirty-two units of this weight (MY)—i.e. an error in one letter: *la-med béth* in place of *yod béth*.

13. It is forbidden, but there is no punishment over it.

14. Not literally a mouthful, but a quantity which if put to one side of the mouth, would make the cheek bulge; TB Yoma 73b, 80a.

plained that "eating" applies to [a minimum of] an olive's amount; but it is affliction for a man as long as he has not eaten up to the quantity of a large date, because a man's spirit is not assuaged by less.[6]

Now, the quantity of a date is more than a dry fig[7] and less than the bulk of an egg;[8] and it is equally less than the amount of two olives, since two olives are equal to one egg.[9] The nub of the matter is that in the past, someone expert who measured with scales[10] noted carefully that not even twelve *argents*[11] and more are the amount of a date,[12] and it thus has the law of "half a minimal amount."[13]

There is, likewise, what the Sages taught, that the minimal [punishable] quantity of drink is the mouthful of a man,[14] which is as an egg. For in the past they measured that an egg contains the mouthful of a man; so for less than that there is no prohibition that imposes *karéth* [Divine severance of existence], but it rather has the law of half a minimal amount.[13]

Therefore, if someone is ill, even if there is no absolute danger to his life, if he is very feeble, it is well to give him food and drink bit by bit, in the amounts we have stated. Between every instance of eating and the next, a pause should be made—the amount of time it would take to eat half a loaf of bread,[15] which is the bulk of three eggs, in the view of most authorities—so that the instances of eating should not be joined together to be reckoned as one meal, of one [large] amount. However, between an instance of eating and one of drinking, there is no need to pause, as eating and drinking are not reckoned together in this regard.[16] Between one instance of drinking and another, the pause should be the time it takes to drink a *r'vi'ith*.[17] It is permissible to weigh and measure these things on the Day of Atonement at a time of need. It is better that we should be concerned and take precautions not to eat a minimal amount, than that we should be concerned about the ban on weighing, which is by the ruling of the Sages.

It is likewise of the subject-matter of the precept what they (of blessed memory) taught:[18] that those afflictions which are by the decree of the Sages, such as [the ban on] washing and applying oil to the skin,[19] they imposed, that these should not be done, only when there is no need; but on any person who does them out of necessity, they did not impose the decree: For instance, if someone has a scurf or sores on his head, he may put on oil in his usual way and need not be concerned.[18] Even to safeguard fruit or produce, the Sages of blessed memory said it is permissible to cross through water up to the neck;[18]

שֶׁכֵּן לְדָבָר מִצְוָה, בֵּין בַּהֲלִיכָה בֵּין בַּחֲזָרָה.

וּבְעִנְיַן הַסַּנְדָּל פֵּרְשׁוּ לָנוּ מוֹרֵינוּ יִשְׁמְרֵם אֵל שֶׁסַּנְדָּל הוּא בְּכָל מָקוֹם שֶׁל עוֹר, וְזֶהוּ שֶׁאָסוּר בְּיוֹם הַכִּפּוּרִים, אֲבָל לֹא שֶׁל מִין אַחֵר. וּכְלָלָא דְמִלְּתָא לְפִי קְצָת הַפֵּרוּשִׁים דְּכָל שֶׁהוּא רָאוּי לְעִנְיַן חֲלִיצָה, כְּלוֹמַר שֶׁהוּא שֶׁל עוֹר, הוּא אָסוּר בְּיוֹם הַכִּפּוּרִים וּמֻתָּר לָצֵאת בּוֹ בְּשַׁבָּת בִּרְשׁוּת הָרַבִּים; וְכָל שֶׁאֵינוֹ רָאוּי לַחֲלִיצָה, כְּגוֹן שֶׁל שַׂעַם וְגֶמִי וְהוּצֵי וְכִילֵי וּשְׁאָר מִינֵי עֲשָׂבִים, מֻתָּרִים בְּיוֹם הַכִּפּוּרִים, וּבִלְבַד שֶׁלֹּא יֵצֵא בָהֶם לְמָקוֹם שֶׁאֵינוֹ מְעֹרָב, דְּמַשּׁוּי חַשְׁבִינָן לְהוּ. וּמִן הַמְפָרְשִׁים רַבִּים וְנִכְבָּדִים מַתִּירִין לָצֵאת בְּכֻלָּן בִּרְשׁוּת הָרַבִּים.

וְדִין חוֹלֶה שֶׁיֵּשׁ בּוֹ סַכָּנָה, שֶׁמַּאֲכִילִין אוֹתוֹ עַל־פִּי רוֹפֵא בָקִי, אוֹ עַל־פִּי עַצְמוֹ וַאֲפִלּוּ רוֹפֵא אוֹמֵר אֵינוֹ צָרִיךְ; וְדִין עֻבָּרָה שֶׁהֵרִיחָה, וְדִין מִי שֶׁאֲחָזוֹ בּוּלְמוּס; וְדִין קְטַנִּים בֵּין תִּינוֹק בֵּין תִּינֹקֶת מֵאֵי זֶה זְמַן מְעַנִּין אוֹתָן כָּל הַיּוֹם מִדְּרַבָּנָן, וְכֵן מֵאֵי זֶה זְמַן מְחַנְּכִין אוֹתָן לְשָׁעוֹת; וּכְלָלָא דְמִלְּתָא לְפִי קְצָת מִן הַמְפָרְשִׁים, דְּשְׁתֵּי שָׁנִים קֹדֶם גַּדְלוּת בְּבָרִיא מַשְׁלִימִין מִדְּרַבָּנָן, וּשְׁתֵּי שָׁנִים קֹדֶם לְכָךְ מְחַנְּכִין אוֹתָם לְשָׁעוֹת; וְיֵשׁ שֶׁפֵּרְשׁוּ שָׁנָה אַחַת קֹדֶם גַּדְלוּת מַשְׁלִימִין מִדְּרַבָּנָן בֵּין תִּינוֹק בֵּין תִּינֹקֶת; וְיֵשׁ שֶׁפֵּרְשׁוּ שֶׁאֵין מַשְׁלִימִין מִדְּרַבָּנָן רַק בְּתִינֹקֶת לְבַד, שָׁנָה אַחַת קֹדֶם גַּדְלוּת, אֲבָל תִּינוֹק אֵינוֹ מַשְׁלִים כְּלָל מִדְּרַבָּנָן, וְגַדְלוּת הוּא בְתִינוֹק י"ג שָׁנָה וְיוֹם אֶחָד, וּבְתִינֹקֶת י"ב שָׁנָה וְיוֹם אֶחָד. וְהַמֶּלֶךְ וְהַכַּלָּה בִּרְחִיצָה בְּיוֹם זֶה, מַה דִּינָן.

וְעוֹד אַזְכִּיר לְךָ כָּאן מַה שֶּׁאָמְרוּ זִכְרוֹנָם לִבְרָכָה גַּם־כֵּן בְּעִנְיַן תַּעֲנִית תִּשְׁעָה

---

15. So TB K'rithoth 12b. The illness in question here is one which poses no present mortal danger (this is the basic sense of "no absolute danger" four lines above), but with prolonged fasting the illness may worsen to the point of endangering the patient's life (MY).

16. TB Yoma 73b.

17. Tosefta, Yoma iv; MT hilchoth sh'vithath 'asor ii 4.

18. TB Yoma 87b.

19. In the first paragraph, above, this is given a basis in the repetition of a term in Scripture (notes 3, 4); that, however, is only to give a dimension of authority to what is only a ruling of the Sages.

20. So Rashba (R. Sh'lomoh ibn 'Adreth, evidently our author's master teacher), commentary, TB Yevamoth 102b.

21. See Deuteronomy 25:9, that the ritual involves a shoe.

22. A technical way of enclosing an area so that it is considered as a private domain on the Sabbath, whereupon carrying within it is permissible.

23. So Ramban, commentary, TB Shabbath 66a.

24. Rashba, commentary, TB Yevamoth 102b, s.v. 'ela lav; R. 'Ashér, TB Yoma viii, §8; et al.

25. TB Yoma 83a. The word בּוּלְמוּס, "ravenous hunger" (at the second appearance of the note number), is from the Greek boulimos. Alternatively, its origin is a

then all the more certainly so for a matter of religious duty, whether in going or in returning.[18]

Now, regarding sandals [shoes], our instructors (God protect them) explained to us that the sandal everywhere denotes [footgear made] of leather.[19] This is what is forbidden on the Day of Atonement, and not of any other kind. The crux of the matter, according to some authorities, is that anything suitable to be used in halitzah [the ritual to release a woman from the duty of levirate marriage][21]—i.e. that is of leather—is forbidden on the Day of Atonement, and it is permissible to go out in it on the Sabbath into the public domain; and whatever is not suitable for halitzah—for instance, of cork, reed grass, palm leaves, twisted reeds, or other kinds of grass—is permissible on the Day of Atonement, but on condition that one should not go out in them to a location not enclosed in an 'éruv,[22] for they are considered something carried.[23] Yet many eminent authorities allow going out in any of them into the public domain.[24]

Further, we have the law of a sick person in danger of his life, that he is given food according to the instruction of an expert physician, or according to his own word, even if the physician says he does not need it.[25] Then we have the law of a pregnant woman who sniffed [savory food];[26] the law of a person seized by ravenous hunger;[25] and the law of children, either a young boy or girl—from which time they are to be made to fast the entire day by the ruling of the Sages; and so too, from which age they are to be trained for a few hours.[27] The rule of the matter, according to some of the authorities, is that two years before pubertal maturity they are to complete [the full fast] by the ruling of the Sages, and two years before that they are to be trained for a number of hours.[28] Then there are those who explained that one year before pubertal maturity, they are to complete the fast by the law of the Sages, whether a boy or a girl.[29] But there are others who hold that by the law of the Sages, none but a young girl alone must complete the fast, one year before this maturity, while a young boy need not complete it at all by the ruling of the Sages. This maturity for a boy is at thirteen years and a day, and for a girl at twelve years and a day. Then there is the matter of a king and a bride, in regard to washing on this day, what the law is for them.[30]

I will also mention for you here what the Sages of blessed memory likewise taught about the subject of the fast of the ninth of Av, which is known to be only by the decree of the Sages. Even though these

בְּאָב הַיָּדוּעַ שֶׁהוּא מִדְּרַבָּנָן; וְאַף־עַל־פִּי שֶׁרְחוֹקִים מְאֹד שְׁנֵי הַיָּמִים אֵלֶּה בְּטַעֲמָן וּבְכָל עִנְיָנָם, לְפִי שֶׁשֵּׁם תַּעֲנִית כּוֹלְלָם נִדְבֵּר בּוֹ מְעַט.

וְאוֹדִיעֲךָ שֶׁהֶחְמִירוּ בוֹ חֲכָמִים בְּכָל עִנְיָנוֹ כְּמוֹ בְיוֹם הַכִּפּוּרִים: לְהַפְסִיק מִבְּעוֹד יוֹם, וּבִרְחִיצָה וּבְסִיכָה וּבִנְעִילַת הַסַּנְדָּל וּבְתַשְׁמִישׁ הַמִּטָּה; וְעָבְרוֹת וּמֵנִיקוֹת, שֶׁמִּתְעַנּוֹת בּוֹ כִּשְׁאָר הָעָם, מַה שֶּׁאֵינָן עוֹשִׂין כֵּן בְּכָל שְׁאָר תַּעֲנִיּוֹת, חוּץ מִשָּׁלשׁ תַּעֲנִיּוֹת אֶמְצָעִיּוֹת שֶׁל עֲצִירַת מָטָר, כְּמוֹ שֶׁנִּזְכַּר בְּמַסֶּכֶת תַּעֲנִית בְּסוֹף פֶּרֶק רִאשׁוֹן, דְּאַסִּיק רַב אַשֵׁי הָתָם: נָקוֹט מִיצִיעָתָא בְּיָדָךְ.

וְיֶתֶר פְּרָטֵי מִצְוָה זוֹ, מְבֹאָרִים בְּמַסֶּכֶת יוֹמָא.

וְנוֹהֶגֶת בְּכָל מָקוֹם וּבְכָל זְמַן, בִּזְכָרִים וּנְקֵבוֹת. וְעוֹבֵר עַל זֶה וְאָכַל בְּיוֹם הַכִּפּוּרִים כַּשִּׁעוּר כַּכּוֹתֶבֶת, בִּטֵּל עֲשֵׂה, וְעָבַר עַל לָאו שֶׁיֵּשׁ בּוֹ כָּרֵת, שֶׁנֶּאֱמַר: כִּי כָל הַנֶּפֶשׁ אֲשֶׁר לֹא תְעֻנֶּה בְּעֶצֶם הַיּוֹם הַזֶּה וְנִכְרְתָה. אָכַל אוֹ שָׁתָה כַּשִּׁעוּר זֶה בִּשְׁגָגָה, חַיָּב קָרְבָּן חַטָּאת קְבוּעָה.

[מִצְוַת קָרְבָּן מוּסָף בְּיוֹם עֲשִׂירִי בְּתִשְׁרֵי, שֶׁהוּא נִקְרָא יוֹם הַכִּפּוּרִים]

שיד לְהַקְרִיב קָרְבָּן מוּסָף בֶּעָשׂוֹר לַחֹדֶשׁ הַשְּׁבִיעִי, שֶׁנֶּאֱמַר: אַךְ בֶּעָשׂוֹר לַחֹדֶשׁ וְכוּלֵי וְהִקְרַבְתֶּם אִשֶּׁה לַיָי; וּבְסֵדֶר פִּינְחָס פֵּרַשׁ הַקָּרְבָּן, כְּמוֹ שֶׁכָּתוּב שָׁם: וְהִקְרַבְתֶּם עֹלָה לַיָי רֵיחַ נִיחֹחַ פַּר בֶּן בָּקָר אֶחָד אַיִל אֶחָד כְּבָשִׂים בְּנֵי שָׁנָה שִׁבְעָה, וְגוֹמֵר. וְזֶה הַכָּתוּב שֶׁבְּפִינְחָס הֵבִיא הָרַמְבָּ"ם זִכְרוֹנוֹ לִבְרָכָה בְּמִנְיָנוֹ; וַאֲנִי כָתַבְתִּי הַקּוֹדֵם בַּתּוֹרָה, וְהַכֹּל עוֹלֶה לְעִנְיָן אֶחָד.

מִשָּׁרְשֵׁי מִצְוַת קָרְבָּן הַמּוּסָף וּקְצָת דִּינָיו, כְּבָר כָּתַבְתִּי שָׁם מַה שֶׁיָּדַעְתִּי בְּמוּסַף הַפֶּסַח שֶׁבְּסֵדֶר זֶה [סִי' רצ"ט], וְקֵשֵׁר אֶחָד לְכֻלָּם לְפִי הַדּוֹמֶה.

combination of the Greek *boul*, "ox" (bull) and *laimos*, "throat" denoting (so the *Aruch* explains) a sick state which makes a person ready to eat "as the ox licks up the grass of the field" (Numbers 22:4; see *Aruch haShalém*). R. Benjamin Musafia (*Musaf ha'Aruch*) describes it as "a faintness of the spirit to the extent that a person's hands and feet grow cold, his face turns green, and his senses are numbed, until there is hardly any life left in him." In TB Yoma 83a, Rashi (s.v. *mi she'ahazo*) explains it as "an illness which seizes one on account of hunger, whereby his eyes grow dim and he is in peril of his life; and when his normal appearance returns, he is cured for certain."

26. *Ibid.* 82a-b; MT *hilchoth sh'vithath 'asor* ii 9.
27. I.e. to wait a few hours longer than usual.
28. TB Yoma 82a, version in our standard edition, and Rashi.
29. See MT *ibid.* and Rabad there.
30. TB Yoma 73b, 78b.
31. In good time before the evening that begins the fast day; TB P'sahim 54b.
32. They are equally forbidden on the ninth of Av; TB Ta'anith 30a.
33. TB P'sahim 54b.
34. I.e. we follow that as definitive law; and it teaches that on the first three fast

two days are far apart in their reason and in their entire subject-matter, since the name "fast" encompasses them both, let us speak of it a bit.

Now, I can inform you that the Sages were as stringent about its entire subject-matter as about the Day of Atonement: to stop [eating] when it is yet day;[31] in regard to washing, applying oil to the skin, wearing shoes, and conjugal intimacy;[32] and pregnant women and those who are nursing infants are to fast on it like other people[33]— while the Sages do not so rule about all other fast days, except for the three middle fasts when rain is withheld, as mentioned in the Talmud tractate *Ta'anith* (14a), at the end of the first chapter; for R. Ashi concludes there: "Hold the middle [*baraitha*] in your hand" [as a sure guide to follow].[34]

The remaining details of this precept are explained in the tractate *Yoma*. It applies everywhere, at every time, for both man and woman. If someone transgresses it and eats on the Day of Atonement as the amount of a bulky date, he disobeys a positive precept, and violates a negative precept that entails *karéth* (§316): as it is stated, *For whatever soul it is that shall not be afflicted on this selfsame day, he shall be cut off* (Leviticus 23:29). If someone ate or drank the minimal amount unwittingly, he would be obligated to bring a standard unvarying *hattath* (sin) offering.[35]

[THE PRECEPT OF THE MUSAF OFFERING ON THE DAY
OF ATONEMENT]

314 to sacrifice a *musaf* (additional) offering on the tenth day of the seventh month [the Day of Atonement], as it is stated, *But on the tenth day of this seventh month . . . you shall bring an offering by fire to the Lord* (Leviticus 23:27). In sidrah pinhas, the offering is explained, as it is written there, *and you shall present a burnt-offering to the Lord, a pleasing savor: one young bullock, one ram, seven male lambs of the first year*, etc. (Numbers 29:8). Rambam of blessed memory cited this verse in *sidrah pinhas*, in his listing [of the *mitzvoth*],[1] whereas I have written the earlier [verse] in the Torah; but it all comes to the same thing.

As to the root reason for the *musaf* offering and some of its laws, I have previously written there what I have known—in connection with the *musaf* of Passover in this *sidrah* (§299). One theme, as it seems, unites them all.

[שֶׁלֹּא לַעֲשׂוֹת מְלָאכָה בַּעֲשָׂרָה בְּתִשְׁרִי]

שטו שֶׁלֹּא לַעֲשׂוֹת שׁוּם מְלָאכָה בְּיוֹם הַכִּפּוּרִים, וְהוּא יוֹם עֲשִׂירִי לְחֹדֶשׁ תִּשְׁרֵי, שֶׁנֶּאֱמַר: בֶּעָשׂוֹר לַחֹדֶשׁ הַשְּׁבִיעִי וְגוֹמֵר, וּכְתִיב בַּתְרֵיהּ: וְכָל מְלָאכָה לֹא תַעֲשׂוּ בְּעֶצֶם הַיּוֹם הַזֶּה כִּי יוֹם כִּפּוּרִים הוּא לְכַפֵּר עֲלֵיכֶם; וּמִלַּת "כִּי" הוּא נְתִינַת טַעַם לְבִטּוּל הַמְּלָאכָה, וּכְעִנְיָן שֶׁכָּתַבְתִּי לְמַעְלָה בְּסֵדֶר זֶה בְּמִצְוַת עֲשֵׂה דִשְׁבִיתָה דְכִפּוּרִים, י"ח [סי' שי"ז]; וְגַם כָּל עִנְיַן מִצְוָה זוֹ שָׁם תִּמְצָאֶנּוּ, וְלֹא אֶכְתֹּב לָךְ תּוֹסֶפֶת בַּדָּבָר אֵינוֹ צָרִיךְ.

[שֶׁלֹּא לֶאֱכֹל וְלִשְׁתּוֹת בְּיוֹם הַכִּפּוּרִים]

שטז שֶׁלֹּא לֶאֱכֹל וְלִשְׁתּוֹת בְּיוֹם הַכִּפּוּרִים, שֶׁנֶּאֱמַר: כִּי כָל הַנֶּפֶשׁ אֲשֶׁר לֹא תְעֻנֶּה בְּעֶצֶם הַיּוֹם הַזֶּה וְנִכְרְתָה. כָּל עִנְיַן מִצְוָה זוֹ כָּתַבְתִּי לְמַעְלָה בְּסֵדֶר זֶה, בְּמִצְוַת עֲשֵׂה י"ו [סי' שי"ג]; עַיֵּן שָׁם כִּי קָרוֹב הוּא.

[מִצְוַת שְׁבִיתָה מִמְּלָאכָה בְּיוֹם הַכִּפּוּרִים]

שיז לִשְׁבֹּת מִכָּל מְלָאכָה בְּיוֹם הַכִּפּוּרִים, שֶׁנֶּאֱמַר: שַׁבַּת שַׁבָּתוֹן הוּא לָכֶם, וּכְבָר כָּתַבְתִּי מַה שֶּׁאָמְרוּ זִכְרוֹנָם לִבְרָכָה: הַאי "שַׁבָּתוֹן" עֲשֵׂה הוּא, כְּלוֹמַר שֶׁפֵּרוּשׁוֹ כְּאִלּוּ יֹאמַר שְׁבָתוּ בְּיוֹם זֶה.

מִשָּׁרְשֵׁי הַמִּצְוָה, עַל צַד הַפְּשָׁט, כְּדֵי שֶׁלֹּא נִהְיֶה טְרוּדִים בְּשׁוּם דָּבָר וְנָשִׂים כָּל מַחֲשַׁבְתֵּנוּ וְכָל כַּוָּנוֹתֵינוּ לְבַקֵּשׁ מְחִילָה וּסְלִיחָה מֵאֵת אָדוֹן הַכֹּל בְּיוֹם זֶה, שֶׁהוּא נָכוֹן לִסְלִיחַת הָעֲוֹנוֹת מִיּוֹם שֶׁנִּבְרָא הָעוֹלָם, וּכְמוֹ שֶׁכָּתַבְתִּי בְּאַחֲרֵי-מוֹת בְּמִצְוַת עֲשֵׂה א' [סי' קפ"ה].

מִדִּינֵי הַמִּצְוָה, מַה שֶּׁאָמְרוּ זִכְרוֹנָם לִבְרָכָה שֶׁכָּל דָּבָר שֶׁאָסוּר לַעֲשׂוֹתוֹ בְּשַׁבָּת אַף-עַל-פִּי שֶׁאֵינוֹ מְלָאכָה גְמוּרָה, אָסוּר לַעֲשׂוֹתוֹ בְּיוֹם הַכִּפּוּרִים; כְּלָלוֹ שֶׁל דָּבָר, אֵין בֵּין שַׁבָּת לְיוֹם הַכִּפּוּרִים אֶלָּא שֶׁזְּדוֹן מְלָאכָה בְּשַׁבָּת בִּסְקִילָה, וּבְיוֹם

days which the *beth din* proclaims when rain does not fall, pregnant and nursing women need not fast, as Heaven's wrath is not yet so apparent (hence the fasts are not so serious a matter); but they are to fast on the three later ones that are decreed. As for the seven final ones that may follow, pregnant and nursing women are exempt, since seven fasts would be too much for them. For various views on details see *Shulḥan 'Aruch 'Oraḥ Hayyim* § 575, 5.

35. Explained in § 121.

§314   1. ShM positive precept §48.

§315   1. The original reads, "what I have written above." §315 is a negative precept, and §317 a positive, and in the original, all positive precepts in each *sidrah* were arranged first.

[THE PROHIBITION AGAINST DOING WORK ON THE TENTH OF TISHRI]

315 not to do any work whatever on the Day of Atonement, which is the tenth day of the month of Tishri: for it is stated, *on the tenth day of this seventh month* (Leviticus 23:27), and it is written afterward, *And you shall do no work on this selfsame day, for it is a day of atonement, to make atonement for you* (ibid. 28). Thus the word "for" means that a reason is given for the cessation of work, in keeping with what I will write below[1] in this *sidrah*, in the eighteenth positive precept, about resting from work on the Day of Atonement (§317). The entire subject-matter of this precept you will also find there; I shall not write anything additional for you where the matter is unnecessary.

[THE PROHIBITION AGAINST EATING OR DRINKING ON THE DAY OF ATONEMENT]

316 not to eat or drink on the Day of Atonement, as it is written, *For whatever soul it is that shall not be afflicted on this selfsame day, it shall be cut off* (Leviticus 23:29). The entire subject of this precept I wrote above in this *sidrah*, in the sixteenth positive precept (§313). Look there, for it is nearby.

[THE PRECEPT OF RESTING FROM WORK ON THE DAY OF ATONEMENT]

317 to rest from all work on the Day of Atonement: for it is stated, *it shall be to you a sabbath of* shabbathon, *solemn rest* (Leviticus 23:32), and I have written previously (§297) what the Sages of blessed memory said: This term, *shabbathon*, denotes a positive precept.[1] In other words, its significance is as though it read, "rest on this day."

At the root of the precept, considering the plain meaning, lies the purpose that we should not be distracted by anything at all, but should set all our thought and intention to beseech pardon and forgiveness from the Ruler of all on this day, which was destined for the forgiveness of wrongdoing from the day the world was created—as I wrote in *sidrah aharé moth*, in the first positive precept (§185).

As for the laws of the commandment, there is what the Sages of blessed memory taught:[1] that whatever is forbidden to be done on the Sabbath, even if it is not a complete, absolute labor, is [equally] forbidden to be done on the Day of Atonement. In short: there is no difference between the Sabbath and the Day of Atonement [in this regard]

הַכִּפּוּרִים בְּכָרֵת; וּמִכָּל־מָקוֹם הִתִּירוּ זִכְרוֹנָם לִבְרָכָה לְקַנֵּב הַיָּרָק בְּיוֹם הַכִּפּוּרִים
מִן הַמִּנְחָה וּלְמַעְלָה, כְּדֵי שֶׁנִּמְצָא אוֹתוֹ מוּכָן לָעֶרֶב מִיָּד, מַה שֶּׁאֵינוֹ מֻתָּר בְּשַׁבָּת;
וְנָהֲגוּ הָעָם לְהַחְמִיר בַּדָּבָר וְלִנְהֹג בּוֹ אִסּוּר כְּשַׁבָּת לְכָל דָּבָר; וְיֶתֶר פְּרָטֶיהָ,
מְבֹאָרִים בְּמַסֶּכֶת יוֹמָא.

וְנוֹהֶגֶת בְּכָל מָקוֹם וּבְכָל זְמַן, בִּזְכָרִים וּנְקֵבוֹת. וְעוֹבֵר עָלֶיהָ וְעָשָׂה מְלָאכָה,
בִּטֵּל עֲשֵׂה זֶה, מִלְּבַד שֶׁעָבַר עַל לָאו, וּכְמוֹ שֶׁנִּכְתֹּב בְּסֵדֶר זֶה [סִי׳ שט״ו] בְּעֶזְרַת
הַשֵּׁם.

[מִצְוַת שְׁבִיתָה מִמְּלָאכָה בְּיוֹם רִאשׁוֹן שֶׁל חַג הַסֻּכּוֹת]

שיח לִשְׁבֹּת מִמְּלָאכָה שֶׁאֵינָהּ צֹרֶךְ אֹכֶל נֶפֶשׁ, בְּיוֹם רִאשׁוֹן שֶׁל חַג הַסֻּכּוֹת,
שֶׁנֶּאֱמַר: בַּיּוֹם הָרִאשׁוֹן מִקְרָא קֹדֶשׁ.

מִשָּׁרְשֵׁי מִצְוַת הַשְּׁבִיתָה בְּשַׁבָּת וּבְיָמִים־טוֹבִים, כָּתַבְתִּי בָּהֶן כְּבָר מַה
שֶּׁיָּדַעְתִּי, וְטַעַם אֶחָד לְכֻלָּן. וּקְצָת דִּינֶיהָ נִכְתֹּב בְּלָאו דְּאִסּוּר מְלָאכָה שֶׁבְּסֵדֶר זֶה
[סִי׳ שי״ט] בְּעֶזְרַת הַשֵּׁם.

וְנוֹהֶגֶת בְּכָל מָקוֹם וּבְכָל זְמַן, בִּזְכָרִים וּנְקֵבוֹת. וְעוֹבֵר עָלֶיהָ בִּטֵּל עֲשֵׂה, מִלְּבַד
שֶׁעָבַר עַל לָאו.

[שֶׁלֹּא לַעֲשׂוֹת מְלָאכָה בְּיוֹם רִאשׁוֹן שֶׁל חַג הַסֻּכּוֹת]

שיט שֶׁלֹּא לַעֲשׂוֹת מְלָאכָה שֶׁלֹּא לְצֹרֶךְ אֹכֶל נֶפֶשׁ, בְּיוֹם רִאשׁוֹן שֶׁל חַג
הַסֻּכּוֹת, שֶׁהוּא יוֹם חֲמִשָּׁה־עָשָׂר בְּתִשְׁרֵי, שֶׁנֶּאֱמַר: דַּבֵּר אֶל בְּנֵי יִשְׂרָאֵל לֵאמֹר
בַּחֲמִשָּׁה עָשָׂר יוֹם לַחֹדֶשׁ הַשְּׁבִיעִי וְגוֹמֵר, בַּיּוֹם הָרִאשׁוֹן מִקְרָא קֹדֶשׁ כָּל מְלֶאכֶת
עֲבֹדָה לֹא תַעֲשׂוּ. עִנְיַן אִסּוּר מְלָאכָה בְּיוֹם־טוֹב כְּתַבְתִּיו לְמַעְלָה בְּפֶסַח בְּסֵדֶר זֶה
[סִי׳ רח״צ], וְעִנְיָנָן שָׁוֶה בְּכָל דָּבָר.

§317   1. So ShM positive precept §165.
2. TB M'gillah 7b.
3. TB Shabbath 115a.
4. So MT *hilchoth sh'vithath 'asor* i 3.
5. See §297, note 3, and §321, last paragraph.
6. The original reads, "as we will write, with the Eternal Lord's help," for the reason given in §315, note 1. Our arrangement of the precepts, that of the standard printed editions, follows the order of the verses in Scripture.

§318   1. See §297, beginning, on the interpretation of the verse.
2. The Hebrew reads, "Some of its laws we will write ... in this *sidrah*, with the Eternal Lord's help." See §315, note 1, and §317, note 6.
3. See §297, note 3, and §321, last paragraph.

other than the fact that work willfully done on the Sabbath incurs death by stoning, and on the Day of Atonement, by *karéth* [Divine severance of existence].[2] However, the Sages of blessed memory permitted cleaning and trimming vegetables on the Day of Atonement, from the time of *minhah* (the afternoon prayer) and onward, so that we should find it ready in the evening, immediately[3]—which is not permissible on the Sabbath. Yet the people accepted the practice of being stringent in the matter and to observe the prohibition on it [the Day of Atonement] as on the Sabbath, in everything.[4] The rest of its details are explained in the Talmud tractate *Yoma*.

It is in effect everywhere, at every time, for both man and woman.[5] If a person transgresses it and does work, he disobeys a positive precept, apart from violating a negative precept (§315), as I have written.[6]

[THE PRECEPT OF RESTING FROM WORK ON THE FIRST DAY OF SUKKOTH]

318 to rest from work that is not essential for [preparing] human food, on the first day of the festival of *Sukkoth*: for it is stated, *On the first day shall be a holy convocation* (Leviticus 23 : 35).[1]

As to the root reason for the precepts of resting from work on the Sabbath and festival days, I have already written about them what I have known; there is one reason for them all. Some of its laws we have written in the negative precept of the prohibition on work in this *sidrah*[2] (§298).

It is in force everywhere, at every time, for both man and woman.[3] Anyone who transgresses it disobeys a positive precept, apart from violating a negative precept (§319).

[THE PROHIBITION AGAINST DOING WORK ON THE FIRST DAY OF SUKKOTH]

319 not to do work that is not essential for [preparing] human food, on the first day of the festival of *Sukkoth*, which is the fifteenth day of Tishri: for it is stated, *Speak to the Israelites, saying: On the fifteenth day of this seventh month . . . On the first day shall be a holy convocation; you shall do no laborious work* (Leviticus 23 :34–35). As to the ban on work on a festival day, I wrote of it above, concerning Passover, in this *sidrah* (§298); their subject-matter is the same in every respect.

[מִצְוַת קָרְבַּן מוּסָף בְּכָל יוֹם מִשִּׁבְעַת יְמֵי חַג הַסֻּכּוֹת]

שכ לְהַקְרִיב קָרְבָּן בְּחַג הַסֻּכּוֹת, שֶׁנֶּאֱמַר: שִׁבְעַת יָמִים תַּקְרִיבוּ אִשֶּׁה, וְזֶהוּ מוּסָף הֶחָג; וּבְסֵדֶר פִּינְחָס מַאֲרִיךְ בּוֹ יוֹתֵר וּמְפָרֵשׁ בְּמוּסָף שֶׁל כָּל יוֹם וָיוֹם כַּמָּה בְהֵמוֹת הָיוּ מַקְרִיבִין, כִּי כָל יוֹם וָיוֹם מֵהֶן חָלוּק מֵחֲבֵרוֹ, שֶׁחֶשְׁבּוֹן הַפָּרִים מִתְמַעֲטִים בְּכָל יוֹם (וְאָמְרוּ זִכְרוֹנָם לִבְרָכָה שֶׁבִּזְכוּת מִצְוָה זוֹ יִתְמַעֲטוּ שׂוֹנְאֵיהֶם שֶׁל יִשְׂרָאֵל כְּמוֹ שֶׁהַפָּרִים מִתְמַעֲטִין בְּכָל יוֹם).

וּכְבָר כָּתַבְתִּי בְּקָרְבַּן מוּסַף הַפֶּסַח שֶׁרֹשׁ מַסְפִּיק לְכָל הַמּוּסָפִין, לְפִי דַעְתִּי, עַל צַד הַפְּשָׁט. וְהָרַמְבַּ"ם זִכְרוֹנוֹ לִבְרָכָה הֵבִיא בְמִנְיָנוֹ הַכָּתוּב שֶׁבְּסֵדֶר פִּינְחָס, וַאֲנִי הֵבֵאתִי הַבָּא רִאשׁוֹן בַּתּוֹרָה, וְהַכֹּל עוֹלֶה לְטַעַם אֶחָד.

[מִצְוַת שְׁבִיתָה מִמְּלָאכָה בְּיוֹם שְׁמִינִי שֶׁל סֻכּוֹת]

שכא לִשְׁבֹּת מִמְּלָאכָה שֶׁאֵינָהּ צֹרֶךְ אֹכֶל נֶפֶשׁ בַּיּוֹם הַשְּׁמִינִי שֶׁל חַג הַסֻּכּוֹת, שֶׁנֶּאֱמַר: בַּיּוֹם הַשְּׁמִינִי מִקְרָא קֹדֶשׁ יִהְיֶה לָכֶם; וְהוּא יוֹם כ"ב בְּתִשְׁרֵי. מִשָּׁרְשֵׁי מִצְוַת שְׁבִיתַת הָרֶגֶל, כָּתַבְנוּ לְמַעְלָה. וְעוֹד נִכְתֹּב בָּעִנְיָן בְּעֶזְרַת הַשֵּׁם בְּאִסּוּר מְלָאכָה שֶׁבְּיוֹם זֶה בְּסֵדֶר זֶה [סִי' שכ"ג] וְשָׁם נְבָאֵר שֶׁיּוֹם־טוֹב זֶה הוּא יוֹם־טוֹב בִּפְנֵי עַצְמוֹ.

וְנוֹהֶגֶת בְּכָל מָקוֹם וּבְכָל זְמַן, בִּזְכָרִים וּנְקֵבוֹת; וְאַף־עַל־פִּי שֶׁשְּׁבִיתַת הָרֶגֶל מִמִּצְווֹת שֶׁהַזְּמַן גְּרָמָא הוּא, אַף־עַל־פִּי־כֵן, מִכֵּיוָן שֶׁבַּעֲשִׂיַּת הַמְּלָאכָה יֵשׁ בָּהּ גַּם־כֵּן אִסּוּר לָאו, הַנָּשִׁים חַיָּבוֹת בָּהּ, מִן הַכְּלָל שֶׁבְּיָדֵינוּ: "אִישׁ אוֹ אִשָּׁה כִּי יַעֲשׂוּ מִכָּל חַטֹּאת הָאָדָם", הִשְׁוָה הַכָּתוּב אִשָּׁה לְאִישׁ לְכָל עֳנָשִׁין שֶׁבַּתּוֹרָה. וְעוֹבֵר עַל

---

§320   1. TB Sukkah 55b.

2. The passage in parentheses is not in the oldest manuscripts or in any but the first edition. It may be a later interpolation, but equally likely, it may well be part of the original, preserved only in the first edition, that was omitted elsewhere by a usual scribal error: a jump of the eye between identical phrases.

3. ShM positive precept §50.

§321   1. See §297, beginning, about the term "a holy convocation."

2. I.e. it becomes obligatory at a specific time.

3. And since she must observe the negative precept, on pain of punishment, she must equally observe the positive precept, which is inseparably connected with it.

[THE PRECEPT OF THE MUSAF OFFERING ON EACH DAY
OF SUKKOTH]

320 to sacrifice an offering on the festival of *Sukkoth*: for it is stated, *Seven days you shall bring an offering by fire* (Leviticus 23:36). This is the *musaf* (additional offering) of the festival. In *sidrah pinhas* (Numbers 29:13–35) Scripture describes it more at length, and explains for the *musaf* of each day how many animals they would offer up; because [the *musaf* of] each day was different from [that of] any other. For the number of bullocks became smaller each day (and the Sages of blessed memory said[1] that for the merit of this *mitzvah*, the enemies of Jewry would become diminished, just as the bullocks diminished in number every day).[2]

I have previously written, regarding the *musaf* offering of Passover (§299), a root reason that should be adequate for all the *musaf* offerings, to my mind, from the aspect of the plain meaning. Rambam of blessed memory cited in his listing [of the precepts] the verses in *sidrah pinhas*,[3] whereas I have cited what appears earlier in the Torah; but it all comes to the same thing.

[THE PRECEPT OF RESTING FROM WORK ON THE EIGHTH
DAY OF SUKKOTH]

321 to rest from work that is not a necessity for [the preparation of] human food, on the eighth day of the festival of *Sukkoth*: for it is stated, *on the eighth day it shall be a holy convocation for you*[1] (Leviticus 23:36)—this being the twenty-second of Tishri.

About the root reason for resting from work on a festival we have written above (§297); and we will write further of the matter, with the Eternal Lord's help, in regard to the ban on work for this day, in this *sidrah* (§323). There we will explain that this festive day is a [separate] festival by itself.

It is in force everywhere, at every time, for both man and woman. Even though resting from work is among the precepts that time causes [to become obligatory],[2] nevertheless, since doing work also entails [the violation of] a negative precept, women are therefore obligated to observe it, by the rule we have: *When a man or woman shall commit any sin that men commit* (Numbers 5:6)—Scripture has equated the woman to the man in regard to all punishments in the Torah.[3] If a person transgresses this and does work on this day, he disobeys a

זֶה וְעָשָׂה מְלָאכָה בְּיוֹם זֶה, בִּטֵּל עֲשֵׂה, מִלְּבַד שֶׁעָבַר עַל לָאו, כְּמוֹ שֶׁנִּכְתַּב בְּסֵדֶר זֶה [סִי׳ שכ"ג] בְּעֶזְרַת הַשֵּׁם.

[מִצְוַת קָרְבַּן מוּסָף בְּיוֹם שְׁמִינִי שֶׁל סֻכּוֹת, שֶׁהוּא נִקְרָא שְׁמִינִי עֲצֶרֶת]

שכב לְהַקְרִיב קָרְבַּן מוּסָף בַּיּוֹם הַשְּׁמִינִי מֵחַג הַסֻּכּוֹת, וְזֶהוּ מוּסַף שְׁמִינִי עֲצֶרֶת, שֶׁנֶּאֱמַר: וְהִקְרַבְתֶּם אִשֶּׁה לַיי עֲצֶרֶת הִיא וְגוֹמֵר; וּבְסֵדֶר פִּינְחָס מְפָרֵשׁ אוֹתוֹ בָּאֲרֻכָּה. וּבְבֵאוּר אָמְרוּ זִכְרוֹנָם לִבְרָכָה שֶׁהוּא רֶגֶל בִּפְנֵי עַצְמוֹ וְקָרְבָּן בִּפְנֵי עַצְמוֹ, וְעַל־כֵּן יֵשׁ לָנוּ לִמְנוֹת מוּסָף זֶה מִצְוָה בִּפְנֵי עַצְמָהּ.

מִשָּׁרְשֵׁי מִצְוַת הַמּוּסָף וּמִכָּל עִנְיָנָהּ, כָּתַבְתִּי הַרְבֵּה פְּעָמִים לְמַעְלָה מַה שֶּׁהִשִּׂיגָה יָדִי.

[שֶׁלֹּא לַעֲשׂוֹת מְלָאכָה בְּיוֹם שְׁמִינִי בּוֹ]

שכג שֶׁלֹּא לַעֲשׂוֹת מְלָאכָה בְּיוֹם שְׁמִינִי שֶׁל חַג, וְהוּא יוֹם כ"ב בְּתִשְׁרֵי, שֶׁנֶּאֱמַר: בַּיּוֹם הַשְּׁמִינִי מִקְרָא קֹדֶשׁ...כָּל־מְלֶאכֶת עֲבֹדָה לֹא תַעֲשׂוּ; וְזֶה נִקְרָא חַג הָעֲצֶרֶת; וְאָמְרוּ זִכְרוֹנָם לִבְרָכָה שֶׁהוּא נִקְרָא כֵן לְפִי שֶׁהוּא סוֹף הַמּוֹעֲדִים, וְעַל דֶּרֶךְ מָשָׁל הוּא, כְּאִלּוּ אָמַר הַקָּדוֹשׁ בָּרוּךְ הוּא לְיִשְׂרָאֵל: עַכְּבוּ עִמִּי יוֹם אֶחָד, שֶׁקָּשָׁה עָלַי פְּרִידַתְכֶם.

כְּבָר אָמַרְנוּ הַרְבֵּה פְּעָמִים שֶׁאִסּוּר מְלָאכָה בְּכָל הַמּוֹעֲדִים שָׁוֶה, אָמְנָם יֵשׁ לִי לְהַרְחִיב הַמַּאֲמָר בְּכָאן וּלְהוֹדִיעֲךָ, בְּנִי, בְּעִנְיַן יוֹם־טוֹב זֶה מַה שֶּׁהוֹדִיעוּנוּ בוֹ חֲכָמִים זִכְרוֹנָם לִבְרָכָה, שֶׁהוּא יוֹם־טוֹב בִּפְנֵי עַצְמוֹ, כְּלוֹמַר שֶׁאֵינוֹ מִכְּלַל חַג הַסֻּכּוֹת; וְאַף־עַל־פִּי שֶׁאַתָּה רוֹאֶה כָּל יִשְׂרָאֵל יוֹשְׁבִים בְּסֻכּוֹתֵיהֶם יוֹם אֶחָד מִשְּׁנֵי יָמִים־טוֹבִים שֶׁל חַג הָעֲצֶרֶת זֶה, אֵין הַדָּבָר מִפְּנֵי שֶׁיִּהְיֶה מִכְּלַל הֶחָג, שֶׁהֲרֵי בְּפֵרוּשׁ אָנוּ אוֹמְרִים בְּבִרְכוֹתָיו "אֶת יוֹם שְׁמִינִי חַג הָעֲצֶרֶת", וְאֵין זֵכֶר לְחַג הַסֻּכּוֹת בּוֹ כְּלָל; אֲבָל מִפְּנֵי תַקָּנַת שְׁנֵי יָמִים־טוֹבִים שֶׁל גָּלֻיּוֹת אָנוּ צְרִיכִין לֵישֵׁב

§322   1. Numbers 29:36-38.
        2. TB Yoma 2b, etc.

§323   1. So Rashi on the verse; cf. P'sikta d'R. Kahana, 30 (ed. Buber, 193a; ed. Mandelbaum, 431) and parallel sources. The verb related to 'atzereth is 'atzar: stop, arrest or restrain. Hence the point made here: at the end of the festivals in the month of Tishri, as it were the Almighty restrains His people from leaving Jerusalem for yet one day, since (so to speak) He finds their departure hard to bear.
        2. TB Yoma 2b, etc.
        3. See §301 about the two festival days of the exile.

positive precept, apart from violating a negative precept, as we will write in this *sidrah* (§323), with the Eternal Lord's help.

[THE PRECEPT OF THE MUSAF OFFERING ON THE EIGHTH DAY OF SUKKOTH]

322 to sacrifice a *musaf* (additional) offering on the eighth day of the festival of *Sukkoth*, which is the *musaf* of *Sh'mini 'Atzereth* (the Eighth Day of Assembly): as it is stated, *and you shall bring an offering by fire to the Lord; it is a day of assembly*, etc. (Leviticus 23:36); and in *sidrah pinḥas* Scripture explains it at length.[1] In elucidation, our Sages of blessed memory said[2] that this is a festival by itself, and a [separate] offering by itself. We therefore have to count this *musaf* as a precept in its own right.

Of the root reason for the *musaf*, and about all its subject-matter, I have written many times above what I was able to.

[THE PROHIBITION AGAINST DOING WORK ON THE EIGHTH DAY OF SUKKOTH]

323 not to do any work on the eighth day of the [*Sukkoth*] festival, which is the twenty-second of Tishri: for it is stated, *on the eighth day shall be a holy convocation . . . you shall do no laborious work* (Leviticus 23:36). This is called the Festival of '*atzereth*, the Assembly; and our Sages of blessed memory said that it is so named because it is the end of the holy occasions. By way of parable, it is as though the Holy One, blessed is He, said to the Jewish people, "Tarry yet one day with Me, for your departure is hard for Me to bear."[1]

We have previously said many times that the prohibition on work is the same on all the holy occasions. However, I would enlarge on the subject here and impart to you, my son, what the Sages of blessed memory informed us about it:[2] that this is a separate festival, by itself, i.e. it is not included in the festival of *Sukkoth*. Now, even though you see all Jews sitting in their *sukkoth* (branch-covered booths) on one out of the two festive days of this Festival of '*atzereth* (the Assembly), this is not because it is part of that festival [of *Sukkoth*]—for you see, we distinctly say in its benedictions, "the eighth day, the Festival of the Assembly," and there is no remembrance of the *Sukkoth* festival in it at all. Rather, on account of the institution of the two festival days of the exile [in place of one][3] we have to sit in the *sukkah*

בַּסֻּכָּה שְׁמֹנָה יָמִים, וְלֹא יַסְפִּיקוּ לָנוּ שִׁבְעָה כְּדִין הַתּוֹרָה, וְעַל־כֵּן אָנוּ יוֹשְׁבִים בַּסֻּכָּה בַּיּוֹם הַשְּׁמִינִי שֶׁל חַג הַסֻּכּוֹת.

וְאָמְרוּ זִכְרוֹנָם לִבְרָכָה: מֵיתַב יַתְבִינַן בְּסֻכָּה, כְּדֵי לָצֵאת יְדֵי חוֹבָה; אַחַר שֶׁחִיְּבוּנוּ זִכְרוֹנָם לִבְרָכָה לְהוֹסִיף יוֹם אֶחָד בְּכָל מוֹעֵד וּמוֹעֵד, הוֹסַפְנוּהוּ גַּם־כֵּן בְּסֻכּוֹת וְעָשִׂינוּ יְמֵי סֻכָּה שְׁמֹנָה יָמִים; אֲבָל מִכָּל־מָקוֹם לֹא מְבָרְכִינַן עַל הַסֻּכָּה בְּיוֹם זֶה, אַחַר שֶׁהוּא בֶּאֱמֶת יוֹם מוֹעֵד אַחֵר, שֶׁהֲשַׁתָּא בְּקִיאִין אָנוּ בְּקִבּוּעָא דְּיַרְחָא, וְיוֹתֵר רָאוּי שֶׁנְּבָרֵךְ עַל יוֹם־טוֹב הָעֲצֶרֶת, שֶׁהוּא הָאֲמִתִּי, וְלֹא עַל הָאַחֵר, שֶׁהוּא מִפְּנֵי הַתַּקָּנָה. וְשֶׁמָּא תֹּאמַר: לָמָּה לֹא תִּקְנוּ לְבָרֵךְ עַל שְׁנֵיהֶם, וְנֹאמַר "בְּיוֹם חַג הַסֻּכּוֹת וְחַג הָעֲצֶרֶת הַזֶּה", כְּמוֹ בְּשַׁבָּת וּמוֹעֵד, שֶׁאָנוּ זוֹכְרִים שְׁנֵיהֶם? הָא לֵיתָה, דְּאִלּוּ בְּשַׁבָּת וּמוֹעֵד שְׁנֵיהֶם בְּיוֹם אֶחָד הֵן, אֲבָל שְׁנֵי מוֹעֲדִים אִי אֶפְשָׁר שֶׁיִּהְיוּ בְּיַחַד, וְעַל־כֵּן אֵין רָאוּי לָנוּ לְבָרֵךְ כֵּן; אֲבָל לֵישַׁב בַּסֻּכָּה רָאוּי לָנוּ, שֶׁיְּשִׁיבַת הַסֻּכָּה לֹא גָּרְעָא מִידֵי בְּחַג הָעֲצֶרֶת, וְיֵשׁ בַּדָּבָר מִצְוַת הַתַּקָּנָה שֶׁל שְׁנֵי יָמִים טוֹבִים שֶׁל גָּלֻיּוֹת שֶׁתִּקְנוּ זִכְרוֹנָם לִבְרָכָה בְּכָל מוֹעֵד, כְּמוֹ שֶׁפֵּרַשְׁנוּ לְמַעְלָה.

וְעוֹד אוֹדִיעֲךָ, בְּנִי, מְעַט בְּמַה שֶּׁאָמְרוּ זִכְרוֹנָם לִבְרָכָה בְּעִנְיַן חֻלּוֹ שֶׁל מוֹעֵד, וְהֵם הַיָּמִים הָאֶמְצָעִיִּים שֶׁבְּפֶסַח וְסֻכּוֹת, שֶׁאָסְרוּ זִכְרוֹנָם לִבְרָכָה בַּעֲשִׂיַּת מְלָאכָה מִן הַתּוֹרָה; וְאוּלָם לֹא בָּא מְפֹרָשׁ בַּתּוֹרָה אִי זוֹ מְלָאכָה אֲסוּרָה בָּהֶם אוֹ מֻתֶּרֶת, אֲבָל מִכָּל־מָקוֹם הַתּוֹרָה אָסְרָה בָּהֶם מְלָאכָה, כְּמוֹ שֶׁלָּמְדוּ חֲכָמִים הַדָּבָר מִן הַכָּתוּב (בְּרֹאשׁ מַסֶּכֶת מוֹעֵד קָטָן) [בְּפֶרֶק ב׳ מִמַּסֶּכֶת חֲגִיגָה]: יֵשׁ מֵהֶם שֶׁלָּמְדוּ הַדָּבָר מִמִּקְרָא דְּ"אֶת חַג הַמַּצּוֹת תִּשְׁמֹר", וְהוּא רַבִּי יֹאשִׁיָה, דְּמַשְׁמַע לֵיהּ כָּל יְמֵי חַג הַמַּצּוֹת מֵעֲשִׂיַּת מְלָאכָה, אֲבָל לֹא שֶׁיִּהְיוּ כֻּלָּן שָׁוִין בִּמְלָאכוֹת;

4. TB Sukkah 47a.

5. So MS Vatican 163/1, where the word *she'asurin* ("that is forbidden") is added above the line—evidently omitted in earlier manuscripts by an oversight. In all other extant texts the word is missing; and hence the preceding *she'amru* (for they said) was changed to *she'asru* (for they forbade).

6. So in most editions; but the first edition reads: at the beginning of the tractate Mo'éd Katan. While it may have been present there in a version that our author had, in our Talmud editions it is found there only in the *Rif* (R. Isaac 'Alfasi).

(booth) eight days, and seven, in accord with the Torah's law, is not enough for us. Therefore we sit in the *sukkah* on the eighth day of the *Sukkoth* festival.

So our Sages of blessed memory said:[4] We indeed sit in the *sukkah*, to fulfill the obligation. Since they (of blessed memory) imposed on us the duty to add one day to every single holy occasion, we added it equally to *Sukkoth*, and made eight days the required time for the *sukkah* (booth). But in any case, we say no benediction over the *sukkah* on this day, since it is in truth a different holy occasion. For now we are expertly versed in the determination of the lunar month, and it is [thus] more proper for us to say the benedictions over the Festival day of the Assembly, which it actually is, and not on the other one, which is only involved by virtue of the enactment [of the Sages].[3]

Now, you might ask: Why did the Sages not institute that the benedicitions should be said over both of them? Let us say, "on this day of the festival of *Sukkoth* and the Festival of the Assembly"—as on a Sabbath which occurs on a holy occasion, when we mention both of them? This, however, cannot be: for a Sabbath and a holy occasion can occur together on one day; but it is impossible that two holy occasions should occur together. Therefore it is improper for us to recite the benediction so. It is, however, quite proper for us to sit in the *sukkah*, since sitting in the *sukkah* detracts in no way from the Festival of the Assembly, and the matter concerns the religious obligation of the institution of two festival days in the exile, which the Sages of blessed memory established for every holy occasion, as we explained above (§301).

Let me tell you further, my son, a bit of what the Sages of blessed memory said regarding the intermediate days of a holy occasion, which are the middle days of Passover and *Sukkoth*; for they (of blessed memory) declared doing work then to be forbidden by the law of the Torah.[5] Now, in truth, it is not stated distinctly in the Torah which labor is then forbidden or permitted. Yet in any case, the Torah forbade labor on those days, as the Sages derived the matter from Scripture in the second chapter of the Talmud tractate *Ḥagigah* (18a):[6] One of them learned the matter from the verse, *The feast of unleavened bread shall you keep* (Exodus 23:15); this is R. Josiah, for whom it implies: All the days of the festival of *matzoth* (unleavened bread) you shall keep from doing work—but not that all [the days] should be alike in regard to labors. R. Jonathan, though, derives it by *kal*

וְרַבִּי יוֹנָתָן אַתְיָא לֵיהּ בְּקַל וָחֹמֶר הָתָם מֵרִאשׁוֹן וּשְׁבִיעִי, שֶׁאֵין קְדֻשָּׁה לִפְנֵיהֶם וּלְאַחֲרֵיהֶם וְכוּלֵי.

וְאִיכָּא הָתָם דְּיָלִיף לַהּ מִ"כָּל מְלֶאכֶת עֲבֹדָה לֹא תַעֲשׂוּ", וְהוּא רַבִּי יוֹסֵי הַגְּלִילִי, וְהָכִי פָרִישְׁנָא לֵיהּ לִקְרָא אַלִּיבֵּיהּ: כְּלוֹמַר בַּיּוֹם הָרִאשׁוֹן הוּא אָסוּר כָּל מְלֶאכֶת עֲבוֹדָה חוּץ מִצֹּרֶךְ אֹכֶל נֶפֶשׁ, אֲבָל בְּחֻלּוֹ שֶׁל מוֹעֵד לֹא כָל מְלָאכוֹת שֶׁל עֲבוֹדָה אֲסוּרוֹת בּוֹ, אֲבָל יֵשׁ אֲסוּרוֹת וְיֵשׁ מֻתָּרוֹת, וּמְסָרָן הַכָּתוּב לַחֲכָמִים.

וְרַבִּי עֲקִיבָא יָלִיף לַהּ מִ"אֵלֶּה מוֹעֲדֵי יי מִקְרָאֵי קֹדֶשׁ", דְּמוֹקִים לַהּ אַחֻלּוֹ שֶׁל מוֹעֵד, וּמִדְּכְתִיב בֵּיהּ "מִקְרָאֵי קֹדֶשׁ" מְלַמֵּד שֶׁאָסוּר בַּעֲשִׂיַּת מְלָאכָה; וְאֶפְשָׁר דְּאַלִּיבֵּיהּ הַמְּלָאכוֹת הַמֻּתָּרוֹת בּוֹ נַפְקִי לֵיהּ מִ"עֲצֶרֶת הִיא", כְּלוֹמַר שֶׁיּוֹם שְׁמִינִי הוּא עָצוּר בְּכָל מְלָאכָה וְלֹא הַשְּׁאָר יָמִים; אִי נַמֵּי, נָפִיק לֵיהּ מִ"הַשְּׁבִיעִי" הַכָּתוּב בְּפֶסַח "רְאֵה אָנֹכִי": "שֵׁשֶׁת יָמִים תֹּאכַל מַצּוֹת", שֶׁאָמְרוּ נָם זִכְרוֹנָם לִבְרָכָה: "וּבַיּוֹם הַשְּׁבִיעִי עֲצֶרֶת", הַשְּׁבִיעִי עָצוּר בְּכָל מְלָאכָה וְלֹא הַשִּׁשִּׁי.

וְאֵי זוֹ מְלָאכָה אֲסוּרָה אוֹ מֻתֶּרֶת, מְסָרָן הַכָּתוּב לַחֲכָמִים, וְאַחַר שֶׁהַדָּבָר מָסוּר בְּיָדָם, שֶׁלֹּא אָסְרָה הַתּוֹרָה אֶלָּא בְּמָה שֶׁיֹּאמְרוּ הֵם, חִלְקוּ הַמְּלָאכוֹת כְּפִי רְצוֹנָם וְדַעְתָּם; וְנִמְצָא שֶׁכָּל מְלָאכָה שֶׁאֲסָרוּהָ (זִכְרוֹנָם לִבְרָכָה) אֲסוּרָה לָנוּ מִדְּאוֹרַיְתָא, וַאֲשֶׁר הִתִּירוּ, גַּם־כֵּן מֻתָּר מִן הַתּוֹרָה, כִּי בְּיָדָם נִמְסַר אִסּוּר זֶה לְפִי מַשְׁמָעוּת הַנִּדְרָשׁ בַּכָּתוּב.

וְהֵם אָמְרוּ דֶּרֶךְ כְּלָל כָּל שֶׁכָּל מְלָאכָה שֶׁאִם לֹא יַעֲשֶׂה אוֹתָהּ בַּמּוֹעֵד יִמְּצָא בָהּ הֶפְסֵד הַרְבֵּה, מֻתָּר לַעֲשׂוֹתָהּ, וְזֶהוּ אָמְרָם: מַשְׁקִין בֵּית הַשְּׁלָחִין בַּמּוֹעֵד, כְּלוֹמַר גַּן יָרָק אוֹ כַּיּוֹצֵא בוֹ, שֶׁמַּשְׁקִין אוֹתוֹ תָמִיד, וְאִם לֹא יַשְׁקוּהוּ יִפָּסֵד; לְשׁוֹן שְׁלָחִין

---

7. If on the first and last days of Passover and *Sukkoth*, which are not both preceded and followed by [days of] holiness, work is forbidden, it should all the more certainly be forbidden on the intermediate days, which are both preceded and followed by [days of] holiness.

8. The noun *'atzereth*, "a solemn assembly," is derived from the same root as the verb *'atzar*, "to restrict"; hence it can connote the restriction of work.

9. Since the Writ has informed us that some work, but not all, is forbidden then, and it did not explain which is permitted and which is not (Rashi, TB Ḥagigah 18a, s.v. *ha haré lo'*).

10. TB Mo'éd Katan 2a.

va-ḥomer [reasoning from the less to the more] there, from the first and seventh days, which are not both preceded and followed by holiness, etc. [7]

Then there is one Sage who derives it from the verse, *you shall do no laborious work* (Leviticus 23:7, etc.); this is the view of R. Yosé of Galilee, and thus we interpret the verse according to him: i.e. on the first day, every kind of laborious work is forbidden, except what is necessary for [preparing] human food; however, on the intermediate days of the festival, not all kinds of laborious work are forbidden; rather, some are prohibited, and some permitted, the matter being given over to the Sages [to determine].

R. 'Akiva, though, learns it from the verse, *These are the appointed occasions, holy convocations* (Leviticus 23:4), which he applies to the festivals' intermediate days; and since the term "holy convocations" is written about them, that teaches that it is forbidden to do any work on them. Possibly, according to him, the fact that there are labors permitted then is derived from the phrase, *it is 'atzereth, a solemn assembly* (*ibid.* 36): i.e. on the eighth day all labor is *'atzur*, restricted, [8] but not on the other days. Alternatively, he may infer it from "the seventh" written in regard to Passover in *sidrah r'éh: Six days you shall eat unleavened bread* (Deuteronomy 16:8), whereupon our Sages of blessed memory said [about the phrase that follows], *and on the seventh day there shall be 'atzereth, a solemn assembly*: the seventh has all work *'atzur*, restricted on it, but not the sixth.

Now, as to which labor is forbidden and which permitted, Scripture gave the matter over to the Sages; [9] and since the matter was left in their hands, so that the Torah forbade nothing but what they would so declare, they divided the labors according to their wish and their thinking. Consequently, whatever kind of work they (of blessed memory) prohibited, is forbidden us by the law of the Torah; and what they permitted, is likewise allowed by the law of the Torah— since this prohibition was given over into their hands, according to the inference derived from the Writ.

Well, they said as a general rule that if there is any work which, if not performed during the holy occasion, will entail a large, major loss, it is permissible to do it. This is why they taught: [10] A *beth shalḥin*, a field needing irrigation regularly, may be watered on the intermediate days—in other words, a vegetable garden or anything similar which is

constantly watered, and if it is not irrigated, it will suffer damage;

כְּמוֹ שֶׁלַּהִין, מִלְּשׁוֹן מְשַׁלְהֵי, שֶׁהוּא צָמֵא לְמָיִם.

וְאָמְרוּ זִכְרוֹנָם לִבְרָכָה דִּכְשֶׁהוּא מַשְׁקֶה אוֹתוֹ לֹא יַשְׁקֵהוּ מִמֵּי הַבְּרֵכָה וּמִמֵּי הַגְּשָׁמִים, שֶׁיֵּשׁ בַּדָּבָר טֹרַח הַרְבֵּה, אֲבָל מַשְׁקִין אוֹתוֹ מִן הַמַּעְיָן, כְּלוֹמַר שֶׁמַּמְשִׁיכוֹ וּמַשְׁקֵהוּ בוֹ. הֲרֵי שֶׁהֶחְמִירוּ בָּזֶה קְצָת שֶׁלֹּא לִטְרֹחַ בַּדָּבָר טֹרַח רַב, מִפְּנֵי שֶׁזֶּה אֵינוֹ נַעֲשֶׂה אֶלָּא כְּדֵי שֶׁתִּהְיֶה גִּנָּתוֹ רַעֲנָנָה, דְּשֶׁמָּא תִיבַשׁ כֻּלָּהּ אוֹ מִקְצָתָהּ.

אֲבָל בְּכָל מְלָאכָה הָאֲבֵדָה אוֹ וַדַּאי קְרוֹבָה לְהֶפְסֵד אִם לֹא יַעֲשֶׂנָּה בַּמּוֹעֵד, כְּגוֹן מִי שֶׁיֵּשׁ לוֹ זֵיתִים וְיָרֵא שֶׁלֹּא יִפָּסְדוּ אִם לֹא יוֹצִיאוּ מֵהֶן שַׁמְנָן מִיָּד, אוֹ עֲנָבִים אִם לֹא יִדְרֹךְ אוֹתָם מִיָּד, אוֹ כָל דָּבָר כַּיּוֹצֵא בָהֶן, לֹא הֶחְמִירוּ בָּזֶה וְלֹא חָשׁוּ לְטֹרַח רַב, אֶלָּא עוֹשֶׂה בָהֶם כָּל צְרָכָיו בְּלֹא שׁוּם שִׁנּוּי, כְּדֶרֶךְ שֶׁהוּא עוֹשֶׂה בְּחֹל.

וְכֵן הִתִּירוּ זִכְרוֹנָם לִבְרָכָה לִבְצֹר בַּמּוֹעֵד כֶּרֶם שֶׁהִגִּיעַ זְמַנּוֹ לְהִבָּצֵר. וְעוֹד אָמְרוּ דֶרֶךְ כְּלָל בְּעִנְיָן זֶה, שֶׁהַהֶדְיוֹט תּוֹפֵר כְּדַרְכּוֹ וְהָאֻמָּן מַכְלִיב; וּבְוַדַּאי לֹא בִתְפִירָה לְבַד אָמְרוּ כֵן, אֶלָּא הוּא הַדִּין לְכָל הַמְּלָאכוֹת, לְפִי הַדּוֹמֶה.

וְשָׁאַלְתִּי פִּי מוֹרִי אִם נֹאמַר כֵּן בִּכְתִיבָה, שֶׁיִּכְתֹּב הַהֶדְיוֹט כְּדַרְכּוֹ, וְלֹא הִתִּירוּ לִי. אוּלַי מִפְּנֵי שֶׁמְּצָאֲנוּ בְּפֵרוּשׁ שֶׁאָסְרוּ זִכְרוֹנָם לִבְרָכָה לְהַגִּיהַּ אֲפִלּוּ אוֹת אַחַת בְּסֵפֶר הָעֲזָרָה, נַחְמִיר בִּכְתִיבָה.

וְאָסְרוּ לְכָל אָדָם שֶׁלֹּא יְכַוֵּן מְלַאכְתּוֹ בַּמּוֹעֵד, כְּלוֹמַר שֶׁיַּנִּיחַ מְלַאכְתּוֹ לְדַעַת קֹדֶם הַמּוֹעֵד בְּעִנְיָן שֶׁיַּעֲשֶׂה אוֹתָהּ בַּמּוֹעֵד מִפְּנֵי שֶׁהוּא פָנוּי, כִּי לֹא לַעֲסֹק בִּמְלָאכָה הֻקְבְּעוּ יְמֵי חֻלּוֹ שֶׁל מוֹעֵד, כִּי־אִם לִשְׂמֹחַ לִפְנֵי יְיָ, רְצוֹנִי לוֹמַר

---

11. Literally, it is drawn further. See MT *hilchoth yom tov* vii 2.

12. Or perhaps, that may become a lost cause.

13. This is apparent from TB Mo‘éd Katan 2b, etc.

14. TB Mo‘éd Katan 12b.

15. I.e. a tailor; *ibid.* 8b.

15a. This view is in accord with Rashba, *Responsa* III §273.

16. I.e. from which the *kohen gadol* read aloud on the Day of Atonement; hence it would serve the public need to repair the letter; nevertheless it is forbidden; *ibid.* 18b. (Instead of *b'séfer ha‘azarah*, "in the scroll of the Temple forecourt," our editions of the Talmud, following Rashi, have *b'séfer 'ezra*, "in the scroll of Ezra"—the Scribe—a completely accurate written Torah by which all others were compared and corrected. But see *Dikduké Sof'rim* that this is not the preferable reading.)

the Talmudic term *shalḥin* is like *shalhin,* deriving from *m'shalḥé,* which means thirsty for water.

Yet the Sages of blessed memory taught[10] that when he irrigates it, one should not do so with pond water or rain water, since the matter entails burdensome toil, but it should rather be watered from a spring. In other words, the water is led to flow on,[11] and with this it is irrigated. Thus they were slightly stringent about this, that nothing very tedious or burdensome should be done in the matter, since this may be done only in order that one's garden may remain green; for [otherwise] all or part of it may dry up.

However, in regard to every [other] labor that may mean a loss[12] or that is quite certainly likely to entail a loss if it is not done during the intermediate days—for example, if someone has olives and he fears they may spoil if their oil is not extracted from them at once, or [likewise] grapes, if they are not trodden (pressed) at once, or anything similar to these—about this they were not stringent, and were not concerned about great burdensome toil. Rather, one may do about them whatever is necessary, without any change from the way in which he would do it on an ordinary weekday.[13]

Similarly, our Sages of blessed memory permitted harvesting, on the intermediate days, a vineyard whose time to be harvested has come.[14] Furthermore, they said as a general rule in this matter that an ordinary, unskilled man may do sewing in his usual way, while a craftsman[15] may sew with irregular stitches. Now, certainly they did not mean this about sewing alone, but rather, the law is the same for all kinds of labor, as it would seem.

Well, I asked of my instructors if we should apply this rule to writing—that an unskilled person may write in his ordinary way; and they would not permit this for me.[15a] Perhaps because we find explicitly that our Sages of blessed memory forbade fixing even one character in the Torah scroll of the Temple forecourt,[16] we must be stringent about writing.

They forbade any man from intending (planning) his work for the intermediate festival days—in other words, deliberately leaving his work over before the holy occasion so that he can do it in the intermediate days, because he is free [then].[14] For not for busying oneself with work were the intermediate festival days set apart, but only for rejoicing before the Lord, by which I mean gathering in the houses of study and listening to the agreeable teachings of the Book [of the

לְהִתְקַבֵּץ בְּמִדְרָשׁוֹת וְלִשְׁמֹעַ נֹעַם אִמְרֵי סֵפֶר, הִלְכוֹת הַפֶּסַח בְּפֶסַח וְהִלְכוֹת עֲצֶרֶת בַּעֲצֶרֶת.

וְכָל הַמְכֻוָּן מְלַאכְתּוֹ בַּמּוֹעֵד וְעָשָׂה אוֹתָהּ, בֵּית־דִּין מְאַבְּדִין אוֹתָהּ וּמַפְקִירִין אוֹתָהּ לַכֹּל; וְאִם מֵת אוֹתוֹ שֶׁכִּוֵּן אוֹתָהּ בַּמּוֹעֵד, אֵין קוֹנְסִין בָּנוֹ אַחֲרָיו, וְגַם אֵין מוֹנְעִין הַבֵּן מִלַּעֲשׂוֹת אוֹתָהּ מְלָאכָה בַּמּוֹעֵד, כְּדֵי שֶׁלֹּא תֹאבַד; וְקוֹרֵא אֲנִי עַל זֶה: יָכִין וְצַדִּיק יִלְבָּשׁ.

וְדֶרֶךְ כְּלָל הִתִּירוּ זִכְרוֹנָם לִבְרָכָה לְכָל מִי שֶׁיֵּשׁ לוֹ צֹרֶךְ, כְּלוֹמַר שֶׁאֵין לוֹ מַה יֹּאכַל, לַעֲשׂוֹת כָּל מְלָאכָה; וְכֵן לְבַעַל הַבַּיִת הִתִּירוּ לַעֲשׂוֹת כָּל מְלָאכָה מִי שֶׁאֵין לוֹ מַה יֹּאכַל; וּפֵרוּשׁ אֵין לוֹ מַה יֹּאכַל, לְפִי הַדּוֹמֶה הוּא מִי שֶׁאֵין לוֹ מָעוֹת בַּמֶּה יִקְנֶה צְרָכָיו, וְאַף־עַל־פִּי שֶׁיֵּשׁ לוֹ בַיִת וּכְלֵי תַשְׁמִישׁ, שֶׁאֵין מְחַיְּבִין לוֹ לְאָדָם לִמְכֹּר כֵּלָיו.

וְיֶתֶר פְּרָטֵי חִלּוּקֵי מְלָאכוֹת הַמּוֹעֵד רַבּוּ עַד מְאֹד, וְכֻלָּן יִתְבָּאֲרוּ יָפֶה בְּמַסֶּכֶת מוֹעֵד קָטָן. וּכְלָל זֶה יִהְיֶה בְיָדְךָ: שֶׁהִלְכוֹת מוֹעֵד כְּהִלְכוֹת שְׁבוּתֵי שַׁבָּת, שֶׁאֵין לְךָ לָדַמּוֹת וּלְהוֹצִיא בָהֶן דָּבָר מִדַּבֵּר, כִּי פְעָמִים תִּמְצָא לְרַבּוֹתֵינוּ זִכְרוֹנָם לִבְרָכָה מַתִּירִין מְלָאכָה כְבֵדָה בְּעִנְיָן אֶחָד וּפְעָמִים יַחְמִירוּ עַל הַקַּלָּה בְּעִנְיָן אַחֵר. וְאַל תִּתְמַהּ עַל הַדָּבָר עִם הַהַקְדָּמָה שֶׁהִקְדַּמְתִּי, כִּי הַתּוֹרָה לֹא אָסְרָה וְלֹא הִתִּירָה בְחִלּוּל שֶׁל מוֹעֵד אֶלָּא בְמָה שֶׁיַּסְכִּימוּ הֵם; וְכֵן בְּעִנְיַן שְׁבוּתֵי שַׁבָּת וְיוֹם־טוֹב נִמְצָא בַּגְּמָרָא מְקוֹמוֹת שֶׁהֶעֱמִידוּ דִבְרֵיהֶם זִכְרוֹנָם לִבְרָכָה אֲפִלּוּ בִמְקוֹם תּוֹרָה, וּפְעָמִים מְקִלִּין בָּהֶן בְּמָקוֹם שֶׁרָאוּ טוֹב לְהָקֵל; וְלֹא דָבָר רֵיק בְּכָל דִּבְרֵיהֶם. וּזְכֹר בְּנִי כְּלָל זֶה, שֶׁהִלְכוֹת מוֹעֵד כְּהִלְכוֹת שְׁבוּתֵי שַׁבָּת, שֶׁאֵין דָּנִין בָּהֶן דָּבָר מִדַּבֵּר, וְאַל תִּטְעֶה בוֹ, כִּי גְדוֹלֵי עוֹלָם אֲמָרוּהוּ.

---

17. A Talmudic expression (TB Sanhedrin 101a) given verbatim, although *Shavu'oth* has no intermediate days.

18. TB Mo'éd Katan 12b; MT *hilchoth yom tov* vii 4.

19. *Ibid.* 13a; MT *ibid.*

20. TB Mo'éd Katan 13a.

21. Which may be done by the Torah's law.

21a. I.e. the Sages imposed their ban of *sh'vuth* even where it might prevent the observance of a law of the Torah.

22. I.e. R. Ḥama b. Giora in the name of Rav, R. Daniel b. K'tina, and perhaps 'Abbaye; TB Mo'éd Katan 12a.

Torah]: the laws of Passover on Passover, the laws of *Shavu'oth* on *Shavu'oth*, [and the laws of *Sukkoth* on *Sukkoth*].[17]

If anyone intends (plans) his work for the intermediate days and so does it, the *beth din* (court) is to destroy it or make it ownerless, free for all.[18] However, if the one who planned it for the intermediate days died, his son is not thus penalized after him, nor is the son to be prevented from doing that work on the intermediate days so that it should not be lost [to him entirely].[19] To this we apply the verse, *he may prepare it, but the just shall wear it* (Job 27:17).

Generally the Sages of blessed memory permitted anyone who has a need, i.e. who hasn't anything to eat, to do any kind of work. They likewise permitted a householder to do any kind of work for the need of one who has not what to eat.[20] One who "has not what to eat" would seem to mean a person who hasn't the money with which to buy his needs, even if he has a house and utensils; for a man is not to be required to sell his utensils.

The remaining details about differences among kinds of labor on the intermediate days are very numerous indeed; and they are all well explained in the Talmud tractate *Mo'éd Katan*. But let this rule ever be in your hand: The laws of the intermediate days are like the laws of *sh'vuth*, abstention from certain labors on the Sabbath by the Sages' decree.[21] You cannot compare any one thing to another or derive any one thing from another among them. For at times you will find that our Sages of blessed memory permit some heavy, major labor in one situation, while at other times they are stringent about something light or minor in another situation. But you should not wonder about the matter, in view of the preface with which I began, that the Torah neither forbade nor permitted on the intermediate festival days anything other than what they [the Sages] decided. So too, regarding *sh'vuth*, abstention from certain labors on the Sabbath and festival days,[21] we find instances in the Talmud where the Sages of blessed memory set their rulings firmly even where a Torah law is involved;[21a] and at times they were lenient about them in a case where they saw fit to be lenient. But there is nothing empty (meaningless) in all their words. Then remember, my son, this rule: in the laws of the intermediate days, as in the laws of abstention from work on the Sabbath by the Sages' decree, no one thing is to be deduced from anything else. Do not make any mistake about it, because the great authorities of the world said this.[22]

⟨351⟩

וְדַעַת הָרַמְבַּ"ם זִכְרוֹנוֹ לִבְרָכָה שֶׁכָּל מְלָאכָה בְּחֻלּוֹ שֶׁל מוֹעֵד אֵינָהּ אֶלָּא
מִדִּבְרֵי סוֹפְרִים; וְכָל אוֹתָן הַכְּתוּבִים שֶׁאָמַרְנוּ לְמַעְלָה שֶׁהֵם בְּרֵישׁ מַסֶּכֶת מַשְׁקִין,
יִרְצֶה הָרַב לוֹמַר דְּאַסְמַכְתָּא בְּעָלְמָא נִינְהוּ. וְהָרַמְבַּ"ן זִכְרוֹנוֹ לִבְרָכָה וְרַבִּים עִמּוֹ
אָמְרוּ שֶׁעִקַּר מְלָאכָה אָסוּר בּוֹ מִן הַתּוֹרָה, כְּמוֹ שֶׁכָּתַבְנוּ, וּפְרָטֵי הַמְּלָאכוֹת
וְחִלּוּקֵיהֶן נִמְסְרוּ לַחֲכָמִים זִכְרוֹנָם לִבְרָכָה.

[מִצְוַת נְטִילַת לוּלָב]

שכד מִצְוַת לוּלָב, שֶׁנִּקַּח בְּיוֹם רִאשׁוֹן שֶׁל חַג הַסֻּכּוֹת בְּיָדֵינוּ פְּרִי עֵץ הָדָר,
כַּפּוֹת תְּמָרִים, וַעֲנַף עֵץ עָבוֹת וְעַרְבֵי נַחַל, שֶׁנֶּאֱמַר: וּלְקַחְתֶּם לָכֶם בַּיּוֹם הָרִאשׁוֹן
פְּרִי עֵץ הָדָר כַּפֹּת תְּמָרִים וַעֲנַף עֵץ עָבֹת וְעַרְבֵי נָחַל; וּבָא הַפֵּרוּשׁ כִּי פְּרִי עֵץ
הָדָר זֶה הָאֶתְרוֹג, וְכַפּוֹת תְּמָרִים הוּא הַלּוּלָב, וְנִכְתַּב "כַּפֹּת" חָסֵר, בְּלֹא ו', לִרְמֹז
שֶׁהַחַיָּיב שֶׁנִּקַּח לוּלָב אֶחָד וְלֹא שְׁנַיִם וּשְׁלֹשָׁה אוֹ יוֹתֵר; וַעֲנַף עֵץ עָבוֹת הוּא
הַהֲדַס, וְעַרְבֵי נַחַל הִיא הָעֲרָבָה הַיְדוּעָה בְּיִשְׂרָאֵל.

מִשָּׁרְשֵׁי הַמִּצְוָה, הַקְדָּמָה: כְּבָר כָּתַבְתִּי לְךָ, בְּנִי, כַּמָּה פְעָמִים בְּמַה שֶּׁקָּדַם,
שֶׁהָאָדָם נִפְעָל כְּפִי פְּעֻלּוֹתָיו שֶׁיַּעֲשֶׂה תָמִיד, וְרַעְיוֹנָיו וְכָל עֶשְׁתּוֹנוֹתָיו נִתְפָּשׂוֹת
אַחֲרֵי פֹעַל יָדָיו, אִם טוֹב וְאִם רַע; וְעַל-כֵּן כִּי רָצָה הַמָּקוֹם לְזַכּוֹת עַמּוֹ יִשְׂרָאֵל
אֲשֶׁר בָּחַר, הִרְבָּה לָהֶם מִצְווֹת, לִהְיוֹת נַפְשָׁם מִתְפַּעֶלֶת בָּהֶן לְטוֹבָה תָּמִיד כָּל
הַיּוֹם.

וּמִכְּלַל הַמִּצְווֹת שֶׁצִּוָּנוּ, לְהַתְפִּישׂ מַחֲשַׁבְתֵּנוּ בַּעֲבוֹדָתוֹ בְּטָהֳרָה, הִיא מִצְוַת
הַתְּפִלִּין, לִהְיוֹתָן מוּנָחִין כְּנֶגֶד אֵבְרֵי הָאָדָם הַיְדוּעִים בּוֹ לְמִשְׁכַּן הַשֵּׂכֶל, וְהֵם הַלֵּב
וְהַמֹּחַ, וּמִתּוֹךְ פָּעֳלוּ זֶה, תָּמִיד יְיַחֵד כָּל מַחְשְׁבוֹתָיו לְטוֹב, וְיִזְכֹּר וְיִזָּהֵר תָּמִיד כָּל

---

23. MT *bilchoth yom tov* vii 1.

24. I.e. they lend an overtone of authority to the ruling of the Sages, but do not
give it a basis in Torah law. As others explain it, the Torah thus hints at these laws but
does not expressly command them; hence they are enactments of the Sages.

25. So Ramban, and Rashba as cited in R. Nissim, commentaries to TB Mo'éd
Katan, beginning. Cf. also Ramban on TB 'Avodah Zarah 22a, s.v. *ha de'akshinnan*; and
idem on Leviticus 23:7.

§324   1. TB Sukkah 35a.

Now, it is the view of Rambam of blessed memory[23] that the entire prohibition of work on the intermediate festival days is only by the ruling of the Scribes [the Sages]; as for all those verses of Scripture that we cited above, the master scholar is inclined to say that they are mere supportive derivations.[24] However, Ramban of blessed memory, and many with him, said that the main [basic] forbiddance of work then is by the law of the Torah, as we have written, while the details of the labors and their differences were given over to the Sages [to determine].[25]

[THE PRECEPT OF TAKING UP THE LULAV ON THE FIRST DAY OF SUKKOTH]

324 the precept of the *lulav* (palm branch)—that on the first day of the *Sukkoth* festival we should take in our hand "the fruit of a goodly tree, branches of palm trees, and boughs of thick trees, and willows of the brook": for it is stated, *And you shall take on the first day the fruit of goodly trees, branches of palm trees, and boughs of thick trees, and willows of the brook* (Leviticus 23:40). The explanation was given [in the Oral Tradition][1] that this "fruit of a goodly tree" means an *'ethrog* (citron); "branches of palm trees" means a *lulav*; the Hebrew for "branches" is spelled defectively, without a *vav*, so that it may be read as singular—to imply that the obligation is for us to take one palm branch, not two, three, or more; "and boughs of thick trees" denotes the myrtle; while "willows of the brook" means the willow branch known well among Jewry.

As to the root reason for the precept, [let me begin with] a preface: I have written you previously, my son, many times in the earlier pages, that a man is acted upon (influenced) according to his actions which he does continually; his concepts and all his thoughts are drawn after the activity of his hands, be they good or bad. Therefore, since the omnipresent God wished to bring merit to His people Israel (Jewry) that He chose, He increased and multiplied *mitzvoth*, that their spirit might be influenced by them toward the good, constantly, all the day.

Included among the *mitzvoth* that He commanded us so as to fasten our thought onto His worship and service in purity, is the precept of *t'fillin* (phylacteries), that they should rest against those organs of a man which are known to be the seat of the intelligence, i.e. the heart and the brain. Through this action of his, one will constantly focus all his thoughts toward the good, and he will remember and be careful

הַיּוֹם לְכַוֵּן כָּל מַעֲשָׂיו בְּיֹשֶׁר וּבְצֶדֶק.

וּכְמוֹ־כֵן מִצְוַת הַלּוּלָב עִם שְׁלֹשֶׁת מִינָיו מִזֶּה הַשֹּׁרֶשׁ הִיא: לְפִי שֶׁיְּמֵי הַחַג הֵם יְמֵי שִׂמְחָה גְדוֹלָה לְיִשְׂרָאֵל, כִּי הוּא עֵת אֲסִיפַת הַתְּבוּאוֹת וּפֵרוֹת הָאִילָן [אֶל] הַבַּיִת, וְאָז יִשְׂמְחוּ בְנֵי־אָדָם שִׂמְחָה רַבָּה, וּמִפְּנֵי־כֵן נִקְרָא חַג הָאָסִיף; וְצִוָּה הָאֵל לַעֲמוֹ לַעֲשׂוֹת לְפָנָיו חַג בְּאוֹתוֹ הָעֵת, לְזָכּוֹתָם לִהְיוֹת עִקַּר הַשִּׂמְחָה לִשְׁמוֹ.

וּבִהְיוֹת הַשִּׂמְחָה מוֹשֶׁכֶת הַחֹמֶר הַרְבֵּה וּמְשַׁכַּחַת מִמֶּנּוּ יִרְאַת אֱלֹהִים בָּעֵת הַהִיא, צִוָּנוּ הַשֵּׁם לָקַחַת בֵּין יָדֵינוּ דְּבָרִים הַמַּזְכִּירִים אוֹתָנוּ כִּי כָל שִׂמְחַת לִבֵּנוּ לִשְׁמוֹ וְלִכְבוֹדוֹ; וְהָיָה מֵרְצוֹנוֹ לִהְיוֹת הַמַּזְכִּיר מִין הַמְשַׂמֵּחַ, כְּמוֹ שֶׁהָעֵת עֵת שִׂמְחָה, כִּי צֶדֶק כָּל אִמְרֵי פִיו, וְיָדוּעַ מִצַּד הַטֶּבַע כִּי אַרְבָּעָה הַמִּינִין כֻּלָּם מְשַׂמְּחֵי לֵב רוֹאֵיהֶם.

וְעוֹד יֵשׁ בְּאַרְבָּעָה מִינִין אֵלּוּ עִנְיָן אַחֵר, שֶׁהֵם דּוֹמִים לָאֵיבָרִים שֶׁבָּאָדָם הַיְקָרִים: שֶׁהָאֶתְרוֹג דּוֹמֶה לַלֵּב, שֶׁהוּא מִשְׁכַּן הַשֵּׂכֶל, לִרְמֹז שֶׁיַּעֲבֹד בּוֹרְאוֹ בְשִׂכְלוֹ; וְהַלּוּלָב דּוֹמֶה לַשִּׁדְרָה, שֶׁהִיא הָעִקָּר שֶׁבָּאָדָם, לִרְמֹז שֶׁיַּיְשִׁיר כָּל גּוּפוֹ לַעֲבוֹדָתוֹ בָּרוּךְ הוּא; וְהַהֲדַס דּוֹמֶה לָעֵינַיִם, לִרְמֹז שֶׁלֹּא יָתוּר אַחַר עֵינָיו בְּיוֹם שִׂמְחַת לִבּוֹ; וְהָעֲרָבָה דּוֹמָה לַשְּׂפָתַיִם, שֶׁבָּהֶן יִגְמֹר הָאָדָם כָּל מַעֲשֵׂהוּ בְּדִבּוּר, לִרְמֹז שֶׁיָּשִׂים רֶסֶן בְּפִיו וִיכַוֵּן דְּבָרָיו, וְיִירָא מֵהַשֵּׁם אַף בְּעֵת הַשִּׂמְחָה.

וְטַעַם שֶׁאֵינוּ נוֹהֵג בַּמְּדִינָה אֶלָּא יוֹם אֶחָד, לְפִי שֶׁיָּדוּעַ כִּי עִקַּר הַשִּׂמְחָה בְּיוֹם רִאשׁוֹן הוּא. וְאִם תִּשְׁאַל: שְׁמִינִי עֲצֶרֶת, שֶׁיֵּשׁ בּוֹ שִׂמְחָה גְדוֹלָה לְיִשְׂרָאֵל, לָמָּה לֹא הָיָה נִטָּל בּוֹ? — הַתְּשׁוּבָה, כִּי יוֹם שְׁמִינִי עֲצֶרֶת כֻּלּוֹ לַשֵּׁם, וּכְמוֹ שֶׁאָמְרוּ זִכְרוֹנָם לִבְרָכָה: מָשָׁל לְמֶלֶךְ שֶׁעָשָׂה סְעֻדָּה וְכוּלֵי, כִּדְאִיתָא בַּמִּדְרָשׁ, וְלַבְּסוֹף אָמַר לָהֶם: עַכְּבוּ עִמִּי יוֹם אֶחָד, שֶׁקָּשָׁה עָלַי פְּרִידַתְכֶם; וּלְפִיכָךְ נִקְרָא עֲצֶרֶת; וְאִם־כֵּן אֵין צָרִיךְ זִכָּרוֹן אַחֵר.

2. So Va-yikra Rabbah 30, 14; Tanḥuma, 'emor 19; ed. Buber, 25 (but without the interpretations of the resemblances given here).

3. I.e. when the Sanctuary was extant, following Leviticus 23:40; but after the Sanctuary was destroyed, Rabban Yoḥanan b. Zakkai instituted that the four should be taken up all seven days of the festival, to commemorate the practice at the Sanctuary (Mishnah, Sukkah iii 2); and this has remained the standard procedure.

4. In Midrash haGadol (Numbers 29:36, 518) we find: [We can liken it] to a king who had a happy occasion to celebrate. Said the king to his son, "I know that all the seven days of feasting you busied yourself with the guests. Now let you and me rejoice one day. I will not trouble you greatly, but only for one chicken and one measure of bread." So, all the seven days of the festival, the Israelites were busied with the offerings [on behalf] of the nations of the world.... Once the seven days of the festival ended, the Holy One, blessed is He, told the Israelites, "My sons, I know that all the seven days of the festival, you busied yourselves with the offerings for the nations of the world. Now I and you will rejoice for one day; and I will not trouble you for much, but only *one bullock, one ram* (Numbers 29:36)." (Cf. Tanḥuma, *pinḥas* 16; ed. Buber, 15; Bamidbar ⟨354⟩

all the day to regulate all his deeds in honesty and righteousness.

Similarly, the precept of the *lulav* with its three species is for this root reason. For the days of the festival are days of great rejoicing in Israel, because it is the time of the gathering of the crops and the fruit of the trees into the house; and then people rejoice in great happiness. For this reason it is called the harvest festival. Well, God commanded His people to celebrate a festival in His presence at that time, to make them meritorious, by having the essential rejoicing dedicated to Him.

Now, since joy greatly evokes the physical, material self and makes it forget reverent fear of God at that time, the Eternal Lord commanded us to take in our hands objects which will remind us that all the rejoicing of our heart [should be] for His sake and for His glory. It was His wish, too, that the reminding object should be a joy-giving species, just as the time is a season of happiness; for all the utterances of His word are righteous; and it is known in the ways of nature that all four species gladden the heart of those who behold them.

Moreover, another significance lies in these four species:[2] for they resemble the distinctive organs of a man. The *'ethrog* resembles the heart, the seat of the intelligence, to intimate that one should serve his Creator with his intelligence. The *lulav* is like the spine, the main element in a man, intimating that one should direct his entire body straight toward His worship (blessed is He). The myrtle resembles the eyes, to imply that one should not go straying about following his eyes on the day of his heart's rejoicing. And the willow is like the lips, with which a man completes every utterance of his in speaking— to intimate that one should put a bridle of restraint on his mouth and focus his words, being reverently fearful of the Eternal Lord even at the time of rejoicing.

The reason why it was observed in the regions [of Israel, outside the Sanctuary] for no more than one day,[3] is that it is known that the main rejoicing is on the first day. But you might ask: On *Sh'mini 'Atzereth* (the Eighth Day of Assembly) there is a great joy for Jewry; why is it [the *lulav*] not taken up then? The answer is that the day of *Sh'mini 'Atzereth* is entirely [devoted] to the Eternal Lord. As the Sages of blessed memory said: It can be likened to a parable of a king who made a feast, etc. as we read in the Midrash;[4] and at the end he said to them, "Stay with me yet one day, for your departure is hard for me to bear"; and it is therefore called *'atzereth,* "retention." That

being so, it requires no other remembrance.

וְחַג הַפֶּסַח אֵין צָרִיךְ הַזְכָּרָה בְּלוּלָב, שֶׁהֲרֵי מַצָּה וּמָרוֹר וְגוּפוֹ שֶׁל פֶּסַח בֵּין
יָדָיו, וְעוֹד שֶׁאֵינוֹ זְמַן שִׂמְחָה כְּמוֹ חַג הָאָסִיף; וְחַג הַשָּׁבוּעוֹת גַּם־כֵּן אֵין צָרִיךְ
הַזְכָּרָה אַחֶרֶת, כִּי עִקַּר הָרֶגֶל אֵינוֹ אֶלָּא מִצַּד מַתַּן תּוֹרָתֵנוּ, וְהִיא זִכְרוֹנֵנוּ הַגָּדוֹל
לְיַשֵּׁר כָּל אָרְחוֹתֵינוּ. זֶהוּ הַנִּרְאֶה לִי בְּעִנְיָנִים אֵלּוּ עַל צַד הַפְּשָׁט; וְהֶאֱמַנְתִּי כִּי יֵשׁ
אֶל הַמְקֻבָּלִים סוֹדוֹת נִפְלָאִים בְּמִצְוַת הַלּוּלָב וּשְׁלֹשֶׁת הַמִּינִים.

דִּינֵי הַמִּצְוָה, מַה שֶּׁאָמְרוּ זִכְרוֹנָם לִבְרָכָה שֶׁאַרְבָּעָה מִינִין אֵלּוּ מִצְוָה אַחַת הֵן,
וּמְעַכְּבִין זֶה אֶת זֶה בְּשֶׁאֵין לוֹ, אֲבָל אִם יֵשׁ לוֹ וּנְטָלָן בְּזֶה אַחַר זֶה יָצָא, דְּקַיְמָא
לָן לוּלָב אֵין צָרִיךְ אֶגֶד.

וְנוֹטְלִין לוּלָב אֶחָד וְאֶתְרוֹג אֶחָד וּשְׁנֵי בַדֵּי עֲרָבָה וּשְׁלֹשָׁה בַדֵּי הֲדַס כָּשֵׁר,
כְּלוֹמַר שֶׁיְּהוּ עָלָיו עֲשׂוּיִין תְּלָתָא תְּלָתָא בְּקַנָּא, כְּמוֹ שֶׁמְּפֹרָשׁ בַּגְּמָרָא; וְלָזֶה רָמַז
הַכָּתוּב כְּשֶׁקְּרָאוֹ עָבֹת; וְשִׁעוּר אָרְכּוֹ שֶׁל לוּלָב לְכָל הַפָּחוֹת אַרְבָּעָה טְפָחִים, וַהֲדַס
וַעֲרָבָה שְׁלֹשָׁה טְפָחִים עֲצֵבוֹת, שֶׁהֵן עֶשֶׂר אֶצְבָּעוֹת בְּגוּדָל; וְשִׁעוּר אֶתְרוֹג אֵין
פָּחוֹת מִכְּבֵיצָה.

וְדִין הַדְּבָרִים שֶׁהַלּוּלָב וְהָאֶתְרוֹג וְהָעֲרָבָה וְהַהֲדַס נִפְסָלִין בָּהֶן; וְדִין שֶׁתָּפִין
שֶׁקָּנוּ אֶתְרוֹג בְּשֻׁתָּפוּת, אוֹ אַחִין שֶׁקְּנָאוּהוּ מִתְּפִיסַת הַבַּיִת, שֶׁאִם קָנוּהוּ עַל דַּעַת
לָצֵאת בּוֹ, יוֹצְאִין בּוֹ כָּל אֶחָד מֵהֶם, וְאֵין צְרִיכִין זְכִיָּה זֶה מִזֶּה; כֵּן הוֹרוּ לָנוּ
מוֹרֵינוּ יִשְׁמְרֵם אֵל.

וְדִינֵי הַנַּעֲנוּעַ, שֶׁהַחִיּוּב לְהוֹלִיךְ וּלְהָבִיא וּלְהַעֲלוֹת וּלְהוֹרִיד; וְהָעִנְיָן לְעוֹרֵר
הַנֶּפֶשׁ שֶׁתִּזְכֹּר בְּעֵת הַשִּׂמְחָה כִּי הַכֹּל לַשֵּׁם, מִמַּעְלָה עַד מַטָּה וְאַרְבַּע רוּחוֹת,

---

Rabbah 21, 24.) For the part that follows, though, we find a basis only in Rashi to
Leviticus 23:36 and Numbers 29:36; likely, both Rashi and our text are based on another
Midrash, lost to us.

5. Which, as tradition teaches, took place on that day of the year.

6. Cf. Ramban to Leviticus 23:40.

7. TB M'nahoth 27a, as explained by *Halachoth G'doloth*, cited in *tosafoth* s.v.
lo' shanu.

8. TB Sukkah 34b.

9. *Ibid.* MT *hilchoth lulav* vii 8; on the handbreadth see §53, note 2.

10. TB Sukkah 29b, 32b, 34b.

11. Literally, "the seizure of the house."

12. Rashbam to TB Bava Bathra 137b, s.v. *v'im lav*; Rashba, cited in *Maggid
Mishneh* to MT *hilchoth lulav* viii 11, and in *Hiddushé Ritba* to TB Sukkah 41b. See
Rashba, *Responsa* I §62.

13. TB Sukkah 38a.

The festival of Passover requires no remembrance through the
lulav, since [one has] *matzah*, bitter herbs, and the Passover offering
itself between his hands; moreover, it is not such a time of rejoicing
as the harvest festival. The festival of *Shavu'oth* likewise requires no
other remembrance, since the main theme of the festival derives
only from the giving of our Torah;[5] this is our great remembrance
to set all our paths aright. This is what [significance] seems to me to
lie in these matters, from the aspect of the plain meaning. But I believe
that those who are the recipients of the mystic tradition possess wondrous secrets in regard to the *mitzvah* of *lulav* and the three [other]
species.[6]

As for the laws of the precept, there is what the Sages of blessed
memory said:[7] that these four species constitute one precept, and they
prevent one another [from being acceptable for fulfilling the precept]
when a person does not have [one of them]; but if he has them and he
takes them up one after the other [not together], he fulfills his obligation; for we have a standing rule: a *lulav* does not require binding
[the other three species to it].

We take one *lulav*, one *'ethrog*, two willow branches, and three
branches of an acceptable myrtle, which means that its leaves should
grow arranged in groups of three from a common point on a stem,
as it is explained in the Talmud.[8] Scripture implies this when it describes
it as thick. The length of the *lulav* must measure at least four handbreadths, and the myrtle and willow leaves, three narrow handbreadths,
which are ten thumb-lengths;[9] while the size of the *'ethrog* should
be not less than that of an egg.[8]

Then there is the law about things by which the *lulav*, *'ethrog*,
willow and myrtle branches are disqualified (become unacceptable);[10]
and the law for partners who bought an *'ethrog* in joint ownership,
or brothers who acquired it from the contents of the house (an un-
divided inheritance)[11]—that if they acquired it with the intention of
fulfilling the obligation with it, they acquit themselves of it [the
obligation] each in turn, and they do not need to take formal possession
of it, each from the other. So our master teachers, God protect them,
instructed us.[12]

There are, further, the laws of waving [the *lulav*], the obligation
being to wave it forward, backward, upward and downward.[13]
The purpose is to arouse the spirit, that it may remember during the
⟨357⟩   rejoicing that all is the Eternal Lord's, from above, on high, to below,

שֶׁהַכֹּל נִכְלָל בָּזֶה; וְיֶתֶר פְּרָטֶיהָ, מְבֹאָרִים בְּמַסֶּכֶת סֻכָּה.

וְנוֹהֶגֶת בְּכָל מָקוֹם וּבְכָל זְמַן, בַּזְּכָרִים וְלֹא בַּנְּקֵבוֹת. וְעוֹבֵר עָלֶיהָ וְלֹא נָטַל אַרְבָּעָה מִינִין אֵלּוּ בְּיוֹם רִאשׁוֹן שֶׁל חַג הַסֻּכּוֹת שֶׁלֹּא חָל בְּשַׁבָּת בְּכָל מָקוֹם, וְכֵן בְּכָל שִׁבְעָה בַּמִּקְדָּשׁ, בִּטֵּל עֲשֵׂה זֶה. וּבַמִּקְדָּשׁ הָיָה נָטַל בְּיוֹם רִאשׁוֹן אֲפִלּוּ בְּשַׁבָּת.

[מִצְוַת יְשִׁיבַת סֻכָּה]

שׁכה מִצְוַת סֻכָּה, שֶׁנִּצְטַוֵּינוּ לָשֶׁבֶת בְּסֻכָּה שִׁבְעַת יָמִים, שֶׁנֶּאֱמַר: בַּסֻּכֹּת תֵּשְׁבוּ שִׁבְעַת יָמִים. וְיוֹם רִאשׁוֹן הוּא יוֹם ט״ו בְּתִשְׁרֵי.

מִשָּׁרְשֵׁי הַמִּצְוָה, מַה שֶּׁמְּפֹרָשׁ בַּכָּתוּב, לְמַעַן נִזְכֹּר הַנִּסִּים הַגְּדוֹלִים שֶׁעָשָׂה הָאֵל בָּרוּךְ הוּא לַאֲבוֹתֵינוּ בַּמִּדְבָּר בְּצֵאתָם מִמִּצְרַיִם, שֶׁסִּכְּכָם בְּעַנְנֵי כָבוֹד שֶׁלֹּא יַזִּיק לָהֶם הַשֶּׁמֶשׁ בַּיּוֹם וְקָרַח בַּלַּיְלָה; וְיֵשׁ שֶׁפֵּרְשׁוּ שֶׁסֻּכּוֹת מַמָּשׁ עָשׂוּ בְּנֵי־יִשְׂרָאֵל בַּמִּדְבָּר; וּמִתּוֹךְ זְכִירַת נִפְלְאוֹתָיו שֶׁעָשָׂה עִמָּנוּ וְעִם אֲבוֹתֵינוּ, נִזָּהֵר בְּמִצְווֹתָיו בָּרוּךְ הוּא, וְנִהְיֶה רְאוּיִים לְקַבָּלַת הַטּוֹבָה מֵאִתּוֹ, וְזֶהוּ חֶפְצוֹ בָּרוּךְ הוּא, שֶׁחָפֵץ לְהֵיטִיב.

מִדִּינֵי הַמִּצְוָה, מַה שֶּׁאָמְרוּ זִכְרוֹנָם לִבְרָכָה: סֻכָּה שֶׁהִיא גְּבוֹהָה לְמַעְלָה מֵעֶשְׂרִים אַמָּה פְּסוּלָה, וְכֵן אִם הִיא נְמוּכָה לְמַטָּה מֵעֲשָׂרָה טְפָחִים; וּבְרָחְבָּהּ צָרִיךְ שִׁבְעָה טְפָחִים עַל שִׁבְעָה, וּפָחוֹת מִכֵּן פְּסוּלָה; וּצְרִיכָה שָׁלֹשׁ דְּפָנוֹת, וְצוּרַת פֶּתַח, שֶׁהִיא קָנֶה מִכָּאן וּמִכָּאן וְקָנֶה עַל גַּבֵּיהֶן.

וְדִין צִלָּתָהּ מְרֻבָּה מֵחַמָּתָהּ שֶׁכְּשֵׁרָה, וְאִם לָאו פְּסוּלָה, וְהַמְעֻבָּה כְּמִין בַּיִת כְּשֵׁרָה, וְדִין הָעוֹשֶׂה סֻכָּתוֹ בֵּין הָאִילָנוֹת וְהָאִילָנוֹת דְּפָנוֹת לָהּ, וְדִין הָעוֹשֶׂה סֻכָּתוֹ

---

14. Because it is a positive precept "caused by time," i.e. obligatory when a specific time comes.

15. Because then the obligation is by the law of the Torah; see note 3.

16. See Mishnah, Sukkah iv 4; MT *bilchoth lulav* vii 16.

§325 1. Leviticus 23:43, *that your generations may know that I had the people of Israel dwell in booths when I brought them out of the land of Egypt.*

2. So Targum Onkelos; Mechilta, *b'shallaḥ*; and R. 'Eli'ezer in TB Sukkah 11b.

3. E.g. R. 'Akiva, TB *ibid.*

4. TB Sukkah 2a.

5. Literally, in its width; *ibid.* 3a, 16a.

6. *Ibid.* 6b–7a. As MY notes, this last sentence is patently only a general, but imprecise, statement (evidently to mention a subject for further study by the author's son and his young friends). For it is clear from TB Sukkah 6b that with three complete walls, no form of a door is required; and under certain conditions, two adjacent whole walls and a bit of a third, or two facing whole walls with part of a third and also a rudimentary door, are sufficient.

7. Coming through the roofing, which must consist of material that grew naturally

and in the four directions; for in this, all is included. The rest of its details are explained in the Talmud tractate *Sukkah*.

It is in effect in every place and every time, for men, but not for women. [14] If someone violated this and did not take these four species on a first day of *Sukkoth* that did not fall on a Sabbath, in any location, and so likewise on any of the seven days at the Sanctuary, he would disobey this positive precept. [15] At the Sanctuary they were taken up on the first day even if it was the Sabbath. [16]

325 [THE MITZVAH OF DWELLING IN A SUKKAH] the precept of the *sukkah*—that we were commanded to dwell in a *sukkah* (booth) seven days: as it is stated, *You shall abide in booths seven days* (Leviticus 23:42), the first day being the fifteenth of Tishri.

At the root of the precept lies what is distinctly explained in Scripture: [1] It is in order that we should remember the great miracles which God (blessed is He) wrought for our fathers in the wilderness when they went out of Egypt. For He formed a covering of clouds of glory for them, [2] so that the sun should not injure them by day, or frost at night. And there are those who explained [3] that the Israelites actually made *sukkoth*, booths in the wilderness. Then thus remembering His wonders that He did with us and with our forefathers, we will take care to observe His precepts (blessed is He), and will be worthy of receiving the good reward from Him. This is His desire, blessed is He, as He delights in bestowing good.

Among the laws of the precept, there is what the Sages of blessed memory taught: [4] If a *sukkah* is more than twenty cubits in height, it is disqualified (unacceptable); and so too if it is less than ten handbreadths in height. In its surface area [5] it requires seven handbreadths by seven; and if it is smaller than that, it is unacceptable. It needs to have, moreover, [at least] three walls and the [rudimentary] form of a door, which means a stick (beam) on either side and a stick (beam) on top of them. [6]

There is, too, the law about its shade being more than its sunlight: [7] then it is acceptable; and if not, it is disqualified. [4] If it has a thickened covering, quite like a house, it is acceptable. [8] We have, too, the law if someone makes his *sukkah* among the trees, and the trees constitute its walls; [9] the law if someone makes his *sukkah* atop a wagon or atop [on the deck of] a ship; [10] the law that if someone made a roof of

בְּרֹאשׁ הָעֲגָלָה אוֹ בְּרֹאשׁ הַסְּפִינָה, וְדִין סְכַךְ עַל־גַּבֵּי אַכְסַדְרָה שֶׁיֵּשׁ לָהּ פְּצִימִין, בֵּין מִבִּפְנִים בֵּין מִבַּחוּץ, כְּשֵׁרָה.

וְדִין הַסְּכַךְ שֶׁהַחִיּוּב לַעֲשׂוֹתוֹ מִדָּבָר שֶׁאֵינוֹ מְקַבֵּל טֻמְאָה, כְּגוֹן פְּסֹלֶת גֹּרֶן וָיֶקֶב, אֲבָל לֹא בְדָבָר הַמְּקַבֵּל טֻמְאָה; וְדִין סְכַךְ פָּסוּל בָּאֶמְצַע אוֹ מִן הַצַּד; וְדִין אֲוִיר שְׁלֹשָׁה שֶׁפּוֹסֵל בֵּין בָּאֶמְצַע בֵּין מִן הַצַּד בְּסֻכָּה קְטַנָּה; וְדִין פֵּרַשׂ עָלֶיהָ סָדִין מִפְּנֵי הַחַמָּה אוֹ תַחְתֶּיהָ מִפְּנֵי הַנֶּשֶׁר, שֶׁפְּסוּלָה; פְּרָסָן לְנָאוֹתָהּ, כְּשֵׁרָה, שֶׁכָּל לְנָאוֹתָהּ כְּשֵׁרָה.

וְדִין סְכַךְ עַל־גַּבֵּי סְכַךְ; וְדִין יָשֵׁן בְּכִילָה בְּסֻכָּה, שֶׁאִם יֵשׁ לָהּ גַּג, אֲפִלּוּ גַּג טֶפַח, אָסוּר, וְאִם לָאו מֻתָּר; וְהַיָּשֵׁן תַּחַת הַמִּטָּה בְּסֻכָּה, שֶׁאִם גָּבוֹהָה עֲשָׂרָה טְפָחִים אָסוּר, וְאִם לָאו מֻתָּר; וְאַף־עַל־גַּב דְּבִקְינוֹפוֹת אָסוּר אַף־עַל־גַּב דְּלָא גְּבוֹהַּ עֲשָׂרָה, שֶׁאֲנִי מִטָּה הוֹאִיל וּלְגַבָּהּ הִיא עֲשׂוּיָה; וְהַפּוֹרֵס סָדִין עַל שְׁנֵי נַקְלִיטִין, מֻתָּר לִישֹׁן תַּחְתָּיו, לְפִי שֶׁאֵין לוֹ גַּג, וַהֲרֵי הוּא כְמִי שֶׁעוֹשֶׂה חָלָל בַּאֲצִילֵי יָדָיו, שֶׁזֶּה וַדַּאי מֻתָּר.

וְדִין סֻכָּה גְּזוּלָה שֶׁכְּשֵׁרָה, לְפִי שֶׁאֵין קַרְקַע נִגְזֶלֶת; וַאֲפִלּוּ גָּזַל הָעֵצִים וְעָשָׂה מֵהֶן סֻכָּה, כְּשֵׁרָה, מִתַּקָּנַת חֲכָמִים שֶׁתִּקְּנוּ לְשַׁלֵּם דְּמֵי עֵצִים, וְדִין הַמִּצְטַעֵר, שֶׁפָּטוּר מִן הַסֻּכָּה, שֶׁהַתּוֹרָה אָמְרָה "תֵּשְׁבוּ", כְּעֵין תָּדוּרוּ, וְכָל־שֶׁכֵּן חוֹלֶה, שֶׁפָּטוּר גַּם־כֵּן מִטַּעַם זֶה, וַאֲפִלּוּ מְשַׁמְּשֵׁי חוֹלֶה פְּטוּרִין, וְכָל שְׁלוּחֵי מִצְוָה; וְכֵן חָתָן וְכָל חֲבוּרָתוֹ, דִּמְצְוָה עָבְדֵי.

<hr />

from roots in the soil and was detached; e.g. tree branches.

8. *Ibid.* 22a.

9. *Ibid.* 23b.

10. *Ibid.* 22b–23a.

11. I.e. a courtyard between several houses is used for a *sukkah*, the walls of the houses serving as its walls. One of the houses, though, has not a wall but an open porch facing the courtyard, and the roofing material is begun from the roof of the porch and extended to cover the courtyard. If the porch is more than four cubits deep, the *sukkah* is unacceptable, because the house's wall is too far away from where the *sukkah*'s roofing properly begins (beyond the porch). But if there are vertical poles or anything similar at the edge of the veranda, with less than three handbreadths between one pole and another, that is considered as a wall, and the *sukkah* is acceptable; TB Sukkah 17a. Even if the poles do not extend for the whole length of the porch, and one makes the *sukkah* including that part of the veranda which has no poles (or lattice-work, etc.) it is acceptable; *ibid.* 19a. The first instance is indicated by the words "whether within" in the text; the second case, by the term "without."

12. *Ibid.* 11a, 12a.

13. R. Isaac 'Alfasi, Sukkah i; MT *hilchoth sukkah* v 13. MY notes that this last phrase, "if it is a small *sukkah*," evidently applies in a general way to both the laws on disqualified roofing material and on empty space; for as MH writes, the law about three handbreadths of empty space applies as well to a large *sukkah*.

branches [from] above a veranda (porch) which has poles, whether within or without, it is acceptable.[11]

There is, further, the law about the roofing material: that the obligation is to make it of something that cannot become subject to ritual uncleanness, such as the waste of the threshing-floor [straw from the grain] and the wine-press [twigs from the grapes], but not of anything that can acquire ritual defilement;[12] the law of unacceptable, disqualified roofing in the middle or at the side and the law about a space of three [handbreadths in the roofing], that it disqualifies [the sukkah] whether it is in the middle or at the side—if it is a small sukkah [of minimum size].[13] [Then we have] the law if a person spread a sheet over it [over the roofing] against the sun, or under it on account of bits dropping [from the covering branches]—that it is disqualified; but if he spread them to decorate it, it is acceptable; for whatever [is done] for its decoration, it remains acceptable.[14]

In addition, there is the law about one sukkah atop another;[15] and the law about one who sleeps in a canopied bed[16]—that if it has a roof, even a roof of one handbreadth [in width],[17] it is forbidden, and if not, it is permissible;[18] and if someone sleeps beneath a bed in a sukkah—that if it is ten handbreadths high, he is forbidden, and if not, he is permitted.[18] Even though a bed curtained on four poles is forbidden even if it is not ten handbreadths high, a bed is different because it was made for sleeping on it.[19] If someone spreads a sheet over two bedstead poles[20] it is permissible for him to sleep underneath it, because it has no roof, and hence it is as though he made a separate space [over him] with his forearms, which is certainly permissible.[18]

Moreover, there is the law of a sukkah seized by force: that it is acceptable, because land cannot be taken in robbery.[21] Even if a person took pieces of wood by robbery and made a sukkah of them, it is acceptable, because of the ruling of the Sages, who instituted that the value of the wood should be paid.[22] Then we have the law about a person who finds it painful,[23] that he is free of the obligation of sukkah: for the Torah said, You shall abide (Leviticus 23:42), which is akin to "You shall dwell"; and all the more certainly is a sick person equally free of the obligation, for the same reason.[24] Even those who attend an ill person are not obligated, and so all who are sent on the mission of a mitzvah (religious duty).[24] So too a bridegroom and his entire entourage, for they are carrying out a religious duty.[24]

וְדִין הוֹלְכֵי דְרָכִים וְשׁוֹמְרֵי גַנּוֹת וּפַרְדֵּסִים וְשׁוֹמְרֵי הָעִיר; וְדִין יָרְדוּ גְשָׁמִים;
וְדִין סָכַּת גנב"ש ורקב"ש, שֶׁכְּשֵׁרָה, וְדִין עֲצֵי סָכָּה, שֶׁאֲסוּרִין כָּל שִׁבְעָה
מִדְּאוֹרַיְתָא, וּבַיּוֹם הַשְּׁמִינִי וּתְשִׁיעִי בַּגּוֹלָה אֲסוּרִין מִשּׁוּם מֻקְצֶה, וְנוֹיֵי סֻכָּה
אֲסוּרִין מִשּׁוּם בִּזּוּיֵי מִצְוָה, מִשֵּׁם הָרַמְבַּ"ן זִכְרוֹנוֹ לִבְרָכָה. וְיֶתֶר רֻבֵּי פְּרָטֶיהָ,
מְבֹאָרִים בַּמַּסֶּכְתָּא הַבְּנוּיָה עַל זֶה, וְהִיא מַסֶּכֶת סֻכָּה.

וְנוֹהֶגֶת בְּכָל מָקוֹם וּבְכָל זְמַן, בִּזְכָרִים אֲבָל לֹא בִנְקֵבוֹת. וְעוֹבֵר עַל זֶה וְלֹא
אָכַל אֲכִילָה שֶׁל פַּת בַּסֻּכָּה, אוֹ שֶׁלֹּא יָשַׁן בָּהּ וַאֲפִלּוּ שְׁנַת עֲרַאי, וְהוּא שֶׁלֹּא יִהְיֶה
חוֹלֶה אוֹ מִצְטַעֵר אוֹ פָטוּר מֵחֲמַת הַדְּבָרִים שֶׁאָמַרְנוּ, בִּטֵּל עֲשֵׂה זֶה. וּכְבָר כָּתַבְתִּי
לְמַעְלָה שֶׁבֵּית דִּין כּוֹפִין עַל בִּטּוּל עֲשֵׂה.

וְלַיְלָה הָרִאשׁוֹן חַיָּב כָּל אָדָם מִדְּאוֹרַיְתָא לֶאֱכֹל בָּהּ כְּזַיִת פַּת לְכָל הַפָּחוֹת.
שְׁאָר הַיָּמִים רְשׁוּת, שֶׁאִם רָצָה לֶאֱכֹל חוּץ לַסֻּכָּה אוֹכֵל, וּבִלְבַד שֶׁלֹּא יֹאכַל
אֲכִילַת קֶבַע שֶׁל פַּת אֶלָּא בַסֻּכָּה; וַחֲסִידִים הָרִאשׁוֹנִים לֹא הָיוּ אוֹכְלִין שׁוּם דָּבָר
כִּי־אִם בַּסֻּכָּה.

בְּהַר סִינַי

יֵשׁ בָּהּ כ"ד מִצְווֹת: שֶׁבַע מִצְווֹת עֲשֵׂה וּשְׁבַע־עֶשְׂרֵה מִצְווֹת לֹא־תַעֲשֶׂה.

[שֶׁלֹּא נַעֲבֹד הָאֲדָמָה בַּשָּׁנָה הַשְּׁבִיעִית]

שכו שֶׁלֹּא נַעֲבֹד הָאֲדָמָה בַּשָּׁנָה הַשְּׁבִיעִית, שֶׁהִיא נִקְרֵאת שְׁנַת הַשְּׁמִטָּה,
שֶׁנֶּאֱמַר: וּבַשָּׁנָה הַשְּׁבִיעִית... שָׂדְךָ לֹא תִזְרָע.
שֹׁרֶשׁ מִצְוָה זוֹ וּפְרָטֶיהָ וְכָל עִנְיָנֶיהָ כָּתוּב בְּ"כֶּסֶף תַּלְוֶה" עֲשֵׂה ד' [פָּרָשַׁת

14. TB Sukkah 10a.
15. *Ibid.* 9b.
16. More accurately, a bed with poles at the four corners, which can bear curtains, a canopy, etc.
17. I.e. the bed is canopied, and the curtains slope upward from the two sides toward the middle, until at the top they form a "roof" of one handbreadth in width.
18. TB Sukkah 10b.
19. Therefore, if someone sleeps under it and it is not ten handbreadths above the ground, it is acceptable, because it does not constitute a separate, disqualifying tent; *ibid.*
20. Rising from the center of the head and foot of the bed.
21. Hence it remains the property of the owner; TB Sukkah 31a.
22. But the *sukkah* need not be dismantled so that the wood itself can be returned; hence the *sukkah* is the robber's, and he has only an obligation to pay for the wood; *ibid.*

Then there is the law about those journeying on the roads, watchmen of gardens and orchards, and sentries of a town;[25] the law if
rain fell;[26] the law on the *sukkah* (booth) of a non-Jew, a woman, an
animal [its stall], a Cuthite; a shepherd, a watchman over drying
produce, a city sentry, or a watchman over a field—that it is acceptable.[27] And we have the law about the wood of a *sukkah*: that it is
forbidden [for any use] all seven days by the law of the Torah; and
on the eighth day, and the ninth in the Diaspora, it is forbidden for
use by the law of *muktzeh*.[28] Decorations of a *sukkah* are forbidden
[for any use] because it indicates the scornful treatment of a precept, in
the view of Ramban of blessed memory.[29]

[These] and its numerous other details are clarified in the Talmud
tractate composed about this, i.e. the tractate *Sukkah*. It is in effect
everywhere, at every time, for men, but not for women. If a person
violates this and does not eat a piece of bread in the *sukkah*, or does
not sleep in it even to take a nap[30]—provided he is not sick and does
not find it painful, and is not free of the obligation on account of the
matters we mentioned—he disobeys this positive precept. I wrote
previously, above (§6), that the *beth din* is to bring force to bear over
the disobedience of a positive precept.

On the first night every man is obligated by the law of the Torah
to eat in it an olive's amount of bread at least. The rest of the days, it
is a voluntary matter: If a person wishes to eat outside (away from)
the *sukkah*, he may eat, provided he does not have a set (regular) meal
of bread anywhere but in the *sukkah*.[31] The early men of piety, though,
would eat nothing whatever anywhere but in the *sukkah*.[32]

sidrah b'har
(Leviticus 25–26:2)

It contains twenty-four precepts: seven positive and seventeen negative.

[THE PROHIBITION AGAINST WORKING THE EARTH
DURING THE SABBATICAL YEAR]

326 that we should not work the soil in the seventh year, which is
called the year of *sh'mittah* (release): as it is stated, *But in the seventh
year . . . you shall not sow your field* (Leviticus 25:4).

The root purpose of this precept, its details, and all its subject-

מִשְׁפָּטִים סִי׳ פ״ד], וְקָחֵנּוּ מִשָּׁם. וְעוֹבֵר עַל זֶה וְעָבַד אַדְמָתוֹ בִּזְמַן הַבַּיִת בְּאַחַת
מִן הָעֲבוֹדוֹת הָאֲסוּרוֹת מִדְאוֹרַיְתָא, כְּמוֹ שֶׁאָמַרְנוּ שָׁם, לוֹקֶה.

[שֶׁלֹּא נַעֲבֹד עֲבוֹדָה גַּם בְּאִילָנוֹת]

שכז שֶׁלֹּא נַעֲשֶׂה עֲבוֹדָה גַּם בְּאִילָנוֹת בַּשָּׁנָה הַשְּׁבִיעִית, שֶׁנֶּאֱמַר: וְכַרְמְךָ לֹא
תִזְמֹר; וּלְשׁוֹן סִפְרֵי: "הַזֶּרַע וְהַנָּמִיר", פֵּרוּשׁ: לֹא תִזְרַע וְלֹא תִזְמֹר, "בַּכְּלָל הָיוּ",
כְּלוֹמַר בִּכְלָל שְׁבִיתָה הָיָה, שֶׁכְּבָר אָמַר: וְשָׁבְתָה הָאָרֶץ, וְכֵן: שְׁנַת שַׁבָּתוֹן יִהְיֶה
לָאָרֶץ; "וְלָמָּה יָצְאוּ—לְהַקִּישׁ אֲלֵיהֶם: מַה זֶּרַע וְזָמִיר מְיֻחָדִין, שֶׁהֵן עֲבוֹדָה
בָּאָרֶץ וּבָאִילָן" וְכוּלֵי, כִּדְאִיתָא הָתָם.

עִנְיַן מִצְוָה זוֹ כַּמִּצְוָה הַקּוֹדֶמֶת. וּקְצָת פְּרָטֶיהָ כָּתַבְתִּי גַּם-כֵּן בְּפָרָשַׁת "אִם
כֶּסֶף תַּלְוֶה" [מִשְׁפָּטִים סִי׳ פ״ד], תִּרְאֵנוּ מִשָּׁם.

[שֶׁלֹּא נִקְצֹר סְפִיחִים בַּשָּׁנָה הַשְּׁבִיעִית]

שכח שֶׁלֹּא נִקְצֹר מַה שֶּׁתַּצְמִיחַ הָאָרֶץ מֵעַצְמָהּ בַּשָּׁנָה הַשְּׁבִיעִית, וְלֹא מַה
שֶּׁתַּצְמִיחַ זוֹ בְּשָׁנָה זוֹ מִמַּה שֶׁנִּזְרַע בָּהּ בַּשָּׁנָה הַשִּׁשִּׁית, וְזֶהוּ נִקְרָא סָפִיחַ, שֶׁנֶּאֱמַר:
אֵת סְפִיחַ קְצִירְךָ לֹא תִקְצוֹר, רְצוֹנוֹ לוֹמַר שֶׁלֹּא נִקְצֹר אוֹתוֹ כְּדֶרֶךְ שֶׁאָנוּ קוֹצְרִין
תְּבוּאָתֵנוּ בִּשְׁאָר שָׁנִים; אֲבָל מִכָּל-מָקוֹם אֲכִילָתוֹ הֻתְּרָה לָנוּ, וּבִלְבַד שֶׁנֹּאכְלֵהוּ
דֶּרֶךְ הֶפְקֵר, כְּלוֹמַר בְּלִי הֲכָנָה, וּכְמוֹ שֶׁנִּפָרֵשׁ בַּמִּצְוָה שֶׁלְּפָנֵינוּ; כִּי לֹא תַקְפִּיד
הַתּוֹרָה בִּדְבָרִים אֵלּוּ זוּלָתִי שֶׁיֵּרָאֶה מִמַּעֲשֵׂה הָאָדָם בְּכָל עִנְיַן שָׁנָה זוֹ כְּאִלּוּ אֵין
דָּבָר מְיֻחָד בִּרְשׁוּתוֹ, רַק שֶׁהַכֹּל בִּרְשׁוּת אֲדוֹן הַכֹּל, וּכְמוֹ שֶׁאָמַרְנוּ לְמַעְלָה.

מִשָּׁרְשֵׁי הַמִּצְוָה זוֹ, מַה שֶּׁכָּתַבְנוּ בְּעִנְיָן זֶה בְּ"כֶּסֶף תַּלְוֶה" עָשֹׁה [מִשְׁפָּטִים
סִי׳ פ״ד].

---

23. Literally, *who suffers*—i.e. if he must stay in the *sukkah*, being delicate; or if it
is very cold, etc.

24. TB Sukkah 25a–26a.

25. *Ibid.* 26a.

26. *Ibid.* 28b–29a.

27. *Ibid.* 8b.

28. I.e. set apart for a use having no connection with the festival; hence it is then
forbidden to be used by the ruling of the Sages; *ibid.* 9a, 46b; and see *Maggid Mishneh* to
MT *hilchoth sukkah* vi 15.

29. Ramban, *Milḥamoth haShem*, *bétzah* iv; commentary to TB Shabbath 45a, s.v.
v'ikka l'médak.

30. I.e. if he eats the bread or naps outside the *sukkah*.

31. So TB Sukkah 27a. This means a piece of bread the size of an egg.

32. Rabban Yoḥanan b. Zakkai and Rabban Gamliel; *ibid.* 26b.

matter are written in *sidrah mishpatim*, precept §84; so gather it all from there. If someone violated this and worked his earth at the time the Temple was extant, by one of the labors forbidden by Torah law, as we stated there (§84), he should receive whiplashes.

[THE PROHIBITION ON DOING WORK ON TREES DURING THE SABBATICAL YEAR]

327 that we should do no work on trees as well in the seventh year, for it is stated, *nor shall you prune your vineyard* (Leviticus 25:4). In the language of the Midrash *Sifra*:[1] Sowing and pruning—meaning "you shall not sow" and "nor shall you prune"—were in the general rule; in other words, they were included in the general rule of cessation from work, since Scripture already stated, *the land shall keep a sabbath* (*ibid.* 2), and likewise, *it shall be a year of solemn rest for the land* (*ibid.* 5). Then why were they singled out?[2]—to compare all other labors with them: Just as it is characteristic of sowing and pruning that they are labors of the land and trees, etc.—as it is given there.[3]

The subject-matter of this precept is like that of the previous one. Some of its details I likewise wrote in *sidrah mishpatim* (§84); you can learn it from there.

[THE PROHIBITION AGAINST HARVESTING WHAT GROWS WILD IN THE SABBATICAL YEAR]

328 that we should not harvest what the land may sprout (grow) by itself in the seventh year, nor what it may sprout in this year from that which was sown in it in the sixth year, which is called the spontaneous (wild) growth—for it is stated, *What grows of itself in your harvest you shall not reap* (Leviticus 25:5), which means to say that we should not reap it in the way that we reap our ground crops in the other years; but in any event, it was permitted us to eat it as something ownerless—in other words, without preparation.[1] As we will explain in the precept that lies ahead of us (§329), the Torah is particular in these matters about nothing other than this: that it should appear from a man's behavior in every aspect during this year as though there is nothing specifically in his possession, but only that everything belongs to the [Divine] Ruler of all, as we stated above.

The root purpose of this precept is as I have written of this matter in *sidrah mishpatim* (§84).

Among the laws of the precept, there is what the Sages of blessed

מִדִּינֵי הַמִּצְוָה, מַה שֶּׁאָמְרוּ זִכְרוֹנָם לִבְרָכָה שֶׁאֲפִלּוּ עָבַר אָדָם וְנָטַע שָׂדֵהוּ
בַּשְּׁבִיעִית וְצָמְחָה, פֵּרוֹתֶיהָ מֻתָּרִין בַּאֲכִילָה מִדְּאוֹרַיְתָא, וּבִלְבַד שֶׁלֹּא יִקְצֹר כְּדֶרֶךְ
הַקּוֹצְרִים בְּכָל שְׁאָר שָׁנִים, שֶׁקּוֹצְרִים כָּל הַשָּׂדֶה וּמְעַמְּרִין כְּרִי וְדָשִׁין בַּבָּקָר, אֶלָּא
הַדִּין הוּא מִדְּאוֹרַיְתָא לִקְצֹר מְעַט מְעַט וְלַחְבֹּט וְלֶאֱכֹל; אֲבָל חֲכָמִים גָּזְרוּ לִהְיוֹת
הַסְּפִיחִין אֲסוּרִין בַּאֲכִילָה, מִפְּנֵי עוֹבְרֵי עֲבֵרָה שֶׁיִּזְרְעוּ גִנָּתָם בַּסֵּתֶר וְיֹאמְרוּ
סְפִיחִין הֵן; וּגְזֵרָה זוֹ אֵינָהּ אֶלָּא בִּירָקוֹת וּתְבוּאָה וְקִטְנִיּוֹת, שֶׁדֶּרֶךְ בְּנֵי־אָדָם
לְזָרְעָן, אֲבָל פֵּרוֹת הָאִילָנוֹת וְהָעֲשָׂבִים, שֶׁאֵין דֶּרֶךְ בְּנֵי אָדָם לְזָרְעָן, מֻתָּרִין.

וְנוֹהֶגֶת מִצְוָה זוֹ בִּזְכָרִים וּנְקֵבוֹת בְּאֶרֶץ יִשְׂרָאֵל בִּלְבַד מִן הַתּוֹרָה, וּבִזְמַן
שֶׁיִּשְׂרָאֵל שָׁם; וּלְעִנְיַן שְׁאָר מְקוֹמוֹת, הַכֹּל כְּמוֹ שֶׁכָּתַבְתִּי בְּ״כֶּסֶף תַּלְוֶה״ עֲשֵׂה ד׳
[מִשְׁפָּטִים סִי׳ פ״ד]. וְעוֹבֵר עַל זֶה בִּזְמַן הַבַּיִת וְקָצַר תְּבוּאָה שֶׁזָּרַע כְּדֶרֶךְ
הַקּוֹצְרִים, כְּגוֹן שֶׁקָּצַר אֶת כָּל הַשָּׂדֶה וְהֶעֱמִיר כְּרִי וְדָשׁ בַּבָּקָר, כְּדֶרֶךְ שֶׁבְּנֵי־אָדָם
עוֹשִׂים בִּשְׁאָר שָׁנִים, לוֹקֶה; וְהַמְלַקֵּט מִסְּפִיחֵי תְבוּאוֹת הַנִּזְרָעוֹת, אַף־עַל־פִּי
שֶׁלֹּא קָצַר הַכֹּל בְּיַחַד, מַכִּין אוֹתוֹ מַכַּת מַרְדּוּת, שֶׁחֲכָמִים גָּזְרוּ עֲלֵיהֶן, כְּמוֹ
שֶׁאָמַרְנוּ.

[שֶׁלֹּא נֶאֱסֹף פֵּרוֹת הָאִילָן בַּשְּׁבִיעִית כְּדֶרֶךְ שֶׁאוֹסְפִין אוֹתָן בְּכָל שָׁנָה]

שכט שֶׁלֹּא נֶאֱסֹף מַה שֶּׁיּוֹצִיאוּ הָאִילָנוֹת בַּשָּׁנָה הַשְּׁבִיעִית כְּדֶרֶךְ שֶׁאוֹסְפִין
בְּנֵי־אָדָם פֵּרוֹת אִילָנוֹתֵיהֶן בְּכָל שָׁנָה, אֲבָל יֵשׁ לָנוּ לַעֲשׂוֹת בַּדָּבָר שִׁנּוּי כְּדֵי
לְהַרְאוֹת שֶׁהַכֹּל בְּהֶפְקֵר בְּשָׁנָה זוֹ; וְזֶהוּ פֵּרוּשׁ ״וְאֶת עִנְּבֵי נְזִירֶךָ לֹא תִבְצֹר״,
כְּלוֹמַר שֶׁלֹּא תִבְצֹר כְּדֶרֶךְ הַבּוֹצְרִים, שֶׁכֵּן בָּא עָלָיו הַפֵּרוּשׁ הַמְקֻבָּל, וּכְמוֹ שֶׁאָמְרוּ
זִכְרוֹנָם לִבְרָכָה: מִכָּן אָמְרוּ: תְּאֵנִים שֶׁל שְׁבִיעִית אֵין קוֹצִין אוֹתָן בְּמֻקְצֶה אֲבָל
קוֹצֶה הוּא בְּחַרְבָּה, וְאֵין דּוֹרְכִין עֲנָבִים בְּגַת אֲבָל דּוֹרֵךְ הוּא בַּעֲרֵבָה, וְאֵין עוֹשִׂין
זֵיתִים בְּבַד וּבְקוֹטְבִּי אֲבָל כּוֹתֵשׁ הוּא וּמַכְנִיס לְבוֹדֵדָה.

<hr/>

§327   1. Sifra, *b'har, parashah* 1, 6.

2. I.e to be mentioned separately in this verse.

3. The Midrash continues: so can I include only something which is a labor of the
land and the tree—i.e. labors which aid in their growth, but not activities to save them
from ruin (which remain permissible).

§328   1. Based on ShM negative precept §222, which reads here "without preparation
and without arrangement"; i.e. some may be taken casually, informally, for one's
immediate needs.

2. Mishnah, Sh'vi'ith iv 2; Sifra, *b'har, perek* 1, 3; MT *hilchoth sh'mittah* iv 1.

3. Sifra, *ibid.* Mishnah *ibid.* 5.

4. MT *ibid.* 2, based on Mishnah, Sh'vi'ith ix 1 (*Kessef Mishneh*).

5. See §24, note 2.

memory taught:[2] that even if a man transgressed and planted his field and it sprouted, it is permissible to eat its produce by the law of the Torah, provided he does not harvest it in the way of reapers in all the other years, who harvest the entire field, heap it in a pile, and thresh it with cattle. The law of the Torah is rather to reap a bit at a time, thresh it out by beating, and eat it. However, the Sages ruled it forbidden to eat what grows spontaneously, on account of sinners and transgressors, who would sow their fields in autumn and then say it is spontaneous growth.[3] This decree, though, applies only to vegetables, grains and legumes, which it is customary for people to plant; but the fruit of trees and herbs, which people do not usually plant, are permitted.[4]

This precept applies to both man and woman in the land of Israel only, by the law of the Torah, and this at the time that [all] Jewry is there. As for other locations, it is all as I have written in *sidrah mishpatim*, precept §69. If a person violated this while the Temple was extant and reaped produce that he had planted, in the way of the reapers— for instance, if he harvested the entire field, piled all in a heap and threshed it with cattle, in the way that people did in other years—he should receive whiplashes. If someone gathered some produce that is generally planted, which grew of itself, even if he did not reap all at once, he should be whipped with lashes of disobedience;[5] for the Sages decreed it forbidden, as we stated.

[NOT TO GATHER THE FRUIT OF TREES IN THE SABBATICAL
YEAR AS IT IS GENERALLY GATHERED]

329 that we should not gather what the trees yield in the seventh year, in the way that people gather the fruit of their trees every year; we rather have to make some change in the matter in order to show that all is ownerless this year; this is the significance of the verse, *and the grapes of* n'zirecha (*your undressed vine*) *you shall not gather* (Leviticus 25:5). In other words, do not gather in the manner of the harvesters; for so was the traditional, received interpretation of it given.[1] As the Sages of blessed memory said:[2] Hence it was taught: Figs of the seventh year are not to be cut off with a special fig-knife, but may be cut off by an ordinary knife; grapes are not to be trodden out in a wine-press, but may be trodden in a kneading-basin; olives are not to be treated [squeezed out] in an olive-press and with a crusher,

but one may pound them and put them in a small pressing-basin.

וּפֵרוּשׁ "נְזִירֶךָ" כְּלוֹמַר שֶׁהִנְזַרְתָּ וְהִפְרַשְׁתָּ אוֹתָם מִבְּנֵי־אָדָם וְלֹא עָשִׂיתָ מֵהֶם הֶפְקֵר — לֹא תִבְצֹר אוֹתָם עַד שֶׁתַּפְקִירֵם; כֵּן הוּא דַעַת רַשׁ"י זִכְרוֹנוֹ לִבְרָכָה, כִּי הוּא סוֹבֵר שֶׁהַשּׁוֹמֵר שָׂדֵהוּ וּפֵרוֹתָיו בַּשְּׁבִיעִית, אֵין הַפֵּרוֹת נֶאֱסָרִין; וְכֵן כָּתַב בְּפֵרוּשָׁיו בְּסֻכָּה וּבִיבָמוֹת, וְכֵן הַדָּבָר מִדִּין הַתּוֹרָה בִּרְאָיוֹת נְכוֹנוֹת.

וּמַה שֶּׁאָמְרוּ בְּתוֹרַת כֹּהֲנִים: "וְאֶת עִנְּבֵי נְזִירֶךָ לֹא תִבְצֹר", מִן הַשָּׁמוּר בָּאָרֶץ אִי אַתָּה בוֹצֵר, אֲבָל בוֹצֵר אַתָּה מִן הַמֻּפְקָר — נְפָרֵשׁ לְדַעְתֵּנוּ זֶה "מִן הַשָּׁמוּר בָּאָרֶץ אִי אַתָּה בוֹצֵר", בְּעוֹד שֶׁיְּהֵא שָׁמוּר אָסוּר לְךָ לִבְצֹר מֵהֶם, אֲבָל לֹא שֶׁיֵּאָסְרוּ הַפֵּרוֹת בְּכָךְ.

וְהָרַמְבָּ"ן זִכְרוֹנוֹ לִבְרָכָה פֵּרַשׁ "נְזִירֶךָ": כְּלוֹמַר גֶּפֶן שֶׁלֹּא עֲבַדּוּהוּ וְלֹא זָמְרוּ אוֹתוֹ, כִּי כָל גֶּפֶן שֶׁלֹּא יִזָּמֵר וְלֹא יֵעָבֵד, אָמַר שֶׁיִּקָּרֵא כֵן; וְיֹאמַר הַכָּתוּב שֶׁאֲפִלּוּ כֶּרֶם הַנְּזִירוּת לֹא נִבְצֹר כְּדֶרֶךְ שֶׁבּוֹצְרִין בִּשְׁאָר הַשָּׁנִים, וְכָל־שֶׁכֵּן כֶּרֶם שֶׁנֶּעֱבָד.

שֹׁרֶשׁ מִצְוָה זוֹ עִם מִצְוַת שְׁבִיעִית שֶׁלְּפָנֶיהָ אֶחָד הוּא; וְהִנֵּה כָּתַבְתִּי לְךָ מְקוֹמָהּ אַיֵּה, וְשָׁם תִּמָּצֵא בְּאֵי זֶה מָקוֹם נוֹהֶגֶת וּבְאֵיזֶה זְמָן; וּבַמַּסֶּכְתָּא הַבְּנוּיָה עַל עִנְיָנִים אֵלֶּה, וְהִיא מַסֶּכֶת שְׁבִיעִית, שָׁם יִתְבָּאֲרוּ כָּל דִּינֵי מִצְוֹת אֵלּוּ בַּאֲרִיכָה; תֶּחֱזֶה וְתִלְמַד וּתְלַמֵּד.

[מִצְוַת סְפִירַת שֶׁבַע שַׁבְּתוֹת שָׁנִים]

שֶׁל לִמְנוֹת הַשָּׁנִים שֶׁבַע שֶׁבַע שָׁנִים עַד שְׁנַת הַיּוֹבֵל, בְּאֶרֶץ יִשְׂרָאֵל אַחַר הִתְנַחֲלֵנוּ בָהּ, שֶׁנֶּאֱמַר: וְסָפַרְתָּ לְךָ שֶׁבַע שַׁבְּתֹת שָׁנִים שֶׁבַע שָׁנִים שֶׁבַע פְּעָמִים. וְזֹאת הַמִּצְוָה, כְּלוֹמַר זֹאת הַסְּפִירָה שֶׁל שְׁנֵי שְׁמִטָּה עַד שְׁנַת הַיּוֹבֵל, הִיא נִמְסֶרֶת לְבֵית דִּין הַגָּדוֹל, כְּלוֹמַר הַסַּנְהֶדְרִין. וְכֵן הִיא הַמִּצְוָה: שֶׁהָיוּ מוֹנִין שָׁנָה שָׁנָה וְשָׁבוּעַ שָׁבוּעַ שֶׁל שָׁנִים עַד שְׁנַת הַיּוֹבֵל, כְּמוֹ שֶׁאָנוּ מוֹנִין יְמֵי הָעֹמֶר, וְאַחַר־כָּךְ

§329   1. Sifra, *b'har*, *perek* 1, 3.
        2. *Ibid.* Mishnah, Sh'vi'ith viii 6.
        3. Commentary, Leviticus 25:5.
        4. TB Sukkah 39b, s.v. *'aval*; Yevamoth 122a, s.v. *shel 'azikah*.
        5. The last two paragraphs are based on Ramban to Leviticus 25:5.
        6. *Ibid.*

§330   1. So Sifra, *b'har*, *parashah* 2, 1.
        2. So *ibid.* 2.

The meaning of the word *n'zirecha* ("your undressed vine") is, in other words, what you have separated (*hinzarta*) and set apart from people, and have not made ownerless; of these you shall not gather, until you make them free and ownerless. This is the view of Rashi of blessed memory,[3] for he holds that if a person guards his field and his produce in the seventh year, the produce does not become forbidden; so he wrote in his commentary to the tractates *Sukkah* and *Yevamoth*,[4] and so the matter is by the law of the Torah, by correct and proper proofs.

As to the passage in the Midrash *Sifra*:[1] "and the grapes of *n'zirecha* you shall not gather"—from that which is guarded on the land you may not gather, but you may gather from what was made ownerless— we would explain this to mean, to our mind: from what is guarded on the land you may not gather, i.e. while it is guarded you are forbidden to pick of it; but not that the fruit becomes forbidden thereby.[5]

However, Ramban of blessed memory[6] explained *n'zirecha* to mean a vine that was neither worked on nor pruned; for any grape-vine that was neither worked nor pruned, says he, is thus named. Hence the Writ says that even an unworked, unpruned vineyard we may not harvest in the way that harvesting is done in other years, and all the more certainly not a vineyard that was worked.

The root purpose of this precept is one and the same as that of the precept of the seventh year which precedes it; and there I wrote you its place [in this work] where it is (§84). There you will find [too] in which location it is in effect, and in which time. And in the Mishnah tractate built around these topics, i.e. the tractate *Sh'vi'ith*, all the laws of these *mitzvoth* are clarified at length. May you be worthy to learn and to teach it.

[THE PRECEPT OF COUNTING SEVEN SEPTENNATES— CYCLES OF SEVEN YEARS]

330 to count the years, seven by seven, till the jubilee year, in the land of Israel, after we have taken possession of it: for it is stated, *And you shall count for you seven sabbaths of years, seven times seven years* (Leviticus 25:8). This precept, i.e. this counting of the years of *sh'mittah* (release) till the jubilee year, was given over to the great *beth din*, which means the Sanhedrin (supreme court).[1] Now, such is the precept: they would count year by year, and cycles of seven years by seven, till the jubilee year[2]—just as we count the days of the *'omer*

מְקַדְּשִׁין שְׁנַת הַחֲמִשִּׁים בִּשְׁבִיתַת הָאָרֶץ וְלִקְרוֹת דְּרוֹר לְכָל הָעֲבָדִים וְהַשְּׁפָחוֹת, וְכָל הַקַּרְקָעוֹת חוֹזְרִין לְבַעֲלֵיהֶן.

מִשָּׁרְשֵׁי הַמִּצְוָה עַל צַד הַפְּשָׁט, שֶׁרָצָה הַשֵּׁם לְהוֹדִיעַ לְעַמּוֹ כִּי הַכֹּל שֶׁלּוֹ, וְלַבְּסוֹף יָשׁוּב כָּל דָּבָר לַאֲשֶׁר חָפֵץ הוּא לִתְּנָה בַּתְּחִלָּה, כִּי לוֹ הָאָרֶץ, כְּמוֹ שֶׁכָּתוּב: כִּי לִי הָאָרֶץ. וְעִם מִצְוָה זוֹ שֶׁל סְפִירָה שָׁנָה שָׁנָה יַרְחִיקוּ עַצְמָם שֶׁלֹּא יִגְזְלוּ קַרְקַע חֲבֵרָם וְלֹא יַחְמְדוּהָ בְּלִבָּם, בְּדַעְתָּם כִּי הַכֹּל שָׁב לַאֲשֶׁר חָפֵץ הָאֵל שֶׁתִּהְיֶה לוֹ.

וְעִנְיָן זֶה שֶׁל יוֹבֵל דּוֹמֶה קְצָת לְמַה שֶׁנָּהוּג לַעֲשׂוֹת בְּמַלְכוּתָא דְאַרְעָא, שֶׁלּוֹקְחִין אַדְנוּת מִזְּמַן לִזְמַן מֵעָרֵי הַבְּצוּרוֹת אֲשֶׁר לְשָׂרֵיהֶם, לְהַזְכִּיר לָהֶם יִרְאַת הָאָדוֹן. וְכֵן הַדָּבָר הַזֶּה, שֶׁרָצָה הַשֵּׁם שֶׁיָּשׁוּב כָּל קַרְקַע לַאֲשֶׁר לוֹ אֲחֻזַּת הָאָרֶץ מִמֶּנּוּ בָּרוּךְ הוּא; וְכֵן כָּל עֶבֶד אִישׁ יֵצֵא מִתַּחַת יָדוֹ וְיִהְיֶה בִּרְשׁוּת בּוֹרְאוֹ. וְאוּלָם מַלְכֵי אֶרֶץ יַעֲשׂוּ כֵן לְיִרְאָתָם פֶּן יִמְרְדוּ הַשָּׂרִים בָּהֶם, וְהָאֵל בָּרוּךְ הוּא צִוָּה לְעַמּוֹ כֵן לְזַכּוֹתָם וּלְהֵיטִיב לָהֶם, כִּי הַשֵּׁם חָפֵץ לְהֵיטִיב לָהֶם בְּטוּבוֹ הַגָּדוֹל.

וְעוֹד שָׁמַעְתִּי מֵחֲכָמִים שֶׁיֵּשׁ בְּעִנְיַן הַיּוֹבֵל סוֹד נִפְלָא, וְכִי בוֹ נִרְמָז כָּל יְמֵי עוֹלָם וְשָׁנָיו. גַּם בְּעִנְיַן הַשְּׁבִיעִיּוֹת, שֶׁנִּצְטַוֵּינוּ לִמְנוֹת הַשָּׁנִים שֶׁבַע שֶׁבַע וְלֹא שְׁמֹנֶה שְׁמֹנֶה אוֹ תִשְׁעָה תִשְׁעָה אוֹ פָחוֹת מֵהֶן, גַּם בָּזֶה אָמְרוּ שֶׁיֵּשׁ עִנְיָן שֶׁל חָכְמָה גָדוֹל וְטוֹב; יְדָעוּהוּ הֵם וְלֹא יִרְצוּ לְמָסְרוֹ לְכָל אָדָם.

וְאַף כִּי לֹא נִגְלָה לָנוּ סוֹדָם, הִשְׂגַּחְנוּ בַּדָּבָר זֶה, כִּי הָאָמְנָם הֶקֵּף הַשְּׁבִיעִיּוֹת סָדוּר בְּהַרְבֵּה מִמִּצְוֹותֵינוּ: הִנֵּנוּ מַחֲזִיקִין בִּמְלָאכָה שֵׁשֶׁת יָמִים וּבַשְּׁבִיעִי נִשְׁבַּת, נַעֲבֹד הָאֲדָמָה שֵׁשׁ שָׁנִים וּבַשְּׁבִיעִי נִשְׁבַּת, וְאַחַר שֶׁבַע שְׁבִיעִיּוֹת שֶׁל שָׁנִים גַּם־כֵּן נִשְׁבַּת שָׁנָה אַחַת, וְזֶהוּ הַיּוֹבֵל שֶׁבָּאנוּ עָלָיו. וְהִנֵּה חַג הַפֶּסַח שֶׁהוּא שִׁבְעָה יָמִים, וְחַג הַסֻּכּוֹת כְּמוֹ־כֵן שִׁבְעָה, וְאַחַר הַשִּׁבְעָה נָחָג הָעֲצֶרֶת; וּכְמוֹ־כֵן נִמְנֶה שֶׁבַע

---

3. Leviticus 25:10-13.
4. See Ibn Ezra and Ramban to Leviticus 25:2.
5. I.e. *Sh'mini 'Atzereth* (the Eighth Day of Assembly).

⟨370⟩

(§306); then they would consecrate the fiftieth year, to have the land lie fallow and to proclaim freedom for all male and female [Hebrew] servants; and all properties of land would return to their owners.[3]

At the root of the precept, from the aspect of the plain meaning, lies the reason that the Eternal Lord desired to convey to His people that everything is His, and ultimately everything will return to whomever He wished to give it originally—because the earth is His, as it is written, *for the land is Mine* (Leviticus 25:23). Then with this precept of counting every year, people will keep well away from seizing the land of their fellow-man by robbery or even desiring it in their heart, knowing that all returns to the one whom God wishes to have it.

Well, this matter of the jubilee is somewhat similar to a custom practiced in the earthly kingdom: From time to time, the rule over fortified cities belonging to their [the kings'] noblemen is taken away, to remind them of the reverent fear due the master [royal] ruler. So is this matter: for the Eternal Lord wished that every landed property should return to the one who had the original possession of the land from Him (blessed is He). And so would every man's [Hebrew] slave leave his possession and become part of his Creator's estate. However, kings of the earth would do this in their fear that the noblemen might rebel against them; whereas God, blessed is He, so commanded His people to make them worthy and [thus] do good for them; for the Eternal Lord delights in doing good for them, in His great goodness.

Furthermore, I heard from Torah scholars that in the theme of the jubilee there is a wondrous hidden significance, and through it all the days and years of the world are intimated.[4] So also in the matter of the cycles of seven, that we were commanded to count the years seven by seven, and not eight by eight, nine by nine, or in smaller groups than that—in this too, they said, lies a meaning of great and good wisdom. They knew it, but would not transmit it to every man.

Well, even though their mystic conception was not revealed to us, we have perceived in this matter that in truth, cycles of seven are inset in many of our *mitzvoth*. Here we carry on our work for six days, and on the seventh we rest. We work the earth for six years, and on the seventh we rest. Then, after seven septennates, periods of seven years, we likewise rest one year; and this is the jubilee, which we have reached [now in our listing of the precepts]. Again, the Passover festival is seven days, and the *Sukkoth* festival is seven likewise; and after those seven, the day of Assembly is observed.[5] Similarly,

שַׁבָּתוֹת מִפֶּסַח עַד עֲצֶרֶת, וְאַחַר מִנְיַן הַשִּׁבְעָה נָחַג חַג הָעֲצֶרֶת. וּכְמוֹ־כֵן נִמְצָא
כְרִיתַת בְּרִית, שֶׁהוּא דָבָר הַנַּעֲשֶׂה לְקִיּוּם עִנְיָן, עַל חֶשְׁבּוֹן שִׁבְעָה, כְּמוֹ שֶׁכָּתוּב:
כִּי אֶת שֶׁבַע כְּבָשׂת תִּקַּח מִיָּדִי; וְכֵן בִּלְעָם, שֶׁהָיָה חָכָם, עָשָׂה מִזְבְּחוֹת שִׁבְעָה;
וּכְמוֹ־כֵן לְשׁוֹן שְׁבוּעָה, שֶׁהוּא מָתְרְגָּם קִיּוּם, אָמְרוּ מִן הַחֲכָמִים שֶׁהוּא נִגְזָר
מִלְּשׁוֹן שִׁבְעָה; וְכֵן רַבִּים, לֹא הֶעֱלִיתִים עַתָּה בְּפִי עֵטִי. וְאַתָּה הַבֵּן הַיַּקִּיר תִּזְכֶּה
וְתַחְקֹר וְתַרְבֶּה הַדַּעַת וְתָבִין בַּדְּבָרִים, וְאָנֹכִי כְּבָר הִשְׁלַמְתִּי מְלַאכְתִּי זֹאת לְהָעִיר
רוּחֲךָ בַּשְּׁאֵלָה.

וְאִם תִּשְׁאַל: לָמָּה חִיְּבוּ זִכְרוֹנָם לִבְרָכָה לִמְנוֹת הַשָּׁנִים שֶׁבַע שֶׁבַע מִדִּכְתִיב
"וְסָפַרְתָּ לְךָ", וְלֹא רָאִינוּ מֵעוֹלָם שֶׁיִּמְנֶה הַזָּב יְמֵי סְפִירוֹ וְלֹא הַזָּבָה יְמֵי סְפִירָתָהּ
וְאַף־עַל־פִּי שֶׁכָּתוּב בָּהֶם "וְסָפַר לוֹ", "וְסָפְרָה לָהּ", זוּלָתִי שֶׁחַיָּבִים שֶׁיִּתְּנוּ לֵב
עַל הַיָּמִים, אֲבָל לֹא שֶׁיִּתְחַיְּבוּ לִמְנוֹתָם בְּפֶה וּלְבָרֵךְ עַל מִנְיָנָם?

תְּשׁוּבַת דָּבָר זֶה מַה שֶּׁהִקְדַּמְתִּי לְךָ בְּרֹאשׁ סִפְרִי, כִּי כָל עִנְיַן הַתּוֹרָה תָּלוּי
בַּפֵּרוּשׁ הַמְקֻבָּל; וְכַמָּה כְתוּבִים נִרְאִין בְּהֶפֶךְ זֶה מִזֶּה, וְכַמָּה קֻשְׁיוֹת וְכַמָּה סְתִירוֹת
יִתְחַדְּשׁוּ עַל כָּל מִי שֶׁלֹּא יָדְעוּ, וַאֲשֶׁר יֵדָעֵנוּ עַל בֻּרְיוֹ יִרְאֶה כִּי כָל דְּרָכֶיהָ דַּרְכֵי
נֹעַם וְכָל נְתִיבוֹתֶיהָ אֱמֶת; וְכֵן בָּאָתְנוּ הַקַּבָּלָה שֶׁצִּוּוּי "וְסָפַרְתָּ (לְךָ)" דְּיוֹבֵל צָרִיךְ
מִנְיָן בְּפֶה, וְצִוּוּי הַסְּפִירָה הַכָּתוּב בְּזָב וְזָבָה אֵינוֹ אֶלָּא הַשְׁגָּחָה בַּיָּמִים; וּמִנְהָגָן שֶׁל
יִשְׂרָאֵל בְּכָל מָקוֹם כָּךְ הוּא; וְאַף־עַל־פִּי שֶׁאֵינָם נְבִיאִים, בְּנֵי נְבִיאִים הֵם.

וּכְצֵיץ עִנְיָן זֶה מָצָאנוּ בַּתּוֹרָה בִּלְשׁוֹן זְכִירָה, דִּכְתִיב בְּעִנְיַן עֲמָלֵק זְכִירָה, וְעַל
דְּבַר מִרְיָם זְכִירָה, וּכְתִיב גַּם־כֵּן זְכִירָה בְּעִנְיַן יְצִיאַת מִצְרָיִם; וְעַל זְכִירַת מִצְרַיִם
בָּאָתְנוּ הַקַּבָּלָה לַעֲשׂוֹתָהּ בְּפֶה, וּכְמוֹ שֶׁאָמְרוּ זִכְרוֹנָם לִבְרָכָה "אֱמֶת

---

6. Our author uses the Talmudic name for the festival here: '*atzereth*—which indicates that it parallels *Sh'mini 'Atzereth* as a day of assembly following a festival of seven days.

7. In preparation for receiving an oracular message about the Hebrews.

8. So e.g. Ramban to Numbers 30:3. In the phrase which follows, "and thus many things, which I have not," etc., the second and third of the oldest manuscripts omit the word *lo'*, "not"; and so all the editions after the first. This version, however, seems contraindicated by the words "and thus"—i.e. and so too, etc.

9. A Talmudic expression: TB P'sahim 66b; i.e. their standard, accepted practices and ways of observing the precepts can be taken as a reliable indication of authentic tradition by the Oral Law. Intuitively, by some sixth sense or trace element of prophecy, they would find and retain the correct procedure. This somewhat recalls the teachings in classical Jewish thought that as all who were present at the Revelation at Sinai heard the words of the Almighty directly, they attained then the level of prophets.

10. Respectively, in Deuteronomy 25:17, 24:9, Exodus 13:3.

we count seven weeks from Passover to *Shavu'oth*, and after the counting of the seven, the festival of *Shavu'oth* is observed.[6]

We find equally that making a covenant, a solemn pact, which is done to make a matter permanent, [is also done] by the count of seven—as it is written, *Verily, these seven ewe-lambs shall you take from my hand* (Genesis 21:30). And so Balaam, who was a wise man, made seven altars[7] (Numbers 23:1). Thus also the term for an oath, *sh'vu'ah*, which is translated as a solemn affirmation—some scholars said it is derived from the term *shiv'ah*, "seven";[8] and thus many things, which I have not brought up now with the point of my pen. But you, dear son, may you merit to probe and increase your knowledge, and understand the matters. I, however, have already completed this task of mine, to arouse your spirit with the question.

You might ask, though: Why did the Sages of blessed memory make it obligatory to count [the years] seven by seven, since it is written, *And you shall count for you* (Leviticus 25:8)? Yet we have never seen that a man with a discharge (§178) should count his number of days, nor a woman with a discharge (§182) her number of days. Even though it is written regarding them, *and he shall count for him* (Leviticus 15:13), *and she shall count for her* (ibid. 28), they are merely required to pay attention to the days, but have no obligation to count them orally and say a benediction over the counting.

The answer to this matter is what I previously set down for you, at the beginning of my work: that every subject in the Torah depends on the traditional, received interpretation. Thus many verses appear to be the opposite of one another; many difficulties and contradictions will arise for one who does not know this. But anyone who does know this thoroughly will see that all its ways are ways of pleasantness (Proverbs 3:17) and all its paths are true. So we received the tradition that the order, *you shall count for you*, in regard to the jubilee, requires verbal counting, while the command of counting written for a man and a woman with a discharge means only paying attention to the days. And this is the practice of Israelites everywhere; and though they are not prophets, they are the sons [descendants] of prophets.[9]

We find something akin to this matter in the Torah in the expression of remembering: for "remembering" is written concerning Amalek and in regard to Miriam, and so is remembering also written about the theme of the exodus from Egypt.[10] Yet about remembering Egypt we received the tradition to do so orally; as the Sages of blessed

וְיַצִּיב״ דְּאוֹרַיְתָא, וּשְׁאָר הַזְּכִירוֹת דַּי לָנוּ בָּהֶם בִּזְכִירַת הַלֵּב לְבַד וְהַשְׁגָּחָתֵנוּ עַל הַדְּבָרִים.

מִדִּינֵי הַמִּצְוָה, מַה שֶּׁאָמְרוּ זִכְרוֹנָם לִבְרָכָה שֶׁאֵין חִיּוּב מִצְוַת מִנְיָן זֶה עַד אַחַר כִּבּוּשׁ וְחִלּוּק הָאָרֶץ, שֶׁנֶּאֱמַר: שֵׁשׁ שָׁנִים תִּזְרַע שָׂדֶךָ וְשֵׁשׁ שָׁנִים תִּזְמֹר כַּרְמֶךָ — עַד שֶׁיִּהְיֶה כָּל אֶחָד וְאֶחָד מַכִּיר אַרְצוֹ. וּמִשֶּׁגָּלָה שֵׁבֶט רְאוּבֵן וְגָד וַחֲצִי שֵׁבֶט מְנַשֶּׁה, בָּטְלָה מִצְוָה זוֹ, לְפִי שֶׁבָּטְלוּ הַיּוֹבְלוֹת מֵאוֹתוֹ הַזְּמַן וְאֵילָךְ, שֶׁנֶּאֱמַר: וּקְרָאתֶם דְּרוֹר בָּאָרֶץ לְכָל יֹשְׁבֶיהָ — בִּזְמַן שֶׁכָּל יוֹשְׁבֶיהָ עָלֶיהָ דַּוְקָא, וְגַם שֶׁלֹּא יִהְיוּ מְעֹרָבִים אֶלָּא יוֹשְׁבִים בְּתַקָּנָתָם; וּבִזְמַן שֶׁהַיּוֹבֵל נוֹהֵג בָּאָרֶץ, נוֹהֵג בְּחוּצָה לָאָרֶץ, שֶׁנֶּאֱמַר: יוֹבֵל הִיא, כְּלוֹמַר בְּכָל מָקוֹם. וּבִזְמַן שֶׁהַיּוֹבֵל נוֹהֵג, נוֹהֵג דִּין עֶבֶד עִבְרִי, וְדִין בָּתֵּי עָרֵי חוֹמָה, וְדִין שְׂדֵה חֲרָמִים וּשְׂדֵה אֲחֻזָּה, וּמְקַבְּלִין גֵּר תּוֹשָׁב.

וְנוֹהֶגֶת שְׁבִיעִית בָּאָרֶץ, וְהַשְׁמָטַת כְּסָפִים בְּכָל מָקוֹם, מִן הַתּוֹרָה; וּבִזְמַן שֶׁאֵין הַיּוֹבֵל נוֹהֵג, אֵין נוֹהֲגִין כָּל אֵלּוּ, זוּלָתֵי שְׁמִטַּת קַרְקַע בַּשְּׁבִיעִית, שֶׁנּוֹהֶגֶת בָּאָרֶץ מִדִּבְרֵיהֶם, וְכֵן שְׁמִטַּת כְּסָפִים בַּשְּׁבִיעִית בְּכָל מָקוֹם מִדִּבְרֵיהֶם.

וּשְׁנַת הַשְּׁמִטָּה אֵיזוֹ הִיא, הָכִי אַסִּיקְנָא בְּמַסֶּכֶת עֲבוֹדָה זָרָה בְּמֵימְרֵיהּ דְּרַב הוּנָא בְּרֵיהּ דְּרַבִּי יְהוֹשֻׁעַ בְּפֶרֶק קַמָּא, שֶׁהִיא שְׁנַת י״ז לִפְרָט לְדַעַת רַשִׁ״י זִכְרוֹנוֹ לִבְרָכָה, וּשְׁנַת י״ח לְדַעַת רַבֵּנוּ חֲנַנְאֵל זִכְרוֹנוֹ לִבְרָכָה. וְכָל עִנְיַן שְׁמִטַּת כְּסָפִים יִתְבָּאֵר יָפֶה בְּפֶרֶק אַחֲרוֹן דְּמַסֶּכֶת שְׁבִיעִית; וְיֵתֵר פְּרָטֵי כָּל דִּינֵי שְׁבִיעִית, שָׁם בְּאוֹתָהּ מַסֶּכְתָּא הַבְּנוּיָה עַל זֶה. וְעִנְיַן מִצְוָה זוֹ, שֶׁהִיא לִמְנוֹת הַשָּׁנִים, זְכָרוּהוּ

11. Which follows *Sh'ma yisra'el* in the morning prayers, and mentions the liberation from Egypt; TB B'rachoth 21a.

11a. This must be taken as a general statement, applying to *most* other remembrances. For "remembering Amalek," however, mere thought is not sufficient, as our author states in § 603 (point noted by R. Ya'akov Schatz).

12. Sifra, *b'har, parashah* 1, 2.

13. They settled in the Transjordan, and were exiled well before the rest of the Israelites.

14. I.e. with each tribe settled on its territory; TB 'Arachin 32b.

15. So TB Kiddushin 38b.

16. Literally, a convert inhabitant; i.e. one who has renounced idolatry and wishes to live in the land of Israel.

17. TB 'Arachin 29a.

18. I.e. the law that then the earth must rest.

19. The law that the seventh year releases borrowers from their debts; Deuteronomy 15:1–2.

20. See above, § 84.

21. Cited in *tosafoth*, TB 'Avodah Zarah 9b, s.v. *hai man*.

memory said of the benediction "True and firm,"[11] this is by the law of the Torah. But as for the other remembrances, it is enough for us if we recall them solely in the heart, giving thought to those subjects.[11a]

Among the laws of the precept, there is what the Sages of blessed memory taught:[12] that the duty of the precept of this counting did not go into effect till the conquest and division of the land [of Israel]; for it is stated, *Six years you shall sow your field, and six years you shall prune your vineyard* (Leviticus 25:3)—[not] until each and every one will recognize his land. And once the tribes of Reuben and Gad and half the tribe of Manasseh were exiled,[13] this precept ceased. For the jubilees ceased to be in effect from that time onward; it is stated, *and you shall proclaim liberty in the land to all its inhabitants* (ibid. 10), [which means] specifically at a time when all its inhabitants are [settled] on it, and so too that they should not be mixed or thrown together, but living in their proper order.[14] However, when the jubilee is in effect in the land [of Israel], it is in effect outside the land; for it is stated, *It is a jubilee* (ibid. 11)—i.e. everywhere.[15] Now, when the jubilee is in effect, so do there also prevail the laws of a Hebrew servant, houses of walled cities (§341), a *ḥerem* field (made sacred to the *kohen*] (§355), and an inherited field (§397); and a *gér toshav*[16] is received [into the community].[17]

The seventh [fallow] year[18] applies in the land [of Israel], and the release of money [obligations][19] everywhere, by the law of the Torah. But when the jubilee is not in effect, neither of these is in effect, except for leaving the land fallow in the seventh year, which applies in the land [of Israel] by the ruling of the Sages;[20] and so does the release of monetary obligations remain in effect in the seventh year everywhere by their decree.

As to which is a year of *sh'mittah* (release), it was thus concluded in the Talmud tractate 'Avodah Zarah (9b), by the teaching of R. Huna b. R. Joshua, in the first chapter: that it is the year 5,017 since creation (1257) according to the view of Rashi of blessed memory, and 5,018 (1258) by the view of R. Ḥanan'él of blessed memory.[21] The entire subject of release from money obligations is explained well in the last chapter of the Mishnah tractate Sh'vi'ith. The remaining details of all the laws of the seventh year are there, in that tractate, which is built around this theme. As for the subject-matter of this precept, our Sages of blessed memory mentioned it in the Midrash

זִכְרוֹנָם לִבְרָכָה בְּסִפְרָא וּבִמְקוֹמוֹת אֲחֵרִים. וּכְבָר כָּתַבְתִּי לְמַעֲלָה כִּי זֹאת הַמִּצְוָה מְסוּרָה לְבֵית־דִּין הַגָּדוֹל, דְּהַיְנוּ הַסַּנְהֶדְרִין, שֶׁהֵם הַנִּקְרָאִין עֵינֵי הָעֵדָה, וְשֶׁאֵינָהּ נוֹהֶגֶת אֶלָּא בִּזְמַן שֶׁהַיּוֹבֵל נוֹהֵג.

[מִצְוַת תְּקִיעַת שׁוֹפָר בְּיוֹם הַכִּפּוּרִים שֶׁל יוֹבֵל]

שלא לִתְקֹעַ בְּשׁוֹפָר בַּעֲשִׂירִי בְּתִשְׁרֵי, שֶׁהוּא יוֹם הַכִּפּוּרִים, שֶׁנֶּאֱמַר: וְהַעֲבַרְתָּ שׁוֹפַר תְּרוּעָה... בְּיוֹם הַכִּפֻּרִים תַּעֲבִירוּ שׁוֹפָר בְּכָל אַרְצְכֶם... וּקְרָאתֶם דְּרוֹר וְגוֹמֵר. וְיָדוּעַ שֶׁמִּצְוַת הַתְּקִיעָה בְּיוֹם זֶה הִיא לְפַרְסֵם חֵרוּת כָּל עֶבֶד עִבְרִי, שֶׁיֵּצֵא (בֶּן חוֹרִין) בְּלִי דָמִים; וְאֵין עִנְיָנָהּ כְּעִנְיַן תְּקִיעַת שׁוֹפָר בְּרֹאשׁ הַשָּׁנָה, שֶׁהַתְּקִיעָה הַהִיא אָנוּ עוֹשִׂים לִקְבֹּעַ מַחֲשַׁבְתֵּנוּ עַל עִנְיַן עֲקֵדַת יִצְחָק וּנְצַיֵּר בְּנַפְשֵׁנוּ לַעֲשׂוֹת גַּם בָּנוּ כָּמוֹהוּ לְאַהֲבַת יי, וּמִתּוֹךְ כָּךְ תַּעֲלֶה זִכְרוֹנֵנוּ לִפְנֵי יי לְטוֹב, כְּלוֹמַר שֶׁנִּהְיֶה זַכָּאִים לְפָנָיו; וְזֹאת הַתְּקִיעָה שֶׁל יוֹבֵל הִיא לְפַרְסֵם הַחֵרוּת, כְּמוֹ שֶׁאָמַרְנוּ.

מִשָּׁרְשֵׁי הַמִּצְוָה, לְפִי שֶׁיָּדוּעַ כִּי קוֹל הַשּׁוֹפָר תְּעוֹרֵר לֵב בְּנֵי־אָדָם, אִם לְשָׁלוֹם אִם לְמִלְחָמָה, וְעִנְיַן שִׁלּוּחַ הָעֶבֶד שֶׁעָבַד אֶת אֲדוֹנָיו זְמַן רַב, הוּא קָשֶׁה מְאֹד בְּעֵינֵי אֲדוֹנָיו; עַל־כֵּן לְעוֹרֵר לֵב הַבְּרִיּוֹת עַל הָעִנְיָן וּלְחַזֵּק נַפְשָׁם וּלְהַזְהִירָם עַל הַמִּצְוָה בְּשָׁמְעָם אֶת קוֹל הַשּׁוֹפָר, בִּרְאוֹתָם כִּי דָבָר הַשָּׁוֶה הוּא בְּכָל הָאָרֶץ וְשֶׁהַכֹּל עוֹשִׂים כֵּן, נִצְטַוִּינוּ עַל זֶה; שֶׁאֵין דָּבָר שֶׁיְּחַזֵּק לְבוֹת בְּנֵי אָדָם כְּמוֹ מַעֲשֵׂה הָרַבִּים, וּכְמַאֲמַר הֶחָכָם: צַעַר רַבִּים נֶחָמָה.

גַּם הָעֶבֶד בְּעַצְמוֹ מִתְעוֹרֵר לָצֵאת כְּכָל הָעֲבָדִים מִתַּחַת יְדֵי רַבּוֹ אֲשֶׁר אָהֵב, בְּשָׁמְעוֹ קוֹל הַשּׁוֹפָר; וּמִתּוֹךְ כָּךְ הַמִּצְוָה מִתְקַיֶּמֶת לָשׁוּב הַכֹּל בִּרְשׁוּת אֲדוֹן הַכֹּל.

דִּינֵי הַמִּצְוָה, כְּגוֹן בְּאֵי זֶה שׁוֹפָר תּוֹקְעִין בְּיוֹם זֶה, וְאֵי זוֹ בְרָכָה מְבָרְכִין בּוֹ;

---

1. I.e. without recompensing his master for the years of his labor that he will lose; TB Rosh haShanah 8b.

2. *Ibid.* 16a.

3. The paragraph is based on ShM positive precept §137.

4. Cf. II Samuel 2:28, Jeremiah 4:19.

5. The more familiar version, "the trouble of many is half a consolation," is found in *Mar'éh haMussar*, Offenbach 1716 and R. Judah Aryeh Modena, *Midbar Yebudah*, Venice 1602. Other versions of the thought are to be found in D'varim Rabbah 2, 22, and R. Joseph ibn Caspi, *Kappoth Kessef*, Lamentations 2:13.

Sifra and in other places. I have written previously, above, that this precept was given over to the great *beth din*, the Sanhedrin [to observe], since they [the justices] are called "the eyes of the community"; and that it is in effect at no other time but when the jubilee is in force.

[THE PRECEPT OF SOUNDING THE SHOFAR ON THE DAY
OF ATONEMENT IN A JUBILEE YEAR]

331 to sound the *shofar* on the tenth of Tishri [in a jubilee year], which is the Day of Atonement: as it is written, *Then you shall send forth the blast of the shofar . . . on the day of atonement you shall send forth the shofar throughout all your land. . . . and you shall proclaim liberty,* etc. (Leviticus 25:9–10). It is known that the religious duty of sounding the *shofar* on this day is in order to announce the liberty of every Hebrew servant, that he should go out a free man without making payment.[1] Its significance is not like that of the *shofar*-blowing on *Rosh haShanah*; for we do that sounding [of the ram's horn] to focus our thought on the theme of the binding of Isaac, so that we may imagine ourselves acting like him out of love for the Lord; and as a result, our remembrance will ascend before the Lord for good reward; in other words, we will be meritorious before Him.[2] This *shofar*-blowing of the jubilee, however, is to proclaim the liberation, as we stated.[3]

As for the root purposes of the precept, it is known that the sound of the *shofar* arouses the heart of human beings, whether to peace or to war.[4] Now, the matter of sending out a servant who has served his master a great amount of time, is very difficult in the eyes of his master. Therefore, to inspire the heart of people about the matter, encourage their spirit, and adjure them about the *mitzvah* by having them hear the sound of the *shofar*, so that they will realize that this is something standard throughout the land, and that all do so—[for this reason] we were commanded about it. For there is nothing that will so encourage the heart of human beings as something done by all. As the saying of the wise man goes, "the suffering of many is a consolation."[5]

Moreover, the servant himself will also be aroused to go out, like all the servants, from the possession of his master whom he loves, on hearing the sound of the *shofar*; and as a result, the precept will be fulfilled, that all should return to the domain of the Master Ruler of all.

The laws of the precept are, for example, what kind of *shofar*

וּכְבָר אָמְרוּ זִכְרוֹנָם לִבְרָכָה דֶּרֶךְ כְּלָל בְּמַסֶּכֶת רֹאשׁ הַשָּׁנָה: שָׁוֶה הַיּוֹבֵל לְרֹאשׁ הַשָּׁנָה לִתְקִיעָה וְלַבְּרָכוֹת; וּבְמִצְוַת שׁוֹפָר דְּרֹאשׁ הַשָּׁנָה בְּסֵדֶר פִּינְחָס [סי' ת"ה] נְדַבֵּר בּוֹ קְצָת בְּעֶזְרַת הַשֵּׁם, כְּמִנְהָגֵנוּ.

וּמִכָּל־מָקוֹם, אַף־עַל־פִּי שֶׁאָמְרוּ זִכְרוֹנָם לִבְרָכָה שֶׁשָּׁוִין הֵן, חִלּוּק קְצָת יֵשׁ בֵּינֵיהֶם, דְּבִרֹאשׁ הַשָּׁנָה שֶׁחָל לִהְיוֹת בְּשַׁבָּת לֹא הָיוּ תּוֹקְעִין אֶלָּא בְּבֵית־דִּין, וּבַיּוֹבֵל תּוֹקֵעַ כָּל יָחִיד וְיָחִיד כָּל זְמַן שֶׁבֵּית־דִּין יוֹשְׁבִין, בֵּין בִּפְנֵי בֵית־דִּין בֵּין שֶׁלֹּא בִּפְנֵיהֶם.

וְכֵן מִדִּינֵי הַמִּצְוָה, כְּגוֹן מַה שֶּׁאָמְרוּ זִכְרוֹנָם לִבְרָכָה כִּי מֵרֹאשׁ הַשָּׁנָה וְעַד יוֹם הַכִּפּוּרִים הָיוּ הָעֲבָדִים אוֹכְלִין וְשׁוֹתִין וּשְׂמֵחִין בְּבֵית אֲדוֹנָם, לֹא נִפְטָרִין לְבָתֵּיהֶם וְלֹא הָאָדוֹן מִשְׁתַּעֲבֵּד בָּהֶם; כֵּיוָן שֶׁהִגִּיעַ יוֹם הַכִּפּוּרִים, תָּקְעוּ בֵית־דִּין בַּשׁוֹפָר, נִפְטָרִין לְבָתֵּיהֶם, וּכְמוֹ־כֵן שָׂדוֹת חוֹזְרוֹת לְבַעֲלֵיהֶן. וְרַבִּים מִפְּרָטֵי דִּינֵי יוֹבֵל בַּעֲרָכִין, וְדִינֵי שׁוֹפָר בְּמַסֶּכֶת רֹאשׁ הַשָּׁנָה.

וְנוֹהֶגֶת מִצְוָה זוֹ בְּאֶרֶץ יִשְׂרָאֵל בִּזְמַן שֶׁהַיּוֹבֵל נוֹהֵג, וַהֲרֵי כָתַבְתִּי לְךָ בְּסָמוּךְ אֵי זֶה זְמַן הַיּוֹבֵל נוֹהֵג, וְשֶׁמִּצְוַת יוֹבֵל מְסוּרָה לְבֵית־דִּין. וְאִם עָבְרוּ בֵית־דִּין עַל זֶה וְלֹא תָקְעוּ בַשׁוֹפָר, אַף־עַל־פִּי שֶׁנִּשְׁתַּלְּחוּ הָעֲבָדִים וְהֶחֱזִירוּ הַשָּׂדוֹת לְבַעֲלֵיהֶן מִבְּלִי תְקִיעָה, בִּטְּלוּ מִצְוַת־עֲשֵׂה זֶה.

[מִצְוַת קִדּוּשׁ שְׁנַת הַיּוֹבֵל]

שלב לְקַדֵּשׁ שְׁנַת הַחֲמִשִּׁים כְּמוֹ שְׁנַת הַשְּׁמִטָּה, כְּלוֹמַר בְּבִטּוּל הָעֲבוֹדָה בָּאָרֶץ וְהֶפְקֵר הַצּוֹמֵחַ בָּהּ, שֶׁנֶּאֱמַר: וְקִדַּשְׁתֶּם אֵת שְׁנַת הַחֲמִשִּׁים שָׁנָה, וּבֵאַר הַכָּתוּב שֶׁעִנְיָן הַקְּדֻשָּׁה הוּא שֶׁיִּהְיוּ פֵּרוֹתֶיהָ וּתְבוּאָתָהּ נִפְקָרִים, וְשֶׁיִּהְיוּ הָעֲבָדִים

---

6. See also Rashi to the Mishnah there.
7. So TB Rosh haShanah 30a.
8. *Ibid.* 8b.

is to be sounded on this day, and what benediction is said over it. In the past, our Sages of blessed memory said, as a general rule, in the Talmud tractate *Rosh haShanah* (26b):[6] The jubilee is equivalent to *Rosh haShanah* in regard to the *shofar* blasts and the benedictions. In the precept of the *shofar* of *Rosh haShanah*, in *sidrah pinhas* (§405) we will speak a bit about it, with the Eternal Lord's help, as our custom is.

Nevertheless, even though the Sages of blessed memory said that they are alike, there is a slight difference between them: If *Rosh haShanah* happened to fall on a Sabbath, the *shofar* was sounded nowhere but at the [great] *beth din*; but in a jubilee [if the tenth of Tishri fell on a Sabbath] every single individual would sound it, as long as the [great] *beth din* held sessions—whether in the *beth din*'s presence or not.[7]

So too, among the laws of the precept, there is what the Sages of blessed memory taught:[8] that from *Rosh haShanah* till the Day of Atonement, the servants would eat and drink and make merry in the house of their master. They would neither be dismissed to their homes nor would the master make them work. When the Day of Atonement arrived, the [great] *beth din* sounded the *shofar*, whereupon they would be discharged to their homes; and fields would likewise return to their [original] owners. Many of the details of the laws of jubilee are in the Talmud tractate *'Arachin*, while the laws of *shofar* are in the tractate *Rosh haShanah*.

This precept is in force in the land of Israel at the time that the jubilee is in force. I have written for you shortly before (§330) in which time the jubilee is in effect, and that the precept of the jubilee is entrusted to the [great] *beth din*. If the *beth din* violated it and did not sound the *shofar*, even if the servants were sent off [free] and the fields were returned to their [original] owners without the *shofar* blasts, they would disobey this positive precept.

332 [THE PRECEPT OF SANCTIFYING THE JUBILEE YEAR] to sanctify the fiftieth year like a year of *sh'mittah* (release), i.e. by the cessation of work on the land and the renunciation of ownership of all that grows on it: for it is stated, *And you shall hallow the fiftieth year* (Leviticus 25:10); and the Writ explained that the substance of sanctification is that its fruit and produce should be left free for all, and that the servants should go free from the master's

יוֹצְאִין מִתַּחַת יַד הָאָדוֹן, שֶׁאָמַר הַכָּתוּב אַחַר־כֵּן "וּקְרָאתֶם דְּרוֹר בָּאָרֶץ לְכָל יֹשְׁבֶיהָ", כְּלוֹמַר חֵרוּת לָעֲבָדִים, "כִּי יוֹבֵל הִיא קֹדֶשׁ תִּהְיֶה לָכֶם מִן הַשָּׂדֶה תֹּאכְלוּ אֶת תְּבוּאָתָהּ", כְּלוֹמַר שֶׁתִּהְיֶה הַתְּבוּאָה הֶפְקֵר וְלֹא יַאַסְפָה כָּל אֶחָד וְאֶחָד לִרְשׁוּתוֹ.

מִשָּׁרְשֵׁי הַמִּצְוָה, מַה שֶּׁכָּתַבְתִּי בְּמִצְוֹת הַשָּׁנִים, מִצְוָה רִאשׁוֹנָה שֶׁבַּפָּרָשָׁה זוֹ [סי׳ ש״ל], שֶׁרָצָה הַשֵּׁם לְזַכּוֹת עַמּוֹ בְּקַבָּלַת מַלְכוּתוֹ וְכוּלֵי, כְּמוֹ שֶׁכְּתַבְתִּיו שָׁם, וְכָאן הָיָה מְקוֹמוֹ.

מִדִּינֵי הַמִּצְוָה, מַה שֶּׁאָמְרוּ זִכְרוֹנָם לִבְרָכָה שֶׁכָּל שֶׁאָסוּר בַּשָּׁנָה הַשְּׁבִיעִית מֵעֲבוֹדַת הָאָרֶץ אָסוּר בַּיּוֹבֵל, וְכָל שֶׁמֻּתָּר בָּהּ מֻתָּר בָּהּ, וְהֶחָיּוּב עַל הָעוֹשֶׂה שָׁוֶה בִּשְׁנֵיהֶם; וְדִין הַפֵּרוֹת בַּאֲכִילָה וּבִמְכִירָה וּבִבְעוּר שָׁוֶה בִּשְׁנֵיהֶם; יִתְרָה שְׁבִיעִית עַל הַיּוֹבֵל, שֶׁהִיא מְשַׁמֶּטֶת כְּסָפִים, וְדַוְקָא בְּסוֹפָהּ, וְיִתֵּר יוֹבֵל עַל הַשְּׁבִיעִית, שֶׁמְשַׁמֵּט קַרְקַע וּמוֹצִיא עֲבָדִים, וּבִתְחִלָּתָהּ.

וּשְׁנַת יוֹבֵל אֵינוֹ עוֹלֶה מִמִּנְיַן שְׁנֵי הַשָּׁבוּעַ, אֶלָּא מוֹנִין תֵּשַׁע וְאַרְבָּעִים שָׁנָה, שֶׁהֵן שֶׁבַע שֶׁבַע שָׁנִים שֶׁבַע פְּעָמִים, וְאַחַר שְׁנַת הַשְּׁמִטָּה שֶׁהִיא בַּשְּׁבִיעִי הָאַחֲרוֹן, עוֹשִׂין יוֹבֵל בִּשְׁנַת הַחֲמִשִּׁים; וּשְׁנַת אַחַת וַחֲמִשִּׁים מַתְחִילִים לִמְנוֹת יוֹבֵל אַחֵר, וְהִיא הַתְחָלַת שֵׁשׁ שָׁנִים שֶׁל שָׁבוּעַ.

וְנוֹהֶגֶת מִצְוָה זוֹ בְּאֶרֶץ יִשְׂרָאֵל, וּבִזְמַן שֶׁכָּל יוֹשְׁבֶיהָ עָלֶיהָ, כְּמוֹ שֶׁכָּתַבְתִּי לְמַעְלָה. וּמִן הַדּוֹמֶה שֶׁהָיוּ סַנְהֶדְרִין מִתְקַבְּצִין בְּקִדּוּשׁ הַשָּׁנָה וּמְבָרְכִין עָלֶיהָ "לְקַדֵּשׁ שָׁנִים", וְאַחַר־כָּךְ תּוֹקְעִין בַּשּׁוֹפָר, וְכֵן כָּל יָחִיד וְיָחִיד תּוֹקֵעַ גַּם־כֵּן בִּרְשׁוּתוֹ, וְהַקּוֹל נִשְׁמָע בְּכָל הָאָרֶץ, וְהָעֲבָדִים נִפְטָרִין לְבָתֵּיהֶם, וְהַקַּרְקָעוֹת חוֹזְרִין לְבַעֲלֵיהֶם. וְיֶתֶר פְּרָטֶיהָ, בְּמַסֶּכֶת עֲרָכִין.

וְעוֹבֵר עַל זֶה וְעָבַד אַדְמָתוֹ בַּיּוֹבֵל עֲבוֹדָה הָאֲסוּרָה, וְכֵן אִם לֹא רָצָה לְשַׁלֵּחַ

---

§332 1. MT *hilchoth sh'mittah* x 15-16 (sources in *Kessef Mishneh*).
2. Sifra, *b'har, perek* 3, 2.
3. See *ibid.* 4.
4. Sifre, Deuteronomy §§111–112; Sifra, *b'har, perek* 3, 6.
5. Sifre *ibid.* Sifra *ibid.* TB 'Arachin 28b.
6. So TB N'darim 61a; MT *ibid.* 7.

possession: For Scripture states afterward, *and proclaim liberty throughout the land for all its inhabitants (ibid.)*—in other words, freedom for the servants. *For it is a jubilee; it shall be holy to you; you shall eat its yield out of the field (ibid.* 12): in other words, the produce should be ownerless; everyone should not go and gather it into his domain.

At the root of the precept lies what I wrote about the religious duty of counting the years, the first positive precept in this *sidrah* (§ 330): that the Eternal Lord desired to make His people meritorious through the acceptance of His kingship, and so forth, as I wrote of it there, although its proper place was here.

Among the laws of the precept, there is what the Sages of blessed memory said:[1] that whatever is forbidden in a seventh year of the labors of the land, is forbidden during a jubilee; and whatever is permitted in the one, is permitted in the other;[2] and the penalty for doing [any of the forbidden labors] is the same for both. So is the law about the produce, in regard to eating, selling, and removing it, the same for both of them.[3] The seventh year has a greater effect than the jubilee in that it dissolves money obligations, but this only at its end.[4] And the jubilee has a greater effect than the seventh year in that it releases land [to its original owners] and liberates [Hebrew] servants —and this at its beginning.[5]

The year of the jubilee is not included in the reckoning of the seven-year cycles. Rather, forty-nine years are counted, which are seven times seven years, and after the year of *sh'mittah* (release) in the last septennate (seven-year cycle) the jubilee is observed in the fiftieth year. Then, in the fifty-first year, they begin to reckon another jubilee, this being the start of six years of a septennate.[6]

This precept is in effect in the land of Israel, at the time that all its inhabitants are on it, as I wrote above (§ 330). Apparently the Sanhedrin (supreme court) would gather at the hallowing of the year and would recite over it the benediction to consecrate the years; afterward they would sound the *shofar*, and so would each and every individual sound it likewise in his domain. The peal would be heard throughout the land, and the servants would be discharged to their homes, and landed properties would return to their original owners.

The rest of its details are in the Talmud tractate 'Arachin. If someone violated this and did a forbidden labor on his land in the jubilee, and so too if one did not wish to set his servant free, he would [thus] disobey

this positive precept, apart from transgressing a negative precept,

עָבְדוֹ חָפְשִׁי, בִּטֵּל עֲשֵׂה זֶה, מִלְּבַד שֶׁעָבַר עַל לָאו, וּכְמוֹ שֶׁנִּכְתַּב בְּסֵדֶר זֶה [סי׳
של״ג] בְּעֶזְרַת הַשֵּׁם; וְעָנְשׁוֹ גָּדוֹל מְאֹד, שֶׁהוּא כְּאִלּוּ כּוֹפֵר בְּחִדּוּשׁ הָעוֹלָם.

[שֶׁלֹּא נַעֲבֹד הָאָרֶץ בִּשְׁנַת הַיּוֹבֵל]

שלג שֶׁלֹּא נַעֲבֹד הָאָרֶץ בִּשְׁנַת הַיּוֹבֵל, כְּמוֹ שֶׁנִּמְנַעְנוּ מֵעֲבוֹדָתָהּ בִּשְׁנַת
הַשְּׁמִטָה, שֶׁנֶּאֱמַר בְּיוֹבֵל "לֹא תִזְרָעוּ" כְּמוֹ שֶׁנֶּאֱמַר בִּשְׁמִטָּה "שָׂדְךָ לֹא תִזְרָע";
וּכְמוֹ שֶׁהַשְּׁמִטָּה נֶאֱסַר בָּהּ בֵּין עֲבוֹדַת הָאָרֶץ בֵּין עֲבוֹדַת הָאִילָנוֹת, כָּךְ הַיּוֹבֵל,
וּלְפִיכָךְ אָמַר "לֹא תִזְרָעוּ" עַל הַכְּלָל, יִכְלֹל אֶרֶץ וְאִילָן.

מִשָּׁרְשֵׁי מִצְוַת הַיּוֹבֵל כָּתַבְתִּי (לְמַעְלָה) בְּמִצְוָה רִאשׁוֹנָה שֶׁבְּסֵדֶר זֶה [סי׳
של׳] מַה שֶּׁיָּכֹלְתִּי.

דִּינֶיהָ בְּעִנְיַן עֲבוֹדַת הָאָרֶץ וְהָאִילָנוֹת, כְּמוֹ בִּשְׁבִיעִית; וּבְ"כֶּסֶף תַּלְוֶה" עָשָׂה
ד׳ [מִשְׁפָּטִים סי׳ פ״ד] כָּתַבְתִּי קְצָת מִן הָעִנְיָנִים, לְעוֹרֵר לֵב הַקּוֹרֵא עַל עִנְיְנֵי
הַמִּצְוָה, כְּמִנְהָגִי; עַיֵּן שָׁם אִם תַּחְפֹּץ בּוֹ.

[שֶׁלֹּא נִקְצֹר סְפִיחֵי תְּבוּאוֹת שֶׁל שְׁנַת הַיּוֹבֵל]

שלד שֶׁלֹּא נִקְצֹר וְנִלְקֹט סְפִיחֵי תְּבוּאוֹת שְׁנַת הַיּוֹבֵל כְּמוֹ שֶׁאָדָם קוֹצֵר בִּשְׁאָר
הַשָּׁנִים, אֲבָל יֵשׁ לָנוּ לַעֲשׂוֹת בַּדְּבָרִים שִׁנּוּי. וְכָל הָעִנְיָן כְּמוֹ שֶׁפֵּרַשְׁנוּ בְּסָמוּךְ
בִּסְפִיחֵי שְׁבִיעִית.

[שֶׁלֹּא לֶאֱסֹף פֵּרוֹת הָאִילָנוֹת בִּשְׁנַת הַיּוֹבֵל כְּדֶרֶךְ שֶׁאוֹסְפִין אוֹתָן בִּשְׁאָר
שָׁנִים]

שלה שֶׁלֹּא נֶאֱסֹף פֵּרוֹת הָאִילָנוֹת בִּשְׁנַת הַיּוֹבֵל כְּמוֹ שֶׁאָנוּ אוֹסְפִין אוֹתָן
בִּשְׁאָר הַשָּׁנִים, שֶׁנֶּאֱמַר: וְלֹא תִבְצְרוּ אֶת נְזִרֶיהָ, וְהוּא אַזְהָרָה דֶּרֶךְ כְּלָל לְכָל
פֵּרוֹת הָאִילָן; וְהֻזְהִיר הַכָּתוּב בְּפֵרוֹת בַּיּוֹבֵל בְּפֵרוֹת הָאִילָן אַזְהָרָה בִּפְנֵי עַצְמָהּ וּבִתְבוּאוֹת
אַזְהָרָה בִּפְנֵי עַצְמָהּ, כְּמוֹ בִּשְׁבִיעִית, וּכְמוֹ שֶׁכָּתַבְנוּ לְמַעְלָה; וְהַדִּין בִּשְׁנֵיהֶם,

---

7. Since a main purpose of observing the seventh year and the jubilee is to attest thereby that *the earth is the Lord's* (Psalms 24:1), as our author wrote in regard to the root purpose of §330; and He is the Sovereign Master of the earth because it did not exist forever by its own laws, but rather, He brought it into being by His will, at a certain point in time.

as we will write in this *sidrah* (§333) with the Eternal Lord's help; and his punishment would be very great, for it is as though he denied the creation of the world out of nothing. [7]

[THE PROHIBITION AGAINST FARMING THE LAND IN A JUBILEE YEAR]

333 that we should not work the land in a jubilee year, just as we are restricted from working it in a year of *sh'mittah* (release): for it is stated in regard to the jubilee, *you shall not sow* (Leviticus 25:11), just as it is stated concerning *sh'mittah* [the seventh year, of release] *you shall not sow your field* (ibid. 4). And just as in *sh'mittah*, both work on the land and work on trees is forbidden, so during the jubilee. Therefore it says, *you shall not sow*, generally, including both the land and trees. [1]

As to the root reason for the precept of the jubilee, I wrote above, in the first positive precept of this *sidrah* (§330), what I was able to. Its laws in regard to work on the land and on trees are the same as for the seventh year. In *sidrah mishpatim*, precept §69, I wrote some of these topics to arouse the heart (interest) of the reader toward the contents of the precept, according to my custom. Look there if your interest is drawn to it.

[THAT WE SHOULD NOT HARVEST WILD–GROWING PRODUCE IN A JUBILEE YEAR]

334 that we should not pick and gather the spontaneously growing produce of the jubilee year as a man would do harvesting in the other years; rather, we must make a change in these matters. The entire subject is as we have explained shortly above (§328), regarding wild produce of the seventh year.

[NOT TO GATHER THE FRUIT OF TREES IN THE ORDINARY WAY DURING A JUBILEE YEAR]

335 that we should not gather the fruit of trees in the jubilee year as we gather it in the other years: for it is stated, *nor shall you gather its grapes of the undressed vines* (Leviticus 25:11), which is a general admonition about all fruit of trees. Scripture adjured us in regard to the jubilee about tree fruit with a separate admonition, and about produce of the soil with a separate admonition—just as for the seventh year, as we wrote above (§333). The law for the both, i.e. the seventh

כְּלוֹמַר בַּשְׁמִטָּה וּבַיּוֹבֵל, בַּלָּאוִין אֵלֶּה אֶחָד הוּא, וּמִשֹּׁרֶשׁ אֶחָד יַעֲלֶה הַכֹּל לְפִי הַדּוֹמֶה, וְאֵין צֹרֶךְ לְהַאֲרִיךְ עַל כֵּן.

וּכְבָר כָּתַבְתִּי כִּי כָל זֶה אֵינוֹ נוֹהֵג אֶלָּא בָּאָרֶץ, וְעַל תְּנַאי שֶׁיִּהְיוּ כָל יוֹשְׁבֶיהָ עָלֶיהָ, וְיִהְיֶה כָל שֵׁבֶט וָשֵׁבֶט דָּר בִּמְקוֹמוֹ.

[מִצְוַת עֲשִׂיַּת דִּין בֵּין לוֹקֵחַ וּמוֹכֵר]

שלו שֶׁנָּדִין בְּדִין מִקָּח וּמִמְכָּר כְּעִנְיָן שֶׁצִּוְּתָה הַתּוֹרָה עָלָיו, כְּלוֹמַר שֶׁיֵּשׁ צְדָדִין שֶׁיִּתְקַיֵּם הַמֶּכֶר בֵּין מוֹכֵר לְלוֹקֵחַ וְיֵשׁ צְדָדִין שֶׁאֵין לָהּ קִיּוּם, וְהוּא חוֹבָה עָלֵינוּ לָדוּן בֵּינֵיהֶם כְּמִצְוַת הַתּוֹרָה. וְאַף-עַל-פִּי שֶׁבָּאוּ מִצְווֹת אֲחֵרוֹת עַל זֶה, כְּמוֹ שֶׁכָּתַבְנוּ בְּ"מִשְׁפָּטִים", שֶׁנִּצְטַוֵּינוּ לָדוּן בֵּין טוֹעֵן וְנִטְעָן וּבֵין מַזִּיק וְנִזָּק וְכַיּוֹצֵא בָזֶה, וְכָל מִקָּח וּמִמְכָּר בִּכְלַל טוֹעֵן וְנִטְעָן הוּא, אַף-עַל-פִּי-כֵן בָּאָה הַמִּצְוָה עַל עִנְיַן הַמִּקָּח וּמִמְכָּר מְיֻחֶדֶת מִפְּנֵי שֶׁהוּא דָבָר תְּמִידִי אֶל הַבְּרִיּוֹת, שֶׁאִי-אֶפְשָׁר לִבְנֵי-אָדָם לִחְיוֹת אֲפִלּוּ יוֹם אֶחָד זוּלָתוֹ.

וְאַתְּ מוֹצֵא שֶׁכָּךְ דַּרְכָּהּ שֶׁל תּוֹרָה בְּהַרְבֵּה מְקוֹמוֹת, שֶׁלְּפִי צֹרֶךְ הַדָּבָר אוֹ חֹמֶר שֶׁבּוֹ תִּיחֵד הַמִּצְוָה בּוֹ, וּכְמוֹ-כֵן תִּכְפֹּל הָאַזְהָרוֹת בְּדָבָר פְּעָמִים רַבּוֹת כְּמוֹ שֶׁאַתָּה רוֹאֶה בְּאַזְהָרַת עֲבוֹדָה זָרָה, שֶׁנִּכְפְּלָה בְמ"ד מְקוֹמוֹת, וְיִחֵד הָאַזְהָרָה בְּמֶלֶךְ לְבַדּוֹ לְפִי שֶׁהָיְתָה מְצוּיָה הַרְבֵּה אוֹתָהּ הָעֲבוֹדָה הָרָעָה; וְכֵן בָּאוּ בְעִנְיַן שַׁבָּת י"ב אַזְהָרוֹת בַּתּוֹרָה, וְנִתְיַחֲדָה הָאַזְהָרָה בּוֹ בְּקִצָת מְלָאכוֹת, כְּמוֹ הַבְעָרָה וְהוֹצָאָה; וְאַף-עַל-פִּי שֶׁיֵּשׁ בָּהֶן מִדְרָשׁ אִם לְחַלֵּק יָצְאַת אוֹ לְלָאו, אֵין הַמִּדְרָשׁ לָנוּ סְתִירָה: הַרְבֵּה פָנִים לַתּוֹרָה.

שֹׁרֶשׁ הַדִּינִין יָדוּעַ, כִּי הוּא דָבָר שֶׁשֵּׂכֶל בְּנֵי-אִישׁ מֵעִיד עָלָיו וּמְבַקֵּשׁ אוֹתוֹ,

§336 1. The later editions add ועל זה נאמרה פרשת "וכי תמכרו ממכר" וגו': and for this the Scriptural section was stated, *Now if you sell something to your neighbor, etc.* (Leviticus 25:14). Although this is not in the manuscripts or the first edition, it may well be a correct reading, for otherwise we have no Scriptural verse here for the precept, and our author invariably cites one.

1a. See above, §114.

year and the jubilee, in these negative precepts, is one and the same; and it all grows out from one root reason, as it would seem. Then there is no need to go on at length about them all.

I have written previously (§330) that all this is in effect only in the land [of Israel], and provided that all its inhabitants are on it, each and every tribe dwelling in its place.

.[THE PRECEPT OF EFFECTING JUSTICE BETWEEN BUYER AND SELLER]

336 that we should render judgment about purchase and sale (trade) in the way that the Torah commanded about it; in other words, there are situations where a sale is upheld (valid) between the vendor and the buyer, and there are situations where it has no validity; and an obligation lies on us to judge between them by the commandment of the Torah. Even though other precepts were given about this, as we wrote in *sidrah mishpatim*, that we were commanded to judge between plaintiff and defendant (§58), between a damager and a victim, and so forth, and every [controversy about] a purchase and sale is a case of a plaintiff and defendant, nevertheless this precept was given particularly about purchases and sales because that is a constant matter among people: for it is impossible for people to live even one day without it.[1]

You will find that this is the way of the Torah in many instances: that according to the necessity of a matter or its seriousness, there will be a particular precept about it. And so too, prohibitions about some matter may be redoubled many times, as you see about the admonition against idolatry: It was reiterated in forty-four places, yet an admonition was given especially about Molech alone (§208), because that evil worship was very prevalent. So, likewise, twelve admonitions were given in the Torah regarding the Sabbath, yet about some labors, such as burning a fire (§114) and carrying things out-of-doors (§24), we were especially adjured. Even though there is a particular interpretation about these [verses], whether they were singled out to separate [each major category of labor into a separate violation of the Sabbath][1a] or to [make them merely the violation of] a negative precept,[2] this interpretation forms no contradiction for us, since there are many aspects [of meaning] to the Torah.

The root reason for trials of law and justice is known (evident), ⟨385⟩ because it is something that human intelligence affirms and seeks;

כִּי בְדִין יִתְקַיֵּם יִשׁוּב בֵּין בְּנֵי־אָדָם.

מִדִּינֵי הַמִּצְוָה, מַה שֶּׁאָמְרוּ זִכְרוֹנָם לִבְרָכָה שֶׁדִּינֵי הַמֶּקַח וְהַמִּמְכָּר חֲלוּקִים
לְפִי הַדְּבָרִים הַנִּמְכָּרִים וְהַנִּלְקָחִים: שֶׁהַקַּרְקָעוֹת וְהָעֲבָדִים נִקְנִין בְּכֶסֶף וּבִשְׁטָר
וּבַחֲזָקָה; וּבְכָל אֶחָד מֵאֵלוּ, כֵּיצַד בְּכֶסֶף וְכֵיצַד בִּשְׁטָר וְכֵן בַּחֲזָקָה, יֵשׁ בָּהֶן פְּרָטִים
רַבִּים, כְּמוֹ שֶׁבָּא בְקִדּוּשִׁין בְּפֶרֶק קַמָּא; וְהַמִּטַּלְטְלִין נִקְנִין בִּדְרָכִים אֲחֵרִים: יֵשׁ
מֵהֶן שֶׁנִּקְנִין בְּהַגְבָּהָה, וְזֹאת הַקְּנִיָּה גְדוֹלָה וּמַסְפֶּקֶת לְכָל הַמִּטַּלְטְלִין; וְיֵשׁ מֵהֶן
שֶׁנִּקְנִין בִּקְנִיָּה פְּחוּתָה מִזּוֹ, וְהִיא הַמְּשִׁיכָה; וּמֵהֶן שֶׁנִּקְנִין בִּפְחוּתָה מִזּוֹ, וְהִיא
הַמְּסִירָה.

וְהֵבִיאוּ זִכְרוֹנָם לִבְרָכָה רְאָיָה עַל הֱיוֹת הַמִּטַּלְטְלִין צְרִיכִין אֵלוּ הַקְּנִיּוֹת
וְשֶׁאֵינָן נִקְנִין כְּמוֹ הַקַּרְקָעוֹת, מִדִּכְתִיב: אוֹ קָנֹה מִיַּד עֲמִיתֶךָ, וּפֵרְשׁוּ הֵם זִכְרוֹנָם
לִבְרָכָה מִצַּד הַקַּבָּלָה בְּפֵרוּשׁ "אוֹ קָנֹה מִיַּד": כְּלוֹמַר דָּבָר הַנִּקְנֶה מִיַּד לְיָד; וְגַם־
כֵּן הֵבִיאוּ רְאָיָה עַל קְנִיַּת הַקַּרְקָעוֹת בְּכֶסֶף בִּשְׁטָר וּבַחֲזָקָה מִכְּתוּבִים אֲחֵרִים, כְּמוֹ
שֶׁבָּא שָׁם בְּקִדּוּשִׁין.

וְאֵין סָפֵק כִּי אֵלוּ הַקְּנִיּוֹת כֻּלָּן מִתַּקָּנַת חֲכָמִים הֵן, וְהֵבִיאוּ הַכְּתוּבִים לְסָמֹךְ
בָּהֶם דִּבְרֵיהֶם; וְהָאֱמֶת כִּי חָכְמָתָם הַיְקָרָה הָעֲתִידָה לְהִגָּלוֹת עַל יָדָם הָיְתָה רְמוּזָה
וּגְנוּזָה בְּתוֹךְ הַכְּתוּבִים; וְאַף־עַל־פִּי שֶׁעִקַּר הַכְּתוּבִים אֵינוֹ עַל אוֹתָן אַסְמַכְתּוֹת,
נִלְמָדוֹת הֵן מִתּוֹכָן.

וְאָמְרוּ זִכְרוֹנָם לִבְרָכָה בַּגְּמָרָא: דְּבַר תּוֹרָה מָעוֹת קוֹנוֹת אַף בְּמִטַּלְטְלִין, אֲבָל
טַעַם (הצריכים) [הַצְרִיכָם] הַמְּשִׁיכָה בָּהֶן, גְּזֵרָה שֶׁמָּא יֹאמַר לוֹ מוֹכֵר לַלּוֹקֵחַ:
נִשְׂרְפוּ חִטֶּיךָ בָּעֲלִיָּה. וּמִפְּנֵי שֶׁתַּקָּנַת הַמְּשִׁיכָה בָּהֶם נַעֲשֵׂית עַל זֶה, אָמְרוּ זִכְרוֹנָם
לִבְרָכָה שֶׁאִם הָיוּ הַמִּטַּלְטְלִין בִּרְשׁוּתוֹ שֶׁל לוֹקֵחַ, אַף־עַל־פִּי שֶׁנִּשְׂכַּר אוֹתוֹ מָקוֹם
לַמּוֹכֵר, מִכֵּיוָן שֶׁהָרְשׁוּת הוּא שֶׁל לוֹקֵחַ וְעֵינָיו תָּמִיד עָלָיו, וְאִם יֶאֱרַע שׁוּם מִקְרֶה

---

2. Punishable by whiplashes, and not a major kind of labor, punishable by stoning
to death.

3. I.e. a document in which the vendor attests that his land or servant is given over
to the buyer for his acquisition.

4. I.e. some specific action is done to establish the buyer's status as the new owner:
e.g. he digs in the land or has the slave loosen his shoe; TB Kiddushin 22b, 26a.

5. I.e. the purchaser lifts or picks the object up; TB Bava Bathra 76b.

6. The purchased object is drawn into the buyer's domain, or at least out of the
public domain or thoroughfare into a side street or lane where it is permissible to leave
one's possessions or wares for a while.

7. E.g. the seller gives the reins of an animal to the buyer (see below).

8. TB Bava M'tzi'a 47b. From "and they" to "in other words" (below) is missing
in the oldest manuscripts and in all but the first edition. Rather than a later interpolation
it seems more like a scribal omission between somewhat identical phrases, in all but the
first edition.

for with justice a settled community life can endure among people.

Among the laws of the precept, there is what the Sages of blessed memory taught: that the laws of purchase and sale are differentiated according to the things sold and bought: land and servants being acquired by money, a document (deed),[3] or through demonstration of ownership.[4] Then in each of these [there is the law of how it is acquired]: how with money, how with a document, and so also by the demonstration of ownership. There are many details about these, as we find in the first chapter of the tractate *Kiddushin*. Movable goods, however, are acquired in other ways: Some are acquired by lifting up; this is the paramount way of acquisition, which suffices for all movable goods.[5] Some of them are acquired by a means inferior to this, i.e. drawing or pulling.[6] And some are acquired by something yet inferior to this, i.e. handing over.[7]

Now, the Sages of blessed memory brought proof that movable goods require these ways of acquisition, and they cannot be acquired like landed property: For it is written, *or buy from the hand of your neighbor* (Leviticus 25:14); and they (of blessed memory) explained through the Oral Tradition,[8] interpreting "or buy from the hand": in other words, something that is acquired from hand to hand. Similarly, they brought proof that land is acquired with money, a deed, or the demonstration of ownership, from other verses of Scripture, as we read there in the tractate *Kiddushin* (26a).

There is no doubt, though, that these ways of acquisition are all by the enactment of the Sages,[9] and they cited the Scriptural verses [only] to buttress their words with them. The truth is that their precious wisdom, destined to be revealed through them, was intimated and concealed within the verses; and though the main sense of the verses is not to provide those indications of support [for the rulings of the Sages], they yet can be derived from them.

Now, the Sages of blessed memory said in the *g'mara*:[10] By the law of the Torah, money brings possession of movable goods too;[11] but the reason why they made it necessary to draw them [into one's domain, etc.] is that it is a protective decree: for the vendor might tell the buyer, "Your wheat was burned up in the loft."[12] Now, since the method of drawing or pulling was instituted for them [movable goods] for this reason, they (of blessed memory) said that if the movable goods were [already] in the buyer's domain, even if that place was rented to the seller, since the premises are the buyer's and he

בְּאוֹתָן מִטַּלְטְלִין, גַּם הוּא יָכוֹל לְהַרְגִּיש בָּעִנְיָן כְּמוֹ הַמּוֹכֵר וְיִשְׁתַּדֵּל בַּהַצָּלָה, שֶׁבְּצַד זֶה לֹא יִקְנֶה בִּמְשִׁיכָה אֶלָּא בְכֶסֶף כְּדִין תּוֹרָה. וְכֵן אִם הַלּוֹקֵחַ שׂוֹכֵר אוֹתוֹ מָקוֹם שֶׁהַמִּטַּלְטְלִין בּוֹ, גַּם בְּעִנְיָן זֶה לֹא תִקְנוּ בָהֶם מְשִׁיכָה וּמְסִירָה וְהַגְבָּהָה.

וְאָמְרוּ גַם־כֵּן שֶׁהַקַּרְקַע נִשְׂכָּר עִם הַדְּבָרִים שֶׁהוּא נִלְקָח, וְהוּא כֶסֶף וּשְׁטָר וַחֲזָקָה, שֶׁהַשְּׂכִירוּת קְנִיָּה הִיא לְיוֹמָהּ. וְאָמְרוּ גַם־כֵּן: כְּשֵׁם שֶׁמְּקוֹמוֹ שֶׁל אָדָם קוֹנֶה לוֹ כָּךְ כֵּלָיו קוֹנֶה לוֹ בְכָל מָקוֹם שֶׁיִּהְיֶה לוֹ רְשׁוּת לְהָנִיחַ אוֹתוֹ, וּמִכֵּיוָן שֶׁיִּהְיוּ הַמִּטַּלְטְלִין בְּתוֹךְ הַכְּלִי אֵין אֶחָד מֵהֶם יָכוֹל לַחֲזֹר בּוֹ, אֶלָּא הֲרֵי הֵן כְּמוֹ שֶׁהִגְבִּיהָן אוֹ כְמוֹ שֶׁהוּנְחוּ בְתוֹךְ בֵּיתוֹ; אֲבָל כָּל מָקוֹם שֶׁאֵין לוֹ רְשׁוּת לַלּוֹקֵחַ לְהָנִיחַ שָׁם הַכְּלִי אֵין כֵּלָיו קוֹנֶה לוֹ שָׁם, כְּגוֹן רְשׁוּת הָרַבִּים וְכֵן רְשׁוּת הַמּוֹכֵר. וּמִכָּל־מָקוֹם אָמְרוּ חֲכָמִים לְעִנְיַן רְשׁוּת מוֹכֵר שֶׁאִם אָמַר לוֹ מוֹכֵר לַלּוֹקֵחַ "קְנֵה בִכְלִי זֶה", אוֹ אֲפִלּוּ לֹא אָמַר לוֹ כֵן אֶלָּא שֶׁקָּנָה מִמֶּנּוּ בִּרְשׁוּת הַמּוֹכֵר כְּלִי אֶחָד וְהִגְבִּיהוֹ כְּדֵי לִקְנוֹתוֹ וְאַחַר־כָּךְ קָנָה מִמֶּנּוּ פֵּרוֹת וְהִנִּיחָן בְּתוֹךְ הַכְּלִי, מִיָּד קָנָה אוֹתָן, שֶׁמִּפְּנֵי הַהֲנָאָה שֶׁיֵּשׁ לוֹ לַמּוֹכֵר בִּמְכִירַת הַכְּלִי אֵינוֹ מַקְפִּיד עַל מְקוֹמוֹ שֶׁל כְּלִי, וּכְאִלּוּ הַכְּלִי בִּרְשׁוּת הַלּוֹקֵחַ חַשְׁבִינַן לֵיהּ.

וְהַמְּסִירָה אֵינָה כֵּן, שֶׁאֵין הַמְּסִירָה קוֹנָה אֶלָּא בִּרְשׁוּת הָרַבִּים וּבְחָצֵר שֶׁאֵינָהּ שֶׁל שְׁנֵיהֶם; וְקִנְיַן הַמְּסִירָה הוּא בְמַה שֶּׁאֵין דֶּרֶךְ בְּנֵי־אָדָם לְרֹב גְּדֹלָן לְהַגְבִּיהָן וְלֹא אֲפִלּוּ לְמָשְׁכָן, כְּגוֹן הַסְּפִינוֹת הַגְּדוֹלוֹת וְכַיּוֹצֵא בָהֶן, שֶׁאִי אֶפְשָׁר לִבְנֵי־אָדָם (לזוז) [לְהָזִיז] אוֹתָן כִּי־אִם בְּטֹרַח רַב וּבְרֻבּוּי בְּנֵי־אָדָם.

וְהַמְּשִׁיכָה אֵינָה כֵּן, שֶׁאֵין הַמְּשִׁיכָה עוֹשָׂה קִנְיָן אֶלָּא בְסִמְטָא, וְהוּא מָקוֹם סָמוּךְ לְצַד רְשׁוּת הָרַבִּים, שֶׁדֶּרֶךְ בְּנֵי אָדָם לְהָנִיחַ שָׁם כְּלֵיהֶם, וְכָל הַקּוֹדֵם לְהָנִיחַ

---

9. Our author evidently derives this from TJ Kiddushin i 5 (MY).

10. The later part of the Talmud; TB Bava M'tzi'a 47b.

11. Just as with its payment one gains possession of landed property.

12. I.e. if it becomes the buyer's property when he pays for it, while it is on the seller's premises, the seller will take no care to protect it from fire, etc. (On the bracketed addition, "into one's domain, etc.," see note 6.)

13. TB Bava M'tzi'a 49b.

14. This act of itself would give him acquisition of the goods; see Mishnah, Ma'asér Shéni v 9.

15. TB Bava Kamma 79b.

16. TB Bava Bathra 85a–b; MT hilchoth m'chirah iv 1.

17. TB Bava Bathra 76b (see note 7).

18. MT ibid. iii 3; see also tosafoth, TB Bava Bathra 76a, s.v. s'finah.

always has his eyes on it, so that if anything should happen to those movable goods, he too can be aware of the matter, as well as the seller, and he can strive to save them—for this reason he cannot make them his by drawing [them into his domain, etc.] but only by money, according to the law of the Torah.[13] Similarly, if the buyer leased the place where the movable goods are,[14] for this situation too they did not enact the methods of drawing, handing over, and lifting.

The Sages taught further[15] that land may be leased in those ways by which it is bought and acquired, i.e. by money, a deed, and the demonstration of ownership; because leasing means purchasing for its days [its period]. And they taught in addition:[16] Just as a man's place (domain) can acquire something for him, so can his vessel acquire something for him wherever he has the right to leave it. Then once the movable goods are in the vessel, neither of them can retract; it is rather as though he had lifted them up or as though they had been set down within his house. But wherever the buyer does not have the right to put a vessel down, there his vessels can make nothing his own— for example, in the public domain [thoroughfare], and so also on the seller's premises.[16] However, the Sages taught, regarding the seller's domain, that if the seller told the purchaser, "Acquire it in this vessel," or even if he did not tell him this but the other purchased from him a vessel in the seller's domain and he picked it up in order to make it his, and afterward he bought fruit from him [from the seller] and put it into the vessel, he would acquire it immediately.[16] For on account of the benefit that the seller has by the sale of the vessel, he does not mind about the place that the vessel occupies, and it is thus reckoned as if the vessel were in the buyer's domain.[16]

"Handing over" is not so, however: for such transmission brings possession of an object nowhere but in the public domain or in a courtyard that belongs to neither of them.[17] Acquisition by "handing over" applies to objects which, on account of their large size, it is not usual for people to pick up or even to draw [to themselves]: for example, large ships, and similar entities, which it is impossible for people to budge except with great toil and with a large number of men.[18]

Neither is drawing or pulling [an object into another place] like that. For drawing an object makes it become acquired only in an alley, which is a place close by, at the side of the public domain [thoroughfare], where it is usual for people to leave their vessels and things; and whoever leaves his vessels there first. his fellow-man

שָׁם כֵּלָיו, אֵין חֲבֵרוֹ רַשַּׁאי לְסַלְּקוֹ; וּכְמוֹ־כֵן קוֹנֶה הַמְּשִׁיכָה בֶּחָצֵר (שֶׁאֵינָה)
[שֶׁהִיא] שֶׁל שְׁנֵיהֶם. וְהַהַגְבָּהָה קוֹנֶה בְּכָל מָקוֹם, לְפִי שֶׁבְּגוּפוֹ הוּא מַגְבִּיהַּ, וּבוֹ
הוּא קוֹנֶה, וְגוּפוֹ רְשׁוּתוֹ הוּא בְּכָל מָקוֹם שֶׁהוּא.

וְעוֹד יֵשׁ קְנִיָּה אַחֶרֶת בְּקַרְקָעוֹת וּמִטַּלְטְלִין דְּבַר תּוֹרָה, וְהִיא הַחֲלִיפִין, וְזֹאת
הַקְּנִיָּה הָיְתָה מְרֻגֶּלֶת לְפָנִים בְּיִשְׂרָאֵל. וְעִנְיַן הַחֲלִיפִין הוּא שֶׁאָדָם מַחֲלִיף בְּהֶמְתּוֹ
בְּבֶהֱמַת חֲבֵרוֹ אוֹ כְלִי בִּכְלִי אוֹ כֵלִים בְּקַרְקָעוֹת; וְאָמְרוּ חֲכָמִים בְּכָל אֵלּוּ שֶׁכֵּיוָן
שֶׁמָּשַׁךְ הָאֶחָד הַכְּלִי מֵחֲבֵרוֹ זָכָה חֲבֵרוֹ בְּאוֹתוֹ הַכְּלִי הָאַחֵר שֶׁהוּא רוֹצֶה לִקְנוֹתוֹ
מִמֶּנּוּ, בְּכָל מָקוֹם שֶׁיִּהְיֶה, וְאִם יֶאֱרַע בּוֹ שׁוּם אֲבֵדָה, נֶאֱבַד לְצֹרֶךְ זֶה שֶׁזָּכָה בּוֹ
עַכְשָׁיו בַּחֲלִיפִין.

וְדִין קְנִיַּת הַחֲלִיפִין אֵינוֹ אֶלָּא בְכֵלִים, אֲבָל לֹא בְּפֵרוֹת, שֶׁאֵין הַפֵּרוֹת עוֹשִׂין
חֲלִיפִין, שֶׁהֲרֵי בְּפֵרוּשׁ מָצָאנוּ בְּאוֹתוֹ כָּתוּב שֶׁלָּמַדְנוּ מִמֶּנּוּ הַחֲלִיפִין, שֶׁבִּכְלִי הֵן,
כְּמוֹ שֶׁכָּתוּב: וְזֹאת לְפָנִים בְּיִשְׂרָאֵל ... שָׁלַף אִישׁ נַעֲלוֹ, כְּלוֹמַר בֵּית־יָד שֶׁלּוֹ, וְזֶהוּ
כְלִי. וּמִכָּל־מָקוֹם, אַף־עַל־פִּי שֶׁאֵין הַפֵּרוֹת עוֹשִׂין חֲלִיפִין לִקְנוֹת בָּהֶן כְּמוֹ בִכְלִי,
נִקְנִין הֵן בְּתוֹרַת חֲלִיפִין, כְּלוֹמַר בִּכְלִי יָכוֹל אָדָם לִקְנוֹתָן בְּדֶרֶךְ חֲלִיפִין, שֶׁיִּתֵּן
אָדָם לַחֲבֵרוֹ כְלִי וְיִזְכֶּה בְּפֵרוֹת חֲבֵרוֹ בְּכָל מָקוֹם שֶׁהֵן.

מַה שֶּׁאֵין כֵּן בְּמַטְבֵּעַ, שֶׁהַמַּטְבֵּעַ אֵינוֹ נַעֲשָׂה חֲלִיפִין וְלֹא נִקְנֶה בַּחֲלִיפִין, לְפִי
שֶׁדַּעְתּוֹ שֶׁל אָדָם עַל הַצּוּרָה, וְהַצּוּרָה עֲשׂוּיָה לְהִבָּטֵל בִּרְצוֹן הַמֶּלֶךְ אוֹ גְדוֹלֵי
הַמְּדִינוֹת, וְעַל מַה שֶּׁאֵינוֹ דָבָר קַיָּם אֵין לֵב הַבְּרִיּוֹת סוֹמֵךְ בּוֹ לִקְנוֹת בּוֹ, וְעַל־כֵּן
אֵינוֹ נִקְנֶה בַּחֲלִיפִין וְלֹא נַעֲשָׂה חֲלִיפִין.

אֲבָל מַטְבֵּעַ שֶׁאֵין חֲשִׁיבוּתוֹ מֵחֲמַת הַצּוּרָה נִקְנֶה בַּחֲלִיפִין וְנַעֲשָׂה חֲלִיפִין כְּכָל
שְׁאָר הַמִּטַּלְטְלִין; וְאֵי זֶהוּ, זֶה מַטְבֵּעַ שֶׁפְּסָלַתּוּ מַלְכוּת אוֹ בְּנֵי הַמְּדִינָה, וְכִדְאָמַר
רֵישׁ לָקִישׁ בְּפֶרֶק הַזָּהָב: אֲפִלּוּ כִּיס מָלֵא מָעוֹת, וְתִרְגְּמָא רַבִּי אַבָּא בְּדִינָרָא

---

19. Thus it is not only usual for people to leave their belongings there, but also
fully permissible. TB *Bava Bathra* 76b.

20. The original reads "to neither of them," but it is evidently a scribal error (MY).

21. Inferred from Ruth 4:7 (see next paragraph), which refers to the intention of
Boaz to acquire Naomi's field.

22. MT *hilchoth m'chirah* v 5, based on TB *Bava M'tzi'a* 45–47, etc. (*Kessef
Mishneh, Maggid Mishneh*).

23. TB *Bava M'tzi'a* 47a.

24. Or sleeve; so Targum to Ruth 4:7 (although *na'al* is usually understood as a
shoe).

25. TB *Bava M'tzi'a* 46a (see *tosafoth*, s.v. *'e-la*).

26. Stamped on the coin, which gives it its official value as legal tender; he does not
consider its worth as precious metal; *ibid.* 45b. (In olden times many local city
governments had the right to mint their own coins, under the sovereign powers that
ruled them; or they had to use the coinage of the sovereign powers. The value of a
particular minting would thus vary with the political situation.)

has no right to move them away.[19] Drawing likewise brings ownership in a courtyard that belongs to both of them.[20] Lifting, though, brings ownership everywhere,[19] because he picks it up himself, with his body, and with that he acquires it; and his body is his domain wherever he is.

Now, there is yet another way of acquisition for both land and movable goods, by the law of the Torah, which is exchange or barter; and this way of acquisition was habitual in Israel in times of old.[21] In substance, barter means that a man exchanges his animal for his fellow-man's beast, or one vessel for another, or objects for landed property. Our Sages said concerning all these instances[22] that once one draws a vessel from his fellow [to his place] his fellow gains possession of the other vessel, which he wished to buy from him, wherever it may be; and if any kind of loss occurs to it, the loss is suffered by this man who acquired it now by the exchange.

The law of taking possession by barter applies, however, only to objects of utility, but not to produce, as produce cannot effect an exchange:[23] For we distinctly find in the verse from which we learn the law of barter, that it applies to objects: as it is written, *Now this was the custom in former times in Israel . . . a man drew off his* na'al (Ruth 4:7), i.e. his gauntlet,[24] which was an object. Nevertheless, even though produce cannot effect a barter to bring about the acquisition of an object in exchange for it, it can itself be acquired by the method of barter. In other words, for an object a man can acquire it by way of exchange: A person can give his fellow-man an object of utility and gain possession of the other's produce wherever it is.

This is not the case, though, with coinage: for a coin can neither be used to effect a barter nor can it be acquired by barter[25]—because a man's consideration [of its value] is by the imprinted design,[26] and the imprinted design can be made valueless at the pleasure of the king or the high officers of the states; and on something that is not permanent the heart of human beings does not [truly] rely, to acquire something by it. For this reason it can neither be acquired through barter nor can it effect a barter.

However, a coin whose value is not on account of the imprint may be acquired by barter and can put through a barter, like all other movable goods. Which is this?—this is a coin which the royal government or the country's inhabitants have disqualified.[27] As Resh Lakish said in chapter 4 of the tractate *Bava M'tzi'a* (46b), "even a purse full of coins"; and R. 'Abba[28] understood it to mean two kinds of

נְיָאקָא וְאַנְגְּרָא, חַד פְּסָלַתּוּ מַלְכוּת וְחַד פְּסָלַתּוּ מְדִינָה.

וְאֵין הַכַּוָּנָה בְּאָמְרֵנוּ שֶׁאֵינוֹ נַעֲשֶׂה חֲלִיפִין וְלֹא נִקְנֶה בַּחֲלִיפִין, שֶׁמִּי שֶׁמָּשַׁךְ פֵּרוֹת מֵחֲבֵרוֹ בְּכָךְ-וְכָךְ מָעוֹת לֹא יִתְחַיֵּב לָתֵת לוֹ הַמָּעוֹת, דְּוַדַּאי מִתְחַיֵּב הוּא לְהַשְׁלִים לוֹ מָעוֹתָיו מִכֵּיוָן שֶׁמָּשַׁךְ פֵּרוֹתָיו; אֲבָל הָעִנְיָן הוּא שֶׁאֵינוֹ נַעֲשֶׂה חֲלִיפִין, שֶׁמִּי שֶׁהָיוּ לוֹ שַׂק שֶׁל מָעוֹת מַטְבֵּעַ שֶׁאֵינוֹ נִפְסָל, כְּמוֹ שֶׁאָמַרְנוּ, וּמָשַׁךְ מֵחֲבֵרוֹ כֵּלִים אוֹ בְהֵמָה אוֹ פֵרוֹת, וְאָמַר לַחֲבֵרוֹ "הֲרֵינִי מוֹשֵׁךְ פֵּרוֹת אֵלּוּ חֲלִיפֵי אוֹתוֹ שַׂק שֶׁל מָעוֹת שֶׁיֵּשׁ לִי בַּבַּיִת, שֶׁיֵּשׁ בּוֹ מֵאָה דִינָרִין", אֵין חֲבֵרוֹ זוֹכֶה בְּאוֹתָן דִּינָרִין כְּלָל, וְאִם נֶאֶבְדוּ אַחַר שֶׁמָּשַׁךְ זֶה הַפֵּרוֹת בְּשׁוּם צַד, וַאֲפִלּוּ בְּאֹנֶס, לֹא נֶאֶבְדוּ לוֹ כְּלָל, אֶלָּא חֲבֵרוֹ מְחֻיָּב לָתֵת לוֹ מֵאָה דִינָרִין מִכָּל-מָקוֹם.

וְזֶהוּ שֶׁאָמְרוּ זִכְרוֹנָם לִבְרָכָה: מָשַׁךְ הֵימֶנּוּ פֵּרוֹת וְלֹא נָתַן לוֹ מָעוֹת, אֵינוֹ יָכוֹל לַחֲזוֹר בּוֹ, כְּלוֹמַר מְחֻיָּב הוּא לוֹ לְהַשְׁלִים הַדָּמִים מִכָּל-מָקוֹם, דְּלָאו בְּתוֹרַת חֲלִיפִין אִתְּמַר אֶלָּא בְּתוֹרַת דָּמִים. וְכֵן הוּא מְבֹאָר בְּרֵישׁ פֶּרֶק הַזָּהָב, שֶׁאָמְרוּ שָׁם "הַזָּהָב קוֹנֶה אֶת הַכֶּסֶף"; וּמַקְשֶׁה שָׁם, "אִי הָכִי, 'קוֹנֶה', 'מְחֻיָּב' מִבָּעֵי לֵיהּ", כְּלוֹמַר דְּלָא נָפִיל לְשׁוֹן קִנְיָן אֶלָּא בְּדָבָר יָדוּעַ; אֲבָל זֶה מֵבִיא הוּא לוֹ אִי זֶה דָמִים שֶׁיִּרְצֶה, וּמְתָרֵץ "תְּנֵי מְחֻיָּב", כְּלוֹמַר מְחֻיָּב הוּא לָתֵת לוֹ הַדָּמִים מִכֵּיוָן שֶׁמָּשַׁךְ מִמֶּנּוּ הַפֵּרוֹת, וְאֵינוֹ יָכוֹל לַחֲזוֹר בּוֹ.

אֲבָל הַנּוֹתֵן לַחֲבֵרוֹ מָעוֹת לִקְנוֹת מִמֶּנּוּ פֵּרוֹת, אֵינוֹ מִתְחַיֵּב בַּעַל הַפֵּרוֹת לְתִתָּם לוֹ, שֶׁזּוֹ הִיא תַּקָּנַת חֲכָמִים זִכְרוֹנָם לִבְרָכָה, שֶׁלֹּא לִקְנוֹת בְּכֶסֶף אֶלָּא בִמְשִׁיכָה; אֲבָל מִכָּל-מָקוֹם חִיְּבוּהוּ זִכְרוֹנָם לִבְרָכָה לְקַבֵּל "מִי שֶׁפָּרַע", לְפִי שֶׁחוֹזֵר בִּדְבָרוֹ,

27. Among themselves, the people refuse to honor it as legal tender. In these cases a person evaluates it only as precious metal.

28. So also in four Talmud manuscripts, etc. (*Dikduké Sof'rim*); in our Talmud editions it is R. 'Aḥa.

29. Out of hatred for the king, although it has full value in other provinces (Rashi).

30. TB Bava M'tzi'a 44a.

31. The *beth din* (court) pronounces over him, "He who exacted payment from the members of the generation of the Flood, from the members of the generation of the Dispersal, from the people of Sodom and Gomorrah, and from the Egyptians who drowned in the sea—He shall exact payment from one who does not stand by his word"; then he may refund the money (MT *hilchoth m'chirah* vii 2).

disqualified coins: one, which the government voided; and one, which the province rendered worthless.[29]

Now, when we say that it cannot be used in barter or acquired by barter, it does not mean that if someone drew produce [to him] from his neighbor for such-and-such a price, he is not obligated to give him the money. For he is certainly duty-bound to pay him the money, since he drew his produce [into his own domain, etc.]. The meaning is rather that it cannot serve for barter: If someone has a bag of coins that were not disqualified, as we said, and his fellow-man drew to him vessels, a domestic animal, or produce, and told the other, "I hereby draw this produce in exchange for that bag of money that I have at home, which contains 100 *denarii*," his fellow does not gain possession of those *denarii* at all; and if, after this man drew the produce [into his place] they were lost in any way whatever, even if by accident or force, he does not suffer their loss at all. Rather, his fellow is duty-bound to give him 100 *denarii* in any event.

Hence what the Sages of blessed memory said:[30] If one drew produce from the other [into his place] and did not give him money, he cannot turn about and retract. In other words, he is obligated to pay the other the money under all circumstances, since this was not meant in terms of an exchange but in terms of monetary payment. And so is it elucidated at the beginning of the fourth chapter of the tractate *Bava M'tzi'a* (45b); for it was taught there: Gold brings acquisition of silver; does this not surely mean by exchange?—no: by monetary payment. It is then asked there: If so, it should have said, "the purchaser is obligated [to pay with the silver]." In other words, the expression of "acquisition" fits nothing other than something specific [given in return]; but this man may bring him whatever money he wishes. The answer is then given: Read this as "imposes obligation." This means, then, that one is duty-bound to give the other money once he has drawn produce from him [into his own domain, etc.] and he cannot retract.

However, if someone gives his fellow-man money in order to acquire produce from him, the owner of the produce is not obligated to give it to him. For this is the enactment of the Sages of blessed memory: that acquisition should come not through money but by drawing or pulling [the object into one's place]. In any event, though, they (of blessed memory) required him to accept the imprecation, "He who exacted payment,"[31] because he goes back on his word

וְאַחַר שֶׁעָשָׂה מַעֲשֶׂה עִם חֲבֵרוֹ, שֶׁקִּבֵּל מִמֶּנּוּ מָעוֹת.

וּקְנִיָּה זוֹ שֶׁל חֲלִיפִין, שֶׁהִיא הַנִּקְרֵאת לַחֲכָמִים זִכְרוֹנָם לִבְרָכָה "קִנְיָן", הִיא קְנִיָּה חֲזָקָה בְּכָל דָּבָר, בֵּין בְּמֶכֶר בֵּין בְּמַתָּנָה, וּבְכָל תְּנָאִין שֶׁבֵּין אָדָם לַחֲבֵרוֹ, שֶׁנֶּאֱמַר בָּזֶה: לְקַיֵּם כָּל דָּבָר...וְזֹאת הַתְּעוּדָה בְּיִשְׂרָאֵל.

וְדִין מִי הוּא רָאוּי לְמְכֹּר וְיִתְקַיֵּם מִכְרוֹ אוֹ מִי אֵינוֹ רָאוּי, כְּגוֹן בֶּן־דַּעַת וְשֶׁאֵינוֹ בֶן־דַּעַת; וְדִין מוֹכֵר דְּבָרִים סְתָם וְאֵינוֹ מְפָרֵשׁ כָּל הָעִנְיָנִים שֶׁצָּרִיךְ לְפָרֵשׁ; וְדִין מְשַׁיֵּר בְּמִמְכָּרוֹ שׁוּם דָּבָר בַּגּוּף אוֹ בַּפֵּרוֹת; וְדִין מְצָרִים שֶׁצָּרִיךְ אָדָם לְהַזְכִּיר בְּמֶכֶר קַרְקַע, וְאִם הִזְכִּיר קְצָתָם וְלֹא כֻלָּם הֵיאַךְ תּוֹרָתוֹ; וְדִין מוֹכֵר מָמוֹן שֶׁאֵינוֹ שֶׁלּוֹ מַה דִּינוֹ; וְדִין מִי שֶׁנֶּאֱנַס לְמְכֹּר קַרְקָעוֹ מַה דִּינוֹ, וְהַחִלּוּק שֶׁבֵּין תָּלוּהוּ וַזַּבֵּן אוֹ תָּלוּהוּ וְיָהֵיב.

וְדִין הַמַּתְנֶה עִם חֲבֵרוֹ שֶׁאִם יִרְצֶה לִמְכֹּר לוֹ קַרְקָעוֹ, שֶׁיִּמְכְּרֵהוּ לוֹ; וְדִין הַמּוֹכֵר קַרְקָעוֹ עַל דַּעַת לַעֲשׂוֹת שׁוּם עִנְיָן וְלֹא עָלָה בְיָדוֹ לַעֲשׂוֹתוֹ, אִם יִתְקַיֵּם מִכְרוֹ אִם לֹא — כְּגוֹן הַמּוֹכֵר אוֹתוֹ עַל דַּעַת לַעֲלוֹת לְאֶרֶץ יִשְׂרָאֵל וְלִבְסוֹף לֹא עָלָה שָׁם, וְכֵן כָּל כַּיּוֹצֵא בָזֶה. וְזֶה שֶׁאֲנִי אוֹמֵר "עַל דַּעַת לַעֲשׂוֹת שׁוּם דָּבָר", לֹא שֶׁיְּפָרֵשׁ הַמּוֹכֵר אוֹתוֹ דָּבָר בִּשְׁעַת הַמֶּכֶר, אֶלָּא שֶׁהַבְּרִיּוֹת יוֹדְעוֹת מִתּוֹךְ מַעֲשָׂיו וּדְבָרָיו שֶׁכֵּן חֶפְצוֹ.

וְדִין מְכִירַת הֶקְדֵּשׁוֹת אוֹ בָתֵּי־כְנֵסִיּוֹת כֵּיצַד, וּלְאֵי זֶה עִנְיָן הֻתַּר הַמֶּכֶר בָּהֶן; וְדִין קִנְיַת שְׁטָרוֹת, שֶׁצָּרִיךְ בָּהֶן מְסִירַת הַשְּׁטָר, וּכְתִיבָה מִצַּד אַחֵר, שֶׁיְּפָרֵשׁ בּוֹ שֶׁהוּא מוֹכֵר לוֹ אוֹתוֹ שְׁטָר וְכָל שִׁעְבּוּדָא דְאִית בֵּיהּ.

וְדִין נוֹתֵן מָעוֹת לַחֲבֵרוֹ לִקְנוֹת לוֹ דָבָר וּקְנָאוֹ לְעַצְמוֹ בְּאוֹתָן מָעוֹת, מַה יְהֵא

<hr>

32. I.e. a witless fool; TB K'thuboth 20a, etc.
33. TB Bava Bathra chapters 4-5.
34. *Ibid.* 69b.
35. *Ibid.* chapter 4, beginning, etc.
36. E.g. "what I will inherit from my father" or "this field, when I will buy it"; TB Bava M'tzi'a 16a; MT *hilchoth m'chirah* xxii 5.
37. TB Bava Bathra 47b, 40b (MT *ibid.* x 1-3); *t'luh* ("one was coerced") literally means "if they hanged him"; Rashi (TB 47b) explains: if someone was hanged [i.e. his head was put in a noose and he was thus threatened with death] or was tortured until he made the sale, took the money, and said, "I am agreeable."
38. TB 'Avodah Zarah 72a.
39. TB Kiddushin 49b.
40. So *tosafoth, ibid.* s.v. *d'varim*; Rambam, MT *ibid.* xi 8-9, differs.
41. TB B'choroth 31 a-b; T'murah 32a; 'Arachin 21a, 24a; M'gillah 26a.
42. TB Bava Bathra 76a; MT *hilchoth m'chirah* vi 11.
43. TB Kiddushin 59a, and see *Shulḥan 'Aruch Ḥoshen Mishpat* §183, 3.

after he has performed a specific action in regard to his fellow, in taking money from him.[30]

Now, this way of acquisition, by barter, which is called by the Sages of blessed memory [simply] "acquisition," is a strong, firm method of making something one's own in every situation, be it a sale, a gift, or any conditions [of transaction] between a man and his fellow. For it is stated of this, *to confirm all things . . . and this was the attestation in Israel* (Ruth 4:7).

Then there is the law on who is fit to sell and his sale will be permanent, and who is not fit: for example, a person with intelligence, and one without intelligence.[32] And we have the law if one sells things generally and does not specify all the matters that need to be expressed;[33] the law if a person leaves over [retains] something in what he sells, in an object or in produce;[34] the law about the borders that a man needs to mention in selling land; and if he mentioned some of them but not all, what his disposition should be;[35] the law if someone sells goods or wares that are not his,[36] what the judgment is for that; the law if someone was compelled by force to sell his land, what his judgment is; and the difference [in law] whether one was coerced and he sold it, or he was coerced and he gave it away.[37]

There is, further, the law if one makes an agreement with his fellow-man that if he should wish to sell his land, he will sell it to him;[38] and the law if one sells his land with the intention of carrying out some plan, and it did not work out for him—if his sale remains valid or not: for instance, if he sells it planning to go up to the land of Israel [to settle there], and ultimately he did not go up there;[39] and so anything similar. Now, when I say, "with the intention of carrying out something," it does not mean that the seller expresses this matter at the time of the sale, but that people know from his actions and his words that this is his desire.[40]

There is, in addition, the law on selling consecrated property or synagogues—how it is done, and for what purpose selling them was permitted.[41] And there is the law of buying deeds: that they require handing over the deed, and something [a bill of sale] in writing, on the other hand, specifying that the one sells this deed to the other, with every obligation and power that it entails.[42]

We have, moreover, the law if one gives money to his fellow-man to buy something for him, and he then bought it for himself with that money—what should be done with it;[43] and the law if three

בְּזֶה; וְדִין שְׁלשָׁה שֶׁנָּתְנוּ מָעוֹת לְאֶחָד וְהָלַךְ וְקָנָה בְּמִקְצָת הַדָּמִים, הֵיאַךְ יַחֲלקוּ; וְדִין מַה שֶּׁאָמְרוּ שֶׁבְּאַרְבָּעָה פְּרָקִים בַּשָּׁנָה מָעוֹת קוֹנוֹת לְעִנְיַן קוֹנֶה בְּהֵמָה, וּלְפִיכָךְ אָמְרוּ זִכְרוֹנָם לִבְרָכָה בְּפֶרֶק "אוֹתוֹ וְאֶת בְּנוֹ" שֶׁמַּשְׁחִיטִין אֶת הַטַּבָּח עַל כָּרְחוֹ, וּכְאוֹקִמְתָּא דְרַבִּי אֶלְעָא אָמַר רַבִּי יוֹחָנָן, שֶׁפֵּרֵשׁ דִּבְאַרְבָּעָה פְּרָקִים אֵלּוּ הֶעֱמִידוּ דִבְרֵיהֶם עַל דִּבְרֵי תוֹרָה, וְכִדְאָמַר רַבִּי יִצְחָק אָמַר רַבִּי יוֹחָנָן: דְּבַר תּוֹרָה מָעוֹת קוֹנוֹת.

וְדִין מוֹכֵר בְּהֵמָה וְנִמְצֵאת טְרֵפָה, מַה דִּינוֹ; וְדִין מוֹכֵר אוֹמֵר בְּמָנֶה וְלוֹקֵחַ בַּחֲמִשִּׁים, וְהָלַךְ כָּל אֶחָד וְאֶחָד, וְאַחַר-כָּךְ לְקָחוֹ סְתָם; וְדִין מַה שֶּׁאָמְרוּ שֶׁאֵין אָדָם מַקְנֶה דָבָר שֶׁלֹּא בָא לָעוֹלָם; וְדִין בַּעַל הַמֵּצָר; וְדִין שְׁלוּחוֹ שֶׁל אָדָם וְשֶׁתָּפוּ בְּמִקְחוֹ וּמִמְכָּרוֹ, בְּהֶפְסֵדוֹ וּבִשְׂכָרוֹ; וְיֶתֶר פְּרָטֵי הַמִּצְוָה רַבִּים, יִתְבָּאֲרוּ בְּפֶרֶק רִאשׁוֹן מִקִּדּוּשִׁין וּבְפֶרֶק רְבִיעִי וּשְׁמִינִי וּתְשִׁיעִי מִמְּצִיעָא, וּבְפֶרֶק שְׁלִישִׁי וּרְבִיעִי וַחֲמִישִׁי וְשִׁשִּׁי וּשְׁבִיעִי מִבַּתְרָא, וּקְצָת מֵהֶן בִּמְקוֹמוֹת אֲחֵרִים מִן הַתַּלְמוּד בְּפִזּוּר.

וְנוֹהֶגֶת בְּכָל מָקוֹם וּבְכָל זְמַן בִּזְכָרִים, כִּי לָהֶם לַעֲשׂוֹת דִּין. וּבֵית-דִּין הָעוֹבֵר עַל זֶה וְדָן בֵּין מוֹכֵר וְלוֹקֵחַ שֶׁלֹּא כַּדִּין שֶׁצִּוַּתָּה עַל זֶה תּוֹרָתֵנוּ הַשְּׁלֵמָה, בִּטֵּל עֲשֵׂה זֶה, זוּלָתִי אִם עָשָׂה כֵן מִדַּעַת שְׁנֵיהֶם, שֶׁאִלּוּ בְקַבָּלַת שְׁנֵיהֶם רַשַּׁאי, דְּכָל תְּנַאי שֶׁבְּמָמוֹן קַיָּם.

[שֶׁלֹּא לְהוֹנוֹת בְּמִקָּח וּמִמְכָּר]

שלז שֶׁלֹּא לְהוֹנוֹת אֶחָד מִיִּשְׂרָאֵל, בֵּין זָכָר בֵּין נְקֵבָה, בְּמִקָּח וּבְמִמְכָּר, שֶׁנֶּאֱמַר: וְכִי תִמְכְּרוּ מִמְכָּר לַעֲמִיתֶךָ אוֹ קָנֹה מִיַּד עֲמִיתֶךָ אַל תּוֹנוּ אִישׁ אֶת אָחִיו; וְאָמְרוּ זִכְרוֹנָם לִבְרָכָה בְּסִפְרָא: "אַל תּוֹנוּ אִישׁ אֶת אָחִיו", זוֹ אוֹנָאַת מָמוֹן;

---

44. TB Bava M'tzi'a 74a.

45. These times are at the festivals, when domestic animals were generally bought for meat, for the holiday meals.

46. The butcher would sell portions of meat from an animal before it was ritually slain, and he wished to wait until all its edible flesh was sold before he had it put to death and apportioned the meat to his customers. Under this law, if he failed to find enough customers for all the meat and he wished to retract and return the money already advanced, he could be compelled to have the animal ritually slain; MT *hilchoth m'chirah* ix 7. (Our author follows here R. Isaac 'Alfasi's reading in the Talmud.)

47. Because the people needed the meat then.

48. TB K'thuboth 76b.

49. Tosefta, Kiddushin ii, end.

50. E.g. a crop of produce that has not yet begun to grow; TB Yevamoth 93a, etc.

51. That if one wants to sell his land, he must offer it to this neighbor first; TB Bava M'tzi'a 108a-b.

52. See MT *hilchoth sh'luhin* and *Shulhan 'Aruch Hoshen Mishpat* §§176-198.

gave a person money and he went and bought [something] with some of it, how they should share things out.[44] Then there is the law that the Sages taught: that at four times in the year, money effects acquisition in regard to buying a domestic animals.[45] Therefore they (of blessed memory) said in the fifth chapter of the tractate *Hullin* (83a) that the butcher is to be compelled to carry out the ritual slaying [of the beast] against his will[46]—in accord with the teaching of R. 'Ila'i in the name of R. Yohanan, who explained that at these four periods the Sages made their ruling accord with the law of the Torah;[47] and as R. Yitzhak taught in R. Yohanan's name, by the law of the Torah money makes a thing one's own.

Then there is the law if someone sells a domestic animal and it is found to be fatally ill or wounded, what the judgment is for him;[48] the law if the seller says, "for a hundred," and the buyer says, "for fifty," and each went his way, and afterward he [the buyer] took it without specifying anything;[49] and the law that the Sages taught: that a man cannot sell something which has not come into the world. We have, too, the law of an adjoining neighbor;[51] and the law of a man's agent and his partner in his purchase or his sale, when he loses money or gains.[52]

[These] and other details of the precept, numerous indeed, are explained in the first chapter of the Talmud tractate *Kiddushin*, in chapters 4, 8 and 9 of *Bava M'tzi'a*, and chapters 3–7 of *Bava Bathra*; and some of them are in other places in the Talmud, scattered.

It applies everywhere, at every time, for men, since it is for them to carry out justice. If a *beth din* (court) violated this and judged a case between a vendor and a buyer not in accord with the law that the perfect Torah commanded about it, it would disobey this positive precept—unless it so acted with the consent of both of them: For upon the acceptance of both, it is permitted, since any condition regarding goods and possessions is valid.

[THE PROHIBITION AGAINST WRONGING ANYONE IN BUYING AND SELLING]

337 not to wrong or cheat any Israelite, whether a man or a woman, in buying and selling (trade): for it is stated, *And if you sell anything to your neighbor or buy of your neighbor's hand, you shall not wrong one another* (Leviticus 25:14); and the Sages of blessed memory said in the Midrash *Sifra*:[1] "you shall not wrong one another"—this means

וּבַגְּמָרָא אָמְרוּ זִכְרוֹנָם לִבְרָכָה: "מִיַּד עֲמִיתֶךָ", דָּבָר הַנִּקְנֶה מִיָּד לְיָד, כְּלוֹמַר מְטַלְטְלִין.

וְאֵין כַּוָּנַת הַמִּדְרָשׁ שֶׁלֹּא יַזְהִיר הַכָּתוּב עַל אוֹנָאַת הַקַּרְקָעוֹת כְּמוֹ־כֵן, אֶלָּא הָעִנְיָן הוּא לוֹמַר שֶׁדִּינֵי אוֹנָאָה, כְּגוֹן הַחֲלוּקִין שֶׁאָמְרוּ זִכְרוֹנָם לִבְרָכָה בָּאוֹנָאָה, שֶׁהִיא חוֹזֶרֶת בְּיָתֵר מִשְׁתוּת, וְדִינֶיהָ בְּפָחוֹת מִשְׁתוּת וּבִשְׁתוּת, אֵינָן נוֹהֲגִין בְּקַרְקָעוֹת אֶלָּא בְּמִטַּלְטְלִין.

וְעוֹד דָּרְשׁוּ בָּזֶה הַכָּתוּב: אִם בָּאתָ לִקְנוֹת, קְנֵה מִיִּשְׂרָאֵל, שֶׁנֶּאֱמַר: אוֹ קָנֹה מִיַּד עֲמִיתֶךָ.

וְאוּלַי זֶה שֶׁדִּקְדְּקוּ בְּכָאן לִהְיוֹת דִּינֵי הָאוֹנָאָה בְּמִטַּלְטְלִין לְבַד, לְפִי שֶׁשָּׁנָה הַכָּתוּב בְּלָשׁוֹן זֶה, שֶׁאָמַר "וְכִי תִמְכְּרוּ מִמְכָּר (לַעֲמִיתֶךָ)", דְּמַשְׁמַע כָּל מִמְכָּר, בֵּין קַרְקַע בֵּין מִטַּלְטֵל, וְאַחַר־כֵּן יִחֵד הָאַזְהָרָה בְּמִטַּלְטֵל, שֶׁאָמַר "אוֹ קָנֹה מִיָּד", דְּמַשְׁמַע דַּוְקָא מִטַּלְטֵל, שֶׁהוּא נִקְנֶה מִיָּד לְיָד, לָמְדוּ מִזֶּה לוֹמַר שֶׁיֵּשׁ בְּמִטַּלְטֵל דִּין מְחֻדָּשׁ שֶׁאֵינוֹ בְּקַרְקַע, וְזֶהוּ חֲזָרַת הַמָּמוֹן בְּקָצָת צְדָדִין שֶׁבּוֹ.

אֲבָל עִקַּר הָאַזְהָרָה בֵּין בְּקַרְקַע בֵּין בְּמִטַּלְטֵל הוּא בֶּאֱמֶת, שֶׁהֻזְהַרְנוּ שֶׁלֹּא לְהוֹנוֹת הַבְּרִיּוֹת לְדַעַת; אֲבָל הַחִלּוּק שֶׁבֵּינֵיהֶן הוּא שֶׁאִם נִמְצֵאת אוֹנָאָה בְּמִטַּלְטֵל בְּיָתֵר מִשְׁתוּת, שֶׁיִּבָּטֵל הַמֶּכֶר, שֶׁדַּעַת הַבְּרִיּוֹת שֶׁלֹּא לִסְבֹּל אוֹנָאָה יְתֵרָה מִכֵּן בְּמִטַּלְטְלִין; אֲבָל בְּקַרְקַע, לְפִי שֶׁהַקַּרְקַע דָּבָר קַיָּם לְעוֹלָם, דֶּרֶךְ הַבְּרִיּוֹת לִמְחֹל בּוֹ כָּל אוֹנָאָה אַחַר שֶׁלְּקָחוּהוּ אוֹתוֹ; וּכְעִנְיַן מַה שֶּׁאָמְרוּ זִכְרוֹנָם לִבְרָכָה עַל דֶּרֶךְ הַהַפְלָגָה שֶׁהַקַּרְקַע דָּבָר הַשָּׁוֶה כָּל כֶּסֶף הוּא. וְהָרְאָיָה לִדְבָרֵינוּ אֵלֶּה, כְּלוֹמַר שֶׁאִסּוּר אוֹנָאָה אַף בְּקַרְקַע, שֶׁהֲרֵי עִקַּר אַזְהָרָה זוֹ בַּקַּרְקָעוֹת הוּא דִּכְתִיבָא, וּכְמוֹ שֶׁמְּפֹרָשׁ בַּפָּרָשָׁה. זֶהוּ דַעַת הָרַמְבַּ"ן זִכְרוֹנוֹ לִבְרָכָה בָּעִנְיָן זֶה, וּכְמוֹ שֶׁכָּתַב בְּפֵרוּשׁ הַחֻמָּשׁ.

§337   1. Sifra, *b'har, parashah* 3, 4.
2. TB Bava M'tzi'a 56b.
3. *Ibid.* 50b.
4. Sifra, *b'har, parashah* 3, 1.
5. TB Bava Kamma 14b.
6. Ramban, commentary, Leviticus 25:14.

wronging through goods and wares. In the Talmud,[2] they (of blessed memory) said: "of your neighbor's hand"—[this refers to] something that is acquired from hand to hand, i.e. movable goods.

Now, it is not the intent of the interpretation that Scripture does not adjure us equally against cheating in regard to landed property. It is rather a matter of conveying that [certain] laws about cheating—such as the distinctions that the Sages of blessed memory made about deceitful profit,[3] that it [the property] reverts to the seller if [the overcharge was] more than a sixth, and its laws if it was less than a sixth or [precisely] a sixth—do not apply to landed property but only to movable goods.

They inferred further from this verse:[4] If you come to make a purchase, buy from an Israelite, since it says, or buy of the hand of your neighbor.

Perhaps this specification made here, that the laws about defrauding apply only with movable goods, [was postulated] because Scripture made a change in this expression: For it stated, And if you sell anything to your neighbor, which implies anything to be sold, whether landed or movable; and then it set the admonition particularly about movable goods: for it says, or buy of the hand, implying specifically movable goods, which can be acquired from hand to hand. So they learned from this to rule that there is a new law for movable goods which does not apply to land, namely, returning the wares in some situations.

The main admonition, however, really applies with both land and movable property: for we were adjured not to defraud people deliberately. But the difference between them is that if the cheating about movable goods was found to amount to more than a sixth, the sale is nullified. For it is the way of people not to tolerate cheating beyond that with movable goods. With land, though, since land is something that endures forever, it is the way of people to forgive any overcharge after they have purchased it—in keeping with what the Sages of blessed memory said by way of exaggeration for emphasis:[5] that land is something worth any monetary price. Now, the proof of these words of ours, i.e. that the prohibition against cheating applies with land too, is that here it is principally about landed property that this admonition is written, as it is made explicit in the Scriptural section. This is the view of Ramban of blessed memory in this matter, as he wrote in his commentary to the Pentateuch.[6]

The root reason for the precept is known (evident), for it is

שֹׁרֶשׁ הַמִּצְוָה יָדוּעַ, כִּי הוּא דָבָר שֶׁהַשֵּׂכֶל מֵעִיד עָלָיו, וְאִם לֹא נִכְתַּב, דִּין הוּא
שֶׁיִּכָּתֵב, שֶׁאֵין רָאוּי לָקַחַת מָמוֹן בְּנֵי־אָדָם דֶּרֶךְ שֶׁקֶר וְתַרְמִית, אֶלָּא כָּל אֶחָד
יִזְכֶּה בַעֲמָלוֹ בְּמַה שֶׁיְּחָנֶּנּוּ הָאֱלֹהִים בְּעוֹלָמוֹ בֶּאֱמֶת וּבְיֹשֶׁר; וּלְכָל אֶחָד וְאֶחָד יֵשׁ
בַּדָּבָר הַזֶּה תּוֹעֶלֶת, כִּי כְּמוֹ שֶׁהוּא לֹא יוֹנֶה אֲחֵרִים, גַּם אֲחֵרִים לֹא יוֹנוּ אוֹתוֹ; וְאַף
כִּי יִהְיֶה אֶחָד יוֹדֵעַ לְרַמּוֹת יוֹתֵר מִשְּׁאָר בְּנֵי־אָדָם, אוּלַי בָּנָיו לֹא יִהְיוּ כֵן וִירַמּוּ
אוֹתָם בְּנֵי אָדָם; וְנִמְצָא שֶׁהַדְּבָרִים שָׁוִים לַכֹּל, וְשֶׁהוּא תּוֹעֶלֶת רַב בְּיִשּׁוּבוֹ שֶׁל
עוֹלָם, וְהַשֵּׁם בָּרוּךְ הוּא לָשֶׁבֶת יְצָרוֹ.

מִדִּינֵי הַמִּצְוָה, מַה שֶׁאָמְרוּ זִכְרוֹנָם לִבְרָכָה שֶׁהַמּוֹכֵר וְהַלּוֹקֵחַ שְׁנֵיהֶם מֻזְהָרִים
בָּאַזְהָרָה זוֹ, שֶׁנֶּאֱמַר "וְכִי תִמְכְּרוּ מִמְכָּר ... אוֹ קָנֹה", וְלֹא יֹאמַר הַלּוֹקֵחַ "דֶּרֶךְ
הַמּוֹכֵר לָדַעַת שְׁוִוי מִמְכָּרוֹ, וְאַחַר שֶׁהוּא מוֹכְרוֹ לִי בְּדָמִים קַלִּים אֵין עָלַי עָוֹן",
שֶׁאֵינוֹ כֵן, אֶלָּא שְׁנֵיהֶם בָּאַזְהָרָה; וּכְמוֹ־כֵן שְׁנֵיהֶם הֵן בְּדִינֵי הָאוֹנָאוֹת כְּמוֹ
שֶׁחִלְּקוּם זִכְרוֹנָם לִבְרָכָה, וְכֵן הוּא בַּמִּשְׁנָה: אֶחָד הַמּוֹכֵר וְאֶחָד הַלּוֹקֵחַ יֵשׁ לָהֶם
אוֹנָאָה, וְכָל מִי שֶׁנִּתְאַנָּה מֵהֶן יָכוֹל לַחֲזֹר בּוֹ.

וְאָמְרוּ זִכְרוֹנָם לִבְרָכָה שֶׁשִּׁעוּר הָאוֹנָאָה שֶׁמַּחֲזִירִין אוֹתָהּ וְיִהְיֶה הַמֶּקַּח קַיָּם
הוּא שְׁתוּת הַמֶּקַּח אוֹ שְׁתוּת הַדָּמִים; וְשִׁעוּר הָאוֹנָאָה שֶׁאֵין מַחֲזִירִין שֶׁאֵין אֲפִלּוּ אוֹתָהּ,
וְאֵין צָרִיךְ לוֹמַר שֶׁאֵין מְבַטְּלִין הַמֶּקַּח בִּשְׁבִילָהּ, הוּא פָּחוֹת מִשְּׁתוּת הַמֶּקַּח
וְהַדָּמִים; אֲבָל הָיָה בַדָּבָר שְׁתוּת אֶחָד מֵהֶם, כְּלוֹמַר שְׁתוּת הַמֶּקַּח אוֹ שְׁתוּת
הַדָּמִים, מַחֲזִירִין הָאוֹנָאָה; וְשִׁעוּר הָאוֹנָאָה שֶׁמְּבַטֶּלֶת הַמֶּקַּח כֻּלּוֹ, הוּא כָּל זְמַן
שֶׁהִיא יָתֵר מִשְּׁתוּת הַמֶּקַּח וְהַדָּמִים, שֶׁהֲלָכָה הִיא כִשְׁמוּאֵל, דְּאָמַר בַּגְּמָרָא:
שְׁתוּת מָעוֹת נַמִּי שָׁנִינוּ.

כְּלוֹמַר שֶׁאִם הָאוֹנָאָה אֵינָהּ יְתֵרָה עַל שְׁנִיהֶם, לֹא יִתְבַּטֵּל הַמֶּקַּח אֶלָּא יַחֲזִיר
אוֹנָאָה.

וּמַה שֶׁאָמַרְנוּ שֶׁבְּאוֹנָאָה שֶׁיְּתֵרָה עַל שְׁתוּת יִתְבַּטֵּל הַמֶּקַּח, וְאַף־עַל־פִּי שֶׁזֶּה

---

7. TB Bava M'tzi'a 51a.
8. Literally, for light money (contrast the English idiom: a heavy price).
9. Mishnah, Bava M'tzi'a iv 4 (TB 51a).
10. If the object is worth six, and it is sold for five or seven.
11. If the price paid was six, but the object is worth five or seven.
12. TB Bava M'tzi'a 49b.

something to which the intelligence attests. Had it not been written, justice would have required it to be written. For it is not right to acquire people's property by way of lying and deceit. Rather, everyone should attain by his toil to that which God has graciously bestowed on him, in truth and honesty. For each and every one there will be a gainful benefit in this condition: for just as one will not wrong others, others will equally not wrong him. And even if one person should know how to cheat more than other people, perhaps his sons will not be so, and people will wrong them. Consequently, matters turn out equally for all, and it is of great benefit in the civilizing settlement of the world, which the Eternal Lord, blessed is He, formed to be settled.

Among the laws of the precept, there is what the Sages of blessed memory taught:[7] that the vendor and buyer are both adjured by this admonition: for it is stated, *And if you sell anything . . . or buy*; and the purchaser is not to say, "It is the way of a vendor to know the value of what he is selling, and since he is selling it to me for a slight price,[8] I bear no sin." For it is not so: both are subject to the admonition; and both are likewise subject to the laws about wronging, as the Sages of blessed memory differentiated them. And so it is [taught] in the Mishnah:[9] The law against defrauding applies to the seller and the buyer alike. Hence, whichever of them is cheated, he can undo the transaction.

Now, the Sages of blessed memory taught that the amount of fraudulent charge which must be returned, leaving the purchase valid, is a sixth of [the value of] the object bought[10] or a sixth of the money.[11] The amount of fraud that is not even itself returnable—and needless to say, the purchase is not invalidated on its account—is less than a sixth of the bought object's value and of the money. If, however, the matter involved a sixth of one of them—i.e. a sixth of the item purchased or a sixth of the money—the amount of the wrong is to be returned. And fraud is sufficient to invalidate the entire purchase as long as it amounts to more than a sixth of the purchased object's value or the money. For the definitive law follows Samuel, who said in the Talmud,[12] "We learned [this law about] a sixth of the money too."

In other words, then, if the cheating does not amount to more [than a sixth] of either, the purchase is not nullified, but the extra, fraudulent charge should be returned.

Now, when we say that if the amount of cheating is more than a

הָלַךְ לְבֵיתוֹ בִּמְעוֹתָיו וְזֶה בְּפֵירוֹתָיו — דַּוְקָא שֶׁבָּא לַחֲזֹר בּוֹ מִי שֶׁנִּתְאַנֶּה; אֲבָל בָּא לַחֲזֹר בּוֹ (המאונה) [הַמְּאַנֶּה] מֵחֲמַת שֶׁנִּתְיַקְּרוּ הַפֵּרוֹת בֵּינְתַיִם אוֹ בְּטַעֲנָה אַחֶרֶת, אֵין שׁוֹמְעִין לוֹ, מִשּׁוּם דְּאָמַר לֵיהּ מִי שֶׁנִּתְאַנֶּה: אִי לָאו דְּאוֹנִיתָן לָא מָצֵית הֲדָרַת בָּךְ, וְהַשְׁתָּא מָצֵית הֲדָרַת בָּךְ? וְכֵן הוּא הַלָּשׁוֹן בַּגְּמָרָא, וְרַב חִסְדָּא הוּא דְּאָמְרָהּ לִשְׁמַעְתְּתָא (בְּפֶרֶק הַסְּפִינָה, וְרַב אַלְפָס זִכְרוֹנוֹ לִבְרָכָה פָּסְקָהּ בְּבִטּוּל מֶקַח וּפֵרוֹת); כְּלוֹמַר דַּאֲמַר לֵיהּ מִי שֶׁנִּתְאַנֶּה (למאונה) [לַמְּאַנֶּה] "בִּשְׁעַת הַמֶּכֶר הָרֶוַח הָיָה עִמְּךָ, וּכְבָר נִתְקַיֵּם מִמְכָּרֵנוּ אוֹ מִקָּחֵנוּ מֵחֲמָתְךָ; מַה זֶּה שֶׁבָּא לְבַטֵּל אוֹתוֹ — הָאוֹנָאָה שֶׁעָשִׂיתָ לִי — הֲרֵינִי מוֹחֲלָהּ"; כִּי רַבּוֹתֵינוּ לֹא בָּטְלוּ הַדְּבָרִים אֶלָּא מֵחֲמַת הַמְּתְאַנֶּה; מִכֵּיוָן שֶׁהוּא רוֹצֶה בַּדָּבָר, הַדְּבָרִים קַיָּמִים.

וְזֶהוּ שֶׁשָּׁנִינוּ: יָפוֹת וְנִמְצְאוּ רָעוֹת, לוֹקֵחַ יָכוֹל לַחֲזֹר בּוֹ, כְּלוֹמַר וְלֹא מוֹכֵר; רָעוֹת וְנִמְצְאוּ יָפוֹת, מוֹכֵר יָכוֹל לַחֲזֹר בּוֹ, כְּלוֹמַר וְלֹא לוֹקֵחַ.

וְאָמְרוּ זִכְרוֹנָם לִבְרָכָה בְּעִנְיְנֵי הָאוֹנָאָה שֶׁאֵין רָאוּי לִהְיוֹת דִּין הַחֲזָרָה אוֹ הַבִּטּוּל נִמְשָׁךְ לְעוֹלָם, אֶלָּא זְמַן קָצוּב הוּא שֶׁנָּתְנוּ בַּדְּבָרִים, כְּדֵי שֶׁיִּתְקַיְּמוּ עִנְיְנֵי הַמֶּקַח וְהַמִּמְכָּר בֵּין בְּנֵי־אָדָם; וְהַזְּמַן שֶׁנָּתְנוּ אֵינוֹ שָׁוֶה בְּכָל הַדְּבָרִים, וְגַם אֵינוֹ שָׁוֶה בְּלוֹקֵחַ וּבְמוֹכֵר, כִּי בְּכָל סְחוֹרָה שֶׁתִּהְיֶה בְּחִלּוּף הַמַּטְבְּעוֹת נָתְנוּ בָהּ שִׁעוּר כְּדֵי שֶׁיַּרְאֶה אוֹתָהּ הַלּוֹקֵחַ לְשֻׁלְחָנִי אִם הוּא בְּכַרְךְ, וְאִם הוּא בִּכְפָר יִהְיֶה הַשִּׁעוּר עַד יוֹם הַשּׁוּק, שֶׁיַּעֲלֶה לַכַּרְךְ אוֹ לְמָקוֹם שֶׁשֻּׁלְחָנִי שָׁם; וּבִשְׁאָר כָּל הַסְּחוֹרוֹת אֵין חִלּוּק בֵּין כְּפָר לִכְרַךְ, וְהַשִּׁעוּר בָּהֶם הוּא כְּדֵי שֶׁיַּרְאֶה הָאָדָם מַה שֶּׁלָּקַח לַתַּגָּר אוֹ לִקְרוֹבוֹ; וְשִׁעוּר זֶה לְפִי רְאוֹת עֵינֵי הַדַּיָּן, שֶׁאִי אֶפְשָׁר לִקְבֹּעַ בְּעִנְיָן זֶה חֶשְׁבּוֹן שָׁעוֹת.

וְרָבָא נָתַן טַעַם בַּגְּמָרָא בְּחִלּוּק הַמַּטְבֵּעַ מִשְּׁאָר סְחוֹרוֹת, וְאָמַר דֶּרֶךְ כְּלָל:

---

13. Because you defrauded me, should your legal rights be stronger?

14. The part in parentheses is not in the oldest manuscripts or in any but the first edition. It is evidently a later interpolation.

15. TB Bava Bathra 83b.

16. Or, money-changer; i.e. when someone "bought" the coins in exchange for goods, and he needed to ascertain their value; TB Bava M'tzi'a 52a. (In olden times, many city governments had the right to mint their own coins, and ordinary people who did not travel about could hardly know the value of distant coinage.)

17. Ibid. 52b.

sixth, the purchase is to be nullified, even though this one went home with his money and that one with his produce, it specifically means when the defrauded person comes to back out of it. But if the one who cheated comes to retract because the produce rose in price meanwhile, or with some other contention, we pay him no heed. For the one who was cheated can say to him, "Had you not defrauded me, you would not be able to back out; should you *now* be able to retract?"[13] So is the matter expressed in the Talmud, R. Ḥisda being the one who gives this teaching (in the fifth chapter of the tractate *Bava Bathra* (84a); and R. Isaac 'Alfasi of blessed memory so ruled regarding the nullification of the purchase of produce).[14] In other words, the one who was defrauded can say to the cheater, "At the time of the sale, the profit was yours, and our sale or purchase became valid because of you [because you wanted it]. What is this that comes now [as a reason] to undo it?—the fraud that you perpetrated on me? I hereby forgive it." For our Sages rendered the transaction void for no other reason but for the sake of the victim; since he is satisfied with the matter, the transaction remains valid.

This is why we learned:[15] [If one bought produce] of good quality and it was found to be bad, the buyer can back out of it—i.e. but not the vendor; [if he bought produce] of bad quality and it was found to be good, the seller can retract from it—i.e. but not the buyer.

Our Sages of blessed memory taught, further, regarding cheating, that it is not right for the law of returning [the excess charge] or nullification to extend forever, but rather it is a fixed amount of time that they set for these matters, so that transactions of buying and selling should have a permanence among people. The time that they gave is not the same for all matters, nor is it the same for the buyer as for the vendor. For regarding any transaction involving exchange of coins, they set a limit of time enough for the buyer to show it to a banker,[16] if he is in a city. If he is in the country, the time limit is until the market-day when he will go up to the city or to the place where the banker is. With all other merchandise, there is no difference between country and city: The limit for them is enough time for the man to show what he bought to a merchant or to his relative;[17] and this time limit depends on the estimation of the judge, for it is impossible to fix for this matter a set number of hours.

In the Talmud,[17] Rava gave a reason for the distinction made between coinage and other kinds of merchandise. He said, as a general

טַלִּית לְכָל אִינִישׁ קִים לֵיהּ, סֶלַע לְשִׁלְחָנִי הוּא דְקִים לֵיהּ.

עָבַר זֶה הָעֵת וְלֹא חָזַר בּוֹ הַלּוֹקֵחַ, אֲפִלּוּ יֵשׁ בָּאוֹנָאָה יָתֵר מִשְׁתוּת כַּמָּה, אֵין יָכוֹל לַחֲזֹר בּוֹ מִן הַדִּין; אֲבָל אָמְרוּ חֲכָמִים שֶׁמִּמִּדַּת חֲסִידוּת רָאוּי לְהַחֲזִירָהּ לְעוֹלָם.

וְשִׁעוּרִין אֵלּוּ הֵן בַּלּוֹקֵחַ, אֲבָל הַמּוֹכֵר חוֹזֵר בּוֹ לְעוֹלָם, לְפִי שֶׁאֵין הַסְּחוֹרָה בְיָדוֹ כְּדֵי שֶׁיּוּכַל לְמָלֵךְ עָלֶיהָ. וְלֹא נֶאֶמְרוּ דִינִין אֵלּוּ שֶׁכָּתַבְנוּ אֶלָּא בְלוֹקֵחַ מִן הַתַּגָּר, אֲבָל בְּלוֹקֵחַ מִבַּעַל־הַבַּיִת אֵין בּוֹ אוֹנָאָה וְלֹא בִטּוּל מִקָּח בְּתוֹךְ הַזְּמָן הַקָּצוּב שֶׁאָמַרְנוּ, וְלֹא אַחַר־כֵּן; שֶׁלֹּא נֶאֶמְרוּ אֵלּוּ הַדְּבָרִים אֶלָּא בְתַגָּרִים, לְתִקּוּן הָעוֹלָם וּלְיִשּׁוּב הַמְּדִינוֹת, אֲבָל בַּעֲלֵי־בָתִּים אֵין מוֹכְרִין כְּלֵיהֶם אֶלָּא בְיֹקֶר, וּבְנֵי־אָדָם, בְּדַעְתָּם עִנְיָן זֶה שֶׁהוּא בָהֶן, מוֹחֲלִין הַדָּבָר לְעוֹלָם בְּבַעַל־הַבַּיִת.

וְאֵלּוּ דְבָרִים שֶׁאֵין בָּהֶם דִּינֵי אוֹנָאָה לְשׁוּם אָדָם אֲפִלּוּ נִמְכְּרוּ פִי שְׁנַיִם בְּשָׁוְיָן, וְאַף־עַל־פִּי שֶׁיֵּשׁ בָּהֶן אִסּוּר אוֹנָאָה, כְּמוֹ שֶׁכָּתַבְתִּי בְּרֹאשׁ הַמִּצְוָה לְדַעַת הָרַמְבַּ"ן זִכְרוֹנוֹ לִבְרָכָה: הַקַּרְקָעוֹת, וְהָעֲבָדִים — שֶׁהוּקְּשׁוּ לַקַּרְקָעוֹת, כְּמוֹ שֶׁנִּלְמַד בַּגְּמָרָא, מִדִּכְתִיב "וְהִתְנַחַלְתֶּם אֹתָם", וְהַשְּׁטָרוֹת וְהַהֶקְדֵּשׁוֹת, וּכְמוֹ שֶׁאָמְרוּ זִכְרוֹנָם לִבְרָכָה: תָּנוּ רַבָּנָן: "וְכִי תִמְכְּרוּ וְגוֹמֵר אוֹ קָנֹה מִיָּד", דָּבָר הַנִּקְנֶה מִיָּד לְיָד, יָצְאוּ הַקַּרְקָעוֹת שֶׁאֵינָן מִטַּלְטְלִין, וְיָצְאוּ עֲבָדִים שֶׁהוּקְּשׁוּ לַקַּרְקָעוֹת, וְיָצְאוּ שְׁטָרוֹת דְּאָמַר קְרָא "מִמְכָּר", מִי שֶׁגּוּפוֹ קָנוּי, יָצְאוּ אֵלּוּ שֶׁאֵין גּוּפָן קָנוּי אֶלָּא לִרְאָיָה שֶׁבָּהֶן.

מִכָּאן אָמְרוּ: הַמּוֹכֵר שְׁטָרוֹתָיו לַבַּשָּׂם, יֵשׁ לָהֶם אוֹנָאָה; וְהַטַּעַם לְפִי שֶׁאֵין מוֹכְרָן לוֹ לִרְאָיָה שֶׁבָּהֶן אֶלָּא לְהִשְׁתַּמֵּשׁ בַּנְּיָר. וְקָא מַתְמַהּ עָלֶיהָ בַּגְּמָרָא: מַאי קָא מַשְׁמַע לָן, כְּלוֹמַר פְּשִׁיטָא, וְכִי מִגְרַע גָּרַע נְיָר מִכָּל שְׁאָר מִלֵּי; וּמְשַׁנֵּי: לְאַפּוֹקֵי

---

18. So R. Isaac 'Alfasi, Bava M'tzi'a iv, and MT *hilchoth m'chirah* xiii 8, based on TB Bava M'tzi'a 108a.

19. Above, the fifth paragraph.

20. TB Bava M'tzi'a 56a.

21. To wrap his powders in them.

rule, "Every man can be certain about a garment, but only a banker is certain about a coin."

If this period passed and the buyer did not back out, then even if the overcharge amounted to much more than a sixth, he cannot retract under the law. But the Sages said[17] that by the quality of pious kindness, it would be right to let him return it [the purchase] at any time.

Now, these time limits apply to the buyer. The vendor, however, may retract at any time, since the merchandise is not in his hand, so that he can take counsel about it.[3] Moreover, these laws that we have written apply only to one who buys from a merchant; but when a person makes a purchase from an ordinary householder, neither the law of fraud nor the law of nullifying the purchase applies to him, either in the set time that we stated or afterward.[7] For these things were said about none but merchants, for the sake of improving communal life and civilizing human habitation. Householders, however, do not sell their belongings for anything but a high price, and knowing this characteristic of theirs, people are always ready to forgive a householder.

Now, these are the items for which there is no law about fraud for any man, even if they were sold for twice their value[18]—although there is a prohibition against cheating with them, as I wrote at the beginning of the precept,[19] in the view of Ramban of blessed memory: landed property; slaves, who were equated with land, as it was derived in the Talmud,[20] since it is written, *And you may make them an inheritance* (Leviticus 25:46); deeds and consecrated property. As they (of blessed memory) said:[10] Our Sages taught: *And if you sell . . . or buy from the hand* (ibid. 14)—this means something which is acquired from hand to hand; thus landed property is excluded, because it is not movable; slaves are excluded, because they were equated to landed property; and deeds are excluded, because the verse states, *memkar*— something for sale: i.e. something which is bought for itself; so these [deeds] are excluded, since they are bought not for themselves but for the attestation that they contain.

Hence it was ruled:[20] If someone sells his deeds to an apothecary, the law of fraud applies to them. The reason is that he sells them to him not for the evidence in them, but to use the paper.[21] Now, in the Talmud[20] this is questioned: "What is this meant to tell us?" In other words, it is obvious; is paper then inferior to anything else? The answer is thereupon given: It is meant to negate the teaching of

מִדְּרַב כַּהֲנָא, דַּאֲמַר אֵין אוֹנָאָה לִפְרוּטוֹת.

וְהֶקְדֵּשׁוֹת אָמְעִיטוּ מִדִּין אוֹנָאָה מִדִּכְתִיב: עֲמִיתֶךָ.

וְתֵדַע שֶׁכָּל עִנְיְנֵי הָאוֹנָאָה נֶאֶמְרוּ בְשִׁוּוּיֵי הַחֵפֶץ, כְּגוֹן שֶׁמָּכַר שָׁוֶה שֵׁשׁ בְּחָמֵשׁ אוֹ שָׁוֶה חָמֵשׁ בְּשֵׁשׁ וְכַיּוֹצֵא־בָזֶה, אֲבָל (המאונה) [הַמְאַנֶּה] בְּמִדָּתוֹ שֶׁל חֵפֶץ, בְּאָרְכּוֹ וְרָחְבּוֹ, בְּעָבְיוֹ אוֹ בְמִשְׁקָלוֹ, וַאֲפִלּוּ בְּדָבָר מֻעָט, חוֹזֵר; וְהַיְנוּ דַּאֲמַר רָבָא בַּגְּמָרָא: כָּל דָּבָר שֶׁבְּמִדָּה וְשֶׁבְּמִשְׁקָל וְשֶׁבְּמִנְיָן, אֲפִלּוּ פָּחוֹת מִכְּדֵי אוֹנָאָה, חוֹזֵר.

וְהָרוֹצֶה לְהִנָּצֵל מִכָּל חֲמֵשׁ עִנְיָנִים אֵלּוּ שֶׁכָּתַבְנוּ, יָכוֹל לוֹמַר לַלּוֹקֵחַ "חֵפֶץ זֶה שֶׁאֲנִי מוֹכֵר לְךָ, יוֹדֵעַ אֲנִי שֶׁיֵּשׁ בּוֹ אוֹנָאָה עַד כֵּן וְכֵן. אִם תִּרְצֶה לָקַח אוֹתוֹ עַל־מְנָת שֶׁלֹּא יְהֵא לְךָ עָלַי אוֹנָאָה, קָחֶנּוּ, וְאִם לָאו הַנַּח אוֹתוֹ". אֵין לוֹ עָלָיו אוֹנָאָה אַחַר־כֵּן, וְלֹא אֲפִלּוּ תַּרְעֹמֶת דְּבָרִים. וְיֶתֶר פְּרָטֶיהָ, בְּפֶרֶק רְבִיעִי מִמְּצִיעָא.

וְנוֹהֶגֶת בְּכָל מָקוֹם וּבְכָל זְמַן, בִּזְכָרִים וּנְקֵבוֹת. וְעוֹבֵר עַל זֶה וְעָשָׂה אוֹנָאָה לַחֲבֵרוֹ לְדַעַת בְּשָׁתוּת אוֹ יוֹתֵר, עָבַר עַל לַאו זֶה; אֲבָל בְּפָחוֹת מִשָּׁתוּת הִתִּירוּ זִכְרוֹנָם לִבְרָכָה לְהִשְׂתַּכֵּר לַתַּגָּר, מִפְּנֵי תִקּוּן הַיִּשּׁוּב, שֶׁיִּמָּצְאוּ בְנֵי־אָדָם צָרְכֵיהֶם מוּכָנִים בְּכָל מָקוֹם. וְאֵין לוֹקִין עַל לַאו זֶה, לְפִי שֶׁנִּתָּן לְהִשָּׁבוֹן.

[שֶׁלֹּא לְהוֹנוֹת אֶחָד מִיִּשְׂרָאֵל בִּדְבָרִים]

שלח שֶׁלֹּא לְהוֹנוֹת אֶחָד מִיִּשְׂרָאֵל בִּדְבָרִים, כְּלוֹמַר שֶׁלֹּא נֹאמַר לְיִשְׂרָאֵל דְּבָרִים שֶׁיַּכְאִיבוּהוּ וִיצַעֲרוּהוּ וְאֵין בּוֹ כֹּחַ לְהֵעָזֵר מֵהֶם; וּבְפֵרוּשׁ אָמְרוּ זִכְרוֹנָם לִבְרָכָה כֵּיצַד: אִם הָיָה בַעַל תְּשׁוּבָה, לֹא יֹאמַר לוֹ "זְכֹר מַעֲשֶׂיךָ הָרִאשׁוֹנִים"; הָיוּ חֳלָאִים בָּאִין עָלָיו, לֹא יֹאמַר לוֹ כְּדֶרֶךְ שֶׁאָמְרוּ חֲבֵרָיו לְאִיּוֹב: הֲלֹא יִרְאָתְךָ כִּסְלָתֶךָ, וְגוֹמֵר; רָאָה חַמָּרִים מְבַקְּשִׁים תְּבוּאָה, לֹא יֹאמַר לָהֶם "לְכוּ אֵצֶל פְּלוֹנִי"

---

22. For which deeds and documents would be sold as paper. R. Kahana holds that the law about cheating applies when at least an *'issar* is involved — one twenty-fourth of a *denar*, the smallest silver coin.

23. TB Kiddushin 42b.

24. TB Bava M'tzi'a 51b.

25. TB Bava Bathra 90a.

26. I.e. people should be willing and ready to sell goods.

27. The overcharge can be returned.

§338   1. TB Bava M'tzi'a 58b.

2. Meaning that the afflictions came because he was lacking in proper reverent fear of God; similarly, Job 4:7 could be quoted to intimate that had the man been innocent, his misfortune would not have befallen him (*tosafoth*, TB *ibid.* s.v. *ha-lo'*).

R. Kahana, who said that the law of fraud does not apply to a matter of *p'rutoth* (a few trifling pennies).[22]

Consecrated property is excluded from the law of cheating because it is written, *of your neighbor* (Leviticus 25:14).[20]

Now, you should know that all the rules about cheating were said only in regard to the value of the object: for example, if something worth six was sold for five, or something worth five, for six; and so forth. But if a person cheats about the measure of an object—its length or width, its thickness or weight—then even over a small amount one may retract. This is the teaching that Rava gave in the Talmud:[23] Whatever [is sold] by measure, weight or number, even if the fraud was less than the legal amount, one may retract.

Well, if a person wishes to be safe from every suspicion of these matters that we have written, he can say to the buyer, "This object that I am selling you—I know that it involves an overcharge to this-and-this extent. If you wish to buy it on condition that you can have no claim of fraud against me, buy it; and if not, leave it." Afterward he can have no claim of cheating against him, nor even words of complaint.[24]

The rest of its details are in chapter 4 of the tractate *Bava M'tzi'a*. It applies in every place, at every time, for both man and woman. If a person violates it and defrauds his fellow-man deliberately of a sixth or more, he transgresses this negative precept. But less than a sixth, the Sages of blessed memory permitted a merchant to earn,[25] for the sake of improved communal relations—so that people should find their needs ready everywhere.[26] A whipping of lashes is not given, though, for violating this prohibition, since it is given over to rectification.[27]

[THE PROHIBITION AGAINST OPPRESSING A JEW WITH WORDS]

338 not to wrong or oppress any Israelite with words, which is to say that we should not speak any words to an Israelite that will pain and distress him, when he has no power to help himself against them. Our Sages of blessed memory said explicitly how [this might be done]:[1] If the other was a repentant sinner, one should not tell him, "Remember your former activities." If afflictions came upon him, one should not tell him, as Job's friends said to him, "Is not your fear of God your confidence?" (Job 4:6), etc.[2] If one sees donkey-drivers looking

וְהוּא יוֹדֵעַ שֶׁאֵין לוֹ; וְלֹא יֹאמַר לַתַּגָּר "בְּכַמָּה חֵפֶץ זֶה" וְהוּא אֵינוֹ רוֹצֶה לִקַּח. וְעַל זֶה נֶאֱמַר: וְלֹא תוֹנוּ אִישׁ אֶת עֲמִיתוֹ.

שֹׁרֶשׁ מִצְוָה זוֹ יָדוּעַ, כִּי הוּא לָתֵת שָׁלוֹם בֵּין הַבְּרִיּוֹת; וְגָדוֹל הַשָּׁלוֹם, שֶׁבּוֹ הַבְּרָכָה מְצוּיָה בָּעוֹלָם וְקָשָׁה הַמַּחֲלֹקֶת, כַּמָּה קְלָלוֹת וְכַמָּה תַקָּלוֹת תְּלוּיוֹת בּוֹ.

מִדִּינֵי הַמִּצְוָה, כַּמָּה אַזְהָרוֹת וְכַמָּה זֵרוּזִין שֶׁהִזְהִירוּנוּ לִבְרוֹנָם זִכְרוֹנָם בְּעִנְיָן זֶה שֶׁלֹּא לְהַכְאִיב הַבְּרִיּוֹת בְּשׁוּם דָּבָר וְלֹא לְבַיְשָׁם, וְהִפְלִיגוּ בַּדָּבָר עַד שֶׁאָמְרוּ שֶׁלֹּא יִתְלֶה עֵינָיו עַל הַמְּקָח בְּשָׁעָה שֶׁאֵין לוֹ דָּמִים.

וְרָאוּי לְהִזָּהֵר שֶׁאֲפִלּוּ בְּרֶמֶז דְּבָרָיו לֹא יְהִי נִשְׁמָע חֵרוּף לִבְנֵי־אָדָם, כִּי הַתּוֹרָה הִקְפִּידָה הַרְבֵּה בְּאוֹנָאַת הַדְּבָרִים, לְפִי שֶׁהוּא דָּבָר קָשֶׁה מְאֹד לְלֵב הַבְּרִיּוֹת, וְהַרְבֵּה מִבְּנֵי־אָדָם יַקְפִּידוּ עֲלֵיהֶן יוֹתֵר מִן הַמָּמוֹן, וּכְמוֹ שֶׁאָמְרוּ זִכְרוֹנָם לִבְרָכָה: גְּדוֹלָה אוֹנָאַת דְּבָרִים מֵאוֹנָאַת מָמוֹן, שֶׁבְּאוֹנָאַת דְּבָרִים הוּא אוֹמֵר: וְיָרֵאתָ מֵאֱלֹהֶיךָ וְגוֹמֵר.

וְלֹא יִהְיֶה בְּאֶפְשָׁר לִכְתֹּב פְּרָט כָּל הַדְּבָרִים שֶׁיֵּשׁ בָּהֶן צַעַר לַבְּרִיּוֹת; אֲבָל כָּל אֶחָד צָרִיךְ לְהִזָּהֵר כְּפִי מַה שֶּׁיִּרְאֶה, כִּי הַשֵּׁם בָּרוּךְ הוּא הוּא יוֹדֵעַ כָּל פְּסִיעוֹתָיו וְכָל רְמִיזוֹתָיו, כִּי הָאָדָם יִרְאֶה לַעֵינַיִם וְהוּא יִרְאֶה לַלֵּבָב; וְכַמָּה מַעֲשִׂים כָּתְבוּ לָנוּ זִכְרוֹנָם לִבְרָכָה בַּמִּדְרָשִׁים לְלַמֵּד עַל זֶה מוּסָר; וְעִקַּר הָעִנְיָן בְּפֶרֶק רְבִיעִי מִמְּצִיעָא.

וְנוֹהֶגֶת מִצְוָה זוֹ בְּכָל מָקוֹם וּבְכָל זְמָן, בִּזְכָרִים וּנְקֵבוֹת, וַאֲפִלּוּ בַּקְּטַנִּים רָאוּי לְהִזָּהֵר שֶׁלֹּא לְהַכְאִיבָן בִּדְבָרִים יוֹתֵר מִדַּי, זוּלָתִי בְּמַה שֶּׁצְּרִיכִין הַרְבֵּה כְּדֵי שֶׁיִּקְחוּ מוּסָר, וַאֲפִלּוּ בְּבָנָיו וּבְנוֹתָיו וּבְנֵי־בֵיתוֹ שֶׁל אָדָם; וְהַמֵּקַל בָּהֶם שֶׁלֹּא לְצַעֲרָן בְּעִנְיָנִים אֵלֶּה, יִמְצָא חַיִּים בְּרָכָה וְכָבוֹד.

וְעוֹבֵר עַל זֶה וְהִכְאִיב אֶת חֲבֵרוֹ בִּדְבָרִים, בְּאוֹתָן שֶׁפֵּרְשׁוּ חֲכָמִים זִכְרוֹנָם

---

3. Since it would raise false hopes in the merchant and needlessly disappoint him.

4. Cf. Va-yikra Rabbah 9, 9, beginning: Great is peace, for all the blessings are included in it.

5. See Mishnath R. 'Eli'ezer, pp. 80–81.

for grain, he should not tell them, "Go to so-and-so," knowing that this person does not have any. Nor should one ask a merchant, "How much is this object?" when he does not wish to buy.[3] About this it was stated, *And you shall not wrong one another* (Leviticus 25:17).

The root purpose of this precept is known (evident): for it is to promote peace among human beings; and great is peace, for through it, blessing is found in the world;[4] while contention is harsh—so many maledictions and misfortunes devolve from it.[5]

Among the laws of the precept there are many admonitions and many exhortations with which our Sages of blessed memory cautioned us about this matter, not to inflict pain on people by any means at all, nor to shame them. They went so far in the matter as to say[1] that a man should not set his eyes on an object offered for purchase at a time when he has no money.[3]

Well, it is proper to be careful that even by an intimation in one's words, no calumny should be heard against any man. For the Torah was exceedingly particular about a wrong inflicted with words, because this is something very hard for the heart of people to bear, and a great many persons care more about this than about [being wronged] in matters of property. As the Sages of blessed memory said:[1] Wronging with words is more serious than wronging with property; for about wronging with words, Scripture stated, *but you shall fear your God* (Leviticus 25:17).

It would not be possible to write in detail all the words that could bring pain to people. Rather, everyone needs to take care according to what he sees; for the Eternal Lord, blessed is He, knows all his steps and all his hints; *for man looks on the outward appearance, but He looks on the heart* (I Samuel 16:7). Our Sages of blessed memory wrote many tales for us in the Midrashim, to teach ethical lessons about this. The main part of the subject, though, is in tractate *Bava M'tzi'a*, chapter 4.

This precept is in effect everywhere, at every time, for both man and woman. Even toward young children it is right to take care not to pain them unduly with words, except for what is greatly necessary so that they should learn ethics and morals—and this even toward a man's own sons and daughters and members of his household. He who is lenient with them, not to inflict pain on them in these ways, will find life, blessing and honor.

If someone transgresses this and wounds his fellow-man with
⟨409⟩ words, i.e. one of those about whom the Sages of blessed memory

לְבָרְכָה בְּבַעַל תְּשׁוּבָה וּבְחוֹלֶה וּבְכַיּוֹצֵא־בָהֶן, עָבַר עַל לָאו זֶה, אֲבָל אֵין לוֹקִין
עָלָיו לְפִי שֶׁאֵין בּוֹ מַעֲשֶׂה. וְכַמָּה מַלְקִיּוֹת מִבְּלִי רְצוּעָה שֶׁל עֵגֶל בְּיַד הָאָדוֹן
הַמְצַוֶּה עַל זֶה, יִתְבָּרַךְ וְיִתְעַלֶּה.

וְאוּלָם לְפִי הַדּוֹמֶה אֵין בְּמַשְׁמָע שֶׁאִם בָּא יִשְׂרָאֵל אֶחָד וְהִתְחִיל וְהִרְשִׁיעַ
לְצַעֵר חֲבֵרוֹ בִּדְבָרִים הָרָעִים, שֶׁלֹּא יַעֲנֵהוּ הַשּׁוֹמֵעַ, שֶׁאִי אֶפְשָׁר לִהְיוֹת הָאָדָם
כְּאֶבֶן שֶׁאֵין לָהּ הוֹפְכִים, וְעוֹד שֶׁיִּהְיֶה בִּשְׁתִיקָתוֹ כְּמוֹדֶה עַל הַחֵרוּפִין; וּבֶאֱמֶת לֹא
תְצַוֶּה הַתּוֹרָה לִהְיוֹת הָאָדָם שׁוֹתֵק לִמְחָרְפָיו כְּמוֹ לִמְבָרְכָיו, אֲבָל תְּצַוֶּה
אוֹתָנוּ שֶׁנִּתְרַחֵק מִן הַמִּדָּה הַזֹּאת, וְשֶׁלֹּא נַתְחִיל לְהִתְקוֹטֵט וּלְחָרֵף בְּנֵי־אָדָם, וּבְכֵן
יִנָּצֵל אָדָם מִכָּל זֶה, כִּי מִי שֶׁאֵינוֹ בַעַל קְטָטָה לֹא יְחָרְפוּהוּ בְּנֵי־אָדָם, זוּלָתִי
הַשּׁוֹטִים הַגְּמוּרִים, וְאֵין לָתֵת לֵב עַל הַשּׁוֹטִים.

וְאִם אוּלַי יַכְרִיחֵנוּ מְחָרֵף מִבְּנֵי־אָדָם לְהָשִׁיב עַל דְּבָרָיו, רָאוּי לְחָכָם שֶׁיָּשִׁיב
לוֹ דֶרֶךְ סִלְסוּל וּנְעִימוּת וְלֹא יִכְעַס הַרְבֵּה, כִּי כַעַס בְּחֵיק כְּסִילִים יָנוּחַ, וְיִנָּצֵל
עַצְמוֹ אֶל הַשּׁוֹמְעִים מֵחֵרוּפָיו וְיַשְׁלִיךְ הַמַּשָּׂא עַל הַמְחָרֵף; זֶהוּ דֶרֶךְ הַטּוֹבִים
שֶׁבִּבְנֵי־אָדָם.

וְיֵשׁ לָנוּ לִלְמֹד דָּבָר זֶה, שֶׁמַּתָּר לָנוּ לַעֲנוֹת כְּסִיל, לְפִי הַדּוֹמֶה, מֵאֲשֶׁר הִתִּירָה
הַתּוֹרָה הַבָּא בְּמַחְתֶּרֶת לְהַקְדִּים וּלְהָרְגוֹ, שֶׁאֵין סָפֵק שֶׁלֹּא נִתְחַיֵּב הָאָדָם לִסְבֹּל
הַנִּזָקִין מִיַּד חֲבֵרוֹ, כִּי יֵשׁ לוֹ רְשׁוּת לְהִנָּצֵל מִיָּדוֹ, וּכְמוֹ־כֵן מִדִּבְרֵי פִיהוּ אֲשֶׁר מָלֵא
מִרְמוֹת נָתוֹךְ, בְּכָל דָּבָר שֶׁהוּא יָכוֹל לְהִנָּצֵל מִמֶּנּוּ.

וְאוּלָם יֵשׁ כַּת מִבְּנֵי־אָדָם שֶׁעוֹלָה חֲסִידוּתָם כָּל־כָּךְ שֶׁלֹּא יִרְצוּ לְהַכְנִיס עַצְמָם
בְּהוֹרָאָה זוֹ לְהָשִׁיב חוֹרְפֵיהֶם דָּבָר, פֶּן יִגְבַּר עֲלֵיהֶם הַכַּעַס וְיִתְפַּשְּׁטוּ בָעִנְיָן יוֹתֵר
מִדַּי; וַעֲלֵיהֶם אָמְרוּ זִכְרוֹנָם לִבְרָכָה: נֶעֱלָבִין וְאֵינָם עוֹלְבִין, שׁוֹמְעִין חֶרְפָּתָם
וְאֵינָם מְשִׁיבִין, עֲלֵיהֶם הַכָּתוּב אוֹמֵר "וְאֹהֲבָיו כְּצֵאת הַשֶּׁמֶשׁ בִּגְבֻרָתוֹ".

---

6. An expression found in the Talmud: TB Sanhedrin 14a.
7. So TB Sanhedrin 72a, interpreting Exodus 22:1.
8. TB Shabbath 88b, etc. Cf. MT *bilchoth déoth* ii 3.

spoke explicitly—a repentant sinner, a sick man, and so forth—he violates this negative precept; but whiplashes are not given for it, since it involves no physical action. Yet how many lashes [to be given] without a whip of calfskin lie in the power of the Soverign Ruler who gave the commandment about this (be He blessed and exalted).

However, as it would seem, this does not mean that if one Israelite came along and began wickedly to inflict pain on his fellow with evil words, the listener should not answer him. For it is impossible for a man to be as a stone that has no one to turn it over.[6] Moreover, with his silence he would be as though admitting to the calumnies. And in truth the Torah does not order a man to be as a stone, as silent toward his slanderers as toward those who bless him. It rather commands us to move far away from this way of behavior, and that we should not start to quarrel and calumniate people. In this way, a man will be saved from all that: for whoever is not a quarrelsome person, people will not calumniate him—except for utter witless fools, and no attention need be paid to fools.

Now, if some slanderer among people will compel us to reply to his words, it were well for a wise man to answer him in a way of dignity and pleasantness, and not become very angry, *for anger rests in the bosom of fools* (Ecclesiastes 7:9). Let him excuse himself to those who hear the slanders about him, and let him throw the burden onto the calumniator. This is the way of good people in society.

We can learn this point, that we are permitted to answer a fool, as it would seem, from the fact that the Torah permitted us, when someone comes stealthily breaking in, to act first and kill him.[7] For there can be no doubt that a man is not obligated to endure injuries from the hand of his fellow-man, but rather has the right to save himself from the other's hand. Then likewise [may he save himself] from the words of the other's mouth which is filled with cunning and deceit, with every means by which he can rescue himself.

Nevertheless, there is a certain group among people whose kindly piety is of such a high degree that they would not wish to accept this ruling for themselves, to answer their calumniators any word, for fear that anger might overcome them, and they would unburden themselves unduly in the situation. Of them the Sages of blessed memory said:[8] They are humiliated, and do not humiliate; they hear their disgrace, and do not reply; of them does Scripture say, *but those who bear Him love shall be as the sun going forth in its might* (Judges 5:31).

[שֶׁלֹּא נִמְכֹּר שָׂדֶה בְּאֶרֶץ יִשְׂרָאֵל לִצְמִיתוּת]

שלט שֶׁלֹּא נִמְכֹּר שָׂדֶה בְּאֶרֶץ יִשְׂרָאֵל לִצְמִיתוּת, שֶׁנֶּאֱמַר: וְהָאָרֶץ לֹא תִמָּכֵר
לִצְמִתֻת, כְּלוֹמַר שֶׁלֹּא יַתְנוּ בֵּינֵיהֶן מוֹכֵר וְלוֹקֵחַ לַעֲשׂוֹת מִמְכָּרָם לִצְמִיתוּת; וְאַף־
עַל־פִּי שֶׁהַיּוֹבֵל מַפְקִיעָהּ בְּעַל־כָּרְחָם, שֶׁאִי־אֶפְשָׁר לָהֶם לְהַתְנוֹת עַל זֶה, לְפִי
שֶׁהוּא כְּנֶגֶד מִצְוַת הַתּוֹרָה, אַף־עַל־פִּי־כֵן אִם עָשׂוּ כֵן עָבְרוּ עַל הַלָּאו הַזֶּה; זֶהוּ
דַּעַת הָרַמְבַּ"ם זִכְרוֹנוֹ לִבְרָכָה.

וְהָרַמְבַּ"ן זִכְרוֹנוֹ לִבְרָכָה כָּתַב שֶׁדִּבְרֵי הָרַב בָּזֶה בְּעִנְיָן הַמֻּזְכָּר בָּרִאשׁוֹן שֶׁל
תְּמוּרָה, דְּאָמַר רָבָא הָתָם, חוֹלֵק עַל אַבַּיֵּי, דְּכָל מִלְּתָא דְּאָמַר רַחֲמָנָא לָא תַעֲבֵד,
אִי עֲבַד לָא מְהַנֵי וְלָקֵי, מִשּׁוּם דַּעֲבַר אַהַרְמָנָא דְּמַלְכָּא. וְהוּא זִכְרוֹנוֹ לִבְרָכָה פֵּרַשׁ
בְּעִנְיָן אַחֵר: שֶׁמַּזְהִיר אוֹתָנוּ שֶׁלֹּא נַצְמִית הָאָרֶץ בְּיַד הַגּוֹיִם, כְּלוֹמַר שֶׁלֹּא נִמְכְּרֶנָּה
לָהֶם לִצְמִיתוּתם; וּפֵרוּשׁ הַכָּתוּב כֵּן: לֹא תִמָּכֵר לְמִי שֶׁיַּחֲזִיק בָּהּ לְעוֹלָם, וְזֶהוּ הַגּוֹי,
אֲבָל הַיִּשְׂרָאֵל יַחֲזִיר אוֹתָהּ; וְאִם הִתְנָה עִם הַגּוֹי לְהַחֲזִירָהּ, מֻתָּר לְמָכְרָהּ לוֹ.

מִשָּׁרְשֵׁי מִצְוַת הַיּוֹבֵל, מַה שֶׁכָּתַבְתִּי בְּמִצְוַת מִנְיַן שְׁנֵי הַיּוֹבֵל, הָרִאשׁוֹנָה
שֶׁבְּסֵדֶר זֶה [סִי' שׁ"ל].

מִדִּינֵי הַמִּצְוָה, מַה שֶׁאָמְרוּ זִכְרוֹנָם לִבְרָכָה שֶׁהַמּוֹכֵר שָׂדֵהוּ לְשִׁשִּׁים שָׁנָה אוֹ
יוֹתֵר, כָּל זְמַן שֶׁיִּזְכֹּר לוֹ סְכוּם שָׁנִים אֵינוֹ חוֹזֵר בַּיּוֹבֵל, שֶׁאֵין חוֹזֵר בַּיּוֹבֵל אֶלָּא
דָּבָר הַנִּמְכָּר סְתָם אוֹ הַנִּמְכָּר לִצְמִיתוּת, כְּמוֹ שֶׁאָמַרְנוּ לְמַעְלָה, שֶׁשְּׁנֵיהֶם עוֹבְרִים
עַל הַלָּאו כְּשֶׁהַמֶּכֶר נַעֲשָׂה לִצְמִיתוּת וְלֹא הוֹעִילוּ מַעֲשֵׂיהֶם, שֶׁאֵין מַתְנִין לַעֲבֹר
עַל דִּבְרֵי תוֹרָה, שֶׁהַתּוֹרָה אָמְרָה: וְהָאָרֶץ לֹא תִמָּכֵר לִצְמִתֻת; אֲבָל כָּל זְמַן
שֶׁמַּזְכִּירִין בֵּינֵיהֶם סְכוּם שָׁנִים, אֵין זֶה צְמִיתוּת.

וְאוּלַי לָמְדוּ זִכְרוֹנָם לִבְרָכָה דָּבָר זֶה מֵאֲשֶׁר אָמַר הַכָּתוּב "לֹא תִמָּכֵר

§339   1. MT *hilchoth sh'mittah* xi 1.

2. Ramban, commentary (*hassagoth*) to ShM, negative precept §227.

3. Ramban does not accept Rambam's view, reasoning that if Rambam were
correct, the Talmud should have mentioned this in connection with Rava's teaching
(with which 'Abbaye differs), since it is highly relevant.

4. TB Bava M'tzi'a 79a.

4a. In place of *v'ulam*, "(and) actually," the two oldest manuscripts and the first
edition read *v'ulai*, "(and) perhaps." This is not tenable, however, as the deduction
which follows is found in TB *ibid*.

⟨412⟩

[THE PROHIBITION AGAINST SELLING A FIELD PER-
MANENTLY IN THE LAND OF ISRAEL]

339 that we should not sell a field in the land of Israel for all time: for it is stated, *And the land shall not be sold in perpetuity* (Leviticus 25:23). In other words, a vendor and buyer should not stipulate between them to have their sale (transaction) remain in effect forever. Although the jubilee extracts it [from the buyer's possession] against their will, so that they cannot really make this condition, since it runs counter to a precept of the Torah, nevertheless, if they did so, they violated this negative precept. Such is the view of Rambam of blessed memory.[1]

Now, Ramban of blessed memory wrote[2] that the words of the master on this are akin to a teaching noted in the first chapter of the tractate *T'murah* (4b): For Rava said there, differing with 'Abbaye, that as for any matter which the merciful God said you should not do, if someone did it, it is of no avail, but he receives whiplashes, since he disobeyed the Soverign Ruler's authority. But he (of blessed memory) explained it in a different way:[3] that [the Torah] adjures us not to leave the land permanently in the possession of non-Jews. In other words, we should not sell it to them in perpetuity. Then the sense of the verse is this: Do not sell to one who will retain it permanently, i.e. a non-Jew. An Israelite, though, will return it. But if one stipulates the condition with the non-Jew that he is to return it, it is permissible to sell it to him.

At the root of the precept of the jubilee lies the purpose that I wrote about the *mitzvah* of counting the years until the jubilee—the first positive precept in this *sidrah* (§330).

Among the laws of the precept, there is what the Sages of blessed memory taught:[4] that if someone sells his field for sixty years or more—as long as he mentions a number of years—it does not revert [to him] at the jubilee. For nothing reverts at the jubilee but that which was sold without any specifications or sold in perpetuity. As we said above, both transgress the negative precept when the sale is made for all time, yet their action is of no avail, since agreements cannot be made to transgress the words of the Torah. For the Torah said, *the land shall not be sold in perpetuity*. However, as long as they mention between them an amount of years, this is not perpetuity (forever).

Actually[4a] our Sages of blessed memory derived this ruling from the fact that Scripture stated, *shall not be sold in perpetuity*, and did not

לְצְמִתֻת״ וְלֹא אָמַר ״לֹא תִמָּכֵר אֶלָּא עַד הַיּוֹבֵל״, דְּמַשְׁמַע שֶׁכָּל זְמַן שֶׁלֹּא מְכָרָהּ לַחֲלוּטִין, אֵינָהּ חוֹזֶרֶת בַּיּוֹבֵל.

וּבְפֵרוּשׁ כָּתַב הָרַמְבַּ״ן זִכְרוֹנוֹ לִבְרָכָה בְּחִדּוּשָׁיו בְּמַסֶּכֶת מַכּוֹת שֶׁהַמַּתָּנָה (בַּיּוֹבֵל) ״עַל־מְנָת שֶׁלֹּא תַחֲזֹר הַשָּׂדֶה בַּיּוֹבֵל״, שֶׁאֵין תְּנָאוֹ תְּנַאי וְחוֹזֵר הוּא בַּיּוֹבֵל, אַף־עַל־פִּי שֶׁבִּשְׁמִטָּה אֵינוֹ־כֵן, שֶׁהַמַּתָּנָה ״עַל־מְנָת שֶׁלֹּא תִשְׁמֹטֶנּוּ בַּשְּׁבִיעִית״, אֵינוֹ נִשְׁמָט בַּשְּׁבִיעִית, דְּכָל תְּנַאי שֶׁבְּמָמוֹן קַיָּם; וְנָתַן טַעַם לַדָּבָר: לְפִי שֶׁבִּשְׁמִטָּה לֹא הִזְהַר עַל שְׁמִטַּת הַכְּסָפִים כִּי אִם הַמַּלְוֶה, וּכְמוֹ שֶׁכָּתוּב: שָׁמוֹט כָּל בַּעַל מַשֵּׁה יָדוֹ אֲשֶׁר יַשֶּׁה בְרֵעֵהוּ, אֲבָל לֹא הַלֹּוֶה, שֶׁאִם רָצָה לִפְרֹעַ, בְּיָדוֹ הוּא; אֲבָל בְּעִנְיַן הַיּוֹבֵל שְׁנֵיהֶם הֻזְהֲרוּ עָלָיו, מוֹכֵר וְלוֹקֵחַ, וּכְמוֹ שֶׁכָּתַבְנוּ, שֶׁלִּשְׁנֵיהֶם נֶאֱמַר ״לֹא תִמָּכֵר לִצְמִתֻת״, כְּלוֹמַר לֹא יַתְּנוּ בֵּינֵיהֶן, מוֹכֵר וְלוֹקֵחַ, מְכִירַת צְמִיתוּת, כִּי לַיי הָאָרֶץ וְאֵין בְּיַד בְּנֵי־אָדָם לְמָכְרָהּ לַחֲלוּטִין; וּמִכֵּיוָן שֶׁהַחִיּוּב עַל שְׁנֵיהֶם, אֵין בְּיַד אֶחָד מֵהֶם לִמְחֹל עַל הַדָּבָר, אֲבָל עַל כָּרְחָם יָשׁוּב הַקַּרְקַע לַאֲשֶׁר לוֹ אֲחֻזַּת הָאָרֶץ, וְאַף־עַל־פִּי שֶׁהִתְנוּ אֶלֶף פְּעָמִים עַל־מְנָת שֶׁלֹּא יָשׁוּב בַּיּוֹבֵל; וְטַעַם נָכוֹן הוּא.

וְכֵן מִדִּינֵי הַמִּצְוָה מַה שֶּׁאָמְרוּ זִכְרוֹנָם לִבְרָכָה שֶׁהַמּוֹכֵר שָׂדֵה אֲחֻזָּה וְהָיוּ לוֹ שָׂדוֹת אֲחֵרוֹת, כְּלוֹמַר שָׂדוֹת שֶׁקְּנָה הוּא אוֹ נִתְּנוּ לוֹ בְּמַתָּנָה, וּמָכַר מֵאוֹתָן שָׂדוֹת כְּדֵי לִגְאֹל שָׂדֵה אֲחֻזָּתוֹ שֶׁמָּכַר, שֶׁאֵין שׁוֹמְעִין לוֹ, דִּכְתִיב בְּפָרָשַׁת שָׂדֵה אֲחֻזָּה: וּמָצָא כְּדֵי גְאֻלָּתוֹ, וּבָא הַפֵּרוּשׁ עָלָיו: עַד שֶׁיִּמָּצֵא לוֹ דָבָר שֶׁלֹּא הָיָה לוֹ מָצוּי בְּשָׁעָה שֶׁמָּכַר; וְכֵן אִם לָוָה וְרָצָה לִגְאֹל בְּאוֹתָהּ הַלְוָאָה, אֵין שׁוֹמְעִין לוֹ, שֶׁנֶּאֱמַר ״וְהִשִּׂיגָה יָדוֹ״, וְלֹא שֶׁיִּלְוֶה.

וְעִנְיַן שָׂדֵה אֲחֻזָּה יִקָּרְאוּ הַשָּׂדוֹת שֶׁנָּפְלוּ בִירֻשָּׁה לְכָל אֶחָד מִיִּשְׂרָאֵל בְּחִלּוּק הָאָרֶץ, וְכֵן מִי שֶׁזָּכָה וְנוֹסְפָה אֲחֻזָּתוֹ מֵחֲמַת הַסִּבַּת נַחֲלָה עַל־יְדֵי יוֹרֶשֶׁת

---

5. So TB Makkoth 3b.
6. TB 'Arachin 30a–b.
7. He is not permitted to carry out his wish; TB 'Arachin 30a.
8. Ibid. 30b; MT hilchoth sh'mittah xi 17.

say, "shall not be sold except till the jubilee"; for it implies that as long as one did not sell it forever, it does not revert [to him] at the jubilee.

Now, Ramban of blessed memory wrote distinctly in his novellae (commentary) to the tractate *Makkoth* (3b) that if one stipulates [that the sale should be] with the proviso that the field should not revert [to him] at the jubilee, his stipulation is no stipulation, and it does revert at the jubilee—although in *sh'mittah* [a seventh year] it is not so: For if one makes a condition stipulating that [a debt] should not be dissolved by the seventh year, it is not released by the seventh year;[5] for any condition made about goods and wares remains valid. And he gave a reason for the matter: [It is] because in a *sh'mittah* year, none but the lender is adjured about the release of money [obligations]—as it is written, *every creditor shall release what he has lent to his neighbor* (Deuteronomy 15:2)—but not the borrower; for if he wishes to pay it, he has the choice. But in regard to the jubilee, both of them were adjured about it: the seller and the buyer. As we wrote, it is stated to both of them, *the land shall not be sold in perpetuity*; in other words, they shall not stipulate between them, the seller and the buyer, a sale for all time; for *the earth is the Lord's* (Psalms 24:1), and it is not in the power of human beings to sell it permanently. And since the obligation lies on both, neither of them has the power to forgo the matter; rather, whether they want or not, the ground will revert to the one who has the inherited title to the land, even if they stipulated a thousand times the condition that it should not revert at the jubilee. And this is a right and proper reason.

So is there among the laws of the precept what the Sages of blessed memory said:[6] that if someone sold a field of heritage and he had other fields, i.e. fields that he had bought or that had been given him as gifts, and he then sold some of those fields in order to redeem his field of heritage that he had sold, he is not heeded;[7] for it is written in the Scriptural section about a field of heritage, *and he attains the means, finding enough to redeem it* (Leviticus 25:26), and the interpretation was given for it:[8] [he cannot redeem it] until he finds something that was not available to him at the time he sold it. Likewise, if he borrowed money and wished to redeem it with that loan, he is not heeded: for it is stated, *and he attains the means*, not if he borrows money.[8]

As to the meaning of fields of heritage, so are those fields called that were allotted as an inheritance to everyone in Israel when the land was divided; and so also if someone was fortunate to have his inheritance

נַחֲלָה—שֶׁדָּבָר יָדוּעַ הוּא שֶׁלֹּא נֶאֱמַר "וְלֹא תִסֵּב נַחֲלָה" אֶלָּא בְּאוֹתוֹ הַדּוֹר
בִּלְבַד — אֵלּוּ הֵן הַנִּקְרָאִין שְׂדוֹת אֲחֻזָּה; וְנִתְחַדֵּשׁ דִּינָם בַּתּוֹרָה מִשְּׁאָר שָׂדוֹת
לְעִנְיַן הַגְּאֻלָּה, שֶׁשְּׂדֵה אֲחֻזָּה נִגְאָל עַל־יְדֵי הַמּוֹכֵר אוֹ עַל־יְדֵי גּוֹאֲלוֹ לְאַחַר שְׁתֵּי
שָׁנִים, בְּעַל כָּרְחוֹ שֶׁל לוֹקֵחַ; וּשְׁאָר שָׂדוֹת, שֶׁנִּקְרָאִים שְׂדֵה מִקְנָה, אֵינָם נִגְאָלִין
אֶלָּא בִּרְצוֹן הַלּוֹקֵחַ, אֶלָּא יַעַמְדוּ בְּיַד לוֹקֵחַ עַד הַיּוֹבֵל.

וּבְחִלּוּק בָּתִּים מִשָּׂדוֹת, כְּבָר כְּתַבְנוּ לְמַעְלָה בִּמְקוֹמוֹ דִּינָם, כִּי בָּתֵּי הַחֲצֵרִים
דִּינָם כִּשְׂדֵה אֲחֻזָּה, כְּלוֹמַר שֶׁיֵּשׁ לָהֶם גְּאֻלָּה עַל כָּרְחוֹ שֶׁל לוֹקֵחַ, כְּמוֹ שֶׁכָּתוּב
בָּהֶן: גְּאֻלָּה תִהְיֶה לּוֹ; וְיָפֶה כֹחָן מִשָּׂדוֹת, שֶׁהֵן נִגְאָלִין אֲפִלּוּ תּוֹךְ שָׁנָה, כְּדִין בַּיִת
בְּעָרֵי חוֹמָה. וְדִין בָּתֵּי עָרֵי חוֹמָה מְפֹרָשׁ בַּכָּתוּב, וּכְבָר כְּתַבְנוּהוּ לְמַעְלָה גַּם־כֵּן.

וּמֵעִנְיַן הַמִּצְוָה מַה שֶּׁאָמְרוּ זִכְרוֹנָם לִבְרָכָה גַּם־כֵּן, שֶׁהַלּוֹקֵחַ שְׂדֵה אֲחֻזָּה וְנָטַע
בָּהּ אִילָנוֹת וְהִשְׁבִּיחָהּ, כְּשֶׁהִיא חוֹזֶרֶת שָׁמִין שֶׁבַח הָאִילָנוֹת שֶׁבְּתוֹכָהּ לַלּוֹקֵחַ,
שֶׁנֶּאֱמַר: וְיָצָא מִמְכַּר בַּיִת, וּבָא עָלָיו הַפֵּרוּשׁ הַמְקֻבָּל: מִמְכָּר חוֹזֵר, וְאֵין שֶׁבַח
חוֹזֵר.

וּמַה שֶּׁאָמְרוּ זִכְרוֹנָם לִבְרָכָה גַּם־כֵּן שֶׁהַמּוֹכֵר שָׂדֵהוּ, בֵּין שָׂדֶה אֲחֻזָּה אוֹ שָׂדֶה
אַחֵר, אֵין רַשַּׁאי לְגָאֲלָהּ לְפָחוֹת מִשְּׁתֵּי שָׁנִים, וַאֲפִלּוּ בִּרְצוֹן הַלּוֹקֵחַ, שֶׁהַכָּתוּב
צִוָּה שֶׁיַּעֲמֹד הַמֶּכֶר קַיָּם שְׁתֵּי שָׁנִים עַל־כָּל־פָּנִים, שֶׁנֶּאֱמַר: בְּמִסְפַּר שְׁנֵי תְבוּאֹת
יִמְכָּר לָךְ, אַזְהָרָה לַמּוֹכֵר, וְאַזְהָרָה לַלּוֹקֵחַ מִדִּכְתִיב: בְּמִסְפַּר שָׁנִים... תִּקְנֶה,
וּמְעוּט שָׁנִים שְׁנַיִם.

וּמִן הַדּוֹמֶה שֶׁהָעִנְיָן הוּא כְּדֵי שֶׁיִּמְכֹּר כָּל אָדָם קַרְקָעוֹ בְּקֹשִׁי וְאַל יַחְשֹׁב כִּי

---

9. I.e. his wife, if she inherits land from her father.

10. The generation of Israelites in the wilderness, that would conquer and settle the land; TB Bava Bathra 120a.

11. When they return to the original owners, who inherited them as fields of heritage (if the purchasers refused to let them be redeemed before); Leviticus 25:25–28.

12. While in the standard editions this is the next precept, in the original work it occurs earlier; see § 285, note 2.

12a. I.e. after they have been sold.

13. Leviticus 25:29–30.

14. TB Bava M'tzi'a 109a.

15. TB 'Arachin 29b.

16. It should be difficult for him to decide to sell it.

increased on account of the transfer of inherited land through a daughter[9] who became heir to such a possession. For it is a known matter
that the verse, *So shall no inheritance . . . be transferred* (Numbers 36:7)
was stated for none but that generation alone.[10] These, then, are called
fields of heritage; and a new law was given about them in the Torah,
apart from other fields, regarding redemption: For a field of heritage
can be redeemed by the vendor or by his kinsman after two years,
against the will of the purchaser. Other fields, though, which are called
fields of purchase, cannot be redeemed except with the consent of the
buyer; and they can rather remain in the purchaser's possession till
the jubilee.[11]

As to the difference [in law] between houses and fields, I have
written their law previously, above (§340),[12] in its proper place: that
for houses of open (unwalled) towns, the law is the same as for a field
of heritage. This means that they can undergo redemption against
the buyer's will—as it is written of them, *they may be redeemed* (Leviticus
25:31). And they entail a greater right than fields, in that they may be
redeemed even within a year,[12a] as the law is for a house in a walled city.
The law of houses in walled cities is given explicitly in Scripture,[13]
and I have already written it above (§340),[12] as well.

In the subject-matter of the precept, there is what the Sages of
blessed memory also said:[14] that if someone bought a field of heritage,
planted trees in it, and improved it, when it reverts [to the original
owner] the improvement by the trees in it is estimated, to [be paid]
the purchaser. For it is stated, *then the house that was sold shall go out*
(Leviticus 25:33), and the interpretation received in the Oral Tradition
was given for it:[14] what was sold returns, but the improvement does
not revert.

Then there is what the Sages of blessed memory taught as well:[15]
that when a person sells his field, whether a field of heritage or another
plot, he is not allowed to redeem it for at least two years, even with the
purchaser's consent. Scripture ordained that the sale should remain in
effect for two years under all circumstances. For it is stated, *according
to the number of years of crops he shall sell to you* (Leviticus 25:15)—this
is an admonition to the vendor; and there is an admonition to the purchaser since it is written, *According to the number of years . . . you shall
buy* (*ibid.*); and the minimum number of "years" is two.

Well, it would seem that the reason is in order that a man should
⟨417⟩ sell his land reluctantly, with difficulty,[16] and he should not think

לְמָחָר יָשׁוּב וְיִקָּחֶנּוּ לוֹ מִיַּד הַלּוֹקֵחַ, אֲבָל יָדַע שֶׁאֵינוֹ יָכוֹל לֶאֱכֹל מִתְּבוּאוֹתָיו בְּשׁוּם פָּנִים עַד שְׁתֵּי שָׁנִים מִיּוֹם לְיוֹם מֵעֵת הַמְּכִירָה.

וְגַם אָמְרוּ זִכְרוֹנָם לִבְרָכָה גַּם־כֵּן שֶׁצָּרִיךְ שֶׁיֹּאכַל הַלּוֹקֵחַ שְׁתֵּי תְבוּאוֹת בְּאוֹתָן שְׁתֵּי שָׁנִים, שֶׁנֶּאֱמַר "שְׁנֵי תְבוּאֹת", לְפִיכָךְ אִם הָיְתָה אַחַת מִשְּׁתֵּי שָׁנִים אֵלּוּ שְׁנַת שִׁדָּפוֹן וְיֵרָקוֹן אוֹ שְׁנַת שְׁבִיעִית, אֵינָהּ עוֹלָה מִן הַמִּנְיָן; אֲבָל שְׁנַת בּוּרָה, אָמְרוּ זִכְרוֹנָם לִבְרָכָה שֶׁעוֹלָה הִיא מִן הַמִּנְיָן. מְכָרָהּ בִּשְׁנַת הַיּוֹבֵל עַצְמָהּ, אֵין הַמְּכִירָה מְכִירָה, וְחוֹזְרִין הַדָּמִים לִבְעָלָיו. מָכַר הָאִילָנוֹת לְבַד, אֵין נִגְאָלִין לְפָחוֹת מִשְּׁתֵּי שָׁנִים; וְאִם לֹא גְאָלָן בְּתוֹךְ שְׁנֵי יוֹבֵל, אֵינָם חוֹזְרִין בַּיּוֹבֵל, שֶׁנֶּאֱמַר "וְשָׁב לַאֲחֻזָּתוֹ" וְלֹא [לְ]אִילָנוֹת. מָכַר שָׂדֵהוּ לָרִאשׁוֹן וְרִאשׁוֹן לְשֵׁנִי וְשֵׁנִי לִשְׁלִישִׁי, וַאֲפִלּוּ מֵאָה אוֹ יוֹתֵר, הַשָּׂדֶה חוֹזֶרֶת בַּיּוֹבֵל לָרִאשׁוֹן, שֶׁנֶּאֱמַר: לַאֲשֶׁר לוֹ אֲחֻזַּת הָאָרֶץ; וְיֶתֶר פְּרָטֶיהָ, בְּסוֹף עֲרָכִין.

וְנוֹהֶגֶת בִּזְכָרִים וּנְקֵבוֹת בְּאֶרֶץ יִשְׂרָאֵל, בִּזְמַן שֶׁיּוֹשְׁבֶיהָ עָלֶיהָ, כִּי כָל עִנְיְנֵי הַיּוֹבֵל אֵינָם אֶלָּא בִּזְמַן שֶׁיּוֹשְׁבֶיהָ עָלֶיהָ, כְּמוֹ שֶׁכָּתַבְנוּ לְמַעְלָה. וְעוֹבֵר עַל זֶה וּמָכַר שָׂדֵהוּ לִצְמִיתוּת, וְכֵן הַלּוֹקְחוֹ מִמֶּנּוּ בְּעִנְיָן זֶה, שְׁנֵיהֶם לוֹקִין, אַף־עַל־פִּי שֶׁלֹּא הוֹעִילוּ דִבְרֵיהֶם; וְהוּא שֶׁעָשׂוּ מַעֲשֶׂה בַּדָּבָר, שֶׁאֵין לוֹקִין בְּלָאו שֶׁאֵין בּוֹ מַעֲשֶׂה; זֶהוּ דַעַת הָרַמְבַּ"ם זִכְרוֹנוֹ לִבְרָכָה; אֲבָל לְדַעַת הָרַמְבַּ"ן זִכְרוֹנוֹ לִבְרָכָה אֵין בָּזֶה מַלְקוֹת כְּלָל, כְּמוֹ שֶׁכָּתַבְתִּי בְרֹאשׁ הַמִּצְוָה.

[מִצְוַת הָשֵׁב קַרְקַע לְבַעֲלֶיהָ בַּיּוֹבֵל]

שם לְהָשִׁיב כָּל הַקַּרְקָעוֹת, בֵּין בַּיִת אוֹ שָׂדֶה וְכֶרֶם וּפַרְדֵּסִין, בִּשְׁנַת הַיּוֹבֵל לְבַעֲלֵיהֶן בְּלֹא כֶסֶף וּבְלֹא מְחִיר, שֶׁנֶּאֱמַר: וּבְכֹל אֶרֶץ אֲחֻזַּתְכֶם גְּאֻלָּה תִּתְּנוּ

17. I.e. two full years, from the day he sells it to the day he redeems it.
18. And the minimum number of "years" (plural) is two.
19. When the purchaser decided not to cultivate the field; MT *hilchoth sh'mittah* xi 11.
20. TB 'Arachin 14b.
21. MT *ibid.* 15.

that tomorrow he can return and buy it back for himself from the purchaser. He must rather know that he cannot eat (benefit) from his crops under any conditions until two years, from day to day,[17] from the time of the sale.

Moreover, our Sages of blessed memory said[15] that the purchaser must have two crops in those two years: for it is stated, *years of crops*[18] (*ibid.*). Therefore, if one of these two years was a year of blight and grain-disease or a seventh year, it is not included in the number. But as for a year of non-cultivation,[19] the Sages of blessed memory said[15] it is included in the reckoning. If it was sold in a jubilee year itself, the sale is no sale, and the money goes back to its owner.[15] If one sold the trees [of a field] alone, they are not to be redeemed within less than two years; and if they were not redeemed within the years of [until] the jubilee, they do not revert [to the original owner] at the jubilee: for it is stated, *and he shall return to his [field] estate* (Leviticus 25:28), but not to his trees.[20] If a person sold his field to a first buyer, then the first to a second, the second to a third, [and so on up to] even a hundred or more, it returns at the jubilee to the first [original] owner:[21] for it is stated, *to whom the possession of the land belongs* (Leviticus 27:24). The rest of its details are toward the end of the tractate *'Arachin*.

It applies for both man and woman in the land of Israel, at the time that its inhabitants are [settled] on it; for all aspects of the jubilee apply only at a time that its inhabitants are on it, as we wrote above (§330). If someone transgressed this and sold his field for all time, and so whoever bought it from him on these terms—both receive whiplashes, even though their words achieved nothing—but this, provided they did some action about the matter; for whiplashes are not given over a negative precept that involves no physical action. This is the view of Rambam of blessed memory.[1] But in the view of Ramban of blessed memory it entails no whiplashes ever, as I wrote at the beginning of the precept.

[THE PRECEPT OF RETURNING LAND TO ITS ORIGINAL OWNER AT THE JUBILEE]

340 to return all landed properties, whether a house, a field, a vineyard or an orchard, in the jubilee year to their owners, without payment of money or any [other] price: for it is stated, *And in all the land of your possession, you shall grant a redemption for the land* (Leviticus

לָאָרֶץ, כְּלוֹמַר בְּכָל אֶרֶץ יִשְׂרָאֵל שֶׁהִיא אֲחֻזַּתְכֶם, גְּאֻלָּה תִּתְּנוּ לָאָרֶץ. וְעִנְיַן הַגְּאֻלָּה בֵּאֵר הַכָּתוּב שֶׁהִיא חֲזָרַת הַקַּרְקַע לִבְעָלָיו, וּכְמוֹ שֶׁכָּתוּב: בִּשְׁנַת הַיּוֹבֵל הַזֹּאת תָּשֻׁבוּ אִישׁ אֶל אֲחֻזָּתוֹ.

מִשָּׁרְשֵׁי הַמִּצְוָה, מַה שֶּׁכָּתַבְנוּ בְּרֹאשׁ הַסֵּדֶר.

מִדִּינֵי הַמִּצְוָה, קְצָתָם מְבֹאָרִים בַּכָּתוּב: אֵיךְ יִהְיֶה דִּין הַמּוֹכֵר עִם הַקּוֹנֶה כְּשֶׁיִּרְצֶה לִפְדּוֹת נַחֲלָתוֹ הַנִּמְכֶּרֶת, קֹדֶם שְׁנַת הַיּוֹבֵל; וְהַחִלּוּק שֶׁבֵּאֵר הַכָּתוּב שֶׁהוּא בֵּין מוֹכֵר בַּיִת בְּעִיר חוֹמָה לְמוֹכֵר אוֹתוֹ בְּעָרֵי הַפְּרָזוֹת, שֶׁנִּקְרָאת בִּלְשׁוֹן הַכָּתוּב עָרֵי הַחֲצֵרִים, שֶׁדִּין בָּתֵּי עָרֵי הַפְּרָזוֹת כְּדִין הַשָּׂדוֹת.

וְעוֹד אָמְרוּ זִכְרוֹנָם לִבְרָכָה בְּמִצְוָה זוֹ, שֶׁאִם מָכַר בַּיִת בְּבָתֵּי עָרֵי חוֹמָה לְאֶחָד וּמְכָרָהּ הַלּוֹקֵחַ רִאשׁוֹן לְשֵׁנִי בְּתוֹךְ הַשָּׁנָה, מוֹנִין לָרִאשׁוֹן, וְכֵיוָן שֶׁשָּׁלְמָה שָׁנָה לָרִאשׁוֹן הֶחְלַט הַבַּיִת לַשֵּׁנִי: מִפְּנֵי שֶׁעִנְיַן מוֹכֵר בַּיִת בְּבָתֵּי עָרֵי חוֹמָה שֶׁהוּא מֻחְלָט לְשָׁנָה, כְּעִנְיַן קְנָס הוּא שֶׁקְּנָסַהּ הַתּוֹרָה לַמּוֹכֵר, מִפְּנֵי חִבַּת הָאָרֶץ, וּמִכֵּיוָן שֶׁעָמַד זוּלָתוֹ שָׁנָה רָאוּי הוּא שֶׁיֵּחָלֵט גַּם בְּיַד הַשֵּׁנִי; וְעוֹד שֶׁהָרִאשׁוֹן מָכַר לַשֵּׁנִי כָּל זְכוּת שֶׁלּוֹ, וְאִלּוּ עָמְדָה שָׁנָה הָרִאשׁוֹן בְּיַד הָרִאשׁוֹן כְּבָר הָיְתָה מֻחְלֶטֶת בְּיָדוֹ.

וּמַה שֶּׁאָמְרוּ זִכְרוֹנָם לִבְרָכָה גַּם-כֵּן שֶׁאִם הִגִּיעַ יוֹם שְׁנֵים-עָשָׂר חֹדֶשׁ וְלֹא נִמְצָא הַלּוֹקֵחַ לִפְדּוֹת מִמֶּנּוּ, הֲרֵי זֶה מַנִּיחַ מָעוֹתָיו בְּבֵית-דִּין וְשׁוֹבֵר אֶת הַדֶּלֶת וְנִכְנָס לַבַּיִת; וְאֵימָתַי שֶׁיָּבוֹא הַלּוֹקֵחַ, יָבוֹא וְיִטֹּל מָעוֹתָיו.

וּמַה שֶּׁאָמְרוּ שֶׁהַמּוֹכֵר בַּיִת בְּעָרֵי חוֹמָה וְהִגִּיעַ יוֹבֵל בְּתוֹךְ שְׁנַת הַמֶּכֶר, שֶׁאֵינוֹ חוֹזֵר מִיָּד בַּיּוֹבֵל, אֶלָּא דִּינָהּ כְּמוֹ בִּשְׁאָר שָׁנִים שֶׁבְּתוֹךְ שְׁנֵי הַיּוֹבֵל, שֶׁהוּא נֶחְלָט לְשָׁנָה אִם אֵין הַמּוֹכֵר רוֹצֶה לְגָאֳלָהּ.

---

§340   1. Leviticus 25:27.

2. *Ibid.* 29–31.

3. This is the reading of an MS Mosaieff, in ed. Chavel p. 739: *baté 'aré ha-p'razoth.* MS Vatican 163/1 has only *'aré ha-p'razoth*; all other sources read *'aré baté ha-p'razoth*—except MS Parma 741, which has *'aré baté 'aré ha-p'razoth.* Likely, at some early point the reading was as in MS Vatican, and *baté* was added in the margin as a correction; in one copying it was evidently inserted in the wrong place, giving the reading that found its way into the editions; the correct reading was recorded in MS Mosaieff, while MS Parma 741 has an amalgamation of the two.

4. TB 'Arachin 31a–b (and Rashi to the Mishnah).

4a. More literally, the belovedness of the land: i.e. a house in a walled city in the land of Israel should be so beloved and dear to its owner by inheritance that if he sold it, he should go to any length to get it back; and if he did not, the non-revocability of the sale is his penalty.

5. *Ibid.* 31b; MT *hilchoth sh'mittah* xii 7.

6. TB *ibid.*

25:24); in other words, in all the land of Israel, which is your heritage-possession, you shall provide redemption for the land; and Scripture explained the meaning of redemption, that it denotes the reversion of landed property to its original owner. As it is written, *In this year of jubilee, you shall return every man to his heritage-possession.*

The root purpose of the precept is as we have written of the first positive precept in the *sidrah* (§330).

Among the laws of the precept, some are explained in the Writ: how the law is for a vendor [settling] with a buyer when he wishes to redeem his sold property of inheritance before the jubilee year;[1] the difference that Scripture explained,[2] between one who sells a house in a walled city and one who sells it in an open city, which is called in the language of Scripture, *cities of the* ḥatzérim, *villages* (Leviticus 25:31). For the law of houses in open, unwalled cities[3] is as the law for fields.

Our Sages of blessed memory taught further in regard to this precept[4] that if a person sold a house in a walled city to one, and the first purchaser sold it to a second within the year, [the period for redemption] is reckoned as for the first [original owner]: once a year has ended for this first man, the house becomes irrevocably that of the second. For the rule that when a house in a walled city is sold, it is irrevocable at the end of a year, is in the nature of a penalty with which the Torah penalized the vendor, on account of the preciousness of the land;[4a] and since he remained without it for a year, it is right that it should remain irrevocably also in the second [buyer's] possession. Moreover, the first [buyer] sold to the second every right of his; and had it remained a complete year in the first one's possession, it would already have been irretrievably his.

Then there is what the Sages of blessed memory said, as well,[5] that if the day [ending] twelve months arrived and the purchaser is not to be found, to redeem it from him, he [the original owner] can then leave his money at the *beth din* (court), break the door, and enter the house; and whenever the purchaser will appear, he can come and take his money.

Further, we have what the Sages said:[6] that if a person sold a house in a walled city and the jubilee arrived within a year of the sale, it does not revert at once, at the jubilee, but its law is rather as in other years within a jubilee period—that it remains irrevocably sold at one year if the vendor does not wish to redeem it.

מַה שֶּׁאָמְרוּ שֶׁהַמּוֹכֵר בַּיִת בְּעָרֵי הַחֲצֵרִים, שֶׁאִם רָצָה לִגְאֹל מִיָּד, גּוֹאֵל, כְּדִין בַּיִת בְּבָתֵּי עָרֵי חוֹמָה; וְאִם לֹא רָצָה לִגְאֹל מִיָּד, גּוֹאֵל אוֹתָהּ אֲפִלּוּ אַחַר שָׁנָה, כְּדִין שָׂדוֹת—דְּכֹחַ יָפֶה שֶׁבַּשָּׂדוֹת וְשֶׁבְּבָתֵּי עָרֵי חוֹמָה יֵשׁ לָהֶן.

וּמַה שֶּׁאָמְרוּ שֶׁכָּל שֶׁהוּא לִפְנִים מִן הַחוֹמָה, כְּגוֹן גַּנּוֹת מֶרְחֲצָאוֹת וְשׁוֹבָכוֹת, דִּינָם כְּבָתִּים, דְּמִדְּכְתִיב "אֲשֶׁר בָּעִיר" רִבָּה הַכֹּל; אֲבָל אִם הָיוּ שָׂדוֹת בְּתוֹךְ הָעִיר, דִּינוֹ כְּשָׂדוֹת שֶׁחוּץ לָעִיר, שֶׁנֶּאֱמַר "וְקָם הַבַּיִת", כְּלוֹמַר בַּיִת וְכָל הַדּוֹמֶה לַבַּיִת, כְּמוֹ מֶרְחֲצָאוֹת וְשׁוֹבָכוֹת וְאַף פַּרְדֵּסִין, אֲבָל לֹא שָׂדוֹת.

וּבַיִת שֶׁאֵין בּוֹ אַרְבַּע אַמּוֹת עַל אַרְבַּע אַמּוֹת אֵינוֹ נִקְרָא בַיִת, וּלְפִיכָךְ אֵינוֹ נֶחְלָט; וּבִירוּשָׁלַיִם אֵין הַבַּיִת נֶחְלָט בָּהּ; וְעִיר שֶׁגַּגּוֹתֶיהָ חוֹמָתָהּ, אֵין דִּינָהּ כְּמֻקֶּפֶת חוֹמָה, אֶלָּא בָעִינַן שֶׁתִּהְיֶה לָהּ חוֹמָה מִלְּבַד גַּגּוֹתֶיהָ; וּבָעִינַן גַּם־כֵּן שֶׁהֻקְּפָה חוֹמָה תְחִלָּה וְאַחַר־כָּךְ נִתְיַשְּׁבָה, אֲבָל נִתְיַשְּׁבָה וְאַחַר־כָּךְ הֻקְּפָה, אֵין זוֹ עִיר חוֹמָה; וְאֵין סוֹמְכִין אֶלָּא עַל חוֹמָה הַמֻּקֶּפֶת בְּשָׁעָה שֶׁכָּבַשׁ יְהוֹשֻׁעַ אֶת הָאָרֶץ; וְכֵינָן שֶׁגָּלוּ בְּחָרְבָּן רִאשׁוֹן בָּטְלָה קְדֻשַּׁת עִיר חוֹמָה, וּכְשֶׁעָלָה עֶזְרָא בְּבִיאָה שְׁנִיָּה, נִתְקַדְּשׁוּ כָל הֶעָרִים הַמֻּקָּפוֹת חוֹמָה בְּאוֹתוֹ הָעֵת, מִפְּנֵי שֶׁבִּיאָתָן בִּימֵי עֶזְרָא, שֶׁהִיא בִיאָה שְׁנִיָּה, כְּבִיאָתָן בִּימֵי יְהוֹשֻׁעַ: מַה בִּיאָתָן בִּימֵי יְהוֹשֻׁעַ, מָנוּ שְׁמִטִּין וְיוֹבְלוֹת וְקִדְּשׁוּ עָרֵי חוֹמָה וְנִתְחַיְּבוּ בְמַעֲשֵׂר, אַף בִּימֵי עֶזְרָא כֵּן; וְכֵן כְּשֶׁיָּבוֹא מָשִׁיחַ בְּבִיאָה שְׁלִישִׁית, נַתְחִיל לִמְנוֹת שְׁמִטִּין וְיוֹבְלוֹת וְיִתְקַדְּשׁוּ בָּתֵּי עָרֵי חוֹמָה שֶׁיִּהְיוּ מֻקָּפִין בְּאוֹתָהּ הָעֵת, וְיִתְחַיֵּב כָּל מָקוֹם שֶׁנִּכְבַּשׁ בְּמַעַשְׂרוֹת — שֶׁנֶּאֱמַר: וֶהֱבִיאֲךָ יי אֱלֹהֶיךָ וְגוֹמֵר, וְאָמְרוּ: מַקִּישׁ יְרֻשָּׁתְךָ לִירֻשַּׁת אֲבוֹתֶיךָ וְכוּלֵי, וְיֻתַּר פְּרָטֶיהָ, בְּמַסֶּכֶת עֲרָכִין.

7. TB 'Arachin 33a.

8. *Ibid.* 32a.

9. TB Sukkah 3a.

10. TB 'Arachin 32b.

11. So MS Parma 928, *she-gagotheha*; generally, *she-ganotheha*, "whose gardens" — the reading of one MS (in ed. Romm) and ed. Lowe of the Mishnah, 'Arachin ix 6 (TB 32a). Our reading, however, is far more tenable, meaning, according to one explanation in the commentary of R. Gershom (TB ed. Vilna), slanting house-roofs which reach down to the ground; and as Rashi notes, the houses are set close together, so that these sloping roofs take on the appearance of a wall; but the city has no proper separate wall round about.

12. TB M'gillah 3b.

13. Of the Israelites into the Promised Land.

Then there is what the Sages taught:[7] that if one sold a house in an open, unwalled city, if he wishes to redeem it at once, he may redeem it, as the law is for a house in a walled city; and if he does not wish to redeem it at once, he may redeem it even after a year, as the law is for fields. For the privileges of both fields and houses in walled cities apply to it.

We have, too, what the Sages said:[8] that whatever is within the wall [of a city], such as gardens, bath-houses and dovecotes, are under the same law as houses; for since it is written, *that is in the city* (Leviticus 25:30), it thus includes everything. However, if there were fields within the city, their law would be as for fields outside the city: for it is stated, *then the house shall remain (ibid.)*—i.e. a house and whatever is like a house, such as bath-houses and dovecotes, and even orchards, but not fields.

A house that does not measure four cubits by four cubits is not called (considered) a house, and therefore it cannot be sold irrevocably.[9] In Jerusalem the sale of a house does not become irrevocable.[10] A city whose roofs[11] form its wall is not considered a walled city under the law; it is rather required to have a wall apart from its roofs [to qualify];[8] and it is likewise required to have been surrounded by a wall first and then settled; but if it was settled and walled about afterward, it is not [considered] a walled city.[12] So reliance could be placed on none but a wall that surrounded [a city] at the time that Joshua conquered the land.[10] Once [the Israelites] were exiled upon the first destruction [of the Temple] the sanctity of the walled city ceased; and when Ezra went up at the second arrival, all the cities that were walled about at that time became sanctified; for their arrival in Ezra's time, which was the second entry,[13] was like [equal to] their entry in Joshua's time. Just as upon their entry in Joshua's time they reckoned *sh'mittah* [seventh] years and jubilees, sanctified walled cities, and became obligated to give tithes, so also in Ezra's time. And so too when the Messiah will come, at the third entry, we will begin to reckon *sh'mittah* years and jubilees, the houses of those cities that are walled about at that time will be sanctified, and in every conquered location the obligation of tithes will be imposed. For it is stated, *And the Lord your God will bring you into the land which your fathers possessed, and you shall possess it* (Deuteronomy 30:5); and the Sages said:[10] It equates your heritage-possession with that of your fathers, etc.

The rest of its details are in the Talmud tractate *'Arachin*. It applies

וְנוֹהֶגֶת בִּזְכָרִים וּנְקֵבוֹת בְּאֶרֶץ יִשְׂרָאֵל וּבִזְמַן שֶׁהַיּוֹבֵל נוֹהֵג; וּכְבָר כָּתַבְתִּי
לְמַעְלָה בְּאֵי זֶה זְמַן הַיּוֹבֵל נוֹהֵג, וְהוּא בִּזְמַן שֶׁכָּל יִשְׂרָאֵל עַל אַדְמָתָן בְּיִשּׁוּבָן.
וְעוֹבֵר עַל זֶה וְכָבַשׁ הַקַּרְקַע שֶׁבְּיָדוֹ וְלֹא הֶחֱזִירוֹ לִבְעָלָיו, בִּטֵּל עֲשֵׂה זֶה, וְעָנְשׁוֹ
גָּדוֹל, כְּאִלּוּ כֹּפֵר בְּמַעֲשֵׂה בְרֵאשִׁית.

[מִצְוַת פִּדְיוֹן הַנַּחֲלוֹת שֶׁהֵן תּוֹךְ הָעִיר עַד הַשְׁלָמַת שָׁנָה]

שמא שֶׁיִּהְיֶה פִּדְיוֹן הַנַּחֲלוֹת שֶׁהֵן תּוֹךְ הָעִיר הַמֻּקֶּפֶת חוֹמָה, עַד הַשְׁלָמַת
שָׁנָה אַחַת, וְאַחַר הַשָּׁנָה תִּהְיֶה בְּחֶזְקַת הַקּוֹנֶה אוֹתָן וְלֹא יִהְיוּ חוֹזְרוֹת בַּיּוֹבֵל,
שֶׁנֶּאֱמַר: וְאִישׁ כִּי יִמְכֹּר בֵּית מוֹשַׁב עִיר חוֹמָה וְגוֹמֵר. כְּבָר כָּתַבְתִּי לְמַעְלָה שֶׁעִנְיַן
הֱיוֹת בַּיִת בְּעִיר חוֹמָה נֶחְלַט לְשָׁנָה, מִצַּד חִבַּת הָאָרֶץ הוּא, כְּדֵי שֶׁיִּשְׁתַּדֵּל הַמּוֹכְרָהּ
לִגְאֹל אוֹתָהּ מְהֵרָה.

מִדִּינֵי הַמִּצְוָה, מַה שֶּׁאָמְרוּ זִכְרוֹנָם לִבְרָכָה שֶׁהַמּוֹכֵר יָכוֹל לְגָאֲלָהּ בְּכָל עֵת
שֶׁיִּרְצֶה תּוֹךְ שָׁנָה, וּכְשֶׁפּוֹדֶהָ אוֹתָהּ נוֹתֵן לוֹ כָּל הַדָּמִים שֶׁקִּבֵּל בִּמְכִירָתָהּ, וְאֵינוֹ
מְנַכֶּה לוֹ כְּלוּם מֵחֲמַת הַזְּמַן שֶׁדָּר בָּהּ; וְאַף־עַל־פִּי שֶׁבְּעָלְמָא אָסוּר, דְּהַיְנוּ צַד
אֶחָד בְּרִבִּית, הַתּוֹרָה הִתִּירַתּוֹ כָּאן, כִּדְאִיתָא בְּמַסֶּכֶת עֲרָכִין.

וְשֶׁאֵין הַקְּרוֹבִין פּוֹדִין אוֹתָהּ, אֶלָּא הַמּוֹכֵר בְּעַצְמוֹ; וְזֶהוּ דַּעַת הָרַמְבַּ"ם זִכְרוֹנוֹ
לִבְרָכָה, וְלֹא כֵן נִרְאֶה בְּקִדּוּשִׁין. וְאֵינוֹ לֹוֶה וְגוֹאֵל, אֶלָּא יִמְכֹּר נְכָסִים אֲחֵרִים אִם
יֵשׁ לוֹ וְיִגְאָלֶנָּה, אוֹ אִם רָוַח מָעוֹת אוֹ נָתְנוּ לוֹ, יָכוֹל לְגָאֲלָהּ בָּהֶן; וְאֵינוֹ גוֹאֵל
אוֹתָהּ לַחֲצָאִין, כְּלוֹמַר שֶׁיִּפְרַע לוֹ קְצָת הַמָּעוֹת בְּפַעַם אַחַת וּקְצָתָן בְּפַעַם אַחֶרֶת,
כְּמוֹ שֶׁאָמְרוּ זִכְרוֹנָם לִבְרָכָה בְּקִדּוּשִׁין פֶּרֶק קַמָּא; וְאִם מֵת הַלּוֹקֵחַ תּוֹךְ שָׁנָה,
פּוֹדֶה אוֹתָהּ מִיַּד בְּנוֹ; וְאִם מֵת הַמּוֹכֵר, פּוֹדֶה אוֹתָהּ גַּם־כֵּן בְּנוֹ שֶׁל מוֹכֵר מִיַּד

---

14. With every tribe on the territory originally allotted to it; see §330, third
paragraph from end, and § 335, end.

15. See § 332, note 7.

§341

1. This first part is based on ShM positive precept §139.

1a. See § 340, note 4a.

2. TB 'Arachin 31a.

3. Ordinarily it would amount to a loan repaid in full, while the creditor enjoyed
the free use of the house as a form of interest on the loan; and the payment of interest is
forbidden (§ 343).

4. Since the transaction was not a loan but the sale of a house, which was redeemed
by right.

5. MT hilchoth sh'mittah xii 2.

6. Rambam follows the ruling of R. Shésheth there, but an unanswered difficulty
remains there about it (MY); see Leḥem Mishneh to MT hilchoth 'avadim ix 3.

7. TB Kiddushin 20b.

8. TB 'Arachin 31a.

to both man and woman in the land of Israel, at the time that the law of the jubilee is observed; and I have previously written, above (§330), at which time the jubilee is in effect—i.e. when all the Israelites are on their land, in their settlements.[14] If someone violated this and retained the landed property that he held, not returning it to its [original] owner, he would [thus] disobey this positive precept; and his punishment would be very great, as though he had denied the Scriptural account of Creation.[15]

[THE PRECEPT OF REDEEMING HERITAGE LAND IN A WALLED CITY WITHIN A YEAR]

341 that the redemption of landed heritage-properties within a city that is walled about should be [allowed] until the completion of one year, and after the year, they should remain in the firm possession of those who purchased them, and should not revert [to the original owners] at the jubilee: for it is stated, *And if a man sells a dwelling-house in a walled city*, etc. (Leviticus 25:29).[1] I have already written above (§340) that the reason why a house in a walled city becomes irrevocably transferred at a year is on account of the preciousness of the land[1a]—so that the one who sold it should strive to redeem it quickly.

Among the laws of the precept, there is what the Sages of blessed memory taught:[2] that the seller can redeem it at any time he wishes within the year; and when he redeems it, he gives the other all the money he received on selling it, and deducts nothing from it on account of the time that the other lived in it. Even though this would ordinarily be forbidden, since it is one [possible] way of interest,[3] the Torah permitted it here,[4] as we learn in the tractate *'Arachin* (31a).

Relatives of his may not redeem it, but only the vendor himself; this is the view of Rambam of blessed memory[5]—although from the tractate *Kiddushin* (21a) it would not appear to be so.[6] He may not borrow money and redeem it, but only sell other property if he has any, and thus redeem it; or if he earned money, or it was given him, he can redeem it with that.[7] Nor may he redeem it by halves, i.e. that he should pay him some of the money at one time and some at another time, as our Sages of blessed memory said in the first chapter of the tractate *Kiddushin* (20b). If the purchaser died within the year, he may redeem it from the other's son.[8] If the vendor died [within the year]

הַלּוֹקֵחַ; וְיֶתֶר פְּרָטֶיהָ, בְּמַסֶּכֶת עֲרָכִין.

וְנוֹהֶגֶת בְּאֶרֶץ יִשְׂרָאֵל בִּזְכָרִים וּנְקֵבוֹת, בִּזְמַן שֶׁהַיּוֹבֵל נוֹהֵג.

[שֶׁלֹּא לְשַׁנּוֹת מִגְרְשֵׁי עָרֵי הַלְוִיִּם וּשְׂדוֹתֵיהֶם]

שמב שֶׁלֹּא לְשַׁנּוֹת מִגְרְשֵׁי עָרֵי הַלְוִיִּם וּשְׂדוֹתֵיהֶן, כְּלוֹמַר שֶׁלֹּא יַחֲזִירוּ הָעִיר מִגְרָשׁ, וְלֹא הַמִּגְרָשׁ עִיר, וְלֹא הַשָּׂדֶה מִגְרָשׁ, וְלֹא הַמִּגְרָשׁ שָׂדֶה; וְהוּא הַדִּין מִגְרָשׁ עִיר אוֹ עִיר מִגְרָשׁ, שֶׁאֵין לְשַׁנּוֹת בְּעִנְיָנָם דָּבָר.

וְהָעִנְיָן הַזֶּה יָדוּעַ, כִּי הַתּוֹרָה צִוְּתָה שֶׁיִּתְּנוּ שְׁאָר הַשְּׁבָטִים עָרִים יְדוּעִים לְשֵׁבֶט לֵוִי, וְהֵם אַרְבָּעִים וּשְׁמֹנֶה עִיר, עִם שֵׁשׁ עָרֵי מִקְלָט שֶׁהָיוּ בָהֶן, וְצִוְּתָה גַּם־כֵּן לִהְיוֹת בְּאוֹתָן עָרִים אֶלֶף אַמָּה מִגְרָשׁ, כְּלוֹמַר מָקוֹם פָּנוּי לִרְוָחָה וְנוֹי לָעִיר, וְאַלְפַּיִם אַמָּה חוּצָה לָהּ לְצֹרֶךְ שָׂדוֹת וּכְרָמִים; וְגַם זֶה מִנּוֹיֵי הָעִיר וּמִמַּה שֶּׁצָּרִיךְ לָהּ, כְּמוֹ שֶׁמְּפֹרָשׁ בְּסוֹטָה.

וּבָאָה הַמְּנִיעָה בָּזֶה שֶׁלֹּא לְשַׁנּוֹת עִנְיָנִים אֵלֶּה לְעוֹלָם, וְעַל זֶה נֶאֱמַר: וּשְׂדֵה מִגְרַשׁ עָרֵיהֶם לֹא יִמָּכֵר, שֶׁכֵּן בָּא הַפֵּרוּשׁ עַל לְשׁוֹן מְכִירָה זוֹ, כְּלוֹמַר לֹא יְשֻׁנֶּה, דְּאִלּוּ בִמְכִירָה מַמָּשׁ לֹא קָאָמַר, שֶׁהֲרֵי בְּפֵרוּשׁ כְּתִיב "גְּאֻלַּת עוֹלָם תִּהְיֶה לַלְוִיִּם", מִכְּלָל שֶׁרְשׁוּת יֵשׁ לָהֶם לִמְכֹּר.

מִשָּׁרְשֵׁי הַמִּצְוָה, לְפִי שֶׁעָרֵי הַלְוִיִּם הָיוּ נְכוֹנִים לְצָרְכֵי כָל שְׁאָר הַשְּׁבָטִים, כִּי הוּא הַשֵּׁבֶט הַנִּבְחָר לַעֲבוֹדַת הַשֵּׁם, וְכָל עִסְקָם הָיָה בְחָכְמָה, שֶׁלֹּא הָיוּ טְרוּדִים בְּעִסְקֵי עֲבוֹדַת הָאֲדָמָה כִּשְׁאָר שִׁבְטֵי יִשְׂרָאֵל, וַעֲלֵיהֶם נֶאֱמַר: יוֹרוּ מִשְׁפָּטֶיךָ לְיַעֲקֹב וְתוֹרָתְךָ לְיִשְׂרָאֵל; וּמִתּוֹךְ כָּךְ שֶׁהַחָכְמָה בְתוֹכָם הָיָה עֵסֶק כָּל יִשְׂרָאֵל תָּמִיד עִמָּהֶם, מִלְּבַד שֶׁהָיוּ בְתוֹךְ עָרֵיהֶם עָרֵי מִקְלָט הָרוֹצֵחַ, וּמִתּוֹךְ כָּךְ גַּם־כֵּן הָיוּ עֵינֵי כָל יִשְׂרָאֵל עַל עָרֵיהֶם, כִּי לֹא יֵדַע הָאָדָם מַה יֵּלֶד יוֹם.

וְלָכֵן הָיָה בַדִּין לִהְיוֹת אוֹתָן הֶעָרִים אֲשֶׁר יַד הַכֹּל בָּהֶן וְלֵב הַכֹּל עֲלֵיהֶם,

---

9. See §330, third paragraph from end; §335, end.

1. Numbers 35:2–7.
2. TB 'Arachin 33b.
3. From the beginning to here is based on ShM negative precept §228.

the vendor's son may likewise redeem it from the purchaser.[8] The rest of its details are in the tractate 'Arachin.

It is in force in the land of Israel, for both man and woman, at the time that the law of the jubilee is in effect.[9]

[NOT TO ALTER THE OPEN LAND AROUND THE LEVITES' CITIES, OR THEIR FIELDS]

342 not to change the open land about the cities of the Levites and their fields; in other words, a city should not be turned into open land, nor open land into a city; neither should a field be made open land, nor open land made a field.

This is a known (evident) matter: for the Torah commanded that the other tribes should give certain known cities to the tribe of Lévi, these being forty-eight cities, containing six cities of refuge among them; and it likewise commanded that about those cities there should be a thousand cubits of open land—i.e. an open area for space and beauty for the city; then two thousand cubits beyond that,[1] for the purpose of fields and vineyards, this too being for the beautification of the city and for what is essential to it, as explained in the Talmud tractate *Sotah* (27b).

Well, the injunction was given about this not to change these arrangements ever. Hence it was stated, *But the fields of the open land about their cities may not be sold* (Leviticus 25:34); for so was the interpretation given[2] about this reference to selling—i.e. they may not be altered.[3] For this could not mean actual selling, since it is written explicitly here, *the Levites shall have a perpetual right of redemption* (*ibid.* 32): hence we infer that they have the right to sell.

At the root of the precept lies the reason that the cities of the Levites were prepared for the needs of all the other tribes. For this was the tribe chosen for the service of the Eternal Lord, and their entire occupation was with wisdom, since they were not burdened with affairs of agricultural labor like the other tribes of Israel. Of them it was said, *They shall teach Jacob Thy ordinances, and Israel Thy law* (Deuteronomy 33:10). And because of the fact that there was wisdom among them, all the Israelites always had dealings with them, apart from the fact that among their cities were the cities of refuge for an inadvertent killer. As a result, the eyes of all Israel were on their cities: for a man never knows what a day may bring forth (Proverbs 27:1).

⟨427⟩ It was therefore only just that those cities, in which all had an

בְּתַכְלִית הַיֹּפִי וְהֶחָמְדָה, וְשֶׁבַח כָּל עַם יִשְׂרָאֵל בְּכָךְ; וּמִפְּנֵי־כֵן בָּאָה הַצַּוָּאָה
עֲלֵיהֶם שֶׁלֹּא לְשַׁנּוֹת בְּעִנְיָנָם דָּבָר, כִּי אֲדוֹן הַחָכְמָה יִסְּדָן וְתִקְּנָן וְהִגְבִּיל גְּבוּלָם
וַיַּרְא כִּי כֵן טוֹב, וְכָל חִלּוּף אַחַר דְּבָרוֹ אֵינוֹ אֶלָּא גֵרוּעַ וּגְנַאי.

מִדִּינֵי הַמִּצְוָה, מַה שֶּׁאָמְרוּ זִכְרוֹנָם לִבְרָכָה כִּי מִלְּבַד אֵלּוּ הַשְּׁלֹשָׁה אֶלֶף אַמָּה
שֶׁאָמַרְנוּ, שֶׁהֵן בֵּין מִגְרָשׁ וְשָׂדוֹת וּכְרָמִים, נוֹתְנִין לְכָל עִיר בֵּית הַקְּבָרוֹת חוּץ
לַתְּחוּם זֶה, שֶׁנֶּאֱמַר: וּמִגְרְשֵׁיהֶם יִהְיוּ לִבְהֶמְתָּם וְלִרְכֻשָׁם וּלְכֹל חַיָּתָם, וּבָא
הַפֵּרוּשׁ בָּזֶה: לְחַיִּים נִתְּנוּ וְלֹא לִקְבוּרָה.

וּמַה שֶּׁאָמְרוּ גַם־כֵּן שֶׁכֹּהֲנִים וּלְוִיִּים שֶׁמָּכְרוּ שָׂדֶה מִשְּׂדוֹתֵיהֶם אוֹ בַּיִת, אֲפִלּוּ
בְּעִיר חוֹמָה, נִגְאָלִין לְעוֹלָם, וַאֲפִלּוּ מִיַּד הַקְּדֵשׁ, שֶׁנֶּאֱמַר: גְּאֻלַּת עוֹלָם תִּהְיֶה
לַלְוִיִּם; וְיִשְׂרָאֵל שֶׁיָּרַשׁ אֲבִי אִמּוֹ לֵוִי, הֲרֵי זֶה גוֹאֵל כַּלְוִיִּים; וְיֶתֶר פְּרָטֶיהָ,
מְבֹאָרִים בְּסוֹף עֲרָכִין.

וְנוֹהֶגֶת מִצְוָה זוֹ בְּאֶרֶץ יִשְׂרָאֵל, בִּזְמַן שֶׁיִּשְׂרָאֵל שָׁם, בֵּין בַּלְוִיִּים בֵּין
בְּיִשְׂרָאֵלִים, בַּזְּכָרִים וּנְקֵבוֹת: שֶׁהַכֹּל חַיָּבִין שֶׁלֹּא לְשַׁנּוֹת שְׁלֹשָׁה מְקוֹמוֹת
הָאֲמוּרִין, לְעוֹלָם: הָעִיר וְהַמִּגְרָשׁ וּמְקוֹם הַשָּׂדוֹת וְהַכְּרָמִים; וּמִן הַדּוֹמֶה כִּי כָל מִי
שֶׁשִּׁנָּה בָהֶן בְּצֵדִים וְהַתְרָאָה, חַיָּב מַלְקוֹת; וְלֹא יָדַעְתִּי שִׁעוּר לְשִׁנּוּי זֶה כַּמָּה יִהְיֶה
וְיִתְחַיֵּב עָלָיו; חָכָם בְּנִי וְדָעֵהוּ.

וְכָתַב הָרַמְבַּ"ם זִכְרוֹנוֹ לִבְרָכָה עַל מִצְוָה זוֹ: לָמָּה לֹא זָכָה לֵוִי בְּנַחֲלַת אֶרֶץ
יִשְׂרָאֵל וּבְבִזָּתָהּ עִם אֶחָיו, מִפְּנֵי שֶׁהֻבְדַּל לַעֲבֹד הַשֵּׁם וּלְשָׁרְתוֹ וּלְהוֹרוֹת דְּרָכָיו
הַיְשָׁרִים; וּלְפִיכָךְ הֻבְדַּל מִדַּרְכֵי הָעוֹלָם: לֹא עוֹרְכִין מִלְחָמָה כִּשְׁאָר יִשְׂרָאֵל וְלֹא
נוֹחֲלִין וְלֹא זוֹכִין לְעַצְמָן בְּכֹחַ גּוּפָן, אֶלָּא חֵיל יְיָ, שֶׁנֶּאֱמַר: בָּרֵךְ יְיָ חֵילוֹ וְגוֹמֵר;

4. TB Makkoth 12a; MT *hilchoth sh'mittah* xiii 3.

5. I.e. if it was consecrated so that all income or revenue from it should be used for
a holy purpose, such as the upkeep of the Sanctuary.

6. MT *hilchoth sh'mittah* xiii 12-13.

equal interest, with which the heart of all was concerned, should have a perfection of beauty and attractiveness. It would be to the praise and advantage of the entire people of Israel. Therefore the order was given about them that nothing in their arrangement was to be changed. For the Soverign Ruler of all founded and constructed them and set their boundaries, and He saw that thus it was good. Then any alteration beyond His words would be nothing but a detraction and a disgrace.

Among the laws of the precept, there is what the Sages of blessed memory said:[4] that apart from the three thousand cubits that we mentioned, which comprised the open land and the fields and vineyards, every city would be given a cemetery beyond this area. For it is stated, *and their open land shall be for their cattle and for their possessions and for all their beasts* (Numbers 35:3); and the interpretation was given on this:[4] it was given for life, and not for burial.

There is, likewise, what the Sages said:[2] that if *kohanim* or Levites sold one of their fields or a house, even in a walled city, they can always be redeemed, even from a state of consecration;[5] for it is stated, *the Levites shall have a perpetual right of redemption* (Leviticus 25:32). If an Israelite inherited [property] from his mother's father who was a Levite, he can redeem [it] like the Levites.[2] The rest of its details are clarified toward the end of the Talmud tractate *'Arachin*.

This precept is in force in the land of Israel at the time the Israelites are there—for both the Levites and the Israelites, both man and woman: because all are duty-bound not to alter the three places mentioned above: the city, the open land, and the location of the fields and vineyards. And apparently, whoever made any change in them, with witnesses and a [prior] warning, would incur a punishment of whip-lashes. However, I do not know how much the minimal amount of this change must be for him to become punishable. Grow wise, my son, and find it out.

Now, Rambam of blessed memory wrote about this precept:[6] Why did [the tribe of] Levi not attain an inheritance [of territory] in the land of Israel and [a share] of its booty along with its brothers [the other tribes]?—because it was set apart to worship the Eternal Lord and serve Him, and to teach His upright ways. Therefore they were separated from the ways of the world: they would neither engage in war like the other Israelites, nor receive tribal territory, nor would they gain anything for themselves by their own physical prowess, but would only be the legion of the Lord; as it is stated, *Let the Lord*

וְהוּא בָּרוּךְ הוּא זִכָּה לָהֶם חֶלְקוֹ, שֶׁנֶּאֱמַר: אֲנִי חֶלְקְךָ וְנַחֲלָתְךָ וְגוֹמֵר. וְלֹא שֵׁבֶט
לֵוִי בִּלְבַד בִּכְלָל זֶה, אֶלָּא כָל אִישׁ וָאִישׁ מִבָּאֵי הָעוֹלָם אֲשֶׁר נָדְבָה רוּחוֹ לְהַבְדֵּל
לַעֲמֹד לִפְנֵי יי לְעָבְדוֹ, לָדַעַת דְּרָכָיו הַיְשָׁרִים וְהַצַּדִּיקִים וּלְלַמְּדָם לַאֲחֵרִים, פּוֹרֵק
מֵעַל צַוָּארוֹ עֹל חֶשְׁבּוֹנוֹת הָרַבִּים אֲשֶׁר בִּקְּשׁוּ בְּנֵי-הָאָדָם, וַהֲרֵי זֶה נִתְקַדֵּשׁ לִהְיוֹת
קֹדֶשׁ קָדָשִׁים, וְיִהְיֶה יי נַחֲלָתוֹ לְעוֹלְמֵי עוֹלָמִים, וְיִזְכֶּה בָעוֹלָם הַזֶּה בְּדָבָר הַמַּסְפִּיק
לוֹ, כְּמוֹ שֶׁזָּכָה שֵׁבֶט לֵוִי; וְכֵן בְּדָוִד הוּא אוֹמֵר: יי מְנָת חֶלְקִי וְכוֹסִי אַתָּה תּוֹמִיךְ
גּוֹרָלִי.

[שֶׁלֹּא לְהַלְווֹת בְּרִבִּית לְיִשְׂרָאֵל]

שמג שֶׁלֹּא לְהַלְווֹת בְּרִבִּית לְיִשְׂרָאֵל, שֶׁנֶּאֱמַר: אֶת כַּסְפְּךָ לֹא תִתֵּן לוֹ בְּנֶשֶׁךְ
וּבְמַרְבִּית לֹא תִתֵּן אָכְלֶךָ; וְאֵין אֵלּוּ שְׁנֵי לָאוִין, שֶׁהָרִבִּית הוּא הַנֶּשֶׁךְ וְהַנֶּשֶׁךְ הוּא
הָרִבִּית, וּכְמוֹ שֶׁאָמְרוּ זִכְרוֹנָם לִבְרָכָה בַּמִּצִיעָא: אִי אַתָּה מוֹצֵא נֶשֶׁךְ בְּלֹא רִבִּית
וְלֹא רִבִּית בְּלֹא נֶשֶׁךְ, וְלָמָּה חִלְּקָם הַכָּתוּב, כְּלוֹמַר לָמָּה חִלְּקָם וְלֹא כָתַב: אֶת
כַּסְפְּךָ וְאָכְלֶךָ לֹא תִתֵּן לוֹ בְּנֶשֶׁךְ — לַעֲבֹר עָלָיו בִּשְׁנֵי לָאוִין, כְּלוֹמַר לְהַרְבּוֹת
הָאַזְהָרוֹת עָלָיו.

וְזֶה הָעִנְיָן הוּא מִמַּה שֶׁאָמַרְתִּי לְמַעְלָה, כִּי הַתּוֹרָה תִּכְפֹּל הָאַזְהָרוֹת לִפְעָמִים
עַל מַה שֶׁחָפֵץ הָאֵל לְהַרְחִיקֵנוּ מִמֶּנּוּ הַרְבֵּה; וְאֶפְשָׁר שֶׁנֹּאמַר בָּזֶה כְּעֵין מַה
שֶׁאָמְרוּ זִכְרוֹנָם לִבְרָכָה בְּעִנְיָנִים אֲחֵרִים: דִּבְּרָה תוֹרָה כִּלְשׁוֹן בְּנֵי-אָדָם, וּכְמוֹ-כֵן
תָּמִיד הַתּוֹרָה הַהַתְרָאוֹת בְּמַה שֶׁיֵּשׁ עָלֵינוּ לְהִזָּהֵר בּוֹ מְאֹד, כְּדֶרֶךְ בְּנֵי-אָדָם
בְּהַזְהִירָם זֶה אֶת זֶה בְּדָבָר חָמוּר, יִכְפְּלוּ תְנָאָם וְיַרְבּוּ דִבְרֵיהֶם עַל הַדָּבָר, כְּדֵי
שֶׁיְּהֵא הַמֻּזְהָר נִזְכָּר וְזָהִיר עַל הָעִנְיָן עַל-כָּל-פָּנִים. וְאִם אָמְנָה כִּי רְאוּי הָאָדָם

---

7. Expression based on Ecclesiastes 7:29.

8. So that he can earn an adequate living and will not become a public charge or
burden (Ridvaz to MT *ibid.*).

§343
1. The term *neshech* is from a verb meaning "to bite"; *ribbith*, literally, "increase,"
is the standard word in the Talmud to denote interest and usury.

2. The paragraph is based on ShM negative precept §235.

3. TB B'rachoth 31b, etc.

bless His legion, etc. (Deuteronomy 33:11); and He (blessed is He) gave them the right to His portion, as it is stated, *I am your portion and your inheritance*, etc. (Numbers 18:20).

Now [Rambam continues] not the tribe of Lévi alone is included in this, but any and every man among those who have come into the world whose spirit moves him to set himself apart and stand before the Lord, to serve Him, to know His upright and righteous ways and to teach them to others; so he removes from about his neck the yoke of many schemes that people seek out.[7] Then he thus becomes consecrated to be the holiest of the holy; the Lord will be his inheritance for ever and ever; and he will attain in this world a measure that will suffice for him,[8] just as the tribe of Lévi attained it. So David said, *The Lord is the portion of my allotment and my cup; Thou dost sustain my lot* (Psalms 16:5).

343 [THE PROHIBITION AGAINST LENDING AT INTEREST] not to lend at interest to an Israelite: for it is stated, *you shall not give him your money at interest, nor give him your food for increased payment* (Leviticus 25:37); and these are not two separate injunctions, for *ribbith* ("increased payment") and *neshech* ("interest") are one and the same.[1] As the Sages of blessed memory said in the tractate *Bava M'tzi'a* (61a): you will not find *neshech* without *ribbith*, nor *ribbith* without *neshech*; then why did the Writ differentiate them?—in other words, why did it separate them rather than write, "you shall not give him your money or your food at interest"?—to make his act the transgression of two negative precepts—meaning, to increase the injunctions against it.[2]

Now, this point is in accord with what I stated above (§336): that the Torah will reiterate injunctions at times about something from which God wishes to remove us a great distance. We could possibly state about this something like what the Sages of blessed memory said in regard to other matters:[3] The Torah spoke in the language of human beings. Similarly, the Torah constantly gives admonitions about something where we have to be very careful, in the way of people: When they warn one another about something serious, they repeat their stipulation and multiply their words about the matter, so that the person alerted will remember and be vigilant about the matter under all circumstances. And though in truth it were

לְהִזָּהֵר בַּדָּבָר עַד מְאֹד וְאַף־כִּי יִשְׁמַע דְּבָרוֹ בְּרֶמֶז קָטָן, כָּל זֶה מֵחֲסָדָיו הָרַבִּים עַל בְּרִיּוֹתָיו שֶׁפָּעַל לָהֶם הָאַזְהָרוֹת פְּעָמִים רַבִּים בְּקְצָת מְקוֹמוֹת, כַּאֲשֶׁר יְיַסֵּר אִישׁ אֶת בְּנוֹ; עַל־כֵּן נוֹדֶה לִשְׁמוֹ הַגָּדוֹל סֶלָה בְּרֹב הַטּוֹבוֹת אֲשֶׁר גְּמָלָנוּ, בָּרוּךְ הוּא.

מִשָּׁרְשֵׁי הַמִּצְוָה, כָּתַבְתִּי בְּאַזְהָרַת עָרֵב וְעֵדִים וְסוֹפֵר שֶׁלֹּא יִתְעַסְּקוּ (במלות) [בְּמִלְוֶה] רִבִּית, בְּ"כֶסֶף תַּלְוֶה" ב' [מִשְׁפָּטִים סִי' ס"ח], וְקָחֶנּוּ מִשָּׁם.

דִּינֵי הַמִּצְוָה, כְּגוֹן הַחִלּוּקִים שֶׁלִּמְּדוּנוּ זִכְרוֹנָם לִבְרָכָה בְּאַזְהָרָה זוֹ, שֶׁאָמְרוּ שֶׁיֵּשׁ רִבִּית שֶׁהוּא אָסוּר מִן הַתּוֹרָה, וְזֵהוּ שֶׁנִּקְרָא לְרַבּוֹתֵינוּ זִכְרוֹנָם לִבְרָכָה רִבִּית קְצוּצָה; וְיֵשׁ רִבִּית שֶׁהוּא לְמַטָּה מִמֶּנּוּ וְהוּא אָסוּר מִדְּרַבָּנָן, וּקְרָאוּהוּ זִכְרוֹנָם לִבְרָכָה אֲבַק רִבִּית; וְיֵשׁ רִבִּית אַחֶרֶת שֶׁהוּא לְמַטָּה מִשְּׁנֵי אֵלּוּ הָרִאשׁוֹנִים, וְהוּא מִן הַדִּין מֻתָּר, לְפִי שֶׁהוּא רָחוֹק הַרְבֵּה מִן רִבִּית הָאָסוּר מִן הַתּוֹרָה, עַד שֶׁאֵין לִגְזֹר עָלָיו כְּלָל, אֲבָל חֲכָמִים הֶחֱמִירוּ בָּעִנְיָן, בִּרְאוֹתָם הַחֹמֶר שֶׁהֶחֱמִירָה הַתּוֹרָה וְרֹב הָאַזְהָרוֹת בַּדָּבָר הָרִבִּית, וַאֲסָרוּהוּ כְּדֵי שֶׁלֹּא יַעֲרִימוּ בְּנֵי־אָדָם לִטֹּל רִבִּית, לֹא מִפְּנֵי דָבָר אַחֵר.

וְאֵלּוּ הֵן שְׁלֹשָׁה מִינֵי הָרִבִּית שֶׁאָמַרְנוּ: רִבִּית הָאָסוּר דְּבַר תּוֹרָה, הוּא כָּל מִי שֶׁאוֹמֵר לַחֲבֵרוֹ "הַלְוֵנִי מָנֶה וְאֶתֵּן לְךָ מִמֶּנּוּ פְּרוּטָה בְּכָל יוֹם, אוֹ שְׁלֹשִׁים פְּרוּטוֹת בְּחֹדֶשׁ, אוֹ פָּחוֹת אוֹ יָתֵר, עַד שֶׁאֶפְרָעֶנּוּ לְךָ"; וְכֵן כְּשֶׁאָמַר לוֹ "הַלְוֵנִי מֵאָה דִינָרִין בְּמֵאָה וְעֶשְׂרִים לְשָׁנָה"; וְכֵן הַמַּלְוֶה לַחֲבֵרוֹ מָעוֹת וּמִשְׁכֵּן לוֹ בָהֶן בַּיִת אוֹ חָצֵר שֶׁיַּחֲזִיק בָּהֶם וְיַקַּח הַפֵּרוֹת לוֹ מֵעוֹתָיו, מִבְּלִי שֶׁיְנַכֶּה לוֹ כְּלוּם מִן הַהַלְוָאָה — זֶהוּ רִבִּית קְצוּצָה הָאָסוּר מִן הַתּוֹרָה.

וְדֶרֶךְ־כְּלָל אָמְרוּ זִכְרוֹנָם לִבְרָכָה: כָּל אֲגַר "נָטַר לִי" אָסוּר מִן הַתּוֹרָה, וְהוּא שֶׁבָּא מִיַּד לֹוֶה לַמַּלְוֶה, זֵהוּ הָרִבִּית הָאָסוּר דְּבַר תּוֹרָה, וְעָלָיו יֹאמְרוּ זִכְרוֹנָם

4. TB Bava M'tzi'a 61b.

5. Literally, the dust of usury; i.e. while interest is not paid directly, the transaction smacks of usury, or could be so perceived from a certain point of view; *ibid.*

6. I.e. the full original amount, apart from the daily or monthly payments; *ibid.*

7. So R. Isaac 'Alfasi, Bava M'tzi'a v, based on TB 67a.

8. TB Bava M'tzi'a 63b, 65a.

9. So *ibid.* 69b.

right for a man to be very greatly cautious over a word of the Eternal
Lord even if he should hear His word in a small hint—this is all by His
manifold kindness toward His human creatures, that He repeated the
cautions many times in certain instances, as a man would admonish
his son. Let us therefore give thanks to His great name for the multitude
of good favors that He bestowed on us, blessed is He.

At the root of the precept lies the purpose that I wrote about the
admonition to the guarantor, witnesses and scribe: that they should
have no business with a loan at interest—in *sidrah mishpatim* (§68);
so gather it from there.

The laws of the precept are, for example, the distinctions that our
Sages of blessed memory taught us in regard to this injunction; for
they said that there is interest which is forbidden by the law of the
Torah, this being what was called by our Sages of blessed memory
"fixed, specific interest."[4] Then there is usury of a lesser degree than
this, which is forbidden by the ruling of the Sages, that they (of blessed
memory) called a shade of interest.[5] Then there is another kind of
usury, of lower degree than these first two, which should rightly be permissible, since it so very far removed from the interest forbidden by
the Torah that there should be no need to decree against it at all. Yet
the Sages were stringent about the matter, seeing the strictness that the
Torah applied, and the many injunctions about the subject of usury.
Hence they forbade it, so that people should not scheme cunningly
to take interest—not for any other reason.

Now, these are the three kinds of usury that we mentioned:
The usury forbidden by the Torah is if anyone says to his fellow-man,
"Lend me a *maneh*, and I will give you for it a *p'rutah* every day,"
or "thirty *p'rutoth* a month," or less, or more, "until I will pay it[6]
back to you"; and so if he tells him, "Lend me 100 *denarii* for 120,
for a year";[4] and so likewise if someone lends his fellow-man money,
and the other gives him in pledge for it a house or a plot of land, that
he [the lender] should have possession of it and take the income from
it until he will return him his money, without deducting anything
from the loan[7]—this is "fixed, specific interest," forbidden by Torah
law.

As a general rule, the Sages of blessed memory said:[8] Every
payment for "wait for me" [for time to repay the loan] is forbidden by
the Torah. Provided it passes from the hand of the borrower to the
lender, this is the interest forbidden by the Torah's law;[9] and about

לִבְרָכָה: רִבִּית קְצוּצָה יוֹצְאָה בְּדַיָּנִין, כְּלוֹמַר שֶׁבֵּית־דִּין יוֹרְדִין לְנִכְסֵי הַמַּלְוֶה
וּמוֹצִיאִין מִמֶּנּוּ, כְּמוֹ בִּגְזֵלוֹת וַחֲבָלוֹת.

וְיֵשׁ מִן הַמְּפָרְשִׁים שֶׁפֵּרְשׁוּ "יוֹצְאָה בְדַיָּנִין" לְעִנְיָן כְּפִיָּה, כְּלוֹמַר שֶׁכּוֹפִין
בֵּית־דִּין אֶת הַמַּלְוֶה לְהַחֲזִירָהּ בְּשׁוֹטִים, כְּמוֹ שֶׁעוֹשִׂין לְכָל מִי שֶׁיֹּאמַר שֶׁלֹּא
יַעֲשֶׂה מִצְוַת עֲשֵׂה.

כָּל שְׁאָר הָרִבִּיּוֹת שֶׁאֶפְשָׁר לְקַבֵּל חוּץ מֵאֵלּוּ שֶׁאָמַרְנוּ, הֵן נִקְרָאִין רִבִּית דְּרַבָּנָן
וְנִקְרָאִין אֲבַק רִבִּית, וְאֵינָהּ יוֹצְאָה בְּדַיָּנִין; וַאֲסָרוּם חֲכָמִים מִשּׁוּם גְּזֵרָה שֶׁלֹּא
יָבוֹא הָאָדָם לִידֵי רִבִּית דְּאוֹרַיְתָא; וּמֵהֶם כְּגוֹן מַה שֶׁאָמְרוּ זִכְרוֹנָם לִבְרָכָה שֶׁאֵין
מְקַבְּלִין צֹאן בַּרְזֶל מִיִּשְׂרָאֵל; פֵּרוּשׁ צֹאן בַּרְזֶל, הַמְקַבֵּל מָמוֹן מִיִּשְׂרָאֵל עַל תְּנַאי
שֶׁיִּהְיֶה הַקֶּרֶן קַיֶּמֶת לְבַעַל הַמָּמוֹן עַל הַמְּקַבֵּל, וְיִטֹּל חֶלְקוֹ בָּרֶוַח.

וְכֵן אֵין פּוֹסְקִין עַל הַפֵּרוֹת עַד שֶׁיֵּצֵא הַשַּׁעַר, אֲבָל יָצָא הַשַּׁעַר פּוֹסְקִין; אַף־
עַל־פִּי שֶׁאֵין לָזֶה יֵשׁ לָזֶה; וּבַמֶּה דְּבָרִים אֲמוּרִים שֶׁאֵין פּוֹסְקִין לְעוֹלָם עַד שֶׁיֵּצֵא
הַשַּׁעַר, בְּשֶׁלֹּא הָיָה לוֹ כְלוּם מֵאוֹתוֹ הַמִּין שֶׁפָּסַק עָלָיו, אֲבָל הָיָה לוֹ מִמֶּנּוּ כְלוּם,
פּוֹסֵק עָלָיו אַף־עַל־פִּי שֶׁלֹּא יָצָא הַשַּׁעַר עֲדַיִן; וְאַף־עַל־פִּי שֶׁלֹּא הָיָה לוֹ מִמֶּנּוּ
אֶלָּא סְאָה אַחַת פּוֹסֵק עָלָיו כַּמָּה סָאִין (שֶׁהֲלָכָה כִּשְׁמוּאֵל דַּאֲמַר) [כְּבֵהֲלָנְעָא,
דְּאָמְרִינָן] הָכִי בַּגְּמָרָא.

וְזֶה שֶׁאָנוּ אוֹמְרִים שֶׁצָּרִיךְ שֶׁיִּהְיֶה לוֹ מֵאוֹתוֹ הַמִּין, יֵשׁ מִן הַמְּפָרְשִׁים שֶׁאָמְרוּ:
דַּוְקָא מֵאוֹתוֹ הַמִּין מַמָּשׁ צָרִיךְ שֶׁיִּהְיֶה לוֹ, שֶׁאִם הוּא פּוֹסֵק עַל חִטִּין חֲדָשׁוֹת, לֹא
יִפְסֹק אֵלָיו אִם הָיוּ לוֹ חִטִּים יְשָׁנוֹת, אֶלָּא כְּאֵין אוֹתוֹ הַמִּין מַמָּשׁ שֶׁפּוֹסֵק עָלָיו
צָרִיךְ שֶׁיִּהְיֶה לוֹ. וְיֵשׁ מֵהֶם שֶׁאָמְרוּ שֶׁאֵין חִלּוּק בֵּין חָדָשׁ לְיָשָׁן, דְּכָל שֶׁיֵּשׁ לוֹ
מֵאוֹתוֹ הַמִּין, מֻתָּר. וּמִכָּל־מָקוֹם אִם הָיָה לוֹ מֵאוֹתוֹ הַמִּין, אַף־עַל־פִּי שֶׁהוּא

---

10. So MT *hilchoth malveh* iv 3.

11. So Rashi implies, in TB Bava M'tzi'a 61b, s.v. *ad kan ribbith k'tzutzah*; and so *Nimmuké Yoséf* to TB *ibid.* explicitly cites Rashba and R. Nissim.

12. Thus the goods or wares are like "iron sheep" for their owner: They can never "die" or be destroyed for him; whatever happens to them, he must get them back or be paid for them, and if they earn profit he takes a share; TB Bava M'tzi'a 70b.

13. E.g. a man may not give a farmer a sum of money for which the farmer agrees to give him at a later time so many bushels of wheat, making the agreement before a market price is officially established; for if the market price is higher than expected, the man will thus receive interest on his loan; TB Bava M'tzi'a 72b.

14. So that the farmer can obtain the produce from someone else at the price, and thus repay his loan.

15. TB Bava M'tzi'a 72b; MT *hilchoth malveh* ix 1.

16. TB *ibid.* 75a; this follows an emendation suggested by MY. The original reads: for the definitive law follows Samuel, who ruled thus in the Talmud. But we find nothing of this in the Talmud. (In MS Parma 741 כשמואל is missing, and added in the margin by another hand; and in all the manuscripts דאמר is written דאמ׳. Or perhaps it

it the Sages of blessed memory would say: Fixed, specific interest is extracted by judges.[4] In other words, the *beth din* (court) goes down to the property of the lender and takes it away from him, like anything seized by robbery, or damages.[10]

There are some authorities, though, who explained "is extracted by judges" in terms of compulsion; in other words, the *beth din* compels the lender to return it, with whips, as they do with anyone who says he will not observe a positive precept.[11]

All other kinds of interest that it is possible to receive, except these that we described, are called "interest by the Sages' decree" and are called [also] a shade of usury;[5] and these are not extracted by judges. The Sages forbade them as a protective measure, so that a man should not become involved with usury under the Torah's law. Among them there is, for example, what the Sages of blessed memory taught: that "iron sheep" are not to be taken from an Israelite. The term "iron sheep" denotes that one takes goods or wares from an Israelite on condition that the principal will remain the property of the owner of the wares, on the responsibility of the one who receives them, but he will take his share of the profit.[12]

So too should terms [for money given] not be decided about produce until the market price is posted.[13] If the market price was posted, though, they may make terms; even if this one [who takes the money] has not any [produce], another does have.[14] Now, when does this rule hold, that terms [for produce] should never be set until the market price is posted?—when he [who takes the money] has none [of the produce], i.e. of that kind over which he made terms; but if he has any of it at all, he may make terms over it even though the market price has not yet been posted.[15] Even if he has no more of it than one *se'ah*, he may set terms over it for many *se'ah*, as in the case of a loan, about which this is stated in the Talmud.[16]

Now, when we say that it is necessary for him to have some of that kind [of produce], there are some authorities who stated that it is necessary for him to have specifically some of that very kind. If he sets terms with him [his creditor] on new wheat, he should not make the agreement with him if he has old wheat; he rather needs to have some of that very same kind over which he sets terms. There are some, though, who stated that there is no difference between old and new, so that as long as he has of that kind, he is allowed.[17] In any event,

however, if he has of that kind, then even if it lacks one or two labors

מְחֻסָּר מְלָאכָה אַחַת אוֹ שְׁתַּיִם, פּוֹסֵק עִמּוֹ עָלָיו; אֲבָל הָיָה מְחֻסָּר שְׁלֹשָׁה מְלָאכוֹת אֵינוֹ פּוֹסֵק, דְּכֵיוָן שֶׁמְּחֻסָּר שְׁלֹשָׁה מְלָאכוֹת, הֲרֵי זֶה כְּמִי שֶׁאֵין לוֹ מֵאוֹתוֹ הַמִּין כְּלוּם. וּבַגְּמָרָא פֶּרֶק "אֵי זֶהוּ נֶשֶׁךְ" בָּא הַבֵּאוּר בַּאֲרֻכָּה בְּחִלּוּק מְלָאכוֹת אֵלּוּ בְּחִטִּים, וְכֵן בִּכְלֵי יוֹצֵר וּבִדְבָרִים אֲחֵרִים.

וְכֵן מֵעִנְיָן הַמִּצְוָה מַה שֶּׁאָסְרוּ לְהַלְווֹת עַל הַקַּרְקַע מָעוֹת וּלְהַתְנוֹת עִם הַלֹּוֶה "אִם לֹא תַחֲזִיר לִי הַמָּעוֹת מִכָּאן וְעַד יוֹם פְּלוֹנִי, תְּהֵא הַקַּרְקַע שֶׁלִּי", לְפִי שֶׁהַתִּקְנִין הַזֶּה אֵינוֹ מוֹעִיל, מִפְּנֵי שֶׁהוּא אַסְמַכְתָּא — כְּלוֹמַר שֶׁדַּעְתּוֹ שֶׁל אָדָם הָיְתָה סוֹמֶכֶת בְּכָךְ, כְּלוֹמַר שֶׁיַּחֲזִיר הַמָּעוֹת, בִּשְׁעַת הַמַּעֲשֶׂה — וְלֹא הִשִּׂיגָה יָדוֹ לְהַשְׁלִים הַדָּבָר, וּכְעֵין אֹנֶס הוּא, וְכָל כִּי הַאי גַוְנָא יֵשׁ לָחוּשׁ בַּאֲכִילַת הַפֵּרוֹת מִשּׁוּם רִבִּית.

וְהַרְבֵּה דְרָכִים נֶאֶמְרוּ בַגְּמָרָא בְּאַסְמַכְתָּא בְּעִנְיַן רִבִּית וּבְעִנְיָנִים אֲחֵרִים; וְדֶרֶךְ כְּלָל לְמִדָּנִי רַבִּי יִשְׁמְרוּ אֵל בְּעִנְיַן דִּינֵי הָאַסְמַכְתָּא, שֶׁכָּל שֶׁיִּתְנֶה הָאָדָם עִם חֲבֵרוֹ דֶּרֶךְ קְנָס — כְּלוֹמַר אִם לֹא יִהְיֶה כֵן, יֵעָנֵשׁ בְּמָמוֹן כֵּן וְכֵן — זֶה יִקָּרֵא אַסְמַכְתָּא, וְעַל זֶה יֹאמְרוּ זִכְרוֹנָם לִבְרָכָה דְּאַסְמַכְתָּא לָא קָנְיָא; וּבְלָשׁוֹן אַחֶרֶת אָמְרוּהָ זִכְרוֹנָם לִבְרָכָה גַּם־כֵּן: כָּל "דְּאִי" לָא קָנֵי.

אֲבָל כָּל תְּנַאי שֶׁיִּתְנֶה הָאָדָם עִם חֲבֵרוֹ וְיֹאמַר "אִם אַתָּה תַּעֲשֶׂה כֵן, אַף אֲנִי אֶעֱשֶׂה כֵן וְכֵן", כְּדֶרֶךְ בְּנֵי־אָדָם, שֶׁמַּתְנִין בְּלָשׁוֹן זֶה, אֵין זֶה בִכְלַל אַסְמַכְתָּא כְּלָל חָלִילָה, שֶׁאִם־כֵּן הֵיאַךְ נִמְצָא יָדֵינוּ וְרַגְלֵינוּ עַל כָּל תְּנָאֵי בְּנֵי־אָדָם זֶה עִם זֶה, שֶׁכֻּלָּם בְּלָשׁוֹן "אִם" הֵם, דְּאִי אֶפְשָׁר בְּלָאו הָכִי; וְעוֹד, בְּכָל הַתְּנָאִין הַנִּזְכָּרִים בְּעִנְיַן גִּטִּין וְקִדּוּשִׁין, שֶׁכֻּלָּן בְּלָשׁוֹן "אִם", מַה נֹּאמַר בָּהֶן.

אֶלָּא וַדַּאי טַעַם נָכוֹן מַה שֶּׁכָּתַבְנוּ, שֶׁלֹּא נֹאמַר "אַסְמַכְתָּא לָא קָנְיָא" אֶלָּא

כשמ' בהל' was originally כשמעתא בהלואה דאמרינן הכי בגמרא and it was abbreviated כשמ' בהל', דאמ' הכי בגמ', which was subsequently misunderstood.)

17. See *Béth Yoséf* to *Tur Yoreh Dé'ah* §175.

18. TB Bava M'tzi'a 66b.

19. To make a piece of land his, a man must perform an act of acquisition, and must have the voluntary consent of its owner. Here there is no such consent: The owner agreed to cede the land upon failure to repay the loan, only to induce the creditor to grant him the loan; but he had every intention of paying the debt and retaining the land. When it is taken from him in this way, he gives his consent no more than any man who sells his land under duress. Hence eventually the creditor must receive payment for the loan and return the land — which means that if he takes produce from it, that constitutes interest.

20. I.e. enjoying the benefit — use or revenue — from something given the creditor as a pledge.

21. See Rashba, Responsa, I §1149.

22. Literally, how will we find our hands and feet.

[to make it ready for sale] he may set terms with him [the creditor] over it; but if it was lacking three labors, he is then like one who has none at all of that kind. In the fifth chapter of the Talmud tractate *Bava M'tzi'a* (74a) the explanation is given at length about the difference [in law] between these labors with wheat, and so too with potters' vessels, and with other things.

So is it also of the subject matter of the precept that the Sages forbade lending money against land [as collateral], making an agreement with the borrower, "If you do not return the money to me from now until that day, the land is to be mine"; for this kind of acquisition is of no avail, since it is a matter of reliance:[18] in other words, the man's mind relied on this, i.e. that he would return the money, at the time of the transaction, but then he could not attain the means to pay, so that it is akin to [a case of] duress.[19] And in every instance of this kind, we have to be concerned about "eating the fruit,"[20] as an aspect of interest.

Many ways (aspects) were described in the *g'mara* about "reliance" in connection with usurious payment and with other matters. As a general rule, my master teacher, God protect him, taught me about the subject of the laws of reliance, that whatever condition a man makes for his fellow-man by way of a fine or penalty—in other words, if it will not be thus-and-so, he will be penalized through goods or wares thus-and-so—that is called a matter of "reliance";[21] and about this our Sages of blessed memory said that where there is "reliance," there is no acquisition.[18] And they (of blessed memory) expressed it in a different way as well: Any instance of "if" does not bring acquisition.[18]

However, whatever condition a man makes with his fellow-man, saying, "If you do so, I will equally do thus and so," in the usual way of people, who agree on conditions with this expression, this is not at all included among instances of "reliance," perish the thought. For if it were, how could we move hand or foot[22] about any conditions that people make with one another? All are made with the word "if"; it is impossible otherwise. Moreover, all conditions mentioned [in the Talmud] in regard to divorce and marriage are made with the expression of "if"; what should we say about them?

Certainly, then, what we have written is a correct elucidation: that we will apply the rule that where there is "reliance" there is no

acquisition, nowhere but in an instance where people make conditions

‏בַּמֶּה שֶׁיִּתְנוּ בְּנֵי־אָדָם זֶה עִם זֶה דֶּרֶךְ קְנָס, כְּגוֹן "אִם לֹא פְּרַעְתִּיךָ עַד יוֹם פְּלוֹנִי,‏
‏תְּהֵא הַשָּׂדֶה שֶׁלְּךָ" אוֹ הַמַּשְׁכּוֹן אִי זֶה שֶׁיִּהְיֶה, וְכָל כַּיּוֹצֵא־בָזֶה; אֲבָל לֹא בְּכָל‏
‏שְׁאָר הַתְּנָאִים רַבִּים שֶׁמַּתְנִים בְּנֵי־אָדָם, כְּגוֹן "אִם תֵּלֵךְ לְמָקוֹם פְּלוֹנִי, אֶתֵּן לְךָ כֵּן‏
‏וְכֵן" אוֹ "אִם תַּעֲשֶׂה בִּשְׁבִילִי עִנְיָן פְּלוֹנִי, אֶתֵּן לְךָ מָאתַיִם זוּז", וְכָל כַּיּוֹצֵא־בָזֶה.‏
‏וְהָבֵן זֶה בְּנִי וְתֵן לִבְּךָ עָלָיו, כִּי בָזֶה תָּסִיר מֵבִין עֵינֶיךָ עָנָן גָּדוֹל בְּדִבְרֵי הַגְּמָרָא‏
‏בִּמְקוֹמוֹת הַרְבֵּה.‏

‏וּכְמוֹ־כֵן אָמְרוּ זִכְרוֹנָם לִבְרָכָה שֶׁהוּא אֲבַק רִבִּית וְאָסוּר מִדְּרַבָּנָן: רִבִּית‏
‏מְקֻדֶּמֶת וְרִבִּית מְאֻחֶרֶת. כֵּיצַד: נָתַן עֵינָיו לִלְווֹת מִמֶּנּוּ וְהָיָה מְשַׁלֵּחַ לוֹ סִבְלוֹנוֹת‏
‏בִּשְׁבִיל שֶׁיַּלְוֵהוּ, זֶהוּ רִבִּית מְקֻדֶּמֶת; לָוָה מִמֶּנּוּ וְהֶחֱזִיר לוֹ מְעוֹתָיו, וְאַחַר־כָּךְ שָׁלַח‏
‏לוֹ סִבְלוֹנוֹת בִּשְׁבִיל מְעוֹתָיו שֶׁהָיוּ בְּטֵלִין אֶצְלוֹ, זֶהוּ רִבִּית מְאֻחֶרֶת.‏

‏וְכֵן אָמְרוּ קְצָת מִן הַמְּפָרְשִׁים שֶׁהַמַּלְוֶה מָעוֹת לַחֲבֵרוֹ עַל מָקוֹם שֶׁפֵּרוֹתָיו‏
‏מְצוּיִין תָּדִיר, כְּגוֹן חָצֵר וּמֶרְחָץ וְחָנוּת, הֲרֵי זֶה נִכּוּי, בְּלֹא נִכּוּי, הֲרֵי זֶה רִבִּית קְצוּצָה, וּבְנִכּוּי,‏
‏הֲרֵי זֶה אֲבַק רִבִּית; אֲבָל הַמַּלְוֶה מָעוֹת בְּלֹא נִכּוּי עַל מָקוֹם שֶׁאֵין פֵּרוֹתָיו מְצוּיִין‏
‏תָּדִיר, כְּגוֹן שָׂדֶה וְכֶרֶם, שֶׁאֵין פֵּרוֹתָיו מְצוּיִין, כִּי פְעָמִים בָּהֶם הַהוֹצָאָה מְרֻבָּה עַל‏
‏הַשֶּׁבַח, הֲרֵי זֶה אֲבַק רִבִּית; וּבְנִכּוּי הֲרֵי זֶה מֻתָּר.‏

‏וּמֵהֶם שֶׁאָמְרוּ שֶׁאֲפִלּוּ בְּשָׂדֶה וְכֶרֶם וּבְנִכּוּי אֲסָרוּהָ חֲכָמִים זִכְרוֹנָם לִבְרָכָה,‏
‏וְלֹא מָצְאוּ מַשְׁכּוֹנָה מֻתֶּרֶת אֶלָּא מַשְׁכַּנְתָּא דְסוּרָא, שֶׁהָיוּ כוֹתְבִין: בְּמִשְׁלַם שְׁנַיָּא‏
‏אִילֵּין תִּפּוֹק אַרְעָא דָא בְּלֹא כָסֶף.‏

‏וְהָאֱמֶת, לְפִי הַנִּרְאֶה מִדִּבְרֵי הַגְּמָרָא לְרַבּוֹתַי אֵל יִשְׁמְרֵם עִם הַפָּרוּשִׁים‏
‏הַטּוֹבִים, שֶׁכָּל מַשְׁכּוֹנָה בְּנִכּוּי, בֵּין בֵּית דִּירָה וּמֶרְחָץ, שֶׁפֵּרוֹתֵיהֶן מְצוּיִּין, וְכָל־‏

23. TB Bava M'tzi'a 75b.

24. MT *hilchoth malveh* vi 7, as a ruling by his master teachers; *Maggid Mishneh* there notes that this is the view of early *ge'onim*.

25. So "some *ge'onim*" cited in MT *ibid.* 8.

26. Thus it was not a loan at all; the lender actually bought, for the money he advanced, the rights to the property he took, for a set number of years; this is simply a leasing transaction; and the lessee is entitled to his revenue, no matter how much it may exceed the amount he gave the lessor.

with one another by way of penalty; for instance, "If I have not paid you until that certain day, the field shall be yours," or "the pledged object" whatever it may be, and anything similar. But this does not apply to all the many other conditions that people make with one another: for instance, "If you go to that certain place, I will give you this-and-this"; so too, "If you do that certain matter for me, I will give you 200 *zuz*"; and anything like that. Understand this, my son, and give it your attention; for with this you will remove from between your eyes a great cloud over the words of the Talmud, in a great many places.

Our Sages of blessed memory likewise taught[23] that advance interest, or delayed interest, is [considered] a shade of usury, and is forbidden by the decree of the Sages. How is this done? If someone set his sights on borrowing from another, and he would send him presents in order that the other should grant him the loan, this is advance interest. If one borrowed money from another and returned his money to him, and afterward he sent him presents on account of the other's money that had lain idle with him [been available to him], this is delayed interest.

And so some authorities ruled likewise[24] that if someone lends money to his fellow-man in return for a place whose revenue is readily available, such as a courtyard, a bath-house, or a shop, without any deduction [from the loan], this is fixed, specific interest. If it was with a deduction, it is a shade of interest. However, if a person lends money with no deduction [to be made from the loan] in return for a place whose revenue is not readily available, such as a field or a vineyard, whose income is not always forthcoming, since at times the expense is greater than the profit—it is a shade of usury; and with a deduction it is permissible.

There are some, though, who ruled[25] that even with a field or a vineyard, and with a deduction, the Sages of blessed memory prohibited it; and they found no pledge of landed property permissible other than the "pledge of Sura," where they [the people] would write, "At the end of these years, this land shall revert [to its owner] without payment of money."[26]

The truth, however, as it appears from the words of the Talmud to my master teachers, God protect them, along with the good commentaries, is that any pledge of landed property in return for a deduction, whether it is a dwelling-house or a bath-house, whose revenue is

שֶׁכֵּן שָׂדֶה וְכֶרֶם, הַכֹּל בְּנִכּוּי מֻתָּר; וְכֵן נָהֲגוּ בְּאַרְצֵנוּ עַל פִּיהֶם; וְהַחוֹשֵׁשׁ לְדִבְרֵי גְּאוֹנֵי עוֹלָם שֶׁהֶחֱמִירוּ בַּדָּבָר, יִתְבָּרֵךְ מִן הַשָּׁמָיִם.

וְאֵי זֶהוּ הָרִבִּית הָאַחֶרֶת שֶׁאָמַרְנוּ לְמַעְלָה שֶׁאָסְרוּ זִכְרוֹנָם לִבְרָכָה מִפְּנֵי הַעֲרָמַת רִבִּית — כְּגוֹן שֶׁאָמַר אָדָם לַחֲבֵרוֹ "הַלְוֵנִי מָנֶה", וְאָמַר לוֹ "מָנֶה אֵין לִי, חִטִּים בְּמָנֶה יֵשׁ לִי", וְנָתַן לוֹ חִטִּים בְּמָנֶה וְחָזַר וּלְקָחָן מִמֶּנּוּ בְּתִשְׁעִים; זֶה בְּוַדַּאי הָיָה מִן הַדִּין מֻתָּר, אֶלָּא שֶׁאֲסָרוּהוּ חֲכָמִים מִפְּנֵי הַעֲרָמַת רִבִּית, שֶׁהֲרֵי דָבָר זֶה נִרְאֶה הוּא כְּרִבִּית, שֶׁזֶּה נָתַן תִּשְׁעִים דִּינָרִין וְלוֹקֵחַ מֵאָה; אֲבָל אִם עָבַר וְעָשָׂה כֵן, מוֹצִיא מִמֶּנּוּ כָּל הַמֵּאָה, שֶׁאֲפִלּוּ אֲבַק רִבִּית אֵין כָּאן, אֶלָּא מִשּׁוּם גֶּדֶר הוּא שֶׁהֶחֱמִירוּ חֲכָמִים בַּדָּבָר.

וְכֵן מִי שֶׁהָיְתָה שָׂדֶה מְמֻשְׁכֶּנֶת בְּיָדוֹ לֹא יַחֲזֹר (וישכור) [וְיַשְׂכִּיר] אוֹתָהּ לְבַעַל הַשָּׂדֶה, מִפְּנֵי הַעֲרָמַת רִבִּית; וְכַיּוֹצֵא בְעִנְיָנִים אֵלּוּ, כְּמוֹ שֶׁבָּא בַּגְּמָרָא.

וְאַף־עַל־פִּי שֶׁדְּבָרִים אֵלּוּ אָסְרוּ מִשּׁוּם הַעֲרָמַת רִבִּית, יֵשׁ דְּבָרִים אֲחֵרִים שֶׁהֵן כְּעֵין רִבִּית מַמָּשׁ וְהִתִּירוּ אוֹתָן חֲכָמִים, שֶׁלֹּא רָאוּ לָחוּשׁ בָּהֶן וְלִגְזֹר כְּלָל; וְזֶהוּ שֶׁהִתִּירוּ שֶׁיִּמְכֹּר אָדָם חוֹבוֹ בְּפָחוֹת, וְהִתִּירוּ גַם־כֵּן שֶׁיִּתֵּן אָדָם לַחֲבֵרוֹ דִּינָר, שֶׁיֹּאמַר לְיִשְׂרָאֵל אַחֵר שֶׁיַּלְוֵהוּ מָנֶה.

וְדֶרֶךְ כְּלָל אָמְרוּ זִכְרוֹנָם לִבְרָכָה שֶׁלֹּא אָסְרָה תּוֹרָה אֶלָּא רִבִּית הַבָּאָה מִיַּד לֹוֶה לַמַּלְוֶה, וְהָעִנְיָן הוּא לְפִי שֶׁהַתּוֹרָה תִּבְחַר בָּרַב לְעוֹלָם וְתַנִּיחַ הַפְּרָטִים, עַל־כֵּן תַּזְהִיר לַלֹּוֶה וּמַלְוֶה, כִּי כֵן דַּרְכּוֹ שֶׁל עוֹלָם. וְאַף־עַל־פִּי שֶׁאָמְרוּ כֵן וְהוּא הָאֱמֶת, רָאוּי לְכָל בַּעַל נֶפֶשׁ לְהִתְרַחֵק מִכָּל עִנְיָן שֶׁיֵּשׁ בּוֹ הַעֲרָמַת רִבִּית, בְּכָל כֹּחוֹ; וְכָל

<hr/>

27. So *Maggid Mishneh* to MT *ibid.* citing Rashba as the authority; *Nimmuké Yoséf* to TB Bava M'tzi'a 67b equally cites Rashba.

28. A hundred *denarii*; TB Bava M'tzi'a 62b.

29. I.e. ninety *denarii*, because the borrower was pressed for ready money and could not wait to sell it at the market.

30. So MT *hilchoth malveh* v 15; *Maggid Mishneh* cites a stricter view. (In effect, the Sages wished to prevent the development of any trait or tendency to take whatever might be akin to interest, by guile or deceit.)

31. TJ Bava M'tzi'a v 1; MT *ibid.* 14.

regularly available, and all the more certainly a field or vineyard—all
is permissible for a deduction. And so the practice is in our countries,
by their word.[27] Yet if one has serious regard for the words of the
exalted authorities of the world who ruled stringently in the matter,
may he be blessed from Heaven.

Now, which is the other [third] kind of interest that we mentioned
above, that the Sages of blessed memory forbade because [it smacks] of
cunning, deceitful usury?—For instance, if a man asks his fellow-
man, "Lend me a *maneh*,"[28] and the other answers him, "I have not a
maneh, but I do have a *maneh*'s worth of wheat," whereupon he gives
him the wheat for a *maneh*, and then turns about and buys it back
from him for ninety.[29] This should certainly be permissible by normal
logic; but the Sages forbade it because [it smacks] of interest by
guileful deceit. For here this matter looks like usury, since this one
[in effect] gives ninety *denarii* and takes a hundred. However, if he
transgressed and acted so, he may extract from the other [at law]
the entire hundred: for there is not even a shade of usury here; it is
only for the purpose of a barrier that the Sages were [initially] stringent
in the matter.[30]

So likewise, if a field was given in pledge into someone's possession,
he should not turn about and lease it to the owner of the field, on account
of [the prohibition on] usury by guileful deceit;[30] and so anything
like these matters, as we find in the Talmud.

Now, even though these matters were forbidden as a barrier
against usury by guileful deceit, there are other matters that are similar
to actual usury, and yet the Sages permitted them, since they saw no
need to be concerned about them and issue any decree at all. Thus
they permitted a man to sell his debt [amount receivable, promissory
note] at a discount.[31] They likewise permitted a man to give his
fellow a *denar* so that this one should tell another Israelite to lend
him a *maneh*.[9]

As a general rule, they (of blessed memory) said that the Torah
prohibited nothing but interest that goes from the borrower's hand to
the lender.[9] The reason is that the Torah chooses the majority element
and leaves aside the details [of minor exceptions]; therefore it adjures
the borrower and the lender, for such is the way of the world [for
them to arrange the payment of interest]. Yet even though they said
so, and it is the truth, it is fitting for every ethical, scrupulous person

to move well away from every matter that entails any guileful, deceitful

הַמְחַזֵּר וּמְבַקֵּשׁ צְדָדִים לִטֹּל רִבִּית מִיִּשְׂרָאֵל, סוֹפוֹ מִתְרוֹשֵׁשׁ, וּכְמוֹ שֶׁאָמְרוּ
זִכְרוֹנָם לִבְרָכָה, שֶׁכָּל הָעוֹסֵק בְּרִבִּית מִתְמוֹטֵט; גַּם אָמְרוּ שֶׁפְּרוּטָה שֶׁל רִבִּית
גּוֹרֶמֶת לוֹ לָאָדָם לְאַבֵּד כַּמָּה כַּמָּה אוֹצָרוֹת שֶׁל מָמוֹן. וְיֶתֶר רַבֵּי פְרָטֵי הַמִּצְוָה, בְּבָבָא
מְצִיעָא פֶּרֶק "אֵי זֶהוּ נֶשֶׁךְ".

וְנוֹהֶגֶת בְּכָל מָקוֹם וּבְכָל זְמַן, בַּזְּכָרִים וּבַנְּקֵבוֹת. וְעוֹבֵר עַל זֶה וְהִלְוָה בְּרִבִּית
הָאָסוּר מִן הַתּוֹרָה, עָבַר עַל לָאו, וּמוֹצִיאִין אוֹתוֹ מִמֶּנּוּ בְּדַיָּנִין, שֶׁיּוֹרְדִין בֵּית-דִּין
לִנְכָסָיו, כְּדֶרֶךְ שֶׁיּוֹרְדִין לִנְכָסִים בְּגֶזְלוֹ אוֹ בִּנְזָקָיו, כְּדַעַת קְצָת הַמְּפָרְשִׁים; אוֹ
מוֹצִיאִין אוֹתוֹ מִמֶּנּוּ דֶּרֶךְ כְּפִיָּה, כְּדֶרֶךְ שֶׁכּוֹפִין לְיִשְׂרָאֵל שֶׁלֹּא רָצָה לְקַיֵּם מִצְוַת
עֲשֵׂה, כְּדַעַת קְצָת מֵרַבּוֹתֵינוּ יִשְׁמְרֵם אֵל.

וְאִם הִלְוָה בְּרִבִּית הָאָסוּר מִדִּבְרֵיהֶם, שֶׁהוּא הַנִּקְרָא אֲבַק רִבִּית, עָבַר עַל לָאו
דְּרַבָּנָן, וְאֵין רִבִּית זוֹ יוֹצְאָה בְּדַיָּנִין, אֲבָל אִם תָּפַשׂ הַלֹּוֶה מִן הַמַּלְוֶה בִּכְדֵי אוֹתוֹ
רִבִּית, אֵין מוֹצִיאִין מִיָּדוֹ. וְאִם עָבַר וְהִלְוָה בְּרִבִּית שֶׁאָסְרוּ זִכְרוֹנָם לִבְרָכָה מִפְּנֵי
הַעֲרָמַת רִבִּית לְבַד, אֵין צָרִיךְ לוֹמַר שֶׁאֵין מוֹצִיאִין אוֹתוֹ מִן הַמַּלְוֶה אִם לָקַח,
שֶׁאֲפִלּוּ מִן הַלֹּוֶה מוֹצִיאִין אוֹתוֹ וְנוֹתְנִין אוֹתוֹ לַמַּלְוֶה, מִכֵּיוָן שֶׁעָבְרוּ וְהִתְנוּ
בֵּינֵיהֶם בְּכָךְ; דְּמִכֵּיוָן שֶׁלֹּא הֶחֱמִירוּ זִכְרוֹנָם לִבְרָכָה בַּדָּבָר אֶלָּא מִשּׁוּם הַעֲרָמַת
רִבִּית, לֹא חָשְׁשׁוּ בַּדָּבָר בְּדִיעֲבַד, וְדִיעֲבַד נִקְרָא מִכֵּיוָן שֶׁנִּתְקַיְּמוּ הַדְּבָרִים בֵּין
מַלְוֶה לְלֹוֶה.

[שֶׁלֹּא נַעֲבֹד בְּעֶבֶד עִבְרִי עֲבוֹדַת בִּזָּיוֹן כְּמוֹ עֲבוֹדַת כְּנַעֲנִי]

שדם שֶׁלֹּא נַעֲבֹד בְּעֶבֶד עִבְרִי בַּעֲבוֹדָה שֶׁיֵּשׁ בָּהּ בִּזָּיוֹן גָּדוֹל וְהַכְנָעָה שֶׁדֶּרֶךְ
לַעֲבֹד כֵּן בְּעֶבֶד כְּנַעֲנִי, שֶׁנֶּאֱמַר: לֹא תַעֲבֹד בּוֹ עֲבֹדַת עָבֶד; וְאָמְרוּ זִכְרוֹנָם לִבְרָכָה
בַּסִּפְרָא בְּפֵרוּשׁ עִנְיַן זֶה: שֶׁלֹּא יִטֹּל אַחֲרֶיךָ בְּלִינְטָא, וְהוּא כְּלִי שֶׁל בֶּגֶד קָטָן

32. TB Bava M'tzi'a 71a.

33. *Ibid.* 75b.

34. So Rabad, cited by R. 'Ashér to Bava M'tzi'a v, §2.

usury, with all his strength. As for anyone who goes about seeking devious ways to take interest from an Israelite, in the end he will be impoverished. As our Sages of blessed memory declared:[32] whoever engages in usury will collapse. They said too that a penny of interest causes a man to lose many stores of goods.[23]

The remaining numerous details of the precept are in the fifth chapter of the tractate *Bava M'tzi'a*. It is in effect everywhere, at every time, for both man and woman. If a person transgressed this and lent money at an interest that is forbidden by the Torah, he would violate a negative precept, and it should be extracted from him by judges; for the *beth din* should go down to his very property, as they go down to property [to collect] in the case of a robber or one who caused damage—in the view of some authorities;[10] or they extract it from him through coercion, in the way that force would be applied to an Israelite who did not wish to fulfill a positive precept, in the view of some of our master teachers, God protect them.[11]

If someone lent money for a form of interest which is forbidden by the ruling of the Sages, which is called a shade of·usury, he would violate a prohibition of the Sages; but this interest is not extracted from his possession. Yet if the borrower seized from the creditor something equal in value to that interest, it is not extracted from him.[34] If he transgressed and lent money for a kind of interest that the Sages of blessed memory forbade only because [it smacks] of guileful, deceitful usury, there is no need to say that it is not extracted from the creditor if he took it; for it is even extracted from the borrower and given to the creditor, since they transgressed and agreed to this between themselves. For since the Sages of blessed memory were stringent about the matter solely as a barrier against usury by guileful deceit, they were not concerned about the matter after the fact, when the deed was already done. And this is called "after the fact" inasmuch as the terms were agreed upon between the creditor and the borrower.

[THAT WE SHOULD NOT HAVE A HEBREW MANSERVANT
DO CONTEMPTIBLE WORK LIKE A HEATHEN SLAVE]

344 that we should not make a Hebrew servant work at labor that involves great disgrace and servility, in the way that a Canaanite (heathen) slave is made to work: for it is stated, *you shall not make him work as a slave* (Leviticus 25:39). Our Sages of blessed memory said in the Midrash *Sifra*,[1] in explanation of this matter, that he should

שֶׁעוֹשִׂין בְּנֵי־אָדָם לֵישֵׁב עָלָיו בְּכָל מָקוֹם שֶׁהֵם כְּשֶׁהֵם יָגֵעִים, וְדֶרֶךְ הָעֶבֶד הַנִּבְזֶה שֶׁנּוֹטֵל אוֹתוֹ כְלִי וּמוֹלִיכוֹ אַחַר אֲדוֹנָיו; וּכְמוֹ כֵן אָמְרוּ: וְלֹא יִטֹּל לְפָנֶיךָ כֵּלִים לְבֵית הַמֶּרְחָץ. וְהֵם זִכְרוֹנָם לִבְרָכָה בֵּאֲרוּ אֵלּוּ הַמְּלָאכוֹת, וְהוּא הַדִּין שֶׁנִּלְמַד מֵהֶם לְכָל כַּיּוֹצֵא־בָזֶה.

נִמְצָא שֶׁיֵּשׁ לוֹ לְאָדָם שֶׁיִּתֵּן אֶל לִבּוֹ אֵיזוֹ מְלָאכָה יְצַוֶּה לְעַבְדּוֹ עִבְרִי, וְזֶהוּ מִכְּלַל מַה שֶׁאָמְרוּ זִכְרוֹנָם לִבְרָכָה: כָּל הַקּוֹנֶה עֶבֶד עִבְרִי, כְּקוֹנֶה אָדוֹן לְעַצְמוֹ. וּמִכָּל־מָקוֹם מִמָּה שֶׁאָמַר הַכָּתוּב "כְּשָׂכִיר כְּתוֹשָׁב יִהְיֶה עִמָּךְ", יֵשׁ לִלְמֹד שֶׁיָּכֹל אָדָם לְצַוּוֹתוֹ בְּכָל הַדְּבָרִים שֶׁדֶּרֶךְ בְּנֵי־אָדָם לְצַוּוֹת הַשָּׂכִיר וְהַתּוֹשָׁב; וּבֶאֱמֶת הַשָּׂכִיר, שֶׁהוּא אָדָם בֶּן־חוֹרִין, בָּרֹב אֵינֶנּוּ נִשְׂכָּר לִמְלָאכָה בְזוּיָה; וּכְמוֹ־כֵן הַתּוֹשָׁב, שֶׁהוּא אָדָם שֶׁבָּא לָגוּר בְּאֶרֶץ אַחֶרֶת, וְדַרְכָּן שֶׁל תּוֹשָׁבִים לַעֲבֹד בַּעַל־הַבַּיִת שֶׁהֵם מִתְגּוֹרְרִים עִמּוֹ לִרְצוֹנָם, וְעַל־כֵּן לֹא יַעֲשׂוּ מְלָאכָה בְזוּיָה בְיוֹתֵר; וְעַל־כֵּן אָמַר הַכָּתוּב: כְּשָׂכִיר כְּתוֹשָׁב יִהְיֶה עִמָּךְ, שֶׁשְּׁנֵי אֲנָשִׁים אֵלּוּ, אַף־עַל־פִּי שֶׁהֵם עוֹבְדִים, אֵין עֲבוֹדָתָם עֲבוֹדָה בְזוּיָה בְּרֹב הַפְּעָמִים. וְאַף־עַל־פִּי־כֵן צָרִיךְ הָעֶבֶד לִנְהֹג בְּעַצְמוֹ מִנְהַג עַבְדוּת וִיכַבֵּד אֲדוֹנָיו בְּכָל כֹּחוֹ, וְלֹא יִתְגָּאֶה בְּכָל זֶה שֶׁאָמַרְנוּ.

מִשָּׁרְשֵׁי הַמִּצְוָה, כְּדֵי שֶׁיִּתֵּן הָאָדָם אֶל לִבּוֹ כִּי הָאֻמָּה שֶׁלָּנוּ הִיא הַנִּכְבֶּדֶת מִכֻּלָּן, וּמִתּוֹךְ כָּךְ יֶאֱהַב כָּל אֻמָּתוֹ וְתוֹרָתוֹ, וְיִתֵּן אֶל לִבּוֹ כִּי גַם־כֵּן כְּמוֹ שֶׁזֶּה הָעֶבֶד הָעִבְרִי נִמְכַּר לוֹ מִפְּנֵי דָחֳקוֹ, כָּךְ אֶפְשָׁר שֶׁיִּקְרֶה גַם לַקּוֹנֶה אוֹתוֹ אוֹ לְאֶחָד מִבָּנָיו אִם אוּלַי יִגְרֹם לָהֶם הַחֵטְא, וּבְכַבְּדוֹ עַבְדּוֹ יַחְשֹׁב מַחֲשָׁבָה זוֹ בְּלִי סָפֵק, וּמִתּוֹךְ מַחֲשַׁבְתּוֹ זֹאת יִזָּהֵר מֵחֲטֹא לַיָי.

וְעוֹד תּוֹעֶלֶת אַחֵר בַּדָּבָר, שֶׁיְּלַמֵּד הָאָדָם נַפְשׁוֹ בְּמִדַּת הַחֶסֶד וְהָרַחֲמִים וְיִתְרַחֵק מִמִּדַּת הָאַכְזָרִיּוּת הָרָעָה, וּבִהְיוֹתָן נַפְשׁוֹ אֶל הַטּוֹבָה תְּקַבֵּל טוֹב; וְהַשֵּׁם חָפֵץ לְהַעֲנִיק מִבִּרְכוֹתָיו אֶל בְּרִיּוֹתָיו, כְּמוֹ שֶׁכָּתַבְתִּי פְּעָמִים הַרְבֵּה בַּמִּצְוֹות הַקּוֹדְמוֹת.

2. TB Kiddushin 22a.

3. From the beginning to here is based on ShM negative precept §257. The word *linta* (perhaps it should be *lenta*), in the first line on the page, is thus found also in ShM. Our eds. of Sifra read *lintia* (or *lentia*), while in the Talmud the word is *'aluntith* (see Kossovsky, Index, s.v.). The origin of the word is the Greek *lention*, a cloth or towel (Latin *linteum*).

not carry a *linta* after you. This is a small cloth that people would make in order to sit on it wherever they were, when they were tired; and it was the way of a despicable slave to take this cloth and carry it after his master. So they taught likewise:[1] and he is not to carry garments before you to the bath-house. They (of blessed memory) explained these labors, and the law requires us to learn from these about anything similar.

Consequently, it is for a man to give thought to which labor he may order his Hebrew servant to do. This is in accord with the rule that the Sages of blessed memory gave:[2] Whoever buys a Hebrew servant is as one who buys a master for himself. However, from the verse in Scripture, *As a hired servant, as a settler shall he be with you* (ibid. 40), it is to be learned that a man may order him about all things that people usually command a hired servant and a settler. Indeed, a hired servant, being a free man, will mostly not hire himself out for despicable work. And so too a settler, who is a man who comes to live in another land. It is the way of settlers to work for the householders with whom they take lodgings, by their own free will; hence they would not do unduly despicable work. Therefore Scripture states, *As a hired servant, as a settler shall he be with you*: for as regards these two persons, even though they work, their employment is not menial labor for the most part.[3] Nevertheless, the servant must conduct himself in a subservient manner, and he is to respect his master with all his power, and not become proud regarding all that we stated.[1]

At the root of the precept lies the aim that a man should reflect in his heart that our nation is the most honorable of all, and as a result he will love his nation and his Torah. And he will equally reflect that just as this Hebrew servant was sold to him on account of his pressing circumstances, so is it possible that someone may happen to buy him or one of his sons, if sin should perhaps make it happen to them. When he treats his servant with respect, he will undoubtedly entertain this thought; and with this thought, he will take care not to sin toward the Lord.

There is a further benefit in the matter, too: A man will thus train his spirit in the quality of loving-kindness and compassion, and will move far away from the evil quality of cruelty. As he thus prepares his spirit for goodness, it will receive good reward; and the Eternal Lord delights in bestowing of His blessings on His human beings, as

⟨445⟩ I have written many times in the previous *mitzvoth*.

דִּינֵי הַמִּצְוָה, כְּגוֹן מַה שֶּׁדִּקְדְּקוּ לְבָרֲכָה פֶּרֶק קַמָּא דְּקִדּוּשִׁין מִמַּה שֶּׁאָמַר הַכָּתוּב "כִּי טוֹב לוֹ עִמָּךְ": עִמָּךְ בְּמַאֲכָל וְעִמָּךְ בְּמִשְׁתֶּה: שֶׁלֹּא תְהֵא אַתָּה אוֹכֵל פַּת נְקִיָּה וְהוּא אוֹכֵל פַּת קִבָּר, אַתָּה שׁוֹתֶה יַיִן יָשָׁן וְהוּא שׁוֹתֶה יַיִן חָדָשׁ; אַתָּה יָשֵׁן עַל-גַּבֵּי מוֹכִין וְהוּא יָשֵׁן עַל-גַּבֵּי הַתֶּבֶן. וְכֵן אָמְרוּ זִכְרוֹנָם לִבְרָכָה שֶׁלֹּא יָדוּר הָאָדוֹן בַּכְּרָךְ וְהָעֶבֶד בַּכְּפָר, שֶׁנֶּאֱמַר "וְיָצָא מֵעִמָּךְ"; וְיֶתֶר פְּרָטֶיהָ, בִּסְפָרָא וּבְקִדּוּשִׁין.

וְנוֹהֶגֶת בִּזְכָרִים וּנְקֵבוֹת, בִּזְמַן שֶׁהַיּוֹבֵל נוֹהֵג; וּכְבָר כָּתַבְתִּי בְּרֹאשׁ הַסֵּדֶר [סִי' שׁ"ל] בְּאֵיזֶה זְמַן הַיּוֹבֵל נוֹהֵג. וְאַף-עַל-פִּי שֶׁאֵין רָאוּי לְאִשָּׁה שֶׁתִּקְנֶה עֶבֶד, מִפְּנֵי הַחֲשָׁד, בִּכְלַל הַמִּצְוָה הִיא מִכָּל-מָקוֹם.

וְעָבַר עַל מִצְוָה זוֹ וְעָבַד בְּעֶבֶד עִבְרִי בָּעֲבוֹדוֹת הַבְּזוּיוֹת, עָבַר עַל לָאו זֶה; אֲבָל מִן הַדּוֹמֶה שֶׁאֵין בָּזֶה חִיּוּב מַלְקוֹת, לְפִי שֶׁאֵין בּוֹ מַעֲשֶׂה, כִּי בִּדְבָרִים יָנֵּס עֶבֶד לַעֲשׂוֹת מְלַאכְתּוֹ, בְּזוּיָה אוֹ נִכְבֶּדֶת, וּכְבָר כָּתַבְתִּי לְמַעְלָה כִּי כָל לָאו שֶׁאֶפְשָׁר לַעֲבֹר עָלָיו מִבְּלִי מַעֲשֶׂה, אַף-עַל-פִּי שֶׁנַּעֲשָׂה בּוֹ שׁוּם מַעֲשֶׂה, שֶׁאֵין לְחַיְּבוֹ מַלְקוֹת עָלָיו, דְּלָאו שֶׁאֵין בּוֹ מַעֲשֶׂה נִקְרָא מִכָּל-מָקוֹם. זֶה דַּרְכִּי, כַּךְ בְּעֵינַי.

[שֶׁלֹּא נִמְכֹּר עֶבֶד עִבְרִי עַל אֶבֶן הַמֶּקָּח]

שמה שֶׁלֹּא נִמְכֹּר עֶבֶד עִבְרִי כְּדֶרֶךְ שֶׁמּוֹכְרִין הָעֲבָדִים כְּנַעֲנִיִּים, בְּהַכְרָזָה עַל אֶבֶן הַמֶּקָּח, אֶלָּא בְּהַצְנֵעַ וְדֶרֶךְ כָּבוֹד; וְכֵן אָמְרוּ בִּסְפָרָא: "לֹא יִמָּכְרוּ מִמְכֶּרֶת עָבֶד", שֶׁלֹּא יִמְכְּרֵם בְּסִמְטָא וְיַעֲמִידֵם עַל אֶבֶן הַמֶּקָּח.

שֹׁרֶשׁ מִצְוָה זוֹ יָדוּעַ, שֶׁאֵין רָאוּי לוֹ לְאָדָם לְהָקֵל בִּכְבוֹד חֲבֵרוֹ אַף-עַל-פִּי

4. Sifra, b'har, perek 7, 2.

5. Literal translation; i.e. when his period of service ends, he is to leave after having been *with* his master—on a par with him.

6. I.e. of possible immorality between them; TB Bava M'tzi'a 71a.

§ 345   1. Literally, the stone of purchase—a public place used specifically for the sale of slaves.

2. Sifra, b'har, parashah 6, 1. Before this sentence there may be a scribal omission of a few words: שנאמר לא ימכרו ממכרת עבד for Scripture states, *they shall not be sold by the sale of slaves*—for as a rule our author cites first the source in the Writ and then brings a relevant interpretation of the Sages on it. The paragraph is based, however, on ShM negative precept § 258, and there likewise the verse is not cited first.

The laws of the precept are, for example, what the Sages of blessed memory inferred in the first chapter of the Talmud tractate *Kiddushin* (22a) from Scripture's words, *because he fares well with you* (Deuteronomy 15:16): [He should be equal] with you in food, with you in drink—and not that you should eat fine bread while he eats coarse bread; you should drink old wine while he drinks new (raw) wine; you should sleep on down feathers while he sleeps on straw. And so our Sages of blessed memory taught[4] that the master should not live in the city and the servant in the country: for it is stated, *Then he shall go out from with you* (Leviticus 25:41).[5]

The rest of its details are in the Midrash *Sifra* and in the tractate *Kiddushin*. It applies to both man and woman at the time that the law of the jubilee is observed; and I wrote previously, in the first positive precept in the *sidrah* (§330), at which time the law of the jubilee is in effect. Even though it is not proper for a woman to buy a servant, on account of the suspicion,[6] she is included under the precept in any event.

If someone transgressed this precept and made a Hebrew servant do menial, despicable tasks, he would violate this negative precept; but it would seem that it entails no penalty of whiplashes, since [the transgression] requires no physical action: for a servant is admonished by words to do his labor, be it despicable or respectable. And I wrote previously, above (§241), that over any negative precept that it is possible to transgress without physical action, even if some act was done for it, the person is not to be sentenced to whiplashes; for in any event it is called a negative precept that involves no physical action. This is my approach, clear in my eyes.

[THE PROHIBITION OF SELLING A HEBREW MANSERVANT
AT THE SLAVES' SELLING-BLOCK]

345 that we should not sell a Hebrew servant in the way that we sell Canaanite (heathen) slaves, by proclamation at the auction block,[1] but rather discreetly and in a respectable way. So was it taught in the Midrash *Sifra*:[2] *they shall not be sold by the sale of slaves* (Leviticus 25:42)—that they should not be sold in the alley, being stood on the auction block.

The root reason for this precept is known (evident): because

it is not right for a man to belittle the esteem of his fellow-man, even

שֶׁהֱבִיאוּהוּ עֲווֹנוֹתָיו לְמָכֵר, כִּי לֹא יֵדַע אִם אוּלַי לְמָחָר יָבוֹא גַם הוּא לְכָךְ. בֵּאוּר מִצְוָה זוֹ בְּקִדּוּשִׁין, וְדִינֶיהָ כְּלוּלִים בְּעִקָּרֵהּ; אֵין לְהַאֲרִיךְ בָּהֶם.

וְנוֹהֶגֶת בִּזְכָרִים וּנְקֵבוֹת, בִּזְמַן שֶׁהַיּוֹבֵל נוֹהֵג, שֶׁאֵין עֶבֶד עִבְרִי נוֹהֵג אֶלָּא בִּזְמַן הַיּוֹבֵל, כְּמוֹ שֶׁכָּתַבְתִּי לְמַעְלָה. וְעוֹבֵר עַל זֶה וּמָכַר עֶבֶד עִבְרִי כְּדֶרֶךְ שֶׁהָעֲבָדִים כְּנַעֲנִיִּים נִמְכָּרִים, עָבַר עַל לָאו; אֲבָל מִן הַדּוֹמֶה שֶׁאֵין בּוֹ חִיּוּב מַלְקוּת, לְפִי שֶׁאֶפְשָׁר לַעֲבֹר עָלָיו מִבְּלִי מַעֲשֶׂה.

[שֶׁלֹּא לַעֲבֹד בְּעֶבֶד עִבְרִי בַּעֲבוֹדַת פֶּרֶךְ]

שמו שֶׁלֹּא נַעֲבִיד עֶבֶד עִבְרִי בַּעֲבוֹדַת פֶּרֶךְ, שֶׁנֶּאֱמַר: לֹא תִרְדֶּה בוֹ בְּפָרֶךְ; וְאֵי זוֹ הִיא עֲבוֹדַת פֶּרֶךְ, פֵּרְשׁוּ זִכְרוֹנָם לִבְרָכָה שֶׁהִיא עֲבוֹדָה שֶׁאֵין לָהּ קִצְבָּה, וְכֵן עֲבוֹדָה שֶׁאֵין אָדָם צָרִיךְ לָהּ אֶלָּא יַעֲשֶׂנָּה כְּדֵי שֶׁלֹּא יִתְבַּטֵּל הָעֶבֶד; וּכְמוֹ שֶׁאָמְרוּ זִכְרוֹנָם לִבְרָכָה: לֹא יֹאמַר לוֹ "עֲדֹר תַּחַת הַגְּפָנִים עַד שֶׁאָבוֹא", שֶׁהֲרֵי לֹא נָתַן לוֹ קִצְבָּה, אֶלָּא יֹאמַר לוֹ "עֲבֹד עַד שָׁעָה פְּלוֹנִית" אוֹ "עַד מָקוֹם פְּלוֹנִי"; וְאָמְרוּ גַם־כֵּן בְּסִפְרָא: שֶׁלֹּא יֹאמַר לוֹ "הָחֵם לִי כּוֹס זֶה", וְהוּא אֵינוֹ צָרִיךְ לוֹ; וְכֵן כָּל כַּיּוֹצֵא־בָזֶה. אֲבָל הֵבִיאוּ זִכְרוֹנָם לִבְרָכָה בְּמָשָׁל קַלָּה שֶׁבַּמְּלָאכוֹת וְהַנִּמְהֶרֶת לַעֲשׂוֹת, וְכָל־שֶׁכֵּן הָאֲחֵרוֹת.

וְהַכְּלָל, שֶׁלֹּא נַעֲבִידֵהוּ זוּלָתִי בִּהְיוֹת הַצֹּרֶךְ לָנוּ לַעֲשׂוֹת הַמְּלָאכָה הַהִיא שֶׁנִּצַּוֵּהוּ עָלֶיהָ.

פְּרָטֵי הַמִּצְוָה קְצָרִים, וְהִנֵּה כְתַבְתִּי קִצְתָן.

וְנוֹהֶגֶת מִצְוָה זוֹ בִּזְכָרִים וּנְקֵבוֹת, בִּזְמַן שֶׁהַיּוֹבֵל נוֹהֵג. וְאֵין לְחַיֵּב מַלְקוּת עָלֶיהָ, לְפִי שֶׁאֶפְשָׁר לַעֲבֹר עָלֶיהָ בְּדִבּוּר לְבַד מִבְּלִי מַעֲשֶׂה.

וְאַף־עַל־פִּי שֶׁאֵינָהּ נוֹהֶגֶת בַּזְּמַן הַזֶּה, לְפִי שֶׁאֵין קִנְיַן עֶבֶד עִבְרִי נוֹהֵג, מִכָּל־מָקוֹם רָאוּי לוֹ לְאָדָם לְהִזָּהֵר בְּעִנְיַן מִצְוָה זוֹ גַם הַיּוֹם בִּהְיוֹת עֲנִיִּים בְּנֵי־בֵיתוֹ,

---

§346

1. Sifra, *b'har, parashah* 6, 2; MT *hilchoth 'avadim* i 6.

2. Sifra *ibid.*

3. I.e. they chose the lightest and easiest of chores (e.g. "Heat this cup for me") as an illustration so that we will understand that if even this may not be given him when it is "oppressive work" by the Sages' definition (it is not needed, or it is for a time without a set limit), he may certainly not be given anything more difficult or demanding under these conditions.

4. See §330, third paragraph from end; and §335, end.

if his sins have brought him to be sold. For he cannot know if perhaps tomorrow he too will be reduced to this.

The elucidation of this precept is in the Talmud tractate *Kiddushin*, and its laws are subsumed under its main requirement; there is no need to dwell on them at length.

It applies to both man and woman at the time that the law of the jubilee is observed, as I have written above (§330). If a person transgressed this and sold a Hebrew servant in the way that heathen slaves were sold, he would violate a negative precept; but it would seem that there is no penalty of whiplashes for it, since it is possible to transgress it without any physical action.

[NOT TO WORK A HEBREW MANSERVANT AT HARD LABOR]

346 that we should not make a Hebrew servant do crushing, oppressive work: for it is stated, *You shall not rule over him with harshness* (Leviticus 25:43). Now, what is crushing, oppressive work? Our Sages of blessed memory explained [1] that it is labor which has no limit; and so too any work for which a man has no need, but he has it done only so that the servant should not be idle. As the Sages of blessed memory taught: [2] He should not tell him, "Hoe beneath the grapevines until I come"—for here he did not set him a limit; he is rather to tell him, "Work until that hour" or "until this place." And they likewise taught in the Midrash *Sifra* [2] that he should not tell him, "Heat this cup for me," when he does not need it; and thus anything similar to it. But they (of blessed memory) gave as an example the lightest of tasks, and which can be quickly done; and so all the more certainly the others. [3]

The rule, in short, is that we should not put him to work except when we have a need for that task to be done which we set for him. The details of the precept are short, and here I have written some of them.

This precept applies to both man and woman at the time that the law of the jubilee is in effect. [4] But a whipping of lashes is not to be imposed for it, since it is possible to transgress it by words alone, without action.

Now, even though this is not in effect at the present time, since the purchase of a Hebrew slave is not a current practice, in any event it is fitting for a man to be careful about the idea of this precept today

וּלְהִזָּהֵר בָּהּ הַרְבֵּה; וְיִתֵּן אֶל לִבּוֹ כִּי הָעֹשֶׁר וְהָעֲנִיּוּת גַּלְגַּל הוּא שֶׁחוֹזֵר בָּעוֹלָם, וּמֵהַשֵּׁם הוּא, וְיִתְּנֶנּוּ לַאֲשֶׁר יִישַׁר בְּעֵינָיו הַזְּמַן שֶׁיִּרְצֶה, וְלֹא יוֹתֵר וַאֲפִלּוּ רֶגַע; שֶׁגַּם כִּי יִצְבֹּר כֶּעָפָר כֶּסֶף וְיִטְמְנֵהוּ בַקַּרְקַע וְיִקְנֶה קַרְקָעוֹת עַד אֵין מִסְפָּר וְטוֹבָה הַרְבֵּה יִהְיֶה לוֹ, הַכֹּל יֹאבַד מִמֶּנּוּ יַחַד בְּחֶטְאוֹ לַיָי; וְאִם יִצְדַּק, תִּתְקַיֵּם בּוֹ הַטּוֹבָה, כִּי כָל מִין בְּמִינוֹ יִדְבַּק.

[מִצְוַת עֲבוֹדָה בְּעֶבֶד כְּנַעֲנִי לְעוֹלָם]

שמז שֶׁנַּעֲבֹד בְּעֶבֶד כְּנַעֲנִי לְעוֹלָם, כְּלוֹמַר, שֶׁלֹּא נְשַׁחְרֵר אוֹתוֹ לְעוֹלָם וְשֶׁלֹּא יֵצֵא לְחֵרוּת, כִּי־אִם בְּשֵׁן וָעַיִן, כְּמוֹ שֶׁבָּא בַכָּתוּב, אוֹ בְרָאשֵׁי אֵיבָרִים הַדּוֹמִין לָהֶם, כְּלוֹמַר אֵיבָרִים שֶׁאֵינָן חוֹזְרִין, כְּמוֹ שֶׁבָּא עַל זֶה הַפֵּרוּשׁ הַמְקֻבָּל — שֶׁנֶּאֱמַר: לְעוֹלָם בָּהֶם תַּעֲבֹדוּ, וְאָמְרוּ זִכְרוֹנָם לִבְרָכָה בְּפֶרֶק הַשּׁוֹלֵחַ בְּמַסֶּכֶת גִּטִּין: אָמַר רַב יְהוּדָה: כָּל הַמְשַׁחְרֵר עַבְדּוֹ עוֹבֵר בַּעֲשֵׂה, שֶׁנֶּאֱמַר: לְעוֹלָם בָּהֶם תַּעֲבֹדוּ.

וְעֶבֶד כְּנַעֲנִי נִקְרָא אֶחָד מִכָּל הָאֻמּוֹת שֶׁקְּנָאוֹ יִשְׂרָאֵל לְעַבְדוּת, אֲבָל נִתְיַחֲסוּ כָּל עֲבָדִים בְּשֵׁם כְּנַעַן מִפְּנֵי שֶׁכְּנַעַן נִתְקַלֵּל לִהְיוֹת עֶבֶד הוּא וְזַרְעוֹ לְעוֹלָם; וְאַף־עַל־פִּי שֶׁפָּרָשָׁה זוֹ שֶׁנִּצְטַוֵּינוּ בָהּ לְהִשְׁתַּעְבֵּד בָּהֶם תְּדַבֵּר בִּכְנַעֲנִיִּים, כְּמוֹ שֶׁכָּתוּב: מֵאֵת הַגּוֹיִם אֲשֶׁר סְבִיבֹתֵיכֶם מֵהֶם תִּקְנוּ עֶבֶד וְאָמָה, וּכְתִיב לְמַעְלָה מִזֶּה: לָתֵת לָכֶם אֶת אֶרֶץ כְּנַעַן, יָדוּעַ לַחֲכָמִים זִכְרוֹנָם לִבְרָכָה דְּלָאו מִשְׁפַּחַת כְּנַעַן וַאֲשֶׁר בְּאַרְצָם דַּוְקָא נִקְרָאִים עֲבָדִים כְּנַעֲנִיִּים, דְּהוּא הַדִּין לְכָל שְׁאָר הָאֻמּוֹת, שֶׁיֵּשׁ לָהֶם דִּין עֶבֶד כְּנַעֲנִי לְכָל דָּבָר.

וְכֵן יִשְׂרָאֵל שֶׁבָּא עַל שִׁפְחָה כְּנַעֲנִית, כְּלוֹמַר עַל אִשָּׁה מִן הָאֻמּוֹת שֶׁקְּנָה אוֹתָהּ אֶחָד מִיִּשְׂרָאֵל, הֲרֵי הַנּוֹלָד מִמֶּנָּה וּמִיִּשְׂרָאֵל כְּעֶבֶד כְּנַעֲנִי לְכָל דָּבָר, וַאֲפִלּוּ

---

5. In keeping with Mishnah, 'Avoth i 5, "and let poor people be in your household'' (more literally, members of your household); i.e. they should be welcome to visit and frequent your home and enjoy your hospitality. It would then be natural for the head of the house and members of the family to employ these poor or make use of them to help with chores, etc.

6. So TB Shabbath 151b; i.e. those who are wealthy today are high on the wheel of fortune; but turning, it may bring them low, to poverty, tomorrow.

§347   1. Exodus 21:26–27.

2. TB Kiddushin 24a.

3. This first paragraph is based on ShM positive precept §235.

4. Genesis 9:25.

too, if poor people are in his household,[5] and to beware about it greatly. Let him ponder in his heart that the matter of wealth and poverty is a wheel that turns round in the world;[6] it [wealth] is from the Eternal Lord, blessed is He; He gives it to whomever it is right in His sight [to give it] for the time that it pleases him, and not more by even a minute. For even if one will heap up silver like dust (Job 27:16) and will hide it in the earth, and he will buy properties of land without number and will have great good fortune—all will be lost to him together, should he sin to the Lord. Should he be righteous, though, the good fortune will endure for him; for every kind clings to its own kind.

[THE PRECEPT OF KEEPING A HEATHEN SLAVE PER-
MANENTLY]

347 that we should use the labor of a Canaanite (heathen) slave for all time; in other words, we should never liberate him, nor should he go free except for [the loss of] a tooth or an eye, as ordained in the Writ,[1] or for [the loss of one of] the major organs or limbs which are equal to them—in other words, organs or limbs which are never regrown, as the received, traditional explanation was given about it.[2] For it is stated, *you shall make them slaves forever* (Leviticus 25:46); and the Sages taught in the fourth chapter of the Talmud tractate *Gittin* (38b): Said R. Judah: Whoever sets his slave free transgresses a positive precept; for it is stated, *you shall make them slaves forever.*[3]

A Canaanite slave is the term used for one from any of the [heathen] nations whom an Israelite bought as a slave. However, all slaves were ascribed to the patronymic Canaan because Canaan was cursed to be in servitude, both he and his descendants, forever.[4] Even though this Scriptural section, in which we are charged to keep them in servitude, speaks of Canaanites, as it is written, *of the nations that are round about you, of them shall you buy male and female slaves* (Leviticus 25:44), and it is written before this, *to give you the land of Canaan* (ibid. 38), it was known to the Sages of blessed memory that not specifically [those] from the progeny of Canaan and those in their land would be called Canaanite slaves. For the law is the same for all other nations: for them too the law of the Canaanite slave applies in every respect.

So too, if an Israelite was conjugally intimate with a Canaanite slave woman, i.e. a woman of the [heathen] nations whom one of the ⟨451⟩ Israelites bought, then any child born to her and the Israelite is as a

הִיא שִׁפְחָתוֹ שֶׁל אוֹתוֹ יִשְׂרָאֵל שֶׁבָּא עָלֶיהָ; וְכֵן אֶחָד מִן הָאֻמּוֹת שֶׁבָּא עַל שִׁפְחָה כְּנַעֲנִית שֶׁלָּנוּ, הֲרֵי הַבֵּן עֶבֶד כְּנַעֲנִי—שֶׁנֶּאֱמַר: אֲשֶׁר הוֹלִידוּ בְּאַרְצְכֶם; אֲבָל עֶבֶד שֶׁלָּנוּ שֶׁבָּא עַל אַחַת מִן הָאֻמּוֹת, אֵין הַבֵּן עֶבֶד, שֶׁהָעֶבֶד אֵין לוֹ יְחוּס.

וּבְגֵר תּוֹשָׁב, כְּלוֹמַר גּוֹי שֶׁקִּבֵּל שֶׁלֹּא לַעֲבֹד עֲבוֹדָה זָרָה וְהוּא שׁוֹכֵן בְּאַרְצֵנוּ, שֶׁמָּכַר עַצְמוֹ לְיִשְׂרָאֵל, הֲרֵי דִּינוֹ כְּעֶבֶד כְּנַעֲנִי.

וְאָמְרוּ זִכְרוֹנָם לִבְרָכָה בְּעִנְיַן עֶבֶד כְּנַעֲנִי, שֶׁמְּטַפֵּל בּוֹ אֲדֹנָיו עַד שָׁנָה: אִם רוֹצֶה לִכְפֹּר בַּעֲבוֹדָה זָרָה וּלְהַנִּיחָהּ וְשֶׁיִּמּוֹל וְיִטְבֹּל לְשֵׁם עַבְדוּת וְיִתְחַיֵּב בְּמִצְווֹת שֶׁהַנָּשִׁים יִשְׂרְאֵלִיּוֹת חַיָּבוֹת בָּהֶן, מוּטָב; וְאִם לָאו, אָסוּר לָנוּ לְהַשְׁהוֹתָם בְּבֵיתֵנוּ יוֹתֵר מִי"ב חֹדֶשׁ, אֶלָּא מוֹכְרִין אוֹתָן מִיָּד. וְעַל אֵלֶּה הָעֲבָדִים שֶׁמָּלוּ וְטָבְלוּ לְשֵׁם עַבְדוּת נִצְטַוִּינוּ לַעֲבֹד בָּהֶן לְעוֹלָם.

וּמִשָּׁרְשֵׁי הַמִּצְוָה, לְפִי שֶׁעַם יִשְׂרָאֵל הֵם מִבְחַר הַמִּין הָאֱנוֹשִׁי וְנִבְרְאוּ לְהַכִּיר בּוֹרְאָם וְלַעֲבֹד לְפָנָיו, וּרְאוּיִּים לִהְיוֹת לָהֶם עֲבָדִים לְשַׁמֵּשׁ אוֹתָם; וְאִם אֵין לָהֶם עֲבָדִים מִן הָאֻמּוֹת, עַל־כָּל־פָּנִים יִצְטָרְכוּ לְהִשְׁתַּעְבֶּד בַּאֲחֵיהֶם, וְלֹא יוּכְלוּ לְהִשְׁתַּדֵּל בַּעֲבוֹדָתוֹ בָּרוּךְ הוּא; עַל־כֵּן נִצְטַוִּינוּ לְהַחֲזִיק בְּאֵלּוּ לְתַשְׁמִישֵׁנוּ אַחַר שֶׁהֻכְשְׁרוּ וְנֶעֶקְרָה עֲבוֹדָה זָרָה מִפִּיהֶם וְלֹא יִהְיוּ לְמוֹקֵשׁ בְּבָתֵּינוּ.

וְזֶהוּ שֶׁאָמַר הַכָּתוּב אַחַר־כֵּן: וּבַאֲחֵיכֶם בְּנֵי יִשְׂרָאֵל אִישׁ בְּאָחִיו לֹא תִרְדֶּה, כְּלוֹמַר וּבְכֵן לֹא תִצְטָרְכוּ לְהִשְׁתַּעְבֵּד בַּאֲחֵיכֶם וְתִהְיוּ כֻּלְּכֶם נְכוֹנִים לַעֲבוֹדַת הַשֵּׁם. וְאַף־עַל־פִּי שֶׁיֵּשׁ בְּמַשְׁמָעוֹת הַכָּתוּב שֶׁיָּבוֹא לְהַזְהִיר שֶׁלֹּא לְהִשְׁתַּעְבֵּד בַּעֲבוֹדַת פֶּרֶךְ בְּעֶבֶד עִבְרִי, שִׁבְעִים פָּנִים לַכְּתוּבִים.

5. So TB Yevamoth 22a.

6. MT *hilchoth gérushin* x 19.

7. MT *hilchoth 'avadim* ix 3, based on TB Yevamoth 78b (*Kessef Mishneh*).

8. His sons do not automatically have his status.

9. MT *ibid.* 2, based on TB Yevamoth 45a (*Kessef Mishneh*).

10. TB Yevamoth 48b.

Canaanite slave in every respect,[5] even if she is the slave of that Israelite who was thus intimate with her.[6] So likewise, if someone from the nations was thus intimate with a Canaanite woman slave of ours, the son is a Canaanite slave: for it is stated, *which they have begotten in your land* (Leviticus 25:45).[7] But if a [heathen] slave of ours was conjugally intimate with a woman from the nations, the son is not a slave: for a slave has no lineage.[8]

The same holds true for a *gér toshav*, which [term] denotes a heathen who accepted [the obligation] not to worship idols, and dwells in our land [of Israel], who sold himself to an Israelite—he is under the same law as a Canaanite (heathen) slave.[9]

Our Sages of blessed memory taught[10] regarding a Canaanite slave that his master is to devote himself to him up to [the end of] a year. If he wishes to renounce idolatry and abandon it, and then undergo circumcision and ritual immersion for the state of servitude, so to accept the duty of those precepts which Israelite women are obligated to observe, well and good. If not, we are forbidden to retain them in our homes more than twelve months, but they must rather be sold at once. It is about those slaves who undergo circumcision and ritual immersion for the purpose of servitude, that we were commanded to make bondservants of them forever.

Now, at the root of the precept lies the reason that the people Israel are the chosen of the human race, created to acknowledge their Creator and worship before Him. They are therefore worthy to have servants to attend upon them; and if they had no servants from the nations, they would in any case need to make servants of their brethren, who would then be unable to devote their efforts to His worship (blessed is He). Therefore we were commanded to maintain possession of these for our service after they shall have been made acceptable, idolatry having been rooted out of their mouths, so that they should not be a snare in our homes.

This is why Scripture states afterward, *but over your brethren the people of Israel, one over another, you shall not rule with harshness* (Leviticus 25:46). In other words, in this way you will have no need to make servants of your brethren, and you will all be ready for the service and worship of the Eternal Lord. Even though it lies in the sense of the verse that it comes to caution [us] not to make a Hebrew servant do harsh, crushing labor, there are seventy aspects [of meaning] to the verses of Scripture.

וּמֵהֱיוֹת יְסוֹד הַמִּצְוָה כְּדֵי שֶׁיַּרְבּוּ בְנֵי־אָדָם בַּעֲבוֹדַת בּוֹרְאָם בָּרוּךְ הוּא, הִתִּירוּ
חֲכָמִים זִכְרוֹנָם לִבְרָכָה לַעֲבֹר עַל מִצְוָה זוֹ בְּכָל עֵת שֶׁבִּטּוּל מִצְוָה זוֹ יִהְיֶה גּוֹרֵם
לְמִצְוָה אַחֶרֶת, וַאֲפִלּוּ בִּשְׁבִיל מִצְוָה דְרַבָּנָן אִם הִיא מִצְוָה דְרַבִּים, כְּגוֹן שֶׁלֹּא הָיוּ
עֲשָׂרָה בְּבֵית הַכְּנֶסֶת וּצְרִיכִין לְשַׁחְרֵר הָעֶבֶד וּלְהַשְׁלִים הַמִּנְיָן.

וְאַל יִקְשֶׁה עָלֶיךָ: וְאֵיךְ נִדְחָה מִצְוַת עֲשֵׂה זוֹ דְאוֹרַיְתָא בִּשְׁבִיל מִצְוָה דְרַבָּנָן?
כִּי מִפְּנֵי שֶׁיְּסוֹד הַמִּצְוָה אֵינוּ אֶלָּא כְדֵי לְהַרְבּוֹת עֲבוֹדָתוֹ בָּרוּךְ הוּא, אַחַר
שֶׁבְּשִׁחְרוּרוֹ עַכְשָׁיו נַעֲשֵׂית מִצְוָה, וְעוֹד שֶׁגַּם הוּא מִתְרַבֶּה בְגוּפוֹ בְּמִצְווֹת שֶׁלֹּא
הָיָה חַיָּב קֹדֶם הַשִּׁחְרוּר, בֵּין זֶה וָזֶה אָמְרוּ זִכְרוֹנָם לִבְרָכָה שֶׁמֻּתָּר לְשַׁחְרְרוֹ, שֶׁכֵּן
קִבְּלוּ הָעִנְיָן.

מִדִּינֵי הַמִּצְוָה, מַה שֶּׁאָמְרוּ זִכְרוֹנָם לִבְרָכָה שֶׁהוּא קוֹנֶה עַצְמוֹ בְּכֶסֶף וּבִשְׁטַר־
שִׁחְרוּר וּבְרָאשֵׁי אֵבָרִים שֶׁאֵינָן חוֹזְרִין, וְהֵם כ"ד אֵיבָרִים; וְאַף־עַל־פִּי שֶׁדִּינוּ
לָצֵאת בְּרָאשֵׁי אֵבָרִים שֶׁאֵינָן חוֹזְרִין, צָרִיךְ גֵּט שִׁחְרוּר מִן הָאָדוֹן, וְכוֹפִין אֶת
רַבּוֹ לִכְתֹּב לוֹ אַחַר שֶׁחִסְּרוֹ מֵאֶחָד מכ"ד אֵיבָרִים הַיְדוּעִים.

וְאָמְרוּ זִכְרוֹנָם לִבְרָכָה שֶׁהַמּוֹכֵר עַבְדּוֹ לְגוֹיִים אוֹ לְכוּתִיִּים אוֹ אֲפִלּוּ לְגֵר
תּוֹשָׁב, יָצָא בֶן־חוֹרִין; וְכֵן יִשְׂרָאֵל הַדָּר בָּאָרֶץ שֶׁמְּכָרוֹ לְיִשְׂרָאֵל הַדָּר בְּחוּצָה־
לָאָרֶץ כְּדֵי שֶׁיּוֹצִיאֶנּוּ מִן הָאָרֶץ, יָצָא בֶן־חוֹרִין. וּכְמוֹ־כֵן אָמְרוּ זִכְרוֹנָם לִבְרָכָה
שֶׁאִם הִשִּׂיא רַבּוֹ לְעֶבֶד בַּת חוֹרִין, אוֹ הִנִּיחַ לוֹ תְּפִלִּין בְּרֹאשׁוֹ, אוֹ שֶׁאָמַר לוֹ רַבּוֹ
לִקְרוֹת שְׁלֹשָׁה פְסוּקִים בְּסֵפֶר תּוֹרָה בִּפְנֵי הַצִּבּוּר, וְכָל כַּיּוֹצֵא בְאֵלּוּ הַדְּבָרִים
שֶׁאֵינָן חַיָּבִין בָּהֶן אֶלָּא בְנֵי חוֹרִין, יָצָא לְחֵרוּת בְּכָךְ, וְכוֹפִין אֶת רַבּוֹ אַחַר־כָּךְ

---

11. TB B'rachoth 47b. (The need of a *minyan* for congregational prayer is a
requirement of the Sages.)

12. TB Kiddushin 22b.

13. *Ibid.* 24a.

14. *Ibid.* 25a.

15. *Ibid.* 24b.

16. So R. Yeruḥam, cited in *Shulḥan 'Aruch Yoreh Dē'ah* §267, 27 (gloss).

17. TB Gittin 43b–44a.

18. Members of the sect of Samaritans, ranked as Gentiles in TB Ḥullin 6a.

19. As a penalty for the master, since the sale would end the slave's observance of
those precepts that are obligatory for a woman (see six paragraphs above).

20. TB Gittin 40a.

21. See note 16.

Yet since the fundamental reason for the precept is that people should be able to increase their worship of their Creator, blessed is He, the Sages of blessed memory permitted the transgression of this precept at any time when ignoring this precept can cause another *mitzvah* [to be observed]—and this even for a *mitzvah* imposed by the Sages, if it is a precept for many [a congregation]: for instance, if there were not ten people in the synagogue and it was necessary to liberate a slave so as to complete the *minyan* (quorum for prayer).[11]

Now, let this not be a difficulty for you: How can we thrust aside this positive precept ordained by the Torah for the sake of a *mitzvah* established by the Sages? For the fundamental reason for the precept is nothing else but to increase and add to His worship (blessed is He), whereas by setting him free now a *mitzvah* will [actually] be observed, and moreover he too enlarges his personal observance to include *mitzvoth* for which he was not obligated before the emancipation. In view of both this and that, the Sages of blessed memory ruled[11] that it is permissible to set him free; for so they received the matter [in the Oral Tradition].

Among the laws of the precept, there is what the Sages of blessed memory taught: that he can acquire ownership of himself through money, a document of manumission (emancipation),[12] or [as compensation] for [the loss of one of] the major limbs or organs that do not grow back,[13] which are twenty-four limbs and organs.[14] Now, although the law is that he goes free [in compensation] for [the loss of one of] the major limbs or organs that do not grow back, he requires a document of manumission from his master,[15] and his master is to be compelled to write it for him[16] after he has made him lacking in one of the twenty-four known limbs and organs.

Our Sages of blessed memory taught, too,[17] that if someone sells his slave to heathens, Cuthites,[18] or even to a *gér toshav*, he goes out a free man.[19] So too, if an Israelite who lives in the land [of Israel] sells him to an Israelite who lives outside the land, so as to remove him from the land, he goes out a free man.[17] Likewise, they (of blessed memory) taught that if his master marries a slave off to a free woman, if he places *t'fillin* (phylacteries) on his head, or if his master tells him to read three verses in a Torah scroll before a congregation, and so anything similar to these matters, in which none but free men are obligated, he goes out to freedom through this,[20] and his master is afterward compelled to write him a writ of manumission.[21] There-

לִכְתֹּב לוֹ גֵּט שִׁחְרוּר; וּלְפִיכָךְ צָרִיךְ הָרַב לְהִזָּהֵר שֶׁלֹּא לַעֲשׂוֹת לוֹ מִכָּל אֵלּוּ
הַדְּבָרִים כְּלָל, כְּדֵי שֶׁלֹּא יְבַטֵּל מִצְוַת עֲשֵׂה זֶה, אֶלָּא־אִם־כֵּן עָשָׂה כֵן לִדְבַר מִצְוָה,
כְּמוֹ שֶׁפֵּרַשְׁנוּ. וְדִינֵי כְּתִיבַת גֵּט הַשִּׁחְרוּר וְתוֹרָתוֹ, וְיֶתֶר פְּרָטֶיהָ, בְּקִדּוּשִׁין וְגִטִּין.

וְנוֹהֶגֶת בְּכָל מָקוֹם וּבְכָל זְמַן, בִּזְכָרִים וּנְקֵבוֹת; אַף־עַל־פִּי שֶׁהַנְּקֵבוֹת אֲסוּר
לָהֶן לִקְנוֹת לָהֶן עֲבָדִים, מִפְּנֵי הַחֲשָׁד, מִכָּל־מָקוֹם אִם קָנוּ אוֹתָם, אָסוּר לָהֶן
לְשַׁחְרְרָן, אֶלָּא יִמְכְּרוּ אוֹתָם. וְעוֹבֵר עַל זֶה וְשִׁחְרֵר עַבְדּוֹ שֶׁלֹּא לִדְבַר מִצְוָה כְּמוֹ
שֶׁאָמַרְנוּ, בִּטֵּל עֲשֵׂה זֶה.

[שֶׁלֹּא לְהַנִּיחַ לְגוֹי לַעֲבֹד בְּעֶבֶד עִבְרִי הַנִּמְכָּר לוֹ]

שמח שֶׁלֹּא נַנִּיחַ הַגּוֹי הַשּׁוֹכֵן בְּאַרְצוֹתֵינוּ לְהַעֲבִיד בְּעֶבֶד עִבְרִי שֶׁמָּכַר עַצְמוֹ
לוֹ, בַּעֲבוֹדַת פֶּרֶךְ, שֶׁנֶּאֱמַר: לֹא יִרְדֶּנּוּ בְּפֶרֶךְ לְעֵינֶיךָ; וְלֹא נֹאמַר: אַחַר שֶׁזֶּה
הָעִבְרִי עָבַר עַל נַפְשׁוֹ וּמָכַר עַצְמוֹ לְגוֹי, נַנִּיחֶנּוּ לִסְבֹּל כָּל עֲבוֹדָה.

וְאָמְרוּ בְּסִפְרָא: "לֹא יִרְדֶּנּוּ בְּפֶרֶךְ לְעֵינֶיךָ", אֵין אַתָּה מְצֻוֶּה אֶלָּא לְעֵינֶיךָ;
כְּלוֹמַר שֶׁאֵין אָנוּ חַיָּבִים לַחֲזֹר עָלָיו וּלְהִכָּנֵס בְּבֵית הַגּוֹי לִרְאוֹת אִם יַעֲבִידֶנּוּ
בְּפֶרֶךְ אִם לֹא, אֶלָּא כָּל זְמַן שֶׁנִּרְאָה הַדָּבָר נִמְנָעֶנּוּ מִמֶּנּוּ.

שֹׁרֶשׁ מִצְוָה זוֹ, נִגְלֶה הוּא לְכָל רוֹאֵי הַשָּׁמֶשׁ. דִּינֶיהָ כְּלוּלִים בְּעִקָּרָהּ.

וְנוֹהֶגֶת בִּזְכָרִים וּנְקֵבוֹת, בִּזְמַן שֶׁיָּדֵינוּ תַּקִּיפָה עַל הָאֻמּוֹת, שֶׁיֵּשׁ בָּנוּ כֹּחַ
עֲלֵיהֶם לְצַוּוֹתָם לַעֲשׂוֹת דָּבָר אוֹ שֶׁלֹּא לַעֲשׂוֹתוֹ. וְעוֹבֵר עַל זֶה וְרָאָה הַגּוֹי מַעֲבִיד
הַיִּשְׂרָאֵל בַּעֲבוֹדַת פֶּרֶךְ, וְיֵשׁ כֹּחַ בְּיָדוֹ לְמָנְעוֹ וְלֹא מְנָעוֹ, עוֹבֵר עַל לָאו זֶה, אֲבָל
אֵין מַלְקִין אוֹתוֹ עָלָיו, לְפִי שֶׁאֵין בּוֹ מַעֲשֶׂה.

---

22. See § 344, note 6.

§348　　1. The paragraph is based on ShM negative precept §260.
　　　　2. Sifra, *b'har*, *perek* 8, 8.

fore a master has to take care not to do any of these things at all, so that he will not disobey this positive precept—unless he does so for the sake of a *mitzvah*, as we explained.

The laws on writing a document of manumission and its proper form, and the rest of its details, are in the tractates *Gittin* and *Kiddushin*. It applies everywhere, at everytime, for both man and woman. Although women are forbidden to buy male slaves, on account of suspicion,[22] nevertheless, if they did purchase them, they are forbidden to set them free, but should rather sell them. If someone transgressed this and liberated his slave not for the sake of a *mitzvah* as we described, he would disobey this positive precept.

[NOT TO LET A HEATHEN PUT A HEBREW MANSERVANT TO HARSH WORK]

348 that we should not allow a heathen who dwells in our lands to make a Hebrew servant who sold himself to him, do crushing, oppressive work: for it is stated, *he shall not rule with harshness over him in your sight* (Leviticus 25:53). We should not say, "Since this Hebrew has sinned against himself and sold himself to a heathen, let us leave him to endure all the labor."[1]

It was taught in the Midrash *Sifra*:[2] "he shall not rule with harshness over him in your sight"—you are commanded no further than "in your sight." In other words, we are not obligated to follow him about and enter the heathen's house to see if he is working him harshly or not; rather, at any time that we may see this matter, we are to prevent him from it.

The root reason for this precept is clear to all who see the sun. Its laws are included in its central thought [given above].

It applies to both man and woman, at a time that our hand is mighty over the nations, when we have power over them to command them to do something or not do it. If someone transgressed this, seeing a heathen make an Israelite do crushing, oppressive work, when he had the power in his hand to prevent him, and he did not prevent him, he would [thus] violate this negative precept. But he would not be given whiplashes for it, since it [his transgression] entailed no physical action.

[שֶׁלֹּא נִשְׁתַּחֲוֶה עַל אֶבֶן מַשְׂכִּית אֲפִלּוּ לַשֵּׁם]

שמט שֶׁלֹּא נִשְׁתַּחֲוֶה עַל אֶבֶן מַשְׂכִּית, אֲפִלּוּ לַיָי בָּרוּךְ הוּא, שֶׁנֶּאֱמַר: וְאֶבֶן מַשְׂכִּית לֹא תִתְּנוּ בְּאַרְצְכֶם לְהִשְׁתַּחֲוֹת עָלֶיהָ; וְאֶבֶן מַשְׂכִּית תִּקָּרֵא אֶבֶן מְצֻיֶּרֶת, וְכֵן אַבְנֵי גָזִית מְגוֹרָרוֹת בִּמְגֵרָה בִּכְלַל אִסּוּר אֶבֶן מַשְׂכִּית.

וּמִשָּׁרְשֵׁי הַמִּצְוָה, כָּתַב הָרַמְבַּ"ם זִכְרוֹנוֹ לִבְרָכָה שֶׁהוּא לְפִי שֶׁהָיוּ עוֹשִׂין כֵּן לַעֲבוֹדָה זָרָה: יָשִׂימוּ אֲבָנִים מְצֻיָּרוֹת נָאֶה לִפְנֵי הַצֶּלֶם, וְהָיוּ מִשְׁתַּחֲוִים עָלֶיהָ לְפָנָיו. וְאֶפְשַׁר לוֹמַר גַּם־כֵּן שֶׁהַטַּעַם מִפְּנֵי שֶׁנִּרְאֶה כְּמִשְׁתַּחֲוֶה לָאֶבֶן עַצְמָהּ; אַחַר שֶׁהֱכִינוּהָ וְצִיְּרוּהָ וְהִיא נָאֶה, יֵשׁ מָקוֹם לַחֲשָׁד.

אֲבָל הַמִּשְׁתַּחֲוֶה עַל גַּבֵּי בְגָדִים נָאִים, אֵין שָׁם מָקוֹם לַחֲשָׁד, שֶׁהַבֶּגֶד דָּבָר שֶׁהוּא כָּלֶה בִּמְהֵרָה, וְלֹא יַעֲשֵׂנּוּ בְרִיָּה אֱלוֹהוֹ; אֲבָל הָאֶבֶן, שֶׁהוּא דָבָר קַיָּם וְיֵשׁ לָהּ שַׂר בַּשָּׁמַיִם — וּכְמוֹ שֶׁאָמְרוּ זִכְרוֹנָם לִבְרָכָה בְּחֻלִּין: הָא דַאֲמַר לְהַר, הָא דַאֲמַר לְגַדָּא דְהַר — יִפֹּל בָּהֶם הַחַשָׁד, וְהַתּוֹרָה תַּרְחִיק הָאָדָם הַרְבֵּה מִלַּעֲשׂוֹת דָּבָר שֶׁיֵּחָשֵׁד בּוֹ; וְעוֹד, שֶׁלֹּא יִכָּשְׁלוּ אַחֲרָיו.

מִדִּינֵי הַמִּצְוָה, מַה שֶּׁאָמְרוּ זִכְרוֹנָם לִבְרָכָה שֶׁאֵין חִיּוּב מַלְקוּת בָּזֶה אֶלָּא בִּפְשׁוּט יָדַיִם וְרַגְלַיִם, שֶׁנִּמְצָא כֻלּוֹ מוּטָל עַל הָאֶבֶן, שֶׁכֵּן בָּא הַפֵּרוּשׁ הַמְקֻבָּל, שֶׁזּוֹ הִיא הִשְׁתַּחֲוָיָה הָאֲמוּרָה בַּתּוֹרָה; אֲבָל בְּלֹא פְשׁוּט יָדַיִם וְרַגְלַיִם אֵין בּוֹ מַלְקוֹת, אֲבָל מַכִּין הָעוֹשֶׂה כֵן מַכַּת מַרְדוּת. וּלְעִנְיַן עֲבוֹדָה זָרָה אֵין חִלּוּק בִּפְשׁוּט יָדַיִם וְרַגְלַיִם, אֶלָּא מִשָּׁעָה שֶׁיִּכְבֹּשׁ הָאָדָם פָּנָיו בַּקַּרְקַע לְפָנֶיהָ, נִסְקָל.

וּמַה שֶּׁאָמְרוּ שֶׁאִם פָּרַס מַחְצְלָאוֹת עַל רִצְפַּת הָאֲבָנִים וְכִסָּה אוֹתָן, מֻתָּר לְהִשְׁתַּחֲווֹת עֲלֵיהֶם; וּמַה שֶּׁאָמְרוּ זִכְרוֹנָם לִבְרָכָה דְּבְכָל מָקוֹם הוּא הָאִסּוּר חוּץ

---

§349   1. The Hebrew now adds, "and *e-ven maskith* is what a figured stone is called" (as the term is generally translated and rendered here, and as R. Abraham ibn Ezra and Rashbam explain it).

2. Our author derives this perhaps from the law that while this injunction applied to the land of Israel, it did not apply in the Sanctuary court (see four paragraphs below), and there, according to TB Yoma 43b (and Rashi), the floor was paved with smooth rectangular stones in regular rows (MY).

3. ShM negative precept §12.

4. His object of worship.

5. I.e. even if he intends no wrong, others may think as a result that idol-worship of this sort is permissible.

6. TB M'gillah 22b.

7. I.e. of something forbidden by the Sages; MT *hilchoth 'avodath kochavim* vi 8 (see *Kessef Mishneh*); see also §24, note 14.

8. TB Horayoth 4a.

9. MT *ibid.* 7.

[THE PROHIBITION AGAINST PROSTRATING OURSELVES
ON A FIGURED STONE]

349 that we should not prostrate ourselves in worship on a figured stone, even to the Eternal Lord, blessed is He: for it is stated, *and you shall not place any figured stone in your land, to bow down on it* (Leviticus 26:1).[1] So also, hewn stones dressed (smoothed) with a scraper are included under the prohibition against a figured stone.[2]

As for the root purpose of the precept, Rambam of blessed memory wrote[3] that it is because they [the heathen] would do this for idolatry. They would place stones figured with beautiful workmanship before the idol, and would prostrate themselves on that before him. It is possible to say also that the reason is that it appears as though one were prostrating himself [in worship] to the stone itself. Since it was prepared and inscribed with a picture, and it is beautiful, there is room for the suspicion.

If a person prostrates himself on pretty cloths, though, there is no room there for suspicion: for a cloth is something which rapidly wears away, and no human being would make it his god.[4] Stone, however, is an enduring material, and it has a guardian angel in heaven; as the Sages of blessed memory said in the Talmud tractate *Ḥullin* (40a): "in one case he spoke to the mountain; in the other case he spoke to the spirit of the mountain." Hence suspicion can fall on them; and the Torah would keep a man very far from doing anything about which he could become suspect [of idol-worship]. And furthermore—so that others should not come to grief in his wake.[5]

Among the laws of the precept there is what the Sages of blessed memory taught:[6] that no penalty of whiplashes is incurred for anything but having the hands and feet outspread, so that the person is entirely prostrate on the stone. For so the traditional, received explanation was given, that this is the "bowing down" stated in the Torah. Without the spreading of hands and feet, though, no whipping is incurred. But one who does this is given whiplashes for disobedience.[7] In regard to idolatry, however, the spreading of hands and feet makes no matter. Rather, from the time a man presses his face to the ground before it, he is to be stoned to death.[8]

Then there is what the Sages said:[9] that if a person placed mats on a floor of stones, covering them, it is permissible to prostrate oneself on them. There is, too what they (of blessed memory) said:[6] that the prohibition applies everywhere except at the Sanctuary,

מִן הַמִּקְדָּשׁ, שֶׁמֻּתָּר לְהִשְׁתַּחֲוֹת לַיי עַל הָאֲבָנִים, שֶׁנֶּאֱמַר "לֹא תִתְּנוּ בְּאַרְצְכֶם", בְּאַרְצְכֶם אִי אַתֶּם מִשְׁתַּחֲוִים, אֲבָל אַתֶּם מִשְׁתַּחֲוִים עַל הָאֲבָנִים הַמְפֻצָּלוֹת בַּמִּקְדָּשׁ.

וְזֶה הָעִנְיָן לְפִי הַדּוֹמֶה מִן הַטַּעַם שֶׁאָמַרְתִּי, כִּי יֵחָשְׁדוּ בְּנֵי-אָדָם הַמִּשְׁתַּחֲוֶה שֶׁלֹּא יַעֲשֶׂה הָאֲבָנִים אֱלוֹהַּ, וּמִפְּנֵי שֶׁהַבַּיִת הַקָּדוֹשׁ נִבְחַר לַעֲבוֹדַת הַשֵּׁם בָּרוּךְ הוּא, וּמְפֻרְסָם לְכָל הָעוֹלָם כַּשֶּׁמֶשׁ בַּחֲצִי הַשָּׁמַיִם שֶׁאֵין עֲבוֹדָה שָׁם בִּלְתִּי לַיי לְבַדּוֹ, אֵין שָׁם מָקוֹם לַחֲשָׁד. אֲבָל אִם כְּטַעַם הָרַמְבַּ"ם זִכְרוֹנוֹ לִבְרָכָה, שֶׁהוּא לְהַרְחִיק עֲבוֹדָה זָרָה שֶׁהָיוּ עוֹשִׂין לָהּ כֵּן, כָּל-שֶׁכֵּן שֶׁהָיָה רָאוּי לְהַרְחִיק כָּל הַדּוֹמֶה לָהּ מִמְּקוֹם הַמִּקְדָּשׁ, שֶׁלֹּא לְפַגֵּל מַחֲשֶׁבֶת הַמִּשְׁתַּחֲוֶה לַשֵּׁם בְּזִכְרוֹ אוֹתָם. וְאוּלָם יָדַעְתִּי כִּי יֵשׁ לְרַבֵּנוּ טַעַם נָכוֹן בְּכָל אֲשֶׁר יִפְנֶה, וְנֶעֱלָם לִפְעָמִים מֵחֶסְרוֹן הַשּׁוֹמֵעַ.

וְיֶתֶר פְּרָטֵי הַמִּצְוָה, בִּגְמָרָא מְגִלָּה.

וְנוֹהֶגֶת בְּכָל מָקוֹם וּבְכָל זְמַן, בִּזְכָרִים וּנְקֵבוֹת. וְעוֹבֵר עַל זֶה וְהִשְׁתַּחֲוָה עַל הָאֲבָנִים בְּפִשּׁוּט יָדַיִם וְרַגְלַיִם, לוֹקֶה; וְשׁוֹמֵר מִצְוָה, אַשְׁרָיו.

☙ אִם בְּחֻקֹּתַי

יֵשׁ בָּהּ י"ב מִצְווֹת, ז' מִצְווֹת עֲשֵׂה וְה' מִצְווֹת לֹא-תַעֲשֶׂה

[מִצְוַת מַעֲרִיךְ אָדָם שֶׁיִּתֵּן דָּמָיו הַקְּצוּבִין בַּתּוֹרָה]

שׁנ לָדוּן בְּעֶרְכֵי אָדָם, כְּלוֹמַר מִי שֶׁאָמַר "עֶרְכִּי עָלַי" אוֹ "עֶרֶךְ פְּלוֹנִי עָלַי" שֶׁיִּתֵּן לַכֹּהֵן כְּפִי הָעֵרֶךְ שֶׁאָמַר, וְלֹא פָחוֹת, כְּמוֹ שֶׁבָּא בַּכָּתוּב מְפֹרָשׁ בְּזָכָר וּנְקֵבָה וּלְפִי חֶשְׁבּוֹן הַשָּׁנִים, שֶׁנֶּאֱמַר: אִישׁ כִּי יַפְלִא נֶדֶר בְּעֶרְכְּךָ נְפָשֹׁת לַיי.

---

10. I.e. a pavement of stones set evenly; see note 2. (The word *m'futzaloth*, "smooth scraped," from the root *pa-tzél*—see Genesis 30: 37—is used by Rambam in this sense.)

11. Expression based on Proverbs 29:18.

where it is permitted to prostrate oneself to the Lord on the stones; for it is stated, *you shall not place in your land* (Leviticus 26:1): in your land you may not prostrate yourself, but you are to do so on the smooth scraped stones[10] in the Sanctuary.

Now, this distinction, as it would seem, is for the reason I stated: that a person who thus bows down can be suspected that perhaps he might have made a divine entity of the stones. But since the holy Temple was chosen for the service of the Eternal Lord, blessed is He, and it is widely known in all the world, as clear as the sun in mid-sky, that there is no service or worship there except to the Lord alone, no room for suspicion exists there. If, however, it is for the reason of Rambam of blessed memory, that it is in order to keep idolatry far removed, since they [the heathen] would thus serve it [an idol, in worship], then it would be all the more certainly proper to remove anything similar to it from the hallowed place, so as not to befoul the thought of one who prostrates himself to the Lord by reminding him of them. Nevertheless, I know that our master teacher has a right and proper reason wherever he turns, although it is inscrutable at times on account of a shortcoming in the listener.

The remaining details of the precept are in the Talmud tractate *M'gillah* (22a). It is in effect in every place, at every time, for both man and woman. If a person violated this and bowed down on stones, [prostrating himself] with hands and feet outspread, he should receive whiplashes. But happy is he who keeps a *mitzvah*.[11]

sidrah b' ḥukothai
(Leviticus 26:3–27:34)

It contains twelve precepts: seven positive and five negative precepts.

[THE PRECEPT OF ONE WHO VOWS A PERSON'S VALUA-
TION, THAT HE SHOULD GIVE HIS PRESCRIBED PRICE]

350 to carry out the valuation of a man; in other words, if a person said, "My valuation be upon me," or "The valuation of so-and-so be upon me," he should give the *kohen* the valuation in accord with what he said [vowed], and not less, as it is distinctly given in the Writ for both man and woman, according to the number of years (age)—as it is stated, *When a man shall utter a clear vow of persons to the Lord, at the valuation* (Leviticus 27:2).

וְעִנְיַן הָעֲרָכִין הוּא מִכְּלַל נִדְרֵי הֶקְדֵּשׁ, וּלְפִיכָךְ חַיָּבִין עֲלֵיהֶן מִשּׁוּם "לֹא יַחֵל
דְּבָרוֹ" וּמִשּׁוּם "לֹא תְאַחֵר לְשַׁלְּמוֹ" וּמִשּׁוּם "כְּכָל הַיֹּצֵא מִפִּיו יַעֲשֶׂה".

מִשָּׁרְשֵׁי הַמִּצְוָה, לְפִי שֶׁהָאָדָם לֹא יִשְׁתַּתֵּף בָּעֶלְיוֹנִים זוּלָתִי בְדִבּוּר, וְהוּא כָּל
הַחֵלֶק הַנִּכְבָּד שֶׁבּוֹ, וְזֶה יִקָּרֵא בָאָדָם נֶפֶשׁ חַיָּה, כִּדְמְתַרְגֵּם אַנְקְלוֹס: וַהֲוַת בְּאָדָם
לְרוּחַ מְמַלְּלָא; כִּי שְׁאָר חֶלְקֵי הַגּוּף מֵתִים הֵם, וְאִם יַפְסִיד הָאָדָם זֶה הַחֵלֶק הַטּוֹב,
יִשָּׁאֵר הַגּוּף מֵת וְכִכְלִי אֵין חֵפֶץ בּוֹ; עַל-כֵּן נִתְחַיֵּב לְקַיֵּם דִּבּוּרוֹ בַּמֶּה שֶׁהוּא
מִשְׁתַּמֵּשׁ בּוֹ בְּדִבְרֵי שָׁמַיִם מִכָּל-מָקוֹם, כְּגוֹן בְּהֶקְדֵּשׁוֹת וּבְכָל דִּבְרֵי הַצְּדָקוֹת.

וּבְיֶתֶר כָּל עִנְיְנֵי הָעוֹלָם, אַף-עַל-פִּי שֶׁלֹּא נִתְיַחֲדוּ בָהֶן עֲשֵׂה וְלָאו, צִוּוּ חֲכָמִים
וְהִזְהִירוּ כַּמָּה אַזְהָרוֹת שֶׁלֹּא יְשַׁנֶּה אָדָם בְּדִבּוּרוֹ; גַּם תִּקְּנוּ לְקַלֵּל הַמְשַׁנֶּה בְדִבּוּרוֹ
כָּל זְמַן שֶׁנַּעֲשָׂה בָעִנְיָן מַעֲשֶׂה, וְזֶהוּ עִנְיַן "מִי שֶׁפָּרַע" הַנִּזְכָּר לָהֶם בְּהַרְבֵּה
מְקוֹמוֹת, שֶׁאָמְרוּ בוֹ: דְּבָרִים וּמָעוֹת קָאִי〈בַּאֲבָל אָמְרוּ וְכוּלֵי, כְּמוֹ שֶׁבָּא בַגְּמָרָא
בְּפֶרֶק הַזָּהָב; וּכְבָר הֶאֱרַכְתִּי הַרְבֵּה בְּשָׁרְשֵׁי שְׁבוּעוֹת וּנְדָרִים בְּסֵדֶר "וַיִּשְׁמַע
יִתְרוֹ" לֹא תַעֲשֶׂה ה' [סִי' ל'].

מִדִּינֵי הַמִּצְוָה, מַה שֶּׁאָמְרוּ זִכְרוֹנָם לִבְרָכָה שֶׁשָּׁנִים אֵלוּ הָאֲמוּרִים בָּעֲרָכִין,
כָּךְ קִבַּלְנוּ, שֶׁהֵם שָׁנִים הַנִּמְנִין מִיּוֹם לְיוֹם, כְּלוֹמַר מִיּוֹם הַלֵּדָה; וְכָל הַשְּׁקָלִים
הָאֲמוּרִים שָׁם גַּם-כֵּן, הֵם שִׁקְלֵי הַקֹּדֶשׁ; וְשֶׁקֶל הַקֹּדֶשׁ יָדַעְנוּ בַּקַּבָּלָה שֶׁהוּא מִשְׁקַל
שְׁלֹשׁ מֵאוֹת וְעֶשְׂרִים שְׂעוֹרוֹת שֶׁל כֶּסֶף טָהוֹר, וּכְבָר הוֹסִיפוּ חֲכָמִים עָלָיו
וְעָשׂוּ מִשְׁקָלוֹ כְּמִשְׁקַל הַמַּטְבֵּעַ הַנִּקְרָא סֶלַע בִּזְמַן בַּיִת-שֵׁנִי, שֶׁהוּא מִשְׁקַל שְׁלֹשׁ
מֵאוֹת וְאַרְבַּע וּשְׁמוֹנִים שְׂעוֹרָה בֵּינוֹנִית.

וְסֶלַע זֶה, אָמְרוּ זִכְרוֹנָם לִבְרָכָה שֶׁהוּא אַרְבַּע דִּינָר, וְהַדִּינָר שֵׁשׁ מָעִין, וּמָעָה

§350   1. Since the expression in Scripture about valuations is, *When a man shall utter a clear vow*, etc. (Leviticus 27:2).

2. So Sifra, *b'ḥukothai, parashah* 3, 4.

3. In his translation of Genesis 2:7.

4. See §336, note 31.

5. I.e. if two have agreed verbally on some business transaction, and money has consequently changed hands; i.e. action was taken.

6. I.e. the Mishnah teaches that the man has the legal right to break his word, but the Sages said (ruled) that the imprecation (§336, note 31) is pronounced over him. In the Hebrew text, the word *ka'i* ("involve") is found in the manuscripts and the first edition; it is subsequently found as *kani* ("effect possession"); the next word, *v'aval*, is likewise in the manuscripts, but from the first edition on it appears as *'aval* ("but"). The passage would then mean: . . . about which they said, "Words and money effect possession," but they said, etc. As this is halachically untenable (possession is effected only by a suitable action), MY emends *kani* to *lo kani*: "Words and money do not effect possession," etc. The version of the manuscripts is awkward in its phrasing, and my rendering is more conjectural than certain, whereas the emended version is very plausible, and may be correct—which would mean that the manuscript version is the

The subject of valuations is part of the general topic of vows of consecration.[1] Therefore punishment is incurred over them for violating the injunctions, *he shall not break his word* (Numbers 30:3, §407), *you shall not be slack to pay it* (Deuteronomy 23:22, §574),[2] and *he shall do according to all that proceeds out of his mouth* (Numbers 30:3, §406).

At the root of the precept lies the reason that a man becomes partner in the supernal realm in no other way but through speech. This is the entire honorable, distinguished part of him. This is called in man the "living spirit"; as Onkelos renders it,[3] "there was in man a *speaking* spirit." For all other parts of the body die and perish. But if a man should lose this good part, the body will remain [already] dead, as an instrument for which there is no desire. Therefore was he given the obligation to fulfill his word, his speech, which he uses for matters of Heaven, under all circumstances: for example, regarding consecrations, and all matters of charity.

Now, in all other matters of the world, even though no positive or negative precept was given about them specifically, the Sages ordained and gave many admonitions that a man should never deviate from his word. Moreover, they instituted an imprecation for one who would deviate from his word, as long as it is done in regard to some activity. This is the imprecation, "He who exacted punishment,"[4] mentioned by them in many instances, wherein they said concerning it [that] words and money [once exchanged][5] involve [the teaching of the Mishnah], "But they said," etc.[6]—as we read in the Talmud, in the fourth chapter of *Bava M'tzi'a* (44a). I wrote previously at great length about the root reasons for [the precepts of] oaths and vows, in the fifth negative precept of *sidrah yithro* (§30).

Among the laws of the precept there is what the Sages of blessed memory taught:[7] that those years [of age] mentioned regarding valuations, as we received [the teaching in the Oral Tradition], mean years counted from day to day, i.e. from the day of birth; and likewise, all shekels mentioned there are holy shekels.[8] As for the holy shekel, we know through the Oral Tradition that it has the weight of 320 kernels of barley, [and is made] of pure silver. Long ago, however, our Sages enlarged it and made its weight equal to that of a coin called a *sela* at the time of the second Temple, which had a weight of 384 medium-sized kernels of barley.[9]

Now, this *sela*, our Sages of blessed memory said, was [worth] four *denarii*, a *denar* being six *ma'ah*; and a *ma'ah* was what, in Moses'

הִיא הַנִּקְרֵאת בִּימֵי מֹשֶׁה גֵּרָה — כִּדְמְתַרְגֵּם אָנְקְלוֹס גֵּרָה, מָעָה — וּמִשְׁקָלָהּ י"ו שְׂעוֹרוֹת.

וּמַה שֶּׁאָמְרוּ גַּם־כֵּן בְּעִנְיָן זֶה שֶׁאֵין חִלּוּק בַּעֲרָכִין בֵּין יָפֶה אוֹ כָעוּר אוֹ חוֹלֶה אוֹ סוּמָא אוֹ גִדֵּם, אֶלָּא הַכֹּל נֶעֱרָכִין לְפִי הַשָּׁנִים כְּמוֹ שֶׁצִּוְּתָה הַתּוֹרָה בָּהֶן; וּמַה שֶּׁאָמְרוּ שֶׁהַדָּמִים אֵינָם כַּעֲרָכִין, שֶׁהָאוֹמֵר "דְּמֵי פְלוֹנִי עָלַי" נוֹתֵן כַּמָּה שֶׁהוּא שָׁוֶה, וְאֵין מַשְׁגִּיחִין בַּשָּׁנִים כְּלָל, שֶׁלֹּא צִוְּתָה הַתּוֹרָה לָתֵת עֶרֶךְ לְפִי הַשָּׁנִים אֶלָּא בְּמַעֲרִיךְ דַּוְקָא, כְּמוֹ שֶׁפֵּרַשְׁנוּ.

וְהָעֲרָכִין וְהַדָּמִים סְתָמָן לְבֶדֶק הַבַּיִת, וְנוֹתְנִין הַכֹּל (לְעוֹלָם) בַּלִּשְׁכָּה שֶׁהָיְתָה מוּכֶנֶת בַּמִּקְדָּשׁ לְקָדְשֵׁי בֶדֶק הַבַּיִת.

וְדִין טוּמְטוּם וְאַנְדְּרוֹגִינוֹס וְגוֹי וְעֶבֶד שֶׁהֶעֱרִיכוּ אוֹ שֶׁנֶּעֶרְכוּ; וְדִין הַגּוֹסֵס, שֶׁאֵין לוֹ לֹא עֶרֶךְ וְלֹא דָמִים; וְדִין הַיּוֹצֵא לַהֵרָג, וְדִין הַמַּעֲרִיךְ אֵבֶר אֶחָד, וְדִין הָאוֹמֵר "מִשְׁקָלִי עָלַי", וְדִין הָאוֹמֵר "קוֹמָתִי עָלַי" אוֹ "מְלֹא קוֹמָתִי עָלַי", וְהָאוֹמֵר "הֲרֵי עָלַי כֶּסֶף וְזָהָב", וְלֹא פֵרַשׁ מֵאֵי זֶה מַטְבֵּעַ, וְדִין מִי שֶׁהֶעֱרִיךְ וְלֹא הִשִּׂיגָה יָדוֹ לִפְרֹעַ מַה שֶּׁהֶעֱרִיךְ, כֵּיצַד מְסַדְּרִין לוֹ.

וְזֶה שֶׁאָמְרוּ חֲכָמִים בְּעִנְיָן זֶה: חַיָּבֵי עֲרָכִין וְדָמִים מְמַשְׁכְּנִין אוֹתָם, וְאֵין מַחְזִירִין לָהֶם הַמַּשְׁכּוֹן בַּיּוֹם וּבַלַּיְלָה; וּמוֹכְרִין כָּל הַנִּמְצָא לָהֶם מִן הַקַּרְקַע וּמִן הַמִּטַּלְטְלִין, אֲפִלּוּ כְסוּת וּכְלֵי תַשְׁמִישׁ, וְאֵין צָרִיךְ לוֹמַר עֲבָדִים וּבְהֵמוֹת; וְאֵין מוֹכְרִין לָהֶם לֹא כְסוּת נְשׁוֹתֵיהֶם וּבְנֵיהֶם וּבְנוֹתֵיהֶם, וְלֹא אֲפִלּוּ בְּגָדִים שֶׁצְּבָעָן לִשְׁמָן, וְלֹא סַנְדָּלִים חֲדָשִׁים שֶׁלְּקָחָן לִשְׁמָן קֹדֶם שֶׁהֶעֱרִיךְ; וְכֵן הַמַּקְדִּישׁ כָּל נְכָסָיו, לֹא הִקְדִּישׁ אֶת אֵלּוּ.

וְעִנְיַן הַסִּדּוּר הוּא, שֶׁנּוֹתְנִין לוֹ, לָזֶה שֶׁיֵּשׁ עָלָיו עֲרָכִין אוֹ דָמִים, מְזוֹן שְׁלֹשִׁים

---

result of scribal errors. Without a firm basis to decide, however, I have let it stand.

7. TB 'Arachin 18b.
8. Leviticus 27:3, 25.
9. MT hilchoth sh'kalim i 2 (sources in *Kessef Mishneh*).
10. *Ibid.* 3.
11. TB 'Arachin 2a.
12. Leviticus 27:3–7.
13. Literally, money—i.e. a person's monetary value, if he were sold as a slave.
14. So TB 'Arachin 24a, T'murah 31b; Sifra, *b'hukothai*, *parashah* 4, 8; TJ Sh'kalim iv 4.
15. MT hilchoth 'arachin i 10.
16. TB 'Arachin 5b; MT *ibid.* 6.
17. I.e. another vowed to give their valuation.
18. TB 'Arachin 6b.
19. *Ibid.* 20a.
20. *Ibid.* 18a.
21. TB M'nahoth 106b.

days, was called a *gérah*—as Onkelos translates *gérah* as *ma'ah*; and its weight was sixteen kernels of barley.[10]

Then there is what the Sages likewise taught on this subject,[11] that there is no difference in valuation whether a person is handsome or ugly, ill or blind or one-handed; rather, all are given a valuation according to the years [of age], as the Torah ordained about them.[12] There is, too, what they stated:[12] that "value"[13] is not the same as "valuation" (*'arachin*); for if someone said, "The value of so-and-so be upon me" [to pay], he gives how much the other is worth, and no attention is paid to years [of age] at all. For the Torah commanded to give the valuation according to years only if a person specifically vows the "valuation," as we explained.

General, unspecified vows of valuation or value are to be given for keeping the Temple in repair;[14] and the whole is always put into the treasury that was maintained at the Sanctuary for the funds consecrated for Temple repairs.[15]

There is, further, the law about a *tumtum* [one of uncertain gender], a hermaphrodite,[11] a non-Jew,[16] or a [heathen] slave[11] who vowed a valuation or were evaluated;[17] the law of an expiring man—that his valuation and his value are nil;[18] the law about a person who goes forth [sentenced] to be put to death;[18] the law if a person vows the valuation of one organ or limb;[19] the law if someone says, "My weight be upon me" [to pay]; the law if one says, "My height be upon me," or "My full height be upon me";[20] and if one says, "I hereby take it upon myself [to give in consecration] silver and gold," and does not specify from which coin;[21] and the law if a person vowed a valuation and he did not have the means to pay the valuation he chose—how matters are arranged for him.[22]

It is about this situation that the Sages said:[22] Of those who owe valuations or values, objects are taken in pledge, and the pledged object is returned to them neither in the day nor at night; whatever is found in their possession is sold, be it landed property or movable goods— even clothing and utensils, and needless to say, slaves and livestock. However, clothes of their wives, sons or daughters are not to be sold for them, nor even clothing that he dyed with them in mind, nor new sandals (shoes) if he but bought them on their behalf before he vowed the valuation.[22] So likewise, if a person consecrates all his possessions, he has not consecrated these.[22]

⟨465⟩   This, in substance, is the arrangement: The one who bears the

יוֹם וּכְסוּת שְׁנֵים-עָשָׂר חֹדֶשׁ מִכְּסוּת הָרְאוּיָה לוֹ, וְסַנְדָּלָיו וּתְפִלָּיו, אֲבָל לֹא שְׁאָר
סְפָרִים, וּמִטָּה וּמַצָּע הָרְאוּיִּים לוֹ; אֲבָל לְאִשְׁתּוֹ וּלְבָנָיו, אַף-עַל-פִּי שֶׁהוּא חַיָּב
בִּמְזוֹנוֹתֵיהֶם וּבִכְסוּתָם, אֵין נוֹתְנִין לָהֶם מָזוֹן וּכְסוּת; וּכְשֶׁנּוֹתְנִין לוֹ לְבַדּוֹ כְּסוּת
שְׁנֵים-עָשָׂר חֹדֶשׁ, דַּוְקָא מִכְּסוּת הָרְאוּיָה לוֹ, אֲבָל הָיָה לָבוּשׁ כְּלֵי מֶשִׁי וּבְגָדִים
מְזֻהָבִין, מַעֲבִירִין אוֹתָם מֵעָלָיו, וְנוֹתְנִין לוֹ כְּסוּת הָרְאוּיָה לְאִישׁ כְּמוֹתוֹ לְחוֹל,
אֲבָל לֹא לְשַׁבָּתוֹת וְיָמִים טוֹבִים.

וְאִם הָיָה אֻמָּן, נוֹתְנִין לוֹ כְּלֵי אֻמָּנוּתוֹ, שְׁנֵי כְּלֵי אֻמָּנוּת מִכָּל מִין וָמִין; כֵּיצַד:
אִם הָיָה חָרָשׁ, נוֹתְנִין לוֹ שְׁנֵי מַעֲצָדוֹת וּשְׁנֵי מְגֵרוֹת; וְאִם הָיוּ לוֹ כֵּלִים מְרֻבִּים
מִמִּין אֶחָד וּמוּעָטִין מִמִּין אַחֵר, אֵין מוֹכְרִין מִן הַמְרֻבֶּה כְּדֵי לִקַּח לוֹ מִן הַמּוּעָט,
אֶלָּא נוֹתְנִין לוֹ שְׁנֵי כֵלִים מִן הַמְרֻבִּים וְכָל שֶׁיֵּשׁ לוֹ מִן הַמּוּעָט. וְאִם הָיָה חַמָּר אוֹ
סַפָּן, אֵין נוֹתְנִין לוֹ הַבְּהֵמָה אוֹ הַסְּפִינָה, אַף-עַל-פִּי שֶׁאֵין לָהֶם מְזוֹנוֹת אֶלָּא
מֵהֶם.

וְכֵן אִם הָיָה תַּלְמִיד-חָכָם וְאֵין לוֹ בַּמֶּה שֶׁיִּתְפַּרְנֵס כִּי-אִם בִּשְׂכַר לִמּוּדוֹ, אָמְרוּ
הַמְפָרְשִׁים שֶׁאֵין מַנִּיחִין לוֹ סְפָרָיו, שֶׁאֵין זֶה גַם-כֵּן בִּכְלַל כְּלֵי אֻמָּנוּת. וּמִכָּאן יֵשׁ
לִי רְאָיָה שֶׁעַל הַתַּלְמִיד לְהָבִיא סֵפֶר לָרַב. וְיֵשׁ מִן הַמְפָרְשִׁים שֶׁאָמְרוּ שֶׁאוֹתָהּ
מַסֶּכְתָּא שֶׁהוּא לוֹמֵד בְּאוֹתָהּ שָׁעָה, מַנִּיחִין לוֹ; וְיָפֶה אָמְרוּ, מִשּׁוּם כְּבוֹד תּוֹרָה.

וּמַה שֶׁאָמְרוּ זִכְרוֹנָם לִבְרָכָה שֶׁנִּשְׁאָלִין עַל הָעֲרָכִין וְעַל הַדָּמִים כְּדֶרֶךְ
שֶׁנִּשְׁאָלִים עַל שְׁאָר נְדָרִים וְהֶקְדֵּשׁוֹת; וְאָמְרוּ גַם-כֵּן שֶׁאִם הָיוּ בְנִכְסֵי הַמַּעֲרִיךְ
בְּהֵמוֹת אוֹ עֲבָדִים וּמַרְגָּלִיּוֹת וְאָמְרוּ הַתַּגָּרִים: אִם יִלָּקַח זֶה לְעֶבֶד זֶה כְּסוּת
בִּשְׁלִשִׁים, מַשְׁבִּיחַ בּוֹ יוֹתֵר מִשִּׁשִּׁים; וְאִם תַּמְתִּינוּ לִבְהֵמָה זוֹ עַד חֹדֶשׁ יָמִים,
מַשְׁבַּחַת הִיא כִפְלַיִם בְּדָמֶיהָ; וּמַרְגָּלִית זוֹ, אִם מַעֲלִין אוֹתָהּ לְמָקוֹם פְּלוֹנִי, תִּשְׁוֶה
מָמוֹן רַב — אֵין שׁוֹמְעִין לָהֶם כְּלָל, אֶלָּא מוֹכְרִין הַכֹּל בִּמְקוֹמָם וּבִשְׁעָתָן,
שֶׁנֶּאֱמַר: וְנָתַן אֶת הָעֶרְכְּךָ בַּיּוֹם הַהוּא קֹדֶשׁ לַיָי, וּבָא הַפֵּרוּשׁ עָלָיו שֶׁזֶּה הַכָּתוּב

---

22. TB 'Arachin 23b–24a.

23. I.e. other than the Scriptural portions on parchment which are placed within the t'fillin.

24. TB Bava M'tzi'a 113b.

25. Literally, the commentators—i.e. the authors of the commentaries on the Talmud, who constitute the early authorities (rishonim) in Jewish law.

26. Otherwise his own volumes would be his indispensable work-tools.

27. Both views are cited in Nimmuké Yoséf, TB Bava M'tzi'a ix, toward the end.

28. MT hilchoth 'arachin i 17, based on TB 'Arachin 23a.

29. See §30, paragraphs 18–20.

30. TB 'Arachin 24a.

obligation of a valuation or value is given food for thirty days and
clothing for twelve months, of a sort suitable for him, his sandals
(shoes) and his *t'fillin* (phylacteries), but no other sacred writings;[23]
and a bed and mattress suitable for him. As regards his wife and children,
however, even though he has the obligation to provide their food and
clothing, no food or garments are given them;[22] and when he alone
is given clothing for twelve months, it is specifically garments appropriate for him; but if he was dressed in silk raiment or gilded clothes,
they are removed from him. He is given clothing suitable for a man
like him for the weekdays, but not for the Sabbath and festival days.[24]

If he was a craftsman, he would be given the tools of his craft, two
working tools of every kind. How so? If he was a carpenter, he would
be given two adzes and two *m'géroth* (planes, or saws). If he had many
tools of one kind and few of another kind, some of the plentiful kind
are not to be sold in order to buy him of the scanty kind; he is rather
given two tools of the plentiful kind and whatever he has of the scanty
kind. If he was a donkey-driver or a boatman, he is not given the
beast or the ship, even though he has sustenance from nothing other
than them.

So too, if he was a Torah scholar and he had no other way of earning
a livelihood but from payment for his teaching, the authorities[25]
ruled that his volumes should not be left him, since they are not included in the category of work-tools. Well, hence I have a proof that it
is for the student to bring a text volume to the teacher.[26] However,
there are some among the authorities who said that the particular
Talmud tractate which he is studying at the time is to be left him;[27]
and they spoke well, for the sake of the honor of the Torah.

Then there is what the Sages of blessed memory said:[28] that a
release from vows of valuation and value may be sought, in the way
that it can be sought for other vows and acts of consecration.[29] And
they likewise said[30] that if among the property of the one who vowed
a valuation there were domestic animals, slaves or pearls, and merchants
said that if a garment for thirty [*denarii*] were bought for that slave his
value would increase with it by more than sixty, or, "If you wait
with this animal up to a full month, it will improve to twice its value,"
or, "If this pearl will be taken up to that certain location, it will be
worth a great sum"—they are not to be heeded at all, but everything
is rather to be sold in its place and at its time [then and there]. For it is

stated, *and he shall give the valuation in that day, as a holy thing to the*

מְלַמֵּד עַל כָּל דְּבַר הַקֹּדֶשׁ שֶׁאֵין מְפַרְנְסִין אוֹתָן, וְאֵין מַמְתִּינִין לָהֶם לְיוֹם הַשּׁוּק,
וְאֵין מוֹלִיכִין אוֹתָם מִמָּקוֹם לְמָקוֹם; וְזֶה הַכְּלָל: שֶׁאֵין לְךָ בָּהֶם אֶלָּא מְקוֹמָן
וְשַׁעֲתָן בִּלְבָד. וּבַמֶּה דְּבָרִים אֲמוּרִים, בְּמִטַּלְטְלִין, אֲבָל הַקַּרְקָעוֹת, מַכְרִיזִין
עֲלֵיהֶם שִׁשִּׁים יוֹם רְצוּפִים בֹּקֶר וָעֶרֶב, וְאַחַר־כָּךְ מוֹכְרִין אוֹתָם.

וְהוֹאִיל וְאָתָא לִידָן עִנְיַן סִדּוּר, נִכְתֹּב כָּאן מַה שֶּׁאָמְרוּ זִכְרוֹנָם לִבְרָכָה בְּעִנְיַן
סִדּוּר בְּבַעַל־חוֹב, בְּפֶרֶק הַמְקַבֵּל שָׂדֶה מֵחֲבֵרוֹ בְּבָבָא מְצִיעָא, דְּאַמְרִינַן הָתָם: תָּנֵי
תַנָּא קַמֵּיהּ דְּרַב נַחְמָן בַּר יִצְחָק: כְּדֶרֶךְ שֶׁמְּסַדְּרִין בַּעֲרָכִין, כָּךְ מְסַדְּרִין בְּבַעַל־
חוֹב; וְהֵבִיאוּ שָׁם בָּזֶה הַרְבֵּה קָשִׁיּוֹת וְתֵרוּצִין, וְסוֹף הָעִנְיָן מֵבִיא בַּגְּמָרָא מַעֲשֶׂה
דְּאֵלְיָהוּ, דְּאַשְׁכְּחֵיהּ רַבָּה בַּר אֲבוּהּ דַּהֲוָה קָאִים בְּבֵית הַקְּבָרוֹת שֶׁל גּוֹיִם. אָמַר
לֵיהּ: מַה הוּא שֶׁיְּסַדְּרוּ בְּבַעַל־חוֹב; וְרַשִׁ"י זִכְרוֹנוֹ לִבְרָכָה וַאֲחֵרִים גָּרְסֵי: מִנַּיִן
שֶׁיְּסַדְּרוּ בְּבַעַל־חוֹב, כְּלוֹמַר דִּפְשִׁיטָא לֵיהּ לְרַבָּה בַּר אֲבוּהּ דִּמְסַדְּרִין, אֲבָל הָיָה
שׁוֹאֵל מֵאֵלְיָהוּ: מֵאֵיזֶה מִקְרָא אָנוּ לְמֵדִין אוֹתוֹ; וְאַהֲדַר לֵיהּ אֵלְיָהוּ דְּהָכִי הוּא
דְּגַמְרִינַן: מִיכָה מִיכָה מֵעֲרָכִין, כְּלוֹמַר דִּכְתִיב גַּבֵּי הַלְוָאָה: וְכִי יָמוּךְ אָחִיךָ וּמָטָה
יָדוֹ עִמָּךְ וְהֶחֱזַקְתָּ בּוֹ, דְּהַיְנוּ הַלְוָאָה, כְּדִכְתִיב בְּסוֹפֵיהּ: אַל תִּקַּח מֵאִתּוֹ נֶשֶׁךְ
וְתַרְבִּית וְגוֹמֵר, וּכְתִיב בַּעֲרָכִין "וְאִם מָךְ הוּא מֵעֶרְכֶּךָ", וּבָא הַפֵּרוּשׁ הַמְקֻבָּל:
הַחֲיֵהוּ מֵעֶרְכֶּךָ.

וְגַמְרִינַן מִיכָה מִיכָה לְסַדֵּר בְּבַעַל־חוֹב כְּדֶרֶךְ שֶׁמְּסַדְּרִין בַּעֲרָכִין, וְאֵין לְפַקְפֵּק
אַחַר דְּבָרֵי אֵלְיָהוּ, וְכֵן פָּסְקוּ כָּל הַגְּאוֹנִים וְרַבֵּנוּ אַלְפָּסִי. וְאַף־עַל־גַּב דְּרַבִּי יַעֲקֹב
מִשְּׁמֵיהּ דְּרַבִּי פְדָת וְרַבִּי יִרְמְיָה מִשְּׁמֵהּ דְּאָלְפָא אָמְרוּ דֶּרֶךְ פְּשִׁיטוּת בַּגְּמָרָא דְּאֵין
מְסַדְּרִין בְּבַעַל־חוֹב, אָנוּ אֵין לָנוּ אַחַר דְּבָרֵי אֵלְיָהוּ פִּקְפּוּק; וְאַף־עַל־פִּי שֶׁמָּצָאנוּ

31. I.e. their value then and there, *ibid.*
32. *Ibid.* 21b.
33. I.e. a scholar versed in the teachings of the Sages of the Mishnah.
34. TB Bava M'tzi'a 114a.
35. In our editions this is not in Rashi but in *tosafoth*, TB Bava M'tzi'a 114a, s.v. *ma-hu*, in the name of *Halachoth G'doloth.*
36. Thus, because the same Hebrew verb appears in Scripture in connection with both subjects, they are considered equivalent, for the same law to apply to both.
37. In *tosafoth*, cited in note 35; "his work," below, is his *Séfer haYashar*, q.v.

⟨468⟩

Lord (Leviticus 27:23); and the interpretation was given for it [in the Oral Tradition][30] that this verse teaches regarding all things conse-crated, that they are not to be sustained and are not to be held in waiting for the market day, nor taken from place to place. In short, you have nothing of them but their place and their moment alone.[31] Now, where where do these words apply?—to movable goods; as for landed properties, however, proclamation is made about them for sixty consecutive days, morning and evening, and then they are sold.[32]

Now, since the subject of arrangement has come to hand, let us write here what the Sages of blessed memory said regarding the ar-rangement for a debtor, in the ninth chapter of the Talmud tractate *Bava M'tzi'a* (113b). It was stated there: A master of tannaitic learning[33] taught in R. Naḥman b. Yitzḥak's presence: In the way that an arrange-ment is made in cases of valuation, so are matters arranged for a debtor. Many difficulties were raised about this, and answers and resolutions were given; and at the end of the discussion the Talmud relates an incident about Elijah:[34] that Rabbah b. Abbuha met him standing in a heathen graveyard, whereupon he asked him, "What is [the law on whether] to arrange matters for a debtor?" Rashi of blessed memory and others have the reading, "Whence do we learn that matters should be arranged for a debtor?"[35] In other words, it was clear and obvious to Rabbah b. Abbuha how matters are arranged but he was asking Elijah from which verse we derive it. And Elijah answered him that we derive it from valuations through a common verb of becoming poor. In other words, it is written with regard to a loan, *And if your brother yamuch, becomes poor, and he cannot maintain himself with you, then you shall uphold him* (Leviticus 25:35), i.e. with a loan—as it is written afterward, *Do not take from him interest or increase*, etc. (*ibid.* 36); and in the section on valuations it is written, *But if he is too poor* (moch) *for the valuation* (Leviticus 27:8); and the traditional interpretation was given for it:[30] let him live despite the obligation of the valuation.[36]

So we learn through a common verb of becoming poor to arrange matters for a debtor in the way that they are arranged concerning a valuation. Well, doubt is not to be cast on the words of Elijah. And so all the *ge'onim* and R. Isaac 'Alfasi ruled. Even though R. Ya'akov in the name of R. P'dath and R. Jeremiah in the name of 'Alpha said flatly in the Talmud that this arrangement is not made for a debtor, after the words of Elijah we can have no doubtful thoughts. And al-though we find that Rabbénu Tam[37] wrote the view that the arrange-

לְרַבֵּנוּ תָּם שֶׁכָּתַב כְּמַאן דַּאֲמַר אֵין מְסַדְּרִין, וּרְאָיוֹתָיו בְּסִפְרוֹ, אַחֲרֵי רַבִּים לְהַטּוֹת.

גַּם הָרַמְבַּ״ם זִכְרוֹנוֹ לִבְרָכָה פָּסַק כִּשְׁאָר הַגְּאוֹנִים דִּמְסַדְּרִין; וּמִכָּל־מָקוֹם, אַף־עַל־פִּי־כֵן כָּתַב דְּאֵין שְׁלִיחַ בֵּית־דִּין מַנִּיחַ לְבַעַל־חוֹב אֶלָּא כֵלִים שֶׁאִי אֶפְשָׁר לוֹ בְּלֹא הֶם, כְּגוֹן מִטָּה וּמַצָּע וּמַה שֶׁהוּא לָבוּשׁ. וְנִרְאֶה שֶׁהֻזְקִיקוּ לָרַב לוֹמַר כֵּן כְּשֶׁרָאָה בְּפֶרֶק זֶה דִּמְקַבֵּל גַּבֵּי שְׁלִיחַ בֵּית־דִּין שֶׁאָמְרוּ בַּמִּשְׁנָה ״הָיוּ לוֹ שְׁנֵי כֵלִים, נוֹטֵל אֶחָד וּמַחֲזִיר אֶחָד, אֶת הַכַּר בַּלַּיְלָה וְאֶת הַמַּחֲרֵשָׁה בַּיּוֹם״, וְלֹא מָנוּ כְלֵי הָאֻמָּנוּת. וְזֶה וַדַּאי מִן הַנִּרְאֶה שֶׁאֵינוֹ הֶכְרֵחַ גָּדוֹל, דְּכֵיוָן דְּקַיְמָא לָן דִּמְסַדְּרִין בּוֹ כְּדֶרֶךְ שֶׁמְּסַדְּרִין בַּעֲרָכִין, שָׁוִין הֵם בְּכָל דָּבָר; וְאַף־עַל־גַּב דְּלָא חָשִׁיב לְהוּ בַּמִּשְׁנָה, אֵין בְּכָךְ כְּלוּם, דְּלָאו כִּי רוֹכְלָא חָשִׁיב וְתָנֵי בְּכָל מָקוֹם, וְנָקֵט כַּר וּמַחֲרֵשָׁה וְהוּא הַדִּין לְכָל מַה שֶׁרָאוּי לְהַנִּיחַ לוֹ.

וּכְלָלָא דְמִלְּתָא, לְפִי הַנִּרְאֶה וְהַמֻּסְכָּם לְרֹב גְּאוֹנֵי הָעוֹלָם אֲשֶׁר יָצָא לָהֶם שֵׁם בַּתּוֹרָה, שֶׁמְּסַדְּרִין בְּבַעַל־חוֹב כְּדֶרֶךְ שֶׁמְּסַדְּרִין בַּעֲרָכִין בְּשָׁוֶה, וְיֵשׁ לָהֶם עַל מַה שֶּׁיִּסְמְכוּ מִדִּבְרֵי הַגְּמָרָא וּמִדְּאֵלְיָהוּ זָכוּר לַטּוֹב, כִּדְכַתְבִינָן.

וְאִם תִּשְׁאַל: וְהֵיכִי מְסַדְּרִין לוֹ כְּסוּתוֹ, וַהֲרֵי אָמְרוּ בַּגְּמָרָא ״מִגְנֵיהּ ״מִגְּנֵיהּ ״אַפְלוּ מִגְּלִימָא דְעַל כַּתְפֵיהּ״? אֶפְשָׁר לוֹמַר דְּלִשׁוֹן גְּזֵמָא הוּא; אִי נַמִּי, מִגְּלִימָא הַחֲשׁוּבָה בְּיוֹתֵר, כְּגוֹן כְּלֵי מֶשִׁי וְזָהָב, מֵאוֹתָהּ הוּא דְּאָמְרִינַן שֶׁאֵינָהּ בִּכְלַל הַסִּדּוּר.

וְיֶתֶר רָבֵּי דִינֵי עֲרָכִין, מְבֹאָרִים בַּמַּסֶּכְתָּא הַבְּנוּיָה עַל זֶה, וְהִיא מַסֶּכֶת עֲרָכִין.

וְנוֹהֶגֶת מִצְוַת עֲרָכִין בְּכָל מָקוֹם וּבְכָל זְמַן, בִּזְכָרִים וּנְקֵבוֹת, כְּלוֹמַר נוֹהֶגֶת לְעִנְיָן שֶׁאִם נָתַן עֶרְכּוֹ אוֹ הֶעֱרִיכוֹ, עֶרְכָּן נִתְפָּס וְהוּא קֹדֶשׁ. וּמִכָּל־מָקוֹם אָמְרוּ חֲכָמִים דְּבַזְּמַן הַזֶּה לַכַּתְּחִלָּה אֵין מַעֲרִיכִין, וְכִדְאַמְרִינַן בְּמַסֶּכֶת עֲבוֹדָה זָרָה פֶּרֶק קַמָּא: אֵין מַקְדִּישִׁין וְאֵין מַעֲרִיכִין וְאֵין מַחֲרִימִין בַּזְּמַן הַזֶּה; וְאִם הִקְדִּישׁ אוֹ הֶעֱרִיךְ אוֹ

38. MT *hilchoth malveh* i 7.

39. *Ibid.* iii 6.

40. TB Bava M'tzi'a 113a.

41. I.e. about a person with a debt or obligation that he absolutely must pay; TB Bava Kamma 11b.

42. Seven paragraphs above.

ment is not made, and his proofs are in his work, the majority are to be followed.

Rambam too, of blessed memory, ruled like the other great authorities that the arrangement is made.[38] However, he wrote that the deputy of the *beth din* is to leave the debtor nothing but those objects without which he cannot be, such as a bed, mattress, and what he wears.[39] Now, it seems that the master scholar was impelled to say this when he saw in this ninth chapter of *Bava M'tzi'a* (113a), in regard to the *beth din's* deputy, that it was taught in the Mishnah:[40] "If he [the debtor] had two objects, he should take one and return one: the bolster at night, and the plow by day"—and work-tools were not listed. Yet it would certainly seem that this is not a greatly decisive proof: for since we have a standing rule that the arrangement is made for him in the way that it is made in a case of valuation, they are identical in every respect; and even if it is not listed in the Mishnah, that is of no matter; for it does not, like an itinerant merchant, list and teach everything at every instance. Thus it mentioned the bolster and the plow, and the law is the same for whatever it is proper to leave him.

The crux of the matter, as it appears to be, and as it is agreed upon by most of the great authorities of the world who have become renowned in Torah, is that matters are arranged for a debtor as they are arranged in a case of valuation, equally. They have a basis on which to rely in the words of the Talmud and of Elijah, be he remembered for good, as we have written.

Yet you might ask: But how can it be arranged for him to have his clothing? It was clearly taught in the Talmud:[41] from him, and even from the cloak (shirt) on his shoulder! It is possible to say, though, that this is an expression of exaggeration [for emphasis]; or else, [it means] from an overly valuable cloak, such as a garment of silk and gold—of that kind which we said[42] is not included in the arrangement.

The rest of the numerous laws about valuations are clarified in the Talmud tractate built about this [subject]—the tractate *'Arachin.*

The precept of valuations is in effect everywhere, at every time, for both man and woman. This is to say that it is in effect in the sense that if people vow their evaluation, the obligation takes hold, and [the amount] is consecrated. However, the Sages said that at the present time [when there is no Sanctuary], initially valuations should not be vowed. As it was taught in the first chapter of the tractate *'Avodah Zarah* (13a): One should vow no consecration, valuation, or *ḥerem*

הַחֲרִים, בְּהֵמָה תֵּעָקֵר, פֵּרוֹת כְּסוּת, כֵּלִים יֵרָקְבוּ, מָעוֹת וּכְלֵי מַתָּכוֹת יוֹלִיכֵם לְיַם־הַמֶּלַח. וְאֵי זֶהוּ עִקּוּר — נוֹעֵל דֶּלֶת בְּפָנֶיהָ וְהִיא מֵתָה מֵאֵלֶיהָ.

וְזֶה הַהֶקְדֵּשׁ פֵּרוּשׁוֹ הֶקְדֵּשׁ לְבֶדֶק הַבַּיִת, דְּהָא גַבֵּי עֲרָכִין תָּנֵי לֵיהּ, דִּסְתָמָן נַמֵּי הֲוֵי לְבֶדֶק הַבַּיִת. וְאַף־עַל־גַּב דְּאָמַר שְׁמוּאֵל בַּעֲרָכִין "הֶקְדֵּשׁ שָׁוֶה מָנֶה שֶׁחִלְּלוֹ עַל שָׁוֶה פְרוּטָה, מְחֻלָּל", וְהַיְנוּ נַמֵּי הֶקְדֵּשׁ לְבֶדֶק הַבַּיִת, דְּאִלּוּ הֶקְדֵּשׁ דַּעֲנָיִים וַדַּאי אֵינוֹ בַּר חִלּוּל, אֶלָּא פּוֹרְעִין אוֹתוֹ מְשֻׁלָּם; וְלָאו דַּוְקָא דְקָאָמַר שְׁמוּאֵל שֶׁחִלְּלוֹ דִיעֲבַד, דְּהוּא הַדִּין דְּקָא סָבַר דִּמְחַלְּלִין אוֹתוֹ עַל שָׁוֶה פְרוּטָה לְכַתְּחִלָּה, כִּדְמוֹכַח בִּגְמָרָא מְבוֹרָר — לָא קַשְׁיָא מִידֵי: הַהִיא בְּהָא דְּאָמְרִינַן הָכָא "בְּהֵמָה תֵּעָקֵר", וְכוּלֵי, דְּהָכָא קָתָנֵי דִּינָא, וּשְׁמוּאֵל קָאָמַר תַּקַּנְתָּא; וְהָכִי נִרְאָה דְתַרְצִינְהוּ רַבֵּנוּ אַלְפָסִי זִכְרוֹנוֹ לִבְרָכָה בְּהִלְכוֹתָיו בְּפֶרֶק קַמָּא דַּעֲבוֹדָה זָרָה, דְּמַיְתֵי לְהוּ הָתָם תַּרְוַיְהוּ בַּהֲדֵי הֲדָדֵי.

וְעוֹבֵר עַל זֶה וְהֶאֱרִיךְ בִּזְמַן הַבַּיִת וְלֹא הִשְׁלִים לָתֵת כָּעֵרֶךְ הַקָּצוּב בַּתּוֹרָה, אוֹ שֶׁלֹּא עָשָׂה בַּדָּבָר בַּזְמַן הַזֶּה מַה שֶּׁאָמְרוּ זִכְרוֹנָם לִבְרָכָה מִדִּינָא, לְאַבֵּד הַכֹּל, אוֹ מַה שֶּׁאָמַר שְׁמוּאֵל בְּתַקַּנְתָּא, בִּטֵּל עָשֵׂה זֶה, וְעָנְשׁוֹ גָּדוֹל מְאֹד, שֶׁמָּעַל מַעַל בַּיָי; וְאִם עָבְרוּ עָלָיו שְׁלֹשָׁה רְגָלִים אַחַר שֶׁהֶאֱרִיךְ, יֵשׁ בַּדָּבָר עוֹד עֹנֶשׁ אַחֵר, שֶׁעוֹבֵר מִשּׁוּם "בַּל תְּאַחֵר".

וְיֵשׁ שֶׁפֵּרְשׁוּ שֶׁמִּיָּד עוֹבֵר גַּם־כֵּן מִשּׁוּם "בַּל תְּאַחֵר", דְּבְכָל מִידֵי דְאִיהוּ חַיָּב נַפְשֵׁיהּ וַחֲזֵי לְשַׁלּוֹמֵי כִצְדָקָה וְכַיּוֹצֵא־בָהּ, לְאַלְתָּר אִית בֵּיהּ מִשּׁוּם "בַּל תְּאַחֵר";

---

43. To be thrown away beyond recall.

44. Hence this would seem to contradict the ruling in TB 'Avodah Zarah 13a that anything consecrated or vowed, etc. must be destroyed when the Sanctuary is not extant, and there is thus no way for him to carry out his word and have the Sanctuary benefit from his consecration or vow. Ordinarily, then, whatever was consecrated or vowed must be destroyed; hence Sh'mu'el's amendment.

45. To spare a person the loss of what he consecrated or vowed.

46. So too R. Nissim explains it (TB 'Avodah Zarah i).

47. Passover, *Shavu'oth* and *Sukkoth*, when the Israelites had to make a pilgrimage to the Sanctuary (at the time that it existed).

48. So R. Nissim, TB Rosh haShanah i, beginning, s.v. *utz'dakah*.

(ban of devotement) at the present time; but if someone did consecrate an animal, vow its value, or vow it in *hérem*, it is to be destroyed; if it was produce, clothing or objects, they are [to be left] to decay; if it was money or metal utensils, they should be taken to the Dead Sea. [43] What is the process of destroying [the animal]?—the door is locked before it, and it dies of itself.

Now, the meaning of this consecration is a sacred designation [of something] toward the maintenance of the Temple in repair; for here it is mentioned along with valuations, which generally, when unspecified, are also used for repairs in the Temple. Sh'mu'el did say in the tractate *'Arachin* (29a) that if a consecrated object worth a *maneh* [= 19,200 *p'rutoth*] was exchanged for something worth a *p'rutah* to make it non-holy, the exchange would take effect; and this also means something consecrated for keeping the Temple in repair: for if it were something consecrated for the poor, it does not allow for an exchange to make it non-holy, but must rather be given or paid in full. And Sh'mu'el did not mean particularly if it was already so exchanged, after the fact; for the truth is that he holds that initially it may be exchanged for something worth a *p'rutah*, as it is shown clearly in the Talmud. [44] Nevertheless, this presents no difficulty at all in regard to our teaching here that the animal is to be destroyed, etc. For here the basic law was taught, while Sh'mu'el stated a way of reclamation. [45] And so it would seem that R. Isaac 'Alfasi of blessed memory resolves the matter in his compendium of definitive law, in the first chapter of *'Avodah Zarah*, since he quotes them both, one after the other. [46]

If a person transgressed this, vowing a valuation at the time the Temple stood and not giving in full the valuation set by the Torah; or if he did not carry out in the matter at the present time what the Sages ruled under the law, to destroy it all, or what Sh'mu'el stated as a way of reclamation—he would [thus] disobey this positive precept, and his penalty would be very great: For he would thus commit a breach of holiness toward the Lord. If after he vowed the valuation, three pilgrimage festivals [47] passed by for him, the matter would entail a further penalty: for he would thus transgress the injunction, *you shall not be slack to pay it* (Deuteronomy 23:22, §574). [48]

However, there are those who explained that he would also violate at once the injunction not to be slack in paying: For in everything about which a person obligates himself, which he ought to pay, such as charity and so forth, the injunction not to be slack in paying applies

לְאַפּוֹקֵי קָרְבָּן, דְּלָאו אִיהוּ חַיָּב נַפְשֵׁיהּ, דְּלָא עַבְרִינָן עֲלֵהּ עַד שְׁלֹשָׁה רְגָלִים, וְכִדְבָרֵי רַבִּי שִׁמְעוֹן: עַד שָׁלֹשׁ רְגָלִים, וְחַג הַמַּצּוֹת תְּחִלָּה.

וְיֵשׁ שֶׁאָמְרוּ שֶׁאֲפִלּוּ בִּצְדָקָה, וְכָל-שֶׁכֵּן בִּשְׁאָר נְדָרִים גַּם-כֵּן, אֵין עוֹבְרִין מִשּׁוּם "בַּל תְּאַחֵר" עַד אַחַר שָׁלֹשׁ רְגָלִים, וְכִדְאַשְׁכְּחָן בַּגְּמָרָא גַּבֵּי לֶקֶט שִׁכְחָה וּפֵאָה; וְאֵין מְחַלְּקִין בֵּין חַיָּב נַפְשֵׁיהּ לְלָא חַיָּב נַפְשֵׁיהּ. וּמַה שֶּׁאָמְרוּ בַּגְּמָרָא בְּרֹאשׁ הַשָּׁנָה: וּצְדָקָה מְחַיַּב עֲלֵהּ לְאַלְתַּר, כְּלוֹמַר מְחַיָּב בָּהּ בַּעֲשֵׂה.

[שֶׁלֹּא נָמִיר הַקֳּדָשִׁים]

שנא שֶׁלֹּא נָמִיר הַקֳּדָשִׁים, כְּלוֹמַר בְּהֵמָה שֶׁהִקְדִּישָׁהּ לַמִּזְבֵּחַ, שֶׁלֹּא יְמִירוּהָ אַחַר-כֵּן בִּבְהֵמָה אַחֶרֶת, אֶלָּא תִקְרַב הִיא בְעַצְמָהּ; וְעַל זֶה נֶאֱמַר: לֹא יַחֲלִיפֶנּוּ וְלֹא יָמִיר אֹתוֹ; וּמִכֵּיוָן שֶׁהֱמִירוּהָ, כְּלוֹמַר שֶׁאָמְרוּ "זוֹ תַּחַת זוֹ" אוֹ "זוֹ תְּמוּרַת זוֹ", וְכַיּוֹצֵא בִלְשׁוֹנוֹת אֵלּוּ, שֶׁזֶּהוּ עִנְיַן הַתְּמוּרָה, אַף-עַל-פִּי שֶׁאֵין שָׁם מַעֲשֶׂה, יֵשׁ בַּדָּבָר חִיּוּב מַלְקוֹת; וַאֲפִלּוּ הָיָה בַדָּבָר שֶׁגָּגָה קְצָת, יֵשׁ בּוֹ חִיּוּב מַלְקוֹת. כֵּיצַד: הַמִּתְכַּוֵּן לוֹמַר "הֲרֵי זוֹ תְּמוּרַת עוֹלָה שֶׁיֵּשׁ לִי", וְאָמַר "תְּמוּרַת שְׁלָמִים שֶׁיֵּשׁ לִי", הֲרֵי זוֹ תְמוּרָה, וְלוֹקֶה, דְּמִכָּל-מָקוֹם מֵזִיד הוּא בַתְּמוּרָה; אֲבָל אִם הָיְתָה מַחֲשַׁבְתּוֹ שֶׁמֵּתָּר לְהָמִיר, וַדַּאי אֵינוֹ לוֹקֶה: חֲדָא דְשׁוֹגֵג הוּא, וְעוֹד דְּלָא מַלְקִינַן אֶלָּא בְעֵדִים וְהַתְרָאָה, וַהֲרֵי אֵין כָּאן הַתְרָאָה.

---

49. So *tosafoth, ibid.* 4a, s.v. *tz'dakoth;* and *Rashba,* cited by R. Nissim, *ibid.*

50. By a vow to give his valuation to the Sanctuary or charity to the poor, a person imposes an obligation on himself; but to bring an offering to the Sanctuary is a duty imposed by the Torah. See further on this in §575.

51. I.e. from the time he makes his vow, a Passover, *Shavu'oth* and *Sukkoth* must pass by, in that order, for him to incur guilt over the injunction against tardiness; TB Rosh haShanah 4b.

52. Rashba (see note 49).

53. So the oldest manuscript reads, as we have it in the Talmud.

54. I.e. the positive precept, *What has passed your lips you shall observe and do* (Deuteronomy 23:24); but the negative precept about tardiness is transgressed only after the three festivals.

§351   1. So TB T'murah 26b.
2. So MT *hilchoth t'murah* i 2 (see *Kessef Mishneh*).

immediately.[49] This, however, excludes [the obligation to bring] an offering, where a person has not obligated himself;[50] then it is not transgressed until three pilgrimage festivals |have passed]; in the view of R. Shim'on: until three pilgrimage festivals, starting with Passover.[51]

Yet there are those who ruled[52] that even over charity, and all the more certainly over other vows, as well, the injunction not to be slack in paying is not transgressed until after three pilgrim festivals—as we find in the Talmud regarding gleanings (§218), forgotten sheaves (§592) and the leftover part of a field (§216); and no distinction is made whether one did or did not impose an obligation on himself. But what the Sages said in the Talmud tractate *Rosh haShanah* (6a): As for charity, there is penalty for it immediately[53]—that is to say one incurs punishment over it on account of a positive precept.[54]

[THE PROHIBITION AGAINST EXCHANGING ANIMALS
CONSECRATED FOR HOLY OFFERINGS]

351 that we should not exchange holy offerings; in other words, an animal that was consecrated for the altar is not to be exchanged afterward for another animal, but is to be itself offered up. About this it is stated, *He shall not subsitute anything for it, nor exchange it* (Leviticus 27:10). Once it was exchanged—in other words, if it was said, "This be instead of that" or "This be in exchange for that,"[1] or anything similar to these expressions, which is the method of exchanging—even though there was no physical action, the matter entails a punishment of whiplashes.

Even if there was some element of inadvertency in the matter, it imposes the punishment of whiplashes. How so?—If a person intended to say, "Let this be a substitue for the 'olah (burnt-offering) that I have," and he said, "a substitute for the sh'lamim (peace-offering) that I have," it is an act of substitution, and he is given lashes; for in any event, he was deliberate in intending a substitution. If, however, it was his thought that it is permissible to make a substitution, then he would certainly receive no whiplashes:[2] first, because he acted unwittingly; and furthermore, because a whipping is not given unless there were witnesses and a [prior] warning, and here there was clearly no warning.

You might ask, though: Why should whiplashes be suffered for

וְאִם תִּשְׁאַל: וְלָמָּה לוֹקִין עַל הַתְּמוּרָה, וַהֲרֵי הוּא לָאו שֶׁנִּתָּק לַעֲשֵׂה, וְהוּא שֶׁאִם הֵמִיר יְהֵא הוּא וּתְמוּרָתוֹ קֹדֶשׁ — כְּבָר פֵּרְשׁוּ חֲכָמִים זִכְרוֹנָם לִבְרָכָה טַעַם הַדָּבָר וְאָמְרוּ: מִפְּנֵי שֶׁיֵּשׁ בָּהּ שְׁנֵי לָאוִין, כְּמוֹ שֶׁכָּתַבְתִּי בְּסֵדֶר זֶה עֲשֵׂה ב' [סִ' שנ"ב], וְלָא אָתֵי עֲשֵׂה עָקַר תְּרֵי לָאוֵי.

וְעוֹד אָמְרוּ טַעַם אַחֵר, לְפִי שֶׁאֵין לָאו דִּתְמוּרָה שָׁוֶה לַעֲשֵׂה שֶׁבָּהּ: שֶׁהַצִּבּוּר, וְכֵן הַשֻּׁתָּפִין, אֵין עוֹשִׂין תְּמוּרָה אִם הֵמִירוּ, וְאַף־עַל־פִּי שֶׁהֵם מֻזְהָרִים שֶׁלֹּא יָמִירוּ; וּמִכֵּיוָן שֶׁאֵין הַלָּאו שָׁוֶה לַעֲשֵׂה, לֹא נֹאמַר בָּזֶה שֶׁיְּהֵא דִינוֹ כְּלָאו שֶׁנִּתָּק לַעֲשֵׂה.

וְאִם תִּשְׁאַל עוֹד: וְלָמָּה לוֹקִין עַל לָאו זֶה, אַחַר שֶׁאֶפְשָׁר לַעֲבֹר עָלָיו מִבְּלִי מַעֲשֶׂה, בְּדִבּוּר לְבַד, וּכְלָלָא הוּא דְקַיְמָא לָן: כָּל לָאו שֶׁאֵין בּוֹ מַעֲשֶׂה, אֵין לוֹקִין עָלָיו — הַתְּשׁוּבָה כְּבָר כְּתַבְנוּהָ בִּמְקוֹמוֹת הַרְבֵּה, כִּי בְּפֵרוּשׁ הוֹצִיאוּ זִכְרוֹנָם לִבְרָכָה מִכְּלָל זֶה נִשְׁבַּע וּמֵמִיר וּמְקַלֵּל חֲבֵרוֹ בַשֵּׁם, שֶׁהַתּוֹרָה הֶחְמִירָה בָּהֶם הַרְבֵּה, לְחַיֵּב בָּהֶם מַלְקוּת אַף־עַל־פִּי שֶׁאֵין בָּהֶם מַעֲשֶׂה.

וְאַל תִּתְהַרְהֵר דְּמִשּׁוּם עֲקִימַת שְׂפָתַיִם הוּא דְהַוְיָא מַעֲשֶׂה, דְּהָא אַסִּיקְנָא בַּגְּמָרָא בְּסַנְהֶדְרִין דְּלָא הַוְיָא מַעֲשֶׂה; אֲבָל וַדַּאי בְּלֹא מַעֲשֶׂה כְּלָל אִיכָּא מַלְקוּת בִּשְׁלֹשָׁה אֵלֶּה שֶׁזָּכַרְנוּ (וּמוֹצִיא שֵׁם רַע וְעֵד זוֹמֵם: מֵהֶם שֶׁהַמַּלְקוּת מְפֹרָשׁ בַּתּוֹרָה בָּהֶם, כְּגוֹן מוֹצִיא שֵׁם רַע וְעֵד זוֹמֵם; וּמֵהֶם דְּנָפִיק לָן מִקְרָא, כְּגוֹן נִשְׁבַּע, כִּדְיַלְּפִינָן בִּשְׁבוּעוֹת פֶּרֶק שְׁבוּעוֹת שְׁתַּיִם; וּמֵהֶם שֶׁאָמְרוּ קְצָת מְפָרְשִׁים מִשּׁוּם מַעֲשֶׂה דְנָפִיק מִנֵּיהּ בַּסּוֹף, כְּגוֹן הָא דְמֵמִיר, שֶׁהַבְּהֵמָה נַעֲשֵׂית קֹדֶשׁ בְּדִבּוּרוֹ, וְנֶהֱנֶה מִמֶּנָּה מָעַל בָּהּ).

---

3. I.e. why offering up both animals as holy sacrifices does not make up for the transgression of the negative precept; TB T'murah 4b.

4. *Ibid.* variant reading in *Shittah M'kubetzeth* (ed. Vilna, margin), note 5; MT *ibid.* 1.

5. I.e. their words do not make the second animal consecrated.

6. So TB Sh'vu'oth 21a, Makkoth 16a, T'murah 3a.

7. Regarding the chastity of one's bride, because Scripture (Deuteronomy 22:18) specifies the penalty; TB K'thuboth 46b.

8. The penalty is indicated by Deuteronomy 2:2; TB Makkoth 2b.

a substitution? Surely it is a negative precept given over to a positive precept for rectification, namely, that if one makes the exchange, *both it and its substitute shall be holy* (Leviticus 27:10)? Long ago, however, the Sages of blessed memory explained the reason for the matter,[3] saying it is because there are two negative precepts about it, as I will write in the second positive precept of this *sidrah* (§352), and a positive precept cannot come along and uproot two negative precepts.

Moreover, they gave another reason:[4] It is because the negative precept about exchange does not correspond exactly to the positive precept about it. For the public, and so also partners, do not achieve an effective substitution if they make an exchange,[5] although they are enjoined not to make the exchange. And since the negative does not correspond exactly to the positive precept, we do not say in this instance that its law should be that of a negative precept given over to a positive one for correction.

Yet you might ask further: But why are whiplashes received over this negative precept, when it is possible to transgress it without any physical action, but by speech alone; and there is a standing rule that we have: over any negative precept that involves no physical action, a whipping is not incurred? The answer is something we have previously written many times: that the Sages expressly excluded from this rule swearing [in vain] (§30), exchanging [a consecrated animal], and cursing one's fellow-man by the Divine name (§231).[6] For the Torah was exceedingly stringent about them, making them punishable by lashes of the whip although they involve no physical action.

Now, do not ponder that [perhaps] because of the twisting [moving] of the lips there is physical action: for it was concluded in the Talmud tractate *Sanhedrin* (65a) that this is not a physical activity. Yet quite certainly, although there is no physical act involved, there is a sentence of whiplashes for the three [transgressions] that we mentioned, (spreading an evil name,[7] and a scheming witness [§524]. There are some of them for which flogging is specified in the Torah: for example, one who spreads an evil name, and a scheming witness.[8] For some of them, it is inferred from a Scriptural verse: for example, swearing [in vain], as we learn in the third chapter of the tractate *Sh'vu'oth* (21a). Then there are those about which some authorities said that it is because of the deed that ultimately ensues from it: for instance, the exchange [of a consecrated animal]—because the [sub-

‏שֹׁרֶשׁ הַמִּצְוָה וּקְצָת דִּינֶיהָ, הַכֹּל כָּתוּב בְּסֵדֶר זֶה עֲשֵׂה ב' [סִי' שנ"ב].‏

‏וְנוֹהֵג אִסּוּר זֶה בְּכָל מָקוֹם וּבְכָל זְמָן, בַּזְּכָרִים וּנְקֵבוֹת: שֶׁאֲפִלּוּ בַּזְּמָן הַזֶּה, אִם עָבַר אָדָם וְהִקְדִּישׁ בְּהֵמָה לַמִּזְבֵּחַ וְאַחַר־כָּךְ הֱמִירָהּ בְּעֶדֶרִים וְהִתְרָאָה, חַיָּב מַלְקוֹת.‏

‏[מִצְוַת הַמֵּמִיר בֶּהֱמַת קָרְבָּן בִּבְהֵמָה אַחֶרֶת שֶׁתִּהְיֶינָה שְׁתֵּיהֶן קֹדֶשׁ]‏

‏שנב לִהְיוֹת הַתְּמוּרָה קֹדֶשׁ, כְּלוֹמַר הַמֵּמִיר בֶּהֱמַת קָרְבָּנוֹ בִּבְהֵמָה אַחֶרֶת, כְּגוֹן שֶׁאָמַר: זוֹ תִּהְיֶה לַקָּרְבָּן תְּמוּרַת זוֹ, שֶׁתִּהְיֶינָה שְׁתֵּיהֶן הִיא וְהַתְּמוּרָה שֶׁתֵּיהֶן קֹדֶשׁ, שֶׁנֶּאֱמַר: וְהָיָה הוּא וּתְמוּרָתוֹ יִהְיֶה קֹדֶשׁ. וְזֶה הַכָּתוּב מִצְוַת־עֲשֵׂה הוּא, כְּלוֹמַר שֶׁתְּצַוֶּה אוֹתָנוּ הַתּוֹרָה לִהְיוֹת הַתְּמוּרָה קְדוֹשָׁה וְלִנְהֹג קֹדֶשׁ בִּשְׁתֵּיהֶן.‏

‏וְהָרְאָיָה שֶׁזֶּה מִצְוַת עֲשֵׂה הוּא אָמְרָם זִכְרוֹנָם לִבְרָכָה בְּמַסֶּכֶת תְּמוּרָה בְּעִנְיַן מֵמִיר: לָא אָתֵי עֲשֵׂה עָקַר תְּרֵי לָאוֵי, כְּלוֹמַר שֶׁהַמֵּנִיעָה בַתְּמוּרָה נִכְפְּלָה שְׁתֵּי פְעָמִים, שֶׁנֶּאֱמַר: לֹא יַחֲלִיפֶנּוּ וְלֹא יָמִיר אֹתוֹ, וְלֹא אָתֵי עֲשֵׂה דְּ"וְהָיָה הוּא וּתְמוּרָתוֹ" עָקַר תְּרֵי לָאוִין אֵלּוּ. הִנֵּה הִתְבָּאֵר מַה שֶּׁרָצִינוּ, דְּמִצְוַת עֲשֵׂה הוּא.‏

‏מִשָּׁרְשֵׁי הַמִּצְוָה, שֶׁרָצָה הַשֵּׁם בָּרוּךְ הוּא לְהָטִיל מוֹרָא בְּלֵב בְּנֵי־אָדָם בְּכָל עִנְיְנֵי הַקֹּדֶשׁ, וּכְמוֹ שֶׁכָּתַבְתִּי בְּבִנְיַן הַבַּיִת הַקָּדוֹשׁ וְכֵלָיו בְּסֵדֶר "וְיִקְחוּ לִי תְרוּמָה" עֲשֵׂה א' [סִי' צ"ה], שָׁם תִּרְאֶה עַל צַד הַפְּשָׁט קְצָנָתֵנוּ בַּחֹמֶר הַגָּדוֹל הָרָאוּי לָנוּ לִנְהֹג בַּקֹּדֶשׁ. וְעַל־כֵּן, כְּדֵי לִקְבֹּעַ בְּלִבֵּנוּ מוֹרָאַת עִנְיַן הַקֹּדֶשׁ, צִוָּה הַכָּתוּב לְבַל נְשַׁנֶּה הַדְּבָרִים, אֶלָּא מִכֵּיוָן שֶׁנִּתְקַדְּשָׁה הַבְּהֵמָה, תִּהְיֶה בִקְדֻשָּׁתָהּ‏

<hr />

9. So TB T'murah 3b.

10. Before the parenthesis (that begins ten lines above) instead of ‏בשלשה אלה‏ ‏שזכרנו‏ "for the three [transgressions] that we mentioned," all the editions read ‏בקצת‏ ‏עבירות והן שלשה הנזכרות‏ "for a few transgressions, these being the three that were mentioned"; and then the words given here in parenthesis follow. As they are absent in the oldest manuscripts, this is all probably a later interpolation.

§352   1. So that whiplashes should not be given, because the negative precept is given over to a positive one for rectification. See §351, third paragraph.

2. So ShM positive precept §87. On the paragraph after this cf. *Guide* III 46.

stituted] beast becomes hallowed by his words,[9] and whoever derives any benefit from it commits a breach of holiness with it.)[10]

The root reason for the precept and some of its laws are all [to be found] written in this *sidrah*, in the second positive precept (§352). This prohibition is in effect everywhere, at every time, for both man and woman. For even at the present time, if a man transgressed, consecrating an animal for the altar and then exchanging it, with witnesses and a [prior] warning, he would be punishable by lashes of the whip.

[THAT IF ONE EXCHANGES AN ANIMAL CONSECRATED
FOR AN OFFERING, BOTH ANIMALS ARE CONSECRATED]

352 that a substituted animal should be sacred; in other words, if someone exchanges the animal for his offering for another animal—for instance, if he said, "Let this be for the offering in exchange for that"— both it and the substitute should be sacred: for it is stated, *then both it and that for which it is exchanged shall be holy* (Leviticus 27:10), and this verse constitutes a positive precept. In other words, the Torah thus commands us that the substituted animal should be sacred, and both are to be treated as hallowed.

Now, the proof that this is a positive precept is the statement of the Sages of blessed memory in the Talmud tractate *T'murah* (4b) in regard to one who makes a substitution: A positive precept cannot come along and uproot two negative precepts.[1] This means that the restriction about substitution was given two times: for it is stated, *He shall not substitute anything for it, nor exchange it* (Leviticus 27:10); then the positive precept, "both it and that for which it is exchanged shall be holy," cannot come and uproot these two injunctions. Thus what we wanted has been made clear: that it is a positive precept.[2]

At the root of the precept lies the reason that the Eternal Lord, blessed is He, wished to put fear in the heart of people about all matters of holiness, as I wrote about the construction of the holy Temple and its vessels and objects, in the first positive precept of *sidrah t'rumah* (§95). There you will see, following the plain meaning, our thoughts about the great seriousness with which it is proper for us to relate to holiness. Therefore, to set firmly in our heart a reverent fear for the essence of holiness, Scripture ordained that we are not to change things. Rather, once a domestic animal has been consecrated, it is to remain in its sacredness for time without limit, and we should not

לְעוֹלָם, וְלֹא נַחְשֹׁב לְהַפְקִיעָהּ מִקְּדֻשָּׁתָהּ וּלְהַחֲלִיפָהּ בִּבְהֵמָה אַחֶרֶת; וְאִם יוֹצִיא הַדָּבָר מִפִּיו, שֶׁתִּתְהַפֵּךְ מַחֲשַׁבְתּוֹ וְכָל מַעֲשֵׂהוּ וְתִהְיֶינָה שְׁתֵּיהֶן קֹדֶשׁ, כִּי הוּא בָא בְמַעֲשָׂיו לְהַפְקִיעַ קְדֻשָּׁה, וְתִהְיֶה לְהֵפֶךְ, שֶׁתִּתְפַּשֵּׁט יוֹתֵר וְתִתְפַּשֵּׁט הַכֹּל.

וְהָרַמְבַּ"ם זִכְרוֹנוֹ לִבְרָכָה כָּתַב בְּטַעַם מִצְוָה זוֹ: וּבְמַה שֶּׁנִּצְטַוֵּינוּ לְהוֹסִיף חֹמֶשׁ בִּפְדִיוֹן הַקֹּדֶשׁ, שֶׁיָּרְדָה הַתּוֹרָה לְסוֹף מַחֲשֶׁבֶת הָאָדָם וְיִצְרוֹ רַע, שֶׁטִּבְעוֹ לְהַרְבּוֹת קִנְיָנָיו וְלָחוּס עַל מָמוֹנוֹ; וְאַף־עַל־פִּי שֶׁנָּדַר וְהִקְדִּישׁ, אֶפְשָׁר שֶׁיַּחֲזֹר בּוֹ וְיִנָּחֵם וְיִרְצֶה לִפְדּוֹתוֹ בְּפָחוֹת מִשָּׁוְיוֹ; לְפִיכָךְ יוֹסִיף חֹמֶשׁ. וּכְמוֹ־כֵן יַחֲלִיף בְּהֵמָה שֶׁהִקְדִּישׁ בִּפְחוּתָה מִמֶּנָּה, וְאִם יֻתַּן לוֹ רְשׁוּת לְהַחֲלִיף רַע בְּטוֹב, יַחֲלִיף טוֹב בְּרַע; וּלְפִיכָךְ סָתַם הַכָּתוּב הַדֶּלֶת בְּפָנָיו.

וְעוֹד הֶאֱרִיךְ בְּעִנְיָן זֶה וְכָתַב: אַף־עַל־פִּי שֶׁכָּל חֻקֵּי הַתּוֹרָה גְּזֵרוֹת הֵן, רָאוּי אַתָּה לְהִתְבּוֹנֵן בָּהֶן (עַל) [וְכָל] שֶׁאַתָּה יָכוֹל לִתֵּן בּוֹ טַעַם, תֵּן. וְיִזָּכֵר הָרַב לְטוֹבָה שֶׁסִּיַּע יָדִי עִם דְּבָרָיו בִּמְלַאכְתִּי זֹאת.

מִדִּינֵי הַמִּצְוָה, מַה שֶּׁאָמְרוּ זִכְרוֹנָם לִבְרָכָה: הַמֵּמִיר בְּכִלְאַיִם אוֹ בִּטְרֵפָה וְיוֹצֵא־דֹפֶן אוֹ בְטוּמְטוּם וְאַנְדְּרוֹגִינוֹס, אֵין הַקְּדֻשָּׁה חָלָה עֲלֵיהֶם, וַהֲרֵי זֶה כְּמִי שֶׁהֵמִיר בְּגָמָל אוֹ בַחֲמוֹר, לְפִי שֶׁאֵין בְּמִינָן קָרְבָּן; וּלְפִיכָךְ אֵינוֹ לוֹקֶה. וּבִבְהֵמָה בַּעֲלַת מוּם עוֹשֶׂה תְמוּרָה, לְפִי שֶׁיֵּשׁ בְּמִינָהּ קָרְבָּן.

וּמַה שֶּׁאָמְרוּ שֶׁאֵין אָדָם מֵמִיר בְּהֶמְתּוֹ בְּקָרְבָּן שֶׁאֵינוֹ שֶׁלּוֹ, אֲבָל אִם אָמַר בַּעַל קָרְבָּן "כָּל הָרוֹצֶה לְהָמִיר יָמִיר", מֵמִיר בָּהּ כָּל אָדָם. וְהַמֵּמִיר בָּקָר אוֹ צֹאן בְּצֹאן, אוֹ כְבָשִׂים בְּעִזִּים אוֹ עִזִּים בִּכְבָשִׂים, אוֹ נְקֵבוֹת בִּזְכָרִים וּזְכָרִים בִּנְקֵבוֹת, אוֹ שֶׁהֵמִיר בְּהֵמָה אַחַת בְּמֵאָה אוֹ מֵאָה בְאַחַת, בֵּין בְּבַת־אַחַת בֵּין בְּזוֹ אַחַר זוֹ, הֲרֵי אֵלּוּ תְמוּרָה, וְלוֹקֶה כְחֶשְׁבּוֹן הַבְּהֵמוֹת שֶׁהֵמִיר.

3. MT *hilchoth t'murah* iv 13. He wrote similarly in *Guide, ibid.*
4. To be obeyed implicitly, whether we understand them or not.
5. TB T'murah 17a.
6. *Ibid.* 9a.

think to wrest it from its holiness and replace it by another animal. And if a person should let the matter out of his mouth, let his intention and his entire plan be turned about, and let the both of them be holy. For he came with his deeds to root out holiness; then let the opposite occur: let it spread further and take hold of all.

Rambam of blessed memory wrote on the reason for this precept:[3] As to our being commanded to add a fifth in redeeming something consecrated (§354), it is because the Torah penetrated to the ultimate thinking of a person and his evil inclination—that it is his nature to increase his acquisitions and to be concerned about his possessions. Then even though he vowed and consecrated [something] it is possible that he will change his mind and regret it, and will wish to redeem it for less than its value. Let him therefore add on a fifth. So too, he might exchange a domestic animal that he consecrated for one inferior to it; and if he were given the right to exchange a bad animal for a good one, he will exchange a good one for a bad one. Therefore the Writ locked the door before him.

He continued further, at length, about the subject and wrote: Although all the laws of the Torah are decrees,[4] it would be well for you to delve and meditate on them, and for whatever you are able to give a reason, do so. Well, may the master scholar be remembered for good, because he has supported me with his words in this my labor.

Among the laws of the precept there is what the Sages of blessed memory said:[5] If a person exchanges it for an animal of mixed breed, one fatally wounded or ill, one born by Caesarian section, or for a *tumtum* (an animal of uncertain gender), or for a hermaphroditic beast, they do not become subject to holiness. It is as though he exchanged it for a camel or a donkey, since none of their kind can be an offering. Therefore he would not receive whiplashes. However, with an animal with a disfiguring blemish an exchange can be made, since an offering can be brought of its kind.[5]

Then there is what the Sages taught:[6] that a man cannot substitute his animal for an offering that is not his; but if the owner of the offering said, "Whoever wishes to exchange it may do so," any man can exchange it [the substitution would take effect]. If a person exchanges cattle for sheep or sheep for cattle, sheep for goats or goats for sheep, females for males or males for females; or if he exchanges one animal for a hundred or a hundred for one, whether at once or one after another—the exchange is effective, and he is to be given whippings

וְאֵין הַתְּמוּרָה עוֹשָׂה תְמוּרָה, וְלֹא וְלַד בֶּהֱמַת הַקֹּדֶשׁ עוֹשָׂה תְמוּרָה, שֶׁנֶּאֱמַר:
וְהָיָה הוּא וּתְמוּרָתוֹ יִהְיֶה קֹּדֶשׁ, וְדִקְדְּקוּ זִכְרוֹנָם לִבְרָכָה עִם הַפֵּרוּשׁ הַמְּקֻבָּל:
"הוּא" וְלֹא וְלָדוֹ, "וּתְמוּרָתוֹ" וְלֹא תְמוּרַת תְּמוּרָתוֹ. אֲבָל הַמֵּמִיר בִּבְהֵמָה וְחָזַר
וְהֵמִיר בָּהּ, אֲפִלּוּ אֶלֶף פְּעָמִים, כֻּלָּן תְּמוּרָה וְלוֹקֶה עַל כָּל אֶחָת.

וְהָעוֹפוֹת וְהַמְּנָחוֹת אֵינָם עוֹשִׂין תְּמוּרָה, שֶׁלֹּא נֶאֱמַר בַּכָּתוּב אֶלָּא בְהֵמָה.
וְאֵין קָדְשֵׁי גּוֹיִם עוֹשִׂין תְּמוּרָה מִן הַתּוֹרָה, אֲבָל מִדִּבְרֵהָנָן, גּוֹי שֶׁהֵמִיר, מוּמָר;
וְהַכֹּל מְמִירִין, אֶחָד אֲנָשִׁים וְאֶחָד נָשִׁים — לֹא שֶׁאָדָם רַשַּׁאי לְהָמִיר, אֶלָּא שֶׁאִם
הֵמִיר, מוּמָר, וְסוֹפֵג אֶת הָאַרְבָּעִים; וּמַה שֶּׁאָמְרוּ: כֵּיצַד דִּין הַתְּמוּרָה לִקְרַב, וְדִין
וַלְדוֹתֶיהָ וּוַלְדֵי וְלָדוֹת; וְיֶתֶר פְּרָטֶיהָ, מְבֹאָרִין בְּמַסֶּכֶת תְּמוּרָה.

וְנוֹהֶגֶת בְּכָל מָקוֹם וּבְכָל זְמַן, בִּזְכָרִים וּנְקֵבוֹת. וְעוֹבֵר עָלֶיהָ וְהֵמִיר וְלֹא נָהַג
קְדֻשָּׁה בִּשְׁתֵּי הַבְּהֵמוֹת, כְּלוֹמַר בָּרִאשׁוֹנָה וּבִתְמוּרָתָהּ, בִּטֵּל עֲשֵׂה, מִלְּבַד הָעֹנֶשׁ
שֶׁיֵּשׁ בַּדָּבָר, שֶׁמּוֹעֵל בַּקֹּדֶשׁ.

[מִצְוַת מַעֲרִיךְ בְּהֵמָה שֶׁיִּתֵּן כְּפִי שֶׁיַּעֲרִיכֶנָּה הַכֹּהֵן]

שנג לָדוּן בְּדִין עֶרְכֵי בְהֵמָה כְּמוֹ שֶׁצִּוְּתַנוּ הַתּוֹרָה עָלָיו, שֶׁנֶּאֱמַר: וְהֶעֱמִיד אֶת
הַבְּהֵמָה לִפְנֵי הַכֹּהֵן וְהֶעֱרִיךְ הַכֹּהֵן אֹתָהּ, וְלָתֵת כְּפִי הָעֵרֶךְ שֶׁיַּעֲרִיכֶנָּה הַכֹּהֵן וְלֹא
פָחוֹת, שֶׁאֵין לְפָחוֹת וּלְשַׁקֵּר כַּמָּה שֶׁאָדָם פּוֹתֵחַ פִּיו לַשָּׁמַיִם; וַאֲפִלּוּ בְּדִבְרֵי הֶדְיוֹט
אָסוּר לְשַׁקֵּר, כְּמוֹ שֶׁפֵּרַשְׁתִּי לְמַעְלָה.

וּמִשָּׁרְשֵׁי הַמִּצְוָה, מַה שֶּׁכָּתַבְתִּי בְּדִין עֶרְכֵי אָדָם, בְּרֹאשׁ הַסֵּדֶר.

7. *Ibid.* 12a.
8. *Ibid.* 13a.
9. MT *hilchoth t'murah* i 15, based on TB T'murah 9a (*Kessef Mishneh*).
10. In Leviticus 27:10, TB T'murah 13a.
11. MT *ibid.* 6, following R. Shim'on in TB Z'vahim 45a.
12. TB T'murah 2a.
13. *Ibid.* 17b, 18b, 20b, 21a.

(sets of lashes) according to the number of animals that he exchanged.[6]

A substituted animal cannot be [further] exchanged, nor can the young of a consecrated animal be used in an effective exchange:[7] for it is stated, *then both it and that for which it is exchanged shall be holy* (Leviticus 27:10), from which our Sages of blessed memory deduced,[8] by the traditional, received interpretation, "it, but not its young; that for which it is exchanged, but not a substitute for the substitute." If, however, one makes a substitution for an animal and again makes a substitution for it, [and so] even a thousand times, all are effective exchanges, and he is given whiplashes for each one.[9]

Fowl and meal-offerings cannot be used for an effective exchange, since nothing but a beast is stated in the Writ.[10] Holy offerings of non-Jews cannot be exchanged by the law of the Torah, but by the ruling of the Sages, if a non-Jew makes a substitution, it takes effect.[11] All can put through a substitution, both men and women. This does not mean that a man has the right to make an exchange, but that if he did so, the exchange is effective, and he is to suffer the forty [whiplashes].[12] There is, too, what the Sages said: how the law is for the substitute animal to be offered up, and the law about its young, and the young of its young.[13]

The rest of its details are explained in the Talmud tractate *T'murah*. It applies in every place, at every time, for both man and woman. If someone violated it and made an exchange and then did not treat both animals as holy—i.e. the first one and its substitute—he would thus disobey a positive precept, apart from the penalty that the matter entails because he committed a breach of holiness.

[THE PRECEPT THAT ONE WHO VOWS AN ANIMAL'S
VALUATION SHOULD GIVE AS THE KOHEN VALUES IT]
353 to carry out the law of valuations of animals as the Torah commanded us about it—for it is stated, *then he shall set the animal before the* kohen, *and the* kohen *shall value it* (Leviticus 27:11–12)—and to give according to the valuation that the *kohen* set on it, not less. For there should be no deducting or lying about anything that a man opens his mouth [to vow] to Heaven. And even about ordinary non-sacred matters it is forbidden to lie, as I explained above (§350).

At the root of the precept lies the reason that I wrote about the law of the valuation of a man, at the beginning of the *sidrah* (§350).

Among the laws of the precept there is what the Sages of blessed

מִדִּינֵי הַמִּצְוָה, מַה שֶּׁאָמְרוּ זִכְרוֹנָם לִבְרָכָה שֶׁהַמַּקְדִּישׁ בְּהֵמָה תְּמִימָה לַמִּזְבֵּחַ
וְנָפַל בָּהּ מוּם וְנִפְסְלָה, הֲרֵי זוֹ נֶעֱרֶכֶת וְנִפְדֵּית, וְיָבִיא בְּהֵמָה אַחֶרֶת קָרְבָּן תַּחְתֶּיהָ;
וְעַל זֶה נֶאֱמַר "וְאִם כָּל בְּהֵמָה טְמֵאָה אֲשֶׁר לֹא יַקְרִיבוּ מִמֶּנָּה קָרְבָּן לַיָי וְהֶעֱמִיד
אֶת הַבְּהֵמָה" וְגוֹמֵר, שֶׁכֵּן בָּא עַל זֶה הַפֵּרוּשׁ הַמְּקֻבָּל שֶׁהוֹצִיאָה הַכָּתוּב בִּלְשׁוֹן
טְמֵאָה, וּבֵין שֶׁהִקְדִּישׁ אָדָם בְּהֵמָה טְהוֹרָה לַמִּזְבֵּחַ וְנָפַל בָּהּ מוּם, כְּמוֹ שֶׁאָמַרְנוּ,
אוֹ טְמֵאָה לְבֶדֶק הַבַּיִת, צְרִיכָה הָעֲמָדָה לִפְנֵי הַכֹּהֵן, שֶׁנֶּאֱמַר "וְהֶעֱמִיד אֶת
הַבְּהֵמָה לִפְנֵי הַכֹּהֵן", וְהוּא מַעֲרִיךְ אוֹתָהּ.

וְאִם מֵתָה קֹדֶם שֶׁתֵּעָרֵךְ וְתִפָּדֶה, אֵין מַעֲרִיכִין וְלֹא פּוֹדִין אוֹתָהּ אַחַר שֶׁמֵּתָה.
וְאִם שָׁחַט בָּהּ שְׁנַיִם אוֹ רֹב שְׁנַיִם, אַף־עַל־פִּי שֶׁהִיא כְּמֵתָה לְעִנְיַן שְׁחִיטָה,
כִּדְקָיְמָא לָן, שֶׁכֵּן נִצְטַוָּה מֹשֶׁה עַל רֹב אֶחָד בְּעוֹף וְרֹב שְׁנַיִם בִּבְהֵמָה, הֲרֵי הִיא
כְּחַיָּה לְעִנְיַן עֲרָכִין, וּמְבִיאָהּ לִפְנֵי הַכֹּהֵן וּמַעֲרִיכָהּ. וְיֶתֶר פְּרָטֶיהָ בִּמְקוֹמוֹת
(מתרומה) [מִתְּמוּרָה] וּמְעִילָה.

וְנוֹהֶגֶת מִצְוָה זוֹ בִּזְכָרִים וּנְקֵבוֹת בִּזְמַן הַבַּיִת, אֲבָל בַּזְּמַן הַזֶּה, אָמְרוּ חֲכָמִים
זִכְרוֹנָם לִבְרָכָה שֶׁאֵין מַקְדִּישִׁין וְאֵין מַעֲרִיכִין וְאֵין מַחֲרִימִין, וְאִם הִקְדִּישׁ אוֹ
הֶעֱרִיךְ אוֹ הֶחֱרִים, מִן הַדִּין הוּא שֶׁהַבְּהֵמָה תֵּעָקֵר, וּפֵרוֹת, כְּסוּת וְכֵלִים יֵרָקְבוּ;
אֲבָל אִם רוֹצֶה אִם תַּקָּנָתָן, עָבֵד לְהוּ כִּדְשְׁמוּאֵל, דְּאָמַר: הֶקְדֵּשׁ שָׁוֶה מָנֶה שֶׁחִלְּלוֹ עַל
שָׁוֶה פְּרוּטָה, מְחֻלָּל, כִּדְכָתְבִינָא.

וְכֵיוָן שֶׁכֵּן, יֵשׁ לָנוּ לִכְתֹּב דִּין שֶׁאֵין דִּין הָעֲמָדָה לִפְנֵי הַכֹּהֵן נוֹהֵג עַכְשָׁיו כְּלָל; אֲבָל
מִכָּל־מָקוֹם דִּין עֶרְכֵי בְּהֵמָה נוֹהֵג לְעִנְיַן שֶׁמִּי שֶׁעָבַר וְהֶעֱרִיךְ בְּהֵמָה בַּזְּמַן הַזֶּה,
שֶׁצָּרִיךְ לַעֲשׂוֹת בַּדָּבָר מַה שֶּׁצִּוּוּנוּ חֲכָמִים; וּמִכֵּיוָן דִּבְדִיעֲבַד צְרִיכִין אָנוּ תַּקָּנָה

§353   1. TB M'naḥoth 101a, T'murah 32b.
2. TB T'murah 32a.
3. *Ibid.* 32a–b.
4. I.e. the ritual slaying has thus been completed.
5. TB Ḥullin 28a.
6. *Ibid.* 30a.
7. TB 'Avodah Zarah 13a.

memory taught:[1] that if a person consecrated a whole, unblemished animal for the altar and it suffered a disfiguring blemish so that it became disqualified, it is to be valued and redeemed, and he is then to bring another animal in its place. About this it is stated, *And if it is any unclean animal, of which they may not bring an offering to the Lord, then he shall set the animal before the* kohen, *etc.* (Leviticus 27:11). For so the traditional interpretation was given about it,[1] that the Torah expressed this with the term, "an unclean animal." So whether a man consecrated a clean (acceptable) animal for the altar and it acquired a blemish, as we stated, or an unclean (unacceptable kind of) animal toward repairs in the Temple, it needs to be set before the *kohen*—as it is stated, *then he shall set the animal before the* kohen—and he is to value it.[2]

If it died before it could be valued and redeemed, it is not to be valued and redeemed after its death.[3] If one ritually slew it by cutting the two [the gullet and the windpipe] or most of the two, even though it is considered as dead in regard to ritual slaying[4]—as the standard rule is established for us,[5] that so Moses was commanded, in regard to most of one [the gullet or the windpipe] in fowl and most of the two in a domestic animal—it is like a living creature in regard to valuations.[6] It is brought before a *kohen*, who establishes its value. The rest of its details are in various places in the tractates *T'murah* and *Me'ilah*.

The precept applies to both man and woman, at the time the Temple is extant. At the present time, however, the Sages of blessed memory said[7] that there should be no consecration, vow of valuation, or *hérem* (a proscriptive vow of devotement) (§357); but if someone made a vow of consecration, valuation, or *hérem*, the law requires that an animal should be destroyed, and produce, clothing and objects should be left to decay. If one wishes to make matters right for them, though, he may do with them as Sh'mu'el ruled; for he said: If something consecrated worth a *maneh* [= 19,200 *p'rutoth*] was exchanged for a *p'rutah's* worth to make it non-holy, the exchange is valid—as we have written (§350).

This being so, it remains for us to write that the law of presenting something before the *kohen* [for his evaluation] is not in effect now at all. But in any case, the law of valuations of animals is in effect in this respect: that if a person transgressed and vowed an animal's valuation at the present day, he is required to do in the matter what the Sages

בַּדָּבָר אֲפִלּוּ בַּזְּמַן הַזֶּה, יֵשׁ לִי לְמָנוֹתָהּ, הִיא וְכָל כַּיּוֹצֵא־בָהּ, בִּכְלַל הַמִּצְוֹת הַנּוֹהֲגוֹת בַּזְּמַן הַזֶּה.

[מִצְוַת מַעֲרִיךְ בָּתִּים שֶׁיִּתֵּן בְּעֶרֶךְ שֶׁיַּעֲרִיכֶם הַכֹּהֵן וְתוֹסֶפֶת חֹמֶשׁ]

שנד לָדוּן בְּעֶרְכֵי בָתִּים, כְּלוֹמַר מִי שֶׁהִקְדִּישׁ בֵּיתוֹ וְרָצָה לִפְדּוֹתָהּ מִיַּד הֶקְדֵּשׁ, הוּא אוֹ אִשְׁתּוֹ אוֹ יוֹרְשָׁיו, שֶׁמַּעֲרִיךְ אוֹתָהּ הַכֹּהֵן וְנוֹתֵן לוֹ כְּפִי הָעֵרֶךְ שֶׁיֹּאמַר הוּא, וְעוֹד חֹמֶשׁ, כְּמוֹ שֶׁכָּתוּב: וְאִישׁ כִּי יַקְדִּשׁ אֶת בֵּיתוֹ קֹדֶשׁ וְגוֹמֵר.

מִשָּׁרְשֵׁי הַמִּצְוָה, מַה שֶּׁכָּתַבְתִּי בִתְמוּרָה, עֲשֵׂה ב' בְּסֵדֶר זֶה [סִי' שנ"ב], כִּי הָאֵל רָצָה לְטוֹבָתֵנוּ לָתֵת מוֹרָאַת הַקֹּדֶשׁ בְּלֵב בְּנֵי־אָדָם, וְאַף־עַל־פִּי שֶׁהָיָה מֵחֲסָדָיו הָרַבִּים לָתֵת לָהֶם מָקוֹם לִפְדּוֹתָן, רָצָה שֶׁיּוֹסִיפוּ חֹמֶשׁ בְּפִדְיוֹנָן, כְּדֵי לְהִתְרַחֵק שֶׁלֹּא לִפְחֹת מִדְּמֵי הַהֶקְדֵּשׁ כְּלוּם. וְאַף־עַל־פִּי שֶׁבַּשָּׂדֶה מִקְנָה אֵין בּוֹ חֹמֶשׁ, לְפִי שֶׁאֵינוֹ מָצוּי שֶׁיַּקְדִּישׁ אָדָם שָׂדֵה מִקְנָתוֹ, שֶׁחֲבִיבָה עָלָיו בְּיוֹתֵר, מִכֵּיוָן שֶׁקְּנָאָהּ בִּמְעוֹתָיו, לֹא תַקְפִּיד הַתּוֹרָה לְעוֹלָם בַּמֶּה שֶׁאֵינוֹ מָצוּי.

מִדִּינֵי הַמִּצְוָה, מַה שֶּׁאָמְרוּ זִכְרוֹנָם לִבְרָכָה שֶׁהַמַּקְדִּישׁ בֵּיתוֹ וְכֵן בְּהֵמָה טְמֵאָה אוֹ מִטַּלְטְלִין, שֶׁכָּל אֵלּוּ נֶעֱרָכִין בְּשׁוּוְיֵיהֶן, בֵּין טוֹב בֵּין רַע; וּכְשֶׁבָּאִין הַכֹּהֲנִים לַעֲרֹךְ אוֹתָן, כּוֹפִין הַבְּעָלִים לִפְתֹּחַ רִאשׁוֹן וְלוֹמַר: בְּכֵן וְכֵן אֲנִי נוֹטְלָהּ לְעַצְמִי, וְהַדָּמִים נוֹפְלִין לְבֶדֶק הַבַּיִת; אֲבָל בַּזְּמַן הַזֶּה, אָמְרוּ זִכְרוֹנָם לִבְרָכָה שֶׁאֵין מַקְדִּישִׁין; וְנִרְאֶה וַדַּאי שֶׁאִם עָבַר וְהִקְדִּישׁ אֶת בֵּיתוֹ בַּזְּמַן הַזֶּה לְבֶדֶק הַבַּיִת, שֶׁמַּעֲרִיכִין אוֹתָהּ בְּשׁוּוְיָהּ, וְעָבִיד כְּתַקַּנְתָּא דִשְׁמוּאֵל, אוֹ מַשְׁלִיךְ כָּל שׁוּוְיָהּ לְיָם הַמֶּלַח.

---

§354   1. So Sifra, b'ḥukothai, perek 10, 2.

2. If a man consecrated a field that he had purchased, and afterward he wished to redeem it; TB 'Arachin 14b.

3. MT hilchoth 'arachin v 3 (see Ridvaz).

4. Ibid. based on TB 'Arachin 27a.

5. TB 'Avodah Zarah 13a.

6. TB 'Arachin 29a; see §350, paragraph 19.

7. I.e. lose it beyond recovery.

ordained. And since after the fact, having done it, we need an act of rectification for it even at the present time, I have to list it, and every-thing similar to it, among the precepts that are in effect at the present time.

[THAT IF ONE VOWS THE EVALUATION OF A HOUSE
HE SHOULD GIVE THE KOHEN'S VALUATION PLUS A
FIFTH]

354 to carry out the law of evaluation of houses; in other words, if someone consecrated his house, and he wished to redeem it from its consecrated state—he himself, his wife, or his heirs[1]—the *kohen* should determine its value, and he should pay him according to the valuation that he stated, plus another fifth: as it is written, *And when a man shall consecrate his house, holy,* etc. (Leviticus 27:14).

At the root of the precept lies what I wrote about the exchange [of an animal consecrated for an offering] in the second positive pre-cept of this *sidrah* (§352): that God desired, for our good, to inculcate a reverent fear of sanctity in the heart of humans. Even though it was a measure of His abounding kindness to give them a way to redeem it, He wished them to add a fifth in its redemption, so that one should keep away from deducting anything from the value of something consecrated. Even though there is no [requirement of an additional] fifth for a field of purchase,[2] that is because it is not usual for a man to consecrate his field of purchase, because he cherishes it greatly, since he bought it with his money. And the Torah is never particular about something that is not usual.

Among the laws of the precept, there is what the Sages of blessed memory said:[3] that if a person consecrates his house, and so likewise an unclean (impermissible) animal or movable goods, all these are evaluated at their actual worth, whether they are good or bad. When the *kohanim* come to evaluate them, they compel the owner to open [the estimation] first by saying, "At such-and-such a price would I buy it for myself"; and the money goes toward maintaining the Temple in repair.[4] At the present time, however, the Sages of blessed memory said that there should be no consecration.[5] Yet it seems cer-tain that if someone transgressed and consecrated his house at the present time toward repairs in the Temple, it is to be evaluated at its worth, and he should act according to the amendment of Sh'mu'el,[6] or he should throw its full value into the Dead Sea.[7]

וּבֵין שֶׁהָיָה הַבַּיִת בְּעָרֵי חוֹמָה בֵּין שֶׁהָיָה בְּעָרֵי הַחֲצֵרִים, לְעוֹלָם יְכוֹלִים
הַבְּעָלִים אוֹ יוֹרְשִׁים לִגְאֹל אוֹתָם מִיַּד הַהֶקְדֵּשׁ; אֲבָל גְּאָלוֹ אָדָם אַחֵר, אִם הָיָה
בְּבָתֵּי עָרֵי חוֹמָה וְקָם בְּיַד הַגּוֹאֵל שְׁנֵים-עָשָׂר חֹדֶשׁ, נֶחְלַט; וְאִם הָיָה בְּבָתֵּי
הַחֲצֵרִים וְהִגִּיעַ יוֹבֵל וְהוּא בְּיַד הַגּוֹאֵל, חוֹזֵר לִבְעָלָיו בַּיּוֹבֵל.

וּמִמַּה שֶׁאָמַר הַכָּתוּב "כִּי יַקְדִּישׁ אֶת בֵּיתוֹ" וְלֹא אָמַר "בַּיִת", דִּקְדְּקוּ זִכְרוֹנָם
לִבְרָכָה: מַה בֵּיתוֹ בִּרְשׁוּתוֹ, אַף כָּל דָּבָר שֶׁאָדָם רוֹצֶה לְהַקְדִּישׁ צָרִיךְ שֶׁיְּהֵא
בִּרְשׁוּתוֹ; אֲבָל אִם אֵינוֹ בִּרְשׁוּתוֹ, אַף-עַל-פִּי שֶׁהוּא שֶׁלּוֹ אֵינוֹ יָכוֹל לְהַקְדִּישׁוֹ. וְכֵן
אָמְרוּ זִכְרוֹנָם לִבְרָכָה: גָּזַל וְלֹא נִתְיָאֲשׁוּ הַבְּעָלִים, שְׁנֵיהֶן אֵינָם יְכוֹלִים לְהַקְדִּישׁ:
זֶה לְפִי שֶׁאֵינוֹ שֶׁלּוֹ, וְזֶה לְפִי שֶׁאֵינוֹ בִּרְשׁוּתוֹ. וְדַוְקָא בְּמִטַּלְטְלִין, אֲבָל קַרְקַע
בְּחֶזְקַת בְּעָלֶיהָ עוֹמֶדֶת; וַאֲפִלּוּ מִטַּלְטְלִין שֶׁהִפְקִידָן, כָּל שֶׁיָּכוֹל לְהוֹצִיאָן בְּדַיָּנִין,
יָכוֹל לְהַקְדִּישָׁן; וְיֶתֶר פְּרָטֶיהָ, בְּמַסֶּכֶת עֲרָכִין.

וְנוֹהֶגֶת בִּזְמַן שֶׁהַיּוֹבֵל נוֹהֵג, שֶׁאֵין דִּין עֶרְכֵי בָתִּים נוֹהֵג, כְּלוֹמַר לְהַקְדִּישׁ בַּיִת
לְכַתְּחִלָּה, אֶלָּא בִּזְמַן שֶׁהַיּוֹבֵל נוֹהֵג. וְעוֹבֵר עַל זֶה וְהִקְדִּישׁ בֵּיתוֹ וְלֹא נָתַן הָעֶרֶךְ
בִּזְמַן הַבַּיִת כַּמִּשְׁפָּט הַכָּתוּב בַּפָּרָשָׁה, אוֹ שֶׁלֹּא תִקֵּן הַדָּבָר בַּזְּמַן הַזֶּה כְּמוֹ
שֶׁאָמַרְנוּ, בִּטֵּל עֲשֵׂה, וְעוֹד יֵשׁ לוֹ עֹנֶשׁ שֶׁמּוֹעֵל בַּקֹּדֶשׁ.

[מִצְוַת מַעֲרִיךְ שָׂדֶה שֶׁיִּתֵּן בָּעֶרֶךְ הַקָּצוּב בַּפָּרָשָׁה]

שנה לָדוּן בְּדִין עֶרְכֵי שָׂדוֹת, כְּלוֹמַר הַמַּקְדִּישׁ שָׂדֵהוּ וְרָצָה לִפְדּוֹתוֹ, שֶׁיִּתֵּן
בָּעֶרֶךְ הַקָּצוּב בַּפָּרָשָׁה, "זֶרַע חֹמֶר שְׂעֹרִים בַּחֲמִשִּׁים שֶׁקֶל כָּסֶף" לְכָל שְׁנֵי

---

8. MT *hilchoth 'arachin* v 3-4, based on TB 'Arachin 31b, 33a (and see note 1).

9. Which would apparently convey the same law.

10. TB Bava Kamma 69b, etc.

11. I.e. is not available, accessible to him.

12. *Ibid.* 68b.

13. Since it cannot be removed or hidden, and so the owner can always recover it by legal means; TB Bava M'tzi'a 7a; MT *hilchoth 'arachin* vi 23.

14. See §330, three paragraphs before the end, and §335, end.

15. Apparently derived from TB 'Arachin 29a (MY).

16. Three paragraphs above (notes 6, 7).

Whether the house was in one of the walled cities or in one of the open cities, the owner or his heirs can always redeem it from the state of consecration. However, if another man redeemed it and it was one of the houses in a walled city, and it then remained twelve months in the redeemer's possession, it would be irrevocably his. If it was one of the houses in open cities and the jubilee arrived while it was in the redeemer's possession, it would return to its owner at the jubilee.[8]

Now, from the fact that Scripture states, "shall consecrate 'eth *bétho*, his house," and not "a house,"[9] the Sages of blessed memory deduced:[10] Just as his house is in his possession, so must anything that a man wishes to consecrate be in his possession. But if something is not in his possession,[11] even if it belongs to him he cannot consecrate it. Hence the Sages of blessed memory said:[12] If someone seized something in robbery and the owner did not give up hope for it, neither of them can consecrate it: the one, because it does not belong to him; and the other, because it is not in his possession. This, however, applies specifically to movable goods; but landed property remains in the status of its owner's possession.[13] Yet even movable goods that were given over for safekeeping [and are not willingly returned]— whatever can be extracted through judges can be consecrated. The rest of its details are in the Talmud tractate 'Arachin*.

It is in effect when the law of the jubilee is in effect;[14] for the law of the evaluation of houses—which means that initially a house is consecrated—is in force only at the time that the law of the jubilee is observed.[15] If someone violated this by consecrating his house and not giving the evaluation, at the time of the Temple, in accord with the requirement of Scripture written in this section; or if he did not rectify the matter at the present time in the way we stated[16]—he would disobey a positive precept. In addition, he would incur a penalty for committing a breach of holiness with a consecrated entity.

[THAT IF ONE VOWS A FIELD'S VALUATION, HE SHOULD
GIVE THE VALUE SET BY SCRIPTURE]

355 to carry out the law of valuations of fields; in other words, if a person consecrates his field, then wishes to redeem it, he should give according to the evaluation set in the Scriptural section: *the sowing of a homer of barley shall be valued at fifty shekels of silver* (Leviticus 27:16) for all the years of the jubilee period, which means forty-nine years.

הַיּוֹבֵל, שֶׁהֵם מ"ט שָׁנָה; וּלְפִי הַחֶשְׁבּוֹן מְכַנְּן יִהְיֶה עֶרֶךְ שָׂדֶה הָרָאוּי לִזְרֹעַ חֹמֶר
שְׂעוֹרִים, סֶלַע וּפוּנְדְּיוֹן לְשָׁנָה: לְפִי שֶׁהַשֶּׁקֶל הָאָמוּר בַּתּוֹרָה הוּא הַנִּקְרָא סֶלַע
סְתָם בִּלְשׁוֹן חֲכָמִים, וְהַגֵּרָה הָאֲמוּרָה בַּתּוֹרָה הִיא הַמָּעָה בְּדִבְרֵי חֲכָמִים; וְהוֹסִיפוּ
חֲכָמִים עַל הַשֶּׁקֶל, הַנִּקְרָא סֶלַע כְּמוֹ שֶׁאָמַרְנוּ, שְׁתוּת; וְהַסֶּלַע זֶה שָׁוֶה אַרְבָּעָה
דִינָרִין, וְהַדִּינָר שֵׁשׁ מָעִין וְהַמָּעָה שְׁנֵי פוּנְדְּיוֹנִין; נִמְצָא לְכָל שָׁנָה סֶלַע וּפוּנְדְּיוֹן,
שֶׁאַף־עַל־פִּי שֶׁהַסֶּלַע מ"ח פוּנְדְּיוֹנִין לְפִי חֶשְׁבּוֹנֵנוּ זֶה, מִכָּל־מָקוֹם הָרוֹצֶה לִקַּח
סֶלַע מִן הַשֻּׁלְחָנִי, מ"ט פוּנְדְּיוֹנִין הוּא צָרִיךְ לָתֵת, כְּדֵי שֶׁיַּרְוִיחַ בּוֹ הַשֻּׁלְחָנִי
פוּנְדְּיוֹן אֶחָד; וְאַחַר שֶׁהוּא צָרִיךְ לָתֵת מ"ט פוּנְדְּיוֹנִין, כְּפִי הַחֶשְׁבּוֹן שֶׁיְּקַחֵם
הַמַּקְדִּישׁ מִן הַשֻּׁלְחָנִי מְחַשְּׁבִין לוֹ, שֶׁיַּד הֶקְדֵּשׁ עַל הָעֶלְיוֹנָה לְעוֹלָם.

וְאֶחָד הַמַּקְדִּישׁ שָׂדֶה טוֹבָה שֶׁאֵין בְּכָל אֶרֶץ־יִשְׂרָאֵל כְּמוֹתָהּ, אוֹ שָׂדֶה רָעָה
שֶׁאֵין כְּמוֹתָהּ לְרֹעַ, כָּזֶה מַעֲרִיכִין אוֹתָהּ, שֶׁלֹּא רָצָה הַכָּתוּב לַחֲלֹק בְּעִנְיָן זֶה,
וְהִשְׁוָה כָּל הַקַּרְקָעוֹת לְעֶרֶךְ אֶחָד.

וְאַחַר שֶׁפֵּרַשְׁנוּ הַשְּׁקָלִים, רָאוּי שֶׁנְּפָרֵשׁ שִׁעוּר הַחֹמֶר, כַּמָּה הוּא. דַּע שֶׁהַחֹמֶר
הוּא מִדָּה אַחַת שֶׁנִּקְרֵאת כּוֹר, וְהַכּוֹר הוּא שְׁנֵי לְתָכִים, וְהַלֶּתֶךְ ט"ו סְאִין; נִמְצָא
הַחֹמֶר שְׁלֹשִׁים סְאִין, שֶׁהֵן י' אֵיפָה, שֶׁהָאֵיפָה שָׁלֹשׁ סְאִין, יָדוּעַ הַדָּבָר; וּכְבָר
יָדַעְנוּ גַם־כֵּן מִדִּבְרֵי רַבּוֹתֵינוּ זִכְרוֹנָם לִבְרָכָה שֶׁיֵּשׁ מָקוֹם שֶׁיֵּשׁ בּוֹ חֲמִשִּׁים אַמָּה עַל
חֲמִשִּׁים אַמָּה הוּא בֵּית־סְאָה, כְּלוֹמַר שֶׁהוּא מִזְרַע סְאָה שְׂעוֹרִים, וְהֵן אַלְפַּיִם
וַחֲמֵשׁ מֵאוֹת אַמָּה בַּתַּשְׁבֹּרֶת. נִמְצָא שֶׁמָּקוֹם הָרָאוּי לִזְרֹעַ חֹמֶר שְׂעוֹרִים, שֶׁהוּא
שְׁלֹשִׁים סְאִין, יֵשׁ בּוֹ חֲמִשָּׁה וְשִׁבְעִים אֶלֶף אַמָּה בַּתַּשְׁבֹּרֶת.

וְכֵיצַד דֶּרֶךְ הַחֶשְׁבּוֹן בְּעֶרְכֵי שָׂדוֹת: שָׂדֶה אֲחֻזָּה חָלוּק בְּעִנְיָנֵנוּ מִשָּׂדֶה מִקְנָה,
וּכְשֶׁמּוֹדְדִין אוֹתָהּ אֵין מוֹדְדִין בָּהּ אֶלָּא מְקוֹמוֹת הָרְאוּיִין לִזְרִיעָה, וְעֶרְכָּהּ הוּא
הַקָּצוּב בַּתּוֹרָה: זֶרַע חֹמֶר שְׂעוֹרִים בַּחֲמִשִּׁים שֶׁקֶל כֶּסֶף, כְּמוֹ שֶׁבֵּאַרְנוּ, בֵּין יָפָה
בֵּין רָעָה, וּמוֹסִיף חֹמֶשׁ עַל הָעֶרֶךְ הַזֶּה הַקָּצוּב.

§355   1. I.e. the *sela tzori* (*sela* of Tyre), which weighed and was worth 19.2 grams of pure silver.

2. To make it equal a *sela*; MT *hilchoth 'arachin* iv 3, based on TB Bava Bathra 90a.

3. And since the rate is fifty shekels (in the verse) for forty-nine years, it becomes one and one forty-ninth shekel per year; but since the shekel, or *sela*, is worth forty-eight *pundyons*, one forty-ninth of a shekel would be slightly less than a *pundyon*.

4. I.e. it has all the advantages; hence it is entitled to the extra *pundyon*, like a money-changer. The entire reckoning here is based on MT *hilchoth 'arachin* iv 3, which is based in turn on Mishnah, Sh'kalim i 10 and TB Kiddushin 12a, etc.

5. TB 'Arachin 14a; MT *ibid.* 2.

6. According to one view, it is 248,832 cubic centimeters; according to another view, 430,000.

7. I.e. fifty cubits by fifty cubits (50 × 50) = 2500 square cubits; TB 'Eruvin 23b.   ⟨490⟩

By the exact reckoning, the valuation of a field suitable for sowing a *homer* of barley would be a *sela* and a *pundyon* per year; for the shekel in the Torah is what is simply called a *sela* in the language of the Sages;[1] while the *gérah* mentioned in the Torah is the *ma'ah* in the vocabulary of the Sages; and the Sages added to the shekel—called a *sela*, as we said—one sixth.[2] The *sela* is worth four *denarii*; the *denar* is six *ma'ah*; while the *ma'ah* is worth two *pundyons*. Consequently, [the rate] for every year is a *sela* and a *pundyon*. For although the *sela* is forty-eight *pundyons* by this reckoning of ours,[3] nevertheless, when a person wants to buy a *sela* from a money-changer, it is forty-nine *pundyons* that he must give, so that the money-changer should earn one *pundyon*. And since he would need to give forty-nine *pundyons*, we calculate it for him according to the amount with which the person consecrating it would buy it from the money-changer. For the realm of the sacred always has the upper hand.[4]

It is all one whether a person consecrates a fine field, the like of which is not [to be found] in all the land of Israel, or a poor field, whose equal in meagerness is not [to be found]—it is thus evaluated.[5] For the Writ did not wish to differentiate in this matter, and it made all properties equal, subject to one evaluation.

Having explained the shekel, it would be fitting for us to explain the quantity of a *homer*, how much it is. Know that the *homer* is a certain measure called a *kor*;[6] the *kor* is two measures named *lethech*, the *lethech* being fifteen *se'ah*. Hence the *homer* is thirty *se'ah*, which is ten *'éphah*; for the *'éphah* is three *se'ah*—it is a known matter. We have likewise known previously from the words of our Sages of blessed memory that an area containing fifty cubits by fifty cubits is a *béth se'ah*, i.e. it is a planting area [that can grow] a *se'ah* of barley—this being 2,500 square cubits[7] in surface measure. Consequently, an area capable of being sown [to grow] a *homer* of barley, which is thirty *se'ah*, would contain 75;000 square cubits in surface measure.[8]

Now, what is the way of reckoning the valuation of fields? A field of heritage is different in its treatment from a field of purchase.[9] When it [the former] is measured, none but those areas in it that are fit for sowing are measured;[10] and its valuation is the one fixed in the Torah: the sowing *of a homer of barley shall be valued at fifty shekels of silver* (Leviticus 27:16), as we explained, whether it is good (fertile) or poor (barren); and a fifth is to be added on to this fixed valuation.[11]

Let this rule be in your hand about every fifth mentioned in the

וּכְלָל זֶה יִהְיֶה בְּיָדְךָ בְּכָל חֹמֶשׁ הָאָמוּר בַּתּוֹרָה, שֶׁהוּא רְבִיעַ הַקֶּרֶן, כְּדֵי שֶׁיְהֵא
הַקֶּרֶן עִם הַחֹמֶשׁ הַנּוֹסָף עָלָיו, הַכֹּל חֲמִשָּׁה.

וְאִם כָּל הַשָּׂדֶה שֶׁהִקְדִּישׁ אֵינָהּ רְאוּיָה לְזָרְעָהּ כְּלָל, פּוֹדִין אוֹתָהּ בְּשׁוּוּיָהּ. וְאֵי
זוֹ הִיא נִקְרֵאת שְׂדֵה אֲחֻזָּה, זֶה שָׂדֶה שֶׁיְּרָשָׁהּ הָאָדָם מֵאֲבוֹרִשָׁיו; וּשְׂדֵה מִקְנָה הוּא
שָׂדֶה שֶׁלְּקָחָהּ אָדָם מִשֶּׁלּוֹ, אוֹ שֶׁזָּכָה בָּהּ בְּשׁוּם צַד שֶׁלֹּא מֵחֲמַת יְרֻשָׁה.

וְדִין הַמַּקְדִּישׁ שָׂדֶה מִקְנָתוֹ, שֶׁשָּׁמִין אוֹתָהּ בְּשׁוּוּיָהּ, רוֹאִין כַּמָּה שָׁוָה עַד שְׁנַת
הַיּוֹבֵל, וְאִם פְּדָאָהּ הַמַּקְדִּישׁ אֵינוֹ מוֹסִיף בָּהּ חֹמֶשׁ, וּפִדְיוֹנָהּ לְבֶדֶק הַבַּיִת כִּשְׁאָר
עֲרָכִין וְדָמִים, וּכְשֶׁיַּגִּיעַ הַיּוֹבֵל תַּחֲזֹר הַשָּׂדֶה לַבְּעָלִים שֶׁמְּכָרוּהָ; בֵּין שֶׁנִּפְדֵּית מִיַּד
הַגִּזְבָּר עַל יַד שׁוּם אָדָם וְיוֹצְאָה מִתַּחַת יָדוֹ, בֵּין שֶׁלֹּא נִפְדֵּית וְיוֹצְאָה מִיַּד הַקְּדֵשׁ,
חוֹזֵר לְעוֹלָם לַאֲשֶׁר לוֹ אֲחֻזַּת הָאָרֶץ וְאֵינָהּ יוֹצְאָה לַכֹּהֲנִים, לְפִי שֶׁאֵין אָדָם
מַקְדִּישׁ דָּבָר שֶׁאֵינוֹ שֶׁלּוֹ, וְזֶה הַקַּרְקַע לֹא הָיָה לַלּוֹקֵחַ כִּי־אִם עַד שְׁנַת הַיּוֹבֵל.

וְלֹא כֵן שָׂדֶה אֲחֻזָּה, שֶׁאִם הִגִּיעַ הַיּוֹבֵל וְלֹא פְדָאוּהָ הַבְּעָלִים מִיַּד הַקְּדֵשׁ אוֹ
מִיַּד אַחֵר שֶׁקְּנָאָהּ מִן הַהֶקְדֵּשׁ, הַכֹּהֲנִים נוֹתְנִין דָּמֶיהָ, לְפִי שֶׁאֵין הֶקְדֵּשׁ יוֹצֵא בְּלֹא
פִדְיוֹן, וְהִיא אֲחֻזָּה לָהֶם לְעוֹלָם, וְאוֹתָן הַדָּמִים נוֹפְלִין לְהֶקְדֵּשׁ בֶּדֶק הַבַּיִת.

וְכָל שָׂדֶה שֶׁשָּׁמִין אוֹתָהּ לְהֶקְדֵּשׁ לִמְכֹּר אוֹתָהּ בְּדָמֶיהָ, מַכְרִיזִין עָלֶיהָ שְׁשִׁים
יוֹם בַּבֹּקֶר וּבָעֶרֶב, שֶׁהוּא שָׁעָה שֶׁהַפּוֹעֲלִים נִכְנָסִין לִמְלַאכְתָּן וְיוֹצְאִין, כְּדֵי
שֶׁיִּשְׁמְעוּ הַכֹּל בַּדָּבָר, וּמְסַמְּנִין מְצָרָנֶיהָ וְאוֹמְרִין: כָּךְ הִיא יָפָה וּבְכָךְ הִיא שׁוּמָהּ,
וְכָל הָרוֹצֶה לִקַּח יָבוֹא וְיִקַּח; וְיֶתֶר פְּרָטֶיהָ, מְבֹאָרִין מְשֻׁלָּם בַּמַּסֶּכְתָּא הַבְּנוּיָה עַל
זֶה, וְהִיא מַסֶּכֶת עֲרָכִין.

וְנוֹהֶגֶת בִּזְכָרִים וּנְקֵבוֹת בִּזְמַן שֶׁהַיּוֹבֵל נוֹהֵג, אֲבָל בַּזְּמַן הַזֶּה, כְּבָר אָמְרוּ

8. Thirty (30) times 2500 equals 75,000. This paragraph is based on MT *hilchoth 'arachin* iv 4.

9. The two kinds of fields are defined two paragraphs below; see TB 'Arachin 24a, 25a.

10. *Ibid.* 25a.

11. Leviticus 27:19.

12. So TB Bava M'tzi'a 54a.

13. TB 'Arachin 12b.

14. And thus it has passed down from owners to heirs since the land was allotted to the original settlers; see §339, seventh paragraph.

15. TB 'Arachin 14b (and Rashi, s.v. *talmud lomar*).

16. *Ibid.*

17. TB 'Arachin 24a, T'murah 31b.

18. Who generally acquire landed property that does not revert to its owner.

19. TB 'Arachin 26b.

20. Mishnah, 'Arachin vii 3–4 (TB 25a-b); MT *hilchoth 'arachin* iv 19–20. MY notes a difficulty here: According to our text, if a man consecrated his *s'déh ahuzah*, his field of heritage (so that it would be a source of income for Sanctuary repairs) and

Torah: that it is a fourth of the principal, so that the principal with
the fifth added to it should be, all together, five parts.[12]

If the entire field that a person consecrated is not fit for sowing
at all, it is redeemed for its actual worth.[13] Now, which is called a
field of heritage? It is a field that a man inherited from those who
left it to him.[14] A field of purchase is a field that a man bought with
his own means, or which he acquired in some way other than by virtue
of inheritance.

Then there is the law for one who consecrates his field of purchase:
that is evaluated at its actual worth; we see how much it is worth till
the jubilee year.[15] If the one who consecrated it redeems it, he does
not add a fifth to it.[16] The money for its redemption goes for repairs
of the Temple, like other valuations and [similar] money.[17] And when
jubilee arrives, the field is to revert to the owner who sold it. Whether
it was redeemed from the [Temple] treasurer's possession by any
man, whereupon it goes out from his possession, or whether it was
not redeemed, whereupon it leaves the realm of consecration, it always reverts to the one who has the [original] possession of the land
and it does not return to the *kohanim*[18]—because a man cannot consecrate something that is not his, and this land belonged to the purchaser
only till the jubilee year.[19]

This is not the case, though, with a field of heritage. If the jubilee
arrives and the owner has not redeemed it from the realm of consecration, or from the possession of another who bought it from the realm
of consecration, the *kohanim* give its monetary value—since nothing
consecrated can go out without redemption—and it is then a possession
of theirs for all time. Then that money goes to the treasury of the
Sanctuary, for Temple repairs.[20]

If any field is evaluated for the treasury of the Sanctuary, in order
to sell it to realize its monetary value, proclamation is made about it
for sixty days, morning and evening, since that is the time when
laborers go in to their work and then leave it—in order that all should
hear the matter. Its boundaries are delineated, and it is announced,
"It is of this-and-this quality, and it is valued at so much"; and whoever wishes to, may come and buy it.[21] The rest of its details are completely explained in the Talmud tractate built about this, which is
the tractate *'Arachin*.

It applies to both man and woman, at the time that the law of
⟨493⟩ the jubilee is in effect. For the present time, however, our Sages said

חֲכָמִים שֶׁאֵין מַקְדִּישִׁין וְלֹא מַחֲרִימִין וְלֹא מַעֲרִיכִין, כְּמוֹ שֶׁכָּתַבְנוּ לְמַעְלָה.
וּמִכָּל־מָקוֹם אִם עָבַר וְהִקְדִּישׁ קַרְקַע עַצְמוֹ לְבֶדֶק הַבַּיִת, אֶפְשָׁר לֵיהּ בְּתַקָּנָה
כִּדְשְׁמוּאֵל, שֶׁמְּחַלְּלוֹ עַל שָׁוֶה פְרוּטָה אוֹ יוֹתֵר וּמַשְׁלִיכָם לְיָם־הַמֶּלַח; וְאִם אֵינוֹ
רוֹצֶה בְּתַקָּנָה זוֹ, נִרְאֶה וַדַּאי שֶׁיֵּשׁ לוֹ לְהַעֲרִיכוֹ כַּמִּשְׁפָּט שֶׁכָּתַבְנוּ, וּמַשְׁלִיךְ הַדָּמִים
לְיָם־הַמֶּלַח, כְּדֵי שֶׁלֹּא יִהְיוּ לְמִכְשֹׁל לוֹ אוֹ לְבָנָיו; מוּטָב יֹאבְדוּ וְאַל יְכַשְּׁלוּ בָהֶם
בְּנֵי־אָדָם, מִשֶּׁיַּנִּיחֵם בְּקֶרֶן זָוִית לְבֶדֶק הַבַּיִת, כִּי לֶעָתִיד לֹא נֶחְסַר מָמוֹן לְחַזֵּק אֶת
בֵּית אֱלֹהֵינוּ.

[שֶׁלֹּא לְשַׁנּוֹת הַקֳּדָשִׁים מִקָּרְבָּן לְקָרְבָּן]

שנו שֶׁלֹּא לְשַׁנּוֹת הַקֳּדָשִׁים מִקָּרְבָּן לְקָרְבָּן, כְּגוֹן שֶׁנַּחֲזִיר הַשְּׁלָמִים אָשָׁם, אוֹ
הָאָשָׁם שֶׁנַּחֲזִירֵהוּ חַטָּאת; בָּזֶה וְהַדּוֹמֶה לוֹ יֵשׁ בּוֹ לָאו, וְעַל דָּבָר זֶה נֶאֱמַר בְּכָאן
בִּבְכוֹר: לֹא יַקְדִּישׁ אִישׁ אֹתוֹ, כְּלוֹמַר שֶׁלֹּא יַעֲשֶׂה הַבְּכוֹר לֹא עוֹלָה וְלֹא שְׁלָמִים
וְלֹא קָרְבָּן אַחֵר; וּבָאָה הַקַּבָּלָה דְּלָאו דַּוְקָא בִּבְכוֹר הִקְפִּיד הַכָּתוּב, דְּהוּא הַדִּין
לְכָל הֶקְדֵּשׁ מִזְבֵּחַ, שֶׁכֵּן אָמְרוּ בְּסִפְרֵי: אֵין לִי אֶלָּא בְכוֹר; מִנַּיִן לְכָל הַקֳּדָשִׁים
שֶׁאֵין מְשַׁנִּין אוֹתָן מִקְּדֻשָּׁה לִקְדֻשָּׁה — תַּלְמוּד לוֹמַר: בַּבְּהֵמָה לֹא יַקְדִּישׁ אִישׁ
אֹתוֹ, יִרְמֹז בְּכָל בְּהֵמָה קְדוֹשָׁה, בֵּין קָדְשֵׁי קְדֻשָּׁה לְקָדְשֵׁי מִזְבֵּחַ אוֹ אֲפִלּוּ לְבֶדֶק הַבַּיִת,
שֶׁאֵין מְשַׁנִּין אוֹתָהּ מִקְּדֻשָּׁתָהּ, וְעַל הַכֹּל נֶאֱמַר: לֹא יַקְדִּישׁ אִישׁ אֹתוֹ, אֲבָל יַנַּח
כְּמוֹת שֶׁהוּא.

מִשָּׁרְשֵׁי הַמִּצְוָה, מַה שֶּׁכָּתַבְתִּי בְּמִצְוַת עֲשֵׂה ב׳ [סִי׳ שנ"ב] בִּתְמוּרָה, כִּי כָל
זֶה לְמוֹרָאַת הַקֹּדֶשׁ.

מִדִּינֵי הַמִּצְוָה, מַה שֶּׁאָמְרוּ זִכְרוֹנָם לִבְרָכָה שֶׁאִם הִקְדִּישׁ לְבֶדֶק הַהֵיכָל, לֹא

another bought it subsequently from *hekdesh* (the realm of consecration), and until the jubilee the owner did not redeem it to regain possession, on the arrival of the jubilee the field becomes the permanent possession of the *kohanim*—but they must give its monetary value to the Sanctuary treasury, "since nothing consecrated can go out without redemption." For this last stipulation, MY notes, there is no basis in the Mishnah in TB 'Arachin; and indeed, why should the *kohanim* give money for the field in the jubilee year, when the man who bought it subsequent to the owner's consecration paid for it then, redeeming it from the realm of consecration? MY would therefore omit the second *mi-yad* as a scribal error, and the resulting phrase, וְלֹא פְדָאוּהוּ הַבְּעָלִים מִיַּד הֶקְדֵּשׁ אוֹ אַחֵר שֶׁקְּנָאָהּ מִן הַהֶקְדֵּשׁ (though somewhat awkward) would then mean, "and the owner has not redeemed if from *hekdesh*, nor was there anyone else who puchased it from *hekdesh*," etc.

To my humble mind, the words אוֹ מִיַּד אַחֵר שֶׁקְּנָאָהּ מִן הַהֶקְדֵּשׁ "or from the possession of another who bought it from the realm of consecration" (the reading found in all the manuscripts and editions) might perhaps have been inserted by the author as a parenthetical phrase, to call the attention of his son and the young lad's friends (for whom, by his own statement, he originally wrote this work) to another case which

long ago that no consecration, *hérem* (proscriptive devotement) or valuation should be vowed, as we wrote above (§350). In any event, though, if someone transgressed and consecrated land today toward keeping the Temple in repair, he can make use of the amendment of Sh'mu'él,²² by which he exchanges it for something worth a *p'rutah* or more to make it non-holy, and throws that into the Dead Sea.²³ If he does not wish to use this amendment, it seems certain that he must have it evaluated according to the rule that we have written, then throw the money into the Dead Sea,²³ so that it should not be a stumbling-block for him or his children.²⁴ Better that it should be lost and people should not come to grief with it, than that it should be left in some corner for the fund for Temple repairs.²⁵ For in the future we shall not lack wealth to strengthen the house of our God.

[THE PROHIBITION AGAINST CHANGING CONSECRATED ANIMALS FROM ONE KIND OF OFFERING TO ANOTHER]

356 not to change consecrated animals from one offering to another; for example, as we might turn a *sh'lamim* (peace-offering) into an *'asham* (guilt-offering), or if it is an *'asham*, turn it into a *sh'lamim*. About this or anything like it there is a negative precept; in regard to this matter it is stated here about a firstborn animal, *no man shall sanctify it* (Leviticus 27:26): in other words, no one is to make a firstborn animal either an *'olah* (burnt-offering) or a *sh'lamim* or any other offering; and the Oral Tradition teaches that Scripture was not particular about a firstling alone, as the law is the same about all animals consecrated for the altar. For so was it taught in the Midrash *Sifra*:¹ I know this only about a firstborn animal; how do I learn it about all sacred offerings— that they are not to be changed from one category of holiness to another?—Scripture states, *among animals, no man shall sanctify it (ibid.)*, implying [this] about every hallowed [dedicated] animal: Whether it was consecrated for the holy offerings on the altar, or even toward maintaining the Temple in repair, it is not to be transposed from its holiness. It was stated about everything, *no man shall sanctify it*; it should rather be left as it is.²

At the root of the precept lies the purpose I wrote about the second positive precept (§352), concerning substitution for a consecrated animal: that it is all for the aim of a reverent fear toward sanctity.

Among the laws of the precept, there is what the Sages of blessed memory said:³ that if a person consecrated something toward main-

יְשַׁנֶּה לְבֶדֶק מִזְבֵּחַ, וְכֵן כָּל כַּיּוֹצֵא־בָזֶה. וְעוֹד אָמְרוּ גַּם־כֵּן שֶׁאֵין מַעֲרִימִין עַל בֶּהֱמַת הַהֶקְדֵּשׁ לְהַקְדִּישׁ עֲבָרָהּ קְדֻשָּׁה אַחֶרֶת, אֶלָּא הֲרֵי הוּא בִּקְדֻשַּׁת אִמּוֹ, שֶׁוַּלְדוֹת קָדָשִׁים מִמְּעֵי אִמָּן הֵן קְדוֹשִׁים.

מַה שֶּׁאֵין כֵּן בִּבְכוֹר, שֶׁהַבְּכוֹר בִּיצִיאָתוֹ הוּא מִתְקַדֵּשׁ, דִּבְפֶטֶר־רֶחֶם תָּלָה הַכָּתוּב, וּלְפִיכָךְ אֶפְשָׁר לְהָעֲרִים עַל הַבְּכוֹר קֹדֶם שֶׁנּוֹלַד, לְהַקְדִּישׁוֹ קְדֻשָּׁה אַחֶרֶת; וְעַל זֶה נֶאֱמַר: אֲשֶׁר יְבֻכַּר לַיי... לֹא יַקְדִּישׁ אִישׁ אֹתוֹ — מִשֶּׁיְּבֻכַּר אִי אַתָּה מַקְדִּישׁוֹ, אֲבָל אַתָּה מַקְדִּישׁוֹ בַּבֶּטֶן; וּלְפִיכָךְ מִי שֶׁאָמַר ״אִם תֵּלֵד זָכָר הַמְבֻכֶּרֶת, הֲרֵי הוּא עוֹלָה״, יִקְרַב לְעוֹלָה; אֲבָל אֵינוֹ יָכוֹל לַעֲשׂוֹתוֹ זִבְחֵי שְׁלָמִים, לְפִי שֶׁאֵינוֹ יָכוֹל לְהַפְקִיעוֹ מִקְּדֻשָּׁתוֹ, וּקְדֻשַּׁת הַשְּׁלָמִים לְמַטָּה הִיא מִן הַבְּכוֹר, שֶׁהַבְּכוֹר נֶאֱכָל לַכֹּהֲנִים לְבַדָּם, וְהַשְּׁלָמִים לְכָל אָדָם; וְיֶתֶר פְּרָטֶיהָ, בְּפֶרֶק חֲמִישִׁי מִתְּמוּרָה.

וְנוֹהֵג אִסּוּר זֶה בְּכָל מָקוֹם וּבְכָל זְמַן, בִּזְכָרִים וּנְקֵבוֹת: שֶׁאֲפִלּוּ בַּזְּמַן הַזֶּה, שֶׁאֵין מַקְדִּישִׁין, מִי שֶׁעָבַר וְהִקְדִּישׁ בְּהֵמָה לְהַקְדֵּשׁ אֶחָד, אֵינוֹ יָכוֹל לְשַׁנּוֹתָהּ לְהֶקְדֵּשׁ אַחֵר. וְעוֹבֵר עַל זֶה וְשִׁנָּה אוֹתוֹ מִקְּדֻשָּׁה לִקְדֻשָּׁה, כְּגוֹן שֶׁהִקְדִּישׁוֹ לִשְׁלָמִים וְאָמַר אַחַר־כָּךְ שֶׁתְּהֵא קְדוֹשָׁה לְעוֹלָה אוֹ לְקָרְבָּן אַחֵר, עָבַר עַל לָאו זֶה; וְאֵין לוֹקִין עָלָיו, לְפִי שֶׁאֵין בּוֹ מַעֲשֶׂה.

[מִצְוַת דִּין מַחֲרִים מִנְּכָסָיו שֶׁהוּא לַכֹּהֲנִים]

שנז לָדוּן בְּדִינֵי חֲרָמִים, כְּלוֹמַר שֶׁכָּל מִי שֶׁהֶחֱרִים דָּבָר מִנְּכָסָיו סְתָם, כְּגוֹן שֶׁאָמַר ״דָּבָר פְּלוֹנִי מִמַּה שֶׁיֵּשׁ לִי יְהִי חֵרֶם״, שֶׁיִּנָּתֵן אוֹתוֹ דָבָר לַכֹּהֵן, שֶׁנֶּאֱמַר: אַךְ כָּל חֵרֶם אֲשֶׁר יַחֲרִם אִישׁ וְגוֹמֵר — אֶלָּא־אִם־כֵּן אָמַר בְּפֵרוּשׁ שֶׁהַחֵרֶם יִהְיֶה

comes under consideration in this subject—although the ruling that follows does not apply to it. We find something quite similar in §330: as remarked there in note 11a, the rule given in a general statement does not apply to one item in it. Again, in §325 MY points out (note 6) that one statement is imprecise, and the author's purpose would seem to be to merely mention details or subjects in order to draw the attention of his son and the youngster's friends to them—for further study.

21. TB 'Arachin 21b.

22. See §350, paragraph 19.

23. To lose it beyond recovery.

24. By tempting them into using it, whereby they would commit a breach of holiness.

25. I.e. when the Sanctuary will be rebuilt.

§356   1. Sifra, b'ḥukothai, parashah 8, 3.

2. The paragraph is based on ShM negative precept §107.

3. TB T'murah 32a; MT bilchoth t'murah iv 11.

4. The holy chamber, the holy of holies, and the 'ulam (entrance hall) leading to them, in the Sanctuary (§95, fourth paragraph from the end).

taining the *héchal*[4] in repair, he should not change it to apply to repairs
of the altar; and so anything similar. In addition, they likewise taught[5]
that no plan should be made about a consecrated animal to consecrate
its unborn young for another holy purpose, but it should rather have
the same hallowing as its dam (mother); for the young of consecrated
animals are hallowed while yet in the womb of their mother.

This, however, is not the case with a firstborn animal: for a firstling
becomes hallowed at its emergence, since Scripture made it depend on
being the first to leave that womb. It is therefore possible to decide
about a firstling before it is born, to consecrate it for a different holiness.
For this reason it is stated, *which shall become a firstling to the Lord . . . no
man shall sanctify it*: From the time it becomes a firstborn animal you
may not consecrate it, but you may consecrate it while it is in the
womb.[5] Therefore, if someone said, "If this animal carrying its first
young will bear a male, it shall be an '*olah*" (burnt-offering), it is to
be offered up as an '*olah*.[6] But he cannot [similarly] make it a *sh'lamim*
sacrifice, because he cannot wrest it from its holiness;[6] and the holiness
of a *sh'lamim* is of lower degree than that of a firstling, since a firstling
may be eaten by the *kohanim* alone, and the *sh'lamim* by everyone. The
rest of its details are in chapter 5 of the tractate *T'murah*.

This prohibition is in effect everywhere, at every time, for both
man and woman. For even at present, when there should be no consecration,[7] if a person transgressed and consecrated an animal for one
particular holy purpose, he could not transfer it to another holy
purpose. If someone transgressed this and transposed it from one
sanctity to another—for instance, if he consecrated it for a *sh'lamim*, and
afterward he said it should be consecrated for an '*olah* or for another
offering, he would violate this negative precept. Yet whiplashes are
not suffered for it, since it involves no physical action.

[THE PRECEPT THAT IF ONE VOWS A ḤÉREM ON PROP-
ERTY OF HIS, IT GOES TO THE KOHANIM]

357 to carry out the laws of *ḥérem* (a proscriptive vow of devotement); in other words, whoever simply declares something among
his possessions to be *ḥérem*—for instance, if he says, "That certain
item out of what belongs to me shall be *ḥérem*"—that item is to be
given to a *kohen*: For it is stated, *But no ḥérem that a man will vow in
proscription*, etc. (Leviticus 27:28); unless he said distinctly that the

ḥérem (the proscribed item) should be for the Lord, or for the upkeep

לַיי אוֹ לְבֶדֶק הַבַּיִת; שֶׁכָּךְ אָמְרוּ זִכְרוֹנָם לִבְרָכָה: סְתָם חֲרָמִים לַכֹּהֲנִים, וּרְאָיָתָם מִמַּה שֶׁכָּתוּב בְּפֵרוּשׁ בַּפָּרָשָׁה: כִּשְׂדֵה הַחֵרֶם לַכֹּהֵן תִּהְיֶה אֲחֻזָּתוֹ.

מִשָּׁרְשֵׁי הַמִּצְוָה, לְפִי שֶׁיִּשְׂרָאֵל הוּא הָעָם אֲשֶׁר בָּחַר הָאֵל מִכָּל שְׁאָר הָעַמִּים לַעֲבוֹדָתוֹ וּלְהַכִּיר שְׁמוֹ, וְהֵם אֵינָם תַּחַת מֶמְשֶׁלֶת הַמַּזָּלוֹת אֲשֶׁר חָלַק יי לְכָל שְׁאָר הָעַמִּים, אֲבָל הֵם תַּחַת יָדוֹ שֶׁל הַקָּדוֹשׁ בָּרוּךְ הוּא מִבְּלִי אֶמְצָעוּת מַלְאָךְ וּמַזָּל, וּכְמוֹ שֶׁכָּתוּב: כִּי חֵלֶק יי עַמּוֹ יַעֲקֹב חֶבֶל נַחֲלָתוֹ, וּכְמוֹ שֶׁאַתָּה מוֹצֵא כְּשֶׁגְּאָלָם מִמִּצְרַיִם, שֶׁהָיָה נֵס כּוֹלֵל כָּל הָאֻמָּה, שֶׁהוּא בְעַצְמוֹ וּבִכְבוֹדוֹ הוֹצִיאָם מִשָּׁם, כְּמוֹ שֶׁדָּרְשׁוּ זִכְרוֹנָם לִבְרָכָה: "וְעָבַרְתִּי בְאֶרֶץ מִצְרַיִם", אֲנִי וְלֹא מַלְאָךְ, "וְהִכֵּיתִי כָל בְּכוֹר", אֲנִי וְלֹא שָׂרָף, וְגוֹמֵר, כְּמוֹ שֶׁבָּא בַּהַגָּדָה.

וְלָכֵן, בְּכָל עֵת הֱיוֹת יִשְׂרָאֵל מַחֲזִיקִים בְּתוֹרָתוֹ וּמִתְעַטְּרִים בַּעֲבוֹדָתוֹ, לֹא תָנוּחַ בָּהֶם רַק טוֹבָה וְשֶׁפַע בְּרָכָה, וְרוּחַ נְדִיבָה וּטְהוֹרָה תִסְמְכֵם; וְהַהֵפֶךְ, וְהִיא הַמְּאֵרָה וְהַחֵרֶם, עַל אוֹיְבֵיהֶם וְשׂוֹנְאֵיהֶם.

וְעַל-כֵּן, כִּי יִקְצֹר רוּחַ אֶחָד מֵהֶם וְיוֹצִיא מִפִּיו לְשׁוֹן קְלָלָה וְחֵרֶם עַל מָמוֹנוֹ וְקַרְקְעוֹתָיו, שֶׁהֵם תַּחַת הַבְּרָכָה, הוֹדִיעוּ הַכָּתוּב שֶׁאִי-אֶפְשָׁר לוֹ לְהוֹצִיאוֹ מֵרְשׁוּת הַמְּבֹרָךְ לִרְשׁוּת אַחֵר, לְפִי שֶׁכָּל אֲשֶׁר לְיִשְׂרָאֵל, שֶׁהֵם חֵלֶק הַשֵּׁם, לוֹ הוּא, וּמַה שֶּׁקָּנָה עֶבֶד קָנָה רַבּוֹ; אֲבָל מִכָּל-מָקוֹם, אַחַר שֶׁיְּדָעֲנוּ בֶאֱמֶת כִּי כַּוָּנַת הַמַּחֲרִים לְהוֹצִיא אוֹתוֹ הַדָּבָר מֵרְשׁוּתוֹ, רָאוּי לְהַשְׁלִים חֶפְצוֹ, וְיָשׁוּב בִּרְשׁוּת אֲדוֹנָיו וְיִהְיֶה קֹדֶשׁ.

וְזֶהוּ שֶׁאָמַר הַכָּתוּב בְּסָמוּךְ: כָּל חֵרֶם אֲשֶׁר יָחֳרַם מִן הָאָדָם לֹא יִפָּדֶה מוֹת יוּמָת, שֶׁעִנְיָנוּ עַל דֶּרֶךְ הַפְּשָׁט שֶׁהַמַּחֲרִים מִן הָאָדָם שֶׁאֵינוֹ שֶׁלּוֹ, כְּגוֹן הַנִּלְחָמִים

---

5. TB T'murah 25a.

6. *Ibid.* 24b.

7. See § 350, fifth paragraph before the end.

§357   1. TB 'Arachin 28b.

2. Literally, under the hand.

3. Where verbs from the same roots as *ḥérem* occur in Scripture, without exception in the *hiph'il* (and *hoph'al*) conjugation, they invariably have the sense of destroying condemned life and/or property (generally of a vile enemy) in response to the Almighty's firm wish or command; and the life and/or property in question is most strictly forbidden for anyone's use or benefit. (See e.g. Numbers 21:2–3, Deuteronomy 2:34, 3:6, 7:2, 13:16, 20:17, Joshua 8:26, etc.) Then here it should initially mean a vow to treat some item of property rather similarly, i.e. to proscribe any use or benefit from it and solemnly relegate it to destruction.

4. So TB P'saḥim 88b.

of the Temple. For so the Sages of blessed memory said: [1] With general, unspecified vows of ḥérem, [the items go] to kohanim; and you can see (learn) this from what is written explicitly in the Scriptural section: *like a field of ḥérem, its possession shall go to the* kohen (*ibid.* 21).

At the root of the precept lies the reason that the Israelites are the people that God chose above all the other peoples, to serve and worship Him and to recognize His name. They are not under the dominion of the zodiacal constellations, which the Lord allotted to all the other nations, but are rather under the rule[2] of the Holy One, blessed is He, without the mediating agency of any angel or constellation; as it is written, *the portion of the Lord is His people, Jacob the lot of His heritage* (Deuteronomy 32:9); and as you find when He rescued them from Egypt, which [rescue] was a miracle that involved the entire people, that He Himself, in His glory, led them forth from there. As the Sages of blessed memory interpreted: *For I will go through the land of Egypt* (Exodus 12:12)—I, and not an angel; *and I will smite all the firstborn* (*ibid.*)—I, and not a seraph; and so forth, as we read in the [Passover] Haggadah.

Therefore, whenever the Israelites (Jewry) uphold His Torah and adorn themselves with His service and worship, nothing but goodness and an abounding flow of blessing will abide with them, and a spirit of generosity and purity will sustain them, while the opposite, i.e. malediction and ḥérem (proscription for destruction) will lie upon their foes and enemies.

Therefore, if one of them [the Israelites] becomes short-tempered, irritated, and he emits out of his mouth an expression of malediction and ḥérem about his property and lands, which are under the blessing, Scripture has informed him that it is impossible for him to transfer it from the realm of the blessed to another domain.[3] For whatever belongs to Israelites, who are the portion of the Eternal Lord, belongs to Him; whatever a servant acquires, his master acquires.[4] Nevertheless, since we know in truth that the intention of the one who pronounced the ḥérem was to remove that thing from his possession, it is proper to fulfill his desire. Then let it return to the possession of his Master, and be consecrated.

This is why Scripture states shortly afterward, *No object of ḥérem that may be proscribed among men shall be ransomed; he shall surely be put to death* (Leviticus 27:29). For its sense, taken at its plain meaning, is

⟨499⟩ that if one imposes a *ḥérem* on any human being who is not of his

עַל אוֹיְבֵיהֶם שֶׁנּוֹדְרִים נֶדֶר, "אִם נָתֹן תִּתֵּן אֶת הָעָם הַזֶּה בְּיָדִי וְהַחֲרַמְתִּי אֶת
עָרֵיהֶם", שֶׁיָּמוּתוּ, כִּי שְׁאָר הָאֻמּוֹת אֵינָם בְּתוֹךְ מַעְיַן הַבְּרָכוֹת, כְּמוֹ שֶׁאָמַרְנוּ,
וּלְשׁוֹן חֵרֶם נִתְפַּס עֲלֵיהֶן וּפוֹעֵל בָּהֶם; וְכֵן פֵּרַשׁ הַכָּתוּב הַזֶּה (הרמב״ם)
[הָרַמְבַּ״ן] זִכְרוֹנוֹ לִבְרָכָה עַל צַד הַפְּשָׁט; וְאַף־עַל־פִּי שֶׁיֵּשׁ בַּכָּתוּב מִדְרָשׁוֹת
רַבִּים, שִׁבְעִים פָּנִים לַתּוֹרָה, וְכֻלָּם נְכוֹחִים לַמֵּבִין.

וּמִזֶּה הַשֹּׁרֶשׁ הוּא מַה שֶׁאָמְרוּ זִכְרוֹנָם לִבְרָכָה שֶׁכָּל אֲשֶׁר לַלְוִיִּם וְלַכֹּהֲנִים,
בֵּין קַרְקַע בֵּין מִטַּלְטְלִין, אֵין מַחֲרִימִין אוֹתָם: כְּלוֹמַר שֶׁאֲפִלּוּ אָמַר הַכֹּהֵן אוֹ
הַלֵּוִי עַל שָׂדֵהוּ שֶׁיְּהֵא חֵרֶם, אֵין נִתְפַּס בּוֹ כְּלָל, כִּי הוּא כְּשׁוֹכֵן בֵּית אֲדוֹנָיו, מְקוֹם
הַבְּרָכָה וְהַחֶסֶד וְהַטּוֹב, וְכָל יֵשׁ לוֹ לַיָי הוּא, וּבְתוֹךְ הַבְּרָכָה אֵין מָקוֹם לְחֵרֶם
חָלִילָה.

מִדִּינֵי הַמִּצְוָה, מַה שֶׁאָמְרוּ זִכְרוֹנָם לִבְרָכָה: מַה בֵּין חֶרְמֵי כֹהֲנִים לְחֶרְמֵי
שָׁמַיִם, שֶׁחֶרְמֵי שָׁמַיִם הֶקְדֵּשׁ, וְנִפְדִּין בְּשָׁוּיֵיהֶן, וְיִפְּלוּ הַדָּמִים לְבֶדֶק הַבַּיִת,
וְיֵצְאוּ הַנְּכָסִים לְחֻלִּין; וְחֶרְמֵי כֹהֲנִים, כְּלוֹמַר חֵרֶם סְתָם שֶׁהוּא לַכֹּהֲנִים, אֵין לָהֶם
פִּדְיוֹן לְעוֹלָם, אֶלָּא נִתָּנִין לַכֹּהֲנִים כִּתְרוּמָה; וְעַל חֵרֶם כֹּהֲנִים נֶאֱמַר "לֹא יִמָּכֵר
וְלֹא יִגָּאֵל": לֹא יִמָּכֵר לְאַחֵר וְלֹא יִגָּאֵל לַבְּעָלִים.

וְאֶחָד הַמַּחֲרִים קַרְקַע אוֹ מִטַּלְטְלִין, נִתָּנִין לַכֹּהֲנִים שֶׁבָּאוֹתוֹ מִשְׁמָר בְּשָׁעָה
שֶׁמַּחֲרִים; וְחֶרְמֵי כֹהֲנִים, כָּל זְמַן שֶׁהֵם בְּבֵית הַבְּעָלִים הֲרֵי הֵם הֶקְדֵּשׁ לְכָל
דִּבְרֵיהֶם, שֶׁנֶּאֱמַר: כָּל חֵרֶם קֹדֶשׁ קָדָשִׁים הוּא לַיָי; נְתָנָם לַכֹּהֵן, הֲרֵי הֵם כְּחֻלִּין

---

5. TB ʿArachin 28a.

6. MT *hilchoth ʿarachin* vi 4, based on TB ʿArachin 28b (see Rashi and *tosafoth*, s.v. *haramé kohanim*).

7. The *kohanim* were divided into twenty-four "watches" of family groups, each of which served a week at the Sanctuary.

[people]—for instance, those who go to battle against their enemies, who make a vow, "If Thou wilt verily deliver this people into my hand, then I will enact a *ḥérem* (a devotement for utter destruction) upon their cities" (Numbers 21:2)—they then must die. For the other [heathen] nations are not included under the source of blessings, as we said; hence the expression of *ḥérem* takes effect on them and achieves its purpose. So Ramban of blessed memory explained this verse (Leviticus 27:29) by way of the plain meaning; and although there are many hermeneutic interpretations of the verse, there are seventy facets [of meaning] to the Torah, and *all are clear to the one who understands* (Proverbs 8:9).

It is for this root reason that the Sages of blessed memory taught[5] that any property belonging to Levites or *kohanim*, whether landed property or movable goods, cannot be placed under a *ḥérem*. In other words, even if a *kohen* or Levite said about his field that it should be *ḥérem* (proscribed in devotement), it has no effect on it at all. For he is as though living in the house of his [Divine] Master, the place of blessing, loving-kindness and good, and all that belongs to him is the Lord's. And amid blessing there is no room for a destructive proscription, perish the thought.

Among the laws of the precept there is what the Sages of blessed memory taught:[6] what the difference is [in law] between vows of *ḥérem* to the *kohanim* and vows of *ḥérem* to Heaven—that things vowed as *ḥérem* to Heaven are [thus] consecrated, and are to be redeemed for their value, the money going for repairs at the Temple, while the property thus reverts to a non-holy state; but for anything vowed as *ḥérem* to the *kohanim*—in other words, it was a simple, unspecified *ḥérem*, so that it goes to the *kohanim*—there is no redemption ever, but it is rather given to the *kohanim*. And about property under *ḥérem* given to *kohanim* it is stated, *it shall not be sold or redeemed* (Leviticus 27:28): it shall not be sold to anyone else, and it shall not be redeemed by the owner.

Whether a *ḥérem* is put on landed property or movable goods, it is given to the *kohanim* of that watch [that was on duty at the Sanctuary][7] at the time the *ḥérem* was pronounced.[1] And as for any property under *ḥérem* to be given to *kohanim*, as long as it is in the owner's house, it is consecrated property in every respect: for it is stated, *every object of ḥérem is most holy to the Lord* (Leviticus 27:28). Once given to a
kohen, it is like non-holy property in every respect: for it is stated,

לְכָל דִּבְרֵיהֶם, שֶׁנֶּאֱמַר: כָּל חֵרֶם בְּיִשְׂרָאֵל לְךָ יִהְיֶה; וּשְׂדֵה חֶרְמוֹ שֶׁל כֹּהֵן אֵינָהּ חוֹזֶרֶת לַבְּעָלִים הָרִאשׁוֹנִים לְעוֹלָם; וְיֶתֶר פְּרָטֶיהָ, בְּפֶרֶק שְׁמִינִי מֵעֲרָכִין וְרִאשׁוֹן מִנְּדָרִים.

וְנוֹהֶגֶת בִּזְמַן הַבַּיִת בִּזְכָרִים וּנְקֵבוֹת; אֲבָל בַּזְּמַן הַזֶּה, כְּבָר אָמַרְנוּ בְּמִצְוָה רִאשׁוֹנָה שֶׁבְּסֵדֶר זֶה שֶׁאֵין מַחֲרִימִין. אֲבָל אִם עָבַר וְהֶחֱרִים בַּזְּמַן הַזֶּה, כָּתַב הָרַמְבַּ"ם זִכְרוֹנוֹ לִבְרָכָה שֶׁאִם הֶחֱרִים בְּחוּצָה לָאָרֶץ מְטַלְטְלִין סְתָם אוֹ קַרְקַע לַכֹּהֲנִים בְּפֵרוּשׁ, שֶׁהֵם נְתוּנִין לַכֹּהֲנִים הַנִּמְצָאִים בְּאוֹתוֹ מָקוֹם, שֶׁהַקַּרְקַע שֶׁבְּחוּצָה לָאָרֶץ דִּינוֹ כְּמִטַלְטְלִין לְעִנְיָן זֶה; אֲבָל אִם הֶחֱרִים קַרְקַע בְּאֶרֶץ־יִשְׂרָאֵל, אֵינָהּ חֵרֶם, שֶׁאֵין שְׂדֵה חֲרָמִים נוֹהֵג אֶלָּא בִּזְמַן שֶׁהַיּוֹבֵל נוֹהֵג.

וְעוֹבֵר עַל זֶה וְהֶחֱרִים מִנְּכָסָיו וְלֹא נְתָנָם לַכֹּהֵן, אוֹ לְבֶדֶק הַבַּיִת בְּאוֹתָן צְדָדִין שֶׁפֵּרַשְׁנוּ שֶׁנִּתָּנִין לְבֶדֶק הַבַּיִת, בִּטֵּל עֲשֵׂה זֶה, וְעָנְשׁוֹ גָּדוֹל מְאֹד, שֶׁמּוֹעֵל בַּקֹּדֶשׁ.

[שֶׁלֹּא יִמָּכֵר קַרְקַע שֶׁהֶחֱרִים אוֹתָהּ בְּעָלָיו אֶלָּא תִנָּתֵן לַכֹּהֲנִים]

שנח שֶׁלֹּא יִמְכֹּר אָדָם שְׂדֵה הַחֵרֶם, וְכֵן כָּל שְׁאָר קַרְקָעוֹת, וְהוּא הַדִּין לְמִטַלְטְלִין, שֶׁהֶחֱרִימוּ אוֹתָן בַּעֲלֵיהֶם — אֶלָּא יִנָּתְנוּ לַכֹּהֲנִים שֶׁבְּאוֹתוֹ מִשְׁמָר, כְּמוֹ שֶׁכָּתַבְנוּ בְּסֵדֶר זֶה עֲשֵׂה ו' [סִי' שנ"ז]; וַאֲפִלּוּ לְגִזְבָּר הַהֶקְדֵּשׁ אָסוּר לַבְּעָלִים לְמָכְרוֹ, אֶלָּא זוֹכֶה בּוֹ בְּלֹא כְלוּם, כִּי הַשֵּׁם זִכָּה הַחֲרָמִים לַכֹּהֲנִים.

וְזֶה יִהְיֶה בְּסְתָם חֲרָמִים, כְּמוֹ שֶׁאָמַרְנוּ לְמַעְלָה, דְּקָיְמָא לָן כְּמַאן דְּאָמַר סְתָם חֲרָמִין לַכֹּהֲנִים, כְּלוֹמַר מִי שֶׁהֶחֱרִים וְלֹא פֵרַשׁ לְמִי, שֶׁאֵלּוּ מַחֲרִים בְּפֵרוּשׁ לְבֶדֶק

8. TB ʿArachin 29a.

9. Tosefta, ʾArachin iv; and see § 359, third paragraph.

10. Fifth paragraph from end.

11. MT *hilchoth ʿarachin* viii 11.

12. MY would emend this to read: or on landed property, *or to the kohanim* explicitly, etc. — meaning that the law is the same whether the *ḥerem* is pronounced on movable or landed property outside the land of Israel, and whether it is uttered to no specific purpose or recipient, or for the *kohanim* explicitly. While MY is patently right about the law, our text, however, simply follows MT (*ibid.*), arbitrary though it may seem in referring to a *ḥerem* as without specification or to the *kohanim* explicitly.

13. See § 330, third paragraph before the end, and §§ 335, end.

§ 358
1. Third paragraph before end. (See § 357, note 7.)

2. So Sifra, *b'hukothai*, *perek* 12, 4.

3. At the beginning.

Every object of ḥérem *in Israel shall be yours* (Numbers 18:14).[8] A field under *ḥérem* which thus becomes a *kohen*'s never returns to its first [original] owner.[9] The rest of its details are in chapter 8 of the Talmud tractate '*Arachin* and the first chapter of *N'darim*.

It is in force at the time of the Temple, for both man and woman. As to the present time, though, we stated previously, in the first precept of this *sidrah* (§350)[10] that a vow of *ḥérem* is not to be pronounced. But if someone transgresses and utters a proscription of *ḥérem* in the present, Rambam of blessed memory wrote[11] that if one imposed a *ḥérem* outside the land [of Israel] on movable goods without specification, or on landed property to the *kohanim* explicitly, it is to be given to *kohanim* located in that place;[12] for the law on land outside the land [of Israel] is the same as for movable goods in this regard. If, however, one pronounced a *ḥérem* on landed property in the land of Israel, it is not a valid proscription, because the law of a field under *ḥérem* is in effect only at the time that the law of the jubilee is observed.[13]

If a person transgressed this, pronouncing a *ḥérem* on some of his property and then not giving it to a *kohen*, or [not giving it] for keeping the Temple in repair under those circumstances where, as we explained, it was to be given for the upkeep of the Temple, he would thus disobey this positive precept, and his punishment would be very great, since he committed a breach of holiness.

[THAT LAND PUT UNDER A ḤÉREM BY ITS OWNER IS
NOT TO BE SOLD BUT TO BE GIVEN TO THE KOHANIM]

358 that one should not sell a field or equally, any other landed property, under *ḥérem* (a proscriptive vow of devotement); and the same law holds for movable goods whose owner put them under *ḥérem*; but they are [all] rather to be given to the *kohanim* in that watch, as we wrote in the sixth positive precept of this *sidrah* (§357).[1] Even to the treasurer of the Sanctuary funds it is forbidden for the owner to sell it,[2] but he [a *kohen*] must rather gain possession of it for nothing, because the Eternal Lord gave the right to property under *ḥérem* to the *kohanim*.

Now, this applies to simple, unspecified vows of *ḥérem*, as we stated above (§357);[3] for we hold to the view of the Sage who said that property under a simple, unspecified vow of *ḥérem* goes to *kohanim*—i.e.

if someone pronounced a vow of *ḥérem* and did not specify for whom.

הַבַּיִת, לֹא יִזְכּוּ בָהֶם הַכֹּהֲנִים.

וְעַל חֶרְמֵי כֹהֲנִים נֶאֱמַר כָּאן: כָּל חֵרֶם...לֹא יִמָּכֵר, אֲבָל הַכֹּהֲנִים וַדַּאי מוֹכְרִים אוֹתָם כִּרְצוֹנָם, שֶׁחֶרְמֵי כֹהֲנִים אַחַר שֶׁיָּצְאוּ מִיַּד הַבְּעָלִים שֶׁהֶחֱרִימוּם וְהִגִּיעוּ לְיַד הַכֹּהֲנִים, הֲרֵי הֵן כְּחֻלִּין לְכָל דִּבְרֵיהֶם, שֶׁנֶּאֱמַר: כָּל חֵרֶם בְּיִשְׂרָאֵל לְךָ יִהְיֶה; אֲבָל בְּעוֹד שֶׁהֵם תַּחַת יַד הַבְּעָלִים, נֶאֱמַר עֲלֵיהֶם: כָּל חֵרֶם קֹדֶשׁ קָדָשִׁים לַיָי.

וְשֹׁרֶשׁ הַמִּצְוָה וְכָל עִנְיָנָהּ, כָּתוּב לְמַעְלָה עֲשֵׂה ו' [סִי' שנ"ז]; עַיֵּן שָׁם כִּי קָרוֹב הוּא.

[שֶׁלֹּא יִגָּאֵל שְׂדֵה הַחֵרֶם]

שנט שֶׁלֹּא יִגָּאֵל שְׂדֵה הַחֵרֶם, וְהוּא הַדִּין לְכָל שְׁאָר קַרְקָעוֹת וּמְטַלְטְלִין הַמָּחְרָמִים, שֶׁאֵין לָהֶם פִּדְיוֹן, אֶלָּא נִתָּנִין לַכֹּהֲנִים וְהֵם עוֹשִׂים בָּהֶם כָּל חֶפְצָם; וְעַל זֶה נֶאֱמַר: כָּל חֵרֶם וְגוֹמֵר לֹא יִגָּאֵל וְלֹא יִמָּכֵר, וְאָמְרוּ בְסִפְרָא: "לֹא יִמָּכֵר" לְאַחֵר, "וְלֹא יִגָּאֵל" לַבְּעָלִים.

מִשָּׁרְשֵׁי הַמִּצְוָה, כָּתוּב לְמַעְלָה עֲשֵׂה ו' [סִי' שנ"ז].

מִדִּינֵי הַמִּצְוָה, מַה שֶּׁאָמְרוּ זִכְרוֹנָם לִבְרָכָה שֶׁהַמַּחֲרִים לַשָּׁמַיִם, הִקְדִּישׁ, אֲבָל נִפְדֶּה הוּא בְשָׁוְויוֹ וְיִפְּלוּ הַדָּמִים לְבֶדֶק הַבַּיִת, וְיָצְאוּ הַנְּכָסִים לְחֻלִּין; אֲבָל חֶרְמֵי כֹהֲנִים אֵין לָהֶם פִּדְיוֹן לְעוֹלָם, אֶלָּא הֲרֵי הֵם לַכֹּהֲנִים וּלְזַרְעָם לְעוֹלָם. וְכֹהֵן שֶׁזָּכָה בִשְׂדֵה חֲרָמִים וּמְכָרוֹ, חוֹזֶרֶת לוֹ אוֹ לְזַרְעוֹ בַּיּוֹבֵל, שֶׁנֶּאֱמַר: לַכֹּהֵן תִּהְיֶה אֲחֻזָּתוֹ, מְלַמֵּד שֶׁשְּׂדֵה חֶרְמוֹ לוֹ כִּשְׂדֵה אֲחֻזָּתוֹ לְיִשְׂרָאֵל. וְיֶתֶר פְּרָטֶיהָ וְכָל עִנְיָנָהּ, הַכֹּל

§359   1. Sifra, b'ḥukothai, perek 12, 4. (This passage actually reads: "it shall not be sold" to the treasurer — i.e. of the funds of the Sanctuary. But see §358, fourth paragraph before end, that this obviously means even to the treasurer.)

     2. See §357, note 6.

     3. MT ḥilchoth 'arachin vi 7, based on TB 'Arachin 26a (Leḥem Mishneh). About "field of heritage" see §355, sixth paragraph, and note 14.

For if one pronounced the *ḥerem* explicitly for maintaining the Temple in repair, the *kohanim* would not gain the right to it.

About property under *ḥerem* [to be acquired] by *kohanim*, it is stated, *no object of* ḥerem . . . *shall be sold* (Leviticus 27:28). But the *kohanim* may certainly sell it as they wish: for after property under *ḥerem* [to be acquired by] *kohanim* has left the possession of the owner who put it under the proscriptive vow and has become the possession of the *kohanim*, it is non-holy property in every respect: for it is stated, *Every object of* ḥerem *in Israel shall be yours* (Numbers 18:14). However, while it is yet in the owner's possession, it is stated about it, *every object of* ḥerem *is most holy to the Lord* (Leviticus 27:28).

Now the root reason for the precept, and all its subject-matter, are written above, in the sixth positive precept (§357); study it there, for it is close by.

[THE PRECEPT THAT LAND UNDER A VOW OF ḤEREM
IS NOT TO BE REDEEMED]

359 that a field under *ḥerem* (a proscriptive vow of devotement) is not to be redeemed; and the law is the same for all other landed properties and movable goods that are put under *ḥerem*—that they can have no redemption, but are to be given to the *kohanim*. and they may do with them whatever their desire. About this it is stated, *no object of* ḥerem . . . *shall be sold or redeemed* (Leviticus 27:28); and it was taught in the Midrash *Sifra*:[1] "it shall not be sold" to anyone else, "or redeemed" by the owner.

Some part of the root reasons for the precept is written above, in the sixth positive precept (§357).

Among the laws of the precept, there is what the Sages of blessed memory said:[2] that if a person puts something under *ḥerem* for Heaven, he thus consecrates it; but it may be redeemed for its value, and the money goes toward maintaining the Temple in repair, while the property becomes non-holy. However, property under *ḥerem* [assigned to the] *kohanim* can never have any redemption, but rather goes to the *kohanim* and their progeny forever. If a *kohen* gained the right to a field under *ḥerem* and then sold it, it would revert to him or to his descendant at the jubilee: For it is stated, *its possession shall be the* kohen's (Leviticus 27:21), which teaches that his field of *ḥerem* shall be for him as one's field of heritage is for any Israelite.[3]

The rest of its details and its entire subject-matter are all as I have

כְּמוֹ שֶׁכָּתַבְתִּי לְמַעְלָה עָשֶׂה ו' [סִי' שנ"ז], וּמִתְבָּאֵר הַכֹּל בְּמַסֶּכֶת עֲרָכִין.

וְאֵין סָפֵק כִּי שְׁנֵי לָאוִין אֵלּוּ, שֶׁהֵן "לֹא יִמָּכֵר וְלֹא יִגָּאֵל", נוֹהֲגִין הַיּוֹם, וּכְמוֹ שֶׁכָּתַבְתִּי לְמַעְלָה עָשֶׂה ו' לְדַעַת הָרַמְבַּ"ם זִכְרוֹנוֹ לִבְרָכָה, שֶׁהַמַּחֲרִים בַּזְּמַן הַזֶּה קַרְקַע אוֹ מִטַּלְטֵל בְּחוּצָה לָאָרֶץ, שֶׁנּוֹתְנָן לַכֹּהֲנִים, וְאַף־עַל־פִּי שֶׁאֵין נוֹהֵג שְׂדֵה חֲרָמִים בָּאָרֶץ אֶלָּא בִּזְמַן שֶׁהַיּוֹבֵל נוֹהֵג. כֵּן כָּתַב הָרַמְבַּ"ם זִכְרוֹנוֹ לִבְרָכָה בְּסֵפֶר הַפְלָאָה.

[מִצְוַת מַעְשַׂר בְּהֵמָה טְהוֹרָה בְּכָל שָׁנָה]

שׁ**ס** לְעַשֵּׂר כָּל הַבְּהֵמוֹת טְהוֹרוֹת, שֶׁהֵן בָּקָר וָצֹאן וְעִזִּים, הַנּוֹלָדוֹת בַּעֲדָרֵינוּ בְּכָל שָׁנָה וְשָׁנָה, וּלְהָבִיא הַמַּעְשֵׂר לִירוּשָׁלַיִם וּלְאָכְלוֹ שָׁם, אַחַר שֶׁיִּהְיֶה קָרֵב הַחֵלֶב וְהַדָּם מֵהֶם בַּמִּזְבֵּחַ, שֶׁנֶּאֱמַר: וְכָל מַעְשַׂר בָּקָר וָצֹאן כֹּל אֲשֶׁר יַעֲבֹר תַּחַת הַשָּׁבֶט הָעֲשִׂירִי יִהְיֶה קֹדֶשׁ.

וְאָמְרוּ זִכְרוֹנָם לִבְרָכָה בִּבְכוֹרוֹת: כֵּיצַד מְעַשְּׂרִין, כּוֹנְסָן לַדִּיר וְעוֹשֶׂה לָהֶם פֶּתַח קָטָן, כְּדֵי שֶׁלֹּא יִהְיוּ שְׁנַיִם יְכוֹלִים לָצֵאת כְּאַחַת, וּמַעֲמִיד אִמּוֹתֵיהֶן מִבַּחוּץ וְהֵן גּוֹעוֹת, כְּדֵי שֶׁיִּשְׁמְעוּ הַטְּלָאִים קוֹלָם וְיֵצְאוּ מִן הַדִּיר לִקְרָאתָם מֵעַצְמָם וְלֹא מִכֹּחַ אַחֵר, וּמוֹנֶה אוֹתָן בַּשָּׁבֶט: אֶחָד שְׁנַיִם שְׁלֹשָׁה אַרְבָּעָה, וְכֵן עַד עֲשָׂרָה, וְהַיּוֹצֵא עֲשִׂירִי סוֹקְרוֹ בְּסִקְרָא וְאוֹמֵר: הֲרֵי זֶה מַעֲשֵׂר.

מִשָּׁרְשֵׁי הַמִּצְוָה, שֶׁהָאֵל בָּרוּךְ הוּא בָּחַר בְּעַם יִשְׂרָאֵל וְחָפֵץ לְמַעַן צִדְקוֹ לִהְיוֹת כֻּלָּם עוֹסְקֵי תוֹרָתוֹ וְיוֹדְעֵי שְׁמוֹ, וּבְחָכְמָתוֹ מְשָׁכָם בְּמִצְוָה זוֹ לְמַעַן יִלְמְדוּ יִקְחוּ מוּסָר, כִּי יוֹדֵעַ אֱלֹהִים כִּי רֹב בְּנֵי־אָדָם נִמְשָׁכִים אַחַר הַחֹמֶר הַפָּחוּת שֶׁגַּם הוּא בָשָׂר, וְלֹא יִתְּנוּ נַפְשָׁם בַּעֲמַל הַתּוֹרָה וּבְעִסְקָהּ תָּמִיד; עַל־כֵּן סִבֵּב בִּתְבוּנָתוֹ

---

4. Next to last paragraph.

5. MT hilchoth 'arachin viii 11.

1. So TB B'choroth 53a.

2. So TB Z'vaḥim 56b.

3. I.e. with a rod bearing red paint (Rashi to Leviticus 27:32).

written above, in the sixth positive precept (§357). And it is all clarified
in the Talmud tractate 'Arachin. Now, there is no doubt that these
two negative precepts, i.e. [*no object of* hérem] *shall be sold or redeemed,*
apply today, as I wrote above, in the sixth positive precept (§357),[4]
according to the view of Rambam of blessed memory—that if a
person pronounces a vow of hérem at the present time on a plot of
land or movable goods outside the land [of Israel], it is to be given
to the kohanim—this even though the law of a field under hérem is
in effect in the land [of Israel] only at the time that the law of the
jubilee is observed. So Rambam of blessed memory wrote in the
Book of Solemn Utterance.[5]

[THE PRECEPT OF THE TITHE OF PERMISSIBLE DOMESTIC
ANIMALS TO BE GIVEN EVERY YEAR]

360 to tithe (separate a tenth of) all clean (permissible) animals,
namely, cattle, sheep and goats, that are born in our herds and flocks,[1]
every single year, and to bring the tithe (tenth part) to Jerusalem to
eat it there, after their fat and blood shall have been offered up on the
altar.[2] For it is stated, *And all the tithe of the herd or the flock, whatever
passes under the rod, the tenth shall be holy* (Leviticus 27:32).

The Sages of blessed memory recounted in the Talmud tractate
B'choroth (58b) how the tithe was taken: [The herdsman] would gather
them [the animals] into the shed, and make a small opening for them,
such that two could not go out at once. He would then place their dams
(mothers) outside, where they would low and cry [for their young],
in order that the lambs should hear their voices and go out of the shed
toward them of their own accord, and not under any other force.
Then he would count them with the herdsman's rod, "one, two, three,
four," and so till ten; and the one which came out the tenth, [the
herdsman] would mark with a red stripe,[3] saying "This is tithe."

At the root of the precept lies the reason that God, blessed is He,
chose the people Israel and desired, for the sake of making them righteous, that they should be those who occupy themselves with His Torah
and know His name. So in His wisdom He drew them [toward Him]
with this *mitzvah,* that they might learn and accept the moral lesson.
For God knows that most people are drawn after the inferior, lowly
physical element, *being also flesh* (Genesis 6:3), and will not devote
their spirit to toiling in the Torah and being constantly occupied with
⟨507⟩ it. He therefore arranged matters, in His perception, and gave them a

וְנָתַן לָהֶם מָקוֹם שֶׁיֵּדְעוּ הַכֹּל דִּבְרֵי תּוֹרָתוֹ עַל־כָּל־פָּנִים, שֶׁאֵין סָפֵק כִּי כָל אָדָם נִמְשָׁךְ לִקְבֹּעַ דִּירָתוֹ בְּמָקוֹם שֶׁמָּמוֹנוֹ שָׁם.

לָכֵן בַּהַעֲלוֹת כָּל אִישׁ מַעְשַׂר כָּל בָּקָר וָצֹאן שֶׁלּוֹ שָׁנָה שָׁנָה בְּמָקוֹם שֶׁעֶסֶק הַחָכְמָה וְהַתּוֹרָה שָׁם, וְהִיא יְרוּשָׁלַיִם, שֶׁשָּׁם הַסַּנְהֶדְרִין יוֹדְעֵי דַעַת וּמְבִינֵי מַדָּע, וּכְמוֹ־כֵן נַעֲלֶה לְשָׁם מַעְשַׂר תְּבוּאָתֵנוּ בְּאַרְבַּע שְׁנֵי הַשְּׁמִטָּה, כְּמוֹ שֶׁיָּדוּעַ שֶׁמַּעֲשֵׂר שֵׁנִי נֶאֱכָל שָׁם, וְכֵן נֶטַע רְבָעִי, שֶׁנֶּאֱכָל שָׁם, עַל־כָּל־פָּנִים אוֹ יֵלֵךְ שָׁם בַּעַל הַמָּמוֹן עַצְמוֹ לִלְמֹד תּוֹרָה אוֹ יִשְׁלַח לְשָׁם אֶחָד מִבָּנָיו שֶׁיִּלְמַד שָׁם, וְיִהְיֶה נִזּוֹן בְּאוֹתָן פֵּרוֹת.

וּמִתּוֹךְ כָּךְ יִהְיֶה בְּכָל בַּיִת וּבַיִת מִכָּל יִשְׂרָאֵל אִישׁ חָכָם יוֹדֵעַ הַתּוֹרָה, אֲשֶׁר יְלַמֵּד בְּחָכְמָתוֹ כָּל בֵּית אָבִיו, וּבְכֵן תִּמָּלֵא הָאָרֶץ דֵּעָה אֶת יי; כִּי אִם חָכָם אֶחָד לְבַד יִהְיֶה בְּעִיר, אוֹ אֲפִלּוּ עֲשָׂרָה, יִהְיוּ הַרְבֵּה מִבְּנֵי־אָדָם שֶׁבָּעִיר, וְכָל־שֶׁכֵּן הַנָּשִׁים וְהַיְלָדִים, שֶׁלֹּא יָבוֹאוּ לִפְנֵיהֶם פַּעַם בְּשָׁנָה, אוֹ אֲפִלּוּ יִשְׁמְעוּ דִבְרֵיהֶם פַּעַם בְּשָׁבוּעַ, יֵלְכוּ הַבַּיִת וְיַשְׁלִיכוּ כָּל דִּבְרֵי הֶחָכָם אַחֲרֵי גֵוָם; אֲבָל בִּהְיוֹת הַמְלַמֵּד בְּכָל בַּיִת וּבַיִת, שׁוֹכֵן שָׁם עֶרֶב וָבֹקֶר וְצָהֳרַיִם, וְיַזְהִירֵם תָּמִיד, אָז יִהְיוּ כֻלָּם, אֲנָשִׁים וְנָשִׁים וִילָדִים, מֻזְהָרִים וְעוֹמְדִים, וְלֹא יִמָּצֵא בֵינֵיהֶם שׁוּם דְּבַר חֵטְא וְעָוֹן, וְיִזְכּוּ לְמַה שֶּׁכָּתוּב: וְנָתַתִּי מִשְׁכָּנִי בְּתוֹכְכֶם ... וִהְיִיתֶם לִי לְעָם וְאָנֹכִי אֶהְיֶה לָכֶם לֵאלֹהִים.

מִדִּינֵי הַמִּצְוָה, מַה שֶּׁאָמְרוּ זִכְרוֹנָם לִבְרָכָה שֶׁאֵין מְעַשְּׂרִין מִן הַבָּקָר עַל הַצֹּאן וְלֹא מִן הַצֹּאן עַל הַבָּקָר, אֲבָל מְעַשְּׂרִין מִן הַצֹּאן עַל הָעִזִּים וּמִן הָעִזִּים עַל הַצֹּאן, שֶׁשְּׁנֵיהֶם הוֹצִיאָם הַכָּתוּב בִּלְשׁוֹן צֹאן, וּכְמִין אֶחָד נֶחְשָׁבִים. וְאֵין מְעַשְּׂרִין מִן הַנּוֹלָד בְּשָׁנָה זוֹ לְשָׁנָה אַחֶרֶת, כְּמוֹ שֶׁאֵין מְעַשְּׂרִין בִּזְרַע הָאָרֶץ מִן הֶחָדָשׁ עַל הַיָּשָׁן וְלֹא מִן הַיָּשָׁן עַל הֶחָדָשׁ, שֶׁנֶּאֱמַר בָּהּ: הַיֹּצֵא הַשָּׂדֶה שָׁנָה שָׁנָה. אֲבָל מִכָּל־

4. In the first, second, fourth and fifth years; in the third and sixth years the tithe was for the poor; in the seventh year, since the earth was left fallow and all produce was left free and ownerless, no tithes were given by Scriptural law.

5. I.e. tithe from produce, to be eaten by the owners in Jerusalem (§473). The First Tithe, separated in all six years of the *sh'mittah* (seven-year) cycle, was given to the Levites. On the point made in this paragraph (see also the part that follows) cf. Sifre, Deut. §106: *that you may learn to fear the Lord your God* (Deuteronomy 14:23)—this informs us that the tithe brings a person to Torah study. In *tosafoth*, TB Bava Bathra 21a, s.v. *ki mitziyon*, we read: As he remained in Jerusalem until he consumed his Second Tithe, seeing them all engaged in the labor of Heaven and in its service, he would also become intent on the reverent fear of Heaven and would become occupied with Torah study. Similarly in *tosafoth* to the Pentateuch (in *Hadar Z'kénim*) on the above verse: Great is the Second Tithe, because it leads to Torah study. How so? When the Israelites came on pilgrimage at Passover, they would remain there no more than one day, being burdened with the barley harvest; and so at *Shavu'oth* because of the wheat harvest.

location where all would know the words of His Torah under all circumstances. For there is no doubt that a man is drawn to establish his dwelling in the place where his possessions are.

Therefore, as every man would take up the tithe of all his cattle and flocks year after year, to the location where the occupation with wisdom and Torah was to be found, namely Jerusalem, where the Sanhedrin (supreme court justices) were—those who had cognition and understood knowledge; and so we would likewise take up the tithe of our crops in four years out of the *sh'mittah* (seven-year) cycle.[4] As we know, the Second Tithe[5] was eaten there; and so too was a tree's fourth-year fruit eaten there (§247). Then in any event, the owner of the stock would either go there himself to learn Torah, or he would send one of his sons there, that he should study there and be sustained by that produce.

As a result, in every single house of every Israelite, there would be a wise man versed in the Torah, who by his wisdom would teach his father's entire household; and thus *the land shall be full of the knowledge of the Lord* (Isaiah 11:9). For if there were only one wise scholar in a city, or even ten, there would be many people in the city, and even more certainly the women and children, who would not come into their presence once a year; and even if they should hear their words once a week, they would go home and throw all the wise scholar's words out behind their back.[6] However, with an instructor in every single house, living there evening, morning and noon, and constantly cautioning them, then all—men, women and children— would remain cautioned and adjured, and no sinful or iniquitous matter would be found among them. Thus they would merit to attain what is written, *Then I will set My* mishkan *(dwelling-place) among you . . . and I will be your God, and you shall be My people* (Leviticus 26:11–12).[6a]

Among the laws of the precept, there is what the Sages of blessed memory said:[1] that the tithe could not be taken from cattle for sheep,[7] nor from sheep for cattle; but the tithe could be taken from sheep for goats, and so from goats for sheep; for Scripture designated both by the term *tzon* (flock, sheep), and they are considered as one species. The tithe is not to be taken from those born this year for those of another year, just as the tithe of the earth's produce may not be separated from a new crop for an old one, nor from an old crop for a new one; for it is stated about it, *which comes forth from the field year by year* (Deuteronomy 14:22).[8] Nevertheless, if a person transgressed and

מָקוֹם אִם עָבַר וְעִשֵּׂר מִן הַבְּהֵמָה הַיְשָׁנִים עַל הַחֲדָשִׁים אוֹ מִן הַחֲדָשִׁים עַל
הַיְשָׁנִים, כָּתַב הָרַמְבַּ"ם זִכְרוֹנוֹ לִבְרָכָה שֶׁיֵּרָאֶה לּוֹ שֶׁהֵן מַעֲשֵׂר, מִפְּנֵי חֻמְרַת
מַעֲשֵׂר, שֶׁהֲרֵי לָא כְּתִיב "שָׁנָה שָׁנָה" אֶלָּא בְּזֶרַע הָאָרֶץ, וְדַי לָנוּ שֶׁנִּלְמַד מִמֶּנּוּ
לִהְיוֹת מַעֲשֵׂר בְּהֵמָה כָּמוֹהוּ לְעִנְיָן לְכַתְּחִלָּה, אֲבָל לֹא דִיעֲבַד.

וְכֵן מֵעִנְיַן הַמִּצְוָה מַה שֶּׁאָמְרוּ זִכְרוֹנָם לִבְרָכָה שֶׁאֵין הַטְּלָאִים הַנּוֹלָדִים כְּמוֹ
הַטֶּבֶל, שֶׁאָסוּר לֶאֱכֹל מִמֶּנּוּ עַד שֶׁיִּתְעַשֵּׂר, אֶלָּא מֻתָּר לִמְכֹּר וְלִשְׁחֹט מִן הַטְּלָאִים
כָּל מַה שֶׁיִּרְצֶה, וּכְשֶׁיַּגִּיעוּ הַזְּמַנִּים שֶׁקָּבְעוּ חֲכָמִים לְעַשֵּׂר, וְהֵם נִקְרָאִין גֹּרֶן
מַעֲשֵׂר בְּהֵמָה, יְעַשֵּׂר אוֹתָן הַנִּמְצָאִים לוֹ; וּמִשֶּׁהִגִּיעוּ אוֹתָם זְמַנִּים, אָסוּר לוֹ
לִמְכֹּר וְלִשְׁחֹט עַד שֶׁיְּעַשֵּׂר אוֹתָם; וְאִם עָבַר וְשָׁחַט, הֲרֵי זֶה מֻתָּר.

וּשְׁלֹשָׁה זְמַנִּים הֵם שֶׁקָּבְעוּ זִכְרוֹנָם לִבְרָכָה בְּזֶה, וְאֵלּוּ הֵן: יוֹם אַחֲרוֹן שֶׁל חֹדֶשׁ
אֲדָר וְיוֹם ל"ה מִסְּפִירַת הָעֹמֶר וְיוֹם אַחֲרוֹן מֵחֹדֶשׁ אֱלוּל; וְלָמָּה קָבְעוּ זְמַנִּים אֵלּוּ,
שֶׁהֵם סְמוּכִים לַמּוֹעֲדִים — כְּדֵי שֶׁיִּהְיוּ בְּהֵמוֹת מְצוּיוֹת לְעוֹלֵי רְגָלִים, שֶׁאַף־עַל־
פִּי שֶׁמֻּתָּר לִמְכֹּר קֹדֶם מַעֲשֵׂר, כְּמוֹ שֶׁאָמַרְנוּ, מִכָּל־מָקוֹם נִמְנָעִים הָיוּ מִלִּמְכֹּר עַד
שֶׁיְּעַשְּׂרוּ אוֹתָן, כְּדֵי שֶׁיַּעֲשׂוּ בָּהֶן מִצְוָה.

וְדִין הַמּוֹנֶה אוֹתָם וְטָעָה בְּמִנְיָנוֹ וְקָרָא לַשְּׁמִינִי עֲשִׂירִי אוֹ לַשְּׁנֵים־עָשָׂר
עֲשִׂירִי, שֶׁלֹּא נִתְקַדְּשׁוּ; וְאִם טָעָה בַּתְּשִׁיעִי וְאֶחָד־עָשָׂר וּקְרָאָן עֲשִׂירִי, נִתְקַדְּשׁוּ,
מִפְּנֵי שֶׁהֵם סְמוּכִים לַעֲשִׂירִי; וְדָבָר זֶה מִפִּי הַקַּבָּלָה יְדַעְנוּהוּ.

וּמַה שֶּׁאָמְרוּ שֶׁכָּל בְּהֵמָה שֶׁהִיא סָפֵק אִם בַּת־מַעֲשֵׂר הִיא אוֹ אֵינָהּ בַּת־
מַעֲשֵׂר, הֲרֵי הִיא פְּטוּרָה מִן הַמַּעֲשֵׂר; וְהַכֹּל נִכְנָסִין לַדִּיר לְהִתְעַשֵּׂר, בֵּין תְּמִימִים
בֵּין בַּעֲלֵי מוּמִין, חוּץ מִן הַכִּלְאַיִם וְהַטְּרֵפָה וּמְחֻסָּר זְמַן, וְכֵן הַיָּתוֹם שֶׁמֵּתָה אִמּוֹ
אוֹ שֶׁנִּשְׁחֲטָה עִם לֵדָתוֹ, וּדְבָרִים אֵלּוּ מִפִּי הַשְּׁמוּעָה יְדַעְנוּם; וְיֶתֶר פְּרָטֶיהָ, בְּפֶרֶק
אַחֲרוֹן מִבְּכוֹרוֹת.

... Then in order that they should learn to fear the Lord our God, they were commanded to eat the Second Tithe in Jerusalem, so that they should be detained there while the *kohanim* performed the service of the Lord with the offerings and the incense, the Levites sang, and the great Sanhedrin gave decisions on the laws of the Israelites.... Then they would understand the reverent fear of the Lord, because they would be detained there till they had consumed their Second Tithe. Finally, cf. *Moshav Z'kénim* on the above verse (p. 500): *And you shall eat before the Lord your God ... the tithe ... that you may learn to fear the Lord your God always*—This is puzzling: what does one matter have to do with the other? Because the tithe will be there, one will learn to fear? Well, it can be answered that they would give the tithes to their sons to eat in Jerusalem, and there they would learn Torah and reverent fear of the Eternal Lord. For the produce was of great quantity, and a person could not tarry so very long until it would be eaten. Hence he would send his son, and he would study Torah in the interim, until it would be eaten up.

6. Expression based on Neḥemiah 9:26.

6a. In the Hebrew, the second part of the Scriptural text is actually in reverse order: ⟨510⟩

did take the tithe from older animals for younger ones, or from younger animals for older ones, Rambam of blessed memory wrote[9] that it appears to him that they are tithe, because of the severity of the law of the tithe. For you see, "year by year" is written solely about produce of the earth, and it is enough for us to learn from it that the tithe of animals should be like it initially, at the start, but not [necessarily] after the fact, if it was already done.

In the subject-matter of the precept there is likewise what the Sages of blessed memory taught:[10] that lambs which are born are not like untithed produce, of which it is forbidden to eat until it is tithed; it is rather permissible for a person to sell or ritually slay any lambs that one wishes, and when the times come which the Sages set for tithing, which are called "the harvest-time of the animal tithe," he should sct aside the tithe from those that he has. Once those times have arrived, however, he is forbidden to sell or ritually slay any until he separates the tithe from them. Yet if he transgressed and did ritually slay one, it is permissible [to be eaten].[10]

There are three [such] times which the Sages of blessed memory set, namely: the last day of the month of Adar, the thirty-fifth day in the counting of the 'omer, and the last day of the month of Elul.[10] Why did they set these times, which are close to the festivals?[11]—so that animals should be available to the festival pilgrims.[12] For even though it was permissible to sell [animals] before tithing [them], as we said, they would nevertheless refrain from selling any until they took the tithe from them, so that they would perform a *mitzvah* with them.[13]

Then there is the law for one who counted them and made a mistake in his counting, and called the eighth the tenth, or the twelfth the tenth—that these would not become sanctified [as tithe]; but if he erred about the ninth or the eleventh, and called those the tenth, they would become hallowed, because they are close to the tenth. This is something we know through the Oral Tradition.[14]

There is, too, what the Sages said:[15] that if there is doubt about any animal, whether it requires tithing or not, it is free of the obligation of the tithe. All are assembled into the shed to be tithed, whether they are whole in body or blemished, except for any animal of mixed breed, fatally ill or wounded, or lacking in age;[16] and so too an orphaned animal whose dam (mother) died or was ritually slain at its birth.

⟨511⟩ These matters we know through the Oral Tradition.[17] The rest of

וְכָתַב הָרַמְבַּ"ם זִכְרוֹנוֹ לִבְרָכָה שֶׁמִּצְוָה זוֹ נוֹהֶגֶת בֵּין בִּזְכָרִים וּנְקֵבוֹת, בֵּין בְּיִשְׂרָאֵלִים בֵּין בְּכֹהֲנִים וּלְוִיִּים, וּבָאָרֶץ וּבְחוּצָה לָאָרֶץ, בֵּין בִּפְנֵי הַבַּיִת וְשֶׁלֹּא בִּפְנֵי הַבַּיִת; וְזֶהוּ דִין־תּוֹרָה. וְאוּלָם בִּגְזֵרָה מִדְּרַבָּנָן כְּדֵי שֶׁלֹּא יֵאָכֵל שֶׁלֹּא בְמוּם, אַחַר שֶׁאֵין לָנוּ מִקְדָּשׁ, וְנִמְצָא בָא לִידֵי אִסּוּר גָּדוֹל, שֶׁהוּא שׁוֹחֵט קָדָשִׁים בַּחוּץ, אָמְרוּ זִכְרוֹנָם לִבְרָכָה שֶׁאֵינוֹ נוֹהֵג אֶלָּא בִּפְנֵי הַבַּיִת; וּכְשֶׁיִּהְיֶה שָׁם מִקְדָּשׁ בָּנוּי, נוֹהֵג בָּאָרֶץ וּבְחוּצָה לָאָרֶץ. עַד כָּאן לְשׁוֹנוֹ.

וְעוֹד כָּתַב בְּמָקוֹם אַחֵר, שֶׁאִם עָבַר וְעִשֵּׂר בַּזְּמַן הַזֶּה, הֲרֵי זֶה מַעֲשֵׂר, וְיֵאָכֵל בְּמוּמוֹ בְּכָל מָקוֹם, כִּי הוּא כְחֻלִּין גְּמוּרִים. וְהַתְּמִים הַנֶּאֱכָל בִּירוּשָׁלַיִם בִּזְמַן הַבַּיִת, דִּינוֹ שֶׁיֵּאָכֵל לַבְּעָלִים כֻּלּוֹ, כְּפֶסַח, חוּץ מִן הָאֵמוּרִים וְהַדָּם, שֶׁהוּא קָרֵב, כְּמוֹ שֶׁאָמְרוּ לְמַעְלָה.

[שֶׁלֹּא לִמְכֹּר מַעֲשַׂר בְּהֵמָה אֶלָּא יֵאָכֵל בִּירוּשָׁלַיִם]

שסא שֶׁלֹּא נִמְכַּר מַעֲשַׂר בְּהֵמָה בְּשׁוּם צַד אֶלָּא יֹאכְלוּהוּ בְעָלָיו אוֹ מִי שֶׁיִּרְצוּ הֵם, בִּירוּשָׁלַיִם; וְעַל זֶה נֶאֱמַר כָּאן בְּמַעֲשַׂר בְּהֵמָה "לֹא יִגָּאֵל", וְאָמְרוּ בְּסִפְרָא: בְּמַעֲשֵׂר הוּא אוֹמֵר "לֹא יִגָּאֵל" — אֵינוֹ נִמְכָּר לֹא חַי וְלֹא שָׁחוּט וְלֹא תָמִים וְלֹא בַעַל מוּם. וּלְשׁוֹן גְּאֻלָּה יְשַׁמֵּשׁ כָּאן בִּלְשׁוֹן מְכִירָה, לְפִי שֶׁהַגְּאֻלָּה מֵעֵין מְכִירָה הוּא, שֶׁהָאָדָם נוֹתֵן דָּמִים וְלוֹקֵחַ קַרְקַע.

מִשָּׁרְשֵׁי הַמִּצְוָה, מַה שֶׁכָּתַבְתִּי בְּסֵדֶר זֶה בְּמִצְוַת מַעֲשַׂר בָּקָר וָצֹאן, עֲשֵׂה ז' [סִי' שׁ"ס]; וּמִן הַטַּעַם הַהוּא שֶׁתִּרְאֶה שָׁם, נִצְטַוֵּינוּ שֶׁלֹּא לִמְכֹּר הַמַּעֲשֵׂר בְּשׁוּם צַד, אֶלָּא יֵאָכֵל עַל־כָּל־פָּנִים בִּירוּשָׁלַיִם.

מִדִּינֵי הַמִּצְוָה, מַה שֶׁאָמְרוּ זִכְרוֹנָם לִבְרָכָה שֶׁמַּעְשַׂר בְּהֵמָה הָיָה נֶאֱכָל כֻּלּוֹ לַבְּעָלִים בִּירוּשָׁלַיִם, וְאֵין לַכֹּהֲנִים בָּהֶם כְּלוּם; אֲבָל הָיָה נִשְׁחָט בָּעֲזָרָה וּמַקְרִיבִין

and you shall be My people, and I will be your God—which is found in Jeremiah 11:4. There is an appreciable body of evidence, however, that in their commentaries and writings, produced long before the invention of printing made accurate copies of the Writ widely available, the *rishonim* (early authorities and scholars) cited verses of Scripture not from any written text but from memory. Hence it can be safely assumed that our author meant to cite Leviticus 26:12 directly after 26:11, from the same *sidrah* as the Scriptural source of §360, and not the very similar text from Jeremiah 11:4. (Somewhat similarly, in the Scriptural source for §253, Leviticus 19:28, the word בבשרכם "in your flesh" from the second part of the verse was unwittingly substituted for בכם "in yourselves.")

7. I.e. to give, for example, ten oxen as the tithe for 100 sheep.
8. TB P'choroth 53a–b.
9. MT *hilchoth b'choroth* vii 5.
10. TB B'choroth 57b.
11. They are respectively fifteen days before Passover, *Shavu'oth* and *Sukkoth*.

its details are in the last chapter of the Talmud tractate *B'choroth*.

Now, Rambam of blessed memory wrote[18] that this precept applies to both man and woman, whether Israelites, *kohanim* or Levites, both when the Temple exists and when it does not—this by the law of the Torah. There is, however, a decree of the Sages: In order that no one should eat such an unblemished animal[19] now when we have no Sanctuary, whereby one would come to violate a major prohibition, ritually slaying a holy offering outside [the Sanctuary],[20] they (of blessed memory) ruled that it is in effect only when the Temple is extant. But when there is an erected Sanctuary there, it is in effect both in the land and outside the land [of Israel]. Thus far his words.

Elsewhere he wrote further[21] that if a person transgressed and separated [an animal] tithe at the present time, it is a valid tithe, and in a blemished condition it may be eaten anywhere, because it is like perfectly non-holy property. As for a whole, unblemished animal eaten in Jerusalem at the time of the Temple, its law is that it is to be entirely eaten by the owner,[22] like a Passover offering,[23] except for the *'émurim* (certain fatty parts) and the blood, which are offered up, as we stated above.

[THAT THE TITHE OF ANIMALS IS NOT TO BE SOLD BUT ONLY EATEN IN JERUSALEM]

361 that we should not sell an animal of the tithe under any circumstances, but rather, the owner, or whoever he wishes, is to eat it in Jerusalem; for this reason it is stated here, about the animal tithe, *it shall not be redeemed* (Leviticus 27:33); and it was taught in the Midrash *Sifra*:[1] About the [animal] tithe Scripture states, "it shall not be redeemed"—it is not to be sold either alive or ritually slain, either whole in body or blemished. The expression of redemption serves here to denote selling, because redemption is akin to sale, since a man gives money and takes land.[2]

At the root of the precept lies the reason I wrote in this *sidrah*, in the seventh positive precept, about the tithe of cattle and sheep (§360). For this reason, that you will see there, we were commanded not to sell the tithe under any circumstances, but it is rather to be eaten, in any event, in Jerusalem.

Among the laws of the precept there is what the Sages of blessed memory taught:[3] that an animal of the tithe would be entirely eaten by the owner in Jerusalem, the *kohanim* having no share of it at all. It

אֵמוּרָיו וְזוֹרְקִין דָּמוֹ זְרִיקָה אַחַת כְּנֶגֶד הַיְסוֹד.

וְאִם נָפַל בּוֹ מוּם, נֶאֱכָל בְּכָל מָקוֹם, אֲבָל אָסְרוּ חֲכָמִים לְמָכְרוֹ בְּכָל מָקוֹם, וַאֲפִלּוּ הוּא בַעַל מוּם; וַאֲפִלּוּ שָׁחוּט אָסְרוּ לְמָכְרוֹ, גְּזֵרָה שֶׁמָּא יִמְכְּרֶנּוּ חַי; וּלְפִיכָךְ אָמְרוּ שֶׁאֵין שׁוֹקְלִין מִמֶּנּוּ מָנֶה כְּנֶגֶד מָנֶה, מִפְּנֵי שֶׁנִּרְאֶה כְּמוֹכֵר, וְאַף־עַל־פִּי שֶׁדָּבָר זֶה הֻתַּר לַעֲשׂוֹת אֲפִלּוּ בִּבְכוֹר תָּמִים, שֶׁאָמְרוּ זִכְרוֹנָם לִבְרָכָה: כֹּהֲנִים שֶׁנִּמְנוּ עַל הַבְּכוֹר מֻתָּרִין לִשְׁקֹל מָנֶה כְּנֶגֶד מָנֶה.

וּמַה שֶּׁאָמְרוּ זִכְרוֹנָם לִבְרָכָה שֶׁמַּעֲשֵׂר שֶׁבְּהֵמָה שֶׁנִּשְׁחַט, מֻתָּר לִמְכֹּר חֶלְבּוֹ וְגִידָיו וְעוֹרוֹ וְעַצְמוֹתָיו, שֶׁלֹּא אָסְרוּ לִמְכֹּר אֶלָּא בְשָׂרוֹ בִּלְבָד; וְאִם הָיוּ הָעֲצָמוֹת יְקָרִים וְהִבְלִיעַ דְּמֵי הַבָּשָׂר בָּעֲצָמוֹת, מֻתָּר.

וְכָתַב הָרַמְבַּ"ם זִכְרוֹנוֹ לִבְרָכָה שֶׁיֵּרָאֶה לוֹ שֶׁהַמּוֹכֵר מַעֲשֵׂר, לֹא קָנָה לוֹקֵחַ, וּלְפִיכָךְ אֵין לוֹקֵחַ עָלָיו הַמּוֹכְרוֹ, לְפִי שֶׁלֹּא הוֹעִילוּ מַעֲשָׂיו, כְּמוֹ מוֹכֵר חֶרְמֵי כֹהֲנִים, שֶׁלֹּא קָנָה לוֹקֵחַ, וּכְמוֹ מוֹכֵר יְפַת־תֹּאַר, שֶׁלֹּא קָנָה לוֹקֵחַ, כְּמוֹ שֶׁיִּתְבָּאֵר בִּמְקוֹמוֹ. עַד כָּאן. וְיֶתֶר פְּרָטֵי הַמִּצְוָה, יִתְבָּאֲרוּ בְמַסֶּכֶת בְּכוֹרוֹת וּבְמַסֶּכֶת מַעֲשֵׂר שֵׁנִי בִּתְחִלָּתָהּ.

וְנוֹהֵג אִסּוּר זֶה בִזְכָרִים וּנְקֵבוֹת, יִשְׂרָאֵלִים וְכֹהֲנִים וּלְוִיִּם, בְּכָל מָקוֹם וּבְכָל זְמָן. וְאַף־עַל־פִּי שֶׁחֲכָמִים אָסְרוּ לַעֲשֵׂר בְּהֵמָה בַּזְּמַן הַזֶּה, גְּזֵרָה שֶׁמָּא יֹאכְלוּם תְּמִימִים, וְיִהְיֶה בַדָּבָר אִסּוּר כָּרֵת, שֶׁהוּא שְׁחִיטַת קָדָשִׁים בַּחוּץ, כְּמוֹ שֶׁכָּתַבְנוּ לְמַעְלָה, אַף־עַל־פִּי־כֵן מִי שֶׁעָבַר וְעִשֵּׂר בַּזְּמַן הַזֶּה, יֵשׁ בּוֹ קְדֻשַּׁת מַעֲשֵׂר, וְאִם

12. The Israelites fulfilling the Torah's precept to go up to Jerusalem for each of the three festivals.

13. TB B'choroth 58a.

14. *Ibid.* 60a–b; MT *hilchoth b'choroth* viii 1.

15. TB Bava M'tzi'a 6b.

16. Before the eighth day of its life, hence too young to be an offering (Leviticus 22:27).

17. TB B'choroth 57a; MT *ibid.* vi 14.

18. ShM positive precept §78; see §282, note 2, which applies here.

19. I.e. the problem exists only with an animal without blemish, which would thus be fit to be offered up at the Sanctuary; about a blemished animal, see next paragraph.

20. Which is punishable by *kareth* (Divine severance of existence); MT *hilchoth b'choroth* vi 2.

21. MT *hilchoth b'choroth* vi 2, 4.

22. And others whom he may choose to join him; see §361, beginning.

23. And none of the flesh is given to the *kohanim*, unlike other offerings; *ibid.* 4.

§361   1. Sifra, *b'hukothai, perek* 13, 4.

2. In redeeming a field that was sold or consecrated.

3. MT *hilchoth b'choroth* vi 4, based on TB Z'vahim 56b.

4. TB B'choroth 31b; MT *ibid.* 6.

was, however, ritually slain in the Temple court; its *'émurim* [certain fatty parts] were offered up [on the altar]; and its blood would be sprinkled in one fling over against the altar base.

If it acquired a disfiguring blemish, it might be eaten anywhere. But the Sages forbade selling it anywhere, even if it was blemished; and even if it was ritually slain, by a protective decree they forbade selling it, for fear that [otherwise] it might be sold alive.[4] For this reason they said that a portion [of meat from a tithe animal] is not to be weighed against a portion [of other meat to determine its weight],[5] because it would look as though it were being sold—although it was permitted to do this even with a whole, unblemished firstborn animal: for the Sages of blessed memory said:[6] Those *kohanim* that were counted over a firstling [registered to eat it] are allowed to weigh a portion against a portion.

Then there is what the Sages of blessed memory taught:[7] that when a tithe animal was ritually slain, it was permissible to sell its fat, sinews, skin and bones; for they forbade selling no more than its flesh alone. If the bones were expensive, and the price of the flesh was absorbed in [the cost of] the bones, it would be permissible.[7]

Now, Rambam of blessed memory wrote[8] that it seems to him that if someone sold a tithe animal, it would not become the purchaser's property; therefore the one who sold it would not be given whiplashes for it, because his action availed nothing, just as when one sells properties under *ḥérem* assigned to *kohanim* (§§357–58), where the purchaser does not acquire them, and when one sells a female war prize (§533), whom the purchaser does not acquire, as it is explained in its place. Thus far his words.

The remaining details of the precept are clarified in the Talmud tractate *B'choroth* and the Mishnah tractate *Ma'asér Shéni*, at the beginning. This prohibition applies to both man and woman, Israelites, *kohanim* and Levites, at every place and in every time. Even though the Sages forbade separating a tithe from animals, as a protective decree for fear that such whole, unblemished animals might be eaten, and the matter entails a prohibition punishable by *karéth* [Divine severance of existence] since it involves the ritual slaying of holy offerings outside [the Sanctuary], as we wrote above (§360)[9]—nevertheless, if someone transgressed and separated a tithe at the present time, it would be subject to the sanctity of the tithe; and if he should ⟨515⟩ sell it in any way, he would thus violate this negative precept over it,

יִמָּכְרֶנּוּ בְּשׁוּם צַד, יַעֲבֹר עָלָיו הַלָּאו הַזֶּה, שֶׁהוּא "לֹא יִגָּאֵל"; אֲבָל אֵין לוֹקִין
עָלָיו, כְּמוֹ שֶׁאָמַרְנוּ סָמוּךְ בְּשֵׁם הָרַמְבַּ"ם זִכְרוֹנוֹ לִבְרָכָה.

וּתְהִלָּה לְאֵל גָּדוֹל וְנוֹרָא, סִיַּמְנוּ סֵפֶר וַיִּקְרָא.

וְהִנְנִי עוֹדֶנִּי בָא לְהַזְכִּירְךָ בְּמֶה שֶׁהִתְנַצַּלְתִּי הַרְבֵּה פְעָמִים עַל הַשָּׁרָשִׁים אֲשֶׁר
מְלָאַנִי לִבִּי לִכְתֹּב בַּמִּצְוֹת, שֶׁאֵין הַכַּוָּנָה רַק לְחַנֵּךְ הַנְּעָרִים וְלָתֵת אֶל לִבָּם כִּי יֵשׁ
בַּמִּצְוֹת תּוֹעָלוֹת רַבּוֹת גְּלוּיוֹת לְכָל אָדָם, כַּאֲשֶׁר יוּכְלוּן הָבִין בְּיַלְדוּתָם, וְעַל־כֵּן
קָרָאתִי שֵׁם הַסֵּפֶר "חִנּוּךְ"; וְעֹמֶק חָכְמָתָן וְרֹב תּוֹעַלְתָּם, אִם יִזְכּוּ יַשִּׂיגוּ בָם בִּימֵי
זִקְנָתָם. הֲלֹא יָדַעְתָּ כִּי יֵשׁ פְּרִי נִמְצָא אֲשֶׁר בּוֹ כַּמָּה תְרוּפוֹת בְּסֶגֻלָּה וְגַם טוֹב
לְאָכְלָה, וְאִישׁ חָכָם יוֹדֵעַ לְסַפֵּר בְּשִׁבְחֵי תְרוּפוֹתָיו, וַאֲשֶׁר לֹא יֵדַע בְּכָל אֵלֶּה
יֹאמַר שֶׁהוּא טוֹב לְאוֹכְלָיו.

גַּם אֲנִי אֲסַפֵּר הַמֻּשָּׂג אֵלַי בְּמַעֲלוֹת הַמִּצְוֹת בְּאָזְנֵי בְנִי (וחבירי) [וַחֲבֵרָיו]:
יֹאכְלוּ פְרִי מְגָדַי, יִשְׂבְּעוּ תְבוּאָתִי שֶׁאָסַפְתִּי אַחֲרֵי הַקּוֹצְרִים בִּשְׂדֵה רַבּוֹתַי וְדַשְׁתִּי
בְמָדוּשָׁתִי.

וְאַחַת שָׁאַלְתִּי מֵאֵת יי כָּל יְמֵי הֱיוֹתִי: לִהְיוֹת לְרָצוֹן לְפָנָיו שִׂיחָתִי, אֶמְצָא חֵן
בְּעֵינָיו, וְיִקַּח נָא מִיָּדִי מְעַט מִנְחָתִי, אֲשֶׁר הֲכִינוֹתִי בְּעָנְיִי בְּגָלוּתִי. הוּא בַּחֲסָדָיו
יִתֵּן בְּלֵב שׁוֹמְעֵי קוֹלִי, לָדוּן לִזְכוּת אוֹתִי; וְאִם עָשִׂיתִי זֹאת לְהַזְכִּיר שְׁמִי וּלְהַגְדִּיל
תְּהִלָּתִי, אַל יְהִי לִי מוֹשֵׁךְ חֶסֶד וְדוֹרֵשׁ בְּטוֹבָתִי; רַק לְשֵׁם אֵל חַי, אֲשֶׁר לוֹ נָאווּ
תְהִלּוֹת, מַחְסִי וּמְצוּדָתִי, יִתְבָּרֵךְ וְיִתְעַלֶּה, אָמֵן.

---

5. If someone had, for example, a pound of ordinary meat and he wished to know if
a piece of meat from a tithe animal was also a pound, he was forbidden to place the two
on pans of a balance scale; MT *ibid.* derived from TB B'choroth 31a (*Kessef Mishneh*).

　6. TB *ibid.*

　7. TB B'choroth 31b; MT *hilchoth b'choroth* vi 8.

　8. MT *ibid.* 5.

　9. Second paragraph from the end.

Addendum

　1. I.e. of the precepts.

　2. Expression based on Song of Songs 4:16.

　3. Expression based on Ruth 2:7.

　4. Expression based on Psalms 27:4.

　5. Expression based on Genesis 33:10.

　6. Expression based on I Chronicles 22:14.

　7. Expression based on Psalms 109:12.

　8. Expressions based on Psalms 33:1.

　9. Psalms 91:2.

i.e. *it shall not be redeemed.* Yet whiplashes would not be suffered for it, as we have stated shortly above in the name of Rambam of blessed memory.

PRAISE TO THE GREAT AND REVERED GOD,
WE HAVE COMPLETED THE BOOK OF LEVITICUS.

Now, here I yet come to remind you of the apologetic explanation that I have given many times about the root reasons which my heart has emboldened me to write about the precepts: that the intention is no more than to educate the young and to make them aware that there are many benefits in the precepts, evident to every man, which they can understand in their childhood. For this reason I have given the work the name *ḥinnuch*, "Education." As for the depth of their wisdom and the great extent of their benefit,[1] if they will merit, they will comprehend them in their older years. You surely know that a fruit can exist which contains many precious elements for healing, and is also good to eat. A wise man knows to tell the great values of its healing powers; but one who knows nothing of all these would [simply] say it is good for eating.

Then I will likewise relate what I grasp of the noble virtues of the precepts, for the ears of my son and his friends. Let them eat my choice, precious fruit,[2] eat their fill of my grain that I gathered after the reapers[3] in the field of my master teachers and pounded out in my threshing.

One thing have I asked of the Lord all the days of my existence:[4] that my discourse may be pleasing before Him. May I find grace in His sight,[5] and may He take from my hand my little gift-offering that I have prepared in my adversity,[6] in my exile. Let Him in His kindness influence the heart of those who hear my voice to judge me favorably, on the side of merit. If I have done this to commemorate my name, to increase my praise, let there be none to extend kindness to me[7] or seek my welfare; but it was only for the sake of the living God, to whom all praises are becoming[8]—my refuge and my fortress,[9] be He blessed and exalted, *amen.*

KV-512-755